Diving
Deep into the
Ocean of the Mind

Ascension Series:

Diving Deep
into the Ocean of the Mind

Susan V. Whittaker, PhD, DMs

Published by

Wellsong Energetics, LLC.
1525 Norway St NE
Salem, OR 97301

Published by

Wellsong Energetics, LLC. 1525 Norway ST NE Salem, OR 97301

Copyright 2025 by Susan V. Whittaker

First Edition, 2025

ISBN: 978-1-962022-03-3 (Paperback)

Front Cover:
Photo ID 20920933 © Peshkova | Dreamstime.com
Enhanced by: Sajid Khan@sajidcreation0 | Fiverr.com
Bovis Chart: https://photonrevelations.com/bovis-chart/ | Revised 09/05/22, © Gary R. Plapp

The author can be contacted by email at this address: Sue@wsEnergetics.com

To advance the integrity of the practice and art of dowsing and to avoid any potential negative consequences from this book being misused, these charts have been designed and energized to work only with the spirit and intentions of honor and love. Crystal Therapy enthusiasts and practitioners are due to receive compensation for their skills and knowledge. The use of this book for these purposes is approved and encouraged. The author's higher guides will ensure these charts are unreliable when copied or distributed without approval or used in any way that is not in the highest and best good for humanity.

Dowser's Guides by Susan V. Whittaker

Ascension Series

General Dowsing

Allergies
Volume 1
Volume 2

Pets

Chakras

Sentient Entities
Angels Invisible Entities
Aliens Visible Entities
Star Trek

Holistic Health
Issues and Needs
Products and Providers
Remedies
Crystal Sips and Zodiac Teas, For the Body, Mind, and Spirit
The Complete Guide to Crystal Therapy (2 Books)
Diving Deep Into the Pool of the Mind

Dowsing Docs Series

General Practitioners
General Practice, Vol 1
Remedies, Vol 2
Products and Providers, Vol 3

Dentists
Dental Charts for a Holistic Practice

Veterinarians
Volume 1
Volume 2

Homeopaths

Acknowledgements

This book is dedicated to the memory of three remarkable individuals whose works have profoundly shaped my understanding of our origins, our destiny and the coming ascension.

To the late Gerald Clark, a visionary and multifaceted genius, whose accomplishments spanned various disciplines from electrical engineering to film production. Gerald's groundbreaking books, including "The Anunnaki of Nibiru: Mankind's Forgotten Creators, Enslavers, Saviors, and Hidden Architects of the New World Order" and "The 7th Planet, Mercury Rising," provided not just knowledge but a new lens through which to view our past and our path toward ascension. His research into the ancient narratives of Nibiru and the complexities of human history inspired me to explore the deeper truths of our existence.

To the late Zechariah Sitchin, whose seminal work, "The Lost Book of Enki: Memoirs and Prophecies of an Extraterrestrial God," delved into the mythic and the mystical to reveal the narratives that have been hidden from the human consciousness. His writings offered insights into the ancient stories of extraterrestrial influences on Earth, highlighting the intertwined fates of humanity and our celestial ancestors.

Lastly, to Al Bates, author of "God's Story," whose exploration of divine narratives brought to light the overarching purposes and patterns that have guided the development of human civilizations across ages. His work continues to inspire those who seek to understand the divine elements of our history and the spiritual underpinnings of our existence.

Together, these authors have not only enlightened readers with forgotten histories but have also illuminated the reasons behind our creation and the greater cosmic roles we are meant to play. Their courageous explorations into the unknown have provided the foundations for this book, enabling us to dive deep into the ocean of the mind with a clear vision of our origins and a guide to our spiritual evolution.

Dedication

Rosalind Franklin

To Rosalind Franklin, whose brilliant discovery of the DNA double helix structure laid the foundation for modern molecular biology. Your meticulous dedication to science and your unwavering pursuit of truth have unlocked the secrets of life at its most fundamental level. Your legacy inspires us to delve deeper into the mysteries of existence, reminding us that the answers we seek to elevate our vibrations and heal our world often lie within the smallest particles of our being.

Candice Pert

To Candice Pert, whose groundbreaking research in psychoneuroimmunology revealed the profound connection between our emotions and our biology. Your discovery of the molecules of emotion has illuminated the path to understanding how our feelings shape our physical reality, empowering us to heal and elevate our consciousness. Your work continues to inspire us to embrace the power of love, joy, and compassion in raising our vibrations and transforming our lives.

Bruce Lipton

To Bruce Lipton, whose revolutionary insights in cell biology and epigenetics have transformed our understanding of the mind-body connection. Your teachings on the power of our beliefs to influence our genetic expression and overall health have empowered countless individuals to take charge of their destiny. Your wisdom has shown us that by aligning our thoughts and emotions with love and positivity, we can truly raise our vibrations and create a harmonious reality.

Gregg Braden

To Gregg Braden, whose profound explorations into ancient wisdom and modern science have bridged the gap between spirituality and science. Your insights into the power of the human heart, the divine matrix, and the interconnectedness of all things have guided us towards a deeper understanding of our place in the universe. Your work inspires us to harness the energy of love and coherence, helping us to elevate our vibrations and co-create a world of peace and harmony.

Quick Start Guide

Please take the next few minutes to discover how to use this book. There's a unique and essential system of interaction between the charts and their counterparts in the narrative section. You may be eager to start dowsing the charts — and they are powerful and rewarding — but you will find what you want faster and more easily when you understand the whole structure.

While this is indeed a dowsing book, the narrative section is the key to unlocking the meaning behind your pendulum's actions. So, right now, no page or chart is more important than the next few pages:

- Notes from the Author
- Purpose
- How to Use This Book

This book isn't here to affirm you; it's here to transform you.

Expect surprises and understand they are gifts from your higher self.

Most of all, these gifts are guideposts for becoming a better version of yourself and exceeding your conscious mind's beliefs and expectations.

Note from the Author

Diving Deep into the Ocean of the Mind is a different kind of dowsing book. Every user can get great rewards because the universe speaks in personal ways and provides what is most needed at any given moment. The more the book is used, the more pre-arranged gifts and benefits one can receive that will enhance their life journey.

Like all of the author's dowsing books, this one has the highest rating and approval from Raymon Grace, considered the world's best dowser given his ability to change matter thousands of miles away and people's lives, past, present and future.

Whether you use this book for personal development or problem solving it can help you raise your energy for ascension. The Bovis Life Force (CHI) Bioenergy Chart at the back of the book lets you monitor your energy level and gauge how negative thoughts and actions lower personal energy and how positive thoughts and actions raise it.

Typically, newcomers find their energy levels ranging from 14K to 21K, but as they delve deeper into the book's exercises, they can reach the threshold level of 144K—the minimum believed to be necessary for ascension in this lifetime.

The author encourages a flexible approach to using the book. Readers may either follow the guidance of the first chart in the book, the Diving Platform, a metaphorical pathfinder through the book's content, or choose specific areas listed in the table of contents to focus on specific matters such as trauma, stuck emotions, or other personal development topics.

A Daily Journey

As your journey through the book progresses, the author advises readers to regularly re-evaluate their need for further work by asking, "In my highest and best good, is there more I need to work on right now to increase my Bovis Life Force Bioenergy?"

Even after reaching the 144K mark, you can continue working through negative energies and layers of personal issues—likened to the layers of an onion—to maintain and enhance your high vibrational state. This underscores the book's role as a companion in the ongoing journey of self-improvement.

Ascension

The foundation of the belief in ascension expressed in this book is rooted in ancient Sumerian clay tablets. The author draws information from personal insight and stone tablets that speak of Enki, a benevolent Anunnaki who created humans and holds a deep affection for them. According to these tablets, Enki will protect those at or above the 144K energy level during a cataclysmic shift when Nibiru returns to Earth, flipping its poles and challenging those with lower energy levels who cannot survive passage through the Van Allen Radiation Belt.

This understanding not only provides a cosmic scale to the book's teachings but also connects personal energy management to the larger, existential opportunity for moving forward on one's soul journey.

Purpose

Welcome to Diving Deep Into the Ocean of the Mind. This book is not merely a guide. It is a mirror of the soul, a spiritual compass, and a vibrational training ground for those seeking personal transformation and ascension.

Each time you use it, you will be guided by the pendulum's access to higher wisdom as it reveals truths you may not consciously see. When a chart phrase doesn't initially resonate, consider it a key to an unseen door. The hidden truth may sound off-track, humbling or unwelcome, but consciousness is simply too limited to perceive what the soul most needs at every point in the journey. The ego is rooted in memory and identity, and because of this your self-awareness is not the measure of your full capacity and we do not see ourselves as others do. There is always a more evolved version of yourself waiting to be discovered and activated.

This book offers a loving, intuitive approach to clearing emotional and energetic blocks, raising your vibration, and stepping into your fullest potential. Your pendulum becomes the bridge inviting in divine intelligence to reveal what will serve you most whether it is for the body, mind or spirit.

As we enter this critical ascension period, the book emphasizes the importance of reaching 144,000 Bovis Units — a vibrational frequency believed to be necessary to survive and thrive during upcoming energetic shifts, including safe passage through the Van Allen radiation belt.

This concept, rooted in ancient Sumerian teachings about Enki and planetary cataclysms, frames your personal healing journey as part of a much larger soul mission. The more you raise your vibration, the more protected, aligned, and empowered you become.

Let this book be your daily companion, your quantum toolkit, and your map to self-mastery.

How to Use this Book

This book is a living energetic system, not just for reading, but for interacting with higher wisdom. It is designed to guide you in uncovering, clearing, and transforming unseen blocks through intuitive guidance and vibrational truth.

Start here: Use your pendulum to access the Diving Platform, the first chart in the book. It will direct you to one of four major gateways:

- Body

- Mind

- Spirit

- Helpful Tools

From there, you'll be led to a series of master charts in the relevant section. Master charts are energetic maps that help you navigate from a broad theme to a more specific one, and finally to a single word or phrase. This is a "drill-down" system that quickly refines concepts step-by-step and pierces through over 10,000 phrases to the one that is right for you at this moment.

Example of a Drill-Down Path:

If your pendulum first points to the Mind gateway and then selects the Grand Master Chart in the Mind Section, it might then direct you to Developing Intuition. From there, you may be guided to Chart 4 – Developing Intuition, and finally to the item "Yoga."

This final selection is your endpoint in the chart section, but it is not the end of your journey.

Seek Interpretation:

Once your pendulum has guided you to a final phrase or word, do the following:

1. Open the Table of Contents.

2. Follow the path you took (e.g., Mind → Developing Intuition).

3. Locate the narrative section and turn to the indicated page.

4. On that page, you'll find:

- A brief introduction to the topic

- An alphabetical list of terms (e.g., "Yoga" may be item 53)

- A description of the concept and guidance for personal reflection and energy integration

This is where the deep work begins. Reflect on what this selection means for you. Sometimes it will be immediately clear, but it may also seem irrelevant. The applicable meaning or divine direction provided through a phrase can unfold as your reflections, perceptions and mental energy shift.

Trust the Process

Even if a term doesn't seem useful at first, it points to a blind spot, a hidden block, or an emerging strength. The selected phrase can't be wrong. It simply reflects an idea that your conscious mind is ready to explore and adopt.

Alternative Approaches

You can also browse or dowse the table of contents to focus on a specific area. The page numbers lead you to the narrative section. And, at the bottom of the narrative section you will find guidance to the related charts.

If you simply choose a chart and dowse it for a particular phrase, you will need to work backwards from there to find the relevant place in the narrative section that well help you interpret and understand the message presented to you.

Guidance and Descriptions

This section provides general information so the charts can be more versatile and comprehensive. These comments are meant to serve as a starting point when a topic seems unrelated to your life, situation or personality. A sense of irrelevancy is common because the universe often helps from a different perspective or with a hidden purpose in order to raise your energy. You may discover a treasure chest that requires meditation and time for pondering how it can help.

Enjoy the journey.

Table of Charts

(Charts start on page 164)

Table of Descriptions

Chapter 3:
Spirit

Chapter 4:
Helpful Tools

Chapter 1

Body

Body Parts

Raising your consciousness through focusing on and healing the physical body can be a powerful path to spiritual growth. When you ask yourself, "What should I work on right now to raise my consciousness?" and your intuition points you to a specific "body part," it's an opportunity to explore the deeper connection between your body and spirit. This idea emphasizes that by paying attention to and caring for certain areas of your physical self, you can gain insights that help you grow spiritually and raise your vibration.

Once you're guided to a specific body part, you can go further by asking, "What part of this body part needs my attention right now?" This isn't just about physical health—it's about discovering the emotional traumas, stuck feelings, and limiting beliefs that may be stored in your body. Our bodies carry the memories of our life experiences, emotions, and even beliefs that shape how we see the world and our spiritual path.

This approach goes beyond the usual way of thinking about healing, as it blends the physical aspect of our existence with our spiritual journey. It recognizes that the body is more than just a container for the soul—it's like a map of our spiritual growth, with every cell and system reflecting our larger spiritual journey. By listening to what your body needs and addressing those areas, you're not only freeing yourself from physical and emotional issues, but also creating space for higher consciousness and deeper spiritual understanding.

Should the answer be negative, it indicates that there are no immediate concerns regarding body parts on that particular day. However, the philosophy underlying this method suggests that healing is a continuous process, likened to peeling back the layers of an onion. Each layer represents different issues and traumas that have accumulated over time. By revisiting this practice regularly, individuals engage in a deeper exploration and gradual healing of their physical and emotional ailments, promoting overall well-being and harmony within the body.

This process of diving deeper into our body's specific areas to release traumas, emotions, and beliefs is a powerful act of self-love and recognition of our inherent wholeness. It is a journey that aligns us more closely with our true nature, inviting profound transformations that ripple out into all dimensions of our being, ultimately guiding us to a state of balance, harmony, and elevated consciousness. Through this intimate dialogue with our physical selves, we learn to listen more deeply, respond with compassion, and nurture our entire being toward a state of integrated health and spiritual awakening.

When focusing on a specific body part, begin by setting a clear intention and connecting with your emotions. Ask for all negativity within this area—whether trauma, trapped emotions, or limiting beliefs—to be gently removed. Holding your pendulum, allow it to naturally rotate counter-clockwise as it works to clear and release the unwanted energy. Once the pendulum comes to a stop, set a new intention and infuse the space you've just cleared with pure, white, loving light. Let the pendulum rotate clockwise as it fills the void with healing energy. When it stops again, complete the process by sealing the area with intention and emotion. I personally visualize using a golden Fleur de Lis to seal in the white light, ensuring the healing is locked in and protected.

See Chart 3 - Body Parts, Grand Master

Foods that Raise Vibrations

The Role of High-Vibration Foods

In the realm of energy and wellness, the concept of vibrations refers to the frequency at which everything in the universe resonates, including our bodies. Consuming high-vibration foods can significantly impact our physical, emotional, and spiritual well-being. These foods, often fresh, natural, and minimally processed, are packed with vital nutrients that enhance our overall energy levels and promote a positive state of mind. Fruits like blueberries, strawberries, and bananas are rich in antioxidants and vitamins that help combat oxidative stress and inflammation, thus contributing to higher vibrational frequencies. Similarly, leafy greens such as kale, spinach, and Swiss chard are dense in chlorophyll, which oxygenates the blood and enhances cellular function, leading to a more vibrant and energized body.

How High-Vibration Foods Influence Our Well-Being

High-vibration foods not only nourish our physical body but also influence our emotional and spiritual states. For instance, consuming raw honey and chia seeds can provide sustained energy and mental clarity, essential for maintaining a balanced and harmonious life. Foods like almonds, hemp seeds, and walnuts, rich in healthy fats and omega-3 fatty acids, support brain health and improve mood, fostering a sense of well-being and happiness. Incorporating superfoods such as spirulina, chlorella, and seaweed into your diet can elevate your vibrational frequency even further, as they are abundant in essential minerals, proteins, and detoxifying properties. By choosing to eat these high-vibration foods, you align yourself with the natural rhythms of the earth, supporting a lifestyle that is not only healthier but also more attuned to the energy of the universe.

See Chart 59 - Foods that Raise Vibrations, Master Chart

Natural Elements

Being in or near natural elements significantly enhances one's vibration by fostering a deep connection with the Earth's intrinsic energies and promoting physical, mental, and spiritual well-being. For instance, spending time in forests or grasslands allows one to absorb the life force and tranquility these environments offer. The gentle rustling of leaves and the symphony of birdsong create a natural soundscape that soothes the mind and elevates the spirit. Similarly, being near rivers, streams, or waterfalls exposes one to negative ions, which can enhance mood and energy levels. Fresh air in these environments, rich in oxygen, revitalizes the body and sharpens mental clarity, while natural light, whether from sunlight, moonlight, or the mesmerizing displays of auroras and meteor showers, regulates circadian rhythms and boosts serotonin levels.

Natural elements like rock formations, canyons, glaciers, and volcanic ash ground us, reminding us of the Earth's ancient and enduring power. Crystals and natural minerals carry specific vibrations that can align and heal our energetic bodies. Being near the ocean or other water bodies, such as natural lakes, hot springs, or coral reefs, can be incredibly calming and rejuvenating. The rhythmic sound of ocean waves, the sight of sunrises and sunsets over water, and the tactile sensation of sand between the toes all contribute to a profound sense of peace and connectedness. Natural phenomena like rainbows, bioluminescence, and foggy mornings inspire awe and wonder, reminding us of the beauty and magic inherent in the natural world.

Incorporating natural fibers like wool, silk, and organic cotton into our daily lives brings us closer to nature's softness and warmth, promoting comfort and well-being. Consuming organic produce, honey, nuts, and wild berries nourishes the body with pure, unadulterated nutrients, enhancing our physical health and vibration. Even natural events like fire pits, lava flows, and meteor showers have a primal, energizing effect, connecting us to the Earth's dynamic and transformative energies. Engaging with these natural elements not only raises our vibration but also deepens our appreciation and respect for the Earth, fostering a harmonious relationship with the world around us.

See Chart 65 - Natural Elements, Master Chart

Trapped Emotions

In this section, we will explore how to use dowsing with Dr. Bradley Nelson's Emotion Code to release trapped emotions. The steps are designed to make it easier for you to follow and know what to do next when you receive an answer with your pendulum.

Getting Started
Trapped Emotions Process
1. **Ask the Pendulum**: Start by asking your pendulum, "Is there a trapped emotion that can be released now?" If the pendulum indicates "yes," proceed to the next step. If the answer is "no," move on to another chart for something else you can work on today.
2. **Identify the Emotion**: Next, dowse the **Trapped Emotions Master Chart (Chart 70)**. This chart will guide you to one of the areas where trapped emotions are most likely located.
3. **Locate the Specific Emotion**: Once you've identified the area, use one of the 6 charts linked to **Chart 70** to find the specific trapped emotion.
4. **Check for Decoding**: After finding the trapped emotion, go to **Chart 77** and ask, "Do I need to decode more?" Your pendulum will select one of the 5 possible answers.
   - If the pendulum selects one of the first 4 answers, you need to decode more information by using the associated charts.
   - If the answer is "No," move to that chart.
5. **Follow the Directions**: On the chart you've been directed to, follow the steps outlined in the "What to Do" section to release the trapped emotion.
6. **Repeat**: Once you've finished, return to the beginning and ask your pendulum again, "Is there a trapped emotion that can be released now?" If the answer is yes, continue with the process.

By following these steps, you can effectively use dowsing to locate and release trapped emotions, thus enhancing your emotional and energetic well-being. Each chart is designed to guide you through the process methodically, ensuring that you address and clear any stuck emotions systematically.

Releasing Traumas
Releasing traumas is crucial for raising your energy vibration and reaching a higher state of consciousness. Traumas, whether emotional or physical, create energy blockages that prevent

personal and spiritual growth. If you've tried Dr. Bradley Nelson's Emotion Code and it hasn't worked fully, there are other methods to clear these blockages and make the Emotion Code more effective later.

If you are directed to **Chart 85** ("What to Do Chart") and instructed to go to **"Trauma, Ways to Release, Master Chart 86"**, here are some methods that can help you release trauma:

1. **Acupuncture**: Balances the body's energy flow (Qi) to support emotional well-being.
2. **Affirmations**: Positive statements to overcome negative thoughts.
3. **Alexander Technique**: Helps unlearn unhealthy patterns of movement and tension.
4. **Aromatherapy**: Uses essential oils for emotional balance.
5. **Art Therapy**: Uses creativity to express emotions that are hard to verbalize.
6. **Bach Flower Remedies**: Natural extracts that balance emotions and restore harmony.
7. **Bilateral Stimulation**: Left-right rhythmic patterns (like tapping) to process trauma.
8. **Bioenergetics**: Exercises to release tension and trapped emotions from the body.
9. **Breathwork**: Breathing exercises that release emotional stagnation.
10. **Chakra Balancing**: Aligns your body's energy centers for healing.
11. **Cognitive Behavioral Therapy (CBT)**: Aims to change negative thought patterns.
12. **Core Energetics**: Combines body therapy and spiritual development.
13. **Crystal Healing**: Uses crystals' energies to clear emotional and physical blockages.
14. **Dance Therapy**: Uses movement to express and release emotions.
15. **Dynamic Energetic Healing**: Integrates different techniques to release trauma.
16. **EFT (Emotional Freedom Techniques)**: Combines tapping and cognitive therapy.
17. **Emotion Code**: Identifies and releases trapped emotions with muscle testing and magnets.
18. **Equine Therapy**: Healing through interaction with horses.
19. **EMDR (Eye Movement Desensitization and Reprocessing)**: Psychotherapy technique to relieve trauma.
20. **Family Constellations**: Addresses emotional issues rooted in family dynamics.
21. **Fasting**: Purifies mind and body for spiritual clarity.
22. **Forest Bathing**: Immersing in nature to reduce stress.
23. **Gestalt Therapy**: Focuses on present-moment awareness to heal past traumas.
24. **Guided Imagery**: Uses visualization to promote healing.
25. **Holosync**: Audio technology for meditative states and emotional healing.
26. **Hypnotherapy**: Accesses the subconscious mind to release buried emotions.
27. **I Ching**: Uses ancient wisdom for guidance.
28. **Journaling**: Writing down thoughts to process emotions.
29. **Kinesiology**: Muscle testing to identify energy imbalances.
30. **Life Coaching**: A partnership for personal and emotional growth.
31. **Magnet Therapy**: Uses magnetic fields to improve emotional and physical health.
32. **Martial Arts Meditation**: Integrates physical discipline with mental balance.
33. **Meditation and Mindfulness**: Practices for present moment awareness and emotional release.

34. **Mind-Body Bridging**: Restores emotional balance using somatic exercises.
35. **Music**: Expands consciousness and releases emotions through sound.
36. **NLP (Neuro-Linguistic Programming)**: Influences the brain's behavior with language.
37. **Neuroplasticity Exercises**: Exercises to improve brain function and emotional resilience.
38. **Past Life Regression**: Healing by exploring past lives to address present issues.
39. **Polarity Therapy**: Balances energy through touch and counseling.
40. **Pranic Healing**: Cleanses and revitalizes your body's energy field.
41. **Psychodrama**: Acting out emotional issues to resolve them.
42. **Qigong**: Balances energy through movement and focused intention.
43. **Radix Therapy**: Uses breathing and movement to integrate emotional and spiritual aspects.
44. **Reiki**: Balances the energy fields in and around the body.
45. **Rolfing**: Releases tension stored in muscles and connective tissue.
46. **Shamanic Healing**: Uses spirit guides and rituals to heal emotional wounds.
47. **Somatic Experiencing**: Body-focused therapy to heal trauma.
48. **Sound Healing**: Uses vibrations from instruments or voice to release blockages.
49. **Byron Katie's Work**: Questions the thoughts that cause suffering.
50. **Therapeutic Touch**: Healing energy directed to release emotional blockages.
51. **Transactional Analysis**: Improves communication by analyzing social interactions.
52. **Voice Therapy**: Vocal exercises to express and release emotions.
53. **Yoga**: Combines movement, breath, and meditation to release emotional and physical tension.
54. **Zero Balancing**: Releases deep tension through bodywork.

These methods can help clear trauma, raise your vibration, and improve your overall well-being.

See Chart 70 - Trapped Emotions, Master Chart

Chapter 2

Mind

Affirmations for Ancestral Healing

Affirmations for ancestral healing are powerful tools used to address and transform the inherited beliefs and emotional patterns passed down through generations. These positive statements help to reprogram the subconscious mind, replacing limiting and harmful beliefs with empowering and healing thoughts. By consistently repeating these affirmations, individuals can shift their mental and emotional states, fostering a sense of liberation from ancestral burdens. Affirmations act as a bridge between the conscious intention to heal and the subconscious patterns that often dictate behavior and emotional responses.

The need for affirmations in the process of clearing ancestral patterns arises from the deep-seated nature of these inherited influences. Ancestral patterns can be so ingrained that they operate below the level of conscious awareness, affecting decisions, relationships, and overall well-being. Affirmations help bring these patterns to the surface, allowing individuals to consciously acknowledge and release them. They provide a daily practice that reinforces the commitment to healing and transformation, helping to break the cycle of generational trauma. Through affirmations, individuals can honor their ancestors' experiences while creating a new, positive legacy for themselves and future generations.

1. I am a beacon of light for my family's healing.
2. I am a powerful agent of change in my family.
3. I am a powerful force for healing and change.
4. I am a source of healing and harmony in my family.
5. I am a source of love and light for my family.
6. I am connected to the love and wisdom of my ancestors.
7. I am free from the burdens of my ancestry.
8. I am free from the burdens of my family lineage.
9. I am free from the past and open to new possibilities.
10. I am free to create a life of joy and abundance.
11. I am free to create a new legacy of love and abundance.
12. I am grateful for the lessons of my ancestors.
13. I am grateful for the strength and resilience of my ancestors.
14. I am the change my ancestors prayed for.
15. I am the creator of my own destiny.
16. I am the embodiment of my ancestors' dreams and hopes.
17. I am the embodiment of my ancestors' highest dreams.
18. I am worthy of love, joy, and abundance.
19. I am worthy of love, joy, and success.
20. I break free from the limitations of my ancestry.
21. I break the cycle of generational trauma.
22. I choose love and forgiveness in my family.
23. I choose to create a new legacy of love and abundance.
24. I embrace the positive qualities of my ancestors.
25. I embrace the wisdom and strength of my ancestors.

26. I forgive and release all ancestral anger and resentment.
27. I forgive and release all ancestral beliefs around money.
28. I forgive and release all ancestral guilt and shame.
29. I forgive and release all ancestral pain and suffering.
30. I forgive and release all ancestral resentments.
31. I forgive my ancestors and myself for past actions.
32. I forgive my ancestors for their mistakes and limitations.
33. I heal and transform my ancestral wounds.
34. I heal and transform the pain of my lineage.
35. I heal and transform the wounds of my lineage.
36. I honor and bless my ancestors for their journey.
37. I honor and release the patterns of my ancestors.
38. I honor the gifts and talents passed down to me.
39. I honor the sacrifices made by my ancestors.
40. I honor the strength and resilience of my family.
41. I release all inherited fears and anxieties.
42. I release all inherited fears and limitations.
43. I release all inherited guilt and shame.
44. I release all inherited pain and suffering.
45. I release all inherited patterns of fear and limitation.
46. I release all inherited patterns of guilt and shame.
47. I release all inherited patterns of scarcity and lack from my lineage.
48. I release all inherited patterns of struggle and hardship.
49. I release all inherited negative beliefs and imprints around money.
50. I release all negative ancestral imprints from my DNA.

See Chart 94 - Affirmation for Ancestral Healing, Master Chart

Affirmations to Attract Positive Experiences

Affirmations such as "Abundance Flows to Me Effortlessly," "I Am a Magnet for Success," and "My Life Is a Beautiful Journey" serve as powerful tools to elevate one's vibration by aligning thoughts with positive, high-frequency energy. Repeating these affirmations daily can help transform negative thought patterns into empowering beliefs, fostering a mindset of abundance, self-love, and gratitude. By affirming statements like "I Am Grateful for All My Blessings" and "I See Beauty in Everything," individuals can cultivate an attitude of appreciation, which attracts more positive experiences and enhances overall well-being. Embracing affirmations like "I Am Healthy, Wealthy, and Wise" and "My Energy Is Vibrant and Powerful" reinforces a strong, healthy self-image, promoting emotional and physical health. Ultimately, these affirmations help individuals focus on their strengths, potential, and the infinite possibilities available to them, thereby raising their vibration and creating a more joyful, prosperous, and fulfilling life.

1. **Abundance Flows to Me Effortlessly**: I naturally attract wealth and prosperity.

2. **All My Dreams Have Come True**: My deepest desires are fulfilled.

3. **All My Relationships Are Harmonious**: I enjoy peaceful and loving connections.

4. **All That I Seek Is Already Within Me**: I have everything I need inside me.

5. **Amazing Opportunities Always Come My Way**: I am constantly presented with wonderful possibilities.

6. **An Attitude of Gratitude Has Brought Me Closer to My Goals**: Being thankful helps me achieve my dreams.

7. **As I Love Myself, My Relationships Have Improved**: Self-love enhances my connections with others.

8. **Balance in My Life Brings Me Peace**: Equilibrium brings tranquility into my life.

9. **Beautiful Things Always Happen to Me**: I am surrounded by beauty and positivity.

10. **Blessings Surround Me**: I am constantly showered with blessings.

11. **Boundless Energy Flows Through Me**: I am full of vibrant and limitless energy.

12. **Challenges Are Opportunities for Growth**: I see difficulties as chances to grow and learn.

13. **Change Is a Positive Force in My Life**: I embrace change as a catalyst for improvement.

14. **Clarity and Focus Come to Me Easily**: I naturally possess clear vision and concentration.

15. **Compassion Flows Through Me Effortlessly**: I naturally feel and express compassion.

16. **Confidence Radiates from Me**: I exude self-assurance and confidence.

17. **Creativity Flows Through Me Freely**: My creativity is boundless and uninhibited.

18. **Divine Guidance Is Always with Me**: I am always led by divine wisdom.

19. **Each Day Is Filled with Joy**: Every day brings me happiness and joy.

20. **Every Experience Brings Me Closer to My Goals**: All events help me achieve my objectives.

21. **Every Part of My Life Is Aligned with Positivity**: My entire life is filled with positive energy.

22. **Everything I Do Brings Me Joy**: All my actions result in happiness.

23. **Everything I Touch Turns to Gold**: I have the Midas touch, creating value in all I do.

24. **Financial Abundance Is Mine**: I am surrounded by financial success.

25. **Good Health Is Mine**: I am blessed with vibrant health.

26. **Gratitude Fills My Heart**: I am deeply thankful for all my blessings.

27. **Happiness Is My Natural State**: I am inherently joyful and content.

28. **Harmony Surrounds Me**: My environment is filled with harmony and peace.

29. **Healing Energy Flows Through Me**: I am a conduit for healing and restorative energy.

30. **I Accept Myself Completely**: I embrace and love myself fully.

31. **I Am a Beacon of Love and Light**: I radiate love and positivity to those around me.

32. **I Am a Divine Being of Light**: I recognize my divine nature and inner light.

33. **I Am a Magnet for Success**: I attract success effortlessly.

34. **I Am a Money Magnet**: Financial prosperity flows to me with ease.

35. **I Am a Powerful Creator**: I manifest my desires with confidence.

36. **I Am a Source of Inspiration**: I motivate and inspire others.

37. **I Am a Vibrational Match for Abundance**: I align myself with the frequency of prosperity.

38. **I Am Abundant in All Areas of My Life**: Abundance permeates every aspect of my existence.

39. **I Am Aligned with My Highest Self**: I am in harmony with my true self.

40. **I Am Aligned with the Energy of Abundance**: I vibrate at the frequency of prosperity.

41. **I Am Always Growing and Evolving**: I am constantly progressing and improving.

42. **I Am Always in the Right Place at the Right Time**: I am perfectly positioned to achieve my goals.

43. **I Am Always Learning and Growing**: I continuously expand my knowledge and skills.

44. **I Am Always Protected and Safe**: I am surrounded by a shield of protection.

45. **I Am an Amazing Person**: I acknowledge and celebrate my unique qualities.

46. **I Am an Excellent Problem Solver**: I tackle challenges with skill and confidence.

47. **I Am at Peace with Myself**: I feel calm and content within.

48. **I Am Calm and Centered**: I maintain inner peace and balance.

49. **I Am Capable of Achieving Greatness**: I have the ability to reach my highest potential.

50. **I Am Cherished and Loved**: I am deeply valued and loved.

51. **I Am Confident in My Abilities**: I trust in my skills and talents.

52. **I Am Constantly Attracting Abundance**: Prosperity and wealth come to me naturally.

53. **I Am Deserving of All Good Things**: I believe I deserve happiness and success.

54. **I Am Deserving of Love and Respect**: I am worthy of love and admiration.

55. **I Am Destined for Greatness**: My path leads to remarkable achievements.

56. **I Am Empowered to Create Change**: I have the power to make positive transformations.

57. **I Am Filled with Creativity and Inspiration**: My mind is a wellspring of creative ideas.

58. **I Am Filled with Positive Energy**: I am brimming with positivity and light.

59. **I Am Financially Free**: I enjoy the freedom that comes with financial independence.

60. **I Am Grateful for All My Blessings**: I appreciate all the good in my life.

61. **I Am Grateful for Every Moment**: I cherish each moment of my life.

62. **I Am Happy and Content**: I experience profound joy and satisfaction.

63. **I Am Healthy, Wealthy, and Wise**: I embody health, prosperity, and wisdom.

64. **I Am Living My Best Life**: I am experiencing the best version of my life.

65. **I Am Loved and Appreciated**: I feel deeply loved and valued.

66. **I Am Making a Difference**: My actions have a positive impact on the world.

67. **I Am Open to Infinite Possibilities**: I embrace limitless opportunities.

68. **I Am Open to New Opportunities**: I welcome and seek out new possibilities.

69. **I Am Open to Receiving Love**: I accept love into my life with an open heart.

70. **I Am Optimistic About the Future**: I look forward to what lies ahead with positivity.

71. **I Am Peaceful and Calm**: I embody tranquility and serenity.

72. **I Am Powerful and Courageous**: I face challenges with strength and bravery.

73. **I Am Proud of Who I Am**: I take pride in my unique qualities and achievements.

74. **I Am Safe and Secure**: I feel protected and at ease.
75. **I Am Successful in All That I Do**: Success follows me in every endeavor.
76. **I Am Surrounded by Abundance**: My life is filled with wealth and prosperity.
77. **I Am Surrounded by Love**: Love envelops me in every aspect of my life.
78. **I Am Thankful for My Life**: I deeply appreciate my life and all it offers.
79. **I Am Thriving in Every Way**: I am flourishing in all areas of my life.
80. **I Am Valuable and Worthy**: I recognize my worth and value.
81. **I Attract Positive Energy**: Positive energy flows to me effortlessly.
82. **I Attract Positive People into My Life**: I am surrounded by supportive and loving individuals.
83. **I Attract Wealth and Prosperity**: Financial success comes to me easily.
84. **I Believe in Myself**: I have faith in my abilities and potential.
85. **I Can Achieve Anything I Set My Mind To**: I have the determination to succeed in all my endeavors.
86. **I Choose Happiness**: I actively choose joy and positivity.
87. **I Choose Love Over Fear**: I make decisions based on love, not fear.
88. **I Choose to Be Happy**: I actively embrace joy and positivity.
89. **I Deserve All the Good Things Life Has to Offer**: I am worthy of all life's blessings.
90. **I Deserve Love and Joy**: I am worthy of love and happiness.
91. **I Deserve Success**: I am worthy of achieving my goals.
92. **I Embrace My Unique Qualities**: I celebrate what makes me special.
93. **I Enjoy a Life of Abundance**: My life is filled with wealth and prosperity.
94. **I Experience Love Wherever I Go**: Love surrounds me in all aspects of life.
95. **I Forgive Myself and Others Easily**: I release the past and embrace forgiveness.
96. **I Have a Positive Outlook on Life**: I look at life with optimism.
97. **I Have Abundant Energy**: My energy levels are high and vibrant.
98. **I Have All the Resources I Need**: Everything I need is within my reach.
99. **I Have an Abundance of Love to Share**: My heart overflows with love for others.
100. **I Have an Open Heart and Mind**: I am receptive to new ideas and experiences.
101. **I Have Everything I Need to Be Happy**: My life is complete and fulfilling.
102. **I Have Faith in My Abilities**: I trust in my skills and talents.
103. **I Have Faith in the Universe**: I believe the universe supports my dreams.
104. **I Have Inner Peace and Joy**: I am serene and joyful within.
105. **I Have Limitless Potential**: My possibilities are endless.
106. **I Have the Power to Create My Reality**: I shape my life with my thoughts and actions.
107. **I Live a Life Filled with Love**: My life is abundant with love and compassion.
108. **I Live a Life of Purpose**: I live each day with intention and meaning.
109. **I Live in Abundance**: Prosperity flows in every aspect of my life.
110. **I Live in Harmony with the World Around Me**: I am in balance with my environment.
111. **I Live in the Present Moment**: I focus on the here and now.
112. **I Manifest Abundance with Ease**: I attract prosperity effortlessly.

113. **I Manifest My Desires Effortlessly**: My goals come to fruition easily.

114. **I Naturally Attract Good Things into My Life**: Positivity is drawn to me.

115. **I Radiate Love and Positivity**: I emit love and positive energy.

116. **I Radiate Positive Energy**: I exude positivity in all I do.

117. **I Release All Negative Thoughts**: I let go of negativity and embrace positivity.

118. **I See Beauty in Everything**: I find joy and beauty in all aspects of life.

119. **I See the Good in Everyone**: I recognize the positive qualities in others.

120. **I Surround Myself with Positivity**: My environment is filled with positive energy.

121. **I Trust in the Process of Life**: I have faith in the journey.

122. **I Trust the Timing of My Life**: I believe everything happens at the right time.

123. **I Welcome Abundance into My Life**: I am open to receiving prosperity.

124. **Joy Is My Natural State of Being**: I am inherently joyful and content.

125. **Love and Happiness Are My Birthrights**: I am entitled to love and joy.

126. **My Abilities Are Limitless**: I am capable of achieving anything.

127. **My Actions Are Aligned with My Goals**: I act in ways that support my objectives.

128. **My Body Is Healthy and Strong**: I am physically vibrant and resilient.

129. **My Creativity Is Limitless**: My creative potential knows no bounds.

130. **My Dreams Have Manifested**: My aspirations have come true.

131. **My Energy Is Vibrant and Powerful**: I am full of dynamic and powerful energy.

132. **My Finances Are in Perfect Order**: My financial situation is stable and prosperous.

133. **My Goals Are Within My Reach**: I am capable of achieving my ambitions.

134. **My Heart Is Open to Love**: I am receptive to giving and receiving love.

135. **My Heart Is Overflowing with Joy**: I feel immense joy within my heart.

136. **My Home Is Filled with Love and Peace**: My living space is a sanctuary of love and tranquility.

137. **My Life Is a Beautiful Journey**: I embrace the adventure of life.

138. **My Life Is a Reflection of My Thoughts**: My reality mirrors my mindset.

139. **My Life Is a Wonderful Adventure**: Every day is an exciting new experience.

140. **My Life Is Abundant and Fulfilling**: I enjoy a life rich with satisfaction and happiness.

141. **My Life Is Blessed with Love and Joy**: I am surrounded by love and happiness.

142. **My Life Is Filled with Prosperity**: My life is abundant with wealth.

143. **My Life Is Full of Potential**: I have endless opportunities ahead.

144. **My Life Is Full of Wonderful Surprises**: I am delighted by unexpected joys.

145. **My Mind Is Clear and Focused**: I have a sharp and concentrated mind.

146. **My Mind Is a Powerful Magnet for Ideas**: I attract innovative and creative ideas.

147. **My Needs Are Always Met**: The universe provides for all my needs.

148. **My Path Is Always Clear**: I have a clear direction in life.

149. **My Possibilities Are Endless**: I have limitless opportunities available to me.

150. **My Potential Is Limitless**: I can achieve anything I set my mind to.

151. **My Relationships Are Loving and Supportive**: I have nurturing and positive connections.

152. **My Soul Is at Peace**: I am spiritually serene and content.

153. **Peace and Tranquility Are Mine**: I am calm and at peace within.

154. **Positive Energy Surrounds Me**: I am enveloped by positive energy.

155. **Prosperity Flows to Me in Abundance**: Wealth and success come to me easily.

156. **Success and Abundance Are My Birthrights**: I am inherently deserving of prosperity.

157. **Success Is My Natural State**: Achieving my goals is natural for me.

158. **The Universe Supports Me in Every Way**: I am guided and supported by the universe.

159. **Things Always Work Out for Me**: Everything happens in my favor.

160. **Today Is a Day of Positive Experiences**: I embrace the positivity of today.

161. **Unlimited Possibilities Are Available to Me**: I have endless opportunities at my disposal.

See Chart 98 - Affirmations to Attract Positive Experiences, Master Chart

Archetypes

Exploring Personal Archetypes involves identifying dominant archetypes by reflecting on your behavior, thoughts, and emotions. Journaling instances where specific archetypes influence your actions can help you understand your patterns better. Meditation on different archetypes allows you to connect with your inner self, discovering which archetypes feel most aligned with your core being.

In relationships, recognizing how your archetypes interact with those of your partner, friends, or family can provide valuable insights into dynamics and conflicts. Understanding conflicting archetypes helps in resolving disagreements effectively. Studying cultural archetypes in mythology, folklore, and modern media reveals how these patterns shape stories and characters, providing a broader context for understanding human behavior.

Identifying shadow aspects of your archetypes is crucial for personal growth. Recognizing these hidden, often negative aspects allows you to engage in shadow work, integrating these parts of yourself to achieve balance. Using archetypes for personal growth involves aligning your goals with the strengths of your dominant archetypes and leveraging the wisdom of mentors or the courage of heroes to overcome challenges.

Archetype assessment tools like personality tests (e.g., MBTI, Enneagram) and archetype cards can provide insights into your archetypal patterns. In the workplace, identifying how different archetypes influence leadership styles and teamwork can guide career paths aligned with your dominant archetypes, leading to greater fulfillment.

Creative expression through archetypes, such as writing stories or creating art, allows for exploration and embodiment of different archetypes. Role-playing games or activities offer new perspectives and deeper understanding. Integrating archetypes into daily life involves mindfulness practices to observe how archetypes influence decisions and interactions, and using positive affirmations to reinforce their strengths.

In summary, Archetype Identification is a powerful tool for self-awareness and growth. By exploring and understanding your archetypes, you can gain valuable insights into your behavior, relationships, and personal development. This comprehensive approach to identifying and working with archetypes enriches your journey towards a more balanced and fulfilling life.

1. **Adventurer**: A person who seeks out new and exciting experiences.
2. **Advocate**: Someone who supports or promotes a cause or the interests of others.
3. **Alchemist**: A person who transforms or creates something through seemingly magical processes.
4. **Altruist**: A person unselfishly concerned for or devoted to the welfare of others.
5. **Ambassador**: An official representative or promoter of a specified activity.
6. **Angel**: A benevolent and protective figure, often seen as a messenger of good.
7. **Artist**: A creator of art who expresses ideas and emotions through various mediums.
8. **Athlete**: A person trained or skilled in sports or physical activities.
9. **Benefactor**: A person who gives help or money to a person or cause.
10. **Caregiver**: A person who provides care and support for others, especially the sick or elderly.
11. **Challenger**: Someone who questions or disputes others' views or the status quo.
12. **Child**: An archetype representing innocence, wonder, and new beginnings.
13. **Clown**: A comic entertainer who uses humor to bring joy and laughter.
14. **Companion**: A loyal and trustworthy friend or partner.
15. **Conqueror**: Someone who overcomes obstacles and achieves victory.
16. **Creator**: An individual who brings new things into existence, often through imagination and innovation.
17. **Destroyer**: A force that brings about destruction or radical change.
18. **Detective**: A person who investigates and solves mysteries or crimes.
19. **Dreamer**: Someone who has visionary ideas or aspirations, often with a sense of idealism.
20. **Emperor/Empress**: A ruler or sovereign with absolute power and authority.
21. **Engineer**: A person skilled in designing and building complex systems or structures.
22. **Entertainer**: Someone who performs to amuse or interest an audience.
23. **Entrepreneur**: An individual who starts and operates a business, taking on financial risks.
24. **Explorer**: A person who investigates unknown regions or fields of interest.
25. **Father**: A paternal figure who provides guidance, protection, and support.
26. **Fool**: An archetype representing a person who appears simple but often possesses hidden wisdom.
27. **Gambler**: Someone who takes risks, especially for potential gain.
28. **Guide**: A person who leads or directs others on a journey or through a process.
29. **Healer**: An individual who restores health or harmony.
30. **Hero**: A person noted for courageous acts or nobility of character.
31. **Hermit**: Someone who lives in solitude, often for spiritual purposes.
32. **Innocent**: An archetype representing purity, optimism, and uncorrupted nature.
33. **Inventor**: A person who creates new devices or methods.
34. **Judge**: An individual who makes decisions or passes judgments, often in legal contexts.
35. **King/Queen**: A sovereign leader who commands respect and authority.
36. **Lover**: A person who is passionate and devoted, especially in romantic contexts.

37. **Magician**: Someone who uses knowledge and skills to create transformative experiences.
38. **Martyr**: A person who sacrifices something of great value for the sake of principle.
39. **Mentor**: An experienced and trusted advisor.
40. **Mother**: A nurturing figure who provides love, care, and support.
41. **Mystic**: Someone who seeks spiritual truths or experiences beyond ordinary understanding.
42. **Orphan**: An archetype representing abandonment, resilience, and independence.
43. **Outlaw**: A rebel who defies societal norms and conventions.
44. **Peacemaker**: Someone who seeks to resolve conflicts and promote harmony.
45. **Performer**: An individual who acts, sings, or otherwise entertains.
46. **Pioneer**: A person who is among the first to explore or settle a new area or field.
47. **Protector**: Someone who guards and defends others from harm.
48. **Rebel**: A person who resists authority or control.
49. **Ruler**: A leader who governs or directs others.
50. **Sage**: A wise person with profound knowledge and judgment.
51. **Scholar**: Someone dedicated to learning and knowledge.
52. **Seeker**: An individual who actively searches for truth, wisdom, or spiritual enlightenment.
53. **Servant**: A person who performs duties for others.
54. **Shaman**: A healer who practices traditional spiritual and healing methods.
55. **Storyteller**: Someone who conveys events and experiences through narrative.
56. **Student**: A person who is learning or studying.
57. **Teacher**: Someone who imparts knowledge or skills to others.
58. **Trickster**: An archetype known for cleverness and the ability to deceive.
59. **Visionary**: A person with original ideas about what the future could be like.
60. **Warrior**: A person who fights or is skilled in combat.
61. **Wizard**: Someone who practices magic or has extraordinary powers.

See Chart 108 - Archetypes, Master Chart

Blocks to Dowsing, Clearing & Healing

Navigating the path to effective dowsing, clearing, and healing can be obstructed by a wide array of blocks, each acting as a barrier to our spiritual and emotional wellbeing. From Abandonment Issues that tether our hearts to the past, to the complex web of Akashic Record Contracts shaping our soul's journey, these blocks are as varied as they are deep-rooted. Ancestral Karma and Astral Attachments add layers of complexity, entangling us in energies not entirely our own.

Astrological Transits and Aura Tears influence our energy flow, while deeply held Beliefs and Betrayal Wounds can keep us locked in patterns of pain and mistrust.
The roadblocks extend into our energetic anatomy, with Chakra Blockages and a Closed Third Eye limiting our perception and spiritual connection. Collective Consciousness Energies and Cultural Expectations can silently dictate our life's direction, as can Curses or the subtle but pervasive influence of Electromagnetic Frequencies (EMFs). Even our own body's Cellular Memory holds onto traumas, echoing past hurts through our present. Environmental factors like

Pollution and Toxins, alongside Energetic Imbalances and Emotional Traumas, further complicate our healing journey.

Navigating these myriad blocks requires a nuanced understanding of our multidimensional selves and the realization that healing is not a linear path but a journey of uncovering, understanding, and transforming. Each block, from Dependency on Tools to Disbelief in Abilities, Fear-Based Energies, and even Nutritional Deficiencies, offers an opportunity for growth, urging us to confront and release what no longer serves us. As we do, we gradually peel away the layers of Discordant Energy, Misaligned Intentions, and Unforgiveness that shroud our true essence, stepping closer to a state of balance, clarity, and profound healing.

1. **Abandonment Issues**: Feelings of being left behind or deserted by loved ones.
2. **Addictions**: Dependency on substances or behaviors for emotional relief.
3. **Agreements**: Unspoken or spoken commitments that may limit personal freedom.
4. **Akashic Record Contracts**: Spiritual agreements made in the Akashic Records that impact current life experiences.
5. **Ancestral Karma**: Energetic imprints from ancestors affecting current life situations.
6. **Assumptions**: Beliefs taken for granted without evidence or proof.
7. **Astral Attachments**: Energetic entities attached to one's astral body causing imbalance.
8. **Astrological Transits**: Planetary movements affecting personal energy and life events.
9. **Aura Tears**: Breaks or holes in the auric field, leading to energy leaks.
10. **Beliefs**: Convictions or acceptances that certain things are true or real.
11. **Betrayal Wounds**: Emotional scars from experiencing betrayal or trust violations.
12. **Cellular Memory**: Information stored in cells from past experiences affecting current life.
13. **Chakra Blockages**: Obstructions in the energy centers of the body hindering energy flow.
14. **Clear - Death Program**: Removing subconscious programming related to fear of death.
15. **Clear - Illness Program**: Eliminating ingrained beliefs about chronic illness.
16. **Clear - Injury Program**: Releasing subconscious patterns related to injury.
17. **Closed Third Eye**: Blocked intuition and inability to perceive higher spiritual insights.
18. **Collective Consciousness Energies**: Energies influenced by the collective thoughts and emotions of humanity.
19. **Contracts**: Binding agreements that may limit personal freedom or growth.
20. **Control Issues**: Need to dominate or manipulate situations or people.
21. **Cosmic Dissonance**: Misalignment with cosmic energies causing imbalance.
22. **Cultural Expectations**: Societal norms and pressures that influence behavior and beliefs.
23. **Curses**: Negative energy directed at a person to cause harm or misfortune.
24. **Dehydrated**: Lack of adequate hydration affecting physical and energetic health.
25. **Dependency on Tools**: Over-reliance on external aids for spiritual or emotional support.
26. **Dimensional Interferences**: Disruptions from other dimensions affecting personal energy.
27. **Disbelief in Abilities**: Doubting one's own skills or talents.
28. **Discordant Energy**: Chaotic or unbalanced energy within or around a person.
29. **Disempowerment**: Feeling of losing power or control over one's life.
30. **Don't Want Issue Cleared**: Resistance to releasing or resolving an issue.
31. **Doubt**: Lack of confidence or certainty in oneself or situations.

32. **Educational Limitations**: Constraints imposed by formal education or lack thereof.
33. **Ego**: The part of the mind that mediates between the conscious and the unconscious.
34. **Ego Attachments**: Identifying too strongly with the ego, causing imbalance.
35. **Electromagnetic Frequencies (EMFs)**: Disruptive frequencies from electronic devices affecting health.
36. **Elemental Imbalances**: Disharmony among the basic elements (earth, water, fire, air, ether).
37. **Emotional Traumas**: Deep emotional wounds from past experiences.
38. **Emotions**: Feelings that influence thoughts and behaviors.
39. **Energetic Imbalances**: Disruptions in the flow of energy within the body.
40. **Energy Vampires**: Individuals or entities that drain your energy.
41. **Entity Attachments**: Non-physical beings attached to a person's energy field.
42. **Environmental Toxins**: Harmful substances in the environment affecting health.
43. **Etheric Cord Attachments**: Energetic cords connecting you to others in unhealthy ways.
44. **Fear of Failure**: Anxiety about not succeeding or meeting expectations.
45. **Fear of Success**: Anxiety about the consequences of achieving success.
46. **Fear-Based Energies**: Energies stemming from fear, causing limitations.
47. **Feelings**: Emotional responses to experiences.
48. **Genetic Memory**: Inherited information in genes influencing current life.
49. **Geopathic Stress**: Negative energy from the earth affecting well-being.
50. **Heart Wall Emotions**: Emotional barriers around the heart blocking love and connection.
51. **Hexes**: Spells or curses intended to cause harm.
52. **Hidden**: Issues or energies not easily perceived or recognized.
53. **Hidden Programs**: Subconscious beliefs or patterns affecting behavior.
54. **Hidden Vows**: Unconscious promises made in past lives or this life.
55. **Illusions of Separation**: Belief that one is separate from others or the divine.
56. **Jealousy and Envy**: Negative feelings towards others' success or possessions.
57. **Karmic Debt**: Spiritual debt accrued from past actions.
58. **Lack of Boundaries**: Difficulty in setting or maintaining personal limits.
59. **Lack of Grounding**: Feeling disconnected from the earth or reality.
60. **Lack of Self-Love**: Inability to fully accept and love oneself.
61. **Lack of Support**: Feeling unsupported or alone.
62. **Layers**: Multiple levels of issues or energies affecting a person.
63. **Life Lesson Not Learned**: Repeating patterns due to unlearned life lessons.
64. **Loss of Faith**: Doubting one's beliefs or spiritual path.
65. **Mental Blocks**: Cognitive barriers hindering thinking or progress.
66. **Misaligned Chakras**: Energy centers not properly aligned, causing imbalance.
67. **Misaligned Intentions**: Goals or desires not in harmony with one's true self.
68. **Miscommunication with Guides**: Difficulty in receiving clear messages from spiritual guides.
69. **Misuse of Power**: Abusing one's power or authority.
70. **Negative External Influences**: Harmful influences from outside sources.
71. **Negative Imprints**: Unwanted energetic marks left by past experiences.
72. **Negative Lifestyle Habits**: Unhealthy behaviors affecting well-being.
73. **Negative Thought Forms**: Persistent negative thinking patterns.

74. **Not Grounded**: Disconnection from the physical world.
75. **Not Willing to Forgive Others**: Inability to let go of grudges or resentment.
76. **Not Willing to Forgive Self**: Holding onto self-blame or guilt.
77. **Nutritional Deficiencies**: Lack of essential nutrients affecting health.
78. **Oaths and Pledges**: Binding promises affecting current life.
79. **Obligations**: Duties or commitments that may feel burdensome.
80. **Obsessions**: Persistent and intrusive thoughts or behaviors.
81. **Overwhelm and Stress**: Feeling excessively burdened or pressured.
82. **Past Life Imprints**: Energetic marks from past lives affecting the present.
83. **Past Life Trauma**: Unresolved traumas from previous incarnations.
84. **Past Life Vows**: Promises made in past lives influencing the current life.
85. **Past-Life Contracts**: Agreements from past lives affecting current experiences.
86. **Past-Life Issues**: Problems originating in past incarnations.
87. **Past-Life Relationships**: Connections with people from previous lives.
88. **Permissions**: Required consent to proceed with healing or changes.
89. **Physic Cord**: Energetic connections between people affecting well-being.
90. **Physical Ailments**: Bodily conditions or diseases.
91. **Physical Inactivity**: Lack of physical movement affecting health.
92. **Planetary Shifts**: Changes in planetary alignments impacting energy.
93. **Pride and Arrogance**: Excessive self-importance or entitlement.
94. **Program**: Ingrained patterns or behaviors.
95. **Program Rebuilding**: Reconstructing healthier patterns or behaviors.
96. **Promises**: Commitments that may limit or influence actions.
97. **Psychic Attacks**: Negative energy directed at a person to cause harm.
98. **Psychic Cords**: Energetic connections affecting personal energy.
99. **Psychic Debts: Energetic obligations owed to others.**
100. **Rejection Sensitivities**: Heightened sensitivity to perceived rejection.
101. **Religious Beliefs**: Faith-based convictions influencing behavior and thoughts.
102. **Religious Dogmas**: Rigid religious rules or doctrines.
103. **Replace Higher Self Helpers**: Substituting guides assisting the higher self.
104. **Replace Spirit Guides**: Changing the spiritual guides aiding a person.
105. **Request Help - Archangels**: Seeking assistance from archangels.
106. **Request Help - Doctor**: Seeking medical or health professional aid.
107. **Request Help - Energy**: Asking for energetic support or healing.
108. **Request Help - Expert**: Consulting a specialist for guidance or assistance.
109. **Resistance to Change**: Reluctance to adapt to new circumstances.
110. **Skepticism or Doubt**: Lack of belief or trust in abilities or outcomes.
111. **Self-Punishment**: Inflicting harm or suffering on oneself.
112. **Shadow Selves**: Repressed aspects of oneself causing imbalance.
113. **Sleep Deprivation**: Lack of sufficient sleep affecting health and well-being.
114. **Societal Conditioning**: Influence of societal norms and expectations.
115. **Solar and Lunar Influences**: Impact of the sun and moon on personal energy.
116. **Soul Contract**: Spiritual agreements affecting current life experiences.
117. **Soul Fragmentation**: Parts of the soul separated due to trauma.
118. **Soul Loss**: Disconnection from parts of the soul affecting wholeness.
119. **Soul Promises**: Spiritual commitments made by the soul.

120. **Spell**: Energetic manipulation intended to cause specific outcomes.
121. **Spiritual Bypassing**: Avoiding emotional work by focusing only on spirituality.
122. **Spiritual Contracts**: Agreements made on a spiritual level affecting life.
123. **Spiritual Disconnection**: Feeling disconnected from spiritual beliefs or practices.
124. **Subconscious Beliefs**: Deep-seated beliefs held in the subconscious mind.
125. **Suppressed Anger**: Repressed feelings of anger causing emotional blocks.
126. **Take Responsibility**: Accepting accountability for one's actions and life.
127. **Technological Dependencies**: Over-reliance on technology affecting well-being.
128. **Thought Forms**: Manifested energy from persistent thoughts.
129. **Time Loop Cycles**: Repeating patterns of behavior or experiences over time.
130. **Tired**: Feeling exhausted or lacking energy.
131. **Unforgiveness**: Inability to forgive oneself or others.
132. **Unhealed Inner Child**: Unresolved childhood issues affecting adult life.
133. **Unresolved Grief**: Lingering sorrow from past losses.
134. **Unwillingness to Accept Change**: Resistance to new situations or transformations.
135. **Victim Mentality**: Perceiving oneself as a victim of circumstances.
136. **Vows**: Solemn promises or pledges affecting one's life.
137. **Vows of Poverty**: Commitments to live in poverty, often from past lives.

See Chart 112 - Blocks to Dowsing, Clearing & Healing, Master Chart

Colors

Colors have a profound impact on our vibration, either elevating our energy or holding us back. Each color carries a specific frequency that can influence our emotions, thoughts, and overall well-being. For instance, vibrant colors like aquamarine, gold, and sapphire can uplift our spirits and promote positivity, while darker hues like charcoal and midnight blue may induce a more subdued or introspective state. When using this color chart, it is essential to dowse or intuitively ask whether wearing a particular color would be in your highest and best good. If you receive a 'no,' follow up by asking if avoiding that color would be beneficial. This approach ensures that you are aligning with the colors that best support your energetic needs and avoiding those that may not be conducive to your personal growth and well-being.

Colors not only affect our external appearance but also resonate with our internal energy systems, particularly the chakras. Each chakra is associated with a specific color, and by wearing or surrounding ourselves with these colors, we can stimulate and balance these energy centers. For example, wearing red can invigorate the root chakra, promoting feelings of security and groundedness, while green can harmonize the heart chakra, enhancing love and compassion. It's important to recognize that our color preferences and needs may change over time, reflecting shifts in our emotional and energetic states. Regularly checking in with your intuitive guidance or using tools like dowsing can help you stay attuned to the colors that will best support your current state of being.

Furthermore, the impact of colors extends beyond clothing to our environment. The colors we choose for our homes, workplaces, and even our digital interfaces can significantly influence our mood and energy levels. Incorporating colors that align with your desired vibration can create a supportive atmosphere that nurtures your well-being. For instance, decorating your workspace with calming blues or energizing yellows can enhance productivity and creativity. By consciously selecting colors that resonate with your energetic needs, you can create spaces that not only reflect your personal style but also promote harmony and balance.

Incorporating color into your vibrational practice is a simple yet powerful way to enhance your ascension journey. Whether through clothing, accessories, or your living environment, mindful use of color can elevate your energy and support your overall well-being. Trust in your intuition and the guidance you receive from dowsing to make color choices that align with your highest good. By doing so, you can harness the vibrational power of colors to facilitate healing, growth, and transformation.

See Chart 120 - Colors, Master Chart

Colors, What to do With

Colors can profoundly influence our mood, energy, and overall well-being, making it essential to use them intentionally in various aspects of our lives. Incorporate colors in your clothing to uplift your spirit and reflect your personality. In home decor, choose colors that create a welcoming and harmonious environment, while in meditation spaces, use hues that promote peace and concentration. Enhance your living space with colorful bed linens, pillows, and throws for added comfort and aesthetic appeal. Utilize colored lights and candles to set the desired ambiance, and select wall paint that complements the atmosphere you wish to create. Engage in art therapy using a vibrant palette to express and process emotions. Surround yourself with nature's colors for rejuvenation, and make mindful choices in office supplies and digital interfaces to boost productivity and reduce eye strain. In personal care, consider hair color and makeup that highlight your features and express your style. Enjoy colorful foods for their nutritional benefits and visual appeal, and use colored bath salts and oils to enhance relaxation or energy during baths. Whether through yoga mats, window tints, or vehicle colors, thoughtfully integrating colors into your daily life can significantly raise your vibration and promote overall harmony.

1. **Aquariums**: Use specific colors in aquariums to create a calming environment.
2. **Art Therapy**: Incorporate various colors in art therapy to express and process emotions.
3. **Bath Salts and Oils**: Choose bath salts and oils with colors that enhance relaxation or energy.
4. **Bed Linens**: Select bed linens in colors that promote restful sleep or invigorate your mornings.
5. **Book Covers**: Design book covers with colors that attract attention and convey the book's theme.
6. **Candles**: Light candles in colors that match your mood or desired ambiance.
7. **Clothing**: Wear clothing in colors that uplift your spirit and complement your energy.
8. **Colored Baths**: Take baths with colored water to soothe or energize your body and mind.
9. **Colored Glasses**: Use colored glasses to influence your perception and mood.
10. **Colored Lights**: Install colored lights to create specific atmospheres in your living spaces.
11. **Colored Pens and Markers**: Use colored pens and markers to make your writing and drawings more vibrant.
12. **Crystals**: Choose crystals in colors that resonate with your healing needs.

13. **Digital Interfaces**: Customize digital interfaces with colors that are visually pleasing and reduce eye strain.
14. **Drinks**: Opt for drinks with natural colors that boost your energy and health.
15. **Flower Arrangements**: Arrange flowers in colors that enhance the aesthetic and energy of your space.
16. **Hair Color**: Dye your hair in colors that reflect your personality and boost your confidence.
17. **Home Decor**: Decorate your home with colors that create a welcoming and harmonious environment.
18. **Jewelry**: Wear jewelry with colored stones that align with your intentions and desires.
19. **Makeup**: Apply makeup in colors that enhance your features and express your style.
20. **Meditation Spaces**: Decorate your meditation space with colors that promote peace and concentration.
21. **Nature's Colors**: Surround yourself with nature's colors to rejuvenate your mind and body.
22. **Office Supplies**: Choose office supplies in colors that increase productivity and creativity.
23. **Pillows and Throws**: Add pillows and throws in colors that make your living spaces cozy and inviting.
24. **Shoes**: Wear shoes in colors that complement your outfit and boost your mood.
25. **Stationery**: Use stationery in colors that make your correspondence more enjoyable.
26. **Vehicle Colors**: Select vehicle colors that reflect your personality and make you feel good.
27. **Wall Paint**: Paint walls in colors that create the desired ambiance in your home or office.
28. **What You Eat**: Include colorful foods in your diet to enhance nutrition and enjoyment.
29. **Window Tints**: Apply window tints in colors that improve privacy and reduce glare.
30. **Yoga Mats**: Use yoga mats in colors that inspire you and enhance your practice.

See Chart 126 Colors, - What to do with, Master Chart

Cultivate a Positive Mindset

Cultivating a positive mindset is a powerful way to raise your vibration and improve your overall well-being. By focusing on positive thoughts and attitudes, you can transform your energy and attract more uplifting experiences into your life. Practicing gratitude, embracing affirmations, and acknowledging your strengths can help shift your perspective from lack to abundance. Avoiding negative self-talk and comparisons while being kind and patient with yourself can enhance your self-esteem and resilience. Engaging in positive activities, like creating a vision board or helping others, can also boost your mood and energy. Ultimately, a positive mindset enables you to navigate challenges with grace and maintain a higher vibrational frequency, fostering a more joyful and fulfilling life.

1. **Accept compliments**: Embrace praise with gratitude and acknowledgment.
2. **Accept imperfection**: Embrace your flaws and see them as part of your uniqueness.
3. **Acknowledge achievements**: Recognize and celebrate your successes.
4. **Affirmations**: Use positive statements to boost your self-belief.

5. **Appreciate your strengths**: Focus on and value your unique abilities.
6. **Avoid comparisons**: Focus on your journey without measuring against others.
7. **Avoid negative self-talk**: Replace self-criticism with supportive thoughts.
8. **Be grateful**: Cultivate a habit of gratitude for all aspects of life.
9. **Be kind to yourself**: Treat yourself with compassion and care.
10. **Be patient**: Allow time for growth and healing without rushing.
11. **Be respectful**: Show consideration and respect to yourself and others.
12. **Be supportive**: Offer help and encouragement to those around you.
13. **Be understanding**: Practice empathy and understanding in interactions.
14. **Bring flowers**: Brighten your space or someone's day with flowers.
15. **Bring treats to work**: Share joy by bringing treats for colleagues.
16. **Build positive habits**: Establish routines that promote well-being.
17. **Buy a gift**: Show appreciation by gifting something thoughtful.
18. **Buy extra groceries**: Purchase additional groceries to share or donate.
19. **Buy local**: Support local businesses and their positive impact.
20. **Buy someone's coffee**: Perform a kind act by buying coffee for someone.
21. **Celebrate small wins**: Acknowledge and rejoice in small achievements.
22. **Challenge negative thoughts**: Confront and reframe negative thinking.
23. **Change your perspective**: Shift your viewpoint to see things positively.
24. **Clean a public space**: Improve the environment by cleaning communal areas.
25. **Compliment a child**: Boost a child's confidence with sincere praise.
26. **Compliment someone**: Spread positivity by complimenting others.
27. **Connect with loved ones**: Strengthen bonds by spending time with family and friends.
28. **Cook a meal**: Nourish yourself and others with a homemade meal.
29. **Create a vision board**: Visualize and manifest your goals with a vision board.
30. **Create care packages**: Assemble and give care packages to those in need.
31. **Create handmade gifts**: Craft personalized gifts to show appreciation.
32. **Declutter your mind**: Clear mental clutter through mindfulness or journaling.
33. **Declutter your space**: Organize and tidy your living environment.
34. **Develop a growth mindset**: Embrace learning and improvement.
35. **Develop resilience**: Strengthen your ability to recover from setbacks.
36. **Do something creative**: Engage in creative activities to boost your mood.
37. **Do something fun**: Enjoy activities that bring you joy.
38. **Donate art supplies**: Provide materials for creative expression to those in need.
39. **Donate blood**: Save lives by donating blood.
40. **Donate books**: Share knowledge and joy by donating books.
41. **Donate clothes**: Give unused clothing to those who need it.
42. **Donate eyeglasses**: Help others see better by donating glasses.
43. **Donate food**: Provide sustenance to the hungry by donating food.
44. **Donate medical supplies**: Support healthcare with donated medical items.
45. **Donate pet supplies**: Assist animal shelters with needed supplies.
46. **Donate school supplies**: Equip students for success by donating supplies.
47. **Donate toys**: Bring joy to children by donating toys.
48. **Donate to education**: Support educational initiatives and institutions.
49. **Donate to medical research**: Fund research for medical advancements.
50. **Donate to shelters**: Assist shelters with donations to support the homeless.

51. **Drive someone**: Offer transportation to those who need it.
52. **Eat healthily**: Nourish your body with nutritious food.
53. **Embrace change**: Adapt to new situations with a positive outlook.
54. **Encourage creativity**: Inspire others to express themselves creatively.
55. **Encourage others**: Support and uplift those around you.
56. **Encourage recycling**: Promote environmental health by recycling.
57. **Engage in hobbies**: Pursue activities that bring joy and fulfillment.
58. **Engage in positive self-reflection**: Reflect on your strengths and progress.
59. **Establish a morning routine**: Start your day positively with a set routine.
60. **Exercise gratitude**: Regularly practice being thankful.
61. **Exercise regularly**: Maintain physical health through regular activity.
62. **Feed the hungry**: Help those in need by providing food.
63. **Find a positive mantra**: Use uplifting phrases to inspire yourself.
64. **Focus on solutions**: Direct energy toward finding solutions, not problems.
65. **Forgive yourself**: Release guilt and embrace self-compassion.
66. **Get a mentor**: Seek guidance and support from experienced individuals.
67. **Get enough sleep**: Prioritize rest to maintain health and energy.
68. **Give back**: Contribute to your community through acts of service.
69. **Help a coworker**: Offer assistance to colleagues.
70. **Help a student**: Provide support and guidance to students.
71. **Help carry groceries**: Assist others with their shopping bags.
72. **Help during a crisis**: Be there for others in times of need.
73. **Help during a move**: Offer your help to those relocating.
74. **Help others**: Be of service in any way you can.
75. **Identify positive role models**: Look up to and learn from inspiring individuals.
76. **Journal**: Write down your thoughts and experiences to process emotions.
77. **Keep a gratitude journal**: Regularly note things you are thankful for.
78. **Laugh often**: Increase joy and reduce stress through laughter.
79. **Learn from failure**: See failures as opportunities for growth.
80. **Learn something new**: Expand your knowledge and skills.
81. **Limit exposure to negativity**: Avoid negative influences and environments.
82. **Limit social media**: Reduce time spent on social platforms.
83. **Listen actively**: Give full attention when communicating with others.
84. **Listen to uplifting music**: Enhance your mood with positive tunes.
85. **Live in the moment**: Focus on the present and enjoy each moment.
86. **Make time for relaxation**: Ensure you have time to unwind and relax.
87. **Meditate**: Practice meditation to calm the mind and elevate your spirit.
88. **Mindfulness**: Be fully present and aware in each moment.
89. **Monitor your media intake**: Be mindful of the content you consume.
90. **Network with positive people**: Surround yourself with uplifting individuals.
91. **Practice deep breathing**: Use breathing exercises to reduce stress.
92. **Practice empathy**: Understand and share the feelings of others.
93. **Practice patience**: Cultivate patience in all aspects of life.
94. **Practice positive affirmations**: Reinforce positive beliefs about yourself.
95. **Practice self-care**: Take actions that promote your health and well-being.
96. **Practice self-compassion**: Be kind and understanding to yourself.

97. **Practice self-discipline**: Develop control over your actions and decisions.
98. **Prioritize tasks**: Organize tasks by importance to manage time effectively.
99. **Read inspirational books**: Gain motivation and insight from uplifting literature.
100. **Recognize your progress**: Acknowledge how far you have come.
101. **Reflect on positive experiences**: Recall and savor positive moments.
102. **Reframe negative situations**: View challenges as opportunities.
103. **Say positive things to others**: Spread positivity through your words.
104. **Set achievable goals**: Create realistic and attainable objectives.
105. **Set boundaries**: Define and maintain personal limits.
106. **Share positivity**: Spread good vibes in your interactions.
107. **Simplify your life**: Reduce complexity to focus on what matters.
108. **Smile often**: Brighten your day and others' with smiles.
109. **Spend time in nature**: Connect with the natural world for rejuvenation.
110. **Spend time with positive people**: Surround yourself with uplifting friends.
111. **Start a new hobby**: Engage in new activities for enjoyment.
112. **Stay hydrated**: Drink plenty of water to maintain health.
113. **Surround yourself with positivity**: Create an uplifting environment.
114. **Take breaks**: Rest regularly to avoid burnout.
115. **Take care of your body**: Maintain physical health through self-care.
116. **Take responsibility**: Own your actions and their outcomes.
117. **Take risks**: Embrace challenges and step out of your comfort zone.
118. **Talk positively to yourself**: Use affirming language in self-talk.
119. **Talk to a therapist**: Seek professional help when needed.
120. **Think about what you can control**: Focus on aspects within your influence.
121. **Think positive thoughts**: Cultivate a mindset of positivity.
122. **Trust yourself**: Have confidence in your abilities and decisions.
123. **Try new things**: Explore new experiences and opportunities.
124. **Unplug from technology**: Take breaks from screens and devices.
125. **Use humor**: Lighten situations with laughter and joy.
126. **Use positive language**: Speak in an uplifting and encouraging manner.
127. **Value your worth**: Recognize and appreciate your inherent value.
128. **Visualize success**: Imagine achieving your goals.
129. **Visualize your goals**: Picture your desired outcomes vividly.
130. **Volunteer**: Give your time and effort to help others.
131. **Walk in nature**: Enjoy the serenity and beauty of the outdoors.
132. **Watch inspiring movies**: Gain motivation from uplifting films.
133. **Write down your goals**: Clarify your objectives by writing them down.
134. **Write thank-you notes**: Express gratitude through written messages.
135. **Yoga**: Practice yoga to enhance physical and mental well-being.

See Chart 129 - Cultivate a Positive Mindset, Master Chart

Developing Intuition

Developing intuition is an empowering process that enables individuals to tap into their innate wisdom and inner guidance. By enhancing one's intuitive abilities, a person can make more informed decisions, navigate life's challenges with greater ease, and cultivate a deeper connection with their true self. Various practices and techniques can help strengthen intuition, such as meditation, journaling, and mindfulness practices. These methods encourage individuals to quiet the mind, focus on their inner experiences, and become more attuned to subtle signals from their subconscious and higher consciousness.

In addition to traditional practices, there are numerous innovative and holistic approaches to developing intuition. Activities like forest bathing, intuitive dancing, and energy healing provide unique ways to connect with one's inner guidance. Techniques such as hypnotherapy and biofeedback training offer scientifically supported methods to enhance intuitive awareness. By exploring and incorporating a diverse range of practices, individuals can develop a more robust and reliable intuitive sense, ultimately leading to greater personal growth, clarity, and fulfillment.

1. **Active listening**: Fully concentrating, understanding, responding, and remembering what is being said in a conversation.
2. **Affirmations**: Positive statements that can help challenge and overcome self-sabotaging and negative thoughts.
3. **Art therapy**: Using creative processes of making art to improve mental, emotional, and physical well-being.
4. **Automatic writing**: Writing without conscious thought, often believed to be guided by the subconscious or spiritual influences.
5. **Biofeedback training**: A technique that teaches control over physiological functions by providing real-time feedback on body processes.
6. **Body scanning**: A mindfulness practice involving paying attention to sensations in the body, usually from head to toe.
7. **Breathing exercises**: Techniques focused on controlling breath to enhance mental, emotional, and physical health.
8. **Candle gazing**: A meditation practice that involves focusing on the flame of a candle to quiet the mind and enhance concentration.
9. **Chakra balancing**: Techniques aimed at aligning and harmonizing the body's energy centers to promote overall well-being.
10. **Contemplative reading**: Reading with deep reflection and thought to gain insight and understanding.
11. **Crystal healing**: Using crystals and gemstones to promote physical, emotional, and spiritual healing.
12. **Dowsing**: A technique for finding water, minerals, or other hidden objects by using a divining rod or pendulum.
13. **Dream journaling**: Recording dreams to explore and understand subconscious messages and themes.
14. **Emotional freedom techniques (EFT)**: A form of psychological acupressure to optimize emotional health.
15. **Energy healing**: Practices like Reiki or pranic healing that manipulate the body's energy fields to promote healing.
16. **Energy medicine practices**: Techniques that involve working with the body's energy systems to enhance health and well-being.
17. **Essential oils**: Concentrated plant extracts used for aromatherapy and other healing purposes.

18. **Fasting**: Voluntarily abstaining from food for a set period to promote physical and spiritual benefits.
19. **Forest bathing**: Immersing oneself in nature, particularly forests, to improve mental and physical health.
20. **Grounding exercises**: Techniques to connect with the Earth's energy, promoting physical and emotional balance.
21. **Guided imagery**: Visualization techniques designed to promote relaxation and positive outcomes.
22. **Herbal teas for relaxation**: Teas made from herbs known for their calming and stress-reducing properties.
23. **Hypnotherapy**: A therapeutic technique that uses hypnosis to create a state of focused attention and increased suggestibility.
24. **Inner child work**: Therapeutic work focused on healing past traumas and nurturing the inner child within.
25. **Intuitive dancing**: Free-form dancing that encourages expression and connection with inner feelings and intuition.
26. **Journaling**: Writing down thoughts, feelings, and experiences to gain insight and clarity.
27. **Journaling with prompts**: Using specific prompts or questions to guide journaling for deeper self-exploration.
28. **Labyrinth walking**: Walking a labyrinth as a form of meditation and contemplation to gain insight and clarity.
29. **Listening to inner voice**: Tuning into one's inner thoughts and feelings for guidance and direction.
30. **Mandala coloring**: Coloring intricate patterns to promote mindfulness and relaxation.
31. **Mantra chanting**: Repeating specific sounds or phrases to focus the mind and enhance spiritual connection.
32. **Meditation**: A practice of focused attention and awareness to achieve a mentally clear and emotionally calm state.
33. **Mindfulness practices**: Techniques aimed at bringing one's attention to the present moment.
34. **Mirror gazing**: Looking into a mirror to connect with oneself and gain deeper self-awareness.
35. **Muscle testing**: A technique used in kinesiology to test the body's responses to various stimuli for guidance.
36. **Nature walks**: Walking in natural settings to promote relaxation and mental clarity.
37. **Oracle cards**: Cards used for divination and gaining insight into one's life and future.
38. **Pendulum work**: Using a pendulum to gain answers and guidance from the subconscious mind.
39. **Prayer**: Communicating with a higher power for guidance, support, and reflection.
40. **Psychic development classes**: Classes designed to enhance one's psychic and intuitive abilities.
41. **Qi Gong**: A Chinese practice involving coordinated movements, breathing, and meditation to cultivate life energy.
42. **Reiki**: A Japanese technique for stress reduction and relaxation that also promotes healing.

43. **Remote viewing**: The practice of seeking impressions about a distant or unseen target using extrasensory perception.
44. **Rituals and ceremonies**: Structured activities performed with intention to connect with the spiritual realm.
45. **Scrying**: Using reflective surfaces like mirrors or water to gain insight or predict the future.
46. **Sensory deprivation**: Reducing sensory input to heighten awareness of inner thoughts and feelings.
47. **Sensory enhancement techniques**: Practices that sharpen the senses to improve intuitive abilities.
48. **Shamanic journeying**: A practice involving entering altered states of consciousness to interact with the spirit world.
49. **Silent retreats**: Periods of silence to facilitate deep introspection and spiritual growth.
50. **Singing bowls**: Using the sound vibrations of bowls to promote relaxation and healing.
51. **Sound healing**: Using sound vibrations to promote physical, emotional, and spiritual healing.
52. **Spirit guide meditation**: Meditative practices aimed at connecting with spirit guides for insight and guidance.
53. **Tai Chi**: A Chinese martial art practiced for its health benefits, focusing on slow, deliberate movements and meditation.
54. **Tarot reading**: Using tarot cards to gain insight into past, present, and future situations.
55. **Theta healing**: A meditation technique aimed at achieving physical, psychological, and spiritual healing.
56. **Trataka (fixed-gaze meditation)**: Focusing on a single point to enhance concentration and mental clarity.
57. **Tuning forks**: Using the sound frequencies of tuning forks to balance energy fields and promote healing.
58. **Visualization**: Creating mental images to influence physical reality and achieve personal goals.
59. **Yoga**: A physical, mental, and spiritual practice that includes breath control, meditation, and body postures.

See Chart 139 - Developing Intuition, Master Chart

Dream Analysis

Dream analysis is a profound method of uncovering the subconscious mind's hidden messages through the exploration of dreams. It involves various techniques to interpret and understand the symbols, emotions, and themes presented in dreams. By delving into dream analysis, one can gain insights into their inner world, revealing unresolved issues, hidden desires, and potential paths for personal growth. The process of dream analysis can be therapeutic, offering a deeper understanding of oneself and fostering psychological healing. It can also serve as a tool for creativity and problem-solving, allowing individuals to tap into their subconscious wisdom and apply it to their waking lives.

The methods of dream analysis range from classic psychoanalytic approaches to modern techniques that incorporate cultural and personal symbolism. Understanding the archetypes, recurring themes, and emotional content of dreams can lead to significant breakthroughs in self-awareness and emotional well-being. Dream journaling, free association, and guided imagery are some of the common practices used to analyze dreams. Each method provides a unique lens through which to view the dream's content, helping to unravel its deeper meaning. By consistently engaging in dream analysis, individuals can enhance their emotional intelligence, resolve inner conflicts, and achieve a more harmonious state of mind.

1. **Archetype Identification**: Recognizing universal symbols and themes in dreams that represent fundamental human experiences.
2. **Art Interpretation**: Using artistic expression to represent and understand dreams.
3. **Association Techniques**: Linking dream symbols to personal experiences and emotions.
4. **Behavioral Patterns**: Observing and interpreting patterns of behavior within dreams.
5. **Carl Jung's Approach**: A method of dream analysis focusing on archetypes and the collective unconscious.
6. **Color Analysis**: Examining the significance of colors in dreams and their emotional impact.
7. **Creative Journaling**: Writing creatively about dreams to explore their meaning.
8. **Cultural Symbolism**: Understanding dream symbols within the context of cultural beliefs and traditions.
9. **Dream Dictionary Usage**: Referencing dream dictionaries to find common interpretations of dream symbols.
10. **Dream Journaling**: Keeping a detailed record of dreams to identify patterns and themes.
11. **Emotional Mapping**: Charting the emotions experienced in dreams to uncover underlying issues.
12. **Environmental Influence**: Analyzing how one's surroundings influence dreams.
13. **Event Correlation**: Linking dream events to real-life occurrences.
14. **Free Association**: A psychoanalytic technique where individuals say whatever comes to mind in relation to dream symbols.
15. **Freud's Theory**: Sigmund Freud's approach to dream analysis, focusing on unconscious desires and conflicts.
16. **Guided Imagery**: Using mental visualization to explore and interpret dreams.
17. **Historical Context**: Considering historical events and personal history in dream interpretation.
18. **Hypnotherapy Sessions**: Using hypnosis to delve deeper into dream content and meaning.
19. **Identifying Recurring Themes**: Noticing and interpreting themes that repeatedly appear in dreams.
20. **Imagery Rehearsal Therapy**: A technique for changing the narrative of disturbing dreams.
21. **Inner Dialogue**: Engaging in a conversation with characters or elements within a dream.
22. **Interpretation Sessions**: Working with a therapist or analyst to interpret dreams.

23. **Lucid Dreaming Practice**: Developing the ability to control and consciously experience dreams.
24. **Meditation Techniques**: Using meditation to enhance dream recall and insight.
25. **Memory Integration**: Integrating dream memories with waking life experiences.
26. **Metaphor Exploration**: Interpreting dreams through the lens of metaphorical meaning.
27. **Mind Mapping**: Creating visual diagrams to explore connections in dream content.
28. **Mood Tracking**: Monitoring emotional responses to dreams over time.
29. **Mythological Analysis**: Interpreting dreams using mythology and folklore.
30. **Narrative Reconstruction**: Rewriting dream narratives to gain insight and resolution.
31. **Nightmares Analysis**: Understanding and addressing the causes of nightmares.
32. **Object Symbolism**: Interpreting the symbolic meaning of objects in dreams.
33. **Pattern Recognition**: Identifying and understanding patterns in dream content.
34. **Personal Symbol Analysis**: Interpreting symbols based on personal significance.
35. **Pre-Sleep Intentions**: Setting intentions before sleep to influence dream content.
36. **Projection Identification**: Recognizing aspects of oneself projected onto dream characters.
37. **Psychoanalytic Approach**: Using psychoanalytic theories to interpret dreams.
38. **Reality Checks**: Practicing techniques to distinguish between dreams and reality.
39. **Recurring Dream Tracking**: Keeping track of dreams that recur to understand their significance.
40. **Reflective Writing**: Writing reflectively about dreams to uncover deeper meaning.
41. **Relationship Analysis**: Exploring relationships within dreams to gain insights into real-life relationships.
42. **Relaxation Techniques**: Using relaxation methods to improve dream recall and analysis.
43. **REM Sleep Analysis**: Studying the rapid eye movement (REM) phase of sleep when dreaming occurs.
44. **Sensory Details**: Analyzing sensory experiences within dreams.
45. **Shadow Work**: Exploring the darker, hidden aspects of the psyche through dream analysis.
46. **Sleep Environment Optimization**: Creating an optimal sleep environment to enhance dream recall.
47. **Sleep Hygiene**: Maintaining healthy sleep habits to improve dream quality and recall.
48. **Spiritual Interpretation**: Interpreting dreams from a spiritual or metaphysical perspective.
49. **Symbol Analysis**: Analyzing the meaning of symbols within dreams.
50. **Synchronicity Exploration**: Investigating meaningful coincidences related to dreams.
51. **Tarot Card Interpretation**: Using tarot cards to gain insights into dream meanings.
52. **Thematic Analysis**: Identifying and interpreting overarching themes in dreams.
53. **Therapeutic Techniques**: Using various therapeutic methods to analyze and work through dreams.
54. **Trigger Identification**: Recognizing and understanding triggers for certain dreams.
55. **Visualization Techniques**: Using visualization to recall and interpret dreams.
56. **Word Association**: Associating words with dream symbols to uncover hidden meanings.

See Chart 144 - Dream Analysis, Master Chart

Emotional Baggage

Emotional baggage refers to the unresolved emotional turmoil and psychological burdens that individuals carry with them from past experiences. This can include a wide range of negative emotions such as anger, fear, guilt, sadness, and shame, which are often tied to specific events or relationships that have left a lasting impact. These unresolved emotions can manifest in various ways, affecting a person's thoughts, behaviors, and overall well-being. Emotional baggage can weigh heavily on an individual, influencing their reactions and interactions in current situations. It often leads to patterns of negative thinking and behavior that can hinder personal growth and the ability to form healthy relationships.

Clearing emotional baggage is crucial for several reasons. Firstly, it allows individuals to break free from the past and live more fully in the present. By addressing and releasing these pent-up emotions, people can alleviate the constant undercurrent of stress and anxiety that emotional baggage can cause. This process fosters emotional healing, leading to improved mental health and well-being. Moreover, clearing emotional baggage enables individuals to build healthier relationships and make better life choices, unencumbered by the shadows of past traumas and disappointments. Ultimately, letting go of emotional baggage paves the way for personal transformation and the ability to achieve one's fullest potential, free from the constraints of past wounds.

1. **The Abandoned**: Someone who feels left alone or deserted, often experiencing deep emotional pain and a sense of rejection due to being left by someone they trusted or loved.
2. **The Abandoned Child**: A child who feels deserted by their caregivers, leading to deep feelings of hurt, rejection, and loneliness.
3. **The Abandoned Friend**: An individual who feels left behind or ignored by a close friend, leading to feelings of betrayal and sadness.
4. **The Abandoned Partner**: Someone who feels deserted by their romantic partner, leading to feelings of hurt, rejection, and loneliness.
5. **The Abused**: An individual who has been subjected to harmful or violent behavior, resulting in physical, emotional, or psychological trauma.
6. **The Angry Monster**: A person whose anger is intense and uncontrollable, often leading to destructive or harmful behavior towards themselves or others.
7. **The Anxious Achiever**: Someone who is driven to succeed but constantly feels anxious and fearful of failure, leading to high stress and pressure.
8. **The Anxious Adult**: An adult who frequently experiences anxiety, worrying about various aspects of life, often impacting their ability to function normally.
9. **The Anxious Overthinker**: A person who excessively thinks and worries about situations, leading to heightened anxiety and often paralysis by analysis.
10. **The Ashamed**: Someone who feels deep regret and humiliation over their actions, beliefs, or characteristics, often leading to low self-esteem and self-worth.
11. **The Betrayed**: An individual who feels profoundly hurt and deceived by someone they trusted, resulting in feelings of anger, sadness, and mistrust.
12. **The Blamed**: Someone who is frequently held responsible for mistakes or problems, leading to feelings of guilt, frustration, and inadequacy.
13. **The Bullied**: An individual who has been persistently targeted by aggressive behavior, resulting in emotional or physical harm and feelings of powerlessness.

14. **The Bully**: A person who habitually seeks to harm or intimidate others, often driven by their insecurities, anger, or need for control.
15. **The Condemned**: Someone who feels judged and sentenced harshly by others, leading to feelings of hopelessness, shame, and isolation.
16. **The Criticized**: An individual who often receives negative feedback or disapproval, leading to feelings of inadequacy and self-doubt.
17. **The Cynic**: A person who has a negative outlook on life and often distrusts the motives of others, leading to feelings of bitterness and detachment.
18. **The Depressed Dreamer**: Someone who has aspirations and dreams but feels weighed down by feelings of depression, making it hard to pursue their goals.
19. **The Desperate**: An individual who feels a sense of urgency and hopelessness, often leading to frantic or irrational actions in an attempt to change their situation.
20. **The Disappointed**: Someone who feels let down and disheartened by unmet expectations or unfulfilled hopes, leading to feelings of sadness and frustration.
21. **The Dismissed Employee**: An individual who feels disregarded and undervalued at work, leading to feelings of frustration and low self-worth.
22. **The Distrusted**: An individual who feels that others do not trust them, leading to feelings of isolation, hurt, and self-doubt.
23. **The Doubter**: A person who frequently questions their abilities, decisions, or worth, leading to hesitation and a lack of confidence.
24. **The Embarrassed**: Someone who feels self-conscious and ashamed due to a mistake or awkward situation, often leading to feelings of discomfort and humiliation.
25. **The Envious**: An individual who feels discontent or resentment towards others because of their possessions, achievements, or qualities.
26. **The Excluded**: Someone who feels left out or not included in social groups or activities, leading to feelings of loneliness and rejection.
27. **The Failure**: A person who perceives themselves as unsuccessful or inadequate, often leading to feelings of shame and hopelessness.
28. **The Fearful**: An individual who frequently experiences fear or anxiety about various aspects of life, impacting their ability to function normally.
29. **The Forgotten**: Someone who feels ignored or overlooked, often leading to feelings of loneliness and insignificance.
30. **The Frustrated**: An individual who feels upset or annoyed due to obstacles or unmet goals, often leading to feelings of helplessness and irritation.
31. **The Grieving**: Someone who is experiencing profound sorrow and pain due to a significant loss, such as the death of a loved one.
32. **The Guilty**: An individual who feels remorse and responsibility for a wrong action or decision, often leading to feelings of self-blame and regret.
33. **The Helpless**: Someone who feels powerless and unable to change their situation, leading to feelings of despair and frustration.
34. **The Hopeless**: An individual who feels a lack of optimism and belief in a positive future, often leading to feelings of despair and depression.
35. **The Humiliated**: Someone who feels deeply ashamed and embarrassed by their actions or experiences, often leading to feelings of worthlessness and vulnerability.
36. **The Hurt**: An individual who feels emotional pain due to negative experiences or actions by others, leading to feelings of sadness and betrayal.

37. **The Ignored**: Someone who feels unnoticed and disregarded by others, leading to feelings of insignificance and loneliness.
38. **The Inadequate**: An individual who feels insufficient or not good enough in various aspects of life, leading to feelings of low self-esteem and self-worth.
39. **The Insecure**: Someone who lacks confidence in themselves and their abilities, leading to feelings of anxiety and self-doubt.
40. **The Invalidating Parent**: A parent who disregards or diminishes their child's feelings and experiences, leading to feelings of inadequacy and low self-esteem in the child.
41. **The Invalidating Partner**: A romantic partner who dismisses or undermines their partner's feelings and experiences, leading to feelings of worthlessness and frustration.
42. **The Isolated**: An individual who feels separated from others, often leading to feelings of loneliness and detachment.
43. **The Jealous**: Someone who feels envious and resentful towards others due to their achievements or possessions, often leading to feelings of insecurity and bitterness.
44. **The Judged**: An individual who feels criticized and evaluated harshly by others, leading to feelings of inadequacy and self-consciousness.
45. **The Lonely**: Someone who feels a lack of companionship and connection with others, leading to feelings of sadness and isolation.
46. **The Lost**: An individual who feels directionless and uncertain about their life path, leading to feelings of confusion and despair.
47. **The Low Self-Esteem**: Someone who has a negative perception of their own worth and abilities, leading to feelings of inadequacy and insecurity.
48. **The Manipulated**: An individual who feels controlled and used by others for their own gain, leading to feelings of powerlessness and betrayal.
49. **The Mistrusted**: Someone who feels that others do not have faith in their abilities or intentions, leading to feelings of isolation and hurt.
50. **The Misunderstood**: An individual who feels that others do not understand their thoughts, feelings, or actions, leading to feelings of frustration and loneliness.
51. **The Neglected**: Someone who feels uncared for and ignored, often leading to feelings of abandonment and low self-worth.
52. **The Neglectful Friend**: A friend who consistently fails to support or be there for their friend, leading to feelings of abandonment and hurt.
53. **The Neglectful Parent**: A parent who fails to provide adequate care and attention to their child, often leading to feelings of abandonment and low self-worth in the child.
54. **The Needy**: An individual who feels a constant need for attention, validation, and support from others, often leading to feelings of insecurity and dependency.
55. **The Non-Performer**: Someone who feels that they are not meeting expectations or achieving their potential, leading to feelings of inadequacy and failure.
56. **The Not-Good-Enough**: An individual who feels that they do not meet standards or expectations, leading to feelings of inadequacy and low self-esteem.
57. **The Numb**: Someone who feels emotionally detached and unable to experience feelings, often as a coping mechanism for trauma or stress.
58. **The Overachiever**: An individual who pushes themselves to achieve excessively, often driven by a fear of failure and a need for validation.
59. **The Overbearing Parent/Teacher**: Someone who exerts excessive control and pressure over others, often leading to feelings of resentment and rebellion.

60. **The Overprotective Parent**: A parent who excessively shields their child from potential harm or failure, often leading to feelings of restriction and inadequacy in the child.
61. **The Overwhelmed**: An individual who feels swamped by their responsibilities and unable to cope, leading to feelings of stress and anxiety.
62. **The Passive-Aggressive**: Someone who expresses their negative feelings indirectly rather than openly, often leading to misunderstandings and conflicts.
63. **The Perfectionist**: An individual who strives for flawlessness and sets excessively high standards, often leading to feelings of inadequacy and frustration.
64. **The Persecuted**: Someone who feels harassed and oppressed by others, often leading to feelings of helplessness and anger.
65. **The Pessimist**: An individual who has a negative outlook on life and expects the worst, often leading to feelings of hopelessness and despair.
66. **The Pressured**: Someone who feels constant stress and demands from others or themselves, leading to feelings of anxiety and overwhelm.
67. **The Procrastinator**: An individual who habitually delays tasks, often leading to feelings of guilt and stress.
68. **The Rejected**: Someone who feels unwanted and dismissed by others, leading to feelings of hurt and loneliness.
69. **The Regretful**: An individual who feels sorrow and remorse over past actions or decisions, often leading to feelings of guilt and self-blame.
70. **The Resentful**: Someone who feels bitterness and anger towards others due to perceived wrongs or unfair treatment.
71. **The Sad**: An individual who feels deep sorrow and unhappiness, often impacting their overall well-being and outlook on life.
72. **The Scared Child**: Someone who experiences fear and anxiety reminiscent of childhood insecurities, often feeling vulnerable and unsafe.
73. **The Scapegoat**: An individual who is unfairly blamed for problems or mistakes, often leading to feelings of injustice and resentment.
74. **The Self-Blamer**: Someone who frequently holds themselves responsible for negative outcomes, leading to feelings of guilt and low self-esteem.
75. **The Self-Doubter**: An individual who constantly questions their abilities and decisions, leading to feelings of insecurity and hesitation.
76. **The Self-Hater**: Someone who harbors intense dislike and criticism towards themselves, often leading to feelings of worthlessness and depression.
77. **The Shamed**: An individual who feels deep humiliation and embarrassment over their actions, often leading to feelings of low self-worth.
78. **The Shunned**: Someone who is deliberately excluded and ignored by others, leading to feelings of rejection and loneliness.
79. **The Skeptic**: An individual who doubts and questions the validity of things, often leading to feelings of distrust and detachment.
80. **The Stressed**: Someone who feels overwhelmed and pressured by life's demands, leading to physical and emotional strain.
81. **The Suppressed**: An individual who feels their thoughts, feelings, or desires are stifled and restrained, leading to feelings of frustration and helplessness.

82. **The Tense**: Someone who feels tight and anxious, often due to stress or fear, impacting their ability to relax and function normally.
83. **The Traumatized**: An individual who has experienced a deeply distressing or disturbing event, leading to long-lasting emotional and psychological effects.
84. **The Traumatized Sibling**: A sibling who has undergone a traumatic event, impacting their emotional and psychological health and their relationship with family members.
85. **The Traumatized Spouse**: A spouse who has experienced significant emotional or psychological trauma, leading to lasting negative effects on their well-being and relationship.
86. **The Unappreciated**: Someone who feels their efforts and contributions are not recognized or valued, leading to feelings of neglect and low self-esteem.
87. **The Unheard**: An individual who feels that their voice and opinions are ignored or dismissed, leading to feelings of frustration and insignificance.
88. **The Unloved**: Someone who feels a lack of affection and care from others, leading to feelings of loneliness and low self-worth.
89. **The Unlucky**: An individual who feels that they frequently experience misfortune and bad luck, leading to feelings of frustration and helplessness.
90. **The Unmotivated**: Someone who lacks the drive and enthusiasm to pursue goals or activities, often leading to feelings of stagnation and dissatisfaction.
91. **The Unnoticed**: An individual who feels overlooked and unacknowledged by others, leading to feelings of invisibility and insignificance.
92. **The Unpopular**: Someone who feels that they are not well-liked or accepted by others, leading to feelings of rejection and low self-esteem.
93. **The Unrecognized**: An individual who feels that their achievements and efforts are not acknowledged, leading to feelings of frustration and disappointment.
94. **The Unreliable**: Someone who feels that they cannot be depended upon, leading to feelings of guilt and low self-worth.
95. **The Unwanted**: An individual who feels that they are not desired or valued by others, leading to feelings of rejection and loneliness.
96. **The Unworthy**: Someone who feels that they do not deserve love, success, or happiness, leading to feelings of low self-esteem and self-worth.
97. **The Untrusting Friend**: A friend who struggles to trust others, often due to past betrayals or hurts, leading to strained relationships and feelings of isolation.
98. **The Victim**: An individual who feels that they have been harmed or wronged by others, often leading to feelings of helplessness and resentment.
99. **The Worrywart**: Someone who excessively worries about various aspects of life, leading to chronic anxiety and stress.
100. **The Worrier**: An individual who constantly frets and fears about potential problems or dangers, impacting their ability to relax and enjoy life.
101. **What People Did**: Refers to actions taken by others that have caused emotional pain or trauma, leading to lasting negative impacts on an individual's mental health.
102. **What People Did Not Do**: Refers to the lack of actions or support from others that have resulted in feelings of neglect, abandonment, or unmet needs.

See Chart 148 - Emotional Baggage, Master Chart

Emotional Boundaries

Emotional boundaries are essential components of healthy relationships and personal well-being. They serve as invisible lines that define acceptable behaviors, emotional responses, and personal space, ensuring that interactions remain respectful and mutually beneficial. By setting clear emotional boundaries, individuals can protect their emotional health, prevent burnout, and maintain a sense of autonomy. These boundaries help people manage their emotions, enabling them to respond to others with empathy and compassion without being overwhelmed or manipulated. In essence, emotional boundaries create a safe space for individuals to express themselves authentically, fostering trust and mutual respect in relationships.

The importance of emotional boundaries extends beyond individual interactions to broader social dynamics. Without them, relationships can become unbalanced, leading to issues such as codependency, resentment, and emotional exhaustion. Healthy emotional boundaries promote self-respect and empower individuals to take responsibility for their own emotions and actions, rather than projecting them onto others. They also facilitate effective communication, as individuals are more likely to express their needs and limits clearly. Ultimately, emotional boundaries are vital for creating a balanced life, where personal growth and well-being are prioritized, and healthy, supportive relationships can thrive.

1. **Acceptance**: Recognizing and affirming others as they are without trying to change them.
2. **Accountability**: Taking responsibility for one's actions and behaviors.
3. **Affection**: Showing warmth, fondness, and love towards others.
4. **Appreciation**: Recognizing and valuing the contributions and efforts of others.
5. **Attention**: Giving focused time and interest to others.
6. **Authenticity**: Being true to one's own personality, values, and spirit.
7. **Autonomy**: Respecting the independence and personal space of others.
8. **Balance**: Maintaining a healthy distribution of time and energy among different areas of life.
9. **Care**: Providing physical and emotional support to others.
10. **Clarity**: Communicating in a clear and understandable manner.
11. **Comfort**: Creating an environment where others feel safe and at ease.
12. **Communication**: Exchanging information, thoughts, and feelings effectively.
13. **Compassion**: Showing empathy and concern for the suffering of others.
14. **Confidence**: Trusting in one's abilities and judgments.
15. **Consistency**: Maintaining steady behavior and treatment towards others.
16. **Consideration**: Being thoughtful of others' feelings and circumstances.
17. **Control**: Exercising appropriate power over one's own actions and reactions.
18. **Cooperation**: Working together towards a common goal.
19. **Courage**: Facing challenges and difficulties with bravery.
20. **Creativity**: Encouraging and valuing original ideas and expressions.
21. **Dependability**: Being reliable and trustworthy.
22. **Dignity**: Respecting the inherent worth of oneself and others.
23. **Encouragement**: Offering support and motivation to others.
24. **Fairness**: Treating others equally and justly.
25. **Faithfulness**: Being loyal and steadfast in relationships.
26. **Flexibility**: Being open to change and adaptable.

27. **Freedom**: Allowing oneself and others to make choices without undue restriction.
28. **Friendship**: Valuing and nurturing personal relationships.
29. **Generosity**: Willingly giving time, resources, and energy to others.
30. **Gratitude**: Expressing thankfulness and appreciation.
31. **Growth**: Supporting personal and interpersonal development.
32. **Honesty**: Being truthful and transparent in interactions.
33. **Hope**: Maintaining a positive outlook and optimism for the future.
34. **Humor**: Using laughter and light-heartedness to foster connection and joy.
35. **Inclusion**: Ensuring others feel accepted and valued within a group.
36. **Independence**: Respecting others' need to be self-sufficient.
37. **Integrity**: Adhering to moral and ethical principles.
38. **Intimacy**: Allowing emotional closeness and vulnerability.
39. **Kindness**: Acting with goodwill and compassion.
40. **Love**: Demonstrating deep affection and care.
41. **Loyalty**: Being faithful and devoted to others.
42. **Mindfulness**: Being present and attentive in the moment.
43. **Patience**: Showing tolerance and understanding towards others.
44. **Peace**: Promoting tranquility and harmony.
45. **Positivity**: Maintaining an optimistic and constructive attitude.
46. **Privacy**: Respecting others' need for personal space and confidentiality.
47. **Respect**: Showing regard and consideration for others.
48. **Responsibility**: Being accountable for one's actions and their impact on others.
49. **Safety**: Creating an environment free from harm and danger.
50. **Security**: Ensuring a stable and protected environment.
51. **Self-care**: Attending to one's own physical, emotional, and mental health.
52. **Self-respect**: Valuing and honoring oneself.
53. **Sensitivity**: Being aware of and responsive to the feelings of others.
54. **Space**: Allowing physical and emotional room for oneself and others.
55. **Stability**: Maintaining consistency and reliability in actions and relationships.
56. **Support**: Providing assistance and encouragement.
57. **Sympathy**: Sharing and understanding the feelings of others.
58. **Tact**: Handling difficult situations with sensitivity and diplomacy.
59. **Trust**: Believing in the reliability and integrity of others.
60. **Understanding**: Comprehending and empathizing with others' perspectives.
61. **Validation**: Acknowledging and affirming others' feelings and experiences.

See Chart 154 - Emotional Boundaries, Master Chart

Emotional Level

Checking someone's emotional level using this chart provides a clear and focused measure of their emotional state, separate from their overall vibrational frequency as indicated by the Bovis Unit chart. The emotional level chart ranges from -10 to 10, with negative values representing lower, more challenging emotional states such as sadness, anger, or despair, and positive values indicating higher, more positive emotional states like joy, love, or contentment. A score of 0 suggests a neutral emotional state, neither positive nor negative. By regularly assessing emotional levels with this chart, individuals can gain insight into their emotional well-being and identify areas needing attention or improvement. This tool can help track emotional progress and guide interventions to elevate and stabilize emotions for a more balanced and fulfilling life.

See Chart 158 - Emotional Level

Emotional Regulation

Emotional regulation is a critical skill that involves recognizing, understanding, and managing one's emotions in a healthy and constructive manner. It encompasses a variety of techniques and strategies, such as mindfulness practices, cognitive restructuring, and relaxation techniques, which help individuals navigate their emotional landscapes effectively. Emotional regulation enables a person to respond to emotional triggers with composure and thoughtfulness rather than impulsivity, leading to more balanced and harmonious interactions with others. By mastering emotional regulation, individuals can maintain emotional equilibrium, reduce stress, and enhance their overall well-being, contributing to a more fulfilling and joyful life.

Raising one's vibration involves elevating one's energy levels to experience greater states of consciousness, peace, and spiritual connection. Emotional regulation plays a pivotal role in this process, as unmanaged emotions such as anger, anxiety, and sadness can create energetic blockages that hinder the flow of positive energy. By effectively regulating emotions, individuals can release these blockages and foster a state of inner calm and positivity. This, in turn, allows for a higher vibrational state, making it easier to attract positive experiences, connect with one's higher self, and achieve a sense of spiritual harmony. Emotional regulation not only improves mental and emotional health but also serves as a foundational practice for those seeking to elevate their spiritual vibrations and live a more enlightened life.

1. **Acceptance**: The ability to embrace reality without judgment or resistance.
2. **Adaptability**: The capacity to adjust to new conditions or changes in the environment.
3. **Affection**: A gentle feeling of fondness or liking.
4. **Alertness**: The state of being watchful and ready to respond.
5. **Assertiveness**: The quality of being self-assured and confident without being aggressive.
6. **Attentiveness**: The trait of paying close attention to something.
7. **Authenticity**: The quality of being genuine or true to one's own personality and values.
8. **Balance**: The ability to maintain mental and emotional stability.
9. **Calmness**: The state of being free from agitation or strong emotions.
10. **Clarity**: The quality of being coherent and easily understood.
11. **Comfort**: A state of physical ease and freedom from pain or constraint.
12. **Compassion**: Sympathetic concern for the sufferings or misfortunes of others.
13. **Composure**: The state of being calm and in control of oneself.
14. **Confidence**: A feeling or belief in one's own abilities or qualities.
15. **Consistency**: The quality of always acting or behaving in the same way.
16. **Control**: The power to influence or direct behavior and events.
17. **Courage**: The ability to do something that frightens one.
18. **Creativity**: The use of imagination or original ideas to create something.
19. **Curiosity**: A strong desire to know or learn something.

20. **Determination**: Firmness of purpose; resoluteness.
21. **Dignity**: The state or quality of being worthy of honor or respect.
22. **Discipline**: The practice of training oneself to obey rules or a code of behavior.
23. **Empathy**: The ability to understand and share the feelings of another.
24. **Equanimity**: Mental calmness, composure, and evenness of temper.
25. **Flexibility**: The quality of bending easily without breaking.
26. **Forgiveness**: The action or process of forgiving or being forgiven.
27. **Generosity**: The quality of being kind and generous.
28. **Gratification**: Pleasure, especially when gained from the satisfaction of a desire.
29. **Gratitude**: The quality of being thankful; readiness to show appreciation.
30. **Harmony**: The quality of forming a pleasing and consistent whole.
31. **Healing**: The process of making or becoming sound or healthy again.
32. **Honesty**: The quality of being honest.
33. **Hopefulness**: The feeling or state of being full of hope.
34. **Humility**: A modest or low view of one's own importance.
35. **Insightfulness**: Having or showing an accurate and deep understanding.
36. **Integrity**: The quality of being honest and having strong moral principles.
37. **Intuition**: The ability to understand something immediately, without the need for conscious reasoning.
38. **Joy**: A feeling of great pleasure and happiness.
39. **Kindness**: The quality of being friendly, generous, and considerate.
40. **Mindfulness**: The quality or state of being conscious or aware of something.
41. **Mindset**: The established set of attitudes held by someone.
42. **Moderation**: The avoidance of excess or extremes.
43. **Motivation**: The reason or reasons one has for acting or behaving in a particular way.
44. **Openness**: Lack of restriction; accessibility.
45. **Optimism**: Hopefulness and confidence about the future or the successful outcome of something.
46. **Patience**: The capacity to accept or tolerate delay, trouble, or suffering without getting angry or upset.
47. **Peace**: Freedom from disturbance; tranquility.
48. **Perseverance**: Persistence in doing something despite difficulty or delay in achieving success.
49. **Perspective**: A particular attitude toward or way of regarding something; a point of view.
50. **Positivity**: The practice of being or tendency to be positive or optimistic in attitude.
51. **Pragmatism**: A practical approach to problems and affairs.
52. **Presence**: The state or fact of existing, occurring, or being present in a place or thing.
53. **Privacy**: The state or condition of being free from being observed or disturbed by other people.
54. **Reassurance**: The action of removing someone's doubts or fears.
55. **Reflection**: Serious thought or consideration.
56. **Resilience**: The capacity to recover quickly from difficulties.
57. **Resourcefulness**: The ability to find quick and clever ways to overcome difficulties.
58. **Respect**: A feeling of deep admiration for someone or something elicited by their abilities, qualities, or achievements.

59. **Responsibility**: The state or fact of having a duty to deal with something or of having control over someone.
60. **Safety**: The condition of being protected from or unlikely to cause danger, risk, or injury.
61. **Security**: The state of being free from danger or threat.
62. **Self-awareness**: Conscious knowledge of one's own character, feelings, motives, and desires.
63. **Self-care**: The practice of taking action to preserve or improve one's own health.
64. **Self-respect**: Pride and confidence in oneself; a feeling that one is behaving with honor and dignity.
65. **Sensitivity**: The quality of being sensitive.
66. **Serenity**: The state of being calm, peaceful, and untroubled.
67. **Space**: The freedom to think or act without being constrained.
68. **Stability**: The state of being stable.
69. **Support**: Bear all or part of the weight of; hold up.
70. **Sympathy**: Feelings of pity and sorrow for someone else's misfortune.
71. **Tact**: Sensitivity in dealing with others or with difficult issues.
72. **Thoughtfulness**: Consideration for the needs of other people.
73. **Trust**: Firm belief in the reliability, truth, ability, or strength of someone or something.
74. **Understanding**: The ability to understand something; comprehension.
75. **Validation**: Recognition or affirmation that a person or their feelings or opinions are valid or worthwhile.

See Chart 159 - Emotional Regulation, Master Chart

Empowerment and Self-Assertion

Empowerment Involves Recognizing And Embracing One's Own Strengths, Abilities, And Potential. It Is About Taking Control Of One's Life, Making Informed Decisions, And Acting In Ways That Promote Personal Growth And Well-Being. Empowerment Encourages Individuals To Believe In Themselves, Overcome Obstacles, And Strive For Success In Various Aspects Of Life. By Building Self-Confidence And Resilience, Empowerment Helps People To Navigate Challenges With A Positive Mindset And A Sense Of Purpose. This Process Often Involves Setting Clear Goals, Practicing Positive Self-Talk, And Surrounding Oneself With Supportive And Encouraging Relationships.

Self-Assertion, On The Other Hand, Is The Ability To Communicate One's Needs, Desires, And Boundaries Effectively And Respectfully. It Involves Standing Up For Oneself Without Being Aggressive Or Passive, Ensuring That One's Voice Is Heard And Valued. Self-Assertion Is Essential For Maintaining Healthy Relationships And Personal Integrity. It Requires Confidence, Clarity, And The Willingness To Advocate For One's Rights And Beliefs. Practicing Self-Assertion Helps Individuals To Establish Boundaries, Protect Their Well-Being, And Foster Mutual Respect In Interactions With Others. By Being Assertive, People Can Achieve Greater Satisfaction And Fulfillment In Both Personal And Professional Spheres.

1. **Accept Compliments Graciously**: to receive praise with humility and appreciation.
2. **Advocate for Your Needs**: to actively support and stand up for your own requirements and desires.
3. **Affirm Your Worth**: to recognize and declare your own value and importance.
4. **Apologize When Necessary**: to express regret for mistakes or wrongdoings appropriately.
5. **Ask for Help When Needed**: to seek assistance when required for support or guidance.
6. **Assert Your Boundaries**: to clearly communicate and uphold personal limits and expectations.
7. **Balance Your Needs with Others**: to equitably consider your own needs alongside those of others.
8. **Be Accountable for Your Actions**: to take responsibility for your behaviors and their consequences.
9. **Build Self-Confidence**: to develop a strong belief in your own abilities and worth.
10. **Celebrate Your Achievements**: to acknowledge and rejoice in your successes and accomplishments.
11. **Challenge Limiting Beliefs**: to confront and overcome self-restricting thoughts and assumptions.
12. **Communicate Assertively**: to express yourself directly and respectfully without undermining others.
13. **Cultivate Positive Self-Talk**: to encourage supportive and affirmative inner dialogue.
14. **Develop a Growth Mindset**: to embrace the belief that abilities and intelligence can be developed.
15. **Embrace Change**: to accept and adapt to new situations and transformations.
16. **Embrace Your Strengths**: to recognize and utilize your personal talents and abilities.
17. **Engage in Self-Care**: to take deliberate actions to maintain physical, emotional, and mental health.
18. **Establish Clear Goals**: to set specific, measurable, achievable, relevant, and time-bound objectives.
19. **Express Gratitude**: to show appreciation for positive aspects and experiences in life.
20. **Express Your Opinions**: to share your thoughts and beliefs openly and honestly.
21. **Face Your Fears**: to confront and address your anxieties and insecurities.
22. **Focus on Personal Growth**: to prioritize and invest in your own development and improvement.
23. **Focus on Solutions**: to concentrate on finding resolutions rather than dwelling on problems.
24. **Foster Resilience**: to build the capacity to recover quickly from difficulties and setbacks.
25. **Forgive Yourself and Others**: to release feelings of resentment and grant pardon for mistakes.
26. **Gain New Skills**: to learn and acquire additional abilities and competencies.
27. **Give Constructive Feedback**: to provide helpful and positive criticism aimed at improvement.
28. **Identify and Pursue Passions**: to recognize and actively follow interests and hobbies.
29. **Join Supportive Groups**: to become a member of communities that provide encouragement and assistance.

30. **Keep a Journal**: to regularly write down thoughts, feelings, and experiences for reflection.
31. **Learn to Delegate**: to assign responsibilities to others effectively.
32. **Learn to Say No**: to refuse requests that do not align with your priorities or capacity.
33. **Let Go of Past Mistakes**: to release regret and move forward from previous errors.
34. **Maintain a Support Network**: to keep strong connections with people who offer support and encouragement.
35. **Meditate for Clarity**: to practice mindfulness or meditation to gain mental focus and calmness.
36. **Network with Like-Minded Individuals**: to build connections with people who share similar interests and goals.
37. **Practice Assertive Communication**: to express yourself clearly and respectfully while honoring your own needs.
38. **Practice Gratitude**: to regularly reflect on and appreciate positive aspects of life.
39. **Practice Mindfulness**: to stay present and fully engage with the current moment.
40. **Prioritize Personal Growth**: to make your own development and improvement a top priority.
41. **Protect Your Energy**: to safeguard your physical, emotional, and mental well-being.
42. **Pursue Continuous Learning**: to seek ongoing education and skill development.
43. **Recognize Your Accomplishments**: to acknowledge and appreciate your own successes.
44. **Reflect on Your Progress**: to regularly assess and contemplate your growth and achievements.
45. **Seek Professional Development**: to engage in activities that enhance your career skills and knowledge.
46. **Set Boundaries with Toxic People**: to establish limits to protect yourself from harmful interactions.
47. **Set Healthy Boundaries**: to define and maintain limits that promote your well-being.
48. **Share Your Talents**: to use your skills and abilities to benefit others.
49. **Speak Your Truth**: to communicate your genuine thoughts and feelings honestly.
50. **Stand Up for Yourself**: to defend your rights and assert your needs.
51. **Stay Organized**: to keep your environment and tasks orderly and managed.
52. **Stay True to Your Values**: to consistently act in accordance with your beliefs and principles.
53. **Step Out of Your Comfort Zone**: to take risks and try new things beyond your usual routine.
54. **Surround Yourself with Positivity**: to be in the company of encouraging and supportive people.
55. **Take Care of Your Physical Health**: to maintain your body through healthy habits and practices.
56. **Take Responsibility for Your Actions**: to own your behaviors and their outcomes.
57. **Take Time for Hobbies**: to engage in activities that bring joy and relaxation.
58. **Trust Your Intuition**: to have confidence in your inner guidance and feelings.
59. **Value Your Time**: to use your time wisely and respectfully.
60. **Visualize Success**: to mentally picture achieving your goals and aspirations.

61. **Volunteer for Causes You Care About**: to offer your time and effort to meaningful initiatives.
62. **Walk Away from Negativity**: to distance yourself from negative influences and environments.
63. **Work on Self-Discipline**: to develop the ability to control and direct your own actions.
64. **Write Down Your Goals**: to clearly articulate and document your objectives.

See Chart 164 - Empowerment and Self-Assertion, Master Chart

Exploring Subconscious Patterns

Exploring subconscious patterns is crucial for raising vibration as these hidden patterns significantly influence our thoughts, emotions, and behaviors. These patterns often stem from past experiences, traumas, or conditioning, and can create obstacles in our lives without our conscious awareness. By identifying and understanding these patterns, we can begin to address and transform them, leading to greater emotional freedom and mental clarity. This process of self-discovery helps to uncover the root causes of negative behaviors and thought patterns, allowing for healing and personal growth. As we clear these subconscious blocks, our energy becomes more aligned and coherent, facilitating a higher vibrational state.

Raising vibration is essential for overall well-being and spiritual growth. Higher vibrational states are associated with positive emotions, such as love, joy, and peace, which attract more positive experiences and relationships into our lives. Conversely, lower vibrational states, often rooted in fear, guilt, or shame, can perpetuate cycles of negativity and limit our potential. By exploring and addressing subconscious patterns, we release these lower vibrational energies and make room for higher frequencies to emerge. This not only enhances our personal and spiritual development but also positively impacts our interactions and connections with others, fostering a more harmonious and fulfilling life.

1. **Abandonment Issues**: Persistent fear of being abandoned or left behind, often stemming from past experiences of loss or neglect.
2. **Addictive Behaviors**: Engaging in activities or substances compulsively and uncontrollably, often as a way to cope with stress or emotional pain.
3. **Anger Suppression**: The act of consciously or unconsciously holding back feelings of anger, which can lead to emotional and physical health issues.
4. **Approval Seeking**: A constant need for validation and acceptance from others, often at the expense of one's own needs or desires.
5. **Avoidance of Intimacy**: Fear of getting close to others or forming deep connections, often due to past hurts or fear of vulnerability.
6. **Blame Shifting**: Redirecting responsibility for one's actions or feelings onto others, avoiding accountability and personal growth.
7. **Body Image Distortions**: Having a distorted perception of one's physical appearance, often leading to low self-esteem and unhealthy behaviors.
8. **Catastrophizing**: Exaggerating the potential negative outcomes of a situation, leading to increased anxiety and stress.
9. **Chronic Dissatisfaction**: A persistent feeling of discontent or unhappiness, regardless of circumstances or achievements.

10. **Codependency**: A dysfunctional relationship pattern where one person relies excessively on another for emotional support and validation.
11. **Compulsive Behaviors**: Performing actions repetitively and uncontrollably, often to alleviate anxiety or distress.
12. **Control Issues**: A need to control situations or people to feel safe or secure, often leading to strained relationships and stress.
13. **Criticism of Self and Others**: Frequently judging oneself and others harshly, which can erode self-esteem and interpersonal connections.
14. **Denial of Emotions**: Refusing to acknowledge or express one's true feelings, often leading to emotional numbness and unresolved issues.
15. **Dependency on Others for Validation**: Relying on external affirmation to feel worthy or valued, often leading to insecurity and low self-esteem.
16. **Difficulty Setting Boundaries**: Struggling to establish and maintain healthy limits in relationships, leading to feelings of being overwhelmed or taken advantage of.
17. **Displacement of Anger**: Redirecting anger from its original source to a safer or more convenient target, often without resolving the underlying issue.
18. **Distrust of Others**: A pervasive suspicion of other people's intentions, often resulting from past betrayals or trauma.
19. **Emotional Detachment**: A state of disengaging from one's emotions or relationships, often as a defense mechanism against hurt or disappointment.
20. **Emotional Numbness**: An inability to feel or express emotions, often resulting from prolonged stress or trauma.
21. **Envy and Jealousy**: Feelings of resentment or bitterness towards others' success or possessions, often stemming from a sense of inadequacy.
22. **Excessive Guilt**: Feeling an overwhelming sense of responsibility or remorse for perceived wrongdoings, often disproportionate to the situation.
23. **Fear of Abandonment**: A deep-seated fear of being left alone or deserted, often leading to clingy or needy behaviors in relationships.
24. **Fear of Change**: Anxiety or resistance towards new experiences or alterations in routine, often due to fear of the unknown or loss of control.
25. **Fear of Confrontation**: Avoiding conflicts or difficult discussions, often out of fear of rejection or negative outcomes.
26. **Fear of Failure**: An intense dread of not meeting expectations or achieving goals, which can paralyze efforts and hinder progress.
27. **Fear of Intimacy**: Reluctance to form close, meaningful relationships due to fear of vulnerability or past hurts.
28. **Fear of Rejection**: A pervasive fear of being turned away or not accepted, often leading to avoidance of social situations or new opportunities.
29. **Fear of Success**: Anxiety about achieving goals or reaching a high level of success, often due to fear of increased expectations or responsibilities.
30. **Fixation on Past Mistakes**: Obsessing over past errors or failures, which can prevent moving forward and learning from experiences.
31. **Guilt Manipulation**: Using guilt to influence or control others' behavior, often to gain power or avoid accountability.
32. **Hypercriticism**: Excessive or severe criticism towards oneself or others, often stemming from unrealistic expectations or perfectionism.

33. **Hypersensitivity**: Overreacting emotionally to minor stimuli or criticisms, often due to underlying insecurity or past trauma.

34. **Idealization of Others**: Viewing others as perfect or without flaws, often leading to disappointment when reality does not meet expectations.

35. **Imposter Syndrome**: Persistent doubt about one's abilities or accomplishments, often feeling like a fraud despite evidence of success.

36. **Inability to Forgive**: Holding onto grudges or resentment, which can prevent emotional healing and maintain negative energy.

37. **Insecurity**: A lack of confidence or self-assurance, often resulting in anxiety and a need for constant reassurance.

38. **Internalized Shame**: Deep feelings of unworthiness or defectiveness, often rooted in early life experiences or trauma.

39. **Jealousy**: Feelings of insecurity or resentment towards others' achievements or relationships, often stemming from low self-esteem.

40. **Judgmental Thinking**: Quickly forming negative opinions about oneself or others, often based on superficial or incomplete information.

41. **Lack of Assertiveness**: Difficulty expressing one's needs or desires confidently, often leading to passive or submissive behavior.

42. **Lack of Self-Compassion**: Inability to treat oneself with kindness or understanding, often leading to harsh self-criticism and low self-esteem.

43. **Lack of Trust**: Difficulty believing in the reliability or integrity of others, often due to past betrayals or disappointments.

44. **Low Self-Esteem**: A poor self-image or lack of confidence in one's abilities and worth, often leading to self-sabotaging behaviors.

45. **Martyr Complex**: A tendency to sacrifice one's own needs for others, often seeking validation through suffering or self-denial.

46. **Minimizing Achievements**: Downplaying or dismissing one's successes, often due to a lack of self-worth or fear of standing out.

47. **Negative Self-Talk**: Constantly thinking or speaking negatively about oneself, which can erode self-esteem and reinforce limiting beliefs.

48. **Need for Control**: A strong desire to manage or dictate situations and people, often as a way to feel secure or avoid vulnerability.

49. **Need for External Validation**: Relying on others' approval or recognition to feel good about oneself, often leading to dependency and insecurity.

50. **Obsessive Thinking**: Persistent, intrusive thoughts that dominate one's mind, often causing anxiety and preventing focus on the present.

51. **Over-Apologizing**: Frequently saying sorry for minor or imagined offenses, often as a way to avoid conflict or gain acceptance.

52. **Over-Dependence**: Relying excessively on others for support or guidance, often due to a lack of confidence in one's own abilities.

53. **Over-Giving**: Consistently prioritizing others' needs over one's own, often leading to burnout and resentment.

54. **Over-Identification with Roles**: Defining oneself primarily by a specific role or identity, often limiting personal growth and self-discovery.

55. **Over-Thinking**: Excessive rumination on problems or decisions, often leading to anxiety and difficulty taking action.

56. **Passive-Aggressive Behavior**: Expressing negative feelings indirectly, often through procrastination, sarcasm, or stubbornness.
57. **People-Pleasing**: Prioritizing others' approval and happiness over one's own needs, often leading to self-neglect and resentment.
58. **Perfectionism**: Striving for flawlessness and setting excessively high standards, often leading to stress and dissatisfaction.
59. **Projection of Fears**: Attributing one's own fears or insecurities onto others, often as a defense mechanism to avoid self-reflection.
60. **Procrastination**: Delaying tasks or decisions unnecessarily, often due to fear of failure or overwhelm.
61. **Repressed Anger**: Suppressing feelings of anger, which can lead to emotional and physical health issues over time.
62. **Resentment Accumulation**: Harboring feelings of bitterness or anger towards others, often due to unresolved conflicts or perceived injustices.
63. **Resistance to Change**: Reluctance or refusal to adapt to new situations or perspectives, often due to fear of the unknown or comfort in routine.
64. **Risk Aversion**: Avoiding potential risks or new experiences, often due to fear of failure or loss.
65. **Sabotaging Relationships**: Engaging in behaviors that undermine or destroy relationships, often due to fear of intimacy or abandonment.
66. **Self-Blame**: Holding oneself responsible for negative outcomes or situations, often disproportionate to actual responsibility.
67. **Self-Criticism**: Harshly judging oneself for perceived flaws or failures, often leading to low self-esteem and negative self-image.
68. **Self-Doubt**: Lacking confidence in one's abilities or decisions, often leading to hesitation and missed opportunities.
69. **Self-Isolation**: Withdrawing from social interactions, often as a defense mechanism against perceived threats or rejection.
70. **Self-Neglect**: Failing to take care of one's physical, emotional, or mental needs, often due to low self-worth or prioritizing others.
71. **Self-Pity**: Feeling sorry for oneself and focusing on one's own misfortunes, often leading to a victim mentality.
72. **Self-Sabotage**: Engaging in behaviors that hinder one's success or well-being, often due to underlying fears or limiting beliefs.
73. **Sensitivity to Criticism**: Reacting strongly to negative feedback or perceived slights, often due to insecurity or low self-esteem.
74. **Shame-Based Thinking**: Viewing oneself as fundamentally flawed or unworthy, often due to internalized negative beliefs or past experiences.
75. **Social Anxiety**: Intense fear or discomfort in social situations, often due to fear of judgment or rejection.
76. **Suppression of Desires**: Ignoring or denying one's true wants and needs, often due to fear of rejection or societal expectations.
77. **Toxic Comparison**: Comparing oneself negatively to others, often leading to feelings of inadequacy and low self-worth.
78. **Unhealthy Coping Mechanisms**: Relying on harmful behaviors or substances to manage stress or emotional pain, often leading to further issues.

79. **Unresolved Grief**: Incomplete processing of loss or trauma, often leading to prolonged emotional pain and difficulty moving forward.
80. **Unworthiness**: Believing oneself to be inherently undeserving of love, success, or happiness, often leading to self-sabotaging behaviors.
81. **Victim Mentality**: Viewing oneself as a victim of circumstances, often leading to a sense of powerlessness and lack of responsibility.
82. **Withdrawal from Conflict**: Avoiding disagreements or confrontations, often due to fear of negative outcomes or discomfort.
83. **Worrying Excessively**: Chronic, uncontrollable worrying about potential negative outcomes, often leading to anxiety and stress.

See Chart 168 - Exploring Subconscious Patterns, Master Chart

Families

Family members, while often a source of support and love, can sometimes hold back an individual's vibrational energy through their words, actions, or even their own energy. This influence can stem from longstanding family dynamics, unresolved conflicts, or negative patterns of behavior that create an environment of low energy. For instance, constant criticism, negativity, or lack of emotional support from family members can lower one's self-esteem and energy levels, making it difficult to maintain a high vibration. Additionally, the energy we absorb from those closest to us can affect our emotional and spiritual well-being, sometimes without our conscious awareness.

Recognizing which family members might be contributing to a lower vibrational state is crucial. By identifying these influences, individuals can take proactive steps to protect their energy.

Sending gratitude to these family members for the lessons they bring can help release any emotional hold they have, transforming negative energy into positive. Working around these individuals means setting healthy boundaries, limiting exposure to negative interactions, and engaging in practices that reinforce personal energy, such as meditation, affirmations, and spending time with more supportive and uplifting people. Ultimately, awareness and intentional action can help maintain a high vibrational state, even in the presence of challenging family dynamics.

See Chart 173 - Families, Master Chart

Forgiveness

Offering forgiveness is a multifaceted process that can significantly impact emotional healing and personal growth. The act of forgiveness is not just about reconciling with others, but also about fostering inner peace and understanding.

1. **Understanding and Acceptance**: Start by acknowledging the situation and accepting apologies, whether they are perfect or flawed. Accepting responsibility where applicable and recognizing the immutable nature of the past are foundational steps. This involves understanding the limitations of human behavior and acknowledging our shared

humanity. Accepting what cannot change and the inherent imperfections in everyone can shift perspectives and reduce feelings of bitterness.

2. **Emotional Processing**: Addressing unresolved emotions is crucial. This might involve acknowledging and expressing your own pain and feelings, perhaps through communicating these feelings or through therapeutic practices. Engaging in physical activities can help release built-up tension, while practices like meditation on forgiveness and creative outlets can offer emotional release and help reframe negative thoughts.

3. **Constructive Practices**: Engaging in constructive communication and collaborative problem-solving can mend relationships and foster understanding. Creating rituals for letting go, such as writing forgiveness letters or establishing personal mantras, can solidify your intentions and help in emotionally moving on. Regular practices like mindfulness, loving-kindness meditation, and gratitude can cultivate an environment within oneself that is conducive to forgiveness.

4. **Perspective and Growth**: It is helpful to focus on the bigger picture and consider the growth opportunities arising from difficult situations. Recognize the freedom and peace that forgiving can bring into your life and use the experience as a catalyst for personal development. Viewing the situation through a lens of empathy and compassion rather than anger or revenge can transform resentment into understanding.

5. **Support and Self-Care**: Establishing a support system, seeking professional therapy or counseling, and engaging in self-care are all critical in maintaining emotional health through the process of forgiveness. Self-care might include setting clear boundaries or seeking spiritual guidance to align one's actions with personal values and emotional needs.

6. **Long-Term Practices**: Make a conscious decision to forgive and prioritize peace in your interactions and daily life. Practice daily forgiveness to maintain this mindset and prevent old wounds from reopening. It's also important to give it time—forgiveness is a process, not a one-time act.

Through these varied approaches, forgiveness can transition from being a daunting obligation to a liberating practice that enhances emotional resilience and interpersonal relationships. Each step, whether small or significant, is a stride towards healing and emotional freedom.

1. **Accept an Apology:** Embrace the apology given to you.
2. **Accept an Imperfect Apology:** Understand that not all apologies are perfect.
3. **Accept Responsibility:** Take responsibility if it's yours.
4. **Accept What Cannot Change:** Acknowledge what cannot be changed.
5. **Acknowledge Shared Humanity:** Recognize our common humanity.
6. **Acknowledge the Pain:** Validate the pain you feel.
7. **Acknowledge Your Feelings:** Recognize your own feelings.
8. **Address Unresolved Emotions:** Confront lingering emotions.
9. **Celebrate Your Ability to Forgive:** Appreciate your capacity to forgive.
10. **Challenge Negative Thoughts About the Situation**: Question your negative thoughts.
11. **Choose to Let Go:** Decide to release the past.
12. **Choose Understanding Over Anger:** Opt for understanding instead of anger.
13. **Communicate Your Feelings:** Express how you feel.

14. **Consider the Bigger Picture:** Look at the broader perspective.
15. **Create a Forgiveness Mantra:** Develop a personal forgiveness phrase.
16. **Create a Ritual for Letting Go:** Establish a ritual for letting go.
17. **Engage in Collaborative Problem-Solving:** Work together to solve problems.
18. **Engage in Constructive Communication:** Communicate constructively.
19. **Engage in Physical Activity to Release Tension:** Use physical activity to release tension.
20. **Engage in Self-Care:** Practice self-care.
21. **Establish a Support System:** Build a support system.
22. **Focus on Compassion:** Concentrate on being compassionate.
23. **Focus on Empathy:** Emphasize understanding others' feelings.
24. **Focus on Healing:** Prioritize your healing.
25. **Focus on Positive Memories:** Remember positive memories.
26. **Focus on the Present:** Stay in the present moment.
27. **Focus on What Forgiveness Brings You:** Think about the benefits of forgiveness.
28. **Forgive Yourself:** Allow yourself to be forgiven.
29. **Give Feedback:** Provide constructive feedback.
30. **Give It Time:** Allow time for the process.
31. **Identify the Growth Opportunity:** Find the growth opportunity in the situation.
32. **Keep an Open Mind:** Maintain an open mind.
33. **Lean in Slightly:** Approach the situation with openness.
34. **Let Go of Grudges:** Release any grudges.
35. **Limit Exposure to Negative Influences:** Reduce negative influences in your life.
36. **Limit Rumination:** Decrease excessive thinking.
37. **Listen for Ideas, Not Just Words:** Listen for underlying ideas.
38. **Make a Conscious Decision to Forgive:** Decide intentionally to forgive.
39. **Meditate on Forgiveness:** Meditate with forgiveness in mind.
40. **Offer an Apology:** Give a sincere apology.
41. **Practice Acts of Kindness:** Engage in kind acts.
42. **Practice Daily Forgiveness:** Forgive daily.
43. **Practice Empathy:** Show empathy towards others.
44. **Practice Generosity:** Be generous.
45. **Practice Gratitude:** Practice being grateful.
46. **Practice Loving-Kindness Meditation:** Meditate on loving-kindness.
47. **Practice Mindfulness:** Be mindful in the present moment.
48. **Practice Patience:** Cultivate patience.
49. **Practice Tolerance:** Develop tolerance.
50. **Prioritize Peace:** Make peace a priority.
51. **Recognize Everyone Makes Mistakes:** Accept that mistakes happen.
52. **Recognize the Freedom Forgiveness Offers:** See the freedom in forgiveness.
53. **Recognize the Power of Forgiveness:** Understand the power of forgiveness.
54. **Reflect on the Situation:** Think deeply about the situation.
55. **Reframe the Narrative:** Change the way you view the story.
56. **Release Control Over the Past:** Let go of past control.
57. **Release the Need for Revenge**: Let go of seeking revenge.
58. **Remember the Benefits of Forgiving:** Recall the benefits of forgiveness.

59. **Remember the Context:** Keep the context in mind.
60. **Remember the Value of the Relationship:** Appreciate the relationship's value.

See Chart 177 - Forgiveness, Best Ways to Offer, Master Chart

Inner Critic

The inner critic is an internal voice that often embodies self-doubt, negativity, and harsh judgment. It can be a relentless and unforgiving presence in one's mind, constantly undermining confidence and self-worth. This voice is typically formed from past experiences, societal expectations, and internalized criticisms from others. The inner critic might say things like, "You're not good enough," "You'll never succeed," or "Why even try?" These negative messages can become deeply ingrained, influencing thoughts, feelings, and behaviors in profound ways. The inner critic's pervasive negativity can lead to self-sabotage, depression, anxiety, and a general sense of unfulfillment.

Stopping the inner critic is crucial for raising one's vibration and achieving a higher state of consciousness. The constant barrage of negativity from the inner critic can lower one's vibrational frequency, keeping them stuck in a state of fear, doubt, and low self-esteem. By silencing this inner voice, individuals can create space for positive self-talk, self-compassion, and empowerment. This shift not only enhances mental and emotional well-being but also aligns one with higher frequencies of love, joy, and peace. As one's vibration rises, they become more attuned to positive energies, fostering greater resilience, creativity, and a deeper connection to their higher self and the universe. Embracing a higher vibration allows for a more fulfilling and harmonious life, free from the limiting constraints of the inner critic.

1. **Abrasive**: Harsh and rough in manner.
2. **Abusive**: Engaging in harsh or insulting behavior.
3. **Accusing**: Blaming or pointing out faults.
4. **Alarmist**: Causing unnecessary worry or fear.
5. **Antagonistic**: Hostile and opposed.
6. **Apprehensive**: Fearful or anxious about the future.
7. **Argumentative**: Prone to arguing or disputing.
8. **Belittling**: Making someone or something seem less important.
9. **Blaming**: Holding someone responsible for a fault or wrong.
10. **Bossy**: Domineering and overly authoritative.
11. **Brutal**: Extremely harsh or cruel.
12. **Callous**: Emotionally hardened and insensitive.
13. **Captious**: Inclined to find fault and raise petty objections.
14. **Carping**: Constantly finding fault in trivial matters.
15. **Caustic**: Bitterly sarcastic and critical.
16. **Cavalier**: Showing a lack of proper concern.
17. **Censorious**: Severely critical of others.
18. **Cold-hearted**: Lacking compassion or empathy.
19. **Combative**: Eager to fight or argue.
20. **Condemning**: Expressing strong disapproval.
21. **Condescending**: Acting superior to others.

22. **Confounding**: Causing confusion and frustration.
23. **Contradictory**: Inclined to contradict or oppose.
24. **Critical**: Expressing adverse or disapproving judgments.
25. **Cruel**: Willfully causing pain or suffering.
26. **Cynical**: Distrustful of human sincerity or integrity.
27. **Demeaning**: Causing someone to lose dignity and respect.
28. **Demoralizing**: Causing a loss of confidence or hope.
29. **Deprecating**: Expressing disapproval or belittlement.
30. **Deriding**: Expressing contempt or ridicule.
31. **Derisive**: Mocking and ridiculing.
32. **Destructive**: Causing great harm or damage.
33. **Deterring**: Discouraging someone from doing something.
34. **Disapproving**: Expressing an unfavorable opinion.
35. **Disbelieving**: Unable or unwilling to believe.
36. **Disdainful**: Showing contempt or lack of respect.
37. **Disheartening**: Causing someone to lose determination.
38. **Disparaging**: Belittling or degrading.
39. **Dismissive**: Showing indifference or disregard.
40. **Distrustful**: Inclined to doubt or mistrust.
41. **Downbeat**: Gloomy and pessimistic.
42. **Doubtful**: Feeling uncertain or lacking conviction.
43. **Fault-finding**: Inclined to find faults or defects.
44. **Fearful**: Full of fear or worry.
45. **Forceful**: Strong and assertive.
46. **Frightening**: Making someone afraid or anxious.
47. **Gloomy**: Dark and pessimistic.
48. **Harsh**: Severe and unkind.
49. **Hostile**: Unfriendly and antagonistic.
50. **Hypercritical**: Excessively and unreasonably critical.
51. **Inconsiderate**: Thoughtless and unkind.
52. **Incredulous**: Unwilling or unable to believe.
53. **Insensitive**: Showing a lack of concern for others' feelings.
54. **Intimidating**: Frightening or overawing someone.
55. **Judgmental**: Inclined to make harsh judgments.
56. **Lamenting**: Expressing sorrow or regret.
57. **Lecturing**: Giving a lengthy reprimand or scolding.
58. **Mocking**: Teasing or ridiculing.
59. **Negative**: Lacking in positivity or optimism.
60. **Nitpicking**: Finding small and unimportant faults.
61. **Oppressive**: Harsh and authoritarian.
62. **Overbearing**: Domineering and arrogant.
63. **Pessimistic**: Expecting the worst to happen.
64. **Prejudiced**: Holding biased opinions without reason.
65. **Rebuffing**: Rejecting bluntly or unkindly.
66. **Rebuking**: Expressing sharp disapproval.
67. **Rejecting**: Refusing to accept or acknowledge.

68. **Relentless**: Unyielding in severity or strictness.
69. **Remorseless**: Without regret or guilt.
70. **Reproachful**: Expressing disapproval or disappointment.
71. **Ridiculing**: Making fun of in a cruel way.
72. **Sarcastic**: Using irony to mock or convey contempt.
73. **Sardonic**: Grimly mocking or cynical.
74. **Scathing**: Bitterly severe in criticism.
75. **Scornful**: Feeling or expressing contempt.
76. **Self-deprecating**: Critical of oneself, often humorously.
77. **Self-doubting**: Lacking confidence in oneself.
78. **Self-judging**: Harshly evaluating oneself.
79. **Self-loathing**: Intense dislike of oneself.
80. **Severe**: Very strict or harsh.
81. **Skeptical**: Doubtful about something.
82. **Sneering**: Contemptuously mocking.
83. **Stern**: Serious and unrelenting.
84. **Strict**: Demanding exact adherence to rules.
85. **Suspicious**: Inclined to suspect wrongdoing.
86. **Taunting**: Provoking or mocking.
87. **Threatening**: Intimidating or menacing.
88. **Unforgiving**: Not willing to forgive.
89. **Unkind**: Not kind or considerate.
90. **Unrelenting**: Not giving up or yielding.
91. **Unsympathetic**: Lacking compassion or sympathy.
92. **Unyielding**: Firm and inflexible.
93. **Vindictive**: Seeking revenge.
94. **Vitriolic**: Filled with bitter criticism.
95. **Vicious**: Deliberately cruel or violent.
96. **Warning**: Giving cautionary advice.
97. **Withering**: Intending to make someone feel humiliated.
98. **Worrisome**: Causing worry or anxiety.
99. **Zealous**: Intensely enthusiastic or passionate.
100. **Zero-tolerant**: Showing no tolerance for mistakes or faults.

See Chart 183 - Inner Critic, Master Chart

Inner Peace and Tranquility

Inner peace and tranquility are states of being that transcend the tumultuous nature of daily life, allowing individuals to find a profound sense of calm and balance within themselves. These states are often characterized by a deep-seated feeling of contentment, acceptance, and harmony with the world around us. Achieving inner peace involves cultivating a mindset that remains unaffected by external chaos and stress. This journey often includes practices such as meditation, mindfulness, and self-reflection, which help individuals connect with their inner selves and develop resilience against life's challenges. Inner peace is not about escaping reality but embracing it with a calm and composed mind, allowing one to respond to situations with clarity and compassion.

Tranquility, closely related to inner peace, is the serene state of being free from agitation and disturbance. It is a sense of stillness and quiet that permeates one's mind and environment. This state can be nurtured through various activities such as spending time in nature, engaging in creative pursuits, or practicing yoga and other relaxation techniques. Tranquility allows individuals to slow down, appreciate the present moment, and detach from the constant rush and noise of modern life. By creating pockets of tranquility in our daily routines, we can enhance our overall well-being, reduce stress, and foster a more balanced and peaceful existence. Together, inner peace and tranquility form the foundation of a fulfilling and harmonious life, enabling us to navigate life's ups and downs with grace and equanimity.

1. **Affirmations**: Positive statements to reinforce self-belief and calm.
2. **Alexander Technique**: Improving posture and movement for overall well-being.
3. **Aikido**: A Japanese martial art focused on harmony and peaceful resolution.
4. **Aromatherapy**: Using essential oils to promote relaxation and peace.
5. **Art Therapy**: Expressing emotions and thoughts through creative arts.
6. **Ayurveda**: An ancient Indian system of medicine for balance and health.
7. **Binaural Beats**: Using sound frequencies to alter brainwave patterns.
8. **Body Scan Meditation**: Focusing on different body parts to promote relaxation.
9. **Breathing Exercises**: Techniques to focus and calm the mind.
10. **Bubble Baths**: Soaking in warm water to relax muscles and mind.
11. **Chanting**: Repetitive sounds to create a meditative state.
12. **Chakra Balancing**: Aligning the body's energy centers for harmony.
13. **Coaching**: Working with a coach to achieve personal goals and reduce stress.
14. **Color Therapy**: Using colors to affect mood and energy.
15. **Community Service**: Helping others to create a sense of purpose and calm.
16. **Creative Writing**: Expressing thoughts and emotions through writing.
17. **Crystal Healing**: Using crystals to balance and heal energy.
18. **Cupping Therapy**: Using suction cups on the skin to relieve tension.
19. **Dance**: Moving rhythmically to express oneself and reduce stress.
20. **Dance Therapy**: Expressing through movement to release stress.
21. **Dowsing**: Using tools to find energetic imbalances.
22. **Dream Analysis**: Understanding dreams to uncover subconscious thoughts.
23. **Ecotherapy**: Engaging with nature for therapeutic benefits.
24. **EMDR**: A therapy to alleviate distress from traumatic memories.
25. **Emotional Freedom Techniques (EFT)**: Tapping on meridian points to reduce anxiety.
26. **Energy Medicine**: Techniques to balance the body's energy systems.
27. **Equine Therapy**: Using interactions with horses for emotional healing.
28. **Essential Oils**: Using plant extracts for emotional and physical well-being.
29. **Facial Reflexology**: Applying pressure to facial points to promote relaxation.
30. **Feldenkrais Method**: Awareness through movement to improve physical and mental health.
31. **Floatation Therapy**: Floating in sensory-deprivation tanks to relax.
32. **Forest Bathing**: Immersing in nature for mental clarity and peace.

33. **Gong Bath**: Immersing in the sound of gongs for deep relaxation.
34. **Gratitude Journaling**: Writing down things you're thankful for.
35. **Gratitude Meditation**: Meditating on things you're grateful for.
36. **Guided Imagery**: Visualization techniques to reduce stress.
37. **Hand Mudras**: Specific hand positions to influence energy flow.
38. **Healing Touch**: Using hands to promote physical and emotional healing.
39. **Herbal Remedies**: Using plants to promote relaxation and healing.
40. **Hiking**: Walking in nature to improve physical and mental well-being.
41. **Holistic Nutrition**: Eating to nourish the body and mind.
42. **Homeopathy**: Using natural substances to stimulate healing.
43. **Hypnotherapy**: Using hypnosis to access the subconscious mind for healing.
44. **Intuitive Eating**: Listening to your body's hunger and fullness signals.
45. **Japa Meditation**: Repetition of a mantra to calm the mind.
46. **Journaling**: Writing thoughts and feelings to understand and release them.
47. **Kundalini Yoga**: A form of yoga focusing on awakening energy at the base of the spine.
48. **Labyrinth Therapy**: Walking a labyrinth for meditative and therapeutic benefits.
49. **Labyrinth Walking**: Walking a maze for meditation and clarity.
50. **Laughter Yoga**: Combining laughter exercises with yoga breathing.
51. **Light Language**: Using sacred sounds and symbols for healing.
52. **Light Therapy**: Using light to improve mood and energy.
53. **Mandalas**: Creating or coloring mandalas for meditation and focus.
54. **Mantra Meditation**: Repeating a word or phrase to focus the mind.
55. **Massage Therapy**: Manipulating muscles to relieve tension and promote relaxation.
56. **Meditation**: Practicing mindfulness to achieve mental clarity and calm.
57. **Mindful Eating**: Paying full attention to the eating experience.
58. **Mindfulness**: Being present in the moment without judgment.
59. **Music Therapy**: Using music to address emotional and psychological needs.
60. **Nature Walks**: Walking in nature to calm the mind and body.
61. **Neurofeedback**: Using real-time brain activity feedback to improve mental states.
62. **NLP (Neuro-Linguistic Programming)**: Techniques to change patterns of thought and behavior.
63. **Pet Therapy**: Interaction with pets to reduce stress and improve mood.
64. **Qi Gong**: A Chinese practice involving movement, breath, and meditation.
65. **Reiki**: A Japanese technique for stress reduction and relaxation.
66. **Singing Bowls**: Using sound vibrations to balance energy.
67. **Sound Therapy**: Using sound frequencies to improve health and well-being.
68. **Tai Chi**: A Chinese martial art focused on slow, deliberate movements.
69. **Tea Ceremony**: Mindful preparation and consumption of tea.
70. **Therapeutic Touch**: Using hands to balance energy fields.
71. **Transcendental Meditation**: A technique for detaching from anxiety and promoting harmony.
72. **Visualization**: Imagining peaceful scenes to relax the mind.
73. **Walking Meditation**: Mindful walking to achieve calm and focus.
74. **Water Therapy**: Using water for its soothing and healing properties.
75. **Yoga**: Physical, mental, and spiritual practice for balance and peace.

76. **Zen Gardening**: Creating and tending to a zen garden to find tranquility.

See Chart 189 - Inner Peace and Tranquility, Master Chart

Listening

Listening is crucial to raising your vibration because it fosters deeper connections, enhances understanding, and promotes emotional well-being. By truly listening to others, we cultivate empathy and compassion, which are essential for a higher vibrational state. Listening allows us to be fully present, reducing stress and increasing our ability to respond thoughtfully rather than react impulsively. It also helps us to align with our inner peace and harmony, creating a positive ripple effect in our interactions and overall energy.

1. **Acknowledge Non-Verbal Cues**: Recognize body language and facial expressions.
2. **Ask Clarifying Questions**: Seek additional information for better understanding.
3. **Ask Open-Ended Questions**: Encourage expansive responses.
4. **Avoid Distractions**: Eliminate potential interruptions.
5. **Avoid Interruptions**: Allow the speaker to finish their thoughts.
6. **Be Fully Present**: Focus entirely on the speaker.
7. **Be Patient**: Give the speaker time to express themselves.
8. **Body Language Awareness**: Be aware of your own body language.
9. **Clarify Perceptions**: Ensure you understand the speaker's perspective.
10. **Confirm Assumptions**: Verify any assumptions you have made.
11. **Confirm Understanding**: Make sure you comprehend the message.
12. **Control Emotional Responses**: Manage your emotions while listening.
13. **Demonstrate Interest**: Show that you are engaged and interested.
14. **Encourage the Speaker**: Motivate the speaker to continue.
15. **Engage with the Topic**: Actively involve yourself in the discussion.
16. **Express Empathy**: Show that you understand the speaker's feelings.
17. **Follow Up on Conversations**: Continue the dialogue later if needed.
18. **Listen Without Judging**: Avoid making judgments while listening.
19. **Maintain Appropriate Eye Contact**: Make eye contact to show attention.
20. **Manage Internal Dialogue**: Quiet your inner thoughts to focus on the speaker.
21. **Mindful Listening**: Listen with full awareness.
22. **Minimize External Noise**: Reduce background noise to hear better.
23. **Mirror Speaker's Emotions**: Reflect the speaker's emotions back to them.
24. **Nod and Smile Appropriately**: Use non-verbal affirmations.
25. **Note-Taking**: Write down important points.
26. **Paraphrase to Confirm Understanding**: Repeat the speaker's message in your own words.
27. **Patient Listening**: Wait for the speaker to finish without rushing.
28. **Prioritize Listening Over Speaking**: Focus more on listening than talking.
29. **Read Between the Lines**: Understand underlying meanings.
30. **Reflect Feelings**: Acknowledge the speaker's emotions.
31. **Reflective Listening**: Repeat back what you heard to confirm understanding.
32. **Remain Neutral**: Stay unbiased while listening.
33. **Repeat Key Information**: Echo important points.

34. **Respond Appropriately**: Provide suitable responses.
35. **Show Appreciation for the Speaker**: Thank the speaker for sharing.
36. **Summarize the Conversation**: Recap the main points.
37. **Use Affirmative Gestures**: Use gestures to show agreement and understanding.
38. **Wait Before Replying**: Pause before responding to ensure thoughtful replies.

See Chart 194 - Listening, Master Chart

Living Authentically

Living authentically is of paramount importance because it aligns one's actions and behaviors with their true self, fostering a sense of inner peace and fulfillment. When individuals live authentically, they cultivate a deep sense of self-awareness and self-acceptance, embracing their strengths and weaknesses alike. This authenticity allows for more genuine interactions and relationships, as others can sense the honesty and integrity in one's actions. By being true to oneself, individuals can pursue their passions and dreams without fear of judgment or failure, leading to a more meaningful and purpose-driven life. This alignment with one's true self not only reduces inner conflicts and stress but also promotes mental and emotional well-being, creating a foundation for a balanced and harmonious life.

Raising one's vibration through authentic living is transformative. Authenticity fosters a higher state of consciousness, as individuals are no longer weighed down by the need to conform to societal expectations or suppress their true feelings. This liberation allows for a greater flow of positive energy, attracting more uplifting experiences and relationships. When people live authentically, they emit a frequency of truth and integrity, which resonates with others on a similar wavelength, thereby creating a supportive and empowering community. Moreover, authenticity encourages continuous personal growth and self-improvement, as individuals are more likely to seek out opportunities that align with their true selves. This ongoing journey of self-discovery and authenticity ultimately leads to a higher vibrational state, characterized by love, joy, and inner peace, profoundly enhancing one's overall quality of life and spiritual well-being.

1. **Accept compliments**: Take praise graciously without downplaying your achievements.
2. **Accept constructive criticism gracefully**: Learn and grow from feedback provided by others.
3. **Acknowledge your strengths**: Recognize and appreciate your abilities and talents.
4. **Admit your mistakes and learn from them**: Take responsibility and grow from your errors.
5. **Appreciate your uniqueness**: Value what makes you different from others.
6. **Avoid comparing yourself to others**: Focus on your own journey without measuring against others.
7. **Avoid gossip and negative talk**: Steer clear of spreading or indulging in harmful conversations.
8. **Be accountable to yourself**: Take ownership of your actions and their consequences.
9. **Be a role model for authenticity**: Inspire others by living your truth.
10. **Be compassionate towards yourself and others**: Show kindness and understanding in all interactions.

11. **Be honest in your relationships**: Ensure transparency and truthfulness with those you care about.
12. **Be kind to yourself and others**: Practice gentleness and generosity.
13. **Be open to feedback**: Willingly accept insights from others to improve.
14. **Be open to new experiences and opportunities**: Embrace chances for growth and discovery.
15. **Be open to vulnerability**: Allow yourself to be seen and known, even in your imperfections.
16. **Be true to your word**: Honor your commitments and promises.
17. **Be yourself unapologetically**: Embrace your true self without fear of judgment.
18. **Celebrate diversity and individuality**: Respect and honor the differences in everyone.
19. **Celebrate your successes without downplaying them**: Acknowledge and be proud of your achievements.
20. **Challenge your fears**: Confront and overcome what scares you.
21. **Communicate openly and effectively**: Share your thoughts and listen to others.
22. **Cultivate mindfulness and meditation**: Practice being present and aware.
23. **Cultivate positive habits**: Develop routines that enhance your well-being.
24. **Embrace change and adaptability**: Be flexible and open to new directions.
25. **Embrace creativity**: Explore and express your creative side.
26. **Embrace your flaws and imperfections**: Accept that they are part of who you are.
27. **Engage in activities that bring you joy**: Pursue what makes you happy.
28. **Engage in self-reflection**: Regularly assess and understand your thoughts and behaviors.
29. **Express your emotions openly and honestly**: Share how you feel authentically.
30. **Find balance between work and play**: Ensure you have a healthy mix of responsibilities and leisure.
31. **Find joy in simple things**: Appreciate the small pleasures in life.
32. **Find your own definition of success**: Create your personal standard for achievement.
33. **Follow your dreams despite obstacles**: Pursue your aspirations even when it's challenging.
34. **Follow your own path, not the one others expect of you**: Live according to your own choices and desires.
35. **Foster meaningful connections**: Build deep and genuine relationships.
36. **Forgive yourself and others**: Let go of grudges and self-blame.
37. **Honor your body and its needs**: Take care of your physical health and well-being.
38. **Honor your commitments**: Follow through on your promises and obligations.
39. **Honor your heritage and background**: Respect and celebrate your cultural and familial roots.
40. **Invest in your personal growth**: Dedicate time and resources to self-improvement.
41. **Let go of perfectionism**: Accept that imperfection is a natural part of life.
42. **Let go of what no longer serves you**: Release things that hinder your growth.
43. **Listen to your inner voice**: Pay attention to your internal guidance.
44. **Listen to your intuition and trust it**: Believe in your gut feelings.
45. **Live according to your values**: Align your actions with your core beliefs.
46. **Live in the present moment**: Focus on the here and now.
47. **Live with a sense of adventure**: Approach life with curiosity and excitement.

48. **Live with a sense of humor**: Find laughter and joy in life.
49. **Live with integrity**: Act in ways that are morally and ethically sound.
50. **Live with passion and enthusiasm**: Pursue life with energy and zeal.
51. **Live with purpose and intention**: Be deliberate and meaningful in your actions.
52. **Live with an open heart**: Be receptive and loving in your interactions.
53. **Live with authenticity in all interactions**: Be genuine in every aspect of your life.
54. **Practice gratitude daily**: Regularly acknowledge and appreciate what you have.
55. **Practice patience with yourself and others**: Exercise understanding and tolerance.
56. **Practice self-care regularly**: Consistently take care of your mental, emotional, and physical health.
57. **Prioritize your needs and well-being**: Put yourself first when necessary.
58. **Pursue knowledge and learning**: Seek to continuously expand your understanding and skills.
59. **Pursue your passions without apology**: Follow what excites and fulfills you.
60. **Respect others' authenticity**: Honor the truth and uniqueness of those around you.
61. **Respect yourself and your limits**: Acknowledge and adhere to your boundaries.
62. **Seek authenticity in all interactions**: Strive for genuineness in every encounter.
63. **Seek growth and improvement**: Continuously work towards becoming a better version of yourself.
64. **Seek inner peace**: Find calm and tranquility within.
65. **Set boundaries and enforce them**: Clearly define and protect your personal limits.
66. **Share your story and experiences**: Let others learn from your journey.
67. **Share your unique talents and gifts**: Offer what makes you special to the world.
68. **Speak your truth even when it's difficult**: Be honest and straightforward, even when it's tough.
69. **Stand up for what you believe in**: Advocate for your principles and values.
70. **Surround yourself with supportive people**: Build a network of encouragement and positivity.
71. **Take responsibility for your actions**: Own your behaviors and their impacts.
72. **Trust the process of life**: Have faith in how things unfold.
73. **Trust your own judgment**: Rely on your decision-making abilities.
74. **Trust yourself**: Believe in your capabilities and instincts.
75. **Value integrity**: Hold honesty and strong moral principles in high regard.

See Chart 197 - Living Authentically, Master Chart

Manifestation and Law of Attraction

Manifestation and the Law of Attraction are powerful practices that involve using various methods to bring your desires and goals into reality. By focusing your thoughts, energy, and actions on what you want to attract, you can align yourself with the universe to create a life filled with abundance, joy, and success. Techniques like affirmations, visualization, and gratitude journaling help reinforce positive thinking and keep your goals at the forefront of your mind. Engaging in daily rituals, setting clear intentions, and surrounding yourself with positive influences can significantly enhance your ability to manifest your desires.

There are numerous ways to practice manifestation and the Law of Attraction, each offering unique benefits and approaches. From creating vision boards and using crystals to participating in group manifestations and attending spiritual retreats, the methods are diverse and can be tailored to fit individual preferences and needs. Whether you choose to use sound healing, engage in positive self-talk, or practice gratitude walks, incorporating these techniques into your daily life can help you maintain a high vibration and stay aligned with your goals. Consistency, mindfulness, and a positive mindset are key components in effectively harnessing the Law of Attraction to manifest your dreams.

1. **Act As If**: Behave as if you've already achieved your goals.
2. **Affirmations**: Repeat positive statements about what you want to manifest.
3. **Art Therapy**: Use art to express and visualize your desires.
4. **Astrology**: Align your actions with astrological events.
5. **Body Code**: Address physical and energetic blockages.
6. **Bowenwork**: Use Bowenwork techniques to support physical alignment.
7. **Chakra Balancing**: Balance your chakras to enhance manifestation.
8. **Color Therapy**: Use colors to influence your mood and energy.
9. **Creating Routines**: Establish routines that support your goals.
10. **Creating Space**: Physically and mentally create space for new opportunities.
11. **Crystals Healing**: Use crystals like citrine or pyrite to amplify manifestation.
12. **Cymatics**: Use sound and vibration to influence your manifestation.
13. **Daily Affirmation Cards**: Draw a daily affirmation card.
14. **Daily Challenges**: Set and complete daily manifestation challenges.
15. **Daily Goals**: Set and achieve small daily goals.
16. **Daily Rituals**: Establish daily rituals that support your manifestation.
17. **Dance and Movement**: Use dance to raise your vibration.
18. **Decluttering**: Remove physical clutter to create mental clarity.
19. **EFT Tapping**: Tap on meridian points to release limiting beliefs.
20. **Energy Alignment**: Align your energy with your desires through practices like Reiki.
21. **Energy Clearing**: Remove negative energy from your space.
22. **Energy Medicine**: Use energy medicine practices to align your energy.
23. **Energy Visualization**: Visualize your energy field aligning with your desires.
24. **Emotion Code**: Release trapped emotions that hinder manifestation.
25. **Essential Oils**: Use oils like lavender or frankincense to enhance your mood.
26. **Feedback Loop**: Regularly review and adjust your manifestation strategies.
27. **Feng Shui**: Arrange your space to support positive energy flow.
28. **Full Moon Rituals**: Perform rituals during the full moon for release and intention setting.
29. **Goal Setting**: Clearly define your goals and set actionable steps.
30. **Gratitude Journaling**: Write down things you're grateful for daily.
31. **Gratitude Rituals**: Incorporate gratitude into your daily routine.
32. **Gratitude Walks**: Take walks and focus on things you're grateful for.
33. **Group Manifestation**: Manifest with a group for amplified energy.
34. **Guided Visualization**: Use guided visualization recordings.
35. **Homeopathy**: Use homeopathic remedies to support your goals.
36. **Hypnotherapy**: Use hypnosis to reprogram your subconscious.
37. **Intention Setting**: Set clear intentions for what you want to attract.

38. **Intuition Development**: Strengthen your intuition to guide your manifestation.
39. **Law of Attraction Apps**: Use apps designed to help you stay focused on your goals.
40. **Life Coaching**: Work with a coach to clarify and achieve your goals.
41. **Listening to Affirmations**: Use audio affirmations to reinforce positive thoughts.
42. **Listening to LOA Podcasts**: Gain insights from experts via podcasts.
43. **Listening to Uplifting Music**: Use music to boost your mood and energy.
44. **Manifestation Games**: Play games that reinforce positive thinking.
45. **Manifestation Journal**: Keep a journal dedicated to your manifestation journey.
46. **Meditation**: Focus your mind and visualize your goals clearly.
47. **Mentorship**: Seek guidance from a mentor who practices LOA.
48. **Mind Mapping**: Create mind maps of your goals and desires.
49. **Mind Movies**: Create a video montage of your goals with uplifting music.
50. **Mindfulness**: Stay present and focused on your goals.
51. **Mirror Work**: Speak affirmations while looking into a mirror.
52. **Nature Connection**: Spend time in nature to ground yourself.
53. **New Moon Rituals**: Set intentions during the new moon.
54. **Numerology**: Use numbers to gain insight into your desires.
55. **Pendulum Dowsing**: Use a pendulum to get clarity on your desires.
56. **Positive Environment**: Surround yourself with positivity.
57. **Positive Media**: Consume positive and inspirational media.
58. **Positive Role Models**: Learn from those who have successfully manifested their desires.
59. **Positive Self-Talk**: Talk to yourself in a positive and encouraging way.
60. **Positive Thinking**: Replace negative thoughts with positive ones.
61. **Prayer**: Communicate your desires through prayer.
62. **Reading LOA Books**: Read books about the Law of Attraction for inspiration.
63. **Sage Smudging**: Clear negative energy with sage.
64. **Self-Care**: Prioritize self-care to maintain high energy.
65. **Sound Healing**: Use sound frequencies to align your energy.
66. **Spiritual Ceremonies**: Participate in ceremonies that align with your beliefs.
67. **Spiritual Retreats**: Attend retreats to deepen your manifestation practice.
68. **Scripting**: Write about your desires as if they've already happened.
69. **Storytelling**: Tell positive stories about your future.
70. **Subconscious Reprogramming**: Use techniques to reprogram your subconscious mind.
71. **Tuning Forks**: Use tuning forks to balance your energy.
72. **Vision Boards**: Create a visual representation of your goals and desires.
73. **Vision Statement**: Write a detailed statement of your vision.
74. **Water Manifestation**: Speak intentions into water before drinking it.
75. **Writing Letters to the Universe**: Write letters to the universe expressing your desires.

See Chart 203 - Manifestation and Law of Attraction, Master Chart

Negative Beliefs

Letting go of negative beliefs is crucial to raising your vibration because these beliefs create emotional and mental barriers that prevent you from experiencing joy, peace, and fulfillment. Negative beliefs keep you stuck in a low vibrational state, where fear, doubt, and self-criticism dominate your thoughts and actions. By releasing these limiting thoughts, you open yourself to positive energy, higher consciousness, and a more harmonious life. Releasing negative beliefs allows you to embrace your true potential, cultivate self-love, and attract more positive experiences into your life. This transformation not only enhances your well-being but also positively impacts those around you, creating a ripple effect of higher vibrations.

1. **Change Is Dangerous**: Believing that any change will lead to negative outcomes.
2. **Happiness Is Temporary**: Thinking that happiness is fleeting and will not last.
3. **I am a Failure**: Viewing oneself as inherently unsuccessful.
4. **I am Lazy**: Seeing oneself as unwilling to work or exert effort.
5. **I am Stupid**: Believing oneself to be unintelligent.
6. **I am Worthless**: Feeling that one has no value or worth.
7. **I Can Never Get Ahead**: Thinking that progress or success is impossible.
8. **I Can't Do Anything Right**: Believing that one is incapable of doing things correctly.
9. **I Can't Trust Anyone**: Feeling that no one is trustworthy.
10. **I Don't Belong Anywhere**: Believing that one does not fit in anywhere.
11. **I Don't Deserve Happiness**: Feeling unworthy of happiness.
12. **I Don't Deserve Success**: Believing that one is not entitled to succeed.
13. **I Don't Matter**: Feeling insignificant or unimportant.
14. **I Must Be Perfect to Be Loved**: Believing that love is contingent on perfection.
15. **I Must Earn My Worth**: Feeling that one must prove their value through actions.
16. **I Must Not Make Mistakes**: Believing that mistakes are unacceptable.
17. **I Must Not Show Weakness**: Thinking that showing vulnerability is wrong.
18. **I Must Suffer to Earn Love**: Believing that love must be earned through suffering.
19. **I Never Do Anything Right**: Feeling that one is always wrong or incompetent.
20. **I Should Never Have Been Born**: Believing that one's existence is a mistake.
21. **I'll Never Be Good Enough**: Feeling perpetually inadequate.
22. **I'll Never Be Happy**: Believing that happiness is unattainable.
23. **I'm A Burden to Others**: Thinking that one is a constant burden to others.
24. **I'm Always the Problem**: Believing that one is always the cause of issues.
25. **I'm Destined to Fail**: Feeling that failure is inevitable.
26. **I'm Invisible**: Believing that one is unnoticed or unimportant.
27. **I'm Not Capable of Being Loved**: Feeling unworthy of love.
28. **I'm Not Good Enough**: Believing that one is insufficient.
29. **I'm Not Interesting**: Thinking that one is boring or dull.
30. **I'm Not Smart Enough**: Feeling intellectually inadequate.
31. **I'm Not Strong Enough to Face My Fears**: Believing that one lacks the strength to confront fears.
32. **I'm Not Worthy of Attention**: Feeling undeserving of attention.
33. **I'm Too Weak to Change**: Believing that one lacks the strength to make changes.
34. **It's My Fault When Things Go Wrong**: Feeling responsible for all negative outcomes.
35. **Love Is Conditional**: Believing that love must be earned through certain conditions.

36. **Money does not Come Easy**: Thinking that financial success is difficult to achieve.
37. **Money is the Root of All Evil**: Believing that money inherently causes bad things.
38. **My Needs are Not Important**: Feeling that one's needs are insignificant.
39. **My Opinions Are Not Valuable**: Believing that one's opinions lack worth.
40. **My Voice Doesn't Count**: Feeling that one's voice or input is unimportant.
41. **No One Loves Me**: Believing that one is unloved.
42. **No One Understands Me**: Feeling misunderstood by everyone.
43. **No One Will Ever Love Me**: Believing that one is incapable of being loved.
44. **No Point in Even Trying**: Thinking that efforts are futile.
45. **People Are Inherently Untrustworthy**: Believing that people cannot be trusted.
46. **People Will Always Leave Me**: Feeling that everyone will eventually abandon you.
47. **Showing Emotions is a Sign Of Weakness**: Believing that expressing emotions indicates weakness.

See Chart 208 - Negative Beliefs, Master Chart

Neuroplasticity

Gregg Braden, a renowned author and speaker, emphasizes the power of neuroplasticity—the brain's ability to reorganize itself by forming new neural connections throughout life. This concept highlights how our thoughts, experiences, and activities can physically alter the brain. To harness the potential of neuroplasticity, Braden suggests focusing on several key areas. **Cognitive Activities** (Chart 215), such as puzzles and learning new skills, stimulate brain function and enhance cognitive abilities. **Creative Activities** (Chart 222), such as art, music, and writing, stimulate the brain's creative centers and encourage innovative thinking. **Lifestyle Choices** (Chart 227), like proper nutrition, adequate sleep, and stress management, are crucial for maintaining optimal brain function and supporting neuroplasticity. **Mindset and Attitude** (Chart 233), including maintaining a positive outlook and embracing challenges, play a significant role in shaping brain plasticity by fostering resilience and adaptability. **Physical Activities** (Chart 236), including exercise and movement, boost brain health by increasing blood flow and promoting the release of growth factors. Lastly, **Social Engagement** (Chart 242), involving meaningful interactions and relationships, strengthens neural networks and promotes emotional well-being. By integrating these areas into our daily lives, we can effectively enhance our brain's capacity to learn, adapt, and thrive.

See Chart 213 - Neuroplasticity, Grand Master Chart

Problem Solving: Ways to Respond

In the landscape of human relationships, conflicts and misunderstandings are inevitable, yet they also present opportunities for profound growth and deeper connection. Navigating these challenges with grace and wisdom often requires a multifaceted approach, embodying practices such as acceptance, acknowledgment, and adaptation. These practices allow for a flexible and open-hearted stance towards resolution. Communication stands as a pillar in this process, where phrases like "Can we talk about why this happened?" or "I need some time to process this" foster a safe space for honesty and clarity. Emphasizing the need for empathy through statements like

"I felt hurt by what you did" coupled with a willingness to forgive and heal paves the way for genuine understanding and reconciliation.

Using these responses can help you raise your vibrations by promoting a mindset of empathy, understanding, and positive action. Each response is designed to address conflicts or misunderstandings in a constructive and respectful manner, which helps to diffuse negative emotions and replace them with higher-vibration emotions such as compassion, gratitude, and love. For example, responses like "I don't want to argue; I want to understand" or "Can we talk about why this happened?" encourage open and honest communication, clearing up misunderstandings and preventing the buildup of negative emotions. By seeking to understand the other person's perspective, you foster a sense of empathy and connection, which are key components of higher vibrational states.

In moments where emotions run high, grounding practices like breathing and pausing become invaluable, guiding us back to a place of calm and presence. Engaging in reflective listening and seeking to understand rather than to be understood encourages mutual respect that can bridge even the widest of gaps. The aspiration to evolve and grow together, acknowledging "I think we both need to make some changes," reflects a commitment to the relationship's health and the individual journeys within it. Ultimately, embracing love as the guiding principle, aspiring to navigate conflicts with an intention to heal, uplift, and transform, not only enriches our connections but elevates our collective consciousness.

By asking, "In my highest and best good, how should I respond to the situation I'm dealing with right now?" you can transform potentially negative interactions into opportunities for growth, understanding, and deeper connection, all of which contribute to raising your vibrational frequency.

See Chart 247 - Problem Solving: Ways to Respond, Master Chart

Random Acts of Kindness

Random acts of kindness have a profound ability to raise your vibrations by cultivating positive emotions and fostering a sense of connection and purpose. When you engage in kind acts, such as adopting a pet, cooking a meal for someone, or forgiving mistakes, you not only make a positive impact on others but also on yourself. These actions generate feelings of joy, satisfaction, and fulfillment, which are high-vibration emotions that elevate your overall energy. For example, adopting a pet can bring immense love and companionship into your life, while cooking a meal for someone shows care and appreciation, enhancing your sense of community and belonging.

Moreover, simple gestures like smiling at a stranger, writing a positive review, or picking up litter contribute to a positive environment and inspire others to act kindly as well. These small, thoughtful actions create a ripple effect of positivity that can uplift the collective energy of those around you. By choosing to be inclusive, donating to various causes, and supporting local artists or new businesses, you foster a sense of generosity and support, which further enhances your vibrational state. Engaging in these random acts of kindness helps to shift your focus away from personal worries and towards the well-being of others, promoting a mindset of abundance and gratitude. In turn, this not only raises your vibrations but also contributes to creating a more compassionate and connected world.

See Chart 260 - Random Acts of Kindness, Master Chart

Resilience and Coping Strategies

Resilience and coping strategies are vital tools for navigating the inevitable challenges and stressors of life. Developing these skills involves a multifaceted approach, beginning with Accepting Change and fostering Adaptability. This flexibility allows individuals to respond more effectively to unexpected events and transitions. Engaging in healthy practices such as a Balanced Diet, Exercise, and Maintaining Hydration supports physical resilience, while techniques like Breathing Exercises, Meditation, and Mindfulness aid in managing stress and maintaining emotional balance. Cultivating a support network through Open Communication, Nurturing Relationships, and Social Connections provides essential emotional and psychological backing during tough times. Additionally, prioritizing Self-Care, engaging in Hobbies, and practicing Relaxation Techniques contribute to overall well-being, reinforcing one's ability to cope with life's demands.

On a deeper level, building resilience involves internal practices such as Challenging Negative Thoughts, Practicing Acceptance, and fostering Compassionate Self-Talk. These cognitive strategies help reframe stressors and promote a more optimistic outlook. Reflective Practices, Journaling, and Expressive Writing allow for emotional processing and self-awareness, while Problem-Solving Skills and Setting Achievable Goals enhance one's ability to handle difficulties constructively. Spiritual Practices, Quality Time with Loved Ones, and activities like Yoga and Music Therapy offer holistic benefits, nurturing the mind, body, and spirit. Seeking Professional Help and participating in Support Groups provide additional layers of support and guidance. Ultimately, resilience and coping strategies form a robust foundation for managing life's ups and downs, empowering individuals to thrive despite adversity.

1. **Accepting Change**: Embracing and adapting to new circumstances, rather than resisting them.
2. **Adaptability**: The ability to adjust to new conditions or changes in the environment.
3. **Assertive Communication**: Expressing oneself confidently and clearly while respecting others.
4. **Balanced Diet**: Consuming a variety of nutrients to maintain health and energy levels.
5. **Breathing Exercises**: Techniques to control and regulate breathing for stress reduction.
6. **Building a Support Network**: Creating a group of reliable friends and family for emotional and practical support.
7. **Challenging Negative Thoughts**: Identifying and questioning irrational or harmful thoughts.
8. **Cognitive Behavioral Therapy (CBT)**: A therapeutic approach to changing negative thought patterns and behaviors.
9. **Commitment to Goals**: Setting and adhering to personal and professional objectives.
10. **Compassionate Self-Talk**: Speaking to oneself with kindness and understanding.
11. **Connecting with Nature**: Spending time outdoors to reduce stress and enhance well-being.

12. **Creativity**: Using imagination to generate new ideas or solutions.
13. **Cultivating Gratitude**: Fostering an attitude of thankfulness and appreciation.
14. **Deep Relaxation Techniques**: Methods such as progressive muscle relaxation to achieve a state of deep calm.
15. **Developing Empathy**: Understanding and sharing the feelings of others.
16. **Digital Detox**: Taking a break from digital devices to reduce stress and increase mindfulness.
17. **Discovering Purpose**: Identifying and pursuing what gives one's life meaning and direction.
18. **Emotional Regulation**: Managing and responding to emotional experiences in a healthy way.
19. **Engaging in Hobbies**: Participating in enjoyable activities to relax and unwind.
20. **Exercise**: Physical activity to improve health and reduce stress.
21. **Expressive Writing**: Writing to explore and express thoughts and feelings.
22. **Family Support**: Relying on family members for emotional and practical assistance.
23. **Finding Humor**: Using humor to lighten the mood and cope with stress.
24. **Flexible Thinking**: Adapting one's thinking to new information and situations.
25. **Forgiveness**: Letting go of anger and resentment towards oneself or others.
26. **Fostering Optimism**: Encouraging a positive outlook on life.
27. **Healthy Sleep Patterns**: Maintaining consistent and restorative sleep habits.
28. **Helping Others**: Offering assistance and support to those in need.
29. **Hydration**: Drinking adequate water to maintain bodily functions and energy.
30. **Journaling**: Writing regularly to reflect on experiences and emotions.
31. **Laughter**: Using humor to enhance mood and reduce stress.
32. **Learning from Failures**: Using mistakes as opportunities for growth and improvement.
33. **Limiting Alcohol Consumption**: Reducing or avoiding alcohol intake for better health.
34. **Limiting Caffeine Intake**: Managing caffeine consumption to avoid negative health effects.
35. **Maintaining Boundaries**: Setting and respecting personal limits in relationships and activities.
36. **Managing Expectations**: Setting realistic goals and expectations to reduce disappointment.
37. **Managing Finances**: Planning and controlling financial resources to reduce stress.
38. **Managing Stress**: Using strategies to cope with and reduce stress levels.
39. **Meditation**: Practicing mindfulness or focused concentration to calm the mind.
40. **Mindfulness**: Being fully present and engaged in the current moment.
41. **Music Therapy**: Using music to improve mental health and well-being.
42. **Networking**: Building professional and social connections for support and opportunities.
43. **Nurturing Relationships**: Investing time and effort into meaningful connections with others.
44. **Open Communication**: Sharing thoughts and feelings honestly and openly.
45. **Positive Affirmations**: Repeating encouraging statements to boost confidence and positivity.
46. **Practicing Acceptance**: Embracing situations as they are, without resistance.

47. **Practicing Kindness**: Acting with consideration and compassion towards others.
48. **Prioritizing Self-Care**: Taking time to care for one's own health and well-being.
49. **Problem-Solving Skills**: Developing strategies to effectively address and resolve issues.
50. **Progressive Muscle Relaxation**: A technique for reducing muscle tension and stress.
51. **Pursuing Passions**: Engaging in activities that excite and fulfill one's interests.
52. **Quality Time with Loved Ones**: Spending meaningful time with friends and family.
53. **Reading Inspirational Materials**: Engaging with content that motivates and uplifts.
54. **Reflective Practices**: Taking time to reflect on experiences and learn from them.
55. **Regular Physical Activity**: Engaging in consistent exercise to maintain physical health.
56. **Relaxation Techniques**: Methods to calm the mind and body.
57. **Seeking Professional Help**: Consulting with therapists or counselors for support.
58. **Setting Achievable Goals**: Establishing realistic and attainable objectives.
59. **Social Connections**: Building and maintaining relationships with others.
60. **Spiritual Practices**: Engaging in activities that nurture the spirit.
61. **Staying Informed**: Keeping up-to-date with relevant information and knowledge.
62. **Stress Management Techniques**: Employing methods to control and reduce stress.
63. **Support Groups**: Participating in groups with shared experiences for mutual support.
64. **Taking Breaks**: Allowing time for rest and recovery during tasks.
65. **Time Management**: Organizing and planning time effectively.
66. **Trusting Intuition**: Relying on one's inner guidance and instincts.
67. **Utilizing Humor**: Incorporating humor into daily life to manage stress.
68. **Volunteering**: Offering time and effort to help others without compensation.
69. **Visualization**: Using mental imagery to achieve relaxation or goals.
70. **Walking**: Engaging in walking as a form of exercise and relaxation.
71. **Work-Life Balance**: Maintaining a healthy balance between work responsibilities and personal life.
72. **Yoga**: Practicing yoga to enhance physical and mental well-being.
73. **Zeroing in on Strengths**: Focusing on and utilizing one's positive attributes.
74. **Zone of Control Awareness**: Recognizing and focusing on aspects of life within one's control.
75. **Zoning Out for Rest**: Taking time to disengage and relax mentally.

See Chart 266 - Resilience and Coping Strategies, Master Chart

Secondary Gains

Secondary gain refers to the indirect benefits that individuals receive from maintaining certain behaviors or conditions, often those that are perceived as negative or undesirable. These gains are typically unconscious and serve as a form of psychological reinforcement that makes it difficult for individuals to change their behaviors or circumstances. For example, someone might avoid social interactions due to anxiety but gain increased support and sympathy from others, which inadvertently reinforces their avoidance behavior. Secondary gains can include avoiding responsibilities, receiving compassion, gaining control over others, or experiencing temporary relief from stress. While these benefits may provide short-term comfort, they can hinder personal growth and the ability to achieve a higher state of well-being.

Releasing secondary gains is essential for raising one's vibration and achieving a higher level of consciousness. When individuals cling to these gains, they remain trapped in a cycle of avoidance and dependency, which prevents them from confronting and overcoming their underlying issues. By identifying and letting go of secondary gains, individuals can break free from limiting patterns and embrace personal responsibility, empowerment, and self-awareness. This process allows them to face challenges head-on, develop healthier coping mechanisms, and ultimately raise their vibrational frequency. Higher vibration is associated with increased emotional resilience, inner peace, and a greater sense of connection to the universe, all of which contribute to a more fulfilling and enlightened life.

1. **Avoid Responsibilities**: Dodging tasks and duties that are perceived as burdensome or overwhelming.
2. **Avoid Social Interactions**: Evading social engagements to reduce stress or anxiety associated with socializing.
3. **Avoid Unpleasant Tasks**: Steering clear of tasks that are seen as difficult, uncomfortable, or boring.
4. **Avoidance of Conflict**: Staying away from situations that might lead to disagreements or confrontations.
5. **Compassion from Others**: Receiving empathy and kindness from people in response to one's struggles or hardships.
6. **Control Over Others**: Gaining influence or authority over others' actions or decisions.
7. **Distraction from Personal Issues**: Using external situations to divert attention away from internal problems or emotions.
8. **Escape from Reality**: Finding relief from the pressures and stresses of real life through avoidance behaviors.
9. **Escape from Stress**: Avoiding situations or responsibilities that are perceived as stressful.
10. **Excuse for Poor Performance**: Using avoidance or other secondary gains to justify not performing well in various aspects of life.
11. **Fear Avoidance**: Steering clear of situations or activities that provoke fear or anxiety.
12. **Financial Benefits**: Receiving monetary gain or assistance due to one's circumstances or actions.
13. **Free Time**: Gaining additional time for oneself by avoiding responsibilities or commitments.
14. **Gain Sympathy**: Attracting sympathy and understanding from others due to one's situation or behavior.
15. **Get Attention**: Drawing attention from others to oneself, often through negative means.
16. **Get Away from a Situation**: Exiting a scenario that is uncomfortable or undesirable.
17. **Get Away from Someone**: Avoiding a person who is perceived as problematic or toxic.
18. **Get Out of Commitments**: Finding reasons or excuses to withdraw from previously made obligations.

19. **Get Out of Responsibilities**: Escaping duties or tasks that are seen as too challenging or overwhelming.
20. **Get Out of Work**: Avoiding job-related responsibilities or tasks.
21. **Increased Support**: Receiving more help or assistance from others due to one's situation.
22. **Justification for Anger**: Using one's circumstances as a reason to express or feel justified in their anger.
23. **Justification for Behavior**: Rationalizing one's actions or behavior based on their situation or experiences.
24. **Justification for Laziness**: Using one's situation to justify lack of effort or inactivity.
25. **Justification for Procrastination**: Finding reasons to delay or avoid completing tasks.
26. **Justification for Unhealthy Habits**: Rationalizing harmful behaviors or habits due to one's circumstances.
27. **Less Accountability**: Reducing the level of responsibility or accountability for one's actions.
28. **Less Stress**: Lowering stress levels by avoiding responsibilities or difficult situations.
29. **Manipulation of Others**: Influencing or controlling others to achieve desired outcomes or gain.
30. **Monetary Compensation**: Receiving financial rewards or compensation due to one's situation.
31. **More Rest**: Gaining additional rest or relaxation time by avoiding responsibilities.
32. **Not Facing Fears**: Avoiding confronting one's fears or anxieties.
33. **Not Having to Change**: Staying in a comfortable or familiar situation without needing to make changes.
34. **Not Meeting Expectations**: Avoiding the pressure of meeting others' expectations or standards.
35. **Not Taking Risks**: Staying within a comfort zone to avoid the uncertainty and potential failure associated with taking risks.
36. **Pity from Others**: Eliciting pity or sympathy from others due to one's situation.
37. **Power Over Others**: Gaining dominance or influence over others.
38. **Protection from Failure**: Avoiding situations that could lead to failure or disappointment.
39. **Receive Gifts**: Getting tangible rewards or gifts due to one's situation.
40. **Receive Praise**: Receiving compliments or positive feedback from others.
41. **Relief from Pressure**: Alleviating pressure by avoiding demanding tasks or situations.
42. **Remaining in Comfort Zone**: Staying in a safe, familiar environment without venturing into new or challenging areas.
43. **Security of the Known**: Feeling safe and secure in familiar surroundings and routines.
44. **Sense of Importance**: Feeling valued or important due to one's circumstances or behavior.
45. **Sense of Safety**: Feeling secure and protected from perceived threats or dangers.
46. **Temporary Relief**: Experiencing short-term relief from stress or pressure by avoiding responsibilities.
47. **Time for Hobbies**: Gaining extra time to engage in personal interests and hobbies.
48. **Time for Leisure**: Having more free time for relaxation and leisure activities.
49. **Time Off Work**: Taking a break from job-related duties and responsibilities.

50. **Validation of Feelings**: Receiving acknowledgment and validation of one's emotions from others.
51. **Victimhood**: Adopting a victim mentality to gain sympathy, avoid responsibilities, or justify behavior.

See Chart 272 - Secondary Gain, Master Chart

Self-Care

Self-care is a powerful tool in raising your vibration as it encompasses practices that nurture your physical, mental, and emotional well-being. When you engage in self-care, you are consciously choosing to honor and respect yourself, which in turn sends positive signals to your body and mind. This act of self-love creates a harmonious internal environment, reducing stress and promoting relaxation. As stress levels decrease, your energy flow becomes more balanced and aligned, allowing you to connect more deeply with your higher self and the universe. Regular self-care practices, such as mindful eating, exercise, and adequate rest, ensure that your body is well-nourished and energized, providing a strong foundation for higher vibrational frequencies.

In addition to physical self-care, nurturing your emotional and mental health is crucial for raising your vibration. Practices like meditation, journaling, and spending time in nature help clear your mind of negative thoughts and emotions, creating space for positive energy to flow. By addressing and healing emotional wounds, you release trapped emotions that may be lowering your vibrational frequency. Self-care rituals such as affirmations, gratitude exercises, and creative expression further enhance your emotional well-being, fostering a sense of inner peace and joy. As you cultivate a loving and compassionate relationship with yourself, you naturally elevate your vibration, attracting more positivity and harmony into your life.

See Chart 281 - Self-Care, Master Chart

Self-Compassion

Self-compassion is the practice of treating oneself with the same kindness, understanding, and empathy that one would offer to a friend. It involves recognizing our imperfections, allowing ourselves to rest, and appreciating both our bodies and efforts. Engaging in self-compassion means asking for help when needed, avoiding negative self-talk, and being gentle with ourselves during difficult times. It's about celebrating small wins, cherishing our uniqueness, and comforting ourselves in moments of distress. Connecting with our inner child, cultivating self-awareness, and embracing our emotions are all key aspects of self-compassion, as is the practice of letting go of perfectionism and setting realistic goals.

Furthermore, self-compassion involves activities like meditating for clarity, nurturing our passions, and protecting our energy. It is important to reflect on our progress, respect our boundaries, and prioritize our well-being. By engaging in practices such as writing letters to ourselves, visualizing our success, and spending time in nature, we can foster a deep sense of self-love and acceptance. Self-compassion encourages us to take breaks, rest when tired, and appreciate the simple joys in life. Ultimately, it is about treating ourselves with the same kindness and respect we would offer to someone we care about, thereby fostering a healthier and more balanced life.

1. **Accept Your Flaws**: Recognize and embrace your imperfections as a part of your unique self.
2. **Allow Yourself to Rest**: Give yourself permission to take breaks and rejuvenate.
3. **Appreciate Your Body**: Acknowledge and be thankful for your physical form and what it allows you to do.
4. **Appreciate Your Efforts**: Recognize and value the hard work you put into your tasks and endeavors.
5. **Ask for Help When Needed**: Seek assistance from others when you are struggling or need support.
6. **Avoid Negative Self-Talk**: Refrain from speaking to yourself in a critical or harsh manner.
7. **Be Gentle with Yourself**: Treat yourself with kindness and compassion, especially during tough times.
8. **Be Kind to Your Mind**: Engage in activities and thoughts that promote mental well-being.
9. **Celebrate Small Wins**: Acknowledge and take pride in minor accomplishments along your journey.
10. **Cherish Your Uniqueness**: Value the qualities and traits that make you different from others.
11. **Comfort Yourself in Distress**: Provide yourself with soothing and calming practices when you are upset.
12. **Connect with Your Inner Child**: Revisit and nurture the playful and innocent aspects of your younger self.
13. **Cultivate Self-Awareness**: Develop an understanding of your thoughts, emotions, and behaviors.
14. **Cultivate Self-Compassion**: Practice kindness and empathy towards yourself, especially during failures.
15. **Declutter Your Mind**: Clear away mental clutter to improve focus and clarity.
16. **Develop a Growth Mindset**: Embrace challenges and view failures as opportunities for learning.
17. **Embrace Your Emotions**: Accept and process your feelings without judgment.
18. **Embrace Your Journey**: Appreciate the path you are on, with all its ups and downs.
19. **Encourage Yourself Daily**: Give yourself positive affirmations and support every day.
20. **Engage in Positive Affirmations**: Regularly practice affirmations that promote self-worth and confidence.
21. **Enjoy Moments of Solitude**: Take pleasure in spending time alone for reflection and peace.
22. **Express Gratitude Regularly**: Frequently acknowledge and give thanks for the good things in your life.
23. **Focus on What You Can Control**: Direct your energy towards aspects of your life that you have influence over.
24. **Forgive Your Mistakes**: Let go of past errors and understand that they are part of the learning process.

25. **Give Yourself Permission to Feel**: Allow yourself to experience emotions fully without suppression.
26. **Go Easy on Yourself**: Avoid being overly harsh or demanding on yourself.
27. **Honor Your Needs**: Recognize and prioritize your personal requirements for well-being.
28. **Improve Through Learning**: Continuously seek knowledge and skills for personal growth.
29. **Indulge in Self-Care**: Take time to engage in activities that nurture and rejuvenate you.
30. **Journal Your Thoughts**: Write down your thoughts and feelings to understand and process them better.
31. **Laugh at Your Imperfections**: Find humor in your flaws and accept them as part of being human.
32. **Learn to Say No**: Establish boundaries by declining requests that do not serve your well-being.
33. **Let Go of Perfectionism**: Release the need to be perfect and accept yourself as you are.
34. **Listen to Your Body**: Pay attention to your physical signals and respond accordingly.
35. **Make Peace with the Past**: Accept and reconcile with past events to move forward.
36. **Meditate for Clarity**: Practice meditation to gain mental clarity and calmness.
37. **Nourish Your Soul**: Engage in activities that feed your spirit and bring you joy.
38. **Nurture Your Passions**: Pursue and develop interests that ignite your enthusiasm.
39. **Offer Yourself Compassion**: Be kind and understanding towards yourself in moments of difficulty.
40. **Practice Mindfulness**: Stay present and fully engage with the current moment.
41. **Practice Self-Forgiveness**: Forgive yourself for past mistakes and move forward with a lighter heart.
42. **Prioritize Self-Reflection**: Take time to reflect on your actions, thoughts, and feelings for self-improvement.
43. **Prioritize Your Well-Being**: Put your physical, mental, and emotional health first.
44. **Protect Your Energy**: Set boundaries to safeguard your emotional and mental energy.
45. **Recognize Your Achievements**: Acknowledge and celebrate your accomplishments.
46. **Reflect on Your Progress**: Regularly review and appreciate the progress you have made.
47. **Release Self-Judgment**: Let go of harsh self-criticism and be gentle with yourself.
48. **Respect Your Boundaries**: Honor the limits you set for yourself to maintain balance and well-being.
49. **Respect Your Emotions**: Validate your feelings and understand that they are a natural part of your experience.
50. **Rest When Tired**: Allow yourself to rest and recharge when you are feeling fatigued.
51. **Reward Yourself**: Treat yourself with rewards for your efforts and accomplishments.
52. **Seek Joy in Simple Things**: Find happiness in the small, everyday moments.
53. **Set Realistic Goals**: Establish achievable and practical objectives for yourself.
54. **Show Yourself Love**: Engage in self-love practices to nurture your emotional health.
55. **Simplify Your Life**: Reduce complexity in your life to focus on what truly matters.
56. **Smile at Your Reflections**: Smile at yourself in the mirror to boost self-esteem and positivity.

57. **Speak Kindly to Yourself**: Use gentle and supportive language when talking to yourself.
58. **Spend Time in Nature**: Connect with nature to rejuvenate and find peace.
59. **Surround Yourself with Positivity**: Keep positive influences and supportive people around you.
60. **Take Breaks**: Take regular breaks to rest and recharge.
61. **Take Care of Your Body**: Maintain your physical health through proper nutrition, exercise, and rest.
62. **Take Deep Breaths**: Practice deep breathing to reduce stress and calm your mind.
63. **Take Time for Hobbies**: Engage in activities you enjoy to boost your happiness and creativity.
64. **Treat Yourself as a Friend**: Show yourself the same kindness and compassion you would offer a friend.
65. **Treat Yourself with Respect**: Value and honor yourself in all aspects of life.
66. **Trust in Your Abilities**: Have confidence in your skills and strengths.
67. **Understand Your Limits**: Recognize and respect your boundaries and limitations.
68. **Validate Your Feelings**: Acknowledge and accept your emotions as they are.
69. **Value Your Time**: Use your time wisely and for things that matter to you.
70. **Visualize Your Success**: Imagine and affirm your achievements and goals.
71. **Walk Away from Negativity**: Distance yourself from negative influences and environments.
72. **Welcome Self-Discovery**: Embrace the journey of understanding yourself better.
73. **Write Letters to Yourself**: Write supportive and encouraging letters to yourself.
74. **Write Positive Notes**: Create notes with positive affirmations and reminders.
75. **Write Your Own Story**: Take control of your narrative and define your own path.
76.

See Chart 290 - Self-Compassion, Master Chart

Self-Love

Self-love is a transformative practice that significantly raises your vibration by fostering a deep sense of self-acceptance and compassion. When you engage in self-love, you prioritize activities that nourish your mind, body, and soul, creating a foundation of positivity and well-being. Hydrating often, eating healthily, and exercising regularly are simple yet powerful ways to show love to your physical body, which directly impacts your energy levels and overall vibration. By setting personal goals and celebrating your successes, you build confidence and a sense of accomplishment, further elevating your mood and vibrational frequency. Engaging in creative pursuits like sketching, singing, or dancing freely allows you to express your authentic self, releasing any pent-up emotions and inviting joy into your life.

Moreover, self-love involves nurturing your mental and emotional health by setting boundaries, practicing mindfulness, and seeking supportive relationships. Spending time alone, meditating, and keeping a dream diary help you explore and understand your inner world, promoting a sense of peace and clarity. Acts of self-compassion, such as speaking kindly to yourself and forgiving yourself, dissolve negative self-talk and replace it with loving affirmations, boosting your self-esteem and vibrational energy. Participating in communal activities like attending live events, joining clubs, or volunteering connects you with like-minded individuals and fosters a sense of belonging and support. These practices create a positive feedback loop, where the more you love and care for yourself, the higher your vibration becomes, attracting even more positivity and abundance into your life.

See Chart 295 - Self-Love, Master Chart

Self-Sabotage

Self-sabotage is a behavior pattern where individuals consciously or unconsciously hinder their own success and personal growth. This self-defeating behavior can manifest in various ways, such as procrastination, negative self-talk, or engaging in unhealthy relationships. People who self-sabotage often struggle with feelings of inadequacy, fear of failure, or fear of success. These underlying fears and insecurities drive them to create obstacles in their own path, ultimately preventing them from achieving their goals and fulfilling their potential. The cycle of self-sabotage can be difficult to break, as it often becomes ingrained in one's behavior and thought patterns over time.

Addressing self-sabotage requires self-awareness and a commitment to change. It begins with recognizing and acknowledging the behaviors and thought processes that contribute to self-sabotage. From there, individuals can work on developing healthier habits and coping mechanisms, such as setting realistic goals, practicing self-compassion, and seeking support from others. Therapy or counseling can also be beneficial in uncovering the root causes of self-sabotaging behavior and providing strategies to overcome it. By actively working to replace self-sabotaging actions with positive, goal-oriented behaviors, individuals can break free from the cycle and move towards a more fulfilling and successful life.

1. **Avoiding Responsibility**: Failing to take ownership of one's actions or duties, leading to missed opportunities and lack of progress.
2. **Blaming Others**: Shifting the fault for one's own mistakes or failures onto others, preventing personal growth and accountability.
3. **Burning Bridges**: Damaging relationships and connections that could provide support and opportunities in the future.
4. **Choosing Unhealthy Relationships**: Engaging with people who negatively impact one's well-being and hinder personal development.
5. **Complaining Excessively**: Focusing on problems rather than solutions, which can foster a negative mindset and impede progress.
6. **Comparing Yourself to Others**: Measuring one's worth against others, leading to feelings of inadequacy and discouragement.
7. **Consistently Being Late**: Habitually arriving late, which can damage one's reputation and relationships.
8. **Creating Drama**: Engaging in unnecessary conflict or complications that distract from important goals.
9. **Criticizing Yourself Harshly**: Being overly critical of oneself, which can damage self-esteem and motivation.
10. **Delaying Decisions**: Postponing important decisions, leading to missed opportunities and stagnation.

11. **Denying Problems**: Refusing to acknowledge issues, which prevents finding solutions and making progress.
12. **Disregarding Feedback**: Ignoring constructive criticism that could help improve performance and outcomes.
13. **Disrespecting Boundaries**: Overstepping personal or professional boundaries, causing strain in relationships and environments.
14. **Engaging in Negative Self-Talk**: Internalizing and repeating negative thoughts about oneself, undermining confidence and self-worth.
15. **Exaggerating Problems**: Blowing issues out of proportion, which can lead to unnecessary stress and inaction.
16. **Expecting Perfection**: Setting unattainable standards that can result in constant disappointment and procrastination.
17. **Focusing on Failures**: Dwelling on past mistakes rather than learning from them and moving forward.
18. **Giving Up Easily**: Abandoning efforts prematurely when faced with challenges, preventing success.
19. **Holding Grudges**: Harboring resentment that can poison relationships and mental well-being.
20. **Ignoring Advice**: Dismissing helpful suggestions from others that could lead to better decisions and outcomes.
21. **Ignoring Self-Care**: Neglecting one's physical and mental health, leading to burnout and decreased productivity.
22. **Impulsiveness**: Making hasty decisions without considering the consequences, often resulting in negative outcomes.
23. **Indulging in Excessive Fear**: Allowing fear to dominate decisions and actions, limiting opportunities for growth.
24. **Lacking Discipline**: Failing to maintain focus and consistency in efforts, leading to unachieved goals.
25. **Lying to Yourself**: Avoiding the truth about one's actions or feelings, preventing genuine self-improvement.
26. **Making Excuses**: Rationalizing failures instead of taking responsibility and making necessary changes.
27. **Mismanaging Time**: Poorly allocating time, leading to inefficiency and uncompleted tasks.
28. **Neglecting Personal Growth**: Failing to pursue learning and development opportunities that enhance skills and knowledge.
29. **Neglecting Physical Health**: Ignoring the importance of exercise, nutrition, and rest, resulting in poor overall health.
30. **Not Asking for Help**: Refusing to seek assistance when needed, which can lead to overwhelm and failure.
31. **Not Setting Goals**: Failing to establish clear objectives, resulting in a lack of direction and purpose.
32. **Not Taking Breaks**: Overworking without rest, leading to burnout and reduced effectiveness.
33. **Obsessing Over Mistakes**: Fixating on errors instead of learning from them and moving on.

34. **Overcommitting**: Taking on too many tasks, leading to stress and inability to perform well.
35. **Overworking**: Excessively working to the detriment of health and well-being, often as a means to avoid dealing with other issues.
36. **People-Pleasing**: Prioritizing others' approval over one's own needs and goals, resulting in neglect of personal aspirations.
37. **Perfectionism**: Striving for flawlessness, which can lead to procrastination and dissatisfaction.
38. **Procrastinating**: Delaying tasks unnecessarily, resulting in stress and lower quality work.
39. **Projecting Insecurities**: Attributing one's own insecurities to others, which can damage relationships and self-esteem.
40. **Pursuing Unrealistic Goals**: Setting unattainable objectives, leading to frustration and a sense of failure.
41. **Refusing Change**: Resisting new ideas or methods, which can prevent progress and adaptation.
42. **Refusing to Delegate**: Insisting on doing everything oneself, leading to overwhelm and inefficiency.
43. **Rejecting Compliments**: Dismissing positive feedback, which can undermine self-esteem and confidence.
44. **Resisting Learning**: Avoiding new knowledge or skills, which can hinder personal and professional growth.
45. **Resisting New Experiences**: Shying away from unfamiliar situations, limiting opportunities for development and enjoyment.
46. **Resisting Positive Change**: Opposing beneficial changes out of fear or stubbornness, maintaining the status quo.
47. **Sabotaging Relationships**: Engaging in behaviors that harm relationships, leading to isolation and support loss.
48. **Seeking Validation**: Constantly needing others' approval, which can lead to dependency and lack of self-assurance.
49. **Self-Doubt**: Lacking confidence in one's abilities, preventing the pursuit of opportunities.
50. **Self-Harm**: Engaging in harmful behaviors towards oneself, reflecting deep-seated issues and perpetuating pain.
51. **Setting Unrealistic Expectations**: Expecting too much from oneself or others, leading to disappointment and frustration.
52. **Shaming Yourself**: Engaging in self-blame and guilt, which can damage self-esteem and hinder progress.
53. **Skipping Meals**: Neglecting nutrition, which can affect physical and mental health.
54. **Staying in Toxic Environments**: Remaining in harmful situations that negatively impact well-being.
55. **Staying Up Late**: Not getting enough rest, leading to decreased productivity and health issues.
56. **Suppressing Emotions**: Ignoring or hiding feelings, which can lead to emotional distress and health problems.

57. **Taking Unnecessary Risks**: Engaging in dangerous behaviors without considering the consequences.
58. **Underestimating Abilities**: Not recognizing one's potential, leading to missed opportunities.
59. **Underperforming**: Not putting in the necessary effort, resulting in poor outcomes and lost opportunities.
60. **Undervaluing Achievements**: Not acknowledging or appreciating one's successes, which can undermine motivation and self-worth.
61. **Using Substances**: Relying on drugs or alcohol to cope, which can lead to addiction and other serious issues.
62. **Wasting Opportunities**: Not taking advantage of chances for growth or success, leading to regret.
63. **Withholding Effort**: Not putting in the necessary work, leading to subpar results and unfulfilled potential.
64. **Withholding Love**: Not allowing oneself to give or receive love, leading to loneliness and isolation.
65. **Withholding Trust**: Not trusting others, which can hinder relationship-building and support networks.
66. **Working Inefficiently**: Not using time or resources effectively, leading to poor productivity and outcomes.
67. **Worrying Excessively**: Spending too much time fretting about potential problems, which can lead to inaction and stress.
68. **Yielding to Peer Pressure**: Allowing others to influence one's decisions negatively, leading to actions against one's best interests.
69. **Yielding to Temptations**: Giving in to short-term desires that can derail long-term goals.
70. **You Attract People Who Put You Down**: Surrounding yourself with individuals who undermine your confidence and self-worth.
71. **You Believe You Don't Deserve Success**: Holding a belief that you're unworthy of achievement, which can prevent you from pursuing goals.
72. **You Keep Your Ideas to Yourself**: Not sharing thoughts or innovations, which can limit opportunities for collaboration and growth.
73. **You Let Fear Control You**: Allowing fear to dictate your actions, preventing progress and taking risks.
74. **You Settle for Less**: Accepting less than you deserve or are capable of, leading to unfulfilled potential.
75. **You Stay in Your Comfort Zone**: Avoiding challenges and new experiences, which can limit growth and achievement.

See Chart 300 - Self-Sabotage, Master Chart

Shadow Issues

Shadow issues are the hidden or suppressed aspects of ourselves that we often avoid acknowledging. These can manifest as negative behaviors, thoughts, or feelings that we project onto others or internalize, causing self-sabotage and hindering personal growth. Originating from past traumas, unhealed wounds, and unmet needs, shadow issues influence our actions and relationships in ways we might not fully understand. They represent the parts of our psyche that we deem unacceptable or unworthy, and thus, push into the unconscious. However, ignoring these aspects can lead to a variety of problems, including anxiety, depression, and strained relationships.

Addressing shadow issues involves bringing these hidden parts into conscious awareness and integrating them into our sense of self. This process, often referred to as shadow work, requires self-reflection, honesty, and compassion. By recognizing and accepting our shadow aspects, we can heal old wounds, release limiting beliefs, and transform negative patterns. This journey allows us to reclaim the energy spent on repression and use it for personal growth and empowerment. Embracing our shadow not only fosters a deeper understanding of ourselves but also enhances our capacity for empathy and connection with others. Through this transformative work, we can achieve greater wholeness and authenticity in our lives.

1. **Always Being Right**: Insisting on your correctness in every situation, often ignoring or dismissing others' perspectives.
2. **Always Having Drama**: Constantly creating or being involved in conflict or emotional upheavals.
3. **Always Wanting Revenge**: Harboring a constant desire to get back at those who have wronged you.
4. **Avoiding Responsibility**: Refusing to take accountability for your actions or obligations.
5. **Blaming Others**: Assigning fault to others for your own problems or failures.
6. **Competing**: Feeling the need to outdo others in every situation.
7. **Controlling Behavior**: Attempting to dictate or manage the actions and decisions of others.
8. **Creating Chaos**: Generating confusion and disorder in your environment or relationships.
9. **Criticizing Others**: Regularly finding fault with others and expressing disapproval.
10. **Defensiveness**: Reacting to feedback or criticism with protective or dismissive behavior.
11. **Denial of Problems**: Refusing to acknowledge or accept the existence of issues in your life.
12. **Desiring Approval**: Seeking constant validation and acceptance from others.
13. **Disengaging from Life**: Withdrawing from activities, responsibilities, and social interactions.
14. **Doubting Self**: Lacking confidence in your abilities and decisions.
15. **Exposing Everyone**: Revealing others' flaws, secrets, or mistakes, often to elevate yourself.
16. **Fear of Abandonment**: Being terrified of being left alone or unloved.
17. **Fear of Failure**: Avoiding risks or challenges due to the fear of not succeeding.
18. **Fear of Intimacy**: Avoiding close emotional connections due to fear of vulnerability.
19. **Feeling Inadequate**: Believing you are not good enough or lack value.
20. **Feeling Like a Victim**: Perceiving yourself as always being wronged or powerless.
21. **Fighting**: Engaging in constant arguments or confrontations.
22. **Hiding**: Concealing your true self or avoiding visibility to feel safe.

23. **Insecurity**: Lacking confidence and feeling uncertain about yourself or your worth.
24. **Judging Others**: Making harsh or unfair evaluations of others' actions or character.
25. **Lack of Trust**: Finding it difficult to rely on or believe in others.
26. **Manipulation**: Influencing or controlling others for personal gain or advantage.
27. **Needing to Be Different**: Feeling compelled to stand out or be unique to feel valued.
28. **Needing to Be Poor**: Subconsciously maintaining a state of financial lack.
29. **Needing to Be Safe**: Prioritizing safety and security over growth or change.
30. **Needing to Be Sick**: Subconsciously maintaining illness or ailments.
31. **Needing to Be the Same**: Conforming to norms to avoid standing out or facing rejection.
32. **Needing to Numb Feelings**: Using substances or behaviors to avoid emotional pain.
33. **Not Being Happy**: Persistently feeling discontent or unfulfilled.
34. **Not Being Visible**: Avoiding attention or recognition to remain unnoticed.
35. **Not Healing**: Resisting recovery or improvement from physical or emotional wounds.
36. **Not Learning**: Refusing to grow or acquire new knowledge or skills.
37. **Not Trusting Others**: Struggling to place faith or confidence in people.
38. **Not Working**: Avoiding employment or productive activities.
39. **Perfectionism**: Setting unattainably high standards for yourself and others.
40. **Pleasing Others**: Prioritizing others' happiness and approval over your own needs.
41. **Preventing Others from Getting Too Close**: Keeping emotional distance to avoid vulnerability.
42. **Procrastination**: Delaying or avoiding tasks and responsibilities.
43. **Proving Why You Can't Do Something**: Justifying your inability to achieve or change.
44. **Pushing Others Away**: Creating distance in relationships to avoid closeness.
45. **Rebelling**: Opposing authority or norms to assert independence.
46. **Resisting Change**: Avoiding or fighting against new situations or transformations.
47. **Retreating**: Withdrawing from challenges or social interactions to feel secure.
48. **Seeking Attention**: Desiring to be the focus of others' interest and concern.
49. **Seeking Validation**: Looking for others' approval to feel worthy or accepted.
50. **Struggling with Everyone**: Experiencing ongoing conflict and friction in relationships.

See Chart 305 - Shadow Issues, Master Chart

Subjects for Exploration

Embarking on a journey to elevate your consciousness is a profound quest that intertwines the essence of your being with the universe's infinite wisdom. This explorative path offers a kaleidoscopic array of topics, each a doorway to deeper self-awareness and universal connection.

From achieving inner peace and understanding the transformative Age of Aquarius to harnessing the elements like Air for inspiration and delving into Altered States of Consciousness, every subject serves as a stepping stone towards a more enlightened self. You'll traverse the ancient wisdom of Civilizations long past, communicate with Angelic beings, resolve Anger, and learn from Animal Guides, all while reducing Anxiety and using Aromatherapy to soothe the mind.

Art Therapy provides insights into the soul, Ascension Symptoms guide your spiritual journey, and Astral Projection offers a unique perspective on existence. Astrological Influences and Aura Reading align you with the cosmos, while Authentic Expression and Balance and Harmony cultivate your inner and outer world equilibrium. This holistic approach, enriched by dowsing, enables you to tap into your subconscious, offering a tailored exploration of profound topics like Biofeedback for Awareness, the significance of Bird Messages, and the cyclic nature of Birth and Rebirth. Each aspect, from Boundary Setting to exploring the Cosmic Awareness, Creative Inspiration, and Crystal Energies, is designed to amplify your vibrational frequency, fostering a deep sense of connection, gratitude, and joy. By engaging with these Matters for Exploration, you open yourself to a transformational journey, not just seeking to raise your consciousness but to profoundly enrich your life with wisdom, love, and a palpable sense of interconnectedness with all that is.

1. **Achieving Inner Peace:** Discovering the tranquility within to navigate life's storms with serenity.
2. **Age of Aquarius:** Exploring the era of heightened consciousness and harmony in human relations.
3. **Air for Inspiration:** Drawing upon the element of air to fuel creativity and fresh perspectives.
4. **Altered States of Consciousness:** Venturing beyond ordinary awareness to access deeper insights and spiritual realms.
5. **Ancient Civilizations:** Unearthing wisdom from past cultures to illuminate present and future paths.
6. **Angelic Communications:** Connecting with angelic beings for guidance and protection on your spiritual journey.
7. **Anger Resolution:** Transforming anger into positive action and deeper understanding of self and others.
8. **Animal Guides:** Seeking wisdom from animal spirits to guide and enrich your life journey.
9. **Anxiety Reduction:** Cultivating calmness and resilience in the face of life's uncertainties.
10. **Aromatherapy for the Mind:** Using the power of scent to elevate mood and awaken higher states of consciousness.
11. **Art Therapy Insights:** Exploring emotions and subconscious through creative expression for healing and self-discovery.
12. **Ascension Symptoms:** Navigating the physical and emotional shifts associated with spiritual awakening.
13. **Astral Projection:** Experiencing out-of-body journeys to explore spiritual dimensions and gain new perspectives.
14. **Astrological Influences:** Understanding cosmic alignments and their impact on personal growth and life path.
15. **Aura Reading:** Discerning the energy fields around living beings to understand emotional and spiritual states.
16. **Authentic Expression:** Embracing and communicating your true self with the world.
17. **Balance and Harmony:** Finding equilibrium in all aspects of life for holistic well-being.
18. **Biofeedback for Awareness:** Using technology to enhance mindfulness and control over physiological states.

19. **Bird Messages:** Interpreting messages from avian encounters as spiritual signs or guidance.
20. **Birth and Rebirth:** Embracing the cycles of endings and new beginnings as opportunities for growth.
21. **Boundary Setting:** Establishing healthy limits in relationships for self-care and mutual respect.
22. **Building Confidence:** Strengthening self-belief to pursue goals and face challenges with courage.
23. **Celebrations of the Soul:** Honoring life's milestones and achievements as part of the spiritual journey.
24. **Centering Practices:** Cultivating inner stillness and presence amidst life's chaos.
25. **Ceremonies for Life Changes:** Marking transitions and intentions with ritual for deeper meaning and connection.
26. **Chakra Balancing:** Aligning the energy centers for physical, emotional, and spiritual harmony.
27. **Challenges as Opportunities:** Viewing obstacles as chances for growth and learning.
28. **Chanting for Vibrational Change:** Using the power of voice to transform energy and consciousness.
29. **Clairaudience Techniques:** Developing the ability to hear beyond the physical for spiritual messages.
30. **Clairsentience Development:** Honing intuitive feeling for deeper empathy and understanding.
31. **Clairvoyance Exploration:** Cultivating the gift of spiritual vision to see beyond the visible.
32. **Cognitive Behavioral Techniques:** Applying psychological tools for positive mental health and growth.
33. **Coincidences as Messages:** Interpreting serendipitous events as guidance from the universe.
34. **Collective Unconscious:** Connecting with the shared human psyche for universal wisdom and archetypes.
35. **Color Therapy:** Utilizing colors' healing properties to influence mood and energy.
36. **Communing with Nature:** Deepening connection with the natural world for grounding and inspiration.
37. **Community Building:** Fostering supportive networks for shared growth and collective well-being.
38. **Contrast and Duality:** Appreciating life's polarities as catalysts for deeper understanding and balance.
39. **Cosmic Awareness:** Expanding consciousness to embrace the interconnectedness of all existence.
40. **Courage to Change:** Embracing the strength to transform oneself and one's life circumstances.
41. **Creative Inspiration:** Tapping into the muse within and around to manifest art and innovation.
42. **Crystal Energies:** Harnessing the vibrational power of crystals for healing and spiritual growth.

43. **Cultivating Gratitude:** Fostering a sense of thankfulness as a pathway to abundance and joy.
44. **Cultivating Joy:** Seeking and embracing moments of happiness as essential to the soul's nourishment.
45. **Cultivating Presence:** Being fully in the moment to enhance life's experiences and spiritual connection.
46. **Cultural Awareness:** Exploring diverse cultures to broaden understanding and foster global harmony.
47. **Dance as Expression:** Using movement as a language of the soul for emotional release and joy.
48. **Death and Transformation:** Embracing endings as essential for growth and new beginnings.
49. **Developing Compassion:** Expanding the heart's capacity to empathize and connect deeply with all beings.
50. **Dream Interpretation:** Unlocking the messages in dreams for guidance and insight into the subconscious.
51. **Drum Circles for Connection:** Engaging in rhythmic harmony to unite individuals and elevate collective energy.
52. **Duality to Non-Duality:** Transcending binary thinking to embrace the oneness of existence.
53. **Earth as Support:** Recognizing and honoring the Earth as a nurturing foundation for life and spiritual practice.
54. **Elemental Energies:** Working with the elements (earth, air, fire, water) for harmony and insight.
55. **Embracing the Future:** Openly accepting what's to come with optimism and readiness for growth.
56. **Emotional Healing:** Addressing and resolving past hurts for a liberated and vibrant heart.
57. **Empaths and Sensitives:** Navigating the world as a highly sensitive individual with boundaries and grace.
58. **Energy Healing Techniques:** Employing various modalities to manipulate and restore the body's energetic balance.
59. **Energy Protection:** Shielding oneself from negative influences for spiritual integrity and well-being.
60. **Energy Vortexes:** Exploring places of powerful energy for transformation and connection to the divine.
61. **Enhancing Empathy:** Developing the ability to understand and share the feelings of another.
62. **Enhancing Focus:** Cultivating concentration and clarity for effectiveness in all aspects of life.
63. **Environmental Consciousness:** Fostering awareness and action towards the health of our planet.
64. **Ether and Spirituality:** Delving into the fifth element as a bridge to higher realms and consciousness.
65. **Exploring the Void:** Venturing into the unknown and formless space for profound discovery and rebirth.

66. **Faith Beyond Belief:** Embracing a deep trust in the universe and the journey of the soul.
67. **Fasting for Clarity:** Using abstention from food as a tool for mental, physical, and spiritual purification.
68. **Fear vs. Love:** Choosing love over fear as a guiding principle in life's decisions and relationships.
69. **Feng Shui for Well-being:** Arranging physical spaces to enhance energy flow and personal harmony.
70. **Fire as Transformer:** Utilizing the element of fire for change, purification, and renewal.
71. **Forgiveness Processes:** Releasing the bonds of resentment for freedom and peace.
72. **Grasping the Infinite:** Contemplating the boundless nature of the universe and our place within it.
73. **Grounding Techniques:** Connecting with the Earth to stabilize energy and maintain presence.
74. **Heart Coherence:** Achieving a state of harmony between the heart and mind for holistic wellness.
75. **Hermitic Insights:** Discovering wisdom in solitude and the contemplative life.
76. **Hero's Journey:** Embracing life's adventures as paths to personal growth and self-discovery.
77. **Historical Consciousness Shifts:** Reflecting on pivotal moments in history that have transformed collective awareness.
78. **Holotropic Breathwork:** Using controlled breathing for emotional release and transcendence.
79. **Hope in Darkness:** Finding light and possibility in the midst of challenges and uncertainty.
80. **Humanitarian Efforts:** Contributing to the welfare of humanity for a more compassionate world.
81. **Hypnotherapy for Change:** Utilizing trance states to reprogram the subconscious for positive transformation.
82. **I Ching Interpretations:** Consulting ancient wisdom for guidance and decision-making.
83. Illusions of the Ego: Recognizing and transcending egoic delusions for true freedom and unity.
84. **Improving Memory:** Enhancing cognitive recall for learning and personal development.
85. **Indigo, Crystal, and Rainbow Children:** Understanding and supporting the unique gifts of spiritually advanced souls.
86. **Interconnectedness:** Acknowledging the deep ties that bind all life and existence.
87. **Interdimensional Travel:** Exploring the possibility of journeying beyond the physical dimensions.
88. **Intuition Development:** Honing the inner voice as a guide for life's choices and spiritual path.
89. **Joy as Purpose:** Embracing joy not just as an emotion but as a central aim of life.
90. **Karma and Dharma:** Navigating the laws of cause and effect and one's duty in the world for spiritual alignment.
91. **Kundalini Awakening:** Awakening the dormant spiritual energy within for enlightenment and transformation.
92. **Lessons of Life:** Learning from every experience as opportunities for growth and understanding.

93. **Letting Go of the Past:** Releasing attachments to former experiences for a liberated present and future.
94. **Ley Lines Exploration:** Investigating the alignments of ancient sites and their energetic significance.
95. **Life After Death:** Contemplating the continuity of consciousness beyond physical existence.
96. **Light Language:** Communicating with divine light frequencies for healing and activation.
97. **Lightworkers and Starseeds:** Supporting those who are here to uplift and heal the planet through their innate gifts.
98. **Living in the Present:** Emphasizing mindfulness and presence as keys to fulfillment and awareness.
99. **Love as the Ultimate Truth:** Recognizing love as the fundamental force and goal of the spiritual journey.
100. **Lucid Dreaming:** Gaining awareness within dreams to explore the subconscious and spiritual realms.
101. **Manifesting Desires:** Harnessing the power of intention and visualization to bring dreams into reality.
102. **Manifesting Reality:** Understanding the co-creative process of reality manifestation through thought, belief, and action.
103. **Martial Arts Meditation:** Integrating physical discipline with mental and spiritual practices for balance and enlightenment.
104. **Meditation Techniques:** Exploring various forms of meditation for inner peace, clarity, and spiritual connection.
105. **Mind-Body Connection:** Acknowledging and nurturing the interdependence of physical and mental health.
106. **Mindfulness Practices:** Cultivating awareness of the present moment for enhanced living and spiritual growth.
107. **Monastic Life Lessons:** Drawing wisdom from monastic traditions for simplicity, focus, and spiritual dedication.
108. **Moon Phases and Emotions:** Understanding the lunar cycles' influence on emotions and behavior.
109. **Morphic Resonance:** Exploring the hypothesis that natural systems inherit a collective memory.
110. **Multidimensional Being:** Embracing the complexity and depth of our existence beyond the physical realm.
111. **Music and Consciousness:** Experiencing music as a medium for emotional expression and consciousness expansion.
112. **Mystical Traditions:** Delving into the teachings and practices of mystical paths for deeper spiritual insights.
113. **Mythological Archetypes:** Exploring universal figures and stories that resonate across cultures and time for personal insight.
114. **Nature Spirits:** Connecting with the spirits of the natural world for guidance and companionship.
115. **Near-Death Experiences:** Investigating the transformative insights and spiritual awakenings resulting from near-death experiences.

116. **Neuroplasticity Exercises:** Utilizing brain training practices to enhance mental agility and consciousness.
117. **Non-Attachment:** Practicing detachment from outcomes and material possessions for inner freedom and peace.
118. **Numerology for Personal Growth:** Employing the symbolism and energy of numbers to understand life paths and personal traits.
119. **Oracles and Divination:** Seeking guidance through various forms of divination for insight and direction.
120. **Overcoming Fears:** Addressing and releasing fears as barriers to personal and spiritual growth.
121. **Overcoming Grief:** Navigating the process of loss and mourning to find healing and renewed purpose.
122. **Pain as Teacher:** Recognizing pain as a catalyst for profound personal transformation and empathy.
123. **Past Life Memories:** Exploring memories of past lives for insights into current challenges and talents.
124. **Pastoral Counseling:** Integrating spiritual guidance with psychological support for holistic healing.
125. **Peace Amidst Chaos:** Cultivating inner tranquility in the face of external turmoil and uncertainty.
126. **Planetary Alignments:** Investigating the influence of planetary positions on personal and collective energies.
127. **Plant Consciousness:** Engaging with the consciousness of plants for wisdom, healing, and connection.
128. **Prayer as Conscious Practice:** Utilizing prayer as a means of communication with the divine for support and guidance.
129. **Prophecies and Predictions:** Examining historical and contemporary prophecies for insights into the human journey.
130. **Psychic Abilities:** Developing and understanding psychic senses for guidance and enhanced awareness.
131. **Qi Gong for Energy Flow:** Practicing Qi Gong to harmonize and strengthen the body's energy systems.
132. **Quantum Consciousness:** Exploring the quantum aspects of consciousness and reality.
133. **Quantum Entanglement:** Delving into the phenomenon of interconnectedness at the quantum level as a metaphor for spiritual unity.
134. **Reincarnation Beliefs:** Contemplating the cycle of birth, death, and rebirth for spiritual understanding and karma.
135. **Remote Viewing:** Using psychic ability to perceive distant or unseen targets for exploration and information gathering.
136. **Resolving Conflict:** Applying wisdom and compassion to resolve interpersonal disputes and foster harmony.
137. **Retreats for Renewal:** Participating in retreats for rest, reflection, and spiritual rejuvenation.
138. **Rituals for Transformation:** Creating and engaging in rituals as powerful tools for marking transitions and manifesting intentions.

139. **Rune Stones Insights:** Gaining insights and guidance through the ancient practice of rune casting.
140. **Sacred Geometry:** Studying the spiritual significance of geometric shapes and patterns in the natural and constructed world.
141. **Sacred Pilgrimages:** Undertaking journeys to sacred sites for spiritual awakening and connection.
142. **Sacred Spaces:** Creating and honoring physical spaces dedicated to spiritual practice and reflection.
143. **Sacred Texts Insights:** Drawing wisdom and inspiration from sacred scriptures across various traditions.
144. **Self-Love Practices:** Cultivating a loving and compassionate relationship with oneself as a foundation for well-being and growth.
145. **Service to Others:** Recognizing the importance of altruism and service in spiritual development and societal health.
146. **Shamanic Journeying:** Engaging in shamanic practices to connect with spiritual realms and gain guidance.
147. **Singing Bowls Harmonics:** Experiencing the healing vibrations of singing bowls for balance and meditation.
148. **Social Justice and Equality:** Advocating for fairness and equality as expressions of spiritual values in action.
149. **Solar Flares and Consciousness:** Investigating the impact of solar activity on human consciousness and behavior.
150. **Soul Groups and Contracts:** Exploring connections with soul groups and pre-life agreements for mutual growth and fulfillment.
151. **Sound Healing:** Utilizing the therapeutic potential of sound frequencies to heal and harmonize the body and spirit.
152. **Spiritual Awakening:** Embracing the process of becoming more conscious of spiritual realities and one's true nature.
153. **Spiritual Evolution:** Committing to personal and collective spiritual growth and evolution.
154. **Spiritual Guides:** Connecting with and learning from spiritual guides for direction and enlightenment.
155. **Spiritual Practices Across Cultures:** Exploring and honoring the diverse spiritual traditions and practices around the world.
156. **Stewardship of the Earth:** Taking responsibility for the care and protection of the planet as a sacred duty.
157. **Storytelling Traditions:** Appreciating the power of stories to convey wisdom, values, and cultural heritage.
158. **Strengthening Relationships:** Building deeper and more meaningful connections with others through understanding and empathy.
159. **Stress Management:** Developing strategies to cope with stress for a healthier and more balanced life.
160. **Subconscious Beliefs:** Uncovering and transforming limiting beliefs that reside in the subconscious mind.
161. **Synchronicities and Signs:** Recognizing and interpreting the significance of synchronicities and signs as guidance.

162. **Tantra for Consciousness:** Exploring tantra as a path to spiritual connection and heightened awareness.
163. **Tarot for Self-Discovery:** Using tarot cards as tools for introspection and understanding life's journey.
164. **Telepathy Practices:** Developing the ability to communicate thoughts and emotions directly without verbal or physical means.
165. **The Akashic Records:** Accessing the Akashic Records for insights into past, present, and future potentials.
166. **The Art of Surrender:** Learning to let go and trust in the flow of life for peace and fulfillment.
167. **The Circle of Life:** Contemplating the cyclical nature of existence and our role within it.
168. **The Cycle of Destruction:** Understanding the role of destruction and dissolution in the process of renewal and growth.
169. **The Eternal Soul:** Reflecting on the soul's immortality and its journey through various lifetimes.
170. **The Field of Potentiality:** Exploring the infinite possibilities that exist within the quantum field for manifestation and creativity.
171. **The Gift of Giving:** Recognizing the joy and spiritual growth that come from selflessly giving to others.
172. **The Human Experience:** Appreciating the unique challenges and opportunities of living as a human being on Earth.
173. **The Illusion of Separation:** Dissolving the perceived barriers between self and others, embracing the interconnectedness of all.
174. **The Journey Home:** Understanding life as a journey back to the source, to our true spiritual essence.
175. b Practicing the art of allowing as a form of acceptance and trust in the universe's flow.
176. **The Law of Attraction:** Harnessing the principle that like attracts like to draw desired experiences into one's life.
177. **The Law of Detachment:** Embracing detachment to create space for outcomes to unfold naturally and without resistance.
178. **The Middle Path:** Finding balance and moderation in all things as a way to harmony and enlightenment.
179. **The Mystery of Creation:** Contemplating the origins and purposes of existence and our role within it.
180. **The Power of Now:** Emphasizing the importance of living fully in the present moment for peace and clarity.
181. **The Power of Silence:** Discovering the transformative and healing properties of silence in one's life and practice.
182. **The Power of Thought:** Acknowledging thoughts as creative forces that shape our reality and experiences.
183. **The Reality of Oneness:** Recognizing the underlying unity of all existence beyond apparent differences and divisions.
184. **The Shift in Consciousness:** Participating in the collective movement towards higher awareness and spiritual awakening.
185. **The True Self:** Uncovering and embodying the authentic self beyond social masks and egoic identities.

186. **The Web of Life:** Acknowledging our interdependence with all life forms and the ecosystem.
187. **Timelessness:** Exploring the concept of eternity and the transcendence of linear time.
188. **Totem Animals:** Connecting with totem animals as spiritual allies and guides.
189. **Transcending the Ego:** Moving beyond ego-based consciousness to embrace a higher sense of self and unity.
190. **Transpersonal Psychology:** Integrating spiritual experiences within the framework of psychology for holistic healing.
191. **Trust in the Universe:** Cultivating trust in the universe's wisdom and timing for guidance and support.
192. **Unity Consciousness:** Embracing a state of awareness that sees and honors the unity in all diversity.
193. **Universal Love:** Experiencing and expressing unconditional love as the highest form of connection and truth.
194. **Vibrational Medicine:** Utilizing the principle that everything is energy to heal and balance the body, mind, and spirit.
195. **Vulnerability as Strength:** Embracing openness and vulnerability as pathways to genuine connection and growth.
196. **Water as Cleanser:** Using water as a spiritual and physical cleanser for purification and renewal.
197. **Wisdom of Insecurity:** Finding security in the acceptance of life's inherent uncertainties and changes.
198. **Witness Consciousness:** Cultivating the ability to observe thoughts and emotions without attachment for insight and liberation.

See Chart 309 - Subjects for Exploration, Master Chart

Thoughts That Hinder an Abundance Mindset

Thoughts that hinder an abundance mindset often stem from deep-seated beliefs and perceptions about scarcity, self-worth, and potential. These thoughts can manifest as a constant focus on lack, fear of failure, and a persistent feeling of not being enough. When our minds are preoccupied with what we don't have, it becomes challenging to recognize and appreciate the abundance already present in our lives. This scarcity mindset limits our ability to envision a future filled with prosperity and success. It restricts our actions and decisions, causing us to miss opportunities that could lead to greater abundance. Bruce Lipton, in his book "The Biology of Belief," explains how our beliefs, often programmed from childhood, shape our reality. He states, "Our positive and negative beliefs not only impact our health but also our emotional state and our ability to succeed in life."

Negative self-talk and limiting beliefs are major barriers to an abundance mindset. These include thoughts such as "I will never have enough," "I don't deserve success," or "Opportunities are for others, not for me." Such beliefs create a self-fulfilling prophecy, where the lack of confidence and fear of inadequacy prevent us from taking risks and seizing opportunities. Lipton highlights that these subconscious programs can be reprogrammed to foster a more positive outlook. By consciously changing our thoughts and beliefs, we can shift from a scarcity mindset to one of abundance. He asserts, "When you change your beliefs, you change your reality." Embracing this perspective involves recognizing and challenging limiting beliefs, practicing gratitude, and visualizing success, thereby creating a mental environment where abundance can flourish.

See Chart 319 - Thoughts that Hinder an Abundance Mindset, Master Chart

Vibrational Interferences

Clearing Vibrational Interferences such as addiction cycles, dense energy fields, extraterrestrial interference, karmic patterns, and physical trauma residue is essential for raising your vibration. These interferences can anchor you in lower vibrational states, creating energetic blockages and preventing the free flow of positive energy. By removing these obstacles, you can elevate your vibrational frequency, leading to greater emotional, mental, and spiritual well-being. This process allows for a higher state of consciousness, enabling you to experience more joy, clarity, and alignment with your true self.

Releasing vibrational interferences like depression clouds, false beliefs, lack of boundaries, and psychic attacks can significantly enhance your vibrational state. These interferences often manifest as negative thought patterns and emotional disturbances that drain your energy and lower your vibrational frequency. By addressing and clearing these detrimental influences, you create space for positive energies to flow freely, fostering an environment of inner peace and heightened awareness. This shift not only boosts your overall vibration but also supports a healthier, more balanced, and fulfilling life.

See Chart 323 - Vibrational Interferences, Master Chart

Visualization Techniques

Visualization techniques are powerful tools that harness the power of the mind to improve mental, emotional, and physical well-being. By creating vivid mental images, individuals can influence their thoughts, feelings, and behaviors, leading to positive outcomes in various aspects of life. For example, abundance visualization helps cultivate a mindset of plenty and gratitude, attracting prosperity and joy. Similarly, career success visualization enables individuals to see themselves achieving their professional goals, enhancing motivation, focus, and self-belief. These techniques engage all senses, making the imagined scenarios feel real and attainable, which in turn helps in manifesting these visions into reality.

Incorporating visualization into daily routines can lead to significant improvements in overall well-being. Techniques like emotional healing visualization and self-love visualization promote emotional resilience and self-compassion, essential for mental health. Health and wellness visualization focuses on enhancing physical vitality, while stress relief visualization provides a mental escape from daily pressures, fostering relaxation and peace. Whether it's grounding visualization to increase stability, intuition enhancement visualization to boost insight, or manifestation visualization to achieve dreams, these practices offer a holistic approach to personal development. By regularly engaging in these visualizations, individuals can create a positive mental environment that supports growth, healing, and the achievement of their aspirations.

1. Abundance Visualization
Steps:
1. **Find a Quiet Space**: Sit or lie down in a comfortable position in a quiet space.
2. **Relax Your Body**: Close your eyes and take a few deep breaths, allowing your body to relax.
3. **Visualize Abundance**: Imagine an unlimited source of abundance flowing towards you. Picture wealth, health, and happiness coming into your life.
4. **Engage All Senses**: Visualize the abundance in vivid detail, engaging all your senses to make it feel real.
5. **Feel the Emotions**: Focus on the feelings of gratitude, joy, and contentment as you visualize this abundance.
6. **Return to Reality**: Slowly bring your awareness back to your surroundings, taking a few deep breaths and opening your eyes.

Benefits:
- Enhances feelings of gratitude and contentment
- Attracts positive outcomes and opportunities
- Reduces stress and anxiety related to scarcity

2. Acceptance Visualization
Steps:
1. **Find a Quiet Space**: Sit or lie down in a comfortable position in a quiet space.
2. **Relax Your Body**: Close your eyes and take a few deep breaths, allowing your body to relax.
3. **Visualize Acceptance**: Picture yourself accepting a difficult situation or aspect of yourself with compassion and understanding.
4. **Engage All Senses**: Visualize the situation or aspect clearly, engaging all your senses.
5. **Feel the Emotions**: Focus on the feelings of peace and acceptance that come with letting go of resistance.
6. **Return to Reality**: Slowly bring your awareness back to your surroundings, taking a few deep breaths and opening your eyes.

Benefits:
- Promotes emotional healing and resilience
- Reduces stress and inner conflict
- Enhances self-compassion and understanding

3. Affirmation Visualization
Steps:
1. **Find a Quiet Space**: Sit or lie down in a comfortable position in a quiet space.
2. **Relax Your Body**: Close your eyes and take a few deep breaths, allowing your body to relax.
3. **Visualize Your Goals**: Imagine achieving your goals and living your ideal life. Picture every detail vividly.
4. **Engage All Senses**: Visualize the environment, the people, and the activities involved in achieving your goals. Engage all your senses.

5. **Repeat Affirmations**: While visualizing, repeat positive affirmations to reinforce your vision. For example, "I am successful and fulfilled."
6. **Return to Reality**: Slowly bring your awareness back to your surroundings, taking a few deep breaths and opening your eyes.

Benefits:
- Reinforces positive thinking and self-belief
- Helps in achieving goals and aspirations
- Enhances motivation and confidence

4. Aura Cleansing Visualization

Steps:
1. **Find a Quiet Space**: Sit or lie down in a comfortable position in a quiet space.
2. **Relax Your Body**: Close your eyes and take a few deep breaths, allowing your body to relax.
3. **Visualize Cleansing Light**: Imagine a bright, cleansing light surrounding and penetrating your aura, clearing away any negative or stagnant energy.
4. **Engage All Senses**: Visualize the light in vivid detail, engaging all your senses to make it feel real.
5. **Feel the Emotions**: Focus on the feelings of lightness, clarity, and renewal as your aura is cleansed.
6. **Return to Reality**: Slowly bring your awareness back to your surroundings, taking a few deep breaths and opening your eyes.

Benefits:
- Clears negative energy and enhances clarity
- Promotes emotional and spiritual well-being
- Increases feelings of lightness and renewal

5. Beach Visualization

Steps:
1. **Find a Quiet Space**: Sit or lie down in a comfortable position in a quiet space.
2. **Relax Your Body**: Close your eyes and take a few deep breaths, allowing your body to relax.
3. **Visualize a Beach Scene**: Imagine yourself on a beautiful, serene beach. Picture the sand, the waves, and the sky in vivid detail.
4. **Engage All Senses**: Feel the warmth of the sun, hear the sound of the waves, smell the salty air, and see the vibrant colors.
5. **Feel the Emotions**: Focus on the feelings of peace, relaxation, and joy that the beach scene brings.
6. **Return to Reality**: Slowly bring your awareness back to your surroundings, taking a few deep breaths and opening your eyes.

Benefits:
- Promotes deep relaxation and stress relief
- Enhances feelings of peace and tranquility
- Provides a mental escape from daily stressors

6. Body Scan Visualization

Steps:
1. **Find a Quiet Space**: Sit or lie down in a comfortable position in a quiet space.

2. **Relax Your Body**: Close your eyes and take a few deep breaths, allowing your body to relax.
3. **Scan Your Body**: Mentally scan your body from head to toe, noticing any areas of tension or discomfort.
4. **Visualize Relaxation**: Imagine each area of your body relaxing and releasing tension as you focus on it.
5. **Engage All Senses**: Feel the sensations of relaxation and relief spreading throughout your body.
6. **Return to Reality**: Slowly bring your awareness back to your surroundings, taking a few deep breaths and opening your eyes.

Benefits:
- Reduces physical tension and stress
- Enhances body awareness and relaxation
- Promotes overall well-being

7. Career Success Visualization

Steps:
1. **Find a Quiet Space**: Sit or lie down in a comfortable position in a quiet space.
2. **Relax Your Body**: Close your eyes and take a few deep breaths, allowing your body to relax.
3. **Visualize Career Success**: Imagine yourself achieving success in your career, reaching your professional goals, and receiving recognition.
4. **Engage All Senses**: Visualize the environment, the people, and the activities involved in your career success. Engage all your senses.
5. **Feel the Emotions**: Focus on the feelings of accomplishment, confidence, and pride.
6. **Return to Reality**: Slowly bring your awareness back to your surroundings, taking a few deep breaths and opening your eyes.

Benefits:
- Enhances motivation and focus
- Builds confidence and self-belief
- Helps in achieving professional goals

8. Chakra Balancing Visualization

Steps:
1. **Find a Quiet Space**: Sit or lie down in a comfortable position in a quiet space.
2. **Relax Your Body**: Close your eyes and take a few deep breaths, allowing your body to relax.
3. **Visualize Each Chakra**: Imagine each of your chakras, starting from the root and moving up to the crown, as spinning wheels of energy.
4. **Engage All Senses**: Visualize each chakra in its corresponding color and feel the energy flowing smoothly.
5. **Balance Each Chakra**: Imagine each chakra becoming balanced and aligned, with energy flowing freely.
6. **Return to Reality**: Slowly bring your awareness back to your surroundings, taking a few deep breaths and opening your eyes.

Benefits:
- Enhances energy flow and balance
- Promotes emotional and physical well-being

- Increases spiritual awareness

9. Color Healing Visualization

Steps:

1. **Find a Quiet Space**: Sit or lie down in a comfortable position in a quiet space.
2. **Relax Your Body**: Close your eyes and take a few deep breaths, allowing your body to relax.
3. **Visualize Healing Colors**: Imagine different colors surrounding and penetrating your body, each bringing specific healing properties.
4. **Engage All Senses**: Visualize the colors in vivid detail, engaging all your senses.
5. **Feel the Emotions**: Focus on the feelings of healing, renewal, and balance that the colors bring.
6. **Return to Reality**: Slowly bring your awareness back to your surroundings, taking a few deep breaths and opening your eyes.

Benefits:

- Promotes healing and balance
- Enhances emotional and physical well-being
- Increases energy and vitality

10. Creative Visualization

Steps:

1. **Find a Quiet Space**: Sit or lie down in a comfortable position in a quiet space.
2. **Relax Your Body**: Close your eyes and take a few deep breaths, allowing your body to relax.
3. **Visualize Creative Ideas**: Imagine yourself engaging in creative activities and coming up with new ideas.
4. **Engage All Senses**: Visualize the process of creating, engaging all your senses.
5. **Feel the Emotions**: Focus on the feelings of inspiration, excitement, and satisfaction that come with creativity.
6. **Return to Reality**: Slowly bring your awareness back to your surroundings, taking a few deep breaths and opening your eyes.

Benefits:

- Enhances creativity and inspiration
- Promotes problem-solving and innovation
- Increases motivation and focus

11. Daily Intentions Visualization

Steps:

1. **Find a Quiet Space**: Sit or lie down in a comfortable position in a quiet space.
2. **Relax Your Body**: Close your eyes and take a few deep breaths, allowing your body to relax.
3. **Visualize Daily Goals**: Imagine your goals for the day and visualize yourself achieving them.
4. **Engage All Senses**: Visualize the activities and tasks involved in achieving your daily goals, engaging all your senses.
5. **Feel the Emotions**: Focus on the feelings of accomplishment, satisfaction, and motivation.

6. **Return to Reality**: Slowly bring your awareness back to your surroundings, taking a few deep breaths and opening your eyes.

Benefits:
- Enhances focus and productivity
- Increases motivation and confidence
- Promotes a positive mindset

12. Deep Relaxation Visualization
Steps:
1. **Find a Quiet Space**: Sit or lie down in a comfortable position in a quiet space.
2. **Relax Your Body**: Close your eyes and take a few deep breaths, allowing your body to relax.
3. **Visualize a Relaxing Scene**: Imagine yourself in a peaceful and relaxing place, such as a beach, forest, or garden.
4. **Engage All Senses**: Visualize the scene in vivid detail, engaging all your senses.
5. **Feel the Emotions**: Focus on the feelings of relaxation, peace, and tranquility that the scene brings.
6. **Return to Reality**: Slowly bring your awareness back to your surroundings, taking a few deep breaths and opening your eyes.

Benefits:
- Promotes deep relaxation and stress relief
- Enhances feelings of peace and tranquility
- Provides a mental escape from daily stressors

13. Dream Visualization
Steps:
1. **Find a Quiet Space**: Sit or lie down in a comfortable position in a quiet space.
2. **Relax Your Body**: Close your eyes and take a few deep breaths, allowing your body to relax.
3. **Visualize Your Dreams**: Imagine yourself achieving your dreams and living your ideal life. Picture every detail vividly.
4. **Engage All Senses**: Visualize the environment, the people, and the activities involved in achieving your dreams. Engage all your senses.
5. **Feel the Emotions**: Focus on the feelings of joy, fulfillment, and excitement that come with achieving your dreams.
6. **Return to Reality**: Slowly bring your awareness back to your surroundings, taking a few deep breaths and opening your eyes.

Benefits:
- Enhances motivation and focus
- Builds confidence and self-belief
- Helps in achieving long-term goals

14. Emotional Healing Visualization
Steps:
1. **Find a Quiet Space**: Sit or lie down in a comfortable position in a quiet space.
2. **Relax Your Body**: Close your eyes and take a few deep breaths, allowing your body to relax.

3. **Visualize Healing Emotions**: Imagine healing light surrounding and penetrating any areas of emotional pain or trauma.
4. **Engage All Senses**: Visualize the healing process in vivid detail, engaging all your senses.
5. **Feel the Emotions**: Focus on the feelings of relief, peace, and healing that the visualization brings.
6. **Return to Reality**: Slowly bring your awareness back to your surroundings, taking a few deep breaths and opening your eyes.

Benefits:
- Promotes emotional healing and resilience
- Reduces stress and inner conflict
- Enhances self-compassion and understanding

15. Energy Protection Visualization
Steps:
1. **Find a Quiet Space**: Sit or lie down in a comfortable position in a quiet space.
2. **Relax Your Body**: Close your eyes and take a few deep breaths, allowing your body to relax.
3. **Visualize Protective Energy**: Imagine a protective shield of light surrounding you, keeping out any negative or harmful energy.
4. **Engage All Senses**: Visualize the protective shield in vivid detail, engaging all your senses.
5. **Feel the Emotions**: Focus on the feelings of safety, security, and protection that the visualization brings.
6. **Return to Reality**: Slowly bring your awareness back to your surroundings, taking a few deep breaths and opening your eyes.

Benefits:
- Enhances feelings of safety and security
- Reduces stress and anxiety related to negative energy
- Promotes emotional and spiritual well-being

16. Future Self Visualization
Steps:
1. **Find a Quiet Space**: Sit or lie down in a comfortable position in a quiet space.
2. **Relax Your Body**: Close your eyes and take a few deep breaths, allowing your body to relax.
3. **Visualize Your Future Self**: Imagine yourself in the future, having achieved your goals and living your ideal life. Picture every detail of this future version of yourself.
4. **Engage All Senses**: Visualize the environment, the clothes you are wearing, the activities you are doing, and the people around you. Engage all your senses in this visualization.
5. **Feel the Emotions**: Focus on the emotions you would feel in this future scenario—happiness, fulfillment, confidence, and peace. Allow yourself to fully experience these emotions.
6. **Affirmations**: While visualizing, you can repeat positive affirmations to reinforce your vision. For example, "I am successful and fulfilled," or "I am living my dream life."

7. **Return to Reality**: Slowly bring your awareness back to your surroundings, taking a few deep breaths and opening your eyes.

Benefits:
- Increases motivation and confidence
- Helps in goal setting and achieving aspirations
- Enhances positive thinking and emotional well-being

17. Goal Achievement Visualization
Steps:
1. **Find a Quiet Space**: Sit or lie down in a comfortable position in a quiet space.
2. **Relax Your Body**: Close your eyes and take a few deep breaths, allowing your body to relax.
3. **Visualize Achieving Goals**: Imagine yourself achieving your goals and living your ideal life. Picture every detail vividly.
4. **Engage All Senses**: Visualize the environment, the people, and the activities involved in achieving your goals. Engage all your senses.
5. **Feel the Emotions**: Focus on the feelings of accomplishment, satisfaction, and pride that come with achieving your goals.
6. **Return to Reality**: Slowly bring your awareness back to your surroundings, taking a few deep breaths and opening your eyes.

Benefits:
- Enhances motivation and focus
- Builds confidence and self-belief
- Helps in achieving short-term and long-term goals

18. Gratitude Visualization
Steps:
1. **Find a Quiet Space**: Sit or lie down in a comfortable position in a quiet space.
2. **Relax Your Body**: Close your eyes and take a few deep breaths, allowing your body to relax.
3. **Visualize Things You Are Grateful For**: Imagine all the things in your life that you are grateful for. Picture them vividly.
4. **Engage All Senses**: Visualize the people, places, and experiences you are grateful for, engaging all your senses.
5. **Feel the Emotions**: Focus on the feelings of gratitude, joy, and contentment that come with appreciating these things.
6. **Return to Reality**: Slowly bring your awareness back to your surroundings, taking a few deep breaths and opening your eyes.

Benefits:
- Enhances feelings of gratitude and contentment
- Attracts positive outcomes and opportunities
- Reduces stress and anxiety

19. Grounding Visualization
Steps:
1. **Find a Quiet Space**: Sit or lie down in a comfortable position in a quiet space.

2. **Relax Your Body**: Close your eyes and take a few deep breaths, allowing your body to relax.
3. **Visualize Grounding Energy**: Imagine roots extending from your body into the earth, grounding and stabilizing you.
4. **Engage All Senses**: Visualize the roots in vivid detail, engaging all your senses.
5. **Feel the Emotions**: Focus on the feelings of stability, security, and connection to the earth.
6. **Return to Reality**: Slowly bring your awareness back to your surroundings, taking a few deep breaths and opening your eyes.

Benefits:
- Enhances feelings of stability and security
- Reduces stress and anxiety
- Promotes emotional and physical balance

20. Guided Imagery
Steps:
1. **Find a Quiet Space**: Sit or lie down in a comfortable position in a quiet space.
2. **Relax Your Body**: Close your eyes and take a few deep breaths, allowing your body to relax.
3. **Visualize a Peaceful Scene**: Imagine yourself in a peaceful and serene place, such as a beach, forest, or meadow.
4. **Engage All Senses**: Visualize the scene in vivid detail, engaging all your senses.
5. **Feel the Emotions**: Focus on the feelings of peace, relaxation, and joy that the scene brings.
6. **Return to Reality**: Slowly bring your awareness back to your surroundings, taking a few deep breaths and opening your eyes.

Benefits:
- Promotes deep relaxation and stress relief
- Enhances feelings of peace and tranquility
- Provides a mental escape from daily stressors

21. Health and Wellness Visualization
Steps:
1. **Find a Quiet Space**: Sit or lie down in a comfortable position in a quiet space.
2. **Relax Your Body**: Close your eyes and take a few deep breaths, allowing your body to relax.
3. **Visualize Health and Wellness**: Imagine yourself in a state of perfect health and wellness. Picture your body strong, vibrant, and full of energy.
4. **Engage All Senses**: Visualize the feeling of being healthy and well, engaging all your senses.
5. **Feel the Emotions**: Focus on the feelings of vitality, energy, and joy that come with being healthy.
6. **Return to Reality**: Slowly bring your awareness back to your surroundings, taking a few deep breaths and opening your eyes.

Benefits:
- Enhances physical health and vitality
- Promotes positive thinking and well-being
- Reduces stress and anxiety

22. Healing Light Visualization

Steps:

1. **Find a Quiet Space**: Sit or lie down in a comfortable position in a quiet space.
2. **Relax Your Body**: Close your eyes and take a few deep breaths, allowing your body to relax.
3. **Visualize Healing Light**: Imagine a bright, healing light surrounding and penetrating your body, bringing healing and renewal.
4. **Engage All Senses**: Visualize the healing light in vivid detail, engaging all your senses.
5. **Feel the Emotions**: Focus on the feelings of healing, renewal, and balance that the light brings.
6. **Return to Reality**: Slowly bring your awareness back to your surroundings, taking a few deep breaths and opening your eyes.

Benefits:
- Promotes physical and emotional healing
- Enhances feelings of renewal and balance
- Increases energy and vitality

23. Inner Child Visualization

Steps:

1. **Find a Quiet Space**: Sit or lie down in a comfortable position in a quiet space.
2. **Relax Your Body**: Close your eyes and take a few deep breaths, allowing your body to relax.
3. **Visualize Your Inner Child**: Imagine yourself as a child, connecting with the younger version of yourself.
4. **Engage All Senses**: Visualize your inner child in vivid detail, engaging all your senses.
5. **Feel the Emotions**: Focus on the feelings of love, compassion, and understanding for your inner child.
6. **Return to Reality**: Slowly bring your awareness back to your surroundings, taking a few deep breaths and opening your eyes.

Benefits:
- Promotes emotional healing and self-compassion
- Enhances understanding and acceptance of past experiences
- Increases feelings of love and connection

24. Inner Peace Visualization

Steps:

1. **Find a Quiet Space**: Sit or lie down in a comfortable position in a quiet space.
2. **Relax Your Body**: Close your eyes and take a few deep breaths, allowing your body to relax.
3. **Visualize Inner Peace**: Imagine a state of inner peace and tranquility, free from stress and worry.
4. **Engage All Senses**: Visualize the feeling of inner peace in vivid detail, engaging all your senses.
5. **Feel the Emotions**: Focus on the feelings of calm, serenity, and contentment that come with inner peace.

6. **Return to Reality**: Slowly bring your awareness back to your surroundings, taking a few deep breaths and opening your eyes.

Benefits:
- Enhances feelings of calm and tranquility
- Reduces stress and anxiety
- Promotes emotional and mental well-being

25. Intuition Enhancement Visualization
Steps:
1. **Find a Quiet Space**: Sit or lie down in a comfortable position in a quiet space.
2. **Relax Your Body**: Close your eyes and take a few deep breaths, allowing your body to relax.
3. **Visualize Enhancing Intuition**: Imagine your intuitive abilities growing stronger and more accurate.
4. **Engage All Senses**: Visualize the process of enhancing your intuition in vivid detail, engaging all your senses.
5. **Feel the Emotions**: Focus on the feelings of confidence, clarity, and insight that come with enhanced intuition.
6. **Return to Reality**: Slowly bring your awareness back to your surroundings, taking a few deep breaths and opening your eyes.

Benefits:
- Enhances intuitive abilities and insight
- Promotes confidence and clarity in decision-making
- Increases self-awareness and understanding

26. Joy Visualization
Steps:
1. **Find a Quiet Space**: Sit or lie down in a comfortable position in a quiet space.
2. **Relax Your Body**: Close your eyes and take a few deep breaths, allowing your body to relax.
3. **Visualize Joyful Moments**: Imagine moments of joy and happiness in your life. Picture them vividly.
4. **Engage All Senses**: Visualize the people, places, and experiences that bring you joy, engaging all your senses.
5. **Feel the Emotions**: Focus on the feelings of joy, happiness, and contentment that come with these moments.
6. **Return to Reality**: Slowly bring your awareness back to your surroundings, taking a few deep breaths and opening your eyes.

Benefits:
- Enhances feelings of joy and happiness
- Reduces stress and anxiety
- Promotes emotional well-being and positivity

27. Life Purpose Visualization
Steps:
1. **Find a Quiet Space**: Sit or lie down in a comfortable position in a quiet space.

2. **Relax Your Body**: Close your eyes and take a few deep breaths, allowing your body to relax.
3. **Visualize Your Life Purpose**: Imagine discovering and fulfilling your life purpose. Picture every detail vividly.
4. **Engage All Senses**: Visualize the activities, people, and experiences involved in living your life purpose, engaging all your senses.
5. **Feel the Emotions**: Focus on the feelings of fulfillment, passion, and joy that come with living your life purpose.
6. **Return to Reality**: Slowly bring your awareness back to your surroundings, taking a few deep breaths and opening your eyes.

Benefits:
- Enhances motivation and focus
- Builds confidence and self-belief
- Helps in achieving long-term goals

28. Loving-Kindness Visualization

Steps:
1. **Find a Quiet Space**: Sit or lie down in a comfortable position in a quiet space.
2. **Relax Your Body**: Close your eyes and take a few deep breaths, allowing your body to relax.
3. **Visualize Loving-Kindness**: Imagine sending love and kindness to yourself and others. Picture this loving energy spreading outward.
4. **Engage All Senses**: Visualize the feeling of loving-kindness in vivid detail, engaging all your senses.
5. **Feel the Emotions**: Focus on the feelings of love, compassion, and connection that come with loving-kindness.
6. **Return to Reality**: Slowly bring your awareness back to your surroundings, taking a few deep breaths and opening your eyes.

Benefits:
- Enhances feelings of love and compassion
- Reduces stress and anxiety
- Promotes emotional and spiritual well-being

29. Manifestation Visualization

Steps:
1. **Find a Quiet Space**: Sit or lie down in a comfortable position in a quiet space.
2. **Relax Your Body**: Close your eyes and take a few deep breaths, allowing your body to relax.
3. **Visualize Manifesting Goals**: Imagine yourself achieving your goals and manifesting your desires. Picture every detail vividly.
4. **Engage All Senses**: Visualize the environment, the people, and the activities involved in manifesting your goals, engaging all your senses.
5. **Feel the Emotions**: Focus on the feelings of accomplishment, satisfaction, and joy that come with manifesting your goals.
6. **Return to Reality**: Slowly bring your awareness back to your surroundings, taking a few deep breaths and opening your eyes.

Benefits:
- Enhances motivation and focus

- Builds confidence and self-belief
- Helps in achieving short-term and long-term goals

30. Mindfulness Visualization

Steps:

1. **Find a Quiet Space**: Sit or lie down in a comfortable position in a quiet space.
2. **Relax Your Body**: Close your eyes and take a few deep breaths, allowing your body to relax.
3. **Visualize Being Mindful**: Imagine yourself fully present in the moment, aware of your thoughts, feelings, and surroundings.
4. **Engage All Senses**: Visualize the practice of mindfulness in vivid detail, engaging all your senses.
5. **Feel the Emotions**: Focus on the feelings of calm, clarity, and presence that come with mindfulness.
6. **Return to Reality**: Slowly bring your awareness back to your surroundings, taking a few deep breaths and opening your eyes.

Benefits:

- Enhances focus and concentration
- Reduces stress and anxiety
- Promotes emotional and mental well-being

31. Mountain Visualization

Steps:

1. **Find a Quiet Space**: Sit or lie down in a comfortable position in a quiet space.
2. **Relax Your Body**: Close your eyes and take a few deep breaths, allowing your body to relax.
3. **Visualize a Mountain Scene**: Imagine yourself in a peaceful mountain setting, surrounded by nature and tranquility.
4. **Engage All Senses**: Visualize the mountains, trees, and sky in vivid detail, engaging all your senses.
5. **Feel the Emotions**: Focus on the feelings of peace, strength, and stability that the mountain scene brings.
6. **Return to Reality**: Slowly bring your awareness back to your surroundings, taking a few deep breaths and opening your eyes.

Benefits:

- Promotes deep relaxation and stress relief
- Enhances feelings of peace and tranquility
- Provides a mental escape from daily stressors

32. Nature Visualization

Steps:

1. **Find a Quiet Space**: Sit or lie down in a comfortable position in a quiet space.
2. **Relax Your Body**: Close your eyes and take a few deep breaths, allowing your body to relax.
3. **Visualize a Natural Scene**: Imagine yourself in a beautiful natural setting, such as a forest, meadow, or beach.
4. **Engage All Senses**: Visualize the scene in vivid detail, engaging all your senses.

5. **Feel the Emotions**: Focus on the feelings of peace, relaxation, and joy that the natural setting brings.
6. **Return to Reality**: Slowly bring your awareness back to your surroundings, taking a few deep breaths and opening your eyes.

Benefits:
- Promotes deep relaxation and stress relief
- Enhances feelings of peace and tranquility
- Provides a mental escape from daily stressors

33. Ocean Visualization
Steps:
1. **Find a Quiet Space**: Sit or lie down in a comfortable position in a quiet space.
2. **Relax Your Body**: Close your eyes and take a few deep breaths, allowing your body to relax.
3. **Visualize an Ocean Scene**: Imagine yourself by the ocean, with waves gently crashing and the sun setting on the horizon.
4. **Engage All Senses**: Visualize the ocean scene in vivid detail, engaging all your senses.
5. **Feel the Emotions**: Focus on the feelings of peace, relaxation, and renewal that the ocean brings.
6. **Return to Reality**: Slowly bring your awareness back to your surroundings, taking a few deep breaths and opening your eyes.

Benefits:
- Promotes deep relaxation and stress relief
- Enhances feelings of peace and tranquility
- Provides a mental escape from daily stressors

34. Overcoming Fear Visualization
Steps:
1. **Find a Quiet Space**: Sit or lie down in a comfortable position in a quiet space.
2. **Relax Your Body**: Close your eyes and take a few deep breaths, allowing your body to relax.
3. **Visualize Overcoming Fear**: Imagine yourself facing and overcoming your fears with courage and confidence.
4. **Engage All Senses**: Visualize the process of overcoming fear in vivid detail, engaging all your senses.
5. **Feel the Emotions**: Focus on the feelings of strength, courage, and empowerment that come with overcoming fear.
6. **Return to Reality**: Slowly bring your awareness back to your surroundings, taking a few deep breaths and opening your eyes.

Benefits:
- Enhances confidence and courage
- Reduces anxiety and fear
- Promotes emotional and mental well-being

35. Pain Relief Visualization
Steps:
1. **Find a Quiet Space**: Sit or lie down in a comfortable position in a quiet space.

2. **Relax Your Body**: Close your eyes and take a few deep breaths, allowing your body to relax.
3. **Visualize Relieving Pain**: Imagine a healing light or energy surrounding and penetrating the area of pain, bringing relief and comfort.
4. **Engage All Senses**: Visualize the pain relief process in vivid detail, engaging all your senses.
5. **Feel the Emotions**: Focus on the feelings of relief, comfort, and healing that come with the visualization.
6. **Return to Reality**: Slowly bring your awareness back to your surroundings, taking a few deep breaths and opening your eyes.

Benefits:
- Promotes physical healing and pain relief
- Enhances feelings of comfort and well-being
- Reduces stress and anxiety related to pain

36. Past Healing Visualization

Steps:
1. **Find a Quiet Space**: Sit or lie down in a comfortable position in a quiet space.
2. **Relax Your Body**: Close your eyes and take a few deep breaths, allowing your body to relax.
3. **Visualize Healing the Past**: Imagine a healing light or energy surrounding and penetrating past experiences, bringing healing and resolution.
4. **Engage All Senses**: Visualize the healing process in vivid detail, engaging all your senses.
5. **Feel the Emotions**: Focus on the feelings of healing, resolution, and peace that come with healing the past.
6. **Return to Reality**: Slowly bring your awareness back to your surroundings, taking a few deep breaths and opening your eyes.

Benefits:
- Promotes emotional healing and resolution of past experiences
- Enhances self-compassion and understanding
- Reduces stress and inner conflict

37. Positive Energy Visualization

Steps:
1. **Find a Quiet Space**: Sit or lie down in a comfortable position in a quiet space.
2. **Relax Your Body**: Close your eyes and take a few deep breaths, allowing your body to relax.
3. **Visualize Positive Energy**: Imagine positive energy surrounding and penetrating your body, filling you with light and vitality.
4. **Engage All Senses**: Visualize the positive energy in vivid detail, engaging all your senses.
5. **Feel the Emotions**: Focus on the feelings of vitality, joy, and positivity that come with the visualization.
6. **Return to Reality**: Slowly bring your awareness back to your surroundings, taking a few deep breaths and opening your eyes.

Benefits:
- Enhances feelings of joy and positivity

- Increases energy and vitality
- Promotes emotional and mental well-being

38. Prosperity Visualization
Steps:
1. **Find a Quiet Space**: Sit or lie down in a comfortable position in a quiet space.
2. **Relax Your Body**: Close your eyes and take a few deep breaths, allowing your body to relax.
3. **Visualize Prosperity**: Imagine a flow of prosperity and abundance coming into your life. Picture wealth, health, and happiness.
4. **Engage All Senses**: Visualize the prosperity in vivid detail, engaging all your senses.
5. **Feel the Emotions**: Focus on the feelings of gratitude, joy, and contentment that come with prosperity.
6. **Return to Reality**: Slowly bring your awareness back to your surroundings, taking a few deep breaths and opening your eyes.

Benefits:
- Enhances feelings of gratitude and contentment
- Attracts positive outcomes and opportunities
- Reduces stress and anxiety related to scarcity

39. Protection Visualization
Steps:
1. **Find a Quiet Space**: Sit or lie down in a comfortable position in a quiet space.
2. **Relax Your Body**: Close your eyes and take a few deep breaths, allowing your body to relax.
3. **Visualize Protection**: Imagine a protective shield of light surrounding you, keeping out any negative or harmful energy.
4. **Engage All Senses**: Visualize the protective shield in vivid detail, engaging all your senses.
5. **Feel the Emotions**: Focus on the feelings of safety, security, and protection that the visualization brings.
6. **Return to Reality**: Slowly bring your awareness back to your surroundings, taking a few deep breaths and opening your eyes.

Benefits:
- Enhances feelings of safety and security
- Reduces stress and anxiety related to negative energy
- Promotes emotional and spiritual well-being

40. Relationship Healing Visualization
Steps:
1. **Find a Quiet Space**: Sit or lie down in a comfortable position in a quiet space.
2. **Relax Your Body**: Close your eyes and take a few deep breaths, allowing your body to relax.
3. **Visualize Healing Relationships**: Imagine healing light or energy surrounding and penetrating any troubled relationships, bringing healing and resolution.
4. **Engage All Senses**: Visualize the healing process in vivid detail, engaging all your senses.

5. **Feel the Emotions**: Focus on the feelings of healing, resolution, and peace that come with relationship healing.

6. **Return to Reality**: Slowly bring your awareness back to your surroundings, taking a few deep breaths and opening your eyes.

Benefits:
- Promotes healing and resolution of relationship issues
- Enhances feelings of love and compassion
- Reduces stress and inner conflict

41. Relaxation Visualization
Steps:
1. **Find a Quiet Space**: Sit or lie down in a comfortable position in a quiet space.
2. **Relax Your Body**: Close your eyes and take a few deep breaths, allowing your body to relax.
3. **Visualize Relaxation**: Imagine yourself in a peaceful and relaxing place, such as a beach, forest, or garden.
4. **Engage All Senses**: Visualize the scene in vivid detail, engaging all your senses.
5. **Feel the Emotions**: Focus on the feelings of relaxation, peace, and tranquility that the scene brings.
6. **Return to Reality**: Slowly bring your awareness back to your surroundings, taking a few deep breaths and opening your eyes.

Benefits:
- Promotes deep relaxation and stress relief
- Enhances feelings of peace and tranquility
- Provides a mental escape from daily stressors

42. Self-Compassion Visualization
Steps:
1. **Find a Quiet Space**: Sit or lie down in a comfortable position in a quiet space.
2. **Relax Your Body**: Close your eyes and take a few deep breaths, allowing your body to relax.
3. **Visualize Self-Compassion**: Imagine yourself extending love and compassion to yourself. Picture this loving energy surrounding you.
4. **Engage All Senses**: Visualize the feeling of self-compassion in vivid detail, engaging all your senses.
5. **Feel the Emotions**: Focus on the feelings of love, compassion, and understanding that come with self-compassion.
6. **Return to Reality**: Slowly bring your awareness back to your surroundings, taking a few deep breaths and opening your eyes.

Benefits:
- Enhances self-love and compassion
- Reduces self-criticism and inner conflict
- Promotes emotional and mental well-being

43. Self-Love Visualization
Steps:
1. **Find a Quiet Space**: Sit or lie down in a comfortable position in a quiet space.

2. **Relax Your Body**: Close your eyes and take a few deep breaths, allowing your body to relax.
3. **Visualize Self-Love**: Imagine yourself extending love and care to yourself. Picture this loving energy surrounding you.
4. **Engage All Senses**: Visualize the feeling of self-love in vivid detail, engaging all your senses.
5. **Feel the Emotions**: Focus on the feelings of love, care, and appreciation that come with self-love.
6. **Return to Reality**: Slowly bring your awareness back to your surroundings, taking a few deep breaths and opening your eyes.

Benefits:
- Enhances self-love and appreciation
- Reduces self-criticism and inner conflict
- Promotes emotional and mental well-being

44. Spiritual Connection Visualization

Steps:
1. **Find a Quiet Space**: Sit or lie down in a comfortable position in a quiet space.
2. **Relax Your Body**: Close your eyes and take a few deep breaths, allowing your body to relax.
3. **Visualize Spiritual Connection**: Imagine yourself connecting with a higher power or spiritual source. Picture this connection in vivid detail.
4. **Engage All Senses**: Visualize the feeling of spiritual connection, engaging all your senses.
5. **Feel the Emotions**: Focus on the feelings of peace, love, and connection that come with spiritual connection.
6. **Return to Reality**: Slowly bring your awareness back to your surroundings, taking a few deep breaths and opening your eyes.

Benefits:
- Enhances feelings of peace and connection
- Promotes spiritual growth and well-being
- Reduces stress and anxiety

45. Stress Relief Visualization

Steps:
1. **Find a Quiet Space**: Sit or lie down in a comfortable position in a quiet space.
2. **Relax Your Body**: Close your eyes and take a few deep breaths, allowing your body to relax.
3. **Visualize Relieving Stress**: Imagine a peaceful scene or a soothing light surrounding you, bringing relief from stress.
4. **Engage All Senses**: Visualize the stress relief process in vivid detail, engaging all your senses.
5. **Feel the Emotions**: Focus on the feelings of relaxation, peace, and relief that come with stress relief.
6. **Return to Reality**: Slowly bring your awareness back to your surroundings, taking a few deep breaths and opening your eyes.

Benefits:
- Promotes deep relaxation and stress relief

- Enhances feelings of peace and tranquility
- Reduces physical and emotional tension

46. Success Visualization
Steps:
1. **Find a Quiet Space**: Sit or lie down in a comfortable position in a quiet space.
2. **Relax Your Body**: Close your eyes and take a few deep breaths, allowing your body to relax.
3. **Visualize Success**: Imagine yourself achieving success in your goals and endeavors. Picture every detail vividly.
4. **Engage All Senses**: Visualize the environment, the people, and the activities involved in achieving success, engaging all your senses.
5. **Feel the Emotions**: Focus on the feelings of accomplishment, satisfaction, and pride that come with success.
6. **Return to Reality**: Slowly bring your awareness back to your surroundings, taking a few deep breaths and opening your eyes.

Benefits:
- Enhances motivation and focus
- Builds confidence and self-belief
- Helps in achieving short-term and long-term goals

47. Tranquil Garden Visualization
Steps:
1. **Find a Quiet Space**: Sit or lie down in a comfortable position in a quiet space.
2. **Relax Your Body**: Close your eyes and take a few deep breaths, allowing your body to relax.
3. **Visualize a Tranquil Garden**: Imagine yourself in a peaceful garden, surrounded by beautiful plants and flowers.
4. **Engage All Senses**: Visualize the garden in vivid detail, engaging all your senses.
5. **Feel the Emotions**: Focus on the feelings of peace, relaxation, and joy that the garden brings.
6. **Return to Reality**: Slowly bring your awareness back to your surroundings, taking a few deep breaths and opening your eyes.

Benefits:
- Promotes deep relaxation and stress relief
- Enhances feelings of peace and tranquility
- Provides a mental escape from daily stressors

48. Travel Visualization
Steps:
1. **Find a Quiet Space**: Sit or lie down in a comfortable position in a quiet space.
2. **Relax Your Body**: Close your eyes and take a few deep breaths, allowing your body to relax.
3. **Visualize Traveling**: Imagine yourself traveling to a destination of your choice. Picture every detail vividly.
4. **Engage All Senses**: Visualize the sights, sounds, and experiences of your travel destination, engaging all your senses.

5. **Feel the Emotions**: Focus on the feelings of excitement, joy, and adventure that come with traveling.
6. **Return to Reality**: Slowly bring your awareness back to your surroundings, taking a few deep breaths and opening your eyes.

Benefits:
- Promotes feelings of excitement and adventure
- Provides a mental escape from daily stressors
- Enhances creativity and imagination

49. Vitality Visualization

Steps:
1. **Find a Quiet Space**: Sit or lie down in a comfortable position in a quiet space.
2. **Relax Your Body**: Close your eyes and take a few deep breaths, allowing your body to relax.
3. **Visualize Vitality**: Imagine yourself full of energy and vitality. Picture your body strong, vibrant, and healthy.
4. **Engage All Senses**: Visualize the feeling of vitality in vivid detail, engaging all your senses.
5. **Feel the Emotions**: Focus on the feelings of energy, strength, and joy that come with vitality.
6. **Return to Reality**: Slowly bring your awareness back to your surroundings, taking a few deep breaths and opening your eyes.

Benefits:
- Enhances physical health and vitality
- Promotes positive thinking and well-being
- Increases energy and motivation

50. Weight Loss Visualization

Steps:
1. **Find a Quiet Space**: Sit or lie down in a comfortable position in a quiet space.
2. **Relax Your Body**: Close your eyes and take a few deep breaths, allowing your body to relax.
3. **Visualize Weight Loss**: Imagine yourself at your ideal weight, healthy and fit. Picture every detail vividly.
4. **Engage All Senses**: Visualize the activities, foods, and lifestyle changes involved in achieving weight loss, engaging all your senses.
5. **Feel the Emotions**: Focus on the feelings of accomplishment, confidence, and joy that come with weight loss.
6. **Return to Reality**: Slowly bring your awareness back to your surroundings, taking a few deep breaths and opening your eyes.

Benefits:
- Enhances motivation and focus
- Promotes healthy lifestyle changes
- Builds confidence and self-belief

See Chart 329 - Visualization Techniques, Master Chart

Chapter 3

Spirit

Akashic Record Clearing

Clearing your Akashic Records can significantly raise your vibration by removing energetic blockages and outdated patterns that no longer serve your highest good. The Akashic Records, often described as a cosmic library, hold the energetic imprints of every thought, action, and experience your soul has encountered. By consciously clearing negative imprints, unresolved traumas, and limiting beliefs stored in these records, you release dense, lower-frequency energies from your being. This process allows for a greater influx of high-frequency light and love, elevating your overall vibrational state. As your vibration rises, you align more closely with your higher self, experiencing increased clarity, inner peace, and spiritual connection.

Additionally, raising your vibration through Akashic Record clearing enhances your ability to attract and manifest positive experiences and opportunities in your life. When your energetic field is clear and your vibration is high, you naturally resonate with higher frequencies of abundance, joy, and love. This alignment creates a magnetic pull, drawing in circumstances and relationships that reflect your elevated state. Furthermore, a higher vibration strengthens your intuitive abilities, making it easier to receive guidance from your higher self and spiritual guides. As you continue to clear and elevate your vibration, you move closer to your soul's true potential, living a life of greater purpose and fulfillment.

See Chart 338 - Akashic Record Clearing, Master Chart

Balancing Masculine and Feminine Energies

Balancing masculine and feminine energies is a crucial aspect of achieving inner harmony and overall well-being. Masculine energy is often associated with traits such as assertiveness, logic, action, and strength, while feminine energy encompasses qualities like intuition, nurturing, receptivity, and creativity. When these energies are balanced, they complement each other, creating a state of equilibrium that fosters emotional, mental, and spiritual health. An imbalance can manifest in various ways, such as overworking and burnout (excess masculine energy) or excessive passivity and lack of direction (excess feminine energy). By integrating and harmonizing these energies, individuals can experience a more fulfilling and centered life.

Balancing masculine and feminine energies is also essential for raising one's vibration, which refers to the frequency at which one's energy resonates. Higher vibrations are associated with positive qualities such as love, peace, and joy, whereas lower vibrations align with fear, anger, and sadness. When masculine and feminine energies are in harmony, it facilitates the free flow of energy throughout the body and mind, promoting a higher vibrational state. This balance helps in overcoming emotional blockages, enhancing creativity, and fostering a deeper connection with one's true self. By achieving this energetic equilibrium, individuals can elevate their consciousness, attract positive experiences, and contribute to their overall spiritual growth and evolution.

1. **Affirmations** - Use affirmations that promote balance, such as "I am strong and compassionate" or "I embrace my assertiveness and my nurturing side."
2. **Balancing Activities** - Alternate between activities that are structured (masculine) and those that are more flowing and intuitive (feminine).

3. **Breathwork** - Practice deep, conscious breathing to balance your energies and reduce stress.
4. **Chanting and Mantras** - Use vocal expressions to harmonize and balance energies.
5. **Connecting with Community** - Participate in group activities that encourage both leadership (masculine) and collaboration (feminine).
6. **Connecting with Your Inner Child** - Engage in playful activities to nurture your feminine side while also guiding your inner child with a protective masculine presence.
7. **Creative Expression** - Engage in creative activities like painting, dancing, or writing to awaken your feminine energy.
8. **Dance** - Use dance to express emotions and balance energies.
9. **Energy Healing** - Consider Reiki or other energy healing modalities to balance your chakras and harmonize masculine and feminine energies.
10. **Exploring Emotions** - Allow yourself to feel and express emotions freely (feminine) while also taking action to address their root causes (masculine).
11. **Gardening** - Connect with nature and nurture plants to balance energies.
12. **Journaling** - Reflect on your actions and thoughts to understand where your masculine or feminine energies may be dominant.
13. **Listening to Music** - Choose music that embodies both masculine and feminine qualities to harmonize your energies.
14. **Mind-Body Practices** - Engage in activities like dance or martial arts that integrate physical movement with emotional expression.
15. **Mindful Eating** - Be aware of your food choices and how they nourish (feminine) or energize (masculine) your body.
16. **Mindfulness and Meditation** - Practice mindfulness to become aware of your inner masculine and feminine energies and how they manifest.
17. **Nature Walks** - Spend time in nature to ground yourself and connect with the nurturing feminine energy of the earth.
18. **Partner Work** - Engage in activities with a partner that require both cooperation (feminine) and leadership (masculine).
19. **Physical Exercise** - Strength training or cardio can boost your masculine energy through action and discipline.
20. **Practicing Gratitude** - Cultivate a sense of gratitude for both your masculine and feminine traits.
21. **Reading and Learning** - Study materials that explore the concept of balancing masculine and feminine energies.
22. **Reiki** - Use Reiki healing to balance energy flows within the body.
23. **Setting Boundaries** - Practice setting healthy boundaries to assert your masculine energy while respecting others to nurture your feminine side.
24. **Spiritual Practices** - Incorporate spiritual rituals that honor both the divine masculine and divine feminine within you.
25. **Tai Chi or Qigong** - These practices harmonize energy flow, balancing the yin (feminine) and yang (masculine) within.
26. **Therapy or Counseling** - Seek professional guidance to explore and balance your inner masculine and feminine energies.
27. **Visualization Techniques** - Visualize a harmonious balance between your masculine and feminine energies, seeing them working together synergistically.

28. **Walking Meditation** - Combine mindfulness with physical movement to balance energies.
29. **Yoga** - Engage in yoga poses that emphasize both strength (masculine) and flexibility (feminine).

See Chart 347 - Balancing Masculine and Feminine Energies, Master Chart

Clearing Ancestral Patterns

Clearing ancestral patterns is a profound and transformative process that involves addressing and releasing the inherited emotional, psychological, and energetic imprints passed down through generations. These patterns can manifest as limiting beliefs, recurring negative behaviors, and even physical ailments that are deeply rooted in our family lineage. By recognizing and healing these ancestral influences, we not only liberate ourselves from the burdens of the past but also pave the way for future generations to experience greater freedom, joy, and abundance.

The process of clearing ancestral patterns often begins with awareness and acknowledgment. Understanding that we carry the imprints of our ancestors' experiences can be a powerful first step. This awareness can be cultivated through various means, such as family history research, therapy, meditation, and spiritual practices. Once we have identified these patterns, we can employ a range of healing modalities to release them. These may include energy healing, ritual ceremonies, forgiveness practices, and other holistic approaches. By consciously working to heal and transform these inherited patterns, we honor our ancestors' struggles and sacrifices while reclaiming our own power and potential. Through this journey of ancestral healing, we create a new legacy of love, resilience, and possibility for ourselves and our descendants.

1. **Affirmations for Ancestral Healing**: Positive statements repeated to shift inherited beliefs and patterns, promoting healing within the family lineage.
2. **Ancestral Altars**: Creating altars to honor ancestors and ask for their guidance in releasing negative patterns.
3. **Ancestral Clearing Rituals**: Traditional or personalized rituals to honor and release ancestral burdens, often involving symbolic actions.
4. **Ancestral Healing Meditations**: Guided meditations focusing on healing family lineage and releasing inherited patterns.
5. **Art Therapy**: Creating art as a form of expression and release of ancestral patterns, helping to process and let go of inherited trauma.
6. **Astrology**: Using astrological insights to understand and heal ancestral patterns based on celestial influences and family heritage.
7. **Breathwork**: Techniques like Holotropic Breathwork to access and clear deep-seated ancestral patterns through controlled breathing.
8. **Chakra Balancing**: Focusing on chakras, especially the root chakra, to clear ancestral energies and restore energetic balance.
9. **Crystal Therapy**: Using specific crystals like black tourmaline, smoky quartz, or ancestralite to aid in ancestral healing.
10. **Dance and Movement Therapy**: Expressive movement to release ancestral trauma stored in the body, promoting physical and emotional healing.

11. **DNA Activation Techniques**: Methods to activate and clear ancestral DNA, often involving visualizations or energy work.
12. **Elemental Healing**: Working with the elements (earth, water, fire, air) to release ancestral patterns and restore harmony.
13. **Energy Healing**: Modalities like Reiki, Pranic Healing, or Quantum Healing focusing on clearing ancestral energy blockages.
14. **Energy Meridians and Acupuncture**: Using acupuncture to release blockages related to ancestral patterns by stimulating specific points on the body.
15. **Essential Oils**: Using oils like frankincense, myrrh, and sandalwood for their ancestral healing properties.
16. **Family Constellations Therapy**: A therapeutic approach to understanding and resolving issues rooted in the family system.
17. **Family History Research**: Studying family history to understand and consciously release inherited patterns.
18. **Forgiveness Exercises**: Practices aimed at forgiving ancestors and oneself for past actions and decisions, promoting emotional release.
19. **Generational Trauma Release**: Techniques to identify and heal trauma passed down through generations, breaking the cycle of inherited pain.
20. **Geomancy and Space Clearing**: Clearing the ancestral energy of your living space through geomantic practices and energetic cleansing.
21. **Herbal Remedies**: Using herbs known for their ancestral healing properties, like sage, cedar, or mugwort.
22. **Ho'oponopono**: A Hawaiian practice of reconciliation and forgiveness for ancestral healing, involving the repetition of specific phrases.
23. **Holistic Nutrition**: Adopting dietary changes that support the release of ancestral toxins and imprints, promoting overall well-being.
24. **Inner Child Work**: Healing the inner child to release ancestral wounds carried from childhood, fostering emotional and psychological healing.
25. **Journaling**: Writing exercises to explore and release ancestral stories and patterns, gaining insights and clarity.
26. **Mantras and Chanting**: Using specific mantras or chants to clear ancestral energies and promote healing vibrations.
27. **Mentorship and Coaching**: Working with a mentor or coach specialized in ancestral healing to guide and support the healing process.
28. **Numerology**: Exploring numbers associated with family lineage to identify and clear ancestral influences, gaining deeper understanding.
29. **Past Life Regression**: Exploring past lives to understand and release ancestral influences, often through guided hypnosis.
30. **Plant Medicine Ceremonies**: Participating in ceremonies with plant medicines like Ayahuasca or San Pedro for deep ancestral healing.
31. **Prayer and Intention Setting**: Praying for ancestral healing and setting intentions to release inherited patterns, invoking spiritual support.
32. **Prayer Beads and Rosaries**: Using beads or rosaries to pray and set intentions for ancestral healing, fostering a spiritual connection.
33. **Quantum Healing Hypnosis Technique (QHHT)**: A hypnosis method to explore and heal ancestral patterns, accessing deep subconscious levels.

34. **Shadow Work**: Identifying and integrating shadow aspects related to ancestral patterns, promoting self-awareness and healing.
35. **Shamanic Journeys**: Guided journeys to meet and heal ancestral spirits, often involving drumming or other shamanic practices.
36. **Silent Reflection and Solitude**: Spending time in quiet contemplation to connect with and release ancestral patterns, gaining insights.
37. **Sound Healing**: Using instruments like tuning forks, singing bowls, or drumming to release ancestral imprints and restore energetic balance.
38. **Spiritual Counseling**: Seeking guidance from spiritual counselors or shamans specializing in ancestral healing to navigate the healing process.
39. **Visualization Techniques**: Visualizing the release of ancestral chains or cords binding you to past patterns, promoting energetic freedom.
40. **Yoga and Qigong**: Practicing movements and postures that focus on releasing ancestral energy and restoring balance in the body.

See Chart 350 - Clearing Ancestral Patterns, Master Chart

Consciousness Expansion

Consciousness expansion refers to the deliberate effort to elevate one's awareness and understanding of themselves and the universe. This process involves practices and activities that foster mental, emotional, and spiritual growth. Individuals engaged in consciousness expansion often seek to transcend their ordinary state of awareness, experiencing heightened states of perception and insight. Techniques such as meditation, breathwork, and energy healing are commonly employed to facilitate this journey, allowing individuals to connect more deeply with their inner selves and the world around them. The ultimate goal is to achieve a state of higher consciousness where one can experience greater peace, clarity, and a profound sense of interconnectedness.

Engaging in consciousness expansion can have profound effects on one's life. It can lead to a greater sense of purpose, enhanced emotional well-being, and improved physical health. Practices such as journaling and dream analysis can help uncover subconscious patterns and bring about self-awareness, while activities like yoga and tai chi promote physical harmony and stress reduction. By exploring various modalities like crystals, sound healing, and sacred geometry, individuals can find the methods that resonate most with them, aiding their unique paths of growth. Ultimately, consciousness expansion is a deeply personal journey that opens the door to transformative experiences and a more enriched, enlightened existence.

1. **Affirmations**: Positive statements repeated to oneself to encourage a positive mindset and influence subconscious beliefs.
2. **Art Therapy**: A therapeutic technique utilizing the creative process of making art to improve mental, emotional, and physical well-being.
3. **Astrology**: A belief system that suggests a connection between the positions and movements of celestial bodies and events in human life.
4. **Aura Reading**: The practice of perceiving the energy fields surrounding the human body, which can reflect physical, emotional, and spiritual states.

5. **Breathwork**: Controlled breathing exercises intended to promote relaxation, stress relief, and emotional healing.
6. **Chakra Balancing**: The process of aligning and harmonizing the body's energy centers (chakras) to enhance physical and emotional well-being.
7. **Color Therapy**: The use of colors in various forms to influence mood and promote healing and well-being.
8. **Crystals**: Minerals believed to have healing properties and used to enhance physical, emotional, and spiritual health.
9. **Dancing**: The act of moving rhythmically to music, often used as a form of expression and a way to elevate mood and consciousness.
10. **Dream Analysis**: The interpretation of dreams to gain insights into one's subconscious mind and address unresolved issues.
11. **Earthing**: The practice of making direct physical contact with the earth to balance energy and improve health.
12. **Energy Healing**: A holistic practice that involves channeling healing energy into the patient to restore balance and health.
13. **Feng Shui**: An ancient Chinese practice of arranging the physical environment to promote harmony, balance, and positive energy flow.
14. **Gratitude Practice**: Regularly focusing on and appreciating the positive aspects of life to enhance overall well-being and happiness.
15. **Herbal Remedies**: The use of plant-based substances to promote health and treat various ailments.
16. **Hypnotherapy**: A therapeutic technique that uses guided hypnosis to help individuals access their subconscious mind and address various issues.
17. **Journaling**: The practice of writing down thoughts, feelings, and experiences to gain insight and promote emotional healing.
18. **Kundalini Yoga**: A form of yoga that involves physical postures, breath control, and meditation to awaken spiritual energy.
19. **Labyrinth Walking**: Walking through a labyrinth as a form of meditation and contemplation to promote spiritual insight and relaxation.
20. **Light Therapy**: The use of specific wavelengths of light to treat various conditions, such as seasonal affective disorder (SAD) and skin disorders.
21. **Lucid Dreaming**: The practice of becoming aware that one is dreaming while still in the dream, allowing for control over the dream experience.
22. **Mantras**: Sacred words or sounds repeated during meditation to aid concentration and promote spiritual growth.
23. **Meditation**: A practice of focused attention and mindfulness to achieve a mentally clear and emotionally calm state.
24. **Mindfulness**: The practice of being fully present and engaged in the current moment, aware of thoughts, feelings, and sensations without judgment.
25. **Music Therapy**: The use of music to address physical, emotional, cognitive, and social needs, promoting healing and well-being.
26. **Nature Walks**: Walking in natural environments to reduce stress, improve mood, and enhance overall well-being.
27. **Numerology**: The study of numbers and their mystical significance, often used for personal insight and guidance.

28. **Past Life Regression**: A therapeutic technique that uses hypnosis to recover memories of past lives or incarnations.
29. **Qigong**: An ancient Chinese practice that combines movement, breath control, and meditation to cultivate and balance life energy (qi).
30. **Reiki**: A Japanese healing technique that involves channeling energy through the hands to promote physical and emotional healing.
31. **Sacred Geometry**: The study of geometric shapes and patterns that are believed to have spiritual significance and healing properties.
32. **Shamanic Journeying**: A practice in which a shaman or practitioner enters an altered state of consciousness to interact with the spiritual realm for healing and guidance.
33. **Singing Bowls**: The use of Tibetan or crystal bowls that produce sound vibrations to promote relaxation, meditation, and healing.
34. **Sound Healing**: The use of sound, such as music, tones, and frequencies, to promote physical, emotional, and spiritual healing.
35. **Spiritual Counseling**: Guidance and support that integrates spiritual beliefs and practices to address personal issues and promote growth.
36. **Tai Chi**: A Chinese martial art that combines slow, deliberate movements, meditation, and breathing exercises to improve health and well-being.
37. **Tarot Reading**: The use of tarot cards to gain insight into the past, present, and future, often for personal guidance and self-discovery.
38. **Visualization**: The practice of creating mental images to achieve specific goals, promote relaxation, and enhance overall well-being.
39. **Yoga**: A physical, mental, and spiritual practice that involves postures, breath control, and meditation to promote health and inner peace.

See Chart 353 - Consciousness Expansion, Master Chart

Energetic Protection

Energetic protection practices play a crucial role in maintaining and enhancing one's vibration, which is essential for achieving higher states of consciousness and well-being. By incorporating methods such as Aura Cleansing, Chakra Balancing, Grounding Techniques, and the use of protective Crystals like Black Tourmaline and Selenite, individuals can shield themselves from negative energies that may disrupt their energetic field. Techniques like Affirmations, Breathing Exercises, and Positive Visualization reinforce a positive mindset, further strengthening one's aura against harmful influences. Additionally, ritualistic practices such as Sage Smudging, Salt Baths, and the use of Holy Water, serve to cleanse and purify both personal and environmental energy, creating a harmonious space conducive to higher vibrational frequencies.

Integrating these energetic protection methods into daily routines not only fortifies one's energy field but also enhances spiritual growth and emotional resilience. Practices like Daily Meditation, Yoga, and engaging with Spirit Guides foster a deeper connection to one's inner self and the universal energy. Utilizing tools such as Orgone Devices, Sacred Geometry, and Reiki sessions can harmonize and elevate the energy body, making it more receptive to higher vibrational states. By consistently applying these protective measures, individuals can maintain a balanced and high-frequency energy field, which not only shields them from negative influences but also promotes a state of inner peace, heightened intuition, and overall well-being, ultimately aiding in their journey toward reaching and sustaining a higher vibration.

1. **Affirmations**: Positive statements repeated to reinforce protective beliefs and intentions.
2. **Amulets**: Objects worn or carried to provide protection against negative energies.
3. **Aromatherapy**: The use of essential oils to enhance emotional and physical well-being.
4. **Aura Cleansing**: Techniques used to clear and strengthen the energy field around the body.
5. **Black Tourmaline**: A protective crystal known for its ability to absorb negative energy.
6. **Blue Kyanite**: A crystal that aligns and clears energy channels and protects the aura.
7. **Boundary Setting**: Establishing personal limits to maintain energetic and emotional health.
8. **Breathing Exercises**: Techniques that use breath to balance and protect energy.
9. **Camphor**: A substance used in rituals to cleanse and protect spaces from negative influences.
10. **Candles**: Used in rituals and meditations to focus and amplify protective intentions.
11. **Carrying Crystals**: Keeping protective crystals on your person to shield against negative energy.
12. **Chakra Balancing**: Harmonizing the body's energy centers to ensure balanced and protected energy flow.
13. **Charging Water**: Imbuing water with positive energy and intentions for protection.
14. **Clear Quartz**: A versatile crystal used to amplify energy and provide protection.
15. **Cleansing Rituals**: Practices to remove negative energy from a person or space.
16. **Closing Energy Channels**: Techniques to seal off energy pathways to prevent energy loss or intrusion.
17. **Copper**: A metal known for its grounding and protective properties.
18. **Crystals**: Minerals used for their unique energetic properties to protect and heal.
19. **Daily Meditation**: A regular practice to center, ground, and protect your energy.
20. **Dragon's Blood**: A resin used in incense and rituals for powerful protection and cleansing.
21. **Earth Grounding**: Connecting with the Earth's energy to stabilize and protect your own energy field.
22. **Essential Oils**: Concentrated plant extracts used for their protective and healing properties.
23. **Etheric Shields**: Visualizing or creating energy barriers around your body for protection.
24. **Feng Shui**: An ancient practice of arranging your environment to promote balance and protection.
25. **Flower Essences**: Natural remedies made from flowers to support emotional and energetic well-being.
26. **Frankincense**: An aromatic resin used in rituals to cleanse and protect against negative energy.
27. **Full Moon Baths**: Ritual baths taken during the full moon to cleanse and recharge energy.

28. **Gem Elixirs**: Water infused with the energy of protective crystals.
29. **Golden Light Visualization**: Imagining a golden light surrounding you for protection and healing.
30. **Grounding Techniques**: Practices that connect you to the Earth to stabilize and protect your energy.
31. **Healing Herbs**: Plants used for their protective and healing properties.
32. **Himalayan Salt Lamps**: Lamps made from Himalayan salt that purify the air and provide energetic protection.
33. **Holy Water**: Water that has been blessed and used for protection and cleansing.
34. **Incense**: Aromatic substances burned to purify and protect spaces.
35. **Iron**: A metal traditionally used for protection against negative energies.
36. **Jade**: A crystal known for its protective and healing properties.
37. **Labradorite**: A crystal that protects and strengthens the aura.
38. **Light Codes**: Specific visualizations or symbols used to enhance energetic protection.
39. **Mantras**: Sacred sounds or phrases repeated to invoke protection and positive energy.
40. **Mirrors**: Objects used to reflect and deflect negative energy away from you.
41. **Music Therapy**: The use of music to create a protective and healing environment.
42. **Myrrh**: A resin used in rituals to purify and protect.
43. **Obsidian**: A protective crystal that shields against negative energy.
44. **Orgone Devices**: Tools made from resin, metals, and crystals to balance and protect energy.
45. **Palo Santo**: A sacred wood burned to cleanse and protect spaces.
46. **Personal Space Cleansing**: Techniques to clear negative energy from your immediate environment.
47. **Pineal Gland Activation**: Practices to enhance the pineal gland's protective and intuitive abilities.
48. **Positive Visualization**: Imagining positive outcomes and protective scenarios to influence reality.
49. **Prayer**: Communicating with a higher power to seek protection and guidance.
50. **Protection Grids**: Arrangements of crystals and objects designed to create a protective energy field.
51. **Reiki**: A healing technique that channels energy to protect and balance the body.
52. **Ritual Baths**: Baths with added elements like herbs and salts to cleanse and protect energy.
53. **Rose Quartz**: A crystal that promotes love and emotional protection.
54. **Sacred Geometry**: The use of geometric patterns and symbols for protection and energy alignment.
55. **Sage Smudging**: Burning sage to cleanse and protect spaces and individuals.
56. **Salt Circles**: Creating circles with salt to form a protective barrier.
57. **Salt Lamps**: Lamps made from salt that cleanse the air and provide energetic protection.
58. **Sea Salt**: Used in baths and rituals for its cleansing and protective properties.
59. **Selenite**: A crystal that cleanses and protects energy.
60. **Shielding Techniques**: Methods to create an energy barrier around yourself for protection.

61. **Singing Bowls**: Instruments used to create sound vibrations that cleanse and protect energy.
62. **Sound Baths**: Immersive experiences using sound to cleanse and protect the energy field.
63. **Sound Healing**: The use of sound frequencies to balance and protect energy.
64. **Spirit Guides**: Invoking the assistance of spiritual beings for protection and guidance.
65. **Spiritual Symbols**: Symbols used for their protective and spiritual significance.
66. **Sunlight**: Natural sunlight used to cleanse and recharge energy.
67. **Talisman**: Objects believed to hold magical properties for protection.
68. **Tiger's Eye**: A crystal that provides grounding and protection.
69. **Visualization Techniques**: Using mental imagery to create protective energy fields.
70. **Water Purification**: Using purified water for cleansing and protecting energy.
71. **Wearing Black**: Wearing black clothing to absorb and deflect negative energy.
72. **Wearing Red**: Wearing red clothing to provide energetic protection and grounding.
73. **White Light Meditation**: Visualizing white light surrounding you for protection and healing.
74. **Wind Chimes**: Hanging chimes to create protective sound vibrations.
75. **Yoga**: A practice that balances and protects energy through physical postures and breathwork.

See Chart 356 - Energetic Protection, Master Chart

Gratitude

Gratitude has a remarkable ability to raise your vibration, fostering a profound sense of well-being and positivity. When you consciously practice gratitude, whether through acts of kindness, expressing appreciation verbally, or maintaining a gratitude journal, you begin to shift your focus from what is lacking in your life to the abundance that already exists. This shift in perspective not only enhances your mood but also aligns your energy with higher vibrational frequencies. Simple practices such as daily reflections, morning gratitude affirmations, and evening gratitude rituals help create a consistent flow of positive energy, promoting a more balanced and harmonious state of being.

Incorporating gratitude into your daily routine can be transformative. Engaging in community service, sharing meals with loved ones, or participating in a gratitude meditation group can deepen your sense of connection and fulfillment. Activities like creating a gratitude tree, writing thank you notes, or even joining a gratitude group can foster a supportive environment where positive energy thrives. These practices enable you to appreciate life's small wins and blessings, reinforcing a cycle of positivity that elevates your vibrational state. By regularly acknowledging and celebrating the good in your life, you cultivate an inner atmosphere of joy and contentment, which naturally raises your vibration and enhances your overall quality of life.

Ways to Work with Gratitude

1. **Acts of Kindness:** Perform random acts of kindness to spread gratitude.
2. **Appreciation Messages:** Send messages of appreciation to friends, family, or colleagues.

3. **Blessings List:** Create a list of blessings in your life and review it regularly.
4. **Celebrate Small Wins:** Acknowledge and celebrate small achievements.
5. **Celebration Rituals:** Develop rituals to celebrate milestones and express gratitude.
6. **Community Service:** Participate in community service projects.
7. **Compliment Others:** Give sincere compliments to people around you.
8. **Cooking:** Cook meals mindfully, being grateful for the ingredients and the ability to prepare food.
9. **Crafting:** Engage in crafting activities that symbolize gratitude.
10. **Create a Gratitude Tree:** Make a tree with leaves that represent things you are grateful for.
11. **Create a Vision Board:** Include things you're grateful for on your vision board.
12. **Cultural Appreciation:** Learn about and appreciate different cultures.
13. **Daily Affirmations:** Start your day with positive affirmations related to gratitude.
14. **Daily Gratitude Emails:** Send daily emails to friends or family expressing gratitude.
15. **Daily Reflection:** Spend a few minutes each evening reflecting on the day's positive moments.
16. **Dedicate a Day to Gratitude:** Spend an entire day focusing on gratitude.
17. **Donate to Charity:** Make donations to causes you care about.
18. **Environmental Stewardship:** Take care of the environment as a form of gratitude.
19. **Evening Gratitude:** End each day by writing down three things you're grateful for.
20. **Exercise Gratitude:** Be thankful for your body's abilities and health.
21. **Express Gratitude Verbally:** Make a habit of verbally expressing gratitude to others.
22. **Family Gratitude Time:** Share things you're grateful for during family meals.
23. **Gratitude Affirmation Cards:** Create or purchase cards with gratitude affirmations.
24. **Gratitude Affirmation Mirror: Write gratitude affirmations on your mirror.**
25. **Gratitude Affirmation Videos:** Watch videos with gratitude affirmations.
26. **Gratitude Altar:** Create a small altar with items you are grateful for.
27. **Gratitude Apps:** Use apps designed to help you track and reflect on gratitude.
28. **Gratitude Art:** Create artwork that represents things you're thankful for.
29. **Gratitude Book Club:** Start a book club with a focus on books about gratitude.
30. **Gratitude Calls:** Make calls to express your gratitude to loved ones.
31. **Gratitude Challenges:** Participate in gratitude challenges or create your own.
32. **Gratitude Circle:** Form a circle of friends to share things you're grateful for.
33. **Gratitude Collage:** Make a collage of images and words that represent your gratitude.
34. **Gratitude Dance:** Express gratitude through dance and movement.
35. **Gratitude Drawing:** Draw pictures that represent things you're grateful for.
36. **Gratitude Garden:** Plant a garden with gratitude in mind.
37. **Gratitude Group:** Join or form a group focused on practicing gratitude together.
38. **Gratitude Jar:** Add notes of gratitude to a jar and read them at the end of the year.
39. **Gratitude Journal Prompts:** Use specific prompts to guide your gratitude journaling.
40. **Gratitude Journal:** Write daily entries about things you're grateful for.
41. **Gratitude Letters:** Write letters of gratitude to yourself and others.
42. **Gratitude List:** Make a list of people, experiences, and things you are grateful for.
43. **Gratitude Mantras:** Develop mantras that focus on gratitude.
44. **Gratitude Meditation Group:** Form a group to practice gratitude meditation together.
45. **Gratitude Music Playlist:** Create a playlist of songs that inspire gratitude.

46. **Gratitude Newsletter:** Start a newsletter dedicated to sharing gratitude stories.
47. **Gratitude Partner:** Share your gratitude practice with a friend or partner.
48. **Gratitude Photography:** Take photos of things you're grateful for and create a gratitude album.
49. **Gratitude Poetry:** Write poems about gratitude.
50. **Gratitude Quotes:** Read and reflect on gratitude quotes.
51. **Gratitude Retreat:** Attend or organize a retreat focused on gratitude.
52. **Gratitude Rituals:** Create daily or weekly gratitude rituals.
53. **Gratitude Rocks:** Carry a gratitude rock as a reminder to be thankful.
54. **Gratitude Scavenger Hunt:** Find things around you that you are grateful for.
55. **Gratitude Scrapbook:** Create a scrapbook filled with memories and things you are grateful for.
56. **Gratitude Social Media:** Share gratitude on social media to inspire others.
57. **Gratitude Stories**: Share stories of gratitude with others.
58. **Gratitude Video Diary:** Record video diaries of things you are grateful for.
59. **Gratitude Visualization:** Visualize people, experiences, and things you are grateful for.
60. **Gratitude Walks:** Take walks and mentally note things in nature you are grateful for.
61. **Gratitude Wall:** Create a wall in your home dedicated to things you are grateful for.
62. **Gratitude Workshop:** Attend or host workshops on practicing gratitude.
63. **Gratitude Yoga**: Incorporate gratitude into your yoga practice.
64. **Join a Gratitude Group:** Join or form a group focused on practicing gratitude together.
65. **Meditation:** Practice gratitude meditation focusing on things you're thankful for.
66. **Mindful Breathing:** Practice mindful breathing while focusing on gratitude.
67. **Mindful Eating:** Practice gratitude while eating, appreciating the food and the effort it took to prepare.
68. **Mindfulness:** Practice mindfulness to appreciate the present moment.
69. **Minimalism:** Practice minimalism to appreciate what you have more deeply.
70. **Morning Gratitude:** Start each day by thinking of three things you're grateful for.
71. **Music:** Create a playlist of songs that make you feel grateful.
72. **Nature Appreciation:** Spend time in nature and appreciate its beauty.
73. **Nature Walks:** Take walks in nature, focusing on the beauty and expressing gratitude.
74. **Photography Gratitude Project:** Start a photography project capturing things you are grateful for.
75. **Positive Media:** Consume media that promotes gratitude and positivity.
76. **Positive Reframing:** Reframe negative experiences by finding something to be grateful for in them.
77. **Prayer:** Incorporate gratitude into your prayers or spiritual practices.
78. **Random Acts of Kindness:** Perform random acts of kindness as a way to express gratitude.
79. **Reflect on Past Challenges:** Reflect on past challenges and the growth you experienced.
80. **Seasonal Gratitude:** Focus on things specific to each season to be grateful for.
81. **Self-Gratitude:** Take time to appreciate and express gratitude for yourself and your achievements.
82. **Sharing Meals:** Share meals with others and express gratitude together.
83. **Silent Gratitude:** Spend time in silence, reflecting on things you are grateful for.

84. **Social Media Gratitude Challenge:** Start a social media challenge to share daily gratitude.
85. **Special Occasions:** Use special occasions to express gratitude to those around you.
86. **Support Local Businesses:** Show gratitude by supporting local businesses.
87. **Teach Gratitude:** Teach children or others about the importance of gratitude.
88. **Thank You Notes:** Write thank you notes to people who have made a difference in your life.
89. **Thankful Thursdays:** Dedicate Thursdays to focusing on gratitude.
90. **Travel Gratitude:** Be grateful for the opportunity to travel and explore new places.
91. **Use Gratitude Apps:** Use apps designed to help you track and reflect on gratitude.
92. **Virtual Gratitude Meetings:** Hold virtual meetings with friends or family to share gratitude.
93. **Volunteer:** Help others and reflect on the gratitude you feel for being able to assist.
94. **Write a Gratitude Blog:** Start a blog to document your gratitude journey.
95. **Yoga Gratitude Sequence:** Develop a yoga sequence that focuses on gratitude.

See Chart 361 - Gratitude, Master Chart

Heart-Brain Coherence

Heart-Brain Coherence is a state where the heart and brain operate in harmony, producing synchronized rhythms that have profound effects on emotional and physical health. This coherence is achieved through practices that foster positive emotions, such as gratitude, compassion, and love, which help to align the heart and brain's electromagnetic fields. The benefits of achieving heart-brain coherence are numerous, including reduced anxiety, improved emotional resilience, and enhanced cognitive function. It promotes better decision-making, emotional balance, and overall well-being. Physically, it can lead to lower blood pressure, improved circulation, and a stronger immune system, contributing to a healthier and more resilient body.

In addition to physical health benefits, heart-brain coherence plays a crucial role in personal transformation and emotional well-being. It enhances mental clarity, reduces symptoms of depression, and fosters a sense of inner peace and calmness. By cultivating positive emotional states, individuals can experience heightened emotional intelligence, better stress management, and increased mindfulness. This state of coherence also supports personal growth by enhancing qualities such as authenticity, compassion, and optimism. The practice of achieving heart-brain coherence can ultimately lead to a more fulfilled and purposeful life, characterized by enhanced relationships, greater intuition, and a deep sense of connection with oneself and others.

Achieving heart-brain coherence significantly raises our vibration by fostering a state of alignment and harmony within our energy systems. When the heart and brain synchronize, it generates a powerful electromagnetic field that radiates positive energy, influencing not only our own body but also the environment around us. This elevated state of coherence reduces stress hormones and promotes the production of beneficial neurochemicals, such as oxytocin and serotonin, which enhance feelings of well-being and positivity. By consistently practicing techniques to achieve heart-brain coherence, such as meditation, deep breathing, and focusing on positive emotions, we can elevate our vibrational frequency. This higher vibrational state attracts positive experiences, enhances our intuitive abilities, and promotes spiritual growth, aligning us more closely with our true selves and the universal energy, ultimately leading to a more harmonious and fulfilling life.

Emotional Well-Being

1. **Acceptance**: Fostering a sense of self-acceptance and reducing self-criticism.
2. **Affection**: Enhancing the ability to give and receive affection, improving relationships.
3. **Calmness**: Promoting a state of tranquility and reducing emotional turbulence.
4. **Clarity**: Achieving clear thinking and emotional understanding.
5. **Comfort**: Providing a sense of emotional comfort and stability.
6. **Compassion**: Enhancing the ability to empathize and care for others.
7. **Confidence**: Building self-assurance and emotional stability.
8. **Connection**: Enhancing feelings of connectedness with others.
9. **Contentment**: Fostering a sense of satisfaction and happiness.
10. **Creativity**: Enhancing creative thinking and problem-solving abilities.
11. **Emotional Balance**: Helping achieve a balanced emotional state, reducing mood swings.
12. **Emotional Intelligence**: Enhancing understanding and management of one's emotions and those of others.
13. **Emotional Resilience**: Strengthening the ability to cope with emotional challenges and stressors.
14. **Empathy**: Promoting understanding and sharing the feelings of others.
15. **Enhanced Mood**: Leading to a more consistently positive mood.
16. **Forgiveness**: Increasing the ability to forgive oneself and others, reducing emotional burden.
17. **Gratitude**: Fostering a sense of thankfulness and appreciation.
18. **Harmony**: Achieving a harmonious state within oneself and in relationships.
19. **Hope**: Enhancing a positive outlook and hopefulness for the future.
20. **Improved Relationships**: Enhancing interpersonal relationships by promoting calm and empathy.
21. **Inner Peace**: Promoting a state of inner peace and tranquility.
22. **Joy**: Enhancing feelings of joy and positivity.
23. **Kindness**: Increasing the propensity to act kindly towards oneself and others.
24. **Less Frustration**: Reducing feelings of frustration by promoting calm and balance.
25. **Love**: Enhancing the ability to give and receive love.
26. **Lowered Depression Symptoms**: Alleviating symptoms of depression by fostering positive emotional states.
27. **Mindfulness**: Enhancing the ability to be present and fully engaged.
28. **Optimism**: Promoting an optimistic outlook on life.
29. **Patience**: Enhancing the ability to remain patient and calm.
30. **Peacefulness**: Promoting a peaceful state of mind.
31. **Positive Outlook**: Promoting an optimistic and positive outlook on life.
32. **Reduced Anger**: Helping manage anger by promoting relaxation and emotional control.
33. **Reduced Anxiety**: Lowering anxiety levels by promoting a state of calm and relaxation.
34. **Reduced Guilt**: Reducing feelings of guilt by fostering self-forgiveness and acceptance.
35. **Reduced Loneliness**: Enhancing feelings of connection and reducing loneliness.
36. **Reduced Stress**: Managing stress by creating a calm and balanced emotional state.

37. **Relief**: Providing emotional relief from stress and negative emotions.
38. **Self-Acceptance**: Fostering acceptance of oneself and reducing self-criticism.
39. **Self-Compassion**: Enhancing compassion towards oneself, promoting emotional healing.
40. **Self-Control**: Strengthening the ability to manage emotions and reactions.
41. **Self-Esteem**: Building confidence and a positive self-image.
42. **Self-Worth**: Enhancing feelings of self-worth and value.
43. **Serenity**: Promoting a state of calm and peace.
44. **Social Connection**: Enhancing feelings of social connection and belonging.
45. **Stress Management**: Helping in managing stress by creating a calm and balanced emotional state.
46. **Support**: Increasing the ability to seek and provide emotional support.
47. **Trust**: Building trust in oneself and others.
48. **Understanding**: Enhancing understanding of one's emotions and those of others.
49. **Validation**: Providing a sense of being understood and accepted.
50. **Well-Being**: Promoting overall emotional and psychological well-being.

Health Benefits

1. **Allergy Reduction**: Coherence practices can help lower the body's stress response, which may alleviate allergy symptoms.
2. **Anti-Aging Effects**: Reducing stress through coherence can slow down aging processes in the body.
3. **Antioxidant Production**: Coherence can boost the body's production of antioxidants, combating oxidative stress.
4. **Better Sleep**: Improved relaxation from coherence practices enhances sleep quality.
5. **Blood Pressure Regulation**: Coherence helps maintain healthy blood pressure levels by calming the autonomic nervous system.
6. **Bone Health**: Reduced stress from coherence can positively impact bone density.
7. **Brain Health**: Coherence improves overall brain function by reducing stress and enhancing focus.
8. **Chronic Disease Management**: Coherence practices can help manage chronic conditions by lowering stress levels.
9. **Circulation Improvement**: Achieving coherence enhances blood flow throughout the body.
10. **Cognitive Function**: Regular coherence practices can improve memory, attention, and problem-solving skills.
11. **Detoxification**: Coherence helps the body remove toxins more efficiently.
12. **Digestive Health**: Coherence can enhance digestive function by reducing stress-induced digestive issues.
13. **Emotional Balance**: Helps in achieving a balanced emotional state, reducing mood swings.
14. **Enhanced Empathy**: Promotes a state of coherence, better understanding and sharing feelings of others.
15. **Enhanced Immune Function**: Boosts immune system efficiency, making the body more resilient to illness.
16. **Energy Levels**: Leads to more balanced energy levels by reducing energy drain caused by stress.

17. **Flexibility**: Coherence can improve physical flexibility by promoting relaxation and reducing muscle tension.
18. **Gut Health**: Reduces stress, which can improve gut microbiota balance and overall digestive health.
19. **Happiness**: Promotes a state of well-being and contentment by reducing stress and enhancing positive emotions.
20. **Heart Health**: Supports heart health by reducing stress and improving circulation.
21. **Hormonal Balance**: Coherence practices can help balance hormones by reducing stress.
22. **Increased Resilience**: Enhances the ability to recover from illness or stress by improving overall mental and physical health.
23. **Inflammation Reduction**: Reducing stress through coherence can lower inflammation levels in the body.
24. **Joint Health**: Improved stress management through coherence can reduce joint pain and stiffness.
25. **Liver Function**: Coherence can support liver health by reducing stress and improving detoxification processes.
26. **Lowered Cholesterol**: Coherence practices can help maintain healthy cholesterol levels by reducing stress.
27. **Mental Clarity**: Improved focus and clear thinking from coherence practices.
28. **Metabolic Health**: Supports healthy metabolism by reducing stress and balancing hormone levels.
29. **Migraine Reduction**: Coherence practices can reduce the frequency and severity of migraines.
30. **Mood Improvement**: Regular coherence practices can lead to a more consistently positive mood.
31. **Muscle Relaxation**: Promotes relaxation and reduces muscle tension.
32. **Nervous System Health**: Balances the nervous system by reducing stress and promoting relaxation.
33. **Pain Management**: Helps manage chronic pain by promoting relaxation and reducing pain perception.
34. **Positive Social Interactions**: Enhances interpersonal relationships by promoting calm and empathy.
35. **Reduced Anxiety**: Lowers anxiety levels by promoting a state of calm and relaxation.
36. **Reduced Inflammation**: Stress reduction through coherence practices lowers inflammation levels in the body.
37. **Reduced Stress Hormones**: Coherence practices can lower the levels of stress hormones like cortisol.
38. **Respiratory Health**: Improves breathing and respiratory function by promoting relaxation.
39. **Self-Healing**: Enhances the body's natural ability to heal by reducing stress and promoting balance.
40. **Skin Health**: Reduces stress, which can improve skin conditions like acne and eczema.
41. **Spinal Health**: Promotes relaxation and reduces muscle tension, improving spinal health.
42. **Strengthened Immunity**: Boosts the immune system's ability to fight off infections.
43. **Stress Reduction**: Helps in managing stress by promoting a state of calm and relaxation.
44. **Vision Health**: Coherence can help maintain healthy eyesight by reducing stress.

45. **Weight Management**: Supports healthy weight management by reducing stress and improving metabolic health.
46. **Wound Healing**: Enhances the body's ability to heal wounds by promoting relaxation and reducing stress.
47. **Youthful Appearance**: Promotes a youthful appearance by reducing stress and improving overall health.
48. **Zinc Absorption**: Coherence can improve the body's ability to absorb zinc, important for immune function.
49. **Zest for Life**: Enhances overall enthusiasm and energy for living by promoting well-being.
50. **Zen State**: Achieving a calm, peaceful, and balanced state of mind through coherence practices.

Personal Transformation

1. **Authenticity**: Enhances the ability to be true to oneself and live authentically.
2. **Better Decision Making**: Enhances decision-making skills by promoting clear and focused thinking.
3. **Clarity**: Achieves mental clarity, aiding in better understanding and decision-making.
4. **Clarity of Purpose**: Helps in identifying and pursuing personal goals and purpose.
5. **Commitment**: Strengthens the ability to commit to goals and personal growth.
6. **Compassion**: Enhances the ability to empathize and care for others.
7. **Confidence**: Builds self-assurance and emotional stability.
8. **Connection**: Deepens connections with oneself and others.
9. **Contentment**: Fosters a sense of satisfaction and happiness.
10. **Courage**: Increases the courage to face personal challenges and growth.
11. **Creativity**: Enhances creative thinking and problem-solving abilities.
12. **Determination**: Strengthens the resolve to achieve personal goals.
13. **Emotional Intelligence**: Enhances understanding and management of one's emotions and those of others.
14. **Empowerment**: Promotes a sense of control and empowerment in one's life.
15. **Enhanced Creativity**: Fosters a state of mind conducive to creative thinking and problem-solving.
16. **Enhanced Relationships**: Improves relationships by promoting empathy and understanding.
17. **Focus**: Improves concentration and mental clarity, aiding in more effective focus.
18. **Greater Intuition**: Strengthens intuitive abilities and inner guidance.
19. **Growth Mindset**: Promotes a mindset oriented towards learning and growth.
20. **Happiness**: Enhances overall happiness and life satisfaction.
21. **Higher Self-Awareness**: Increases self-awareness, allowing for greater understanding of one's thoughts and emotions.
22. **Improved Focus**: Helps improve concentration and mental clarity.
23. **Improved Learning**: Enhances the ability to learn and retain information.
24. **Improved Self-Control**: Strengthens the ability to manage impulses and reactions.
25. **Inner Peace**: Promotes a state of inner peace and tranquility.
26. **Inspiration**: Increases the ability to inspire and be inspired by others.
27. **Integrity**: Enhances the ability to live in accordance with one's values.

28. **Intuition**: Enhances the ability to trust and follow one's inner guidance.
29. **Increased Motivation**: Boosts motivation by aligning emotions and thoughts with personal goals.
30. **Increased Productivity**: Enhances productivity by promoting focus and reducing distractions.
31. **Joy**: Enhances feelings of joy and positivity.
32. **Life Satisfaction**: Enhances overall satisfaction with life by promoting positive emotions and reducing stress.
33. **Mindfulness**: Enhances the ability to be present and fully engaged in the moment.
34. **Optimism**: Promotes a positive outlook on life.
35. **Patience**: Enhances the ability to remain patient and calm.
36. **Perseverance**: Strengthens the ability to persist in the face of challenges.
37. **Personal Growth**: Supports personal development by fostering a state of balance and self-reflection.
38. **Positive Thinking**: Promotes positive thinking patterns and reduces negative self-talk.
39. **Problem-Solving Skills**: Enhances problem-solving abilities by promoting clear and focused thinking.
40. **Purpose**: Helps in identifying and pursuing personal goals and purpose.
41. **Resilience**: Enhances the ability to cope with and recover from challenges and setbacks.
42. **Self-Acceptance**: Fosters acceptance of oneself and reduces self-criticism.
43. **Self-Awareness**: Increases self-awareness, allowing for greater understanding of one's thoughts and emotions.
44. **Self-Compassion**: Enhances compassion towards oneself, promoting emotional healing.
45. **Self-Confidence**: Builds confidence and a positive self-image.
46. **Self-Discipline**: Strengthens the ability to stay focused on personal goals.
47. **Self-Esteem**: Builds a strong sense of self-worth and value.
48. **Spiritual Growth**: Promotes spiritual development and connection.
49. **Stress Management**: Helps in managing stress effectively.
50. **Well-Being**: Enhances overall well-being and personal fulfillment.

See Chart 367 - Heart-Brain Coherence, Master Chart

Ho'Oponopono

Ho'oponopono is a traditional Hawaiian practice for reconciliation and forgiveness. It involves four key steps, each with a specific purpose:

1. I'm Sorry (Repentance)
- **Purpose:** Acknowledges that you have caused harm or contributed to the situation. This step is about taking responsibility for your actions, thoughts, and feelings that have led to the current state.
- **Description:** You sincerely express remorse for any wrongdoings or harm you may have caused, whether intentionally or unintentionally. This step is the beginning of the healing process.

2. Please Forgive Me (Asking for Forgiveness)
- **Purpose:** Seeks forgiveness for the actions or thoughts that have caused harm. It is about humbling oneself and asking for pardon.

- **Description:** You ask for forgiveness from those you have wronged, whether they are others or even yourself. This step allows you to release guilt and negative feelings associated with the wrongdoing.

3. Thank You (Gratitude)

- **Purpose:** Expresses gratitude for the opportunity to make amends and for the forgiveness received. It is an acknowledgment of the healing process.
- **Description:** You express gratitude for the understanding, forgiveness, and opportunity to correct the mistake. This step helps to reinforce positive feelings and encourages a mindset of thankfulness.

4. I Love You (Love)

- **Purpose:** Affirms love and connection to oneself, others, and the universe. It promotes the healing power of love and restores harmony.
- **Description:** You express love to yourself, others, and the universe. This step helps to rebuild relationships, restore inner peace, and promote overall well-being. Love is considered a powerful healing force in this practice.

These steps collectively help to cleanse negative emotions, restore balance, and promote healing through personal responsibility, forgiveness, gratitude, and love.

Four Steps in the Ho'oponopono Process

Remorse

This initial step involves a deep self-reflection where you recognize and accept that you have caused harm to someone or something, perhaps even the Earth, which in turn has affected you. It acknowledges the interconnectedness of all beings and situations. This can be a painful realization, but it is essential for genuine healing and making amends. Once this awareness is fully embraced, you can move on to the next step:

Forgiveness

Asking for forgiveness can be one of the hardest steps, especially when done in person. It requires sincerity and an open heart, without excuses or justifications. Simply saying, "I'm sorry, but..." is insufficient and may indicate an unwillingness to fully accept responsibility. The plea for forgiveness must come from deep within. If direct communication isn't possible due to estrangement or death, then silently asking for forgiveness is also effective. The next step is:

Gratitude

Expressing gratitude is crucial for healing and growth. You thank the other person, or the Earth, for the lessons they've imparted, even if those lessons were difficult or painful. Recognizing the growth and insights gained from these experiences helps to transform negative situations into opportunities for personal development. A heartfelt "thank you" can bring a sense of peace and closure. This gratitude naturally leads to the final step:

Love

Love is the ultimate healing force. If possible, express love physically through a handshake, a hug, or by planting a tree. If direct physical expression isn't feasible, visualize a positive interaction, such as holding hands or sharing a smile. This step reinforces the connection and harmony between you and the other person or the Earth.

After completing these steps, give the other person time if they are not immediately receptive. Trust that you have done your best. If the person has passed on or the relationship is beyond repair, take comfort in knowing you've gone through a profound journey of self-improvement and healing.

Additional Gains

Practicing Ho'oponopono enhances self-awareness and helps you understand the impact of your actions on others and the world. This leads to greater empathy and compassion.

These simple yet profound steps can effectively help clients resolve misunderstandings or offenses. Although some may view Ho'oponopono as overly simplistic or unscientific, its wisdom lies in its simplicity. We encourage students and clinicians to incorporate Ho'oponopono into their practices. No formal training or certification is required—just follow the four steps.

Before introducing Ho'oponopono to others, try it in your own life. Experience its effects firsthand to understand its potential for fostering peace and reconciliation. We believe you will find it to be a valuable and transformative practice.

The Four Sayings
The four sayings in Ho'oponopono are simple yet powerful affirmations used to facilitate healing and forgiveness. They are:
1. **I'm sorry.**
2. **Please forgive me.**
3. **Thank you.**
4. **I love you.**
Each of these phrases has a specific role in the healing process:
1. **I'm sorry** - This is an acknowledgment of responsibility. It's an admission that something you did or thought may have caused harm or negativity, whether knowingly or unknowingly.
2. **Please forgive me** - This is a request for forgiveness from anyone who was harmed, including yourself. It's about seeking to make amends and clear away any negativity or guilt.
3. **Thank you** - This is an expression of gratitude. It's about thanking the other person, the situation, or yourself for the lessons learned and the opportunity to grow and heal.
4. **I love you** - This is the affirmation of love. It's about restoring balance and harmony by sending out positive, healing energy to yourself, others, and the universe.

See Chart 377 - Ho'oponopono

Life Purpose

Life purpose is the unique and deeply personal journey each individual undertakes to fulfill their highest potential and true self-expression. It involves recognizing and embracing one's passions, talents, and values to make a meaningful impact on the world. Understanding and pursuing one's life purpose often requires introspection, self-discovery, and a willingness to evolve. It is about aligning with one's inner calling, which can manifest in various forms such as a career, creative endeavor, or personal mission. This alignment brings a sense of fulfillment and direction, guiding individuals toward a life that feels authentic and rewarding.

Following your life purpose can significantly raise your vibration by fostering a state of joy, passion, and inner peace. When you engage in activities and pursuits that resonate with your true self, you naturally emit positive energy, attracting similar high-frequency experiences and people into your life. This alignment not only enhances your well-being but also amplifies your ability to manifest your desires and intentions. Living in harmony with your life purpose helps clear emotional and mental blockages, allowing your energy to flow freely and elevating your overall vibrational frequency. As your vibration rises, you become more attuned to higher states of consciousness, enabling you to access deeper levels of spiritual awareness and growth.

See Chart 378 - Life Purpose, Grand Master Chart

Meditation Topics

Meditation is a transformative practice that can significantly raise your vibration, aligning you with higher frequencies of energy and consciousness. By quieting the mind and focusing inward, meditation helps release negative thoughts, emotions, and energies that weigh you down. This process of cleansing and purification allows for a greater flow of positive, high-vibrational energy throughout your being. Regular meditation practice can help you cultivate inner peace, joy, and a deeper sense of connection with yourself and the universe. As you tune into these higher states of consciousness, you naturally elevate your vibrational frequency, which can lead to improved physical, emotional, and spiritual well-being.

Moreover, meditation facilitates a heightened awareness of the present moment, which is essential for raising your vibration. When you are fully present, you can more easily access feelings of gratitude, love, and compassion—emotions that resonate at higher frequencies. Through mindfulness and focused intention, meditation helps you align your thoughts and actions with your highest aspirations, promoting a sense of harmony and balance. This alignment not only raises your vibration but also attracts positive experiences and opportunities into your life. As you continue to meditate and raise your vibration, you become a beacon of light, positively influencing those around you and contributing to the collective consciousness.

See Chart 410 - Meditation Topics, Master Chart

Modalities for Healing

Healing modalities are diverse techniques and practices that aim to improve overall well-being and raise one's vibration, promoting a higher state of consciousness and health. By engaging with these various methods, individuals can address physical, emotional, and energetic imbalances, facilitating profound healing and personal growth. Each modality offers unique benefits, targeting different aspects of the mind-body-spirit connection to create harmony and enhance vibrational frequency.

Integrating multiple healing modalities into your routine can provide a holistic approach to well-being. For instance, acupuncture can stimulate the flow of energy in the body, while practices like Emotional Freedom Techniques (EFT) address emotional blockages. Similarly, modalities like Reiki and Healing Touch work on the energetic body, promoting relaxation and balance. By exploring and combining these methods, you can tailor a healing regimen that resonates with your unique needs, supporting your journey towards optimal health and elevated vibration. Here's a comprehensive list of healing modalities in alphabetical order, along with their definitions:

1. **Acupuncture**: A traditional Chinese medicine technique that involves inserting thin needles into specific points on the body to balance energy flow.
2. **Alexander Technique**: A method that teaches improved posture and movement to enhance physical and mental well-being.
3. **Aromatherapy**: The use of essential oils and plant extracts to promote health and well-being.
4. **Aura Cleansing**: Techniques to clear and balance the energy field surrounding the body.
5. **Ayurveda**: An ancient Indian system of medicine focused on balancing the body's energies (doshas) through diet, herbs, and lifestyle practices.
6. **Bach Flower Remedies**: Natural remedies made from flowers that aim to balance emotions and promote mental well-being.
7. **Bioenergetic Healing**: A form of therapy that works with the body's energy fields to release trauma and improve health.
8. **Biofield Tuning**: A sound therapy method that uses tuning forks to detect and correct distortions in the body's energy field.
9. **Body Code**: A system of energy healing that identifies and corrects imbalances in the body.
10. **Bowenwork**: A gentle, hands-on therapy that uses precise rolling movements over muscles and connective tissue to promote healing.
11. **Breathwork**: Techniques that involve conscious control of breathing to improve physical, mental, and spiritual well-being.
12. **Chakra Balancing**: Practices to align and balance the body's energy centers (chakras).
13. **Color Therapy**: The use of colors to affect mood and health.
14. **Core Energetics**: A body-oriented therapy that combines energy work, bodywork, and psychotherapy to address physical and emotional issues.
15. **Craniosacral Therapy**: A gentle, hands-on technique that evaluates and enhances the function of the craniosacral system.
16. **Crystal Healing**: The use of crystals and gemstones to promote physical, emotional, and spiritual healing.
17. **Eden Energy Medicine**: A method that combines ancient healing techniques with modern scientific understanding of energy to promote health.
18. **EFT (Emotional Freedom Techniques)**: A form of psychological acupressure that uses tapping on acupuncture points to relieve emotional distress.
19. **Emotion Code**: A healing method that identifies and releases trapped emotions that may be causing physical or emotional issues.
20. **Energy Psychology**: A set of techniques that combine psychological and energy healing principles to address emotional issues.
21. **Feldenkrais Method**: A movement-based therapy that improves physical functioning by increasing awareness of body movements.
22. **Flower Essences**: Remedies made from flowers that aim to balance emotional states.

23. **Healing Touch**: A biofield therapy that uses gentle hand techniques to balance and align the human energy field.
24. **Homeopathy**: A system of natural medicine that uses highly diluted substances to trigger the body's natural healing response.
25. **Huna**: A Hawaiian shamanic healing practice that focuses on energy and spiritual healing.
26. **Integrative Energy Therapy (IET)**: A hands-on healing therapy that uses angelic energy to release cellular memories of trauma.
27. **Iridology**: The study of the iris to diagnose health issues and imbalances in the body.
28. **Jin Shin Jyutsu**: An ancient Japanese healing art that uses gentle touch to harmonize energy flow in the body.
29. **Kinesiology (Muscle Testing)**: A technique that uses muscle response testing to identify imbalances and determine treatment.
30. **Light Therapy**: The use of light to treat various health conditions, including seasonal affective disorder and skin conditions.
31. **Lymphatic Drainage**: A gentle massage technique that stimulates the lymphatic system to promote the removal of toxins and waste.
32. **Magnet Therapy**: The use of magnets to improve circulation and reduce pain.
33. **Metamorphic Technique**: A gentle touch therapy that aims to release patterns of limitation and promote self-healing.
34. **Myofascial Release**: A hands-on therapy that targets the connective tissue (fascia) to release tension and improve movement.
35. **Neuromodulation Technique (NMT)**: A mind-body healing method that uses principles of neuroscience to retrain the nervous system.
36. **Polarity Therapy**: A holistic healing system that combines bodywork, diet, exercise, and self-awareness to balance energy flow.
37. **Pranic Healing**: A no-touch energy healing system that uses prana (life energy) to heal physical and emotional ailments.
38. **Qi Gong**: A Chinese practice that combines movement, meditation, and breath control to enhance energy flow and health.
39. **Radionics**: A form of energy medicine that uses devices to diagnose and treat energetic imbalances.
40. **Reflexology**: A therapy that involves applying pressure to specific points on the feet, hands, or ears to promote healing in corresponding body parts.
41. **Reiki**: A Japanese energy healing technique that involves the transfer of universal energy through the hands of the practitioner.
42. **Rolfing Structural Integration**: A form of bodywork that reorganizes the connective tissues to improve posture and movement.
43. **Shiatsu**: A Japanese massage technique that uses finger pressure on acupuncture points to balance energy flow.
44. **Somatic Experiencing**: A body-oriented therapy that addresses trauma and stress-related disorders.
45. **Sound Healing**: The use of sound, such as singing bowls or tuning forks, to promote healing and relaxation.
46. **Tai Chi**: A Chinese martial art that involves slow, flowing movements to improve balance, flexibility, and energy flow.

47. **Theta Healing**: A meditation technique that uses the theta brainwave state to facilitate physical, emotional, and spiritual healing.
48. **Tui Na**: A form of Chinese therapeutic massage that incorporates acupressure and manipulation techniques.
49. **Yoga**: A mind-body practice that combines physical postures, breath control, and meditation to promote overall health and well-being.
50. **Zero Balancing**: A hands-on therapy that integrates body and mind by aligning energy fields within the body.

See Chart 419 - Modalities for Healing, Master Chart

Non-Beneficial Energies

Clearing non-beneficial energies, including energetic, emotional, environmental, geopathic, non-beneficial entities, and technological, is vital for raising your vibration. These energies can cause disruptions in your physical and energetic bodies, lowering your vibrational state and impacting your overall well-being. By addressing these energies through specific practices, you can restore harmony and enhance your vibration. Creating a balanced energetic environment supports a higher state of consciousness and fosters spiritual and emotional growth.

Non-beneficial technological energies, such as electromagnetic fields (EMFs), Wi-Fi, and radiation from modern devices, interfere with the body's natural energy flow, potentially causing stress and health issues. By reducing exposure and using protective measures, you can mitigate these influences and maintain a healthier energetic state. Clearing energetic and emotional blockages, including negative thought patterns and trapped emotions, as well as environmental and geopathic stressors, helps to create a more supportive environment for raising your vibration. Removing non-beneficial entities through spiritual practices further ensures a clean energetic field, allowing you to maintain higher levels of consciousness and well-being.

Energetic & Emotional Non-Beneficial Energies

Energetic and emotional non-beneficial energies encompass a range of negative emotional states and energetic disruptions that can affect an individual's well-being. This category includes trapped emotions, negative thought patterns, psychic attacks, and past life traumas. These energies can create blockages in the body's energy flow, leading to emotional and physical imbalances. Techniques such as energy healing, meditation, and emotional release practices can help clear these blockages, restoring balance and enhancing one's vibrational state.

Environmental Non-Beneficial Energies

Environmental non-beneficial energies are negative influences present in the physical surroundings that can impact health and well-being. These include toxins in the air, water, and soil, as well as electromagnetic pollution from power lines and industrial zones. Geopathic stress, such as earth radiation and disruptions in natural earth grids, also falls under this category. Mitigating these environmental stressors through detoxification, grounding practices, and creating a harmonious living space can improve overall health and elevate one's vibration.

Geopathic Non-Beneficial Energies

Geopathic non-beneficial energies are harmful energies arising from the earth itself, often due to natural or man-made disruptions. These include disturbances in the earth's magnetic field, ley lines, and underground water veins, as well as residual energies from ancient battlefields or industrial pollution zones. Exposure to these energies can lead to physical and emotional distress. Practices like dowsing, using protective crystals, and adjusting one's living environment can help neutralize geopathic stress and create a more supportive energetic environment.

Non-Beneficial Entities

Removing non-beneficial entities from your energetic field is crucial for raising your vibration. Non-beneficial entities, such as dark energy entities, earthbound spirits, and psychic vampires, drain your life force, cloud your judgment, and perpetuate negative emotions and thoughts. These entities attach themselves to your aura or physical body, creating energetic blockages that hinder the flow of positive energy. By identifying and removing these entities, you release the negative influences that have been anchoring you to lower vibrational states. This process not only frees you from their detrimental impacts but also allows your natural, higher vibrational energy to flow more freely, promoting a state of enhanced well-being and spiritual growth.

When you clear non-beneficial entities, you reclaim your personal power and sovereignty. Entities such as demonic attachments, shadow beings, and interdimensional beings can manipulate your emotions, distort your perception of reality, and weaken your energetic boundaries. Their removal leads to a profound sense of liberation and empowerment. As these entities are cleared, you may experience increased mental clarity, emotional balance, and a deeper connection to your higher self and spiritual guides. The absence of these intrusive influences enables you to vibrate at a higher frequency, which is essential for manifesting positive experiences, attracting abundance, and maintaining overall health and harmony. By elevating your vibration, you create a protective energetic environment that is less susceptible to future entity attachments and more conducive to spiritual evolution.

1. **Ancestral Spirits**: Spirits of deceased family members or ancestors.
2. **Animal Spirits, Dark**: Dark or negative energy associated with animal spirits.
3. **Archonic Entities**: Entities associated with archons, sometimes considered malevolent spiritual forces.
4. **Ascended Masters, Dark Side**: Allegedly ascended beings who have turned to negative or dark influences.
5. **Astral Fragments**: Fragments of consciousness or energy in the astral plane.
6. **Astral Parasites**: Energetic parasites or entities that feed on astral energy.
7. **Cambion**: Offspring of a demon and a human.
8. **Created by Curse**: Entities or energies created through curses.
9. **Created by Hex**: Entities or energies created through hexes.
10. **Created by Sorcery**: Entities or energies created through sorcery.
11. **Created by Spell**: Entities or energies created through spells.
12. **Crystallized Astral Fragment**: Solidified or crystallized fragments of astral energy.
13. **Dark Angels**: Angels associated with negative or dark energies.
14. **Dark Cherub**: Cherubic beings associated with negative or dark energies.
15. **Dark Energies**: Negative or malevolent energies.

16. **Dark Energy Device Implant**: Devices or implants emitting dark or negative energy.
17. **Dark Energy Disguised as God**: Dark energies masquerading as divine or spiritual entities.
18. **Dark Energy Ectoplasm**: Dark or negative energy in ectoplasmic form.
19. **Dark Spirits**: Spirits associated with negative or malevolent energies.
20. **Deceased Loved Ones**: Spirits of deceased loved ones or family members.
21. **Demonic Attachments**: Attachments or connections to demonic entities.
22. **Discarnate Spirits**: Spirits without physical bodies.
23. **Disguised as a Channel**: Entities pretending to be channels for spiritual communication.
24. **Disguised as a Higher-Self**: Entities masquerading as higher aspects of one's self.
25. **Disguised as an Angel**: Entities pretending to be benevolent angelic beings.
26. **Djinn / Jinn**: Supernatural creatures or entities in Islamic mythology.
27. **Earthbound Spirit**: Spirits trapped on the earthly plane after death.
28. **Earthbound Spirit of...**: Earthbound spirits associated with specific individuals.
29. **Egregores**: Collective thought forms or group consciousness entities.
30. **Elemental**: Beings associated with the classical elements (earth, air, fire, water).
31. **Elemental Spirits, Air**: Spirits or beings associated with the element of air.
32. **Elemental Spirits, Earth**: Spirits or beings associated with the element of earth.
33. **Elemental Spirits, Fire**: Spirits or beings associated with the element of fire.
34. **Elemental Spirits, Water**: Spirits or beings associated with the element of water.
35. **Entity Attachments**: Attachments or connections to non-physical entities.
36. **ETs**: Extraterrestrial entities or beings.
37. **Evil**: Malevolent or morally corrupt entities.
38. **Fairy / Fae**: Mythical beings or spirits associated with nature and magic.
39. **Ghosts**: Spirits of deceased individuals that remain on the earthly plane.
40. **Guardian Spirits**: Spirits assigned to protect or guide individuals.
41. **Highly Evolved Dark Masters**: Allegedly advanced beings aligned with dark or negative energies.
42. **Implant**: Energetic or technological implants affecting spiritual or energetic fields.
43. **Incubi**: Malevolent spirits in folklore that seduce and harm women.
44. **Incubus**: Malevolent spirits in folklore that seduce and harm men.
45. **Interdimensional Beings**: Beings existing in dimensions beyond the typical physical realm.
46. **Intrusions**: Unwanted or intrusive energetic presences or influences.
47. **Kuei**: Chinese term for wandering spirits or ghosts.
48. **Low Level Entities**: Entities of lower consciousness or spiritual development.
49. **Malevolent Beings**: Entities or beings characterized by harmful intentions.
50. **Malevolent Spirit**: Spirit or entity characterized by harmful or negative intentions.
51. **Member of the Dark Brotherhood**: Alleged members of a secretive group associated with negative energies.
52. **Multiple Souls**: Presence of multiple soul aspects or energies in one individual.

53. **Nature Spirit**: Spirit or being associated with natural elements or forces.

54. **Nephilim**: Offspring of angels and humans, often portrayed as giants.

55. **Parasitic Entities**: Entities that feed off of or drain the energy of other beings.

56. **Perverse Energy**: Distorted or corrupted energy affecting spiritual or energetic fields.

57. **Poltergeists**: Noisy, disruptive spirits often associated with physical disturbances.

58. **Psychic Attack Entities**: Entities or energies involved in psychic attacks.

59. **Psychic Vampires**: Individuals who drain energy from others.

60. **Samskara**: Imprints or impressions left on the psyche from past experiences.

61. **Satantic Forces**: Forces or entities associated with Satanism or dark occult practices.

62. **Shadow Beings**: Dark or shadowy entities often associated with fear or malevolence.

63. **Shadow Energies**: Dark or negative energies associated with suppressed aspects of the self.

64. **Soul Fragments**: Fragmented aspects of the soul or consciousness.

65. **Spirit Guides Dark**: Spirit guides associated with negative or dark energies.

66. **Spirit Visit by…**: Visitations from spirits or entities, specified. On this one if you have a guess who or what it might be, just add those words when you dowse.

67. **Spirit Visitor**: Visiting spirit or entity.

68. **Spirits Dark**: Spirits associated with darkness, negativity, or malevolence.

69. **Succubus**: Female demonic entity in folklore that seduces and harms men.

70. **Terminated Pregnancy**: Energetic residue or implications from an terminated pregnancy.

71. **Thought Forms**: Energetic manifestations of thoughts or intentions.

72. **Total Mind Spirit Possession**: Complete control or influence over an individual's consciousness.

73. **Trickster Spirits**: Mischievous or deceptive spirits known for causing confusion or chaos.

74. **Unborn Twin**: Energies or implications related to an unborn twin.

75. **Vaccination Implant**: Energetic or physiological effects attributed to vaccinations.

76. **Vampires**: Mythical beings or entities that feed on the life force of others.

77. **Virtual Reality Sickness**: Discomfort or disturbances associated with virtual reality experiences.

78. **White Magic**: Beneficial or positive magical practices intended for healing or protection.

79. **Wi-Fi Overload Areas**: Areas with high levels of electromagnetic interference from Wi-Fi signals.

Technological Non-Beneficial Energies

Technological non-beneficial energies refer to the disruptive electromagnetic fields and radiation emitted by modern electronic devices and infrastructure. Examples include EMFs from cell phones, Wi-Fi routers, and smart meters, as well as radiation from devices like microwaves and airport security scanners. These energies can interfere with the body's natural electromagnetic field, potentially causing stress, fatigue, and other health issues. Reducing exposure to these sources and using protective measures can help mitigate their effects and promote a healthier energetic environment.

1. **5G Technology:** Advanced wireless technology that enhances mobile broadband, promising faster speeds and more reliable connections.
2. **Airport Security Scanners:** Devices used in airports to detect prohibited items by scanning passengers and luggage with electromagnetic waves.
3. **Bluetooth Devices:** Wireless technology that allows for short-range communication between devices, such as smartphones, tablets, and computers.
4. **Cell Phones:** Mobile devices that use radio frequencies to connect calls and transmit data wirelessly.
5. **Cell Towers:** Structures equipped with antennas and other equipment to facilitate wireless communication between devices and networks.
6. **Chemtrails:** Release of chemicals and vaccine toxins from aircraft trails affecting health or environment.
7. **Computer Monitor & Computer:** Display screen and processing unit for digital information and tasks.
8. **Digital Assistants (e.g., Amazon Echo, Google Home):** Voice-activated smart devices that provide information, control smart home devices, and perform tasks using artificial intelligence.
9. **Electric Vehicles:** Automobiles powered partially or entirely by electricity. Very dangerous EMFs in these vehicles.
10. **Electromagnetic Fields:** Fields of electric and magnetic energy generated by electrical devices and power sources.
11. **Electromagnetic Radiation:** Energy emitted by electronic devices and systems as waves or particles.
12. **ELF (Extremely Low Frequency):** Low-frequency electromagnetic waves used in communication and other applications.
13. **GPS Devices:** Navigation devices using satellite signals to determine geographic location.
14. **High-voltage Transmission Lines:** Overhead power lines that carry high-voltage electricity.
15. **Home Automation Systems:** Smart systems controlling household functions like lighting, heating, and security.
16. **Induction Cooktops:** Cooking appliances using electromagnetic induction for heating.
17. **Infrared Devices:** Devices emitting or detecting infrared radiation for various applications, including remote controls and thermal imaging.
18. **Laptop:** Portable computer designed for mobility and convenience.
19. **LED Lighting:** Energy-efficient lighting using light-emitting diodes (LEDs).
20. **Microwaves:** Electromagnetic waves used in microwave ovens for heating food.
21. **Neon Lighting:** Gas-discharge lighting using neon or other gases.
22. **Plasma Screens:** Display screens using plasma technology for vibrant colors and high contrast.
23. **Power Lines:** Cables carrying electrical power from generation to distribution networks.
24. **RFID Tags:** Radio-frequency identification tags for tracking and identifying objects.
25. Radio Frequencies: Electromagnetic frequencies used in radio communication and broadcasting.

26. **Satellite Communications:** Communication via satellites orbiting the Earth.
27. **Smart Meters:** Digital meters measuring electricity, gas, or water usage with wireless communication capabilities.
28. **Smart Watches and Fitness Trackers:** Wearable devices monitoring health metrics and providing smartphone connectivity.
29. **Television:** Electronic device for receiving broadcast signals and displaying audiovisual content.
30. **Ultrasound Devices:** Devices using high-frequency sound waves for medical imaging and diagnostic purposes.
31. **Video Game Consoles:** Electronic devices for playing video games on a TV or monitor.
32. **VR Headsets:** Virtual reality head-mounted displays for immersive virtual experiences.
33. **Wi-Fi Routers:** Devices providing wireless internet connectivity within a specified area.
34. **Wireless Charging Stations:** Devices charging electronic devices wirelessly using electromagnetic induction.
35. **Wireless Frequencies:** Radio frequencies used in wireless communication technologies.

See Chart 423 - Non-Beneficial Energies, Grand Master Chart

Personal Blocks to Dowsing

Personal blocks, such as addictions, anxiety, fear, and limiting beliefs, create energetic barriers that disrupt the flow of intuition and spiritual guidance. These blocks not only affect the accuracy and effectiveness of dowsing but also hinder overall well-being and spiritual growth. By recognizing and addressing these blocks, individuals can clear the energetic pathways, allowing for a more profound connection with their higher selves and the universe.

Clearing these blocks involves a multifaceted approach, including practices such as meditation, energy healing, and self-reflection. Techniques like chakra balancing, aura cleansing, and releasing ancestral agreements can help remove the energetic imprints that hold individuals back. Engaging in physical activities, maintaining a healthy diet, and practicing good energy hygiene are also essential for maintaining a balanced and clear energy field. As these blocks are cleared, individuals experience increased clarity, focus, and intuition, leading to more effective dowsing and a significant rise in their vibrational frequency. This elevated state of being not only enhances dowsing capabilities but also attracts positive experiences, promotes emotional and mental well-being, and fosters spiritual enlightenment.

1. **Addictions**: Compulsive engagement in behaviors or consumption of substances that disrupt mental clarity and focus.
2. **Anger**: Intense emotional response that clouds judgment and impairs decision-making.
3. **Anxiety**: Excessive worry or fear that interferes with concentration and intuition.
4. **Astral Debris**: Residual energies from astral travel or other-dimensional experiences that affect energetic balance.

5. **Aura Tears**: Breaks or disruptions in the aura that allow negative energies to affect one's energy field.
6. **Boundaries**: Lack of clear personal boundaries leading to energetic drain and reduced dowsing efficacy.
7. **Burnout**: Physical or emotional exhaustion that diminishes energy levels and focus.
8. **Chemical Imbalance**: Disruptions in the body's chemistry affecting mood and cognitive function.
9. **Chakra Blockages**: Energetic blockages in the chakras that hinder energy flow and intuition.
10. **Chronic Pain**: Persistent pain that distracts from mental clarity and concentration.
11. **Contracts**: Binding agreements or vows, often from past lives, that limit personal freedom and spiritual growth.
12. **Control Issues**: A need to control situations or outcomes that restricts the flow of intuitive insights.
13. **Cultural Conditioning**: Deeply ingrained beliefs and behaviors from cultural upbringing that limit open-mindedness.
14. **Curses**: Negative energetic imprints or intentions from others that impact well-being and clarity.
15. **Depression**: Persistent feelings of sadness and hopelessness that lower energy and focus.
16. **Desire to Escape (Others)**: A tendency to withdraw or escape from challenging situations or relationships.
17. **Desire to Escape (Yours)**: Personal desire to avoid facing difficult emotions or situations.
18. **Detrimental Agreements (Ancestors)**: Agreements made by ancestors that negatively influence current life.
19. **Detrimental Agreements (Future Life)**: Agreements from potential future lives affecting the present.
20. **Detrimental Agreements (Life Between Lives)**: Agreements made in the spiritual realm between incarnations impacting the current life.
21. **Detrimental Agreements (Parallel Life)**: Agreements in parallel lives that affect the present experience.
22. **Detrimental Agreements (Past Life)**: Agreements from past lives that continue to influence current life.
23. **Detrimental Agreements (This Life)**: Current life agreements that restrict growth and freedom.
24. **Disconnection from Nature**: Lack of connection with the natural world leading to energetic imbalance.
25. **Distractions**: External factors that divert attention and disrupt focus.
26. **Ego**: Over-identification with self-importance that obstructs intuitive guidance.
27. **Emotional Overload**: Being overwhelmed by emotions, hindering clear thinking and intuition.
28. **Energetic Cords**: Unwanted energy connections with others that drain personal energy.

29. **Energetic Imbalances**: Misalignment of energy bodies causing disharmony and confusion.
30. **Environmental Stressors**: External physical or energetic conditions that cause stress and distraction.
31. **Fear**: An emotion that paralyzes decision-making and blocks intuitive flow.
32. **Financial Worries**: Concerns about money that occupy mental space and reduce focus.
33. **Guilt**: Feelings of remorse that weigh down emotional and mental energy.
34. **Habits (Emotional)**: Repetitive emotional patterns that interfere with clear intuition.
35. **Habits (Mental)**: Repetitive thought patterns that distract from intuitive insights.
36. **Habits (Physical)**: Physical habits that disrupt energy flow and concentration.
37. **Hormonal Imbalance**: Disruptions in hormones affecting mood and cognitive function.
38. **Implants**: Energetic implants or devices that interfere with natural energy flow and clarity.
39. **Inherited Behaviors**: Behaviors passed down through generations that limit personal growth.
40. **Inherited Beliefs**: Limiting beliefs inherited from family that restrict open-mindedness.
41. **Inherited Trauma**: Traumas passed down through family lines that affect present well-being.
42. **Jealousy**: An emotion that clouds judgment and creates energetic blockages.
43. **Lack of Clear Intention**: Unclear or undefined goals that disrupt focus and purpose.
44. **Lack of Exercise**: Physical inactivity that diminishes energy levels and clarity.
45. **Lack of Focus**: Inability to concentrate, leading to scattered energy and thoughts.
46. **Lack of Grounding**: Disconnection from the earth that causes instability and confusion.
47. **Lack of Spiritual Connection**: Absence of a connection with a higher power or inner guidance.
48. **Limiting Beliefs**: Negative beliefs that limit potential and intuitive abilities.
49. **Low Self-Esteem**: Lack of confidence that hinders trust in one's intuitive insights.
50. **Lost Soul Parts (Ancestors)**: Fragmented soul parts of ancestors affecting current life.
51. **Lost Soul Parts (Future Life)**: Fragmented soul parts from potential future lives impacting the present.
52. **Lost Soul Parts (Life Between Lives)**: Fragmented soul parts from the spiritual realm between lives.
53. **Lost Soul Parts (Parallel Life)**: Fragmented soul parts from parallel lives influencing the present.
54. **Lost Soul Parts (Past Life)**: Fragmented soul parts from past lives affecting current experiences.
55. **Lost Soul Parts (This Life)**: Fragmented soul parts from current life experiences.
56. **Medical Conditions**: Health issues that impact energy and focus.
57. **Medication Side Effects**: Negative effects from medications that impair clarity and focus.
58. **Mental Fog**: Confusion or lack of mental clarity.
59. **Mental Projections**: Thoughts and beliefs projected onto situations, distorting reality.

60. **Misaligned Energies**: Energies that are out of sync with one's true self or purpose.
61. **Money Beliefs**: Limiting beliefs about money that restrict financial well-being.
62. **Negative Beliefs**: Beliefs that create limitations and block positive outcomes.
63. **Negative Emotions (Others)**: Emotions from others that impact personal energy and clarity.
64. **Negative Emotions (Yours)**: Personal negative emotions that cloud judgment and focus.
65. **Negative Family Dynamics**: Unhealthy family interactions that create stress and distraction.
66. **Negative Thought Forms (Others)**: Negative thoughts from others that influence personal energy.
67. **Negative Thought Forms (Yours)**: Personal negative thoughts that create blockages.
68. **Overthinking**: Excessive thinking that obstructs intuitive flow and clarity.
69. **Past Trauma**: Previous traumatic experiences that impact current well-being.
70. **Peace of Mind**: Absence of mental stress and turmoil, essential for clear intuition.
71. **Peer Pressure**: Influence from peers that distracts from personal goals and intuition.
72. **Perfectionism**: An obsession with perfection that hinders progress and intuitive flow.
73. **Physical Exhaustion**: Extreme physical fatigue that depletes energy and focus.
74. **Poor Diet**: Nutritional deficiencies that affect energy levels and mental clarity.
75. **Poor Energy Hygiene**: Neglect of personal energetic cleanliness, leading to imbalances.
76. **Procrastination**: Delaying actions that create stress and hinder progress.
77. **Psychic Attacks (Future Life)**: Energetic attacks from potential future lives affecting the present.
78. **Psychic Attacks (Life Between Lives)**: Energetic attacks from the spiritual realm between lives.
79. **Psychic Attacks (Parallel Life)**: Energetic attacks from parallel lives impacting the present.
80. **Psychic Attacks (Past Life)**: Energetic attacks from past lives affecting current well-being.
81. **Psychic Attacks (This Life)**: Energetic attacks in the present life disrupting clarity and focus.
82. **Psychic Debris**: Residual negative energies from psychic experiences that affect clarity.
83. **Religious Dogma**: Rigid religious beliefs that limit open-mindedness and spiritual growth.
84. **Resentment**: Holding onto anger or bitterness that blocks positive energy flow.
85. **Secondary Gain**: Subconscious benefits from remaining in a negative state, hindering progress.
86. **Self-Doubt**: Lack of confidence in one's abilities that obstructs intuitive insights.
87. **Shame**: Deep feelings of unworthiness that affect energy and clarity.
88. **Sleep Deprivation**: Lack of sleep that impairs cognitive function and focus.
89. **Societal Expectations**: Pressures from society that distract from personal goals and intuition.

90. **Soul Fragments**: Disconnected parts of the soul that need to be reintegrated for wholeness.

91. **Spells**: Negative energetic influences from spells or curses that affect well-being.

92. **Spiritual Interference**: Disruptions from spiritual entities or energies that impact clarity.

93. **Suppressed Emotions**: Repressed feelings that create energetic blockages and confusion.

94. **Toxic Relationships**: Relationships that drain energy and create stress.

95. **Trauma**: Emotional or physical wounds that impact well-being and clarity.

96. **Trust Issues**: Difficulty trusting others or oneself that hinders intuitive guidance.

97. **Unaligned Purpose**: Lack of alignment with one's true purpose, creating confusion and dissatisfaction.

98. **Unhealthy Boundaries**: Inadequate boundaries that lead to energetic drain and distraction.

99. **Unhealed Inner Child**: Unresolved childhood issues that affect current behavior and intuition.

100. **Unresolved Conflicts**: Ongoing conflicts that create stress and mental clutter.

101. **Unresolved Karma**: Negative karma from past actions that impact current experiences.

102. **Victim Mentality**: Belief in being a victim that creates powerlessness and blocks progress.

103. **Voodoo**: Negative influences from voodoo practices that impact well-being.

104. **Vows**: Binding vows or promises that restrict personal freedom and growth.

105. **Work Stress**: Job-related stress that distracts from personal goals and intuition.

106. **World Thought Forms**: Collective negative thoughts and beliefs that influence personal energy.

See Chart 443 - Personal Blocks to Dowsing, Master Chart

Sacred Geometry Patterns and Symbols

Incorporating sacred geometry into your quest for raising vibration can profoundly enhance your spiritual and energetic journey. Symbols like the Flower of Life, Metatron's Cube, and the Sri Yantra are powerful tools for meditation and visualization, facilitating a deeper connection to the universe's underlying structure. The Flower of Life, with its overlapping circles, represents the cycle of creation and the interconnectedness of all life. Meditating on this symbol can help harmonize your energy and align your vibrational frequency with the universal rhythm. Similarly, Metatron's Cube, which contains all five Platonic solids, can be used to balance and cleanse your chakras, promoting overall energetic equilibrium and aiding in the release of negative emotions and blockages.

The geometric shapes of the dodecahedron, icosahedron, and tetrahedron also play significant roles in elevating your vibration. The dodecahedron, associated with the etheric realm, can be used to tap into higher consciousness and spiritual awakening, helping you transcend physical limitations and access higher states of awareness. The icosahedron, linked to water and emotional balance, can support emotional healing and fluidity, allowing you to release past traumas and embrace a more harmonious state of being. The tetrahedron, representing fire and transformation, can ignite your inner drive for personal growth and spiritual evolution, enabling you to manifest your highest potential. By integrating these sacred geometric symbols into your spiritual practice, you can create a powerful resonance with the cosmic order, facilitating profound personal transformation and an elevated vibrational state.

See Chart 450 - Sacred Geometry Patterns and Symbols

Spiritual Awakening

Spiritual awakening is a profound and transformative journey that leads to a deeper understanding of oneself and the universe. Engaging in various practices and activities, such as those listed above, is essential to facilitate and enhance this process. Each practice, from meditation and mindfulness to energy healing and chakra cleansing, serves to clear mental, emotional, and energetic blockages, allowing for a more profound connection with one's inner self and the greater cosmic consciousness. These practices help in cultivating inner peace, expanding consciousness, and fostering a sense of unity with all life. By consciously integrating these activities into daily life, individuals can experience heightened awareness, greater emotional balance, and an overall sense of well-being.

Improving spiritual awakening through these practices is necessary because it leads to a more fulfilled and authentic life. As individuals become more attuned to their inner selves and the energies around them, they can navigate life's challenges with greater ease and clarity. This heightened state of awareness and understanding fosters compassion, empathy, and a sense of purpose, which are crucial for personal growth and collective harmony. Additionally, these practices help in releasing past traumas and negative patterns, enabling individuals to live more freely and joyfully. By continuously engaging in activities that promote spiritual awakening, one can achieve a state of inner harmony and alignment, leading to a more enlightened and empowered existence.

1. **Acceptance**: The act of embracing all experiences and emotions without resistance.
2. **Affirmations**: Positive statements that help to challenge and overcome self-sabotaging and negative thoughts.
3. **Alignment with Purpose**: Living in a way that is consistent with one's true values and goals.
4. **Altruism**: Selfless concern for the well-being of others.
5. **Awareness**: The ability to perceive, feel, and be conscious of events, objects, or sensory patterns.
6. **Balance**: Achieving a state where different elements are in the correct proportions.
7. **Being Present**: Fully engaging with the current moment without distraction or judgment.
8. **Breathwork**: Various breathing exercises or techniques to improve physical, mental, and spiritual well-being.
9. **Chakra Cleansing**: The process of balancing the body's energy centers to promote health and well-being.
10. **Compassion**: A deep awareness of the suffering of others coupled with the wish to relieve it.

11. **Connection with Nature**: Building a relationship with the natural environment to enhance spiritual and emotional health.
12. **Conscious Eating**: Mindful consumption of food with awareness of its nutritional value and impact on the body.
13. **Conscious Relationships**: Engaging in relationships with mindfulness and intentionality, fostering deeper connections.
14. **Consciousness Expansion**: Practices that lead to an increased awareness and understanding of the self and the universe.
15. **Creativity**: The use of imagination or original ideas to create something new.
16. **Crystals**: Minerals believed to have healing properties that can enhance spiritual practices.
17. **Dance**: A form of expression that can elevate mood and release trapped energy.
18. **Deep Breathing**: Breathing techniques that promote relaxation and stress reduction.
19. **Deep Reflection**: Introspective practices that encourage self-awareness and personal growth.
20. **Detachment**: The process of letting go of attachments to outcomes, people, or material possessions.
21. **Devotion**: Profound dedication to a person, deity, or cause.
22. **Digital Detox**: Taking a break from digital devices to reduce stress and improve well-being.
23. **Dream Analysis**: The interpretation of dreams to gain insights into the subconscious mind.
24. **Earth Grounding**: Connecting with the earth's surface to balance energy and promote health.
25. **Emotional Release**: Techniques for expressing and letting go of pent-up emotions.
26. **Energy Healing**: Practices that restore the balance and flow of energy within the body.
27. **Environmental Harmony**: Creating a living space that supports physical, mental, and spiritual well-being.
28. **Essential Oils**: Concentrated plant extracts used for their therapeutic properties.
29. **Forgiveness**: Letting go of resentment and thoughts of revenge toward someone who has wronged you.
30. **Full Moon Rituals**: Ceremonies performed during the full moon to harness its energy for personal growth.
31. **Gratitude Practice**: Regularly acknowledging and appreciating the positive aspects of life.
32. **Guided Meditation**: Meditation led by a guide or instructor to help focus and relax the mind.
33. **Healing Music**: Music specifically designed to promote relaxation and healing.
34. **Herbal Remedies**: The use of plants for medicinal purposes to support health and healing.
35. **Inner Child Work**: Healing the part of oneself that retains the experiences and emotions of childhood.
36. **Inner Peace**: A state of mental and spiritual calm despite the presence of stressors.

37. **Intention Setting**: The practice of stating desired outcomes to focus energy and actions.
38. **Intuitive Development**: Cultivating the ability to understand or know something instinctively.
39. **Journaling**: Writing down thoughts and feelings to explore and understand them better.
40. **Kindness**: Being friendly, generous, and considerate to oneself and others.
41. **Kundalini Yoga**: A practice that combines physical postures, breathing exercises, and meditation to awaken spiritual energy.
42. **Light Work**: Practices aimed at spreading love, light, and positive energy.
43. **Listening to Intuition**: Trusting and following one's inner guidance.
44. **Living Authentically**: Being true to oneself and living according to one's values and beliefs.
45. **Loving-Kindness Meditation**: A meditation practice focused on cultivating compassion and love for oneself and others.
46. **Lucid Dreaming**: The practice of becoming aware that one is dreaming and potentially controlling the dream.
47. **Manifestation**: The process of bringing desires or goals into reality through focused thought and intention.
48. **Mantras**: Repeated words or sounds used in meditation to aid concentration and focus.
49. **Meditation**: A practice where an individual uses techniques to train attention and awareness, achieving a mentally clear and emotionally calm state.
50. **Mindfulness**: The practice of being fully present and engaged in the current moment.
51. **Nature Walks**: Walking in natural settings to promote physical and mental well-being.
52. **Non-Attachment**: The practice of not clinging to material possessions, outcomes, or relationships.
53. **Non-Judgment**: Accepting others and oneself without criticism or evaluation.
54. **Nutritional Awareness**: Being mindful of the nutritional content and health impact of the food one consumes.
55. **Past Life Regression**: A technique used to explore potential past lives to gain insights into current life issues.
56. **Positive Thinking**: The practice of focusing on positive thoughts and outcomes.
57. **Pranayama**: Breathing exercises that regulate energy flow in the body.
58. **Prayer**: Communicating with a higher power for guidance, support, or gratitude.
59. **Reiki**: A form of energy healing that involves transferring universal energy through the palms.
60. **Sacred Geometry**: Using geometric shapes believed to have spiritual significance in meditation and energy work.
61. **Sacred Space Creation**: Designing a space for spiritual practice and reflection.
62. **Self-Care**: Activities and practices that nurture one's physical, mental, and emotional well-being.
63. **Self-Compassion**: Being kind and understanding toward oneself during times of failure or difficulty.
64. **Self-Discovery**: The process of gaining insight into one's own character and potential.

65. **Self-Expression**: Expressing one's thoughts, feelings, and creativity.

66. **Self-Love**: Valuing and caring for oneself with kindness and respect.

67. **Shadow Work**: The process of exploring and integrating the darker aspects of oneself.

68. **Shamanic Journeying**: A practice of entering altered states of consciousness to connect with spiritual realms.

69. **Silence**: Embracing quietness to calm the mind and enhance inner peace.

70. **Singing Bowls**: Instruments used in sound healing to produce harmonic tones.

71. **Sound Healing**: The use of sound frequencies to promote physical and emotional healing.

72. **Spiritual Reading**: Reading texts that offer spiritual guidance and insights.

73. **Surrender**: Letting go of control and trusting the flow of life.

74. **Tai Chi**: A form of exercise and meditation that promotes balance, flexibility, and inner peace.

75. **Tarot**: A tool for divination and self-reflection using a deck of cards.

76. **Visualization**: The practice of creating mental images to achieve desired outcomes.

77. **Volunteering**: Offering time and service to help others and contribute to the community.

78. **Walking Meditation**: Combining walking with meditative awareness to enhance mindfulness.

79. **Yoga**: A practice that combines physical postures, breathing exercises, and meditation to promote overall well-being.

80. **Zen Practices**: Techniques derived from Zen Buddhism that emphasize simplicity, mindfulness, and meditation.

See Chart 451 - Spiritual Awakening, Master Chart

Things Lost, Taken From, or Given Away

Understanding what we have lost, what has been taken from us, or what we have given away is essential for our overall well-being and personal development. These elements often reside in our subconscious mind, influencing our thoughts, emotions, and behaviors without our conscious awareness. As Bruce Lipton emphasizes, "the subconscious mind runs our lives about 95% of the time, and that's a lot of power to give away." When we identify these hidden aspects, we reclaim the personal authority and emotional control that we may have inadvertently lost, allowing us to live more authentically and intentionally.

By examining aspects such as Personal Authority, Emotional Control, Spiritual Connection, and Mental Clarity, we uncover deep-seated beliefs and experiences that have shaped our current state of being. For instance, regaining lost emotional control can enhance our capacity for joy and acceptance, while reconnecting with our spiritual essence can provide a sense of alignment and purpose. Similarly, understanding where we have lost or given away mental clarity can restore our alertness and positivity. Each of these areas, whether related to health and well-being, creative expression, or time and energy management, holds the key to unlocking our full potential and leading a more balanced, empowered life.

Creative Expression

Creative expression can be suppressed by those who dismiss or criticize your creative efforts, leading to a loss of confidence and inspiration. If your creative expression is taken from you, it often results in feeling stifled and unfulfilled. Giving away your creative expression might happen when you prioritize others' expectations over your own creative desires. Dowsing can uncover when and why you lost touch with your creativity, helping to identify and remove these blocks. Reconnecting with your creative self will allow you to express your unique perspective and raise your vibration.

Emotional Control

Emotional control can often be lost, taken, or given away in relationships or situations where someone exerts power over you. This might happen through manipulation, gaslighting, or constant criticism, leading to a loss of confidence and emotional stability. When you give away your emotional control, you allow others to dictate your feelings and reactions. Reclaiming this power involves recognizing these patterns and using tools like dowsing to uncover the roots of these losses in your subconscious. By identifying and addressing these influences, you can begin to restore your emotional autonomy and resilience.

Health and Well-Being

Health and well-being can be compromised by external pressures, toxic relationships, or environments that drain your energy. When others take away your health and well-being, it can manifest as chronic stress, illness, or a general decline in vitality. Giving away your well-being might occur through neglecting self-care due to overcommitment to others' needs or societal demands. Dowsing can help identify the specific causes of these health issues, uncovering subconscious patterns or external influences that have impacted your well-being. By addressing these factors, you can reclaim your health and vitality.

Mental Clarity

Mental clarity can be undermined by those in power through misinformation, distraction, or emotional manipulation. When your mental clarity is taken away, you might struggle with confusion, indecision, and a lack of focus. If you give away your mental clarity, it might be due to internalizing others' negative opinions or failing to set boundaries against mental clutter. Dowsing can reveal the sources of these mental interferences, enabling you to regain control over your thoughts and decisions. Clearing these blockages will help restore your ability to think clearly and make informed choices.

Personal Authority

Personal authority can be lost, taken away, or given away through power imbalances, manipulation, or self-doubt. When others take your personal authority, it can manifest as feeling powerless, being overly controlled, or constantly seeking validation from external sources. Giving away your personal authority often occurs when you prioritize others' expectations or opinions over your own instincts and desires. Dowsing can help uncover the root causes of this disempowerment, whether they stem from past experiences, external influences, or inner conflicts. By addressing these issues, you can reclaim your personal authority, fostering greater self-confidence and autonomy in your life decisions.

Spiritual Connection

Spiritual connection may be taken from you by individuals or institutions that impose limiting beliefs or dogmas. This can result in a sense of disconnection from your higher self and the universe. When you give away your spiritual connection, you might conform to external expectations, losing touch with your own spiritual truths. Dowsing can help uncover when and how this disconnection occurred, revealing hidden influences that have weakened your spiritual bond. By bringing these to light, you can work on restoring your spiritual connection and reclaiming your innate sense of purpose and belonging.

Time and Energy Management

Time and energy management can be taken from you by demanding schedules, unrealistic expectations, or manipulative individuals who monopolize your time. When you lose control over your time and energy, it can lead to burnout and a feeling of being overwhelmed. Giving away your time and energy might occur when you fail to set boundaries or say no to excessive demands. Dowsing can help pinpoint the moments when you lost control over these resources, allowing you to identify and eliminate the factors draining your energy. Regaining control over your time and energy will help you focus on what truly matters and raise your vibration.

Soul Retrieval

Each item represents a potential block or drain on our life force energy, which can hinder our ability to function optimally and maintain a high vibrational state. Addictions, for example, can create repetitive cycles of dependency that cloud our judgment and disconnect us from our higher self. Emotions like anger, anxiety, and fear can lower our vibrational frequency, making it challenging to access higher states of consciousness. Energetic disruptions such as aura tears and chakra blockages prevent the free flow of vital energy throughout our body, leading to physical, emotional, and spiritual imbalances.

Addressing these issues is not just about achieving a state of well-being but also about preparing ourselves for ascension. Ascension refers to the process of raising our consciousness and vibrational frequency to align more closely with higher dimensions of existence. By healing emotional wounds, releasing detrimental agreements from past, present, and future lives, and clearing energetic imbalances, we remove the barriers that keep us tethered to lower vibrational states. This healing process allows us to elevate our energy, making it possible to experience greater clarity, peace, and connection with the divine. Ultimately, by resolving these disruptions, we enhance our ability to navigate life with more grace and ease, fostering a deeper sense of purpose and alignment with our spiritual path.

1. **Addictions:** Compulsive engagement in behaviors or consumption of substances that disrupt mental clarity and focus.
2. **Anger:** A strong feeling of annoyance, displeasure, or hostility.
3. **Anxiety:** A feeling of worry, nervousness, or unease about something with an uncertain outcome.
4. **Astral Debris:** Energetic clutter or negative residues collected in the astral body during astral travels or interactions.
5. **Aura Tears:** Disruptions or holes in the aura, the energy field surrounding the body, often caused by trauma or negative influences.
6. **Boundaries:** Limits that define acceptable behavior and personal space, protecting one's energy and well-being.

7. **Burnout:** Physical or mental collapse caused by overwork or stress, leading to exhaustion and reduced performance.

8. **Chemical Imbalance:** Disruption in the balance of chemicals in the brain, which can affect mood, thoughts, and behavior.

9. **Chakra Blockages:** Obstructions in the energy flow within the chakras, the body's energy centers, leading to physical and emotional issues.

10. **Chronic Pain:** Persistent pain that lasts for weeks, months, or even years, often resistant to medical treatments.

11. **Contracts:** Agreements or commitments, often on a spiritual level, that can bind or influence one's current life experience.

12. **Control Issues:** Difficulty in allowing others to have power or influence, often leading to manipulation or domination.

13. **Cultural Conditioning:** Influences and beliefs imposed by society and culture that shape an individual's behavior and thoughts.

14. **Curses:** Negative energy or spells cast with the intent to harm or bring misfortune.

15. **Depression:** A mood disorder causing persistent feelings of sadness, hopelessness, and loss of interest.

16. **Desire to Escape (Others):** A strong urge to avoid or flee from relationships or social interactions due to discomfort or fear.

17. **Desire to Escape (Yours):** A personal urge to avoid reality or responsibilities, often through daydreaming or substance use.

18. **Detrimental Agreements (Ancestors):** Negative pacts or commitments inherited from ancestral lines that affect one's life.

19. **Detrimental Agreements (Eternal):** Perpetual and harmful commitments that transcend time, impacting multiple lifetimes.

20. **Detrimental Agreements (Future Life):** Negative pacts or commitments made in future lives affecting the present incarnation.

21. **Detrimental Agreements (Life Between Lives):** Harmful agreements made in the spiritual realm between incarnations that affect the current life.

22. **Detrimental Agreements (Parallel Life):** Negative pacts or commitments made in parallel realities or alternate versions of one's life.

23. **Detrimental Agreements (Past Life):** Harmful pacts or commitments made in previous lives that influence the present life.

24. **Detrimental Agreements (This Life):** Negative pacts or commitments made in the current life that affect one's experiences and well-being.

25. **Disconnection from Nature:** A feeling of being isolated or cut off from the natural world, leading to imbalance and stress.

26. **Distractions:** Things that prevent someone from giving full attention to something else, leading to lack of focus.

27. **Ego:** A person's sense of self-esteem or self-importance that can sometimes hinder spiritual growth.

28. **Emotional Overload:** An overwhelming flood of emotions that can lead to stress, confusion, and impaired decision-making.

29. **Energetic Cords:** Invisible connections between people that can transmit energy and emotions, often draining or influencing one's energy.

30. **Energetic Imbalances:** Disruptions or disharmonies in the body's energy flow, leading to physical or emotional issues.

31. **Environmental Stressors:** External factors in one's surroundings that cause stress or negative impact on health and well-being.

32. **Fear:** An unpleasant emotion caused by the belief that someone or something is dangerous or threatening.

33. **Financial Worries:** Concerns about money and financial stability, leading to stress and anxiety.

34. **Guilt:** A feeling of having committed wrong or failed in an obligation, often causing emotional distress.

35. **Habits (Emotional):** Repetitive emotional responses or patterns that can be detrimental to well-being.

36. **Habits (Mental):** Repetitive thought patterns or cognitive behaviors that can be limiting or harmful.

37. **Habits (Physical):** Repetitive physical actions or behaviors that can negatively impact health and well-being.

38. **Hormonal Imbalance:** Disruption in the body's hormonal system, affecting mood, energy levels, and physical health.

39. **Implants:** Energetic or etheric devices placed in the energy body that can disrupt or control one's energy and behavior.

40. **Inherited Behaviors:** Patterns of behavior passed down through generations, often unconsciously adopted.

41. **Inherited Beliefs:** Belief systems passed down from ancestors that can influence current thoughts and actions.

42. **Inherited Trauma:** Traumatic experiences and their effects passed down through generations, affecting descendants.

43. **Jealousy:** A feeling of envy towards someone else's achievements, possessions, or perceived advantages.

44. **Lack of Clear Intention:** Uncertainty or ambiguity in one's goals or desires, leading to confusion and lack of direction.

45. **Lack of Exercise:** Insufficient physical activity, leading to health issues and decreased energy levels.

46. **Lack of Focus:** Difficulty in concentrating or maintaining attention on tasks or goals.

47. **Lack of Grounding:** Feeling disconnected from the physical world, leading to instability and lack of balance.

48. **Lack of Spiritual Connection:** Feeling disconnected from one's spiritual beliefs or practices, leading to a sense of emptiness or loss.

49. **Limiting Beliefs:** Negative or restrictive beliefs that hinder personal growth and potential.

50. **Low Self-Esteem:** A lack of confidence and self-worth, leading to self-doubt and negative self-perception.

51. **Lost Soul Parts (Ancestors):** Fragments of the soul lost by ancestors, affecting the current generation.
52. **Lost Soul Parts (Eternal):** Perpetually lost fragments of the soul affecting the individual across multiple lifetimes.
53. **Lost Soul Parts (Future Life):** Fragments of the soul lost in future lives, impacting the present incarnation.
54. **Lost Soul Parts (Life Between Lives):** Soul fragments lost in the spiritual realm between incarnations, affecting the current life.
55. **Lost Soul Parts (Parallel Life):** Fragments of the soul lost in parallel realities, influencing the present experience.
56. **Lost Soul Parts (Past Life):** Soul fragments lost in previous lives, affecting the current incarnation.
57. **Lost Soul Parts (This Life):** Fragments of the soul lost during the current life, leading to feelings of incompleteness or disconnection.
58. **Medical Conditions:** Diseases or health disorders that can impact physical and emotional well-being.
59. **Medication Side Effects:** Adverse reactions to medications that can cause additional health issues.
60. **Mental Fog:** A state of confusion or lack of mental clarity, often affecting cognitive functions.
61. **Mental Projections:** Thoughts or beliefs projected onto others, often based on personal insecurities or fears.
62. **Misaligned Energies:** Energy that is not in harmony with the body's natural flow, causing imbalance and discomfort.
63. **Negative Beliefs:** Harmful or limiting thoughts that can affect one's mental and emotional health.
64. **Negative Emotions (Others):** Emotional negativity projected by others that can influence one's own emotional state.
65. **Negative Emotions (Yours):** Personal negative emotions that can impact mental and physical health.
66. **Negative Family Dynamics:** Harmful patterns of behavior within a family that can affect members' well-being.
67. **Negative Thought Forms (Others):** Harmful or negative thoughts directed towards someone by others.
68. **Negative Thought Forms (Yours):** Harmful or negative thoughts generated by oneself that can impact well-being.
69. **Overthinking:** Excessive thinking about something, often leading to anxiety and stress.
70. **Past Trauma:** Previous traumatic experiences that continue to affect the present emotional state.
71. **Peace of Mind:** A state of mental and emotional calmness, free from stress and worry.
72. **Peer Pressure:** Influence from peers to conform to their behaviors and beliefs, often leading to stress and conflict.

73. **Perfectionism:** Striving for flawlessness and setting high standards, often leading to stress and dissatisfaction.
74. **Physical Exhaustion:** Extreme physical tiredness, often due to overexertion or lack of rest.
75. **Poor Diet:** Unhealthy eating habits that can negatively impact physical and mental health.
76. **Poor Energy Hygiene:** Neglecting practices that maintain a clean and balanced energy field, leading to energetic imbalances.
77. **Procrastination:** The action of delaying or postponing tasks, often leading to stress and missed opportunities.
78. **Psychic Attacks (Eternal):** Harmful spiritual or energetic attacks that persist across multiple lifetimes.
79. **Psychic Attacks (Future Life):** Energetic or spiritual attacks originating from future incarnations that affect the present.
80. **Psychic Attacks (Life Between Lives):** Harmful spiritual influences experienced in the realm between lives, affecting the current incarnation.
81. **Psychic Attacks (Parallel Life):** Energetic attacks from parallel realities or alternate versions of one's life.
82. **Psychic Attacks (Past Life):** Harmful spiritual or energetic attacks originating from past lives.
83. **Psychic Attacks (This Life):** Energetic or spiritual attacks experienced in the current life.
84. **Psychic Debris:** Residual negative energy or clutter in the energy field, often from interactions or environments.
85. **Religious Dogma:** Rigid and inflexible religious beliefs that can restrict spiritual growth and personal freedom.
86. **Resentment:** Bitter indignation at having been treated unfairly, often leading to prolonged emotional distress.
87. **Secondary Gain:** Unconscious benefits received from having a problem or condition, which may hinder recovery.
88. **Self-Doubt:** Lack of confidence in one's own abilities or decisions.
89. **Shame:** A painful feeling of humiliation or distress caused by the consciousness of wrong or foolish behavior.
90. **Sleep Deprivation:** Lack of sufficient sleep, leading to physical and mental health issues.
91. **Societal Expectations:** Pressures from society to conform to certain behaviors or standards, often leading to stress and conflict.
92. **Soul Fragments:** Parts of the soul that have been lost or separated due to trauma or other experiences.
93. **Spells:** Magical or spiritual practices intended to bring about specific effects, sometimes harmful.
94. **Spiritual Interference:** Negative influences from spiritual sources that disrupt one's spiritual path or growth.

95. **Suppressed Emotions:** Emotions that are not expressed or acknowledged, leading to emotional and physical issues.

96. **Toxic Relationships:** Harmful or damaging relationships that negatively impact one's well-being.

97. **Trauma:** Deeply distressing or disturbing experiences that can have long-lasting effects on mental and emotional health.

98. **Trust Issues:** Difficulty in trusting others, often stemming from past betrayals or trauma.

99. **Unaligned Purpose:** A sense of disconnection from one's true purpose or life path.

100. **Unhealthy Boundaries:** Lack of clear and healthy personal limits, leading to emotional and physical stress.

101. **Unhealed Inner Child:** Wounds or traumas from childhood that have not been addressed, affecting adult behavior and emotions.

102. **Unresolved Conflicts:** Disagreements or issues that have not been resolved, leading to ongoing tension and stress.

103. **Unresolved Karma:** Past actions or deeds that have not been balanced or resolved, affecting the current life.

104. **Victim Mentality:** A mindset in which a person sees themselves as a victim of circumstances, often leading to helplessness and lack of control.

105. **Voodoo:** A form of magical or spiritual practice that can include harmful rituals or curses.

106. **Vows:** Solemn promises or commitments that can bind one's actions or experiences.

107. **Work Stress:** Stress related to one's job or professional responsibilities.

108. **World Thought Forms:** Collective beliefs or energies from society that can influence individual thoughts and behaviors.

See Chart 456 - Things Lost, Taken From, or Given Away, Master Chart

Time Line

The concept of a Time Line in the context of raising your vibration involves acknowledging the multi-dimensional aspects of our existence, spanning across various lifetimes and states of being. When addressing and clearing energetic blockages or unresolved issues, it's crucial to consider how these issues might relate to different segments of our Time Line. These segments include Future Life, Life Between Lives, Parallel Life, Past Life, and Present Life. Each of these phases holds unique energetic imprints that can influence our current state of being and overall vibration. By examining and resolving issues from these various time periods, we can release accumulated negativity, thereby raising our vibrational frequency and promoting a state of higher consciousness and well-being.

For instance, issues originating from a Past Life might manifest as persistent, inexplicable fears or patterns in the Present Life, while unresolved lessons from a Future Life could create a sense of urgency or anticipation. Life Between Lives, the period between incarnations, often holds significant karmic lessons and soul contracts that need acknowledgment and resolution. Parallel Lives, which occur simultaneously with our current existence in different dimensions, can also impact our vibrational state, as unresolved issues in one reality may bleed into another. By methodically dowsing and addressing these different aspects of the Time Line, we ensure a comprehensive clearing of energetic disturbances, thus allowing for a smoother, more harmonious flow of energy that supports our journey towards a higher vibrational state.

See Chart 486 - Time Line

Frequencies

Frequencies play a significant role in raising vibrations and enhancing overall well-being. Specific frequencies, such as 40 Hz, 174 Hz, 285 Hz, 396 Hz, 417 Hz, 432 Hz, 528 Hz, 639 Hz, 741 Hz, 852 Hz, and 963 Hz, are believed to resonate with various aspects of the mind, body, and spirit, promoting healing and harmony. For example, 40 Hz is known to stimulate brain activity and improve cognitive function, while 174 Hz and 285 Hz are associated with pain relief and healing tissue, respectively. The 396 Hz frequency helps in liberating fear and guilt, allowing for a higher state of consciousness. Similarly, 417 Hz aids in facilitating change and clearing negative energy, paving the way for personal transformation and growth.

Other frequencies, such as 432 Hz, are renowned for their natural harmonic tones, often referred to as the "universal frequency," which brings about a sense of peace and well-being. The 528 Hz frequency, also known as the "Miracle Tone," is linked to DNA repair and transformation, promoting a deep sense of inner peace and spiritual enlightenment. Frequencies like 639 Hz enhance communication and relationships, 741 Hz encourages intuition and problem-solving, 852 Hz awakens inner strength and self-realization, and 963 Hz, often called the "frequency of the Gods," connects you to higher realms and the divine. By incorporating these frequencies into daily practices, such as listening to music tuned to these specific hertz, one can elevate their vibrational state, leading to improved physical health, emotional balance, and spiritual awakening.

1. **40 Hz**: Enhances cognitive function and stimulates brain activity, potentially improving memory and focus.
2. **174 Hz**: Associated with pain relief, offering a soothing and calming effect on the body, which can alleviate stress and promote healing.
3. **285 Hz**: Supports tissue repair and rejuvenation, accelerating the body's natural healing processes and restoring energy balance.
4. **396 Hz**: Helps to liberate fear and guilt, clearing emotional blockages and promoting a higher state of consciousness.
5. **417 Hz**: Aids in facilitating change and clearing negative energy, making it easier to move forward and embrace new beginnings.
6. **432 Hz**: Resonates with the natural harmonic tones of the universe, bringing about a sense of peace, harmony, and well-being.
7. **528 Hz**: Known as the "Miracle Tone," is linked to DNA repair and transformation, fostering a deep sense of inner peace and spiritual enlightenment.
8. **639 Hz**: Enhances communication and relationships, encouraging harmony and connection with others.
9. **741 Hz**: Promotes intuition and problem-solving, helping to clear the mind and enhance creativity.

10. **852 Hz**: Awakens inner strength and self-realization, empowering personal growth and spiritual awakening.
11. **963 Hz**: Often called the "frequency of the Gods," connects us to higher realms and the divine, facilitating spiritual enlightenment and a deeper connection with our higher self.

See Chart 487 - Frequencies

Sound Tools

Sound tools have a profound ability to raise vibration by influencing both the energetic and physical bodies. Chimes, crystal singing pyramids, and Himalayan singing bowls produce harmonic frequencies that can penetrate deeply into the body, promoting relaxation and releasing blockages. These tools create resonant sounds that align with the natural frequencies of the body's energy centers, or chakras, facilitating a state of balance and harmony. The gentle, yet powerful vibrations from these instruments can help to clear stagnant energy, reduce stress, and enhance overall well-being, ultimately raising the individual's vibrational frequency.

Instruments like the didgeridoo, drums, flutes, gongs, and tuning forks offer unique vibrational benefits that can elevate consciousness and promote healing. The deep, grounding tones of the didgeridoo and drums connect one to the Earth's natural rhythms, fostering a sense of stability and rootedness. Flutes and gongs, with their ethereal and expansive sounds, can elevate the mind and spirit, encouraging higher states of awareness and meditation. Tuning forks, used on or around the body, provide precise frequencies that can fine-tune the body's energy field, enhancing the flow of vital life force energy. By incorporating these sound tools into regular practice, individuals can experience heightened states of vibrational resonance, leading to greater clarity, peace, and spiritual growth.

See Chart 488 - Sound Tools

Obstacles & Impediments

Understanding Obstacles & Impediments: Enhancing Higher Vibration in Work, Play, and Home Life

Achieving a higher vibration, a state of elevated consciousness and well-being, requires addressing various obstacles and impediments in our daily lives. These obstacles can stem from different areas such as time management, tools, training, communication, thinking, resources, personal factors, emotions, group dynamics, and social interactions. Each category presents unique challenges that can hinder our progress towards a higher vibration.

Time Management

Effective time management is crucial for maintaining a balanced and stress-free life. Obstacles in this area, such as poor scheduling, can lead to a chaotic lifestyle, preventing us from dedicating time to activities that raise our vibration, such as meditation or self-care. By improving our ability to manage time, we can create a structured environment that supports our physical, mental, and spiritual growth.

Tools

The tools we use daily, including both physical equipment and intangible resources like materials and guidance, play a significant role in our efficiency and effectiveness. Inadequate or inappropriate tools can create frustration and impede progress, whether at work, in personal projects, or during leisure activities. Ensuring access to the right tools and understanding their proper use can significantly reduce stress and enhance our ability to perform tasks that contribute to a higher vibration.

Training

Training encompasses the acquisition of knowledge and skills necessary for various aspects of life. A lack of training or ongoing education can leave us feeling unprepared and insecure, affecting our confidence and ability to handle challenges. Embracing continuous learning and development allows us to stay competent and motivated, fostering a sense of achievement and growth that elevates our vibration.

Talk / Communication

Clear and honest communication is vital for building strong relationships and resolving conflicts. Obstacles in communication, such as lack of clarity, reliability, or openness, can lead to misunderstandings and emotional distress. Improving our communication skills can enhance our interactions with others, creating a harmonious environment that supports emotional and mental well-being.

Thinking

Our thought patterns and beliefs shape our perception of the world and influence our actions. Negative or limiting beliefs can create barriers to personal growth and happiness. Cultivating a positive mindset and being open to new perspectives can transform our approach to life's challenges, enabling us to overcome obstacles and raise our vibration.

Resources

Access to adequate resources, including skills, abilities, and physical necessities, is essential for achieving our goals. Scarcity or mismanagement of resources can lead to frustration and hinder progress. By effectively utilizing and managing resources, we can create a supportive environment that facilitates growth and enhances our overall vibration.

Personal Factors

Personal factors, such as emotional stability, self-confidence, and certainty, play a significant role in our ability to navigate life's challenges. Addressing personal issues and developing a strong sense of self can empower us to overcome obstacles and maintain a higher vibration.

Emotions

Emotional well-being is closely linked to our overall vibration. Unresolved emotions, such as abandonment, anxiety, or fear, can create blockages that impede our progress. By acknowledging and processing these emotions, we can release negative energy and elevate our vibration.

Group Dynamics

Interactions within groups, whether at work or in social settings, can influence our vibration. Issues such as lack of responsiveness, cooperation, or trust can create a negative atmosphere. Fostering positive group dynamics through effective communication and mutual support can enhance the collective vibration and create a more harmonious environment.

Social Interactions

Our social interactions and relationships significantly impact our emotional and mental well-being. Obstacles in social interactions, such as distrust, doubt, or conflict, can create stress and lower our vibration. Building healthy, supportive relationships and addressing social challenges can contribute to a more positive and elevated state of being.

By identifying and addressing these obstacles and impediments, we can create a supportive environment that fosters growth and enhances our vibration. Whether at work, during play, or in our home life, overcoming these challenges allows us to live more fully and achieve a higher state of consciousness and well-being.

See Chart 489 - Obstacles & Impediments, Master Chart

Zen Practices

Zen practices are deeply rooted in mindfulness and the present moment, offering powerful tools to raise our vibration. Engaging in activities such as Zazen (sitting meditation), mindful walking (Kinhin), and mindful breathing helps to quiet the mind and bring attention to the now. By focusing on the present, we can let go of past regrets and future anxieties, which often carry lower vibrational energies. This shift in focus allows us to cultivate a sense of inner peace and clarity, elevating our overall energetic frequency. Moreover, Zen practices emphasize simplicity and detachment from material desires, helping us to align more closely with our true nature and the higher vibrations of love, compassion, and gratitude.

Additionally, Zen practices foster a deep connection with our inner selves and the world around us. Activities such as Zen gardening, tea ceremonies, and mindful eating promote a harmonious balance between body, mind, and spirit. By engaging in these practices with full awareness, we can enhance our sensitivity to the subtle energies within and around us. This heightened awareness enables us to release negative emotions and energy blocks, facilitating a smoother flow of positive energy. The regular practice of Zen rituals encourages a state of mindfulness and presence that permeates all aspects of life, leading to a sustained elevation of our vibrational state and a greater sense of well-being.

1. **Calligraphy**: Practicing Zen calligraphy, focusing on the flow of the brush and the present moment.
2. **Chanting**: Reciting Zen chants or mantras to cultivate concentration and tranquility.
3. **Daily Rituals**: Incorporating mindfulness into daily routines and rituals to create a sense of peace and presence.
4. **Gardening**: Engaging in mindful gardening to appreciate simplicity and nature.
5. **Gratitude Journaling**: Keeping a journal to regularly express gratitude, fostering a positive mindset.

6. **Haiku Writing**: Creating Zen-inspired haiku poems to express and contemplate the beauty of the present moment.
7. **Hiking**: Taking mindful hikes in nature, appreciating the beauty and tranquility of the natural world.
8. **Ikebana (Flower Arranging)**: Practicing the art of Japanese flower arranging with mindfulness and presence.
9. **Kinhin (Walking Meditation)**: Engaging in mindful walking, paying attention to each step and breath.
10. **Koan Study**: Contemplating Zen koans to deepen understanding and provoke insight.
11. **Labyrinth Walking**: Walking through a labyrinth with mindfulness, focusing on the journey and inner reflection.
12. **Listening to Zen Music**: Engaging with Zen-inspired music to cultivate peace and mindfulness.
13. **Loving-Kindness Meditation**: Practicing Metta meditation to cultivate compassion and loving-kindness towards oneself and others.
14. **Mala Beads Meditation**: Using mala beads for counting breaths or mantras during meditation.
15. **Mandala Drawing**: Creating mandalas to focus the mind and explore inner thoughts and emotions.
16. **Mindful Bathing**: Taking a bath with full awareness, focusing on the sensations of water and relaxation.
17. **Mindful Breathing**: Focusing on the breath to anchor the mind and cultivate mindfulness.
18. **Mindful Cleaning**: Engaging in cleaning tasks with full attention and care, treating them as a form of meditation.
19. **Mindful Cooking**: Preparing meals mindfully, focusing on the process and the sensory experience.
20. **Mindful Eating**: Eating slowly and mindfully, savoring each bite and appreciating the food.
21. **Mindful Listening**: Engaging in deep listening, fully attentive and present with others.
22. **Mindful Photography**: Taking photos with mindfulness, focusing on the beauty and details of the present moment.
23. **Mindful Reading**: Reading with full attention, savoring the words and their meaning.
24. **Mindful Running**: Running with mindfulness, focusing on the rhythm of breath and the movement of the body.
25. **Mindful Showering**: Showering with full awareness, focusing on the sensations of water and cleansing.
26. **Mindful Stretching**: Practicing gentle stretching or yoga with mindfulness and awareness of the body.
27. **Mindful Tea Drinking**: Drinking tea with mindfulness, savoring the taste and aroma.
28. **Mindful Writing**: Engaging in writing with full attention, focusing on the process and expressing thoughts mindfully.
29. **Nature Journaling**: Keeping a journal to record observations and reflections on nature.

30. **Nature Walks**: Taking mindful walks in nature, appreciating the beauty and tranquility of the natural world.
31. **Painting**: Creating art with a focus on simplicity, spontaneity, and presence.
32. **Qi Gong**: Practicing the ancient Chinese movement practice to balance energy and cultivate mindfulness.
33. **Sand Mandalas**: Creating intricate sand mandalas to practice mindfulness and impermanence.
34. **Singing Bowl Meditation**: Using Tibetan singing bowls to create calming sounds for meditation.
35. **Sitting by a Waterfall**: Sitting by a waterfall to meditate and connect with nature's tranquility.
36. **Sound Healing**: Using sound instruments like gongs or tuning forks to facilitate meditation and healing.
37. **Sumi-e (Ink Painting)**: Practicing the Japanese art of ink painting with mindfulness and simplicity.
38. **Tea Ceremony**: Participating in a traditional tea ceremony, emphasizing mindfulness and presence.
39. **Temple Stays**: Staying at a Zen temple to immerse oneself in Zen practices and lifestyle.
40. **Thich Nhat Hanh's Pebble Meditation**: Using pebbles as focal points for mindfulness meditation.
41. **Tonglen Meditation**: Practicing Tibetan Buddhist meditation to cultivate compassion by breathing in suffering and breathing out compassion.
42. **Trataka (Candle Gazing)**: Focusing on a candle flame to develop concentration and mindfulness.
43. **Volunteering**: Engaging in volunteer work with mindfulness and a spirit of selfless service.
44. **Walking in Silence**: Taking a walk in silence, focusing on the surroundings and the act of walking.
45. **Yoga**: Practicing yoga to cultivate mindfulness, flexibility, and a sense of inner peace.
46. **Zazen (Sitting Meditation)**: Practicing seated meditation to quiet the mind and focus on the breath.
47. **Zen Archery**: Practicing Kyudo (Zen archery) to cultivate focus, patience, and mindfulness.
48. **Zen Gardening**: Creating and maintaining a Zen garden to practice mindfulness and appreciate simplicity.
49. **Zen Painting**: Creating art with a focus on simplicity, spontaneity, and presence.
50. **Zen Poetry**: Writing or reading Zen poetry to express and contemplate the beauty of the present moment.
51. **Zen Puzzles**: Solving Zen puzzles or riddles to cultivate focus and mental clarity.
52. **Zen Rock Stacking**: Stacking rocks mindfully, appreciating balance and impermanence.

53. **Zen Walking Meditation**: Engaging in mindful walking, paying attention to each step and breath.

See Chart 502 - Zen Practices, Master Chart

Chapter 4

Helpful Tools

Diving into the Pool of Helpful Tools

Diving into Helpful Tools provides an essential framework for dowsing practitioners, offering a variety of methods to enhance accuracy and efficiency in their work. These tools are designed to simplify complex information and make it more accessible for anyone engaging in dowsing, whether a beginner or an experienced dowser. Each chart and method presents a unique way of organizing information, allowing users to navigate through challenges and find the answers they seek with clarity.

From traditional charts like the alphabet chart to modern innovations such as the numbers chart, these tools help expand the practitioner's toolkit. They offer flexibility in how information is accessed and used, whether you're seeking guidance on timing, numbers, or specific outcomes. The addition of these tools enables dowsers to tailor their approach to each individual case, ensuring a personalized experience that leads to the best possible results.

Alphabet Chart: The alphabet chart is a versatile tool used by dowsers to spell out answers when a specific response cannot be easily found in the charts. It acts as a communication bridge between the dowser and the subtle energies being accessed, allowing for greater precision in responses. By guiding the pendulum over letters, the dowser can spell out names, places, or concepts that may not be listed in any pre-existing chart. This tool is especially helpful when dealing with new or unfamiliar situations, ensuring that no vital information is missed.

Dosing: Repetitions Chart: The dosing repetitions chart is designed to provide clarity on how often a specific action or treatment should be performed. It helps dowsers determine the precise number of repetitions needed, whether it's the number of times per day, the number of days, weeks, or months, or even when something should be applied "as needed." This tool ensures that the dowser can tailor the frequency and duration of healing protocols to each individual, helping achieve the desired results while avoiding over-application or underuse.

Dosing: Time of Day Chart: The dosing time of day chart is an essential tool for specifying when a treatment, action, or protocol should be administered. It includes options such as before meals, after meals, at regular intervals, or specific times like morning (am), noon, bedtime, or "as needed." More precise timing options, such as every 4, 6, 8, or 12 hours, as well as every other day, provide additional guidance on how to administer treatments for optimal effectiveness. This chart ensures that healing efforts are timed perfectly to align with the body's natural rhythms and the needs of the individual.

Blank Charts: Blank charts provide a blank canvas for dowsers to create custom charts tailored to specific needs. When an existing chart doesn't fully address a particular question or area of focus, the blank chart offers the flexibility to design a new one. This enables the dowser to expand their toolkit, incorporating personalized insights and responses that are unique to their practice or the client's needs.

Numbers Chart: The numbers chart is another powerful tool used to identify numeric values that may be significant in the dowsing process. Whether it's determining a precise number for dosing, identifying quantities, or uncovering hidden numerical significance in a situation, this chart enables clarity where numbers play a role in decision-making. It's particularly useful in applications requiring measurement or frequency adjustments.

Numbers, Ways to Use Them Chart: This chart delves into the various ways numbers can be applied in a dowsing session, beyond simple numeric responses. It explores how numbers relate to time, frequencies, dosing, and measurements, offering deeper insights into how numeric data can guide decision-making in both physical and energetic healing processes. This chart ensures that numbers are utilized in a comprehensive and meaningful way within the practice.

Dowser's Guide Books: These guide books serve as essential references for dowsers, providing a wealth of knowledge and charts across various topics, such as health, energy balancing, and personal growth. The books contain carefully compiled information that dowsers can use to find quick answers to their queries. They act as companions during a session, offering the dowser structured guidance and reliable data for many different areas of inquiry.

Traditional Chinese Medicine Charts: These charts incorporate ancient wisdom into the dowsing practice, mapping out the body's meridians, energy centers, and associated organs. They help the dowser align their work with the flow of chi, the vital energy that Traditional Chinese Medicine focuses on. By referencing these charts, dowsers can pinpoint imbalances in the body's energy systems and provide targeted healing suggestions based on time-tested principles.

When Chart: The when chart is a tool for pinpointing the ideal time for actions or healing processes. Divided into segments like daytime hours, days of the week, months, and even broader historical periods (such as Earth's history or U.S. history), this chart helps determine the best moment for certain decisions, actions, or interventions. Whether timing a healing session or exploring past events, the when chart ensures that energy is aligned with the most favorable time for success.

See Chart 506 - Diving into Helpful Tools, Master Chart

Charts

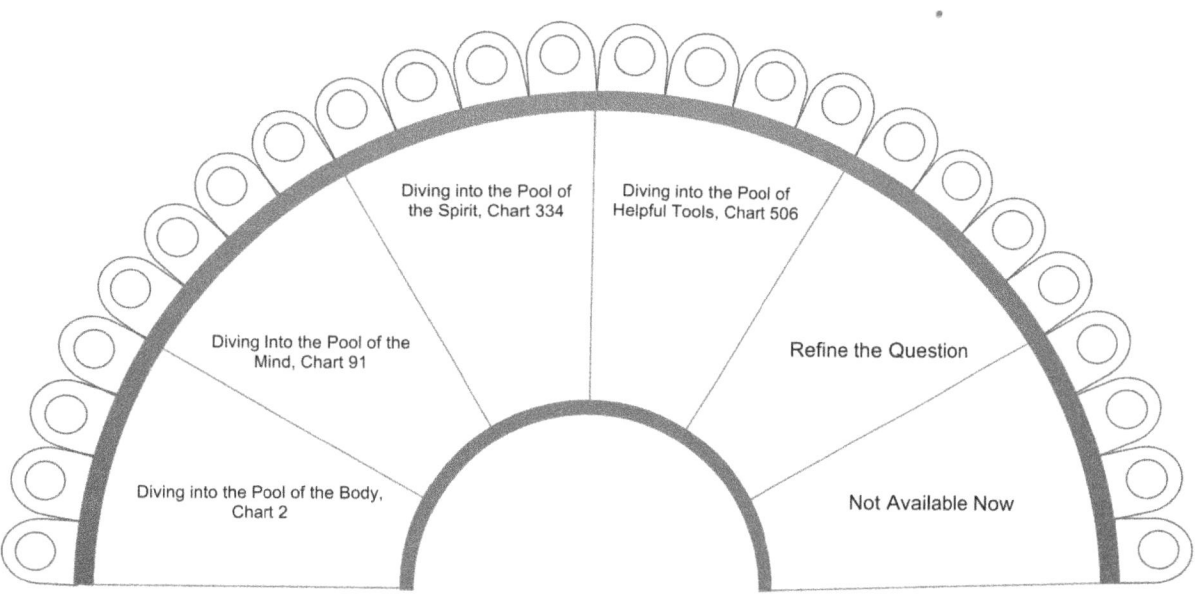

Diving into the Pool of
the Spirit, Chart 334

Diving into the Pool of
Helpful Tools, Chart 506

Diving Into the Pool of the
Mind, Chart 91

Refine the Question

Diving into the Pool of the Body,
Chart 2

Not Available Now

Diving Platforms

Royal Template 6h

Diving Deep into the Pool of the Mind

Chart 1

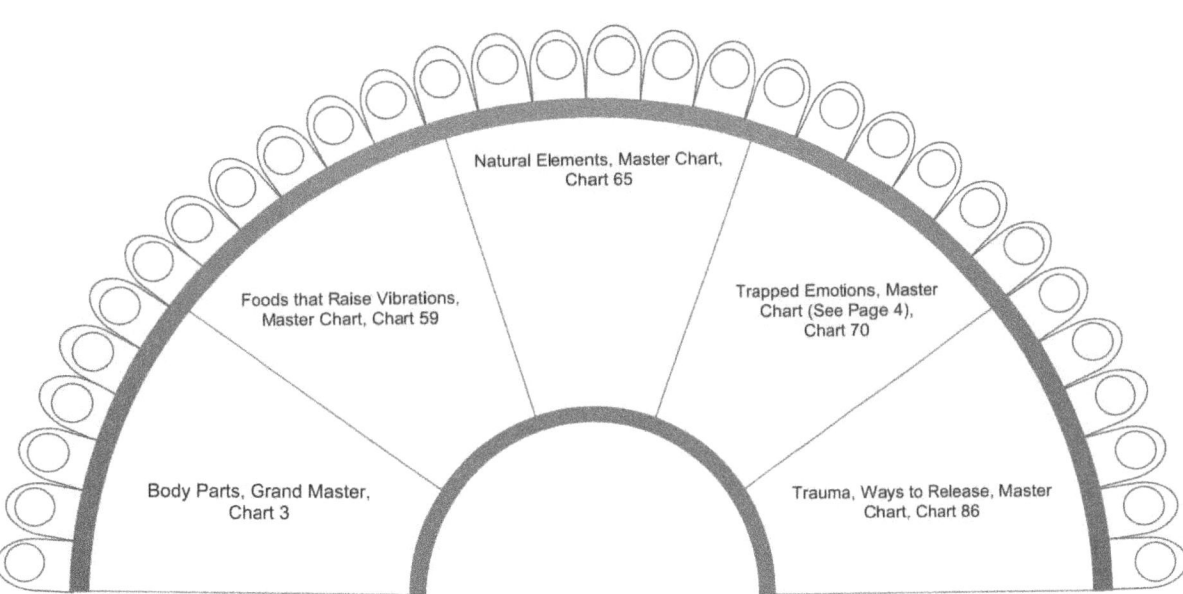

Natural Elements, Master Chart,
Chart 65

Foods that Raise Vibrations,
Master Chart, Chart 59

Trapped Emotions, Master
Chart (See Page 4),
Chart 70

Body Parts, Grand Master,
Chart 3

Trauma, Ways to Release, Master
Chart, Chart 86

Diving into the Pool of the Body

Royal Template 5h

Diving Deep into the Pool of the Mind

Chart 2

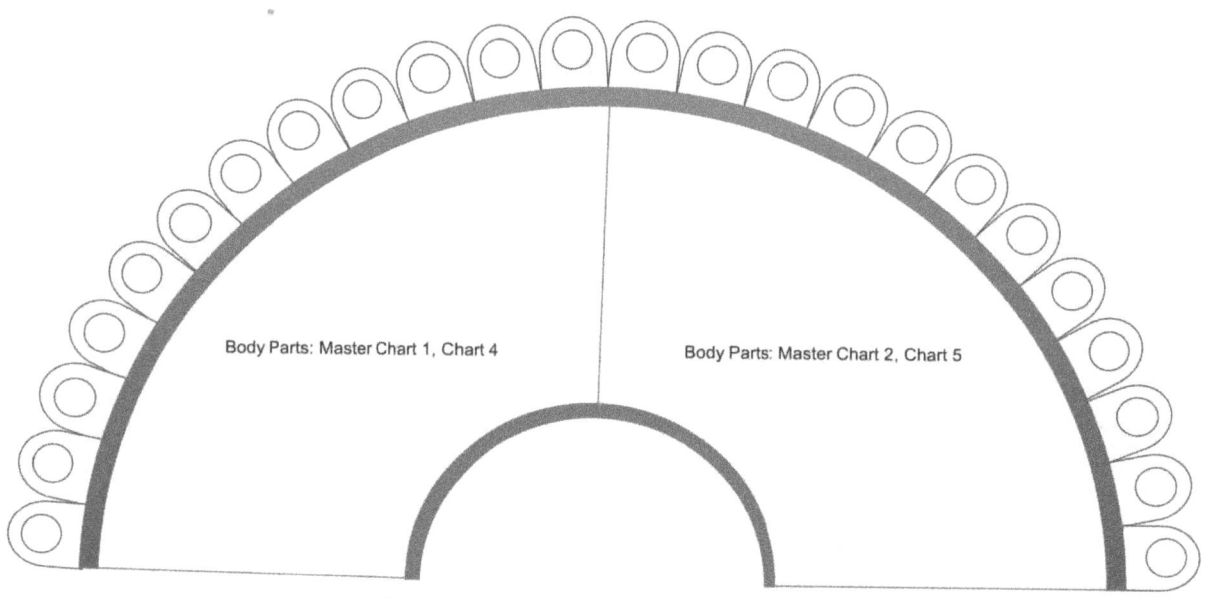

Body Parts: Master Chart 1, Chart 4

Body Parts: Master Chart 2, Chart 5

Body Parts, Grand Master

Royal Template 2

Diving Deep into the Pool of the Mind

Chart 3

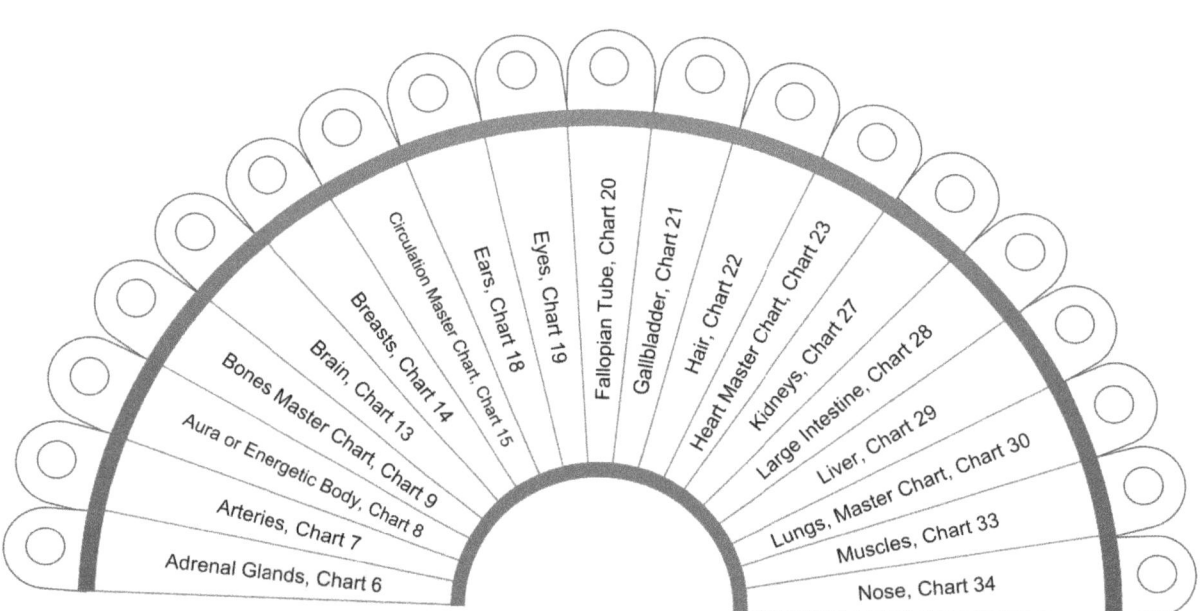

Circulation Master Chart, Chart 15

Breasts, Chart 14

Brain, Chart 13

Bones Master Chart, Chart 9

Aura or Energetic Body, Chart 8

Arteries, Chart 7

Adrenal Glands, Chart 6

Ears, Chart 18

Eyes, Chart 19

Fallopian Tube, Chart 20

Gallbladder, Chart 21

Hair, Chart 22

Heart Master Chart, Chart 23

Kidneys, Chart 27

Large Intestine, Chart 28

Liver, Chart 29

Lungs, Master Chart, Chart 30

Muscles, Chart 33

Nose, Chart 34

Body Parts: Master Chart 1

Royal Template 19

Diving Deep into the Pool of the Mind

Chart 4

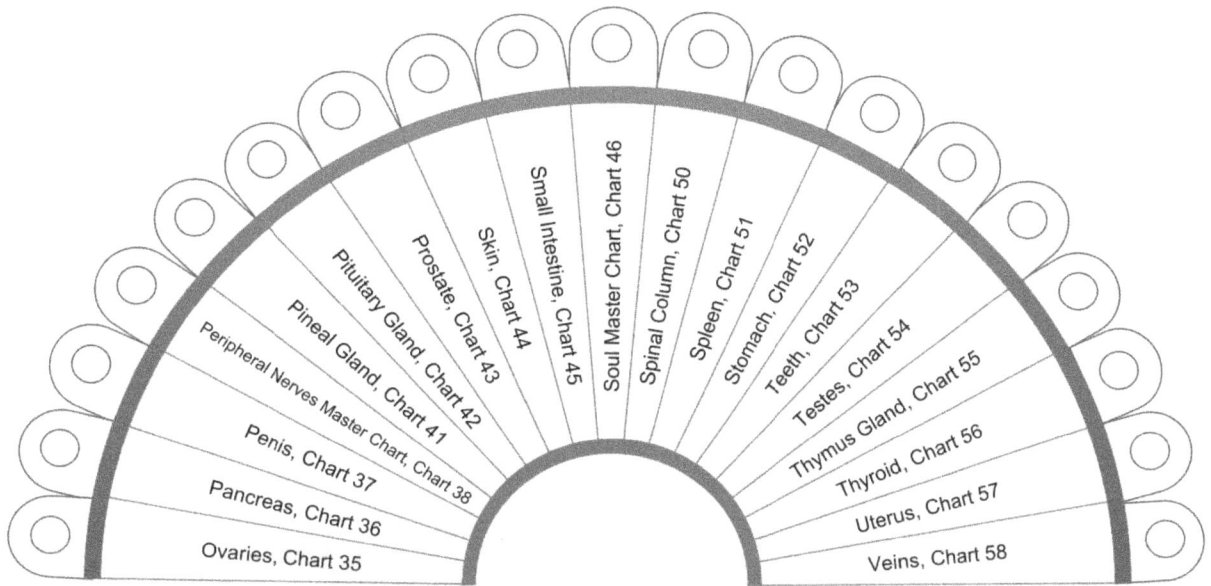

Body Parts: Master Chart 2

Ovaries, Chart 35
Pancreas, Chart 36
Penis, Chart 37
Peripheral Nerves Master Chart, Chart 38
Pineal Gland, Chart 41
Pituitary Gland, Chart 42
Prostate, Chart 43
Skin, Chart 44
Small Intestine, Chart 45
Soul Master Chart, Chart 46
Spinal Column, Chart 50
Spleen, Chart 51
Stomach, Chart 52
Teeth, Chart 53
Testes, Chart 54
Thymus Gland, Chart 55
Thyroid, Chart 56
Uterus, Chart 57
Veins, Chart 58

Royal Template 19

Diving Deep into the Pool of the Mind

Chart 5

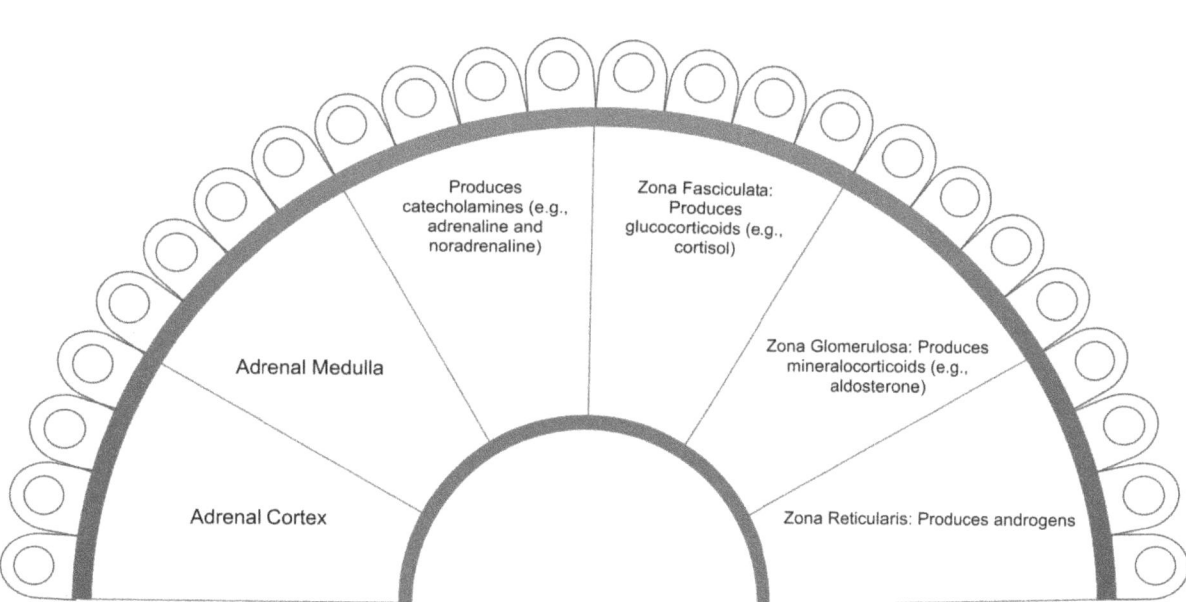

Adrenal Glands

Adrenal Medulla
Adrenal Cortex
Produces catecholamines (e.g., adrenaline and noradrenaline)
Zona Fasciculata: Produces glucocorticoids (e.g., cortisol)
Zona Glomerulosa: Produces mineralocorticoids (e.g., aldosterone)
Zona Reticularis: Produces androgens

Royal Template 6h

Diving Deep into the Pool of the Mind

Chart 6

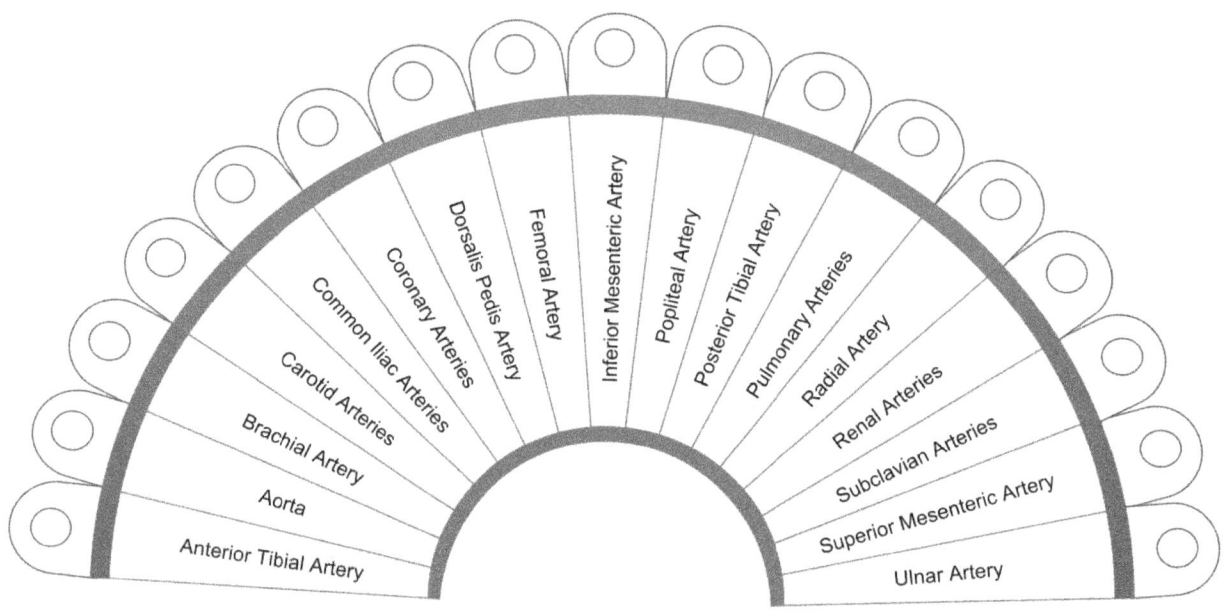

Arteries

Dorsalis Pedis Artery
Femoral Artery
Inferior Mesenteric Artery
Coronary Arteries
Popliteal Artery
Common Iliac Arteries
Posterior Tibial Artery
Carotid Arteries
Pulmonary Arteries
Brachial Artery
Radial Artery
Aorta
Renal Arteries
Anterior Tibial Artery
Subclavian Arteries
Superior Mesenteric Artery
Ulnar Artery

Royal Template 17

Diving Deep into the Pool of the Mind

Chart 7

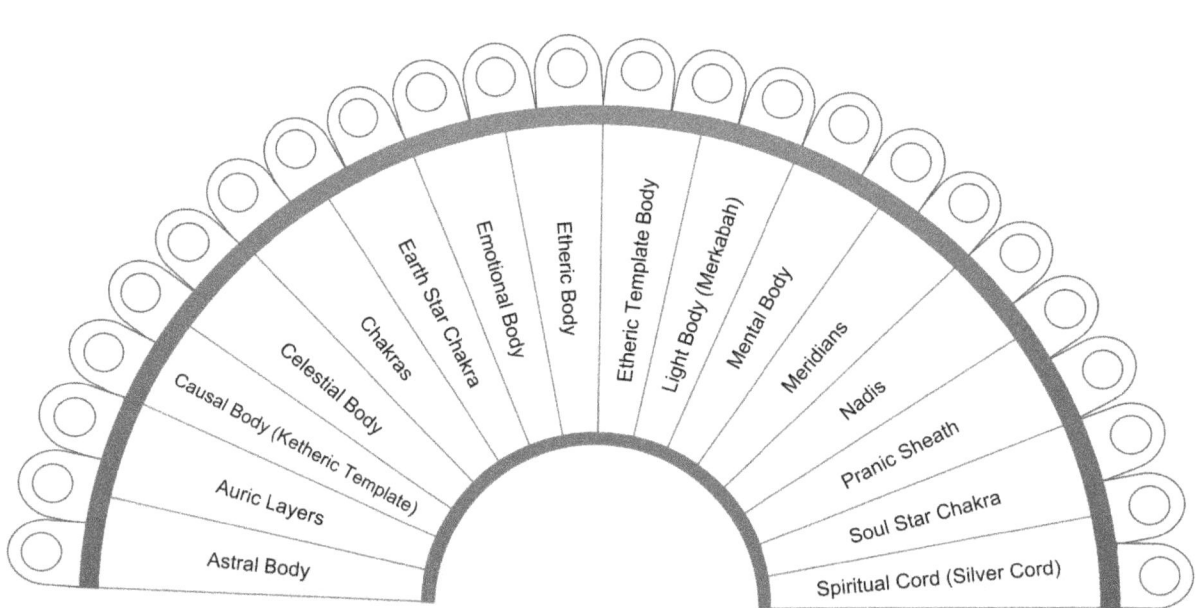

Aura or Energetic Body

Earth Star Chakra
Emotional Body
Etheric Body
Chakras
Etheric Template Body
Celestial Body
Light Body (Merkabah)
Causal Body (Ketheric Template)
Mental Body
Auric Layers
Meridians
Astral Body
Nadis
Pranic Sheath
Soul Star Chakra
Spiritual Cord (Silver Cord)

Royal Template 16

Diving Deep into the Pool of the Mind

Chart 8

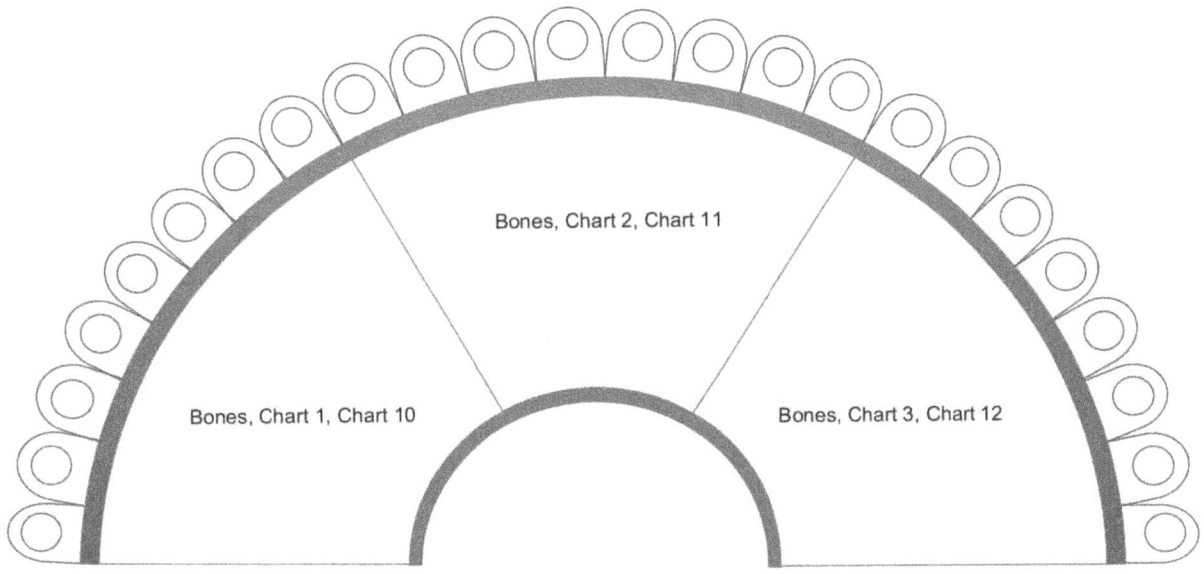

Bones Master Chart

Bones, Chart 2, Chart 11

Bones, Chart 1, Chart 10

Bones, Chart 3, Chart 12

Royal Template 3h

Diving Deep into the Pool of the Mind

Chart 9

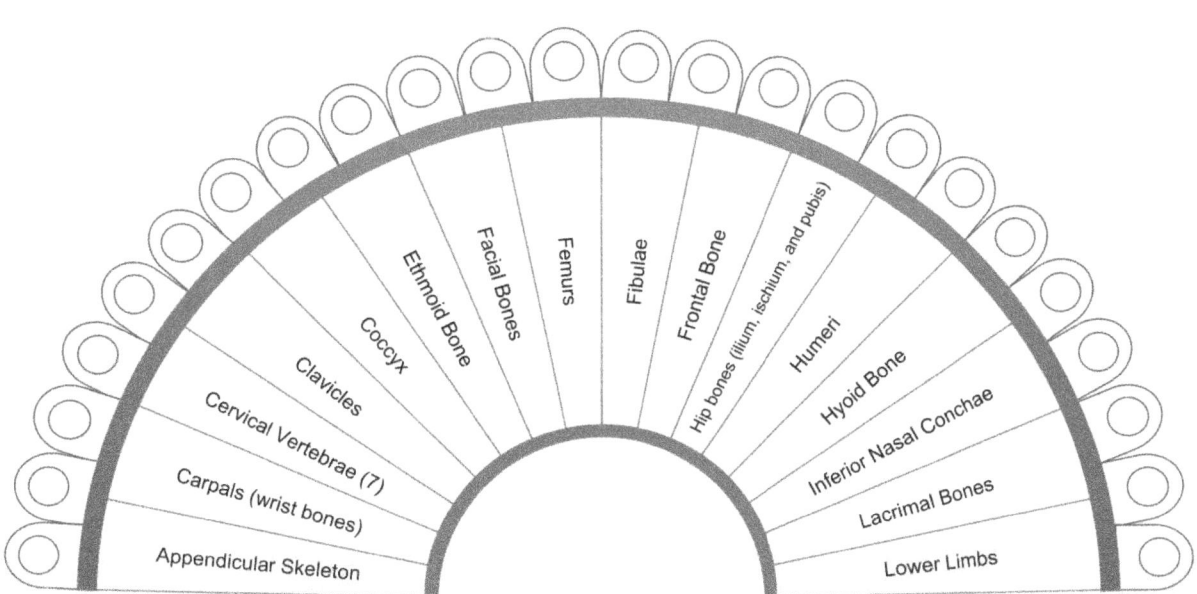

Ethmoid Bone
Facial Bones
Femurs
Fibulae
Frontal Bone
Coccyx
Hip bones (ilium, ischium, and pubis)
Clavicles
Humeri
Cervical Vertebrae (7)
Hyoid Bone
Carpals (wrist bones)
Inferior Nasal Conchae
Appendicular Skeleton
Lacrimal Bones
Lower Limbs

Bones, Chart 1

Royal Template 16

Diving Deep into the Pool of the Mind

Chart 10

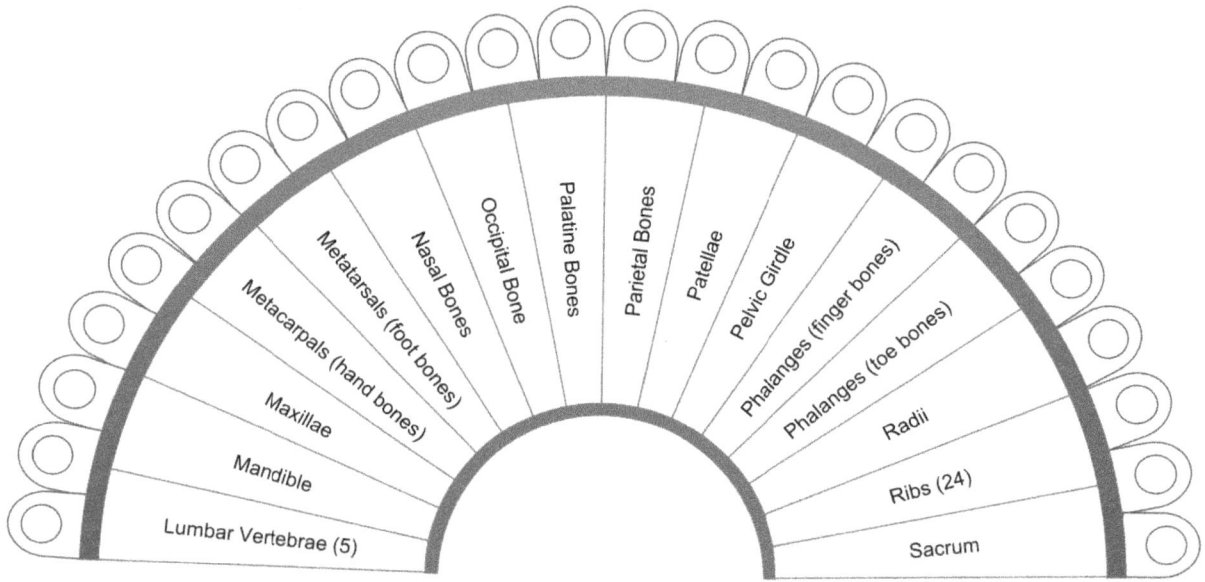

Bones, Chart 2

Royal Template 16

Diving Deep into the Pool of the Mind

Chart 11

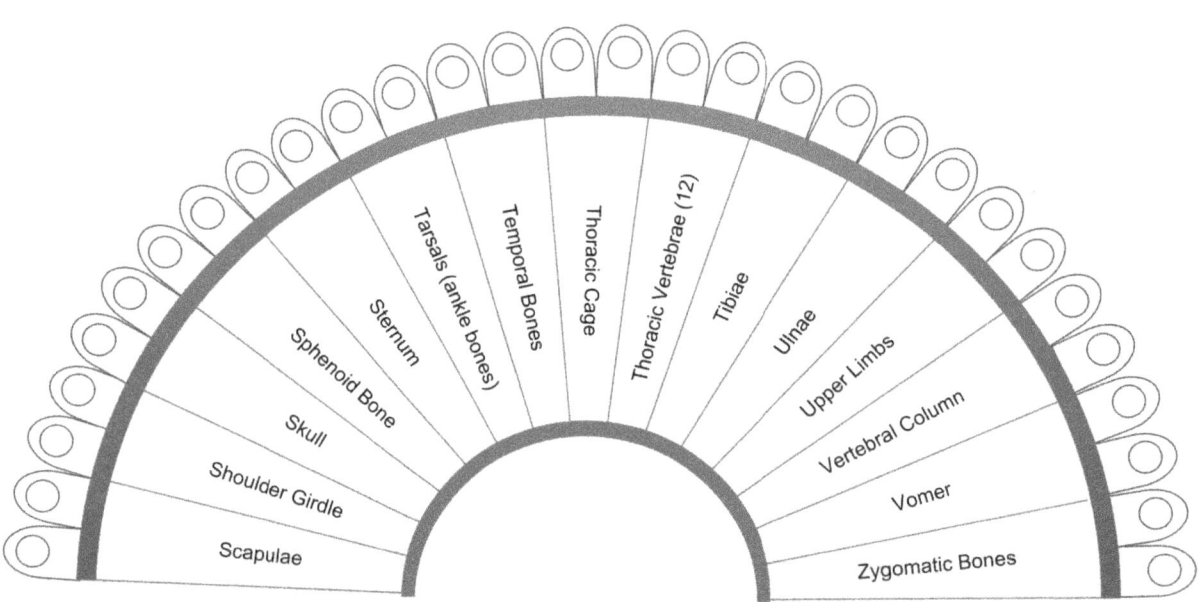

Bones, Chart 3

Royal Template 15

Diving Deep into the Pool of the Mind

Chart 12

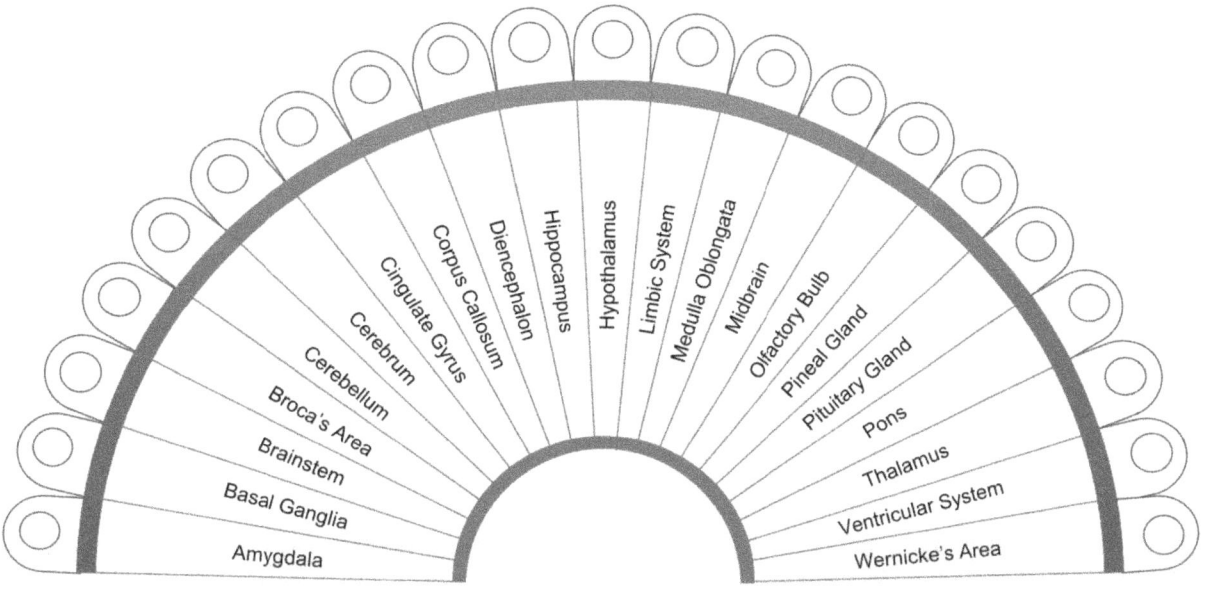

Brain

Royal Template 21

Diving Deep into the Pool of the Mind

Chart 13

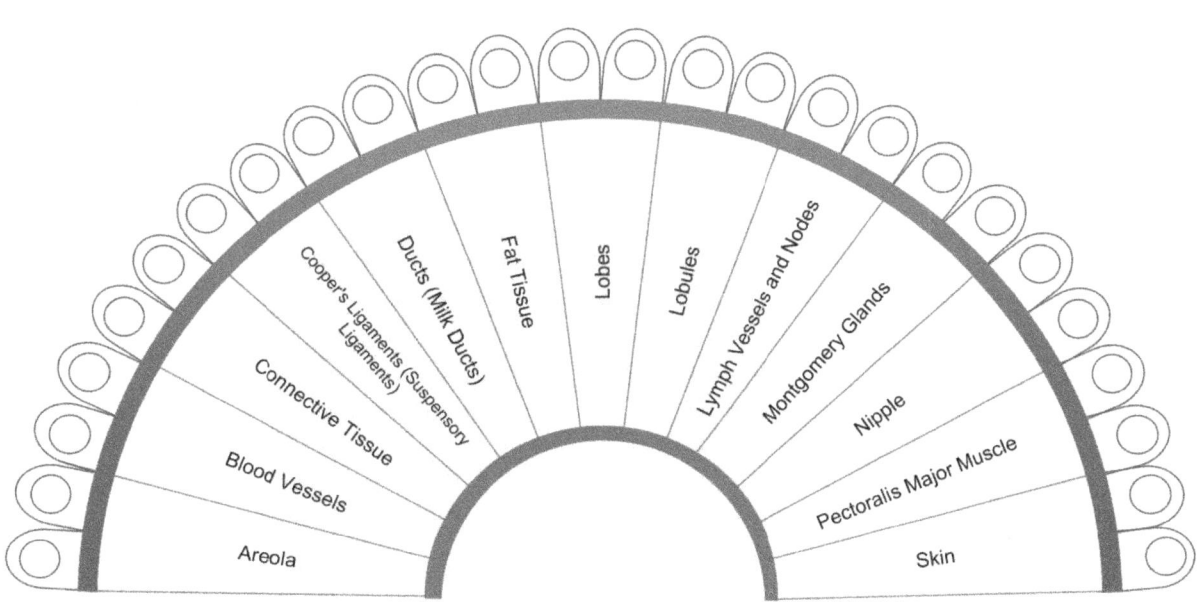

Breasts

Royal Template 13

Diving Deep into the Pool of the Mind

Chart 14

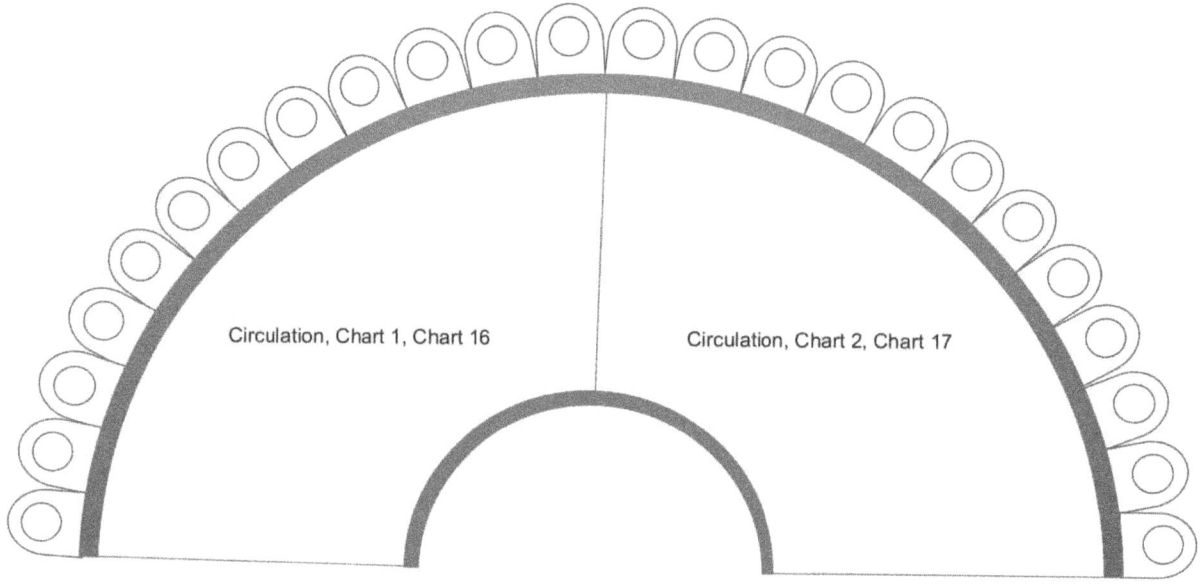

Circulation Master Chart

Circulation, Chart 1, Chart 16

Circulation, Chart 2, Chart 17

Royal Template 2

Diving Deep into the Pool of the Mind

Chart 15

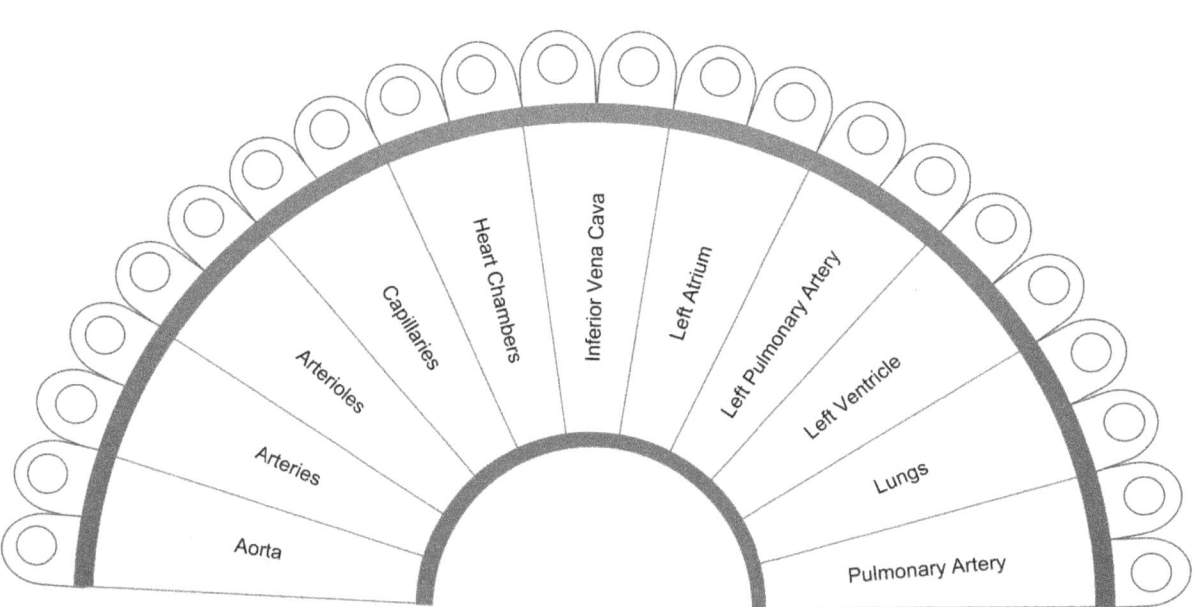

Heart Chambers

Inferior Vena Cava

Left Atrium

Left Pulmonary Artery

Capillaries

Arterioles

Left Ventricle

Arteries

Lungs

Aorta

Pulmonary Artery

Circulation, Chart 1

Royal Template 11

Diving Deep into the Pool of the Mind

Chart 16

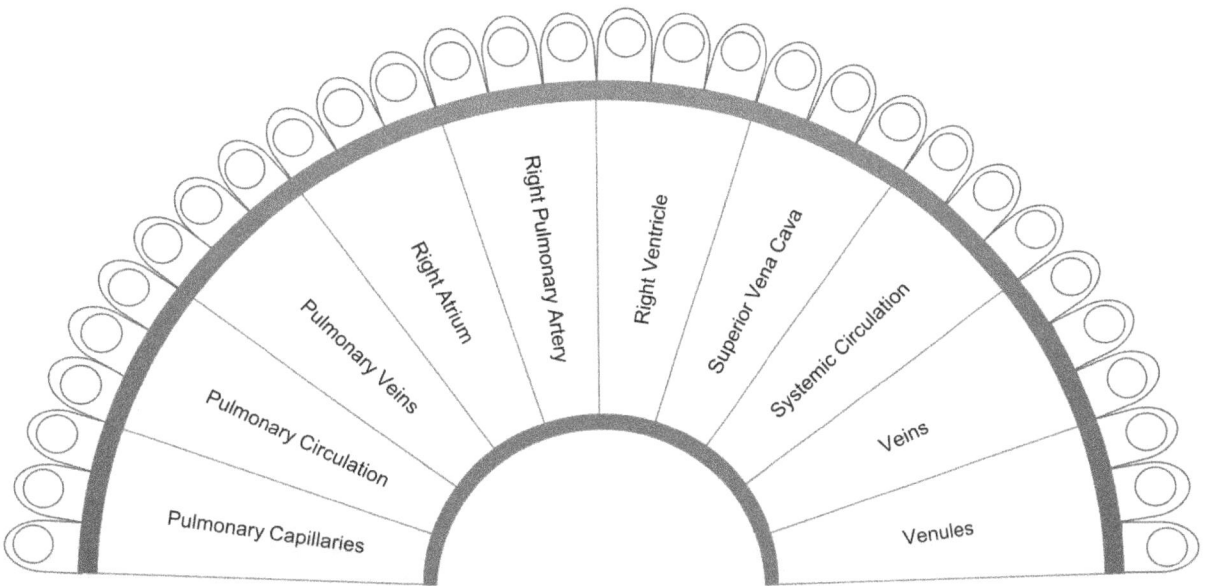

Circulation, Chart 2

Right Pulmonary Artery
Right Ventricle
Right Atrium
Superior Vena Cava
Pulmonary Veins
Systemic Circulation
Pulmonary Circulation
Veins
Pulmonary Capillaries
Venules

Royal Template 10

Diving Deep into the Pool of the Mind

Chart 17

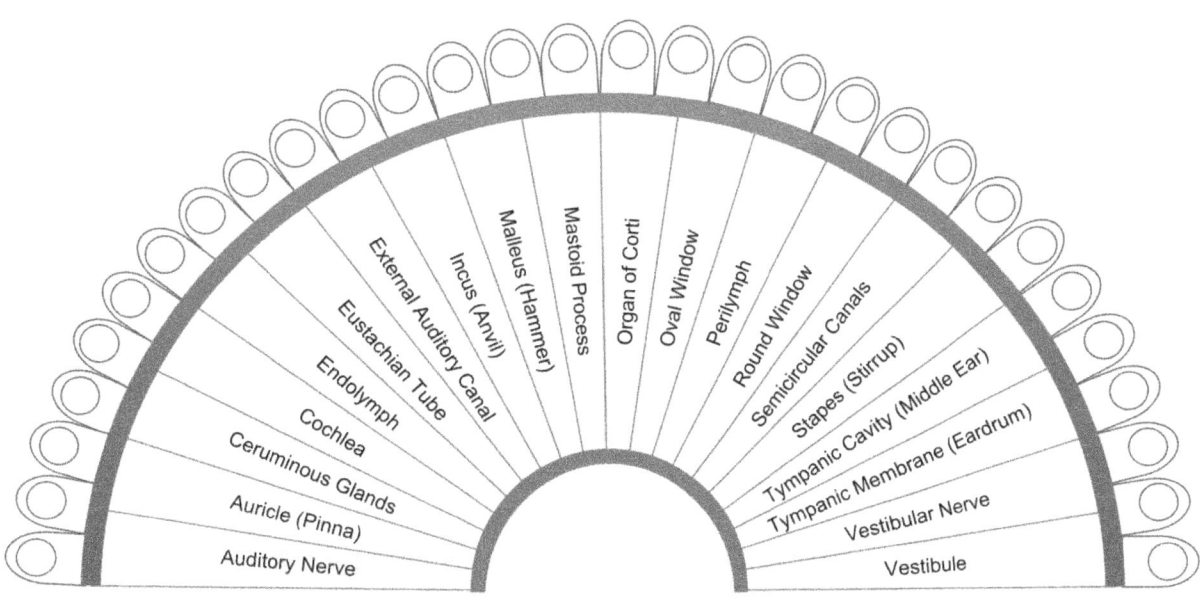

Ears

External Auditory Canal
Incus (Anvil)
Malleus (Hammer)
Mastoid Process
Organ of Corti
Oval Window
Eustachian Tube
Perilymph
Endolymph
Round Window
Cochlea
Semicircular Canals
Ceruminous Glands
Stapes (Stirrup)
Auricle (Pinna)
Tympanic Cavity (Middle Ear)
Tympanic Membrane (Eardrum)
Auditory Nerve
Vestibular Nerve
Vestibule

Royal Template 20

Diving Deep into the Pool of the Mind

Chart 18

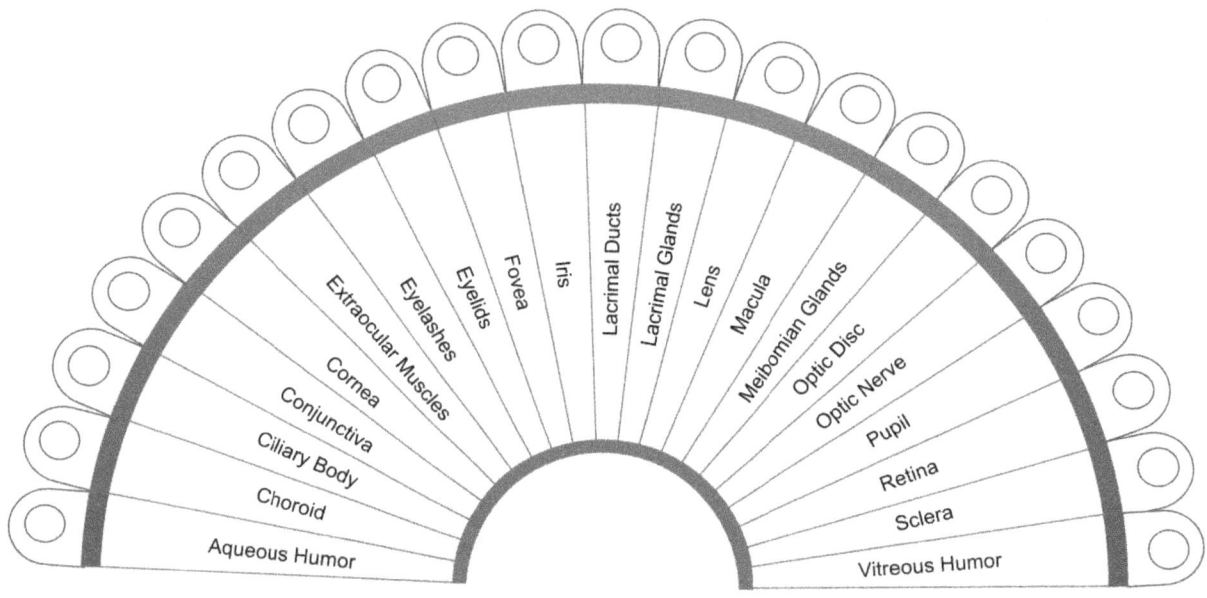

Eyes

Extraocular Muscles · Eyelashes · Eyelids · Fovea · Iris · Lacrimal Ducts · Lacrimal Glands · Lens · Macula · Meibomian Glands · Optic Disc · Optic Nerve · Pupil · Retina · Sclera · Vitreous Humor · Aqueous Humor · Choroid · Ciliary Body · Conjunctiva · Cornea

Royal Template 21

Diving Deep into the Pool of the Mind

Chart 19

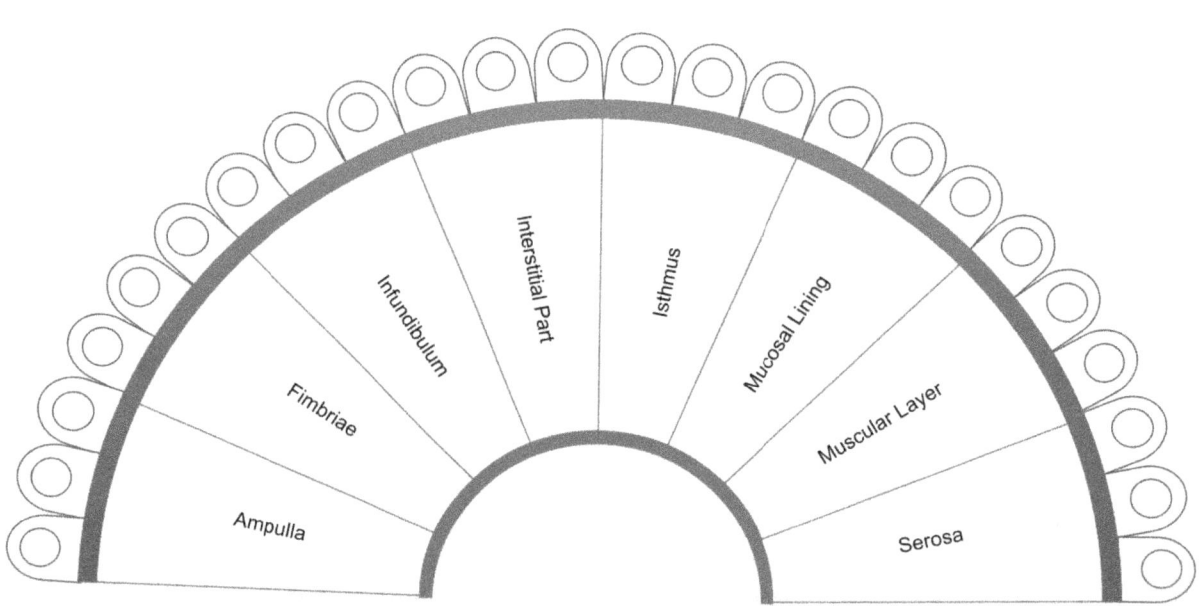

Fallopian Tube

Ampulla · Fimbriae · Infundibulum · Interstitial Part · Isthmus · Mucosal Lining · Muscular Layer · Serosa

Royal Template 8

Diving Deep into the Pool of the Mind

Chart 20

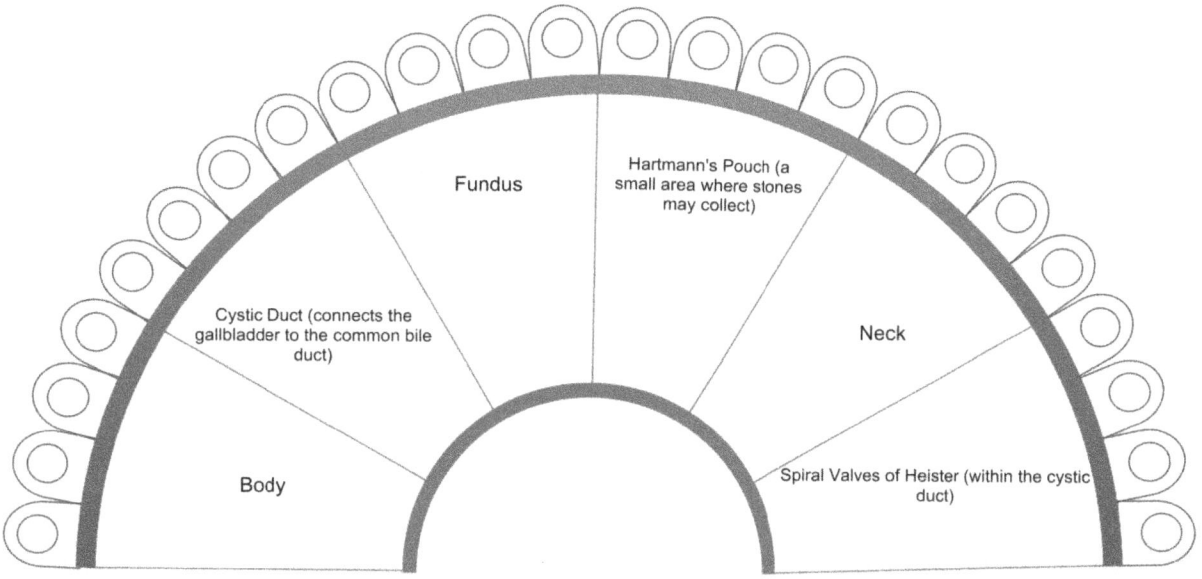

Gallbladder

Fundus

Hartmann's Pouch (a small area where stones may collect)

Cystic Duct (connects the gallbladder to the common bile duct)

Neck

Body

Spiral Valves of Heister (within the cystic duct)

Royal Template 6h

Chart 21

Diving Deep into the Pool of the Mind

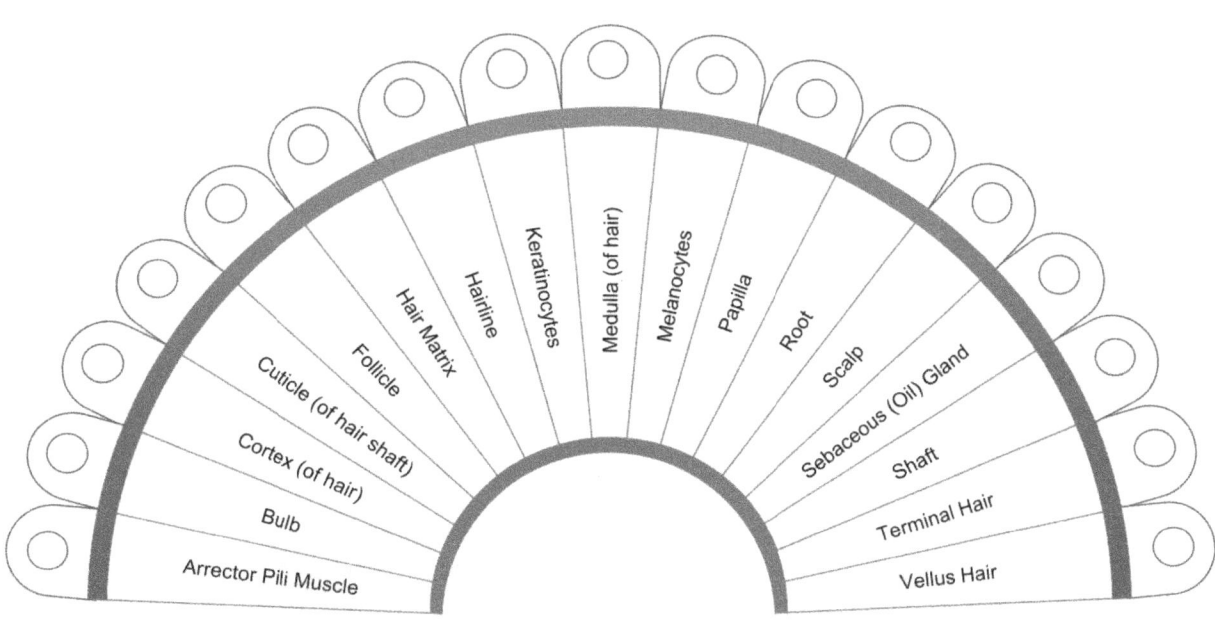

Keratinocytes

Medulla (of hair)

Hairline

Melanocytes

Hair Matrix

Papilla

Follicle

Root

Cuticle (of hair shaft)

Scalp

Cortex (of hair)

Sebaceous (Oil) Gland

Bulb

Shaft

Arrector Pili Muscle

Terminal Hair

Vellus Hair

Hair

Royal Template 17

Chart 22

Diving Deep into the Pool of the Mind

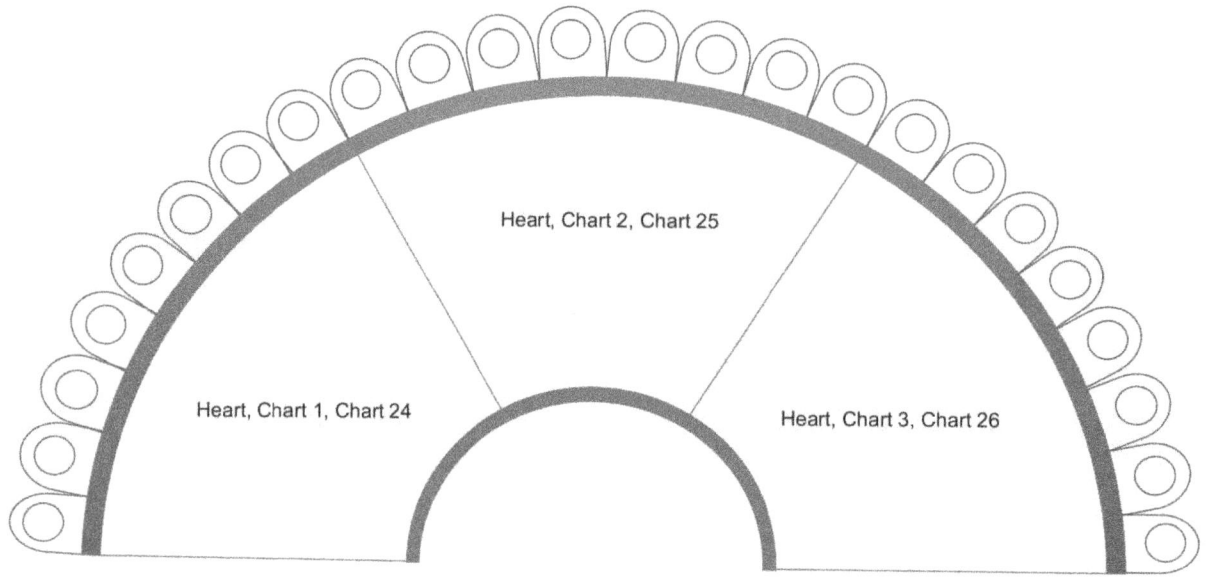

Heart Master Chart

Heart, Chart 2, Chart 25

Heart, Chart 1, Chart 24

Heart, Chart 3, Chart 26

Royal Template 3h

Diving Deep into the Pool of the Mind

Chart 23

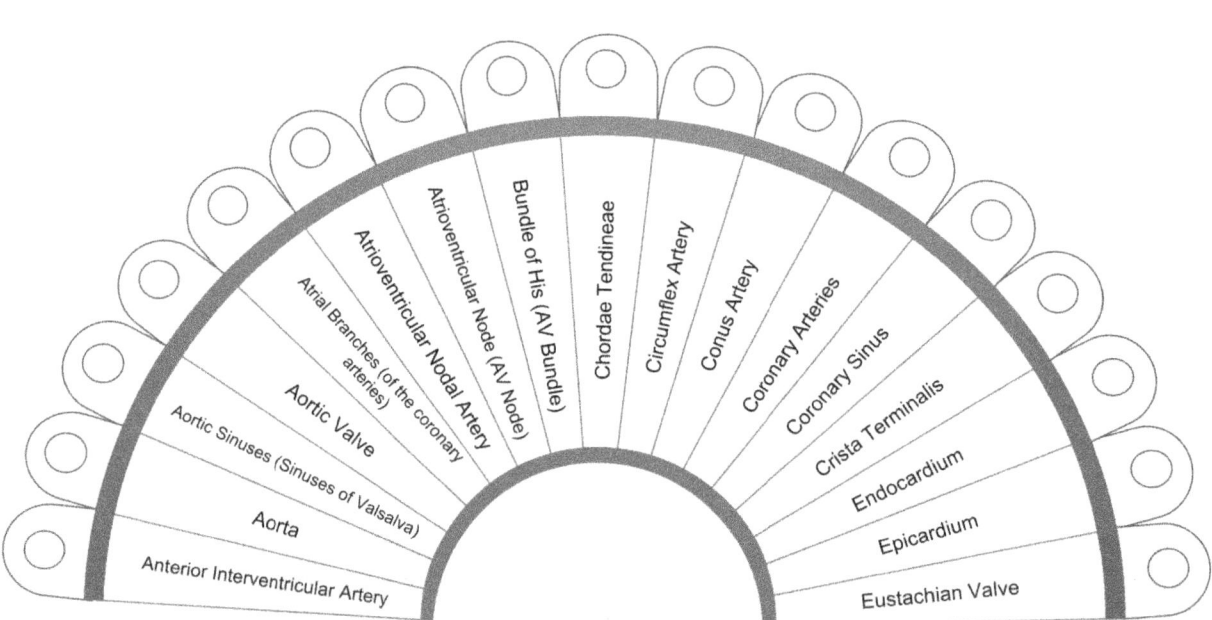

Atrioventricular Nodal Artery
Atrioventricular Node (AV Node)
Bundle of His (AV Bundle)
Chordae Tendineae
Circumflex Artery
Conus Artery
Coronary Arteries
Coronary Sinus
Crista Terminalis
Endocardium
Epicardium
Eustachian Valve
Atrial Branches (of the coronary arteries)
Aortic Valve
Aortic Sinuses (Sinuses of Valsalva)
Aorta
Anterior Interventricular Artery

Heart, Chart 1

Royal Template 17

Diving Deep into the Pool of the Mind

Chart 24

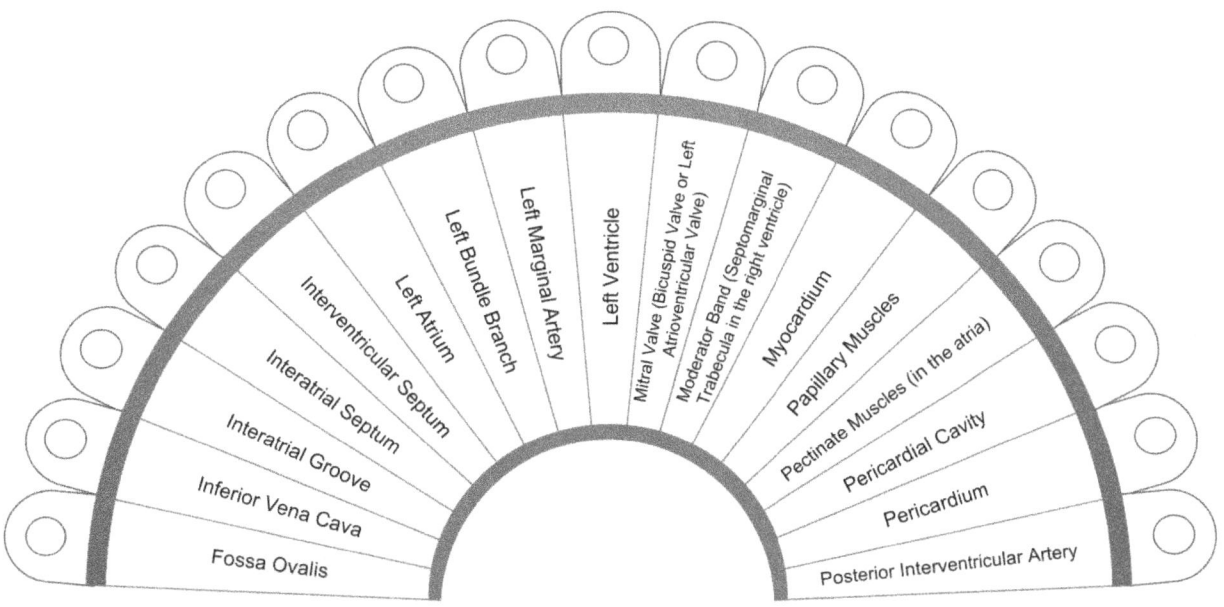

Heart, Chart 2

Left Ventricle
Left Marginal Artery
Left Bundle Branch
Left Atrium
Interventricular Septum
Interatrial Septum
Interatrial Groove
Inferior Vena Cava
Fossa Ovalis
Mitral Valve (Bicuspid Valve or Left Atrioventricular Valve)
Moderator Band (Septomarginal Trabecula in the right ventricle)
Myocardium
Papillary Muscles
Pectinate Muscles (in the atria)
Pericardial Cavity
Pericardium
Posterior Interventricular Artery

Royal Template 17

Diving Deep into the Pool of the Mind

Chart 25

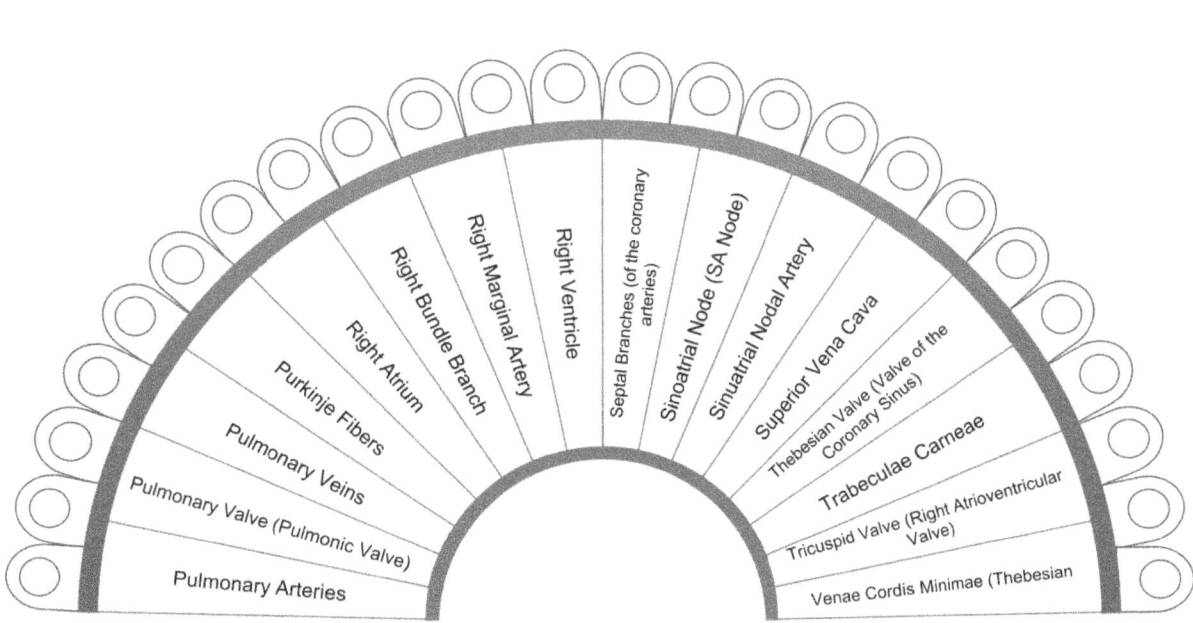

Heart, Chart 3

Right Ventricle
Right Marginal Artery
Right Bundle Branch
Right Atrium
Purkinje Fibers
Pulmonary Veins
Pulmonary Valve (Pulmonic Valve)
Pulmonary Arteries
Septal Branches (of the coronary arteries)
Sinoatrial Node (SA Node)
Sinuatrial Nodal Artery
Superior Vena Cava
Thebesian Valve (Valve of the Coronary Sinus)
Trabeculae Carneae
Tricuspid Valve (Right Atrioventricular Valve)
Venae Cordis Minimae (Thebesian

Royal Template 16

Diving Deep into the Pool of the Mind

Chart 26

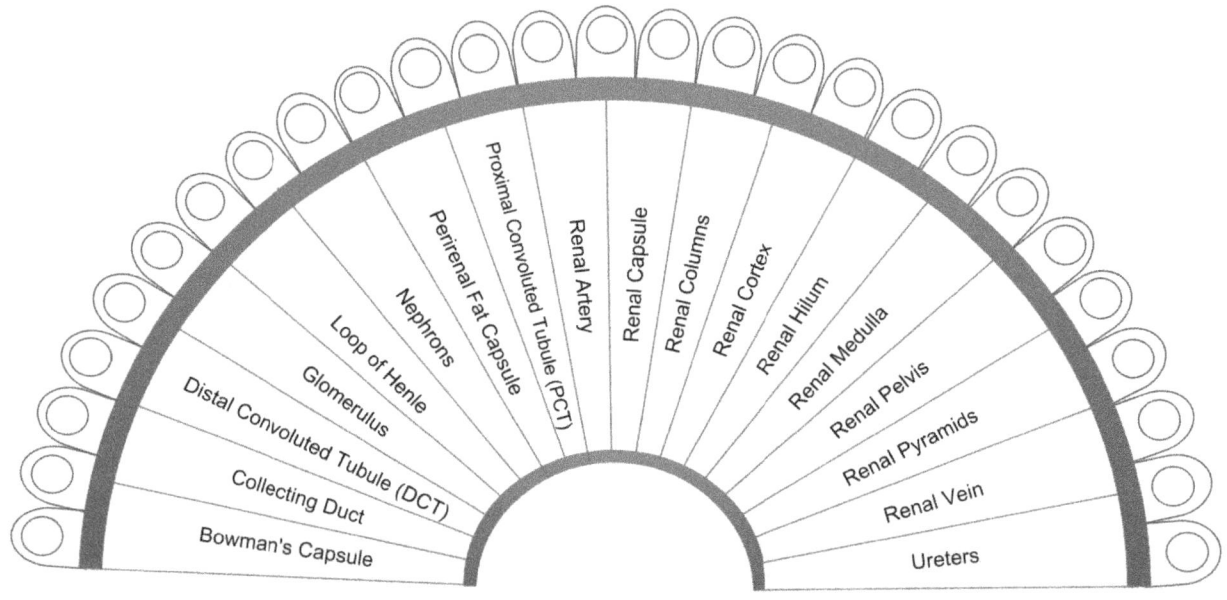

Kidneys

Labels (outer to inner, left side):
- Bowman's Capsule
- Collecting Duct
- Distal Convoluted Tubule (DCT)
- Glomerulus
- Loop of Henle
- Nephrons
- Perirenal Fat Capsule
- Proximal Convoluted Tubule (PCT)
- Renal Artery
- Renal Capsule

Labels (right side):
- Renal Columns
- Renal Cortex
- Renal Hilum
- Renal Medulla
- Renal Pelvis
- Renal Pyramids
- Renal Vein
- Ureters

Royal Template 18

Diving Deep into the Pool of the Mind

Chart 27

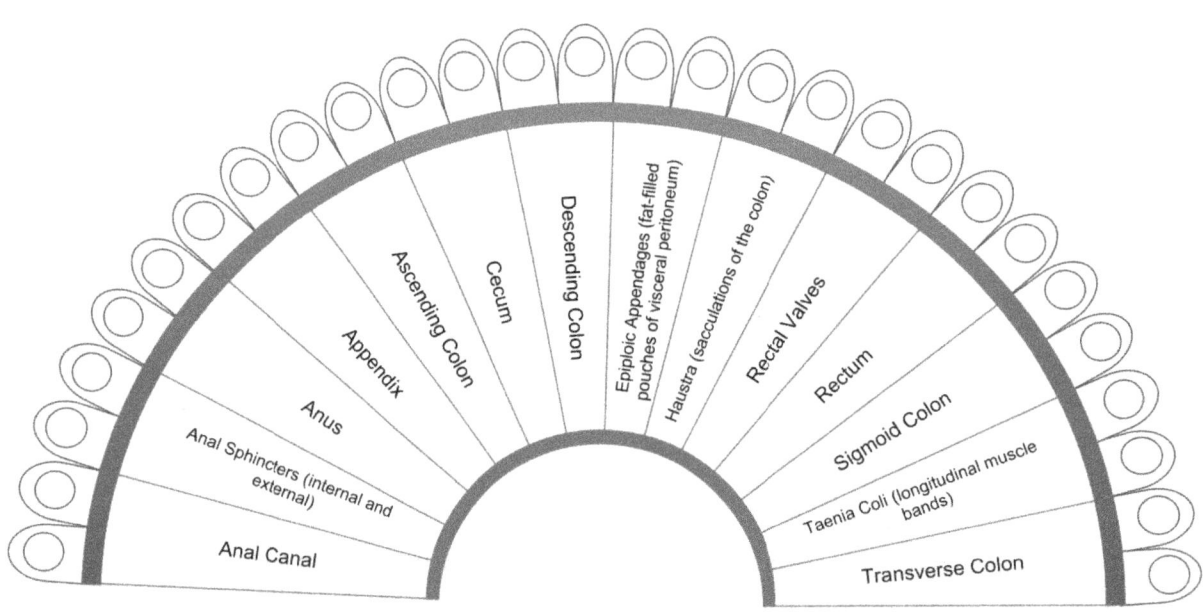

Large Intestine

Labels (left side):
- Anal Canal
- Anal Sphincters (internal and external)
- Anus
- Appendix
- Ascending Colon
- Cecum
- Descending Colon

Labels (right side):
- Epiploic Appendages (fat-filled pouches of visceral peritoneum)
- Haustra (sacculations of the colon)
- Rectal Valves
- Rectum
- Sigmoid Colon
- Taenia Coli (longitudinal muscle bands)
- Transverse Colon

Royal Template 14

Diving Deep into the Pool of the Mind

Chart 28

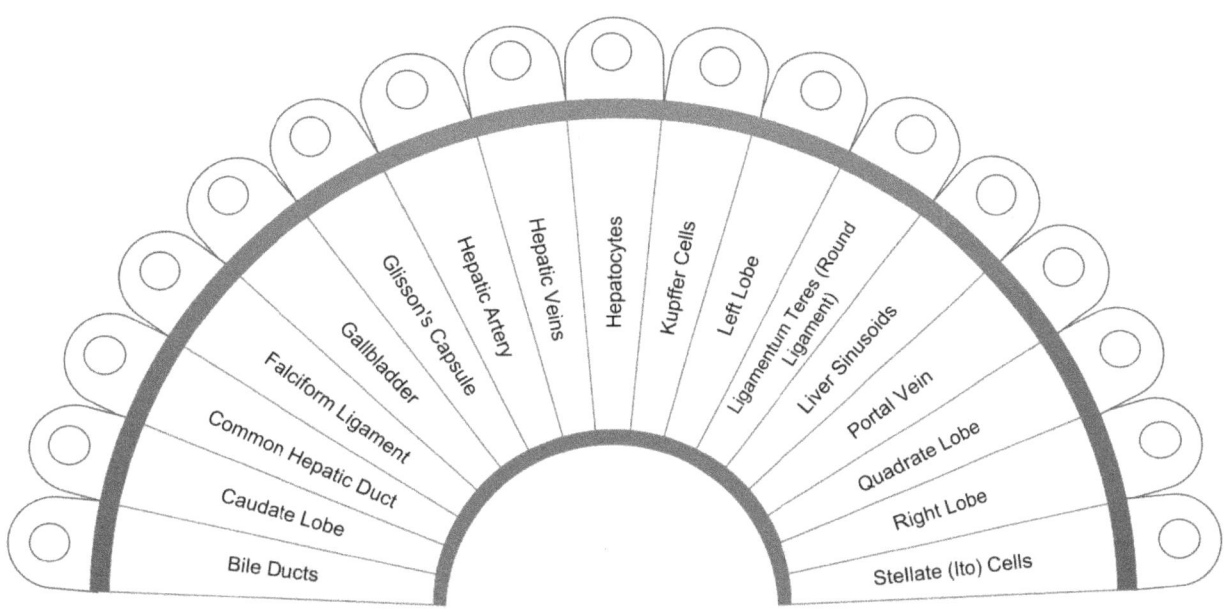

Liver

Glisson's Capsule
Hepatic Artery
Hepatic Veins
Hepatocytes
Kupffer Cells
Left Lobe
Ligamentum Teres (Round Ligament)
Liver Sinusoids
Portal Vein
Quadrate Lobe
Right Lobe
Stellate (Ito) Cells
Gallbladder
Falciform Ligament
Common Hepatic Duct
Caudate Lobe
Bile Ducts

Royal Template 17

Diving Deep into the Pool of the Mind

Chart 29

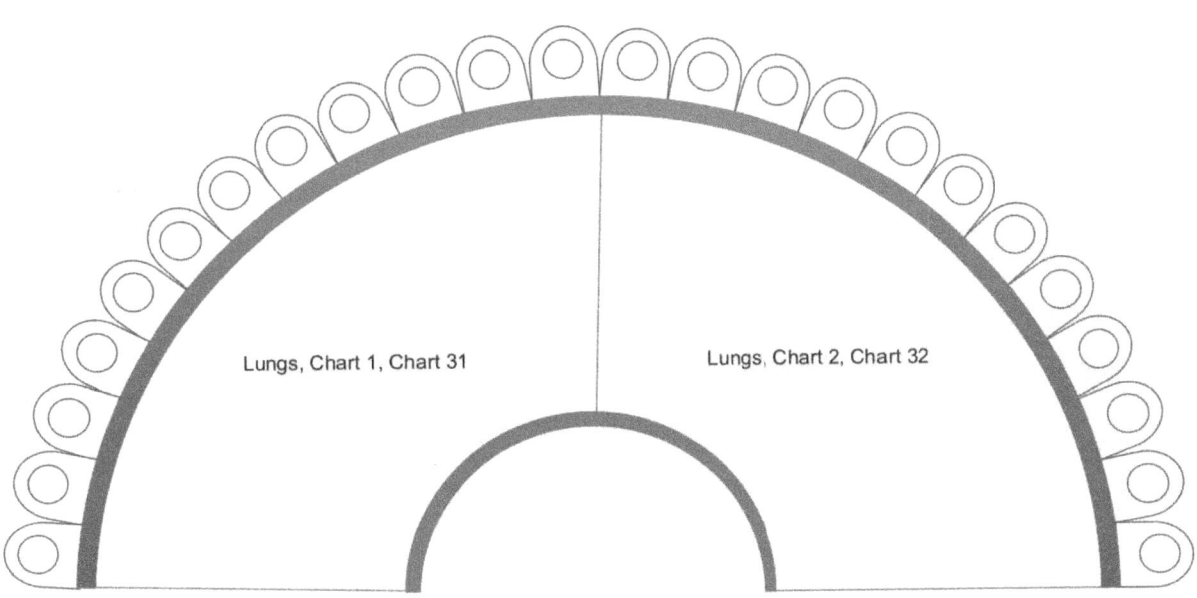

Lungs, Chart 1, Chart 31

Lungs, Chart 2, Chart 32

Lungs, Master Chart

Royal Template 2

Diving Deep into the Pool of the Mind

Chart 30

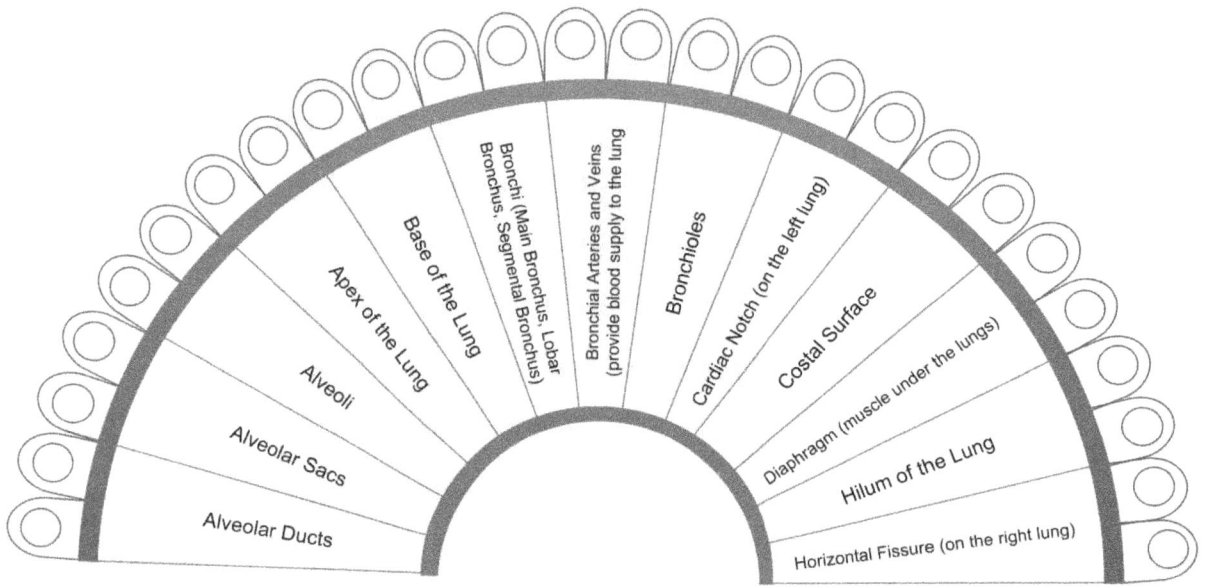

Lungs, Chart 1

The chart shows the following labels radiating outward:
- Alveolar Ducts
- Alveolar Sacs
- Alveoli
- Apex of the Lung
- Base of the Lung
- Bronchi (Main Bronchus, Lobar Bronchus, Segmental Bronchus)
- Bronchial Arteries and Veins (provide blood supply to the lung)
- Bronchioles
- Cardiac Notch (on the left lung)
- Costal Surface
- Diaphragm (muscle under the lungs)
- Hilum of the Lung
- Horizontal Fissure (on the right lung)

Diving Deep into the Pool of the Mind

Chart 31

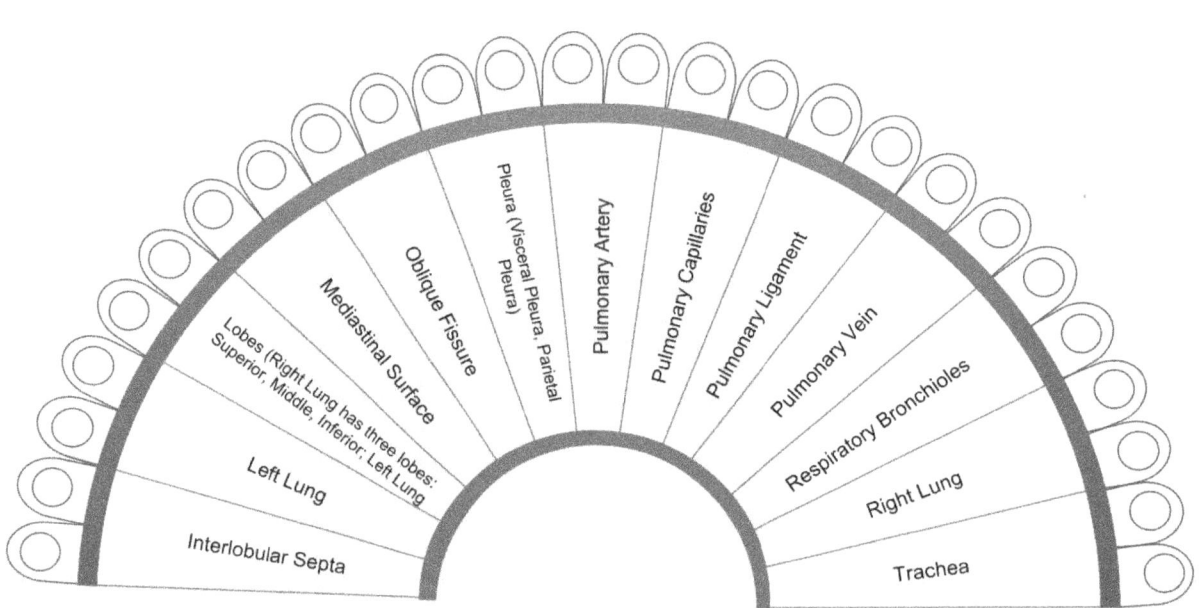

Lungs, Chart 2

The chart shows the following labels radiating outward:
- Interlobular Septa
- Left Lung
- Lobes (Right Lung has three lobes: Superior, Middle, Inferior; Left Lung
- Mediastinal Surface
- Oblique Fissure
- Pleura (Visceral Pleura, Parietal Pleura)
- Pulmonary Artery
- Pulmonary Capillaries
- Pulmonary Ligament
- Pulmonary Vein
- Respiratory Bronchioles
- Right Lung
- Trachea

Diving Deep into the Pool of the Mind

Chart 32

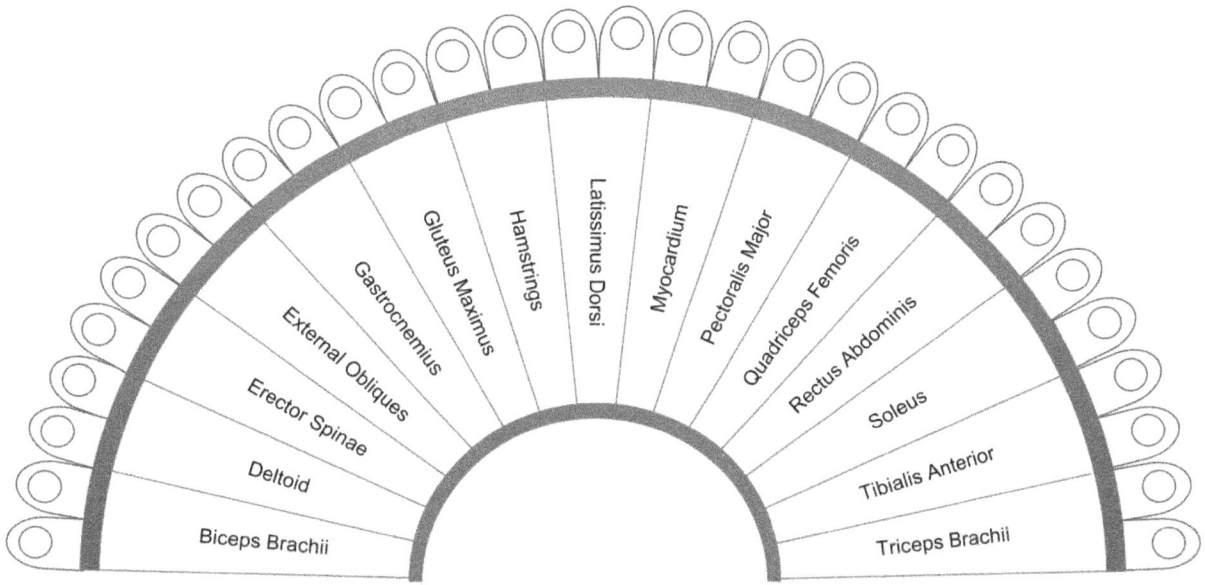

Muscles

Biceps Brachii
Deltoid
Erector Spinae
External Obliques
Gastrocnemius
Gluteus Maximus
Hamstrings
Latissimus Dorsi
Myocardium
Pectoralis Major
Quadriceps Femoris
Rectus Abdominis
Soleus
Tibialis Anterior
Triceps Brachii

Royal Template 15

Diving Deep into the Pool of the Mind

Chart 33

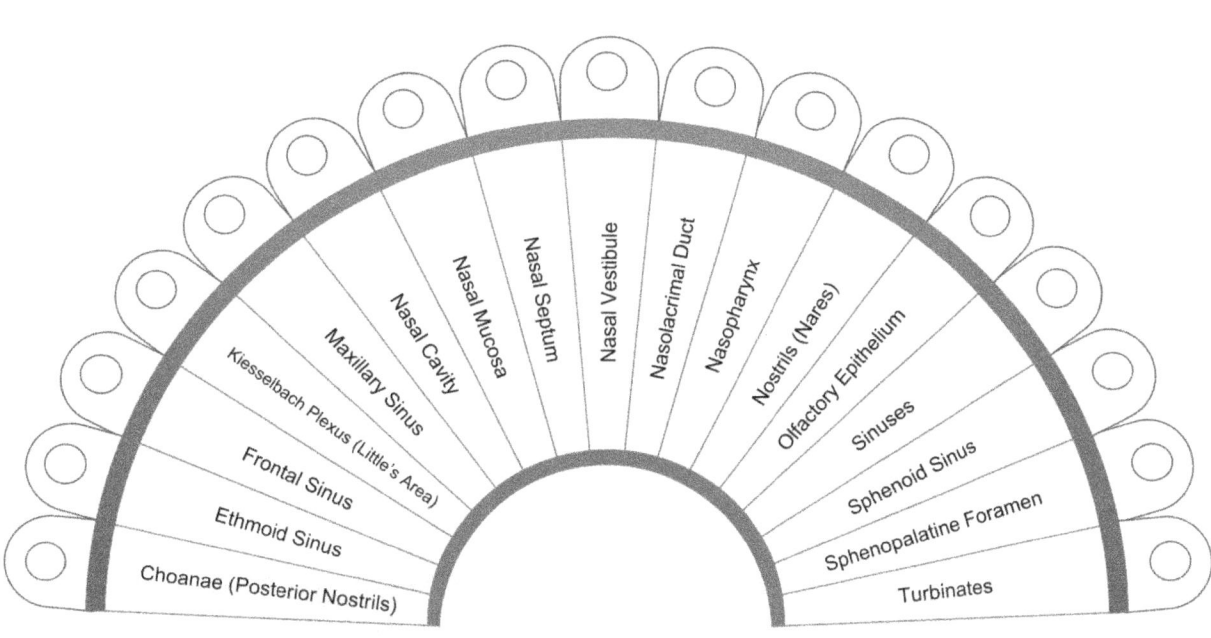

Nose

Choanae (Posterior Nostrils)
Ethmoid Sinus
Frontal Sinus
Kiesselbach Plexus (Little's Area)
Maxillary Sinus
Nasal Cavity
Nasal Mucosa
Nasal Septum
Nasal Vestibule
Nasolacrimal Duct
Nasopharynx
Nostrils (Nares)
Olfactory Epithelium
Sinuses
Sphenoid Sinus
Sphenopalatine Foramen
Turbinates

Royal Template 17

Diving Deep into the Pool of the Mind

Chart 34

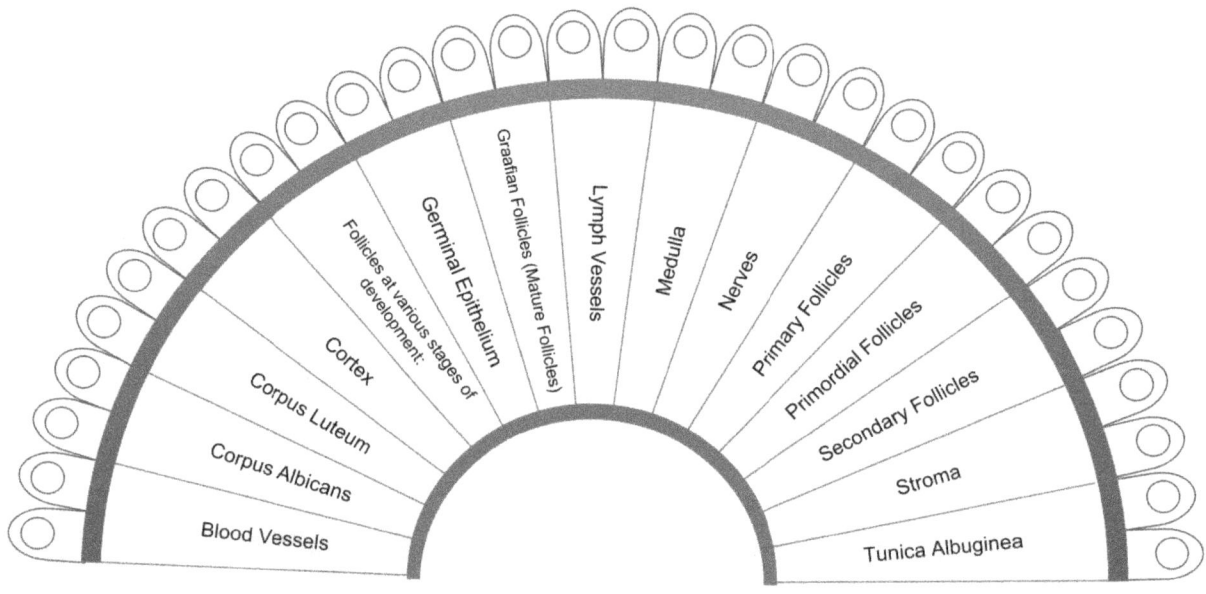

Ovaries

Follicles at various stages of development:
Germinal Epithelium
Graafian Follicles (Mature Follicles)
Lymph Vessels
Medulla
Nerves
Primary Follicles
Primordial Follicles
Secondary Follicles
Stroma
Tunica Albuginea
Cortex
Corpus Luteum
Corpus Albicans
Blood Vessels

Royal Template 15

Diving Deep into the Pool of the Mind

Chart 35

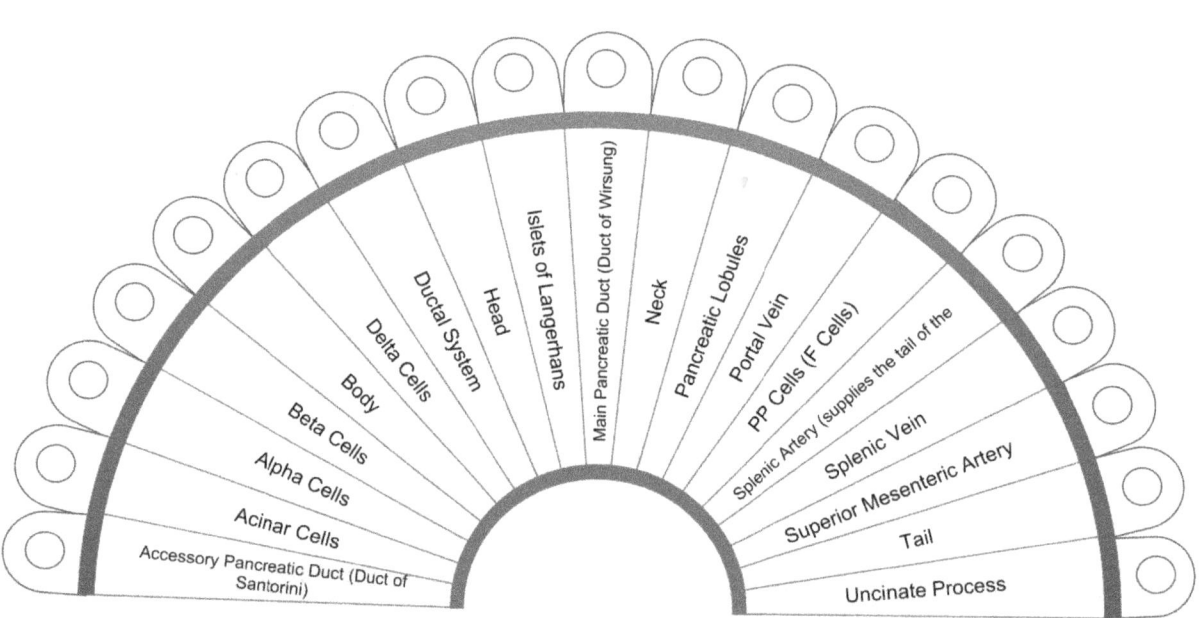

Pancreas

Islets of Langerhans
Main Pancreatic Duct (Duct of Wirsung)
Head
Ductal System
Delta Cells
Body
Beta Cells
Alpha Cells
Acinar Cells
Accessory Pancreatic Duct (Duct of Santorini)
Neck
Pancreatic Lobules
Portal Vein
PP Cells (F Cells)
Splenic Artery (supplies the tail of the
Splenic Vein
Superior Mesenteric Artery
Tail
Uncinate Process

Royal Template 19

Diving Deep into the Pool of the Mind

Chart 36

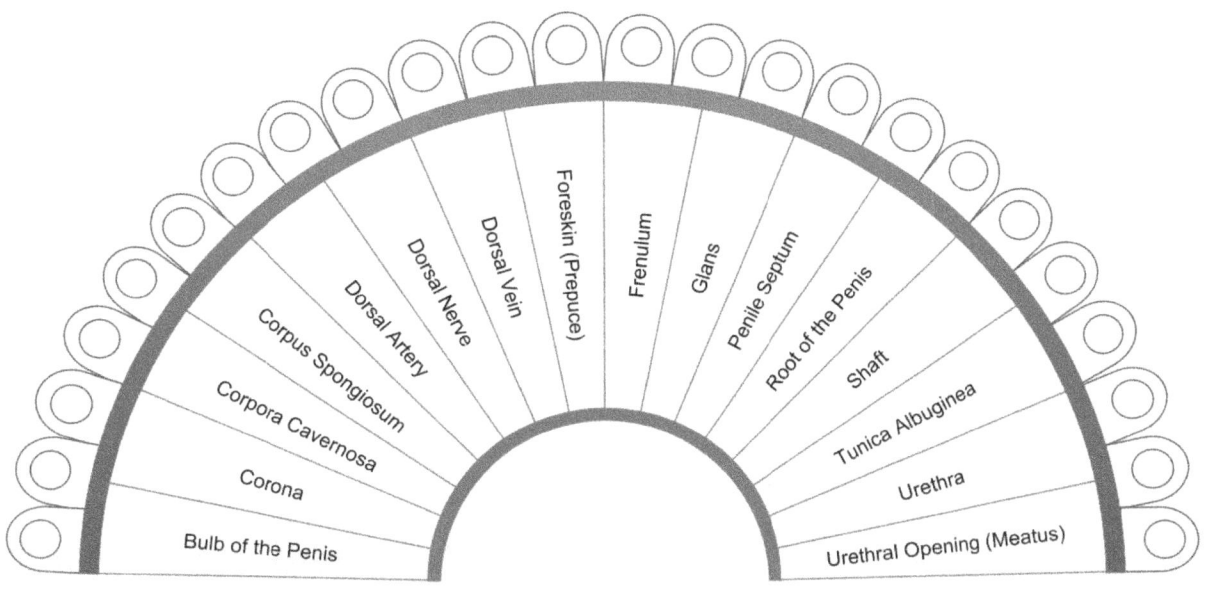

Penis

Royal Template 16

Diving Deep into the Pool of the Mind

Chart 37

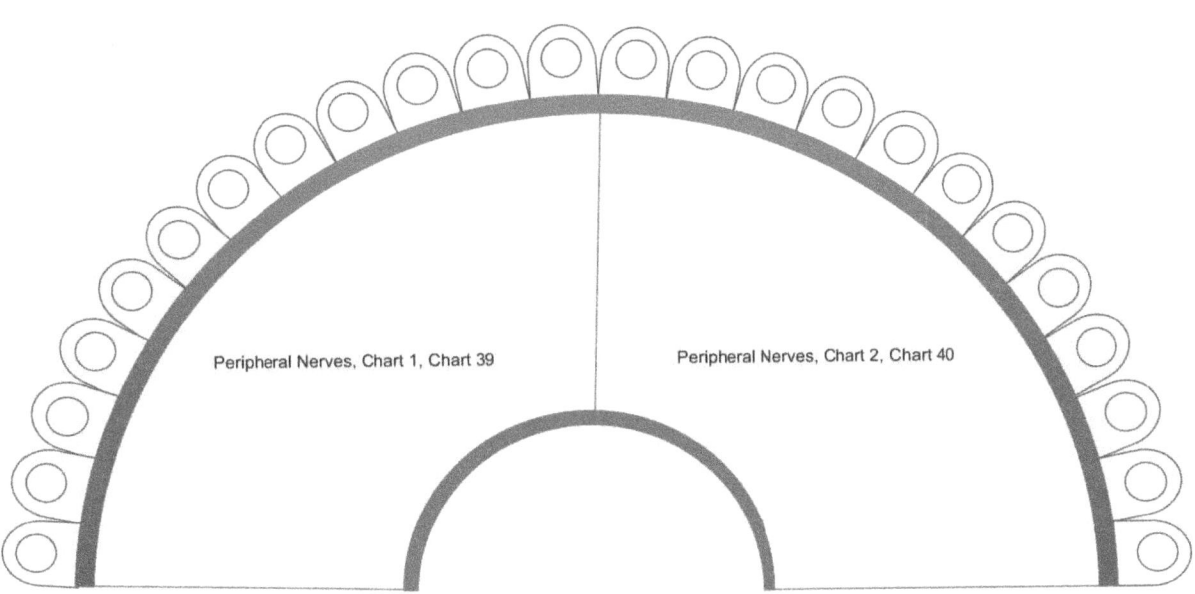

Peripheral Nerves Master Chart

Peripheral Nerves, Chart 1, Chart 39

Peripheral Nerves, Chart 2, Chart 40

Royal Template 2

Diving Deep into the Pool of the Mind

Chart 38

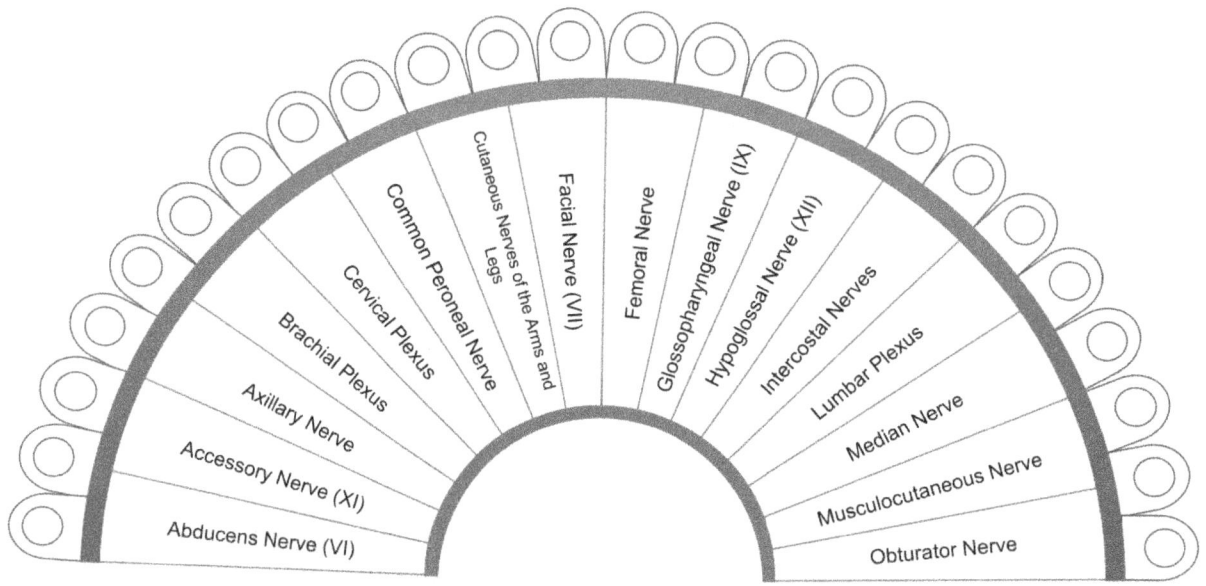

Peripheral Nerves, Chart 1

Royal Template 16

Diving Deep into the Pool of the Mind

Chart 39

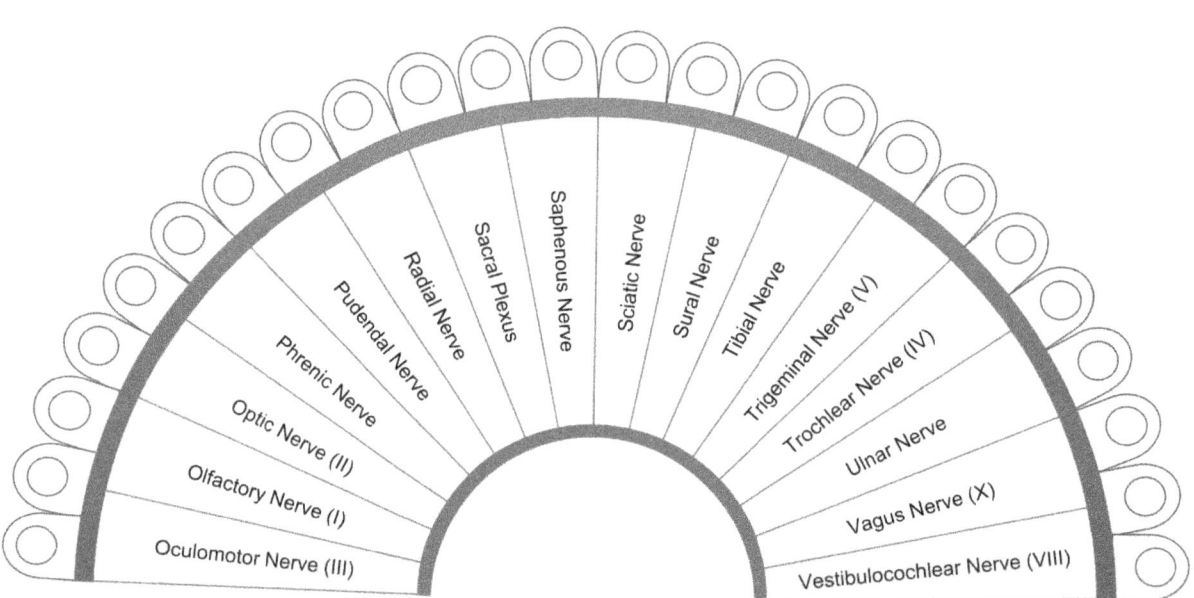

Peripheral Nerves, Chart 2

Royal Template 16

Diving Deep into the Pool of the Mind

Chart 40

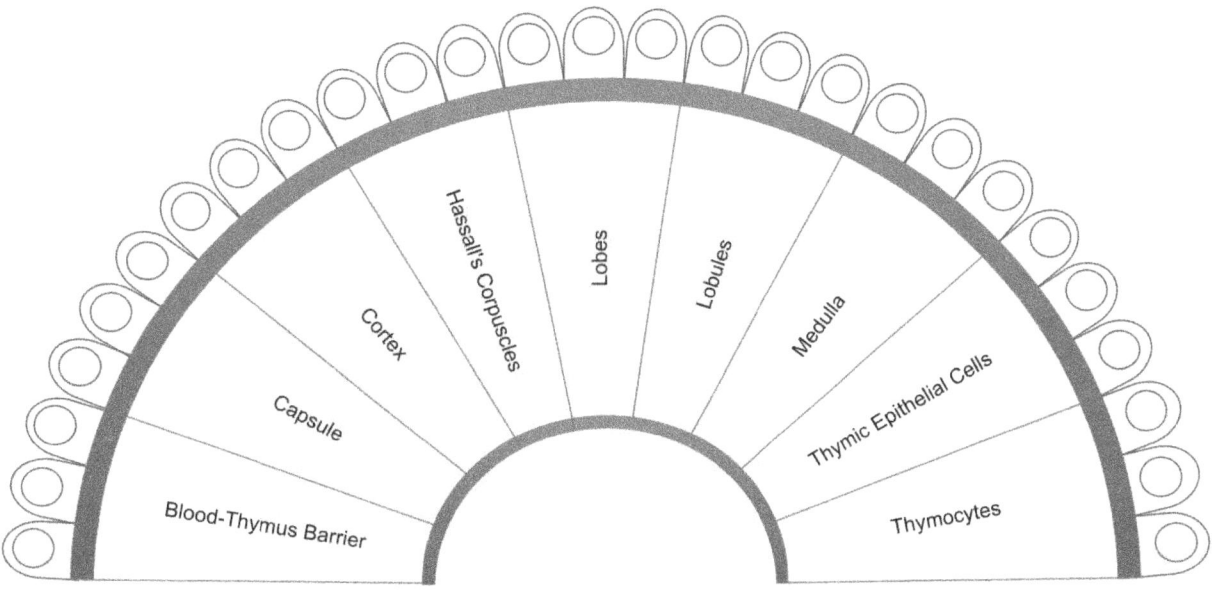

Pineal Gland

Hassall's Corpuscles
Lobes
Cortex
Lobules
Capsule
Medulla
Blood-Thymus Barrier
Thymic Epithelial Cells
Thymocytes

Royal Template 9

Diving Deep into the Pool of the Mind

Chart 41

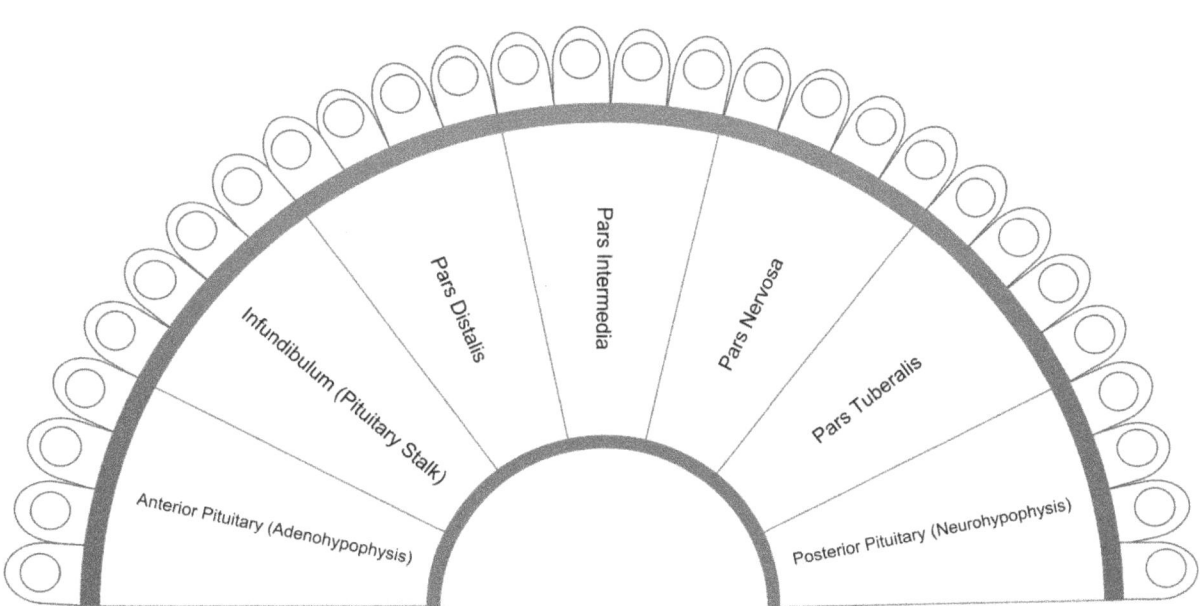

Pituitary Gland

Pars Intermedia
Pars Distalis
Pars Nervosa
Infundibulum (Pituitary Stalk)
Pars Tuberalis
Anterior Pituitary (Adenohypophysis)
Posterior Pituitary (Neurohypophysis)

Royal Template 7

Diving Deep into the Pool of the Mind

Chart 42

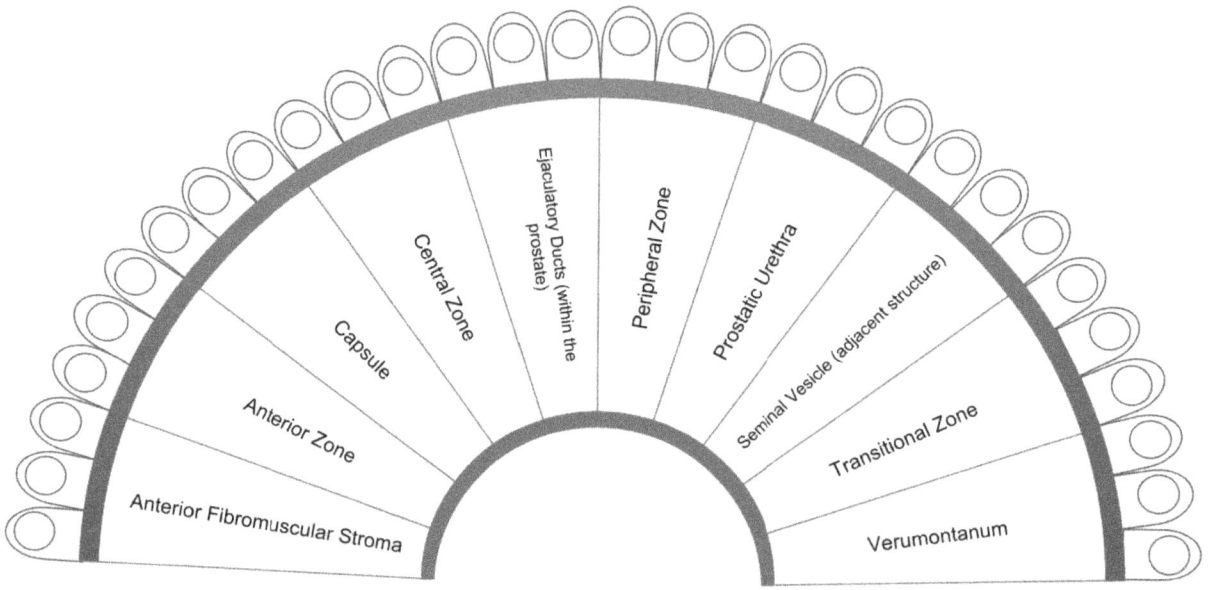

Prostate

Ejaculatory Ducts (within the prostate)
Central Zone
Capsule
Anterior Zone
Anterior Fibromuscular Stroma
Peripheral Zone
Prostatic Urethra
Seminal Vesicle (adjacent structure)
Transitional Zone
Verumontanum

Royal Template 10

Diving Deep into the Pool of the Mind

Chart 43

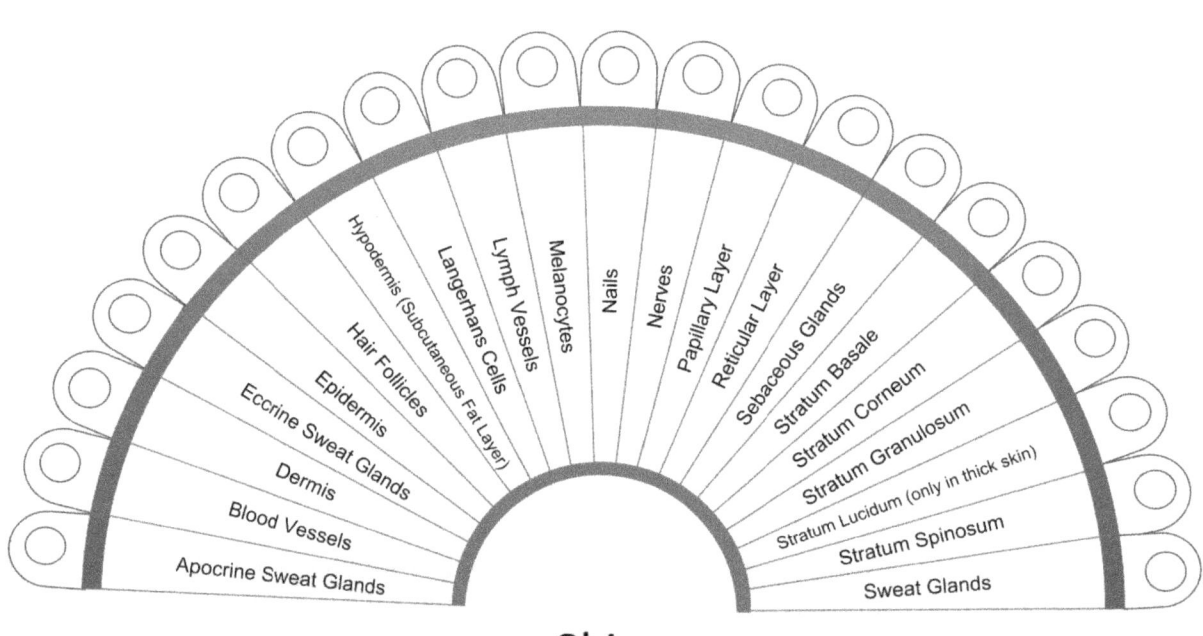

Skin

Hypodermis (Subcutaneous Fat Layer)
Hair Follicles
Epidermis
Eccrine Sweat Glands
Dermis
Blood Vessels
Apocrine Sweat Glands
Langerhans Cells
Lymph Vessels
Melanocytes
Nails
Nerves
Papillary Layer
Reticular Layer
Sebaceous Glands
Stratum Basale
Stratum Corneum
Stratum Granulosum
Stratum Lucidum (only in thick skin)
Stratum Spinosum
Sweat Glands

Royal Template 21

Diving Deep into the Pool of the Mind

Chart 44

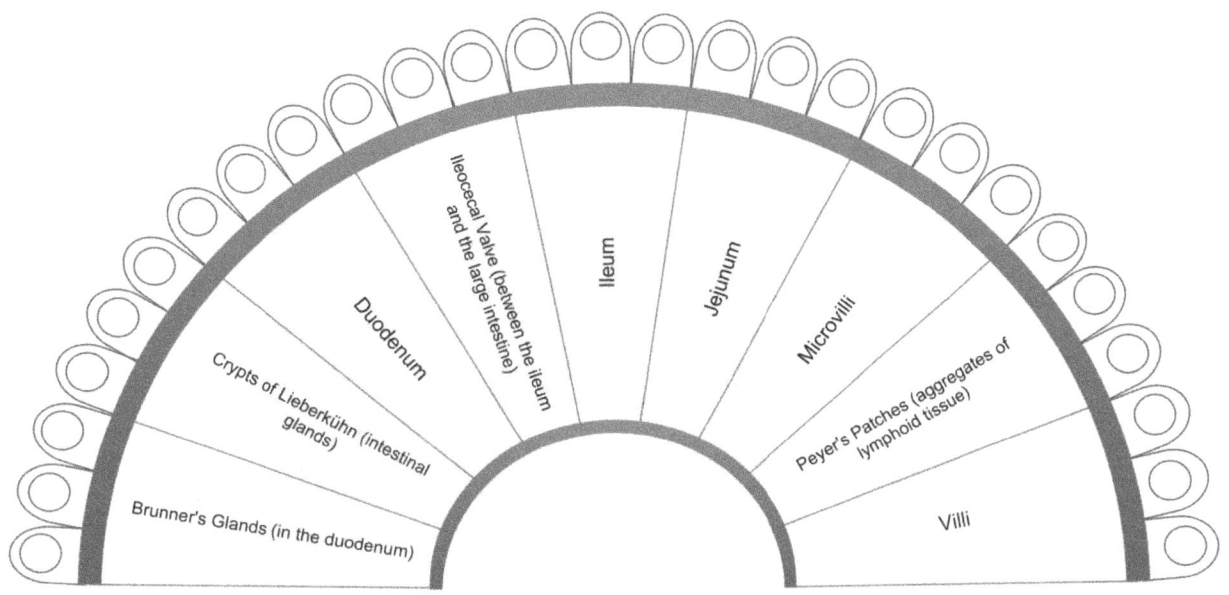

Small Intestine

Duodenum

Crypts of Lieberkühn (intestinal glands)

Brunner's Glands (in the duodenum)

Ileocecal Valve (between the ileum and the large intestine)

Ileum

Jejunum

Microvilli

Peyer's Patches (aggregates of lymphoid tissue)

Villi

Royal Template 9

Diving Deep into the Pool of the Mind

Chart 45

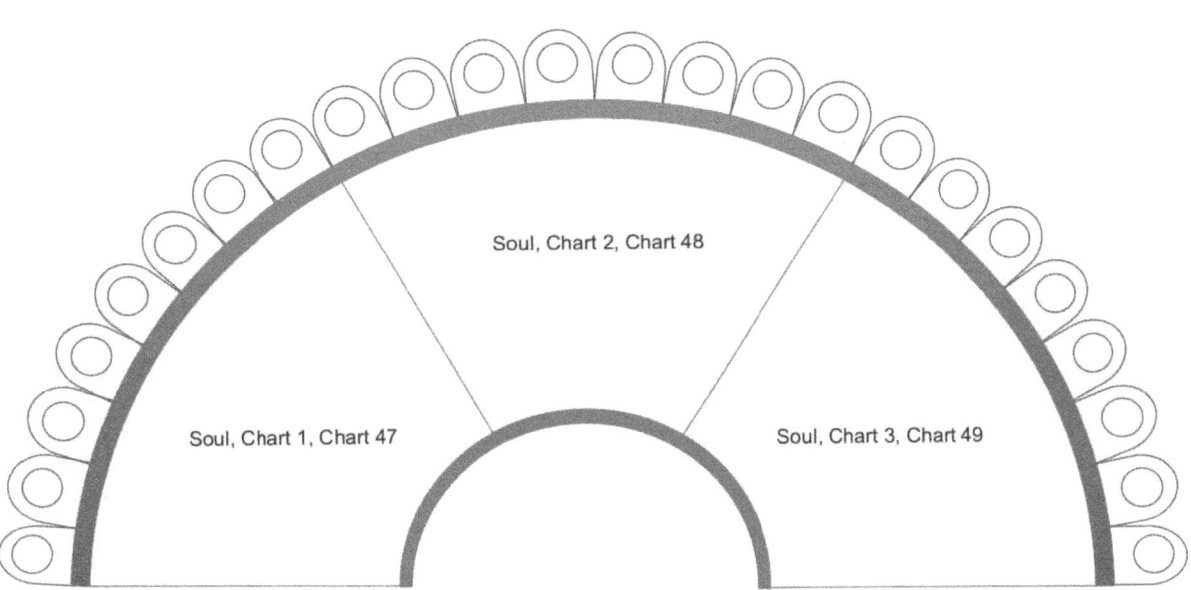

Soul Master Chart

Soul, Chart 2, Chart 48

Soul, Chart 1, Chart 47

Soul, Chart 3, Chart 49

Royal Template 3h

Diving Deep into the Pool of the Mind

Chart 46

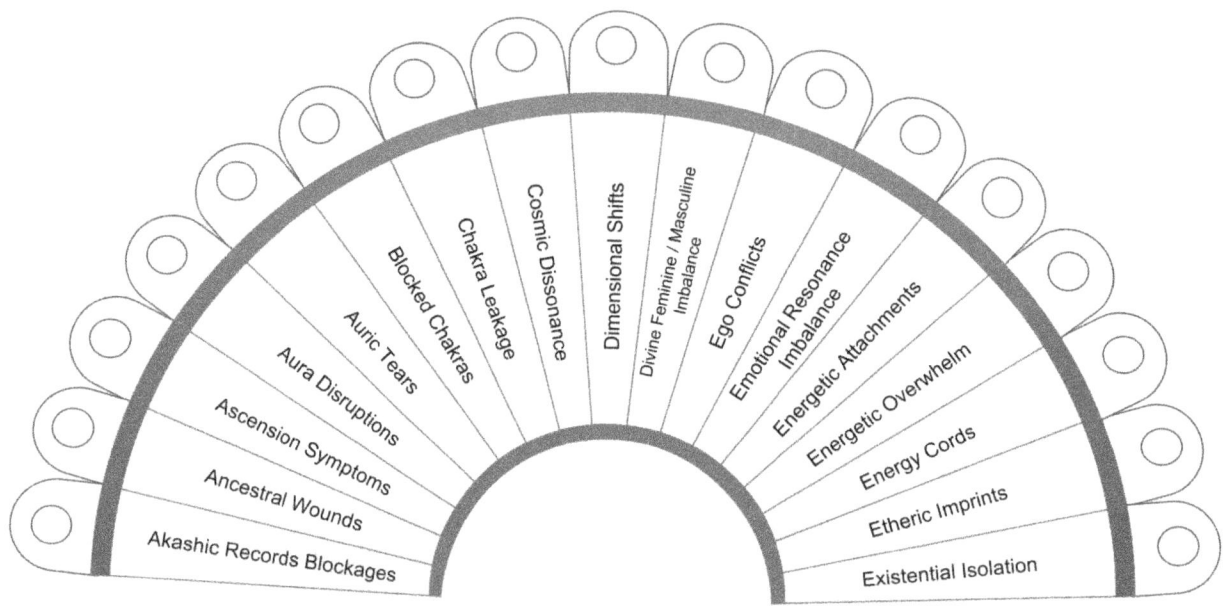

Soul, Chart 1

The chart contains the following labels (left to right):

- Akashic Records Blockages
- Ancestral Wounds
- Ascension Symptoms
- Aura Disruptions
- Auric Tears
- Blocked Chakras
- Chakra Leakage
- Cosmic Dissonance
- Dimensional Shifts
- Divine Feminine / Masculine Imbalance
- Ego Conflicts
- Emotional Resonance Imbalance
- Energetic Attachments
- Energetic Overwhelm
- Energy Cords
- Etheric Imprints
- Existential Isolation

Royal Template 17

Diving Deep into the Pool of the Mind

Chart 47

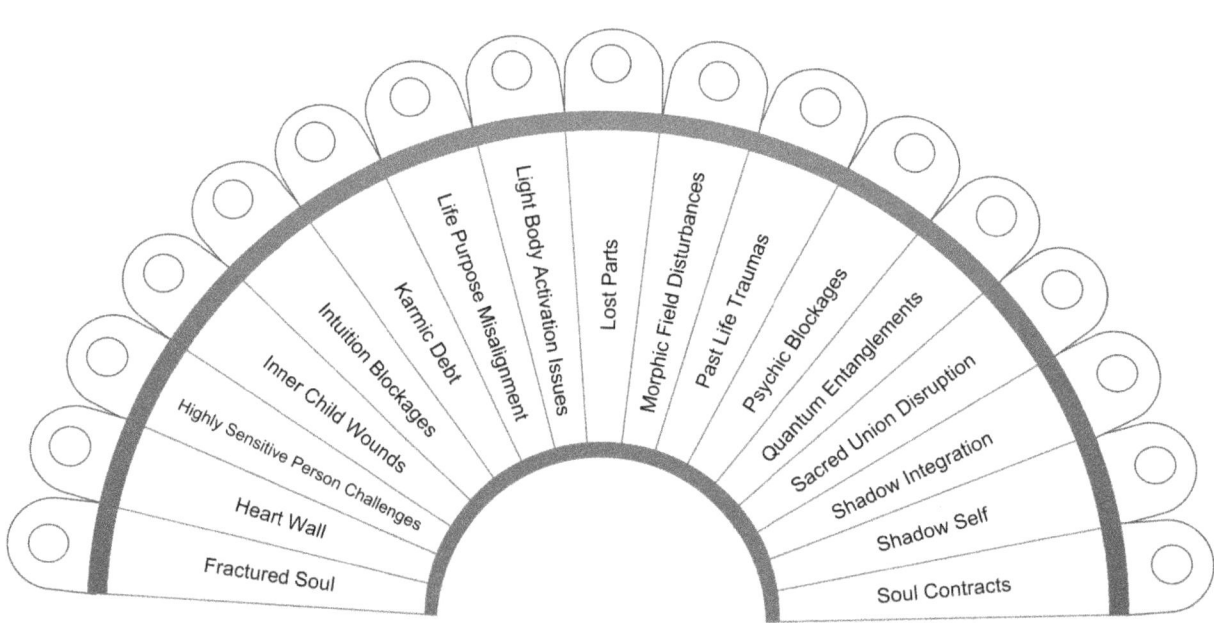

Soul, Chart 2

The chart contains the following labels (left to right):

- Fractured Soul
- Heart Wall
- Highly Sensitive Person Challenges
- Inner Child Wounds
- Intuition Blockages
- Karmic Debt
- Life Purpose Misalignment
- Light Body Activation Issues
- Lost Parts
- Morphic Field Disturbances
- Past Life Traumas
- Psychic Blockages
- Quantum Entanglements
- Sacred Union Disruption
- Shadow Integration
- Shadow Self
- Soul Contracts

Royal Template 17

Diving Deep into the Pool of the Mind

Chart 48

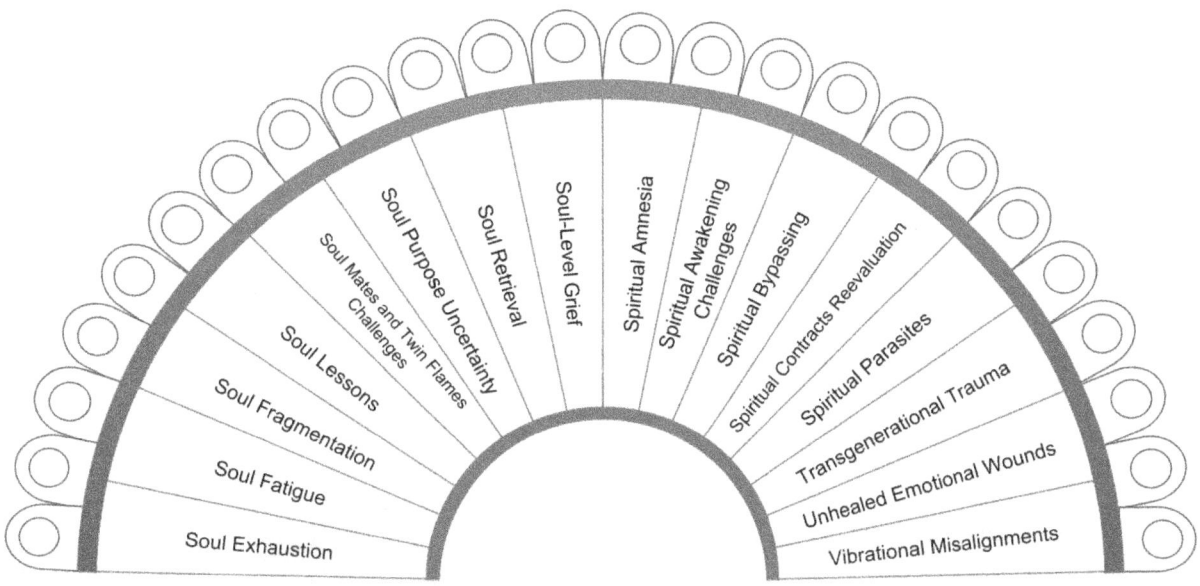

Soul, Chart 3

Soul Exhaustion
Soul Fatigue
Soul Fragmentation
Soul Lessons
Soul Mates and Twin Flames Challenges
Soul Purpose Uncertainty
Soul Retrieval
Soul-Level Grief
Spiritual Amnesia
Spiritual Awakening Challenges
Spiritual Bypassing
Spiritual Contracts Reevaluation
Spiritual Parasites
Transgenerational Trauma
Unhealed Emotional Wounds
Vibrational Misalignments

Royal Template 16

Diving Deep into the Pool of the Mind

Chart 49

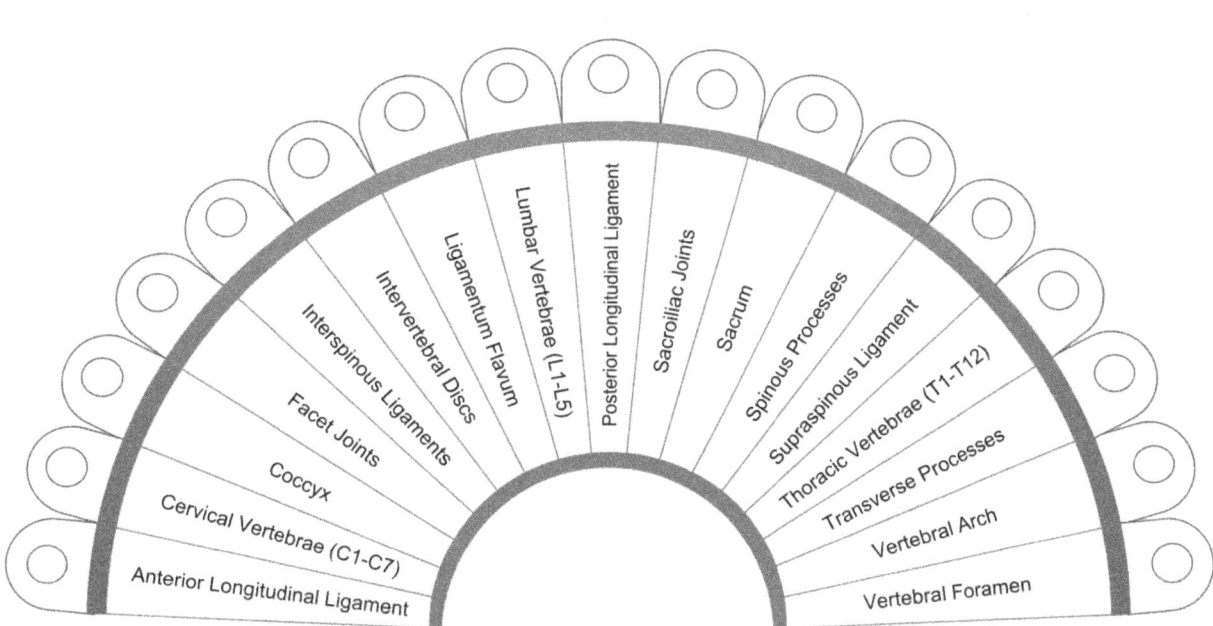

Spinal Column

Anterior Longitudinal Ligament
Cervical Vertebrae (C1-C7)
Coccyx
Facet Joints
Interspinous Ligaments
Intervertebral Discs
Ligamentum Flavum
Lumbar Vertebrae (L1-L5)
Posterior Longitudinal Ligament
Sacroiliac Joints
Sacrum
Spinous Processes
Supraspinous Ligament
Thoracic Vertebrae (T1-T12)
Transverse Processes
Vertebral Arch
Vertebral Foramen

Royal Template 17

Diving Deep into the Pool of the Mind

Chart 50

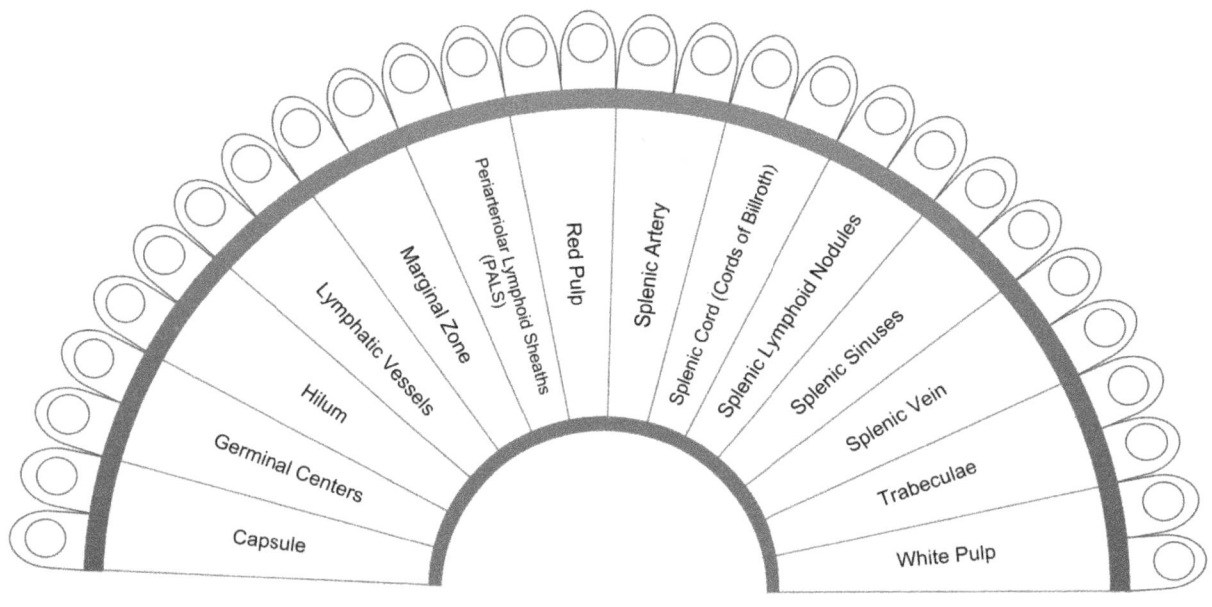

Spleen

Peniarteriolar Lymphoid Sheaths (PALS)
Red Pulp
Splenic Artery
Splenic Cord (Cords of Billroth)
Splenic Lymphoid Nodules
Splenic Sinuses
Splenic Vein
Trabeculae
White Pulp
Marginal Zone
Lymphatic Vessels
Hilum
Germinal Centers
Capsule

Royal Template 14

Diving Deep into the Pool of the Mind

Chart 51

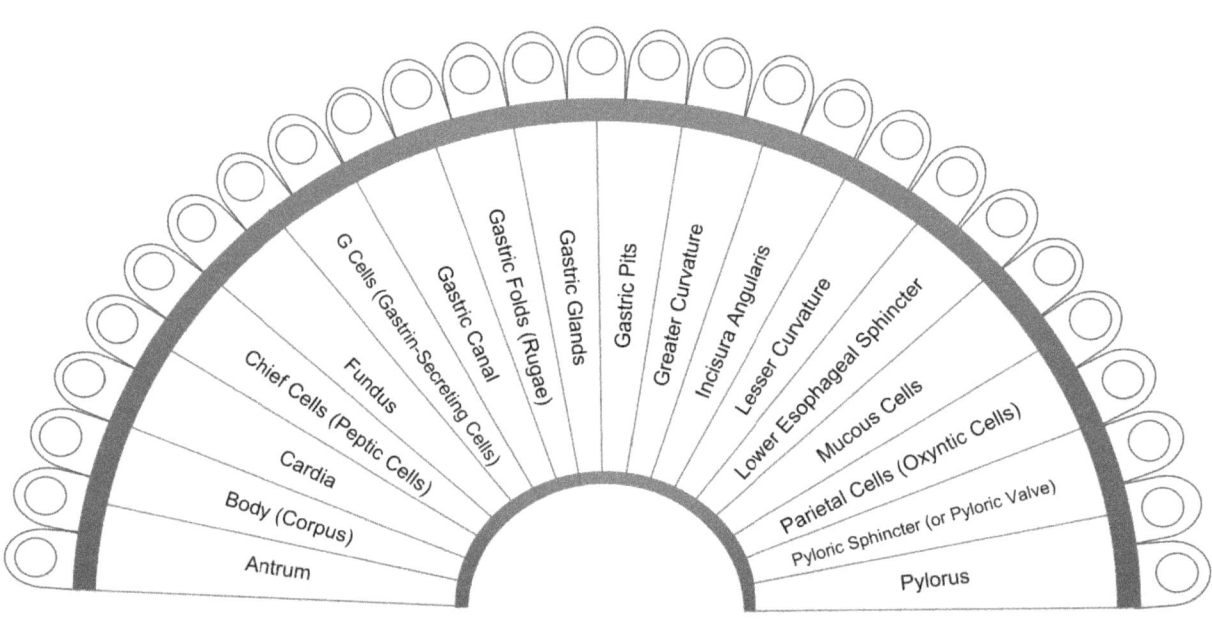

Stomach

G Cells (Gastrin-Secreting Cells)
Gastric Canal
Gastric Folds (Rugae)
Gastric Glands
Gastric Pits
Greater Curvature
Incisura Angularis
Lesser Curvature
Lower Esophageal Sphincter
Mucous Cells
Parietal Cells (Oxyntic Cells)
Pyloric Sphincter (or Pyloric Valve)
Pylorus
Fundus
Chief Cells (Peptic Cells)
Cardia
Body (Corpus)
Antrum

Royal Template 18

Diving Deep into the Pool of the Mind

Chart 52

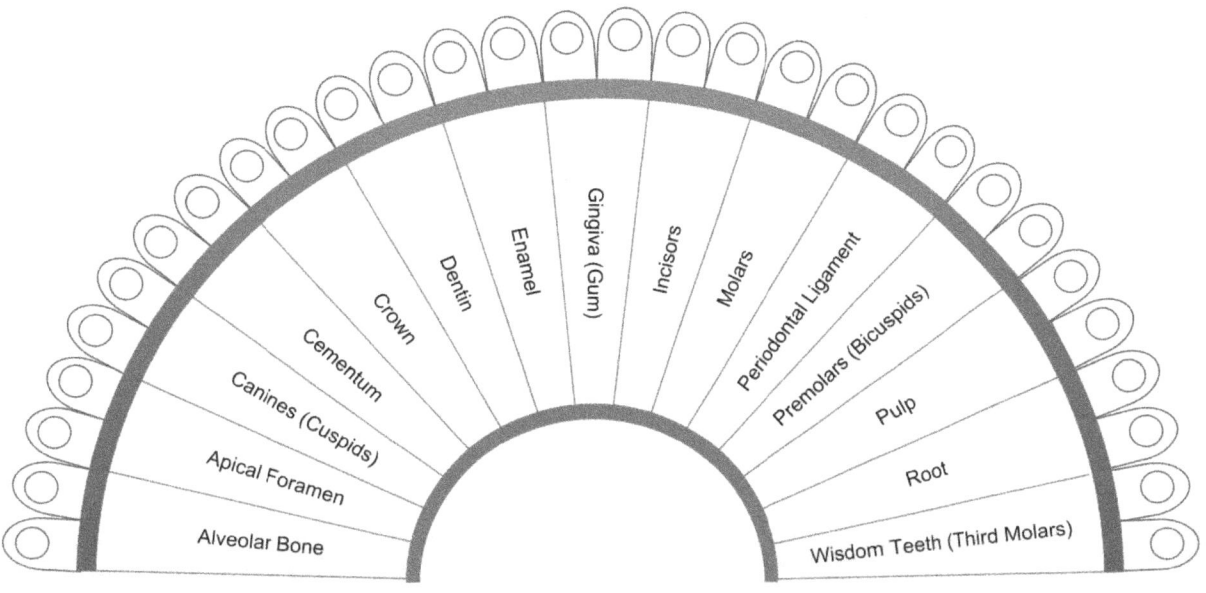

Teeth

Labels (left to right): Alveolar Bone, Apical Foramen, Canines (Cuspids), Cementum, Crown, Dentin, Enamel, Gingiva (Gum), Incisors, Molars, Periodontal Ligament, Premolars (Bicuspids), Pulp, Root, Wisdom Teeth (Third Molars)

Royal Template 15

Diving Deep into the Pool of the Mind

Chart 53

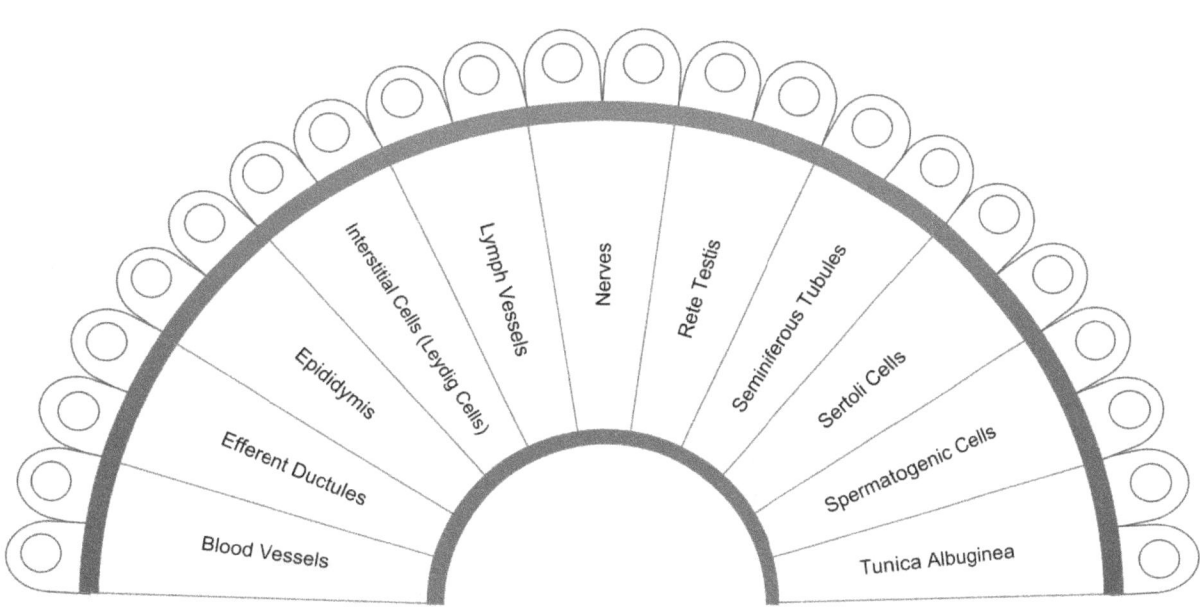

Testes

Labels (left to right): Blood Vessels, Efferent Ductules, Epididymis, Interstitial Cells (Leydig Cells), Lymph Vessels, Nerves, Rete Testis, Seminiferous Tubules, Sertoli Cells, Spermatogenic Cells, Tunica Albuginea

Royal Template 11

Diving Deep into the Pool of the Mind

Chart 54

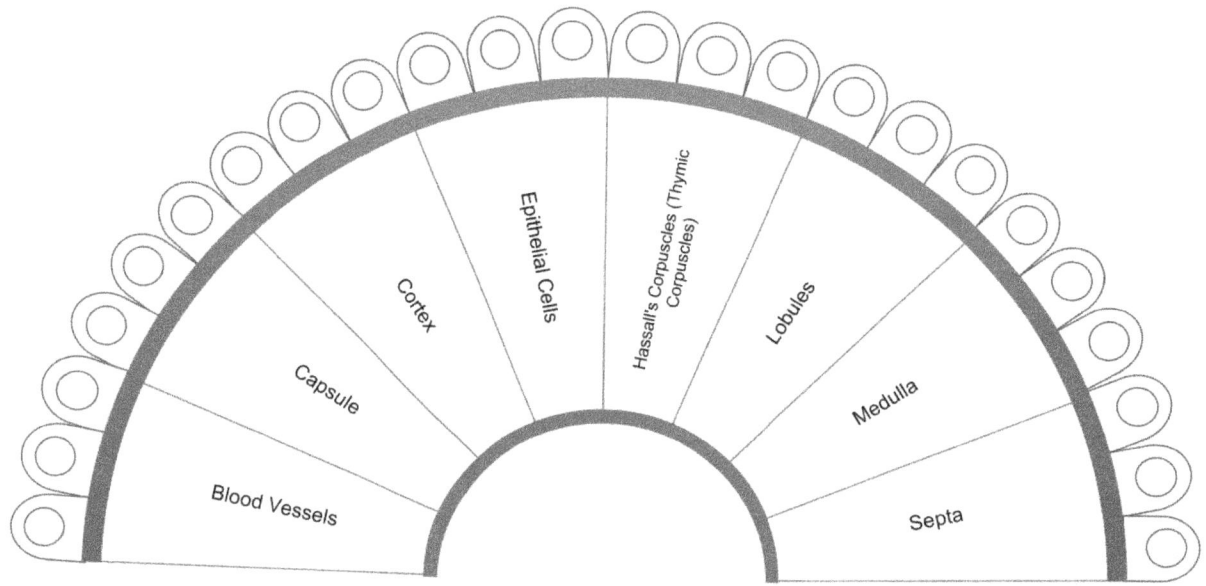

Thymus Gland

Cortex
Epithelial Cells
Hassall's Corpuscles (Thymic Corpuscles)
Lobules
Capsule
Medulla
Blood Vessels
Septa

Royal Template 8

Diving Deep into the Pool of the Mind

Chart 55

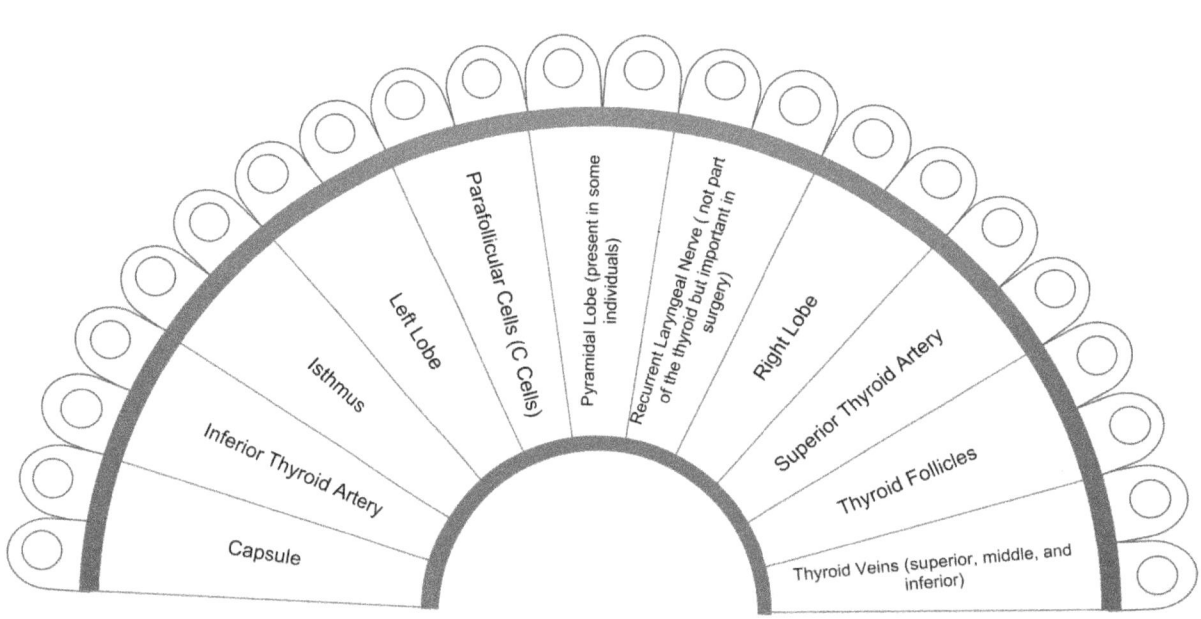

Thyroid

Parafollicular Cells (C Cells)
Pyramidal Lobe (present in some individuals)
Recurrent Laryngeal Nerve (not part of the thyroid but important in surgery)
Left Lobe
Right Lobe
Isthmus
Superior Thyroid Artery
Inferior Thyroid Artery
Thyroid Follicles
Capsule
Thyroid Veins (superior, middle, and inferior)

Royal Template 11

Diving Deep into the Pool of the Mind

Chart 56

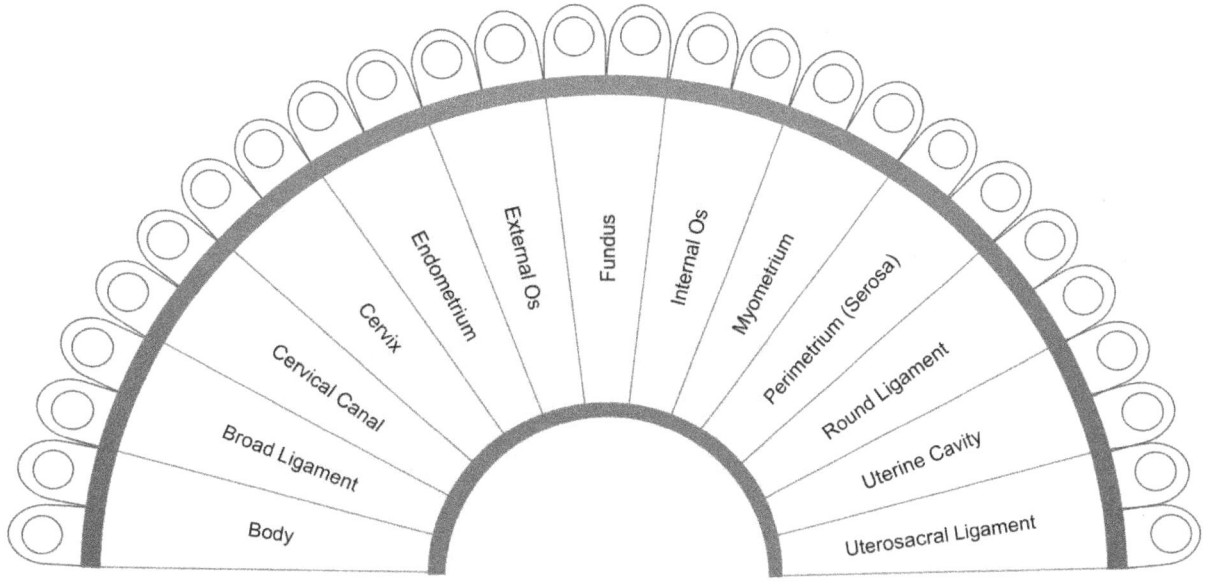

Uterus

Labels (left to right): Body, Broad Ligament, Cervical Canal, Cervix, Endometrium, External Os, Fundus, Internal Os, Myometrium, Perimetrium (Serosa), Round Ligament, Uterine Cavity, Uterosacral Ligament

Royal Template 13

Diving Deep into the Pool of the Mind

Chart 57

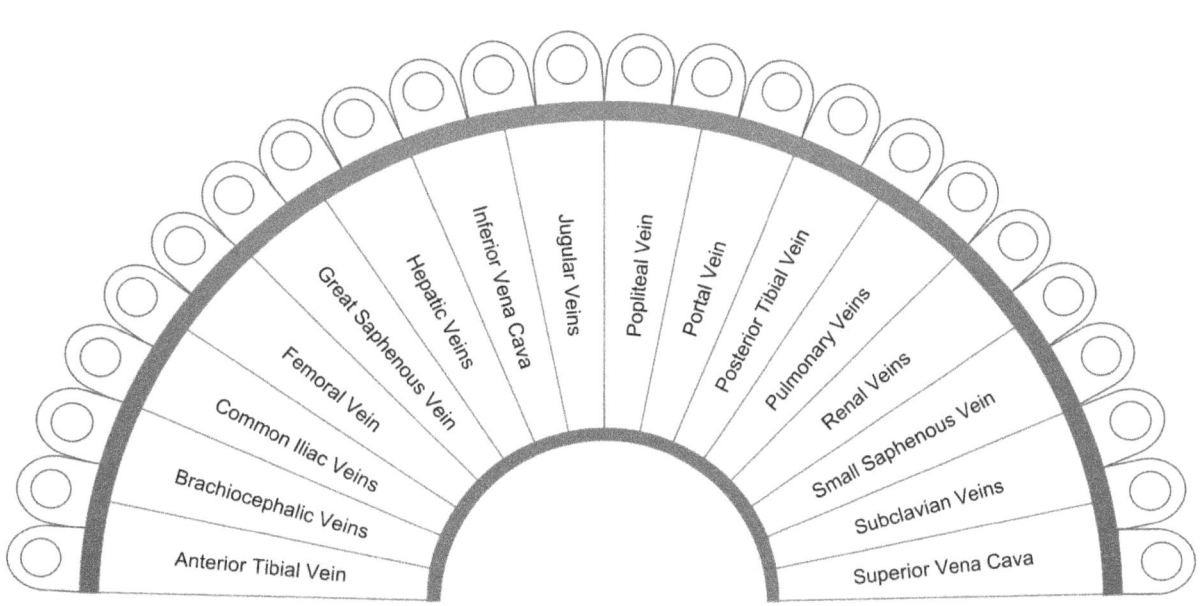

Veins

Labels (left to right): Anterior Tibial Vein, Brachiocephalic Veins, Common Iliac Veins, Femoral Vein, Great Saphenous Vein, Hepatic Veins, Inferior Vena Cava, Jugular Veins, Popliteal Vein, Portal Vein, Posterior Tibial Vein, Pulmonary Veins, Renal Veins, Small Saphenous Vein, Subclavian Veins, Superior Vena Cava

Royal Template 16

Diving Deep into the Pool of the Mind

Chart 58

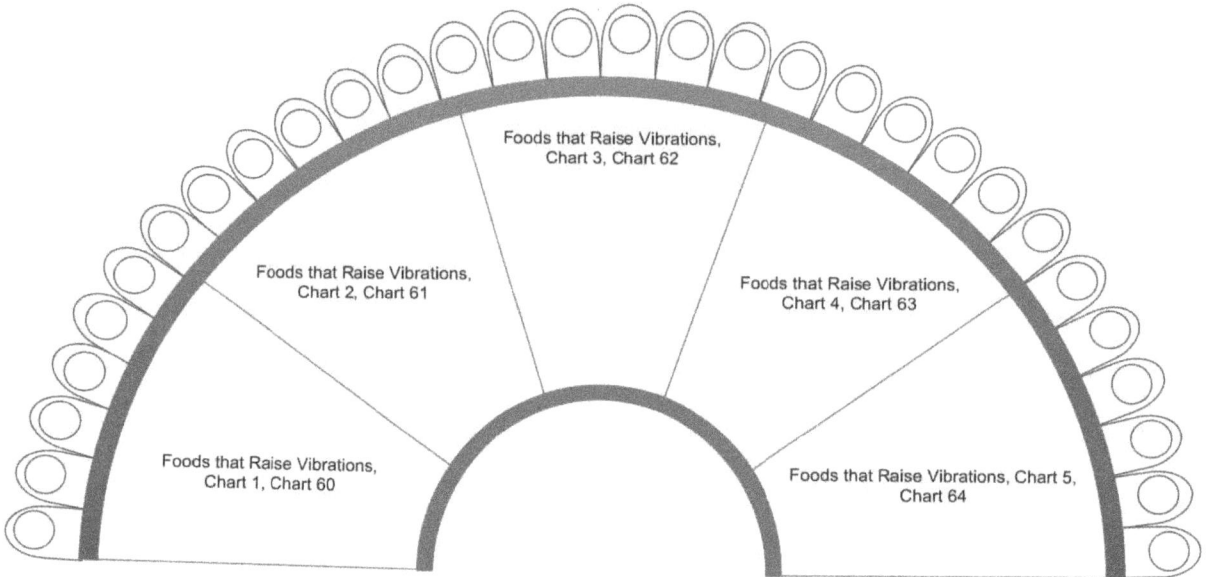

Foods that Raise Vibrations, Master Chart

Foods that Raise Vibrations, Chart 3, Chart 62

Foods that Raise Vibrations, Chart 2, Chart 61

Foods that Raise Vibrations, Chart 4, Chart 63

Foods that Raise Vibrations, Chart 1, Chart 60

Foods that Raise Vibrations, Chart 5, Chart 64

Royal Template 5h

Diving Deep into the Pool of the Mind

Chart 59

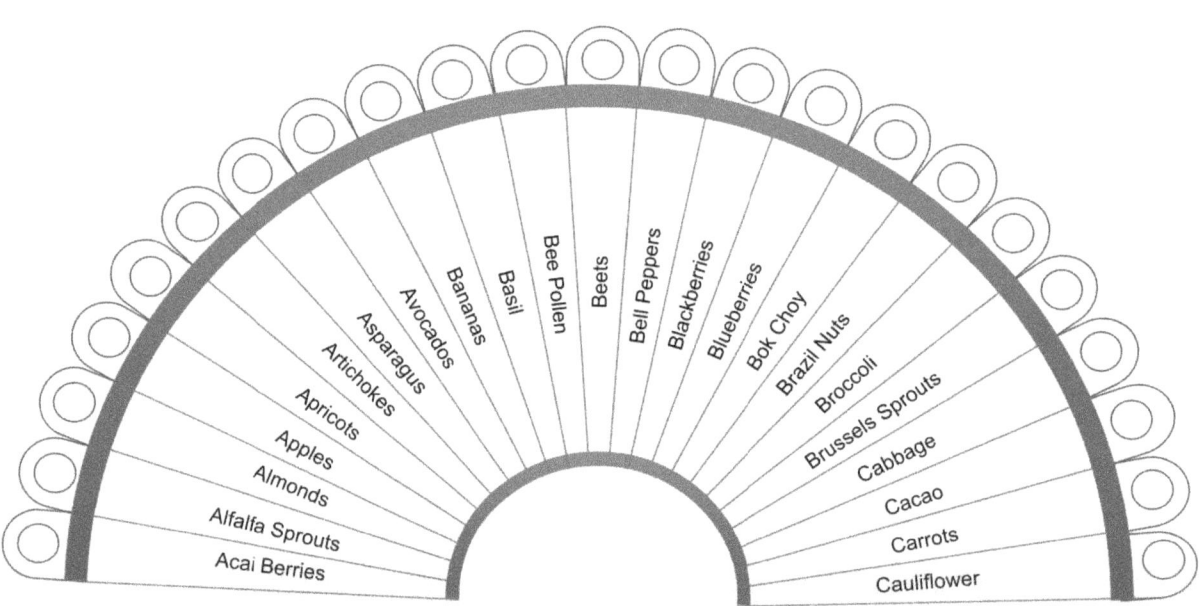

Acai Berries
Alfalfa Sprouts
Almonds
Apples
Apricots
Artichokes
Asparagus
Avocados
Bananas
Basil
Bee Pollen
Beets
Bell Peppers
Blackberries
Blueberries
Bok Choy
Brazil Nuts
Broccoli
Brussels Sprouts
Cabbage
Cacao
Carrots
Cauliflower

Foods that Raise Vibrations, Chart 1

Royal Template 23

Diving Deep into the Pool of the Mind

Chart 60

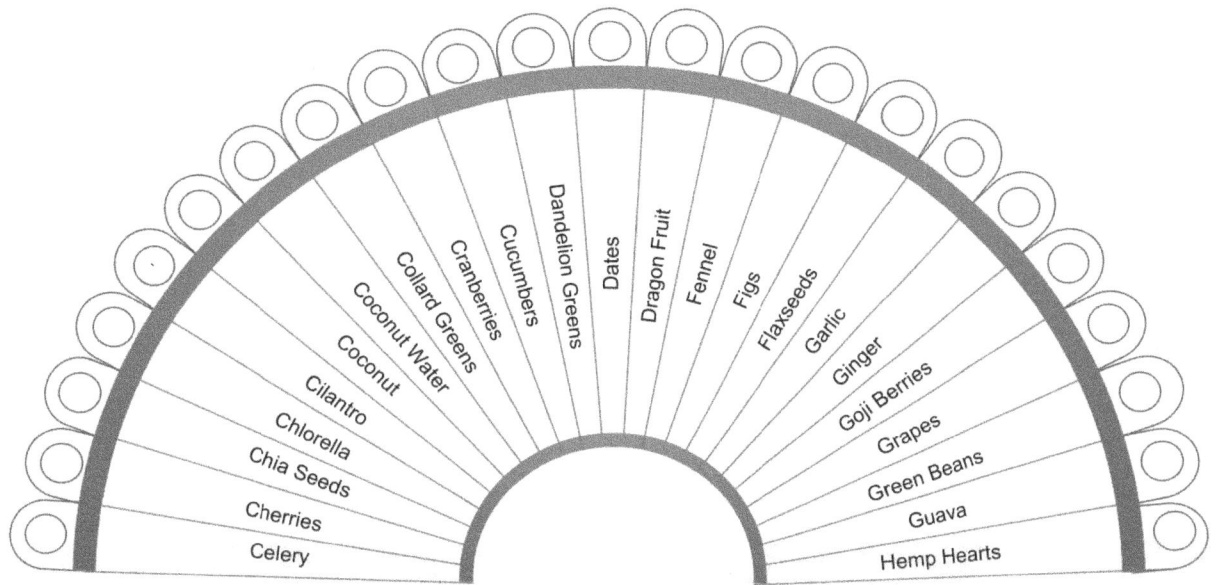

Foods that Raise Vibrations, Chart 2

The chart contains the following items (reading around the fan):

Celery, Cherries, Chia Seeds, Chlorella, Cilantro, Coconut, Coconut Water, Collard Greens, Cranberries, Cucumbers, Dandelion Greens, Dates, Dragon Fruit, Fennel, Figs, Flaxseeds, Garlic, Ginger, Goji Berries, Grapes, Green Beans, Guava, Hemp Hearts

Royal Template 23

Diving Deep into the Pool of the Mind

Chart 61

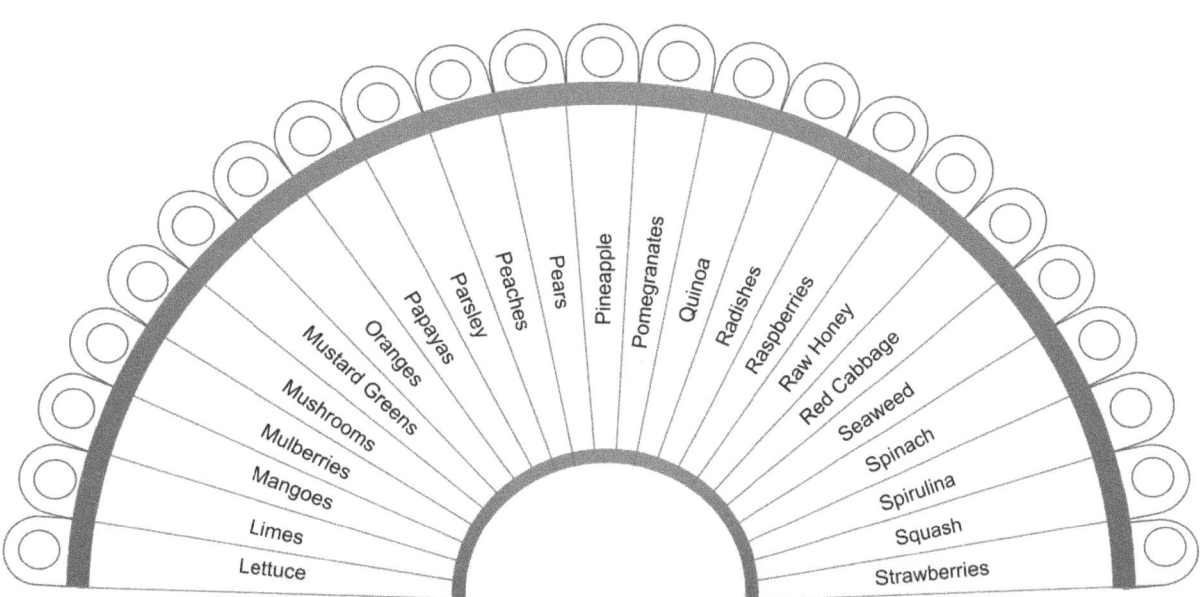

Foods that Raise Vibrations, Chart 3

The chart contains the following items (reading around the fan):

Lettuce, Limes, Mangoes, Mulberries, Mushrooms, Mustard Greens, Oranges, Papayas, Parsley, Peaches, Pears, Pineapple, Pomegranates, Quinoa, Radishes, Raspberries, Raw Honey, Red Cabbage, Seaweed, Spinach, Spirulina, Squash, Strawberries

Royal Template 23

Diving Deep into the Pool of the Mind

Chart 62

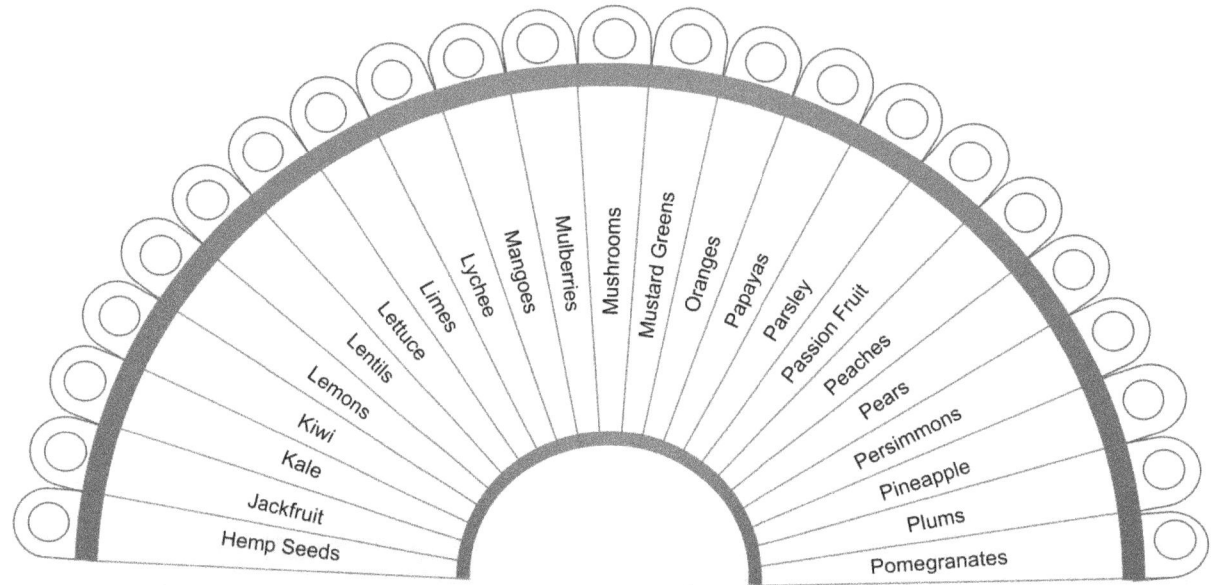

Foods that Raise Vibrations, Chart 4

Hemp Seeds
Jackfruit
Kale
Kiwi
Lemons
Lentils
Lettuce
Limes
Lychee
Mangoes
Mulberries
Mushrooms
Mustard Greens
Oranges
Papayas
Parsley
Passion Fruit
Peaches
Pears
Persimmons
Pineapple
Plums
Pomegranates

Royal Template 23

Diving Deep into the Pool of the Mind

Chart 63

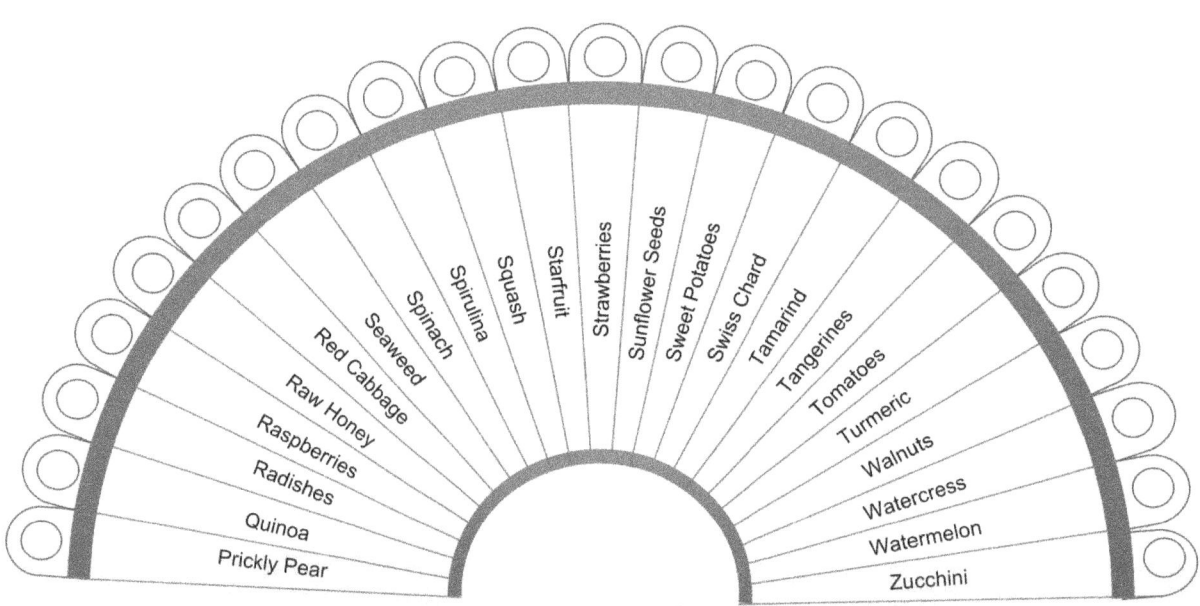

Prickly Pear
Quinoa
Radishes
Raspberries
Raw Honey
Red Cabbage
Seaweed
Spinach
Spirulina
Squash
Starfruit
Strawberries
Sunflower Seeds
Sweet Potatoes
Swiss Chard
Tamarind
Tangerines
Tomatoes
Turmeric
Walnuts
Watercress
Watermelon
Zucchini

Foods that Raise Vibrations, Chart 5

Royal Template 23

Diving Deep into the Pool of the Mind

Chart 64

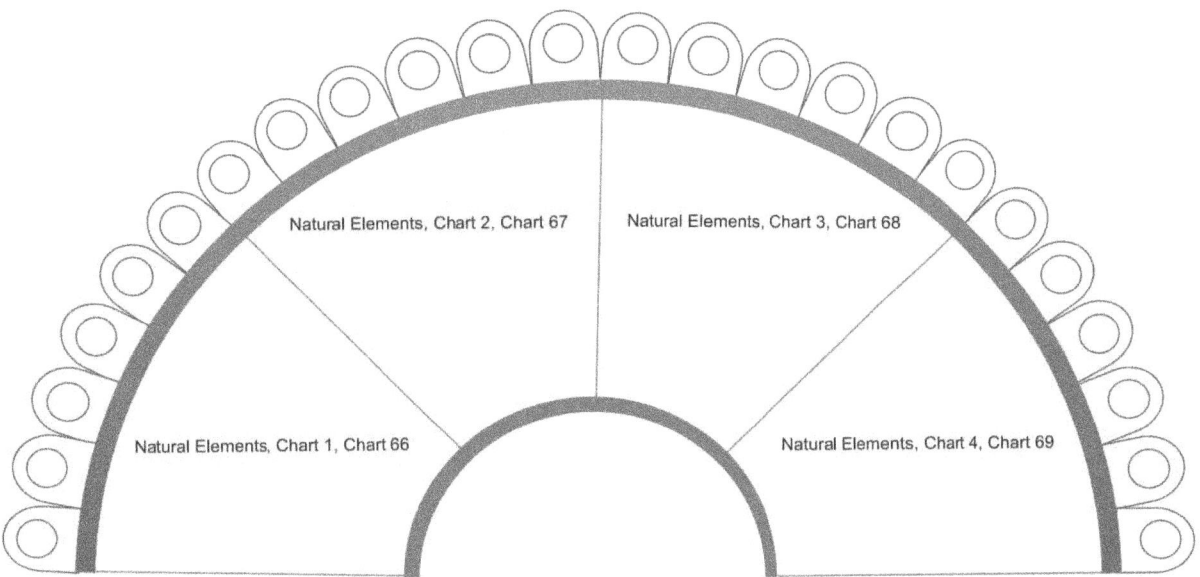

Natural Elements, Master Chart

Natural Elements, Chart 2, Chart 67

Natural Elements, Chart 3, Chart 68

Natural Elements, Chart 1, Chart 66

Natural Elements, Chart 4, Chart 69

Royal Template 4h

Diving Deep into the Pool of the Mind

Chart 65

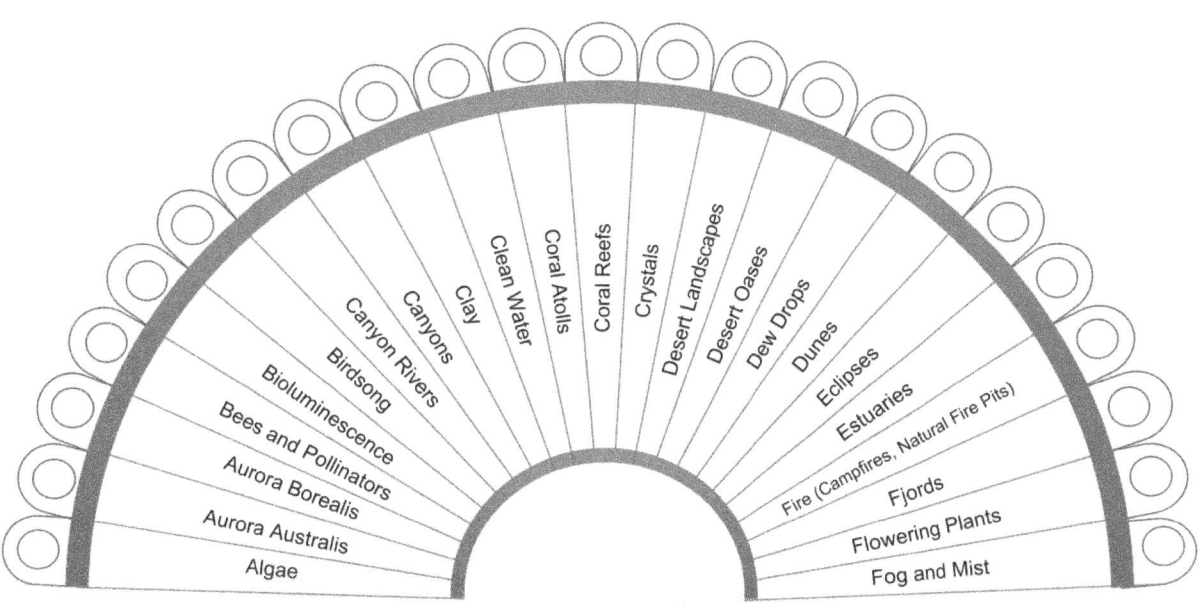

Clean Water
Clay
Canyons
Canyon Rivers
Birdsong
Bioluminescence
Bees and Pollinators
Aurora Borealis
Aurora Australis
Algae

Coral Reefs
Coral Atolls
Crystals
Desert Landscapes
Desert Oases
Dew Drops
Dunes
Eclipses
Estuaries
Fire (Campfires, Natural Fire Pits)
Fjords
Flowering Plants
Fog and Mist

Natural Elements, Chart 1

Royal Template 23

Diving Deep into the Pool of the Mind

Chart 66

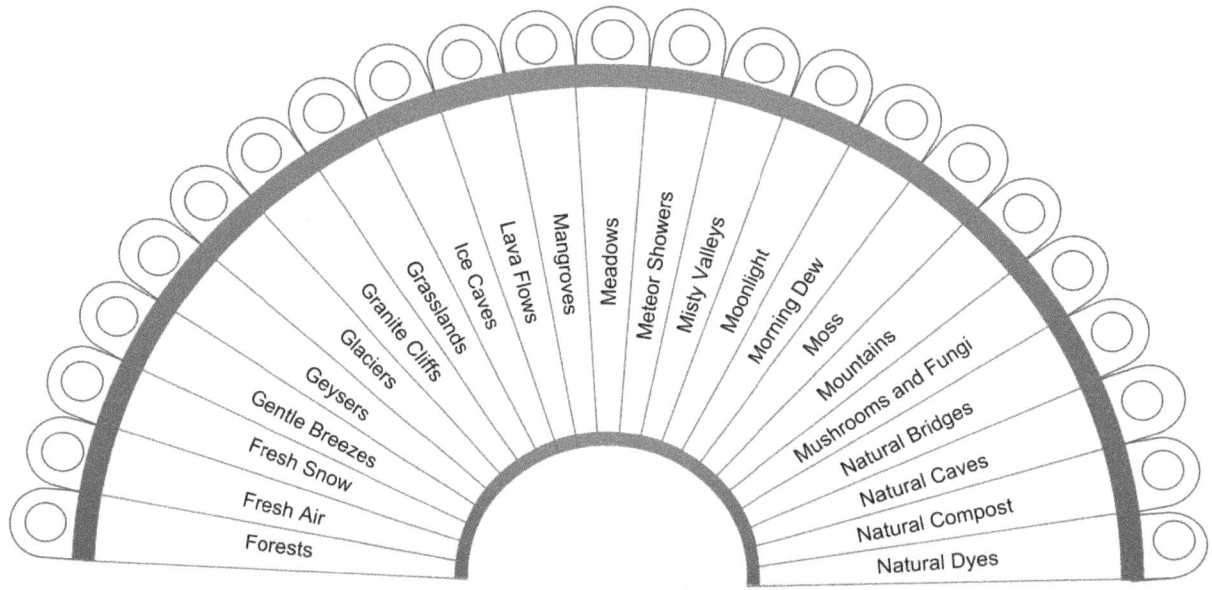

Natural Elements, Chart 2

The fan chart contains the following labels (left to right):

Forests, Fresh Air, Fresh Snow, Gentle Breezes, Geysers, Glaciers, Granite Cliffs, Grasslands, Ice Caves, Lava Flows, Mangroves, Meadows, Meteor Showers, Misty Valleys, Moonlight, Morning Dew, Moss, Mountains, Mushrooms and Fungi, Natural Bridges, Natural Caves, Natural Compost, Natural Dyes

Royal Template 23

Diving Deep into the Pool of the Mind

Chart 67

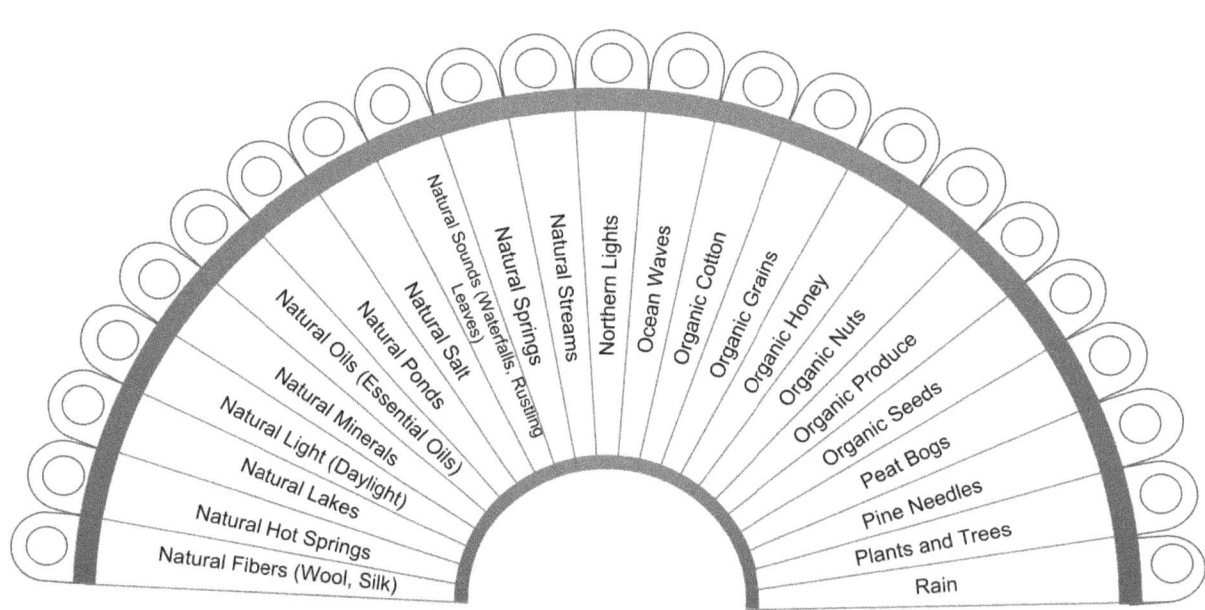

Natural Elements, Chart 3

The fan chart contains the following labels (left to right):

Natural Fibers (Wool, Silk), Natural Hot Springs, Natural Lakes, Natural Light (Daylight), Natural Minerals, Natural Oils (Essential Oils), Natural Ponds, Natural Salt, Natural Springs, Natural Sounds (Waterfalls, Rustling Leaves), Natural Streams, Northern Lights, Ocean Waves, Organic Cotton, Organic Grains, Organic Honey, Organic Nuts, Organic Produce, Organic Seeds, Peat Bogs, Pine Needles, Plants and Trees, Rain

Royal Template 23

Diving Deep into the Pool of the Mind

Chart 68

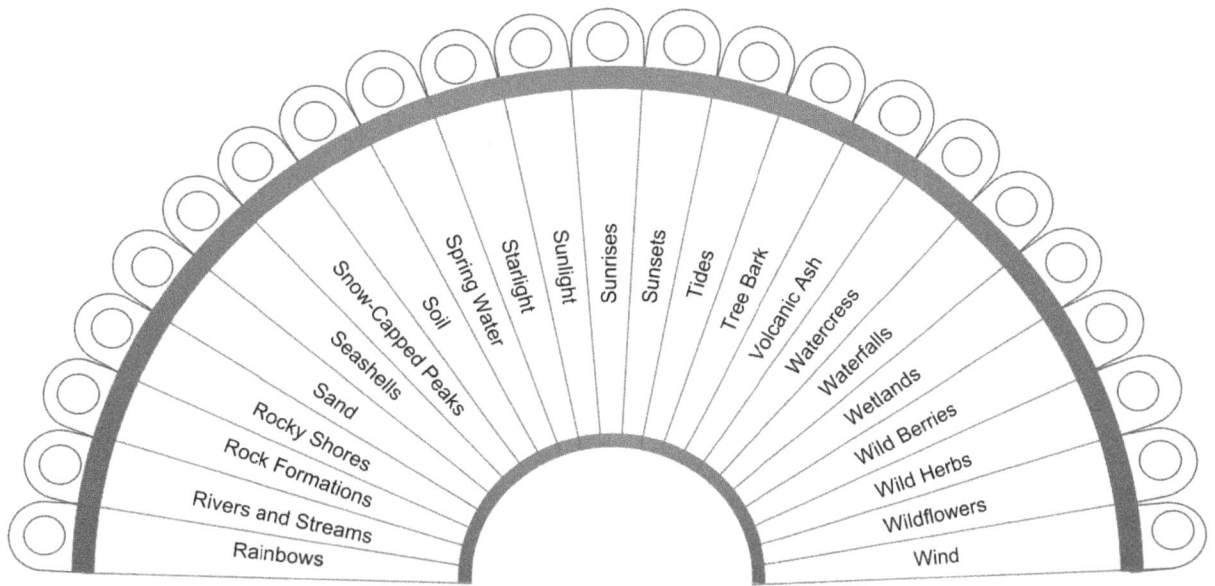

Natural Elements, Chart 4

Labels (left to right): Rainbows, Rivers and Streams, Rock Formations, Rocky Shores, Sand, Seashells, Snow-Capped Peaks, Soil, Spring Water, Starlight, Sunlight, Sunrises, Sunsets, Tides, Tree Bark, Volcanic Ash, Watercress, Waterfalls, Wetlands, Wild Berries, Wild Herbs, Wildflowers, Wind

Diving Deep into the Pool of the Mind

Chart 69

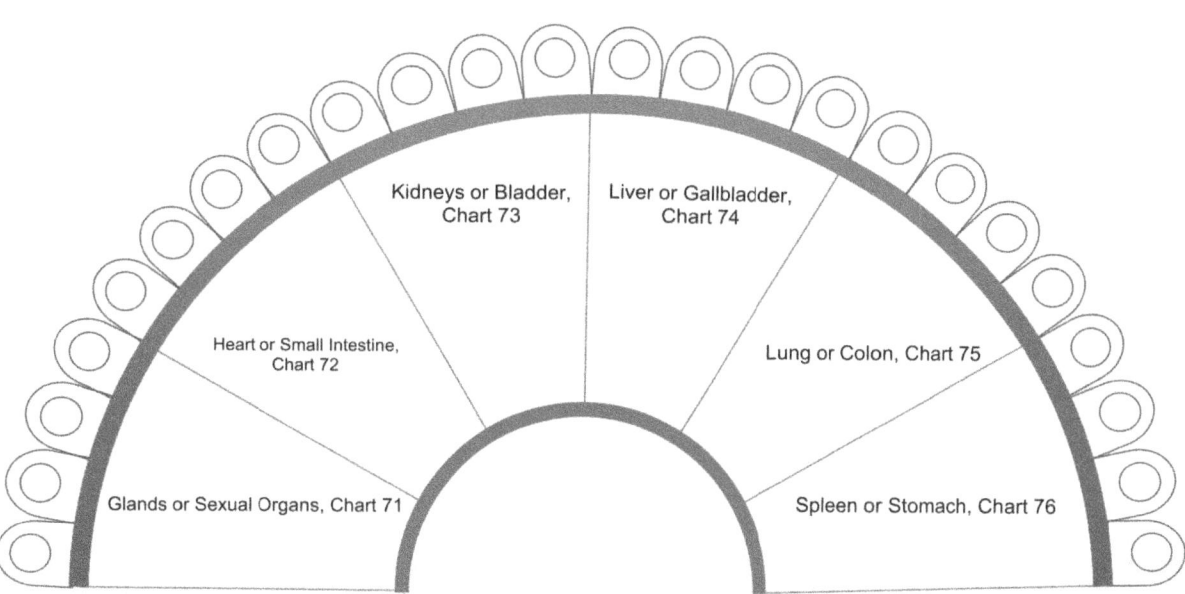

Labels:
- Glands or Sexual Organs, Chart 71
- Heart or Small Intestine, Chart 72
- Kidneys or Bladder, Chart 73
- Liver or Gallbladder, Chart 74
- Lung or Colon, Chart 75
- Spleen or Stomach, Chart 76

Trapped Emotions, Master Chart (See Page 4)

Diving Deep into the Pool of the Mind

Chart 70

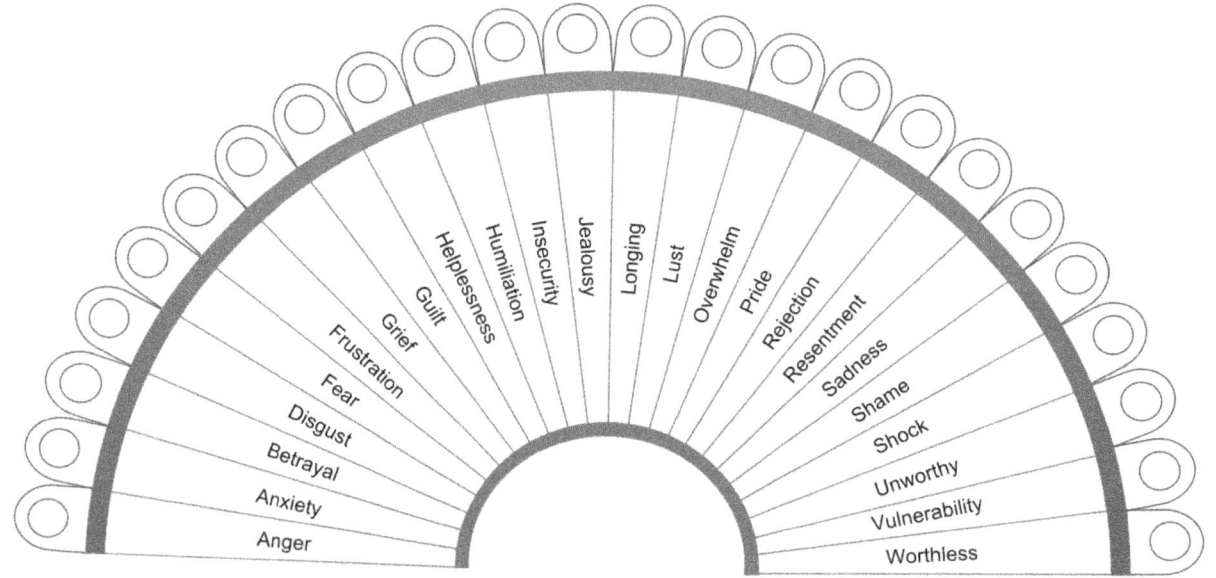

Glands or Sexual Organs

The chart contains the following emotions around the fan (left to right):

Anger, Anxiety, Betrayal, Disgust, Fear, Frustration, Grief, Guilt, Helplessness, Humiliation, Insecurity, Jealousy, Longing, Lust, Overwhelm, Pride, Rejection, Resentment, Sadness, Shame, Shock, Unworthy, Vulnerability, Worthless

Royal Template 24

Diving Deep into the Pool of the Mind

Chart 71

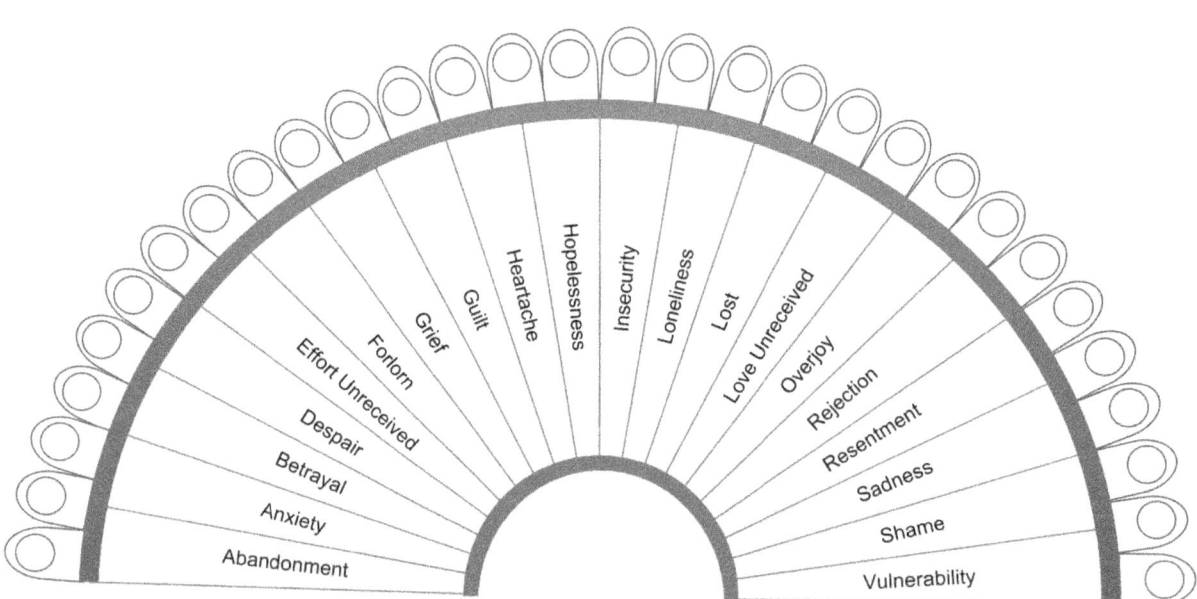

Heart or Small Intestine

The chart contains the following emotions around the fan (left to right):

Abandonment, Anxiety, Betrayal, Despair, Effort Unreceived, Forlorn, Grief, Guilt, Heartache, Hopelessness, Insecurity, Loneliness, Lost, Love Unreceived, Overjoy, Rejection, Resentment, Sadness, Shame, Vulnerability

Royal Template 20

Diving Deep into the Pool of the Mind

Chart 72

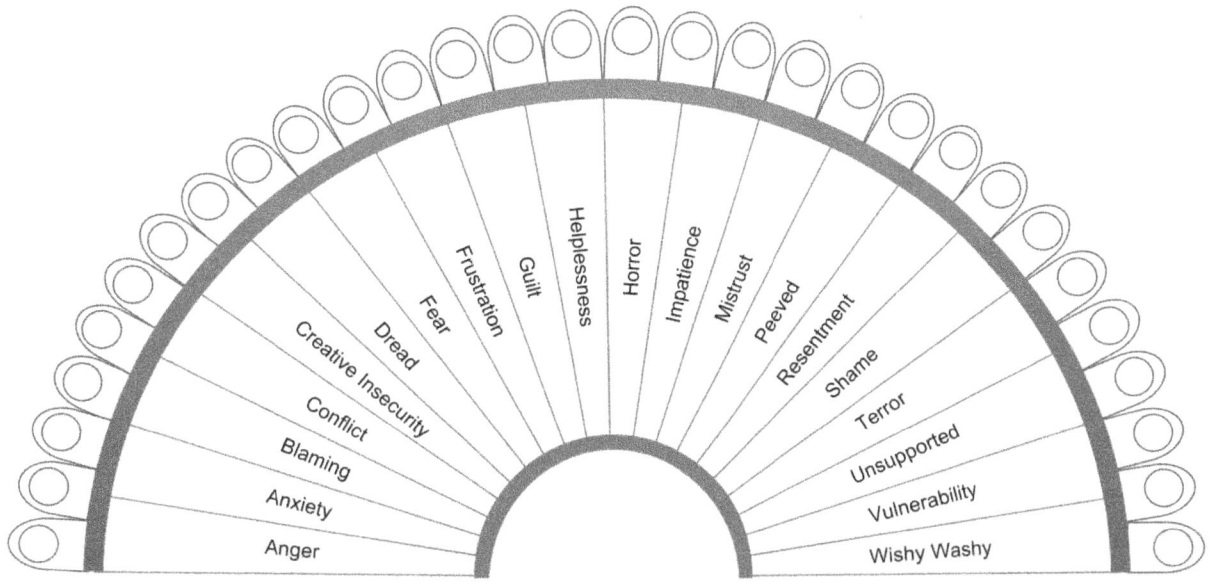

Kidneys or Bladder

Anger, Anxiety, Blaming, Conflict, Creative Insecurity, Dread, Fear, Frustration, Guilt, Helplessness, Horror, Impatience, Mistrust, Peeved, Resentment, Shame, Terror, Unsupported, Vulnerability, Wishy Washy

Royal Template 20

Diving Deep into the Pool of the Mind

Chart 73

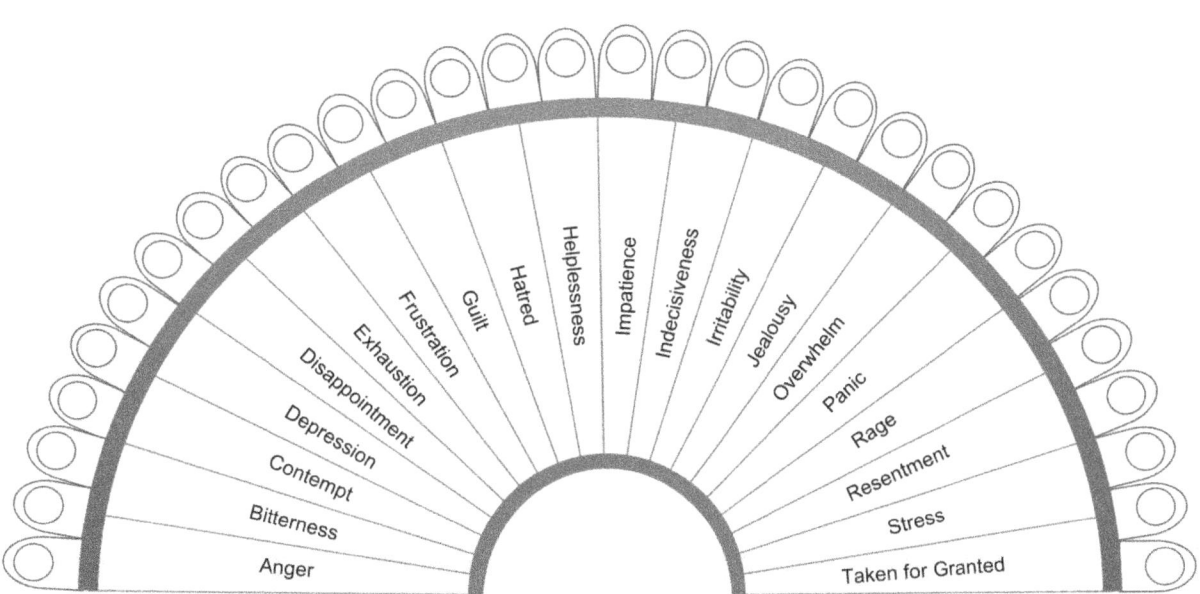

Liver or Gallbladder

Anger, Bitterness, Contempt, Depression, Disappointment, Exhaustion, Frustration, Guilt, Hatred, Helplessness, Impatience, Indecisiveness, Irritability, Jealousy, Overwhelm, Panic, Rage, Resentment, Stress, Taken for Granted

Royal Template 20

Diving Deep into the Pool of the Mind

Chart 74

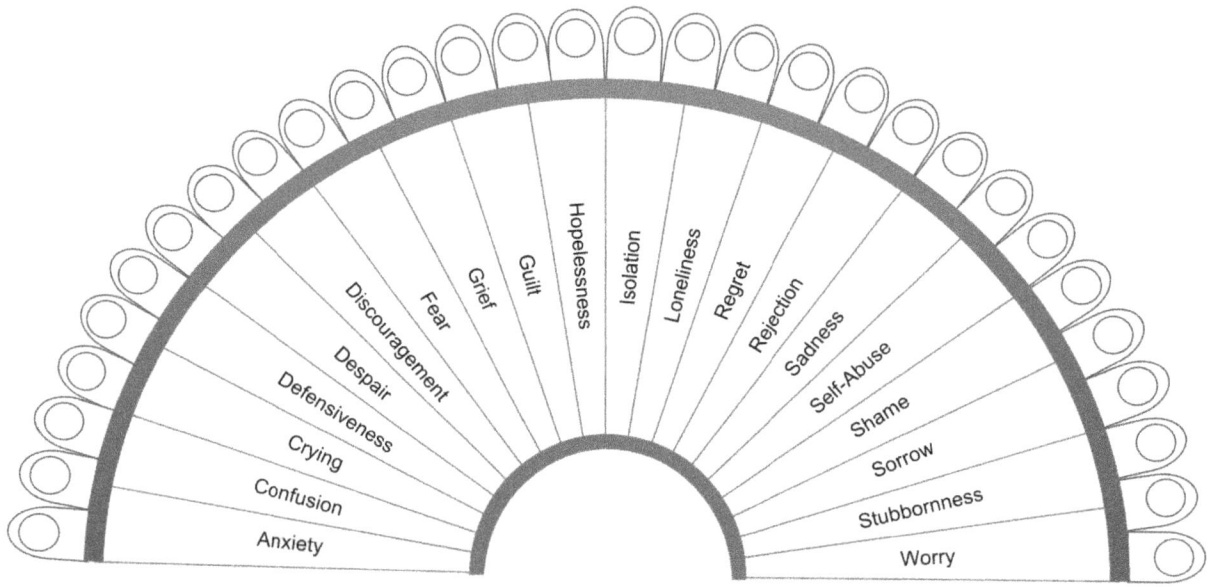

Lung or Colon

The chart contains the following labels, reading clockwise: Anxiety, Confusion, Crying, Defensiveness, Despair, Discouragement, Fear, Grief, Guilt, Hopelessness, Isolation, Loneliness, Regret, Rejection, Sadness, Self-Abuse, Shame, Sorrow, Stubbornness, Worry

Royal Template 20

Diving Deep into the Pool of the Mind

Chart 75

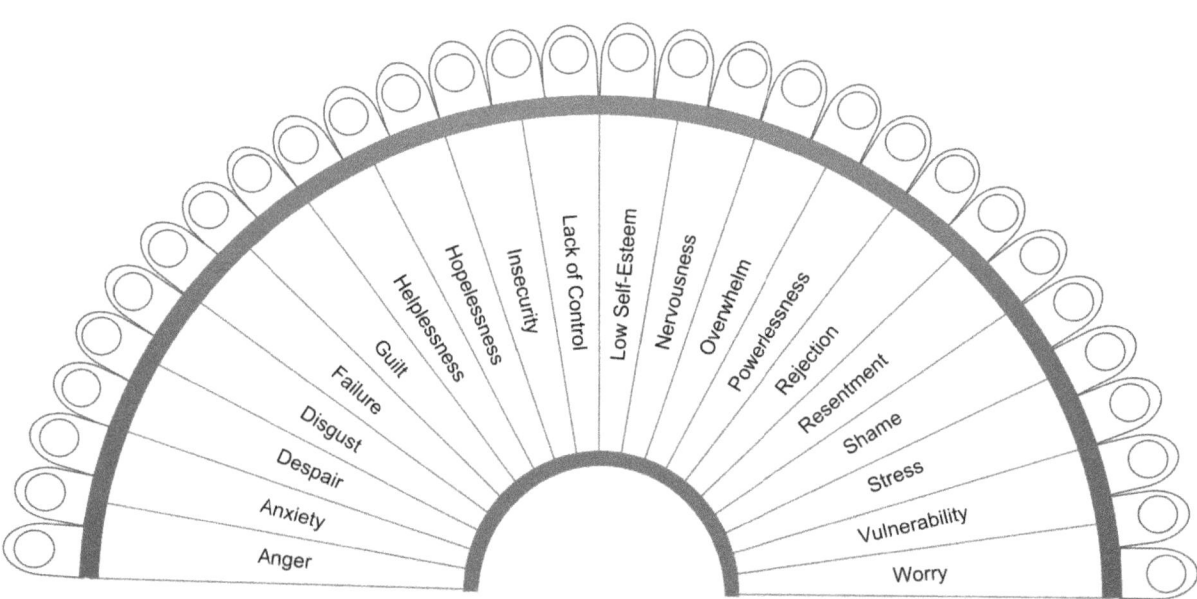

Spleen or Stomach

The chart contains the following labels, reading clockwise: Anger, Anxiety, Despair, Disgust, Failure, Guilt, Helplessness, Hopelessness, Insecurity, Lack of Control, Low Self-Esteem, Nervousness, Overwhelm, Powerlessness, Rejection, Resentment, Shame, Stress, Vulnerability, Worry

Royal Template 20

Diving Deep into the Pool of the Mind

Chart 76

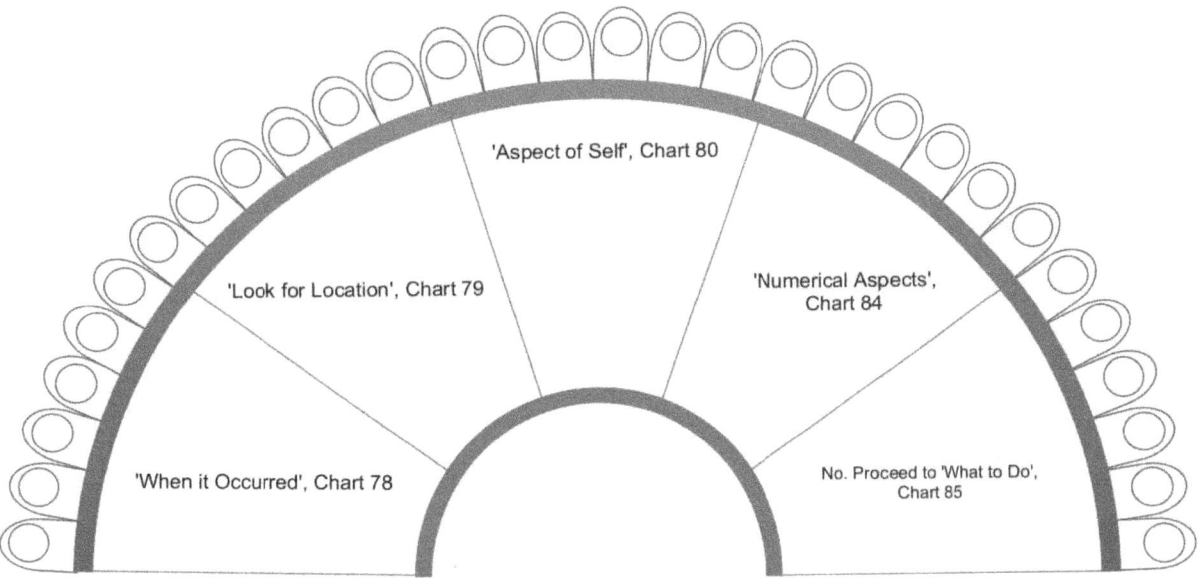

'Aspect of Self', Chart 80

'Look for Location', Chart 79

'Numerical Aspects', Chart 84

'When it Occurred', Chart 78

No. Proceed to 'What to Do', Chart 85

Decode More?

Royal Template 5h

Diving Deep into the Pool of the Mind

Chart 77

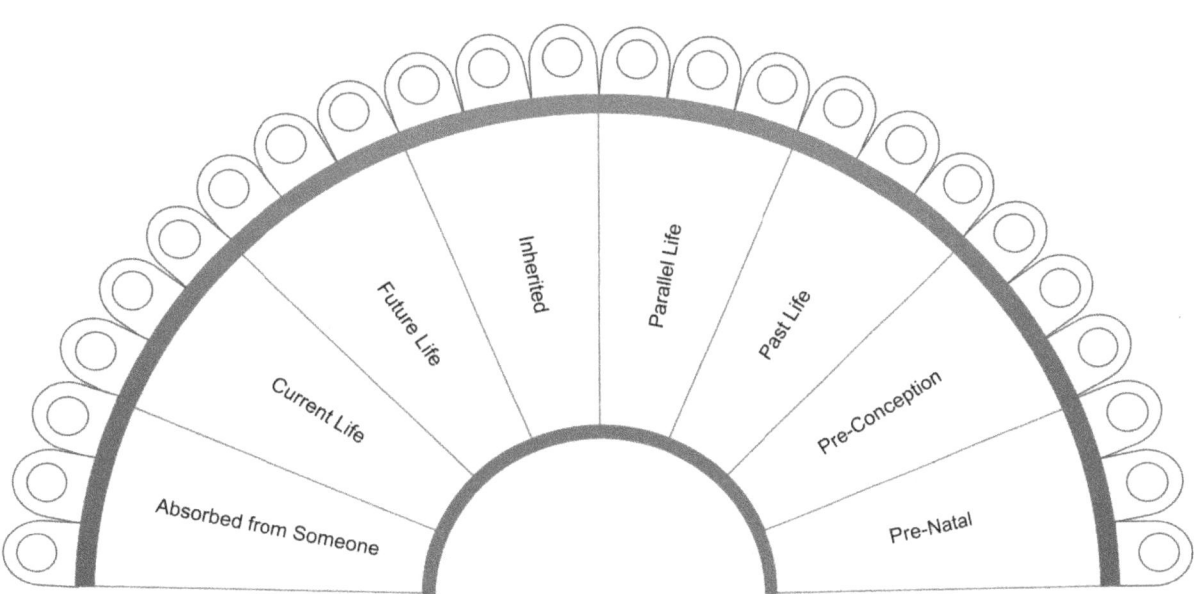

Inherited

Parallel Life

Future Life

Past Life

Current Life

Pre-Conception

Absorbed from Someone

Pre-Natal

When it Occurred

Royal Template 8

Diving Deep into the Pool of the Mind

Chart 78

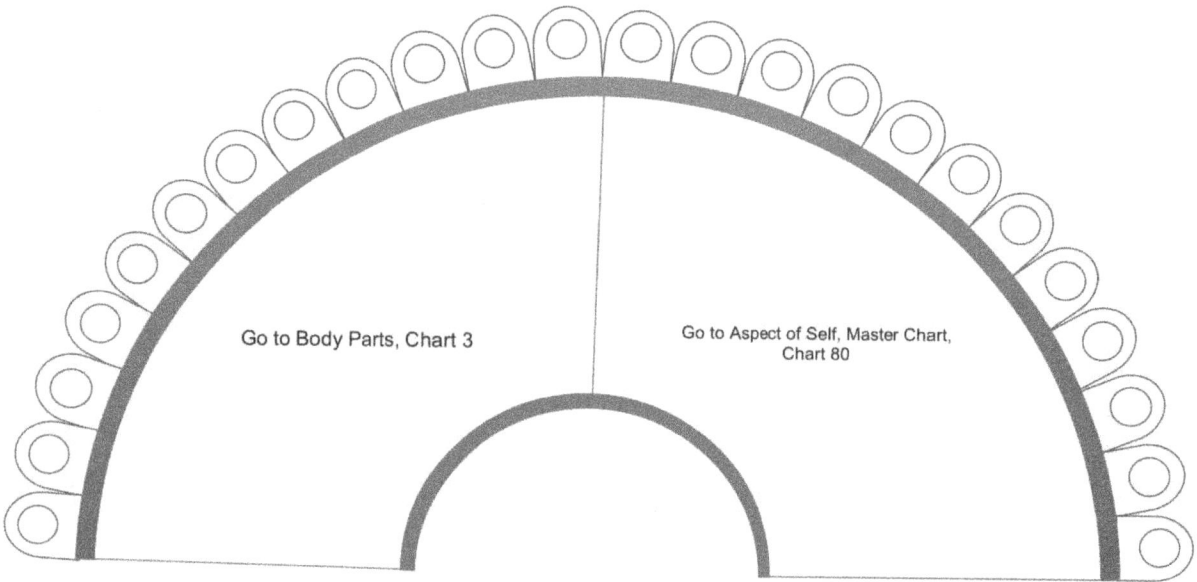

Go to Body Parts, Chart 3

Go to Aspect of Self, Master Chart, Chart 80

Look for Location

Royal Template 2

Diving Deep into the Pool of the Mind

Chart 79

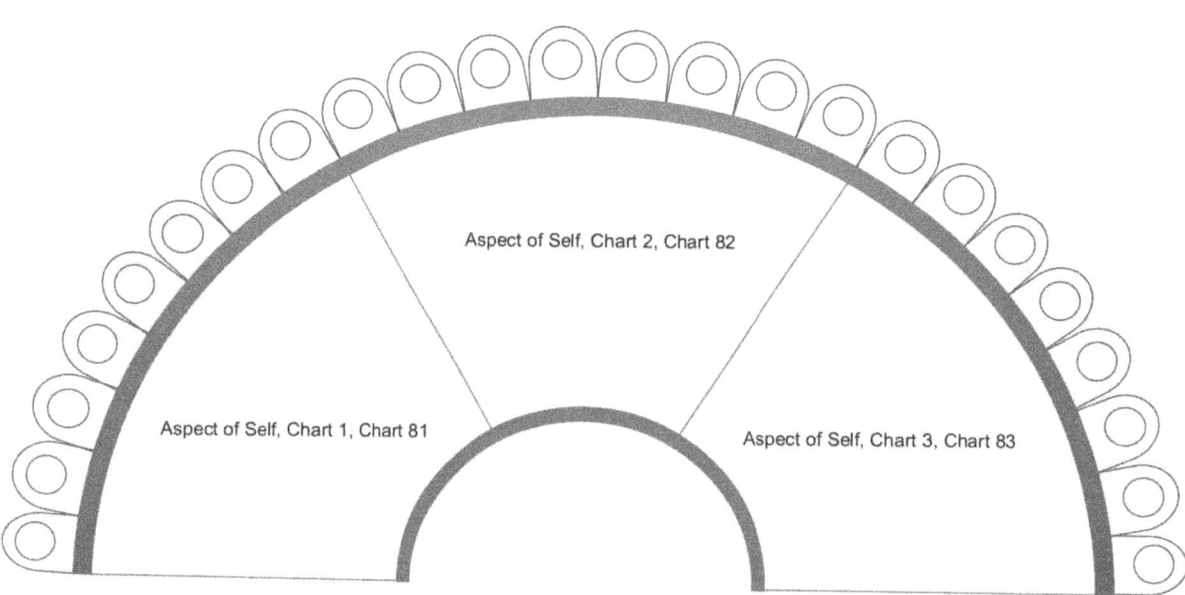

Aspect of Self, Chart 2, Chart 82

Aspect of Self, Chart 1, Chart 81

Aspect of Self, Chart 3, Chart 83

Aspect of Self, Master Chart

Royal Template 3h

Diving Deep into the Pool of the Mind

Chart 80

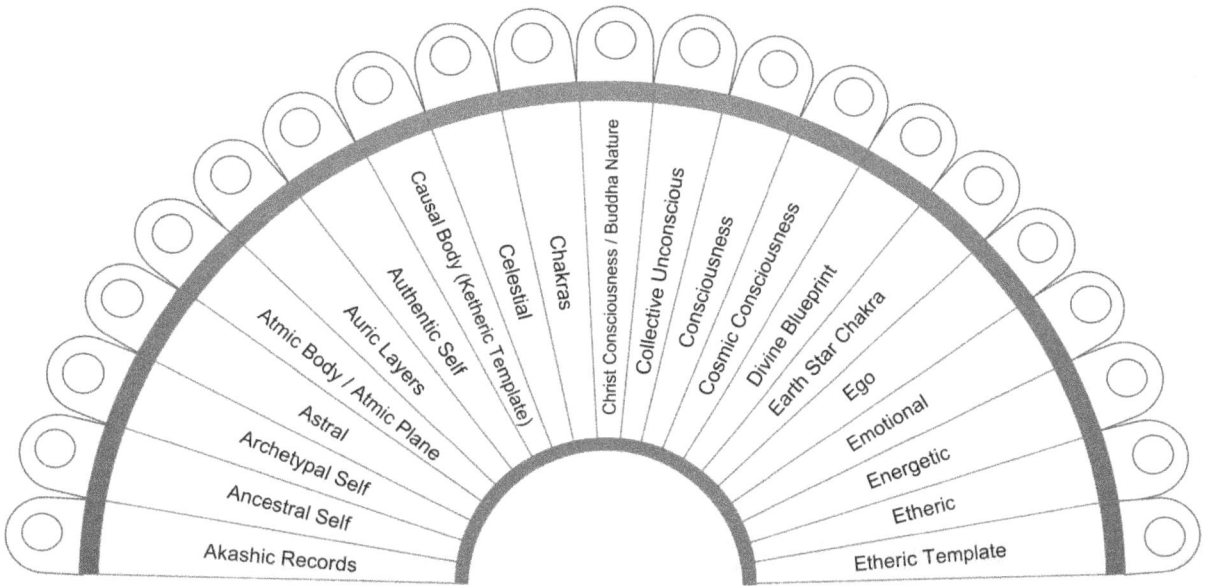

Aspect of Self, Chart 1

Atmic Body / Atmic Plane
Auric Layers
Authentic Self
Causal Body (Ketheric Template)
Celestial
Chakras
Christ Consciousness / Buddha Nature
Collective Unconscious
Consciousness
Cosmic Consciousness
Divine Blueprint
Earth Star Chakra
Ego
Emotional
Energetic
Etheric
Etheric Template
Akashic Records
Ancestral Self
Archetypal Self
Astral

Royal Template 21

Diving Deep into the Pool of the Mind

Chart 81

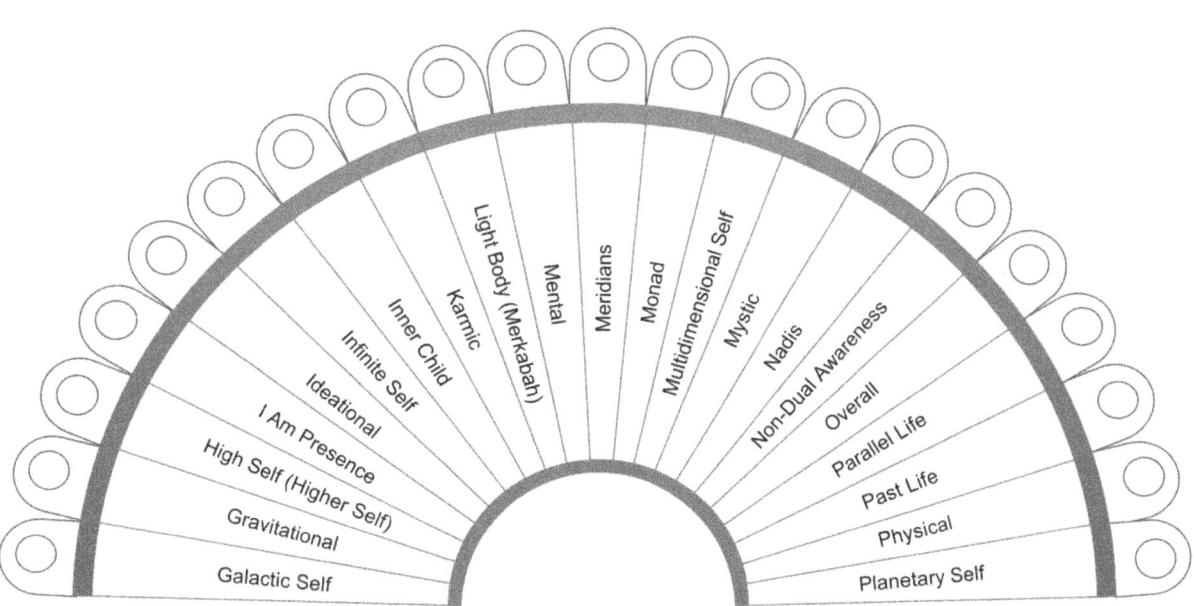

Aspect of Self, Chart 2

Galactic Self
Gravitational
High Self (Higher Self)
I Am Presence
Ideational
Infinite Self
Inner Child
Karmic
Light Body (Merkabah)
Mental
Meridians
Monad
Multidimensional Self
Mystic
Nadis
Non-Dual Awareness
Overall
Parallel Life
Past Life
Physical
Planetary Self

Royal Template 21

Diving Deep into the Pool of the Mind

Chart 82

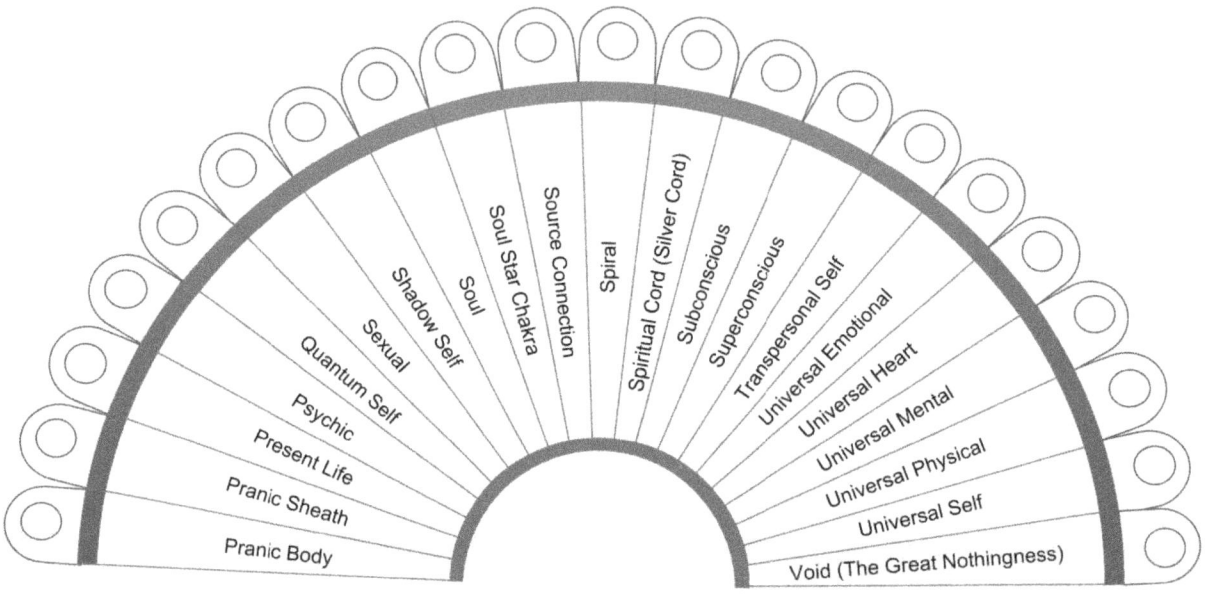

Aspect of Self, Chart 3

The chart contains the following labels (counterclockwise from left):
Pranic Body, Pranic Sheath, Present Life, Psychic, Quantum Self, Sexual, Shadow Self, Soul, Soul Star Chakra, Source Connection, Spiral, Spiritual Cord (Silver Cord), Subconscious, Superconscious, Transpersonal Self, Universal Emotional, Universal Heart, Universal Mental, Universal Physical, Universal Self, Void (The Great Nothingness)

Royal Template 21

Diving Deep into the Pool of the Mind

Chart 83

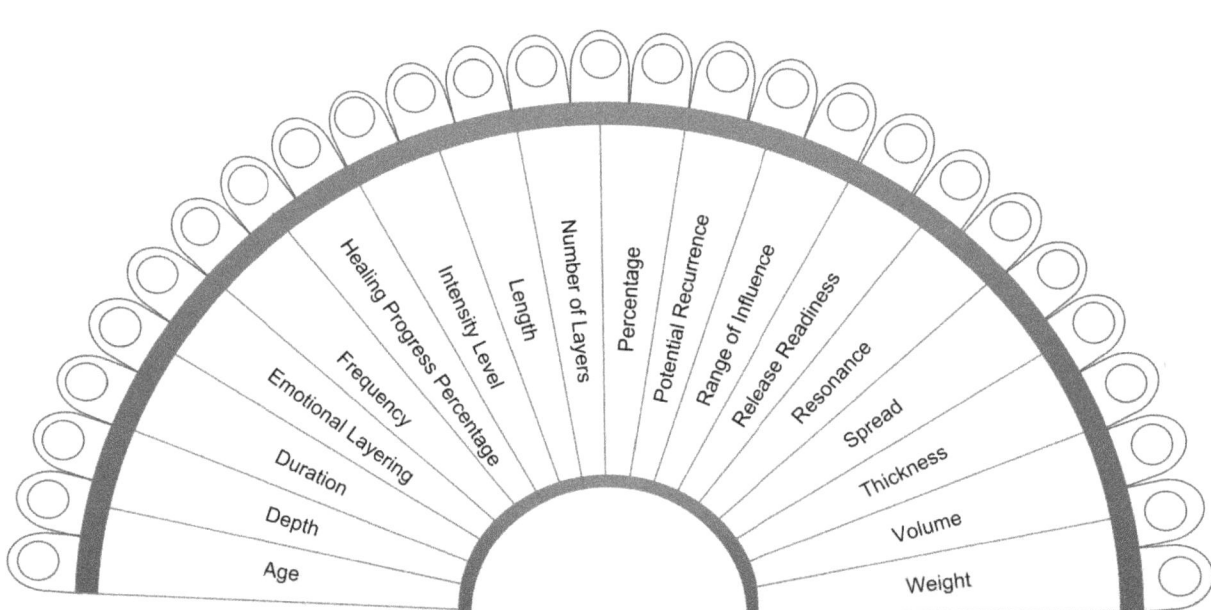

Numerical Aspects

The chart contains the following labels (counterclockwise from left):
Age, Depth, Duration, Emotional Layering, Frequency, Healing Progress Percentage, Intensity Level, Length, Number of Layers, Percentage, Potential Recurrence, Range of Influence, Release Readiness, Resonance, Spread, Thickness, Volume, Weight

Royal Template 18

Diving Deep into the Pool of the Mind

Chart 84

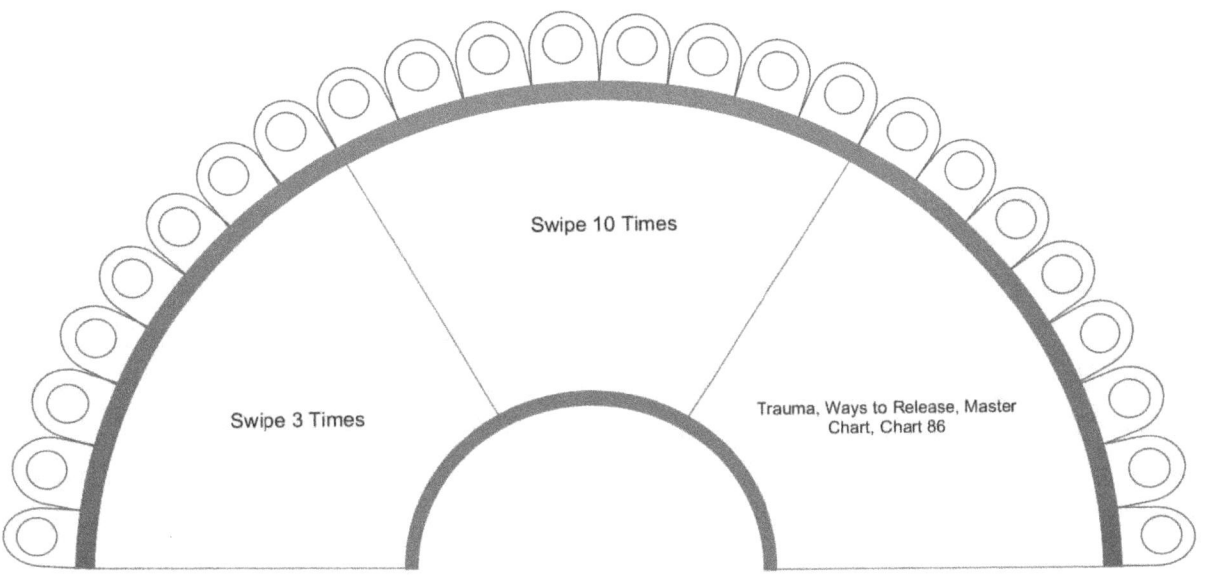

Swipe 10 Times

Swipe 3 Times

Trauma, Ways to Release, Master Chart, Chart 86

What to Do

Royal Template 3h

Diving Deep into the Pool of the Mind

Chart 85

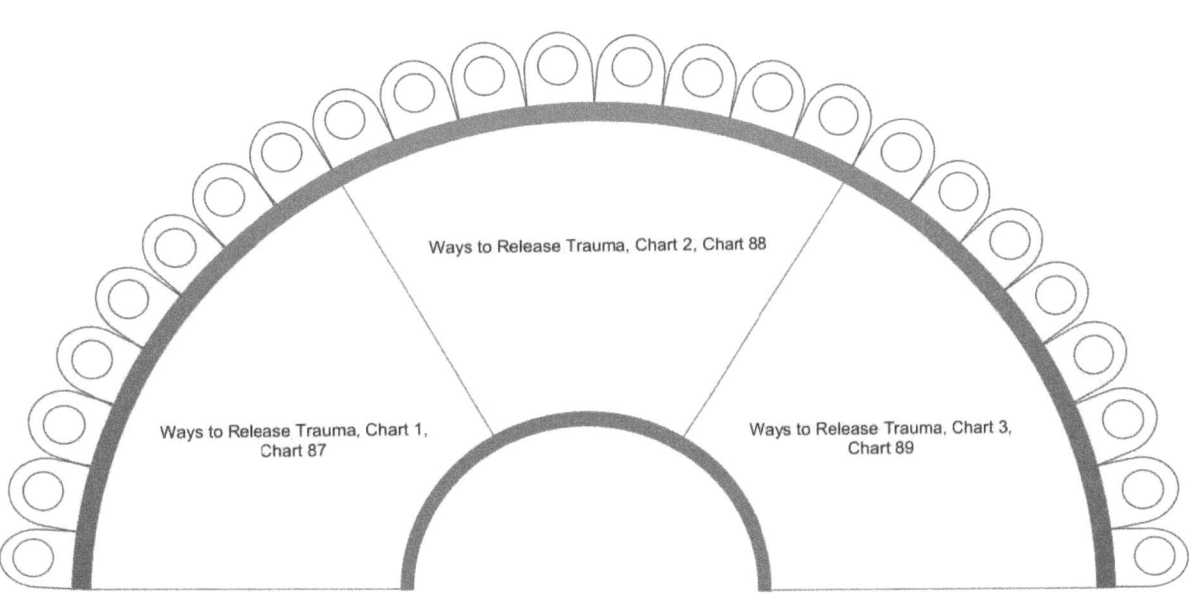

Ways to Release Trauma, Chart 2, Chart 88

Ways to Release Trauma, Chart 1, Chart 87

Ways to Release Trauma, Chart 3, Chart 89

Trauma, Ways to Release, Master Chart

Royal Template 3h

Diving Deep into the Pool of the Mind

Chart 86

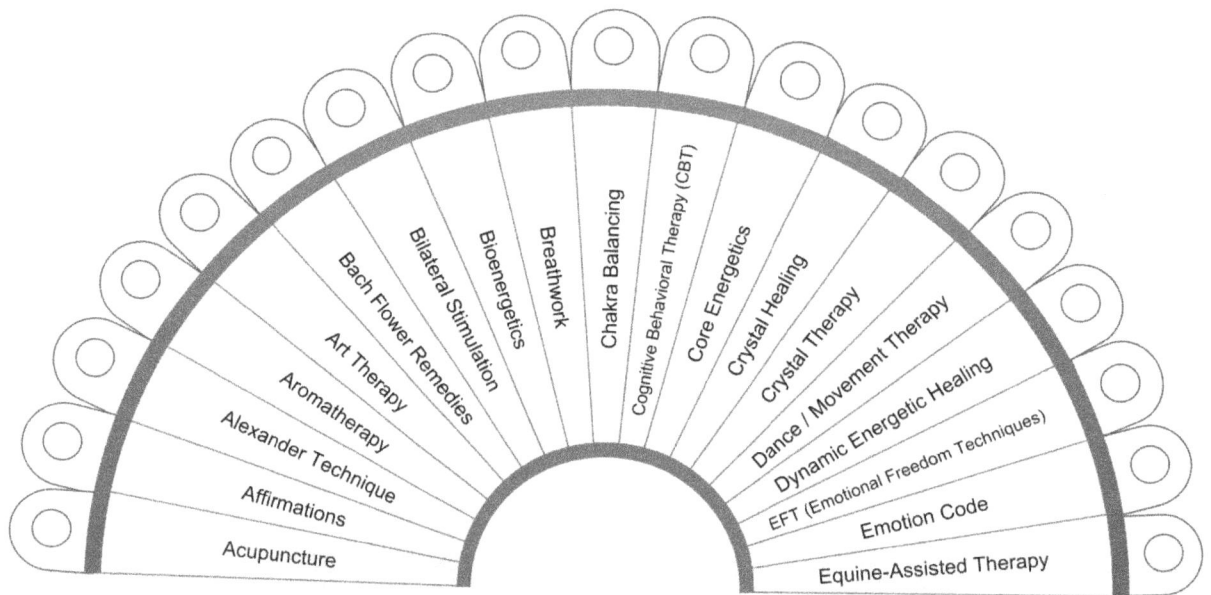

Ways to Release Trauma, Chart 1

The chart contains the following labels (reading around the fan):

- Acupuncture
- Affirmations
- Alexander Technique
- Aromatherapy
- Art Therapy
- Bach Flower Remedies
- Bilateral Stimulation
- Bioenergetics
- Breathwork
- Chakra Balancing
- Cognitive Behavioral Therapy (CBT)
- Core Energetics
- Crystal Healing
- Crystal Therapy
- Dance / Movement Therapy
- Dynamic Energetic Healing
- EFT (Emotional Freedom Techniques)
- Emotion Code
- Equine-Assisted Therapy

Royal Template 19

Diving Deep into the Pool of the Mind

Chart 87

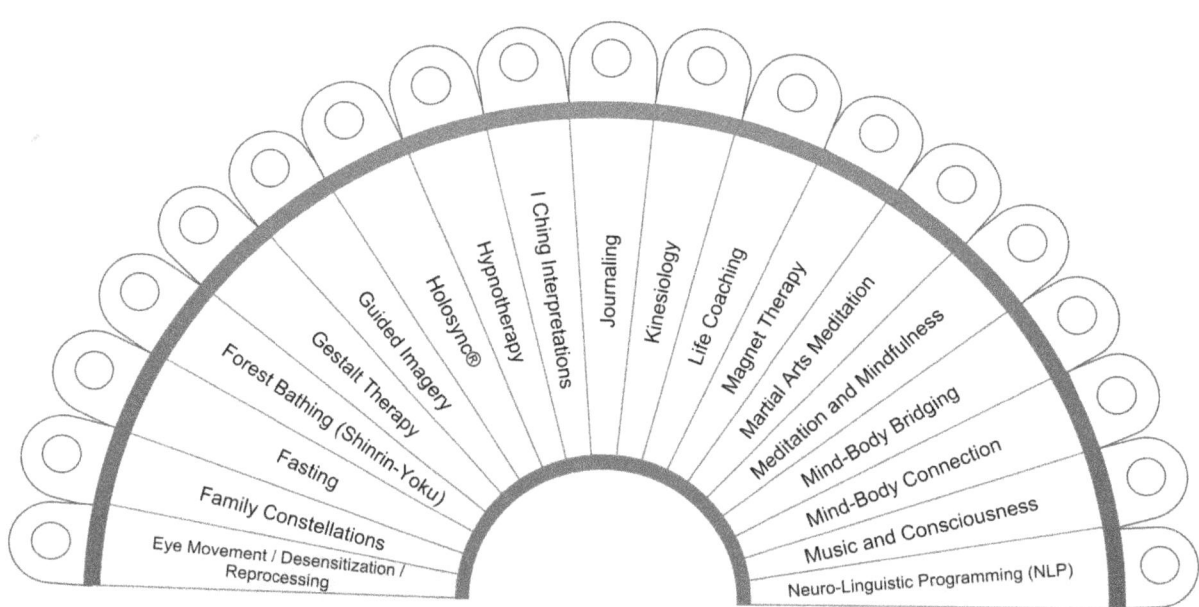

Ways to Release Trauma, Chart 2

The chart contains the following labels (reading around the fan):

- Eye Movement / Desensitization / Reprocessing
- Family Constellations
- Fasting
- Forest Bathing (Shinrin-Yoku)
- Gestalt Therapy
- Guided Imagery
- Holosync®
- Hypnotherapy
- I Ching Interpretations
- Journaling
- Kinesiology
- Life Coaching
- Magnet Therapy
- Martial Arts Meditation
- Meditation and Mindfulness
- Mind-Body Bridging
- Mind-Body Connection
- Music and Consciousness
- Neuro-Linguistic Programming (NLP)

Royal Template 19

Diving Deep into the Pool of the Mind

Chart 88

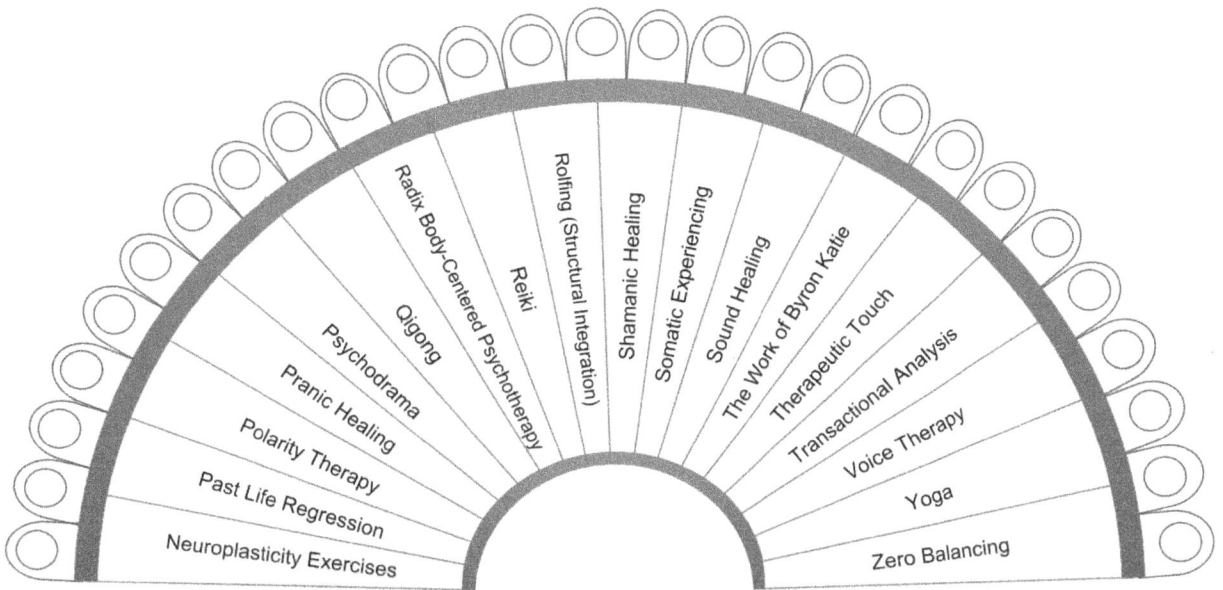

Ways to Release Trauma, Chart 3

The chart lists the following, reading around the fan:

- Neuroplasticity Exercises
- Past Life Regression
- Polarity Therapy
- Pranic Healing
- Psychodrama
- Qigong
- Radix Body-Centered Psychotherapy
- Reiki
- Rolfing (Structural Integration)
- Shamanic Healing
- Somatic Experiencing
- Sound Healing
- The Work of Byron Katie
- Therapeutic Touch
- Transactional Analysis
- Voice Therapy
- Yoga
- Zero Balancing

Royal Template 18

Diving Deep into the Pool of the Mind

Chart 89

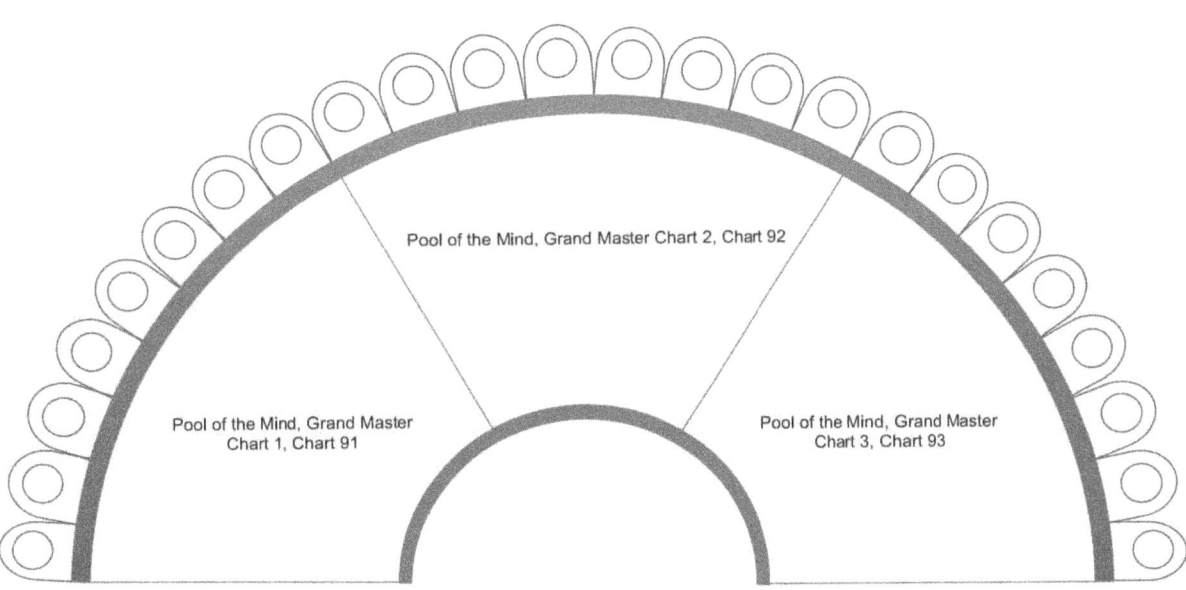

- Pool of the Mind, Grand Master Chart 2, Chart 92
- Pool of the Mind, Grand Master Chart 1, Chart 91
- Pool of the Mind, Grand Master Chart 3, Chart 93

Diving Into the Pool of the Mind

Royal Template 3h

Diving Deep into the Pool of the Mind

Chart 90

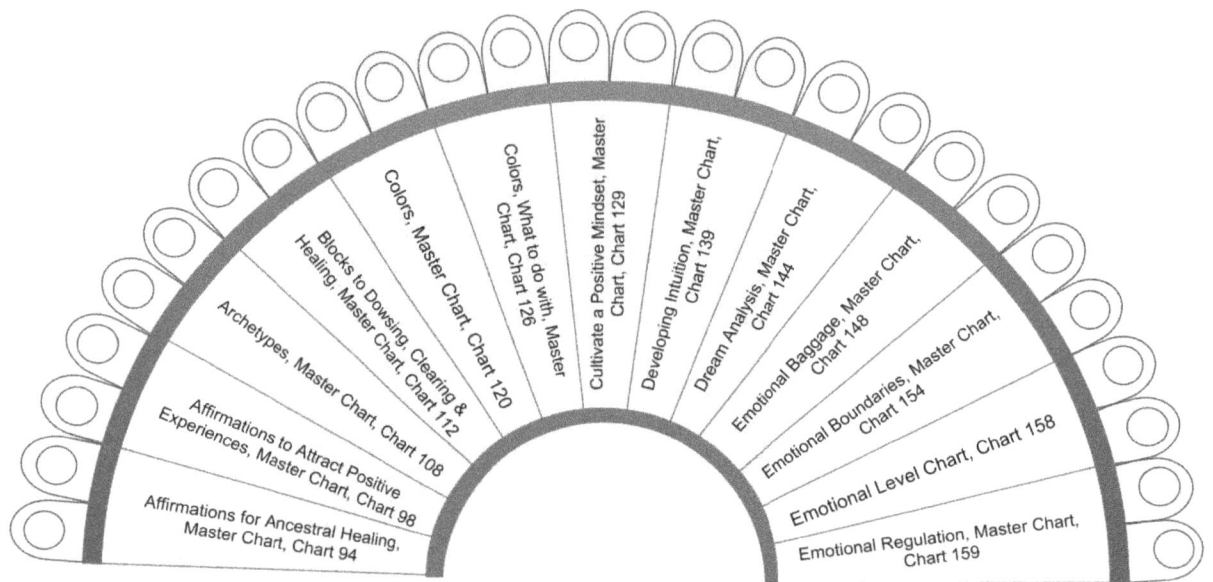

Pool of the Mind, Grand Master Chart 1

Affirmations for Ancestral Healing, Master Chart, Chart 94

Affirmations to Attract Positive Experiences, Master Chart, Chart 98

Archetypes, Master Chart, Chart 108

Blocks to Dowsing, Clearing & Healing, Master Chart, Chart 112

Colors, Master Chart, Chart 120

Colors, What to do with, Master Chart, Chart 126

Cultivate a Positive Mindset, Master Chart, Chart 129

Developing Intuition, Master Chart, Chart 139

Dream Analysis, Master Chart, Chart 144

Emotional Baggage, Master Chart, Chart 148

Emotional Boundaries, Master Chart, Chart 154

Emotional Level Chart, Chart 158

Emotional Regulation, Master Chart, Chart 159

Royal Template 13

Diving Deep into the Pool of the Mind

Chart 91

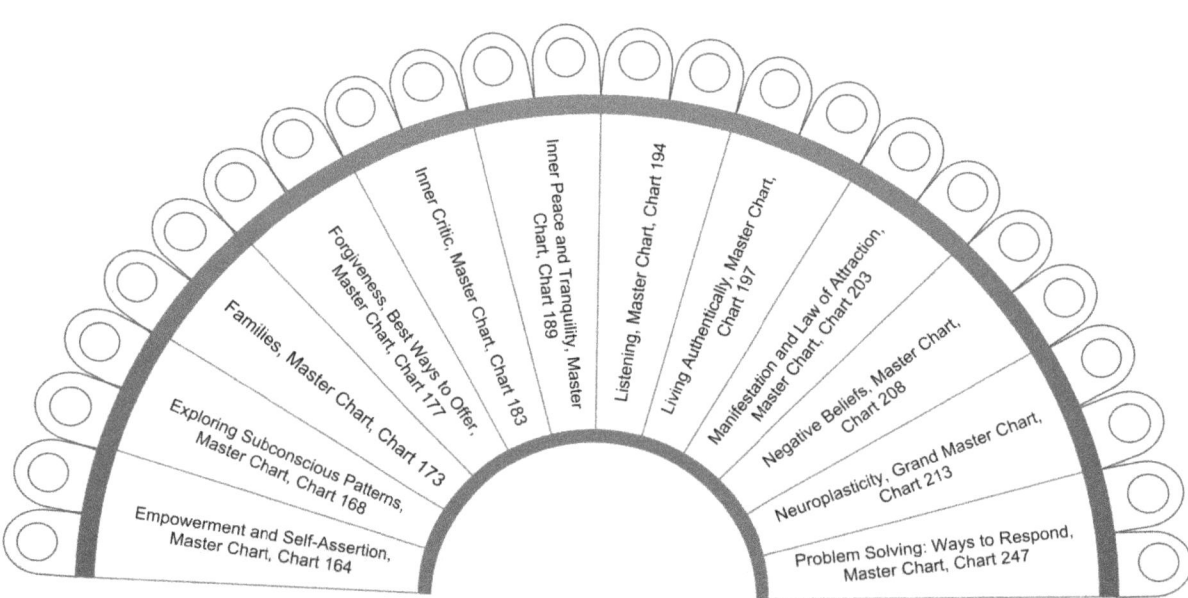

Pool of the Mind, Grand Master Chart 2

Empowerment and Self-Assertion, Master Chart, Chart 164

Exploring Subconscious Patterns, Master Chart, Chart 168

Families, Master Chart, Chart 173

Forgiveness, Best Ways to Offer, Master Chart, Chart 177

Inner Critic, Master Chart, Chart 183

Inner Peace and Tranquility, Master Chart, Chart 189

Listening, Master Chart, Chart 194

Living Authentically, Master Chart, Chart 197

Manifestation and Law of Attraction, Master Chart, Chart 203

Negative Beliefs, Master Chart, Chart 208

Neuroplasticity, Grand Master Chart, Chart 213

Problem Solving: Ways to Respond, Master Chart, Chart 247

Royal Template 12

Diving Deep into the Pool of the Mind

Chart 92

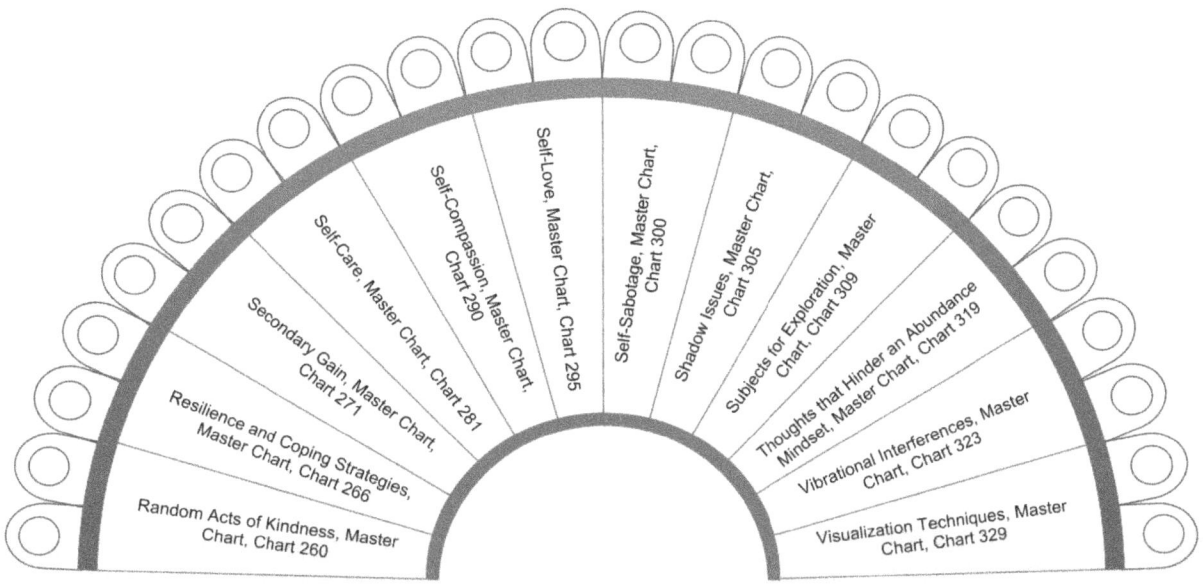

Pool of the Mind, Grand Master Chart 3

Self-Care, Master Chart, Chart 281

Self-Compassion, Master Chart, Chart 290

Self-Love, Master Chart, Chart 295

Self-Sabotage, Master Chart, Chart 300

Shadow Issues, Master Chart, Chart 305

Subjects for Exploration, Master Chart, Chart 309

Thoughts that Hinder an Abundance Mindset, Master Chart, Chart 319

Secondary Gain, Master Chart, Chart 271

Resilience and Coping Strategies, Master Chart, Chart 266

Random Acts of Kindness, Master Chart, Chart 260

Vibrational Interferences, Master Chart, Chart 323

Visualization Techniques, Master Chart, Chart 329

Royal Template 12

Diving Deep into the Pool of the Mind

Chart 93

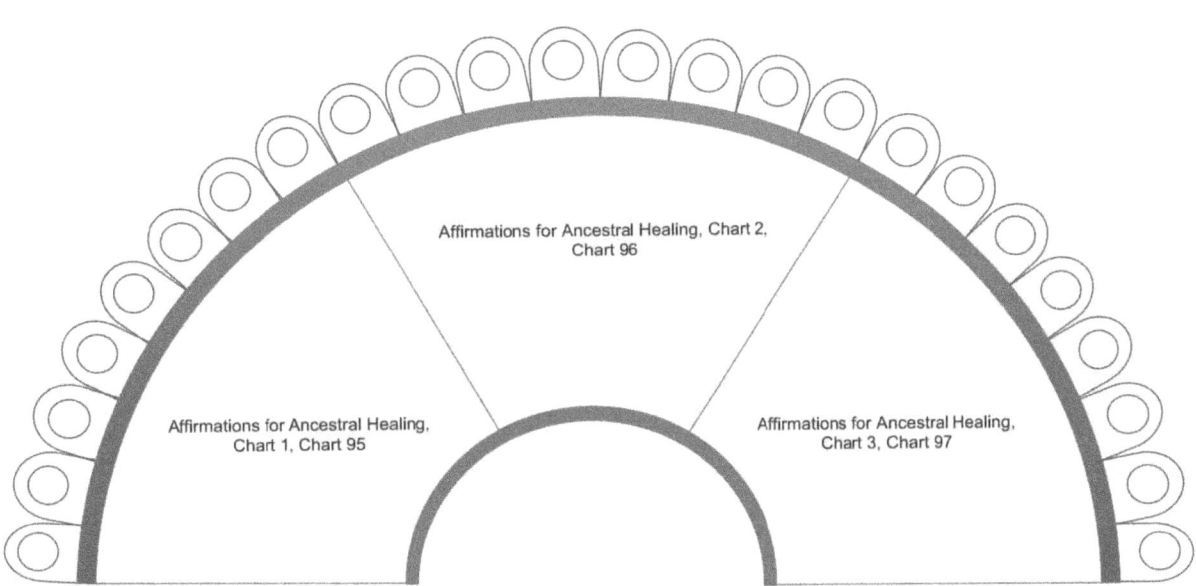

Affirmations for Ancestral Healing, Chart 2, Chart 96

Affirmations for Ancestral Healing, Chart 1, Chart 95

Affirmations for Ancestral Healing, Chart 3, Chart 97

Affirmations for Ancestral Healing, Master Chart

Royal Template 3h

Diving Deep into the Pool of the Mind

Chart 94

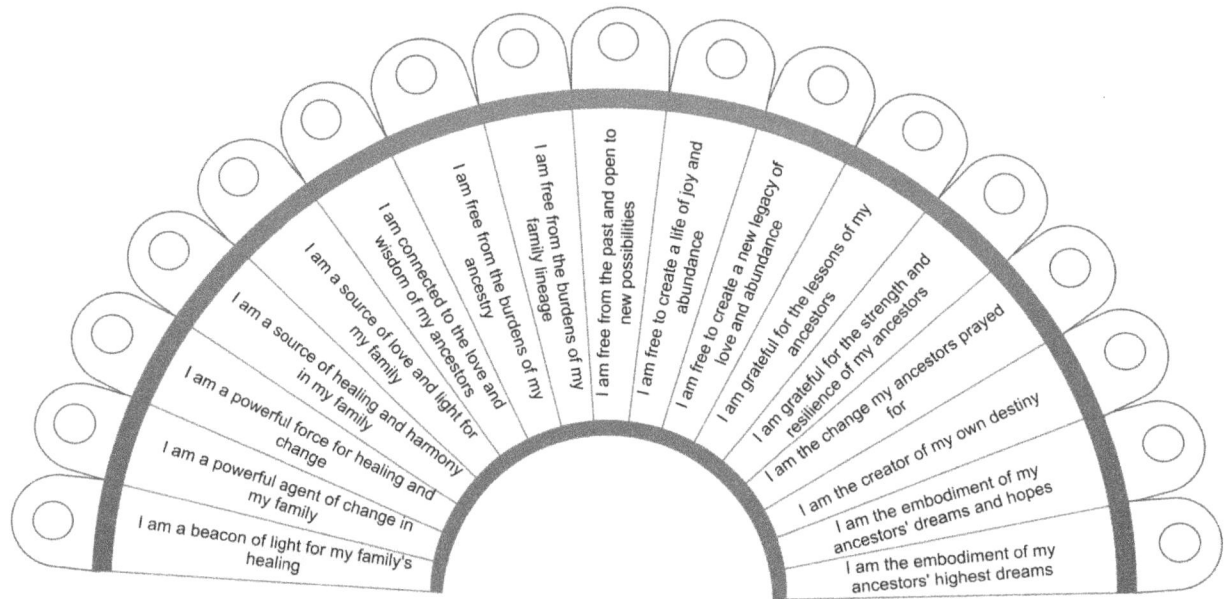

Affirmations for Ancestral Healing, Chart 1

The affirmations on Chart 1 (read clockwise):

- I am a beacon of light for my family's healing
- I am a powerful agent of change in my family
- I am a powerful force for healing and change
- I am a source of healing and harmony in my family
- I am a source of love and light for my family
- I am connected to the love and wisdom of my ancestors
- I am free from the burdens of my ancestry
- I am free from the burdens of my family lineage
- I am free from the past and open to new possibilities
- I am free to create a life of joy and abundance
- I am free to create a new legacy of love and abundance
- I am grateful for the lessons of my ancestors
- I am grateful for the strength and resilience of my ancestors
- I am the change my ancestors prayed for
- I am the creator of my own destiny
- I am the embodiment of my ancestors' dreams and hopes
- I am the embodiment of my ancestors' highest dreams

Royal Template 17

Diving Deep into the Pool of the Mind

Chart 95

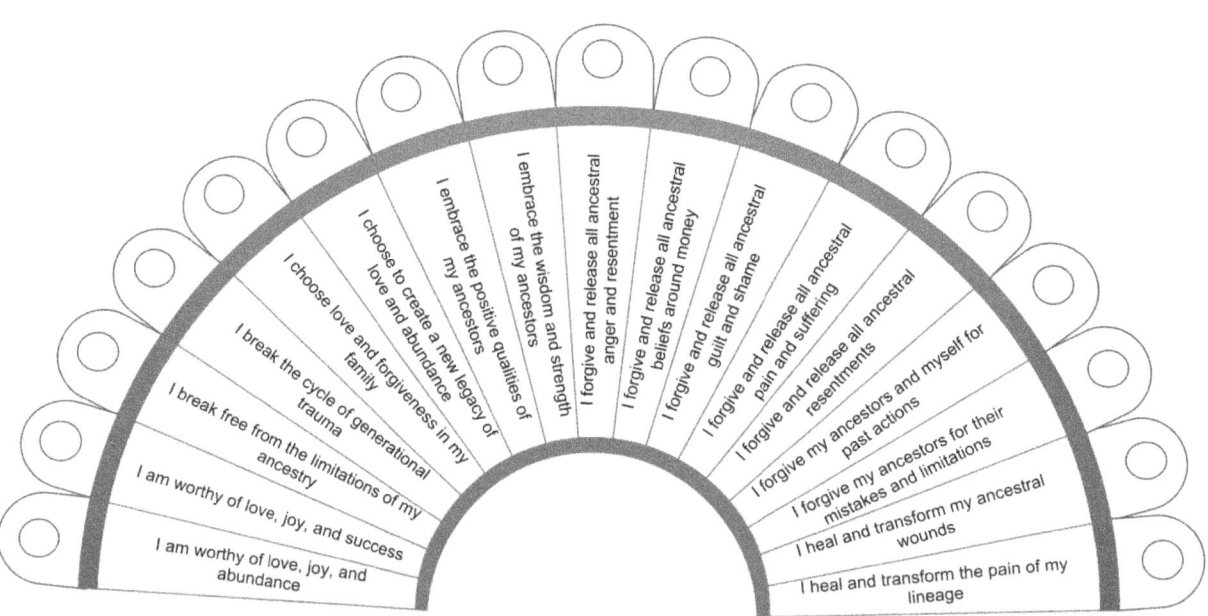

Affirmations for Ancestral Healing, Chart 2

The affirmations on Chart 2 (read clockwise):

- I am worthy of love, joy, and abundance
- I am worthy of love, joy, and success
- I break free from the limitations of my ancestry
- I break the cycle of generational trauma
- I choose love and forgiveness in my family
- I choose to create a new legacy of love and abundance
- I embrace the positive qualities of my ancestors
- I embrace the wisdom and strength of my ancestors
- I forgive and release all ancestral anger and resentment
- I forgive and release all ancestral beliefs around money
- I forgive and release all ancestral guilt and shame
- I forgive and release all ancestral pain and suffering
- I forgive and release all ancestral resentments
- I forgive my ancestors and myself for past actions
- I forgive my ancestors for their mistakes and limitations
- I heal and transform my ancestral wounds
- I heal and transform the pain of my lineage

Royal Template 17

Diving Deep into the Pool of the Mind

Chart 96

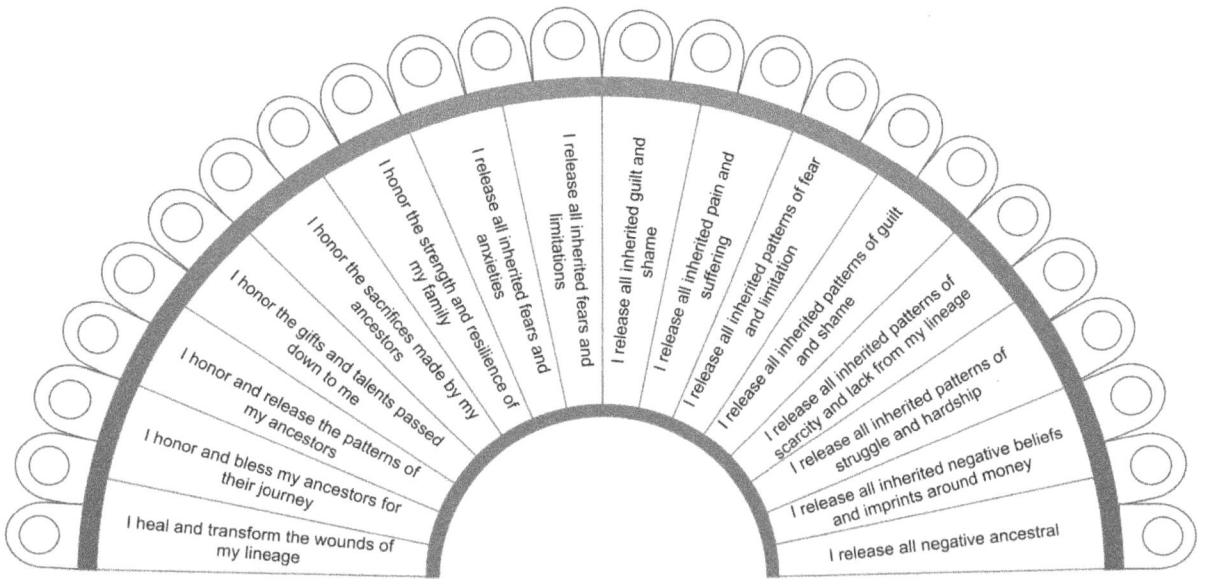

Affirmations for Ancestral Healing, Chart 3

The following affirmations appear on the chart:

- I honor the strength and resilience of my family
- I honor the sacrifices made by my ancestors
- I honor the gifts and talents passed down to me
- I honor and release the patterns of my ancestors
- I honor and bless my ancestors for their journey
- I heal and transform the wounds of my lineage
- I release all inherited fears and anxieties
- I release all inherited guilt and limitations
- I release all inherited fears and limitations
- I release all inherited pain and suffering
- I release all inherited patterns of fear and limitation
- I release all inherited patterns of guilt and shame
- I release all inherited patterns of scarcity and lack from my lineage
- I release all inherited patterns of struggle and hardship
- I release all inherited negative beliefs and imprints around money
- I release all negative ancestral

Royal Template 16

Diving Deep into the Pool of the Mind

Chart 97

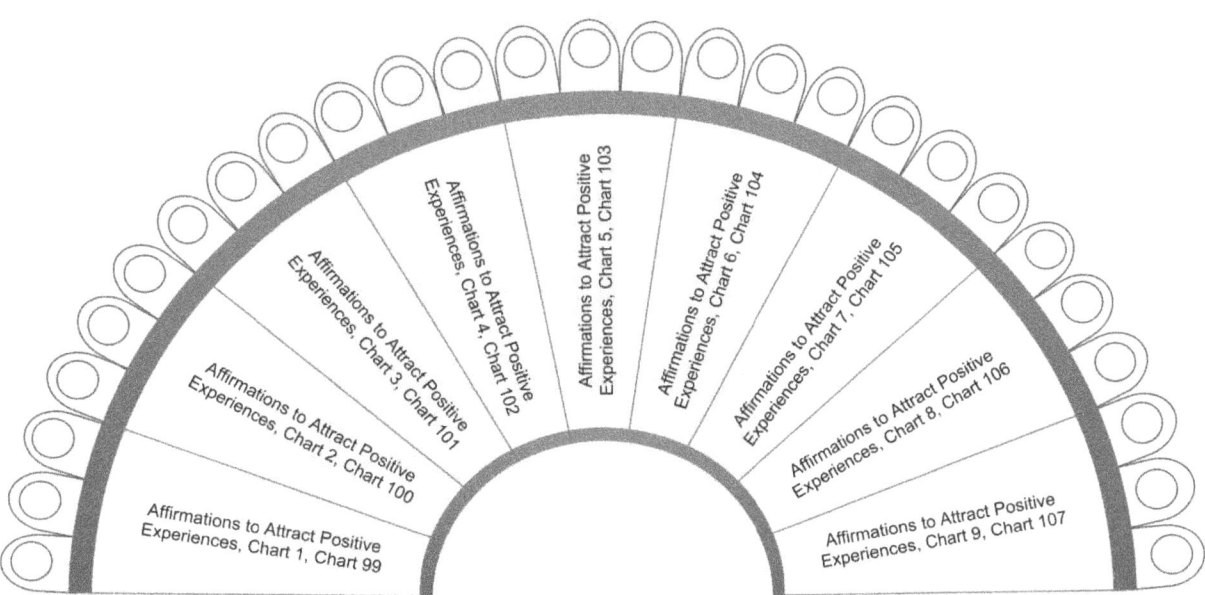

Affirmations to Attract Positive Experiences, Master Chart

The following chart references appear:

- Affirmations to Attract Positive Experiences, Chart 1, Chart 99
- Affirmations to Attract Positive Experiences, Chart 2, Chart 100
- Affirmations to Attract Positive Experiences, Chart 3, Chart 101
- Affirmations to Attract Positive Experiences, Chart 4, Chart 102
- Affirmations to Attract Positive Experiences, Chart 5, Chart 103
- Affirmations to Attract Positive Experiences, Chart 6, Chart 104
- Affirmations to Attract Positive Experiences, Chart 7, Chart 105
- Affirmations to Attract Positive Experiences, Chart 8, Chart 106
- Affirmations to Attract Positive Experiences, Chart 9, Chart 107

Royal Template 9

Diving Deep into the Pool of the Mind

Chart 98

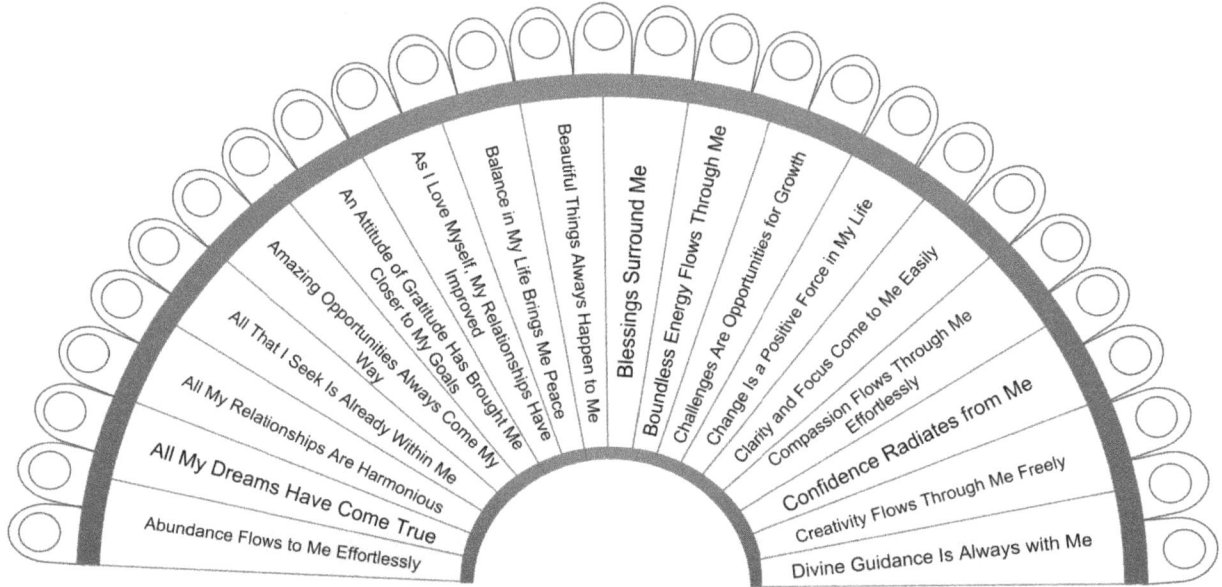

Affirmations to Attract Positive Experiences, Chart 1

Abundance Flows to Me Effortlessly
All My Dreams Have Come True
All My Relationships Are Harmonious
All That I Seek Is Already Within Me
Amazing Opportunities Always Come My Way
An Attitude of Gratitude Has Brought Me Closer to My Goals
As I Love Myself, My Relationships Have Improved
Balance in My Life Brings Me Peace
Beautiful Things Always Happen to Me
Blessings Surround Me
Boundless Energy Flows Through Me
Challenges Are Opportunities for Growth
Change Is a Positive Force in My Life
Clarity and Focus Come to Me Easily
Compassion Flows Through Me Effortlessly
Confidence Radiates from Me
Creativity Flows Through Me Freely
Divine Guidance Is Always with Me

Royal Template 18

Diving Deep into the Pool of the Mind

Chart 99

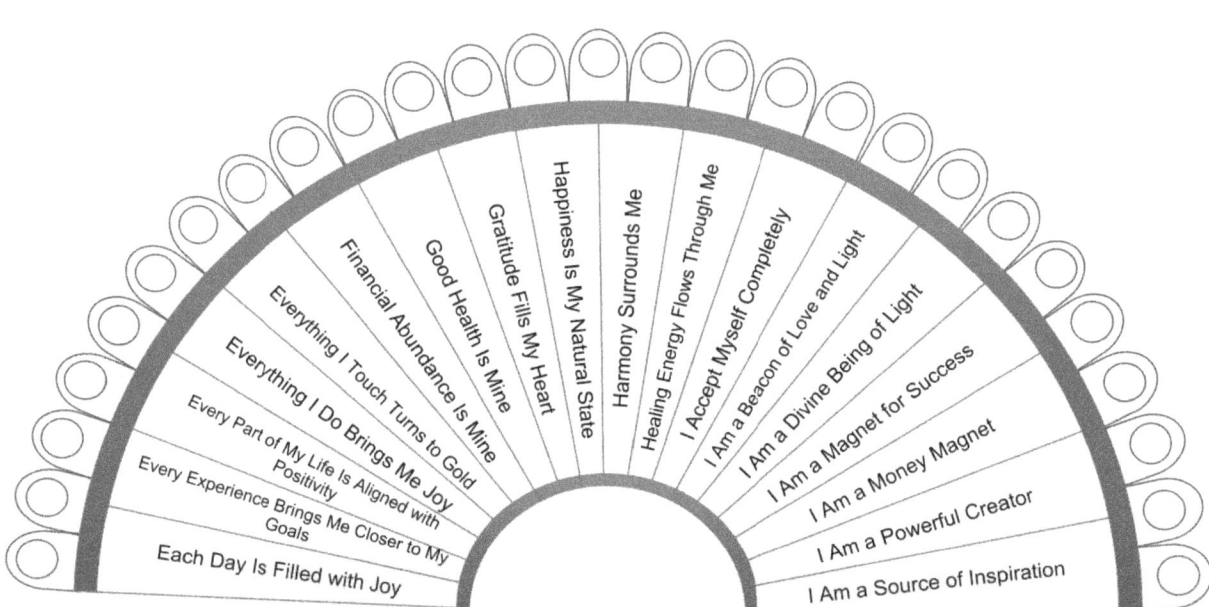

Each Day Is Filled with Joy
Every Experience Brings Me Closer to My Goals
Every Part of My Life Is Aligned with Positivity
Everything I Do Brings Me Joy
Everything I Touch Turns to Gold
Financial Abundance Is Mine
Good Health Is Mine
Gratitude Fills My Heart
Happiness Is My Natural State
Harmony Surrounds Me
Healing Energy Flows Through Me
I Accept Myself Completely
I Am a Beacon of Love and Light
I Am a Divine Being of Light
I Am a Magnet for Success
I Am a Money Magnet
I Am a Powerful Creator
I Am a Source of Inspiration

Affirmations to Attract Positive Experiences, Chart 2

Royal Template 18

Diving Deep into the Pool of the Mind

Chart 100

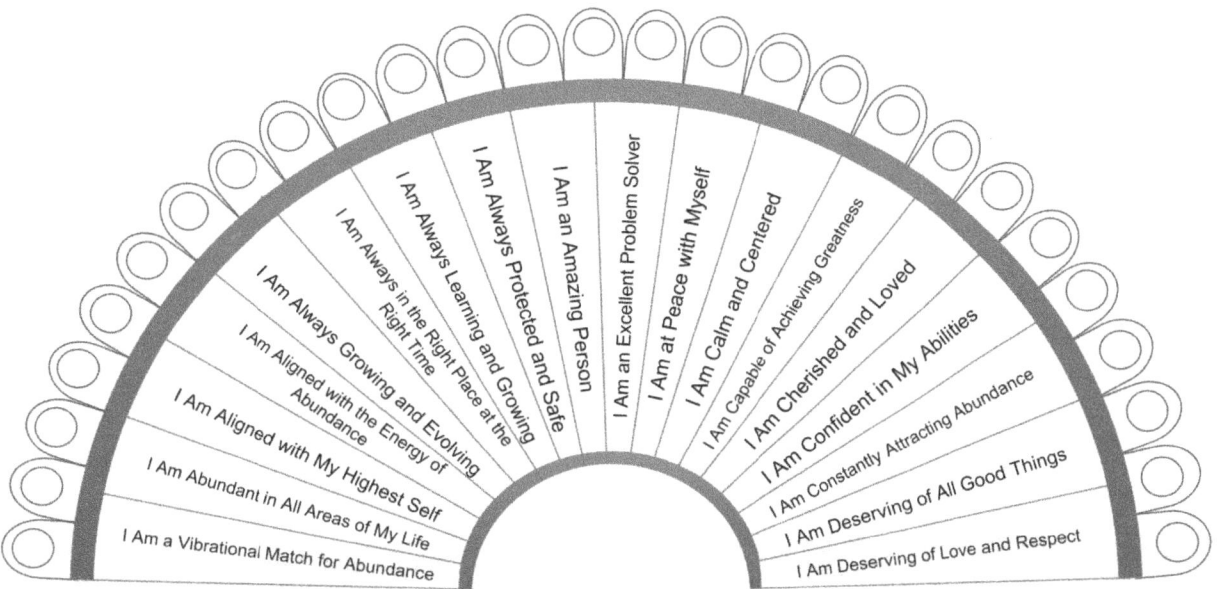

Affirmations to Attract Positive Experiences, Chart 3

Royal Template 18

Diving Deep into the Pool of the Mind

Chart 101

The affirmations on Chart 3 (reading from left to right):

- I Am a Vibrational Match for Abundance
- I Am Abundant in All Areas of My Life
- I Am Aligned with My Highest Self
- I Am Aligned with the Energy of Abundance
- I Am Always Growing and Evolving
- I Am Always in the Right Place at the Right Time
- I Am Always Learning and Growing
- I Am Always Protected and Safe
- I Am an Amazing Person
- I Am an Excellent Problem Solver
- I Am at Peace with Myself
- I Am Calm and Centered
- I Am Capable of Achieving Greatness
- I Am Cherished and Loved
- I Am Confident in My Abilities
- I Am Constantly Attracting Abundance
- I Am Deserving of All Good Things
- I Am Deserving of Love and Respect

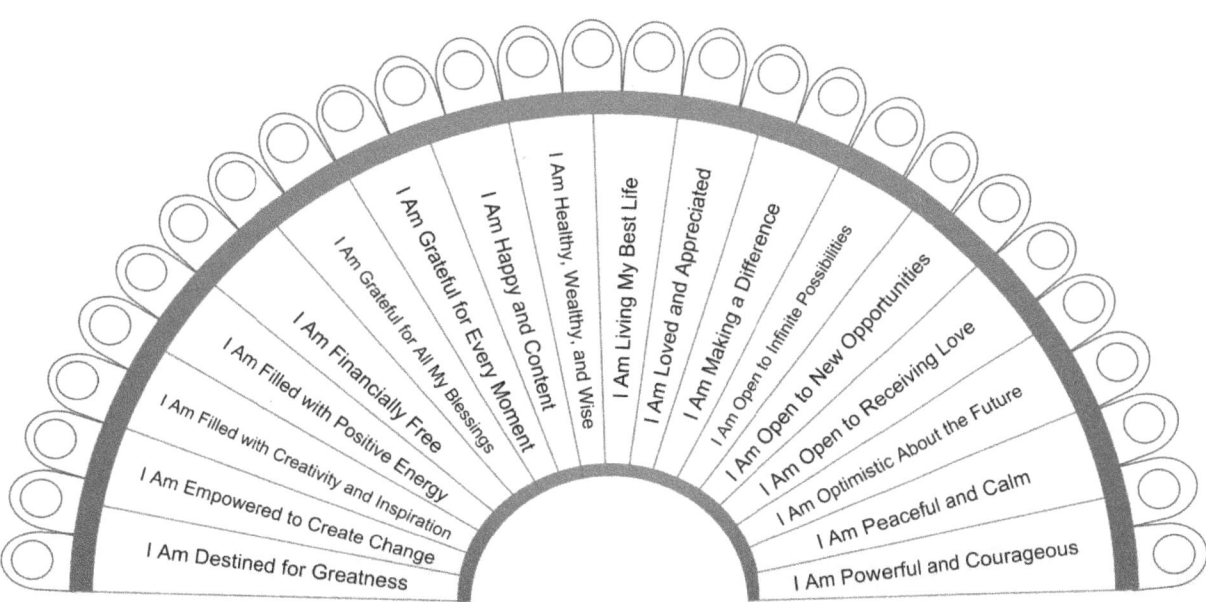

Affirmations to Attract Positive Experiences, Chart 4

Royal Template 18

Diving Deep into the Pool of the Mind

Chart 102

The affirmations on Chart 4 (reading from left to right):

- I Am Destined for Greatness
- I Am Empowered to Create Change
- I Am Filled with Creativity and Inspiration
- I Am Filled with Positive Energy
- I Am Financially Free
- I Am Grateful for All My Blessings
- I Am Grateful for Every Moment
- I Am Happy and Content
- I Am Healthy, Wealthy, and Wise
- I Am Living My Best Life
- I Am Loved and Appreciated
- I Am Making a Difference
- I Am Open to Infinite Possibilities
- I Am Open to New Opportunities
- I Am Open to Receiving Love
- I Am Optimistic About the Future
- I Am Peaceful and Calm
- I Am Powerful and Courageous

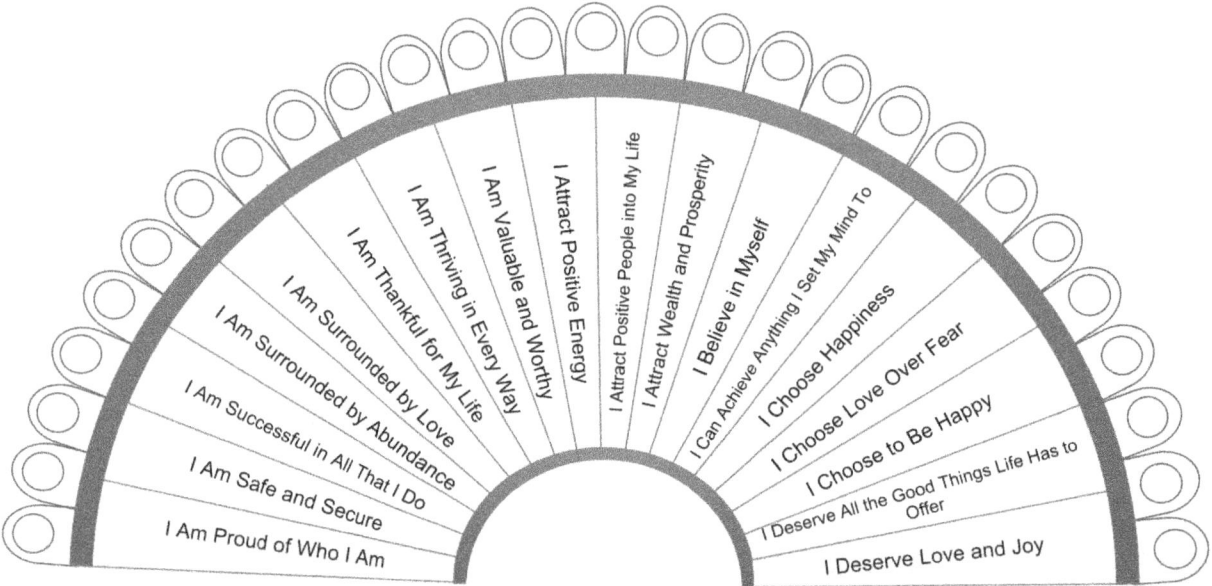

Affirmations to Attract Positive Experiences, Chart 5

Royal Template 18

Diving Deep into the Pool of the Mind

Chart 103

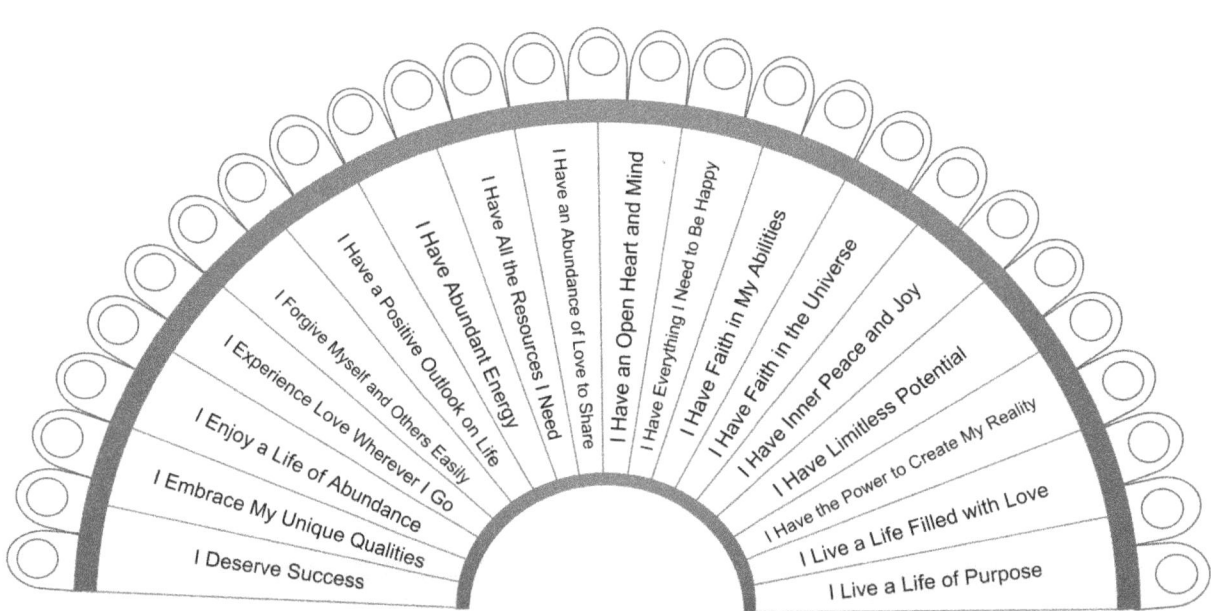

Affirmations to Attract Positive Experiences, Chart 6

Royal Template 18

Diving Deep into the Pool of the Mind

Chart 104

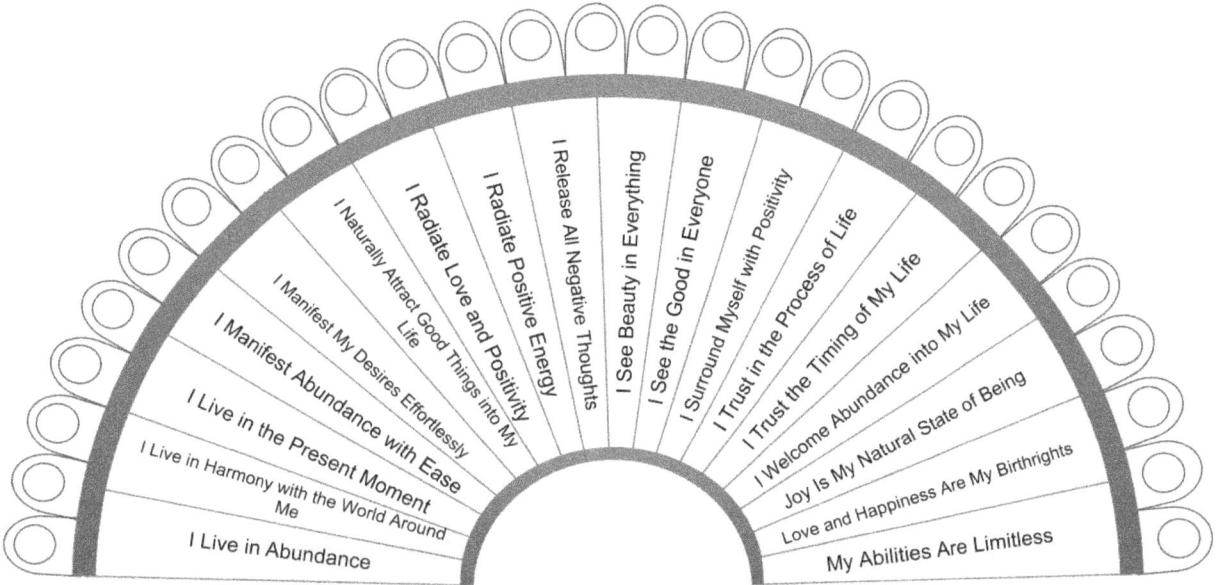

Affirmations to Attract Positive Experiences, Chart 7

I Live in Abundance
I Live in Harmony with the World Around Me
I Live in the Present Moment
I Manifest Abundance with Ease
I Manifest My Desires Effortlessly
I Naturally Attract Good Things into My Life
I Radiate Love and Positivity
I Radiate Positive Energy
I Release All Negative Thoughts
I See Beauty in Everything
I See the Good in Everyone
I Surround Myself with Positivity
I Trust in the Process of Life
I Trust the Timing of My Life
I Welcome Abundance into My Life
Joy Is My Natural State of Being
Love and Happiness Are My Birthrights
My Abilities Are Limitless

Royal Template 18

Diving Deep into the Pool of the Mind

Chart 105

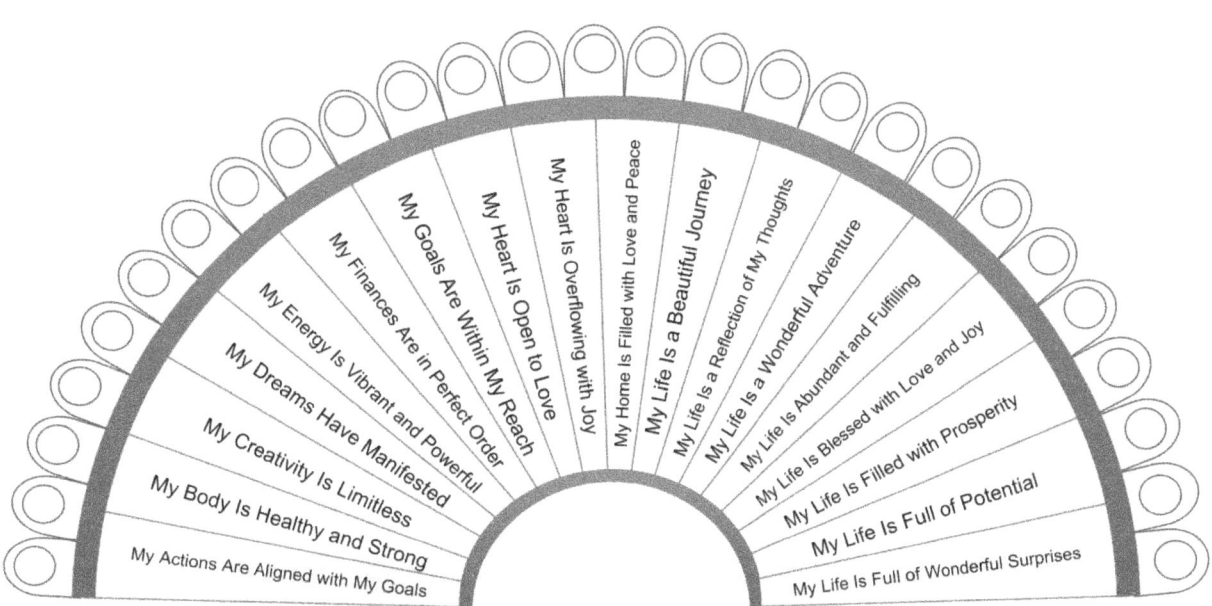

My Actions Are Aligned with My Goals
My Body Is Healthy and Strong
My Creativity Is Limitless
My Dreams Have Manifested
My Energy Is Vibrant and Powerful
My Finances Are in Perfect Order
My Goals Are Within My Reach
My Heart Is Open to Love
My Heart Is Overflowing with Joy
My Heart Is Filled with Love and Peace
My Home Is Filled with Love and Peace
My Life Is a Beautiful Journey
My Life Is a Reflection of My Thoughts
My Life Is a Wonderful Adventure
My Life Is Abundant and Fulfilling
My Life Is Blessed with Love and Joy
My Life Is Filled with Prosperity
My Life Is Full of Potential
My Life Is Full of Wonderful Surprises

Affirmations to Attract Positive Experiences, Chart 8

Royal Template 18

Diving Deep into the Pool of the Mind

Chart 106

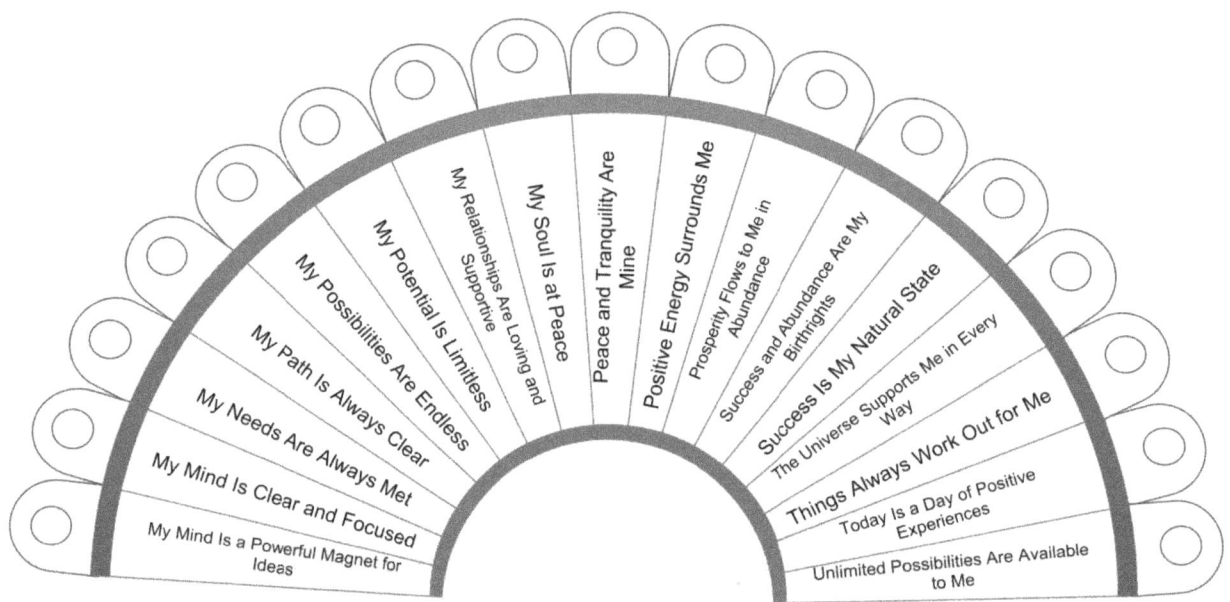

Affirmations to Attract Positive Experiences, Chart 9

My Mind Is a Powerful Magnet for Ideas
My Mind Is Clear and Focused
My Needs Are Always Met
My Path Is Always Clear
My Possibilities Are Endless
My Potential Is Limitless
My Relationships Are Loving and Supportive
My Soul Is at Peace
Peace and Tranquility Are Mine
Positive Energy Surrounds Me
Prosperity Flows to Me in Abundance
Success and Abundance Are My Birthrights
Success Is My Natural State
The Universe Supports Me in Every Way
Things Always Work Out for Me
Today Is a Day of Positive Experiences
Unlimited Possibilities Are Available to Me

© 2025, Susan V Whittaker

Royal Template 17

Diving Deep into the Pool of the Mind

Chart 107

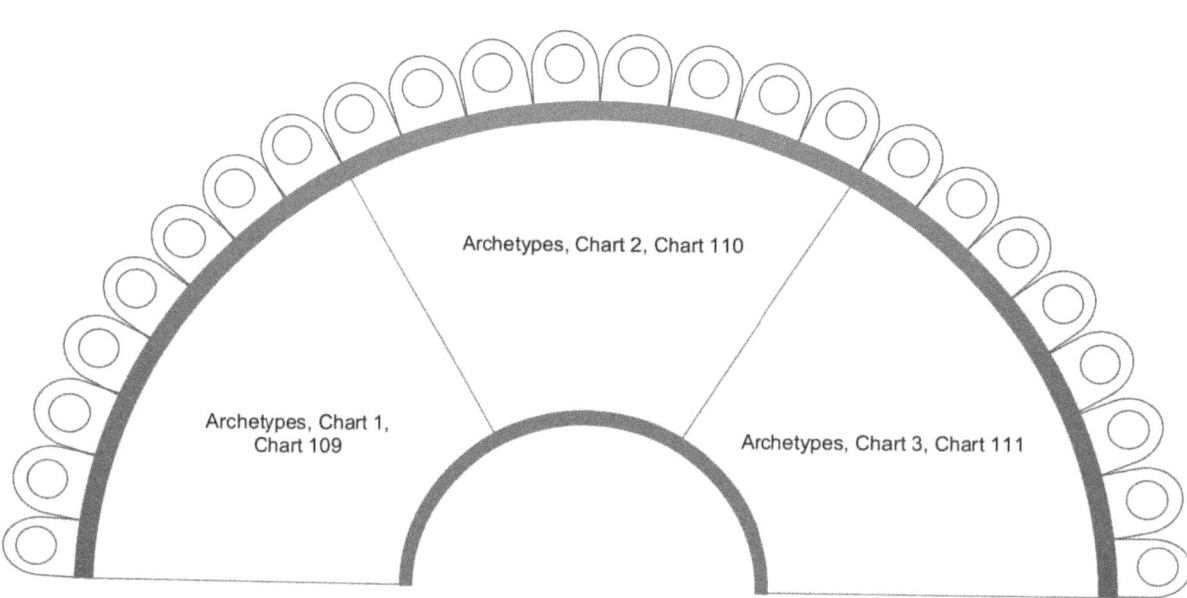

Archetypes, Chart 2, Chart 110

Archetypes, Chart 1, Chart 109

Archetypes, Chart 3, Chart 111

Archetypes, Master Chart

© 2025, Susan V Whittaker

Royal Template 3h

Diving Deep into the Pool of the Mind

Chart 108

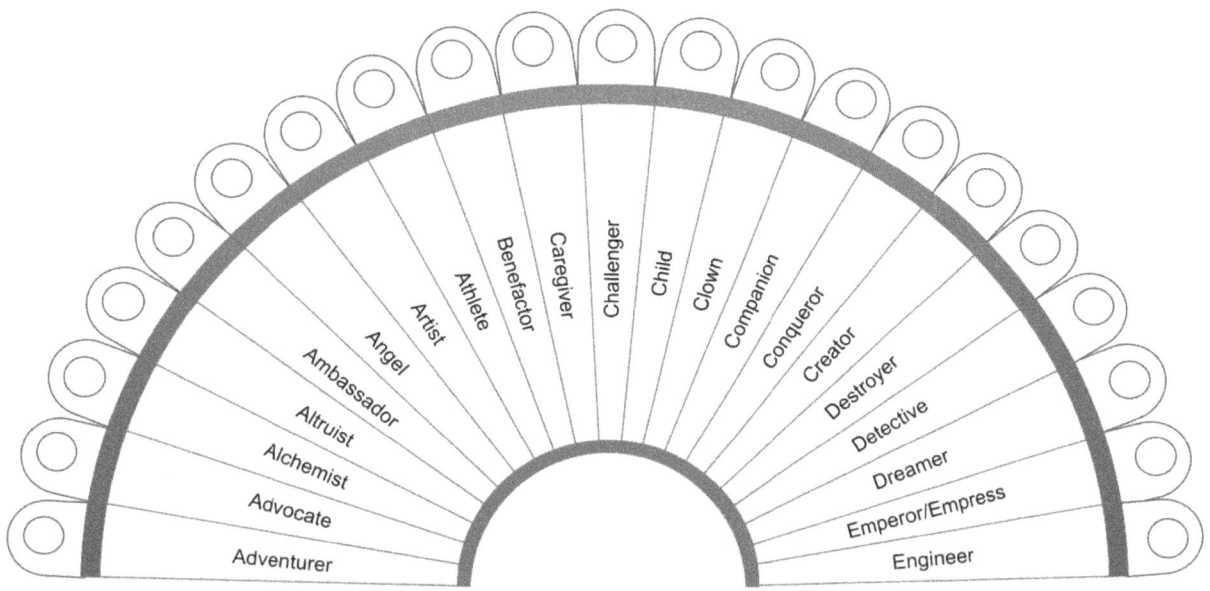

Archetypes, Chart 1

The archetypes shown, reading around the fan:

Adventurer, Advocate, Alchemist, Altruist, Ambassador, Angel, Artist, Athlete, Benefactor, Caregiver, Challenger, Child, Clown, Companion, Conqueror, Creator, Destroyer, Detective, Dreamer, Emperor/Empress, Engineer

Royal Template 21

Diving Deep into the Pool of the Mind

Chart 109

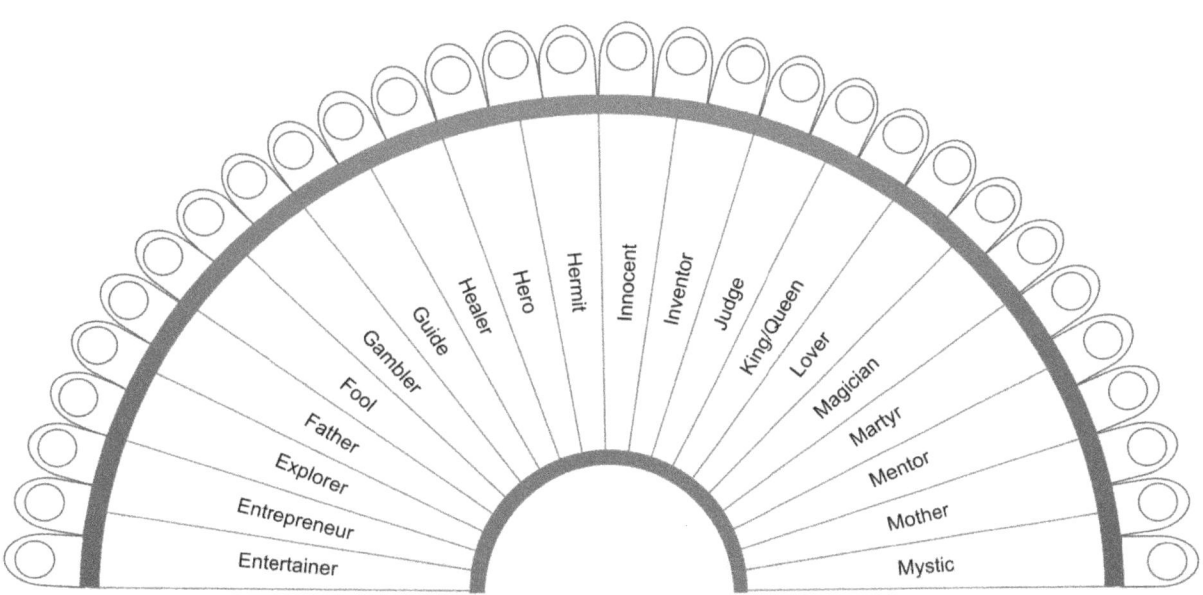

Archetypes, Chart 2

The archetypes shown, reading around the fan:

Entertainer, Entrepreneur, Explorer, Father, Fool, Gambler, Guide, Healer, Hero, Hermit, Innocent, Inventor, Judge, King/Queen, Lover, Magician, Martyr, Mentor, Mother, Mystic

Royal Template 20

Diving Deep into the Pool of the Mind

Chart 110

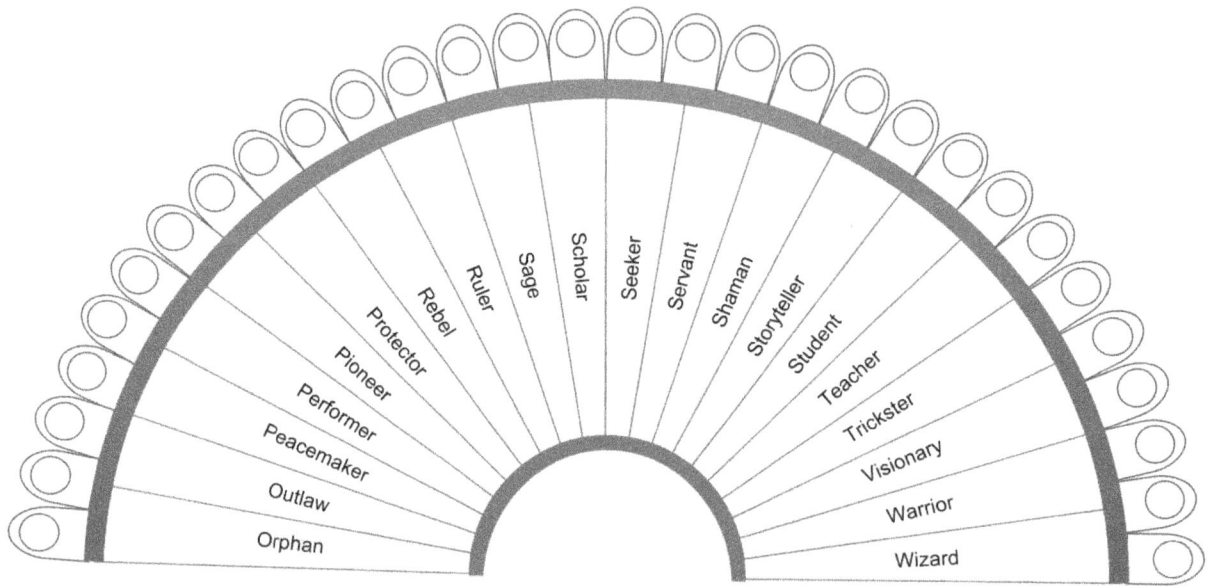

Archetypes, Chart 3

The archetypes shown, reading around the fan:
Orphan, Outlaw, Peacemaker, Performer, Pioneer, Protector, Rebel, Ruler, Sage, Scholar, Seeker, Servant, Shaman, Storyteller, Student, Teacher, Trickster, Visionary, Warrior, Wizard

Royal Template 20

Diving Deep into the Pool of the Mind

Chart 111

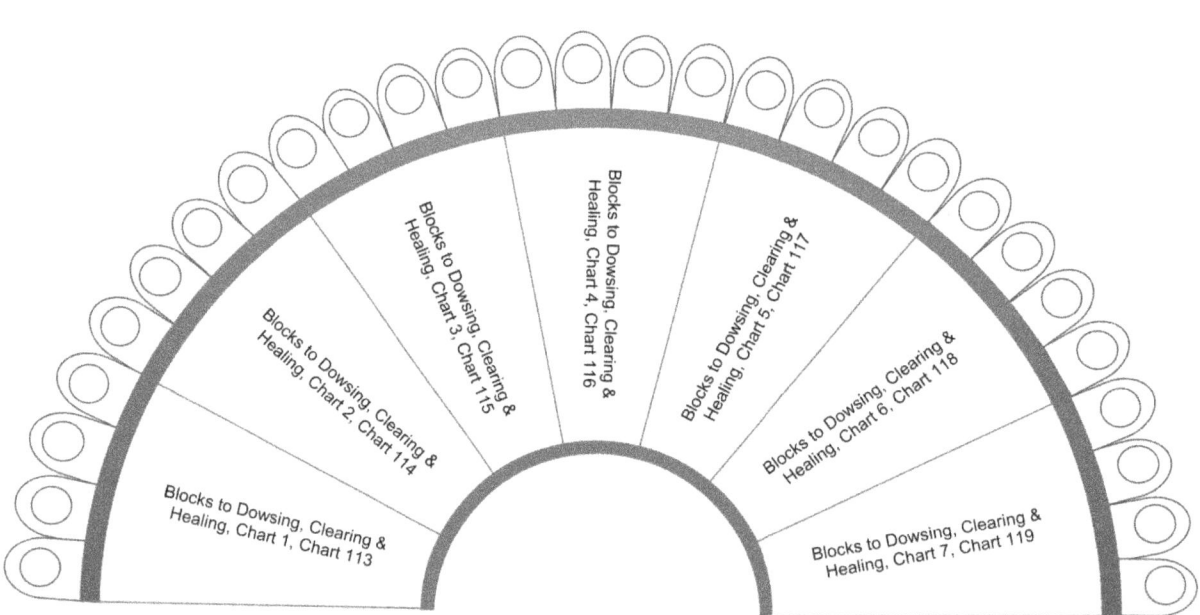

The segments shown, reading around the fan:
Blocks to Dowsing, Clearing & Healing, Chart 1, Chart 113
Blocks to Dowsing, Clearing & Healing, Chart 2, Chart 114
Blocks to Dowsing, Clearing & Healing, Chart 3, Chart 115
Blocks to Dowsing, Clearing & Healing, Chart 4, Chart 116
Blocks to Dowsing, Clearing & Healing, Chart 5, Chart 117
Blocks to Dowsing, Clearing & Healing, Chart 6, Chart 118
Blocks to Dowsing, Clearing & Healing, Chart 7, Chart 119

Blocks to Dowsing, Clearing & Healing, Master Chart

Royal Template 7

Diving Deep into the Pool of the Mind

Chart 112

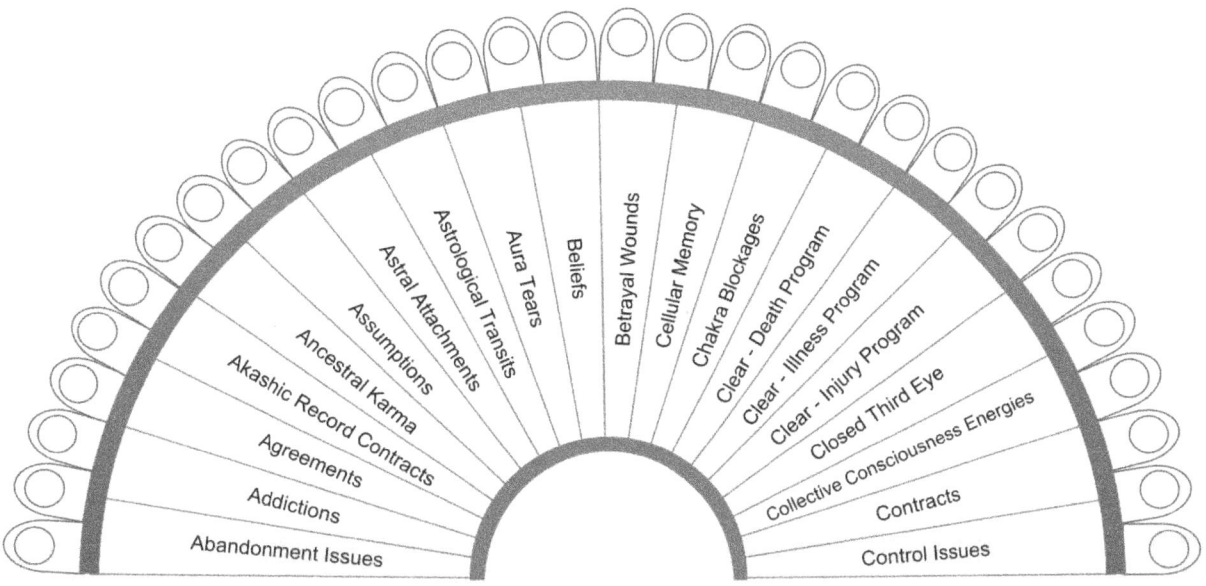

Blocks to Dowsing, Clearing & Healing, Chart 1

Astral Attachments
Astrological Transits
Aura Tears
Beliefs
Betrayal Wounds
Cellular Memory
Chakra Blockages
Clear - Death Program
Clear - Illness Program
Clear - Injury Program
Closed Third Eye
Collective Consciousness Energies
Contracts
Control Issues
Assumptions
Ancestral Karma
Akashic Record Contracts
Agreements
Addictions
Abandonment Issues

Royal Template 20

Diving Deep into the Pool of the Mind

Chart 113

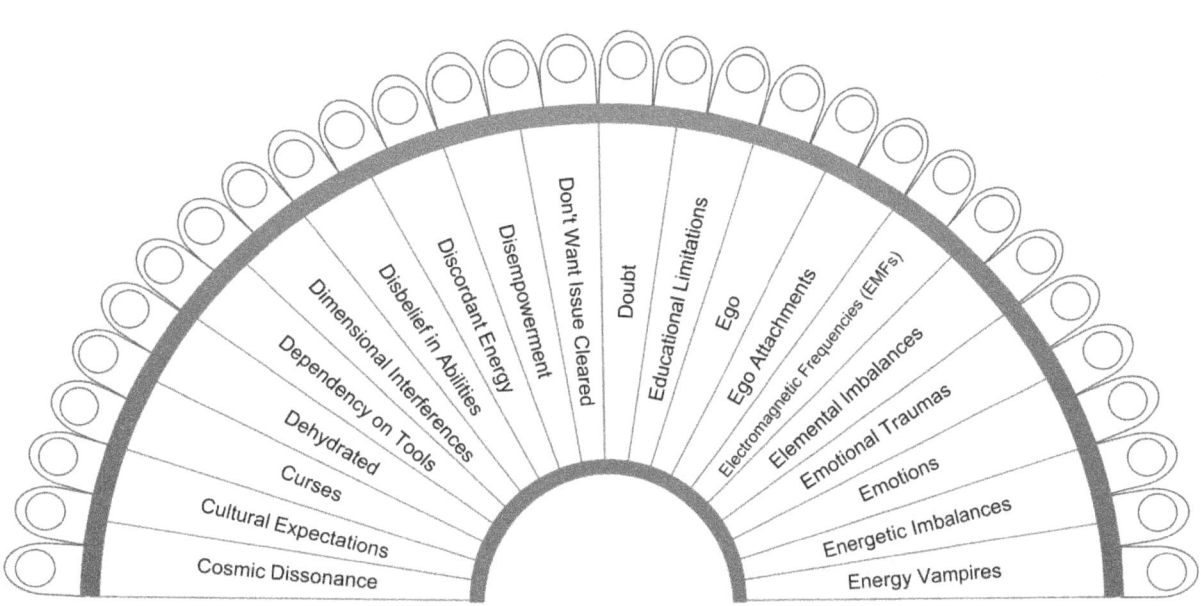

Blocks to Dowsing, Clearing & Healing, Chart 2

Dimensional Interferences
Disbelief in Abilities
Discordant Energy
Disempowerment
Don't Want Issue Cleared
Doubt
Educational Limitations
Ego
Ego Attachments
Electromagnetic Frequencies (EMF's)
Elemental Imbalances
Emotional Traumas
Emotions
Energetic Imbalances
Energy Vampires
Dependency on Tools
Dehydrated
Curses
Cultural Expectations
Cosmic Dissonance

Royal Template 20

Diving Deep into the Pool of the Mind

Chart 114

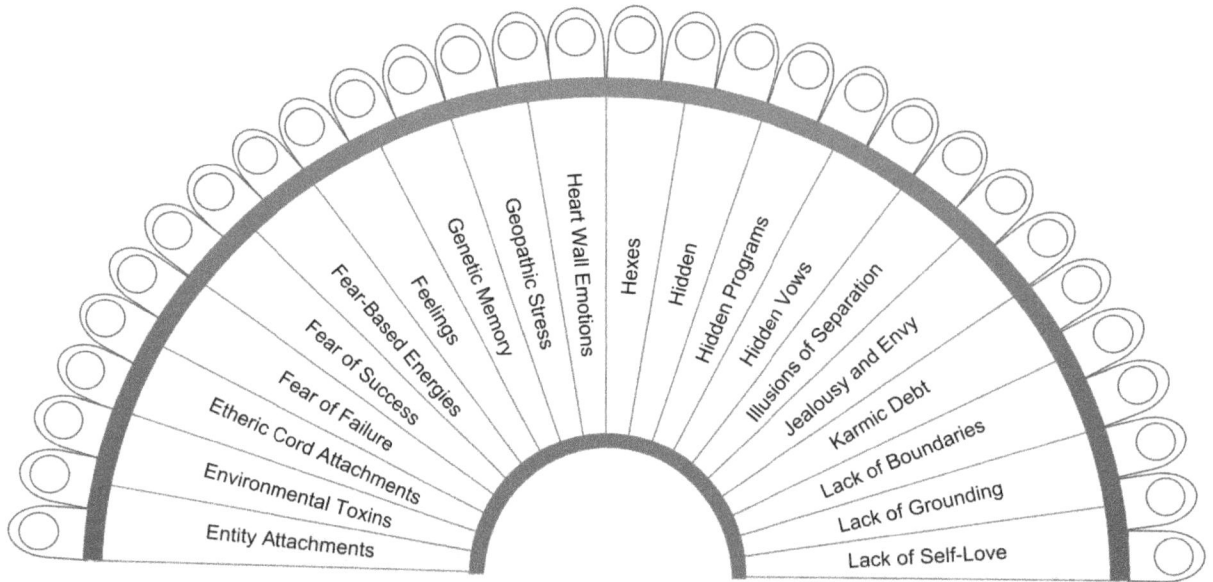

Blocks to Dowsing, Clearing & Healing, Chart 3

The chart contains the following labels (left to right):

- Entity Attachments
- Environmental Toxins
- Etheric Cord Attachments
- Fear of Failure
- Fear of Success
- Fear-Based Energies
- Feelings
- Genetic Memory
- Geopathic Stress
- Heart Wall Emotions
- Hexes
- Hidden
- Hidden Programs
- Hidden Vows
- Illusions of Separation
- Jealousy and Envy
- Karmic Debt
- Lack of Boundaries
- Lack of Grounding
- Lack of Self-Love

Royal Template 20

Diving Deep into the Pool of the Mind

Chart 115

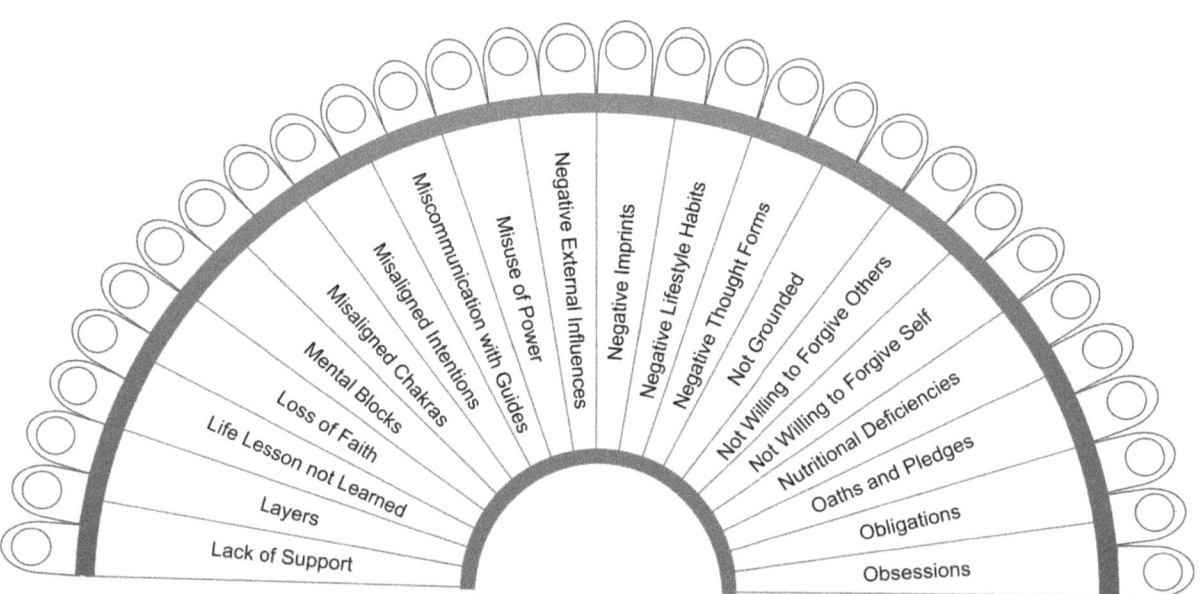

Blocks to Dowsing, Clearing & Healing, Chart 4

The chart contains the following labels (left to right):

- Lack of Support
- Layers
- Life Lesson not Learned
- Loss of Faith
- Mental Blocks
- Misaligned Chakras
- Misaligned Intentions
- Miscommunication with Guides
- Misuse of Power
- Negative External Influences
- Negative Imprints
- Negative Lifestyle Habits
- Negative Thought Forms
- Not Grounded
- Not Willing to Forgive Others
- Not Willing to Forgive Self
- Nutritional Deficiencies
- Oaths and Pledges
- Obligations
- Obsessions

Royal Template 20

Diving Deep into the Pool of the Mind

Chart 116

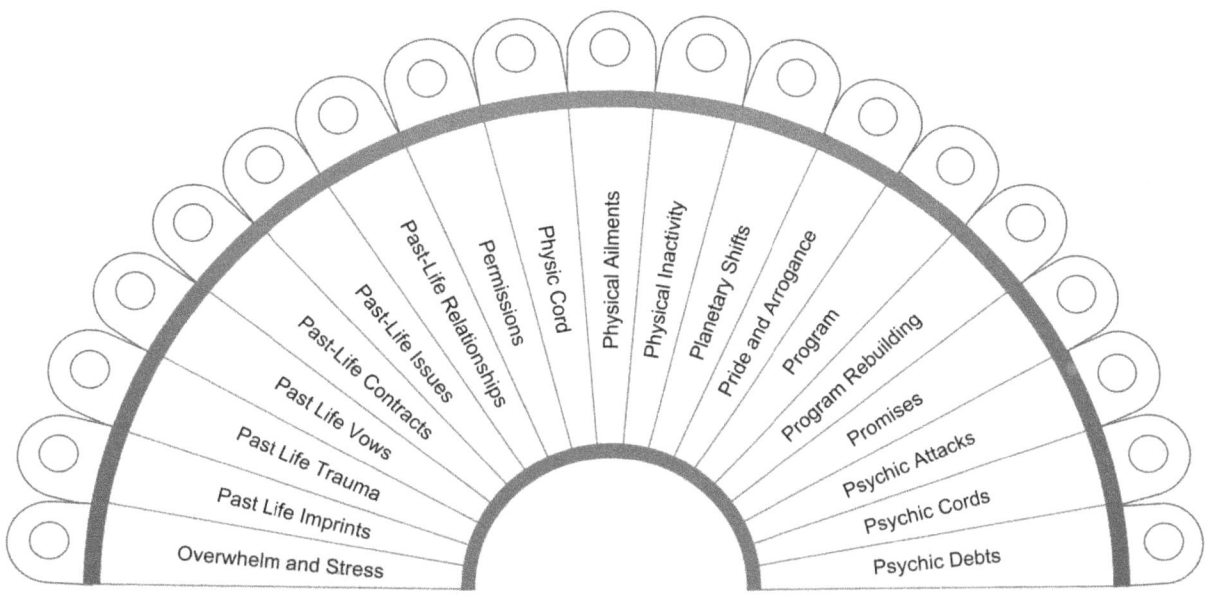

Blocks to Dowsing, Clearing & Healing, Chart 5

The chart contains the following labels (reading around the fan):

- Past-Life Relationships
- Permissions
- Physic Cord
- Physical Ailments
- Physical Inactivity
- Planetary Shifts
- Pride and Arrogance
- Program
- Program Rebuilding
- Promises
- Psychic Attacks
- Psychic Cords
- Psychic Debts
- Past-Life Issues
- Past-Life Contracts
- Past Life Vows
- Past Life Trauma
- Past Life Imprints
- Overwhelm and Stress

Royal Template 19

Diving Deep into the Pool of the Mind

Chart 117

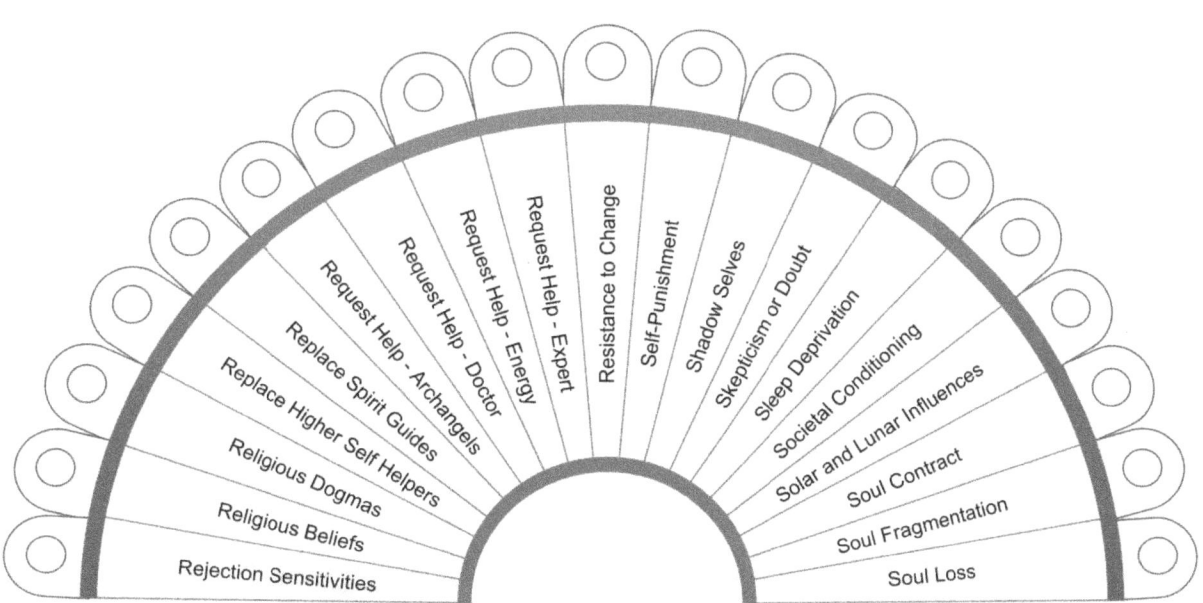

Blocks to Dowsing, Clearing & Healing, Chart 6

The chart contains the following labels (reading around the fan):

- Request Help - Archangels
- Request Help - Doctor
- Request Help - Energy
- Request Help - Expert
- Resistance to Change
- Self-Punishment
- Shadow Selves
- Skepticism or Doubt
- Sleep Deprivation
- Societal Conditioning
- Solar and Lunar Influences
- Soul Contract
- Soul Fragmentation
- Soul Loss
- Replace Spirit Guides
- Replace Higher Self Helpers
- Religious Dogmas
- Religious Beliefs
- Rejection Sensitivities

Royal Template 19

Diving Deep into the Pool of the Mind

Chart 118

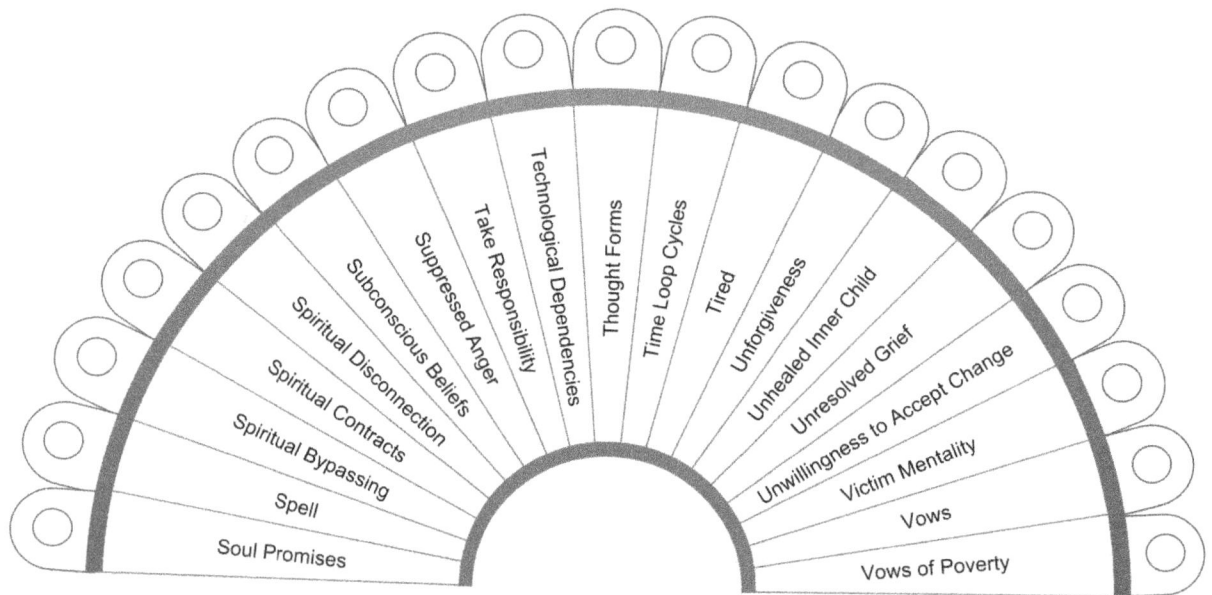

Blocks to Dowsing, Clearing & Healing, Chart 7

Technological Dependencies
Take Responsibility
Suppressed Anger
Subconscious Beliefs
Spiritual Disconnection
Spiritual Contracts
Spiritual Bypassing
Spell
Soul Promises
Thought Forms
Time Loop Cycles
Tired
Unforgiveness
Unhealed Inner Child
Unresolved Grief
Unwillingness to Accept Change
Victim Mentality
Vows
Vows of Poverty

Royal Template 19

Diving Deep into the Pool of the Mind

Chart 119

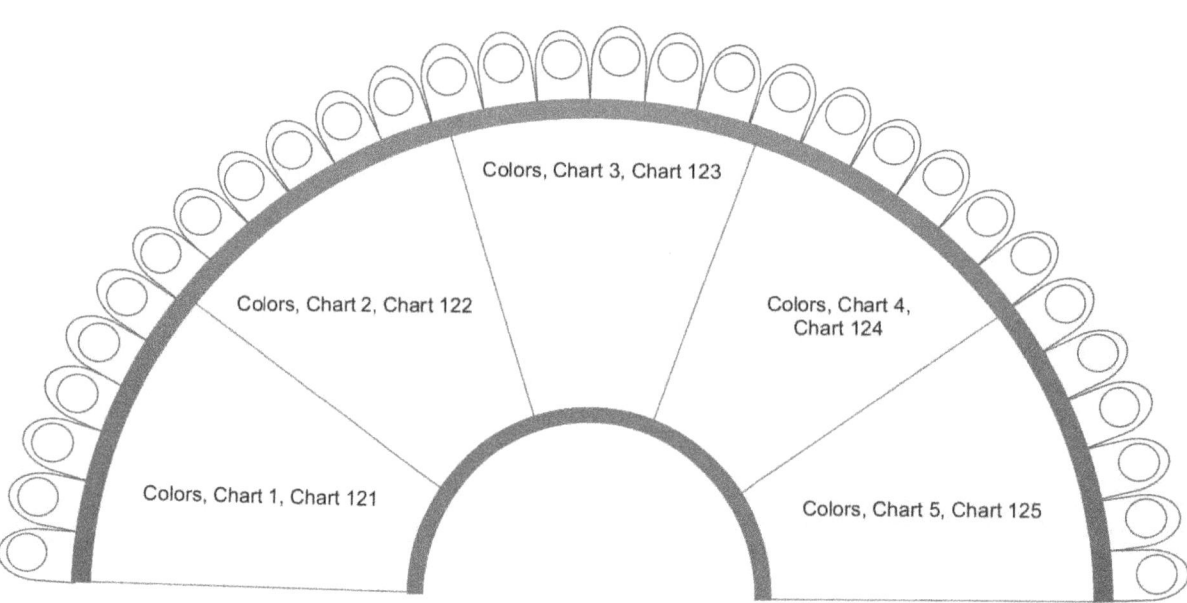

Colors, Chart 3, Chart 123

Colors, Chart 2, Chart 122

Colors, Chart 4, Chart 124

Colors, Chart 1, Chart 121

Colors, Chart 5, Chart 125

Colors, Master Chart

Royal Template 5h

Diving Deep into the Pool of the Mind

Chart 120

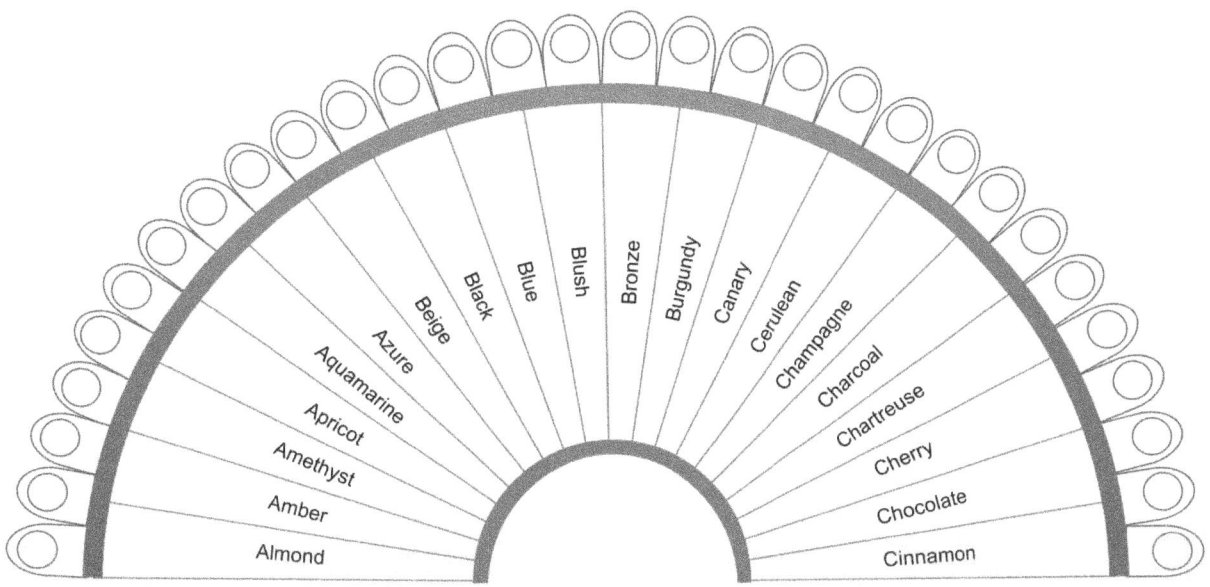

Colors, Chart 1

Royal Template 20

Diving Deep into the Pool of the Mind

Chart 121

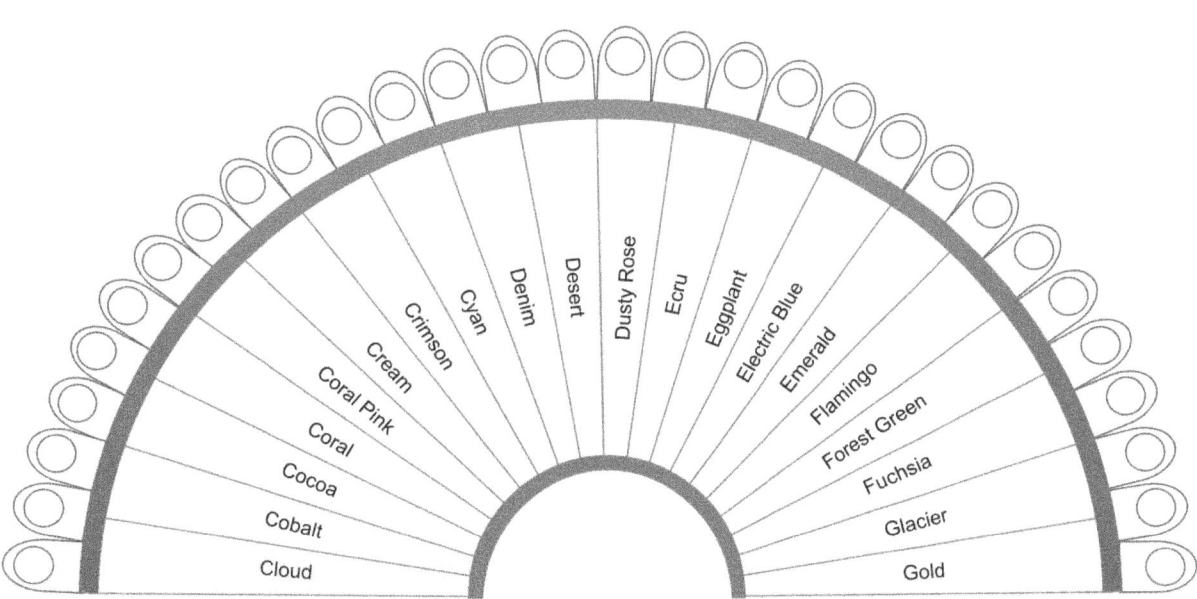

Colors, Chart 2

Royal Template 20

Diving Deep into the Pool of the Mind

Chart 122

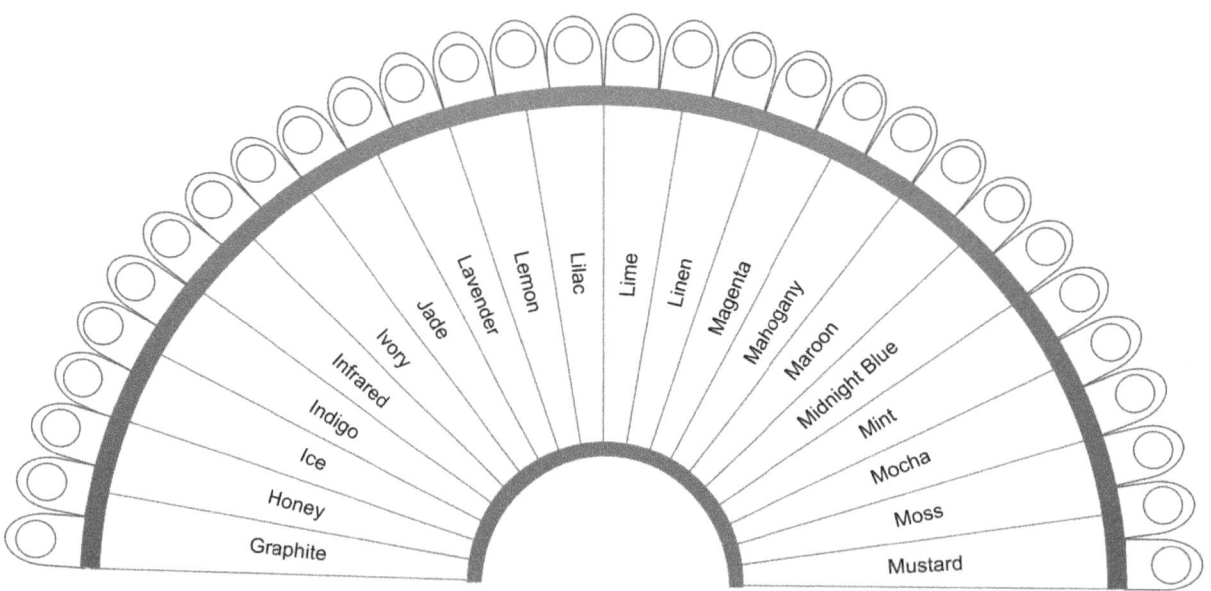

Colors, Chart 3

Royal Template 20

Diving Deep into the Pool of the Mind

Chart 123

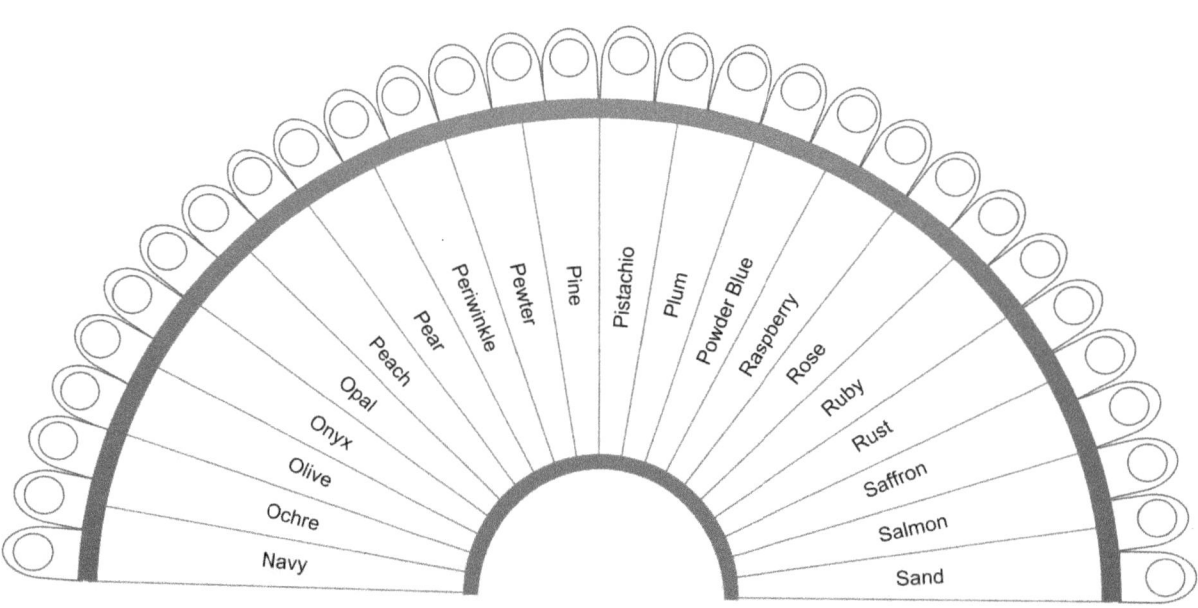

Colors, Chart 4

Royal Template 20

Diving Deep into the Pool of the Mind

Chart 124

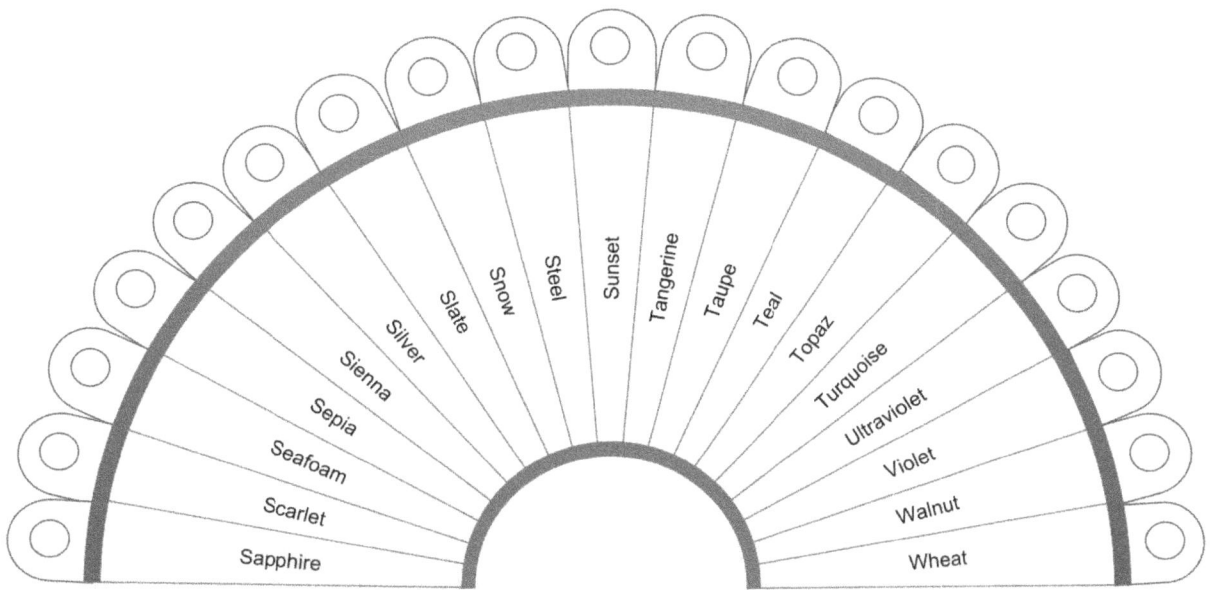

Sapphire
Scarlet
Seafoam
Sepia
Sienna
Silver
Slate
Snow
Steel
Sunset
Tangerine
Taupe
Teal
Topaz
Turquoise
Ultraviolet
Violet
Walnut
Wheat

Colors, Chart 5

Royal Template 19

Diving Deep into the Pool of the Mind

Chart 125

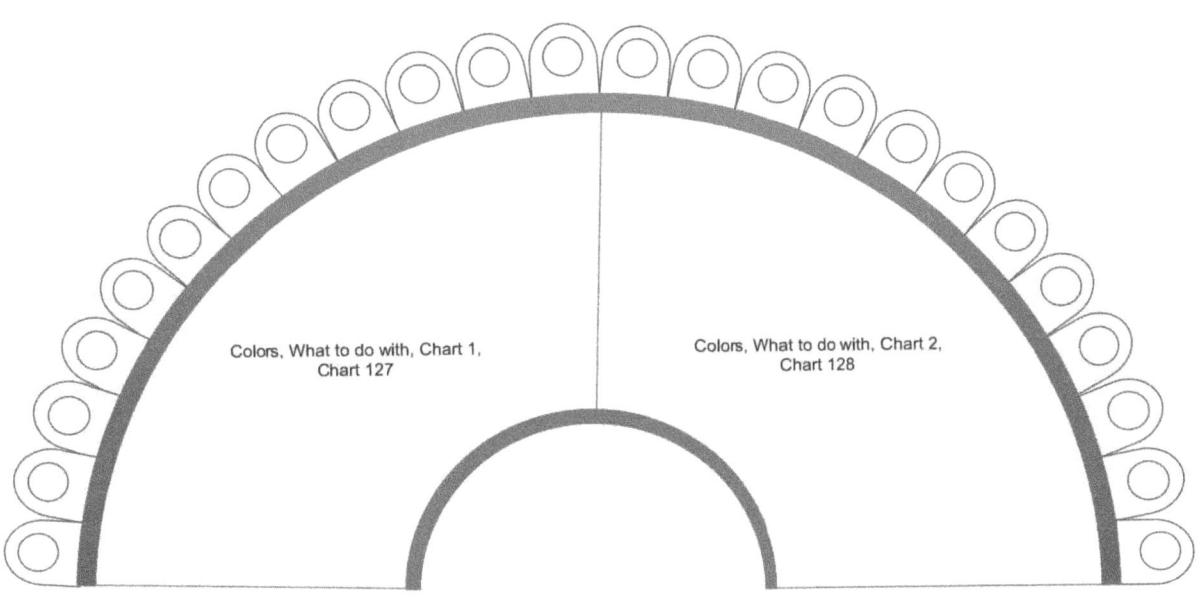

Colors, What to do with, Chart 1, Chart 127

Colors, What to do with, Chart 2, Chart 128

Colors, What to do with, Master Chart

Royal Template 2

Diving Deep into the Pool of the Mind

Chart 126

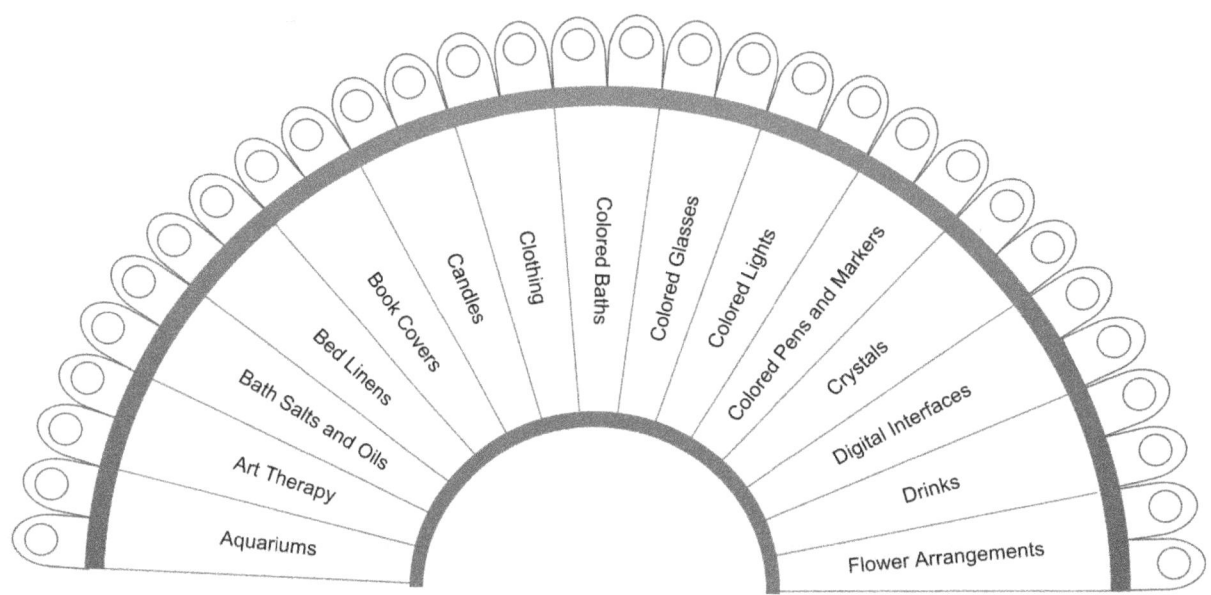

Colors, What to do with, Chart 1

Royal Template 15

Diving Deep into the Pool of the Mind

Chart 127

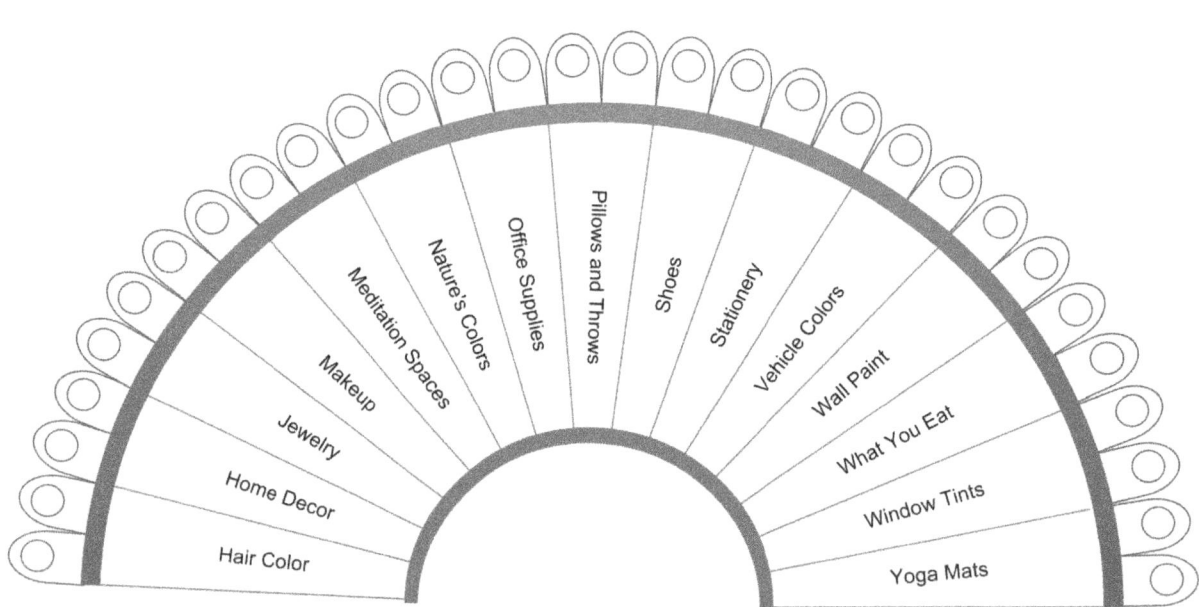

Colors, What to do with, Chart 2

Royal Template 15

Diving Deep into the Pool of the Mind

Chart 128

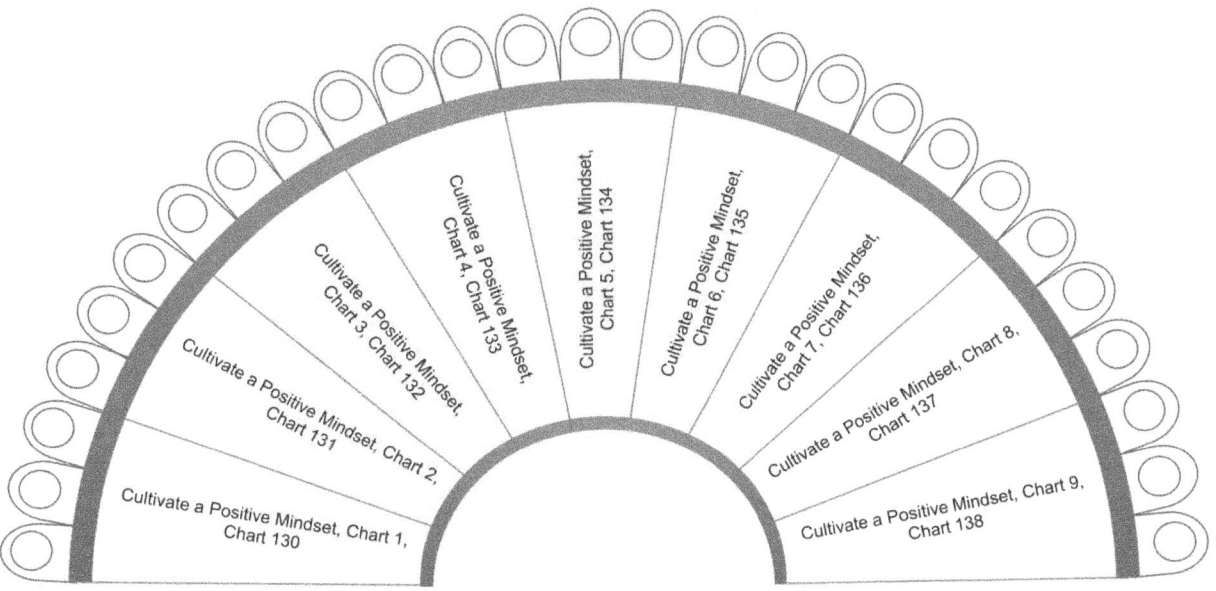

Cultivate a Positive Mindset, Master Chart

Cultivate a Positive Mindset, Chart 1, Chart 130
Cultivate a Positive Mindset, Chart 2, Chart 131
Cultivate a Positive Mindset, Chart 3, Chart 132
Cultivate a Positive Mindset, Chart 4, Chart 133
Cultivate a Positive Mindset, Chart 5, Chart 134
Cultivate a Positive Mindset, Chart 6, Chart 135
Cultivate a Positive Mindset, Chart 7, Chart 136
Cultivate a Positive Mindset, Chart 8, Chart 137
Cultivate a Positive Mindset, Chart 9, Chart 138

Royal Template 9

Diving Deep into the Pool of the Mind

Chart 129

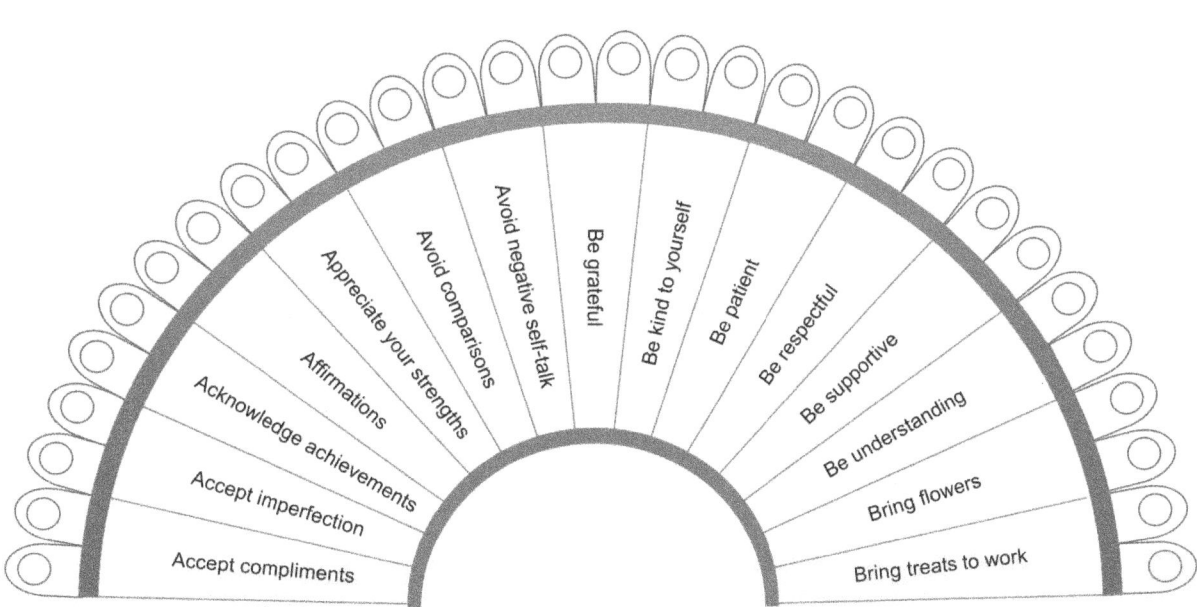

Accept compliments
Accept imperfection
Acknowledge achievements
Affirmations
Appreciate your strengths
Avoid comparisons
Avoid negative self-talk
Be grateful
Be kind to yourself
Be patient
Be respectful
Be supportive
Be understanding
Bring flowers
Bring treats to work

Cultivate a Positive Mindset, Chart 1

Royal Template 15

Diving Deep into the Pool of the Mind

Chart 130

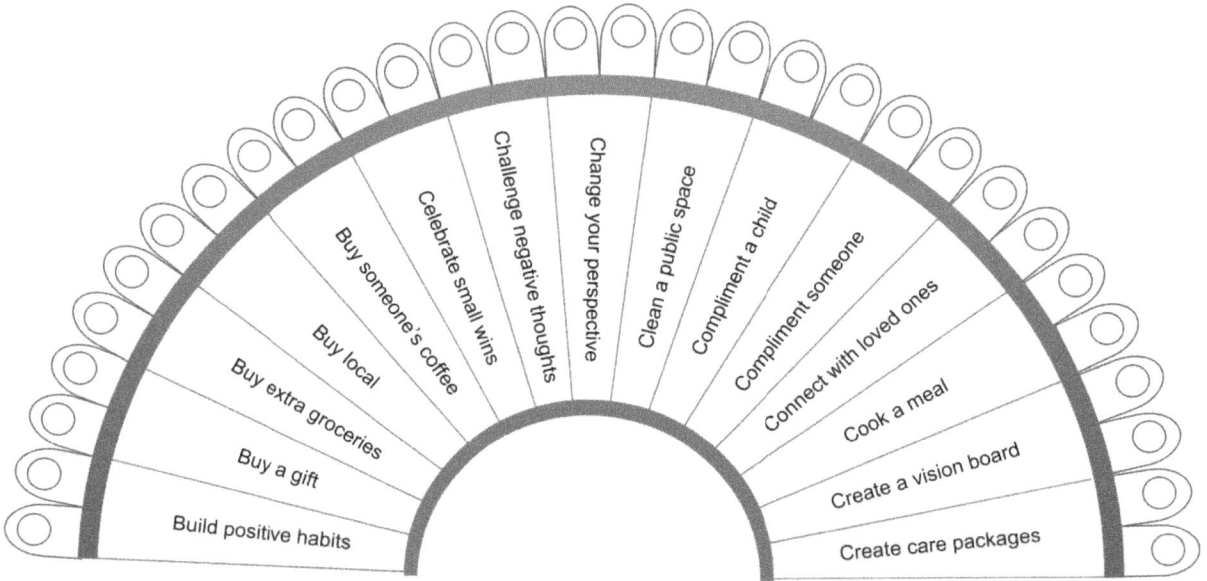

Cultivate a Positive Mindset, Chart 2

The labels on the chart, reading clockwise:
- Build positive habits
- Buy a gift
- Buy extra groceries
- Buy local
- Buy someone's coffee
- Celebrate small wins
- Challenge negative thoughts
- Change your perspective
- Clean a public space
- Compliment a child
- Compliment someone
- Connect with loved ones
- Cook a meal
- Create a vision board
- Create care packages

Royal Template 15

Diving Deep into the Pool of the Mind

Chart 131

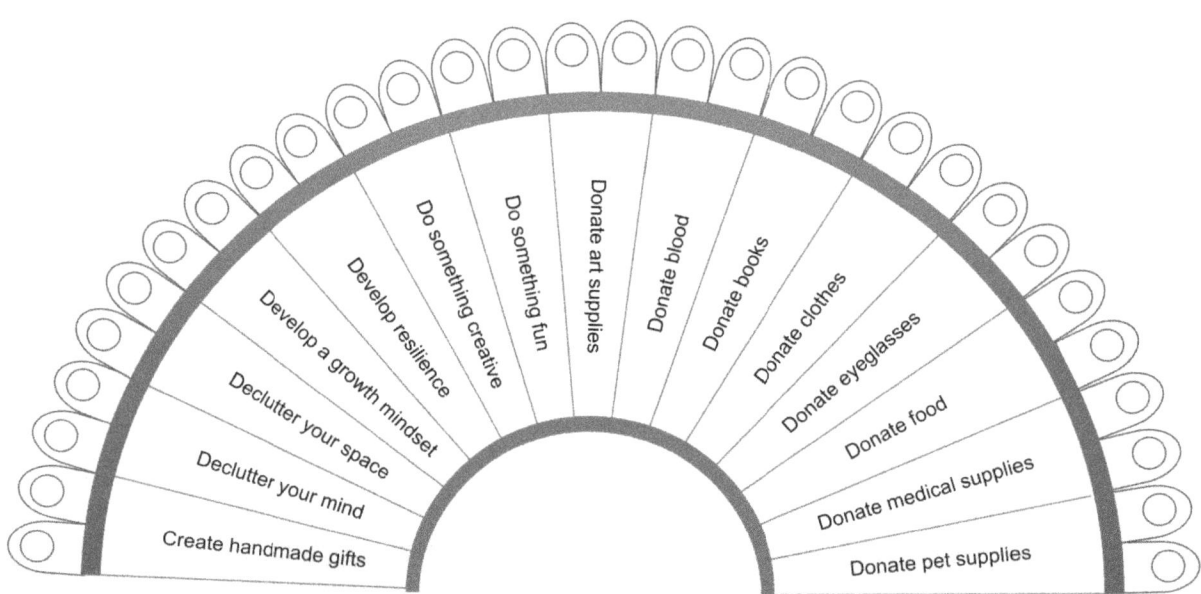

Cultivate a Positive Mindset, Chart 3

The labels on the chart, reading clockwise:
- Create handmade gifts
- Declutter your mind
- Declutter your space
- Develop a growth mindset
- Develop resilience
- Do something creative
- Do something fun
- Donate art supplies
- Donate blood
- Donate books
- Donate clothes
- Donate eyeglasses
- Donate food
- Donate medical supplies
- Donate pet supplies

Royal Template 15

Diving Deep into the Pool of the Mind

Chart 132

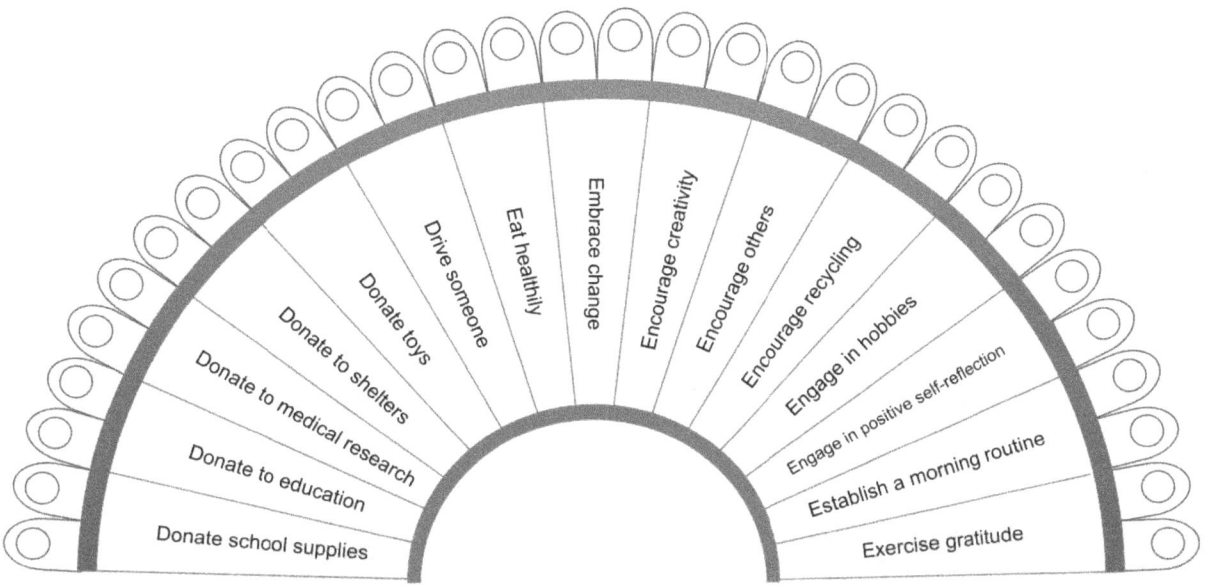

Cultivate a Positive Mindset, Chart 4

Drive someone
Eat healthily
Embrace change
Encourage creativity
Encourage others
Encourage recycling
Engage in hobbies
Engage in positive self-reflection
Establish a morning routine
Exercise gratitude
Donate toys
Donate to shelters
Donate to medical research
Donate to education
Donate school supplies

Royal Template 15

Diving Deep into the Pool of the Mind

Chart 133

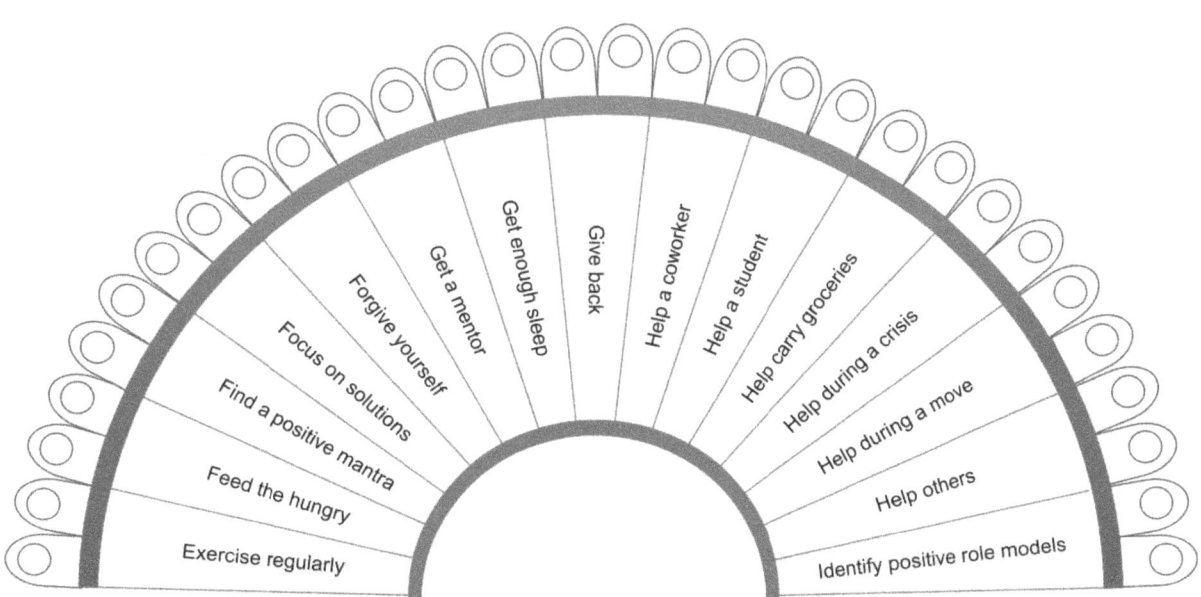

Cultivate a Positive Mindset, Chart 5

Get a mentor
Get enough sleep
Give back
Help a coworker
Help a student
Help carry groceries
Help during a crisis
Help during a move
Help others
Identify positive role models
Forgive yourself
Focus on solutions
Find a positive mantra
Feed the hungry
Exercise regularly

Royal Template 15

Diving Deep into the Pool of the Mind

Chart 134

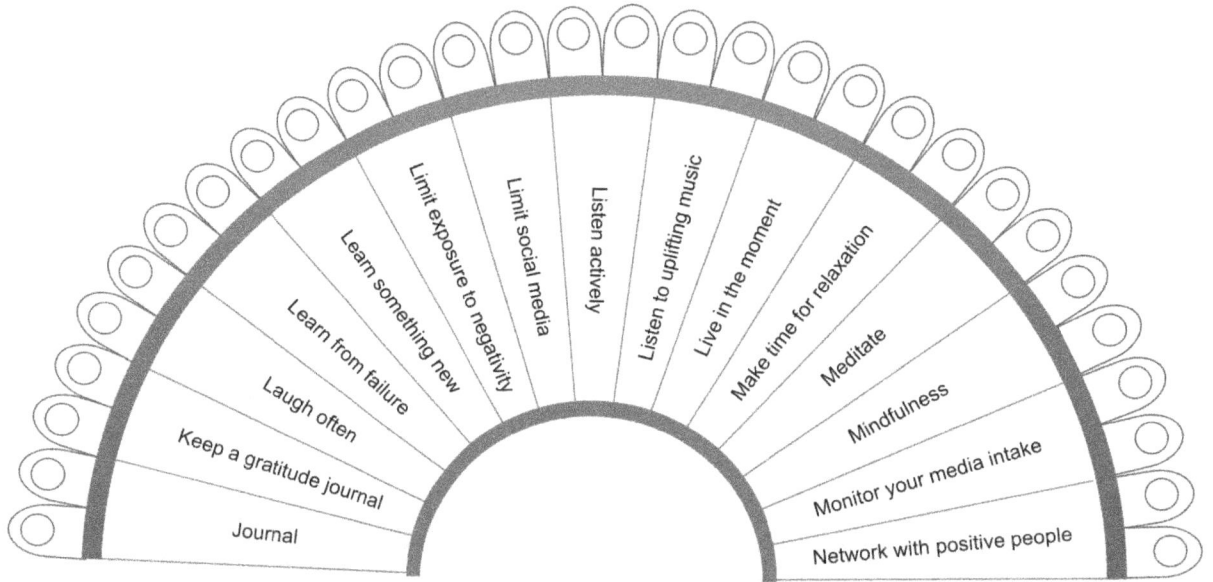

Cultivate a Positive Mindset, Chart 6

Learn something new
Learn from failure
Laugh often
Keep a gratitude journal
Journal
Limit exposure to negativity
Limit social media
Listen actively
Listen to uplifting music
Live in the moment
Make time for relaxation
Meditate
Mindfulness
Monitor your media intake
Network with positive people

Royal Template 15

Diving Deep into the Pool of the Mind

Chart 135

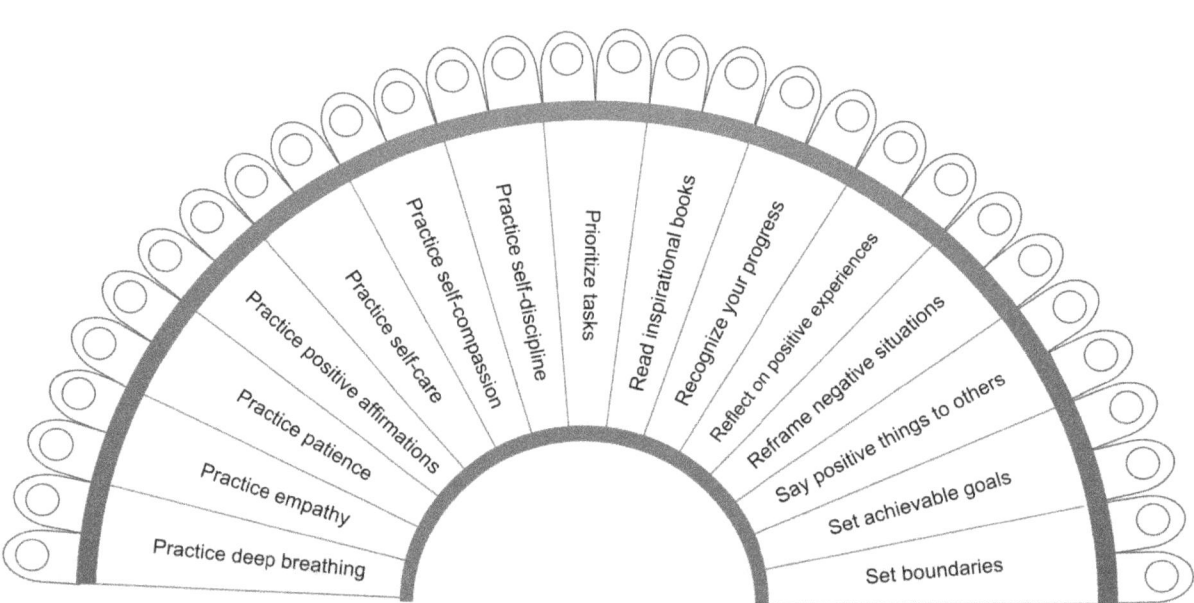

Cultivate a Positive Mindset, Chart 7

Practice positive affirmations
Practice patience
Practice empathy
Practice deep breathing
Practice self-care
Practice self-compassion
Practice self-discipline
Prioritize tasks
Read inspirational books
Recognize your progress
Reflect on positive experiences
Reframe negative situations
Say positive things to others
Set achievable goals
Set boundaries

Royal Template 15

Diving Deep into the Pool of the Mind

Chart 136

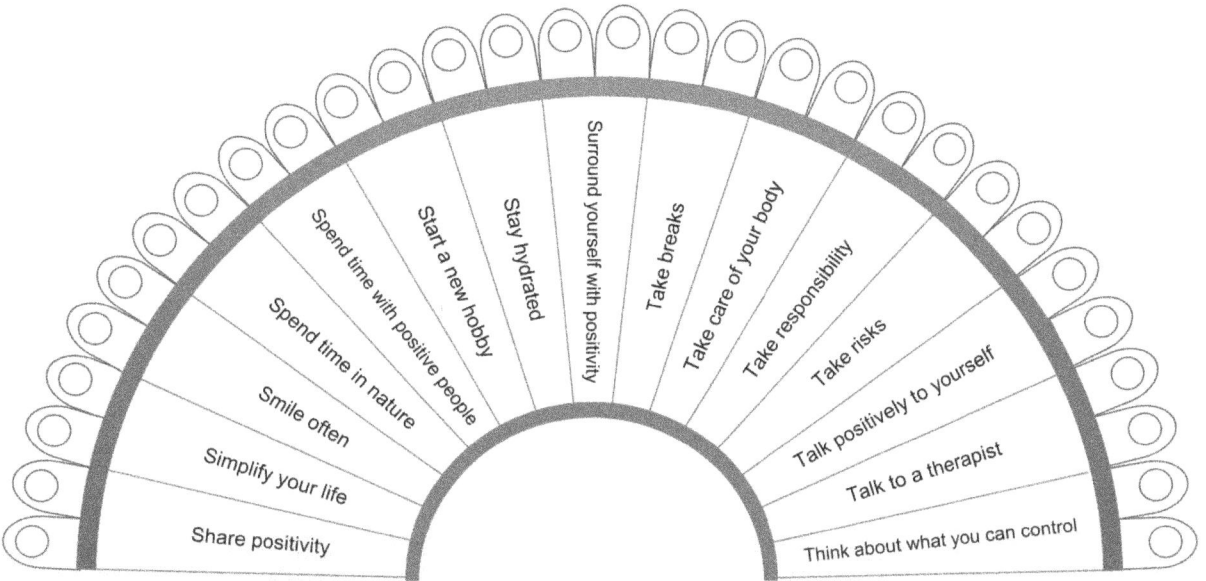

Cultivate a Positive Mindset, Chart 8

Spend time with positive people
Spend time in nature
Smile often
Simplify your life
Share positivity
Start a new hobby
Stay hydrated
Surround yourself with positivity
Take breaks
Take care of your body
Take responsibility
Take risks
Talk positively to yourself
Talk to a therapist
Think about what you can control

Royal Template 15

Diving Deep into the Pool of the Mind

Chart 137

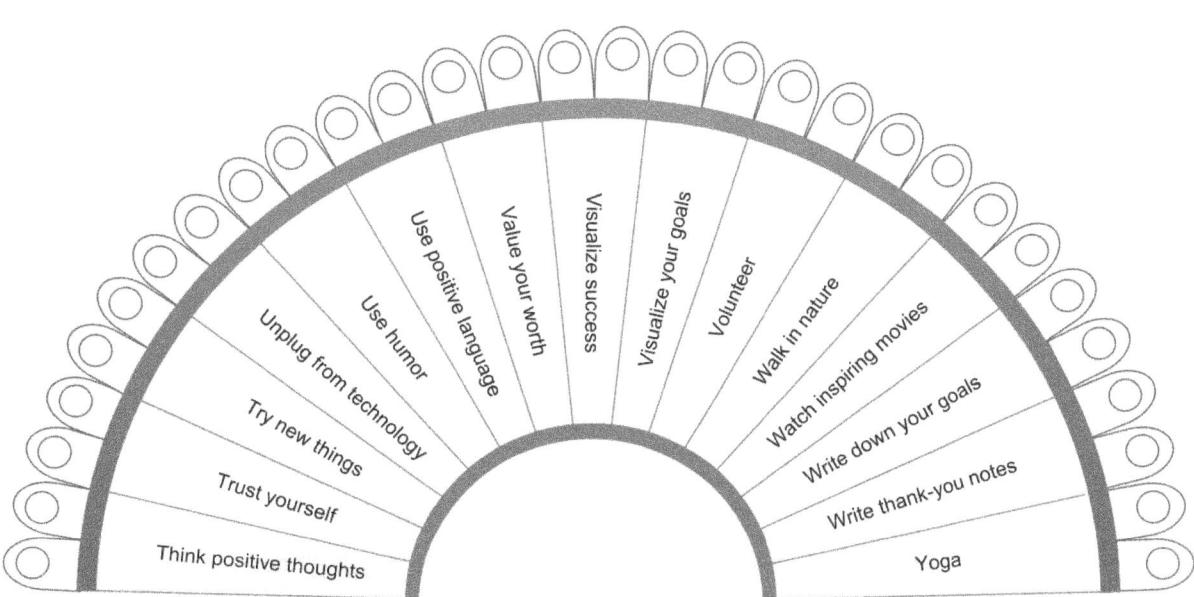

Cultivate a Positive Mindset, Chart 9

Unplug from technology
Try new things
Trust yourself
Think positive thoughts
Use humor
Use positive language
Value your worth
Visualize success
Visualize your goals
Volunteer
Walk in nature
Watch inspiring movies
Write down your goals
Write thank-you notes
Yoga

Royal Template 15

Diving Deep into the Pool of the Mind

Chart 138

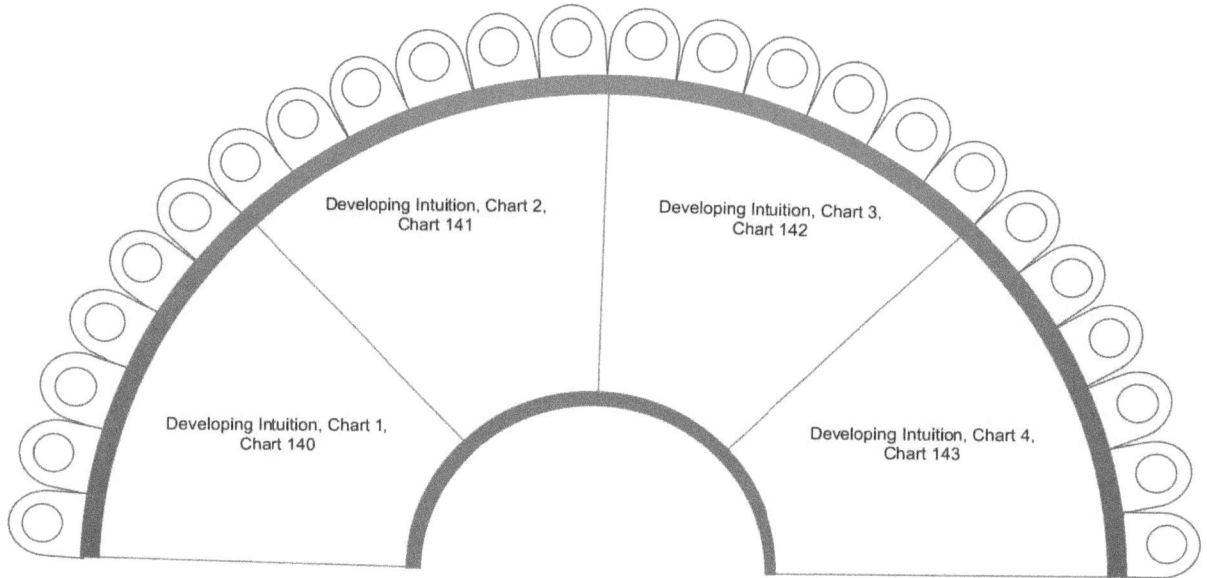

Developing Intuition, Master Chart

Developing Intuition, Chart 2, Chart 141

Developing Intuition, Chart 3, Chart 142

Developing Intuition, Chart 1, Chart 140

Developing Intuition, Chart 4, Chart 143

Royal Template 4h

Diving Deep into the Pool of the Mind

Chart 139

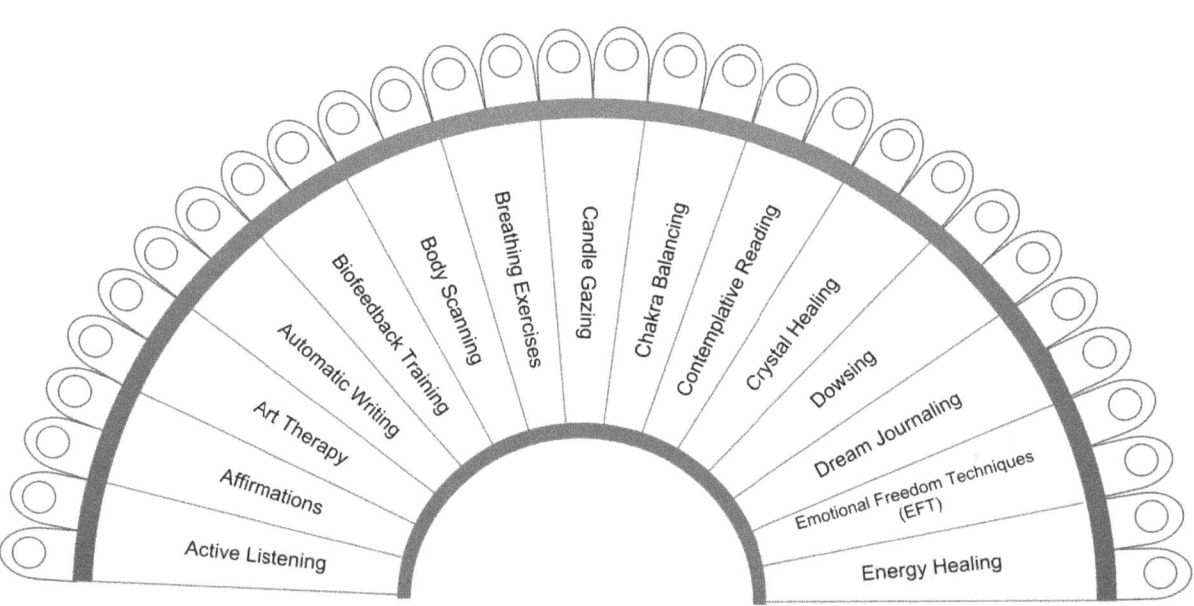

Developing Intuition, Chart 1

Active Listening
Affirmations
Art Therapy
Automatic Writing
Biofeedback Training
Body Scanning
Breathing Exercises
Candle Gazing
Chakra Balancing
Contemplative Reading
Crystal Healing
Dowsing
Dream Journaling
Emotional Freedom Techniques (EFT)
Energy Healing

Royal Template 15

Diving Deep into the Pool of the Mind

Chart 140

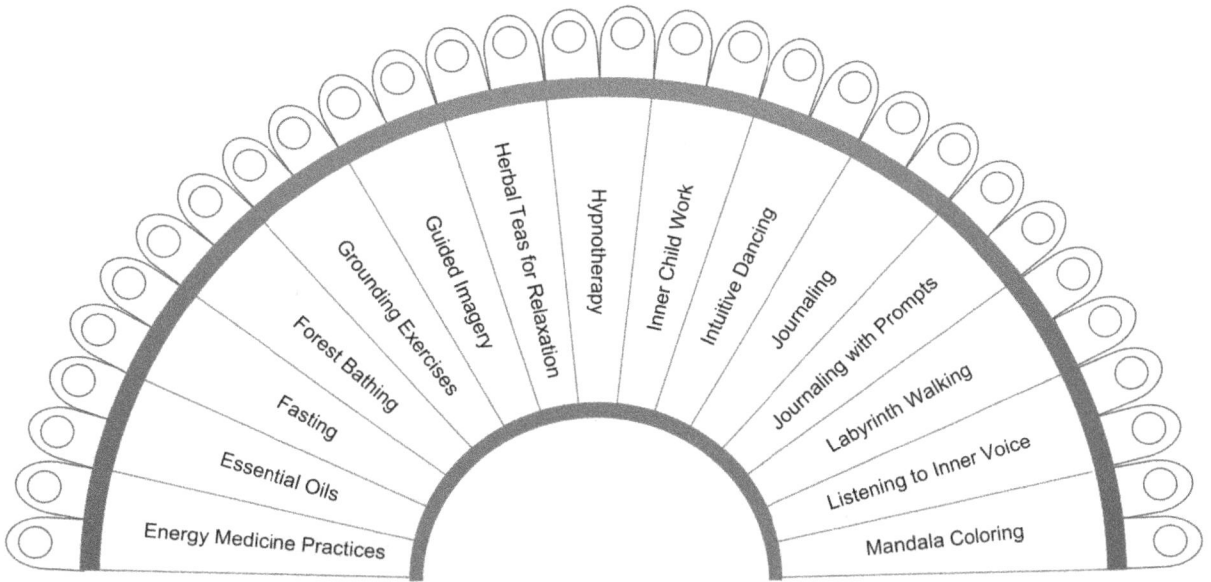

Developing Intuition, Chart 2

Herbal Teas for Relaxation
Hypnotherapy
Guided Imagery
Inner Child Work
Grounding Exercises
Intuitive Dancing
Forest Bathing
Journaling
Fasting
Journaling with Prompts
Essential Oils
Labyrinth Walking
Energy Medicine Practices
Listening to Inner Voice
Mandala Coloring

Royal Template 15

Diving Deep into the Pool of the Mind

Chart 141

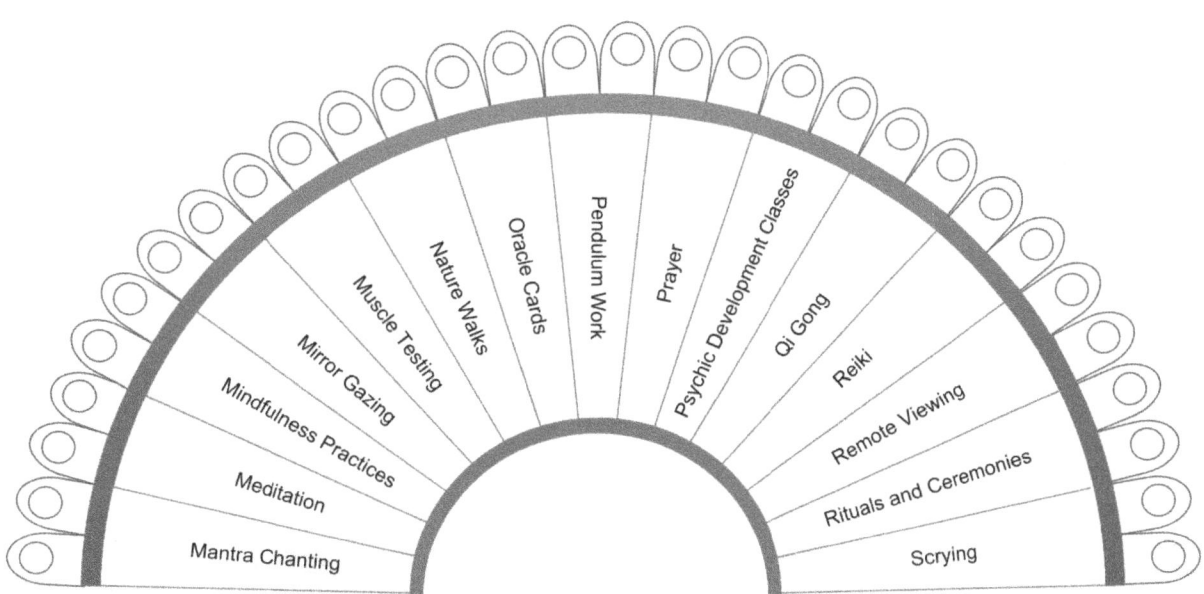

Developing Intuition, Chart 3

Nature Walks
Oracle Cards
Muscle Testing
Pendulum Work
Mirror Gazing
Prayer
Mindfulness Practices
Psychic Development Classes
Qi Gong
Meditation
Reiki
Mantra Chanting
Remote Viewing
Rituals and Ceremonies
Scrying

Royal Template 15

Diving Deep into the Pool of the Mind

Chart 142

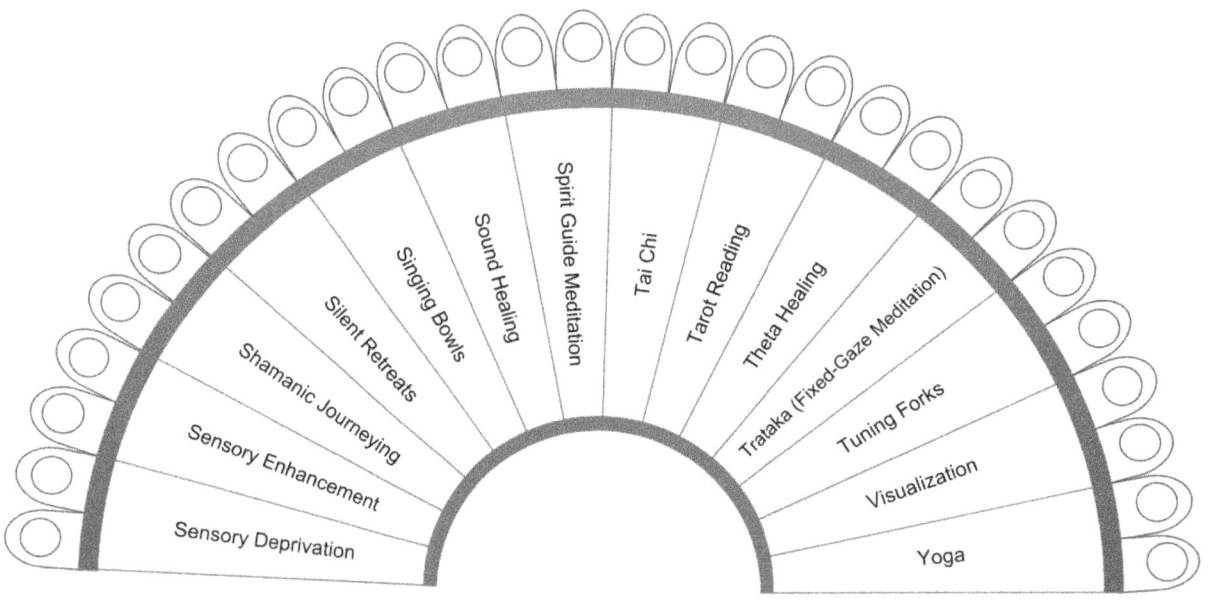

Developing Intuition, Chart 4

Spirit Guide Meditation
Sound Healing
Singing Bowls
Silent Retreats
Shamanic Journeying
Sensory Enhancement
Sensory Deprivation
Tai Chi
Tarot Reading
Theta Healing
Trataka (Fixed-Gaze Meditation)
Tuning Forks
Visualization
Yoga

Royal Template 14

Chart 143

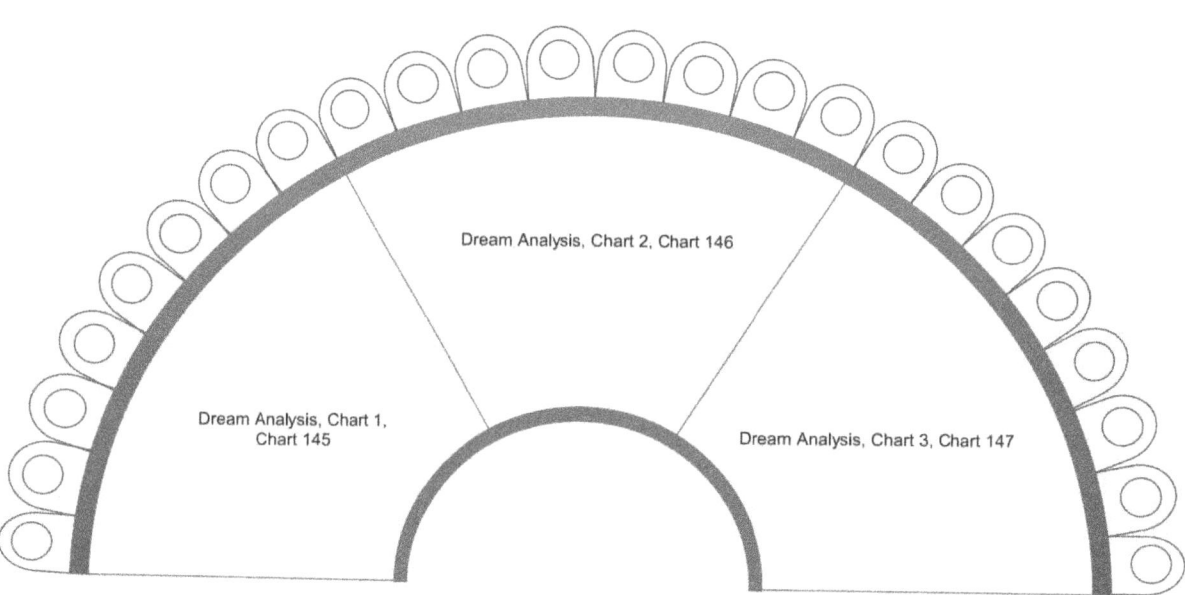

Dream Analysis, Chart 2, Chart 146

Dream Analysis, Chart 1,
Chart 145

Dream Analysis, Chart 3, Chart 147

Dream Analysis, Master Chart

Royal Template 3h

Chart 144

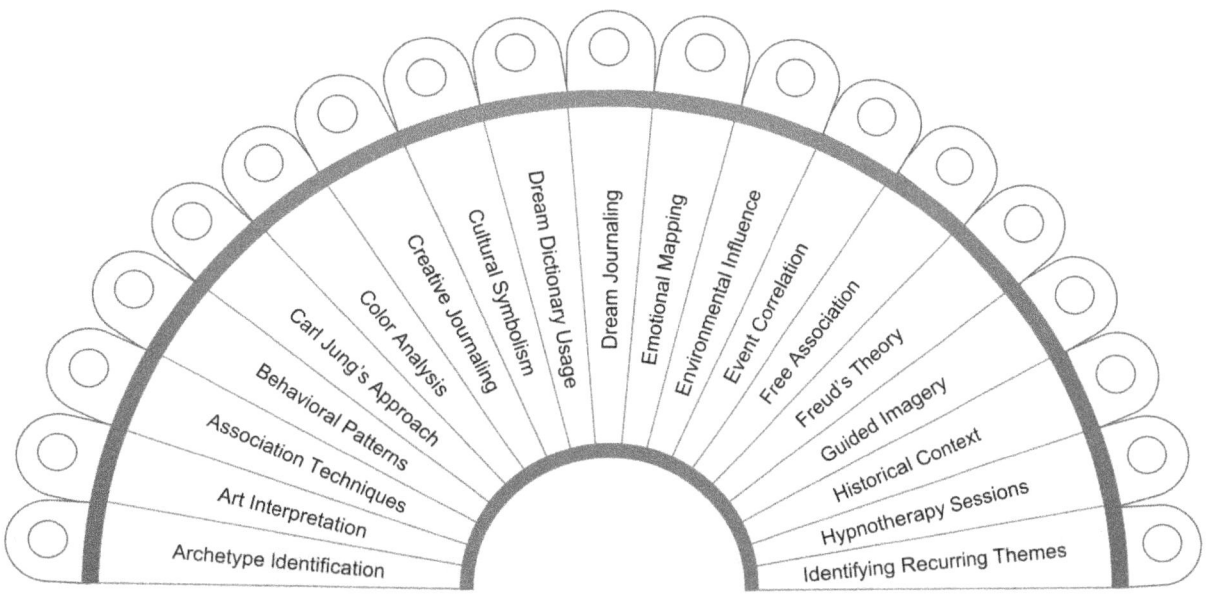

Dream Analysis, Chart 1

Radial labels (clockwise from left):
Archetype Identification, Art Interpretation, Association Techniques, Behavioral Patterns, Carl Jung's Approach, Color Analysis, Creative Journaling, Cultural Symbolism, Dream Dictionary Usage, Dream Journaling, Emotional Mapping, Environmental Influence, Event Correlation, Free Association, Freud's Theory, Guided Imagery, Historical Context, Hypnotherapy Sessions, Identifying Recurring Themes

Diving Deep into the Pool of the Mind

Chart 145

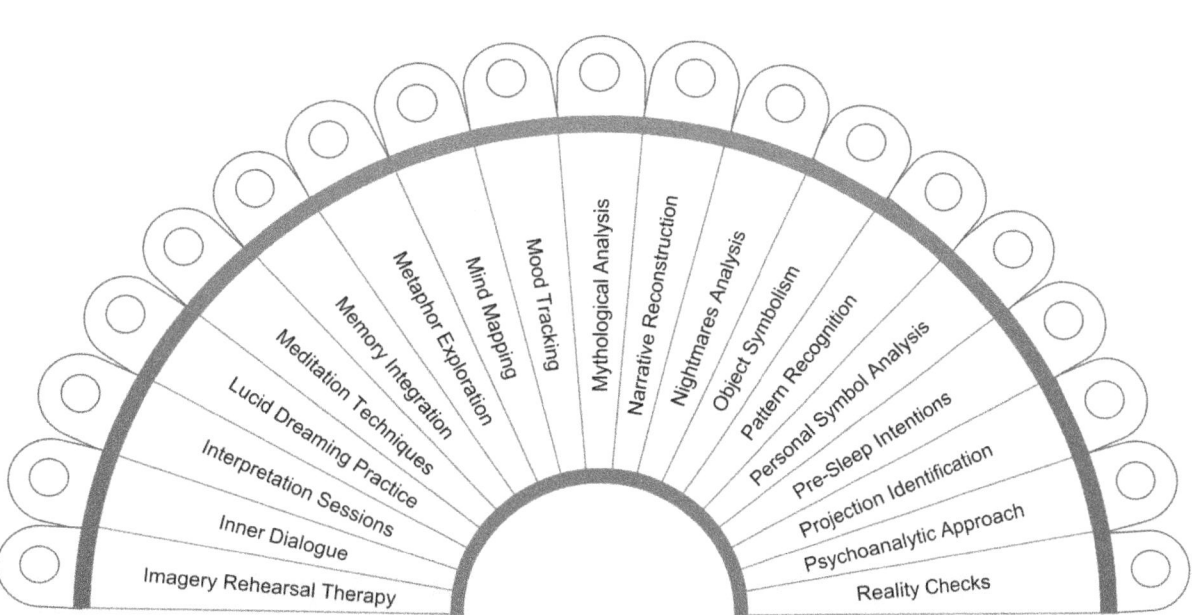

Dream Analysis, Chart 2

Radial labels (clockwise from left):
Imagery Rehearsal Therapy, Inner Dialogue, Interpretation Sessions, Lucid Dreaming Practice, Meditation Techniques, Memory Integration, Metaphor Exploration, Mind Mapping, Mood Tracking, Mythological Analysis, Narrative Reconstruction, Nightmares Analysis, Object Symbolism, Pattern Recognition, Personal Symbol Analysis, Pre-Sleep Intentions, Projection Identification, Psychoanalytic Approach, Reality Checks

Diving Deep into the Pool of the Mind

Chart 146

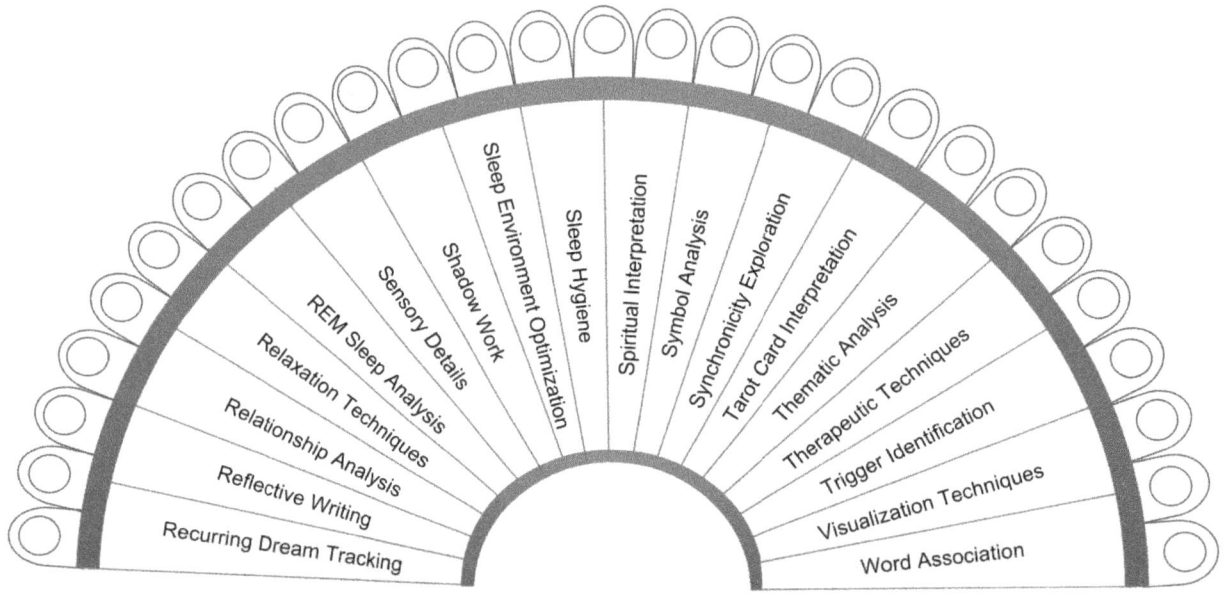

Dream Analysis, Chart 3

Royal Template 18

Diving Deep into the Pool of the Mind

Chart 147

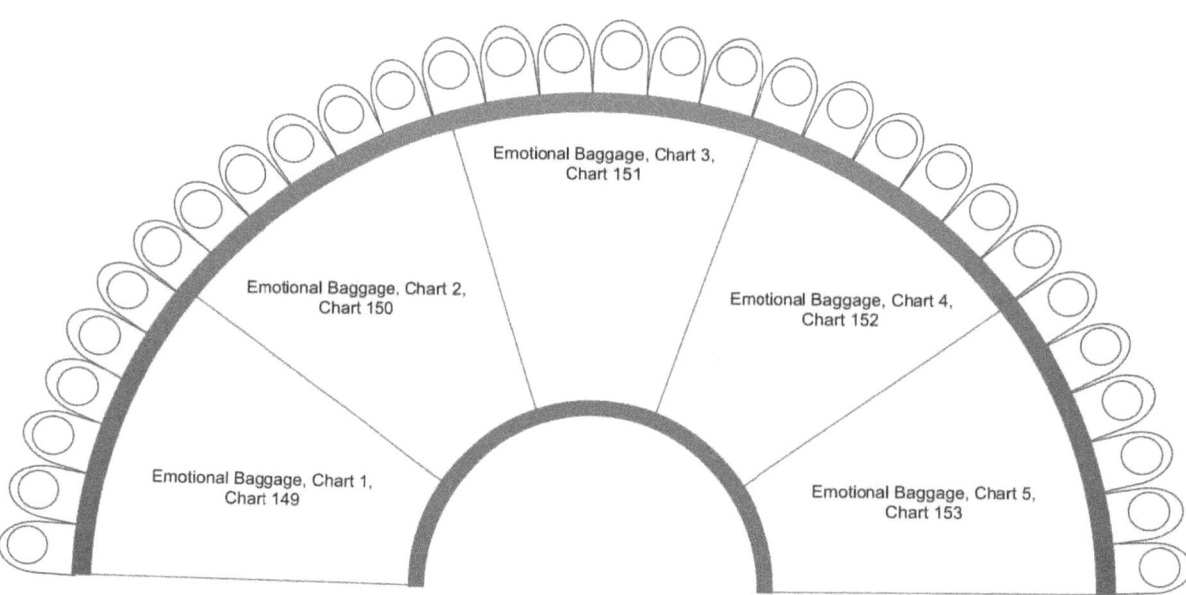

Emotional Baggage, Master Chart

Royal Template 5h

Diving Deep into the Pool of the Mind

Chart 148

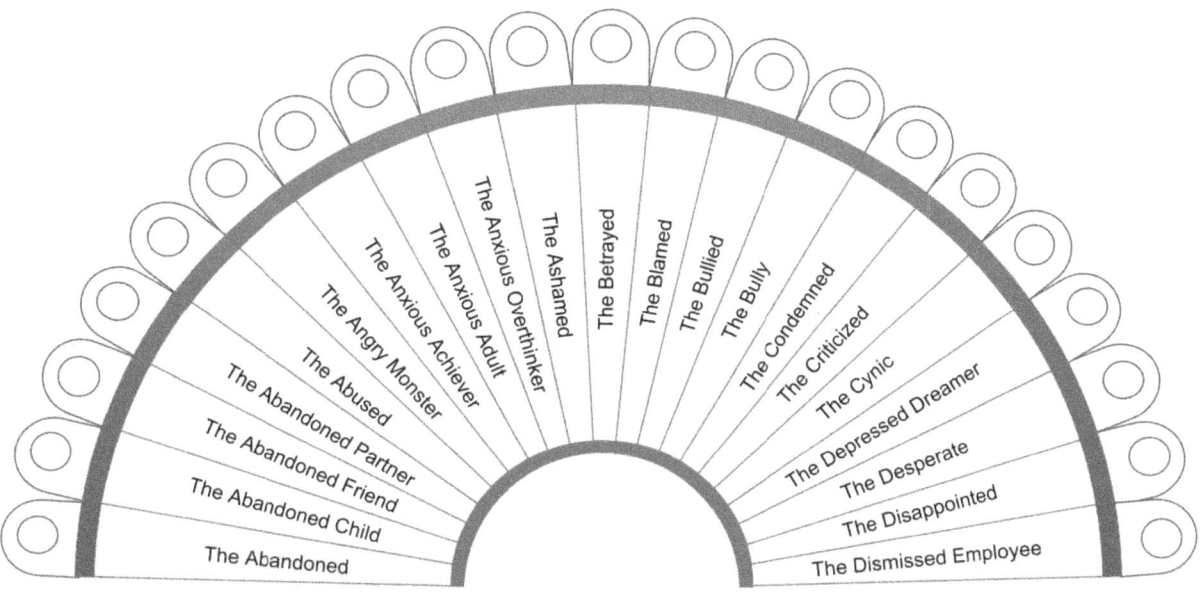

Emotional Baggage, Chart 1

The Anxious Overthinker
The Anxious Achiever
The Anxious Adult
The Angry Monster
The Abused
The Abandoned Partner
The Abandoned Friend
The Abandoned Child
The Abandoned
The Ashamed
The Betrayed
The Blamed
The Bullied
The Bully
The Condemned
The Criticized
The Cynic
The Depressed Dreamer
The Desperate
The Disappointed
The Dismissed Employee

Royal Template 21

Diving Deep into the Pool of the Mind

Chart 149

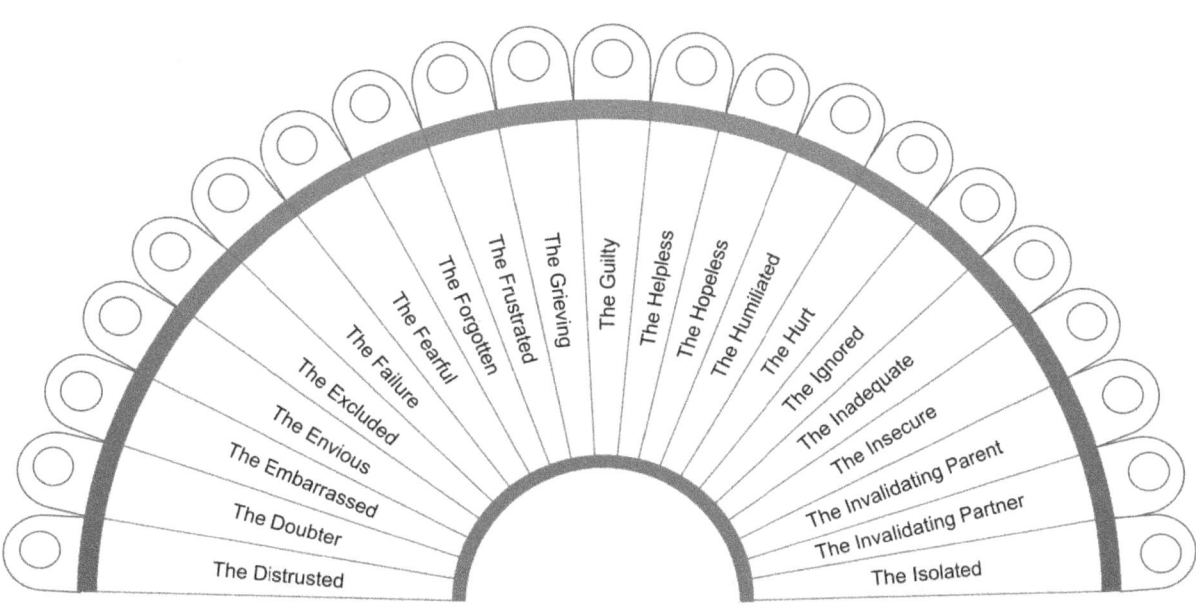

Emotional Baggage, Chart 2

The Fearful
The Failure
The Excluded
The Envious
The Embarrassed
The Doubter
The Distrusted
The Forgotten
The Frustrated
The Grieving
The Guilty
The Helpless
The Hopeless
The Humiliated
The Hurt
The Ignored
The Inadequate
The Insecure
The Invalidating Parent
The Invalidating Partner
The Isolated

Royal Template 21

Diving Deep into the Pool of the Mind

Chart 150

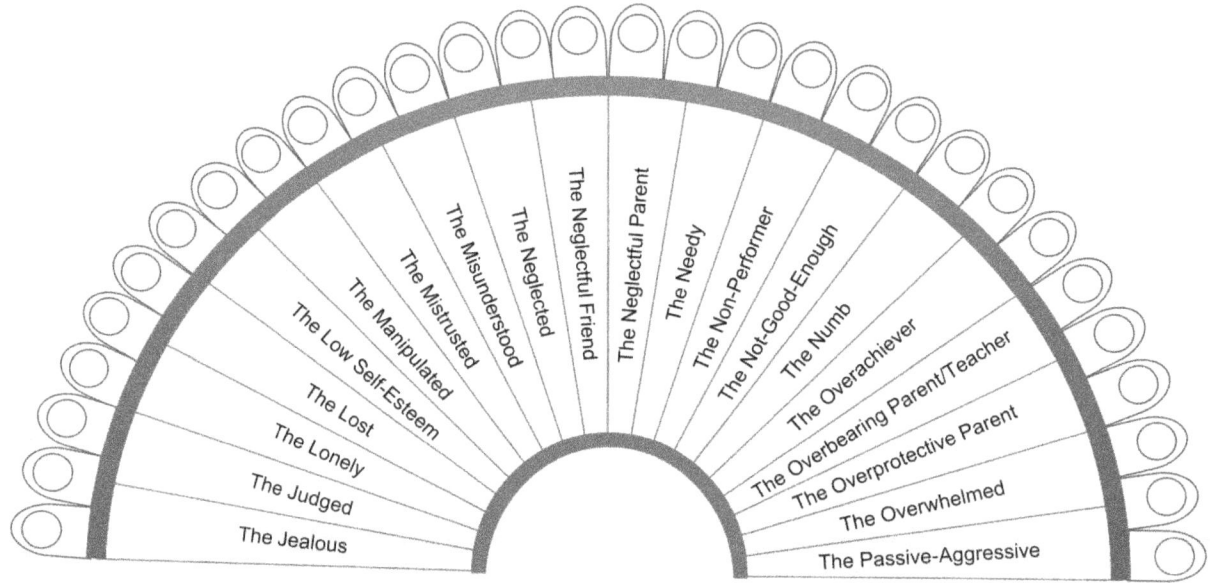

Emotional Baggage, Chart 3

The labels, reading around the fan:
The Jealous
The Judged
The Lonely
The Lost
The Low Self-Esteem
The Manipulated
The Mistrusted
The Misunderstood
The Neglected
The Neglectful Friend
The Neglectful Parent
The Needy
The Non-Performer
The Not-Good-Enough
The Numb
The Overachiever
The Overbearing Parent/Teacher
The Overprotective Parent
The Overwhelmed
The Passive-Aggressive

Royal Template 20

Diving Deep into the Pool of the Mind

Chart 151

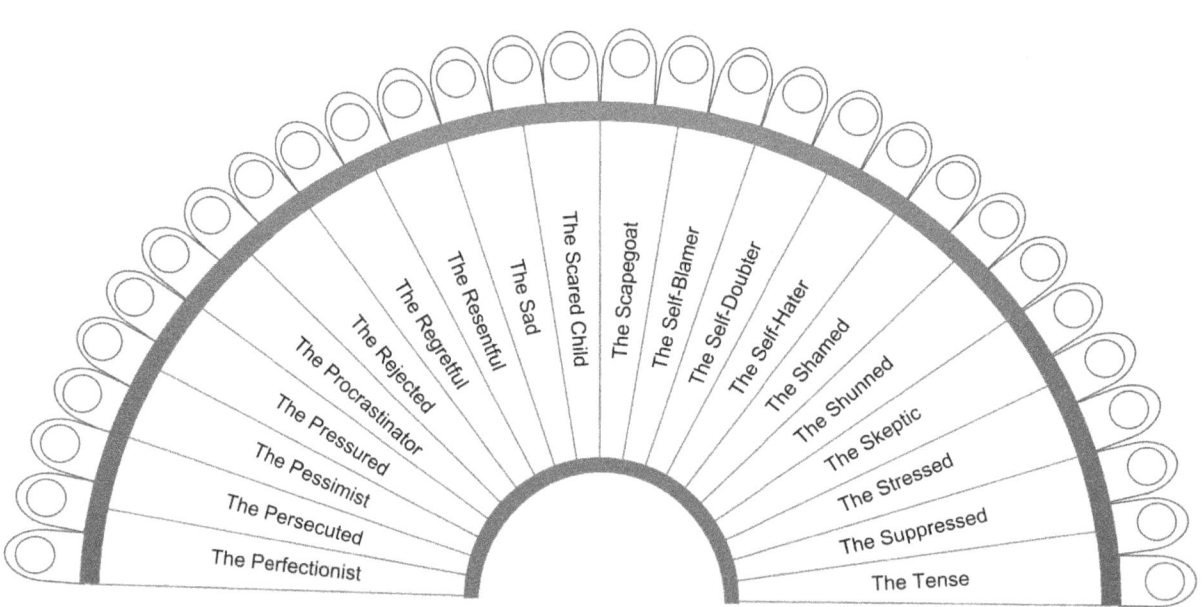

Emotional Baggage, Chart 4

The labels, reading around the fan:
The Perfectionist
The Persecuted
The Pessimist
The Pressured
The Procrastinator
The Rejected
The Regretful
The Resentful
The Sad
The Scared Child
The Scapegoat
The Self-Blamer
The Self-Doubter
The Self-Hater
The Shamed
The Shunned
The Skeptic
The Stressed
The Suppressed
The Tense

Royal Template 20

Diving Deep into the Pool of the Mind

Chart 152

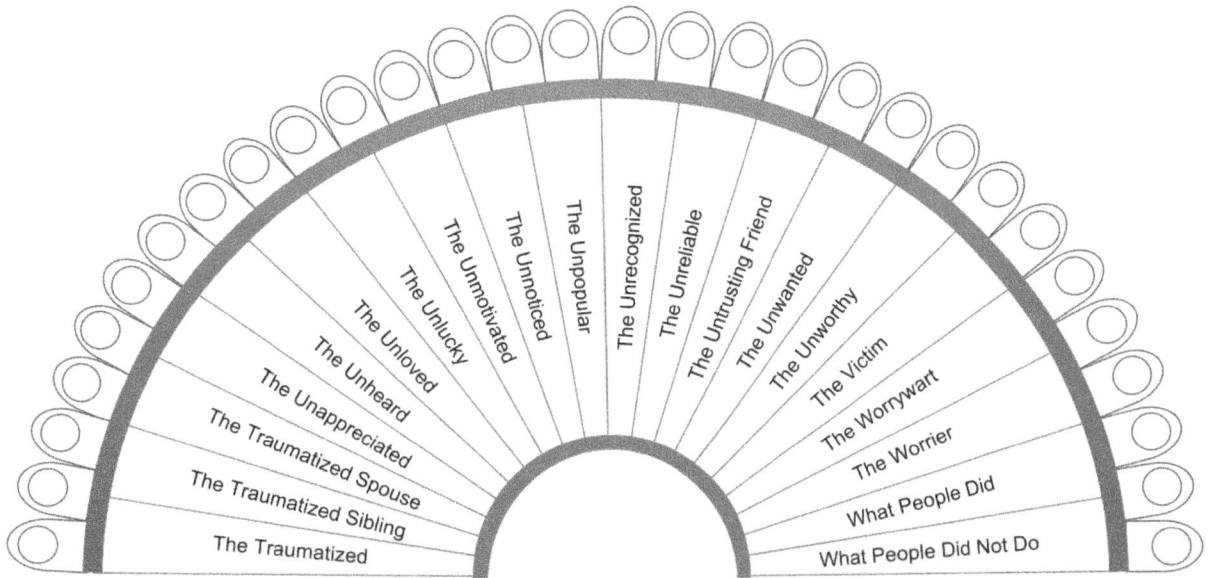

Emotional Baggage, Chart 5

The Unmotivated
The Unlucky
The Unloved
The Unheard
The Unappreciated
The Traumatized Spouse
The Traumatized Sibling
The Traumatized
The Unnoticed
The Unpopular
The Unrecognized
The Unreliable
The Untrusting Friend
The Unwanted
The Unworthy
The Victim
The Worrywart
The Worrier
What People Did
What People Did Not Do

Royal Template 20

Diving Deep into the Pool of the Mind

Chart 153

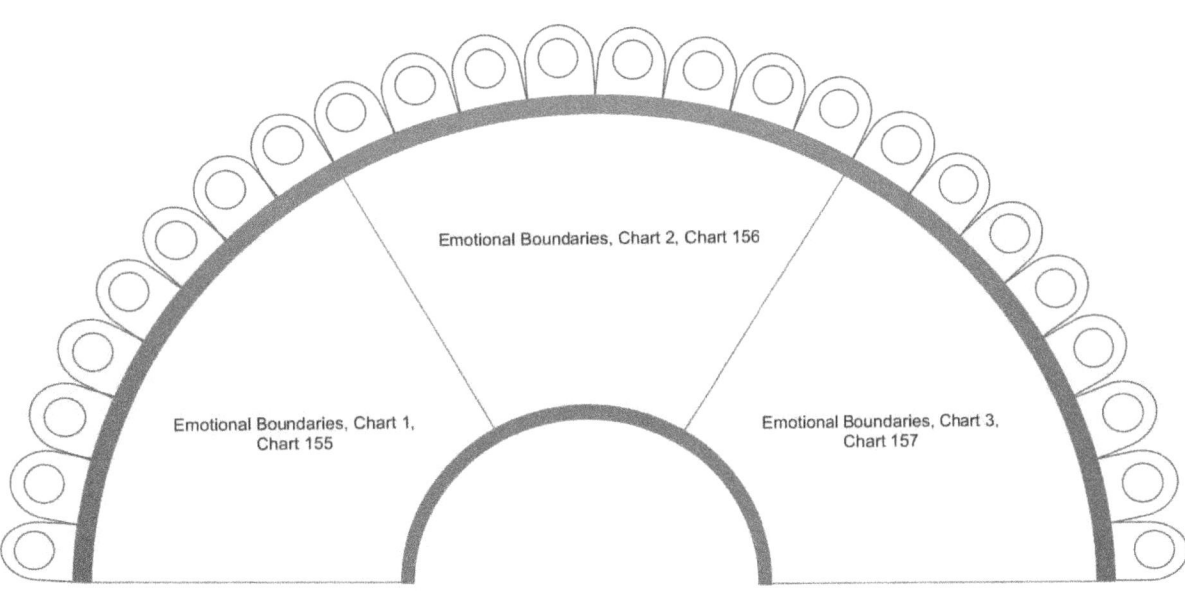

Emotional Boundaries, Chart 2, Chart 156

Emotional Boundaries, Chart 1, Chart 155

Emotional Boundaries, Chart 3, Chart 157

Emotional Boundaries, Master Chart

Royal Template 3h

Diving Deep into the Pool of the Mind

Chart 154

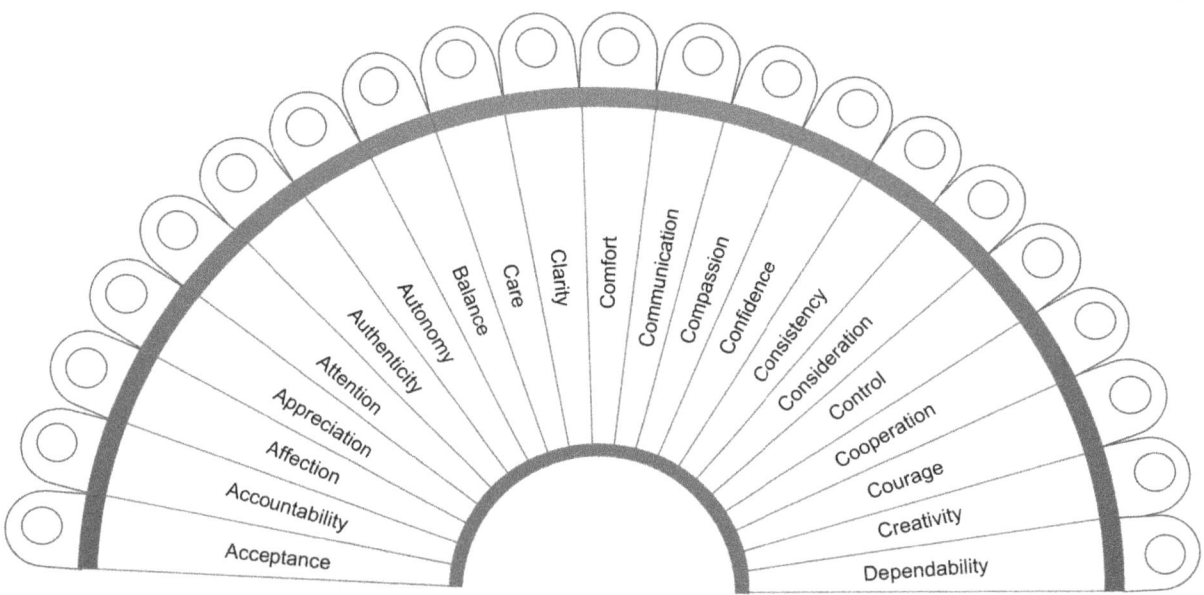

Emotional Boundaries, Chart 1

Acceptance
Accountability
Affection
Appreciation
Attention
Authenticity
Autonomy
Balance
Care
Clarity
Comfort
Communication
Compassion
Confidence
Consistency
Consideration
Control
Cooperation
Courage
Creativity
Dependability

Royal Template 21

Diving Deep into the Pool of the Mind

Chart 155

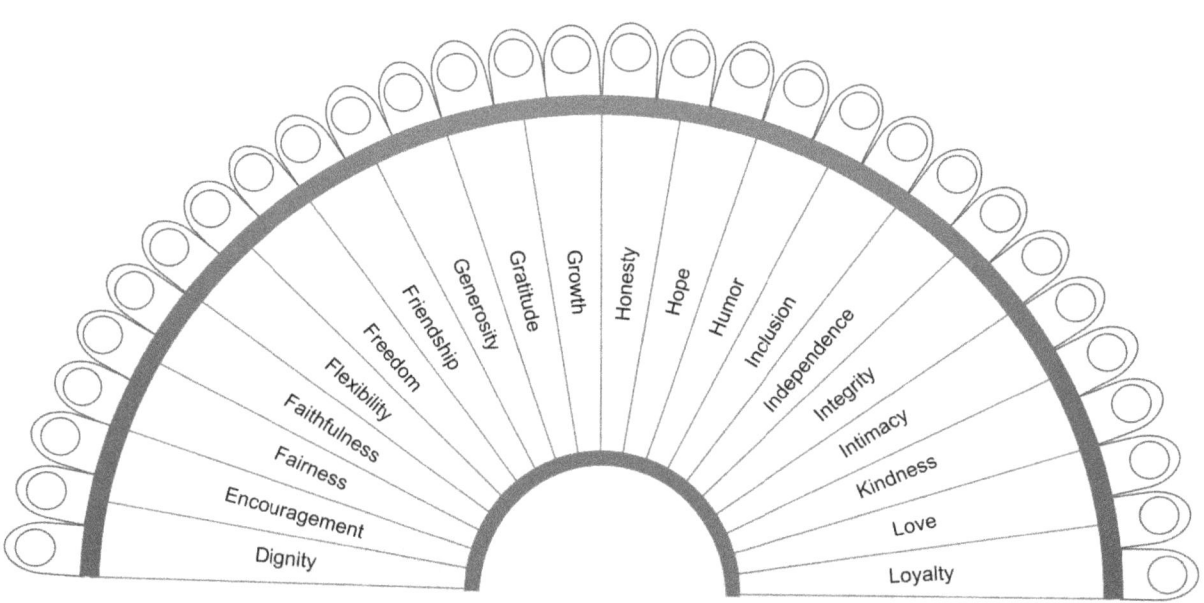

Dignity
Encouragement
Fairness
Faithfulness
Flexibility
Freedom
Friendship
Generosity
Gratitude
Growth
Honesty
Hope
Humor
Inclusion
Independence
Integrity
Intimacy
Kindness
Love
Loyalty

Emotional Boundaries, Chart 2

Royal Template 20

Diving Deep into the Pool of the Mind

Chart 156

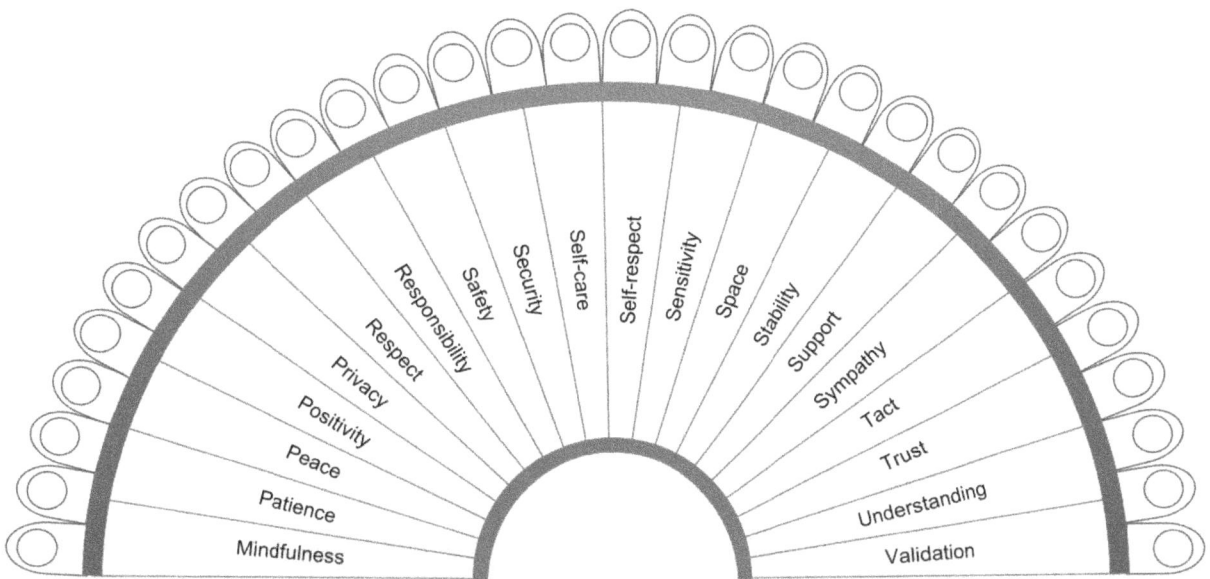

Emotional Boundaries, Chart 3

The chart contains the following labels (left to right):

Mindfulness, Patience, Peace, Positivity, Privacy, Respect, Responsibility, Safety, Security, Self-care, Self-respect, Sensitivity, Space, Stability, Support, Sympathy, Tact, Trust, Understanding, Validation

Royal Template 20

Diving Deep into the Pool of the Mind

Chart 157

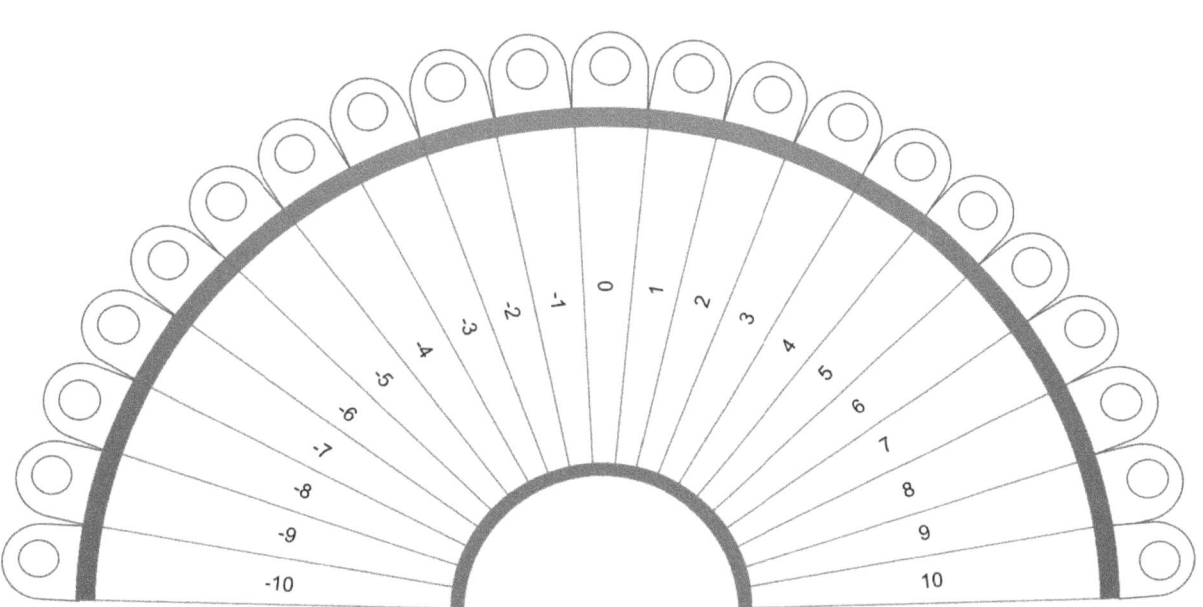

The chart contains the following values (left to right):

-10, -9, -8, -7, -6, -5, -4, -3, -2, -1, 0, 1, 2, 3, 4, 5, 6, 7, 8, 9, 10

Emotional Level Chart

Royal Template 21

Diving Deep into the Pool of the Mind

Chart 158

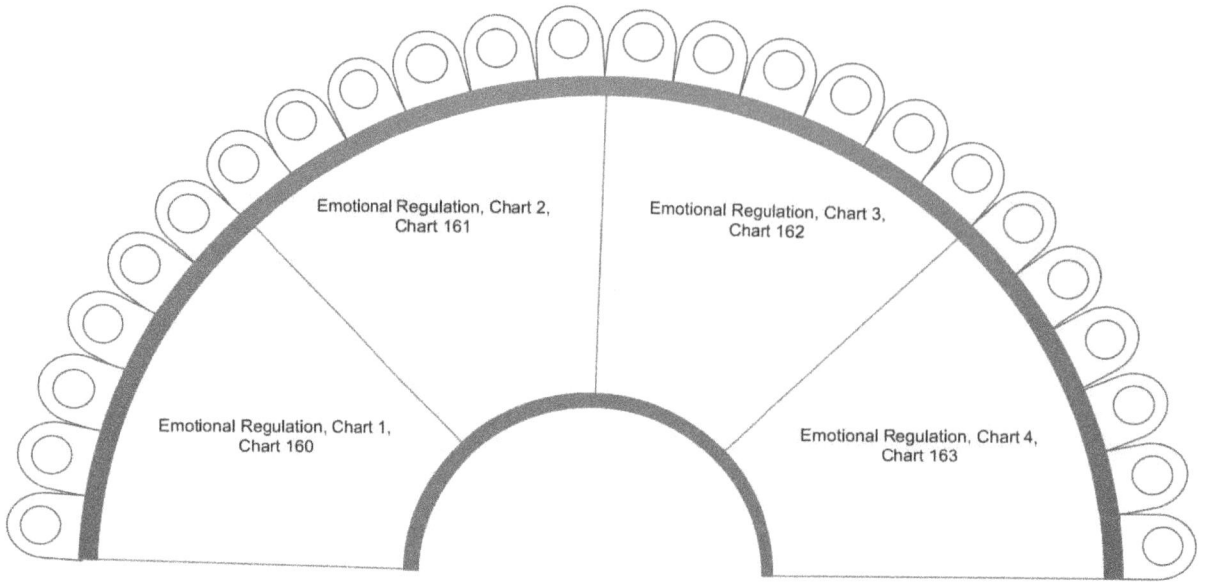

Emotional Regulation, Master Chart

Emotional Regulation, Chart 2, Chart 161

Emotional Regulation, Chart 3, Chart 162

Emotional Regulation, Chart 1, Chart 160

Emotional Regulation, Chart 4, Chart 163

Royal Template 4h

Diving Deep into the Pool of the Mind

Chart 159

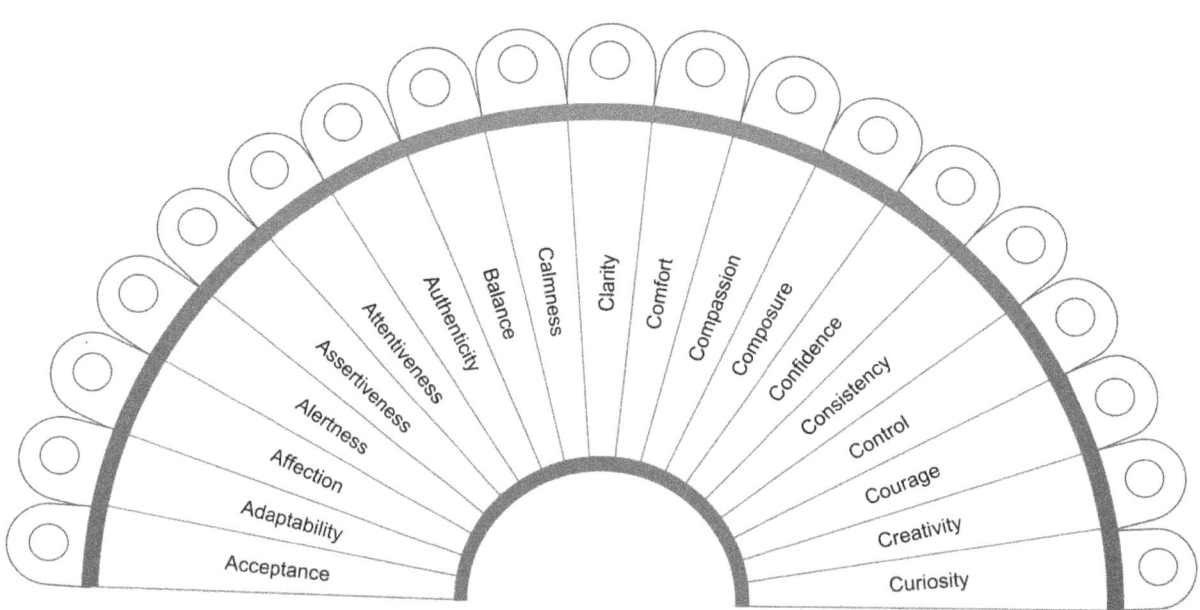

Authenticity
Balance
Calmness
Clarity
Comfort
Compassion
Composure
Confidence
Consistency
Control
Courage
Creativity
Curiosity
Attentiveness
Assertiveness
Alertness
Affection
Adaptability
Acceptance

Emotional Regulation, Chart 1

Royal Template 19

Diving Deep into the Pool of the Mind

Chart 160

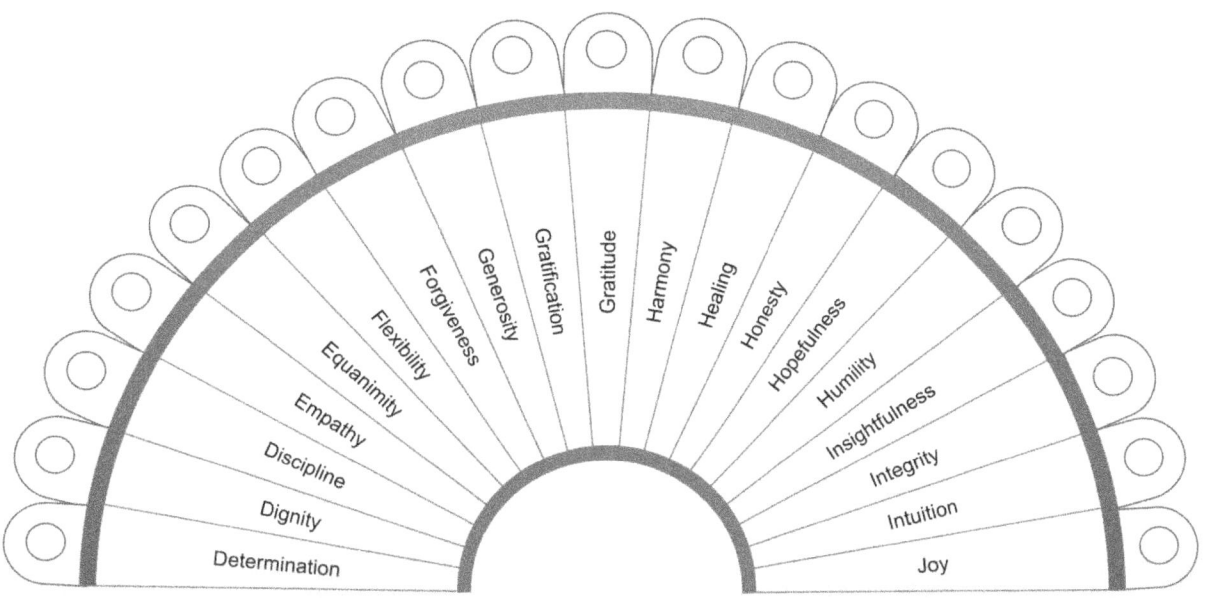

Emotional Regulation, Chart 2

Determination
Dignity
Discipline
Empathy
Equanimity
Flexibility
Forgiveness
Generosity
Gratification
Gratitude
Harmony
Healing
Honesty
Hopefulness
Humility
Insightfulness
Integrity
Intuition
Joy

Royal Template 19

Diving Deep into the Pool of the Mind

Chart 161

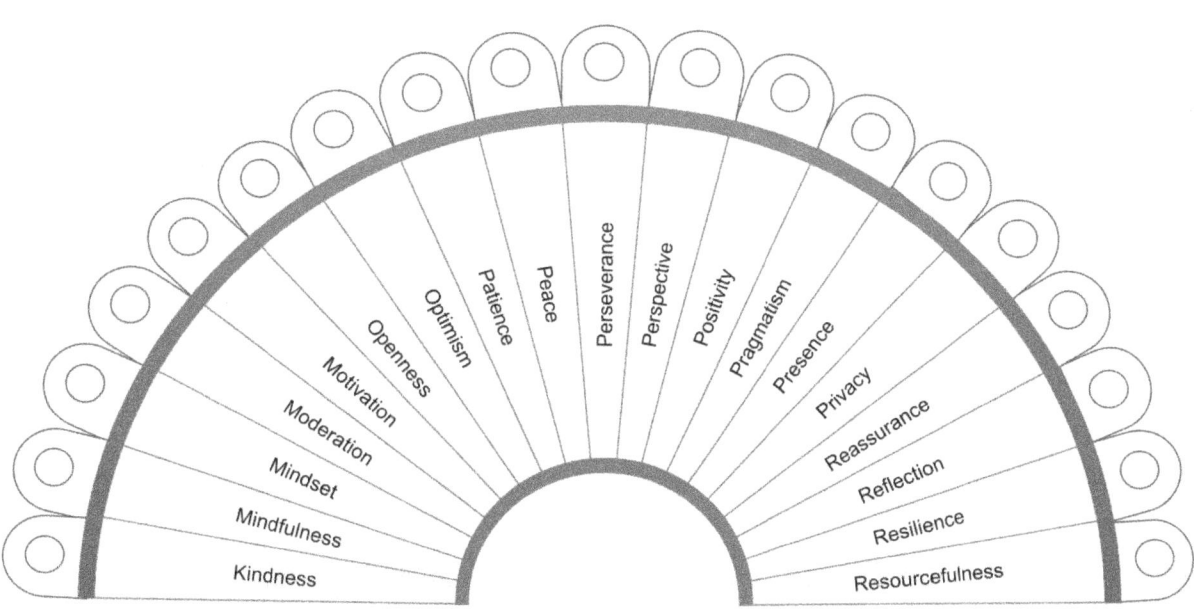

Emotional Regulation, Chart 3

Kindness
Mindfulness
Mindset
Moderation
Motivation
Openness
Optimism
Patience
Peace
Perseverance
Perspective
Positivity
Pragmatism
Presence
Privacy
Reassurance
Reflection
Resilience
Resourcefulness

Royal Template 19

Diving Deep into the Pool of the Mind

Chart 162

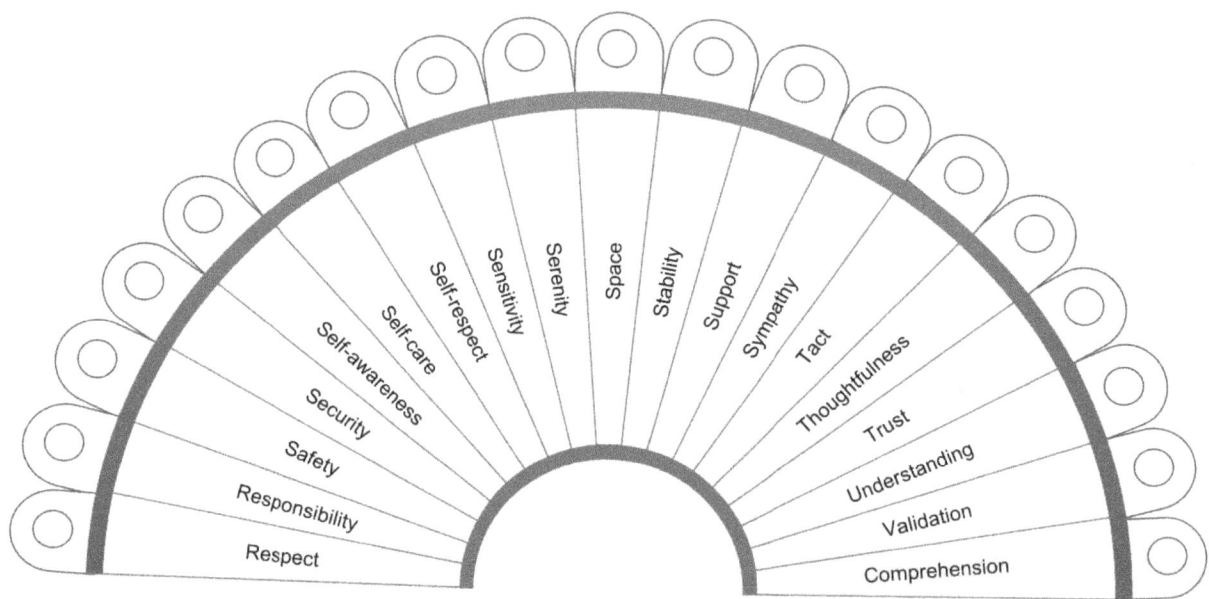

Emotional Regulation, Chart 4

The labels on the fan, reading from left to right:
Respect, Responsibility, Safety, Security, Self-awareness, Self-care, Self-respect, Sensitivity, Serenity, Space, Stability, Support, Sympathy, Tact, Thoughtfulness, Trust, Understanding, Validation, Comprehension

Royal Template 19

Diving Deep into the Pool of the Mind

Chart 163

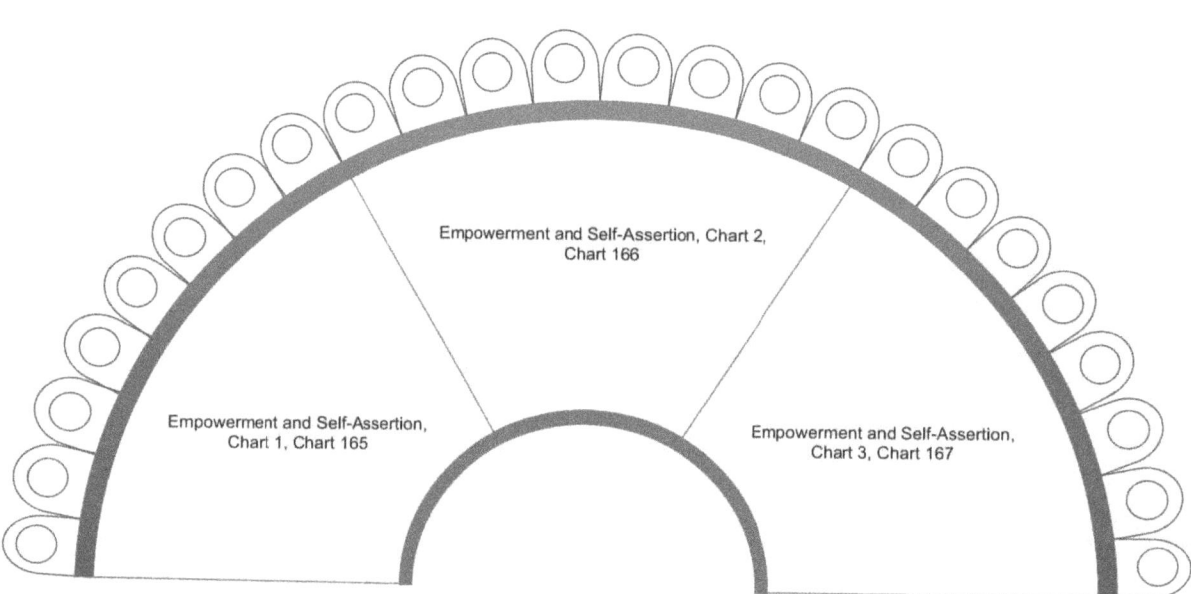

Empowerment and Self-Assertion, Chart 2, Chart 166

Empowerment and Self-Assertion, Chart 1, Chart 165

Empowerment and Self-Assertion, Chart 3, Chart 167

Empowerment and Self-Assertion, Master Chart

Royal Template 3h

Diving Deep into the Pool of the Mind

Chart 164

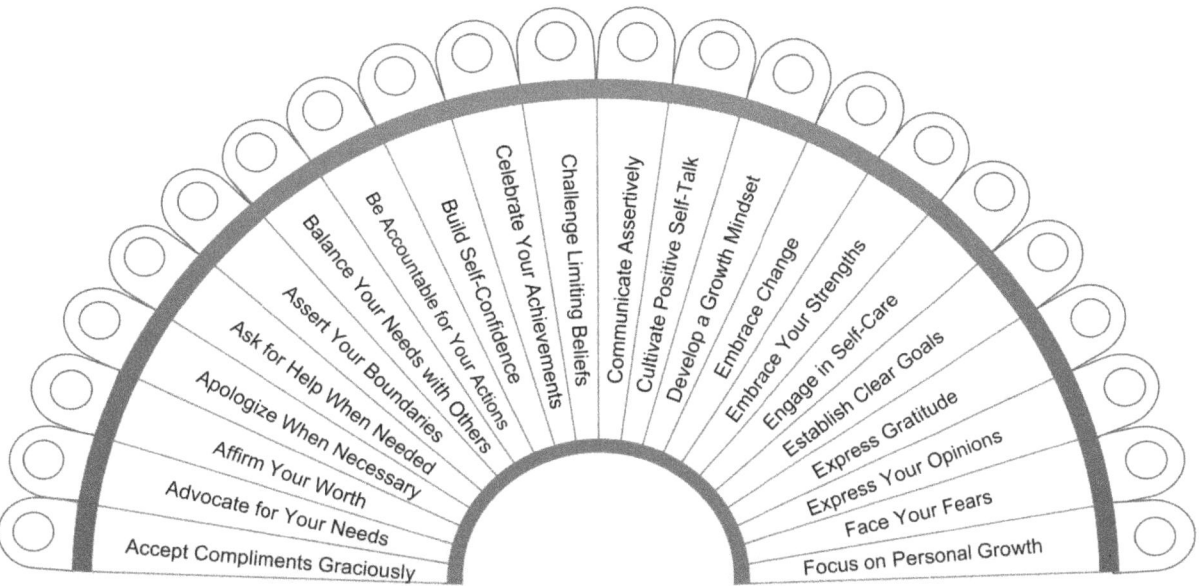

Empowerment and Self-Assertion, Chart 1

Challenge Limiting Beliefs
Celebrate Your Achievements
Build Self-Confidence
Be Accountable for Your Actions
Balance Your Needs with Others
Assert Your Boundaries
Assert Your Needs
Ask for Help When Needed
Apologize When Necessary
Affirm Your Worth
Advocate for Your Needs
Accept Compliments Graciously

Communicate Assertively
Cultivate Positive Self-Talk
Develop a Growth Mindset
Embrace Change
Embrace Your Strengths
Engage in Self-Care
Establish Clear Goals
Express Gratitude
Express Your Opinions
Face Your Fears
Focus on Personal Growth

Royal Template 22

Diving Deep into the Pool of the Mind

Chart 165

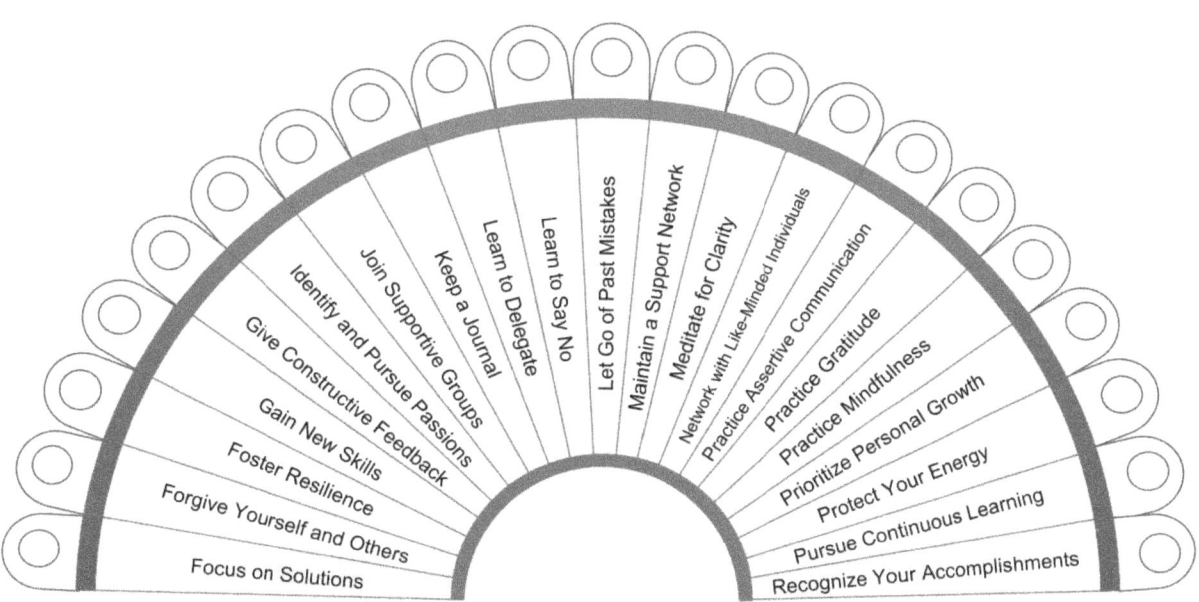

Empowerment and Self-Assertion, Chart 2

Identify and Pursue Passions
Give Constructive Feedback
Gain New Skills
Foster Resilience
Forgive Yourself and Others
Focus on Solutions

Join Supportive Groups
Keep a Journal
Learn to Delegate
Learn to Say No
Let Go of Past Mistakes
Maintain a Support Network
Meditate for Clarity
Network with Like-Minded Individuals
Practice Assertive Communication
Practice Gratitude
Practice Mindfulness
Prioritize Personal Growth
Protect Your Energy
Pursue Continuous Learning
Recognize Your Accomplishments

Royal Template 21

Diving Deep into the Pool of the Mind

Chart 166

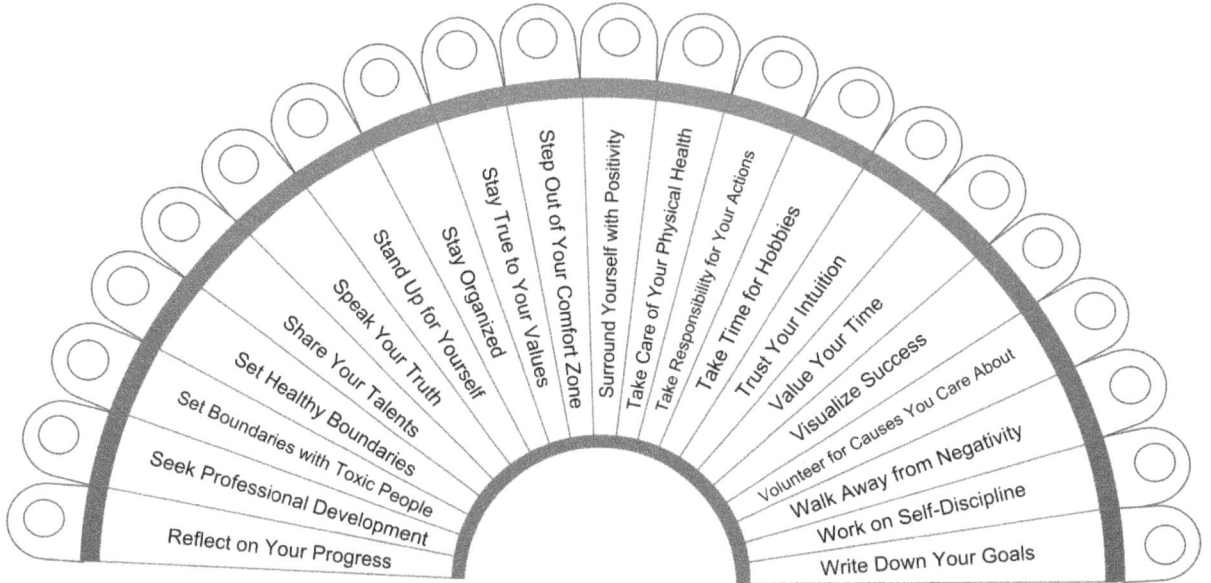

Empowerment and Self-Assertion, Chart 3

© 2025, Susan V Whittaker

Royal Template 21

Diving Deep into the Pool of the Mind

Chart 167

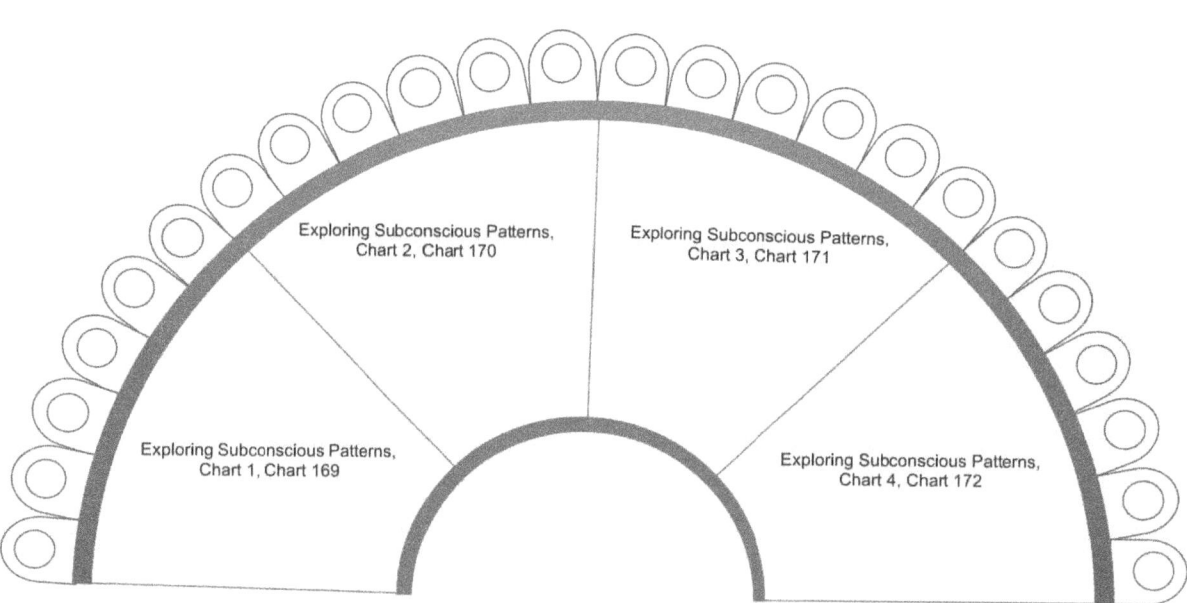

Labels within the chart (outer to inner):

- Exploring Subconscious Patterns, Chart 2, Chart 170
- Exploring Subconscious Patterns, Chart 3, Chart 171
- Exploring Subconscious Patterns, Chart 1, Chart 169
- Exploring Subconscious Patterns, Chart 4, Chart 172

Exploring Subconscious Patterns, Master Chart

© 2025, Susan V Whittaker

Royal Template 4h

Diving Deep into the Pool of the Mind

Chart 168

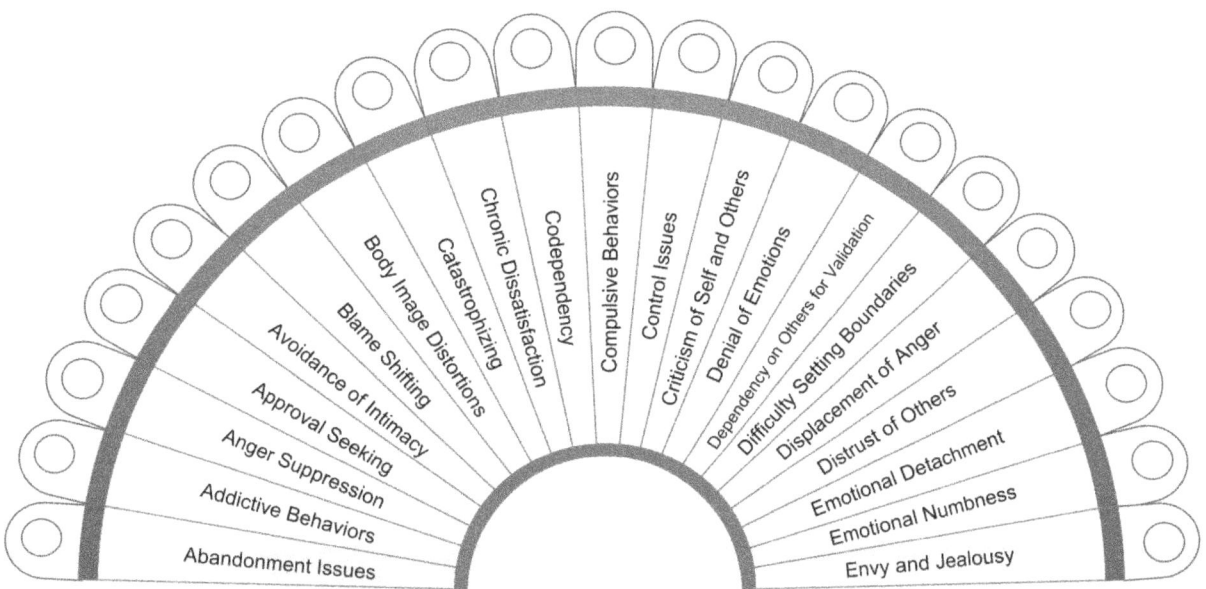

Exploring Subconscious Patterns, Chart 1

The chart contains the following labels (outer ring, left to right):

- Abandonment Issues
- Addictive Behaviors
- Anger Suppression
- Approval Seeking
- Avoidance of Intimacy
- Blame Shifting
- Body Image Distortions
- Catastrophizing
- Chronic Dissatisfaction
- Codependency
- Compulsive Behaviors
- Control Issues
- Criticism of Self and Others
- Denial of Emotions
- Dependency on Others for Validation
- Difficulty Setting Boundaries
- Displacement of Anger
- Distrust of Others
- Emotional Detachment
- Emotional Numbness
- Envy and Jealousy

Royal Template 21

Diving Deep into the Pool of the Mind

Chart 169

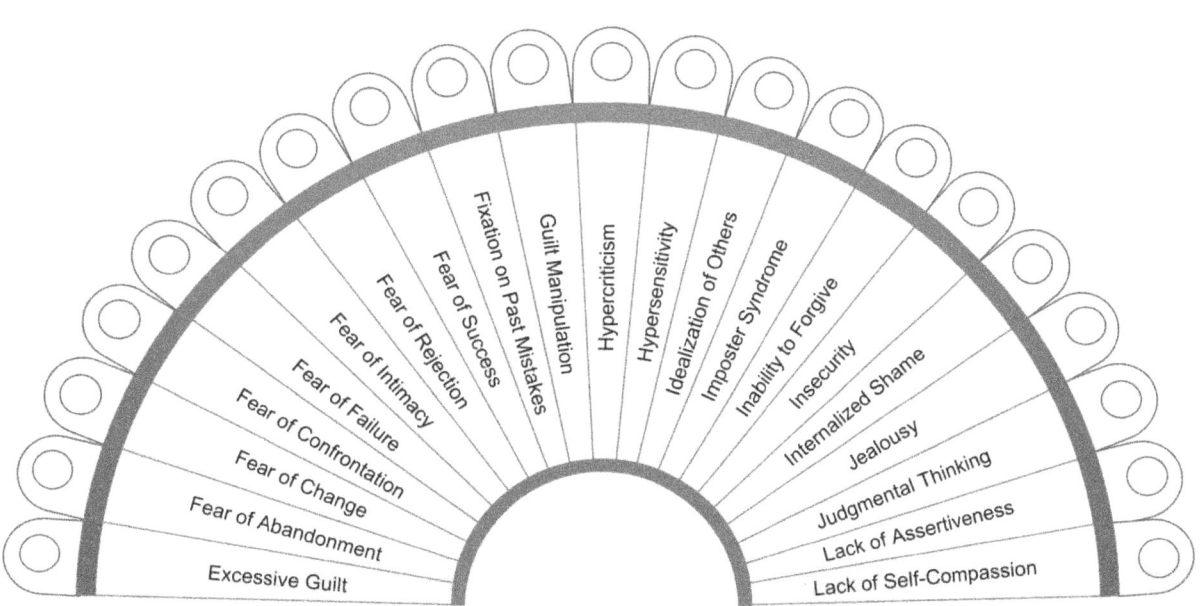

Exploring Subconscious Patterns, Chart 2

The chart contains the following labels (outer ring, left to right):

- Excessive Guilt
- Fear of Abandonment
- Fear of Change
- Fear of Confrontation
- Fear of Failure
- Fear of Intimacy
- Fear of Rejection
- Fear of Success
- Fixation on Past Mistakes
- Guilt Manipulation
- Hypercriticism
- Hypersensitivity
- Idealization of Others
- Imposter Syndrome
- Inability to Forgive
- Insecurity
- Internalized Shame
- Jealousy
- Judgmental Thinking
- Lack of Assertiveness
- Lack of Self-Compassion

Royal Template 21

Diving Deep into the Pool of the Mind

Chart 170

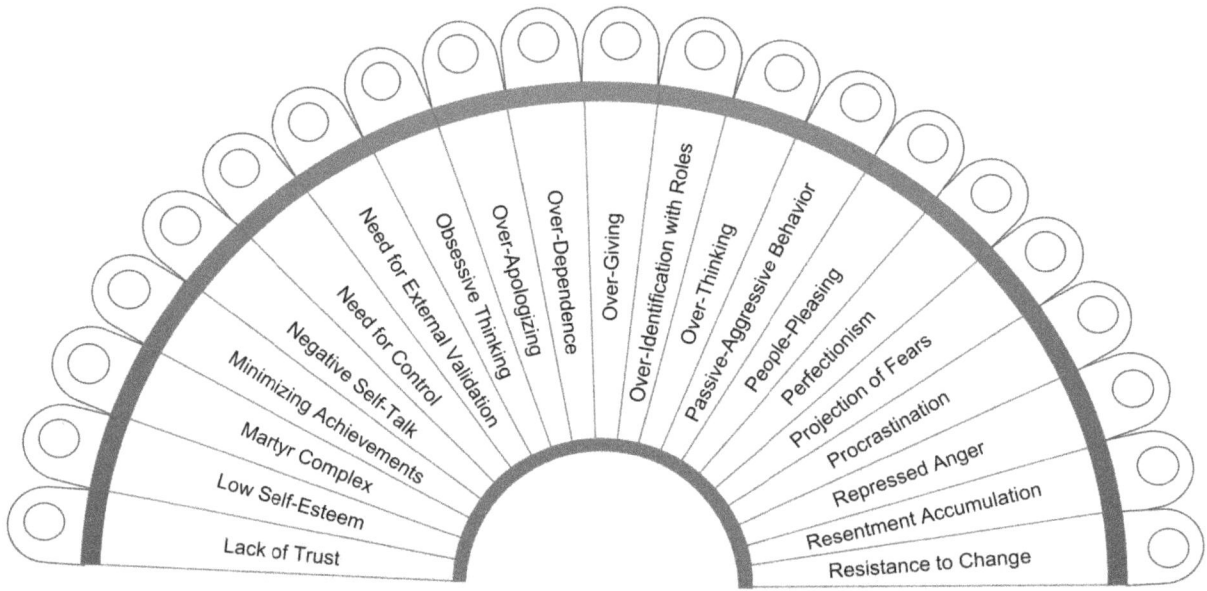

Exploring Subconscious Patterns, Chart 3

Need for External Validation
Need for Control
Negative Self-Talk
Minimizing Achievements
Martyr Complex
Low Self-Esteem
Lack of Trust
Obsessive Thinking
Over-Apologizing
Over-Dependence
Over-Giving
Over-Identification with Roles
Over-Thinking
Passive-Aggressive Behavior
People-Pleasing
Perfectionism
Projection of Fears
Procrastination
Repressed Anger
Resentment Accumulation
Resistance to Change

Royal Template 21

Diving Deep into the Pool of the Mind

Chart 171

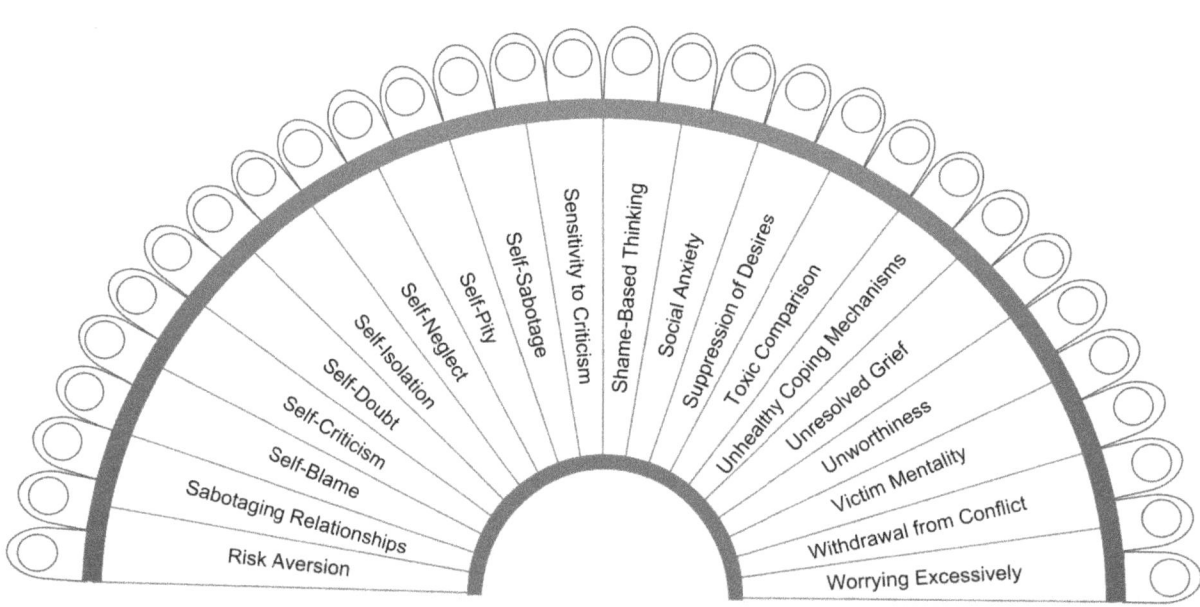

Exploring Subconscious Patterns, Chart 4

Self-Neglect
Self-Isolation
Self-Doubt
Self-Criticism
Self-Blame
Sabotaging Relationships
Risk Aversion
Self-Pity
Self-Sabotage
Sensitivity to Criticism
Shame-Based Thinking
Social Anxiety
Suppression of Desires
Toxic Comparison
Unhealthy Coping Mechanisms
Unresolved Grief
Unworthiness
Victim Mentality
Withdrawal from Conflict
Worrying Excessively

Royal Template 20

Diving Deep into the Pool of the Mind

Chart 172

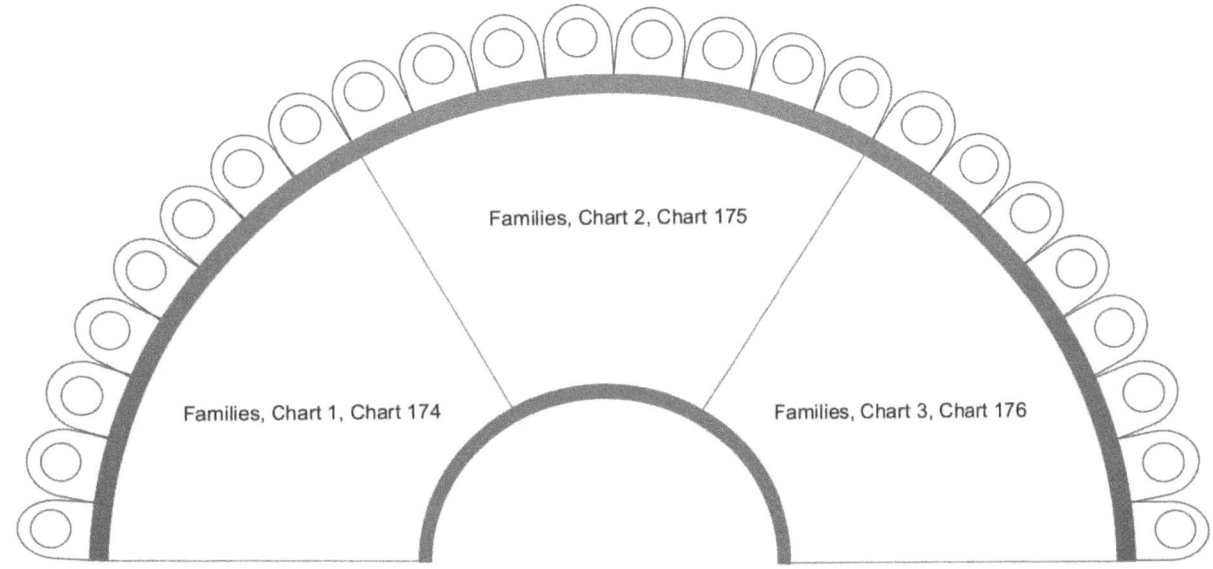

Families, Master Chart

Families, Chart 2, Chart 175

Families, Chart 1, Chart 174

Families, Chart 3, Chart 176

Royal Template 3h

Diving Deep into the Pool of the Mind

Chart 173

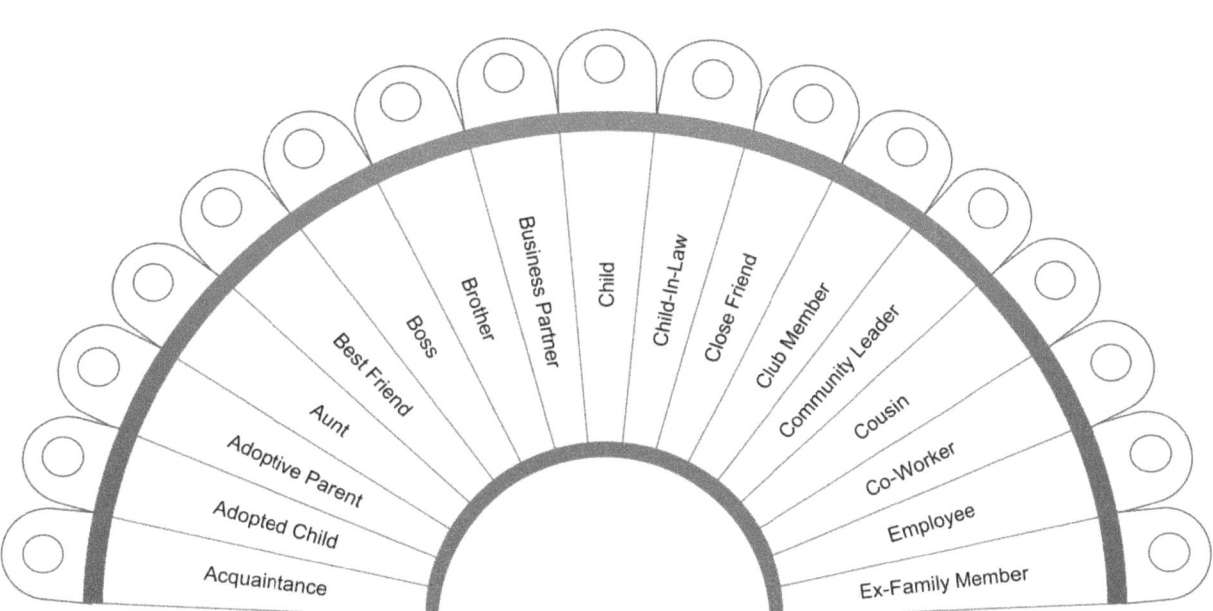

Families, Chart 1

Business Partner
Child
Brother
Child-In-Law
Boss
Close Friend
Best Friend
Club Member
Aunt
Community Leader
Adoptive Parent
Cousin
Adopted Child
Co-Worker
Acquaintance
Employee
Ex-Family Member

Royal Template 17

Diving Deep into the Pool of the Mind

Chart 174

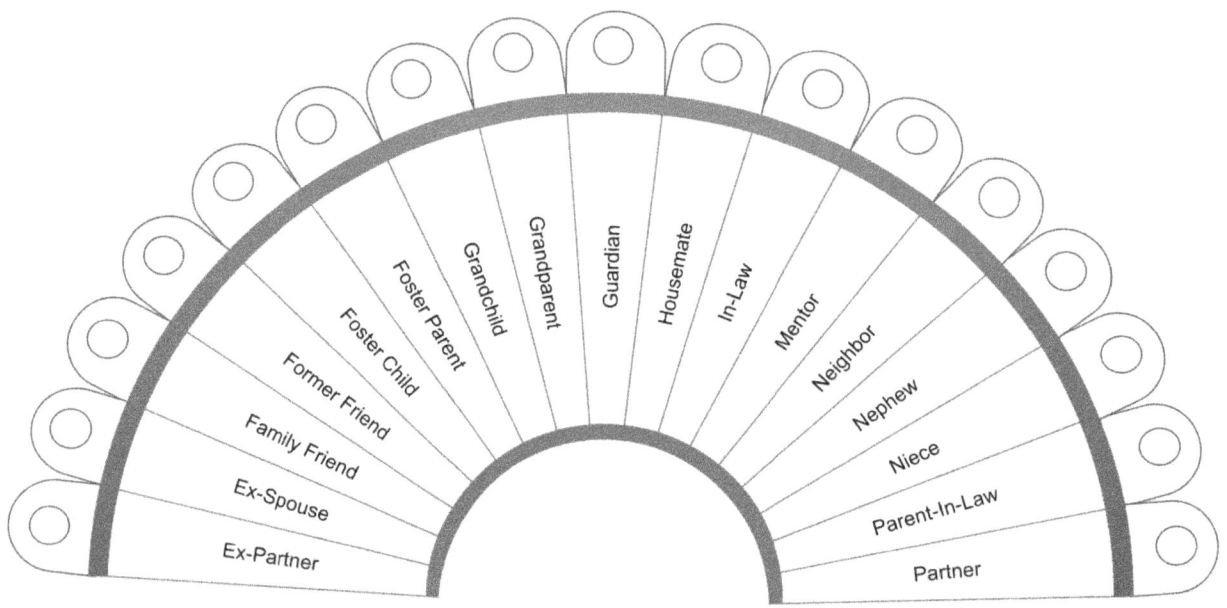

Families, Chart 2

The chart contains the following labels (reading around the fan):
Ex-Partner, Ex-Spouse, Family Friend, Former Friend, Foster Child, Foster Parent, Grandchild, Grandparent, Guardian, Housemate, In-Law, Mentor, Neighbor, Nephew, Niece, Parent-In-Law, Partner

Royal Template 17

Diving Deep into the Pool of the Mind

Chart 175

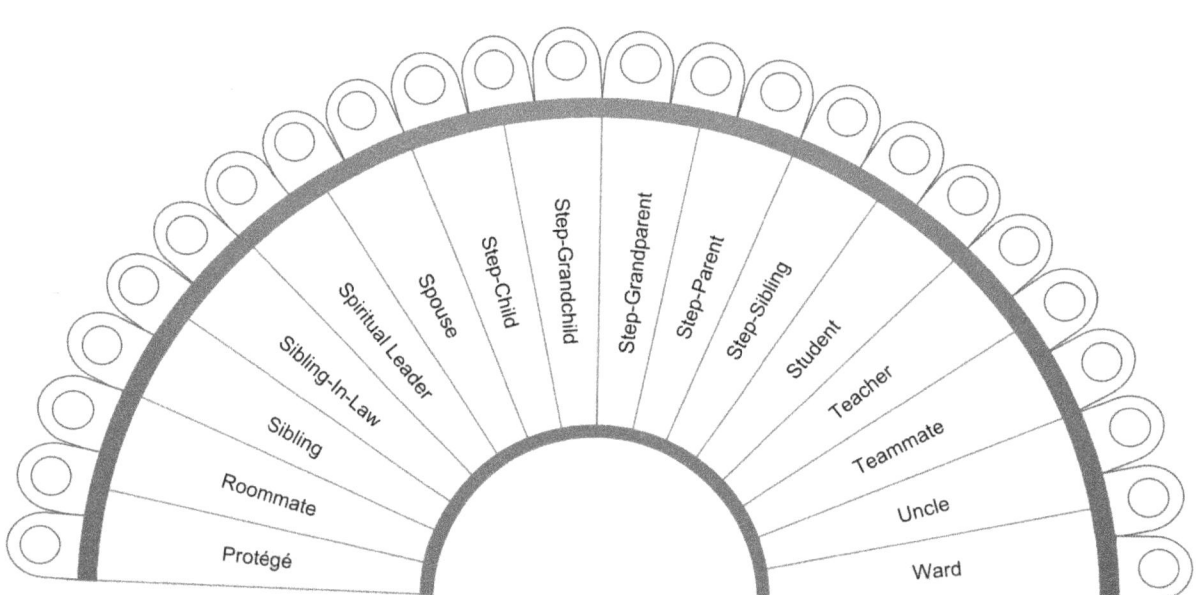

Families, Chart 3

The chart contains the following labels (reading around the fan):
Protégé, Roommate, Sibling, Sibling-In-Law, Spiritual Leader, Spouse, Step-Child, Step-Grandchild, Step-Grandparent, Step-Parent, Step-Sibling, Student, Teacher, Teammate, Uncle, Ward

Royal Template 16

Diving Deep into the Pool of the Mind

Chart 176

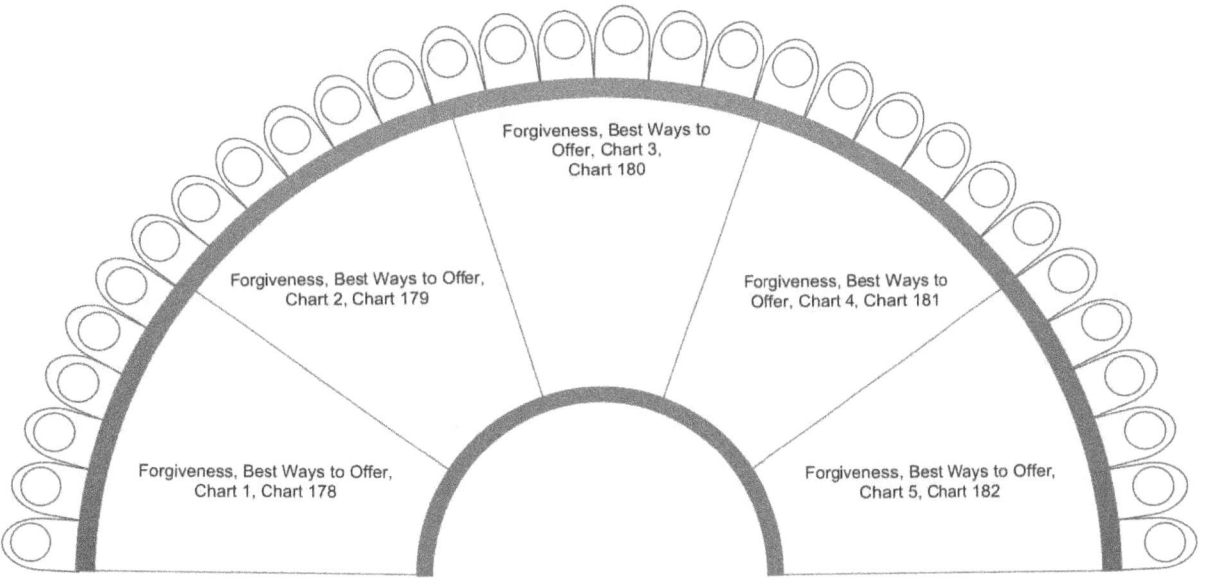

Forgiveness, Best Ways to Offer, Master Chart

Forgiveness, Best Ways to Offer, Chart 3, Chart 180

Forgiveness, Best Ways to Offer, Chart 2, Chart 179

Forgiveness, Best Ways to Offer, Chart 4, Chart 181

Forgiveness, Best Ways to Offer, Chart 1, Chart 178

Forgiveness, Best Ways to Offer, Chart 5, Chart 182

Royal Template 5h

Diving Deep into the Pool of the Mind

Chart 177

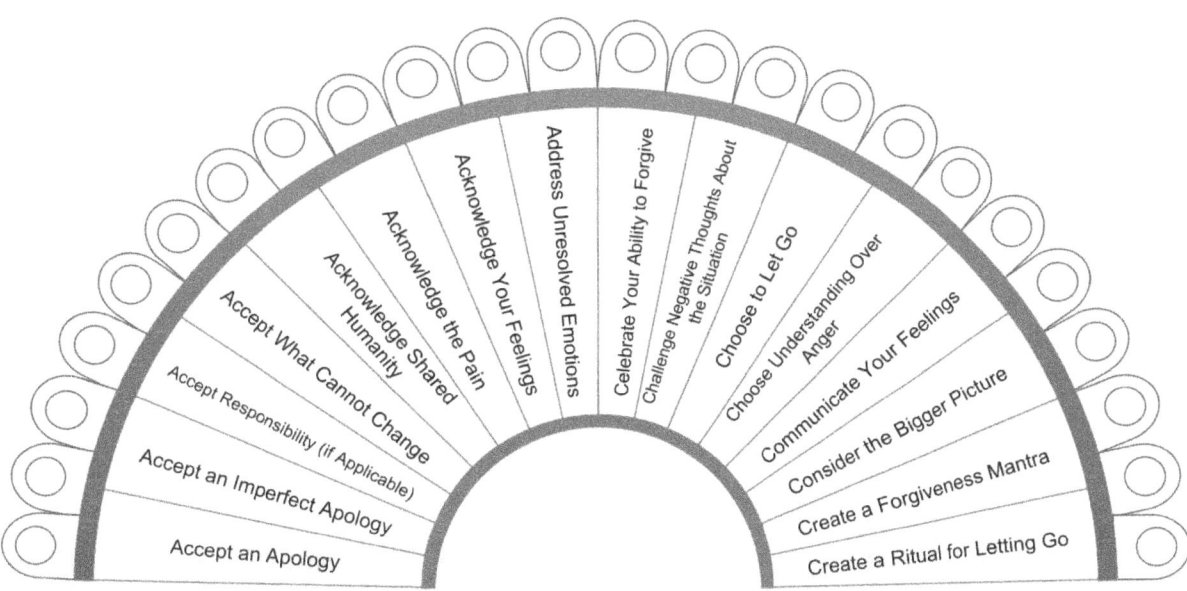

Labels (left to right):
- Accept an Apology
- Accept an Imperfect Apology
- Accept Responsibility (if Applicable)
- Accept What Cannot Change
- Acknowledge Shared Humanity
- Acknowledge the Pain
- Acknowledge Your Feelings
- Address Unresolved Emotions
- Celebrate Your Ability to Forgive
- Challenge Negative Thoughts About the Situation
- Choose to Let Go
- Choose Understanding Over Anger
- Communicate Your Feelings
- Consider the Bigger Picture
- Create a Forgiveness Mantra
- Create a Ritual for Letting Go

Forgiveness, Best Ways to Offer, Chart 1

Royal Template 16

Diving Deep into the Pool of the Mind

Chart 178

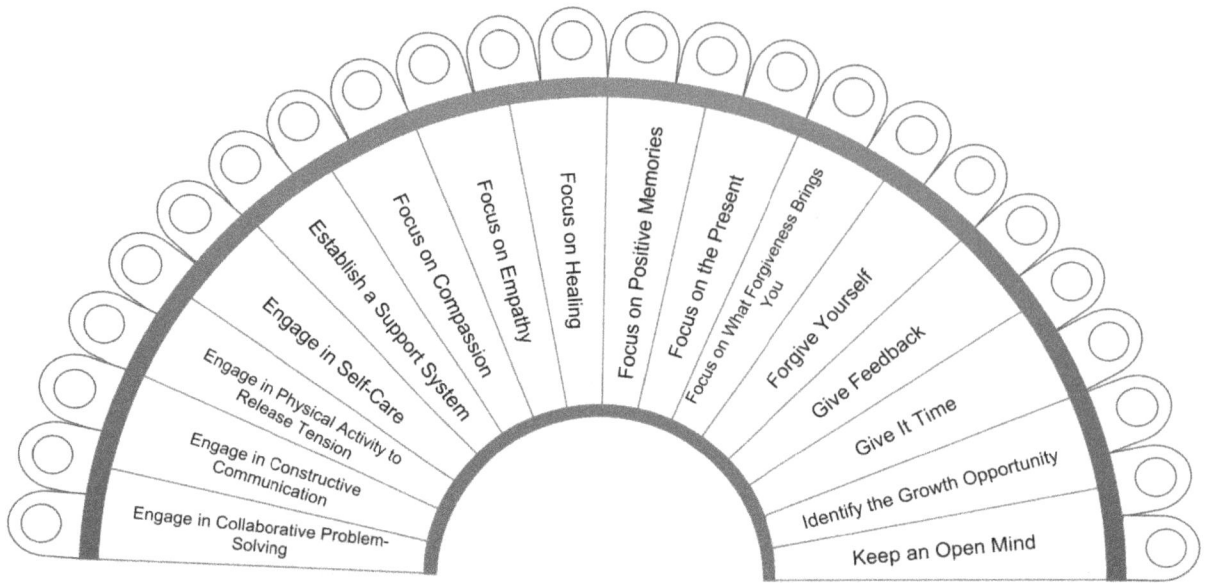

Forgiveness, Best Ways to Offer, Chart 2

© 2025, Susan V Whittaker

Royal Template 16

Diving Deep into the Pool of the Mind

Chart 179

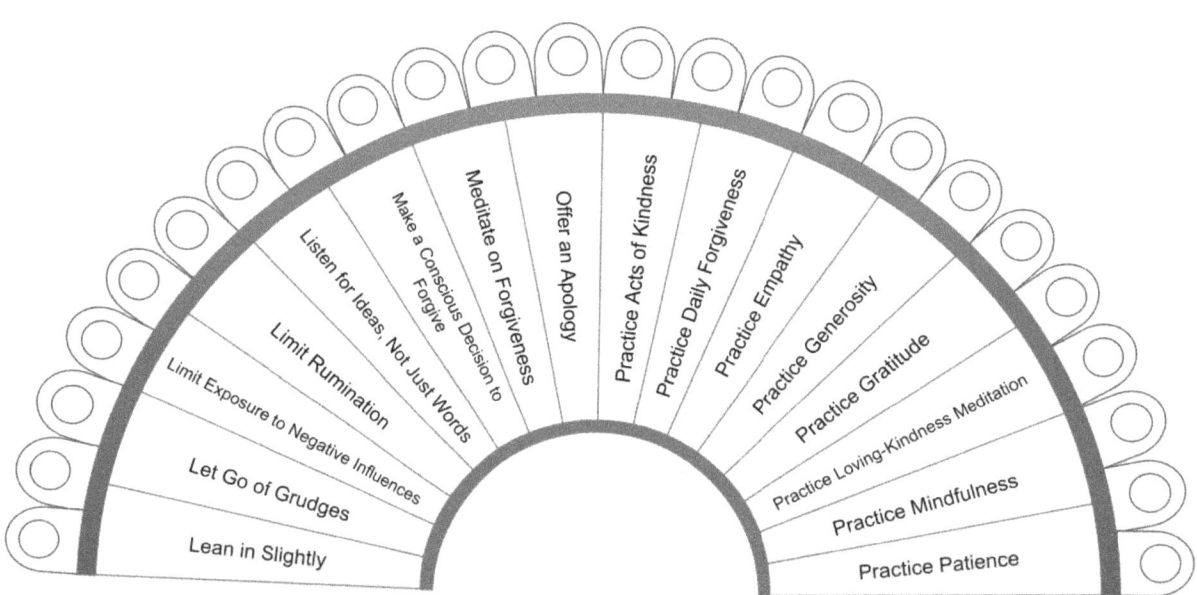

Forgiveness, Best Ways to Offer, Chart 3

© 2025, Susan V Whittaker

Royal Template 16

Diving Deep into the Pool of the Mind

Chart 180

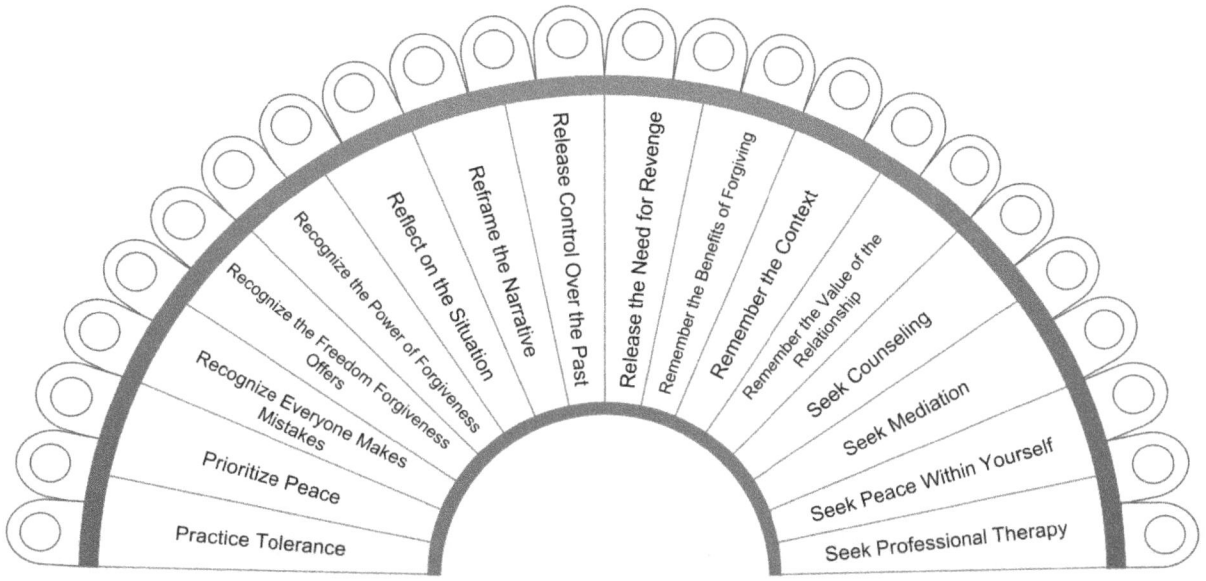

Forgiveness, Best Ways to Offer, Chart 4

The chart contains the following labels radiating from the center:

- Practice Tolerance
- Prioritize Peace
- Recognize Everyone Makes Mistakes
- Recognize the Freedom Forgiveness Offers
- Recognize the Power of Forgiveness
- Reflect on the Situation
- Reframe the Narrative
- Release Control Over the Past
- Release the Need for Revenge
- Remember the Benefits of Forgiving
- Remember the Context
- Remember the Value of the Relationship
- Seek Counseling
- Seek Mediation
- Seek Peace Within Yourself
- Seek Professional Therapy

Royal Template 16

Diving Deep into the Pool of the Mind

Chart 181

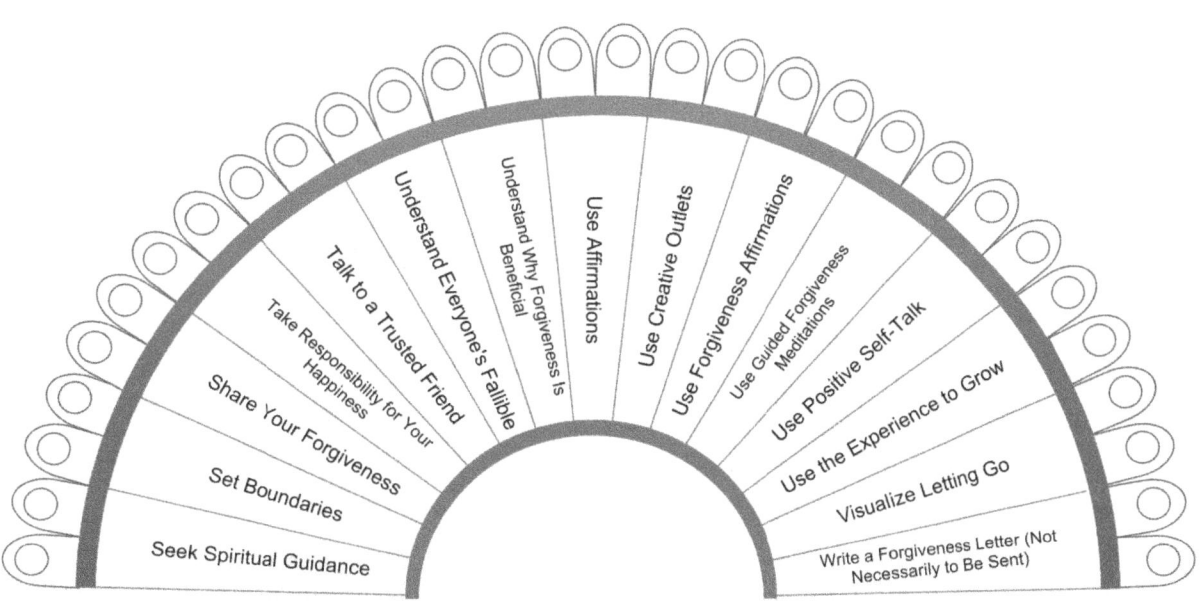

Forgiveness, Best Ways to Offer, Chart 5

The chart contains the following labels radiating from the center:

- Seek Spiritual Guidance
- Set Boundaries
- Share Your Forgiveness
- Take Responsibility for Your Happiness
- Talk to a Trusted Friend
- Understand Everyone's Fallible
- Understand Why Forgiveness Is Beneficial
- Use Affirmations
- Use Creative Outlets
- Use Forgiveness Affirmations
- Use Guided Forgiveness Meditations
- Use Positive Self-Talk
- Use the Experience to Grow
- Visualize Letting Go
- Write a Forgiveness Letter (Not Necessarily to Be Sent)

Royal Template 15

Diving Deep into the Pool of the Mind

Chart 182

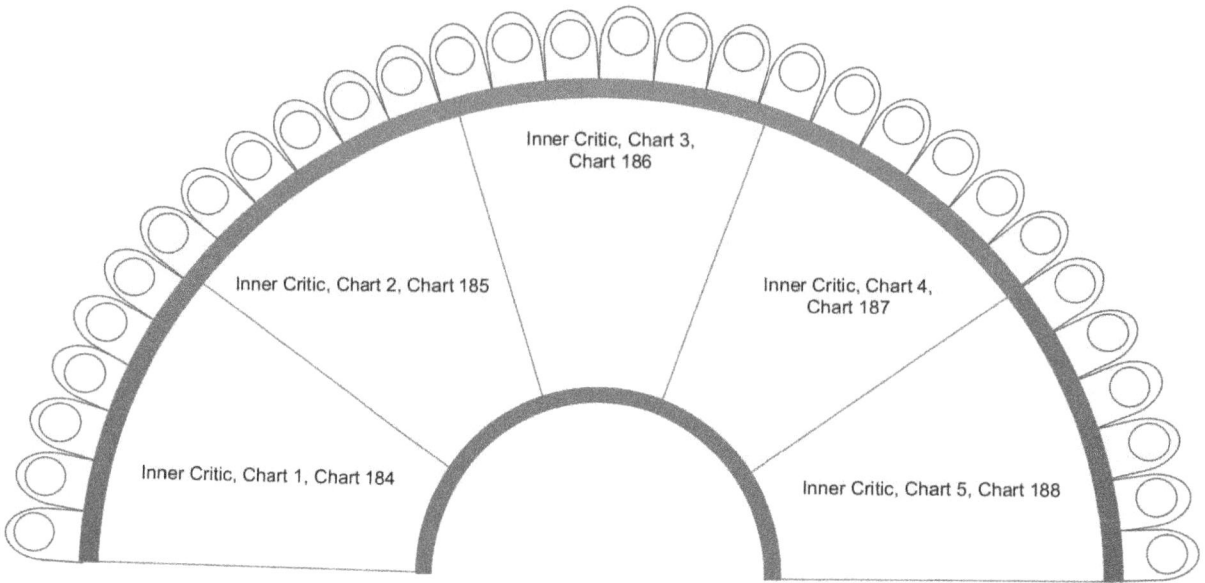

Inner Critic, Master Chart

Inner Critic, Chart 3, Chart 186

Inner Critic, Chart 2, Chart 185

Inner Critic, Chart 4, Chart 187

Inner Critic, Chart 1, Chart 184

Inner Critic, Chart 5, Chart 188

Royal Template 5h

Diving Deep into the Pool of the Mind

Chart 183

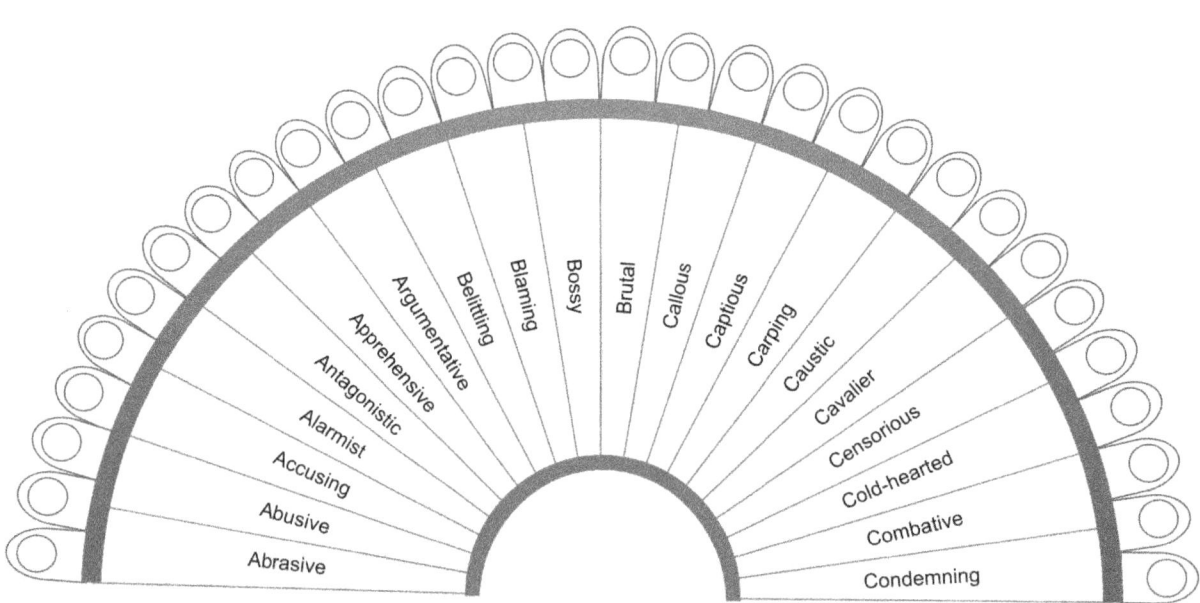

Inner Critic, Chart 1

Argumentative
Apprehensive
Antagonistic
Alarmist
Accusing
Abusive
Abrasive
Belitting
Blaming
Bossy
Brutal
Callous
Captious
Carping
Caustic
Cavalier
Censorious
Cold-hearted
Combative
Condemning

Royal Template 20

Diving Deep into the Pool of the Mind

Chart 184

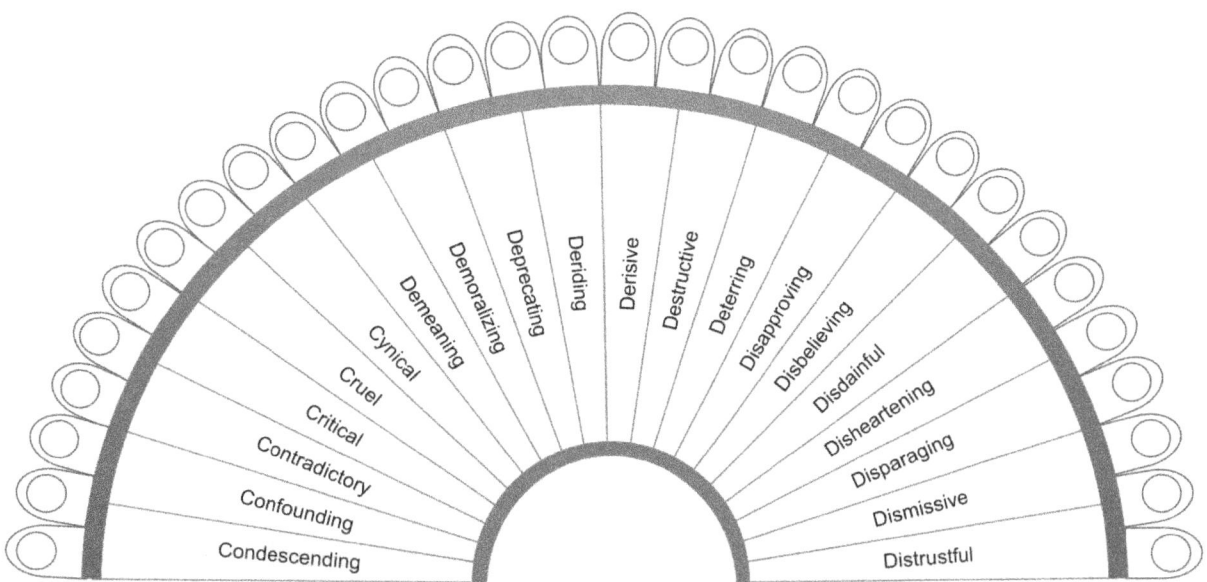

Inner Critic, Chart 2

Condescending
Confounding
Contradictory
Critical
Cruel
Cynical
Demeaning
Demoralizing
Deprecating
Deriding
Derisive
Destructive
Deterring
Disapproving
Disbelieving
Disdainful
Disheartening
Disparaging
Dismissive
Distrustful

Royal Template 20

Diving Deep into the Pool of the Mind

Chart 185

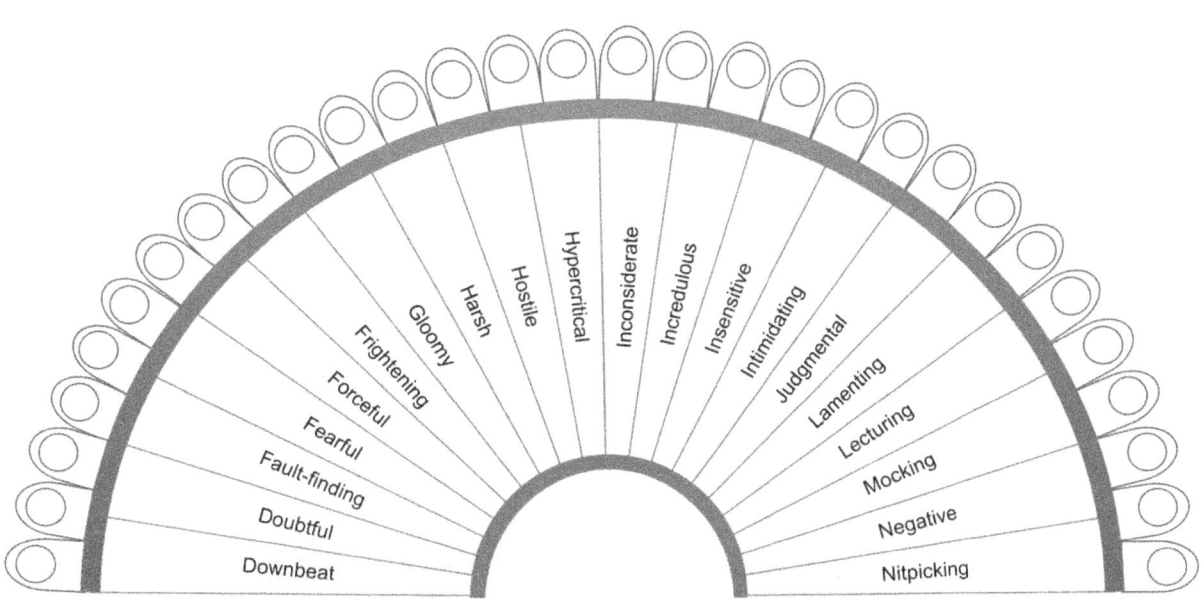

Inner Critic, Chart 3

Downbeat
Doubtful
Fault-finding
Fearful
Forceful
Frightening
Gloomy
Harsh
Hostile
Hypercritical
Inconsiderate
Incredulous
Insensitive
Intimidating
Judgmental
Lamenting
Lecturing
Mocking
Negative
Nitpicking

Royal Template 20

Diving Deep into the Pool of the Mind

Chart 186

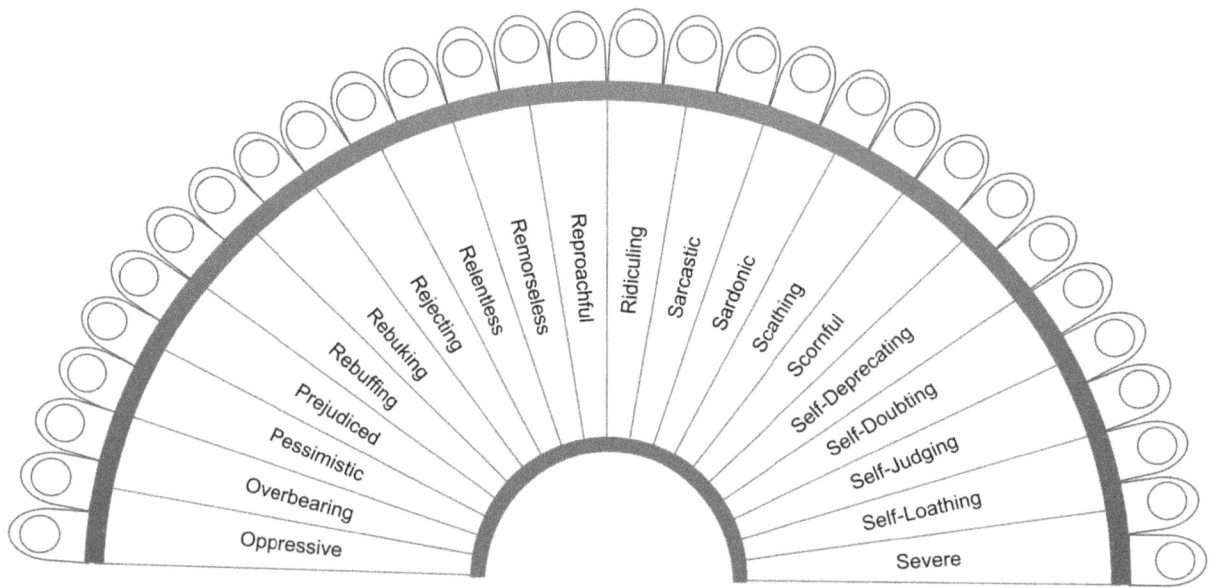

Inner Critic, Chart 4

The chart contains the following labels (clockwise):
Oppressive, Overbearing, Pessimistic, Prejudiced, Rebuffing, Rebuking, Rejecting, Relentless, Remorseless, Reproachful, Ridiculing, Sarcastic, Sardonic, Scathing, Scornful, Self-Deprecating, Self-Doubting, Self-Judging, Self-Loathing, Severe

Royal Template 20

Diving Deep into the Pool of the Mind

Chart 187

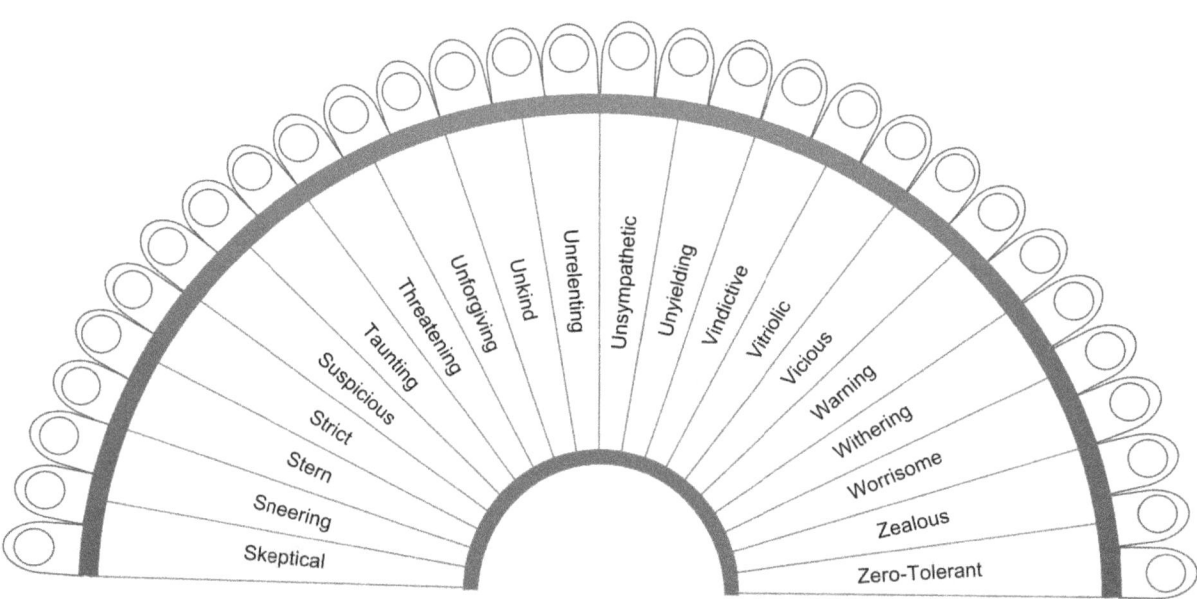

Inner Critic, Chart 5

The chart contains the following labels (clockwise):
Skeptical, Sneering, Stern, Strict, Suspicious, Taunting, Threatening, Unforgiving, Unkind, Unrelenting, Unsympathetic, Unyielding, Vindictive, Vitriolic, Vicious, Warning, Withering, Worrisome, Zealous, Zero-Tolerant

Royal Template 20

Diving Deep into the Pool of the Mind

Chart 188

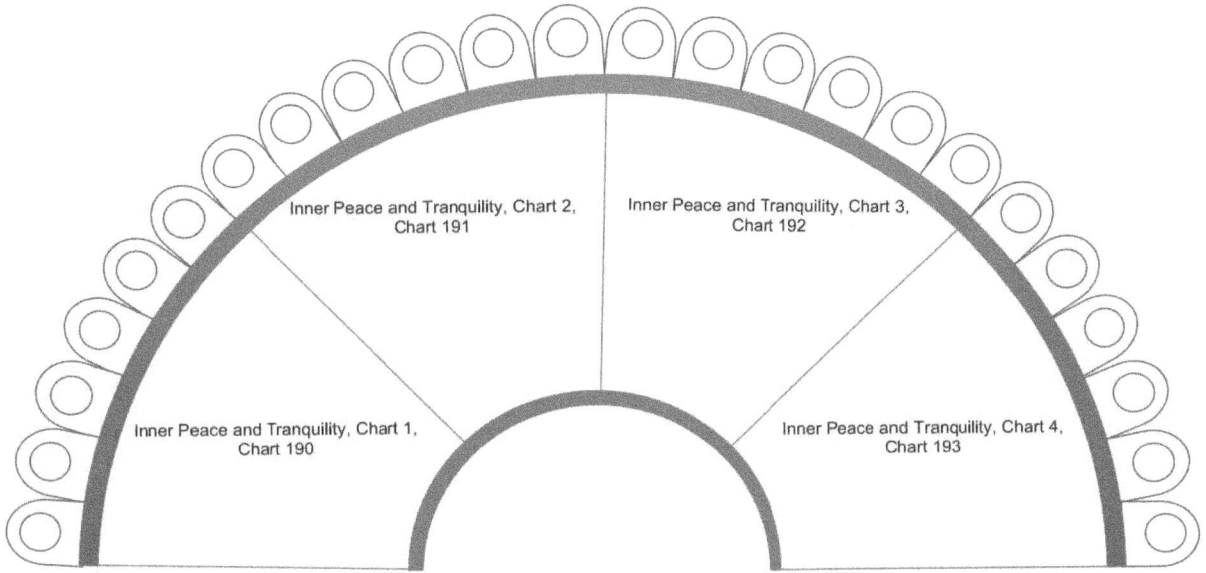

Inner Peace and Tranquility, Master Chart

Inner Peace and Tranquility, Chart 2, Chart 191

Inner Peace and Tranquility, Chart 3, Chart 192

Inner Peace and Tranquility, Chart 1, Chart 190

Inner Peace and Tranquility, Chart 4, Chart 193

Royal Template 4h

Diving Deep into the Pool of the Mind

Chart 189

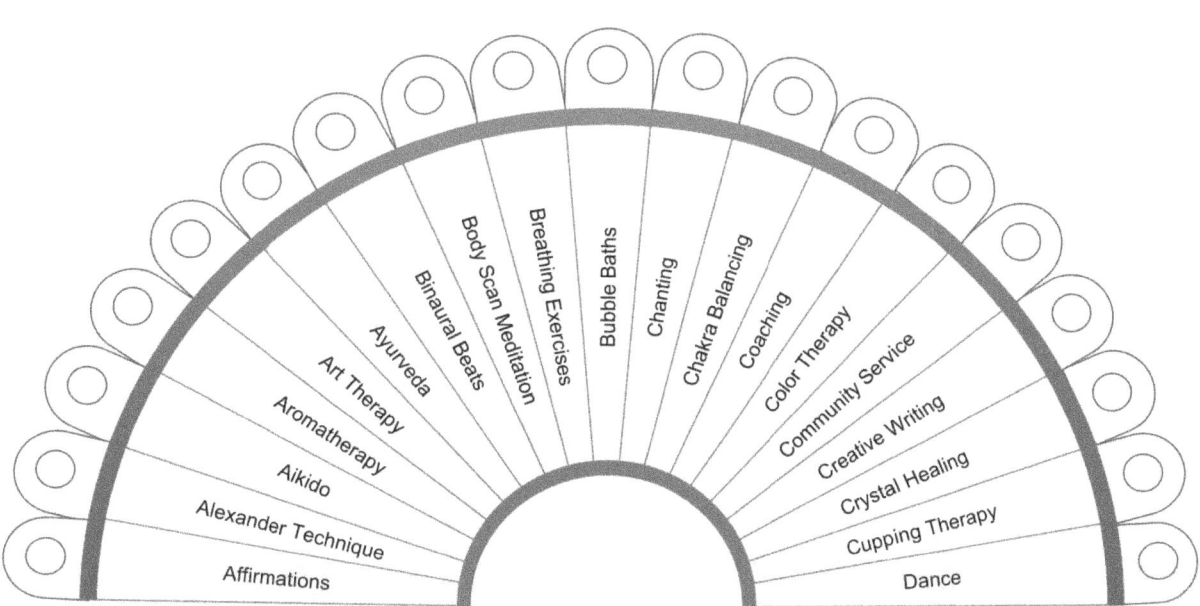

Body Scan Meditation
Binaural Beats
Breathing Exercises
Ayurveda
Bubble Baths
Art Therapy
Chanting
Aromatherapy
Chakra Balancing
Coaching
Aikido
Color Therapy
Community Service
Alexander Technique
Creative Writing
Crystal Healing
Affirmations
Cupping Therapy
Dance

Inner Peace and Tranquility, Chart 1

Royal Template 19

Diving Deep into the Pool of the Mind

Chart 190

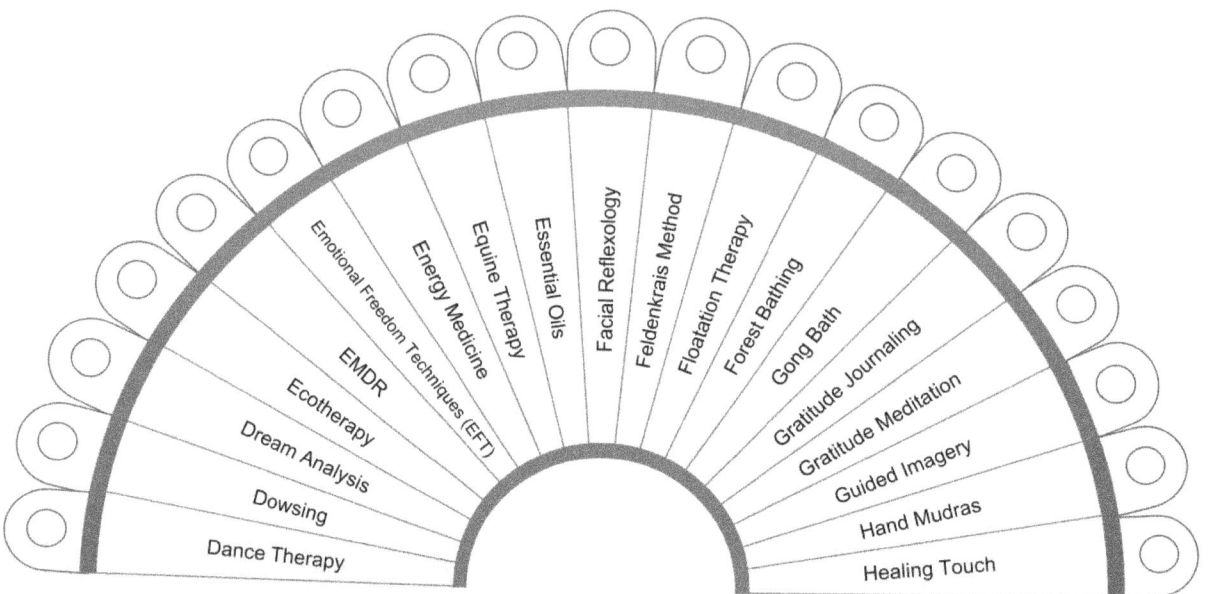

Inner Peace and Tranquility, Chart 2

The chart contains the following labels (arranged radially):

Dance Therapy, Dowsing, Dream Analysis, Ecotherapy, EMDR, Emotional Freedom Techniques (EFT), Energy Medicine, Equine Therapy, Essential Oils, Facial Reflexology, Feldenkrais Method, Floatation Therapy, Forest Bathing, Gong Bath, Gratitude Journaling, Gratitude Meditation, Guided Imagery, Hand Mudras, Healing Touch

Royal Template 19

Diving Deep into the Pool of the Mind

Chart 191

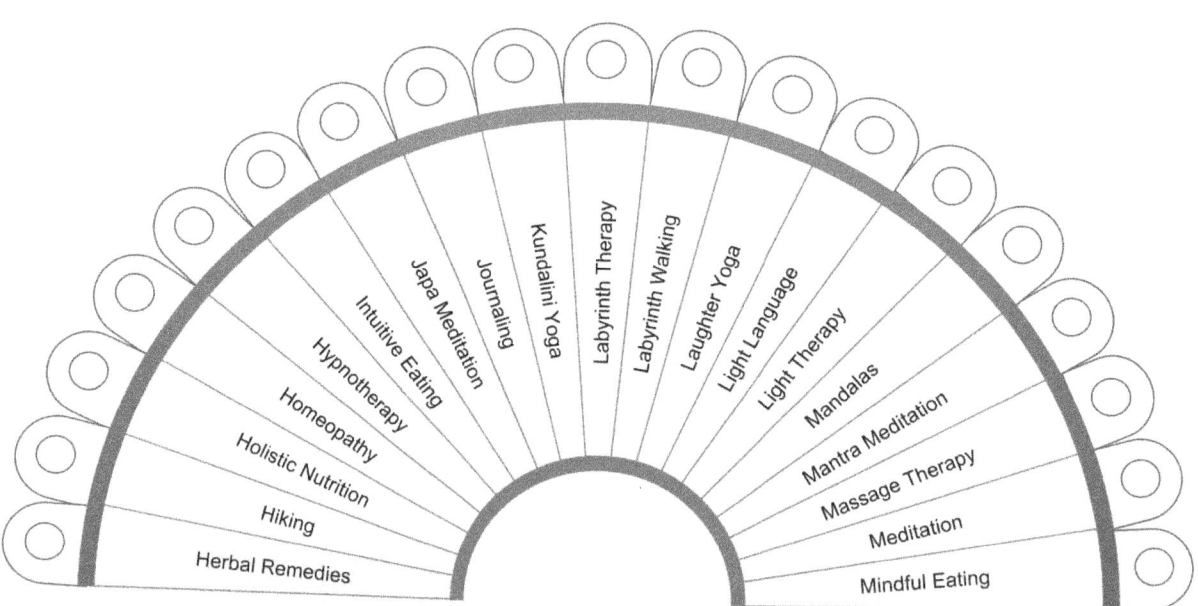

Inner Peace and Tranquility, Chart 3

The chart contains the following labels (arranged radially):

Herbal Remedies, Hiking, Holistic Nutrition, Homeopathy, Hypnotherapy, Intuitive Eating, Japa Meditation, Journaling, Kundalini Yoga, Labyrinth Therapy, Labyrinth Walking, Laughter Yoga, Light Language, Light Therapy, Mandalas, Mantra Meditation, Massage Therapy, Meditation, Mindful Eating

Royal Template 19

Diving Deep into the Pool of the Mind

Chart 192

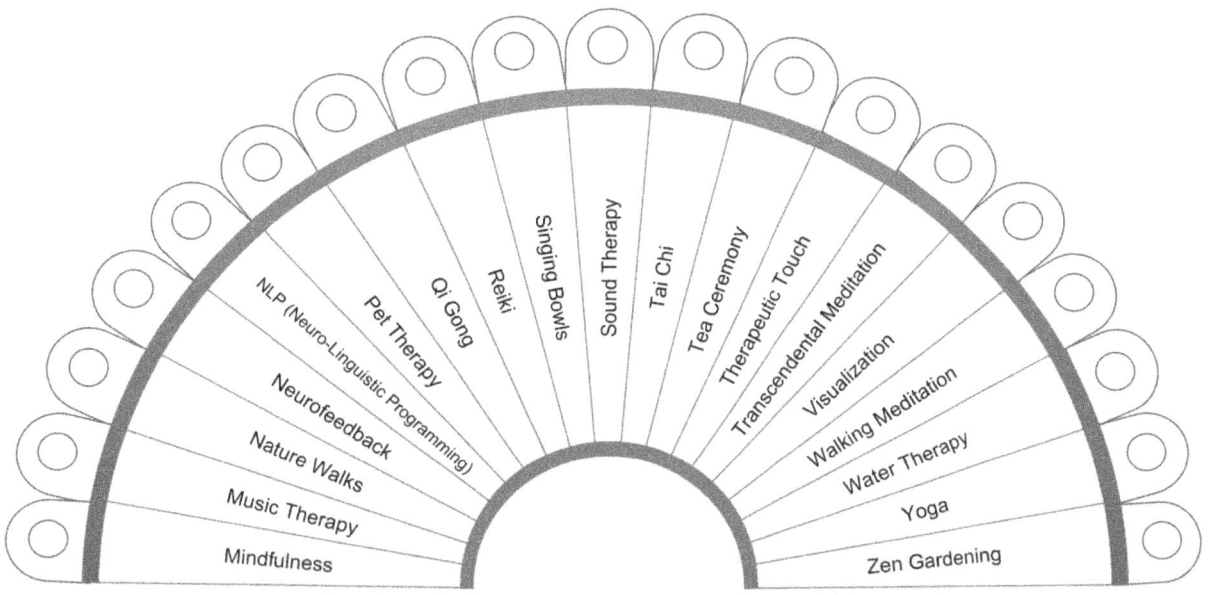

Inner Peace and Tranquility, Chart 4

Labels (left to right): Mindfulness, Music Therapy, Nature Walks, Neurofeedback, NLP (Neuro-Linguistic Programming), Pet Therapy, Qi Gong, Reiki, Singing Bowls, Sound Therapy, Tai Chi, Tea Ceremony, Therapeutic Touch, Transcendental Meditation, Visualization, Walking Meditation, Water Therapy, Yoga, Zen Gardening

Royal Template 19

Diving Deep into the Pool of the Mind

Chart 193

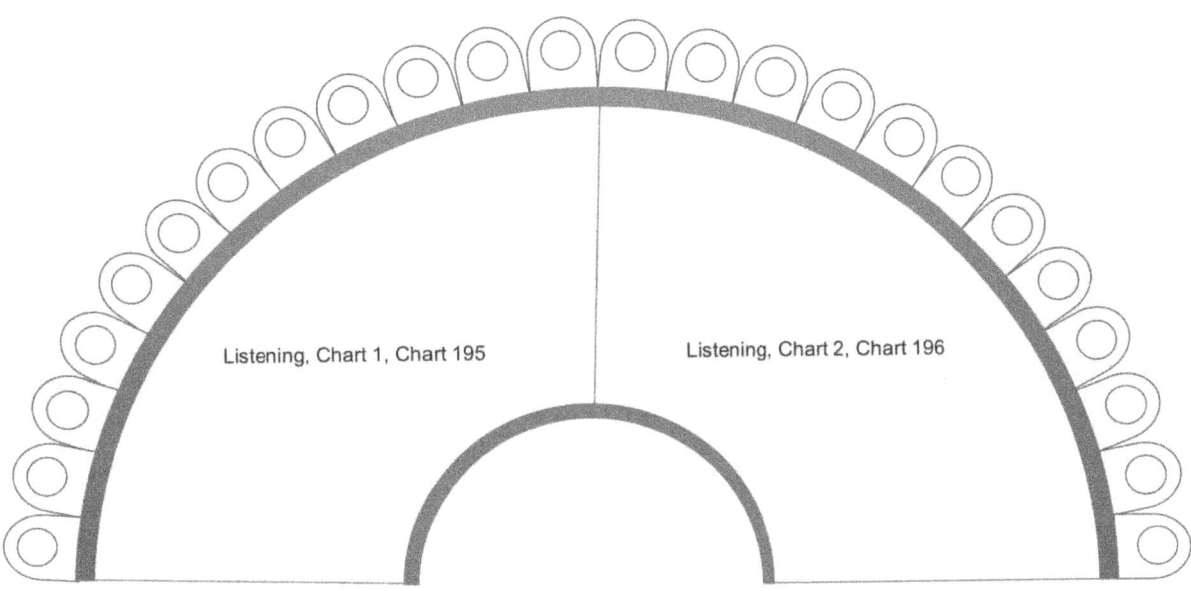

Listening, Chart 1, Chart 195   Listening, Chart 2, Chart 196

Listening, Master Chart

Royal Template 2

Diving Deep into the Pool of the Mind

Chart 194

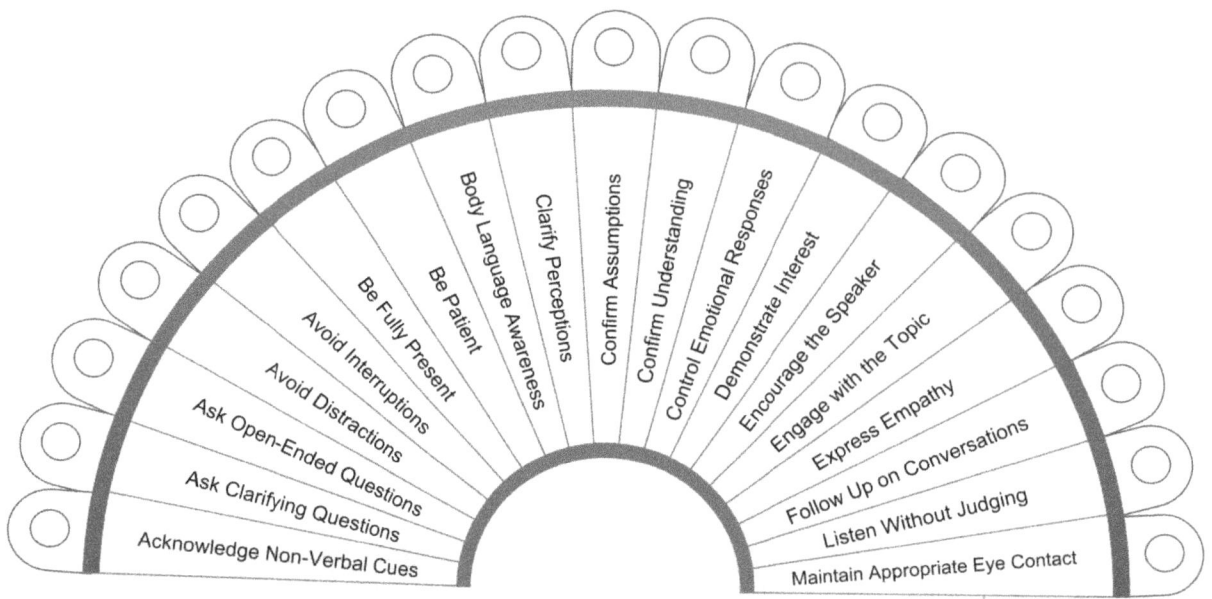

Listening, Chart 1

Body Language Awareness
Be Patient
Be Fully Present
Avoid Interruptions
Avoid Distractions
Ask Open-Ended Questions
Ask Clarifying Questions
Acknowledge Non-Verbal Cues
Clarify Perceptions
Confirm Assumptions
Confirm Understanding
Control Emotional Responses
Demonstrate Interest
Encourage the Speaker
Engage with the Topic
Express Empathy
Follow Up on Conversations
Listen Without Judging
Maintain Appropriate Eye Contact

Royal Template 19

Diving Deep into the Pool of the Mind

Chart 195

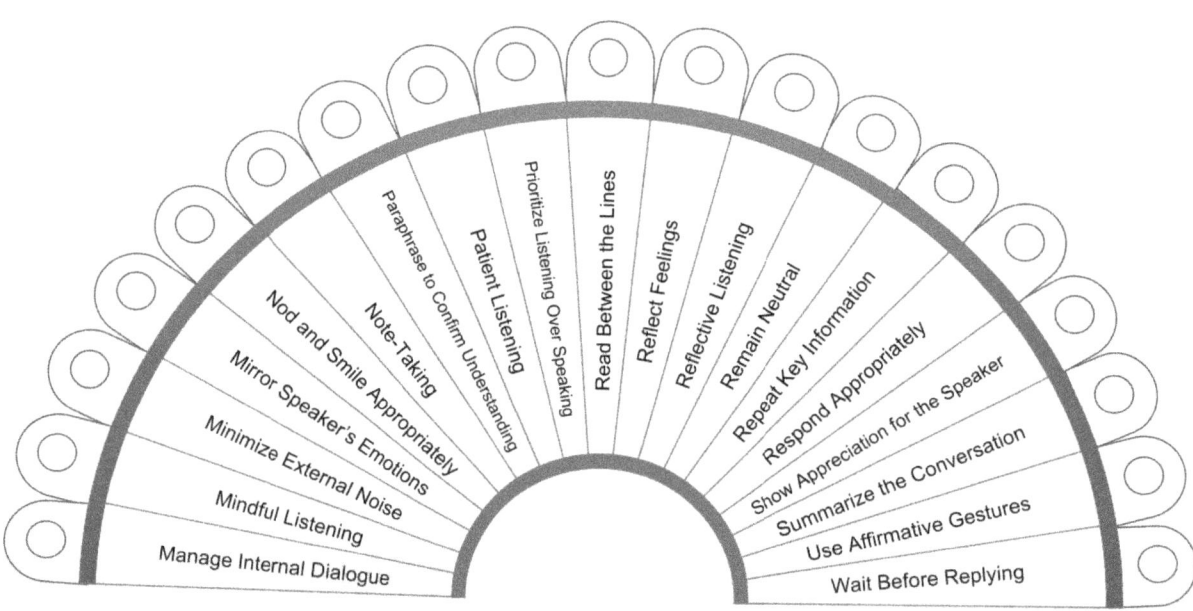

Listening, Chart 2

Prioritize Listening Over Speaking
Paraphrase to Confirm Understanding
Patient Listening
Note-Taking
Nod and Smile Appropriately
Mirror Speaker's Emotions
Minimize External Noise
Mindful Listening
Manage Internal Dialogue
Read Between the Lines
Reflect Feelings
Reflective Listening
Remain Neutral
Repeat Key Information
Respond Appropriately
Show Appreciation for the Speaker
Summarize the Conversation
Use Affirmative Gestures
Wait Before Replying

Royal Template 19

Diving Deep into the Pool of the Mind

Chart 196

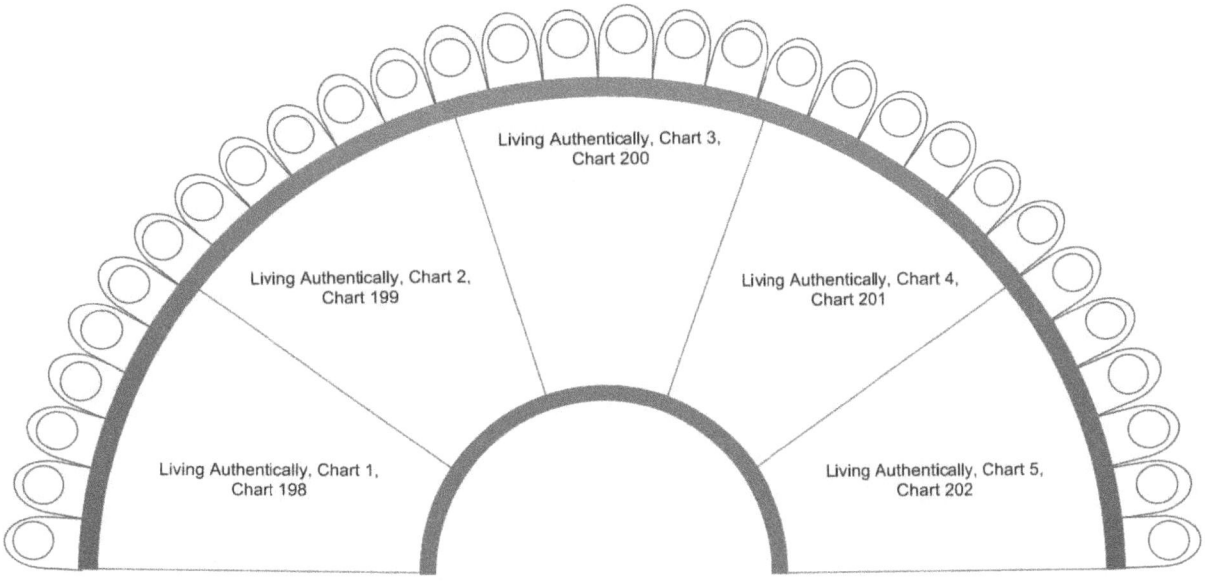

Living Authentically, Master Chart

Living Authentically, Chart 3,
Chart 200

Living Authentically, Chart 2,
Chart 199

Living Authentically, Chart 4,
Chart 201

Living Authentically, Chart 1,
Chart 198

Living Authentically, Chart 5,
Chart 202

Royal Template 5h

Diving Deep into the Pool of the Mind

Chart 197

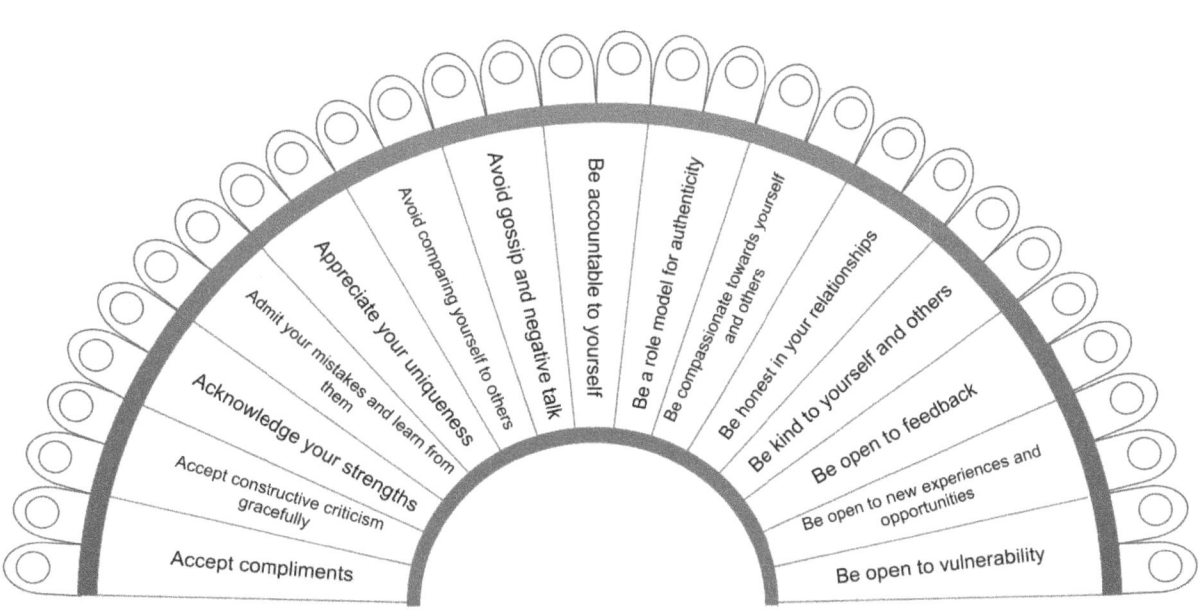

Avoid comparing yourself to others
Appreciate your uniqueness
Avoid gossip and negative talk
Admit your mistakes and learn from them
Be accountable to yourself
Acknowledge your strengths
Be a role model for authenticity
Be compassionate towards yourself and others
Accept constructive criticism gracefully
Be honest in your relationships
Accept compliments
Be kind to yourself and others
Be open to feedback
Be open to new experiences and opportunities
Be open to vulnerability

Living Authentically, Chart 1

Royal Template 15

Diving Deep into the Pool of the Mind

Chart 198

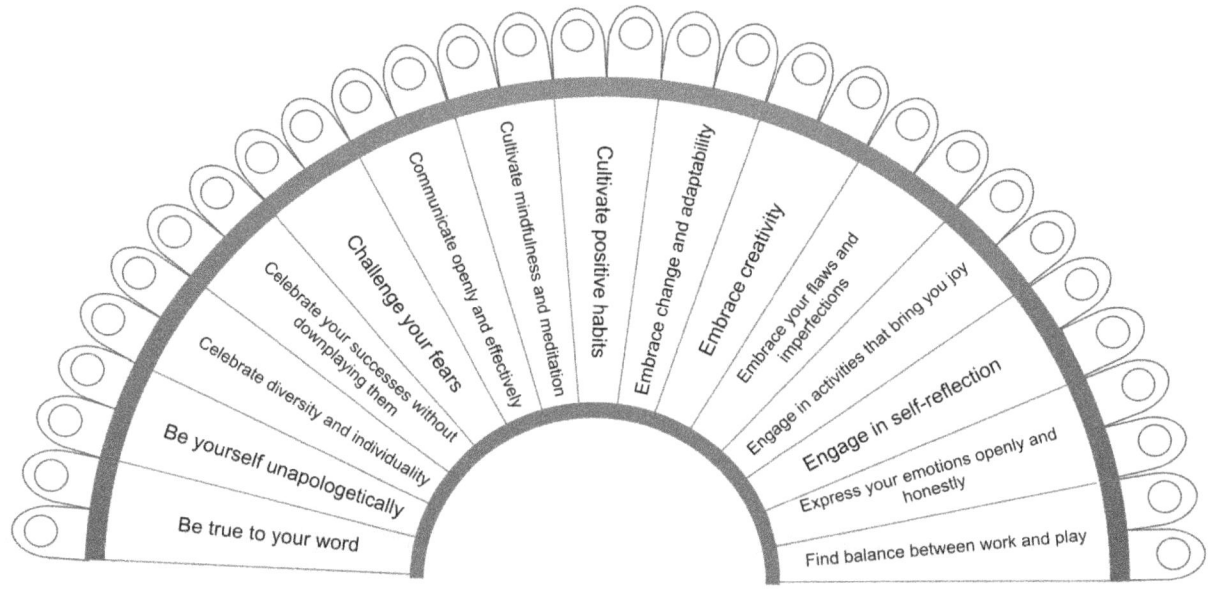

Living Authentically, Chart 2

The chart contains the following entries:

- Be true to your word
- Be yourself unapologetically
- Celebrate diversity and individuality
- Celebrate your successes without downplaying them
- Challenge your fears
- Communicate openly and effectively
- Cultivate mindfulness and meditation
- Cultivate positive habits
- Embrace change and adaptability
- Embrace creativity
- Embrace your flaws and imperfections
- Engage in activities that bring you joy
- Engage in self-reflection
- Express your emotions openly and honestly
- Find balance between work and play

Royal Template 15

Diving Deep into the Pool of the Mind

Chart 199

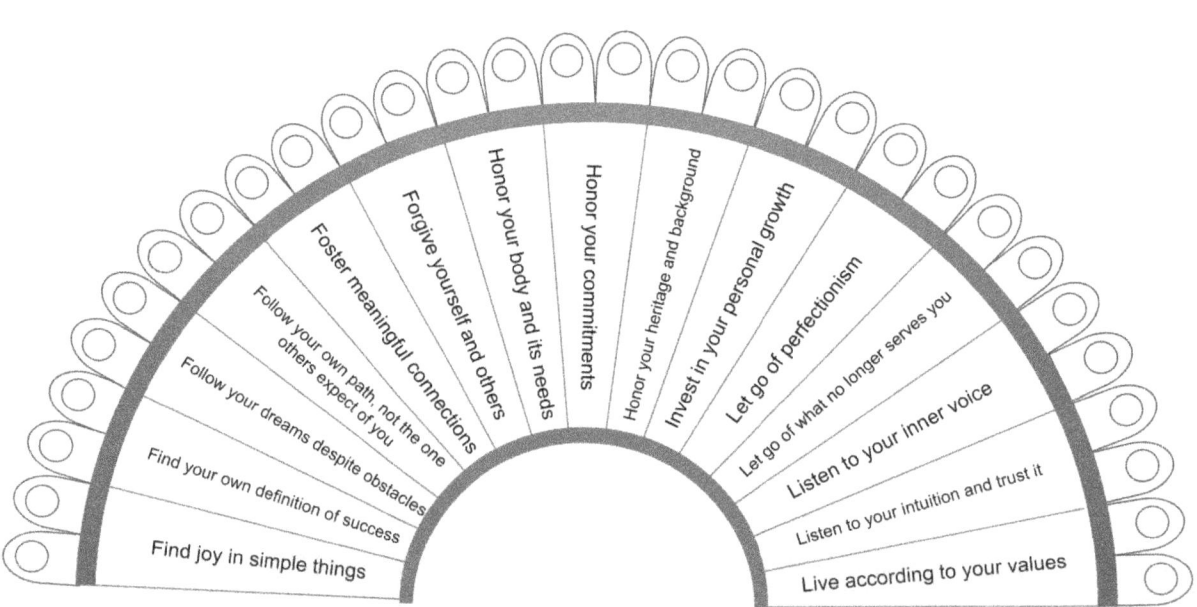

Living Authentically, Chart 3

The chart contains the following entries:

- Find joy in simple things
- Find your own definition of success
- Follow your dreams despite obstacles
- Follow your own path, not the one others expect of you
- Foster meaningful connections
- Forgive yourself and others
- Honor your body and its needs
- Honor your commitments
- Honor your heritage and background
- Invest in your personal growth
- Let go of perfectionism
- Let go of what no longer serves you
- Listen to your inner voice
- Listen to your intuition and trust it
- Live according to your values

Royal Template 15

Diving Deep into the Pool of the Mind

Chart 200

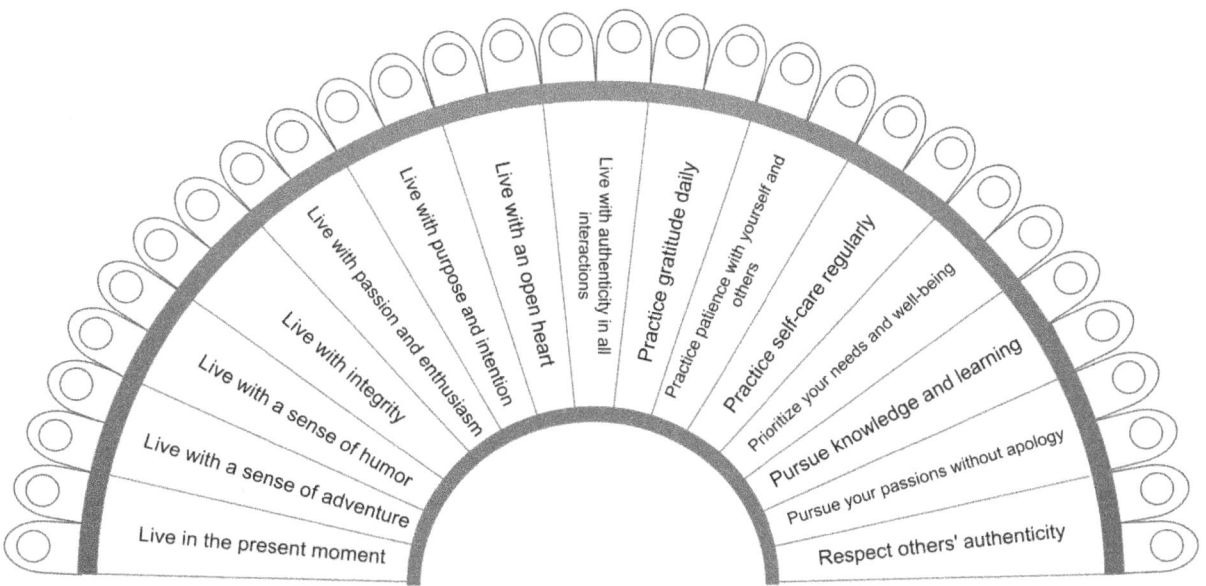

Living Authentically, Chart 4

The chart contains the following radiating labels:

- Live with passion and enthusiasm
- Live with purpose and intention
- Live with an open heart
- Live with authenticity in all interactions
- Practice gratitude daily
- Practice patience with yourself and others
- Practice self-care regularly
- Prioritize your needs and well-being
- Pursue knowledge and learning
- Pursue your passions without apology
- Respect others' authenticity
- Live with integrity
- Live with a sense of humor
- Live with a sense of adventure
- Live in the present moment

Royal Template 15

Diving Deep into the Pool of the Mind

Chart 201

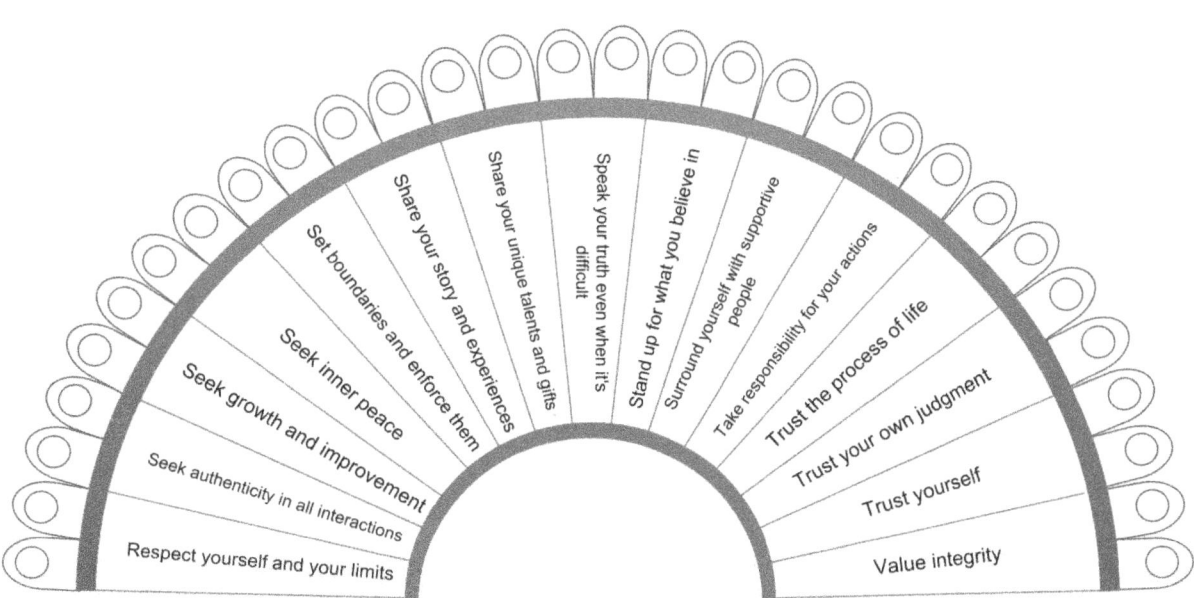

Living Authentically, Chart 5

The chart contains the following radiating labels:

- Set boundaries and enforce them
- Share your story and experiences
- Share your unique talents and gifts
- Speak your truth even when it's difficult
- Stand up for what you believe in
- Surround yourself with supportive people
- Take responsibility for your actions
- Trust the process of life
- Trust your own judgment
- Trust yourself
- Value integrity
- Seek inner peace
- Seek growth and improvement
- Seek authenticity in all interactions
- Respect yourself and your limits

Royal Template 15

Diving Deep into the Pool of the Mind

Chart 202

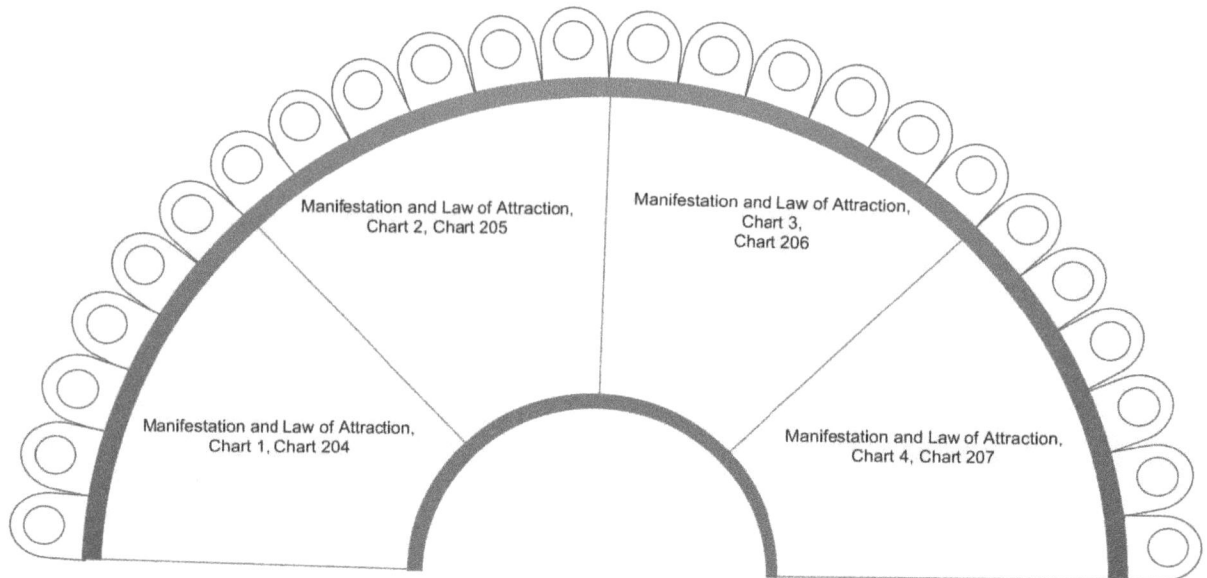

Manifestation and Law of Attraction, Master Chart

Manifestation and Law of Attraction, Chart 2, Chart 205

Manifestation and Law of Attraction, Chart 3, Chart 206

Manifestation and Law of Attraction, Chart 1, Chart 204

Manifestation and Law of Attraction, Chart 4, Chart 207

Royal Template 4h

Diving Deep into the Pool of the Mind

Chart 203

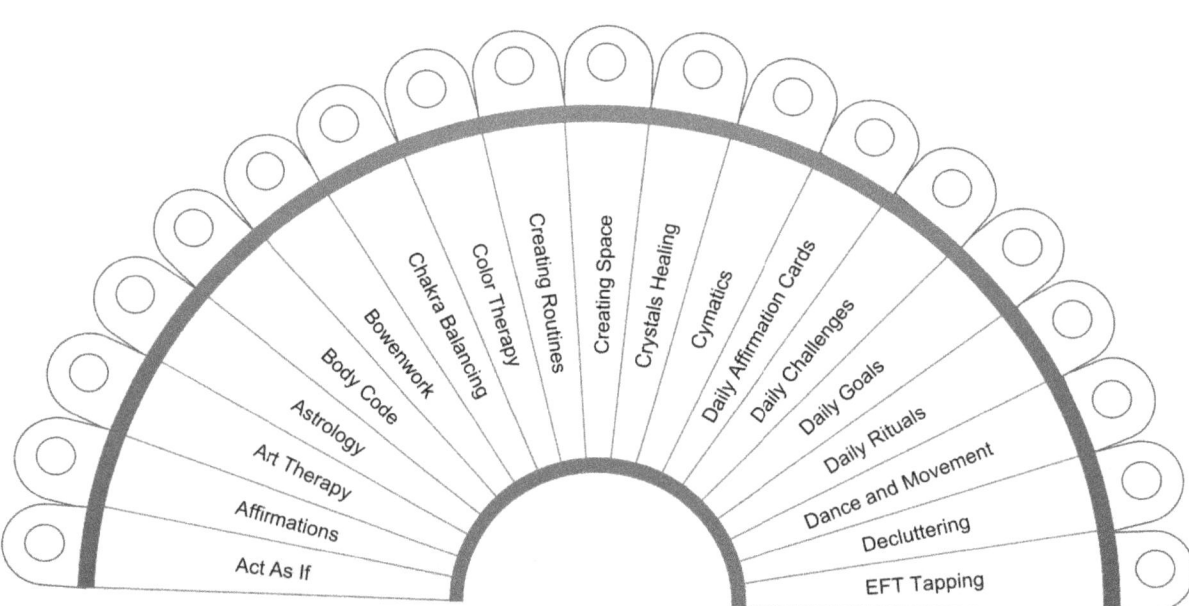

Act As If
Affirmations
Art Therapy
Astrology
Body Code
Bowenwork
Chakra Balancing
Color Therapy
Creating Routines
Creating Space
Crystals Healing
Cymatics
Daily Affirmation Cards
Daily Challenges
Daily Goals
Daily Rituals
Dance and Movement
Decluttering
EFT Tapping

Manifestation and Law of Attraction, Chart 1

Royal Template 19

Diving Deep into the Pool of the Mind

Chart 204

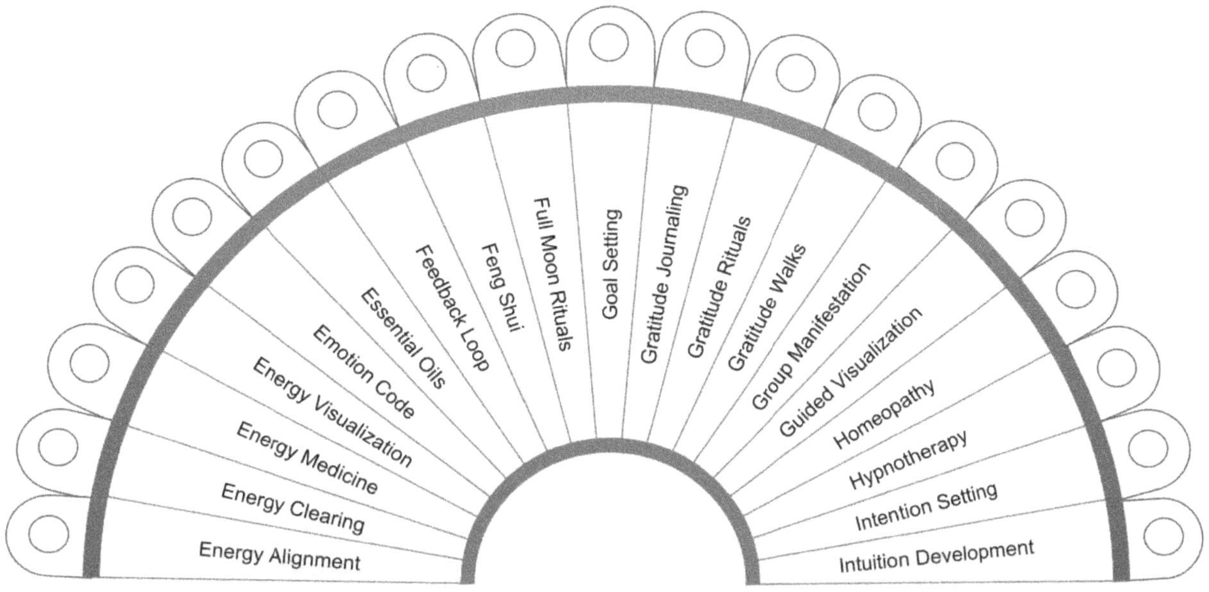
Energy Alignment
Energy Clearing
Energy Medicine
Energy Visualization
Emotion Code
Essential Oils
Feedback Loop
Feng Shui
Full Moon Rituals
Goal Setting
Gratitude Journaling
Gratitude Rituals
Gratitude Walks
Group Manifestation
Guided Visualization
Homeopathy
Hypnotherapy
Intention Setting
Intuition Development

Manifestation and Law of Attraction, Chart 2

Royal Template 19

Chart 205

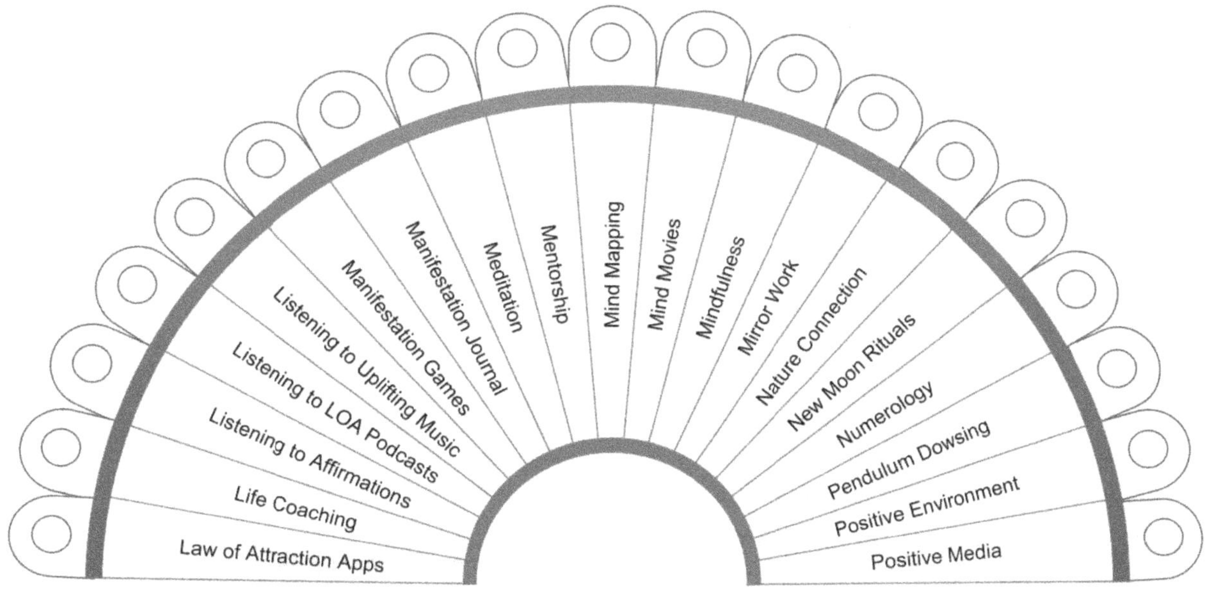
Law of Attraction Apps
Life Coaching
Listening to Affirmations
Listening to LOA Podcasts
Listening to Uplifting Music
Manifestation Games
Manifestation Journal
Meditation
Mentorship
Mind Mapping
Mind Movies
Mindfulness
Mirror Work
Nature Connection
New Moon Rituals
Numerology
Pendulum Dowsing
Positive Environment
Positive Media

Manifestation and Law of Attraction, Chart 3

Royal Template 19

Chart 206

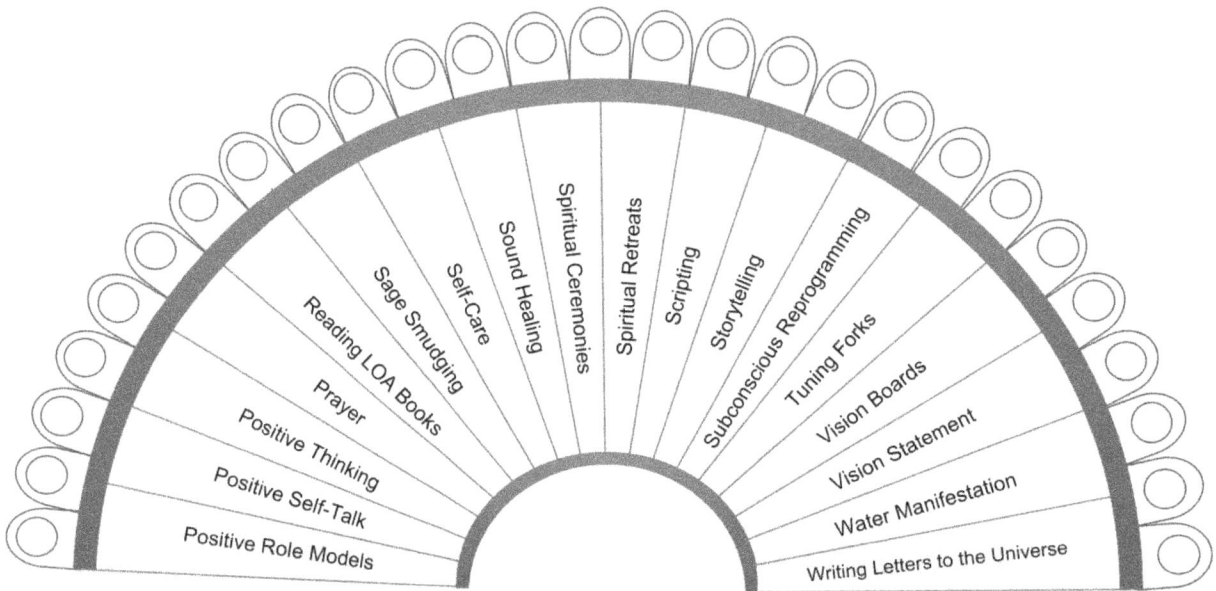

Manifestation and Law of Attraction, Chart 4

Reading LOA Books
Sage Smudging
Self-Care
Sound Healing
Spiritual Ceremonies
Spiritual Retreats
Scripting
Storytelling
Subconscious Reprogramming
Tuning Forks
Vision Boards
Vision Statement
Water Manifestation
Writing Letters to the Universe
Prayer
Positive Thinking
Positive Self-Talk
Positive Role Models

Royal Template 18

Diving Deep into the Pool of the Mind

Chart 207

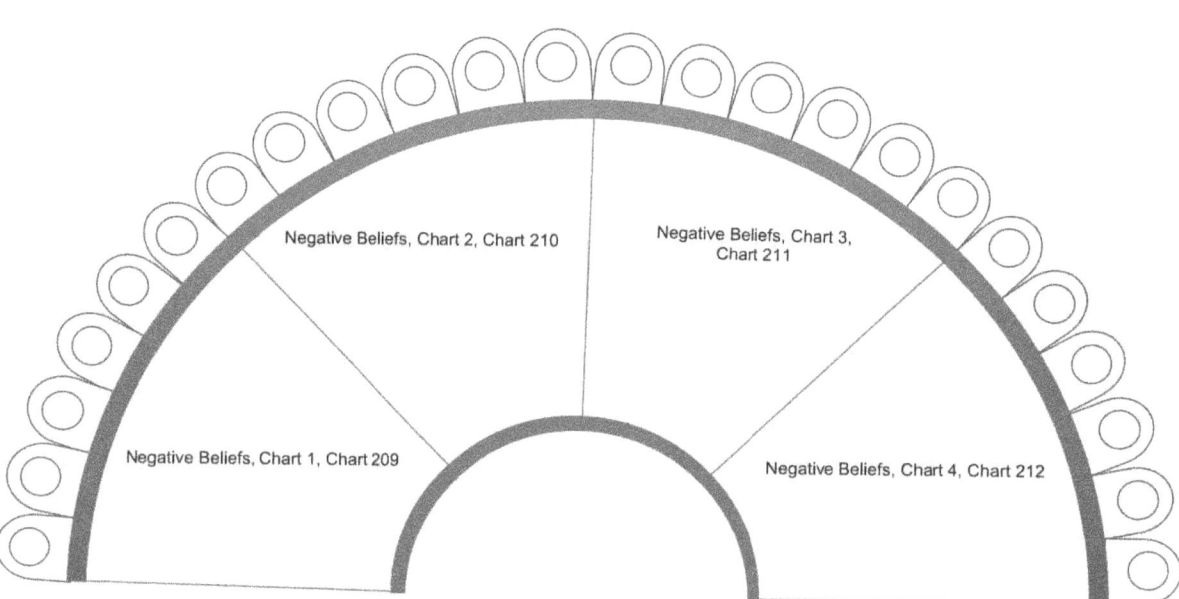

Negative Beliefs, Chart 2, Chart 210

Negative Beliefs, Chart 3, Chart 211

Negative Beliefs, Chart 1, Chart 209

Negative Beliefs, Chart 4, Chart 212

Negative Beliefs, Master Chart

Royal Template 4h

Diving Deep into the Pool of the Mind

Chart 208

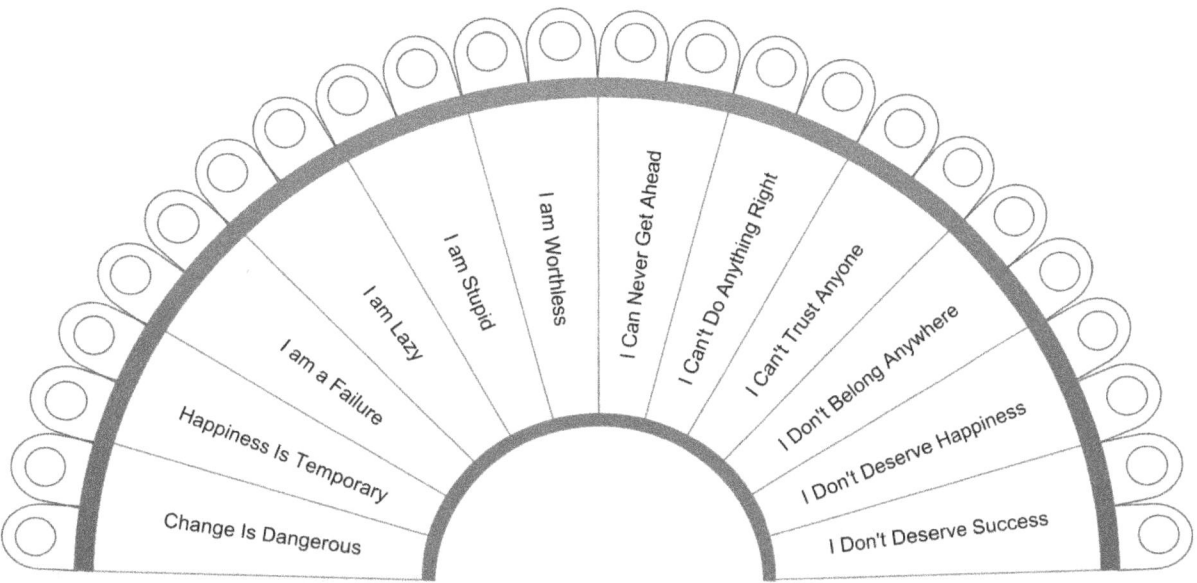

Negative Beliefs, Chart 1

The chart contains the following labels (clockwise from left):

- Change Is Dangerous
- Happiness Is Temporary
- I am a Failure
- I am Lazy
- I am Stupid
- I am Worthless
- I Can Never Get Ahead
- I Can't Do Anything Right
- I Can't Trust Anyone
- I Don't Belong Anywhere
- I Don't Deserve Happiness
- I Don't Deserve Success

Royal Template 12

Diving Deep into the Pool of the Mind

Chart 209

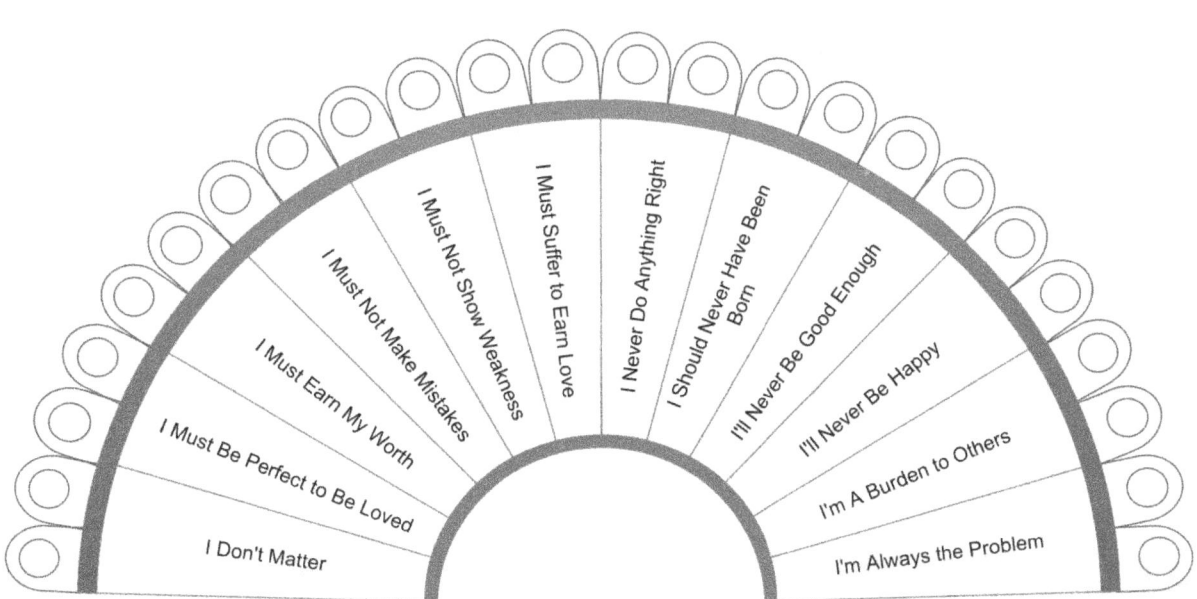

Negative Beliefs, Chart 2

The chart contains the following labels (clockwise from left):

- I Don't Matter
- I Must Be Perfect to Be Loved
- I Must Earn My Worth
- I Must Not Make Mistakes
- I Must Not Show Weakness
- I Must Suffer to Earn Love
- I Never Do Anything Right
- I Should Never Have Been Born
- I'll Never Be Good Enough
- I'll Never Be Happy
- I'm A Burden to Others
- I'm Always the Problem

Royal Template 12

Diving Deep into the Pool of the Mind

Chart 210

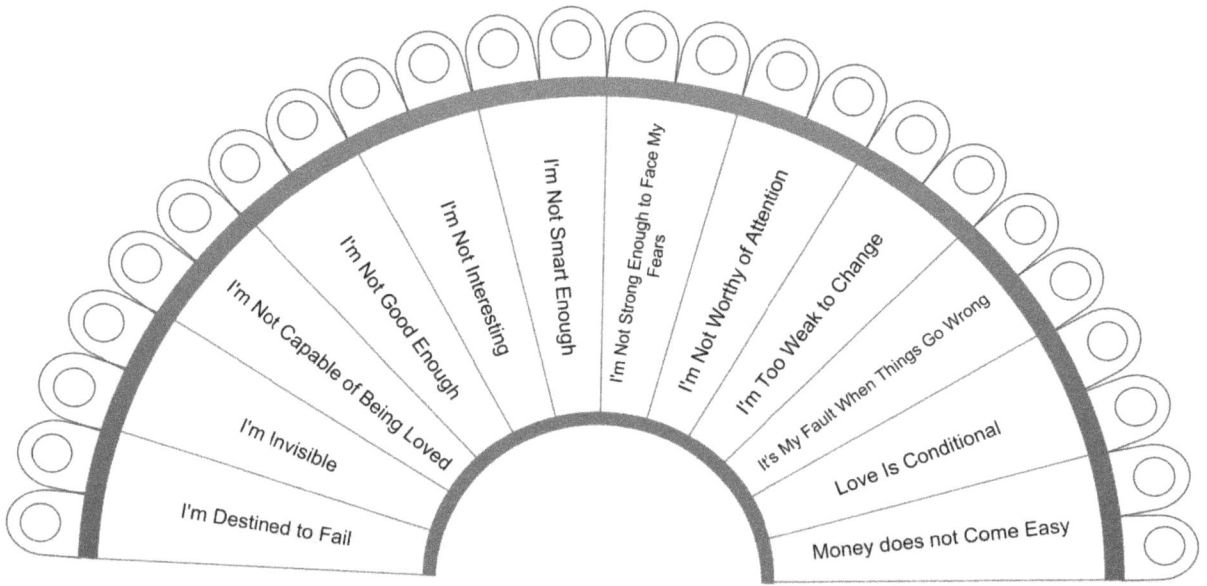

Negative Beliefs, Chart 3

The chart contains the following labels (reading across the fan):

- I'm Destined to Fail
- I'm Invisible
- I'm Not Capable of Being Loved
- I'm Not Good Enough
- I'm Not Interesting
- I'm Not Smart Enough
- I'm Not Strong Enough to Face My Fears
- I'm Not Worthy of Attention
- I'm Too Weak to Change
- It's My Fault When Things Go Wrong
- Love Is Conditional
- Money does not Come Easy

Royal Template 12

Diving Deep into the Pool of the Mind

Chart 211

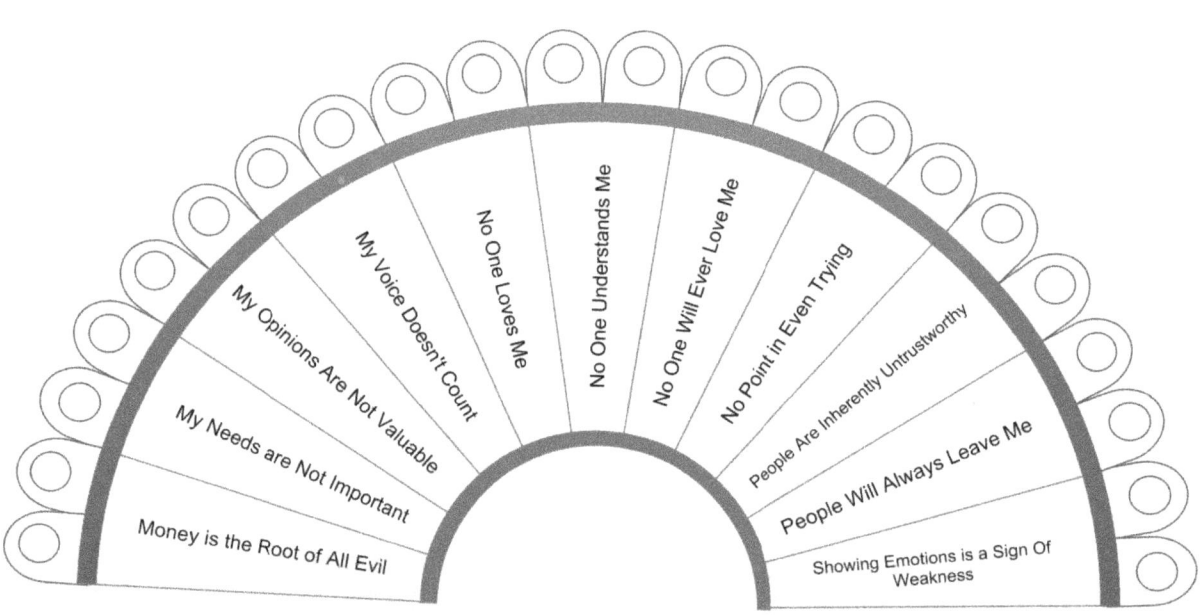

Negative Beliefs, Chart 4

The chart contains the following labels (reading across the fan):

- Money is the Root of All Evil
- My Needs are Not Important
- My Opinions Are Not Valuable
- My Voice Doesn't Count
- No One Loves Me
- No One Understands Me
- No One Will Ever Love Me
- No Point in Even Trying
- People Are Inherently Untrustworthy
- People Will Always Leave Me
- Showing Emotions is a Sign Of Weakness

Royal Template 11

Diving Deep into the Pool of the Mind

Chart 212

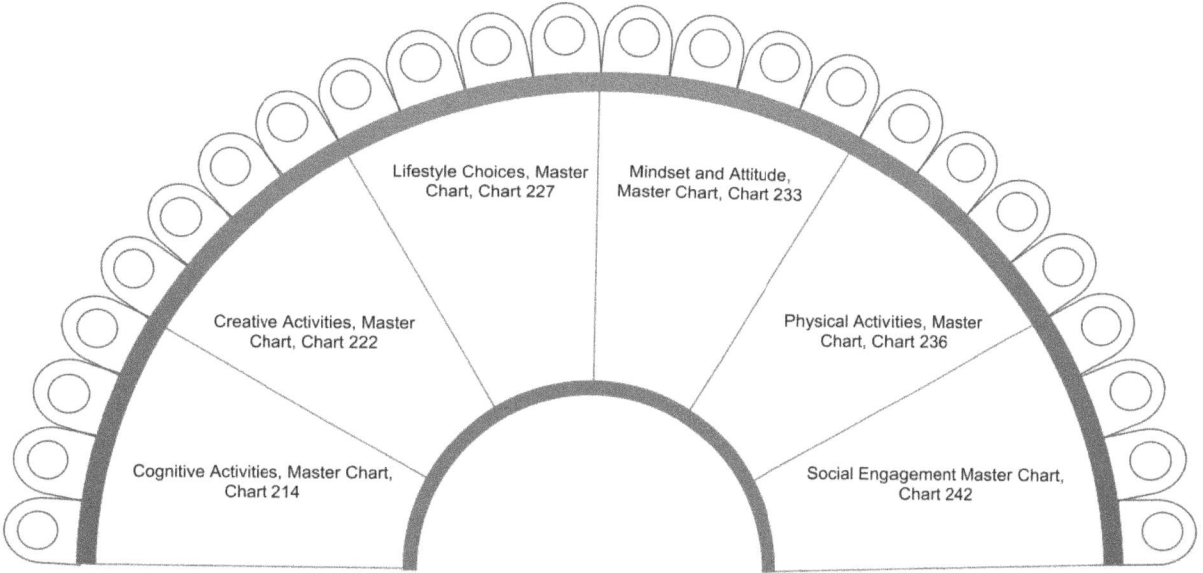

Neuroplasticity, Grand Master Chart

Lifestyle Choices, Master Chart, Chart 227

Mindset and Attitude, Master Chart, Chart 233

Creative Activities, Master Chart, Chart 222

Physical Activities, Master Chart, Chart 236

Cognitive Activities, Master Chart, Chart 214

Social Engagement Master Chart, Chart 242

Royal Template 6h

Diving Deep into the Pool of the Mind

Chart 213

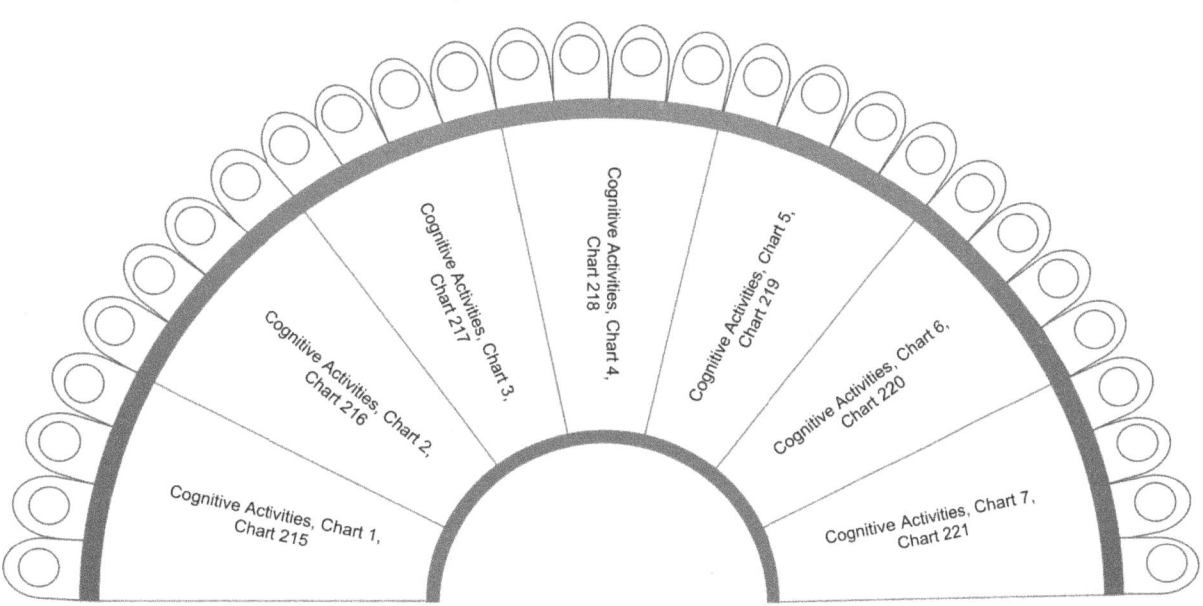

Cognitive Activities, Chart 1, Chart 215

Cognitive Activities, Chart 2, Chart 216

Cognitive Activities, Chart 3, Chart 217

Cognitive Activities, Chart 4, Chart 218

Cognitive Activities, Chart 5, Chart 219

Cognitive Activities, Chart 6, Chart 220

Cognitive Activities, Chart 7, Chart 221

Cognitive Activities, Master Chart

Royal Template 7

Diving Deep into the Pool of the Mind

Chart 214

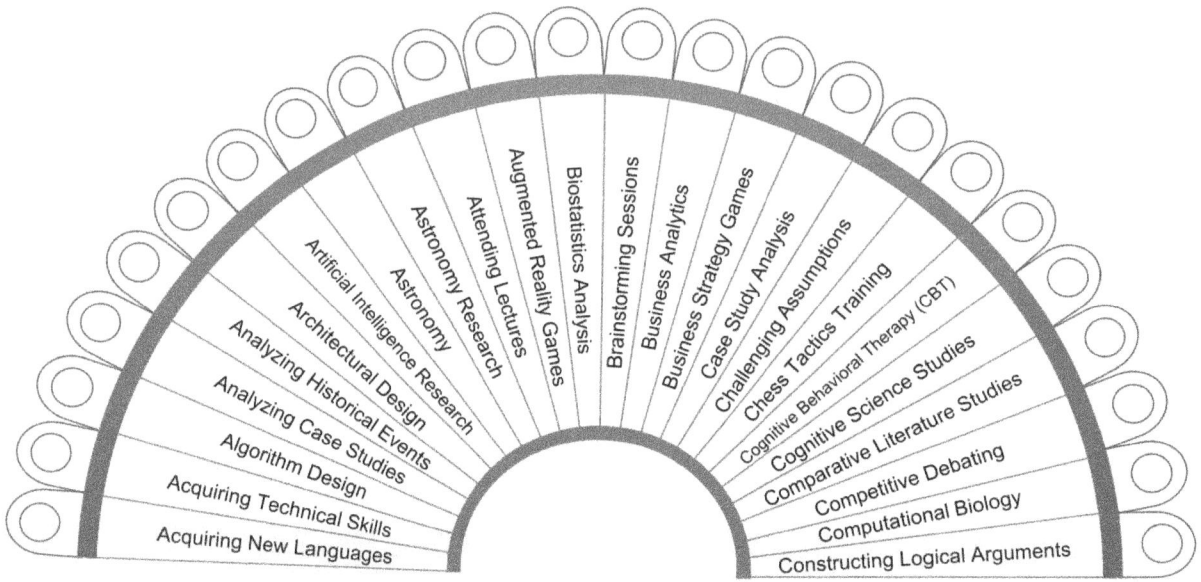

Cognitive Activities, Chart 1

The fan chart contains the following labels (from left to right):

- Acquiring New Languages
- Acquiring Technical Skills
- Algorithm Design
- Analyzing Case Studies
- Analyzing Historical Events
- Architectural Design
- Artificial Intelligence Research
- Astronomy Research
- Attending Lectures
- Augmented Reality Games
- Biostatistics Analysis
- Brainstorming Sessions
- Business Analytics
- Business Strategy Games
- Case Study Analysis
- Challenging Assumptions
- Chess Tactics Training
- Cognitive Behavioral Therapy (CBT)
- Cognitive Science Studies
- Comparative Literature Studies
- Competitive Debating
- Computational Biology
- Constructing Logical Arguments

Royal Template 24

Diving Deep into the Pool of the Mind

Chart 215

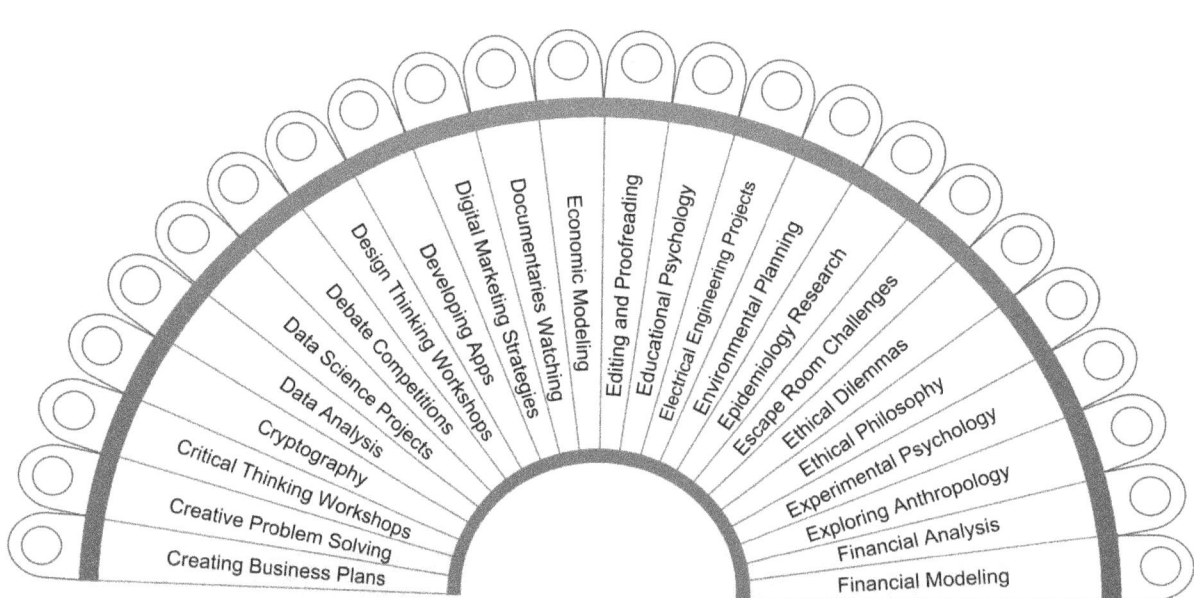

Cognitive Activities, Chart 2

The fan chart contains the following labels (from left to right):

- Creating Business Plans
- Creative Problem Solving
- Critical Thinking Workshops
- Cryptography
- Data Analysis
- Data Science Projects
- Debate Competitions
- Design Thinking Workshops
- Developing Apps
- Digital Marketing Strategies
- Documentaries Watching
- Economic Modeling
- Editing and Proofreading
- Educational Psychology
- Electrical Engineering Projects
- Environmental Planning
- Epidemiology Research
- Escape Room Challenges
- Ethical Dilemmas
- Ethical Philosophy
- Experimental Psychology
- Exploring Anthropology
- Financial Analysis
- Financial Modeling

Royal Template 24

Diving Deep into the Pool of the Mind

Chart 216

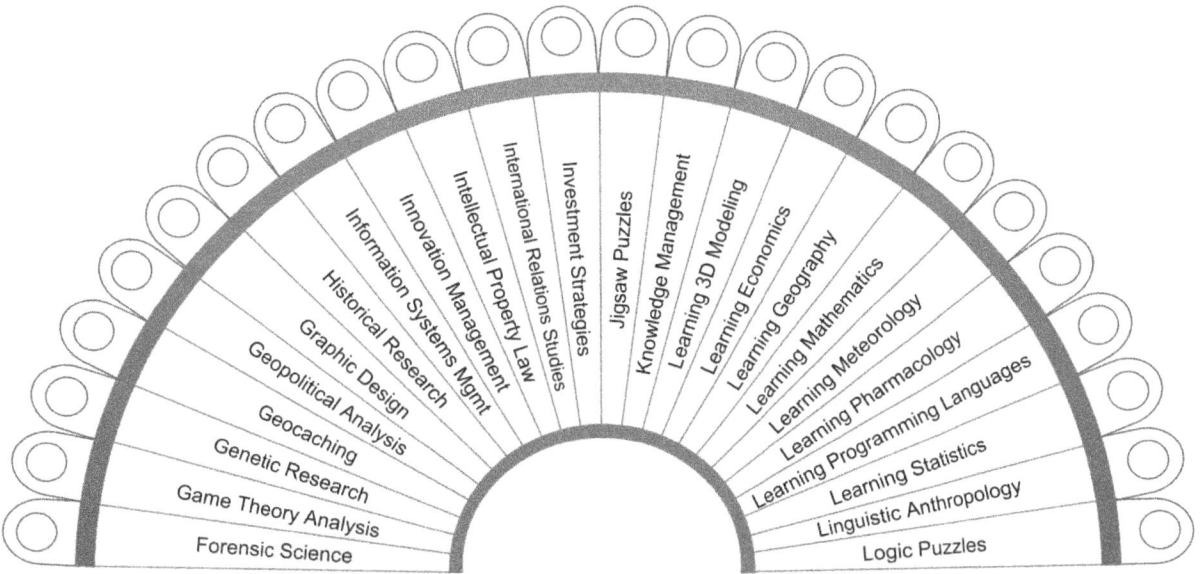

Cognitive Activities, Chart 3

The chart radiates the following labels:

Forensic Science · Game Theory Analysis · Genetic Research · Geocaching · Geopolitical Analysis · Graphic Design · Historical Research · Information Systems Mgmt · Innovation Management · Intellectual Property Law · International Relations Studies · Investment Strategies · Jigsaw Puzzles · Knowledge Management · Learning 3D Modeling · Learning Economics · Learning Geography · Learning Mathematics · Learning Meteorology · Learning Pharmacology · Learning Programming Languages · Learning Statistics · Linguistic Anthropology · Logic Puzzles

Royal Template 24

Diving Deep into the Pool of the Mind

Chart 217

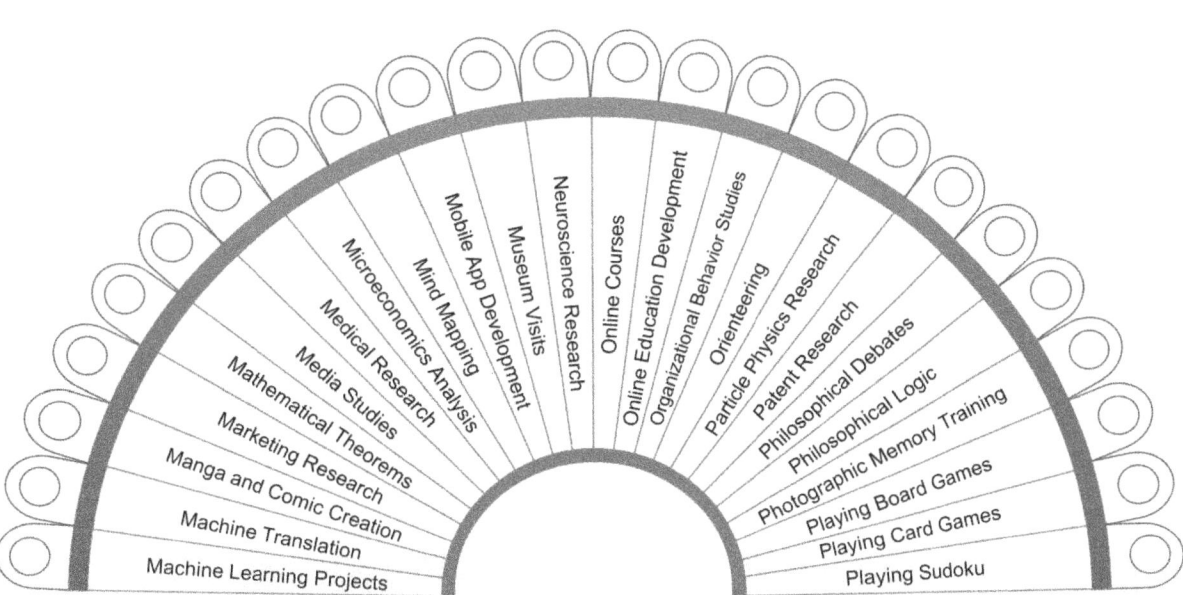

Cognitive Activities, Chart 4

The chart radiates the following labels:

Machine Learning Projects · Machine Translation · Manga and Comic Creation · Marketing Research · Mathematical Theorems · Media Studies · Medical Research · Microeconomics Analysis · Mind Mapping · Mobile App Development · Museum Visits · Neuroscience Research · Online Courses · Online Education Development · Organizational Behavior Studies · Orienteering · Particle Physics Research · Patent Research · Philosophical Debates · Philosophical Logic · Photographic Memory Training · Playing Board Games · Playing Card Games · Playing Sudoku

Royal Template 24

Diving Deep into the Pool of the Mind

Chart 218

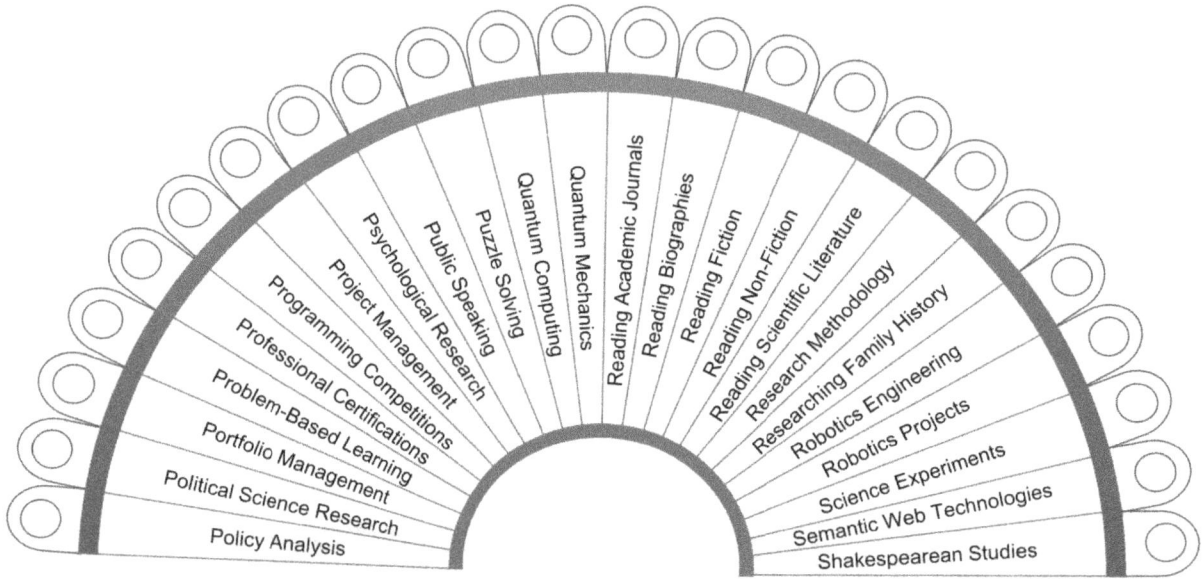

Cognitive Activities, Chart 5

The fan chart contains the following labels (left to right):

- Policy Analysis
- Political Science Research
- Portfolio Management
- Problem-Based Learning
- Professional Certifications
- Programming Competitions
- Project Management
- Psychological Research
- Public Speaking
- Puzzle Solving
- Quantum Computing
- Quantum Mechanics
- Reading Academic Journals
- Reading Biographies
- Reading Fiction
- Reading Non-Fiction
- Reading Scientific Literature
- Research Methodology
- Researching Family History
- Robotics Engineering
- Robotics Projects
- Science Experiments
- Semantic Web Technologies
- Shakespearean Studies

Royal Template 24

Diving Deep into the Pool of the Mind

Chart 219

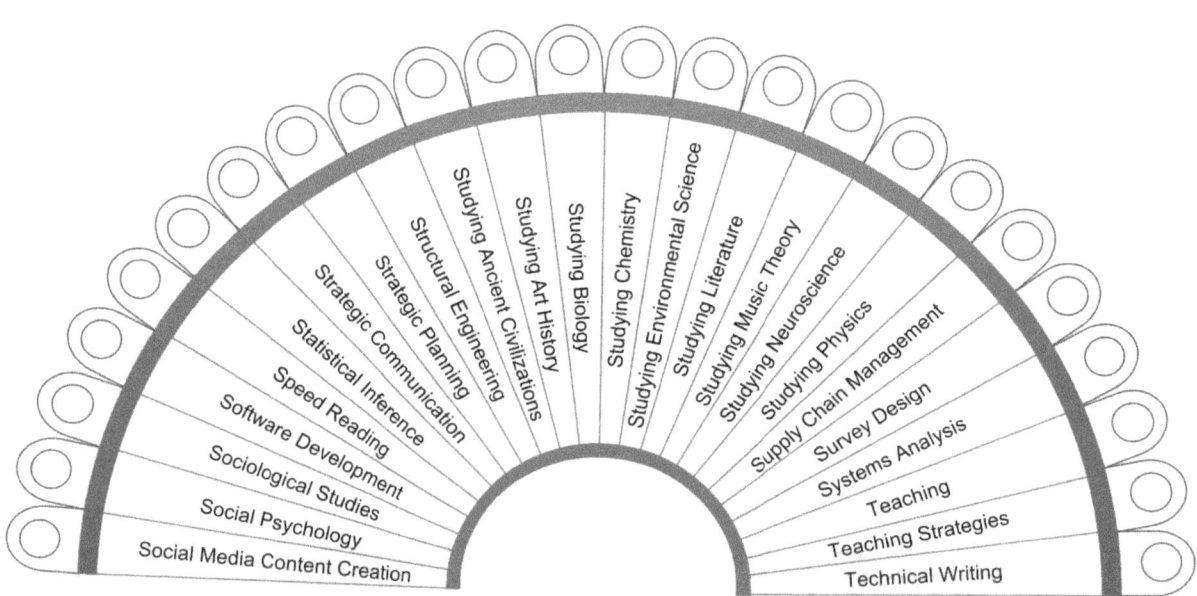

Cognitive Activities, Chart 6

The fan chart contains the following labels (left to right):

- Social Media Content Creation
- Social Psychology
- Sociological Studies
- Software Development
- Speed Reading
- Statistical Inference
- Strategic Communication
- Strategic Planning
- Structural Engineering
- Studying Ancient Civilizations
- Studying Art History
- Studying Biology
- Studying Chemistry
- Studying Environmental Science
- Studying Literature
- Studying Music Theory
- Studying Neuroscience
- Studying Physics
- Supply Chain Management
- Survey Design
- Systems Analysis
- Teaching
- Teaching Strategies
- Technical Writing

Royal Template 24

Diving Deep into the Pool of the Mind

Chart 220

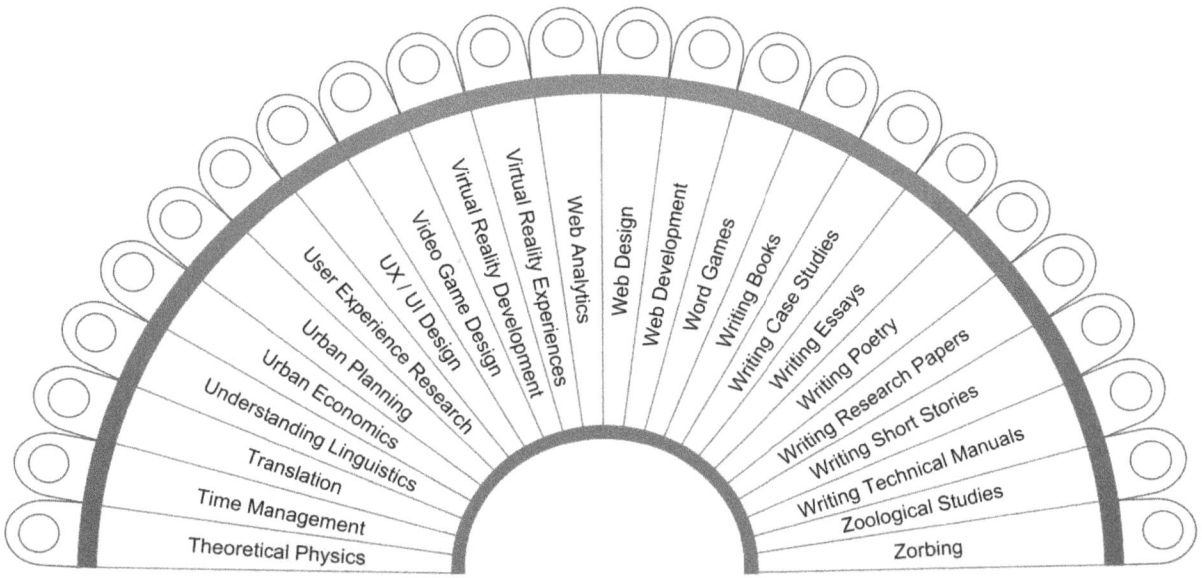

Cognitive Activities, Chart 7

Theoretical Physics
Time Management
Translation
Understanding Linguistics
Urban Economics
Urban Planning
User Experience Research
UX / UI Design
Video Game Design
Virtual Reality Development
Virtual Reality Experiences
Web Analytics
Web Design
Web Development
Word Games
Writing Books
Writing Case Studies
Writing Essays
Writing Poetry
Writing Research Papers
Writing Short Stories
Writing Technical Manuals
Zoological Studies
Zorbing

Royal Template 24

Diving Deep into the Pool of the Mind

Chart 221

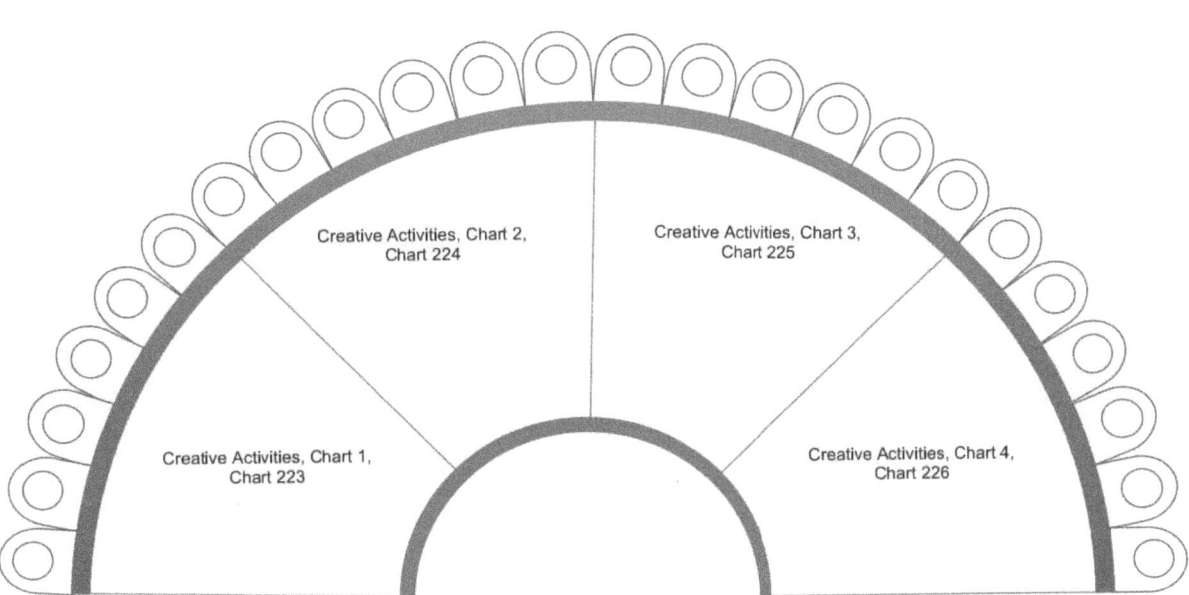

Creative Activities, Chart 2,
Chart 224

Creative Activities, Chart 3,
Chart 225

Creative Activities, Chart 1,
Chart 223

Creative Activities, Chart 4,
Chart 226

Creative Activities, Master Chart

Royal Template 4h

Diving Deep into the Pool of the Mind

Chart 222

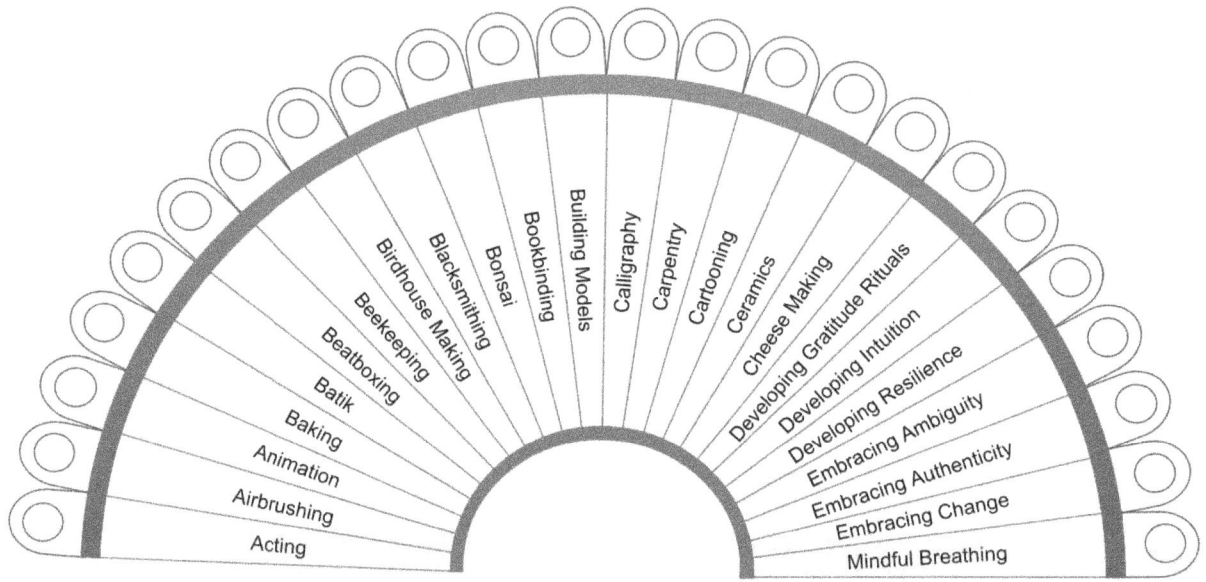

Creative Activities, Chart 1

The fan chart contains the following labels (reading around the arc):

Acting, Airbrushing, Animation, Baking, Batik, Beatboxing, Beekeeping, Birdhouse Making, Blacksmithing, Bonsai, Bookbinding, Building Models, Calligraphy, Carpentry, Cartooning, Ceramics, Cheese Making, Developing Gratitude Rituals, Developing Intuition, Developing Resilience, Embracing Ambiguity, Embracing Authenticity, Embracing Change, Mindful Breathing

Royal Template 24

Diving Deep into the Pool of the Mind

Chart 223

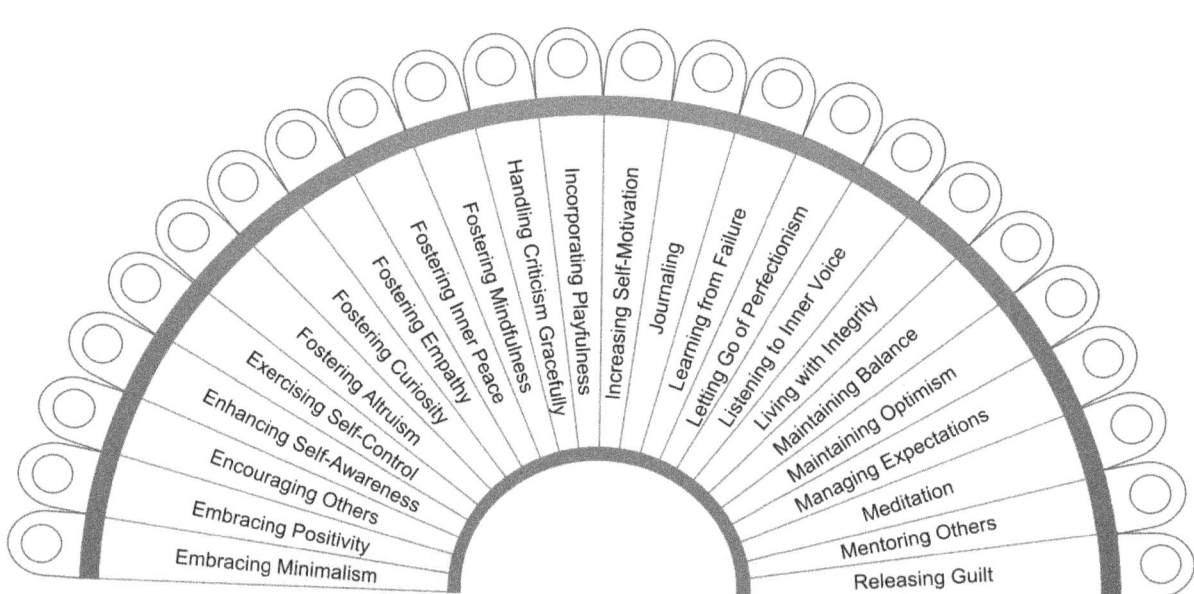

Creative Activities, Chart 2

The fan chart contains the following labels (reading around the arc):

Embracing Minimalism, Embracing Positivity, Encouraging Others, Enhancing Self-Awareness, Exercising Self-Control, Fostering Altruism, Fostering Curiosity, Fostering Empathy, Fostering Inner Peace, Fostering Mindfulness, Handling Criticism Gracefully, Incorporating Playfulness, Increasing Self-Motivation, Journaling, Learning from Failure, Letting Go of Perfectionism, Listening to Inner Voice, Living with Integrity, Maintaining Balance, Maintaining Optimism, Managing Expectations, Meditation, Mentoring Others, Releasing Guilt

Royal Template 24

Diving Deep into the Pool of the Mind

Chart 224

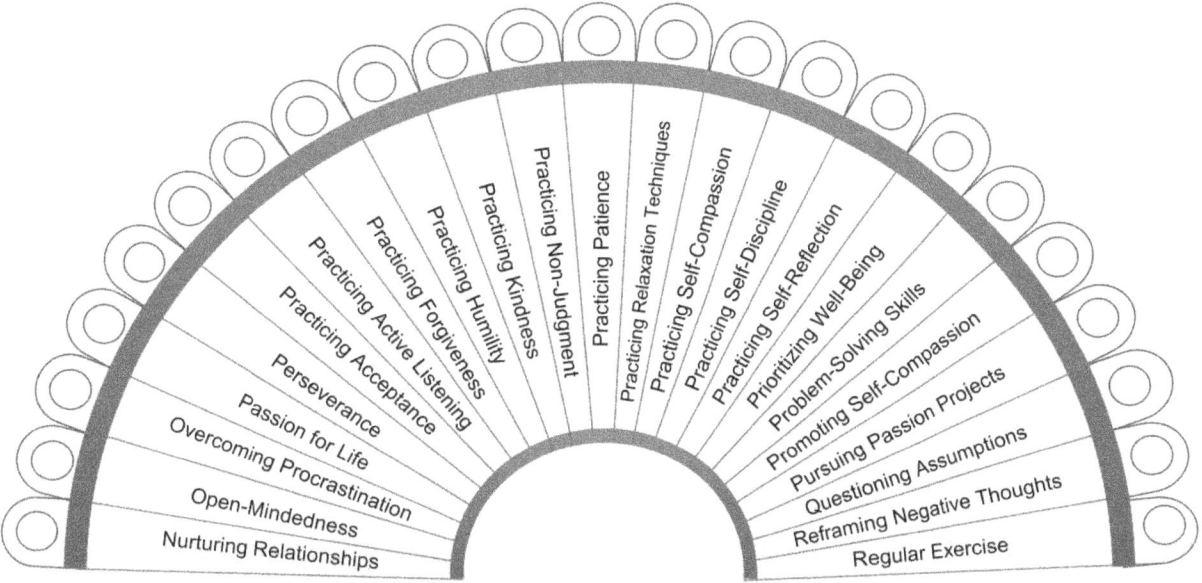

Creative Activities, Chart 3

Practicing Patience
Practicing Non-Judgment
Practicing Kindness
Practicing Humility
Practicing Forgiveness
Practicing Active Listening
Practicing Acceptance
Perseverance
Passion for Life
Overcoming Procrastination
Open-Mindedness
Nurturing Relationships
Practicing Relaxation Techniques
Practicing Self-Compassion
Practicing Self-Discipline
Practicing Self-Reflection
Prioritizing Well-Being
Problem-Solving Skills
Promoting Self-Compassion
Pursuing Passion Projects
Questioning Assumptions
Reframing Negative Thoughts
Regular Exercise

Royal Template 23

Diving Deep into the Pool of the Mind

Chart 225

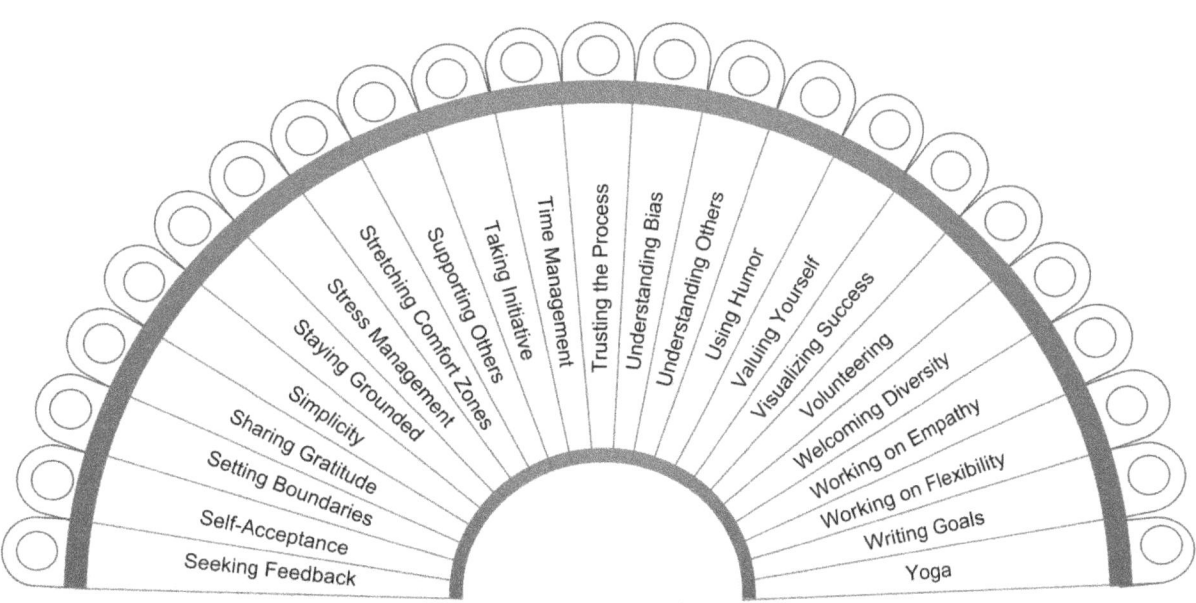

Creative Activities, Chart 4

Time Management
Taking Initiative
Supporting Others
Stretching Comfort Zones
Stress Management
Staying Grounded
Simplicity
Sharing Gratitude
Setting Boundaries
Self-Acceptance
Seeking Feedback
Trusting the Process
Understanding Bias
Understanding Others
Using Humor
Valuing Yourself
Visualizing Success
Volunteering
Welcoming Diversity
Working on Empathy
Working on Flexibility
Writing Goals
Yoga

Royal Template 23

Diving Deep into the Pool of the Mind

Chart 226

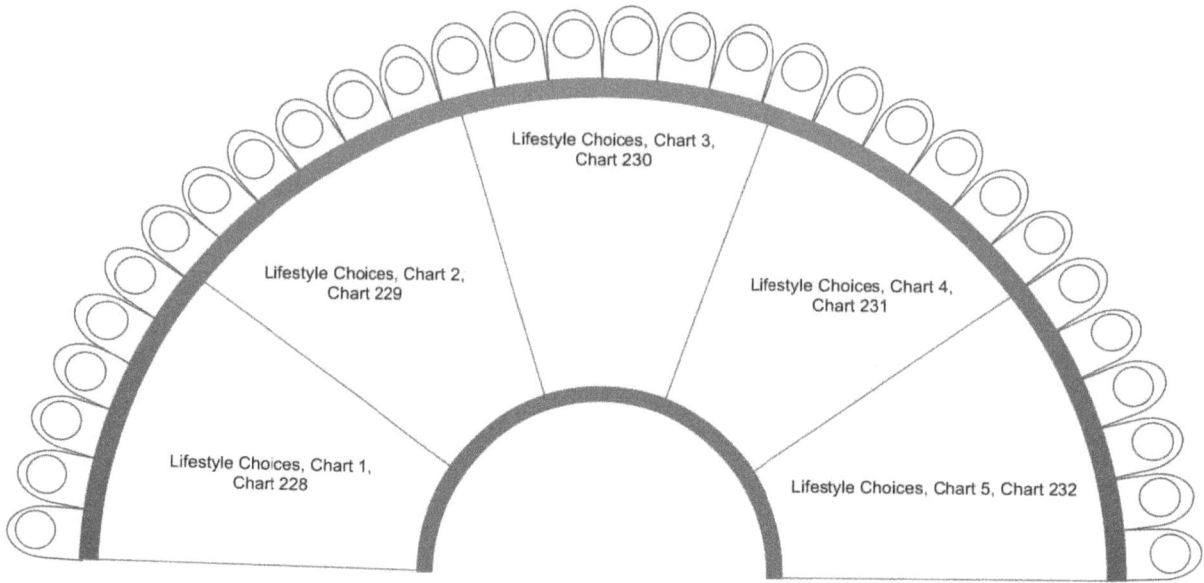

Lifestyle Choices, Master Chart

Lifestyle Choices, Chart 3, Chart 230

Lifestyle Choices, Chart 2, Chart 229

Lifestyle Choices, Chart 4, Chart 231

Lifestyle Choices, Chart 1, Chart 228

Lifestyle Choices, Chart 5, Chart 232

Royal Template 5h

Diving Deep into the Pool of the Mind

Chart 227

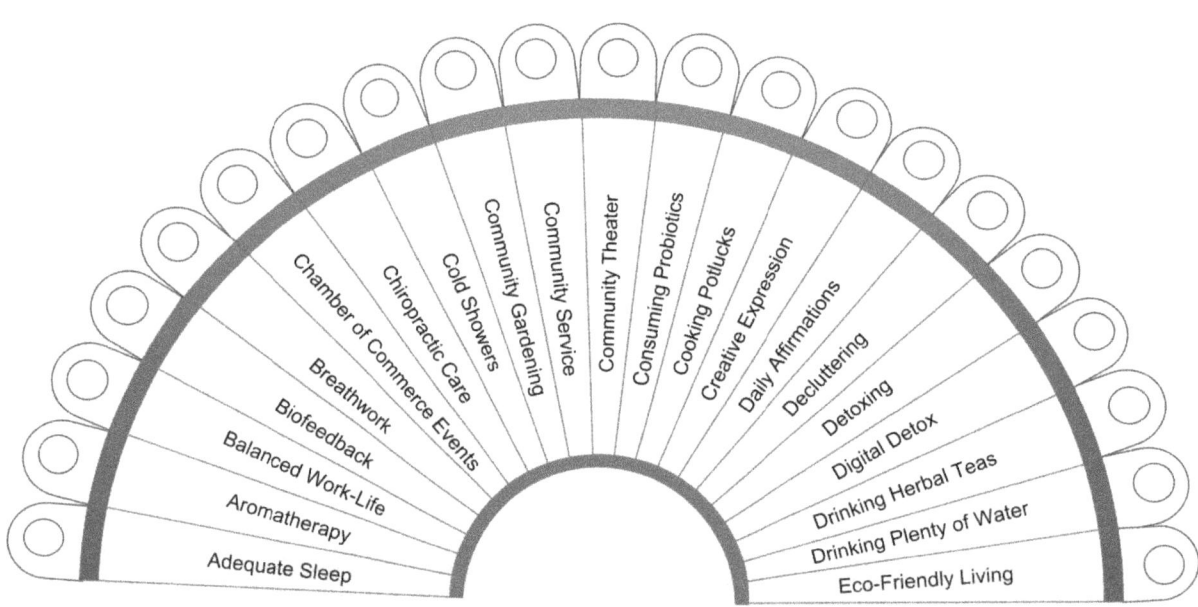

Chamber of Commerce Events
Chiropractic Care
Cold Showers
Community Gardening
Community Service
Community Theater
Consuming Probiotics
Cooking Potlucks
Creative Expression
Daily Affirmations
Decluttering
Detoxing
Digital Detox
Drinking Herbal Teas
Drinking Plenty of Water
Eco-Friendly Living

Breathwork
Biofeedback
Balanced Work-Life
Aromatherapy
Adequate Sleep

Lifestyle Choices, Chart 1

Royal Template 21

Diving Deep into the Pool of the Mind

Chart 228

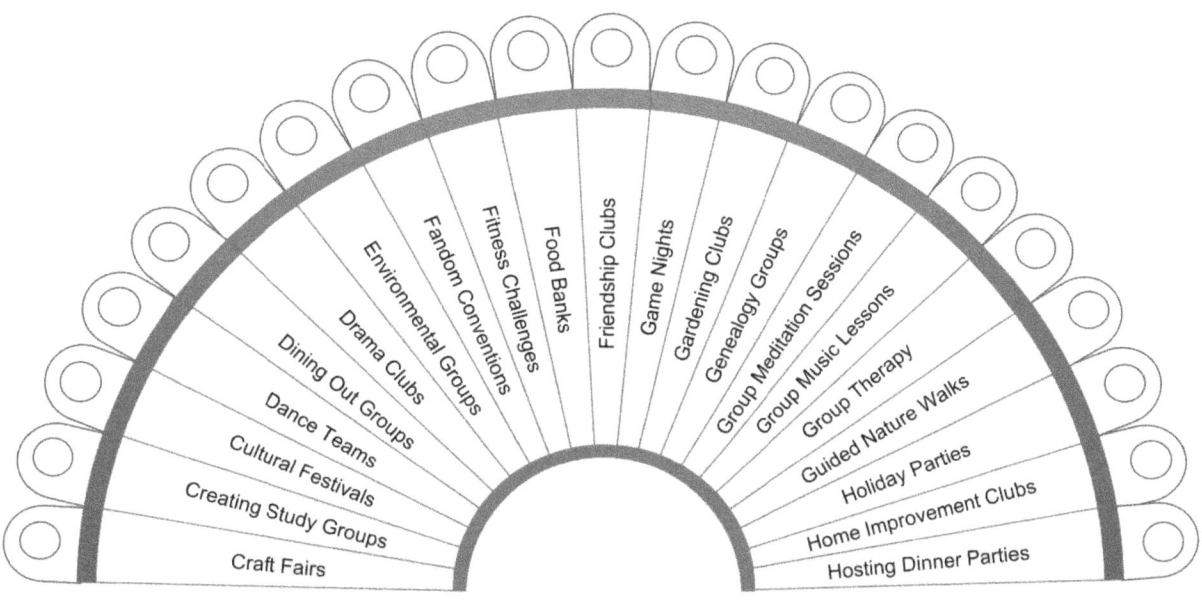

Lifestyle Choices, Chart 2

Craft Fairs
Creating Study Groups
Cultural Festivals
Dance Teams
Dining Out Groups
Drama Clubs
Environmental Groups
Fandom Conventions
Fitness Challenges
Food Banks
Friendship Clubs
Game Nights
Gardening Clubs
Genealogy Groups
Group Meditation Sessions
Group Music Lessons
Group Therapy
Guided Nature Walks
Holiday Parties
Home Improvement Clubs
Hosting Dinner Parties

Royal Template 21

Diving Deep into the Pool of the Mind

Chart 229

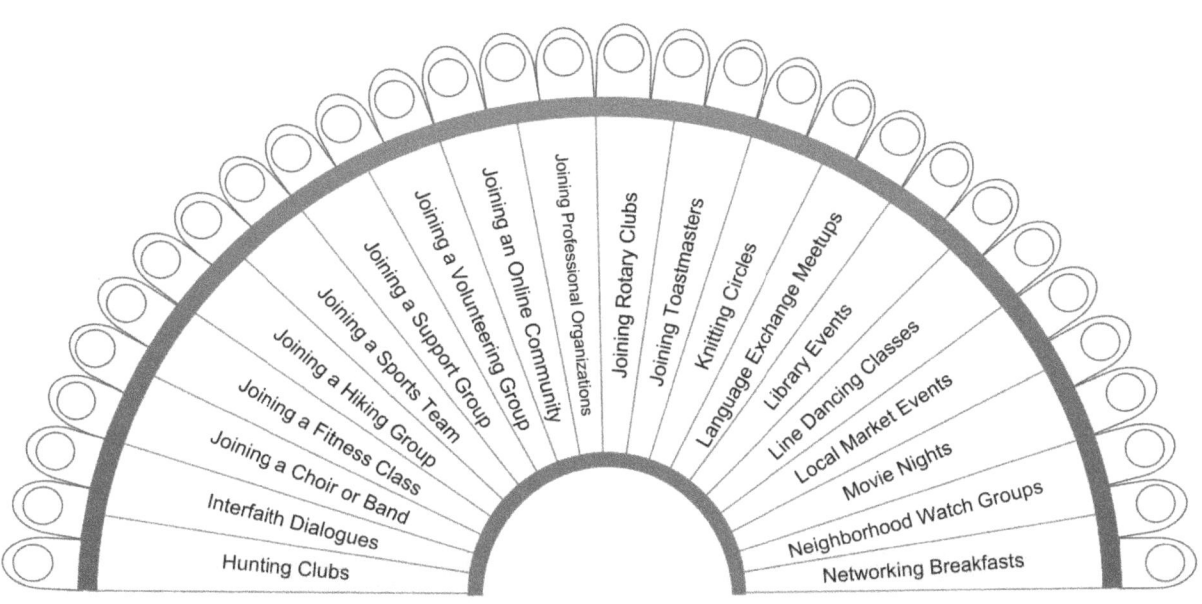

Lifestyle Choices, Chart 3

Hunting Clubs
Interfaith Dialogues
Joining a Choir or Band
Joining a Fitness Class
Joining a Hiking Group
Joining a Sports Team
Joining a Support Group
Joining a Volunteering Group
Joining an Online Community
Joining Professional Organizations
Joining Rotary Clubs
Joining Toastmasters
Knitting Circles
Language Exchange Meetups
Library Events
Line Dancing Classes
Local Market Events
Movie Nights
Neighborhood Watch Groups
Networking Breakfasts

Royal Template 20

Diving Deep into the Pool of the Mind

Chart 230

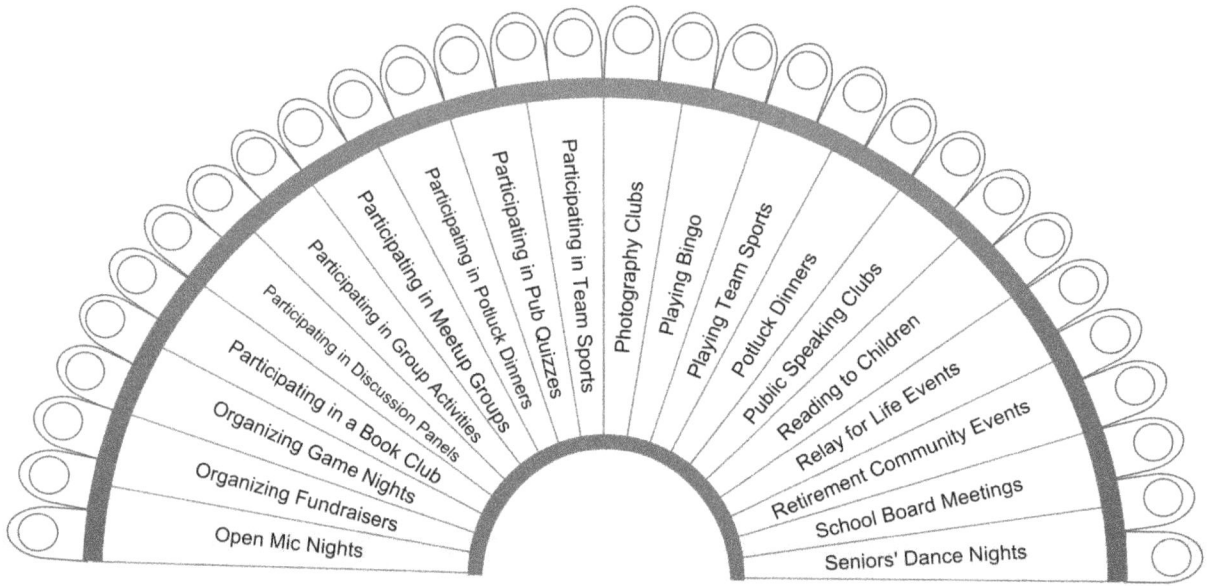

Lifestyle Choices, Chart 4

Participating in Discussion Panels
Participating in Group Activities
Participating in Meetup Groups
Participating in Polluck Dinners
Participating in Pub Quizzes
Participating in Team Sports
Photography Clubs
Playing Bingo
Playing Team Sports
Potluck Dinners
Public Speaking Clubs
Reading to Children
Relay for Life Events
Retirement Community Events
School Board Meetings
Seniors' Dance Nights
Participating in a Book Club
Organizing Game Nights
Organizing Fundraisers
Open Mic Nights

Royal Template 20

Diving Deep into the Pool of the Mind

Chart 231

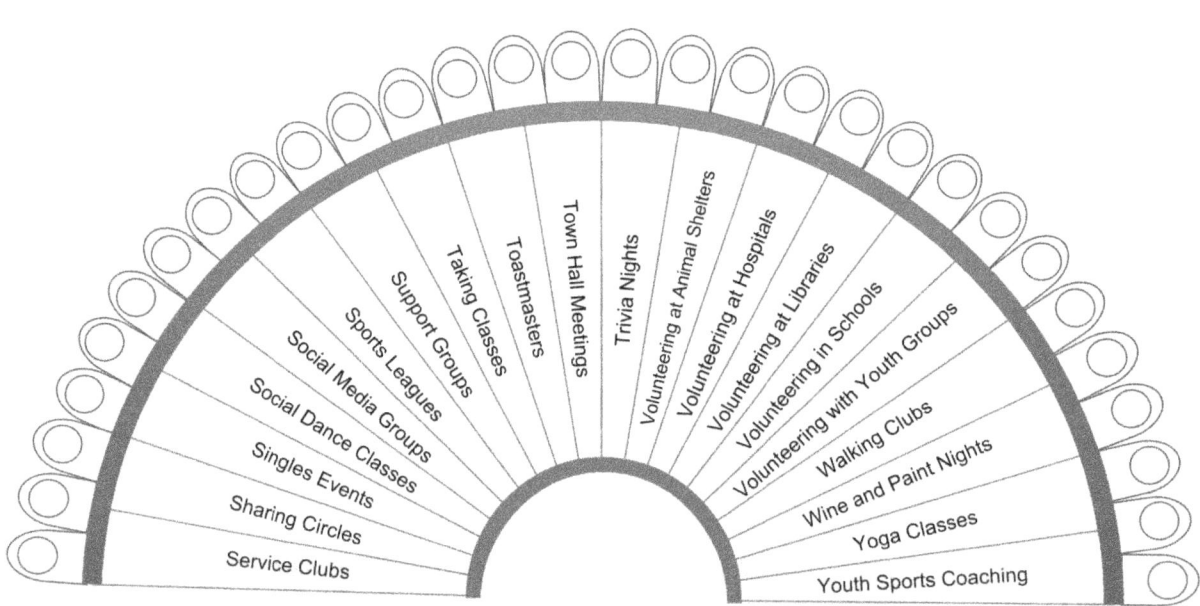

Lifestyle Choices, Chart 5

Town Hall Meetings
Trivia Nights
Volunteering at Animal Shelters
Volunteering at Hospitals
Volunteering at Libraries
Volunteering in Schools
Volunteering with Youth Groups
Walking Clubs
Wine and Paint Nights
Yoga Classes
Youth Sports Coaching
Toastmasters
Taking Classes
Support Groups
Sports Leagues
Social Media Groups
Social Dance Classes
Singles Events
Sharing Circles
Service Clubs

Royal Template 20

Diving Deep into the Pool of the Mind

Chart 232

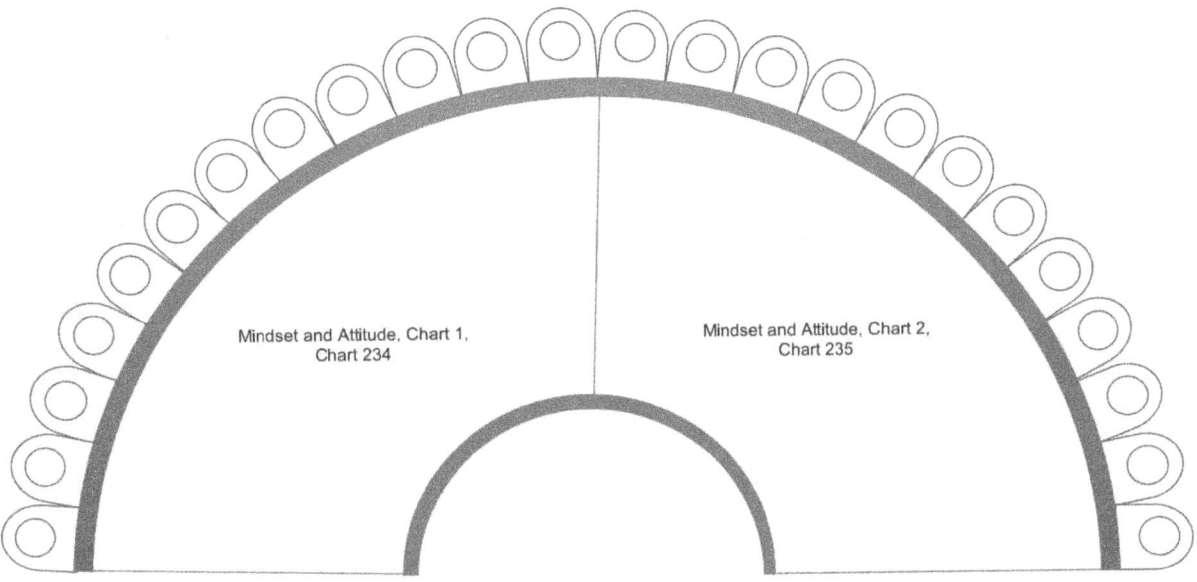

Mindset and Attitude, Master Chart

Mindset and Attitude, Chart 1,
Chart 234

Mindset and Attitude, Chart 2,
Chart 235

Royal Template 2

Diving Deep into the Pool of the Mind

Chart 233

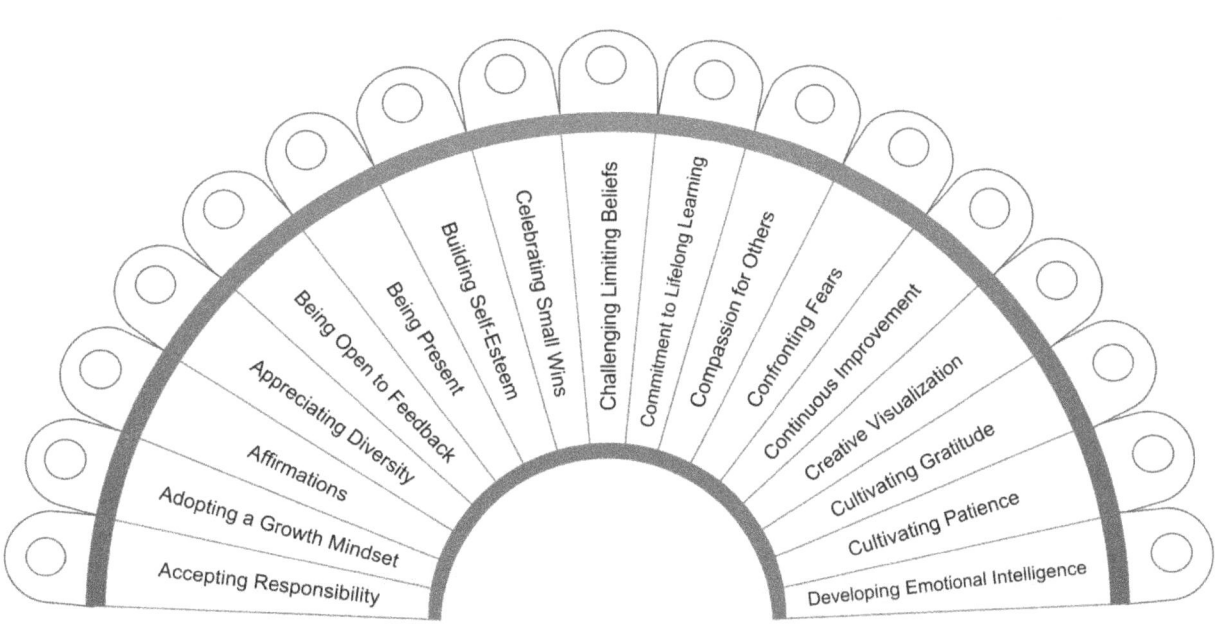

Being Open to Feedback
Being Present
Building Self-Esteem
Celebrating Small Wins
Challenging Limiting Beliefs
Commitment to Lifelong Learning
Compassion for Others
Confronting Fears
Continuous Improvement
Creative Visualization
Cultivating Gratitude
Cultivating Patience
Developing Emotional Intelligence
Appreciating Diversity
Affirmations
Adopting a Growth Mindset
Accepting Responsibility

Mindset and Attitude, Chart 1

Royal Template 17

Diving Deep into the Pool of the Mind

Chart 234

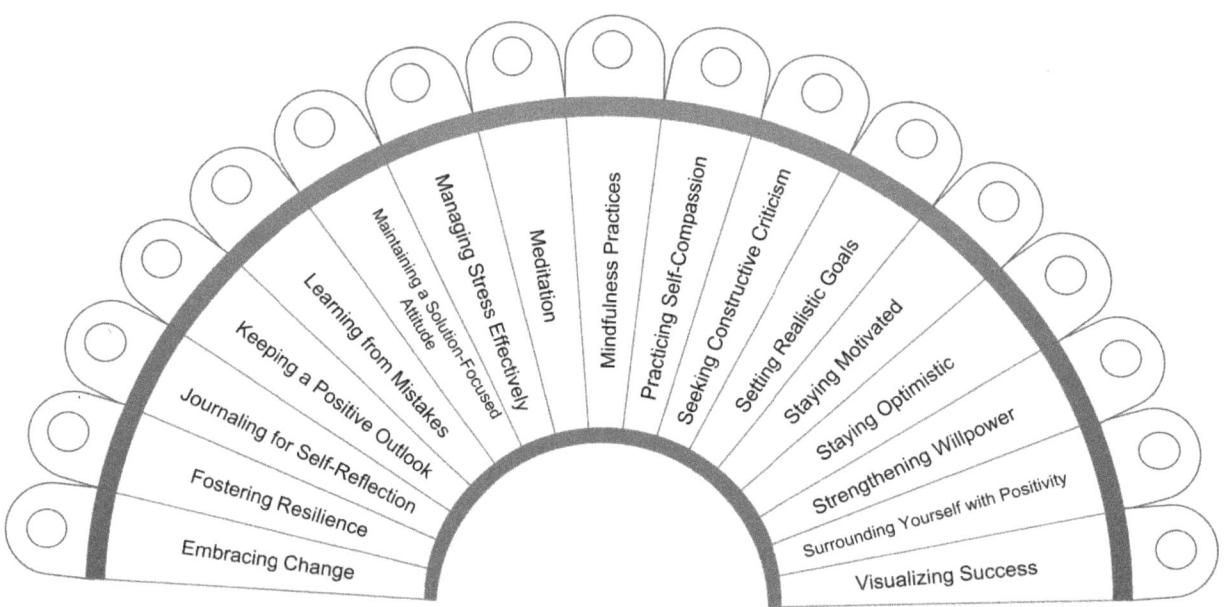

Mindset and Attitude, Chart 2

The fan chart contains the following labels (left to right):

- Embracing Change
- Fostering Resilience
- Journaling for Self-Reflection
- Keeping a Positive Outlook
- Learning from Mistakes
- Maintaining a Solution-Focused Attitude
- Managing Stress Effectively
- Meditation
- Mindfulness Practices
- Practicing Self-Compassion
- Seeking Constructive Criticism
- Setting Realistic Goals
- Staying Motivated
- Staying Optimistic
- Strengthening Willpower
- Surrounding Yourself with Positivity
- Visualizing Success

Royal Template 17

Diving Deep into the Pool of the Mind

Chart 235

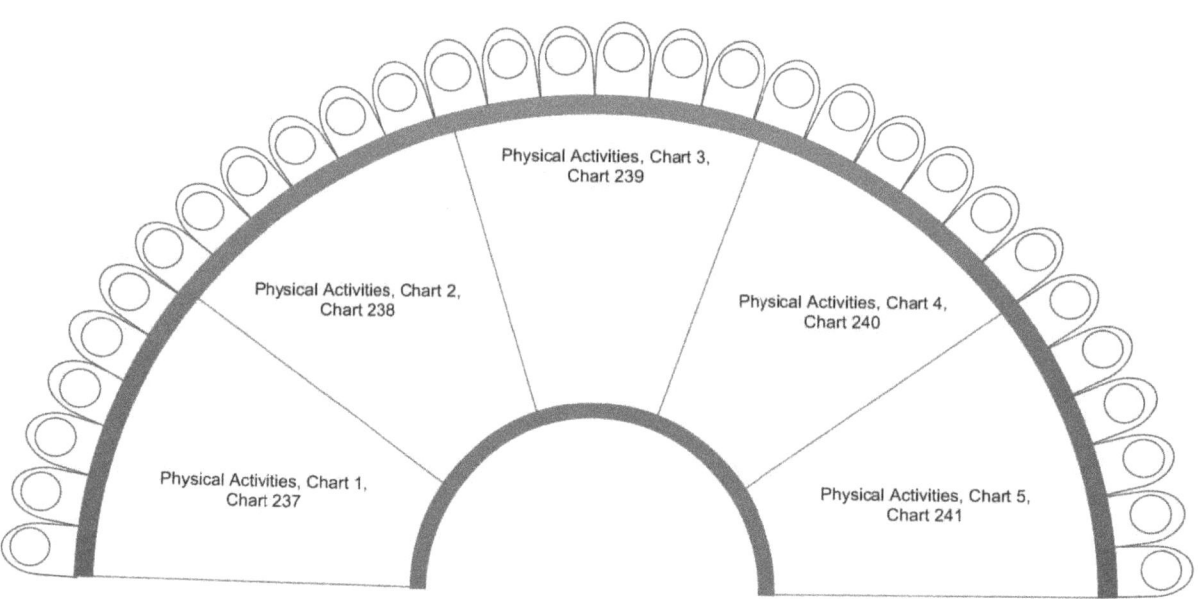

Physical Activities, Master Chart

The fan chart contains the following labels:

- Physical Activities, Chart 1, Chart 237
- Physical Activities, Chart 2, Chart 238
- Physical Activities, Chart 3, Chart 239
- Physical Activities, Chart 4, Chart 240
- Physical Activities, Chart 5, Chart 241

Royal Template 5h

Diving Deep into the Pool of the Mind

Chart 236

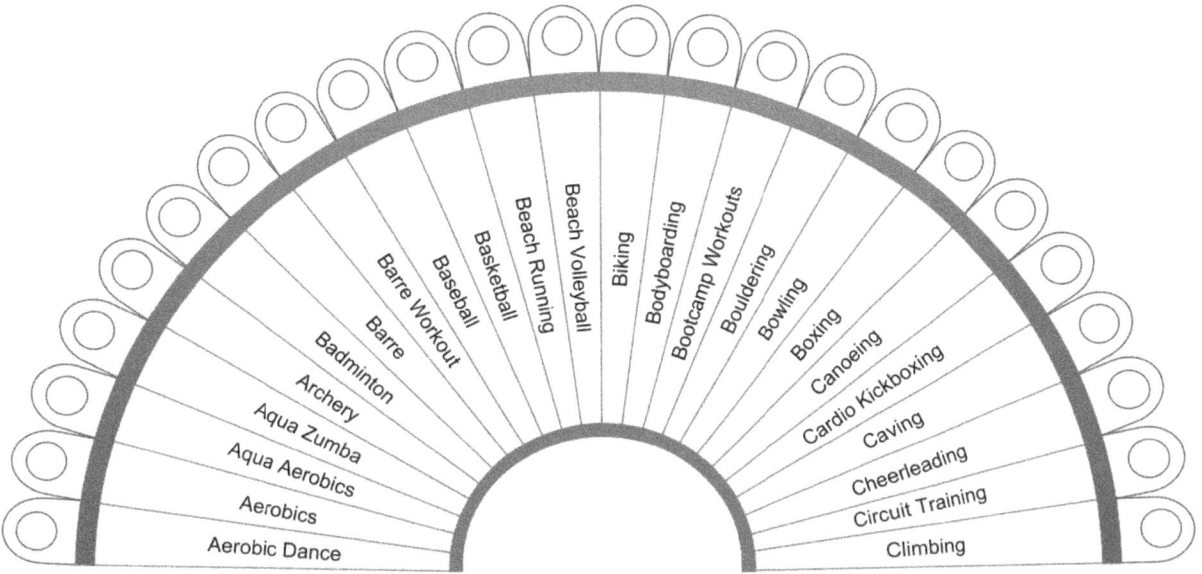

Physical Activities, Chart 1

Royal Template 24

Diving Deep into the Pool of the Mind

Chart 237

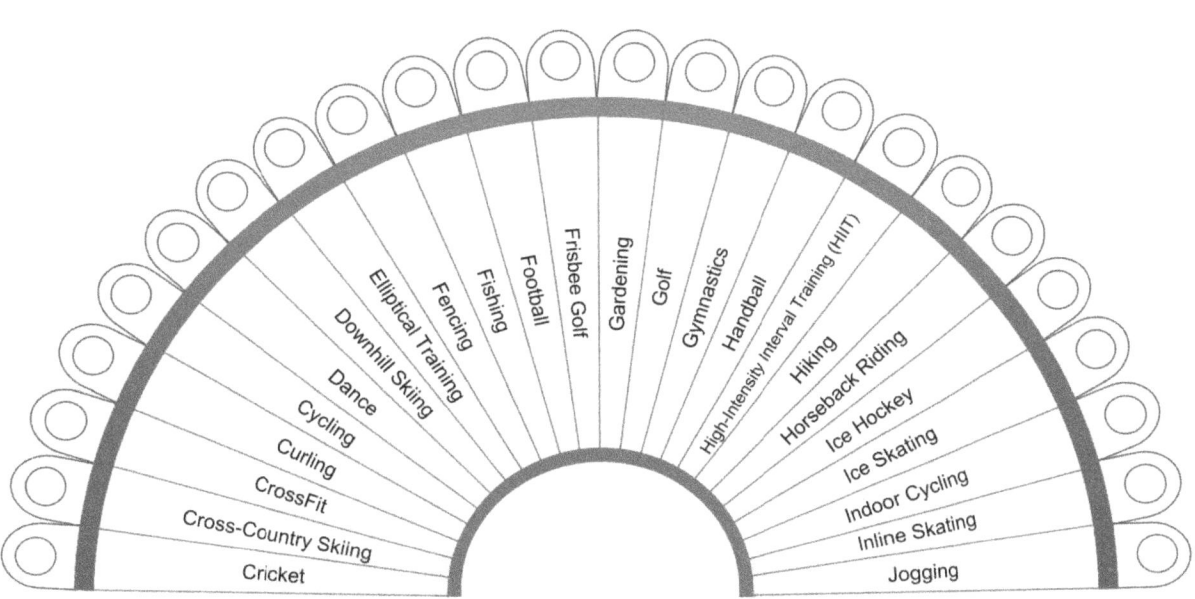

Physical Activities, Chart 2

Royal Template 24

Diving Deep into the Pool of the Mind

Chart 238

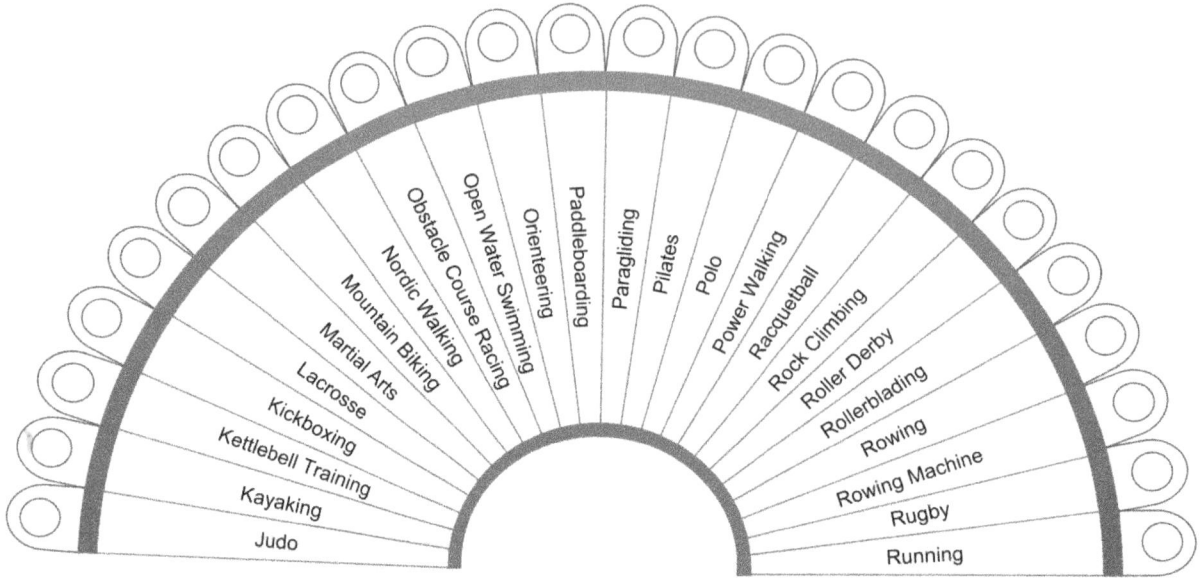

Physical Activities, Chart 3

Judo
Kayaking
Kettlebell Training
Kickboxing
Lacrosse
Martial Arts
Mountain Biking
Nordic Walking
Obstacle Course Racing
Open Water Swimming
Orienteering
Paddleboarding
Paragliding
Pilates
Polo
Power Walking
Racquetball
Rock Climbing
Roller Derby
Rollerblading
Rowing
Rowing Machine
Rugby
Running

Diving Deep into the Pool of the Mind

Chart 239

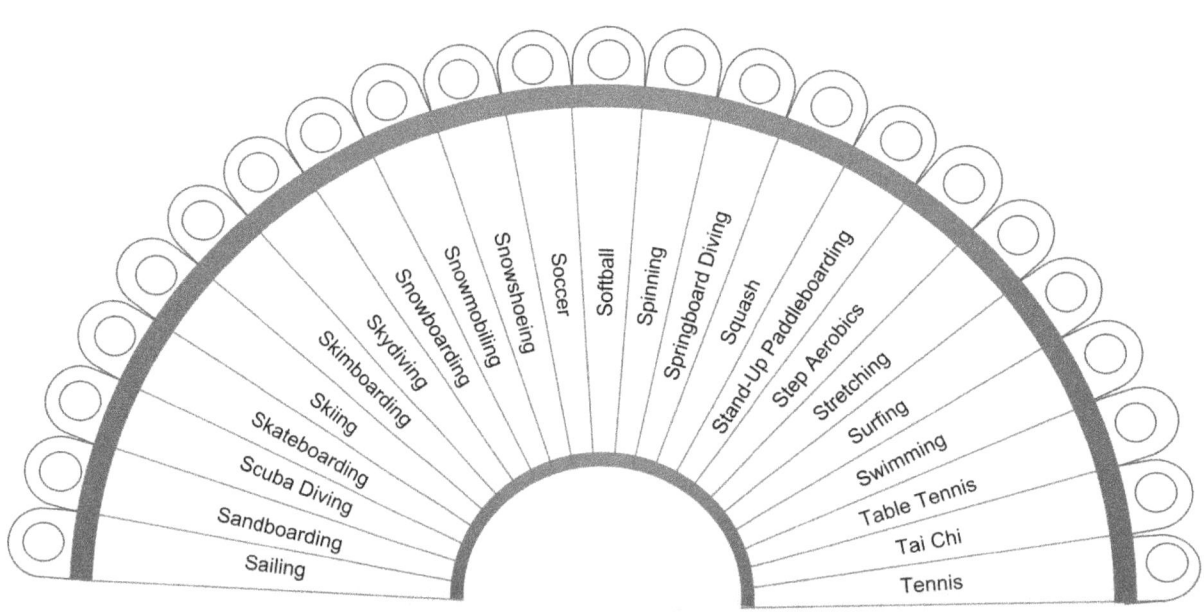

Physical Activities, Chart 4

Sailing
Sandboarding
Scuba Diving
Skateboarding
Skiing
Skimboarding
Skydiving
Snowboarding
Snowmobiling
Snowshoeing
Soccer
Softball
Spinning
Springboard Diving
Squash
Stand-Up Paddleboarding
Step Aerobics
Stretching
Surfing
Swimming
Table Tennis
Tai Chi
Tennis

Diving Deep into the Pool of the Mind

Chart 240

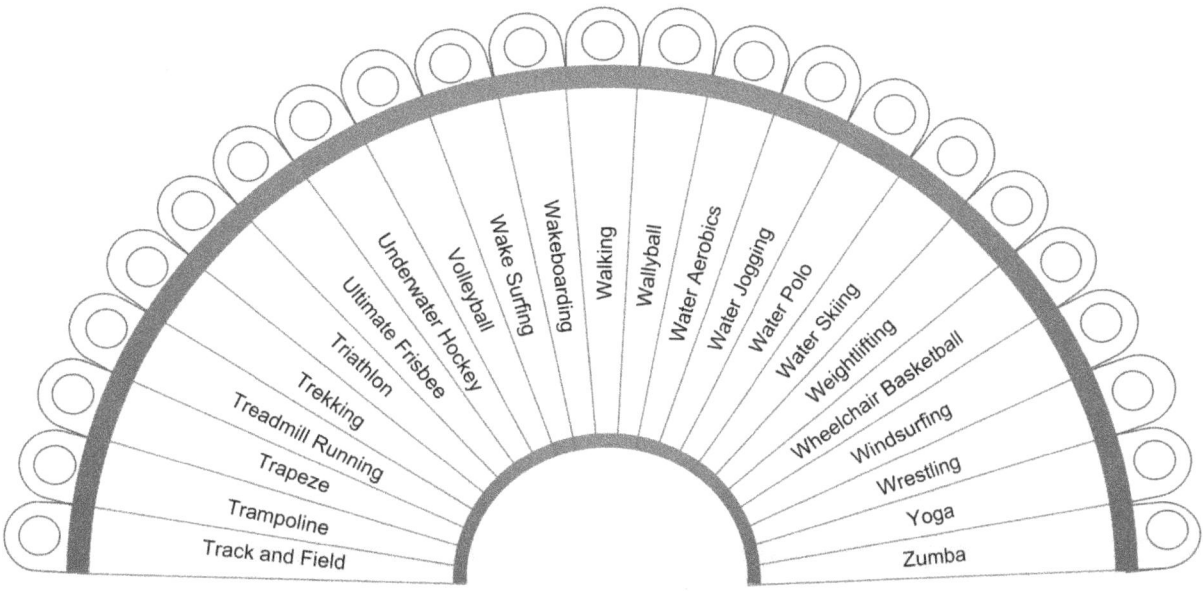

Physical Activities, Chart 5

Track and Field
Trampoline
Trapeze
Treadmill Running
Trekking
Triathlon
Ultimate Frisbee
Underwater Hockey
Volleyball
Wake Surfing
Wakeboarding
Walking
Wallyball
Water Aerobics
Water Jogging
Water Polo
Water Skiing
Weightlifting
Wheelchair Basketball
Windsurfing
Wrestling
Yoga
Zumba

Royal Template 23

Diving Deep into the Pool of the Mind

Chart 241

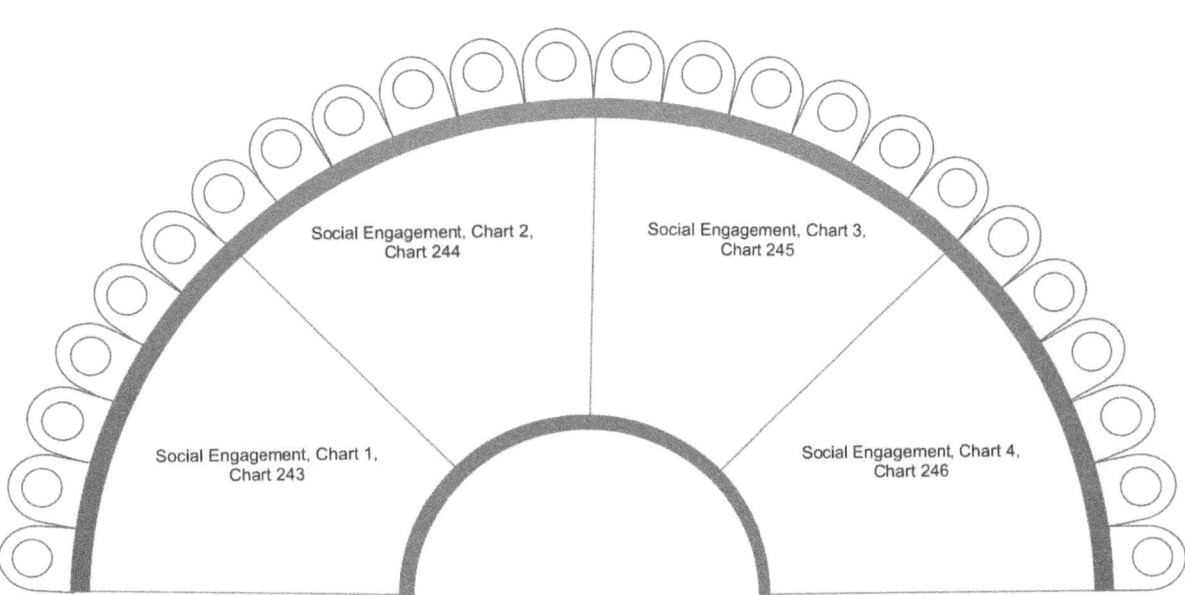

Social Engagement, Chart 2,
Chart 244

Social Engagement, Chart 3,
Chart 245

Social Engagement, Chart 1,
Chart 243

Social Engagement, Chart 4,
Chart 246

Social Engagement Master Chart

Royal Template 4h

Diving Deep into the Pool of the Mind

Chart 242

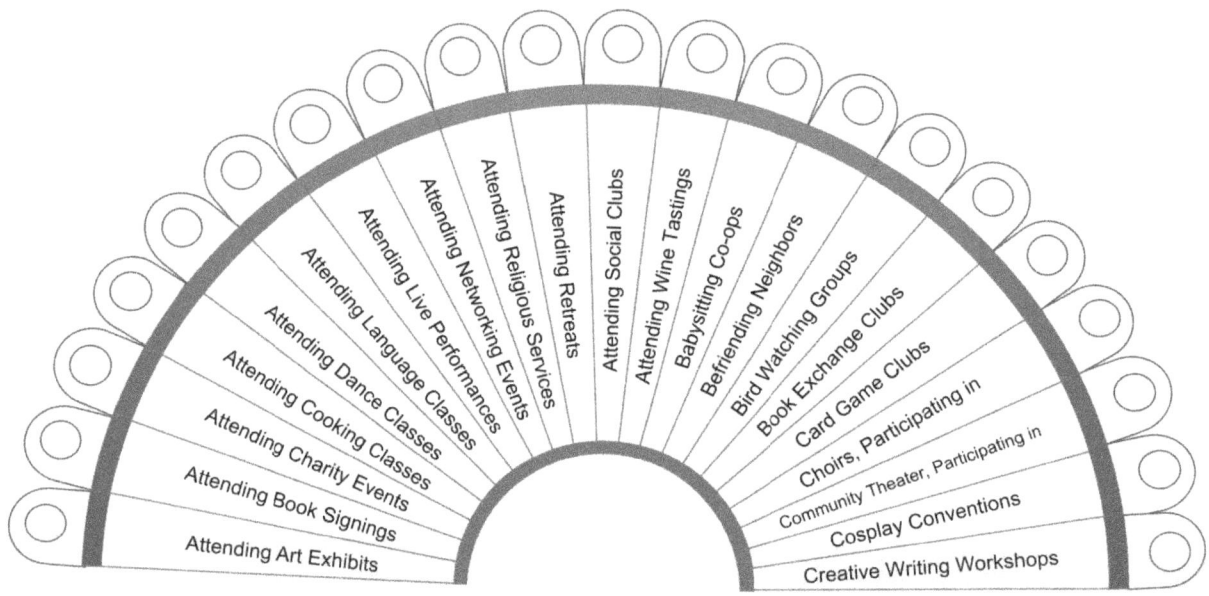

Social Engagement, Chart 1

The chart contains the following labels (reading around the fan):

- Attending Art Exhibits
- Attending Book Signings
- Attending Charity Events
- Attending Cooking Classes
- Attending Dance Classes
- Attending Language Classes
- Attending Live Performances
- Attending Networking Events
- Attending Religious Services
- Attending Retreats
- Attending Social Clubs
- Attending Wine Tastings
- Babysitting Co-ops
- Befriending Neighbors
- Bird Watching Groups
- Book Exchange Clubs
- Card Game Clubs
- Choirs, Participating in
- Community Theater, Participating in
- Cosplay Conventions
- Creative Writing Workshops

Royal Template 21

Diving Deep into the Pool of the Mind

Chart 243

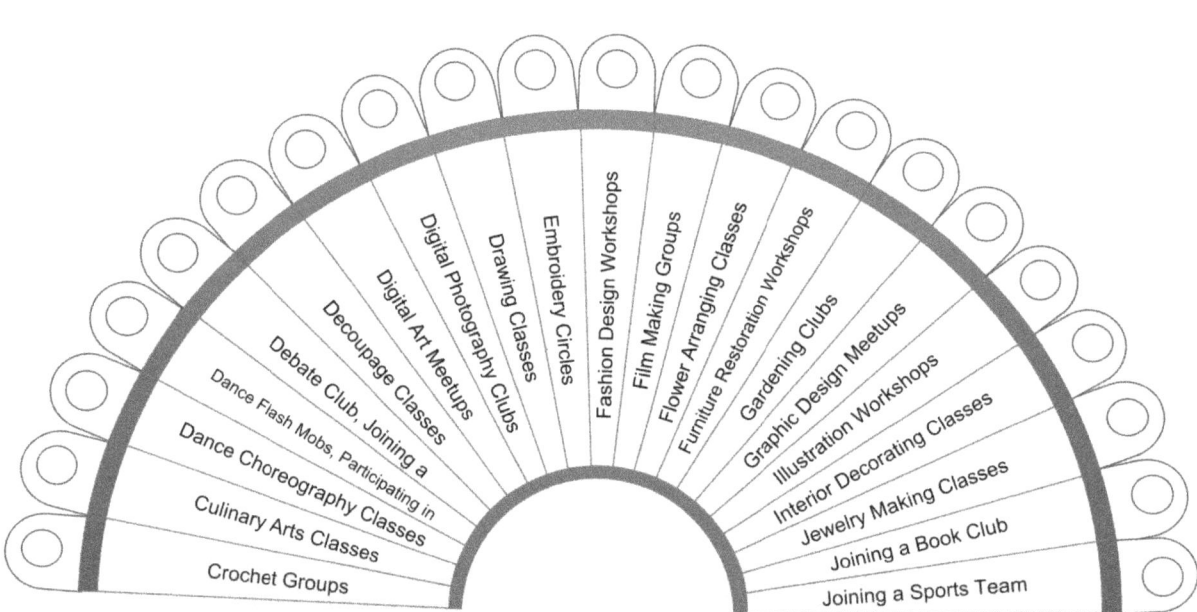

Social Engagement, Chart 2

The chart contains the following labels (reading around the fan):

- Crochet Groups
- Culinary Arts Classes
- Dance Choreography Classes
- Dance Flash Mobs, Participating in
- Debate Club, Joining a
- Decoupage Classes
- Digital Art Meetups
- Digital Photography Clubs
- Drawing Classes
- Embroidery Circles
- Fashion Design Workshops
- Film Making Groups
- Flower Arranging Classes
- Furniture Restoration Workshops
- Gardening Clubs
- Graphic Design Meetups
- Illustration Workshops
- Interior Decorating Classes
- Jewelry Making Classes
- Joining a Book Club
- Joining a Sports Team

Royal Template 21

Diving Deep into the Pool of the Mind

Chart 244

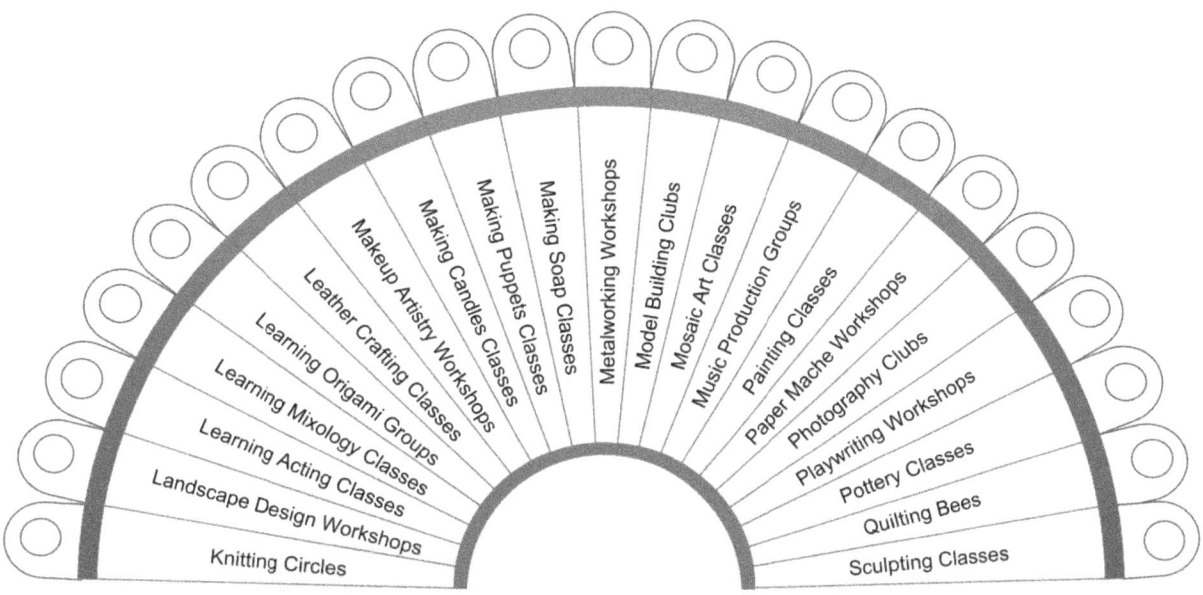

Social Engagement, Chart 3

The chart contains the following labeled segments (reading left to right):

- Knitting Circles
- Landscape Design Workshops
- Learning Acting Classes
- Learning Mixology Classes
- Learning Origami Groups
- Leather Crafting Classes
- Makeup Artistry Workshops
- Making Candles Classes
- Making Puppets Classes
- Making Soap Classes
- Metalworking Workshops
- Model Building Clubs
- Mosaic Art Classes
- Music Production Groups
- Painting Classes
- Paper Mache Workshops
- Photography Clubs
- Playwriting Workshops
- Pottery Classes
- Quilting Bees
- Sculpting Classes

Royal Template 21

Diving Deep into the Pool of the Mind

Chart 245

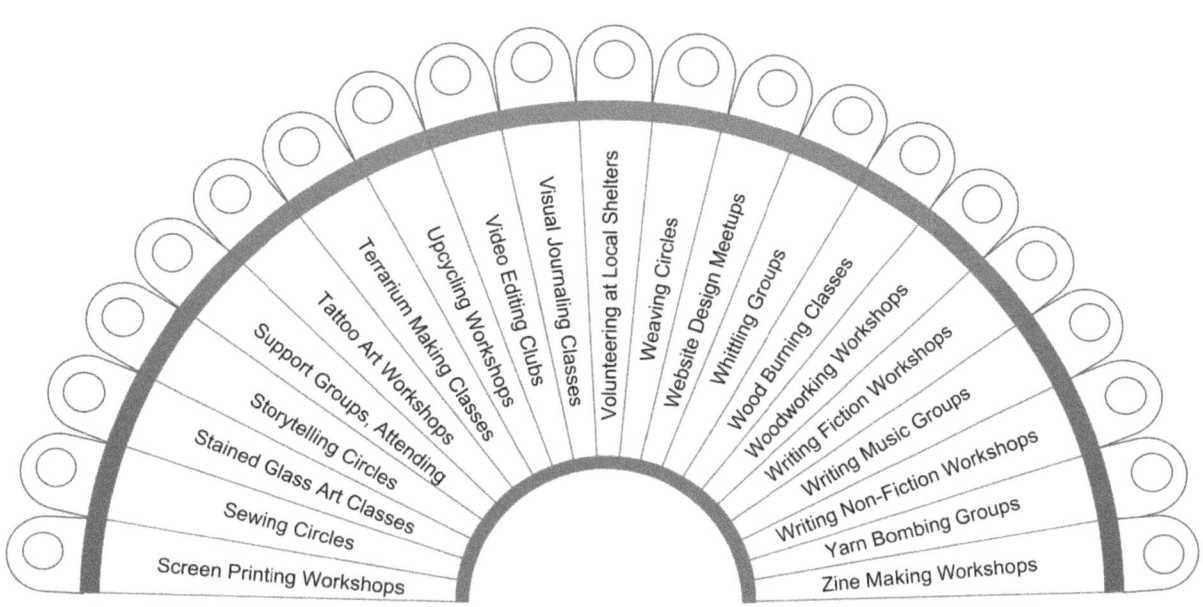

Social Engagement, Chart 4

The chart contains the following labeled segments (reading left to right):

- Screen Printing Workshops
- Sewing Circles
- Stained Glass Art Classes
- Storytelling Circles
- Support Groups, Attending
- Tattoo Art Workshops
- Terrarium Making Classes
- Upcycling Workshops
- Video Editing Clubs
- Visual Journaling Classes
- Volunteering at Local Shelters
- Weaving Circles
- Website Design Meetups
- Whittling Groups
- Wood Burning Classes
- Woodworking Workshops
- Writing Fiction Workshops
- Writing Music Groups
- Writing Non-Fiction Workshops
- Yarn Bombing Groups
- Zine Making Workshops

Royal Template 21

Diving Deep into the Pool of the Mind

Chart 246

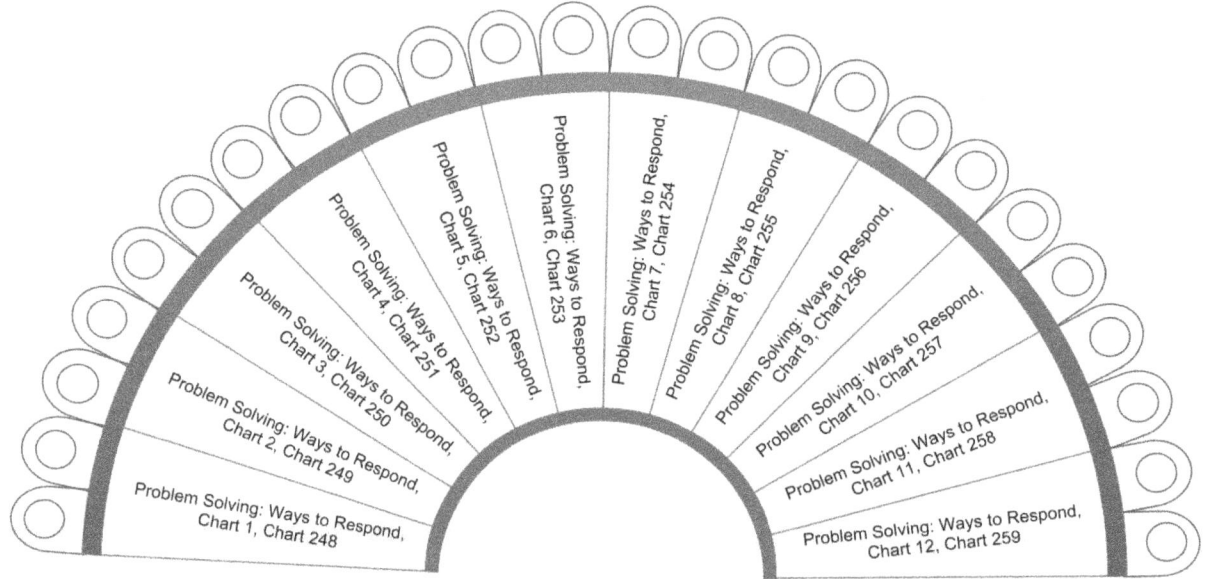

Problem Solving: Ways to Respond, Master Chart

The fan chart contains the following segments (from left to right):

- Problem Solving: Ways to Respond, Chart 1, Chart 248
- Problem Solving: Ways to Respond, Chart 2, Chart 249
- Problem Solving: Ways to Respond, Chart 3, Chart 250
- Problem Solving: Ways to Respond, Chart 4, Chart 251
- Problem Solving: Ways to Respond, Chart 5, Chart 252
- Problem Solving: Ways to Respond, Chart 6, Chart 253
- Problem Solving: Ways to Respond, Chart 7, Chart 254
- Problem Solving: Ways to Respond, Chart 8, Chart 255
- Problem Solving: Ways to Respond, Chart 9, Chart 256
- Problem Solving: Ways to Respond, Chart 10, Chart 257
- Problem Solving: Ways to Respond, Chart 11, Chart 258
- Problem Solving: Ways to Respond, Chart 12, Chart 259

Royal Template 12

Diving Deep into the Pool of the Mind

Chart 247

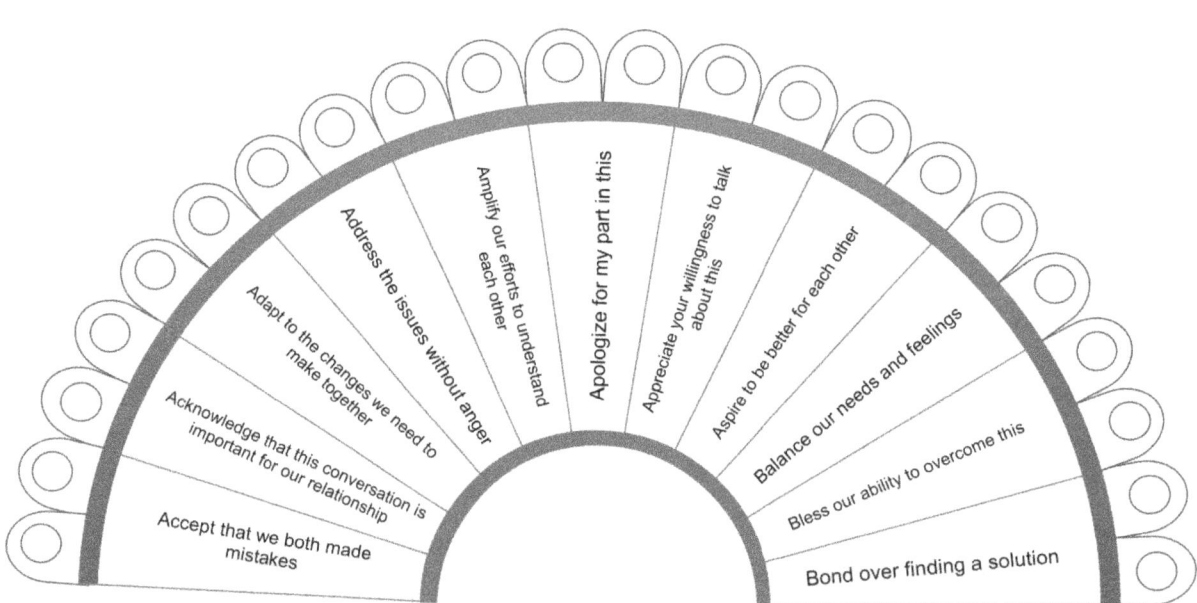

Problem Solving: Ways to Respond, Chart 1

The fan chart contains the following segments (from left to right):

- Accept that we both made mistakes
- Acknowledge that this conversation is important for our relationship
- Adapt to the changes we need to make together
- Address the issues without anger
- Amplify our efforts to understand each other
- Apologize for my part in this
- Appreciate your willingness to talk about this
- Aspire to be better for each other
- Balance our needs and feelings
- Bless our ability to overcome this
- Bond over finding a solution

Royal Template 11

Diving Deep into the Pool of the Mind

Chart 248

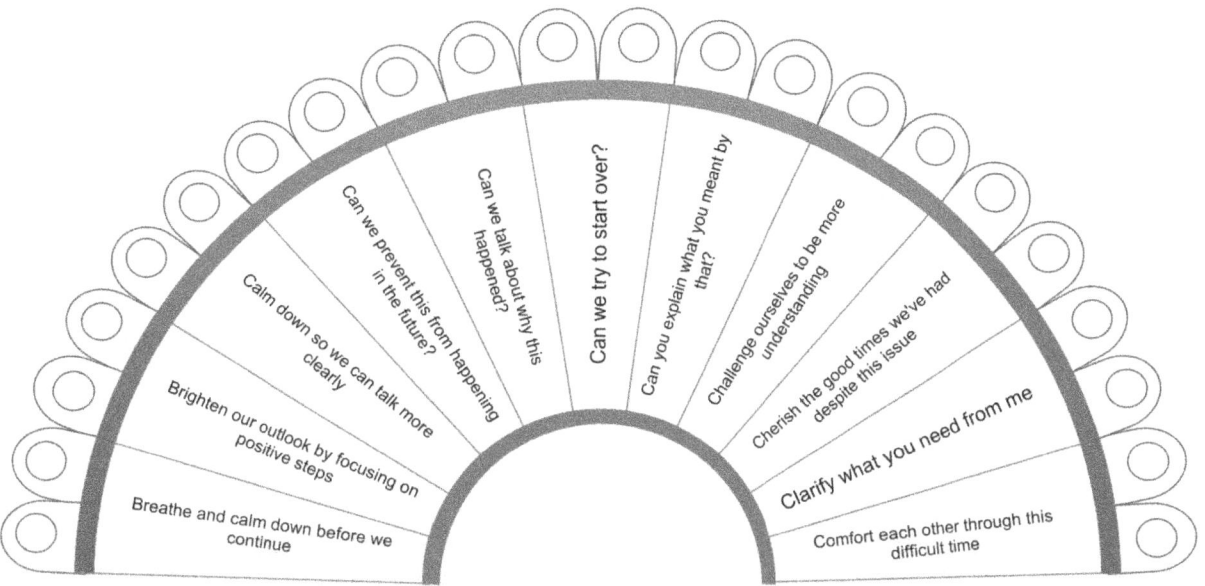

Problem Solving: Ways to Respond, Chart 2

Can we try to start over?

Can we talk about why this happened?

Can you explain what you meant by that?

Can we prevent this from happening in the future?

Challenge ourselves to be more understanding

Calm down so we can talk more clearly

Cherish the good times we've had despite this issue

Brighten our outlook by focusing on positive steps

Clarify what you need from me

Breathe and calm down before we continue

Comfort each other through this difficult time

Royal Template 11

Diving Deep into the Pool of the Mind

Chart 249

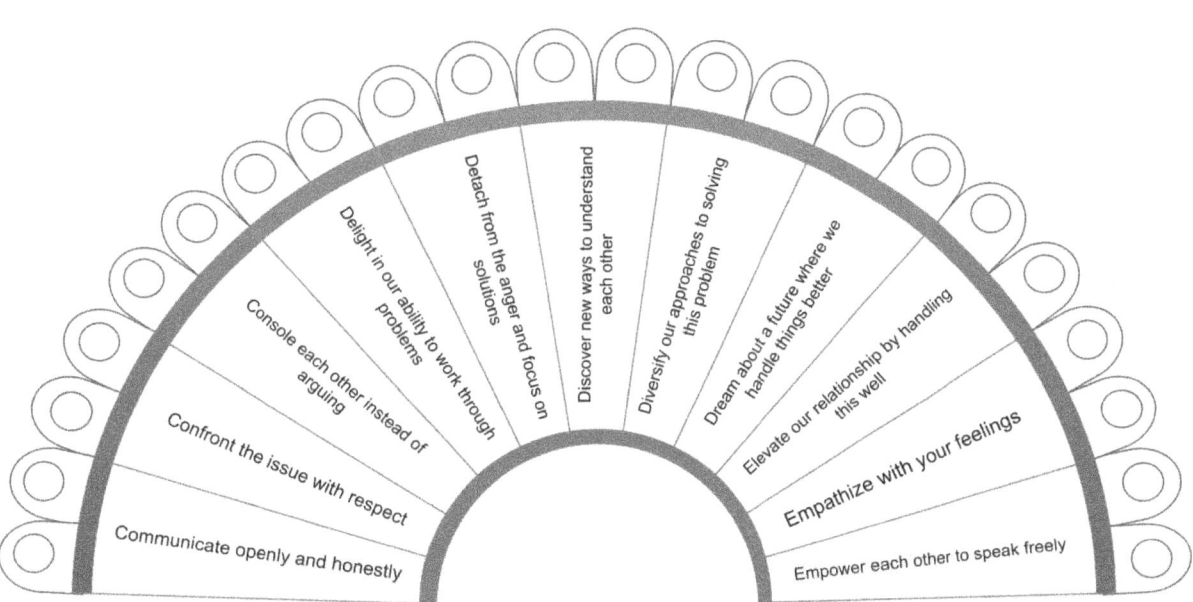

Problem Solving: Ways to Respond, Chart 3

Detach from the anger and focus on solutions

Discover new ways to understand each other

Delight in our ability to work through problems

Diversify our approaches to solving this problem

Console each other instead of arguing

Dream about a future where we handle things better

Confront the issue with respect

Elevate our relationship by handling this well

Empathize with your feelings

Communicate openly and honestly

Empower each other to speak freely

Royal Template 11

Diving Deep into the Pool of the Mind

Chart 250

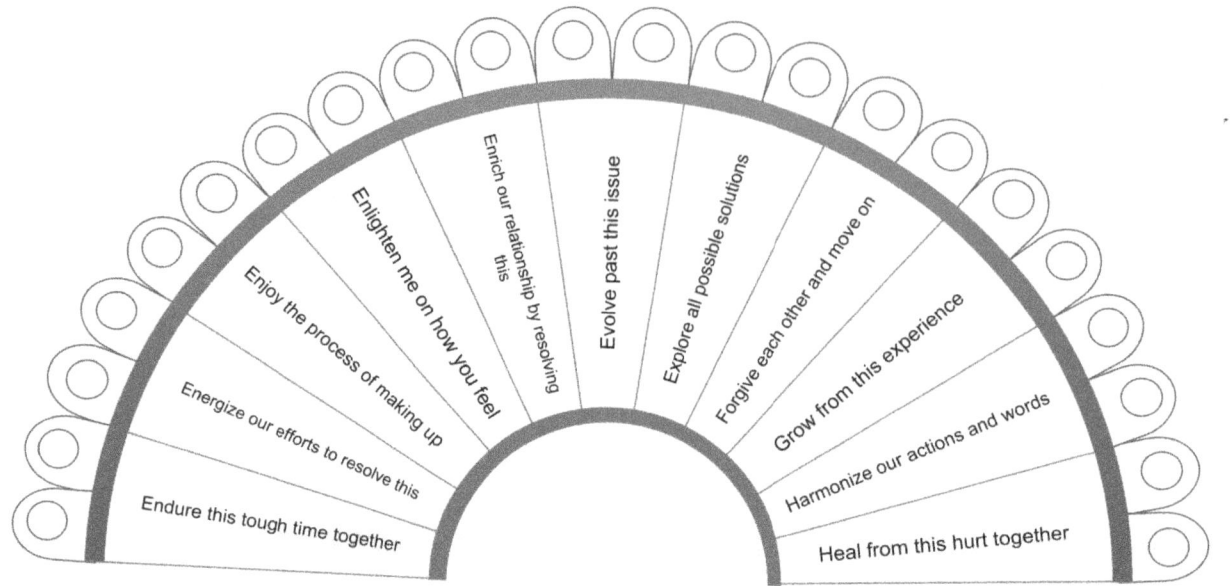

Problem Solving: Ways to Respond, Chart 4

Royal Template 11

Diving Deep into the Pool of the Mind

Chart 251

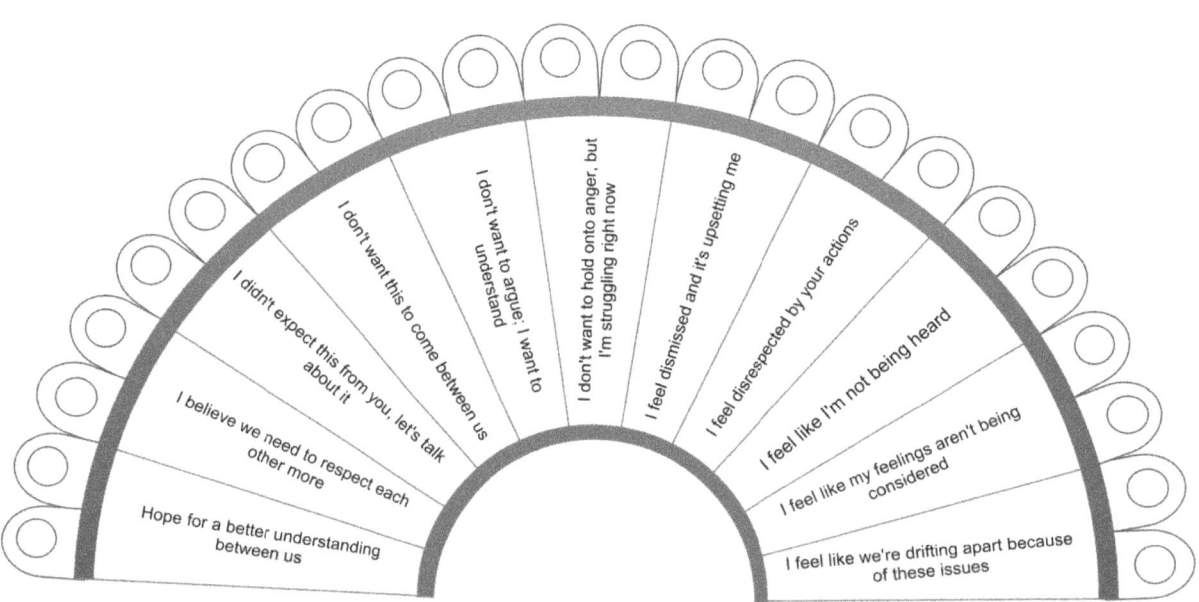

Problem Solving: Ways to Respond, Chart 5

Royal Template 11

Diving Deep into the Pool of the Mind

Chart 252

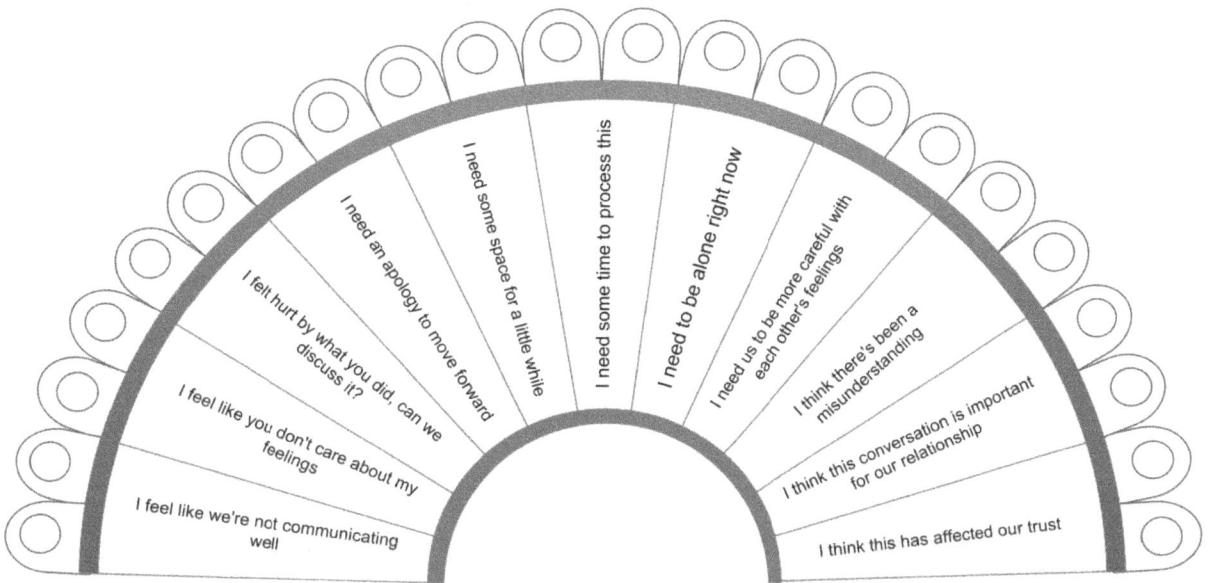

Problem Solving: Ways to Respond, Chart 6

Royal Template 11

Diving Deep into the Pool of the Mind

Chart 253

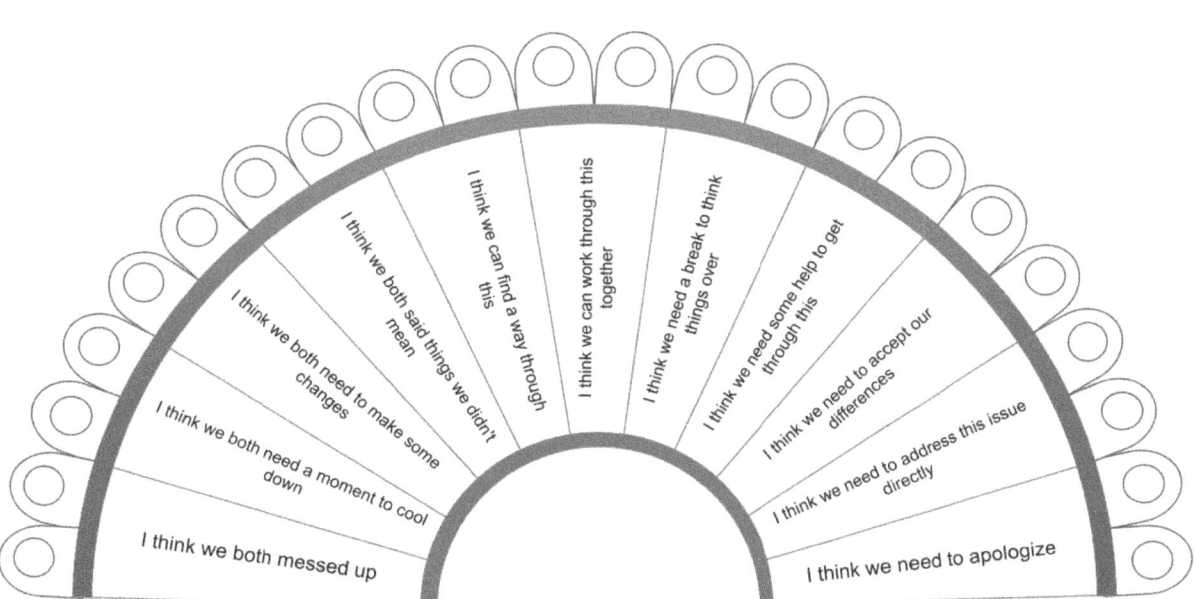

Problem Solving: Ways to Respond, Chart 7

Royal Template 11

Diving Deep into the Pool of the Mind

Chart 254

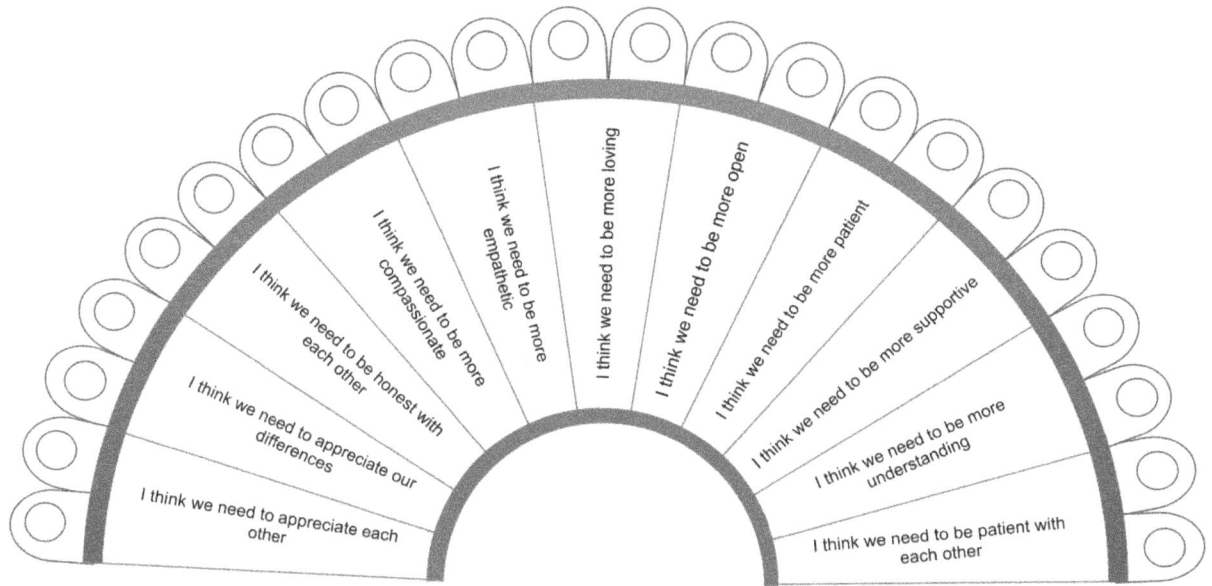

Problem Solving: Ways to Respond, Chart 8

The chart contains the following statements radiating outward:

- I think we need to be more loving
- I think we need to be more empathetic
- I think we need to be more open
- I think we need to be more compassionate
- I think we need to be more patient
- I think we need to be honest with each other
- I think we need to be more supportive
- I think we need to appreciate our differences
- I think we need to be more understanding
- I think we need to appreciate each other
- I think we need to be patient with each other

Royal Template 11

Diving Deep into the Pool of the Mind

Chart 255

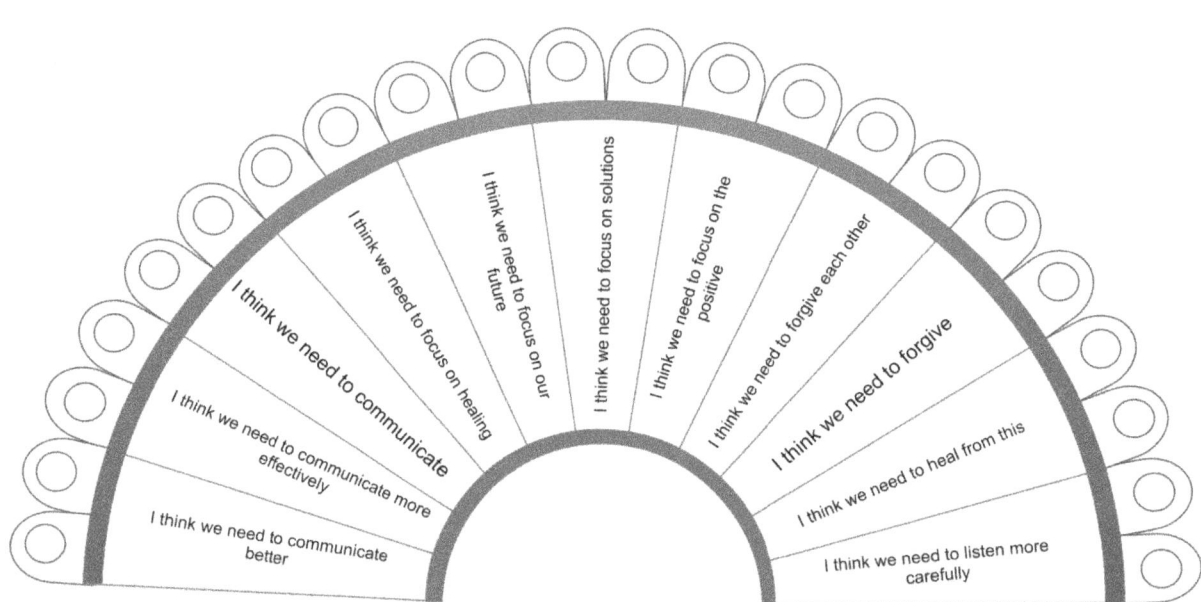

Problem Solving: Ways to Respond, Chart 9

The chart contains the following statements radiating outward:

- I think we need to focus on solutions
- I think we need to focus on our future
- I think we need to focus on the positive
- I think we need to focus on healing
- I think we need to forgive each other
- I think we need to communicate
- I think we need to forgive
- I think we need to communicate more effectively
- I think we need to heal from this
- I think we need to communicate better
- I think we need to listen more carefully

Royal Template 11

Diving Deep into the Pool of the Mind

Chart 256

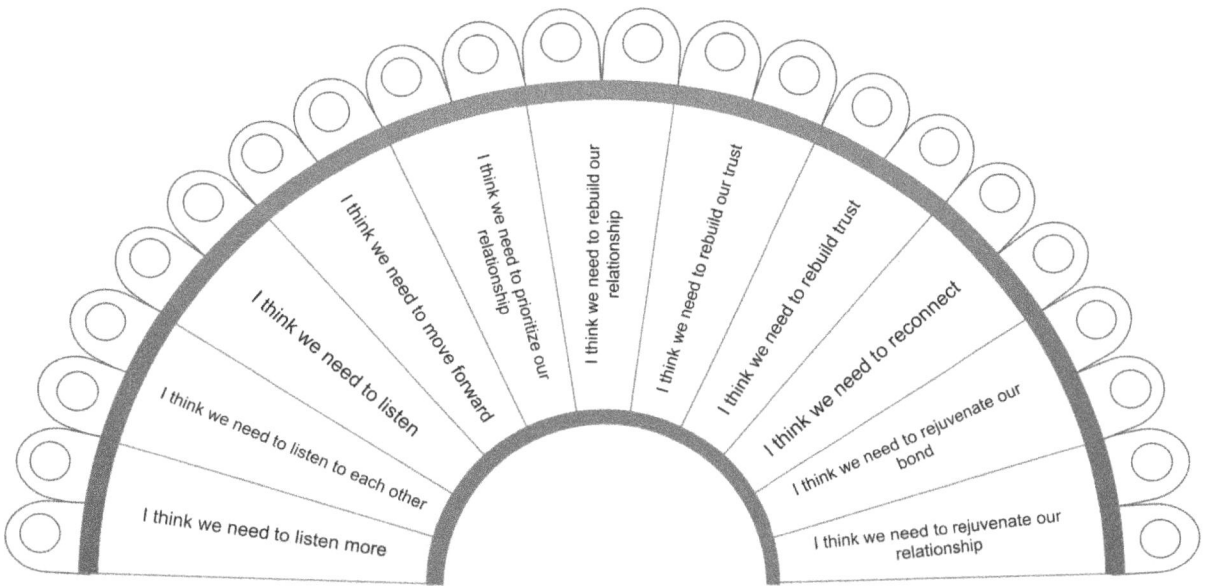

Problem Solving: Ways to Respond, Chart 10

Royal Template 11

Diving Deep into the Pool of the Mind

Chart 257

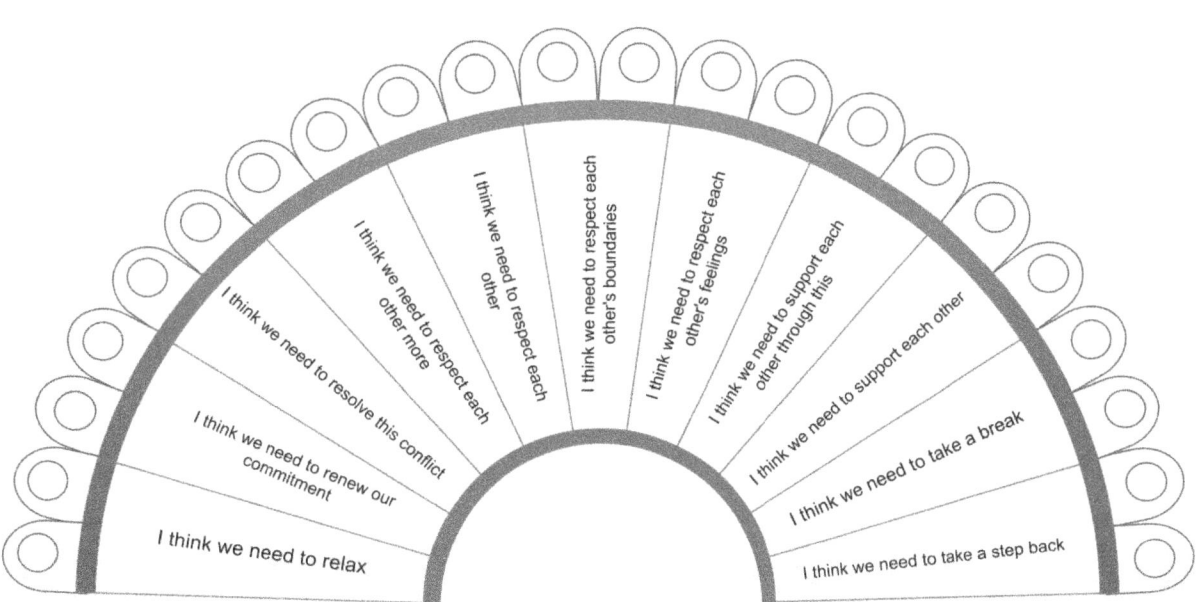

Problem Solving: Ways to Respond, Chart 11

Royal Template 11

Diving Deep into the Pool of the Mind

Chart 258

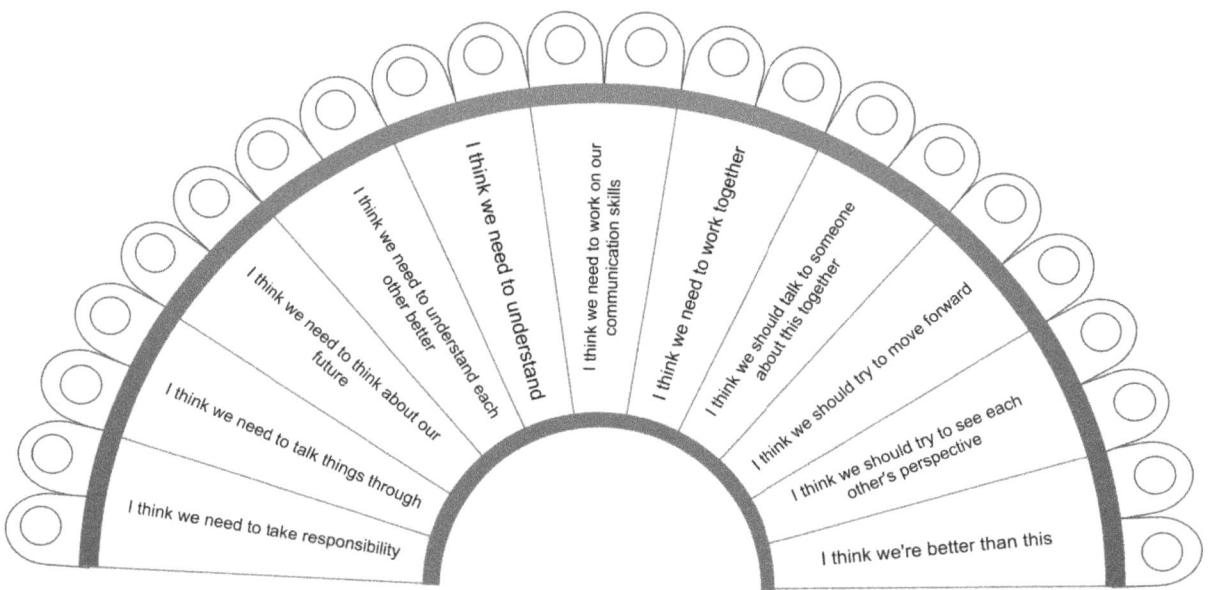

Problem Solving: Ways to Respond, Chart 12

The following text appears on the chart segments:

I think we need to work on our communication skills

I think we need to understand

I think we need to understand each other better

I think we need to think about our future

I think we need to talk things through

I think we need to take responsibility

I think we need to work together

I think we should talk to someone about this together

I think we should try to move forward

I think we should try to see each other's perspective

I think we're better than this

Royal Template 11

Diving Deep into the Pool of the Mind

Chart 259

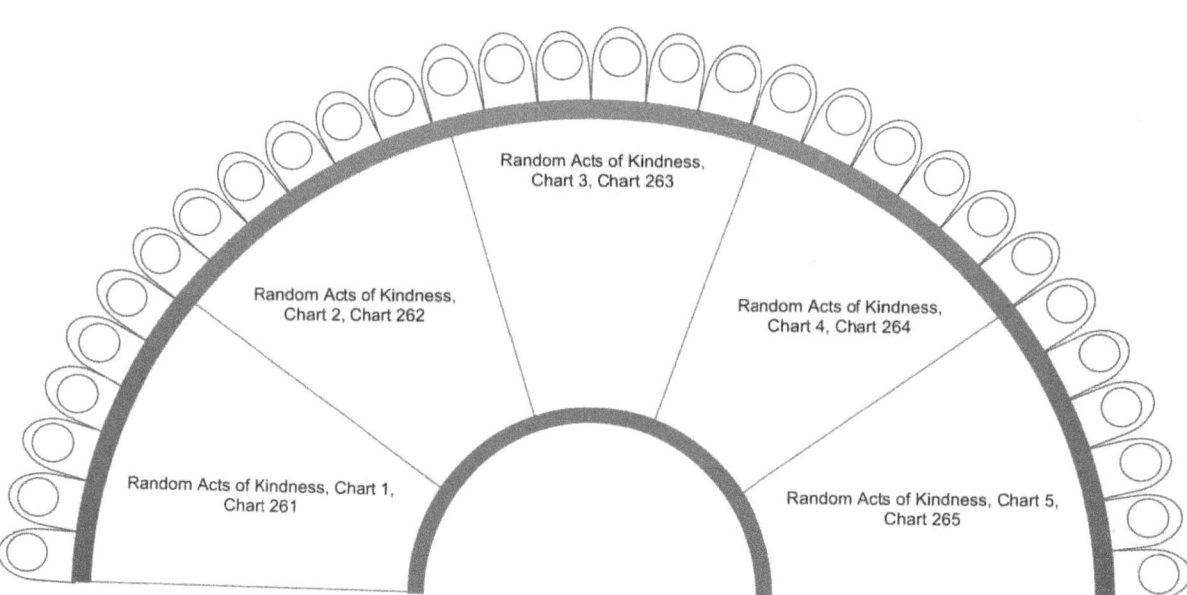

The following text appears on the chart segments:

Random Acts of Kindness, Chart 3, Chart 263

Random Acts of Kindness, Chart 2, Chart 262

Random Acts of Kindness, Chart 4, Chart 264

Random Acts of Kindness, Chart 1, Chart 261

Random Acts of Kindness, Chart 5, Chart 265

Random Acts of Kindness, Master Chart

Royal Template 5h

Diving Deep into the Pool of the Mind

Chart 260

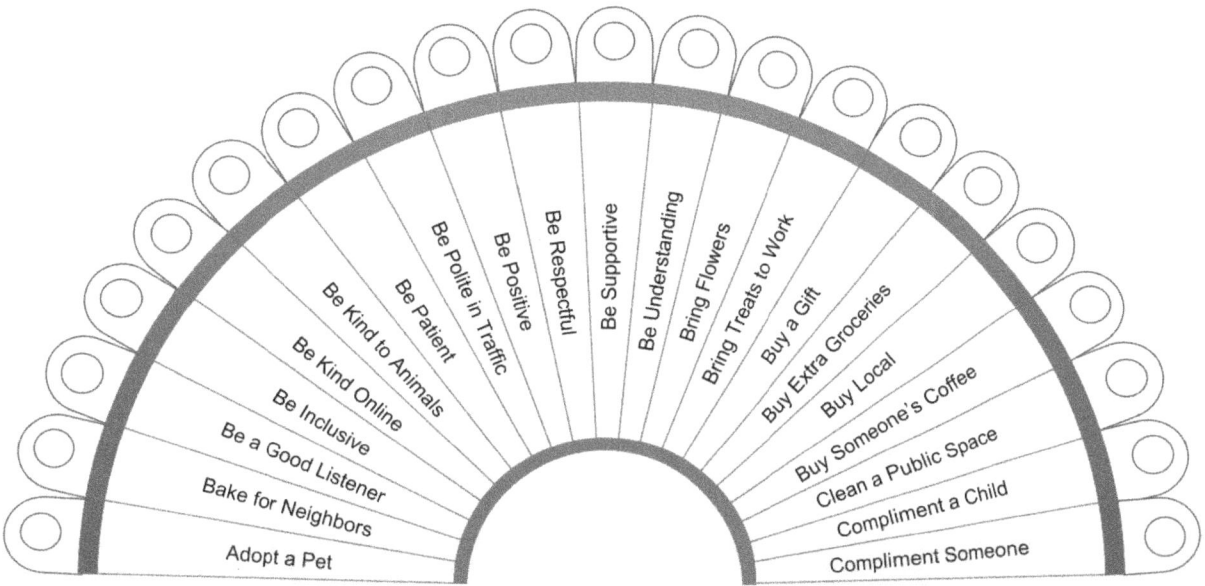

Random Acts of Kindness, Chart 1

Be Polite in Traffic
Be Patient
Be Positive
Be Respectful
Be Supportive
Be Understanding
Bring Flowers
Bring Treats to Work
Buy a Gift
Buy Extra Groceries
Buy Local
Buy Someone's Coffee
Clean a Public Space
Compliment a Child
Compliment Someone
Be Kind to Animals
Be Kind Online
Be Inclusive
Be a Good Listener
Bake for Neighbors
Adopt a Pet

Royal Template 21

Diving Deep into the Pool of the Mind

Chart 261

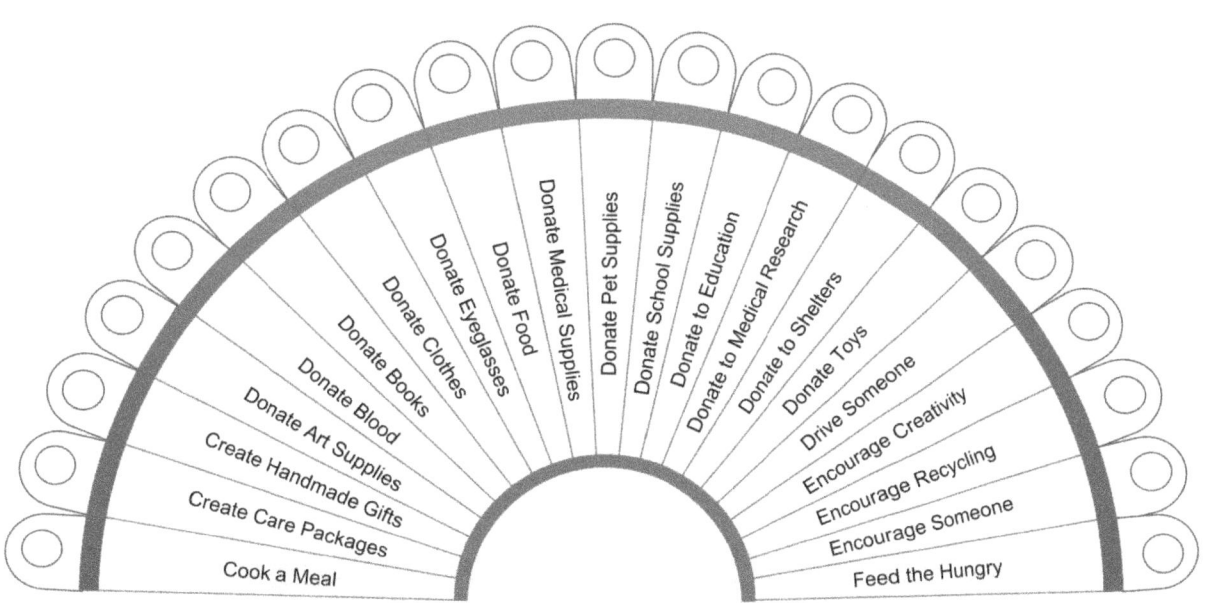

Random Acts of Kindness, Chart 2

Donate Medical Supplies
Donate Pet Supplies
Donate School Supplies
Donate to Education
Donate to Medical Research
Donate to Shelters
Donate Toys
Drive Someone
Encourage Creativity
Encourage Recycling
Encourage Someone
Feed the Hungry
Donate Food
Donate Eyeglasses
Donate Clothes
Donate Books
Donate Blood
Donate Art Supplies
Create Handmade Gifts
Create Care Packages
Cook a Meal

Royal Template 21

Diving Deep into the Pool of the Mind

Chart 262

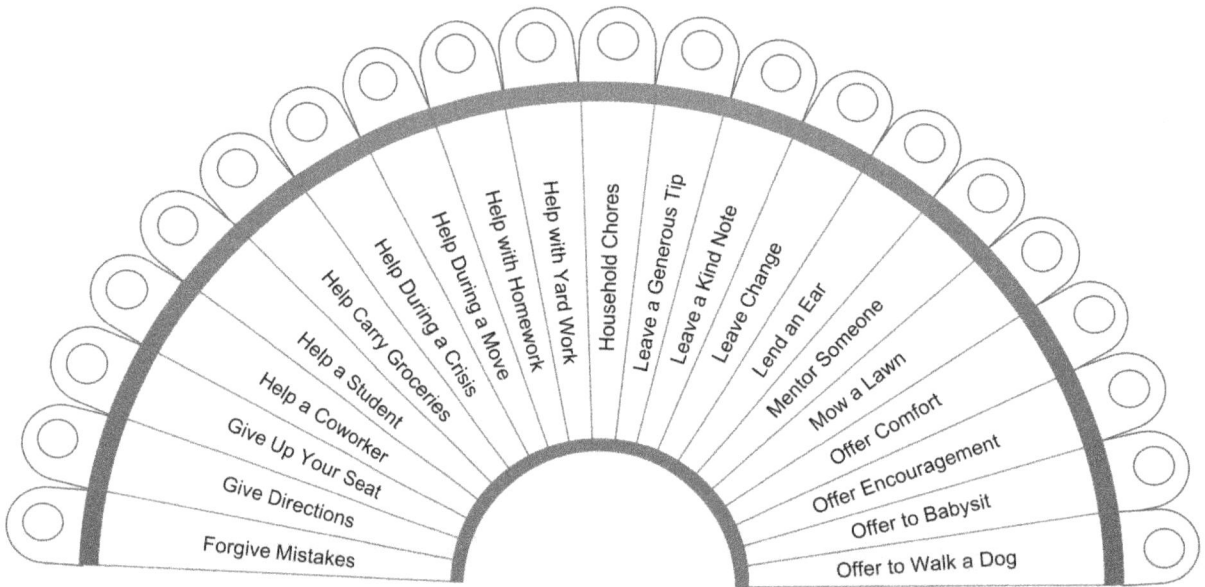

Random Acts of Kindness, Chart 3

The chart contains the following labels (reading around the fan):

- Forgive Mistakes
- Give Directions
- Give Up Your Seat
- Help a Coworker
- Help a Student
- Help Carry Groceries
- Help During a Crisis
- Help During a Move
- Help with Homework
- Help with Yard Work
- Household Chores
- Leave a Generous Tip
- Leave a Kind Note
- Leave Change
- Lend an Ear
- Mentor Someone
- Mow a Lawn
- Offer Comfort
- Offer Encouragement
- Offer to Babysit
- Offer to Walk a Dog

Royal Template 21

Diving Deep into the Pool of the Mind

Chart 263

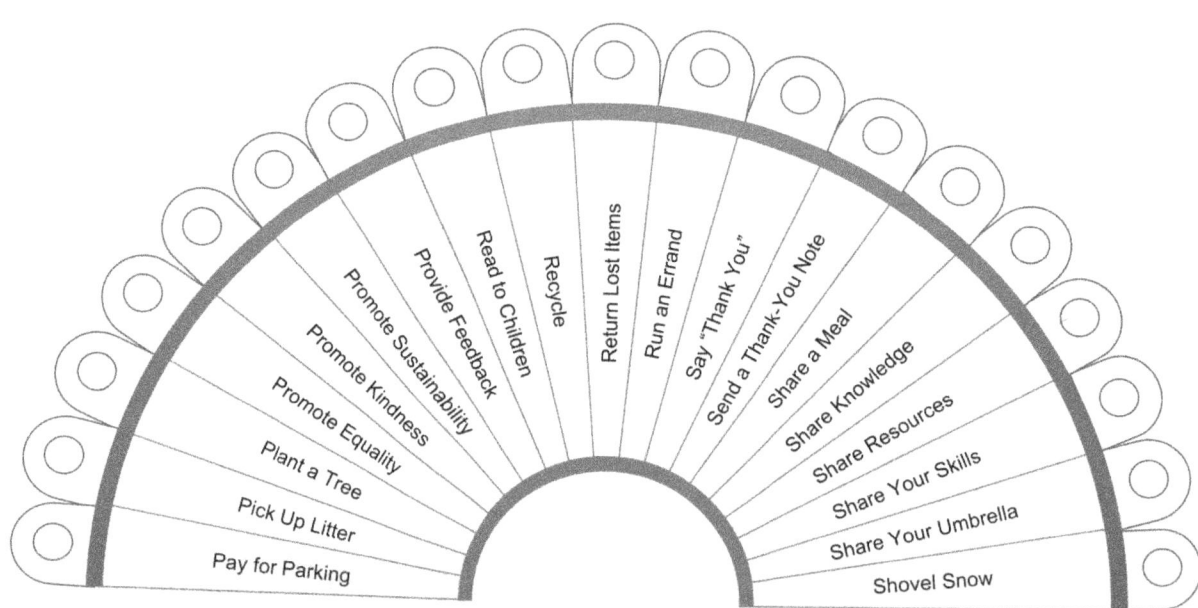

Random Acts of Kindness, Chart 4

The chart contains the following labels (reading around the fan):

- Pay for Parking
- Pick Up Litter
- Plant a Tree
- Promote Equality
- Promote Kindness
- Promote Sustainability
- Provide Feedback
- Read to Children
- Recycle
- Return Lost Items
- Run an Errand
- Say "Thank You"
- Send a Thank-You Note
- Share a Meal
- Share Knowledge
- Share Resources
- Share Your Skills
- Share Your Umbrella
- Shovel Snow

Royal Template 19

Diving Deep into the Pool of the Mind

Chart 264

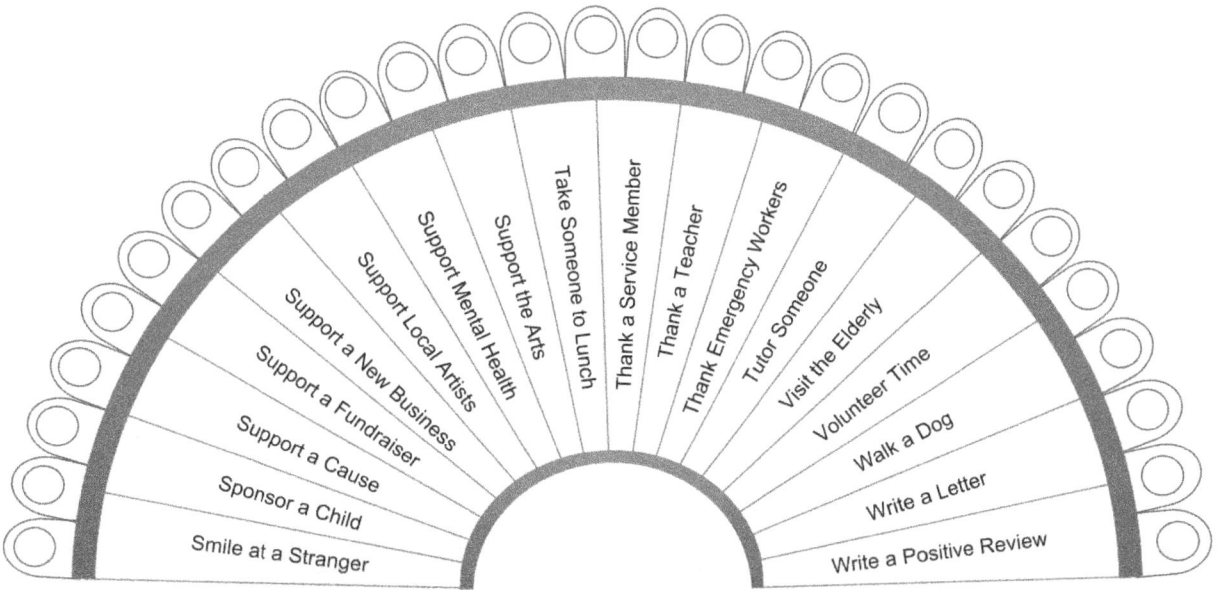

Random Acts of Kindness, Chart 5

Labels (left to right):
- Smile at a Stranger
- Sponsor a Child
- Support a Cause
- Support a Fundraiser
- Support a New Business
- Support Local Artists
- Support Mental Health
- Support the Arts
- Take Someone to Lunch
- Thank a Service Member
- Thank a Teacher
- Thank Emergency Workers
- Tutor Someone
- Visit the Elderly
- Volunteer Time
- Walk a Dog
- Write a Letter
- Write a Positive Review

Royal Template 18

Diving Deep into the Pool of the Mind

Chart 265

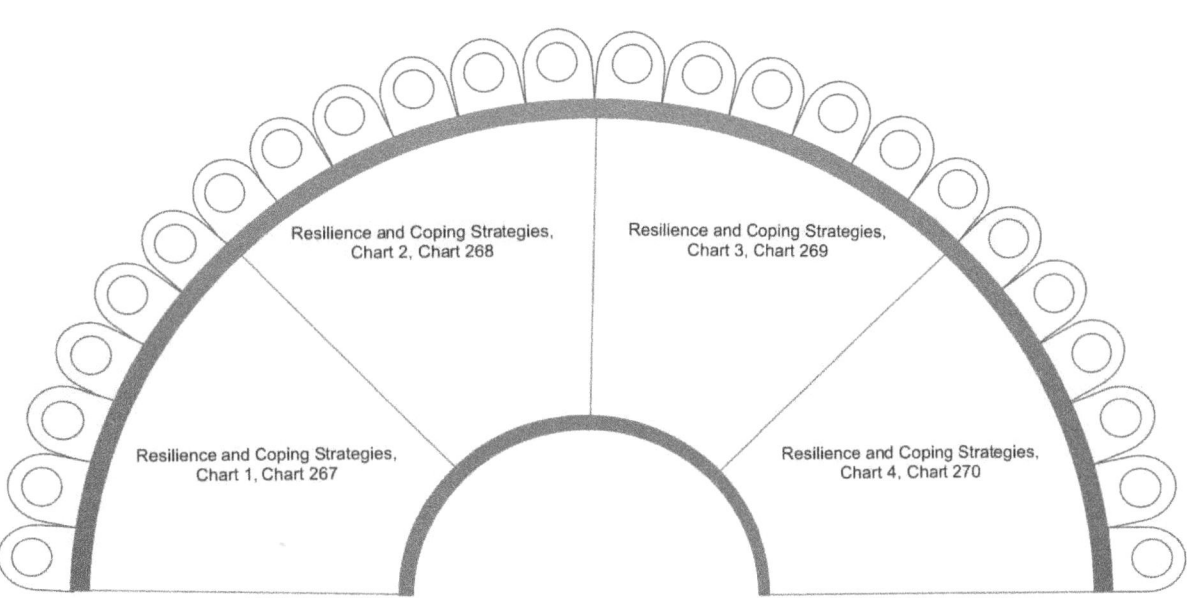

Resilience and Coping Strategies, Master Chart

- Resilience and Coping Strategies, Chart 1, Chart 267
- Resilience and Coping Strategies, Chart 2, Chart 268
- Resilience and Coping Strategies, Chart 3, Chart 269
- Resilience and Coping Strategies, Chart 4, Chart 270

Royal Template 4h

Diving Deep into the Pool of the Mind

Chart 266

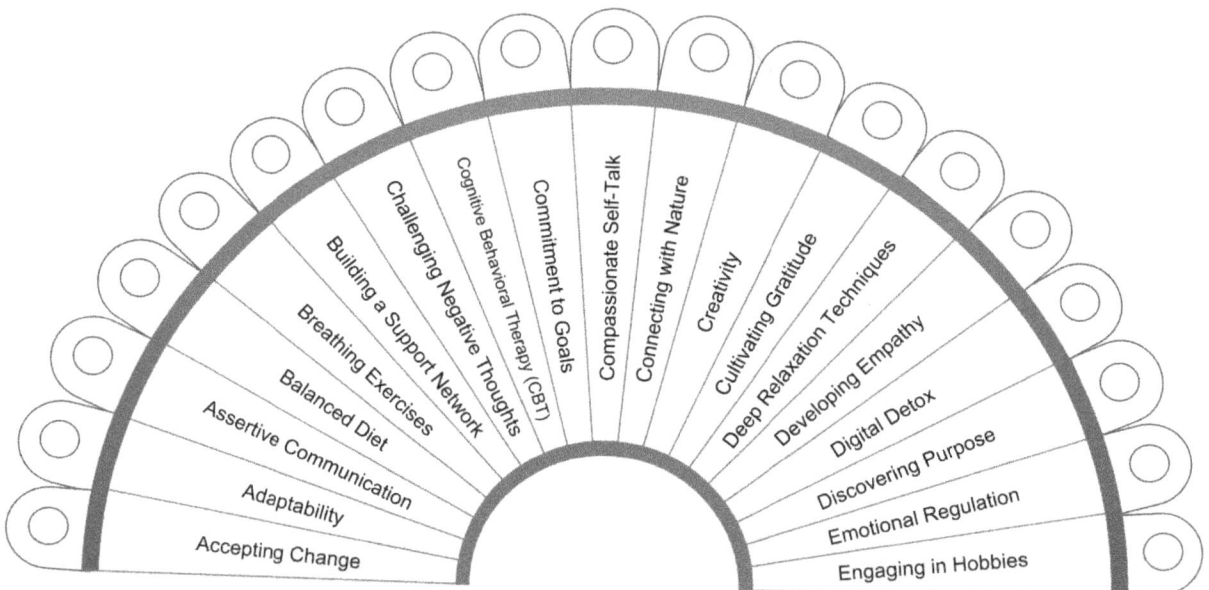

Resilience and Coping Strategies, Chart 1

Royal Template 19

Diving Deep into the Pool of the Mind

Chart 267

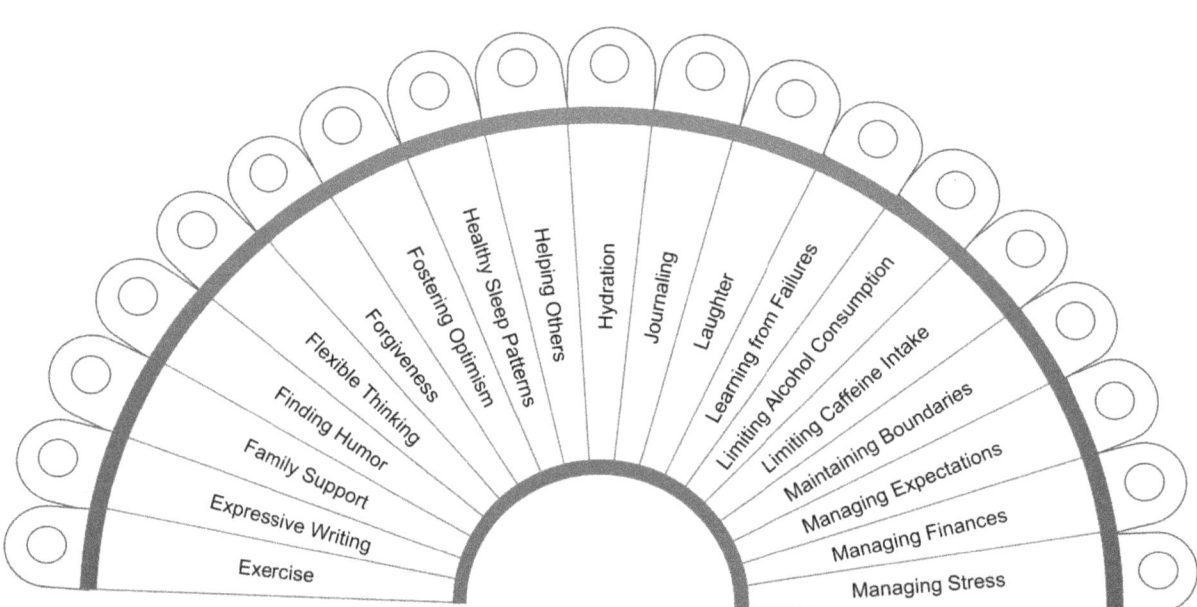

Resilience and Coping Strategies, Chart 2

Royal Template 19

Diving Deep into the Pool of the Mind

Chart 268

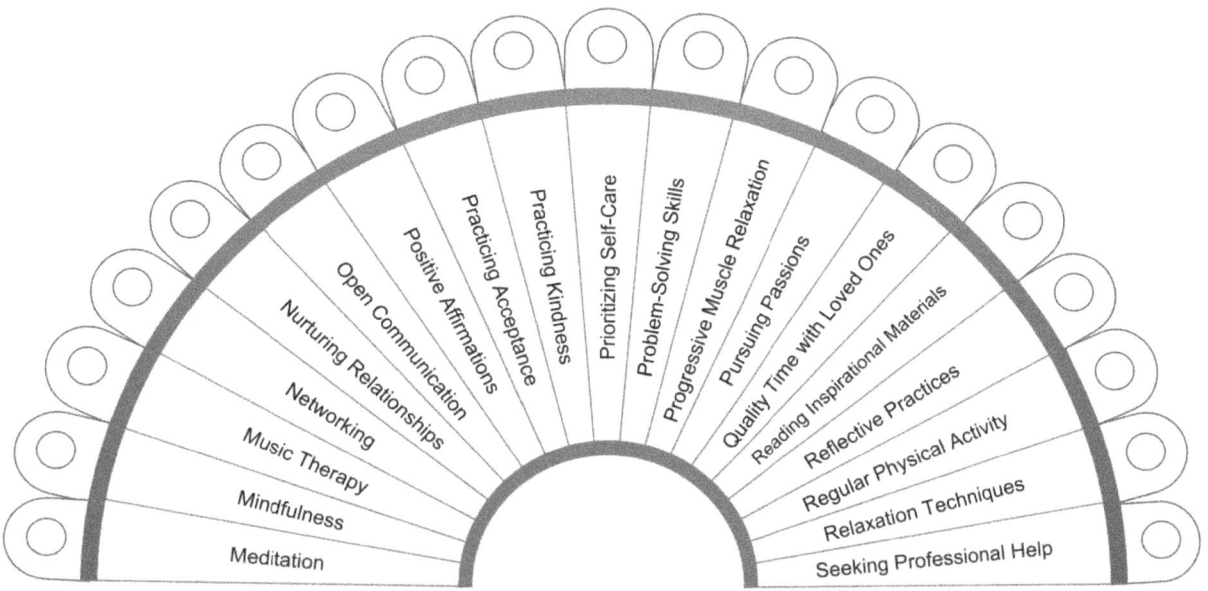

Resilience and Coping Strategies, Chart 3

Royal Template 19

Diving Deep into the Pool of the Mind

Chart 269

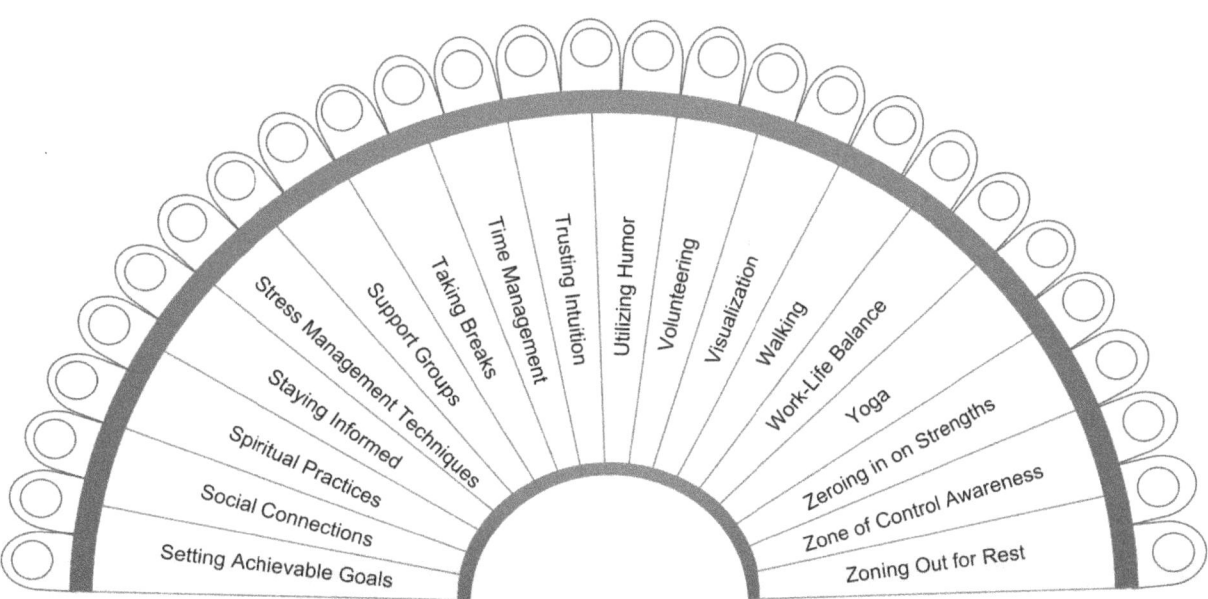

Resilience and Coping Strategies, Chart 4

Royal Template 18

Diving Deep into the Pool of the Mind

Chart 270

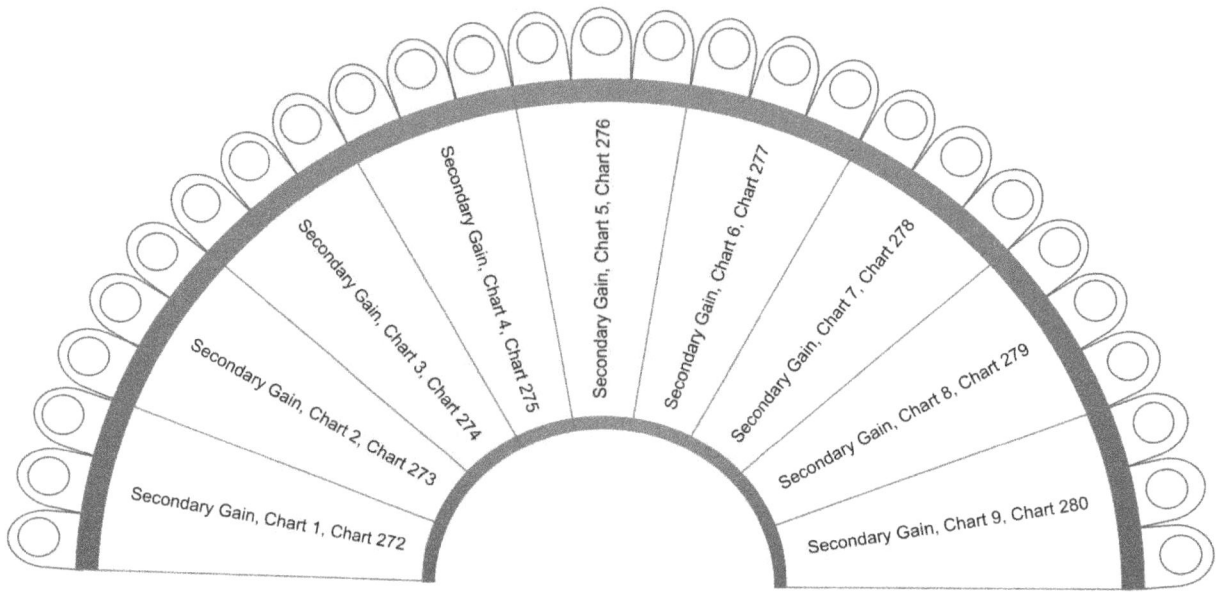

Secondary Gain, Master Chart

Secondary Gain, Chart 1, Chart 272
Secondary Gain, Chart 2, Chart 273
Secondary Gain, Chart 3, Chart 274
Secondary Gain, Chart 4, Chart 275
Secondary Gain, Chart 5, Chart 276
Secondary Gain, Chart 6, Chart 277
Secondary Gain, Chart 7, Chart 278
Secondary Gain, Chart 8, Chart 279
Secondary Gain, Chart 9, Chart 280

Royal Template 9

Diving Deep into the Pool of the Mind

Chart 271

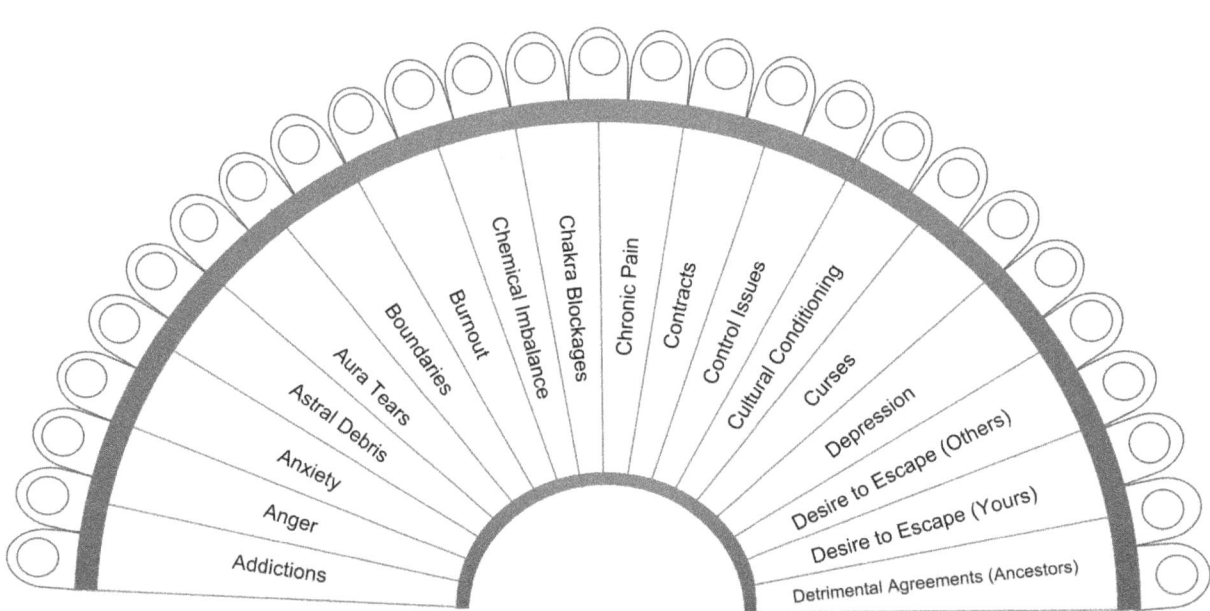

Secondary Gain, Chart 1

Addictions
Anger
Anxiety
Astral Debris
Aura Tears
Boundaries
Burnout
Chemical Imbalance
Chakra Blockages
Chronic Pain
Contracts
Control Issues
Cultural Conditioning
Curses
Depression
Desire to Escape (Others)
Desire to Escape (Yours)
Detrimental Agreements (Ancestors)

Royal Template 18

Diving Deep into the Pool of the Mind

Chart 272

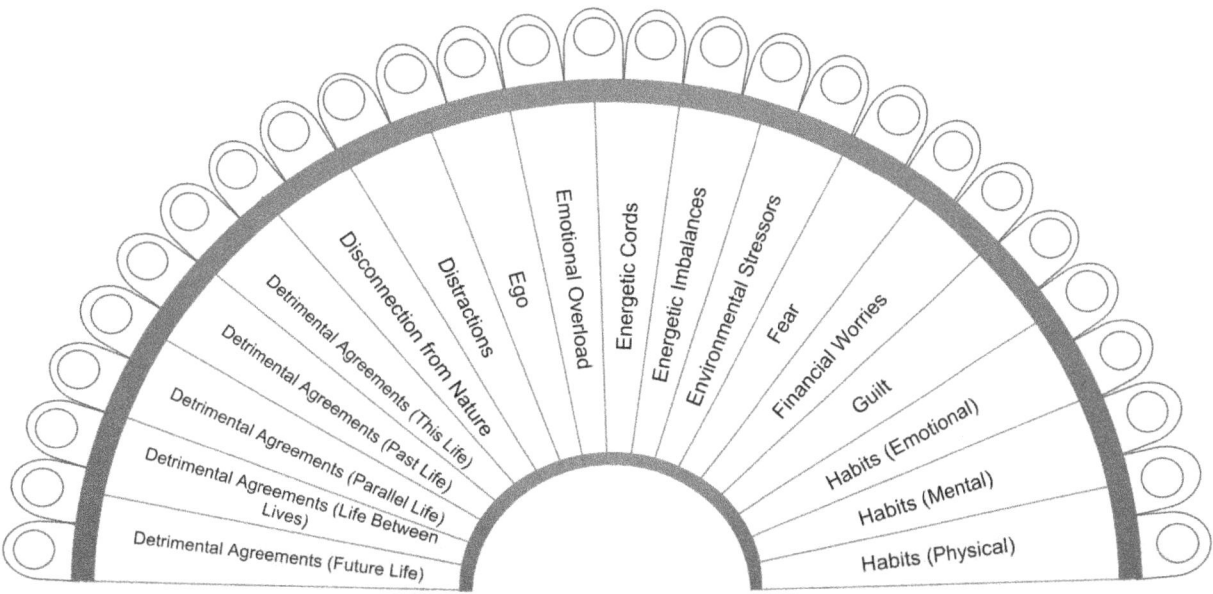

Secondary Gain, Chart 2

The labels on the chart, reading from left to right:

- Detrimental Agreements (Future Life)
- Detrimental Agreements (Life Between Lives)
- Detrimental Agreements (Parallel Life)
- Detrimental Agreements (Past Life)
- Detrimental Agreements (This Life)
- Disconnection from Nature
- Distractions
- Ego
- Emotional Overload
- Energetic Cords
- Energetic Imbalances
- Environmental Stressors
- Fear
- Financial Worries
- Guilt
- Habits (Emotional)
- Habits (Mental)
- Habits (Physical)

Royal Template 18

Diving Deep into the Pool of the Mind

Chart 273

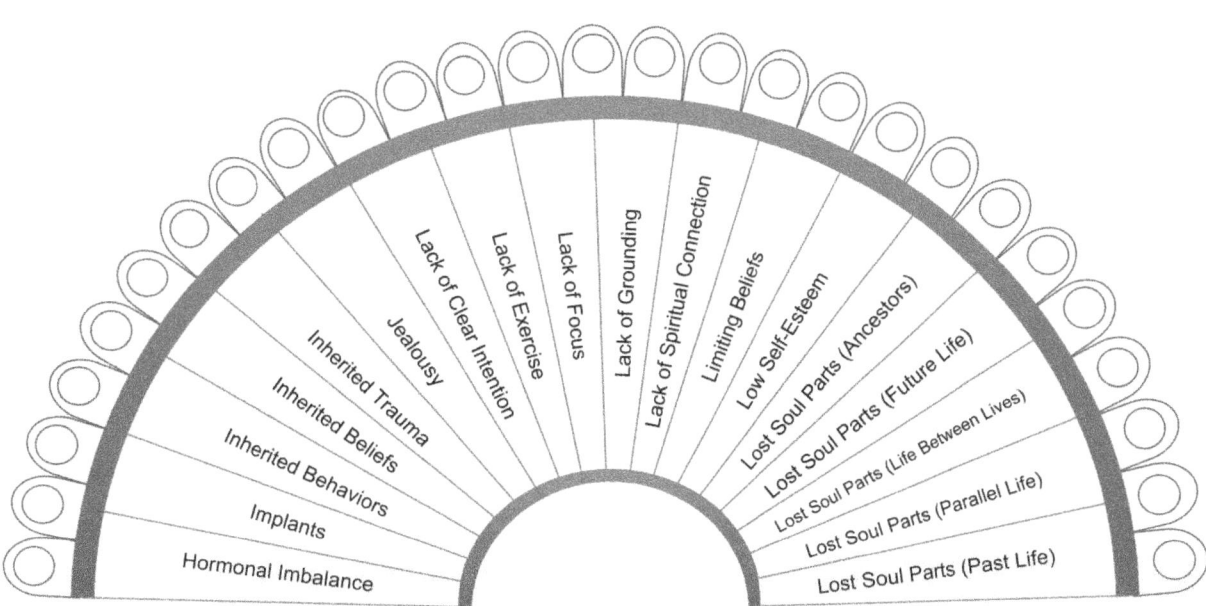

Secondary Gain, Chart 3

The labels on the chart, reading from left to right:

- Hormonal Imbalance
- Implants
- Inherited Behaviors
- Inherited Beliefs
- Inherited Trauma
- Jealousy
- Lack of Clear Intention
- Lack of Exercise
- Lack of Focus
- Lack of Grounding
- Lack of Spiritual Connection
- Limiting Beliefs
- Low Self-Esteem
- Lost Soul Parts (Ancestors)
- Lost Soul Parts (Future Life)
- Lost Soul Parts (Life Between Lives)
- Lost Soul Parts (Parallel Life)
- Lost Soul Parts (Past Life)

Royal Template 18

Diving Deep into the Pool of the Mind

Chart 274

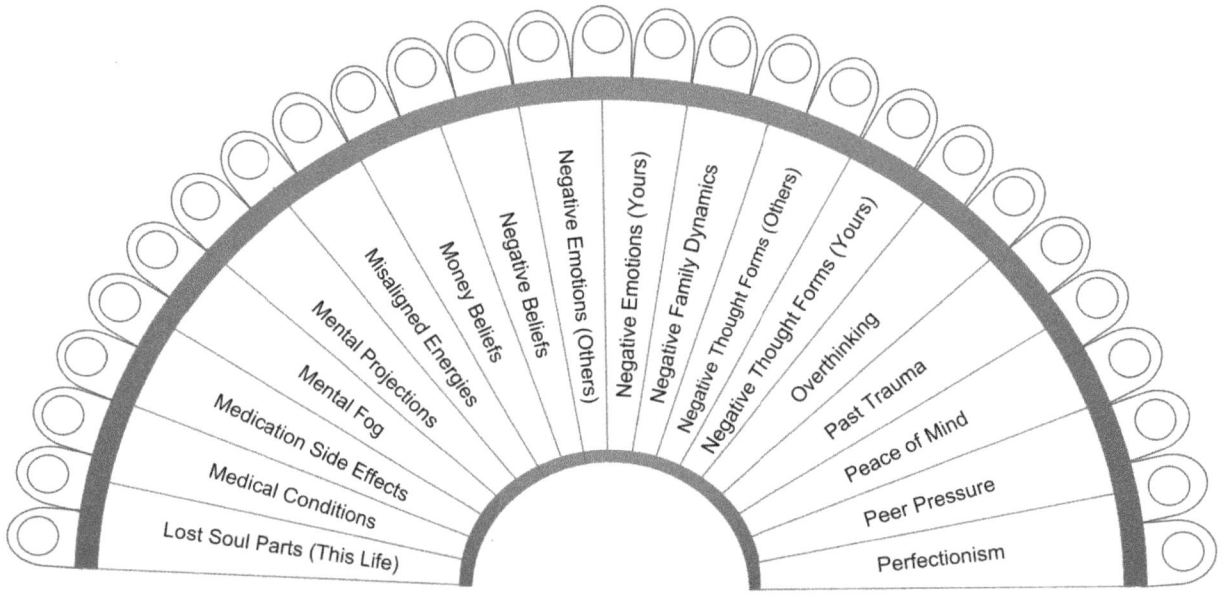

Secondary Gain, Chart 4

Labels (left to right):
- Lost Soul Parts (This Life)
- Medical Conditions
- Medication Side Effects
- Mental Fog
- Mental Projections
- Misaligned Energies
- Money Beliefs
- Negative Beliefs
- Negative Emotions (Others)
- Negative Emotions (Yours)
- Negative Family Dynamics
- Negative Thought Forms (Others)
- Negative Thought Forms (Yours)
- Overthinking
- Past Trauma
- Peace of Mind
- Peer Pressure
- Perfectionism

Royal Template 18

Diving Deep into the Pool of the Mind

Chart 275

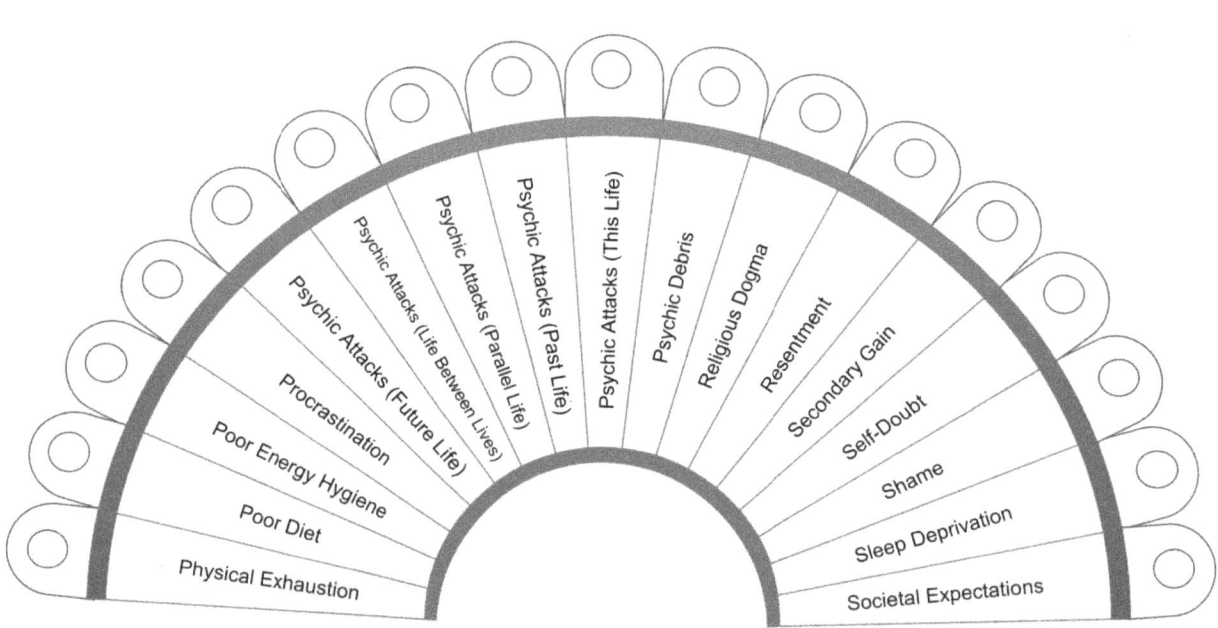

Secondary Gain, Chart 5

Labels (left to right):
- Physical Exhaustion
- Poor Diet
- Poor Energy Hygiene
- Procrastination
- Psychic Attacks (Future Life)
- Psychic Attacks (Life Between Lives)
- Psychic Attacks (Parallel Life)
- Psychic Attacks (Past Life)
- Psychic Attacks (This Life)
- Psychic Debris
- Religious Dogma
- Resentment
- Secondary Gain
- Self-Doubt
- Shame
- Sleep Deprivation
- Societal Expectations

Royal Template 17

Diving Deep into the Pool of the Mind

Chart 276

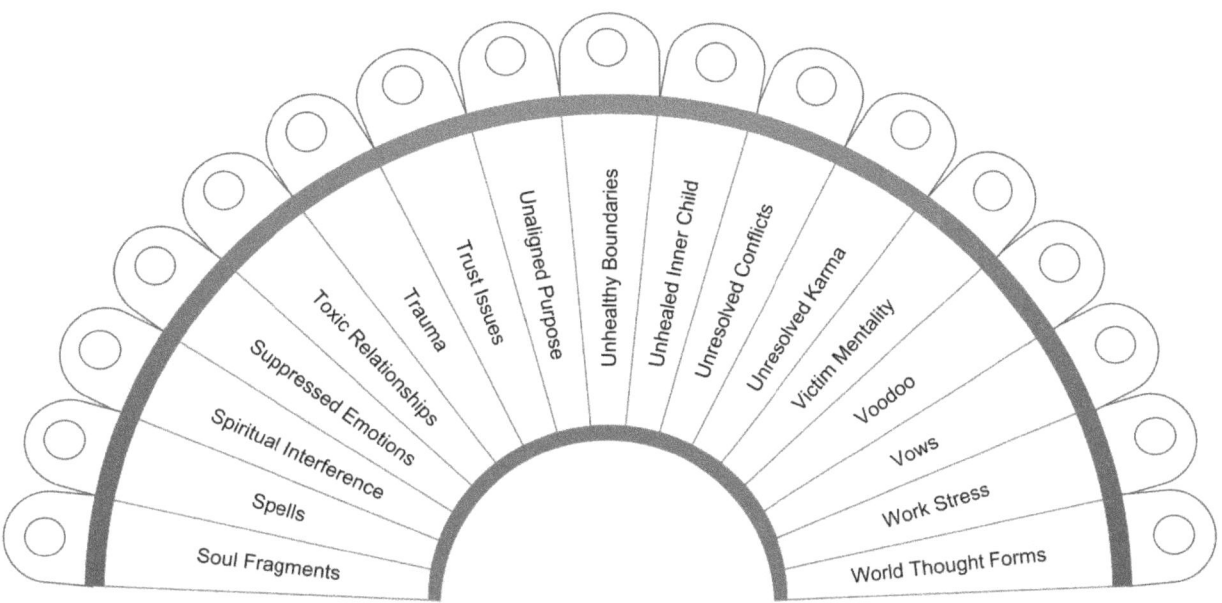

Secondary Gain, Chart 6

Toxic Relationships
Trauma
Trust Issues
Unaligned Purpose
Unhealthy Boundaries
Unhealed Inner Child
Unresolved Conflicts
Unresolved Karma
Victim Mentality
Voodoo
Vows
Work Stress
Suppressed Emotions
Spiritual Interference
Spells
Soul Fragments
World Thought Forms

Royal Template 17

Diving Deep into the Pool of the Mind

Chart 277

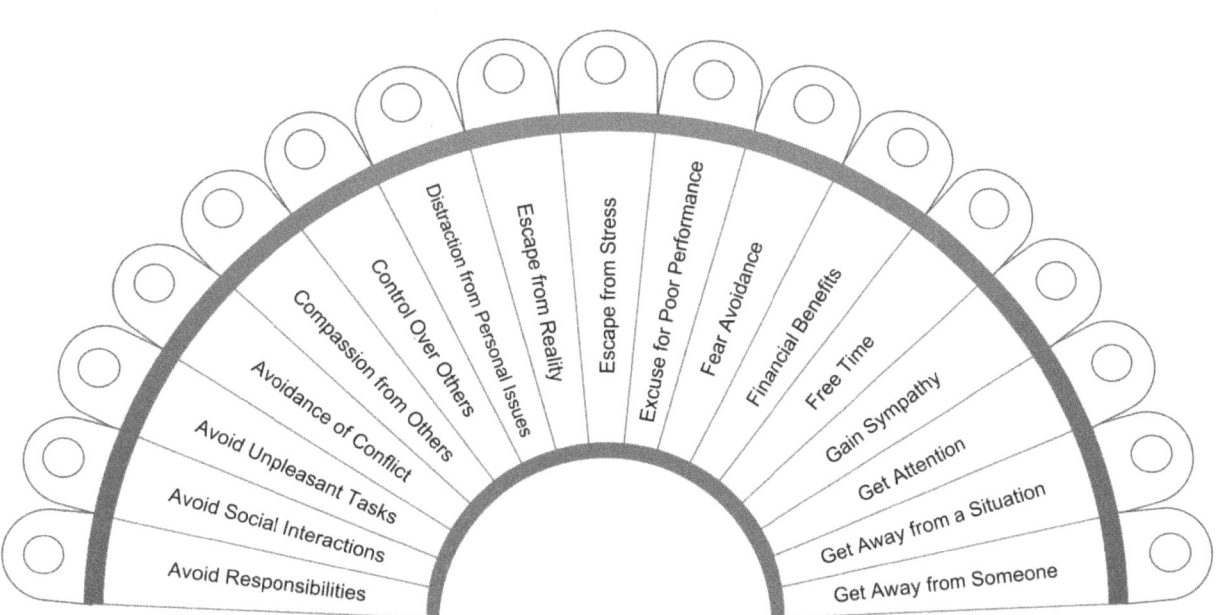

Secondary Gain, Chart 7

Distraction from Personal Issues
Escape from Reality
Escape from Stress
Excuse for Poor Performance
Fear Avoidance
Financial Benefits
Free Time
Gain Sympathy
Get Attention
Get Away from a Situation
Get Away from Someone
Control Over Others
Compassion from Others
Avoidance of Conflict
Avoid Unpleasant Tasks
Avoid Social Interactions
Avoid Responsibilities

Royal Template 17

Diving Deep into the Pool of the Mind

Chart 278

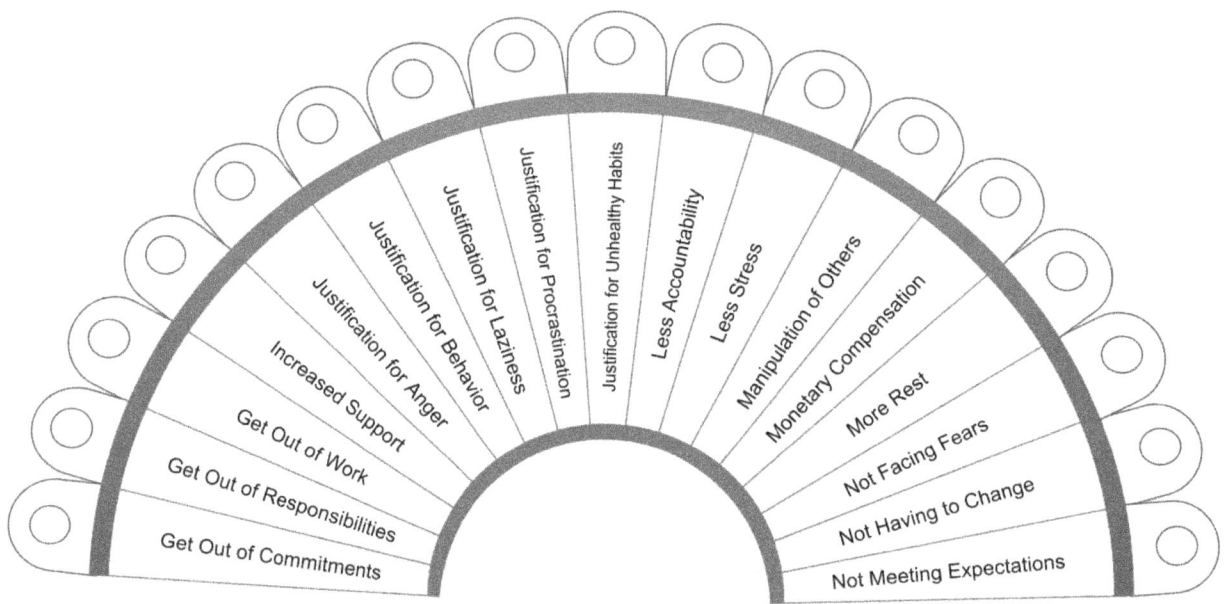

Secondary Gain, Chart 8

Justification for Unhealthy Habits
Justification for Procrastination
Justification for Laziness
Justification for Behavior
Justification for Anger
Increased Support
Get Out of Work
Get Out of Responsibilities
Get Out of Commitments
Less Accountability
Less Stress
Manipulation of Others
Monetary Compensation
More Rest
Not Facing Fears
Not Having to Change
Not Meeting Expectations

Diving Deep into the Pool of the Mind

Chart 279

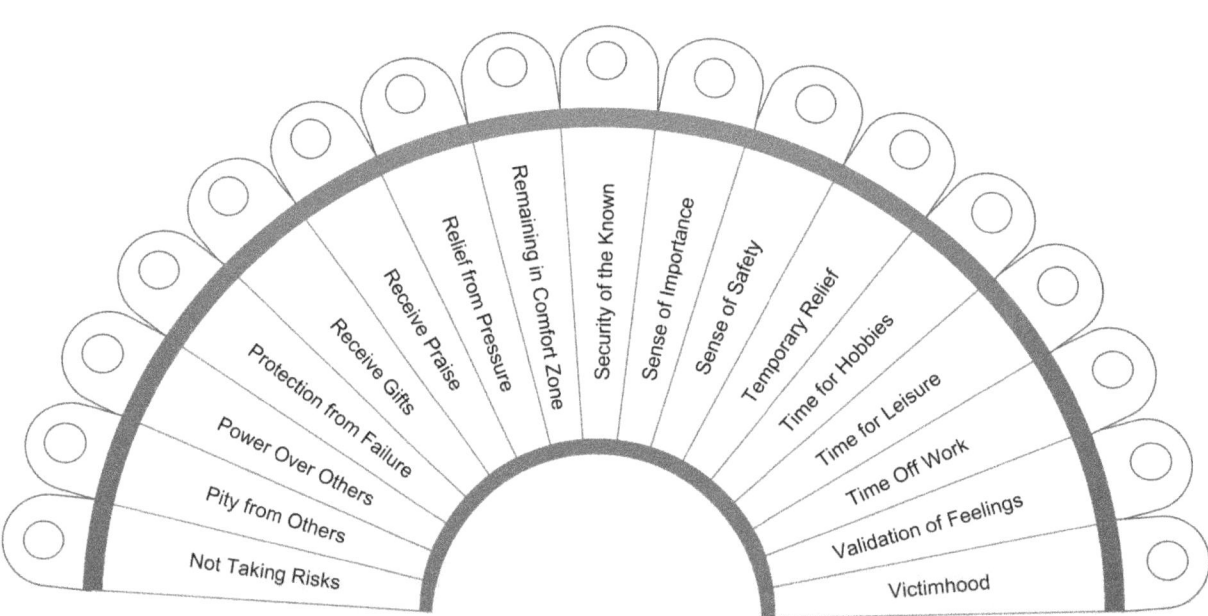

Secondary Gain, Chart 9

Remaining in Comfort Zone
Relief from Pressure
Receive Praise
Receive Gifts
Protection from Failure
Power Over Others
Pity from Others
Not Taking Risks
Security of the Known
Sense of Importance
Sense of Safety
Temporary Relief
Time for Hobbies
Time for Leisure
Time Off Work
Validation of Feelings
Victimhood

Diving Deep into the Pool of the Mind

Chart 280

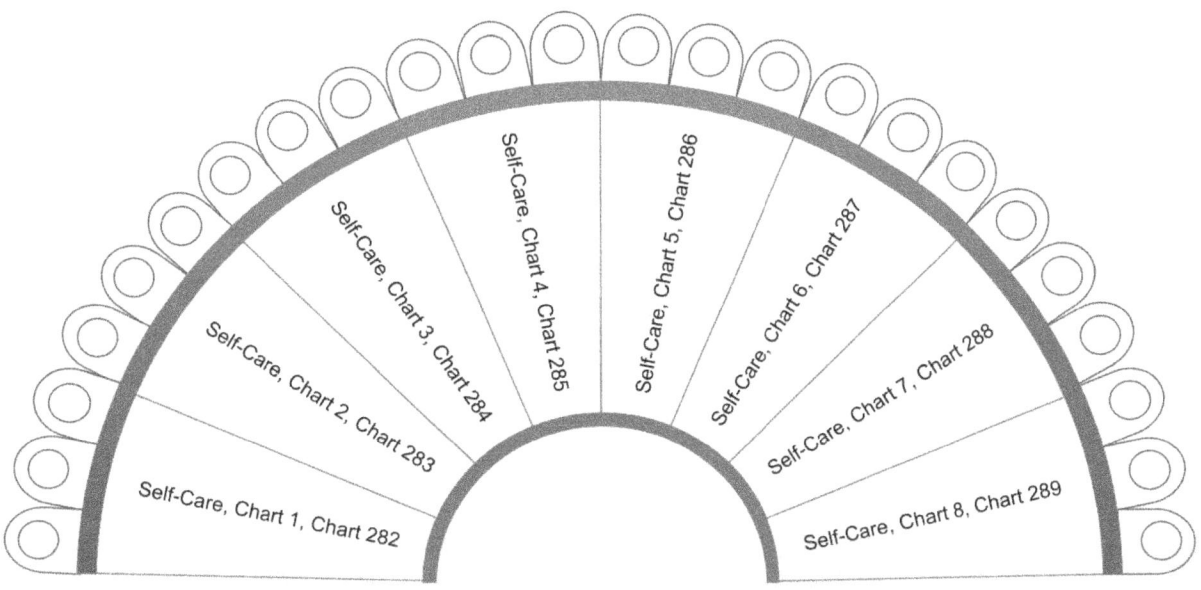

Self-Care, Master Chart

Self-Care, Chart 1, Chart 282
Self-Care, Chart 2, Chart 283
Self-Care, Chart 3, Chart 284
Self-Care, Chart 4, Chart 285
Self-Care, Chart 5, Chart 286
Self-Care, Chart 6, Chart 287
Self-Care, Chart 7, Chart 288
Self-Care, Chart 8, Chart 289

Royal Template 8

Diving Deep into the Pool of the Mind

Chart 281

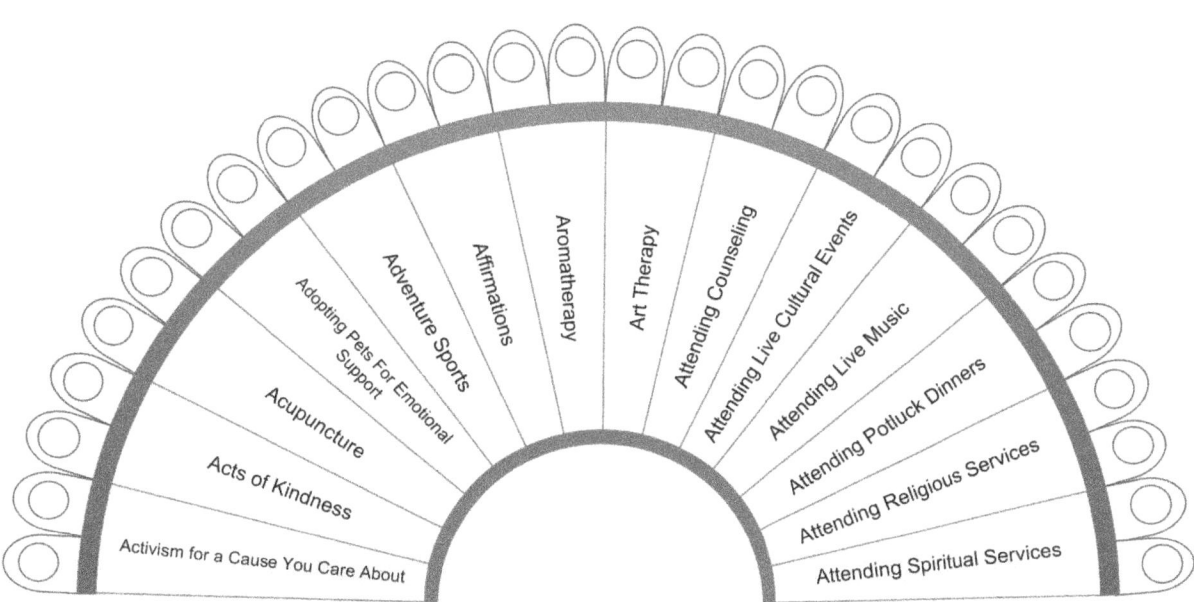

Self-Care, Chart 1

Activism for a Cause You Care About
Acts of Kindness
Acupuncture
Adopting Pets For Emotional Support
Adventure Sports
Affirmations
Aromatherapy
Art Therapy
Attending Counseling
Attending Live Cultural Events
Attending Live Music
Attending Potluck Dinners
Attending Religious Services
Attending Spiritual Services

Royal Template 14

Diving Deep into the Pool of the Mind

Chart 282

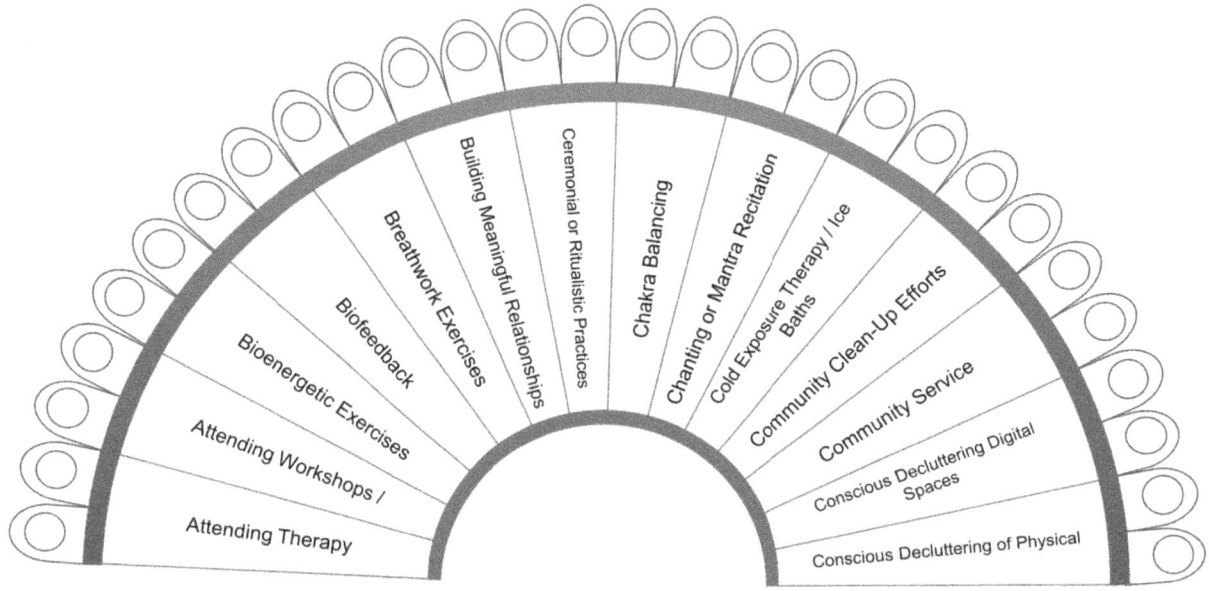

Self-Care, Chart 2

Attending Therapy
Attending Workshops /
Bioenergetic Exercises
Biofeedback
Breathwork Exercises
Building Meaningful Relationships
Ceremonial or Ritualistic Practices
Chakra Balancing
Chanting or Mantra Recitation
Cold Exposure Therapy / Ice Baths
Community Clean-Up Efforts
Community Service
Conscious Decluttering Digital Spaces
Conscious Decluttering of Physical

Royal Template 14

Diving Deep into the Pool of the Mind

Chart 283

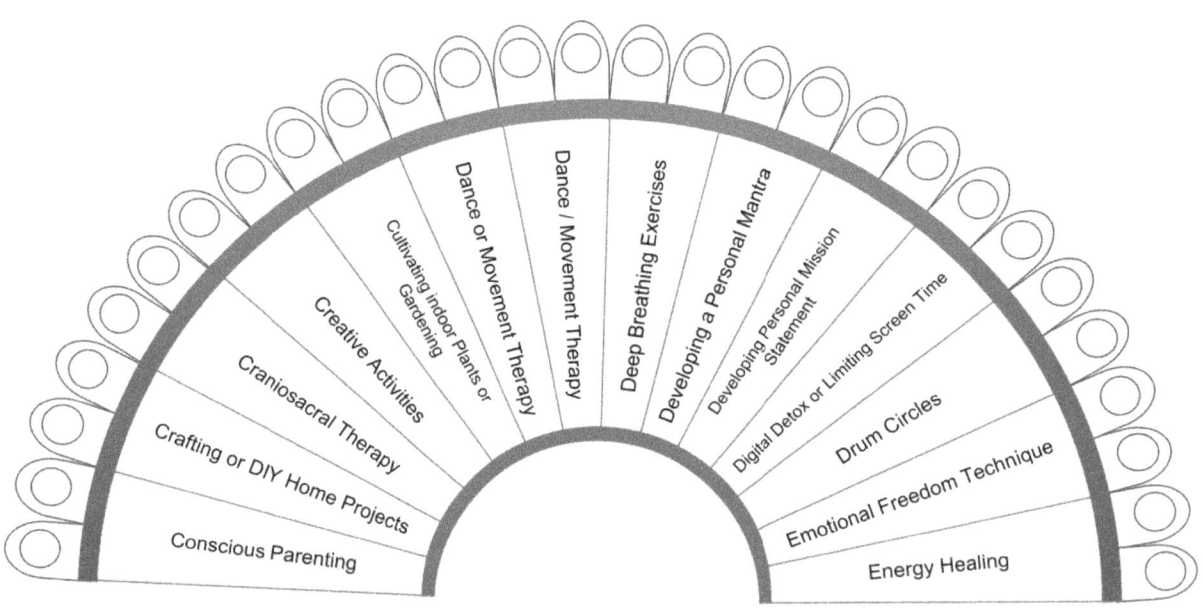

Self-Care, Chart 3

Conscious Parenting
Crafting or DIY Home Projects
Craniosacral Therapy
Creative Activities
Cultivating Indoor Plants or Gardening
Dance or Movement Therapy
Dance / Movement Therapy
Deep Breathing Exercises
Developing a Personal Mantra
Developing Personal Mission Statement
Digital Detox or Limiting Screen Time
Drum Circles
Emotional Freedom Technique
Energy Healing

Royal Template 14

Diving Deep into the Pool of the Mind

Chart 284

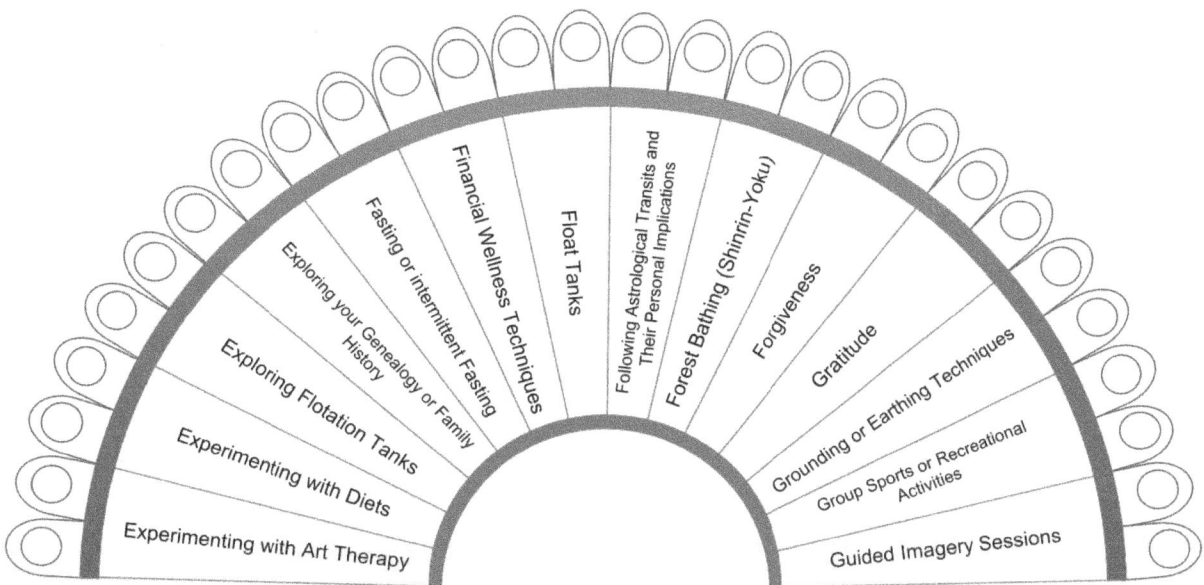

Self-Care, Chart 4

The chart contains the following labels (reading around the fan):

- Experimenting with Art Therapy
- Experimenting with Diets
- Exploring Flotation Tanks
- Exploring your Genealogy or Family History
- Fasting or Intermittent Fasting
- Financial Wellness Techniques
- Float Tanks
- Following Astrological Transits and Their Personal Implications
- Forest Bathing (Shinrin-Yoku)
- Forgiveness
- Gratitude
- Grounding or Earthing Techniques
- Group Sports or Recreational Activities
- Guided Imagery Sessions

Royal Template 14

Diving Deep into the Pool of the Mind

Chart 285

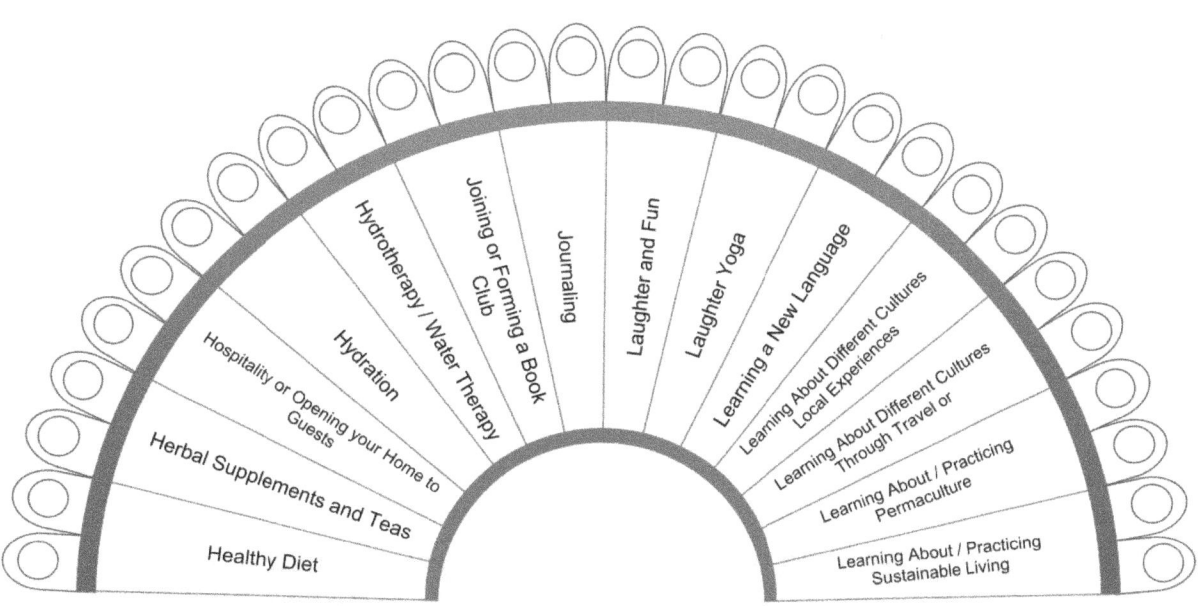

Self-Care, Chart 5

The chart contains the following labels (reading around the fan):

- Healthy Diet
- Herbal Supplements and Teas
- Hospitality or Opening your Home to Guests
- Hydration
- Hydrotherapy / Water Therapy
- Joining or Forming a Book Club
- Journaling
- Laughter and Fun
- Laughter Yoga
- Learning a New Language
- Learning About Different Cultures Local Experiences
- Learning About Different Cultures Through Travel or
- Learning About / Practicing Permaculture
- Learning About / Practicing Sustainable Living

Royal Template 14

Diving Deep into the Pool of the Mind

Chart 286

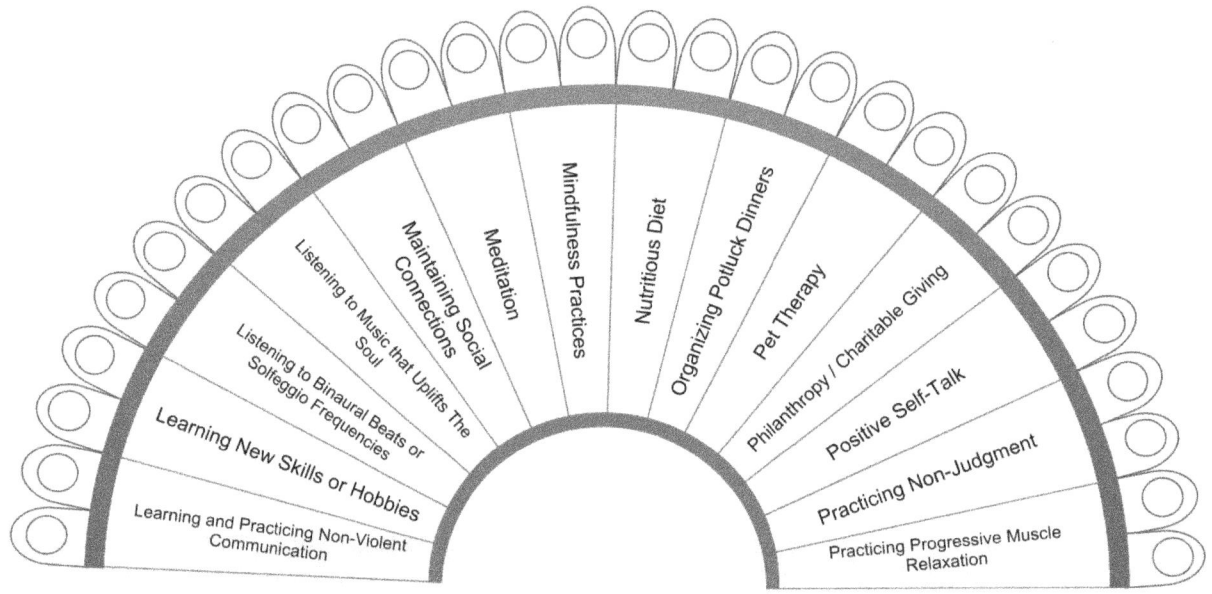

Self-Care, Chart 6

The chart contains the following labeled segments:
- Learning and Practicing Non-Violent Communication
- Learning New Skills or Hobbies
- Listening to Binaural Beats or Solfeggio Frequencies
- Listening to Music that Uplifts The Soul
- Maintaining Social Connections
- Meditation
- Mindfulness Practices
- Nutritious Diet
- Organizing Potluck Dinners
- Pet Therapy
- Philanthropy / Charitable Giving
- Positive Self-Talk
- Practicing Non-Judgment
- Practicing Progressive Muscle Relaxation

Royal Template 14

Diving Deep into the Pool of the Mind

Chart 287

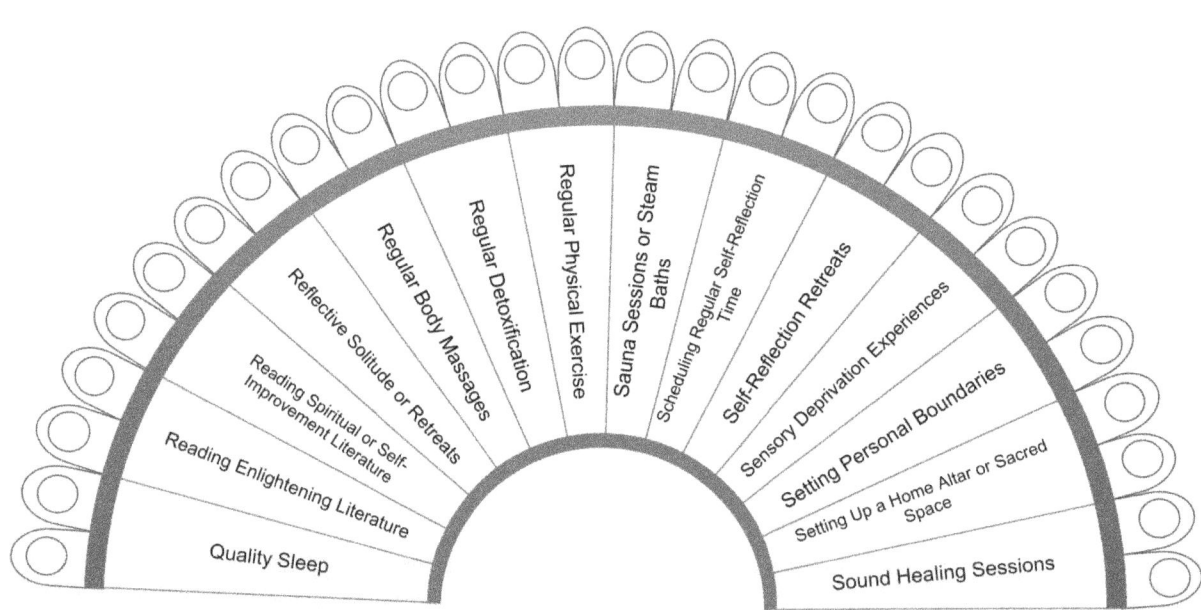

Self-Care, Chart 7

The chart contains the following labeled segments:
- Quality Sleep
- Reading Enlightening Literature
- Reading Spiritual or Self-Improvement Literature
- Reflective Solitude or Retreats
- Regular Body Massages
- Regular Detoxification
- Regular Physical Exercise
- Sauna Sessions or Steam Baths
- Scheduling Regular Self-Reflection Time
- Self-Reflection Retreats
- Sensory Deprivation Experiences
- Setting Personal Boundaries
- Setting Up a Home Altar or Sacred Space
- Sound Healing Sessions

Royal Template 14

Diving Deep into the Pool of the Mind

Chart 288

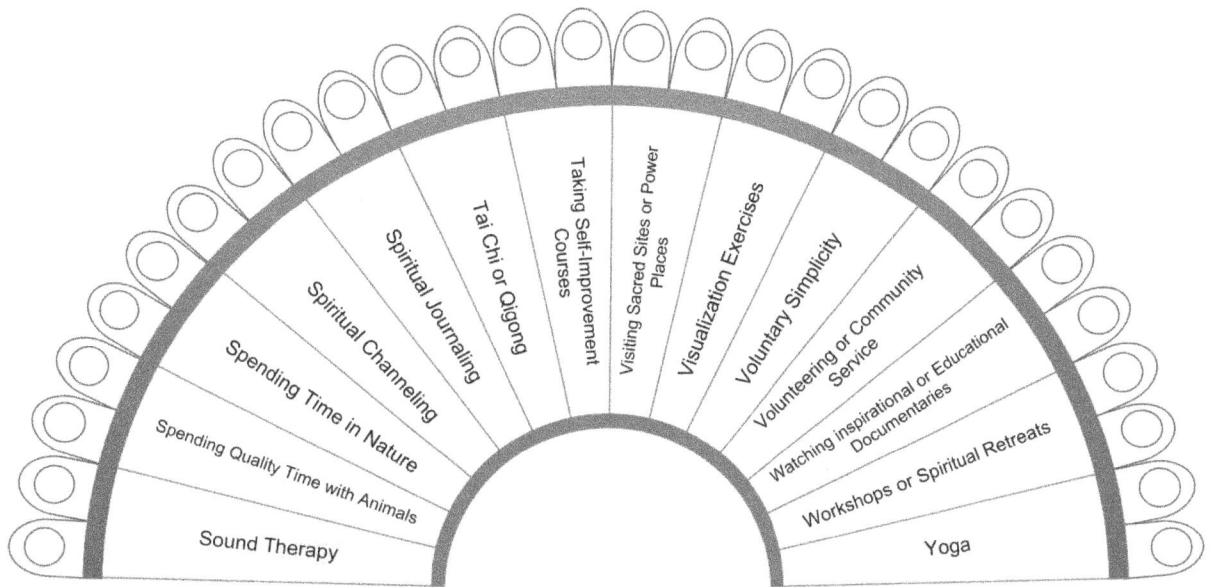

Self-Care, Chart 8

Spending Quality Time with Animals
Spending Time in Nature
Spiritual Channeling
Spiritual Journaling
Tai Chi or Qigong
Taking Self-Improvement Courses
Visiting Sacred Sites or Power Places
Visualization Exercises
Voluntary Simplicity
Volunteering or Community Service
Watching Inspirational or Educational Documentaries
Workshops or Spiritual Retreats
Yoga
Sound Therapy

Royal Template 14

Diving Deep into the Pool of the Mind

Chart 289

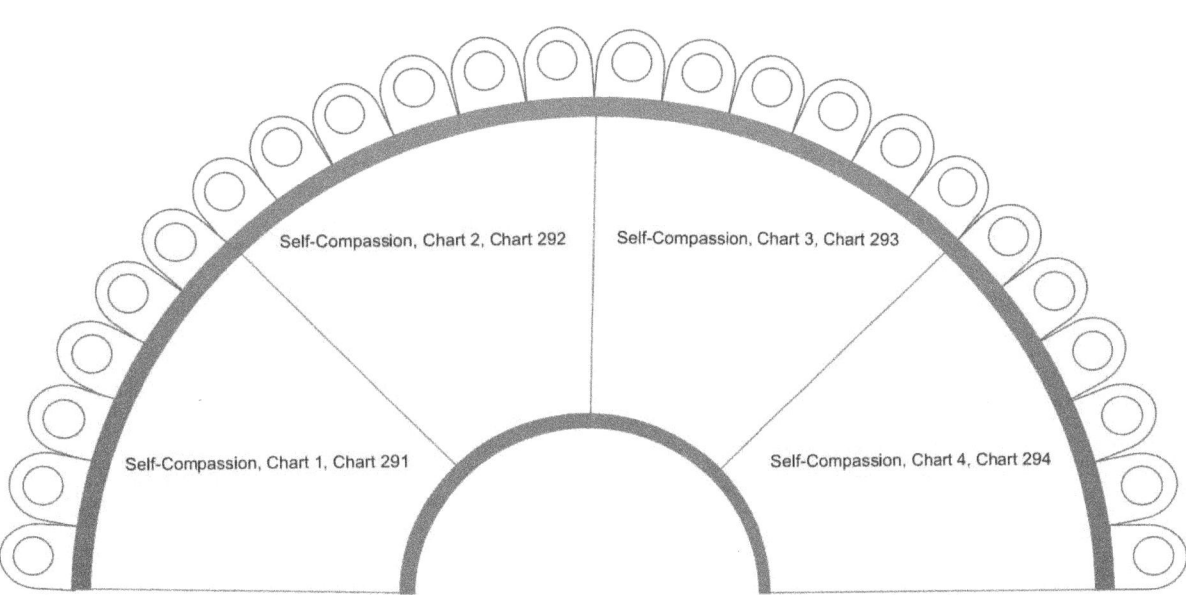

Self-Compassion, Chart 2, Chart 292

Self-Compassion, Chart 3, Chart 293

Self-Compassion, Chart 1, Chart 291

Self-Compassion, Chart 4, Chart 294

Self-Compassion, Master Chart

Royal Template 4h

Diving Deep into the Pool of the Mind

Chart 290

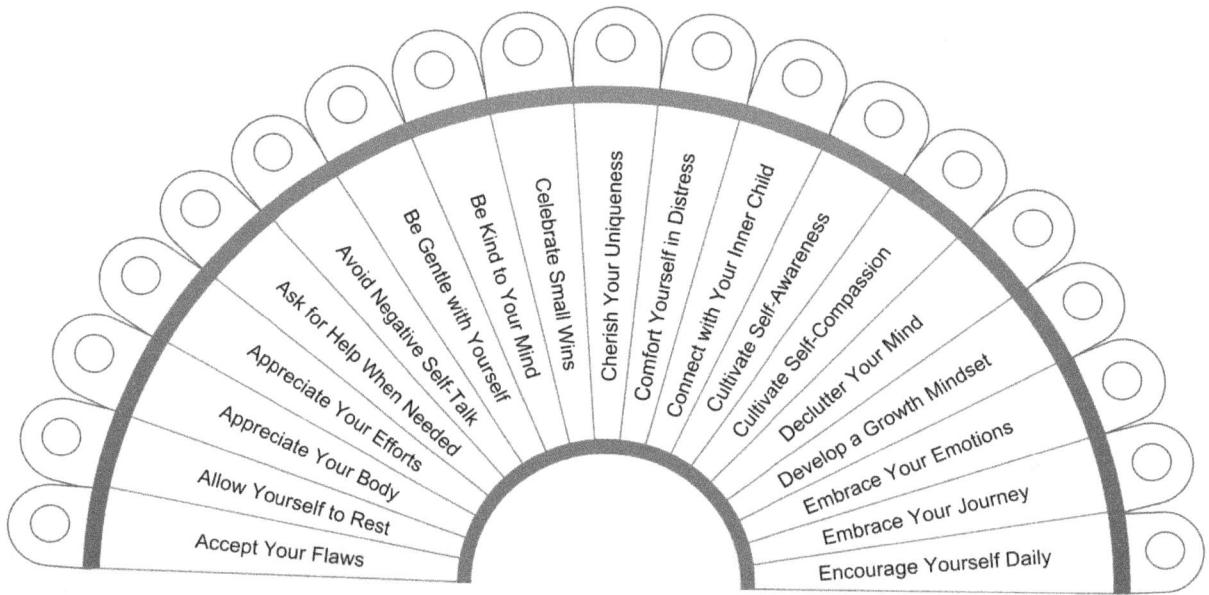

Self-Compassion, Chart 1

The chart contains the following labels (from left to right):

- Accept Your Flaws
- Allow Yourself to Rest
- Appreciate Your Body
- Appreciate Your Efforts
- Ask for Help When Needed
- Avoid Negative Self-Talk
- Be Gentle with Yourself
- Be Kind to Your Mind
- Celebrate Small Wins
- Cherish Your Uniqueness
- Comfort Yourself in Distress
- Connect with Your Inner Child
- Cultivate Self-Awareness
- Cultivate Self-Compassion
- Declutter Your Mind
- Develop a Growth Mindset
- Embrace Your Emotions
- Embrace Your Journey
- Encourage Yourself Daily

Royal Template 19

Diving Deep into the Pool of the Mind

Chart 291

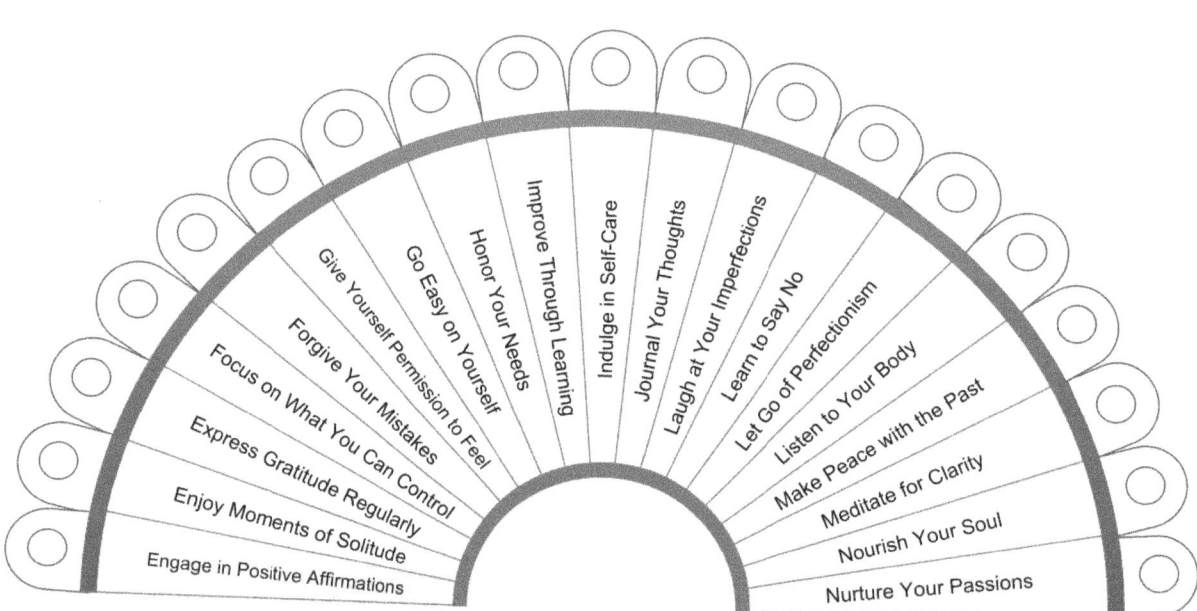

Self-Compassion, Chart 2

The chart contains the following labels (from left to right):

- Engage in Positive Affirmations
- Enjoy Moments of Solitude
- Express Gratitude Regularly
- Focus on What You Can Control
- Forgive Your Mistakes
- Give Yourself Permission to Feel
- Go Easy on Yourself
- Honor Your Needs
- Improve Through Learning
- Indulge in Self-Care
- Journal Your Thoughts
- Laugh at Your Imperfections
- Learn to Say No
- Let Go of Perfectionism
- Listen to Your Body
- Make Peace with the Past
- Meditate for Clarity
- Nourish Your Soul
- Nurture Your Passions

Royal Template 19

Diving Deep into the Pool of the Mind

Chart 292

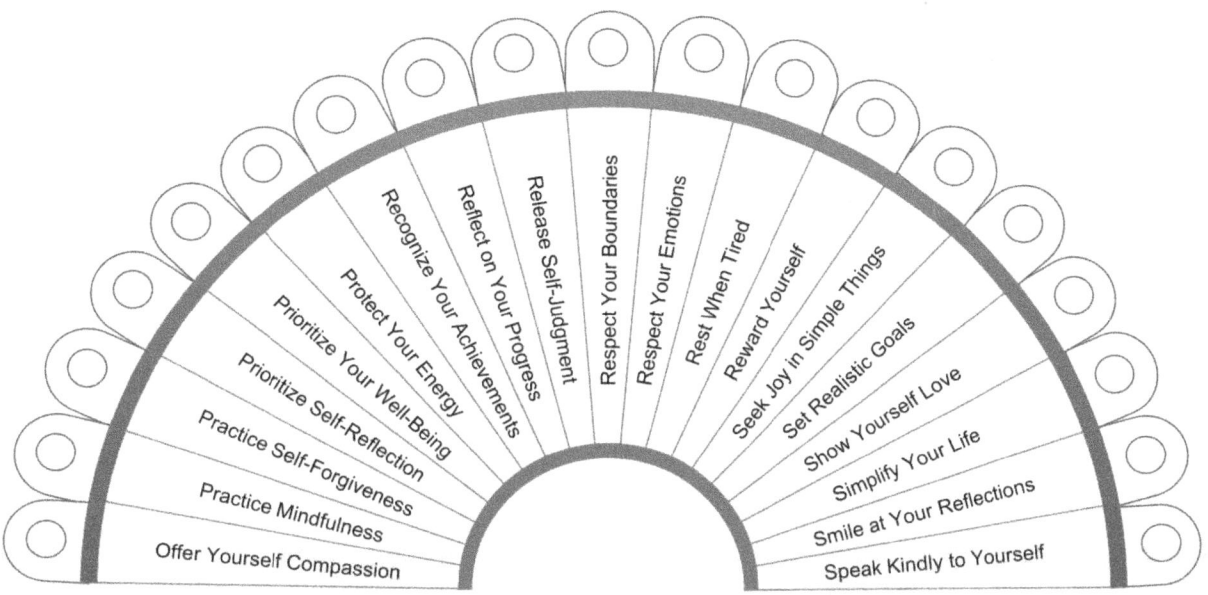

Self-Compassion, Chart 3

Recognize Your Achievements
Reflect on Your Progress
Release Self-Judgment
Respect Your Boundaries
Respect Your Emotions
Rest When Tired
Reward Yourself
Seek Joy in Simple Things
Set Realistic Goals
Show Yourself Love
Simplify Your Life
Smile at Your Reflections
Speak Kindly to Yourself
Protect Your Energy
Prioritize Your Well-Being
Prioritize Self-Reflection
Practice Self-Forgiveness
Practice Mindfulness
Offer Yourself Compassion

Royal Template 19

Diving Deep into the Pool of the Mind

Chart 293

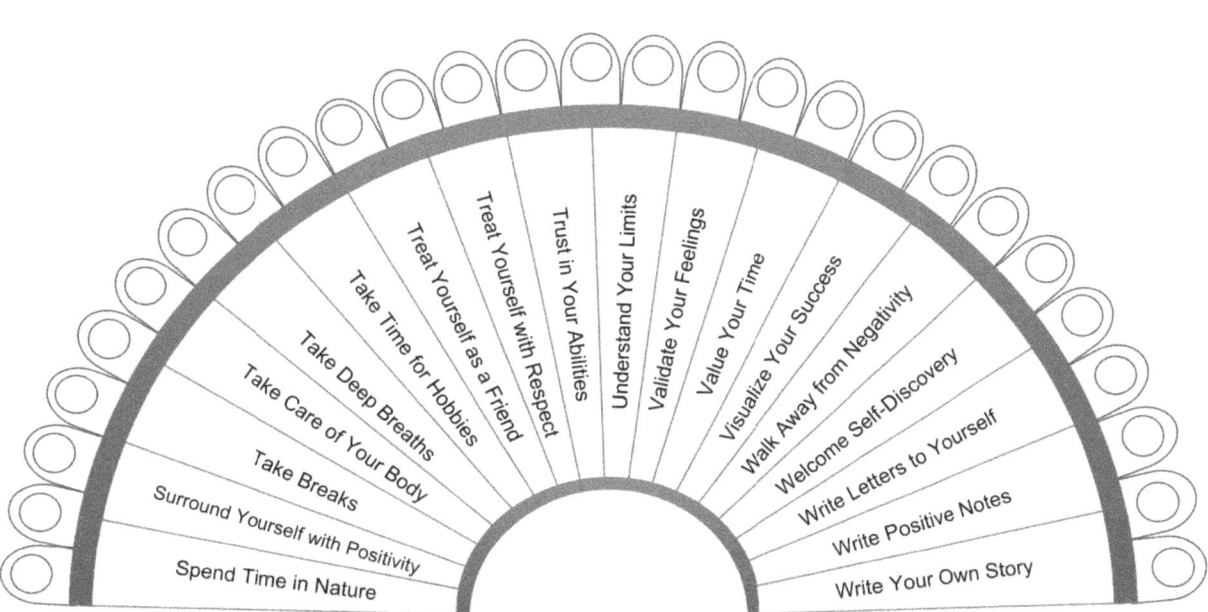

Self-Compassion, Chart 4

Treat Yourself as a Friend
Treat Yourself with Respect
Trust in Your Abilities
Understand Your Limits
Validate Your Feelings
Value Your Time
Visualize Your Success
Walk Away from Negativity
Welcome Self-Discovery
Write Letters to Yourself
Write Positive Notes
Write Your Own Story
Take Time for Hobbies
Take Deep Breaths
Take Care of Your Body
Take Breaks
Surround Yourself with Positivity
Spend Time in Nature

Royal Template 18

Diving Deep into the Pool of the Mind

Chart 294

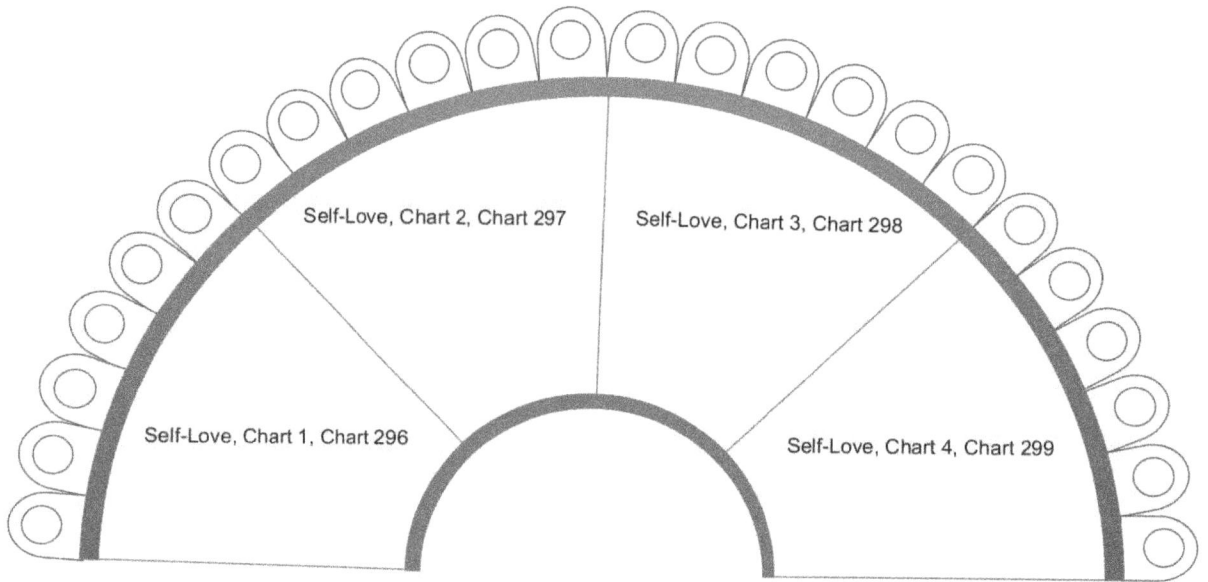

Self-Love, Master Chart

Self-Love, Chart 2, Chart 297

Self-Love, Chart 3, Chart 298

Self-Love, Chart 1, Chart 296

Self-Love, Chart 4, Chart 299

Royal Template 4h

Diving Deep into the Pool of the Mind

Chart 295

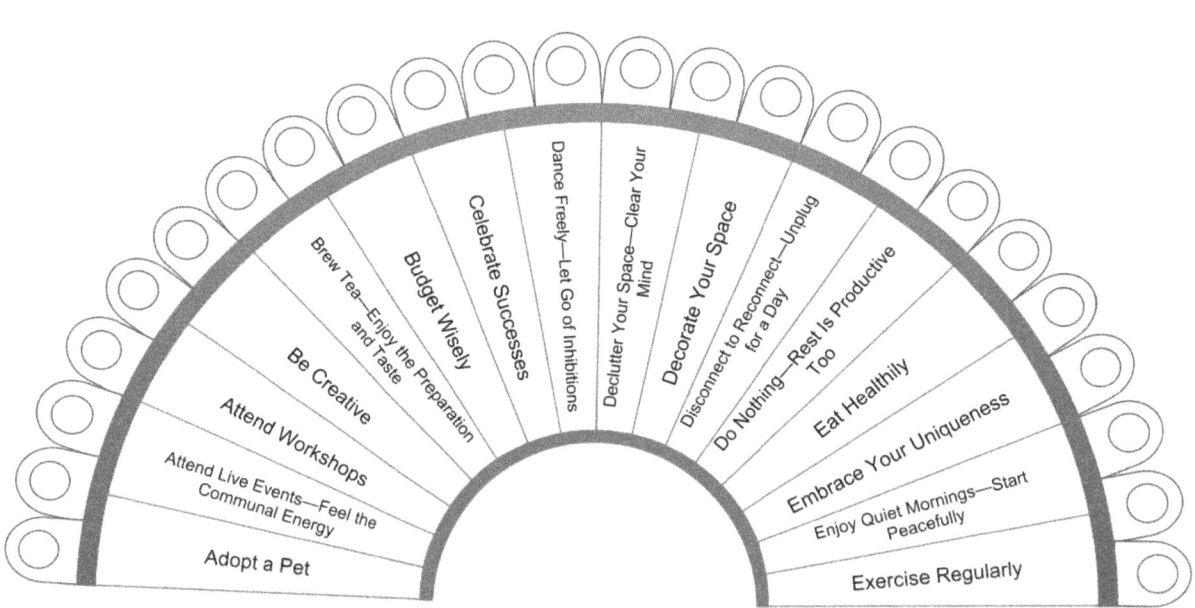

Self-Love, Chart 1

Adopt a Pet
Attend Live Events—Feel the Communal Energy
Attend Workshops
Be Creative
Brew Tea—Enjoy the Preparation and Taste
Budget Wisely
Celebrate Successes
Dance Freely—Let Go of Inhibitions
Declutter Your Space—Clear Your Mind
Decorate Your Space
Disconnect to Reconnect—Unplug for a Day
Do Nothing—Rest Is Productive Too
Eat Healthily
Embrace Your Uniqueness
Enjoy Quiet Mornings—Start Peacefully
Exercise Regularly

Royal Template 16

Diving Deep into the Pool of the Mind

Chart 296

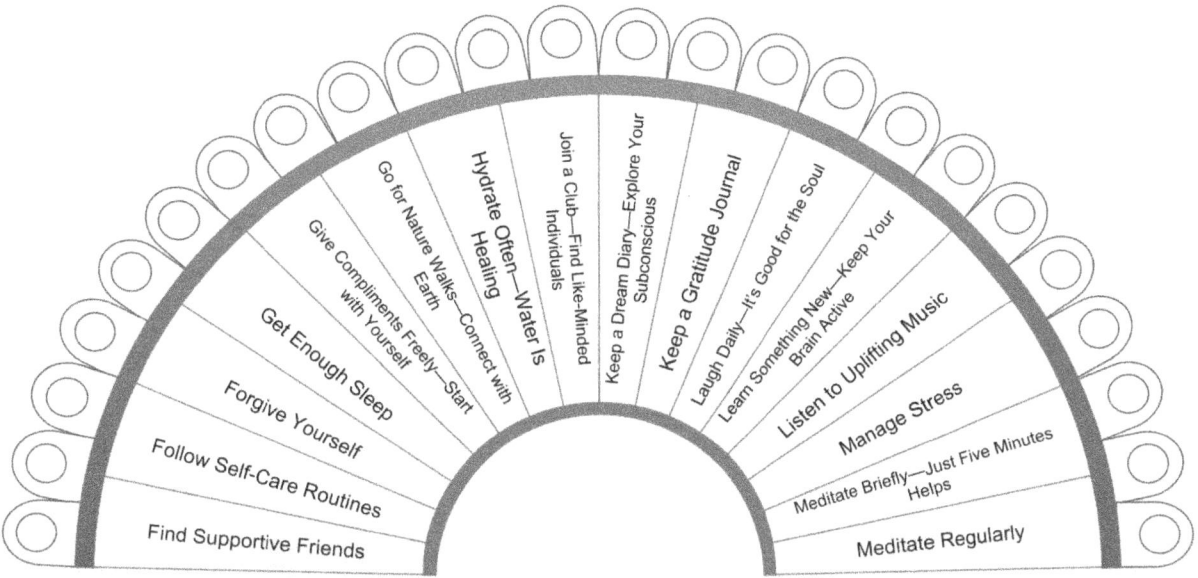

Self-Love, Chart 2

The chart contains the following labels:

- Go for Nature Walks—Connect with Earth
- Give Compliments Freely—Start with Yourself
- Hydrate Often—Water Is Healing
- Join a Club—Find Like-Minded Individuals
- Keep a Dream Diary—Explore Your Subconscious
- Keep a Gratitude Journal
- Laugh Daily—It's Good for the Soul
- Learn Something New—Keep Your Brain Active
- Listen to Uplifting Music
- Manage Stress
- Meditate Briefly—Just Five Minutes Helps
- Meditate Regularly
- Get Enough Sleep
- Forgive Yourself
- Follow Self-Care Routines
- Find Supportive Friends

Royal Template 16

Diving Deep into the Pool of the Mind

Chart 297

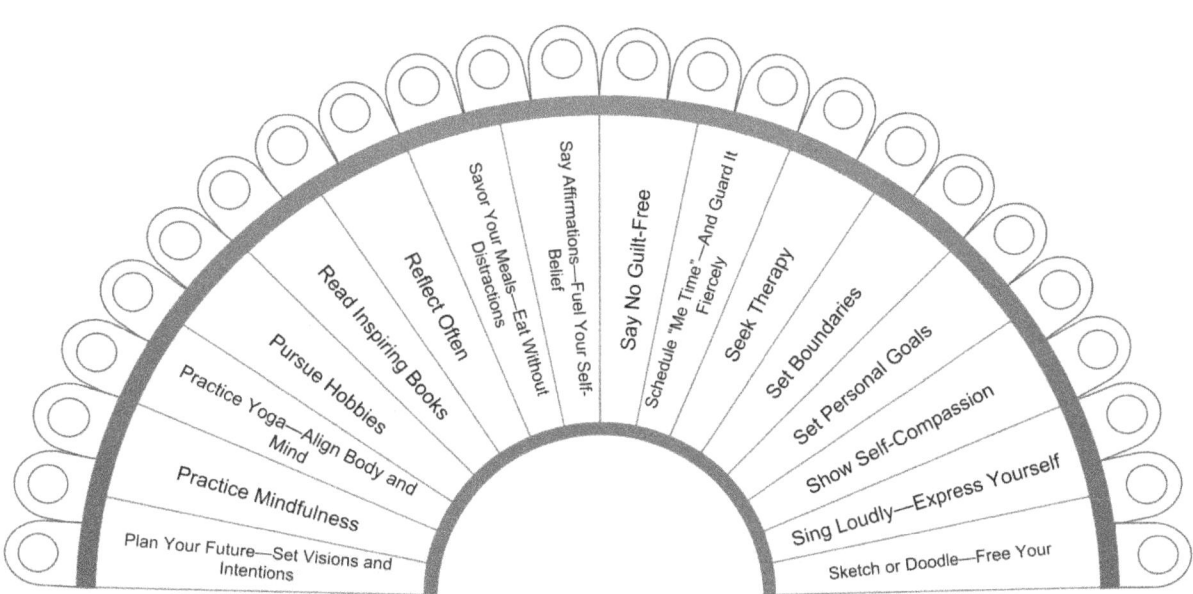

Self-Love, Chart 3

The chart contains the following labels:

- Savor Your Meals—Eat Without Distractions
- Say Affirmations—Fuel Your Self-Belief
- Reflect Often
- Read Inspiring Books
- Pursue Hobbies
- Practice Yoga—Align Body and Mind
- Practice Mindfulness
- Plan Your Future—Set Visions and Intentions
- Say No Guilt-Free
- Schedule "Me Time"—And Guard It Fiercely
- Seek Therapy
- Set Boundaries
- Set Personal Goals
- Show Self-Compassion
- Sing Loudly—Express Yourself
- Sketch or Doodle—Free Your

Royal Template 16

Diving Deep into the Pool of the Mind

Chart 298

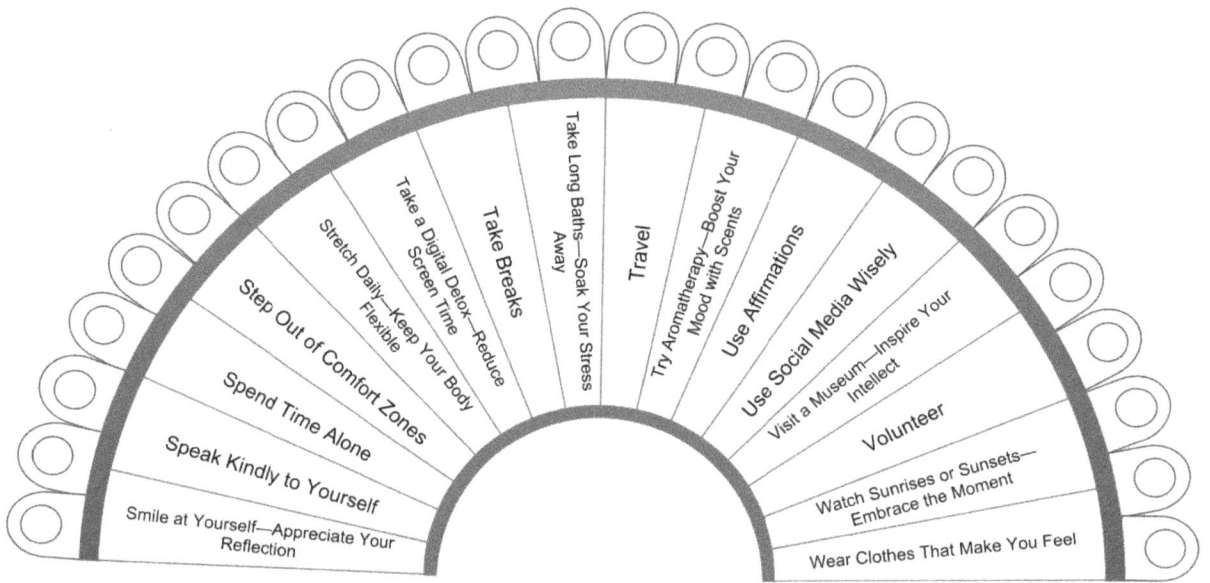

Self-Love, Chart 4

The chart contains the following segments:

- Smile at Yourself—Appreciate Your Reflection
- Speak Kindly to Yourself
- Spend Time Alone
- Step Out of Comfort Zones
- Stretch Daily—Keep Your Body Flexible
- Take a Digital Detox—Reduce Screen Time
- Take Breaks
- Take Long Baths—Soak Your Stress Away
- Travel
- Try Aromatherapy—Boost Your Mood with Scents
- Use Affirmations
- Use Social Media Wisely
- Visit a Museum—Inspire Your Intellect
- Volunteer
- Watch Sunrises or Sunsets—Embrace the Moment
- Wear Clothes That Make You Feel

Royal Template 16

Diving Deep into the Pool of the Mind

Chart 299

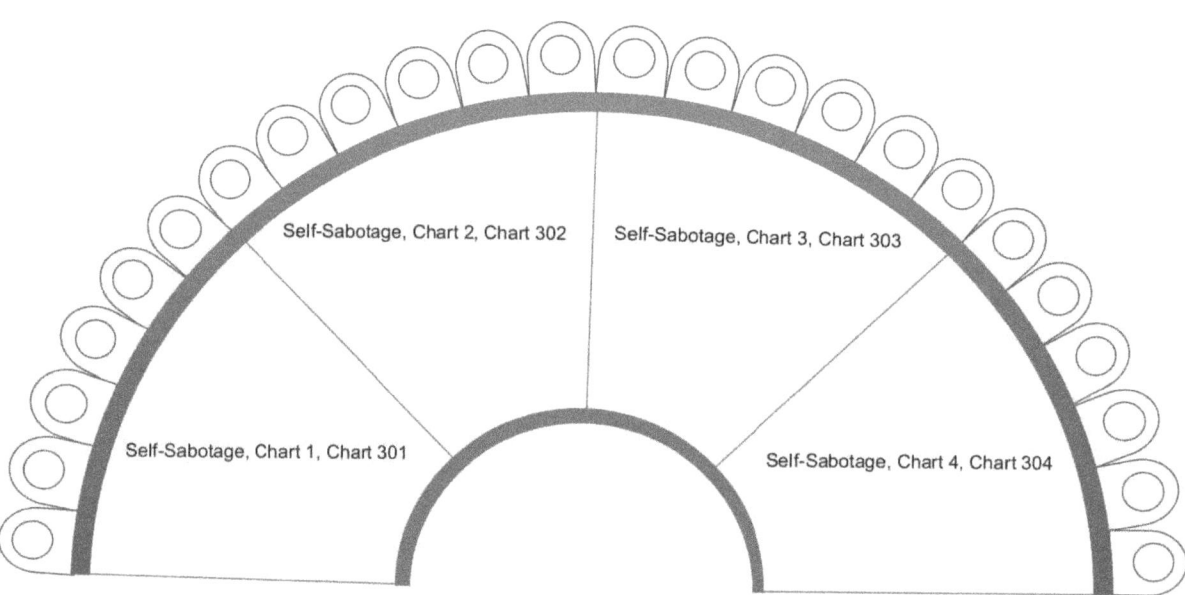

Self-Sabotage, Master Chart

- Self-Sabotage, Chart 1, Chart 301
- Self-Sabotage, Chart 2, Chart 302
- Self-Sabotage, Chart 3, Chart 303
- Self-Sabotage, Chart 4, Chart 304

Royal Template 4h

Diving Deep into the Pool of the Mind

Chart 300

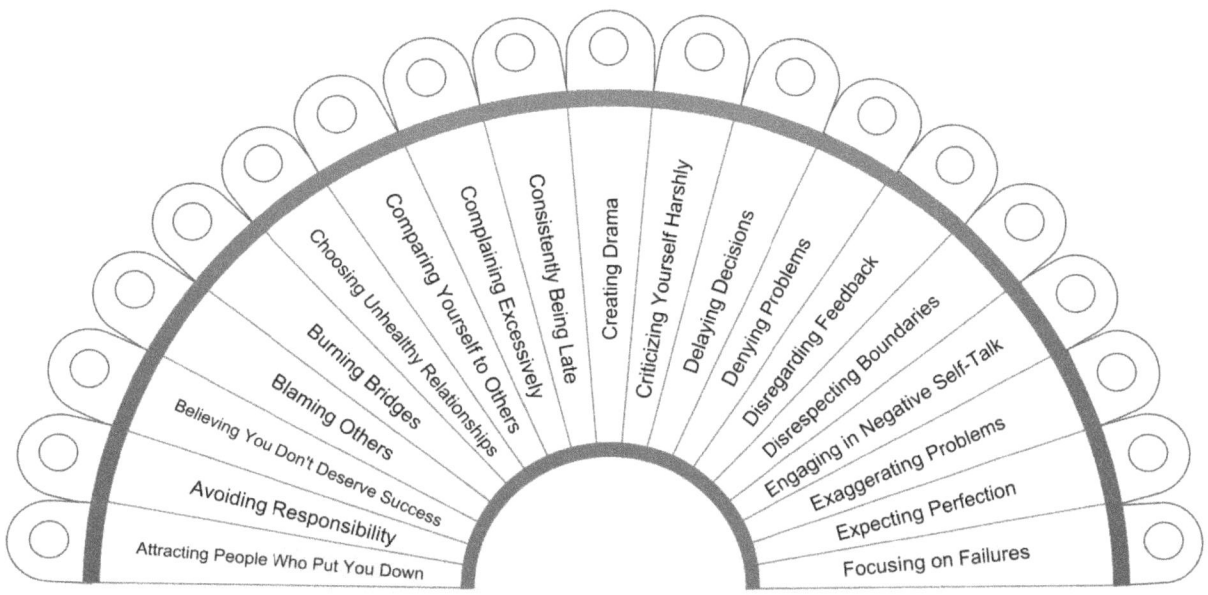

Self-Sabotage, Chart 1

The chart contains the following labels (reading left to right):

- Attracting People Who Put You Down
- Avoiding Responsibility
- Believing You Don't Deserve Success
- Blaming Others
- Burning Bridges
- Choosing Unhealthy Relationships
- Comparing Yourself to Others
- Complaining Excessively
- Consistently Being Late
- Creating Drama
- Criticizing Yourself Harshly
- Delaying Decisions
- Denying Problems
- Disregarding Feedback
- Disrespecting Boundaries
- Engaging in Negative Self-Talk
- Exaggerating Problems
- Expecting Perfection
- Focusing on Failures

Royal Template 19

Diving Deep into the Pool of the Mind

Chart 301

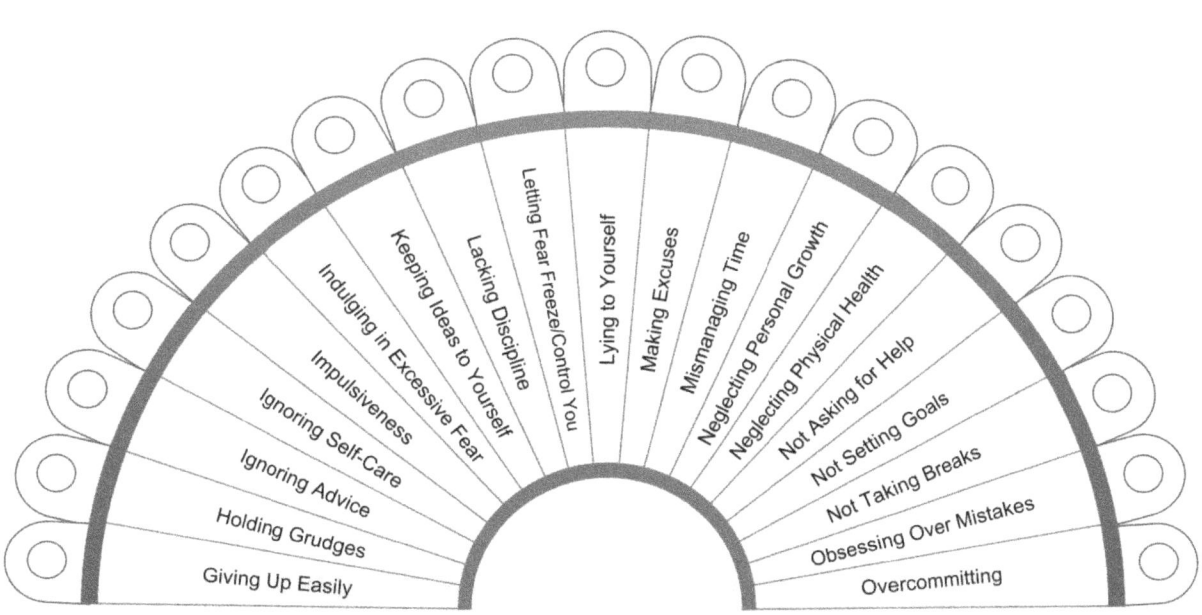

Self-Sabotage, Chart 2

The chart contains the following labels (reading left to right):

- Giving Up Easily
- Holding Grudges
- Ignoring Advice
- Ignoring Self-Care
- Impulsiveness
- Indulging in Excessive Fear
- Keeping Ideas to Yourself
- Lacking Discipline
- Letting Fear Freeze/Control You
- Lying to Yourself
- Making Excuses
- Mismanaging Time
- Neglecting Personal Growth
- Neglecting Physical Health
- Not Asking for Help
- Not Setting Goals
- Not Taking Breaks
- Obsessing Over Mistakes
- Overcommitting

Royal Template 19

Diving Deep into the Pool of the Mind

Chart 302

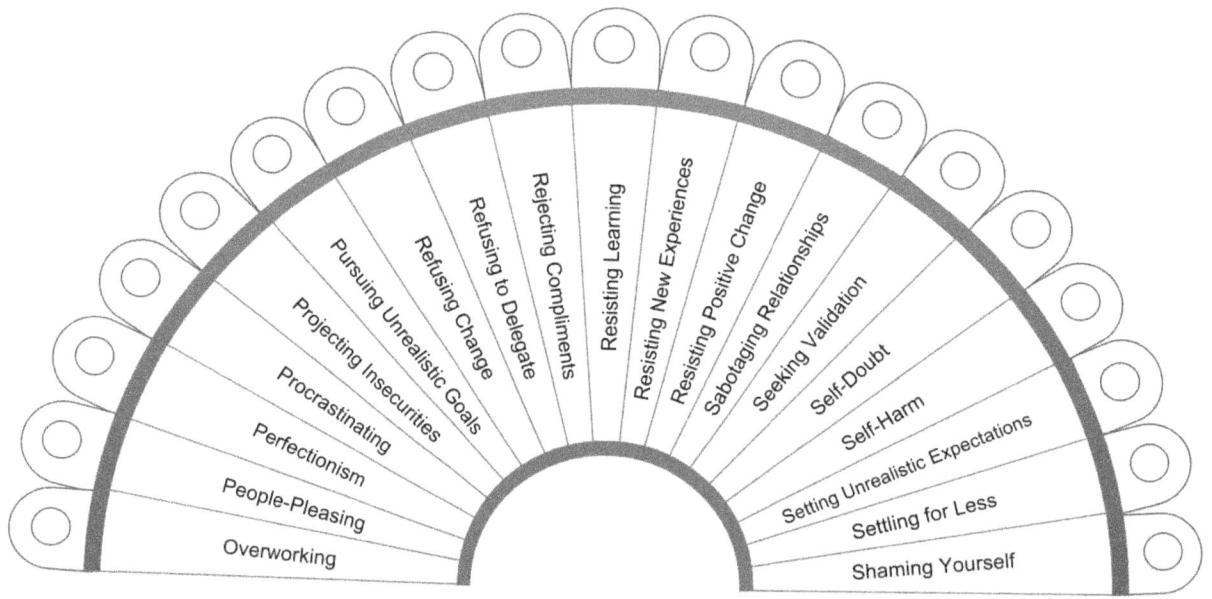

Self-Sabotage, Chart 3

Pursuing Unrealistic Goals
Projecting Insecurities
Procrastinating
Perfectionism
People-Pleasing
Overworking
Refusing Change
Refusing to Delegate
Rejecting Compliments
Resisting Learning
Resisting New Experiences
Resisting Positive Change
Sabotaging Relationships
Seeking Validation
Self-Doubt
Self-Harm
Setting Unrealistic Expectations
Settling for Less
Shaming Yourself

Royal Template 19

Diving Deep into the Pool of the Mind

Chart 303

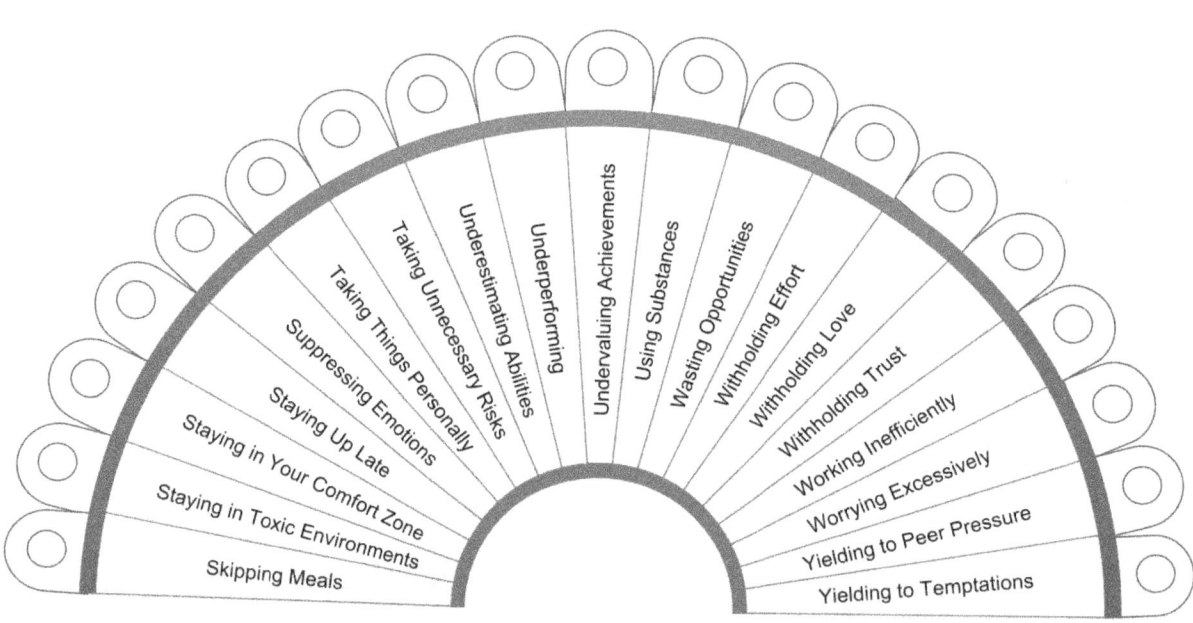

Self-Sabotage, Chart 4

Taking Things Personally
Suppressing Emotions
Staying Up Late
Staying in Your Comfort Zone
Staying in Toxic Environments
Skipping Meals
Taking Unnecessary Risks
Underestimating Abilities
Underperforming
Undervaluing Achievements
Using Substances
Wasting Opportunities
Withholding Effort
Withholding Love
Withholding Trust
Working Inefficiently
Worrying Excessively
Yielding to Peer Pressure
Yielding to Temptations

Royal Template 19

Diving Deep into the Pool of the Mind

Chart 304

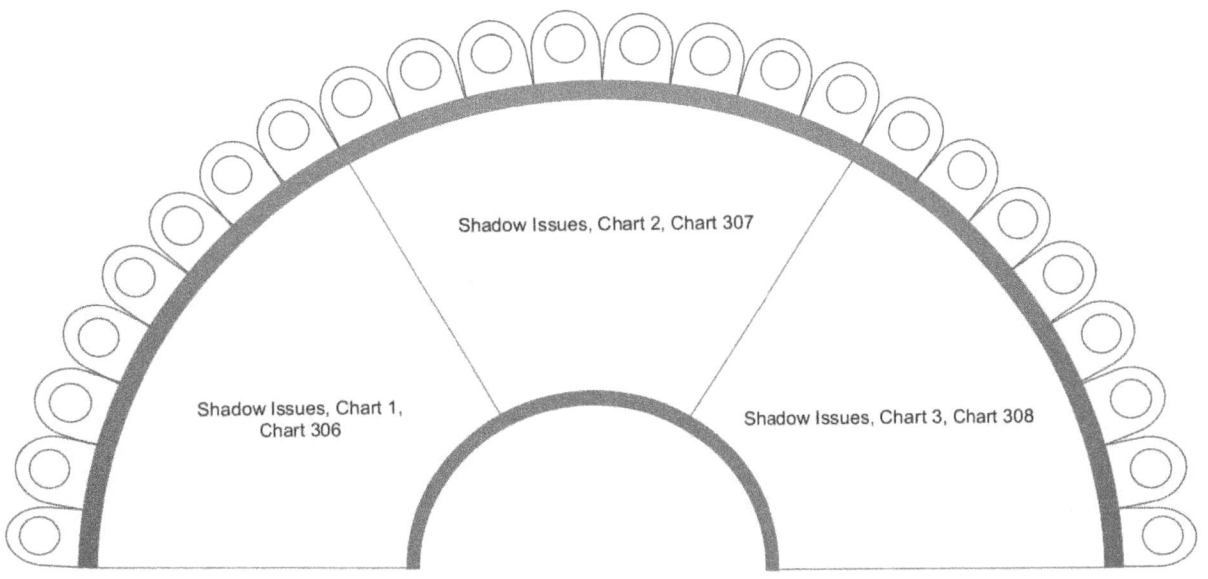

Shadow Issues, Master Chart

Shadow Issues, Chart 2, Chart 307

Shadow Issues, Chart 1, Chart 306

Shadow Issues, Chart 3, Chart 308

Royal Template 3h

Diving Deep into the Pool of the Mind

Chart 305

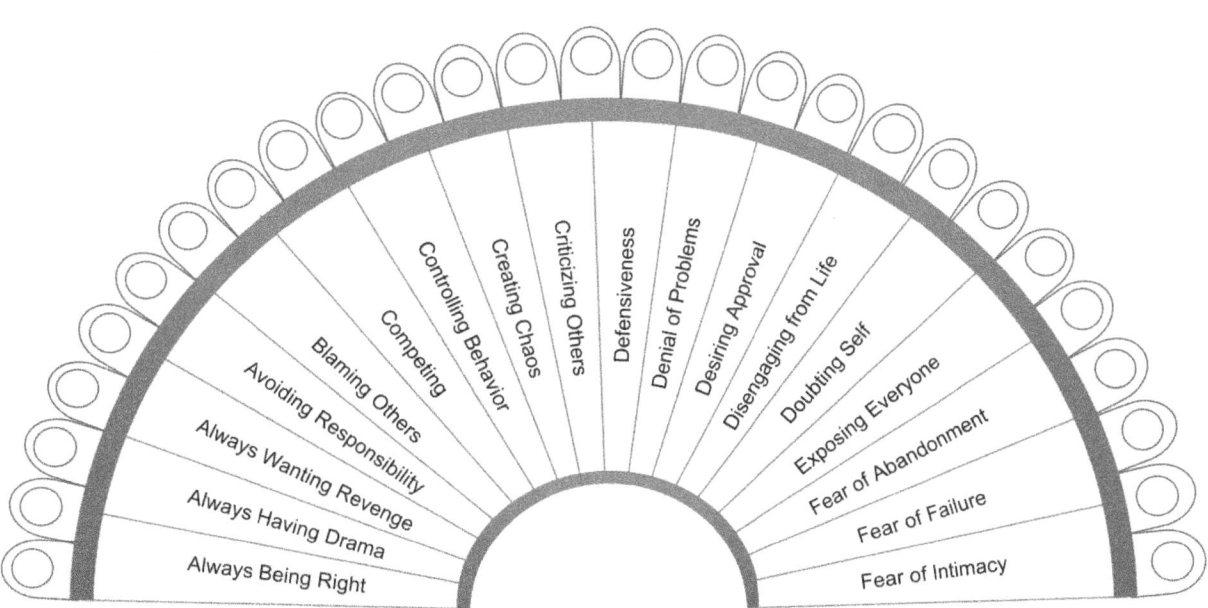

Controlling Behavior
Competing
Blaming Others
Avoiding Responsibility
Always Wanting Revenge
Always Having Drama
Always Being Right
Creating Chaos
Criticizing Others
Defensiveness
Denial of Problems
Desiring Approval
Disengaging from Life
Doubting Self
Exposing Everyone
Fear of Abandonment
Fear of Failure
Fear of Intimacy

Shadow Issues, Chart 1

Royal Template 18

Diving Deep into the Pool of the Mind

Chart 306

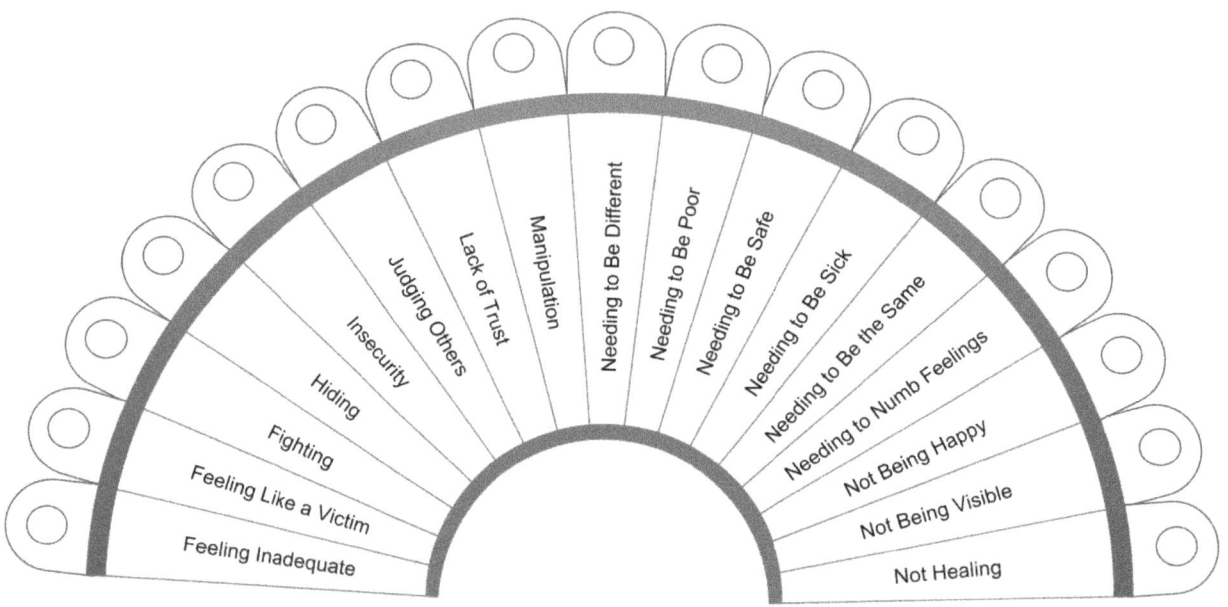

Shadow Issues, Chart 2

Judging Others
Insecurity
Hiding
Fighting
Feeling Like a Victim
Feeling Inadequate
Lack of Trust
Manipulation
Needing to Be Different
Needing to Be Poor
Needing to Be Safe
Needing to Be Sick
Needing to Be the Same
Needing to Numb Feelings
Not Being Happy
Not Being Visible
Not Healing

Royal Template 17

Diving Deep into the Pool of the Mind

Chart 307

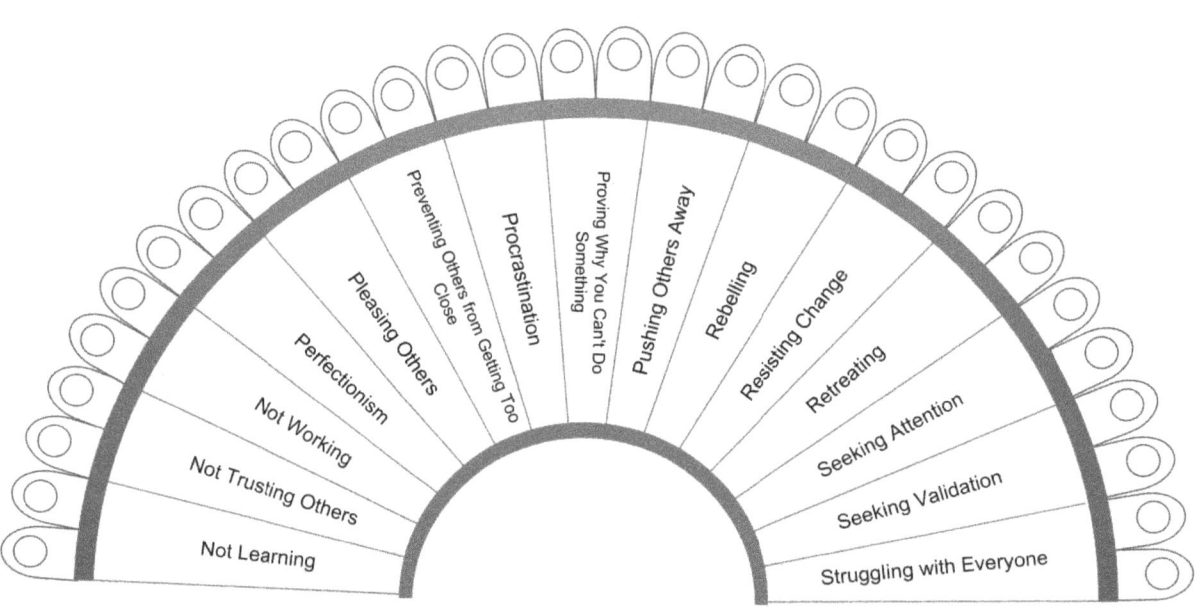

Shadow Issues, Chart 3

Perfectionism
Not Working
Not Trusting Others
Not Learning
Pleasing Others
Preventing Others from Getting Too Close
Procrastination
Proving Why You Can't Do Something
Pushing Others Away
Rebelling
Resisting Change
Retreating
Seeking Attention
Seeking Validation
Struggling with Everyone

Royal Template 15

Diving Deep into the Pool of the Mind

Chart 308

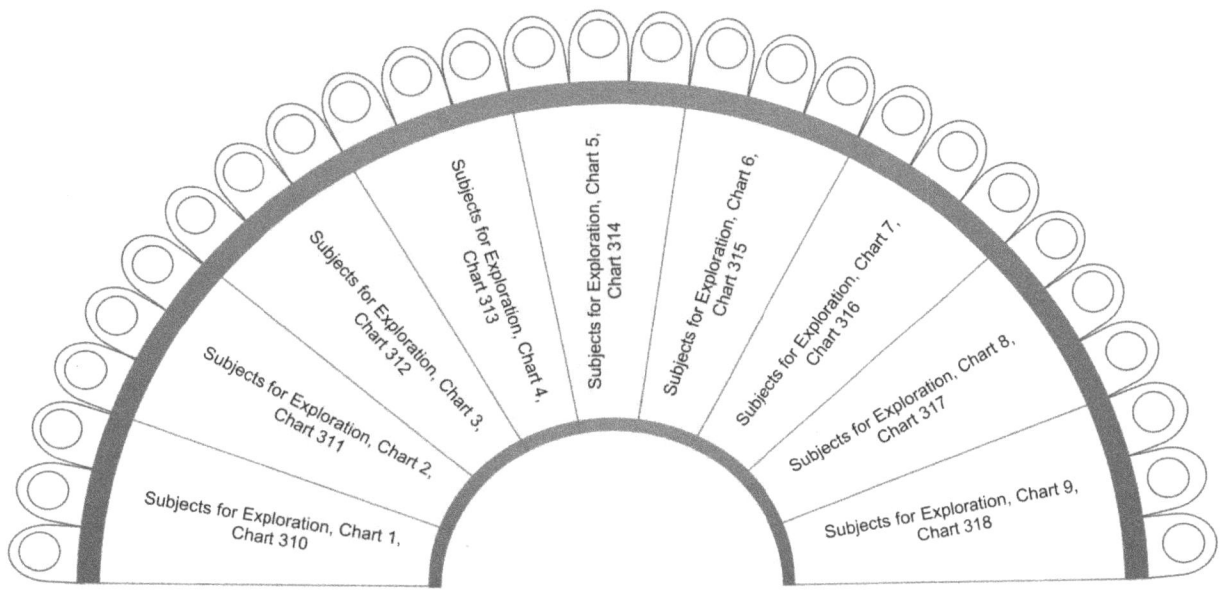

Subjects for Exploration, Master Chart

Subjects for Exploration, Chart 1, Chart 310
Subjects for Exploration, Chart 2, Chart 311
Subjects for Exploration, Chart 3, Chart 312
Subjects for Exploration, Chart 4, Chart 313
Subjects for Exploration, Chart 5, Chart 314
Subjects for Exploration, Chart 6, Chart 315
Subjects for Exploration, Chart 7, Chart 316
Subjects for Exploration, Chart 8, Chart 317
Subjects for Exploration, Chart 9, Chart 318

Royal Template 9

Diving Deep into the Pool of the Mind

Chart 309

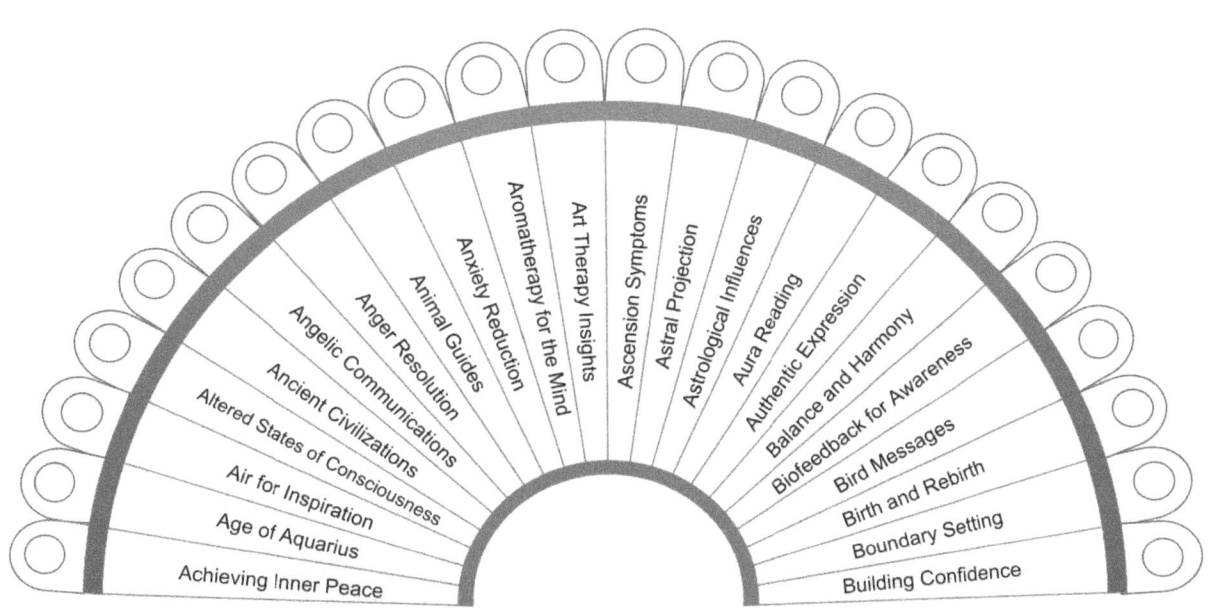

Subjects for Exploration, Chart 1

Achieving Inner Peace
Age of Aquarius
Air for Inspiration
Altered States of Consciousness
Ancient Civilizations
Angelic Communications
Anger Resolution
Animal Guides
Anxiety Reduction
Aromatherapy for the Mind
Art Therapy Insights
Ascension Symptoms
Astral Projection
Astrological Influences
Aura Reading
Authentic Expression
Balance and Harmony
Biofeedback for Awareness
Bird Messages
Birth and Rebirth
Boundary Setting
Building Confidence

Royal Template 22

Diving Deep into the Pool of the Mind

Chart 310

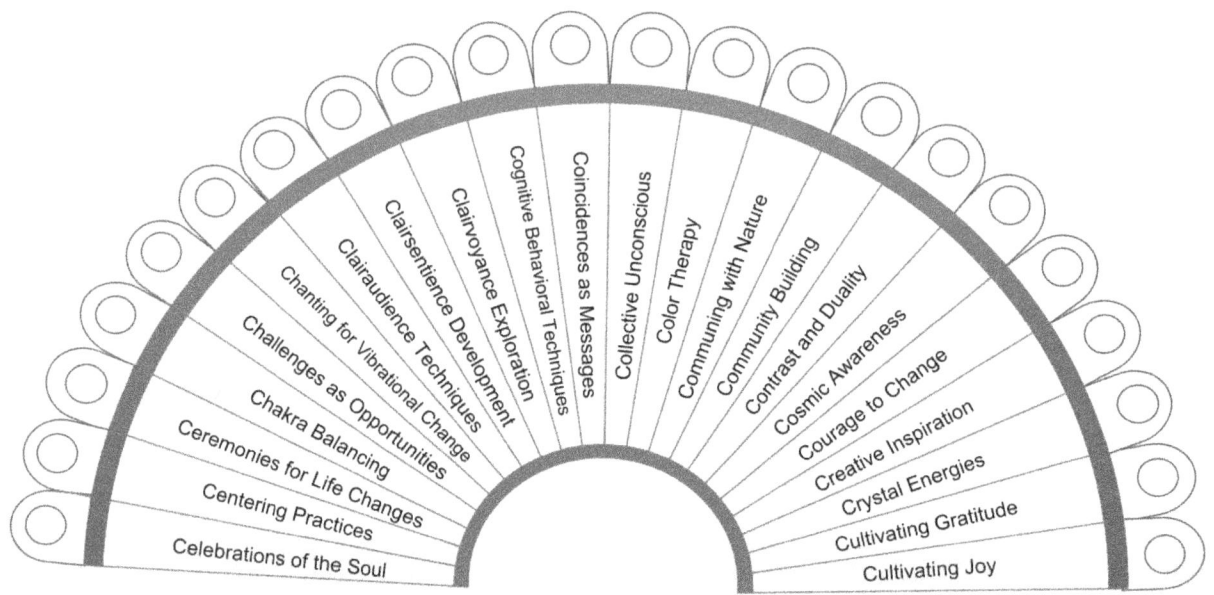

Subjects for Exploration, Chart 2

Celebrations of the Soul
Centering Practices
Ceremonies for Life Changes
Chakra Balancing
Challenges as Opportunities
Chanting for Vibrational Change
Clairaudience Techniques
Clairsentience Development
Clairvoyance Exploration
Cognitive Behavioral Techniques
Coincidences as Messages
Collective Unconscious
Color Therapy
Communing with Nature
Community Building
Contrast and Duality
Cosmic Awareness
Courage to Change
Creative Inspiration
Crystal Energies
Cultivating Gratitude
Cultivating Joy

Royal Template 22

Diving Deep into the Pool of the Mind

Chart 311

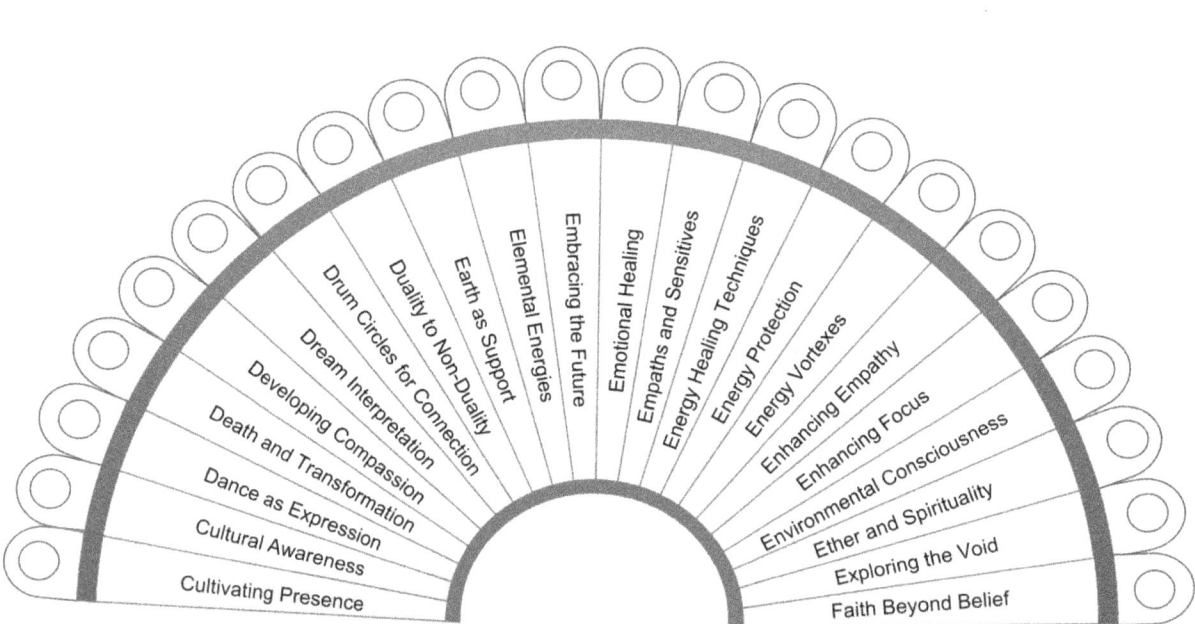

Subjects for Exploration, Chart 3

Cultivating Presence
Cultural Awareness
Dance as Expression
Death and Transformation
Developing Compassion
Dream Interpretation
Drum Circles for Connection
Duality to Non-Duality
Earth as Support
Elemental Energies
Embracing the Future
Emotional Healing
Empaths and Sensitives
Energy Healing Techniques
Energy Protection
Energy Vortexes
Enhancing Empathy
Enhancing Focus
Environmental Consciousness
Ether and Spirituality
Exploring the Void
Faith Beyond Belief

Royal Template 22

Diving Deep into the Pool of the Mind

Chart 312

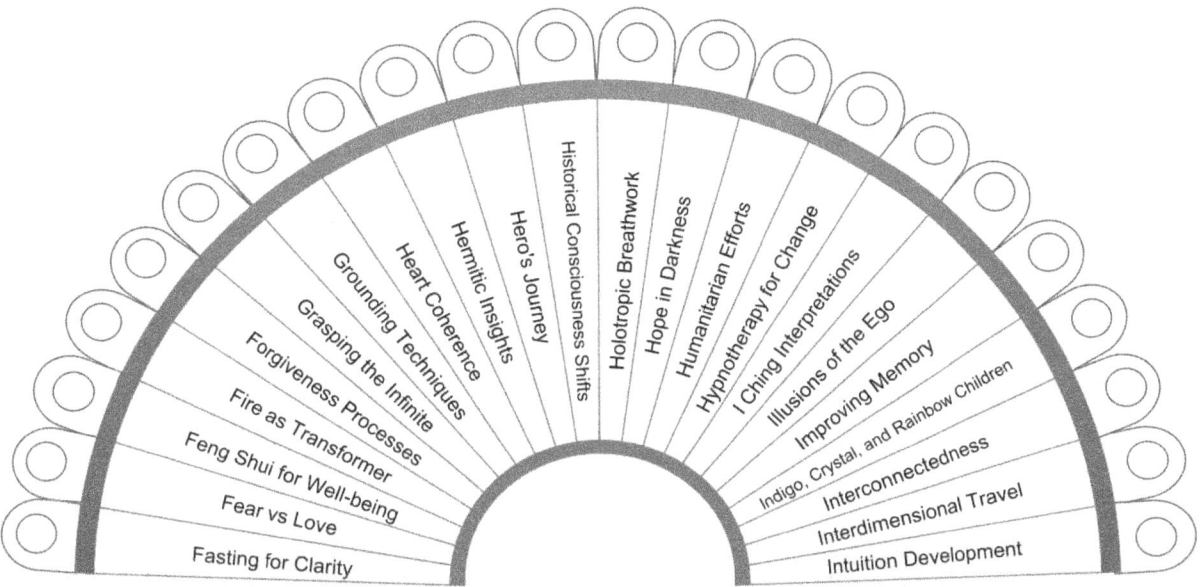

Subjects for Exploration, Chart 4

Historical Consciousness Shifts
Hero's Journey
Hermitic Insights
Heart Coherence
Grounding Techniques
Grasping the Infinite
Forgiveness Processes
Fire as Transformer
Feng Shui for Well-being
Fear vs Love
Fasting for Clarity
Holotropic Breathwork
Hope in Darkness
Humanitarian Efforts
Hypnotherapy for Change
I Ching Interpretations
Illusions of the Ego
Improving Memory
Indigo, Crystal, and Rainbow Children
Interconnectedness
Interdimensional Travel
Intuition Development

Royal Template 22

Diving Deep into the Pool of the Mind

Chart 313

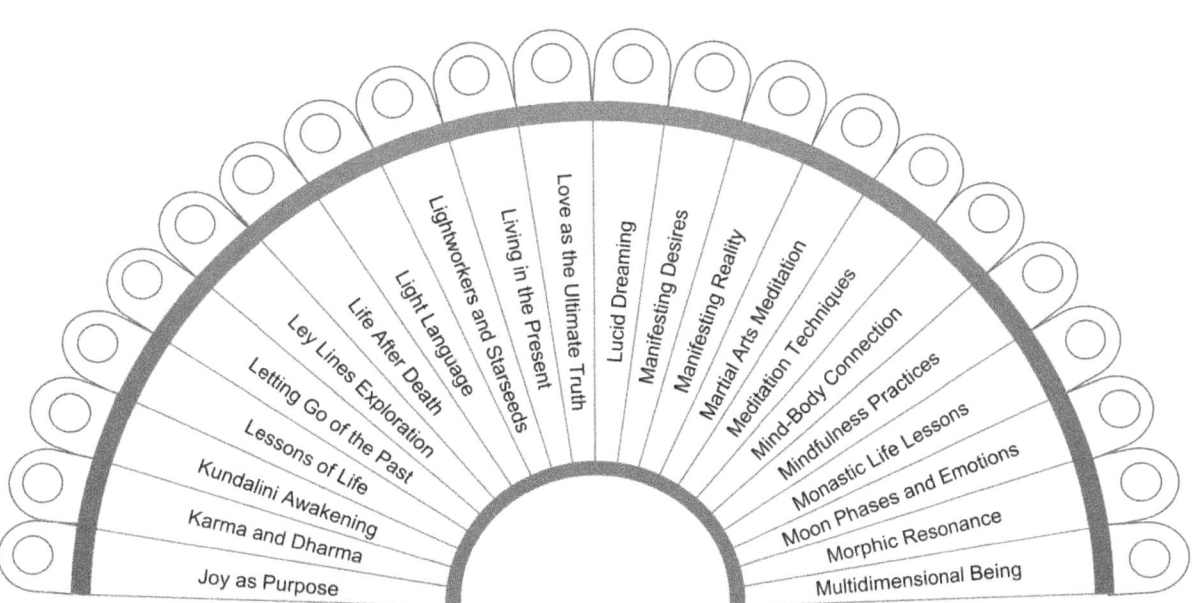

Subjects for Exploration, Chart 5

Love as the Ultimate Truth
Living in the Present
Lightworkers and Starseeds
Light Language
Life After Death
Ley Lines Exploration
Letting Go of the Past
Lessons of Life
Kundalini Awakening
Karma and Dharma
Joy as Purpose
Lucid Dreaming
Manifesting Desires
Manifesting Reality
Martial Arts Meditation
Meditation Techniques
Mind-Body Connection
Mindfulness Practices
Monastic Life Lessons
Moon Phases and Emotions
Morphic Resonance
Multidimensional Being

Royal Template 22

Diving Deep into the Pool of the Mind

Chart 314

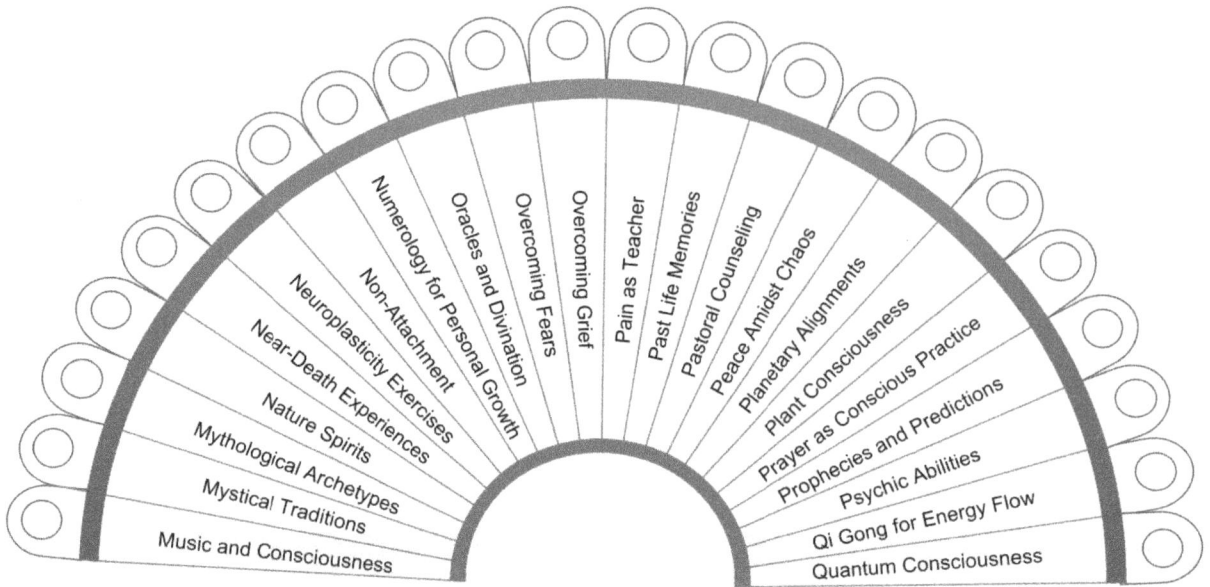

Subjects for Exploration, Chart 6

The chart displays the following subjects (reading around the fan):

- Music and Consciousness
- Mystical Traditions
- Mythological Archetypes
- Nature Spirits
- Near-Death Experiences
- Neuroplasticity Exercises
- Non-Attachment
- Numerology for Personal Growth
- Oracles and Divination
- Overcoming Fears
- Overcoming Grief
- Pain as Teacher
- Past Life Memories
- Pastoral Counseling
- Peace Amidst Chaos
- Planetary Alignments
- Plant Consciousness
- Prayer as Conscious Practice
- Prophecies and Predictions
- Psychic Abilities
- Qi Gong for Energy Flow
- Quantum Consciousness

Royal Template 22

Diving Deep into the Pool of the Mind

Chart 315

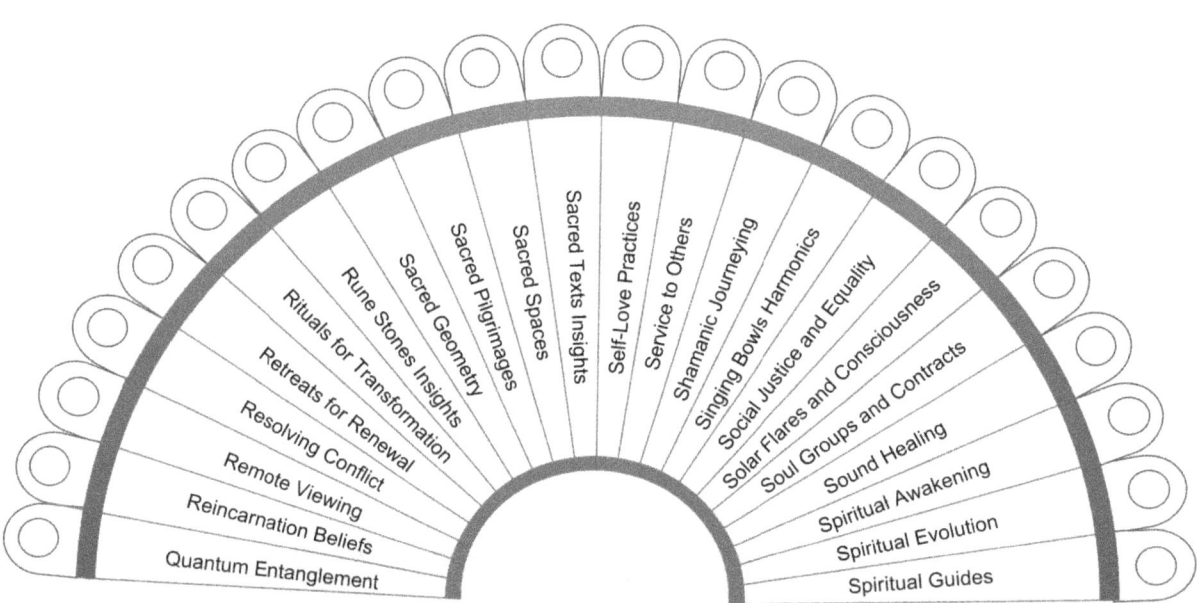

Subjects for Exploration, Chart 7

The chart displays the following subjects (reading around the fan):

- Quantum Entanglement
- Reincarnation Beliefs
- Remote Viewing
- Resolving Conflict
- Retreats for Renewal
- Rituals for Transformation
- Rune Stones Insights
- Sacred Geometry
- Sacred Pilgrimages
- Sacred Spaces
- Sacred Texts Insights
- Self-Love Practices
- Service to Others
- Shamanic Journeying
- Singing Bowls Harmonics
- Social Justice and Equality
- Solar Flares and Consciousness
- Soul Groups and Contracts
- Sound Healing
- Spiritual Awakening
- Spiritual Evolution
- Spiritual Guides

Royal Template 22

Diving Deep into the Pool of the Mind

Chart 316

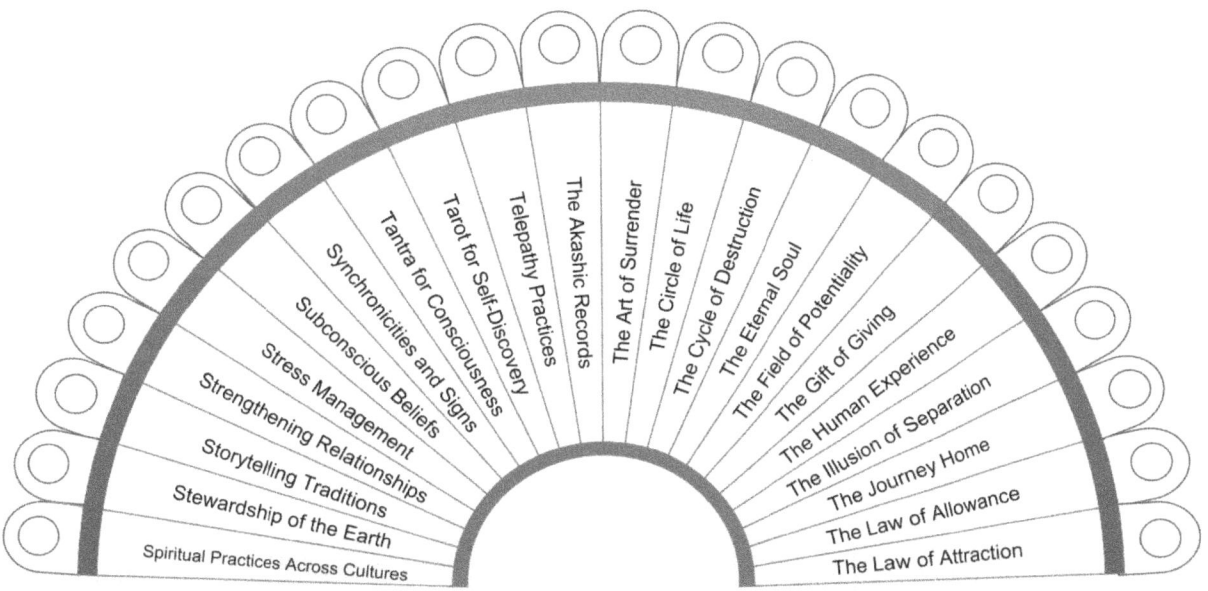

Subjects for Exploration, Chart 8

The Art of Surrender
The Circle of Life
The Cycle of Destruction
The Eternal Soul
The Field of Potentiality
The Gift of Giving
The Human Experience
The Illusion of Separation
The Journey Home
The Law of Allowance
The Law of Attraction

The Akashic Records
Telepathy Practices
Tarot for Self-Discovery
Tantra for Consciousness
Synchronicities and Signs
Subconscious Beliefs
Stress Management
Strengthening Relationships
Storytelling Traditions
Stewardship of the Earth
Spiritual Practices Across Cultures

Royal Template 22

Diving Deep into the Pool of the Mind

Chart 317

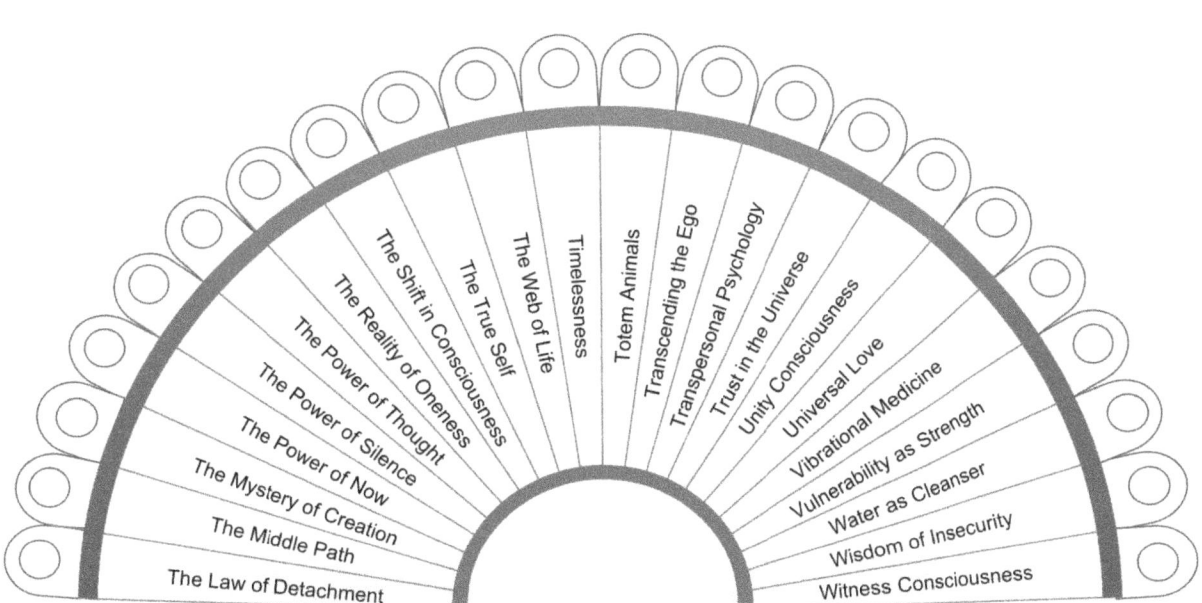

Subjects for Exploration, Chart 9

The Shift in Consciousness
The Reality of Oneness
The Power of Thought
The Power of Silence
The Power of Now
The Mystery of Creation
The Middle Path
The Law of Detachment
The True Self
The Web of Life
Timelessness
Totem Animals
Transcending the Ego
Transpersonal Psychology
Trust in the Universe
Unity Consciousness
Universal Love
Vibrational Medicine
Vulnerability as Strength
Water as Cleanser
Wisdom of Insecurity
Witness Consciousness

Royal Template 22

Diving Deep into the Pool of the Mind

Chart 318

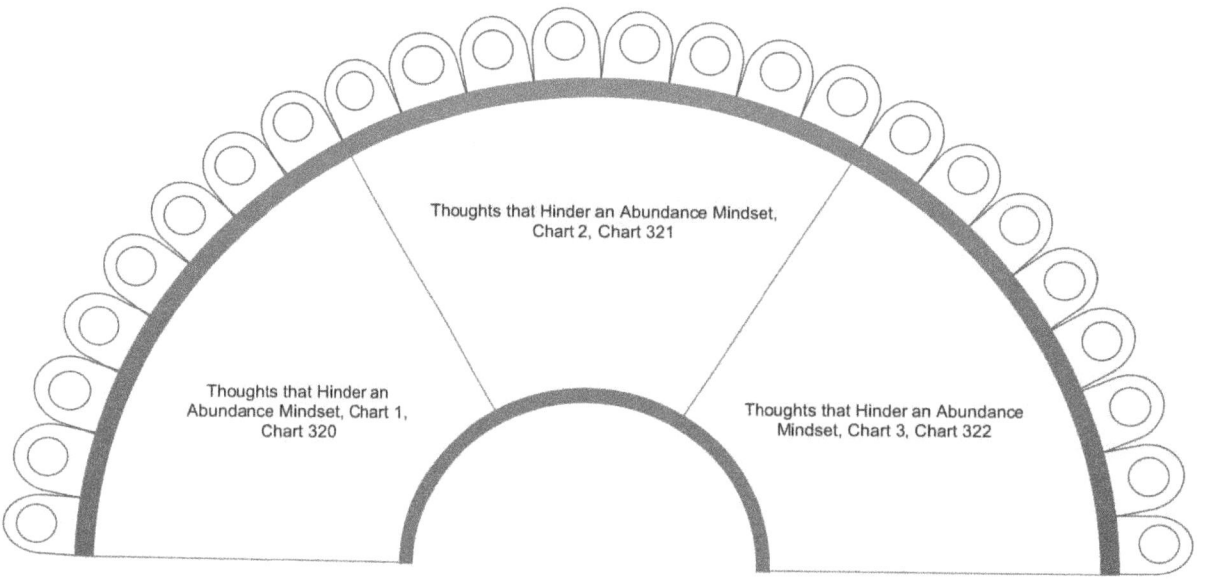

Thoughts that Hinder an Abundance Mindset, Master Chart

Thoughts that Hinder an Abundance Mindset, Chart 2, Chart 321

Thoughts that Hinder an Abundance Mindset, Chart 1, Chart 320

Thoughts that Hinder an Abundance Mindset, Chart 3, Chart 322

Royal Template 3h

Diving Deep into the Pool of the Mind

Chart 319

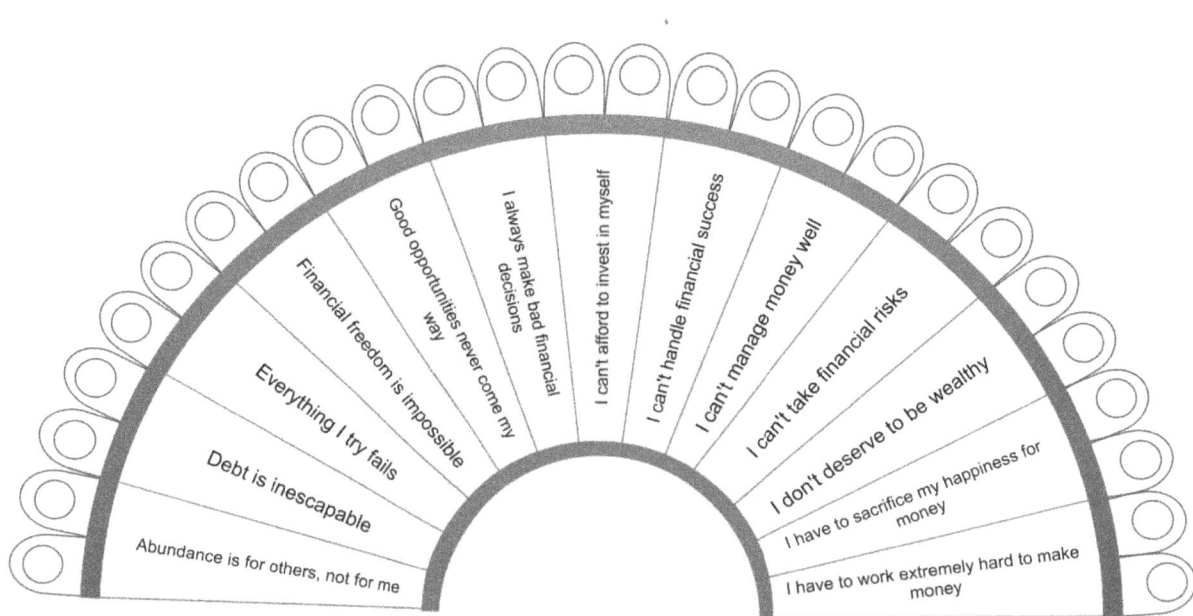

Good opportunities never come my way

I always make bad financial decisions

Financial freedom is impossible

I can't afford to invest in myself

I can't handle financial success

I can't manage money well

Everything I try fails

I can't take financial risks

Debt is inescapable

I don't deserve to be wealthy

I have to sacrifice my happiness for money

Abundance is for others, not for me

I have to work extremely hard to make money

Thoughts that Hinder an Abundance Mindset, Chart 1

Royal Template 13

Diving Deep into the Pool of the Mind

Chart 320

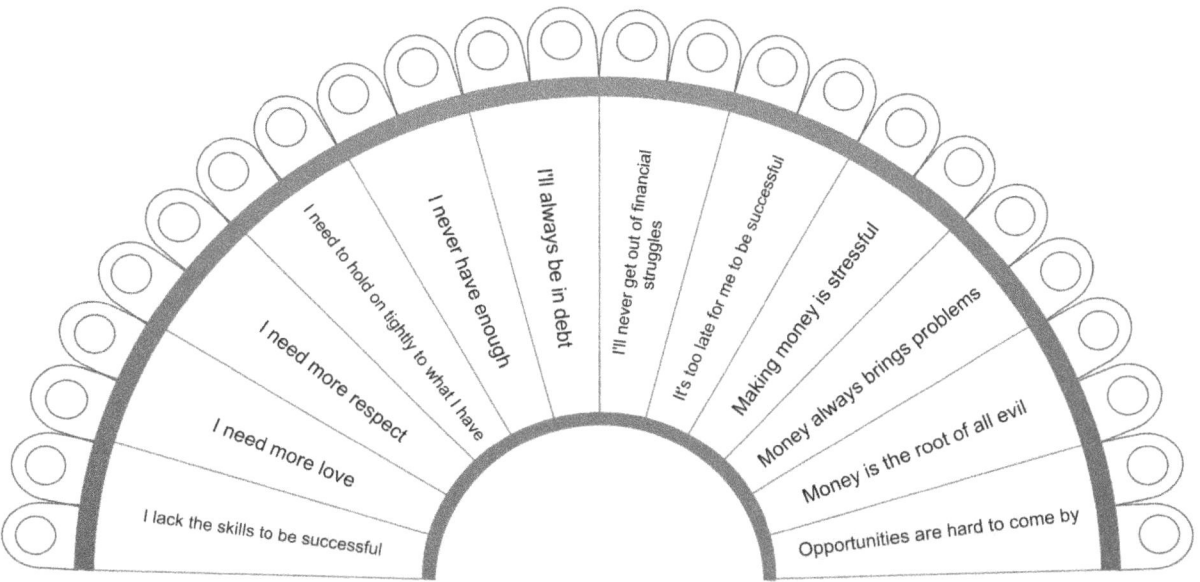

Thoughts that Hinder an Abundance Mindset, Chart 2

The chart contains the following labels (read around the fan):

- I need to hold on tightly to what I have
- I need more respect
- I need more love
- I lack the skills to be successful
- I never have enough
- I'll always be in debt
- I'll never get out of financial struggles
- It's too late for me to be successful
- Making money is stressful
- Money always brings problems
- Money is the root of all evil
- Opportunities are hard to come by

Royal Template 12

Diving Deep into the Pool of the Mind

Chart 321

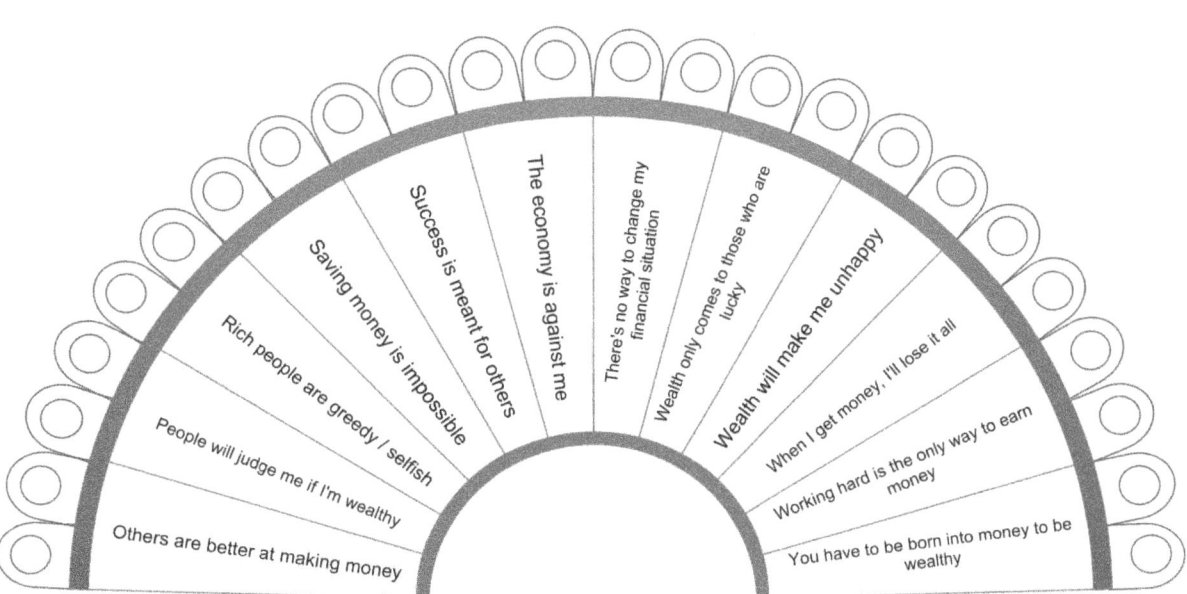

Thoughts that Hinder an Abundance Mindset, Chart 3

The chart contains the following labels (read around the fan):

- Others are better at making money
- People will judge me if I'm wealthy
- Rich people are greedy / selfish
- Saving money is impossible
- Success is meant for others
- The economy is against me
- There's no way to change my financial situation
- Wealth only comes to those who are lucky
- Wealth will make me unhappy
- When I get money, I'll lose it all
- Working hard is the only way to earn money
- You have to be born into money to be wealthy

Royal Template 12

Diving Deep into the Pool of the Mind

Chart 322

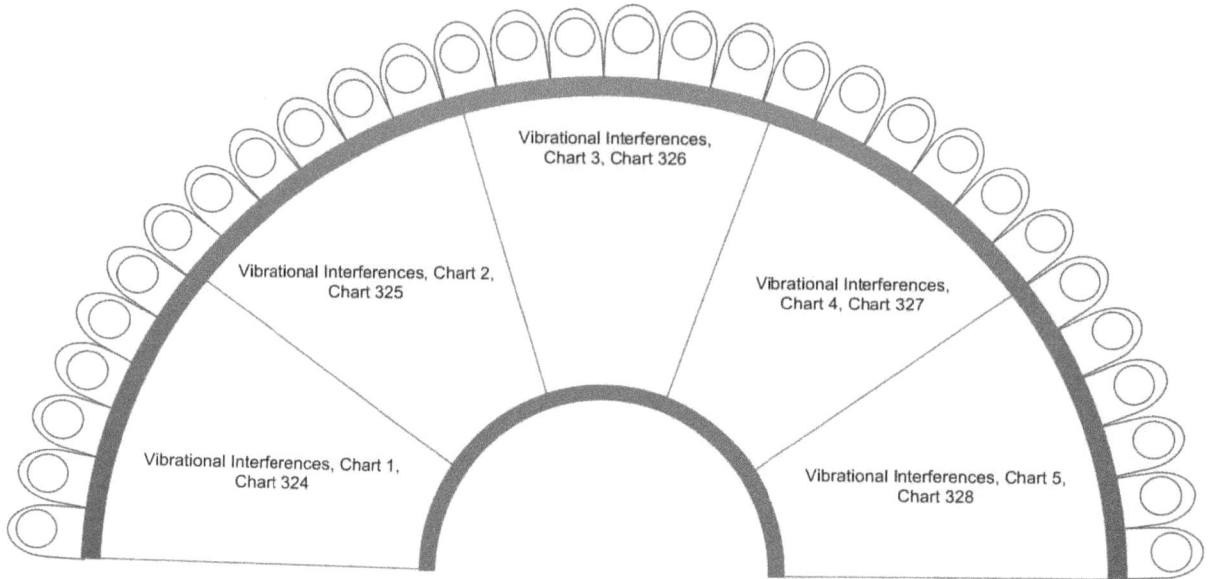

Vibrational Interferences, Master Chart

Vibrational Interferences, Chart 2, Chart 325

Vibrational Interferences, Chart 3, Chart 326

Vibrational Interferences, Chart 4, Chart 327

Vibrational Interferences, Chart 1, Chart 324

Vibrational Interferences, Chart 5, Chart 328

Royal Template 5h

Diving Deep into the Pool of the Mind

Chart 323

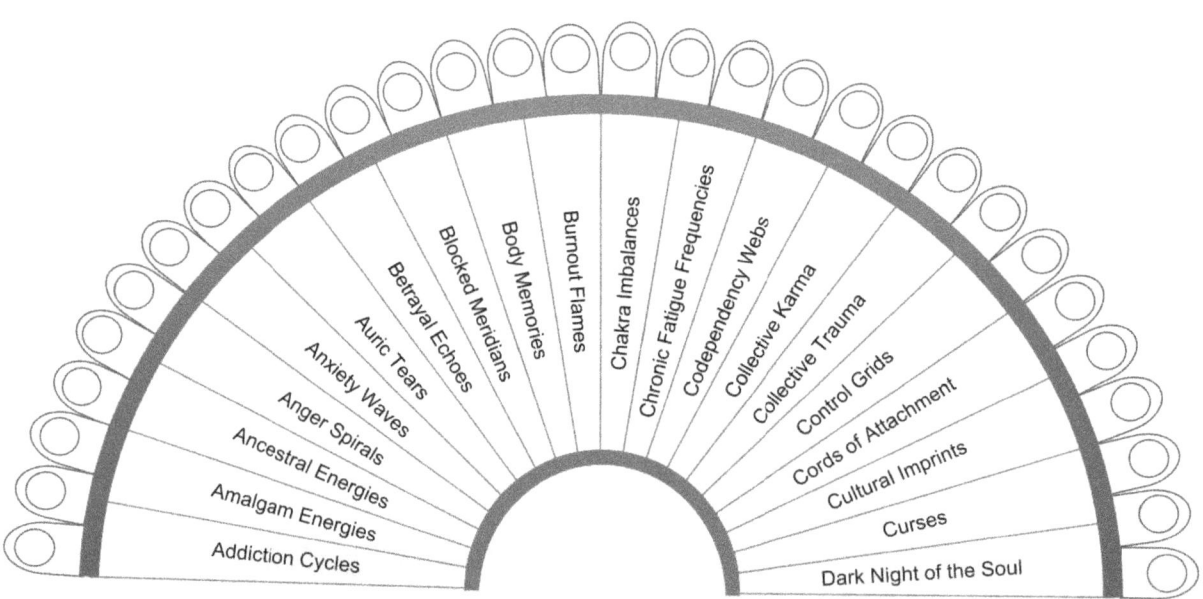

Addiction Cycles
Amalgam Energies
Ancestral Energies
Anger Spirals
Anxiety Waves
Auric Tears
Betrayal Echoes
Blocked Meridians
Body Memories
Burnout Flames
Chakra Imbalances
Chronic Fatigue Frequencies
Codependency Webs
Collective Karma
Collective Trauma
Control Grids
Cords of Attachment
Cultural Imprints
Curses
Dark Night of the Soul

Vibrational Interferences, Chart 1

Royal Template 20

Diving Deep into the Pool of the Mind

Chart 324

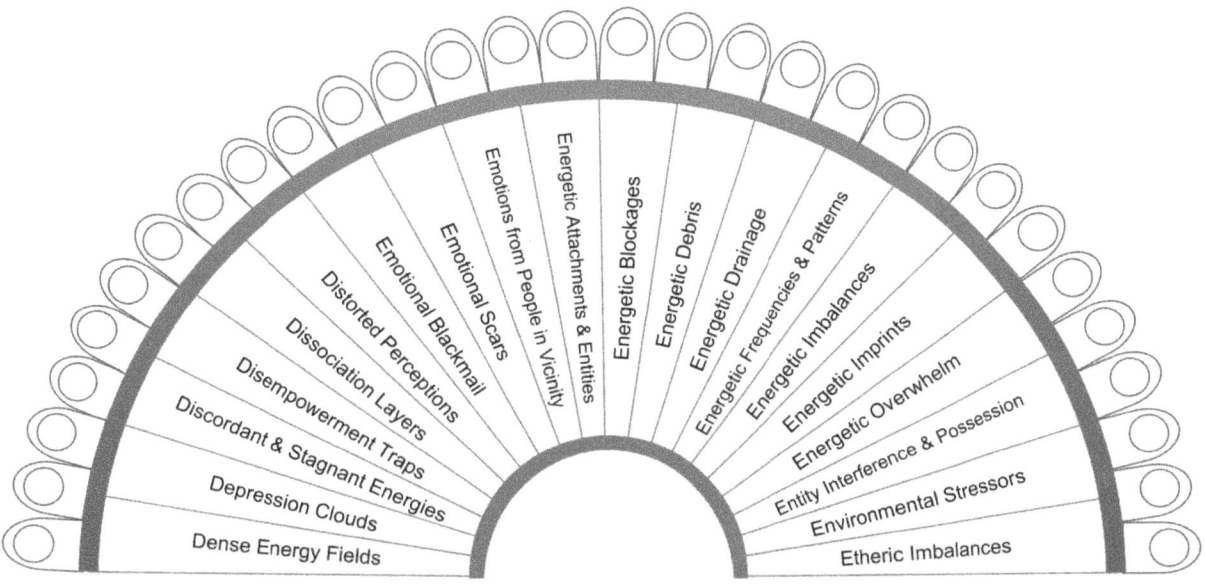

Vibrational Interferences, Chart 2

Labels (left to right):
- Dense Energy Fields
- Depression Clouds
- Discordant & Stagnant Energies
- Disempowerment Traps
- Dissociation Layers
- Distorted Perceptions
- Emotional Blackmail
- Emotional Scars
- Emotions from People in Vicinity
- Energetic Attachments & Entities
- Energetic Blockages
- Energetic Debris
- Energetic Drainage
- Energetic Frequencies & Patterns
- Energetic Imbalances
- Energetic Imprints
- Energetic Overwhelm
- Entity Interference & Possession
- Environmental Stressors
- Etheric Imbalances

Royal Template 20

Diving Deep into the Pool of the Mind

Chart 325

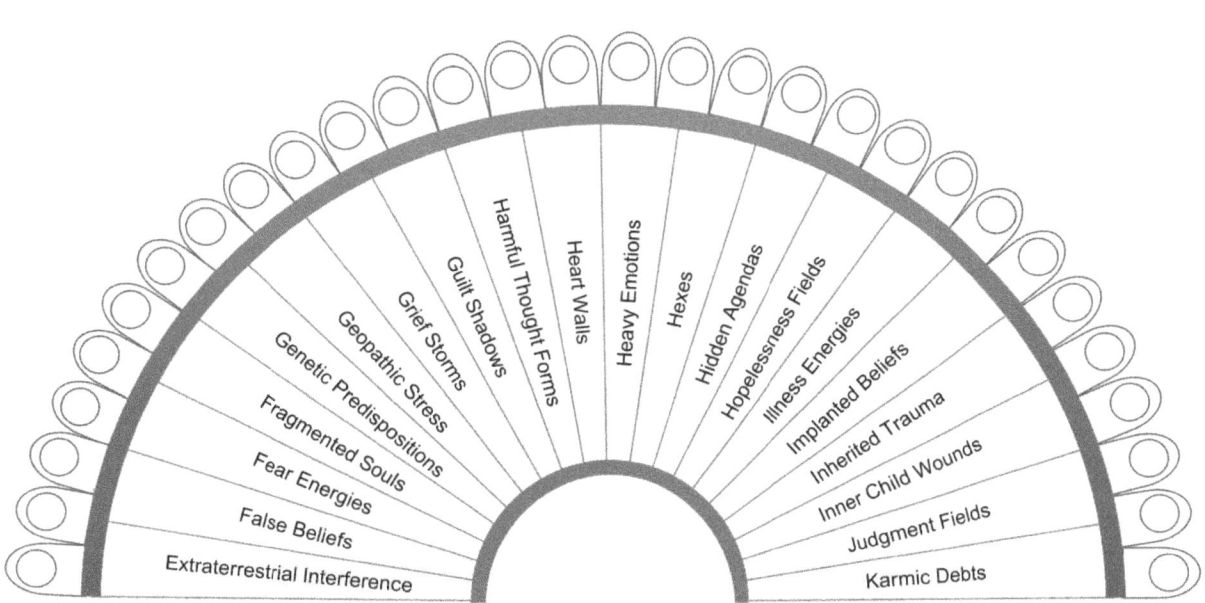

Vibrational Interferences, Chart 3

Labels (left to right):
- Extraterrestrial Interference
- False Beliefs
- Fear Energies
- Fragmented Souls
- Genetic Predispositions
- Geopathic Stress
- Grief Storms
- Guilt Shadows
- Harmful Thought Forms
- Heart Walls
- Heavy Emotions
- Hexes
- Hidden Agendas
- Hopelessness Fields
- Illness Energies
- Implanted Beliefs
- Inherited Trauma
- Inner Child Wounds
- Judgment Fields
- Karmic Debts

Royal Template 20

Diving Deep into the Pool of the Mind

Chart 326

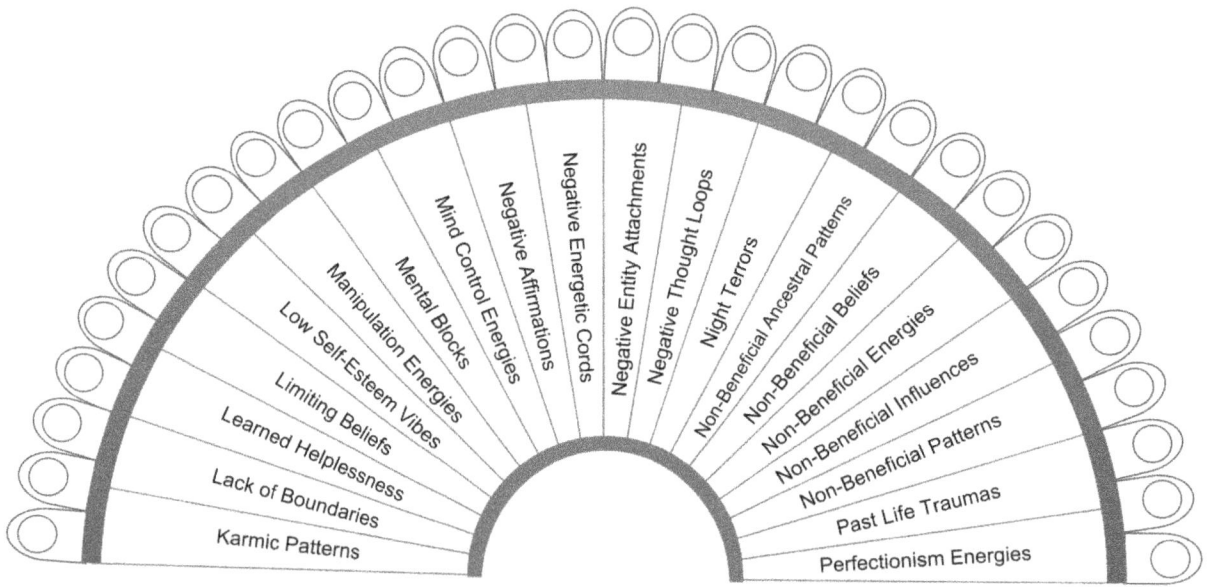

Vibrational Interferences, Chart 4

Mind Control Energies
Negative Affirmations
Negative Energetic Cords
Negative Entity Attachments
Negative Thought Loops
Night Terrors
Non-Beneficial Ancestral Patterns
Non-Beneficial Beliefs
Non-Beneficial Energies
Non-Beneficial Influences
Non-Beneficial Patterns
Past Life Traumas
Perfectionism Energies
Mental Blocks
Manipulation Energies
Low Self-Esteem Vibes
Limiting Beliefs
Learned Helplessness
Lack of Boundaries
Karmic Patterns

Royal Template 20

Diving Deep into the Pool of the Mind

Chart 327

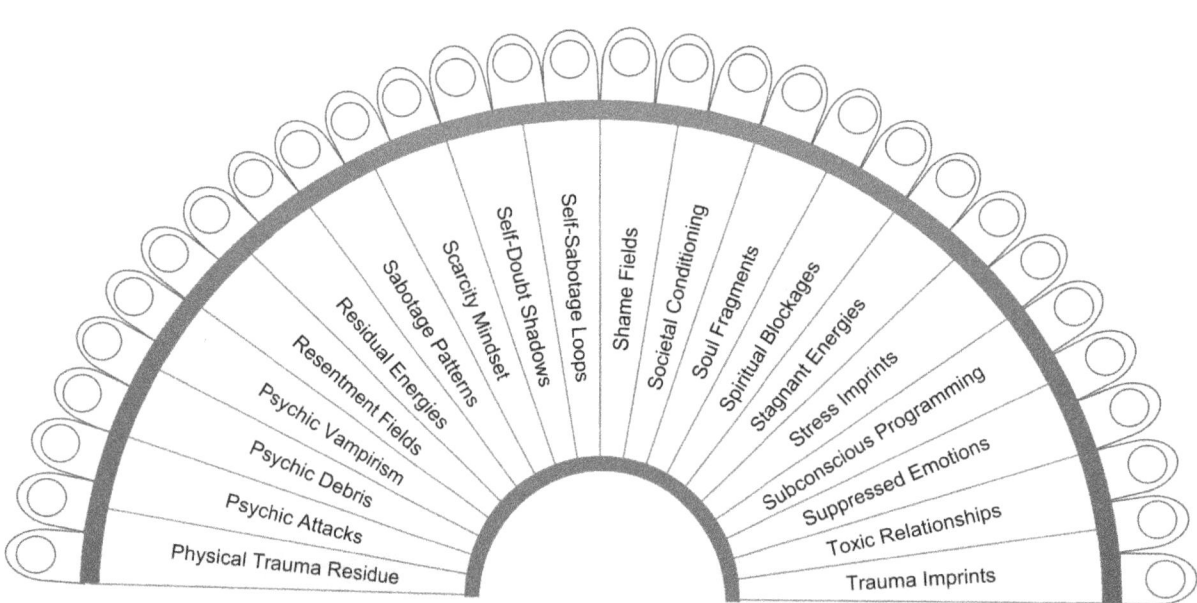

Vibrational Interferences, Chart 5

Sabotage Patterns
Scarcity Mindset
Self-Doubt Shadows
Self-Sabotage Loops
Shame Fields
Societal Conditioning
Soul Fragments
Spiritual Blockages
Stagnant Energies
Stress Imprints
Subconscious Programming
Suppressed Emotions
Toxic Relationships
Trauma Imprints
Residual Energies
Resentment Fields
Psychic Vampirism
Psychic Debris
Psychic Attacks
Physical Trauma Residue

Royal Template 20

Diving Deep into the Pool of the Mind

Chart 328

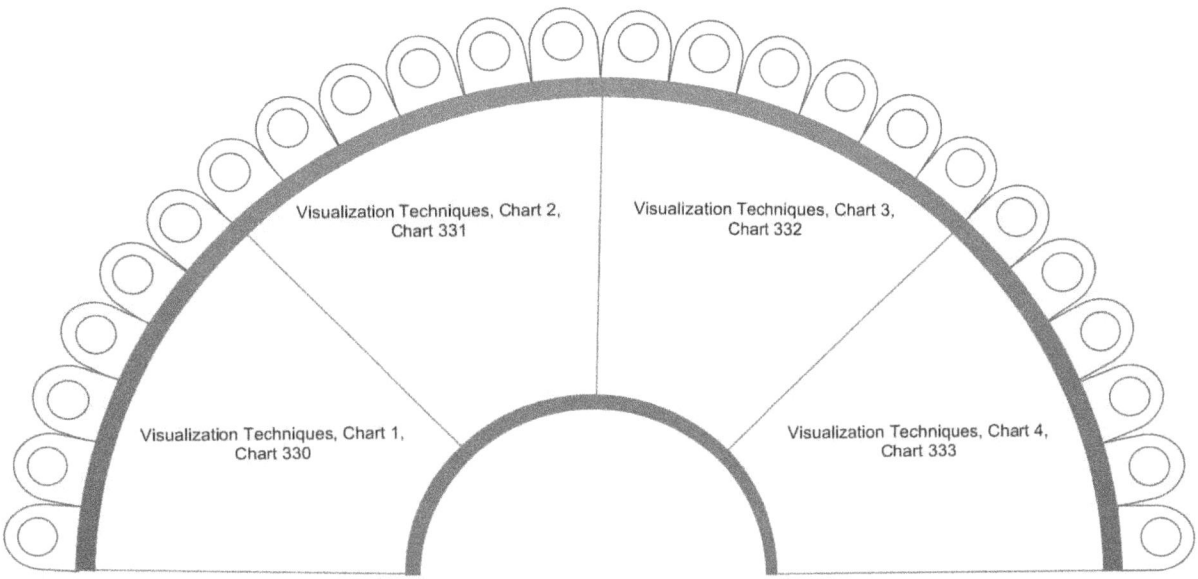

Visualization Techniques, Master Chart

Visualization Techniques, Chart 1, Chart 330
Visualization Techniques, Chart 2, Chart 331
Visualization Techniques, Chart 3, Chart 332
Visualization Techniques, Chart 4, Chart 333

Royal Template 4h

Diving Deep into the Pool of the Mind

Chart 329

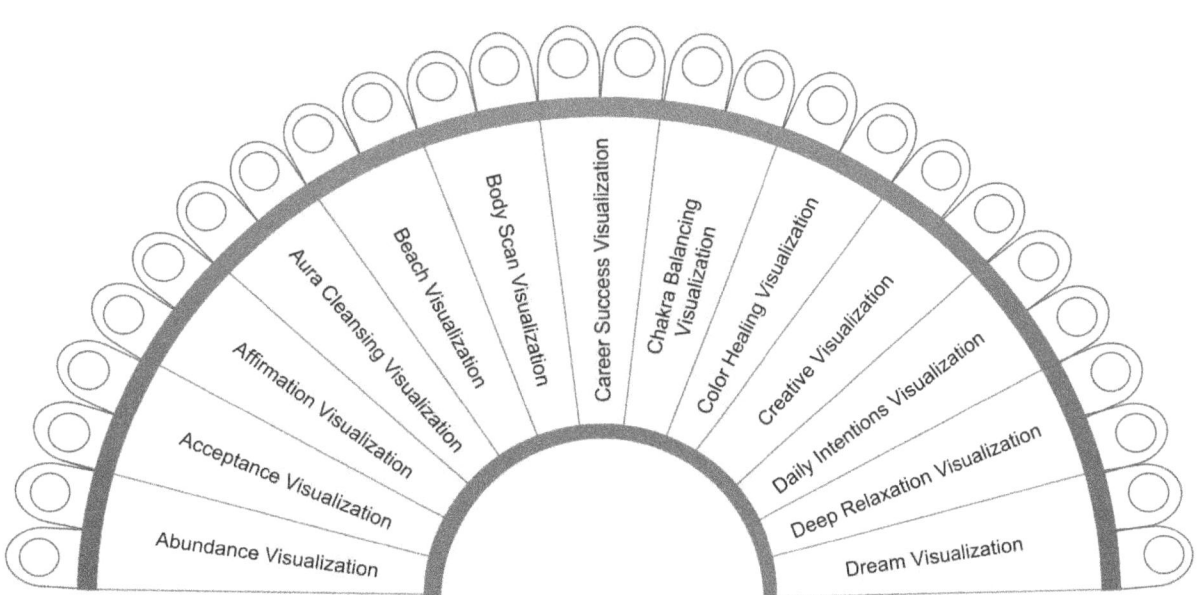

Visualization Techniques, Chart 1

Abundance Visualization
Acceptance Visualization
Affirmation Visualization
Aura Cleansing Visualization
Beach Visualization
Body Scan Visualization
Career Success Visualization
Chakra Balancing Visualization
Color Healing Visualization
Creative Visualization
Daily Intentions Visualization
Deep Relaxation Visualization
Dream Visualization

Royal Template 13

Diving Deep into the Pool of the Mind

Chart 330

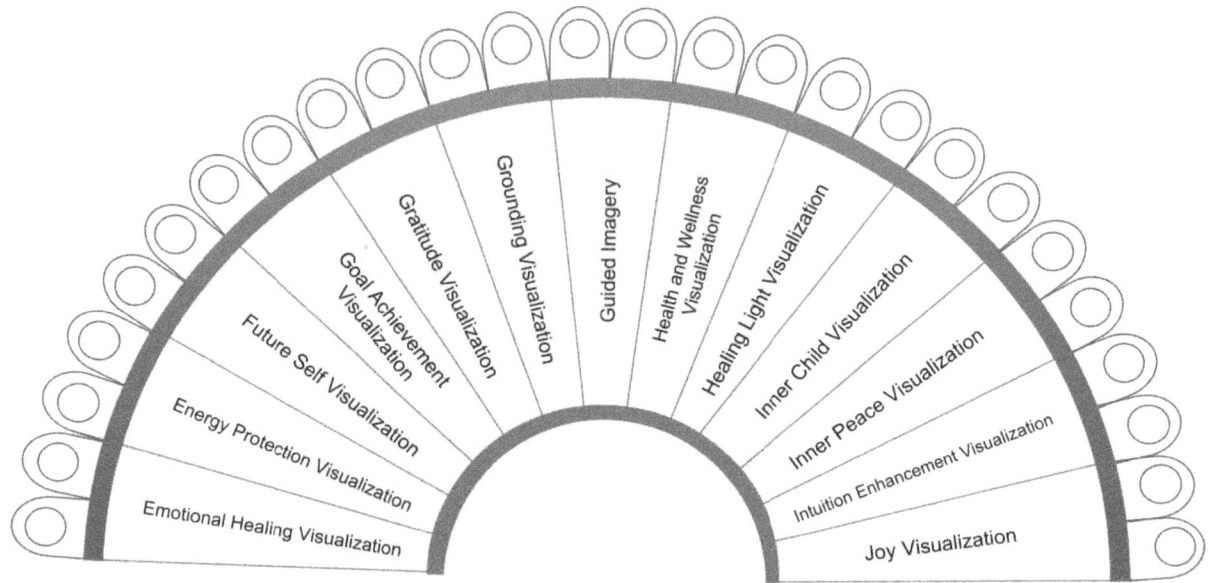

Visualization Techniques, Chart 2

Grounding Visualization
Gratitude Visualization
Goal Achievement Visualization
Future Self Visualization
Energy Protection Visualization
Emotional Healing Visualization
Guided Imagery
Health and Wellness Visualization
Healing Light Visualization
Inner Child Visualization
Inner Peace Visualization
Intuition Enhancement Visualization
Joy Visualization

Royal Template 13

Diving Deep into the Pool of the Mind

Chart 331

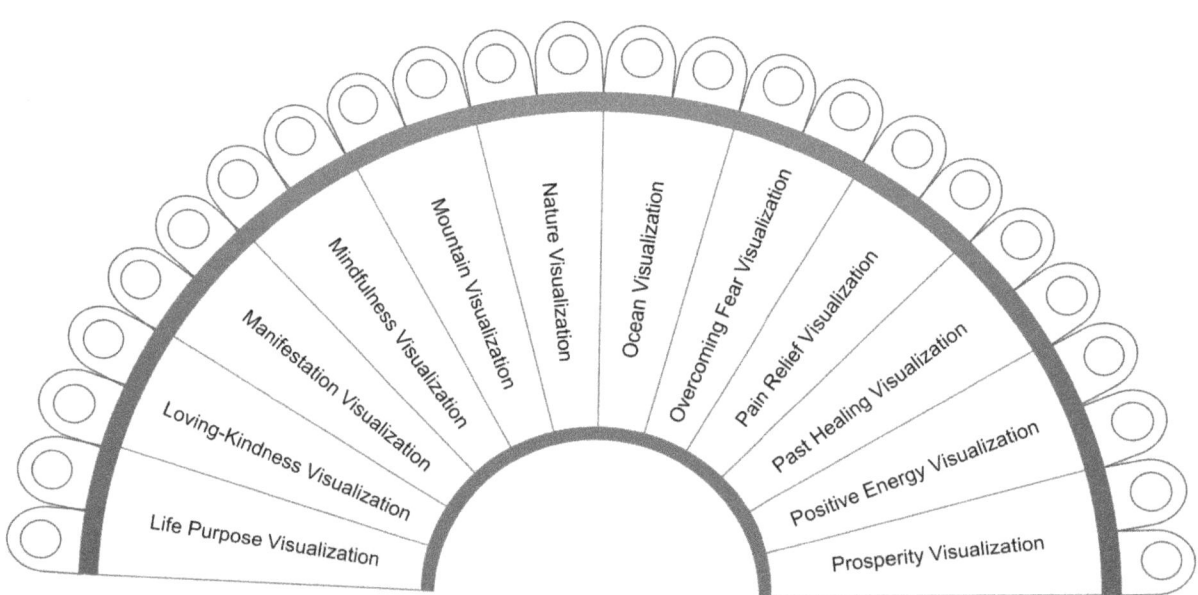

Nature Visualization
Mountain Visualization
Mindfulness Visualization
Manifestation Visualization
Loving-Kindness Visualization
Life Purpose Visualization
Ocean Visualization
Overcoming Fear Visualization
Pain Relief Visualization
Past Healing Visualization
Positive Energy Visualization
Prosperity Visualization

Visualization Techniques, Chart 3

Royal Template 12

Diving Deep into the Pool of the Mind

Chart 332

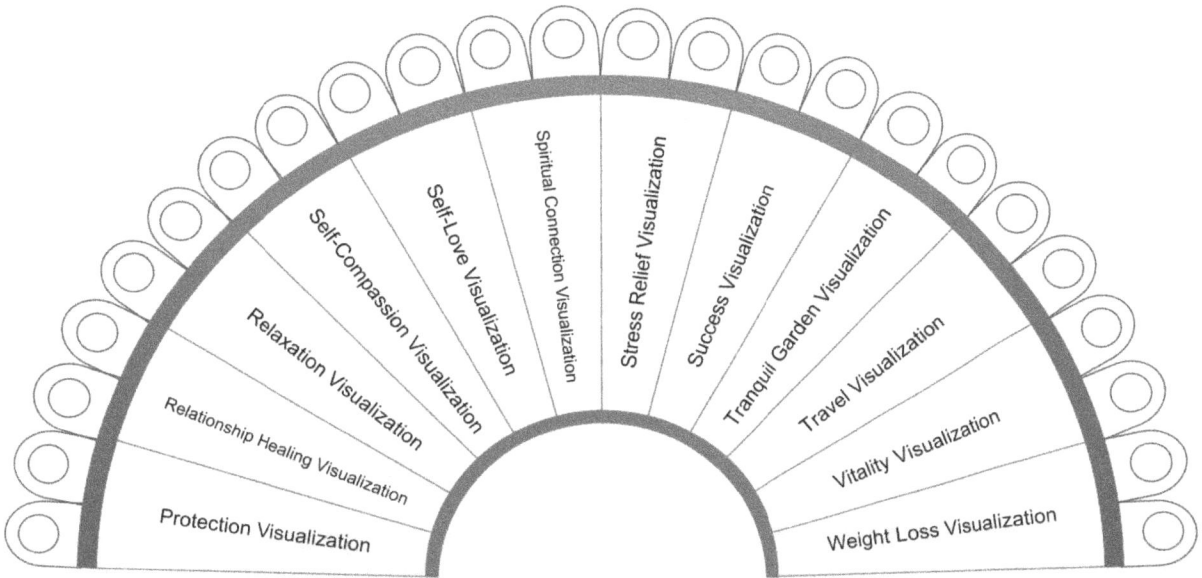

Visualization Techniques, Chart 4

Royal Template 12

Chart 333

Diving Deep into the Pool of the Mind

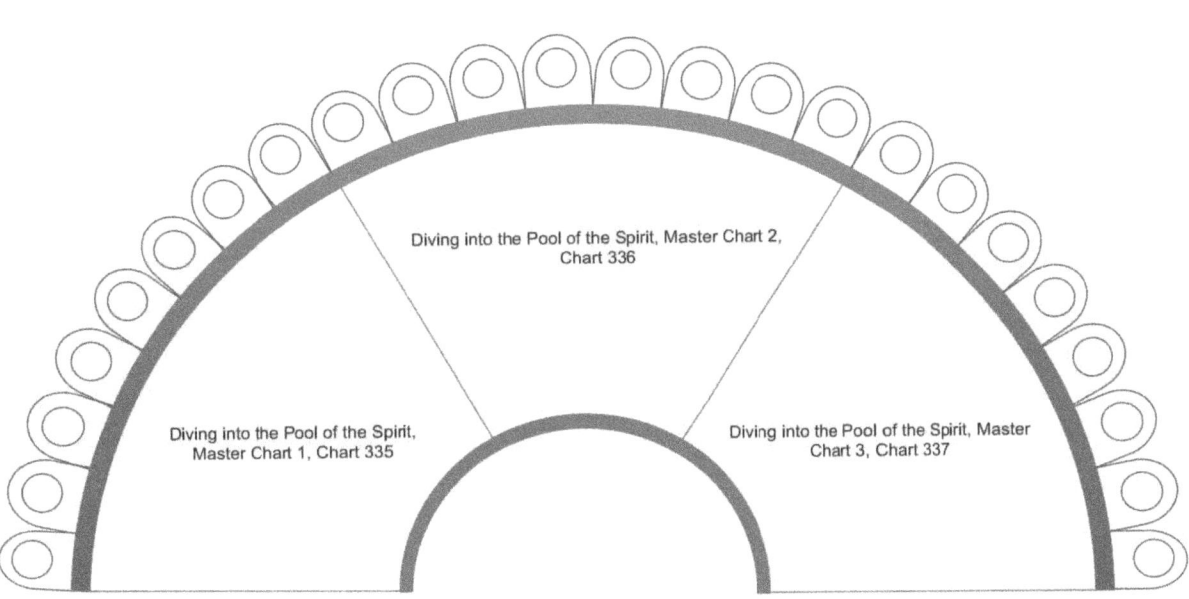

Labels in chart:
- Diving into the Pool of the Spirit, Master Chart 2, Chart 336
- Diving into the Pool of the Spirit, Master Chart 1, Chart 335
- Diving into the Pool of the Spirit, Master Chart 3, Chart 337

Diving into the Pool of the Spirit

Royal Template 3h

Diving Deep into the Pool of the Mind

Chart 334

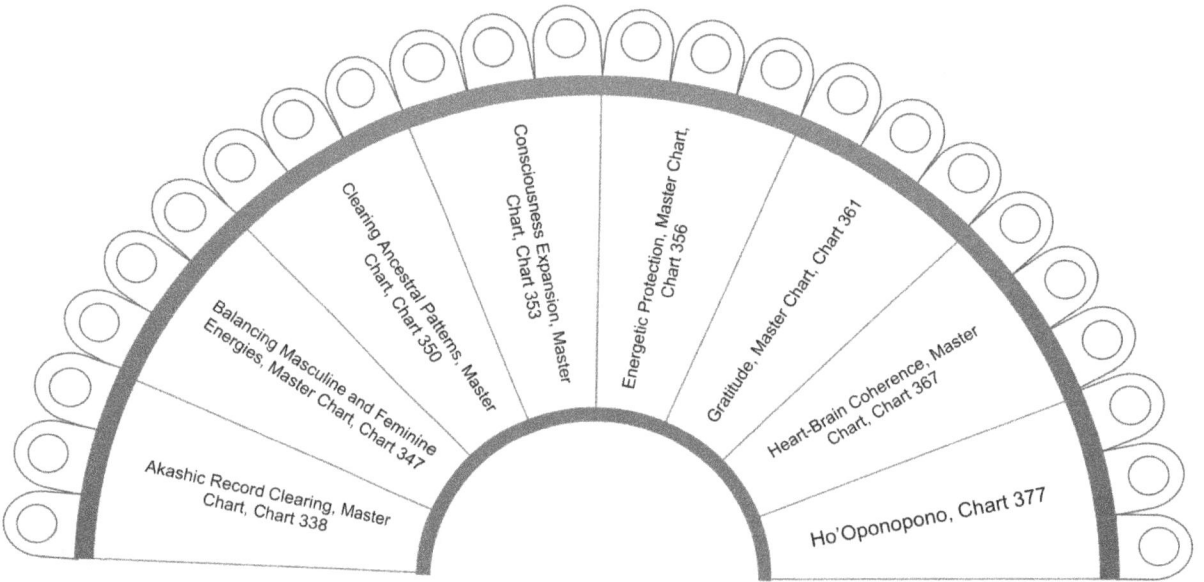

Diving into the Pool of the Spirit, Master Chart 1

The following labels appear around the fan chart:

- Akashic Record Clearing, Master Chart, Chart 338
- Balancing Masculine and Feminine Energies, Master Chart, Chart 347
- Clearing Ancestral Patterns, Master Chart, Chart 350
- Consciousness Expansion, Master Chart, Chart 353
- Energetic Protection, Master Chart, Chart 356
- Gratitude, Master Chart, Chart 361
- Heart-Brain Coherence, Master Chart, Chart 367
- Ho'Oponopono, Chart 377

Royal Template 8

Diving Deep into the Pool of the Mind

Chart 335

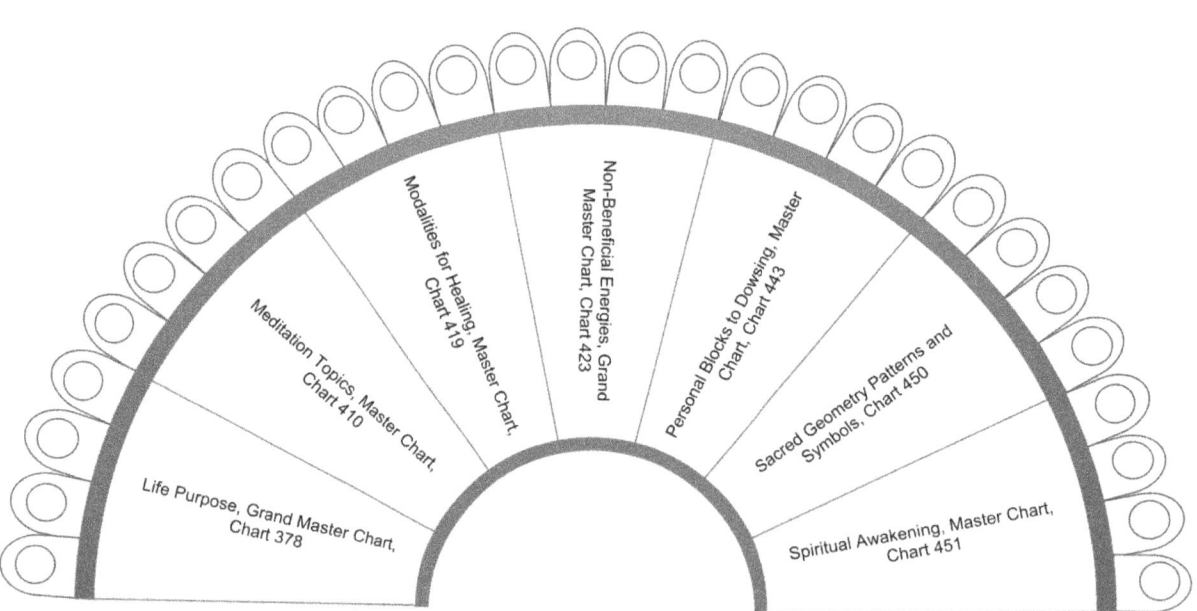

Diving into the Pool of the Spirit, Master Chart 2

The following labels appear around the fan chart:

- Life Purpose, Grand Master Chart, Chart 378
- Meditation Topics, Master Chart, Chart 410
- Modalities for Healing, Master Chart, Chart 419
- Non-Beneficial Energies, Grand Master Chart, Chart 423
- Personal Blocks to Dowsing, Master Chart, Chart 443
- Sacred Geometry Patterns and Symbols, Chart 450
- Spiritual Awakening, Master Chart, Chart 451

Royal Template 7

Diving Deep into the Pool of the Mind

Chart 336

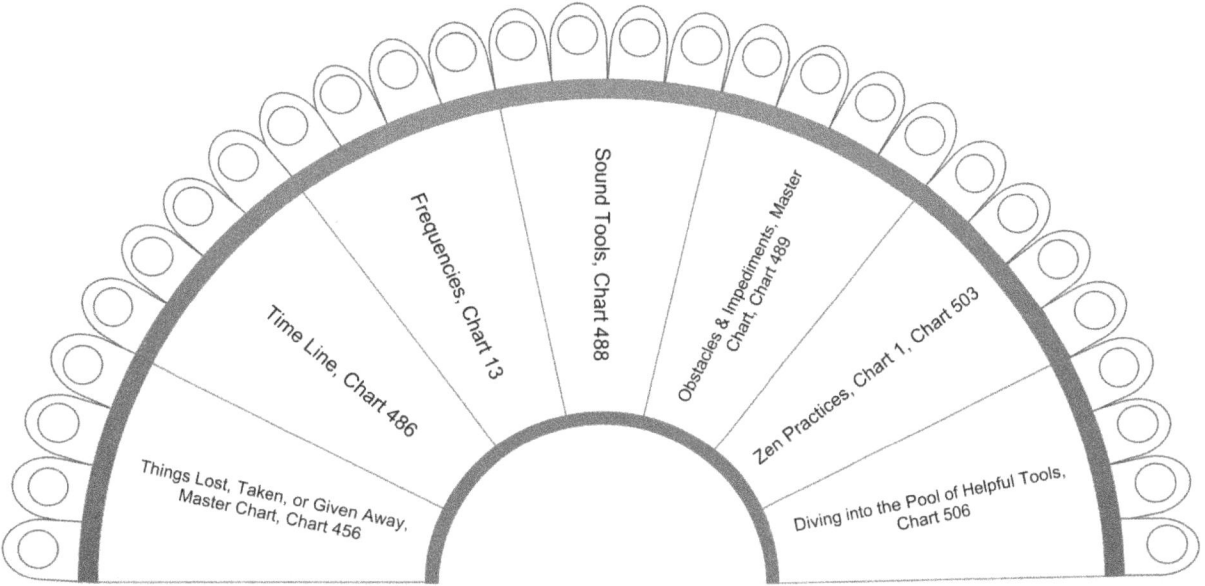

Diving into the Pool of the Spirit, Master Chart 3

Sound Tools, Chart 488

Obstacles & Impediments, Master Chart, Chart 489

Frequencies, Chart 13

Zen Practices, Chart 1, Chart 503

Time Line, Chart 486

Diving into the Pool of Helpful Tools, Chart 506

Things Lost, Taken, or Given Away, Master Chart, Chart 456

© 2025, Susan V Whittaker

Royal Template 7

Chart 337

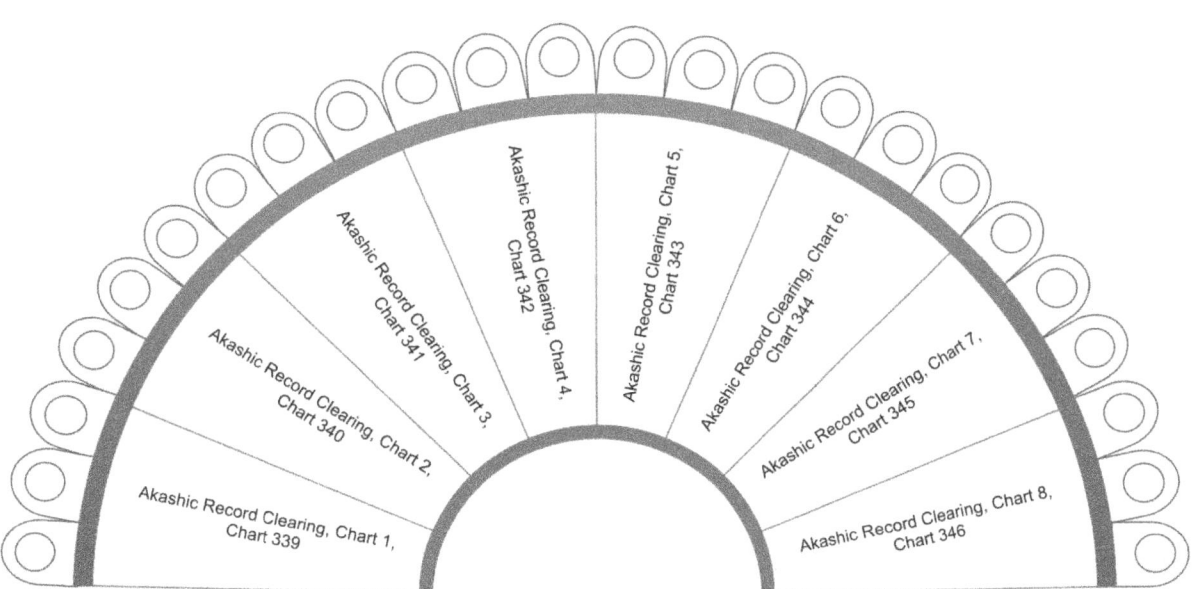

Akashic Record Clearing, Master Chart

Akashic Record Clearing, Chart 5, Chart 343

Akashic Record Clearing, Chart 4, Chart 342

Akashic Record Clearing, Chart 6, Chart 344

Akashic Record Clearing, Chart 3, Chart 341

Akashic Record Clearing, Chart 7, Chart 345

Akashic Record Clearing, Chart 2, Chart 340

Akashic Record Clearing, Chart 1, Chart 339

Akashic Record Clearing, Chart 8, Chart 346

© 2025, Susan V Whittaker

Royal Template 8

Chart 338

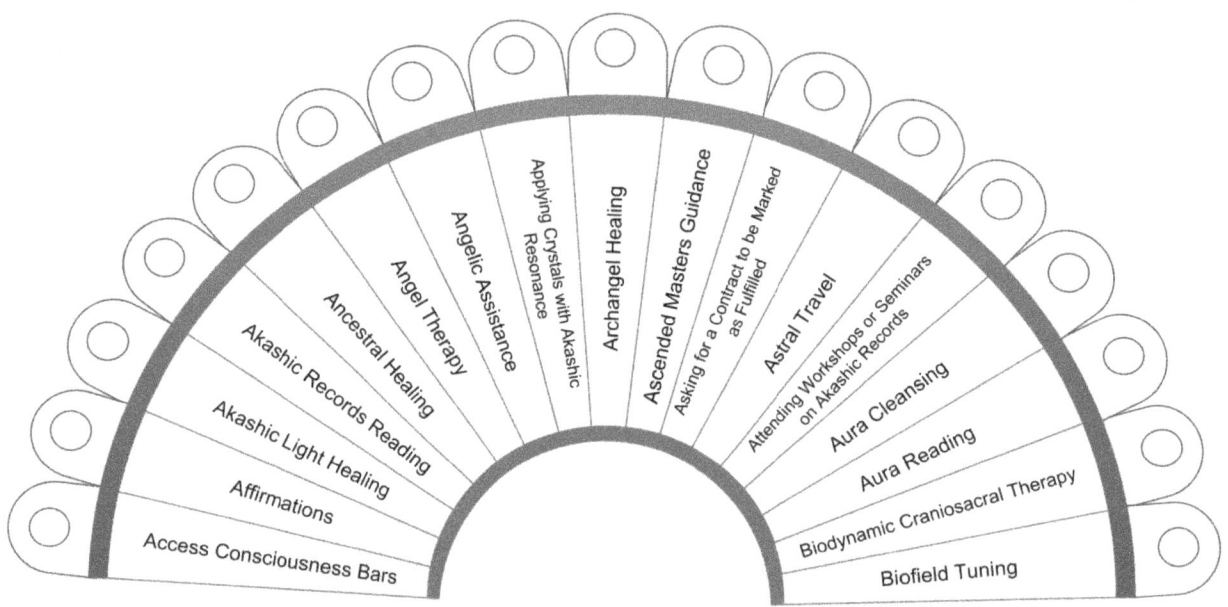

Akashic Record Clearing, Chart 1

Royal Template 17

Diving Deep into the Pool of the Mind

Chart 339

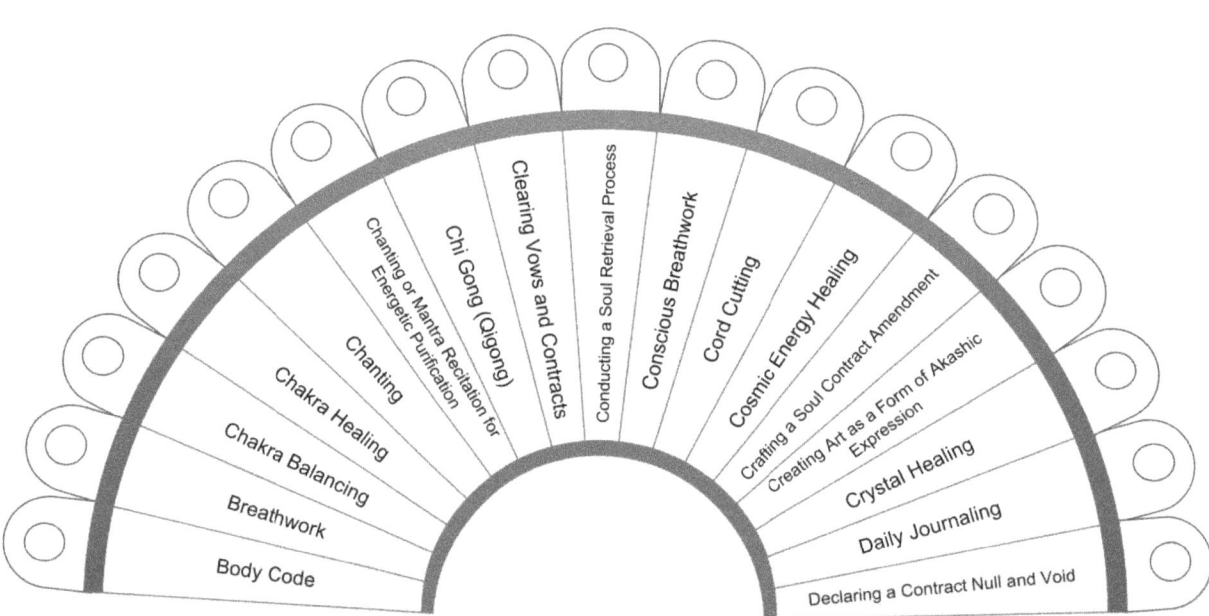

Akashic Record Clearing, Chart 2

Royal Template 17

Diving Deep into the Pool of the Mind

Chart 340

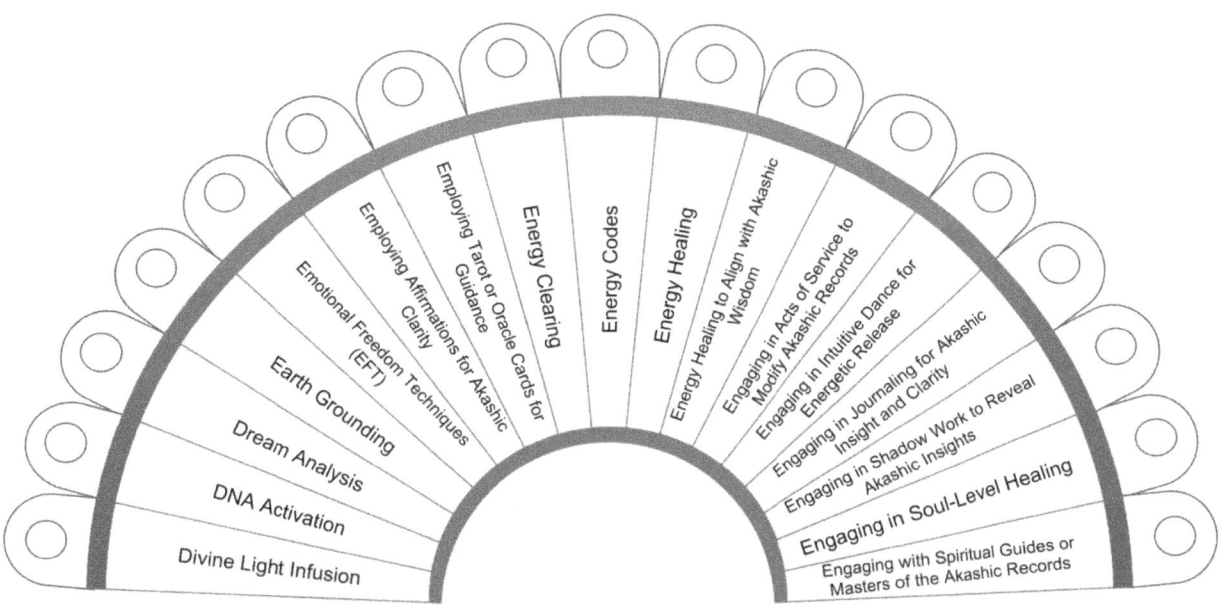

Akashic Record Clearing, Chart 3

Divine Light Infusion
DNA Activation
Dream Analysis
Earth Grounding
Emotional Freedom Techniques (EFT)
Employing Affirmations for Akashic Clarity
Employing Tarot or Oracle Cards for Guidance
Energy Clearing
Energy Codes
Energy Healing
Energy Healing to Align with Akashic Wisdom
Engaging in Acts of Service to Modify Akashic Records
Engaging in Intuitive Dance for Energetic Release
Engaging in Journaling for Akashic Insight and Clarity
Engaging in Shadow Work to Reveal Akashic Insights
Engaging in Soul-Level Healing
Engaging with Spiritual Guides or Masters of the Akashic Records

Royal Template 17

Diving Deep into the Pool of the Mind

Chart 341

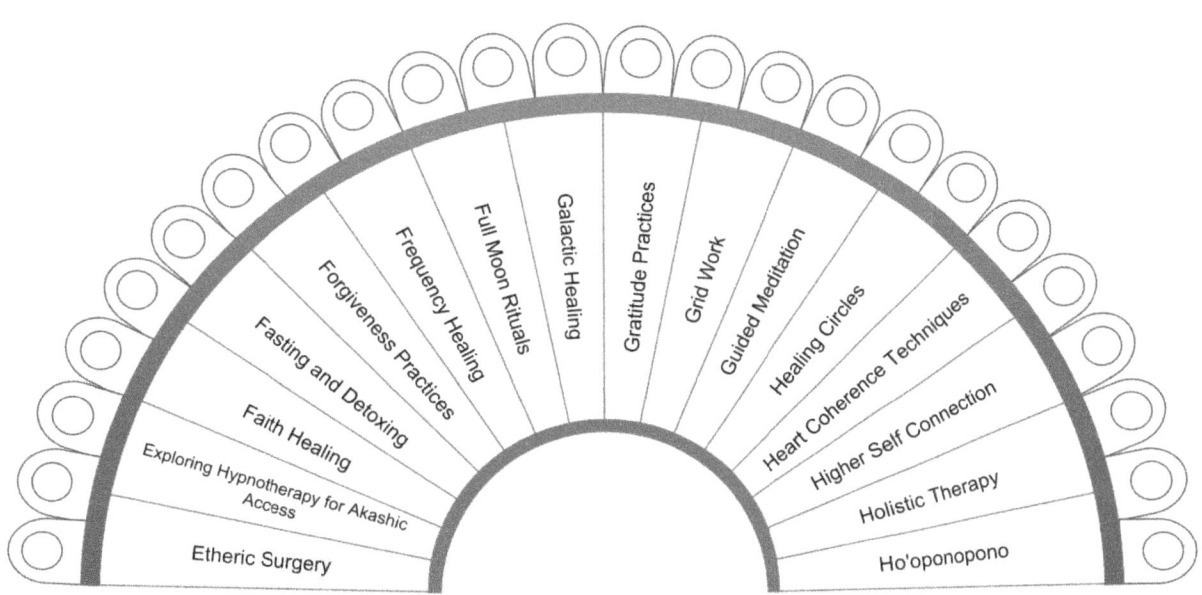

Akashic Record Clearing, Chart 4

Etheric Surgery
Exploring Hypnotherapy for Akashic Access
Faith Healing
Fasting and Detoxing
Forgiveness Practices
Frequency Healing
Full Moon Rituals
Galactic Healing
Gratitude Practices
Grid Work
Guided Meditation
Healing Circles
Heart Coherence Techniques
Higher Self Connection
Holistic Therapy
Ho'oponopono

Royal Template 16

Diving Deep into the Pool of the Mind

Chart 342

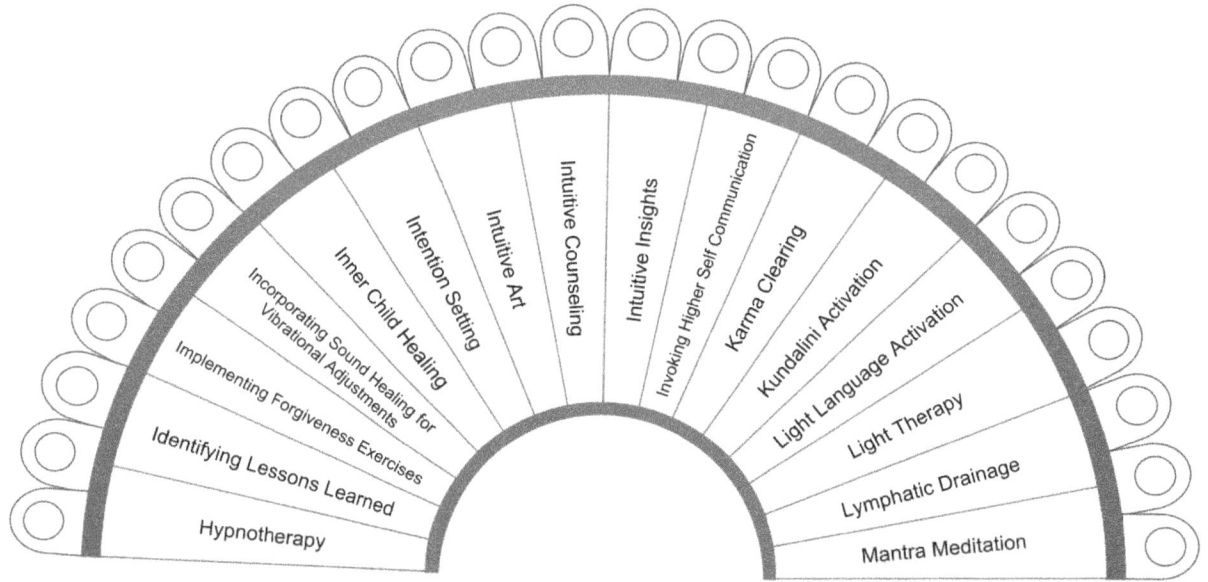

Akashic Record Clearing, Chart 5

Intuitive Insights
Intuitive Counseling
Intuitive Art
Intention Setting
Inner Child Healing
Incorporating Sound Healing for Vibrational Adjustments
Implementing Forgiveness Exercises
Identifying Lessons Learned
Hypnotherapy
Invoking Higher Self Communication
Karma Clearing
Kundalini Activation
Light Language Activation
Light Therapy
Lymphatic Drainage
Mantra Meditation

Royal Template 16

Diving Deep into the Pool of the Mind

Chart 343

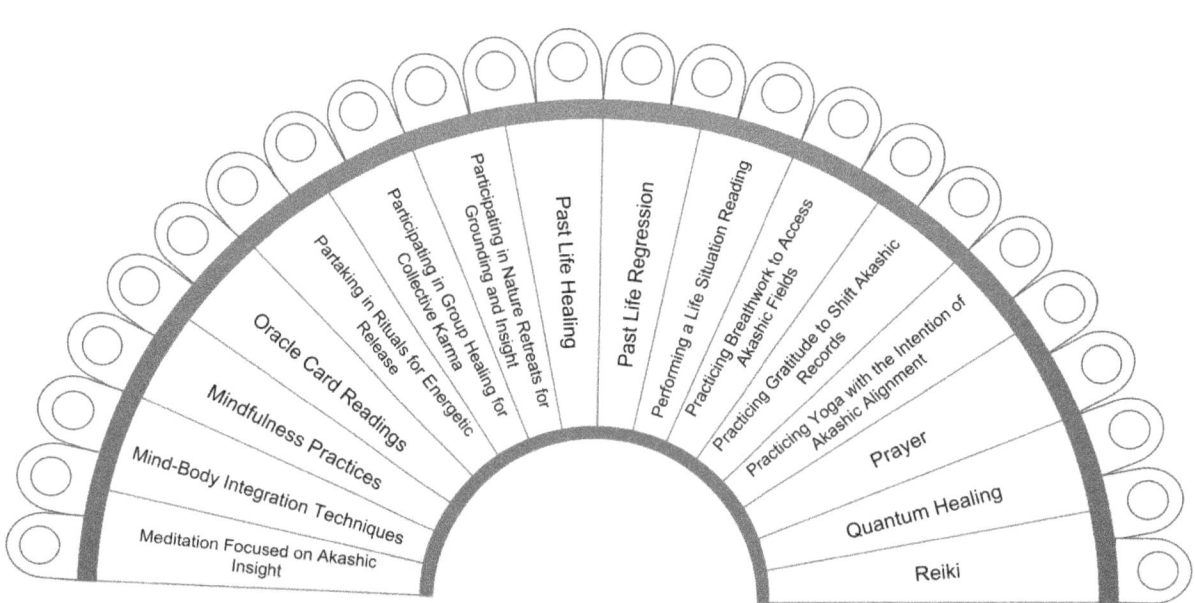

Akashic Record Clearing, Chart 6

Participating in Nature Retreats for Grounding and Insight
Participating in Group Healing for Collective Karma
Partaking in Rituals for Energetic Release
Oracle Card Readings
Mindfulness Practices
Mind-Body Integration Techniques
Meditation Focused on Akashic Insight
Past Life Healing
Past Life Regression
Performing a Life Situation Reading
Practicing Breathwork to Access Akashic Fields
Practicing Gratitude to Shift Akashic Records
Practicing Yoga with the Intention of Akashic Alignment
Prayer
Quantum Healing
Reiki

Royal Template 16

Diving Deep into the Pool of the Mind

Chart 344

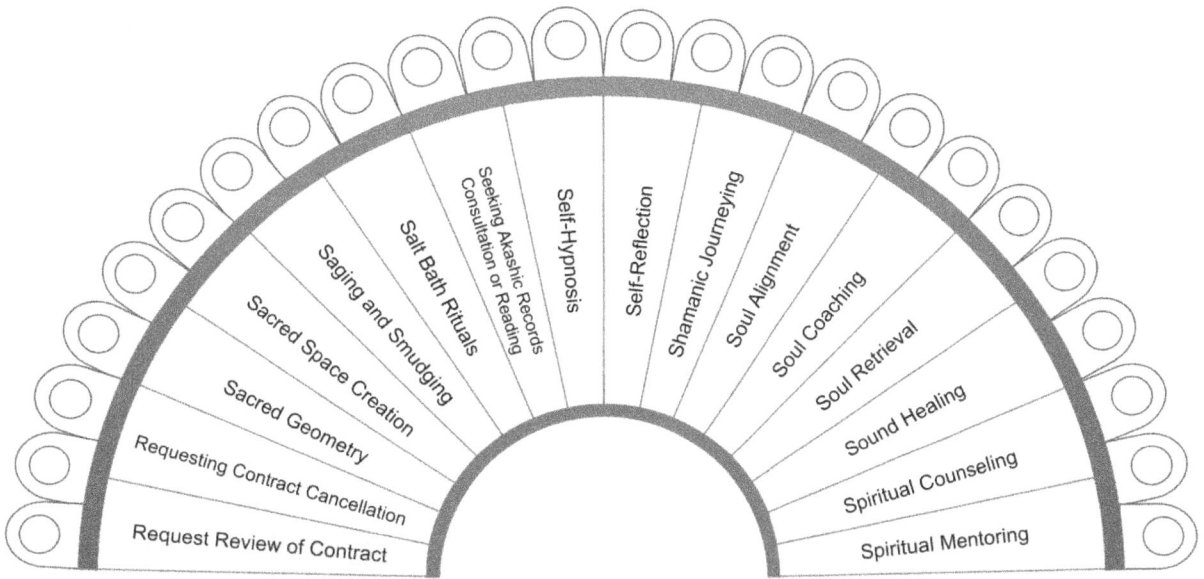

Akashic Record Clearing, Chart 7

The chart contains the following labels (reading around the fan):

- Request Review of Contract
- Requesting Contract Cancellation
- Sacred Geometry
- Sacred Space Creation
- Saging and Smudging
- Salt Bath Rituals
- Seeking Akashic Records Consultation or Reading
- Self-Hypnosis
- Self-Reflection
- Shamanic Journeying
- Soul Alignment
- Soul Coaching
- Soul Retrieval
- Sound Healing
- Spiritual Counseling
- Spiritual Mentoring

Royal Template 16

Diving Deep into the Pool of the Mind

Chart 345

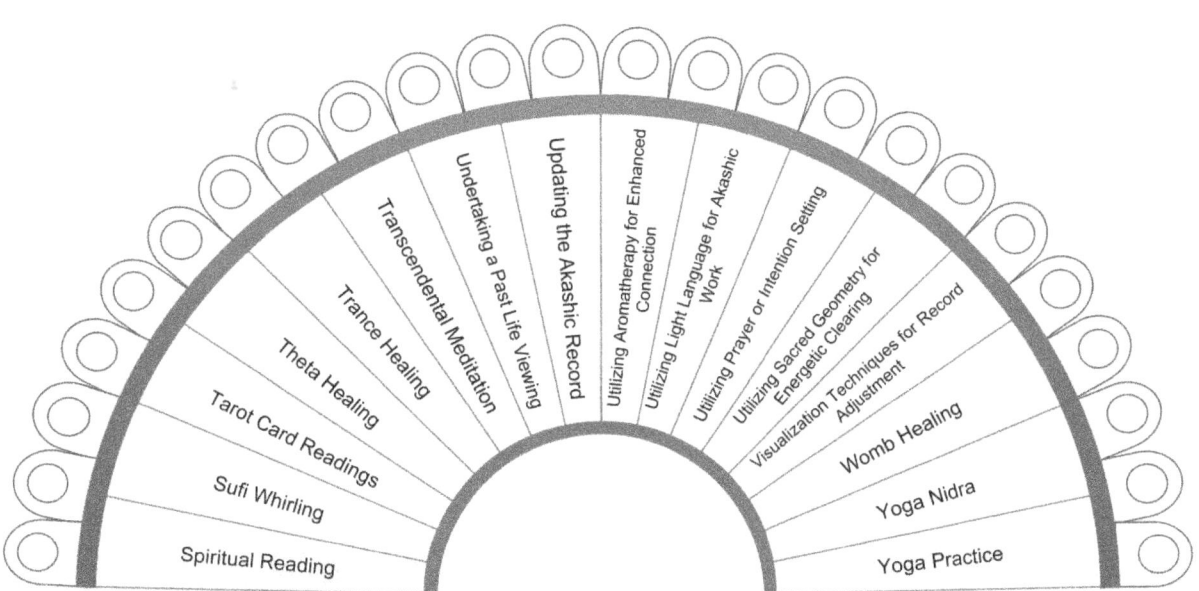

Akashic Record Clearing, Chart 8

The chart contains the following labels (reading around the fan):

- Spiritual Reading
- Sufi Whirling
- Tarot Card Readings
- Theta Healing
- Trance Healing
- Transcendental Meditation
- Undertaking a Past Life Viewing
- Updating the Akashic Record
- Utilizing Aromatherapy for Enhanced Connection
- Utilizing Light Language for Akashic Work
- Utilizing Prayer or Intention Setting
- Utilizing Sacred Geometry for Energetic Clearing
- Visualization Techniques for Record Adjustment
- Womb Healing
- Yoga Nidra
- Yoga Practice

Royal Template 16

Diving Deep into the Pool of the Mind

Chart 346

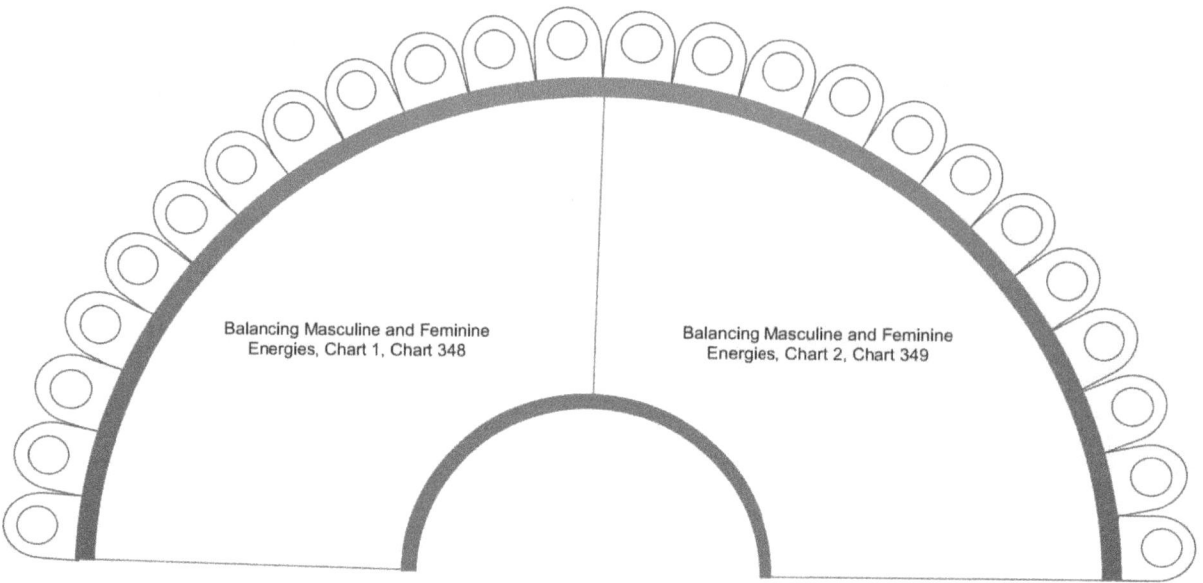

Balancing Masculine and Feminine Energies, Master Chart

Balancing Masculine and Feminine
Energies, Chart 1, Chart 348

Balancing Masculine and Feminine
Energies, Chart 2, Chart 349

Royal Template 2

Diving Deep into the Pool of the Mind

Chart 347

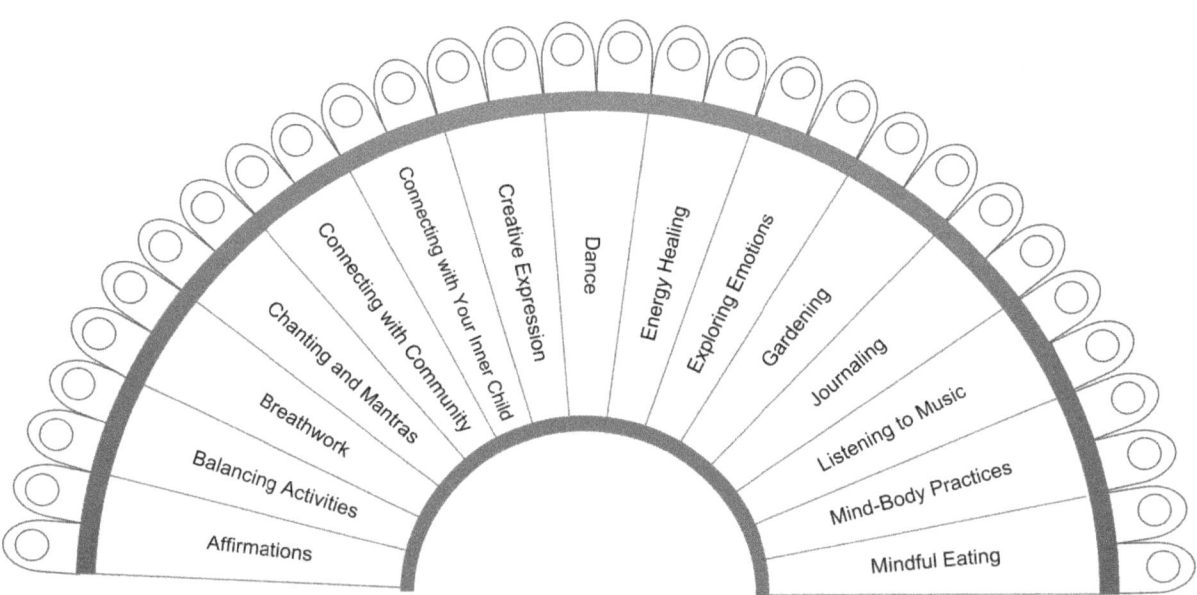

Connecting with Your Inner Child
Connecting with Community
Creative Expression
Chanting and Mantras
Dance
Energy Healing
Breathwork
Exploring Emotions
Balancing Activities
Gardening
Journaling
Affirmations
Listening to Music
Mind-Body Practices
Mindful Eating

Balancing Masculine and Feminine Energies, Chart 1

Royal Template 15

Diving Deep into the Pool of the Mind

Chart 348

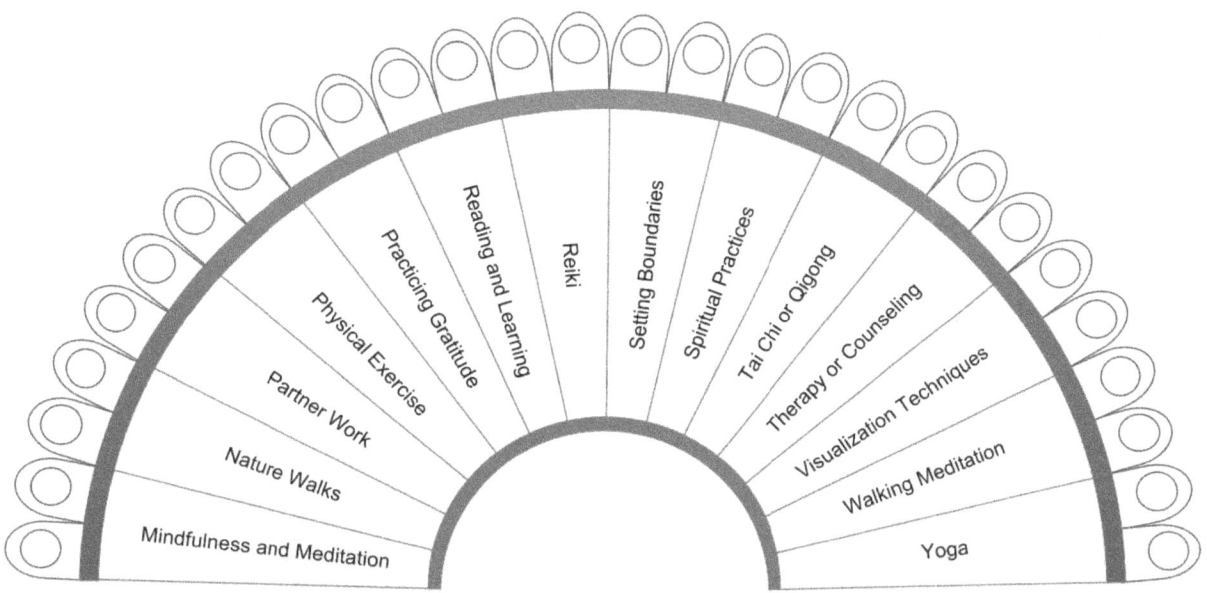

Balancing Masculine and Feminine Energies, Chart 2

Mindfulness and Meditation
Nature Walks
Partner Work
Physical Exercise
Practicing Gratitude
Reading and Learning
Reiki
Setting Boundaries
Spiritual Practices
Tai Chi or Qigong
Therapy or Counseling
Visualization Techniques
Walking Meditation
Yoga

Royal Template 14

Diving Deep into the Pool of the Mind

Chart 349

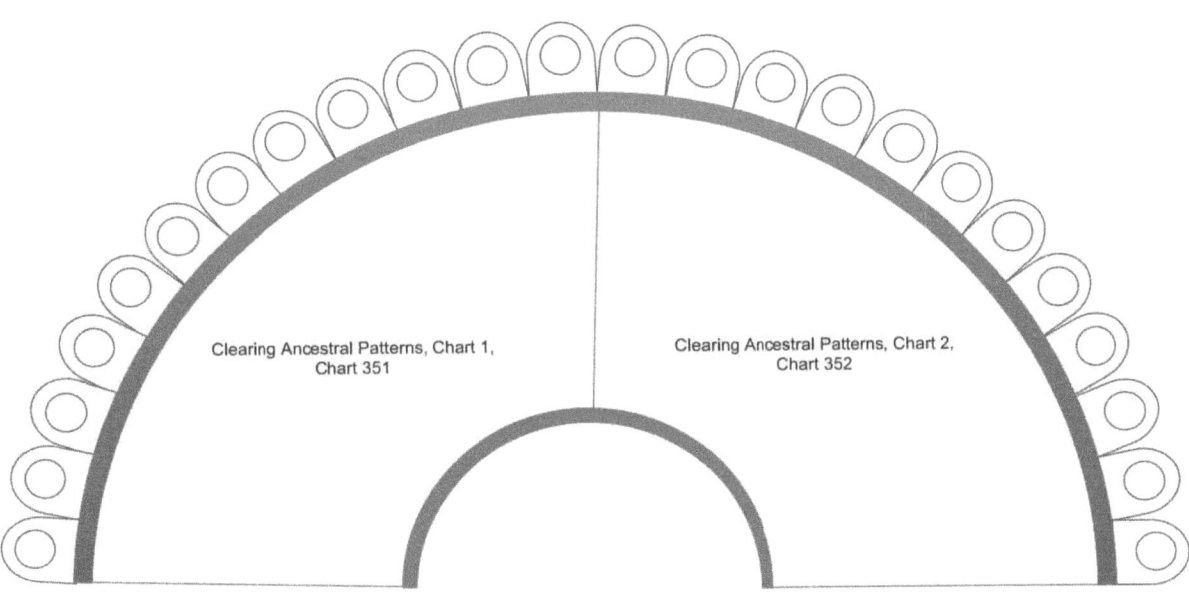

Clearing Ancestral Patterns, Chart 1, Chart 351

Clearing Ancestral Patterns, Chart 2, Chart 352

Clearing Ancestral Patterns, Master Chart

Royal Template 2

Diving Deep into the Pool of the Mind

Chart 350

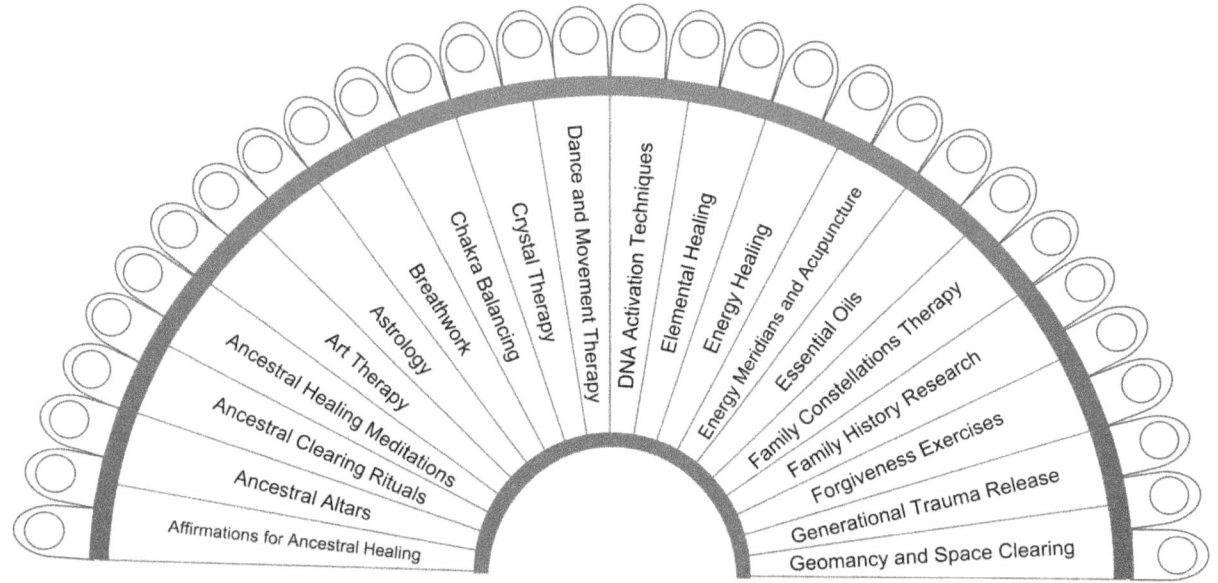

Clearing Ancestral Patterns, Chart 1

The fan chart contains the following labels (reading around the arc):

- Affirmations for Ancestral Healing
- Ancestral Altars
- Ancestral Clearing Rituals
- Ancestral Healing Meditations
- Art Therapy
- Astrology
- Breathwork
- Chakra Balancing
- Crystal Therapy
- Dance and Movement Therapy
- DNA Activation Techniques
- Elemental Healing
- Energy Healing
- Energy Meridians and Acupuncture
- Essential Oils
- Family Constellations Therapy
- Family History Research
- Forgiveness Exercises
- Generational Trauma Release
- Geomancy and Space Clearing

Royal Template 20

Diving Deep into the Pool of the Mind

Chart 351

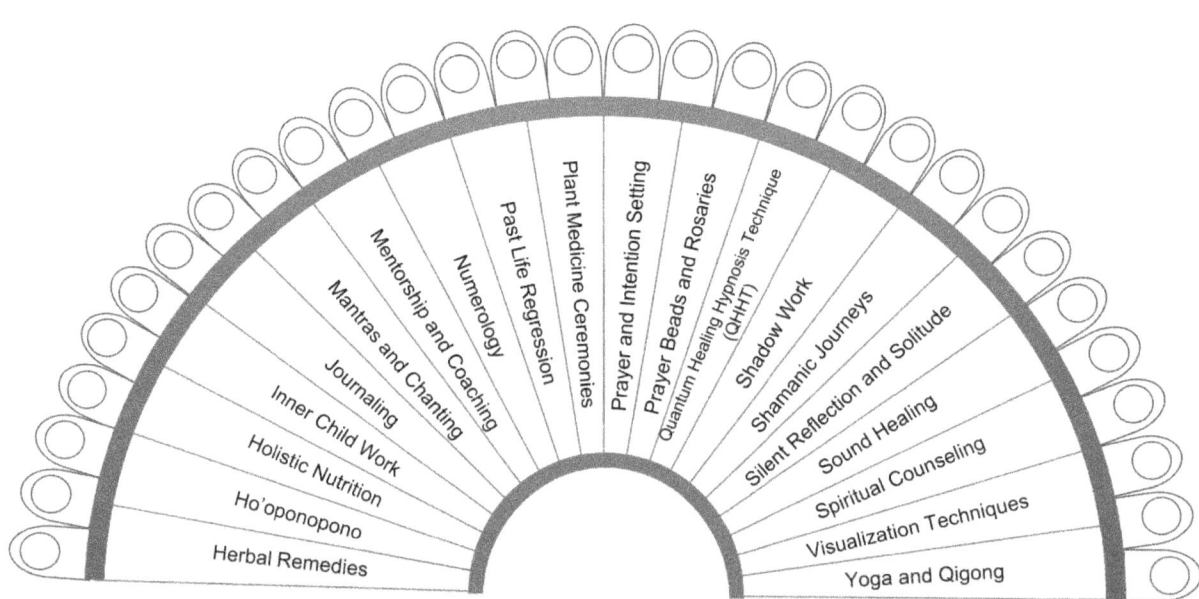

Clearing Ancestral Patterns, Chart 2

The fan chart contains the following labels (reading around the arc):

- Herbal Remedies
- Ho'oponopono
- Holistic Nutrition
- Inner Child Work
- Journaling
- Mantras and Chanting
- Mentorship and Coaching
- Numerology
- Past Life Regression
- Plant Medicine Ceremonies
- Prayer and Intention Setting
- Prayer Beads and Rosaries
- Quantum Healing Hypnosis Technique (QHHT)
- Shadow Work
- Shamanic Journeys
- Silent Reflection and Solitude
- Sound Healing
- Spiritual Counseling
- Visualization Techniques
- Yoga and Qigong

Royal Template 20

Diving Deep into the Pool of the Mind

Chart 352

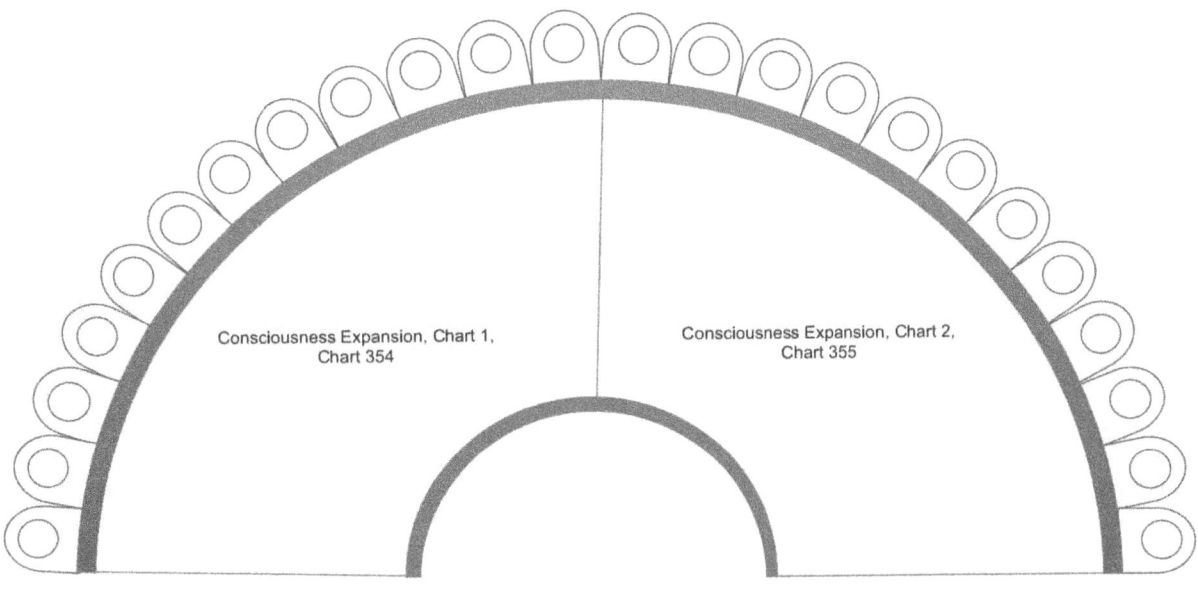

Consciousness Expansion, Master Chart

Consciousness Expansion, Chart 1,
Chart 354

Consciousness Expansion, Chart 2,
Chart 355

Royal Template 2

Diving Deep into the Pool of the Mind

Chart 353

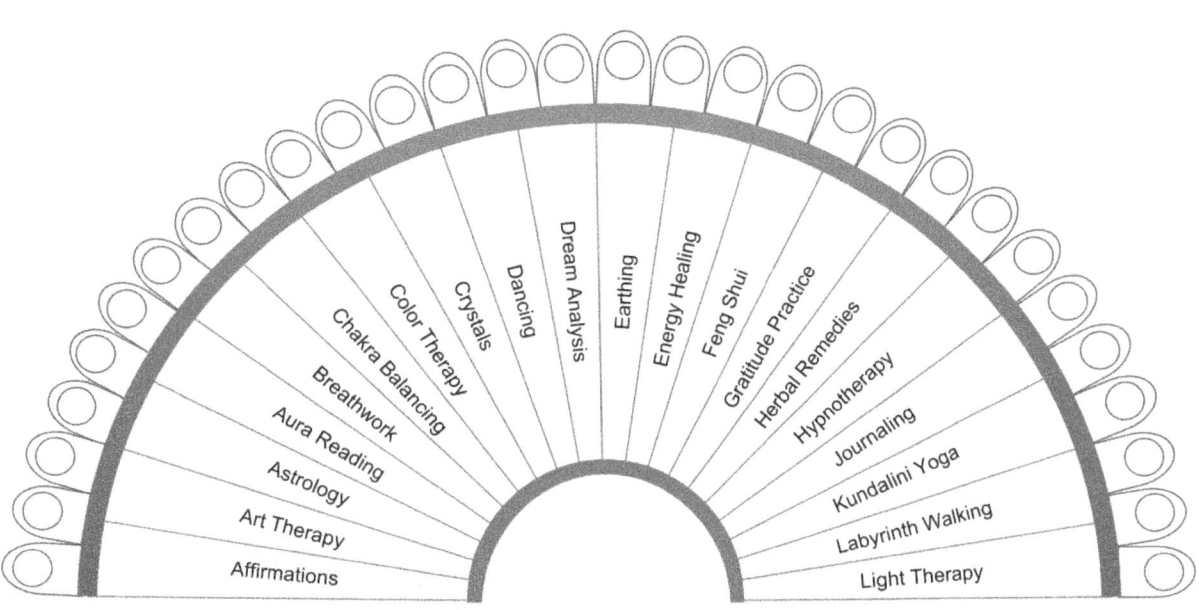

Affirmations
Art Therapy
Astrology
Aura Reading
Breathwork
Chakra Balancing
Color Therapy
Crystals
Dancing
Dream Analysis
Earthing
Energy Healing
Feng Shui
Gratitude Practice
Herbal Remedies
Hypnotherapy
Journaling
Kundalini Yoga
Labyrinth Walking
Light Therapy

Consciousness Expansion, Chart 1

Royal Template 20

Diving Deep into the Pool of the Mind

Chart 354

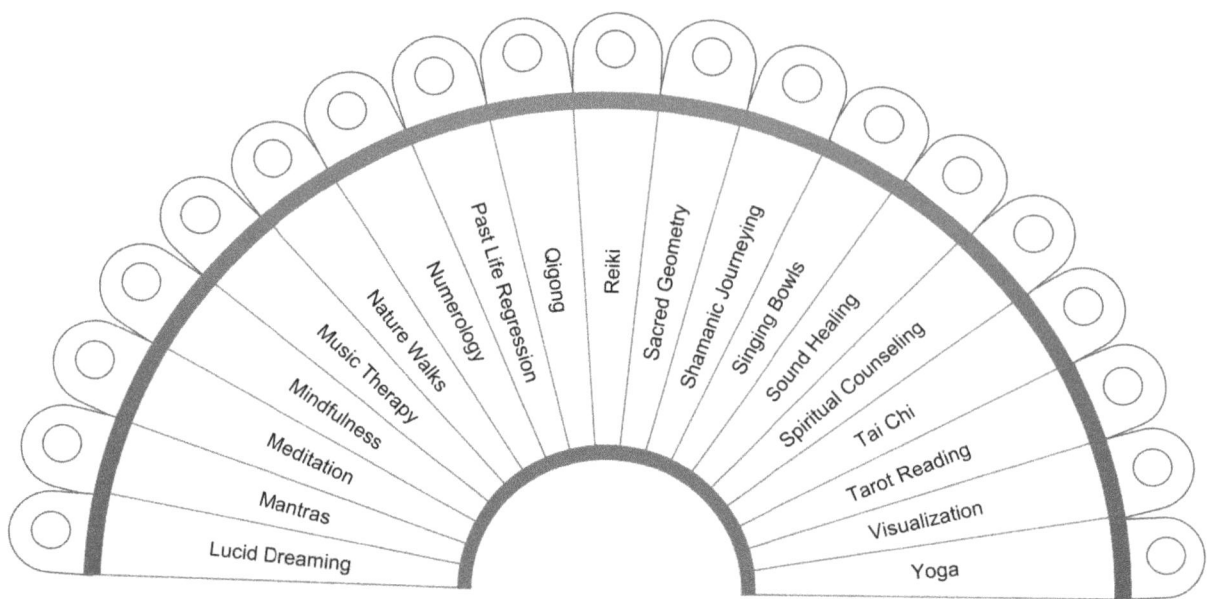

Consciousness Expansion, Chart 2

The chart radial labels (from left to right): Lucid Dreaming, Mantras, Meditation, Mindfulness, Music Therapy, Nature Walks, Numerology, Past Life Regression, Qigong, Reiki, Sacred Geometry, Shamanic Journeying, Singing Bowls, Sound Healing, Spiritual Counseling, Tai Chi, Tarot Reading, Visualization, Yoga

Royal Template 19

Diving Deep into the Pool of the Mind

Chart 355

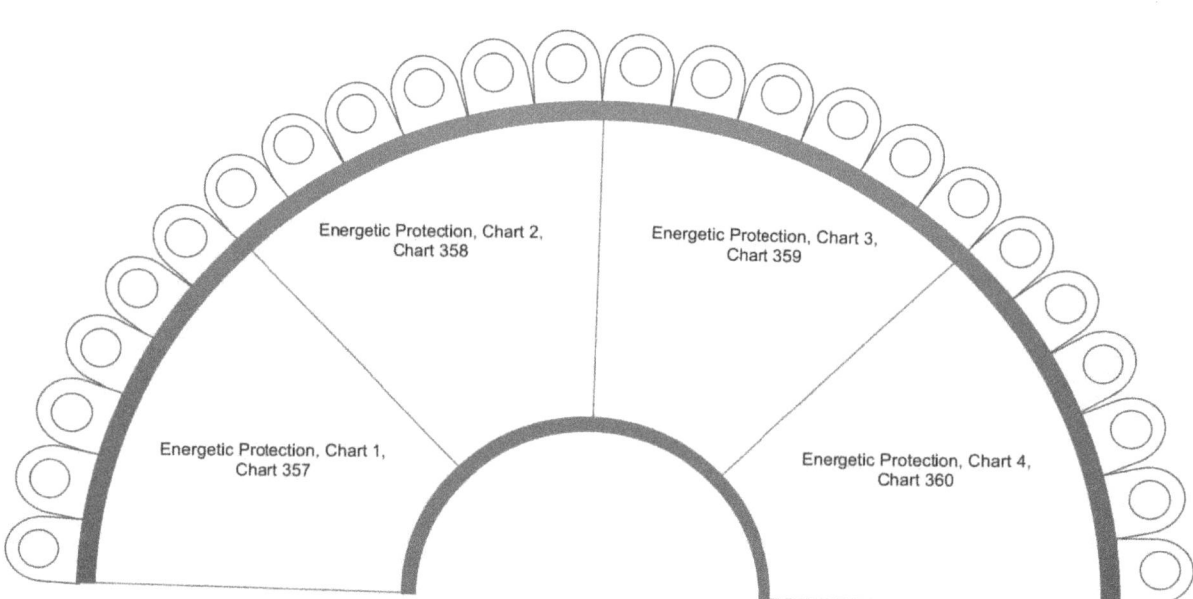

Energetic Protection, Chart 2, Chart 358

Energetic Protection, Chart 3, Chart 359

Energetic Protection, Chart 1, Chart 357

Energetic Protection, Chart 4, Chart 360

Energetic Protection, Master Chart

Royal Template 4h

Diving Deep into the Pool of the Mind

Chart 356

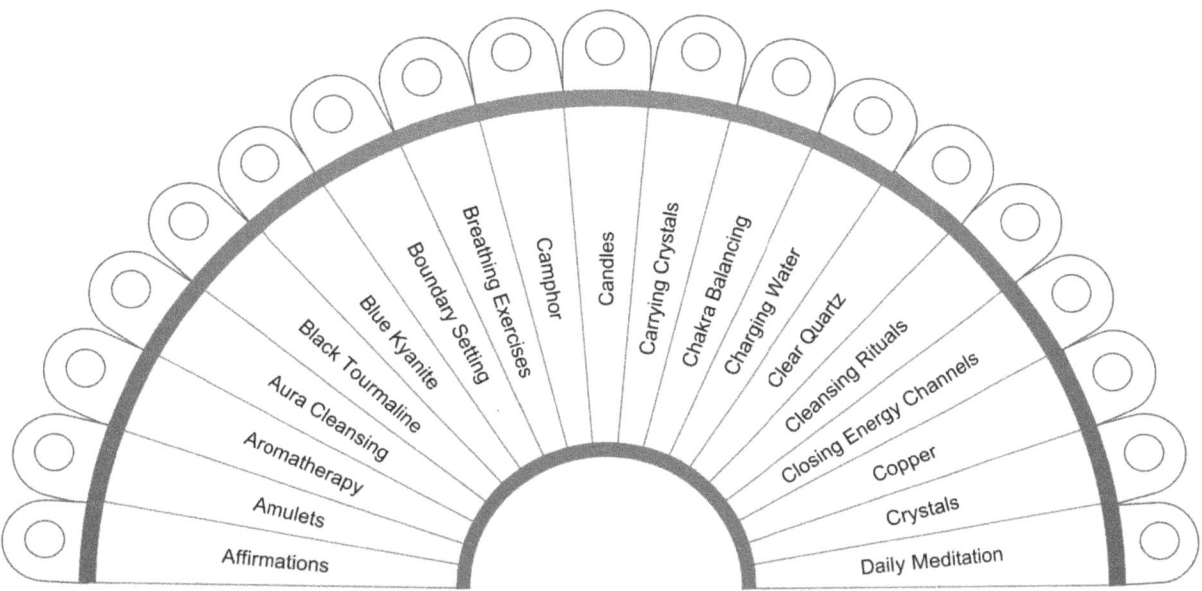

Energetic Protection, Chart 1

Royal Template 19

Diving Deep into the Pool of the Mind

Chart 357

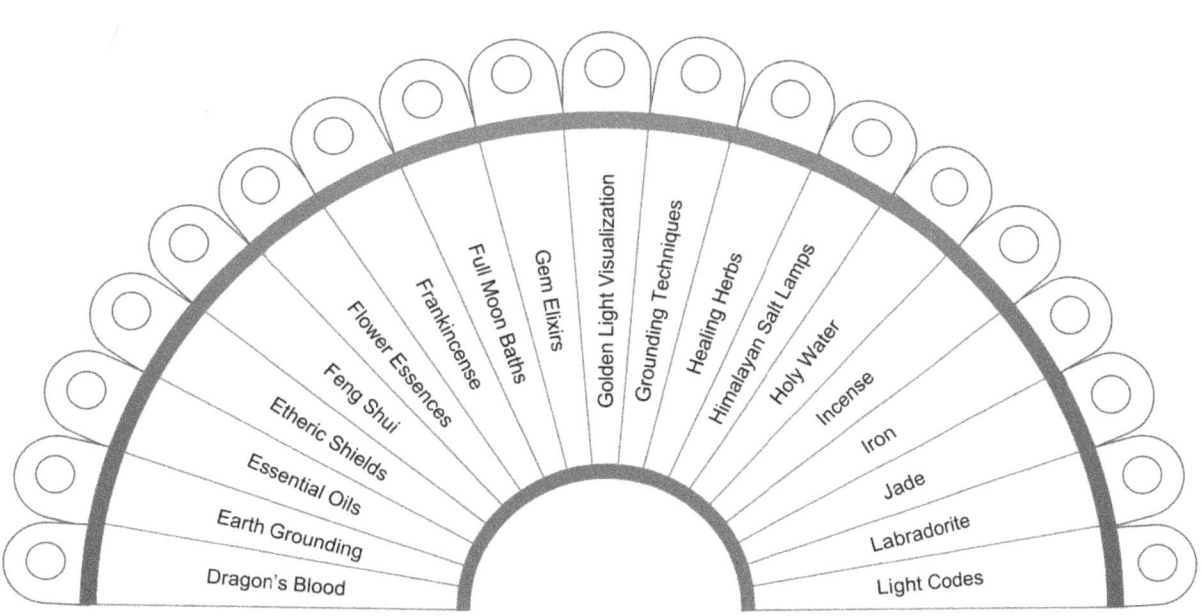

Energetic Protection, Chart 2

Royal Template 19

Diving Deep into the Pool of the Mind

Chart 358

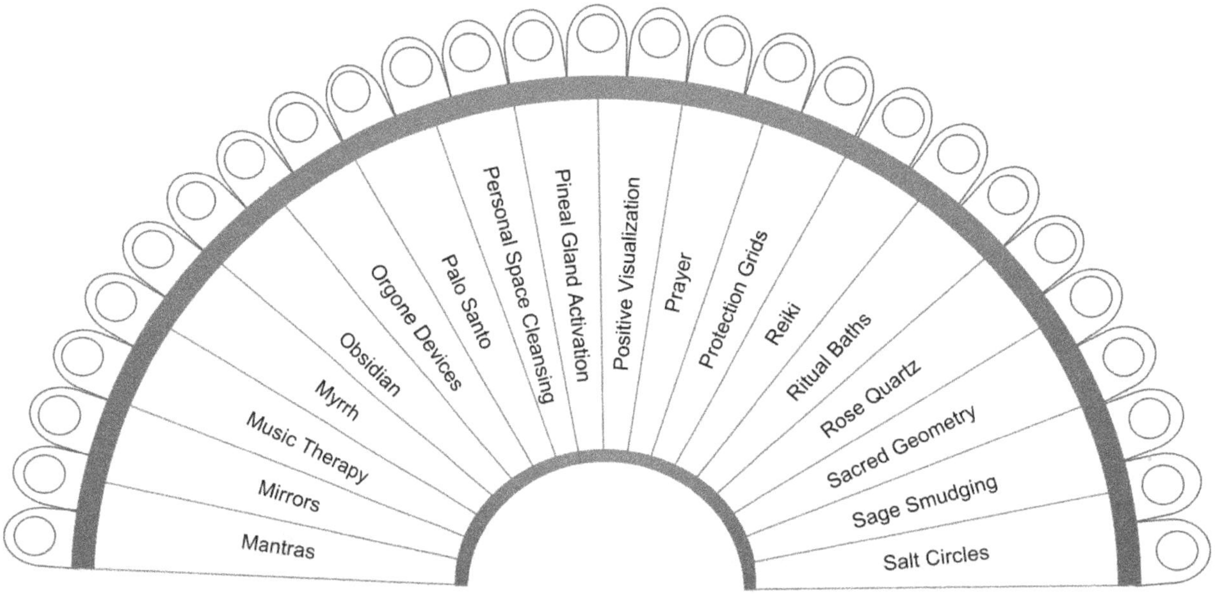
Mantras
Mirrors
Music Therapy
Myrrh
Obsidian
Orgone Devices
Palo Santo
Personal Space Cleansing
Pineal Gland Activation
Positive Visualization
Prayer
Protection Grids
Reiki
Ritual Baths
Rose Quartz
Sacred Geometry
Sage Smudging
Salt Circles

Energetic Protection, Chart 3

Royal Template 18

Chart 359

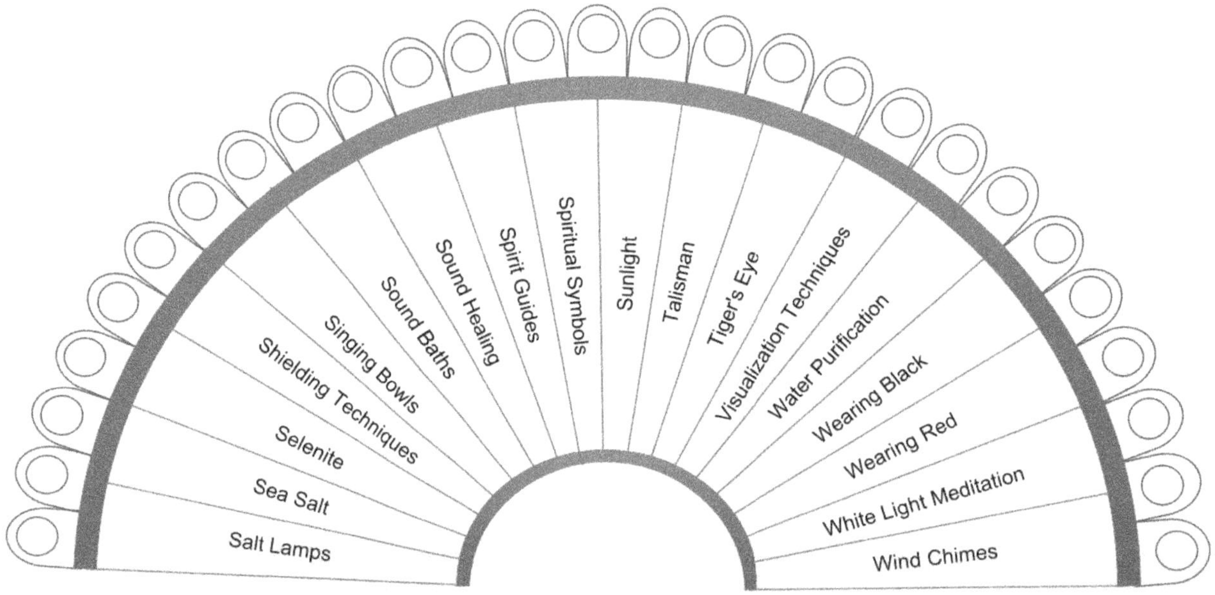
Salt Lamps
Sea Salt
Selenite
Shielding Techniques
Singing Bowls
Sound Baths
Sound Healing
Spirit Guides
Spiritual Symbols
Sunlight
Talisman
Tiger's Eye
Visualization Techniques
Water Purification
Wearing Black
Wearing Red
White Light Meditation
Wind Chimes

Energetic Protection, Chart 4

Royal Template 18

Chart 360

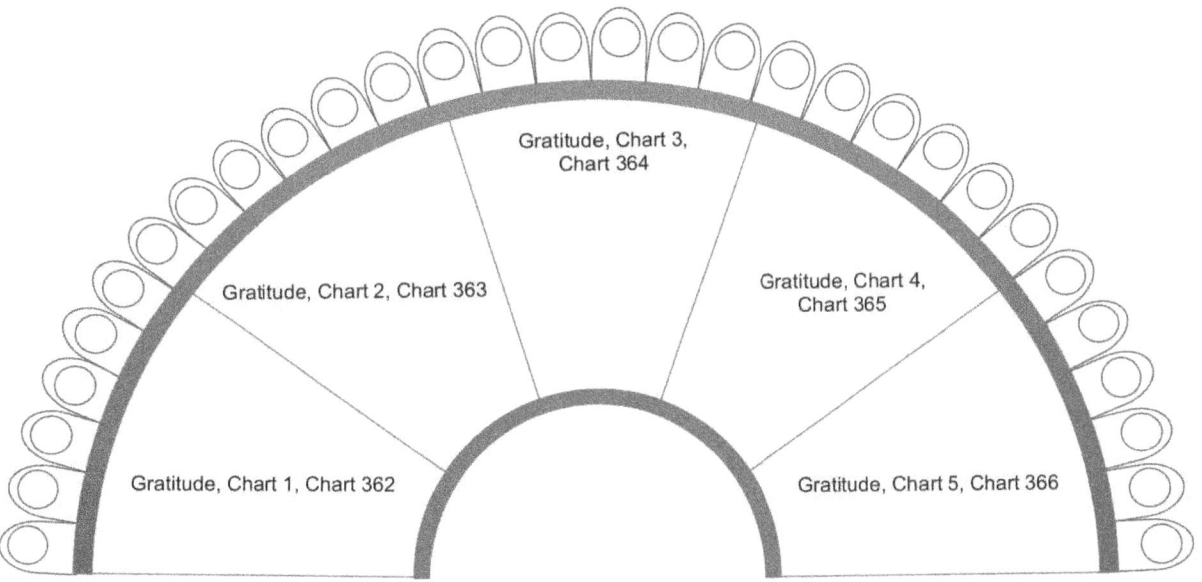

Gratitude, Master Chart

Gratitude, Chart 3, Chart 364

Gratitude, Chart 2, Chart 363

Gratitude, Chart 4, Chart 365

Gratitude, Chart 1, Chart 362

Gratitude, Chart 5, Chart 366

Royal Template 5h

Diving Deep into the Pool of the Mind

Chart 361

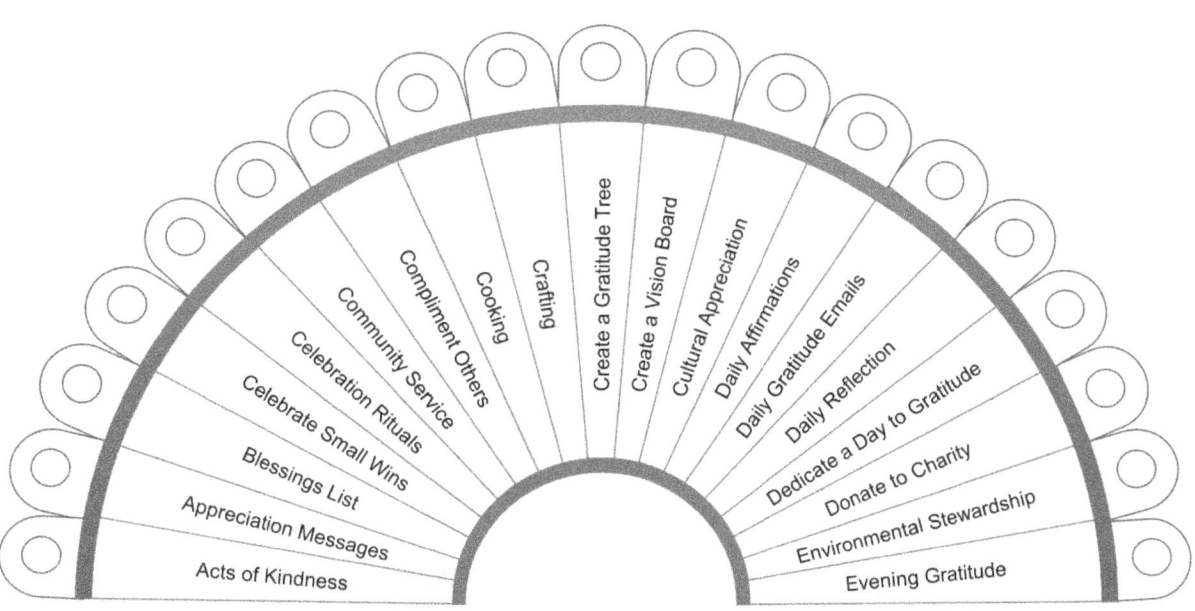

Acts of Kindness
Appreciation Messages
Blessings List
Celebrate Small Wins
Celebration Rituals
Community Service
Compliment Others
Cooking
Crafting
Create a Gratitude Tree
Create a Vision Board
Cultural Appreciation
Daily Affirmations
Daily Gratitude Emails
Daily Reflection
Dedicate a Day to Gratitude
Donate to Charity
Environmental Stewardship
Evening Gratitude

Gratitude, Chart 1

Royal Template 19

Diving Deep into the Pool of the Mind

Chart 362

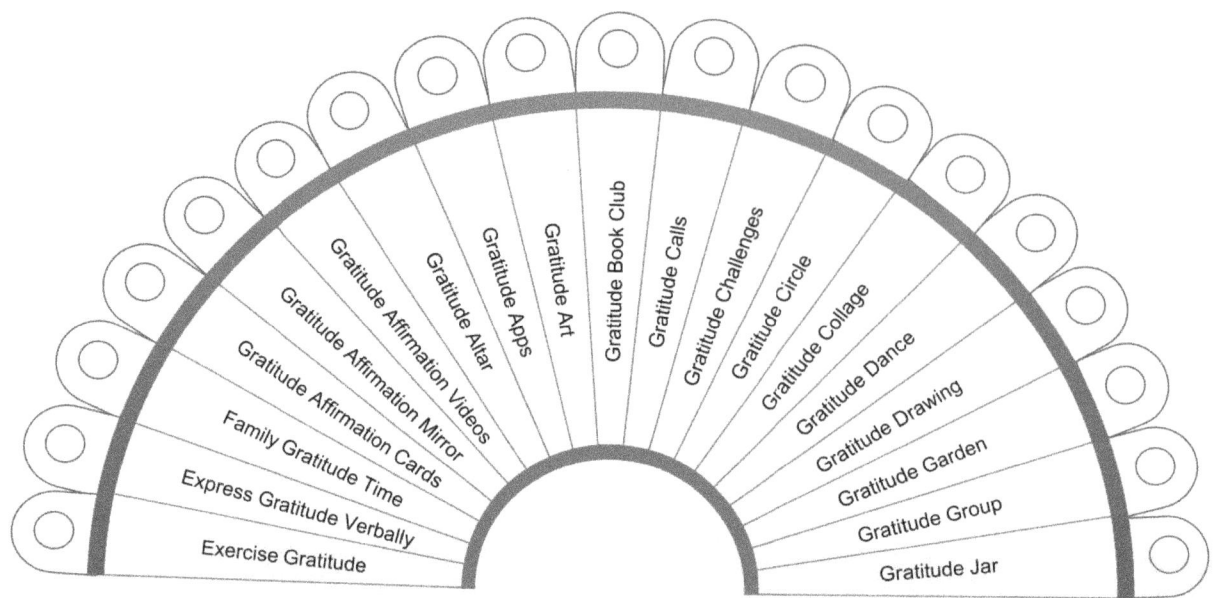

Gratitude, Chart 2

The chart contains the following labels (reading around the fan):

- Exercise Gratitude
- Express Gratitude Verbally
- Family Gratitude Time
- Gratitude Affirmation Cards
- Gratitude Affirmation Mirror
- Gratitude Affirmation Videos
- Gratitude Altar
- Gratitude Apps
- Gratitude Art
- Gratitude Book Club
- Gratitude Calls
- Gratitude Challenges
- Gratitude Circle
- Gratitude Collage
- Gratitude Dance
- Gratitude Drawing
- Gratitude Garden
- Gratitude Group
- Gratitude Jar

Royal Template 19

Diving Deep into the Pool of the Mind

Chart 363

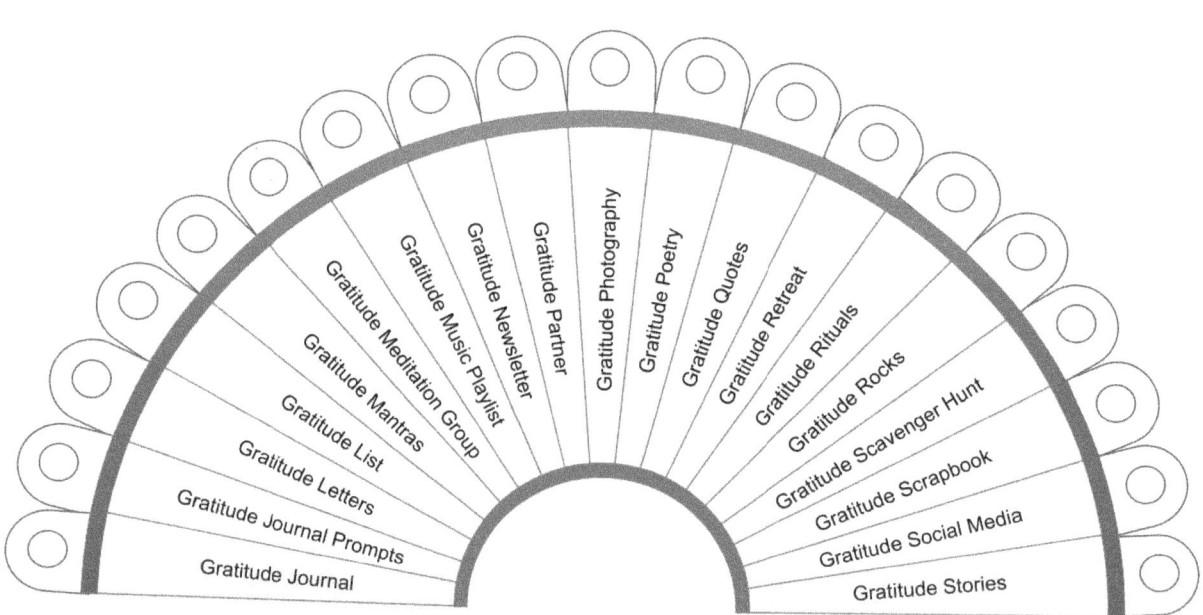

Gratitude, Chart 3

The chart contains the following labels (reading around the fan):

- Gratitude Journal
- Gratitude Journal Prompts
- Gratitude Letters
- Gratitude List
- Gratitude Mantras
- Gratitude Meditation Group
- Gratitude Music Playlist
- Gratitude Newsletter
- Gratitude Partner
- Gratitude Photography
- Gratitude Poetry
- Gratitude Quotes
- Gratitude Retreat
- Gratitude Rituals
- Gratitude Rocks
- Gratitude Scavenger Hunt
- Gratitude Scrapbook
- Gratitude Social Media
- Gratitude Stories

Royal Template 19

Diving Deep into the Pool of the Mind

Chart 364

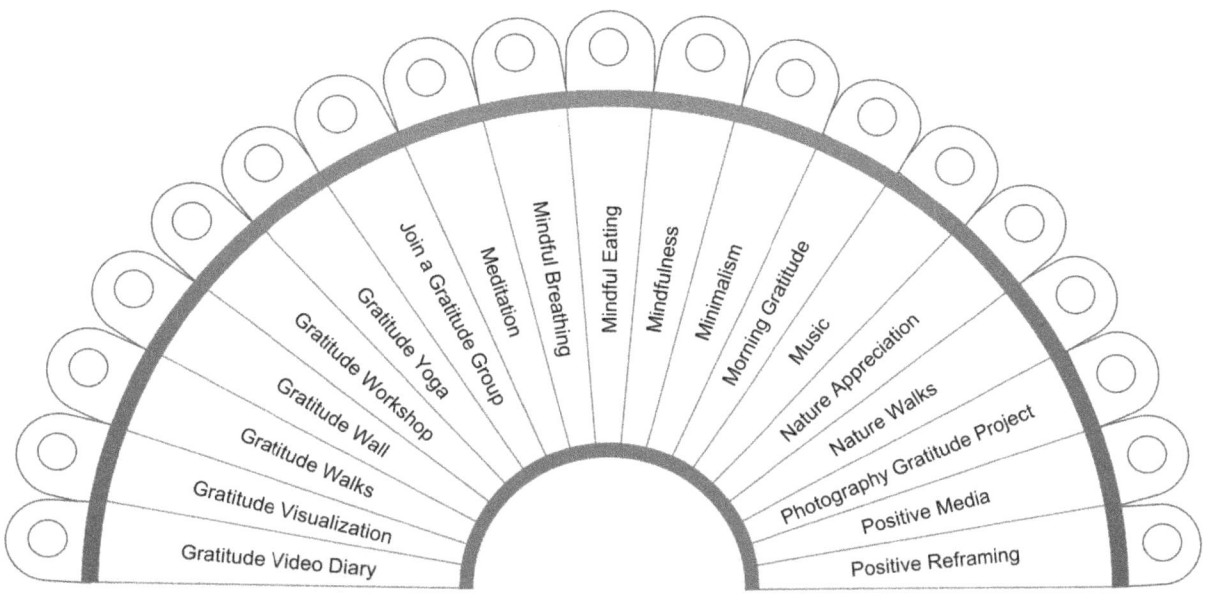

Gratitude, Chart 4

The chart contains the following labels (clockwise from left):

- Gratitude Video Diary
- Gratitude Visualization
- Gratitude Walks
- Gratitude Wall
- Gratitude Workshop
- Gratitude Yoga
- Join a Gratitude Group
- Meditation
- Mindful Breathing
- Mindful Eating
- Mindfulness
- Minimalism
- Morning Gratitude
- Music
- Nature Appreciation
- Nature Walks
- Photography Gratitude Project
- Positive Media
- Positive Reframing

Royal Template 19

Diving Deep into the Pool of the Mind

Chart 365

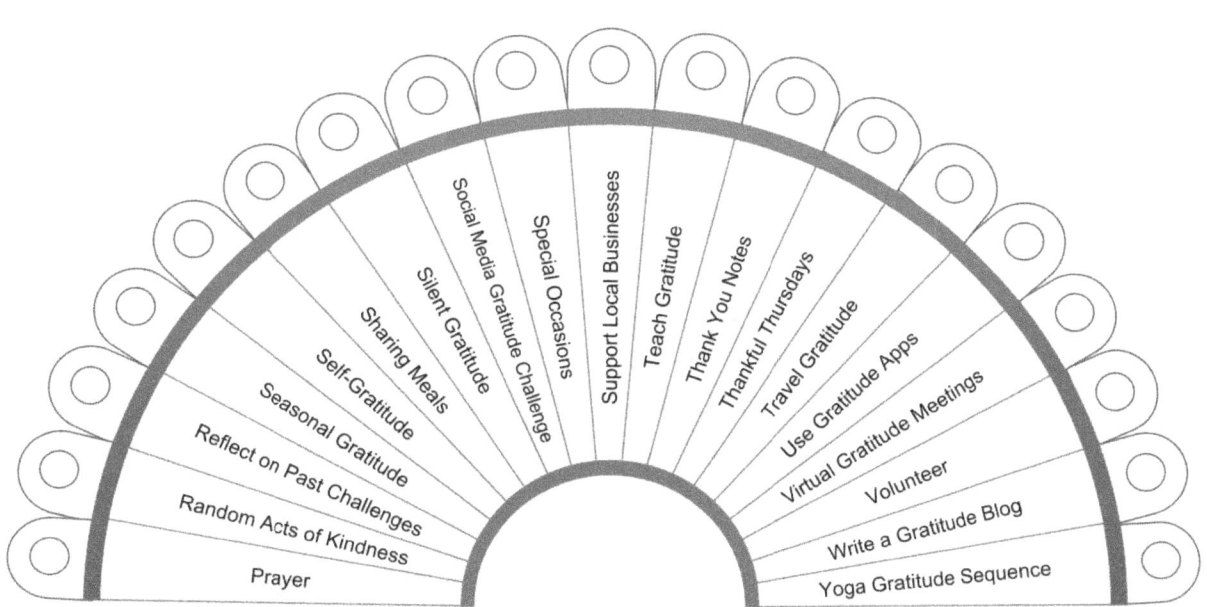

Gratitude, Chart 5

The chart contains the following labels (clockwise from left):

- Prayer
- Random Acts of Kindness
- Reflect on Past Challenges
- Seasonal Gratitude
- Self-Gratitude
- Sharing Meals
- Silent Gratitude
- Social Media Gratitude Challenge
- Special Occasions
- Support Local Businesses
- Teach Gratitude
- Thank You Notes
- Thankful Thursdays
- Travel Gratitude
- Use Gratitude Apps
- Virtual Gratitude Meetings
- Volunteer
- Write a Gratitude Blog
- Yoga Gratitude Sequence

Royal Template 19

Diving Deep into the Pool of the Mind

Chart 366

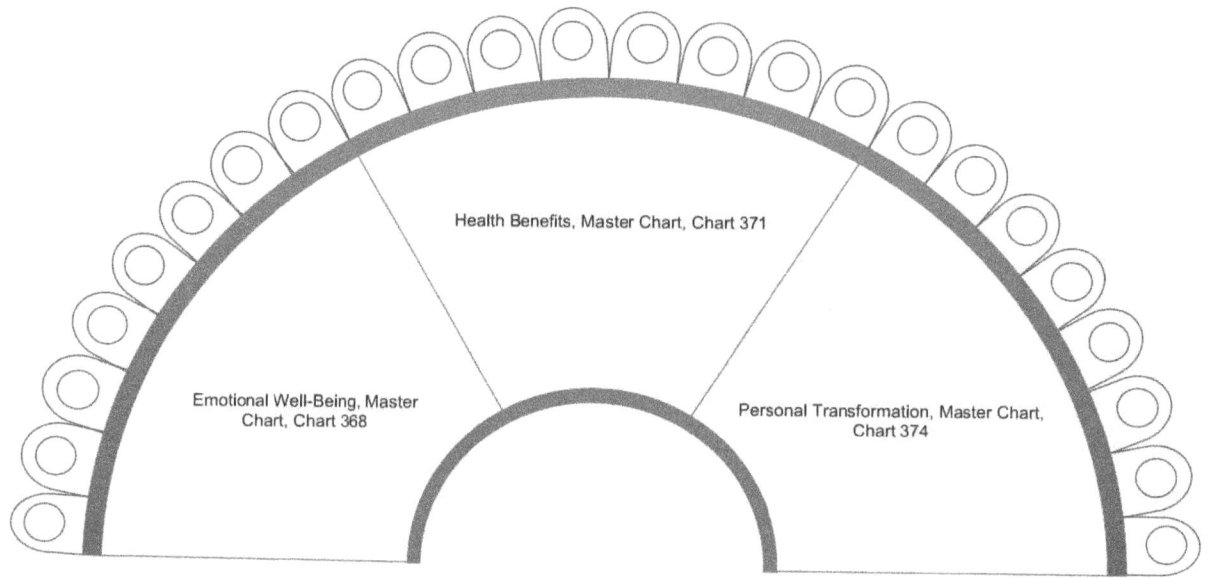

Heart-Brain Coherence, Master Chart

Health Benefits, Master Chart, Chart 371

Emotional Well-Being, Master Chart, Chart 368

Personal Transformation, Master Chart, Chart 374

Royal Template 3h

Diving Deep into the Pool of the Mind

Chart 367

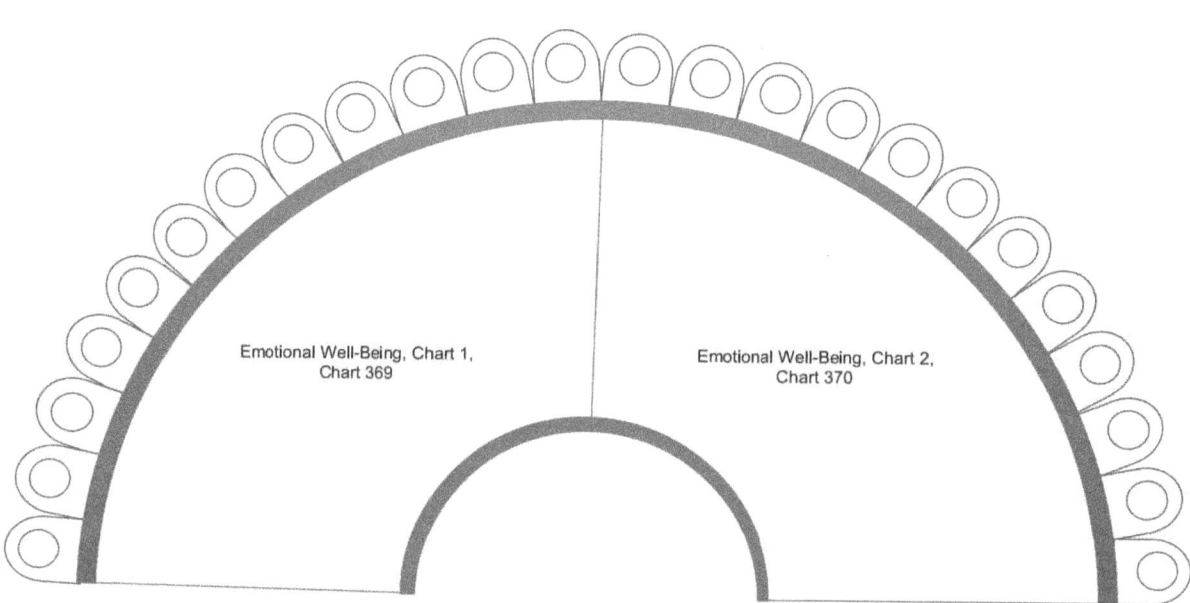

Emotional Well-Being, Master Chart

Emotional Well-Being, Chart 1, Chart 369

Emotional Well-Being, Chart 2, Chart 370

Royal Template 2

Diving Deep into the Pool of the Mind

Chart 368

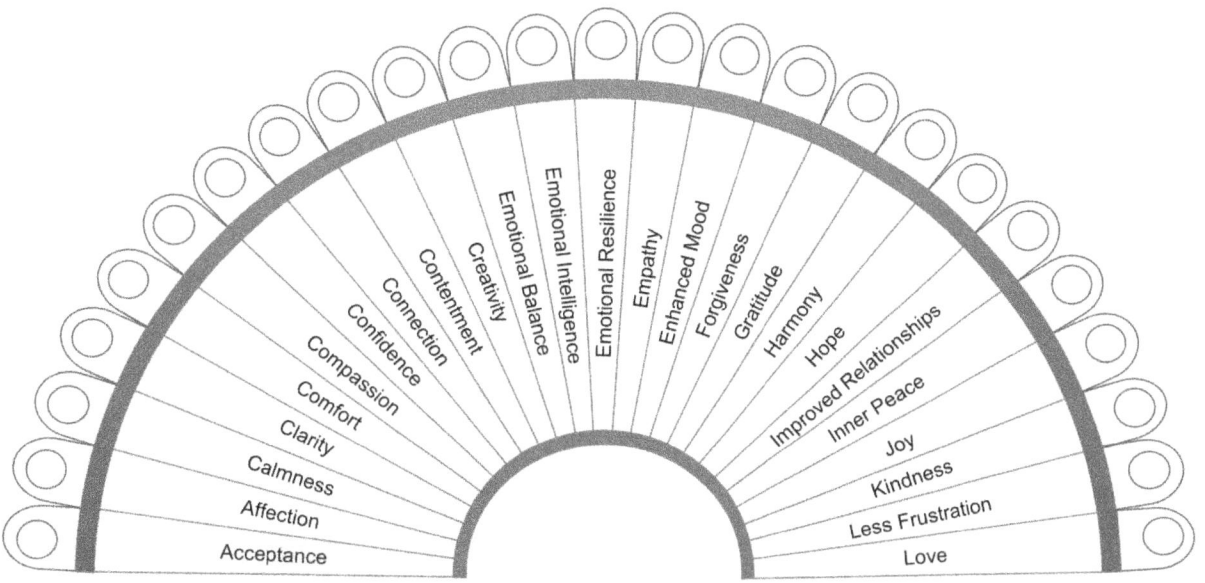

Emotional Well-Being, Chart 1

Acceptance
Affection
Calmness
Clarity
Comfort
Compassion
Confidence
Connection
Contentment
Creativity
Emotional Balance
Emotional Intelligence
Emotional Resilience
Empathy
Enhanced Mood
Forgiveness
Gratitude
Harmony
Hope
Improved Relationships
Inner Peace
Joy
Kindness
Less Frustration
Love

Royal Template 25

Diving Deep into the Pool of the Mind

Chart 369

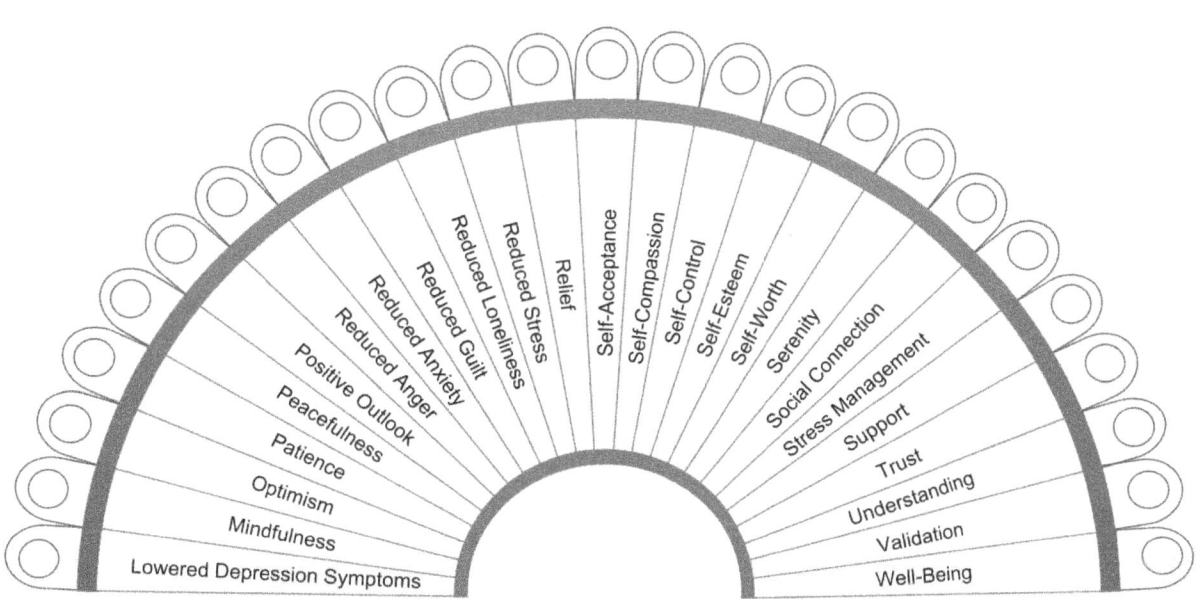

Emotional Well-Being, Chart 2

Lowered Depression Symptoms
Mindfulness
Optimism
Patience
Peacefulness
Positive Outlook
Reduced Anger
Reduced Anxiety
Reduced Guilt
Reduced Loneliness
Reduced Stress
Relief
Self-Acceptance
Self-Compassion
Self-Control
Self-Esteem
Self-Worth
Serenity
Social Connection
Stress Management
Support
Trust
Understanding
Validation
Well-Being

Royal Template 25

Diving Deep into the Pool of the Mind

Chart 370

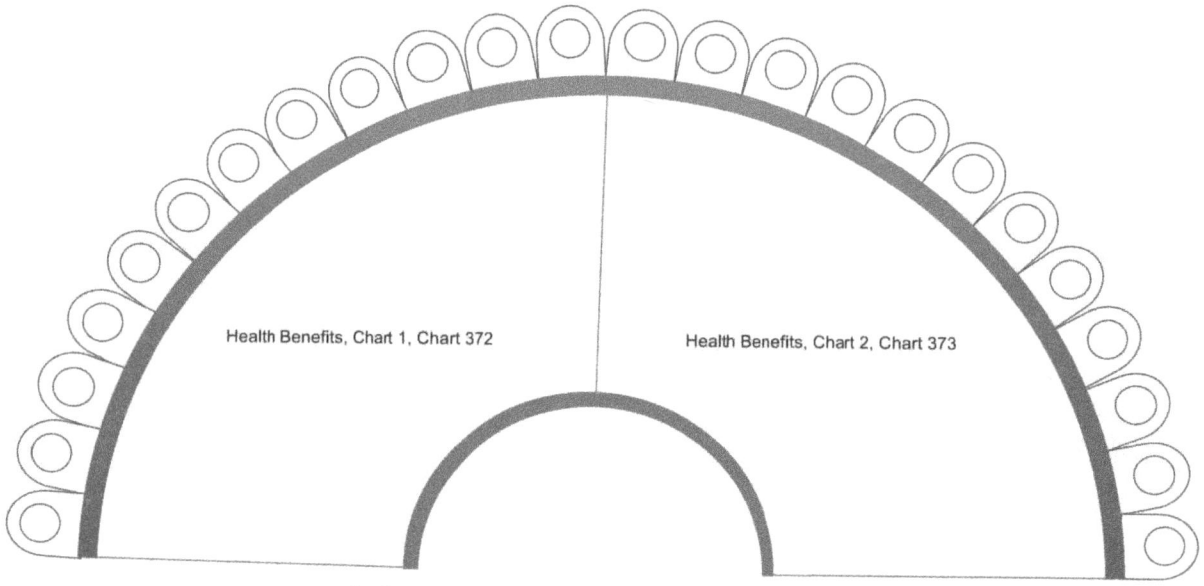

Health Benefits, Chart 1, Chart 372

Health Benefits, Chart 2, Chart 373

Health Benefits, Master Chart

Royal Template 2

Diving Deep into the Pool of the Mind

Chart 371

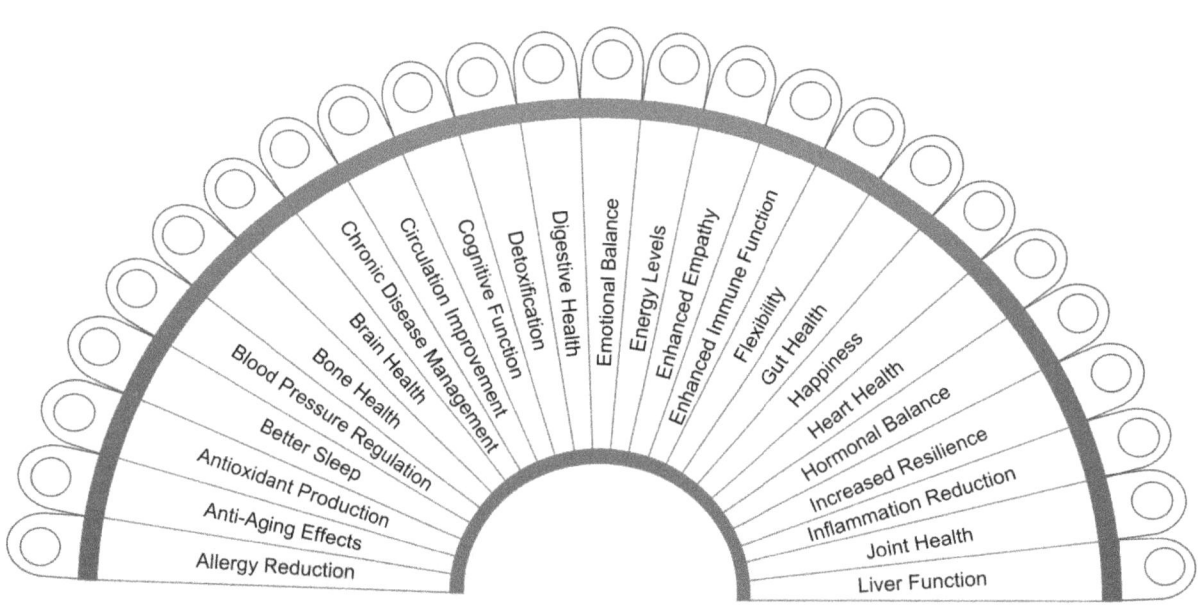

Chronic Disease Management
Circulation Improvement
Cognitive Function
Detoxification
Digestive Health
Emotional Balance
Energy Levels
Enhanced Empathy
Enhanced Immune Function
Flexibility
Gut Health
Happiness
Heart Health
Hormonal Balance
Increased Resilience
Inflammation Reduction
Joint Health
Liver Function
Brain Health
Bone Health
Blood Pressure Regulation
Better Sleep
Antioxidant Production
Anti-Aging Effects
Allergy Reduction

Health Benefits, Chart 1

Royal Template 25

Diving Deep into the Pool of the Mind

Chart 372

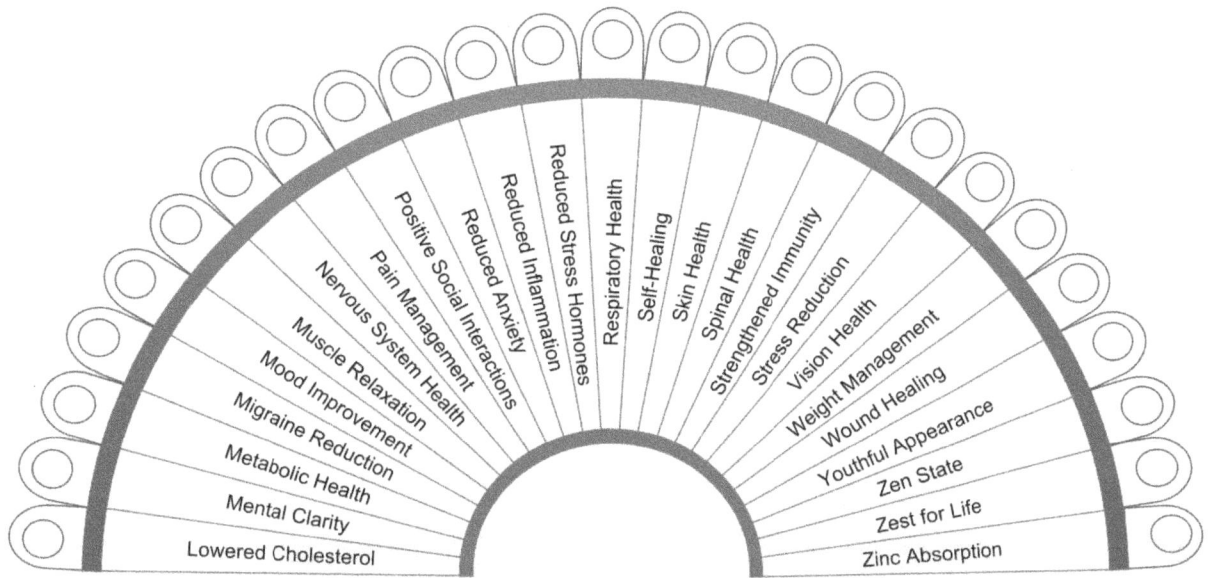

Health Benefits, Chart 2

The labels on the chart, reading left to right:

Lowered Cholesterol
Mental Clarity
Metabolic Health
Migraine Reduction
Mood Improvement
Muscle Relaxation
Nervous System Health
Pain Management
Positive Social Interactions
Reduced Anxiety
Reduced Inflammation
Reduced Stress Hormones
Respiratory Health
Self-Healing
Skin Health
Spinal Health
Strengthened Immunity
Stress Reduction
Vision Health
Weight Management
Wound Healing
Youthful Appearance
Zen State
Zest for Life
Zinc Absorption

Royal Template 25

Diving Deep into the Pool of the Mind

Chart 373

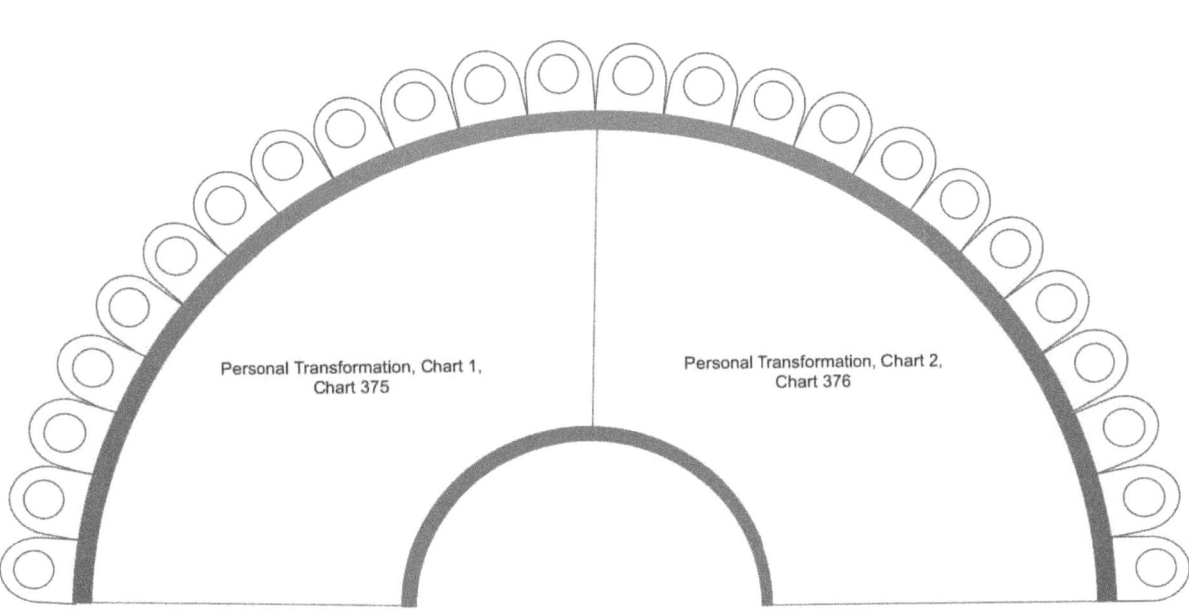

Personal Transformation, Chart 1,
Chart 375

Personal Transformation, Chart 2,
Chart 376

Personal Transformation, Master Chart

Royal Template 2

Diving Deep into the Pool of the Mind

Chart 374

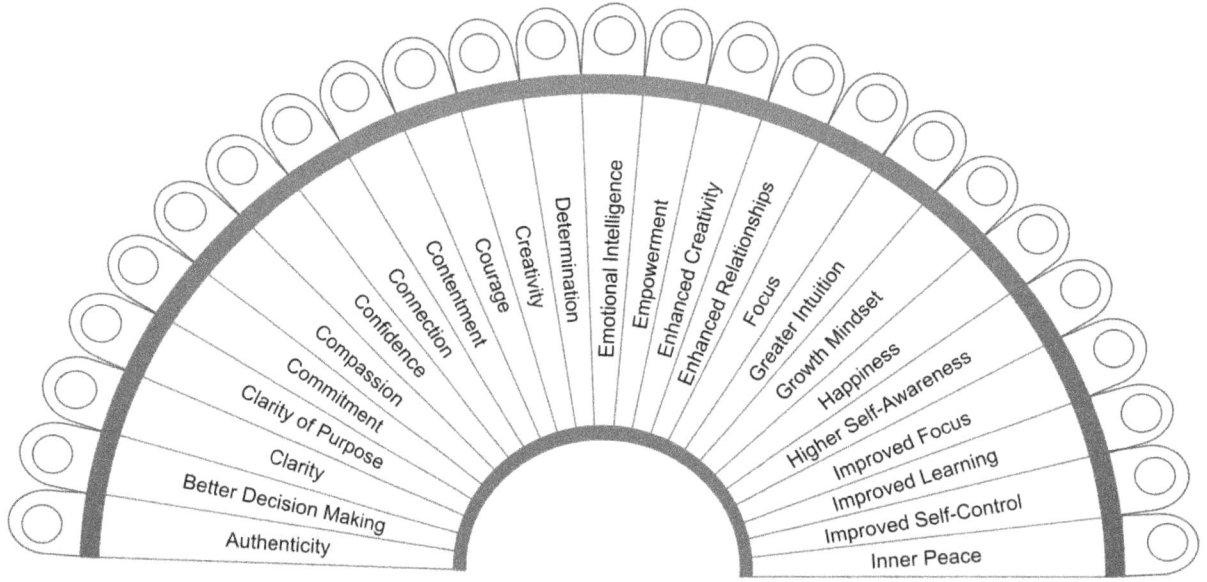

Personal Transformation, Chart 1

The chart contains the following labels (reading around the fan):

Authenticity, Better Decision Making, Clarity, Clarity of Purpose, Commitment, Compassion, Confidence, Connection, Contentment, Courage, Creativity, Determination, Emotional Intelligence, Empowerment, Enhanced Creativity, Enhanced Relationships, Focus, Greater Intuition, Growth Mindset, Happiness, Higher Self-Awareness, Improved Focus, Improved Learning, Improved Self-Control, Inner Peace

Royal Template 25

Diving Deep into the Pool of the Mind

Chart 375

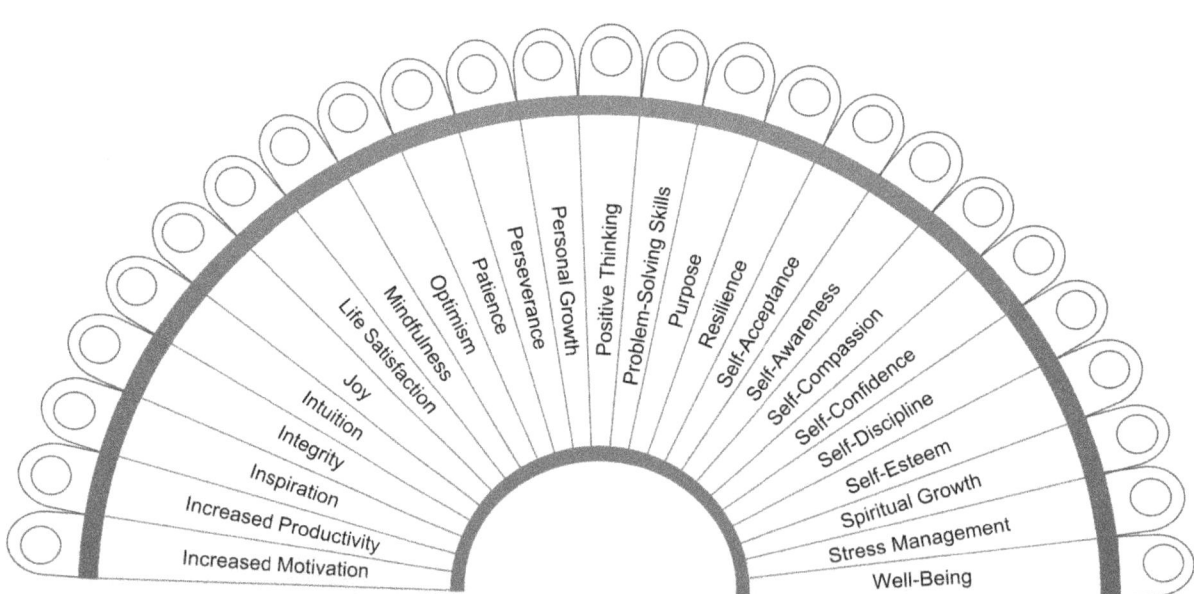

Personal Transformation, Chart 2

The chart contains the following labels (reading around the fan):

Increased Motivation, Increased Productivity, Inspiration, Integrity, Intuition, Joy, Life Satisfaction, Mindfulness, Optimism, Patience, Perseverance, Personal Growth, Positive Thinking, Problem-Solving Skills, Purpose, Resilience, Self-Acceptance, Self-Awareness, Self-Compassion, Self-Confidence, Self-Discipline, Self-Esteem, Spiritual Growth, Stress Management, Well-Being

Royal Template 25

Diving Deep into the Pool of the Mind

Chart 376

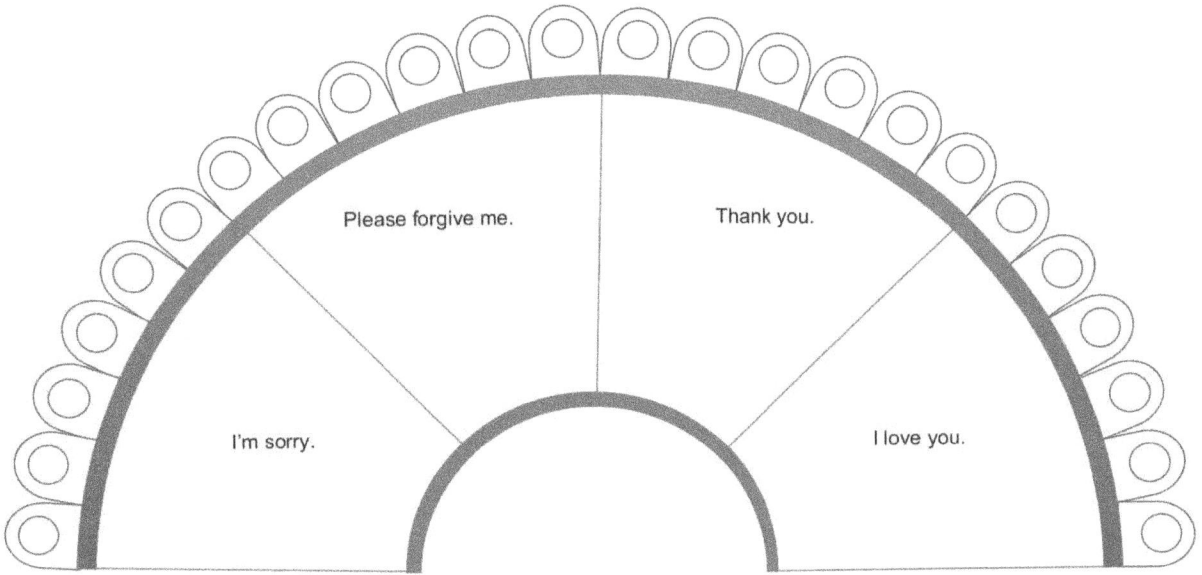

Ho'Oponopono

Please forgive me.

Thank you.

I'm sorry.

I love you.

Royal Template 4h

Chart 377

Diving Deep into the Pool of the Mind

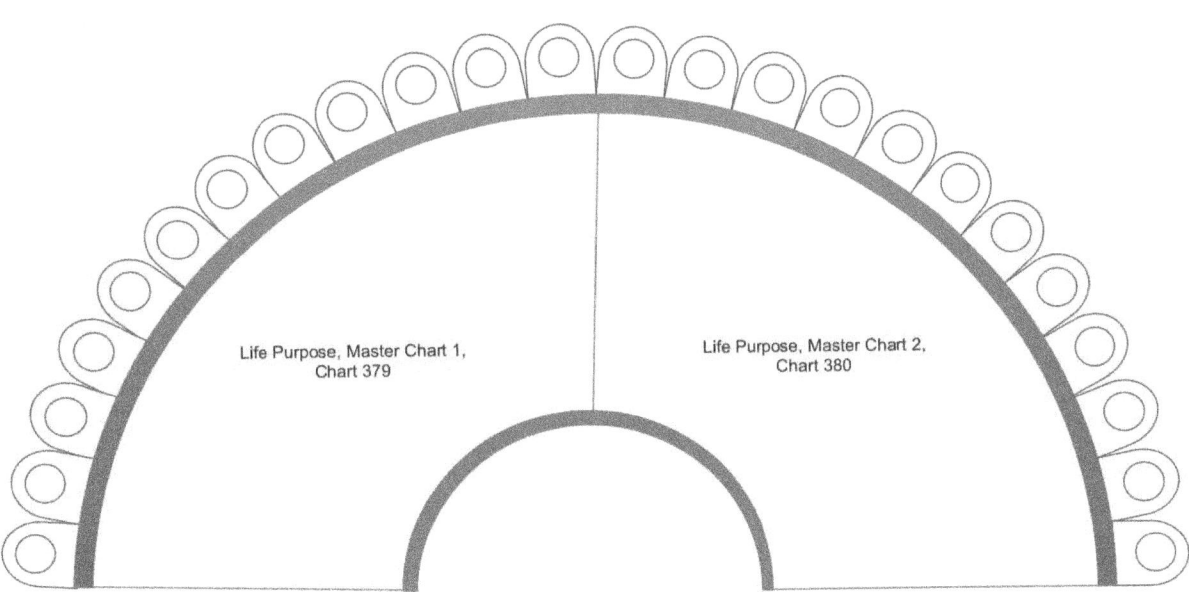

Life Purpose, Master Chart 1, Chart 379

Life Purpose, Master Chart 2, Chart 380

Life Purpose, Grand Master Chart

Royal Template 2

Chart 378

Diving Deep into the Pool of the Mind

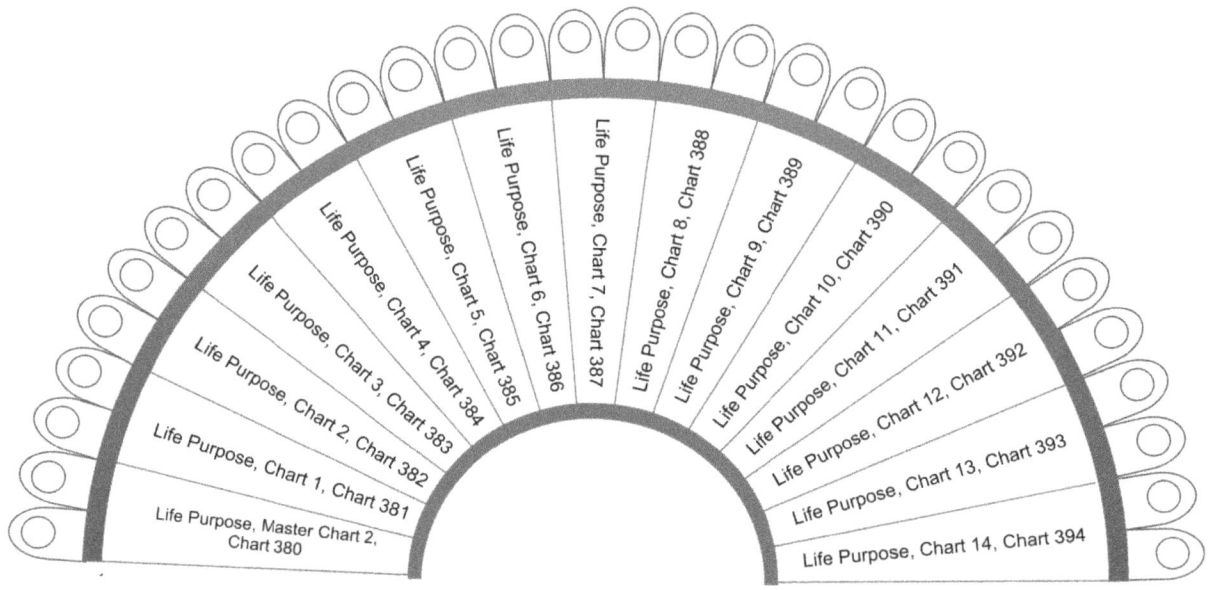

Life Purpose, Master Chart 1

Life Purpose, Master Chart 2, Chart 380
Life Purpose, Chart 1, Chart 381
Life Purpose, Chart 2, Chart 382
Life Purpose, Chart 3, Chart 383
Life Purpose, Chart 4, Chart 384
Life Purpose, Chart 5, Chart 385
Life Purpose, Chart 6, Chart 386
Life Purpose, Chart 7, Chart 387
Life Purpose, Chart 8, Chart 388
Life Purpose, Chart 9, Chart 389
Life Purpose, Chart 10, Chart 390
Life Purpose, Chart 11, Chart 391
Life Purpose, Chart 12, Chart 392
Life Purpose, Chart 13, Chart 393
Life Purpose, Chart 14, Chart 394

Royal Template 15

Diving Deep into the Pool of the Mind

Chart 379

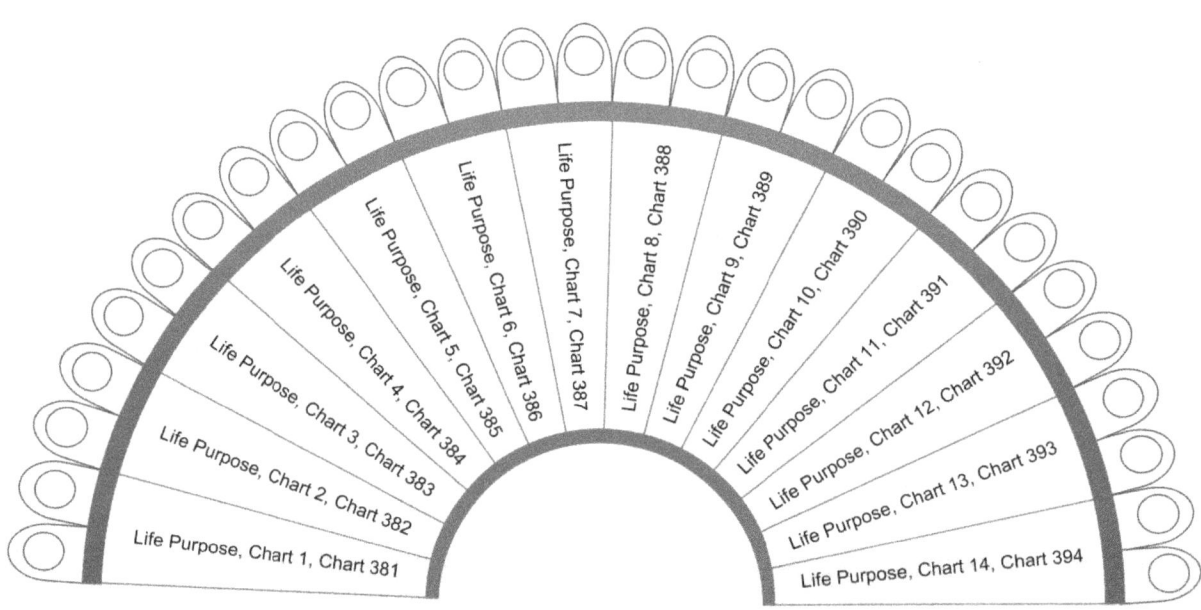

Life Purpose, Master Chart 2

Life Purpose, Chart 1, Chart 381
Life Purpose, Chart 2, Chart 382
Life Purpose, Chart 3, Chart 383
Life Purpose, Chart 4, Chart 384
Life Purpose, Chart 5, Chart 385
Life Purpose, Chart 6, Chart 386
Life Purpose, Chart 7, Chart 387
Life Purpose, Chart 8, Chart 388
Life Purpose, Chart 9, Chart 389
Life Purpose, Chart 10, Chart 390
Life Purpose, Chart 11, Chart 391
Life Purpose, Chart 12, Chart 392
Life Purpose, Chart 13, Chart 393
Life Purpose, Chart 14, Chart 394

Royal Template 14

Diving Deep into the Pool of the Mind

Chart 380

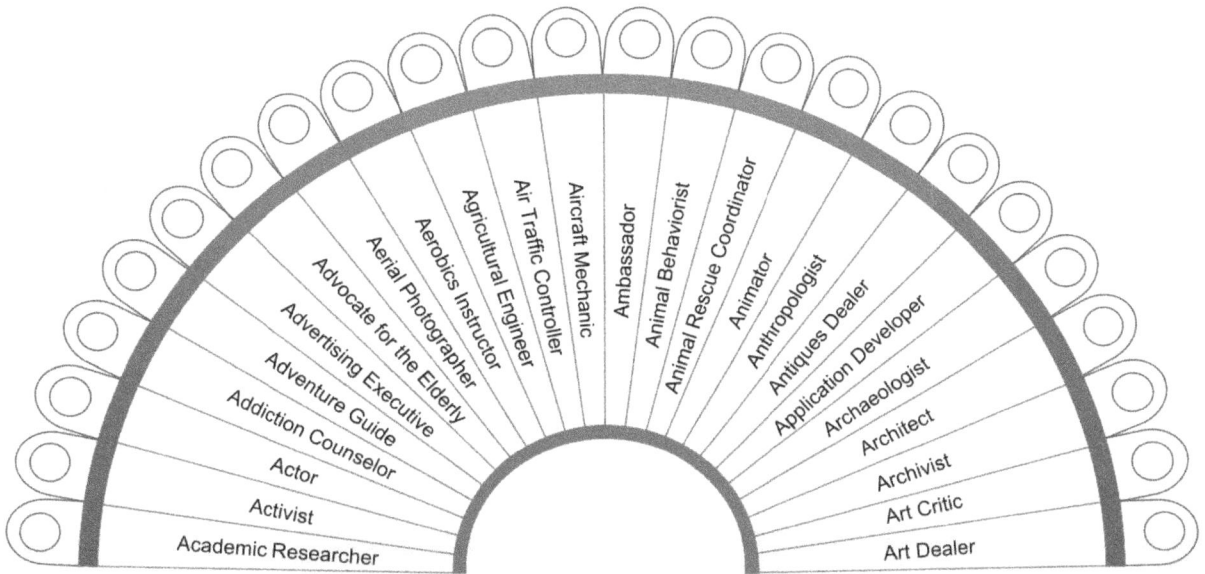

Life Purpose, Chart 1

The chart contains the following labels (left to right):

Academic Researcher, Activist, Actor, Addiction Counselor, Adventure Guide, Advertising Executive, Advocate for the Elderly, Aerial Photographer, Aerobics Instructor, Agricultural Engineer, Air Traffic Controller, Aircraft Mechanic, Ambassador, Animal Behaviorist, Animal Rescue Coordinator, Animator, Anthropologist, Antiques Dealer, Application Developer, Archaeologist, Architect, Archivist, Art Critic, Art Dealer

Royal Template 24

Diving Deep into the Pool of the Mind

Chart 381

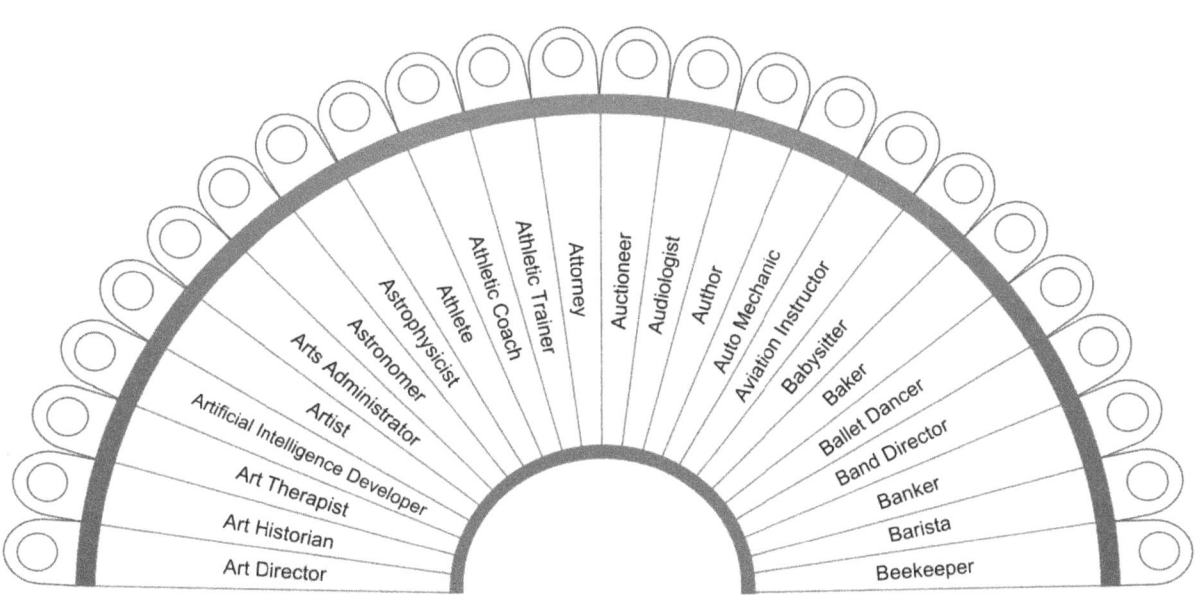

Life Purpose, Chart 2

The chart contains the following labels (left to right):

Art Director, Art Historian, Art Therapist, Artificial Intelligence Developer, Artist, Arts Administrator, Astronomer, Astrophysicist, Athlete, Athletic Coach, Athletic Trainer, Attorney, Auctioneer, Audiologist, Author, Auto Mechanic, Aviation Instructor, Babysitter, Baker, Ballet Dancer, Band Director, Banker, Barista, Beekeeper

Royal Template 24

Diving Deep into the Pool of the Mind

Chart 382

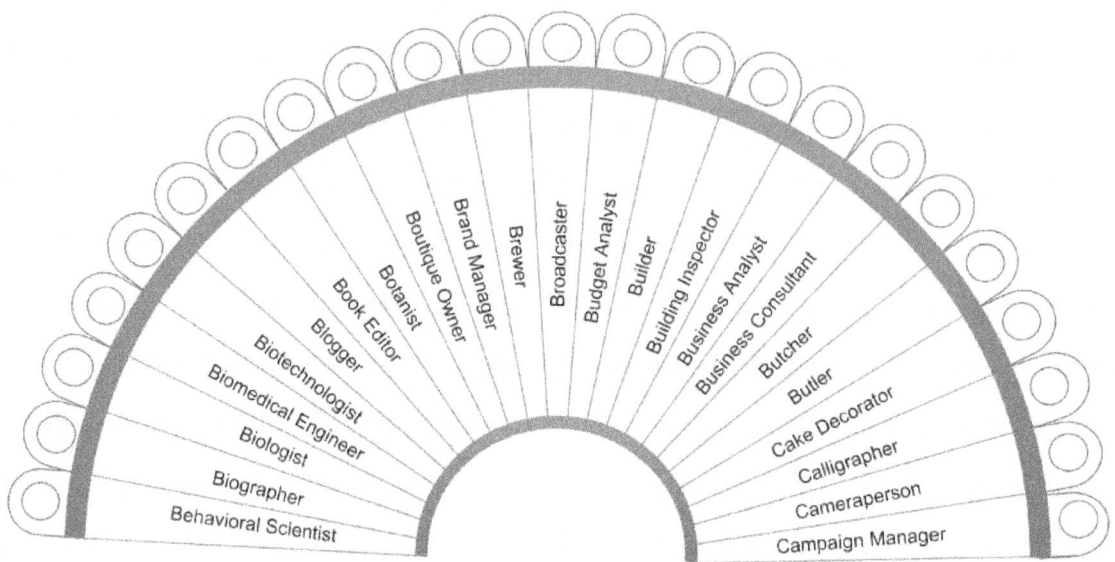

Life Purpose, Chart 3

Behavioral Scientist
Biographer
Biologist
Biomedical Engineer
Biotechnologist
Blogger
Book Editor
Botanist
Boutique Owner
Brand Manager
Brewer
Broadcaster
Budget Analyst
Builder
Building Inspector
Business Analyst
Business Consultant
Butcher
Butler
Cake Decorator
Calligrapher
Cameraperson
Campaign Manager

Diving Deep into the Pool of the Mind

Chart 383

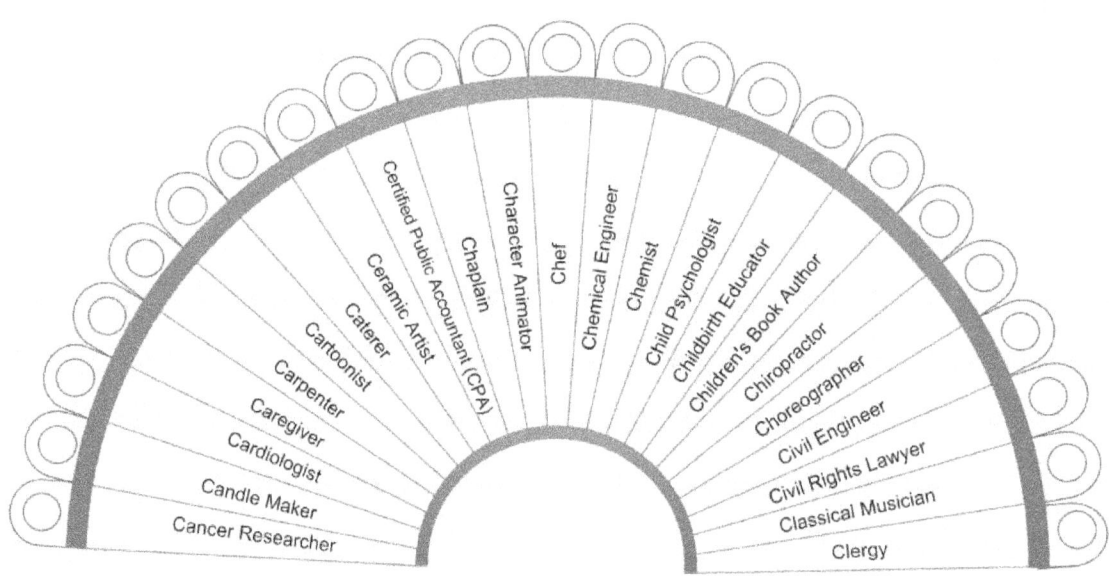

Life Purpose, Chart 4

Cancer Researcher
Candle Maker
Cardiologist
Caregiver
Carpenter
Cartoonist
Caterer
Ceramic Artist
Certified Public Accountant (CPA)
Chaplain
Character Animator
Chef
Chemical Engineer
Chemist
Child Psychologist
Childbirth Educator
Children's Book Author
Chiropractor
Choreographer
Civil Engineer
Civil Rights Lawyer
Classical Musician
Clergy

Diving Deep into the Pool of the Mind

Chart 384

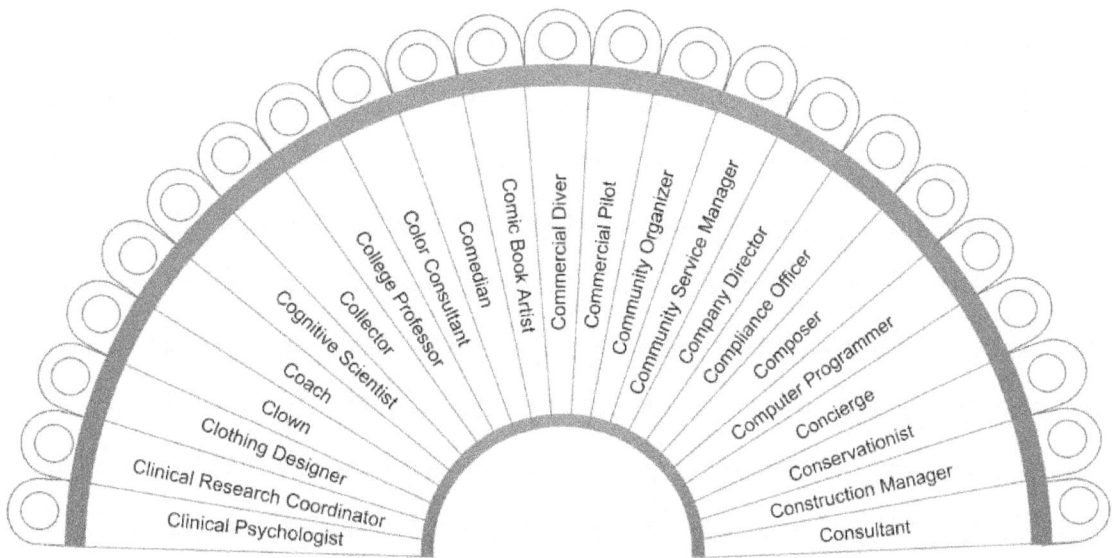

Life Purpose, Chart 5

Clinical Psychologist
Clinical Research Coordinator
Clothing Designer
Clown
Coach
Cognitive Scientist
Collector
College Professor
Color Consultant
Comedian
Comic Book Artist
Commercial Diver
Commercial Pilot
Community Organizer
Community Service Manager
Company Director
Compliance Officer
Composer
Computer Programmer
Concierge
Conservationist
Construction Manager
Consultant

Royal Template 23

Diving Deep into the Pool of the Mind

Chart 385

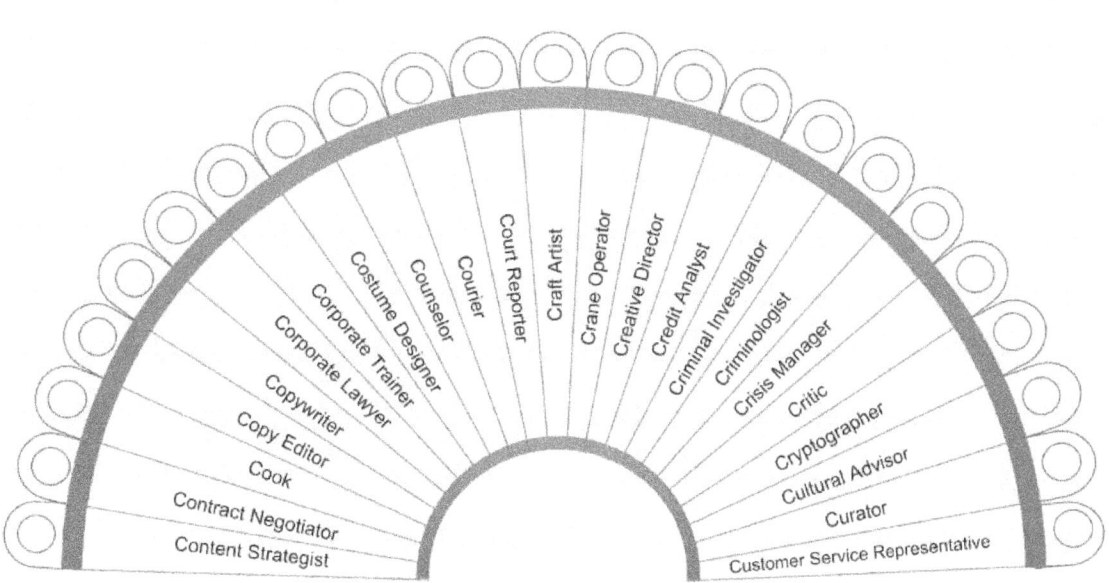

Life Purpose, Chart 6

Content Strategist
Contract Negotiator
Cook
Copy Editor
Copywriter
Corporate Lawyer
Corporate Trainer
Costume Designer
Counselor
Courier
Court Reporter
Craft Artist
Crane Operator
Creative Director
Credit Analyst
Criminal Investigator
Criminologist
Crisis Manager
Critic
Cryptographer
Cultural Advisor
Curator
Customer Service Representative

Royal Template 23

Diving Deep into the Pool of the Mind

Chart 386

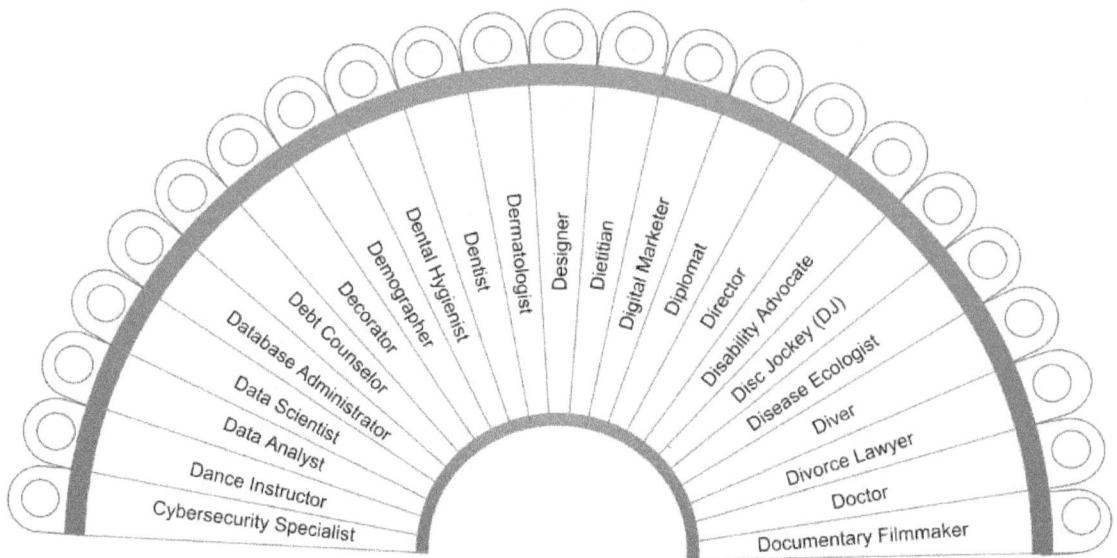

Life Purpose, Chart 7

The chart contains the following labels (clockwise from left):

- Cybersecurity Specialist
- Dance Instructor
- Data Analyst
- Data Scientist
- Database Administrator
- Debt Counselor
- Decorator
- Demographer
- Dental Hygienist
- Dentist
- Dermatologist
- Designer
- Dietitian
- Digital Marketer
- Diplomat
- Director
- Disability Advocate
- Disc Jockey (DJ)
- Disease Ecologist
- Diver
- Divorce Lawyer
- Doctor
- Documentary Filmmaker

Royal Template 23

Diving Deep into the Pool of the Mind

Chart 387

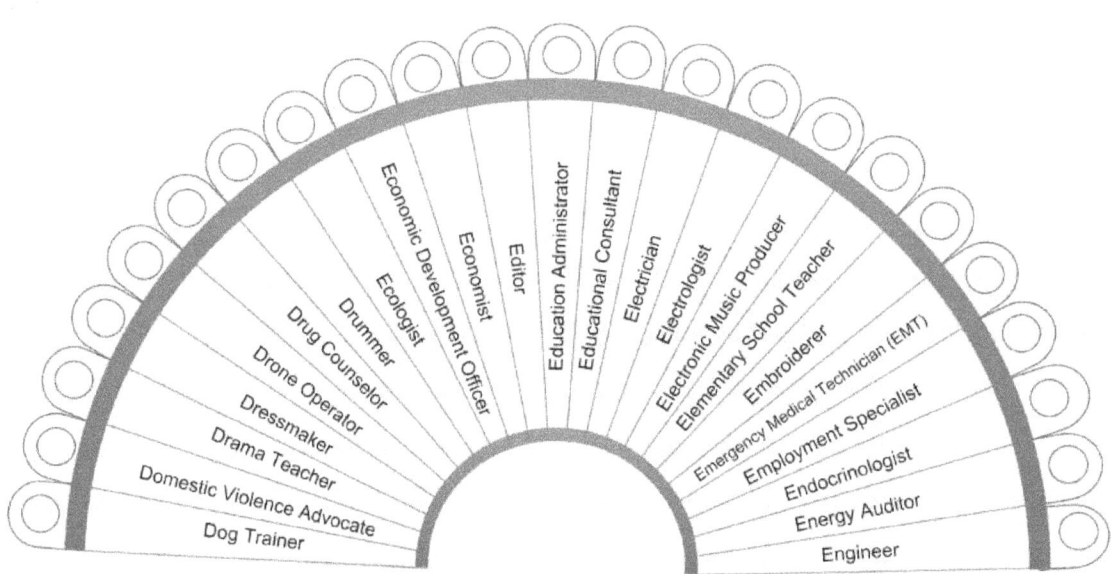

Life Purpose, Chart 8

The chart contains the following labels (clockwise from left):

- Dog Trainer
- Domestic Violence Advocate
- Drama Teacher
- Dressmaker
- Drone Operator
- Drug Counselor
- Drummer
- Ecologist
- Economic Development Officer
- Economist
- Editor
- Education Administrator
- Educational Consultant
- Electrician
- Electrologist
- Electronic Music Producer
- Elementary School Teacher
- Embroiderer
- Emergency Medical Technician (EMT)
- Employment Specialist
- Endocrinologist
- Energy Auditor
- Engineer

Royal Template 23

Diving Deep into the Pool of the Mind

Chart 388

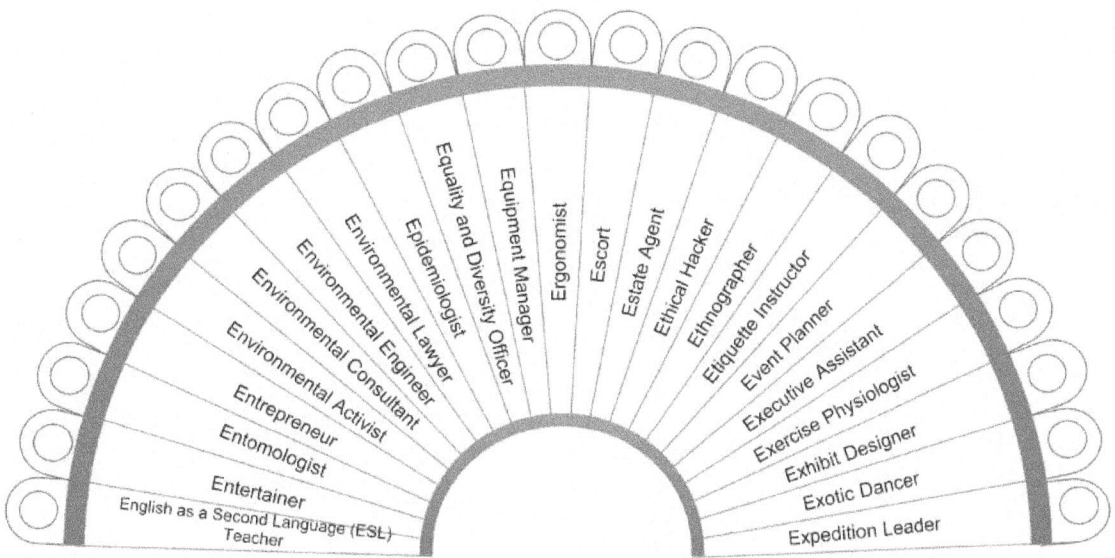

Life Purpose, Chart 9

The chart contains the following labels (reading around the fan):

- English as a Second Language (ESL) Teacher
- Entertainer
- Entomologist
- Entrepreneur
- Environmental Activist
- Environmental Consultant
- Environmental Engineer
- Environmental Lawyer
- Epidemiologist
- Equality and Diversity Officer
- Equipment Manager
- Ergonomist
- Escort
- Estate Agent
- Ethical Hacker
- Ethnographer
- Etiquette Instructor
- Event Planner
- Executive Assistant
- Exercise Physiologist
- Exhibit Designer
- Exotic Dancer
- Expedition Leader

Royal Template 23

Diving Deep into the Pool of the Mind

Chart 389

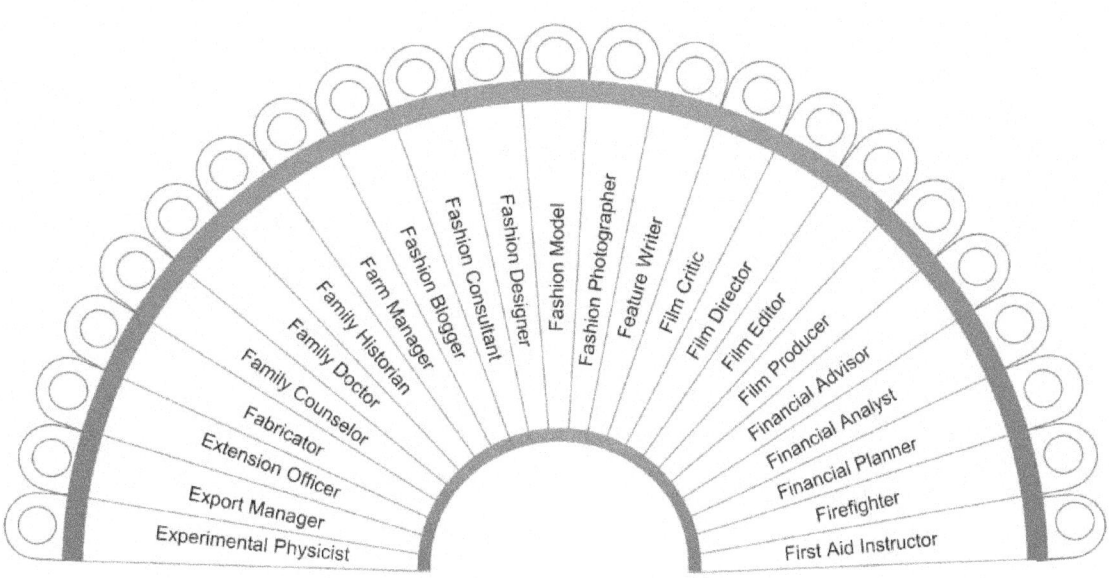

Life Purpose, Chart 10

The chart contains the following labels (reading around the fan):

- Experimental Physicist
- Export Manager
- Extension Officer
- Fabricator
- Family Counselor
- Family Doctor
- Family Historian
- Family Manager
- Farm Manager
- Fashion Blogger
- Fashion Consultant
- Fashion Designer
- Fashion Model
- Fashion Photographer
- Feature Writer
- Film Critic
- Film Director
- Film Editor
- Film Producer
- Financial Advisor
- Financial Analyst
- Financial Planner
- Firefighter
- First Aid Instructor

Royal Template 23

Diving Deep into the Pool of the Mind

Chart 390

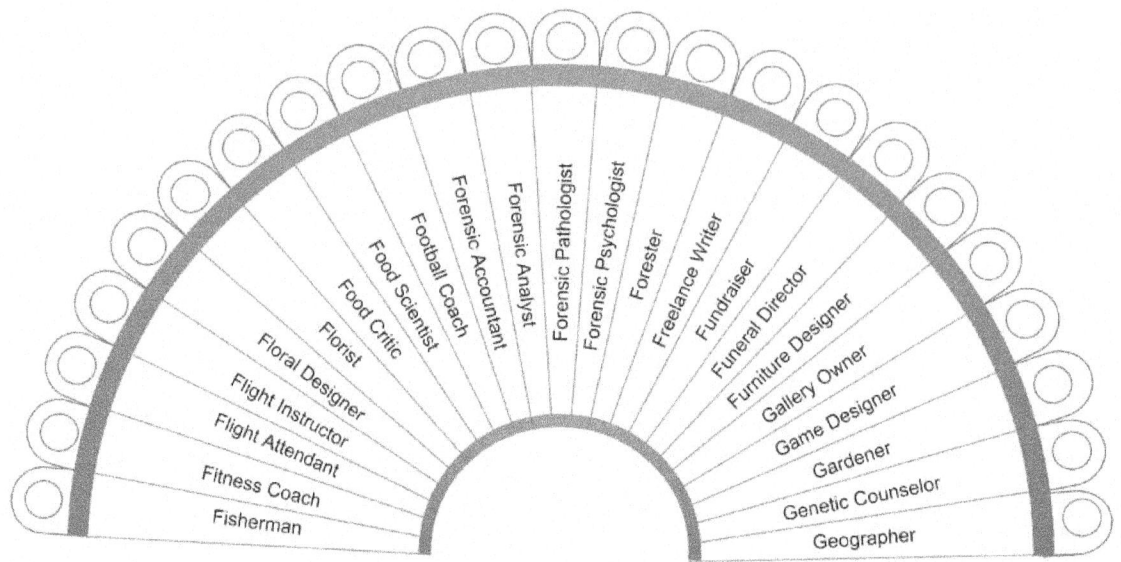

Life Purpose, Chart 11

Fisherman
Fitness Coach
Flight Attendant
Flight Instructor
Floral Designer
Florist
Food Critic
Food Scientist
Football Coach
Forensic Accountant
Forensic Analyst
Forensic Pathologist
Forensic Psychologist
Forester
Freelance Writer
Fundraiser
Funeral Director
Furniture Designer
Gallery Owner
Game Designer
Gardener
Genetic Counselor
Geographer

Royal Template 23

Diving Deep into the Pool of the Mind

Chart 391

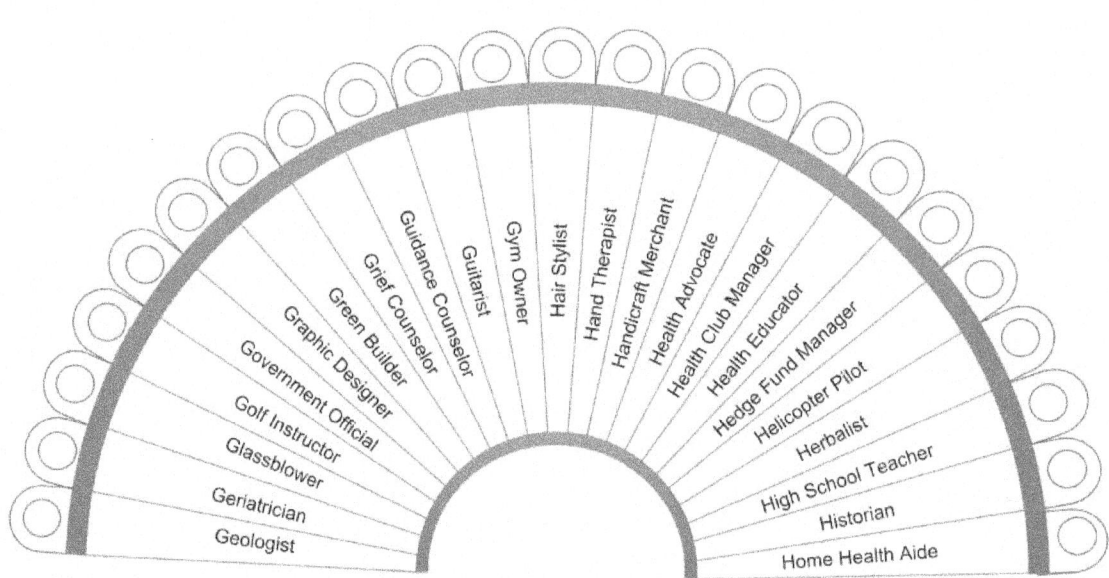

Life Purpose, Chart 12

Geologist
Geriatrician
Glassblower
Golf Instructor
Government Official
Graphic Designer
Green Builder
Grief Counselor
Guidance Counselor
Guitarist
Gym Owner
Hair Stylist
Hand Therapist
Handicraft Merchant
Health Advocate
Health Club Manager
Health Educator
Hedge Fund Manager
Helicopter Pilot
Herbalist
High School Teacher
Historian
Home Health Aide

Royal Template 23

Diving Deep into the Pool of the Mind

Chart 392

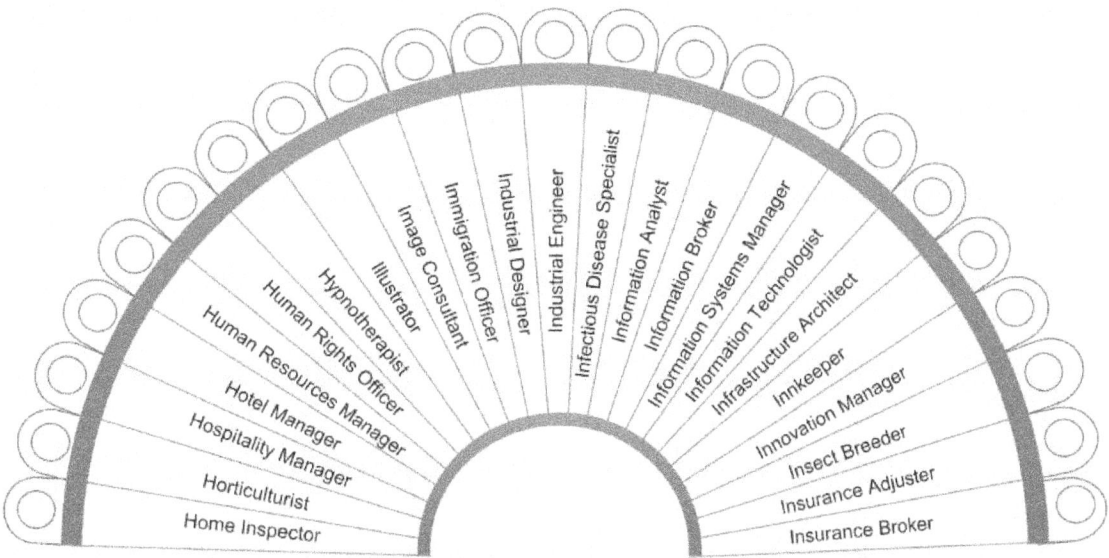

Life Purpose, Chart 13

The chart contains the following labels (left to right):

Home Inspector, Horticulturist, Hospitality Manager, Hotel Manager, Human Resources Manager, Human Rights Officer, Hypnotherapist, Illustrator, Image Consultant, Immigration Officer, Industrial Designer, Industrial Engineer, Infectious Disease Specialist, Information Analyst, Information Broker, Information Systems Manager, Information Technologist, Infrastructure Architect, Innkeeper, Innovation Manager, Insect Breeder, Insurance Adjuster, Insurance Broker

Diving Deep into the Pool of the Mind

Chart 393

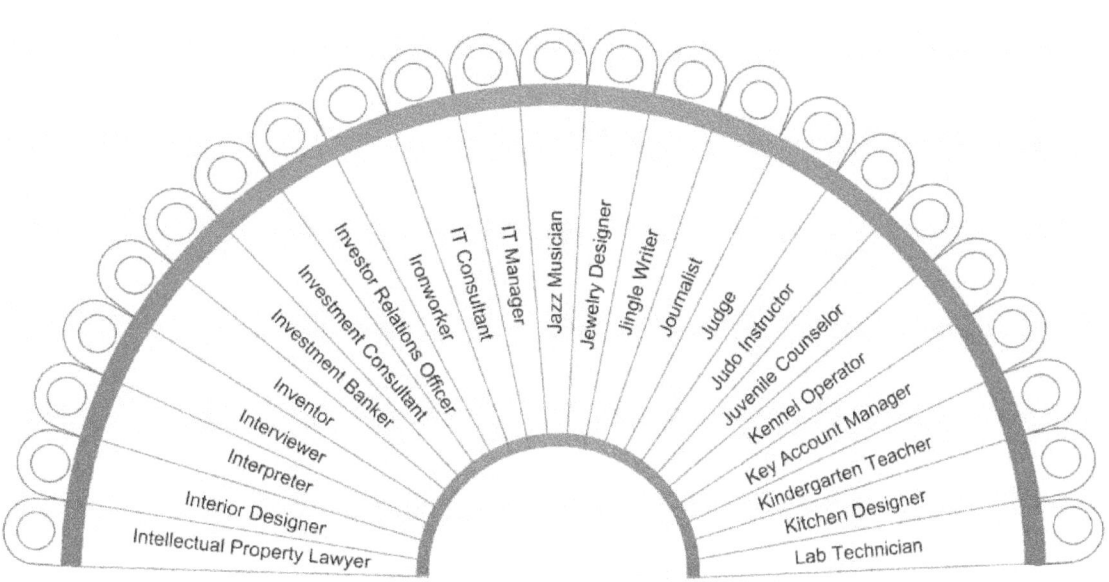

Life Purpose, Chart 14

The chart contains the following labels (left to right):

Intellectual Property Lawyer, Interior Designer, Interpreter, Interviewer, Inventor, Investment Banker, Investment Consultant, Investor Relations Officer, Ironworker, IT Consultant, IT Manager, Jazz Musician, Jewelry Designer, Jingle Writer, Journalist, Judge, Judo Instructor, Juvenile Counselor, Kennel Operator, Key Account Manager, Kindergarten Teacher, Kitchen Designer, Lab Technician

Diving Deep into the Pool of the Mind

Chart 394

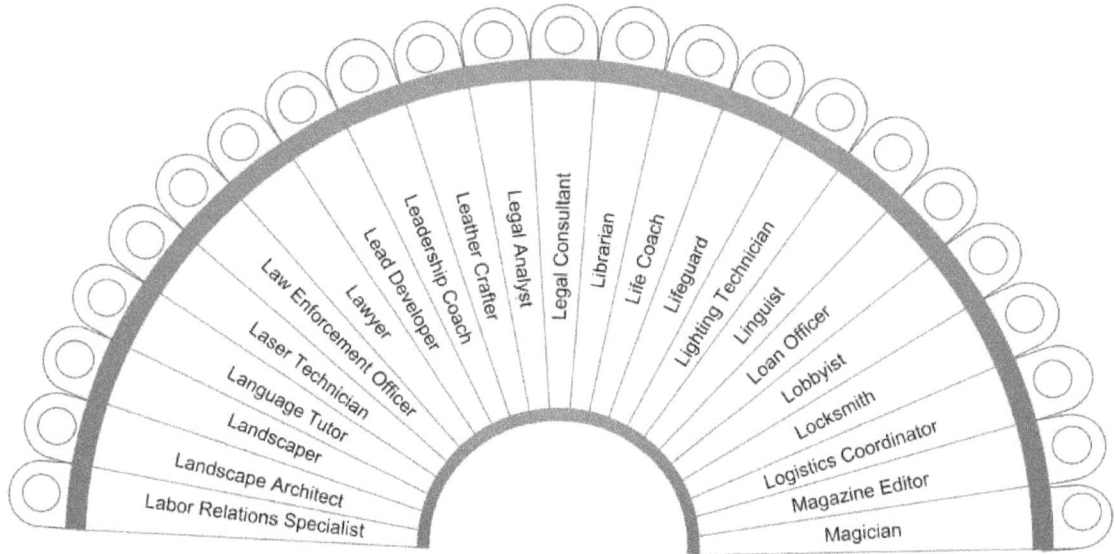

Life Purpose, Chart 15

Leadership Coach
Lead Developer
Lawyer
Law Enforcement Officer
Laser Technician
Language Tutor
Landscaper
Landscape Architect
Labor Relations Specialist
Leather Crafter
Legal Analyst
Legal Consultant
Librarian
Life Coach
Lifeguard
Lighting Technician
Linguist
Loan Officer
Lobbyist
Locksmith
Logistics Coordinator
Magazine Editor
Magician

Royal Template 23

Diving Deep into the Pool of the Mind

Chart 395

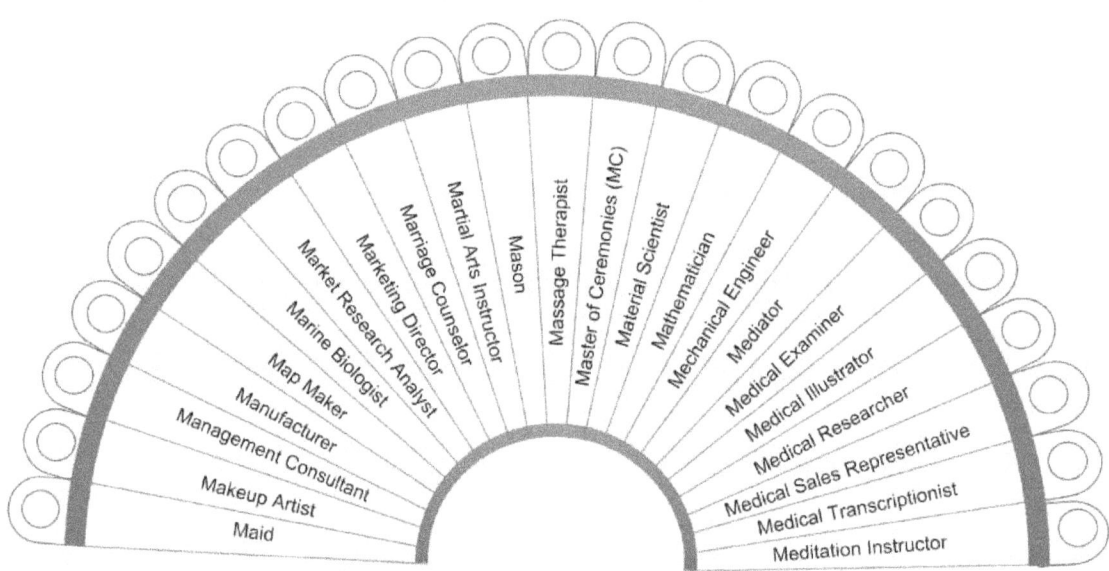

Life Purpose, Chart 16

Market Research Analyst
Marketing Director
Marriage Counselor
Martial Arts Instructor
Mason
Massage Therapist
Master of Ceremonies (MC)
Material Scientist
Mathematician
Mechanical Engineer
Mediator
Medical Examiner
Medical Illustrator
Medical Researcher
Medical Sales Representative
Medical Transcriptionist
Meditation Instructor
Marine Biologist
Map Maker
Manufacturer
Management Consultant
Makeup Artist
Maid

Royal Template 23

Diving Deep into the Pool of the Mind

Chart 396

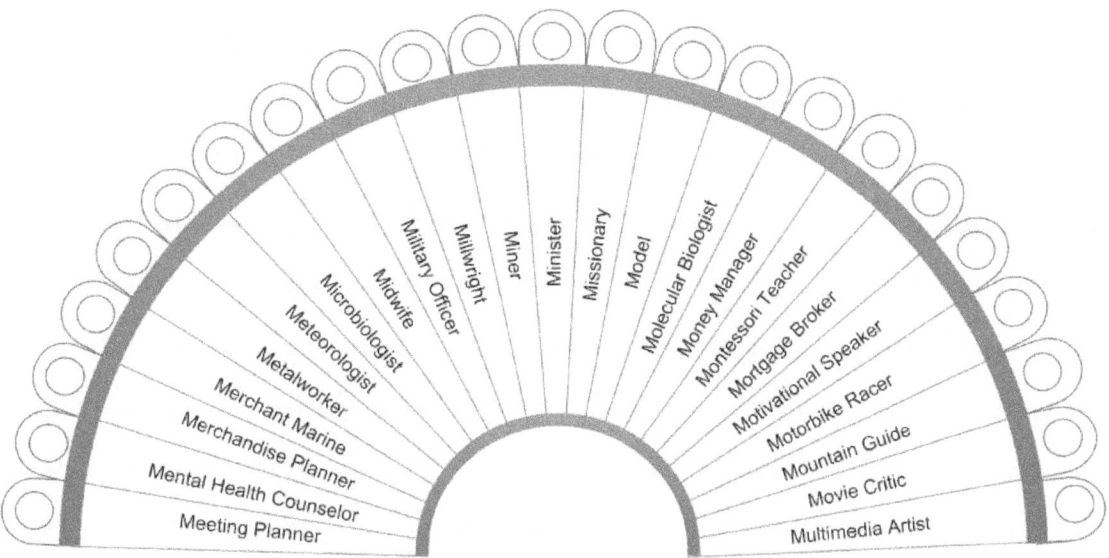

Life Purpose, Chart 17

Meeting Planner
Mental Health Counselor
Merchandise Planner
Merchant Marine
Metalworker
Meteorologist
Microbiologist
Midwife
Military Officer
Millwright
Miner
Minister
Missionary
Model
Molecular Biologist
Money Manager
Montessori Teacher
Mortgage Broker
Motivational Speaker
Motorbike Racer
Mountain Guide
Movie Critic
Multimedia Artist

Royal Template 23

Diving Deep into the Pool of the Mind

Chart 397

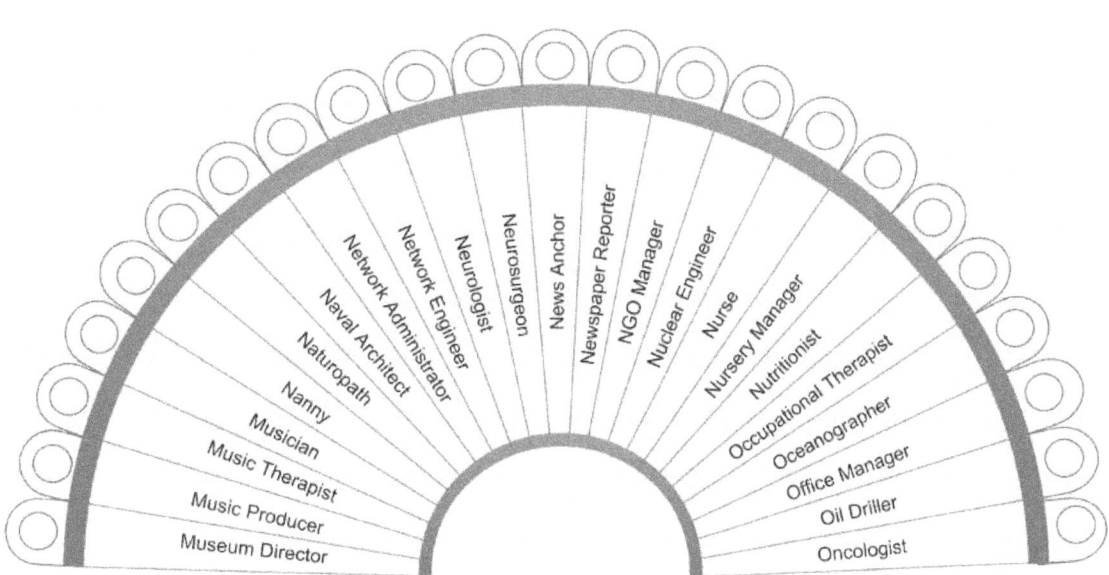

Life Purpose, Chart 18

Museum Director
Music Producer
Music Therapist
Musician
Nanny
Naturopath
Naval Architect
Network Administrator
Network Engineer
Neurologist
Neurosurgeon
News Anchor
Newspaper Reporter
NGO Manager
Nuclear Engineer
Nurse
Nursery Manager
Nutritionist
Occupational Therapist
Oceanographer
Office Manager
Oil Driller
Oncologist

Royal Template 23

Diving Deep into the Pool of the Mind

Chart 398

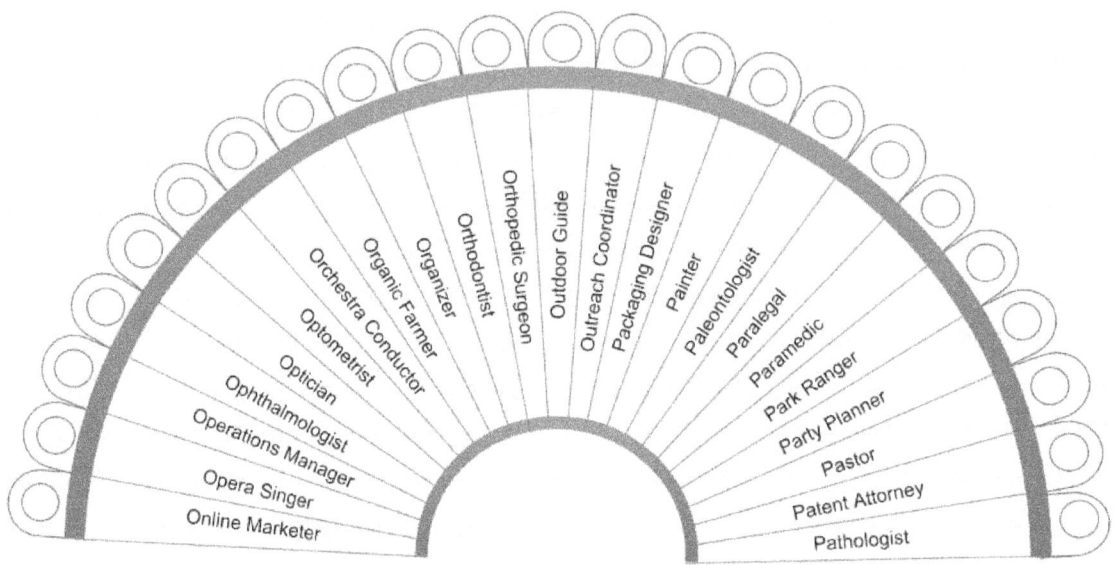

Life Purpose, Chart 19

The chart contains the following labels (reading around the fan):

- Online Marketer
- Opera Singer
- Operations Manager
- Ophthalmologist
- Optician
- Optometrist
- Orchestra Conductor
- Organic Farmer
- Organizer
- Orthodontist
- Orthopedic Surgeon
- Outdoor Guide
- Outreach Coordinator
- Packaging Designer
- Painter
- Paleontologist
- Paralegal
- Paramedic
- Park Ranger
- Party Planner
- Pastor
- Patent Attorney
- Pathologist

Royal Template 23

Diving Deep into the Pool of the Mind

Chart 399

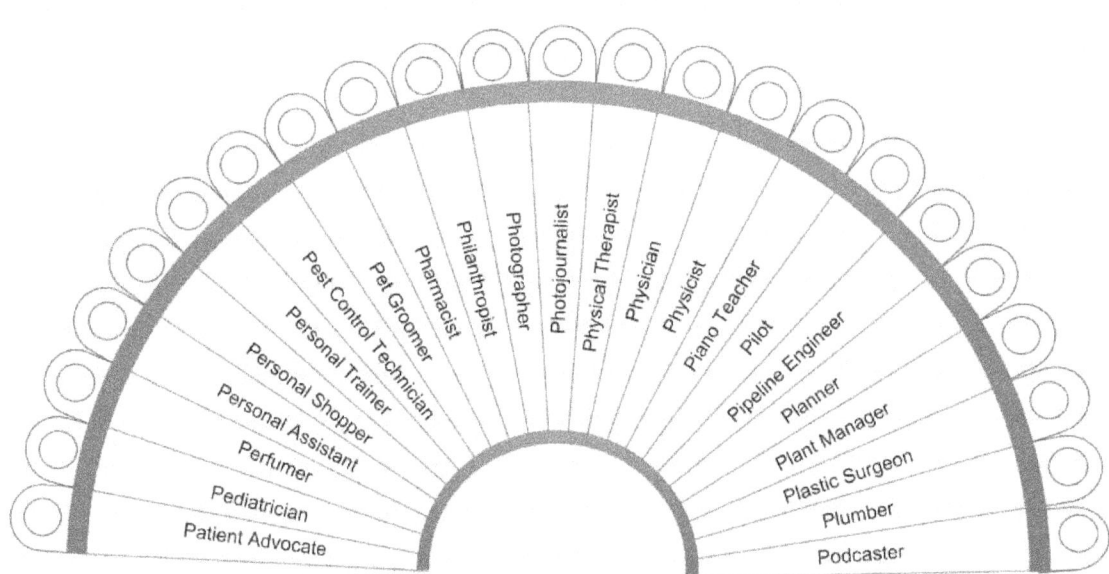

Life Purpose, Chart 20

The chart contains the following labels (reading around the fan):

- Patient Advocate
- Pediatrician
- Perfumer
- Personal Assistant
- Personal Shopper
- Personal Trainer
- Pest Control Technician
- Pet Groomer
- Pharmacist
- Philanthropist
- Photographer
- Photojournalist
- Physical Therapist
- Physician
- Physicist
- Piano Teacher
- Pilot
- Pipeline Engineer
- Planner
- Plant Manager
- Plastic Surgeon
- Plumber
- Podcaster

Royal Template 23

Diving Deep into the Pool of the Mind

Chart 400

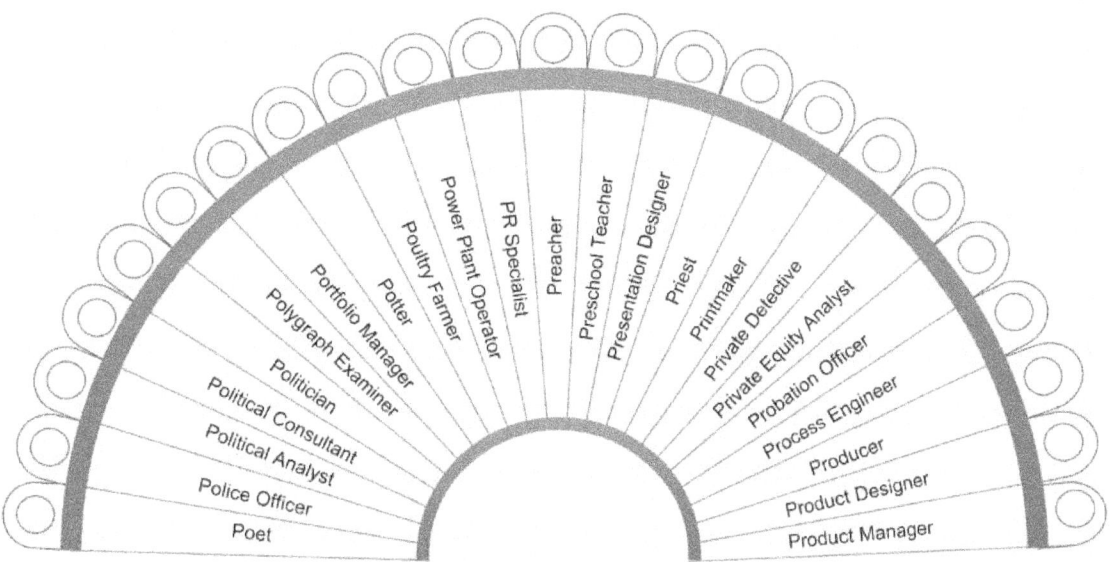

Life Purpose, Chart 21

Power Plant Operator
Poultry Farmer
Potter
Portfolio Manager
Polygraph Examiner
Politician
Political Consultant
Political Analyst
Police Officer
Poet
PR Specialist
Preacher
Preschool Teacher
Presentation Designer
Priest
Printmaker
Private Detective
Private Equity Analyst
Probation Officer
Process Engineer
Producer
Product Designer
Product Manager

Royal Template 23

Diving Deep into the Pool of the Mind

Chart 401

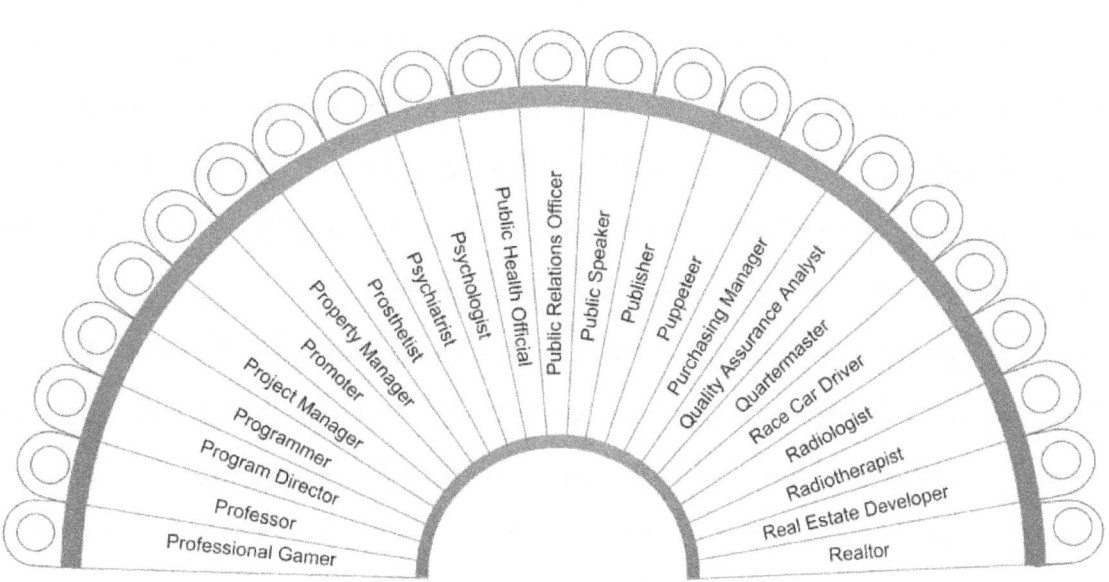

Life Purpose, Chart 22

Property Manager
Prosthetist
Psychiatrist
Psychologist
Public Health Official
Public Relations Officer
Public Speaker
Publisher
Puppeteer
Purchasing Manager
Promoter
Project Manager
Programmer
Program Director
Professor
Professional Gamer
Quality Assurance Analyst
Quartermaster
Race Car Driver
Radiologist
Radiotherapist
Real Estate Developer
Realtor

Royal Template 23

Diving Deep into the Pool of the Mind

Chart 402

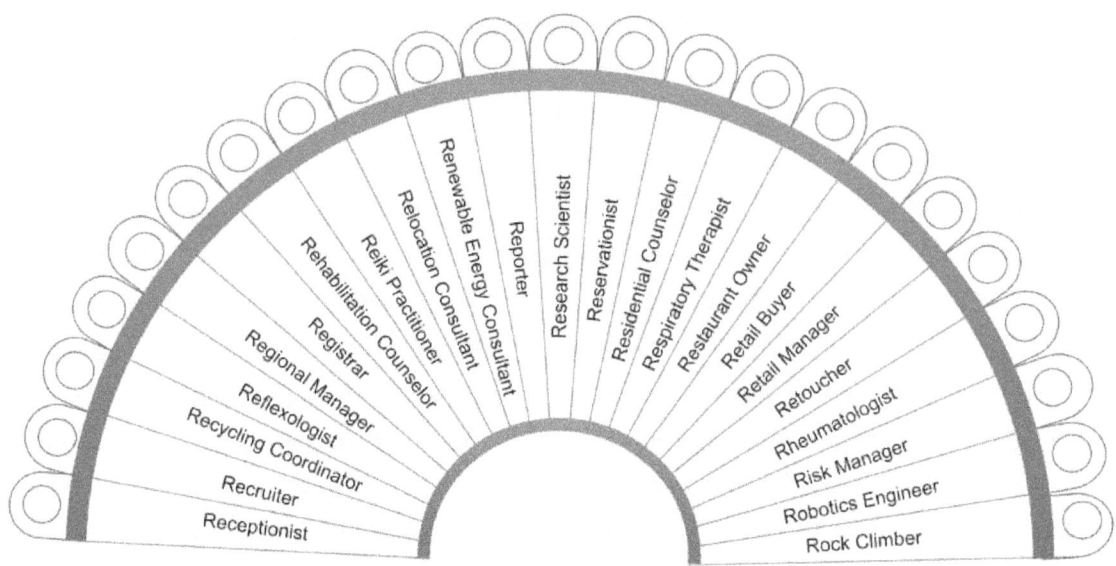

Life Purpose, Chart 23

The chart shows the following labels arranged in a fan pattern (left to right):

Receptionist, Recruiter, Recycling Coordinator, Reflexologist, Regional Manager, Registrar, Rehabilitation Counselor, Reiki Practitioner, Relocation Consultant, Renewable Energy Consultant, Reporter, Research Scientist, Reservationist, Residential Counselor, Respiratory Therapist, Restaurant Owner, Retail Buyer, Retail Manager, Retoucher, Rheumatologist, Risk Manager, Robotics Engineer, Rock Climber

Royal Template 23

Diving Deep into the Pool of the Mind

Chart 403

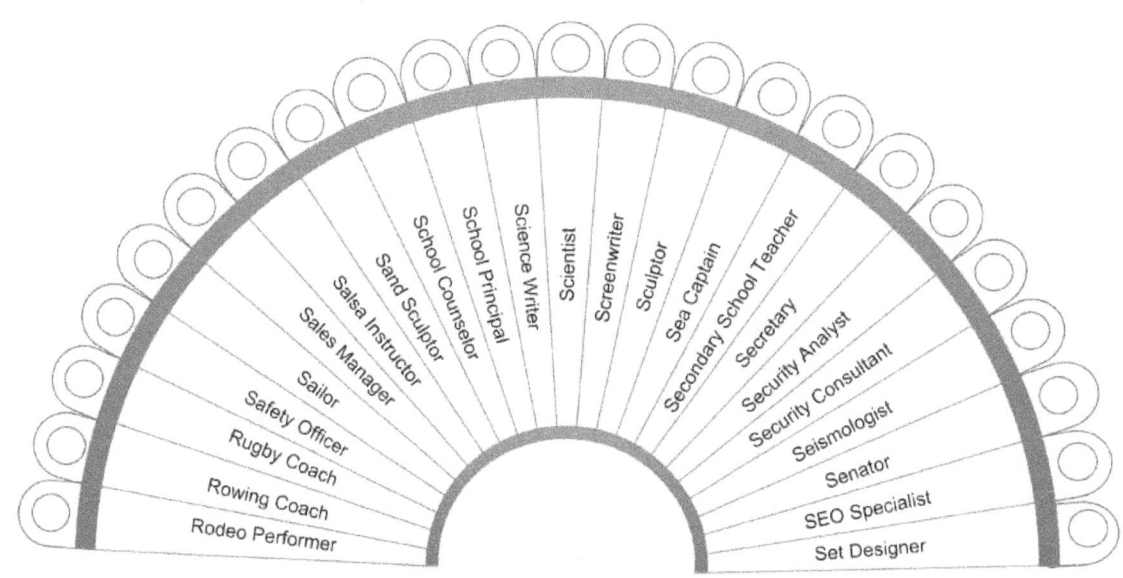

Life Purpose, Chart 24

The chart shows the following labels arranged in a fan pattern (left to right):

Rodeo Performer, Rowing Coach, Rugby Coach, Safety Officer, Sailor, Sales Manager, Salsa Instructor, Sand Sculptor, School Counselor, School Principal, Science Writer, Scientist, Screenwriter, Sculptor, Sea Captain, Secondary School Teacher, Secretary, Security Analyst, Security Consultant, Seismologist, Senator, SEO Specialist, Set Designer

Royal Template 23

Diving Deep into the Pool of the Mind

Chart 404

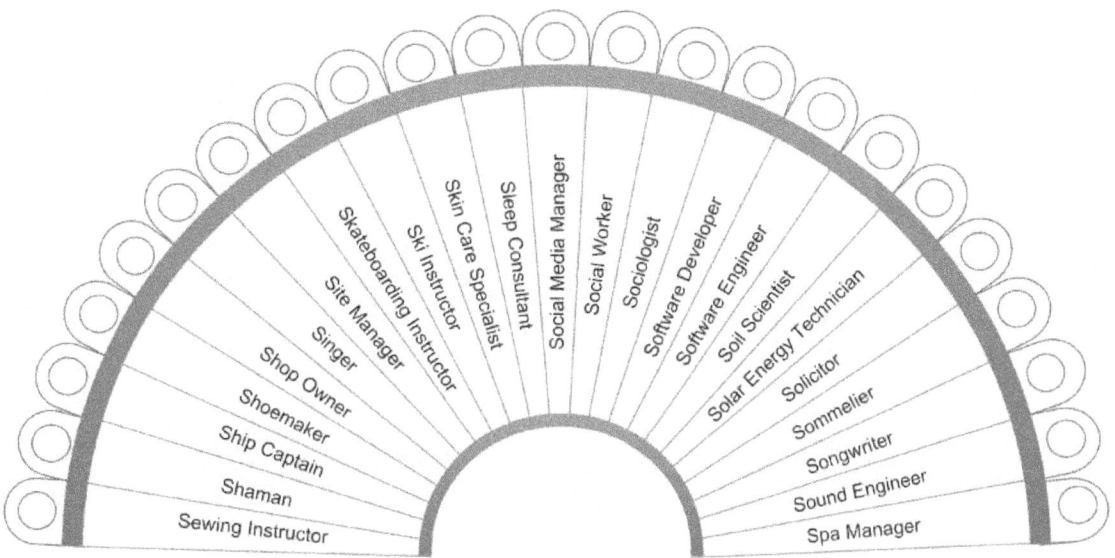

Life Purpose, Chart 25

The chart contains the following labels (reading around the fan):

- Sewing Instructor
- Shaman
- Ship Captain
- Shoemaker
- Shop Owner
- Singer
- Site Manager
- Skateboarding Instructor
- Ski Instructor
- Skin Care Specialist
- Sleep Consultant
- Social Media Manager
- Social Worker
- Sociologist
- Software Developer
- Software Engineer
- Soil Scientist
- Solar Energy Technician
- Solicitor
- Sommelier
- Songwriter
- Sound Engineer
- Spa Manager

Royal Template 23

Diving Deep into the Pool of the Mind

Chart 405

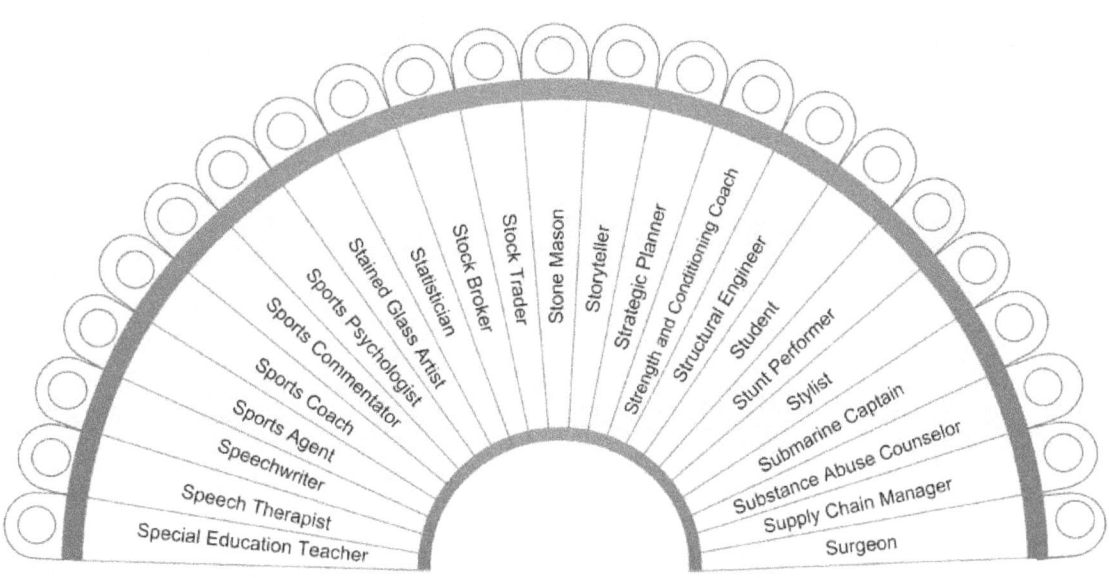

Life Purpose, Chart 26

The chart contains the following labels (reading around the fan):

- Special Education Teacher
- Speech Therapist
- Speechwriter
- Sports Agent
- Sports Coach
- Sports Commentator
- Sports Psychologist
- Stained Glass Artist
- Statistician
- Stock Broker
- Stock Trader
- Stone Mason
- Storyteller
- Strategic Planner
- Strength and Conditioning Coach
- Structural Engineer
- Student
- Stunt Performer
- Stylist
- Submarine Captain
- Substance Abuse Counselor
- Supply Chain Manager
- Surgeon

Royal Template 23

Diving Deep into the Pool of the Mind

Chart 406

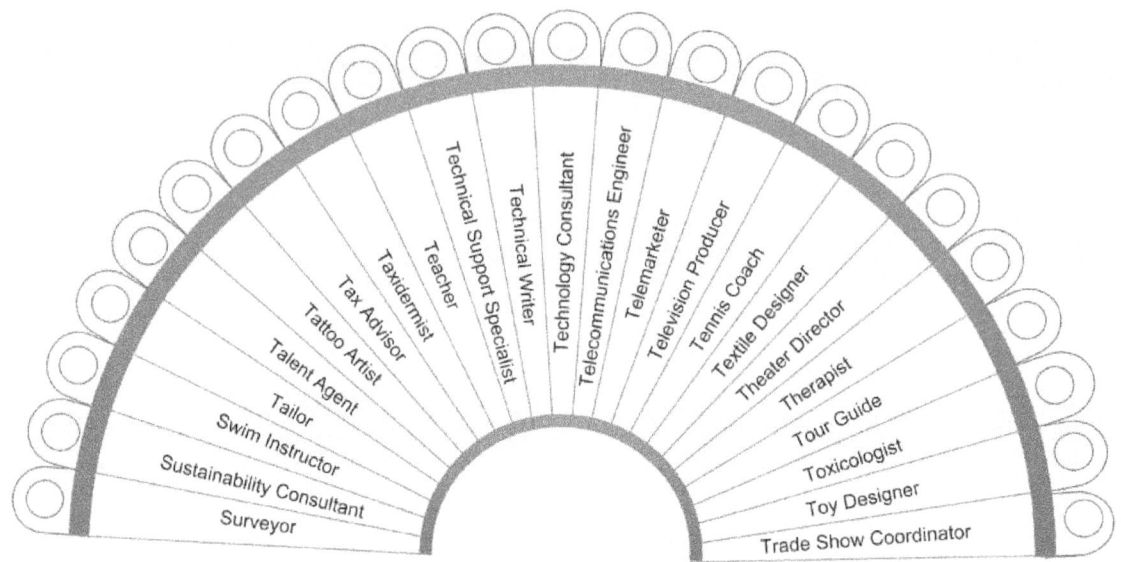

Life Purpose, Chart 27

The chart shows a fan layout with the following occupations (left to right):

Surveyor, Sustainability Consultant, Swim Instructor, Tailor, Talent Agent, Tattoo Artist, Tax Advisor, Taxidermist, Teacher, Technical Support Specialist, Technical Writer, Technology Consultant, Telecommunications Engineer, Telemarketer, Television Producer, Tennis Coach, Textile Designer, Theater Director, Therapist, Tour Guide, Toxicologist, Toy Designer, Trade Show Coordinator

Royal Template 23

Diving Deep into the Pool of the Mind

Chart 407

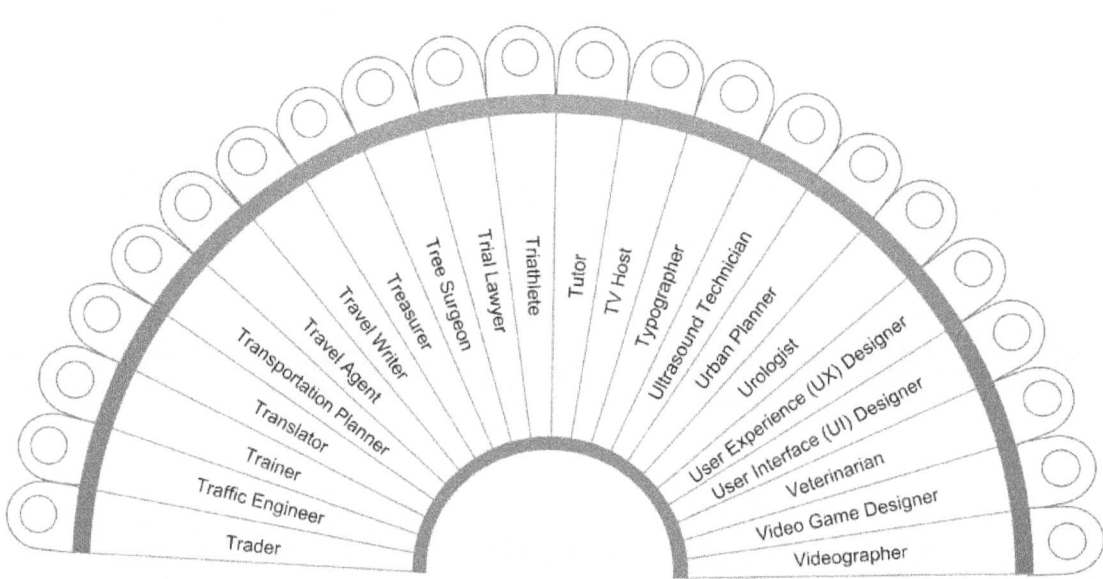

Life Purpose, Chart 28

The chart shows a fan layout with the following occupations (left to right):

Trader, Traffic Engineer, Trainer, Translator, Transportation Planner, Travel Agent, Travel Writer, Treasurer, Tree Surgeon, Triathlete, Trial Lawyer, Tutor, TV Host, Typographer, Ultrasound Technician, Urban Planner, Urologist, User Experience (UX) Designer, User Interface (UI) Designer, Veterinarian, Video Game Designer, Videographer

Royal Template 22

Diving Deep into the Pool of the Mind

Chart 408

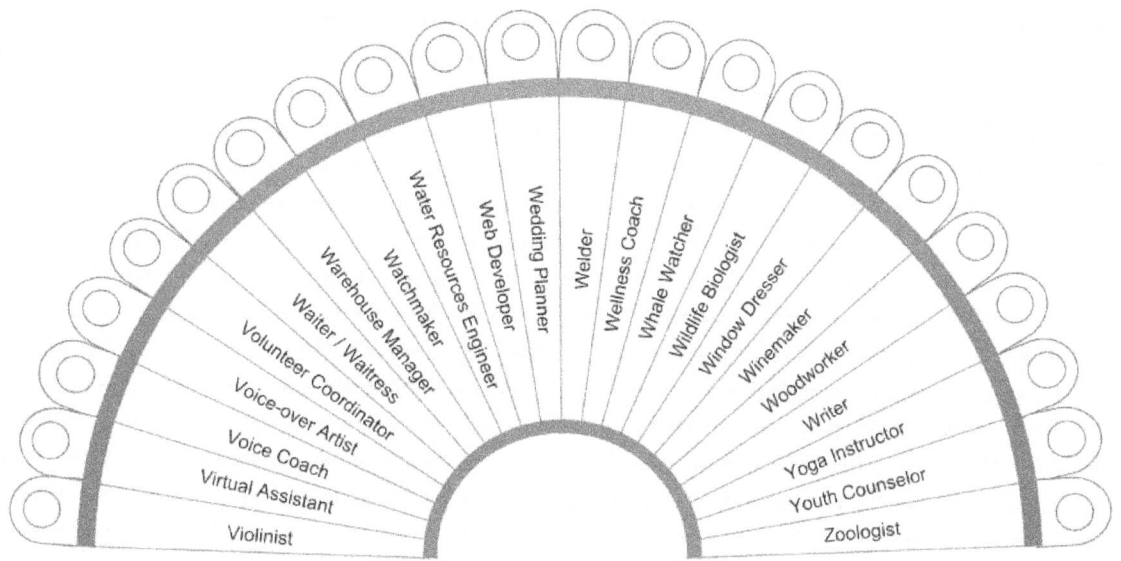

Life Purpose, Chart 29

Water Resources Engineer
Web Developer
Wedding Planner
Welder
Wellness Coach
Whale Watcher
Wildlife Biologist
Window Dresser
Winemaker
Woodworker
Writer
Yoga Instructor
Youth Counselor
Zoologist

Watchmaker
Warehouse Manager
Waiter / Waitress
Volunteer Coordinator
Voice-over Artist
Voice Coach
Virtual Assistant
Violinist

Royal Template 22

Diving Deep into the Pool of the Mind

Chart 409

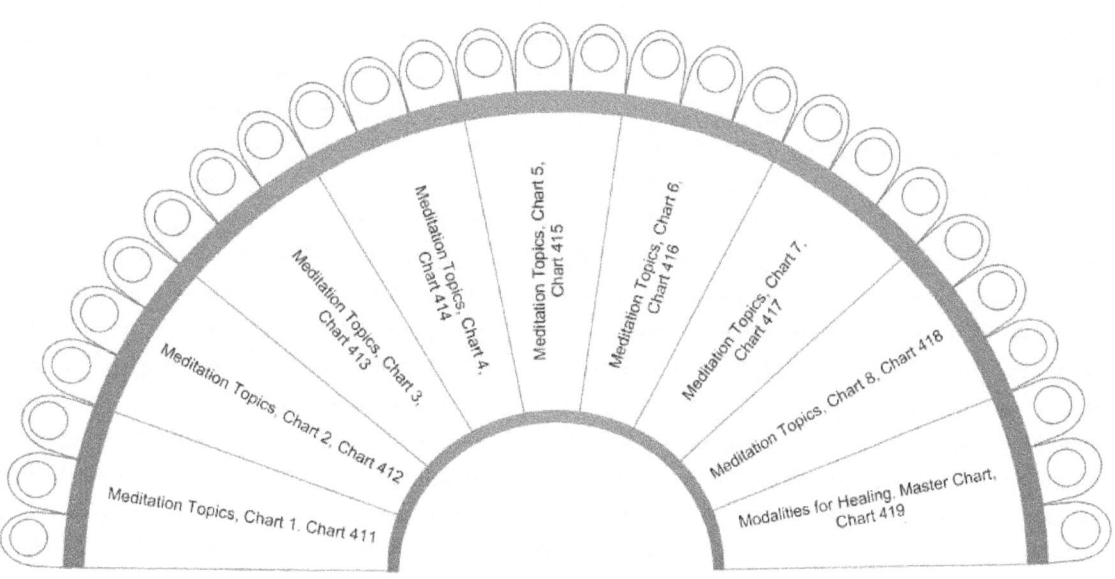

Meditation Topics, Master Chart

Meditation Topics, Chart 1, Chart 411
Meditation Topics, Chart 2, Chart 412
Meditation Topics, Chart 3, Chart 413
Meditation Topics, Chart 4, Chart 414
Meditation Topics, Chart 5, Chart 415
Meditation Topics, Chart 6, Chart 416
Meditation Topics, Chart 7, Chart 417
Meditation Topics, Chart 8, Chart 418
Modalities for Healing, Master Chart, Chart 419

Royal Template 9

Diving Deep into the Pool of the Mind

Chart 410

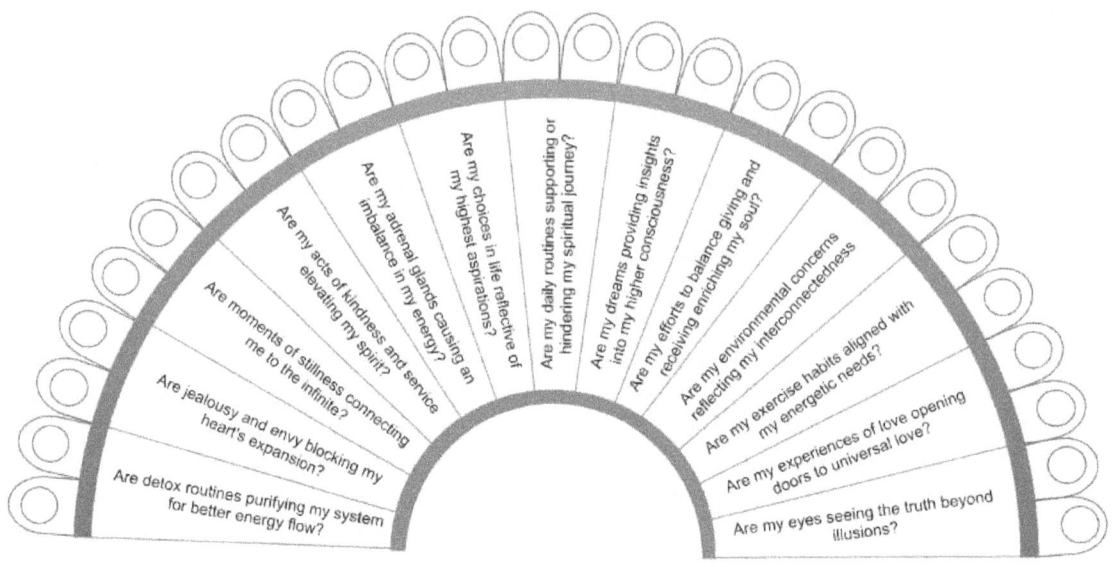

Meditation Topics, Chart 1

Questions (clockwise):
- Are my adrenal glands causing an imbalance in my energy?
- Are my choices in life reflective of my highest aspirations?
- Are my daily routines supporting or hindering my spiritual journey?
- Are my dreams providing insights into my higher consciousness?
- Are my efforts to balance giving and receiving enriching my soul?
- Are my environmental concerns reflecting my interconnectedness?
- Are my exercise habits aligned with my energetic needs?
- Are my experiences of love opening doors to universal love?
- Are my eyes seeing the truth beyond illusions?
- Are my acts of kindness and service elevating my spirit?
- Are moments of stillness connecting me to the infinite?
- Are jealousy and envy blocking my heart's expansion?
- Are detox routines purifying my system for better energy flow?

Royal Template 13

Diving Deep into the Pool of the Mind

Chart 411

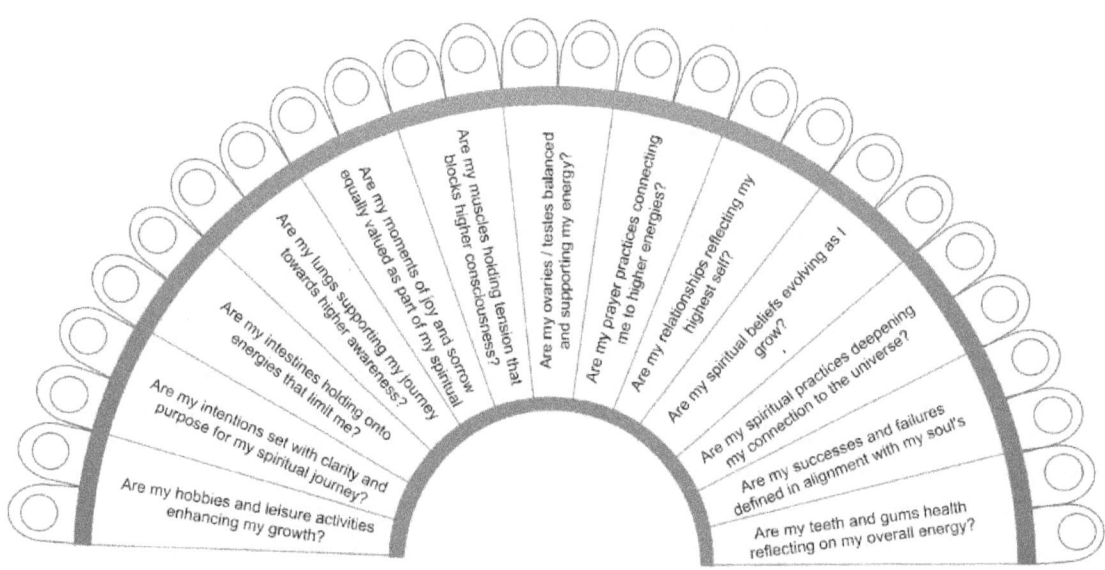

Meditation Topics, Chart 2

Questions (clockwise):
- Are my moments of joy and sorrow equally valued as part of my spiritual journey?
- Are my muscles holding tension that blocks higher consciousness?
- Are my ovaries / testes balanced and supporting my energy?
- Are my prayer practices connecting me to higher energies?
- Are my relationships reflecting my highest self?
- Are my spiritual beliefs evolving as I grow?
- Are my spiritual practices deepening my connection to the universe?
- Are my successes and failures defined in alignment with my soul's
- Are my teeth and gums health reflecting on my overall energy?
- Are my lungs supporting my journey towards higher awareness?
- Are my intestines holding onto energies that limit me?
- Are my intentions set with clarity and purpose for my spiritual journey?
- Are my hobbies and leisure activities enhancing my growth?

Royal Template 13

Diving Deep into the Pool of the Mind

Chart 412

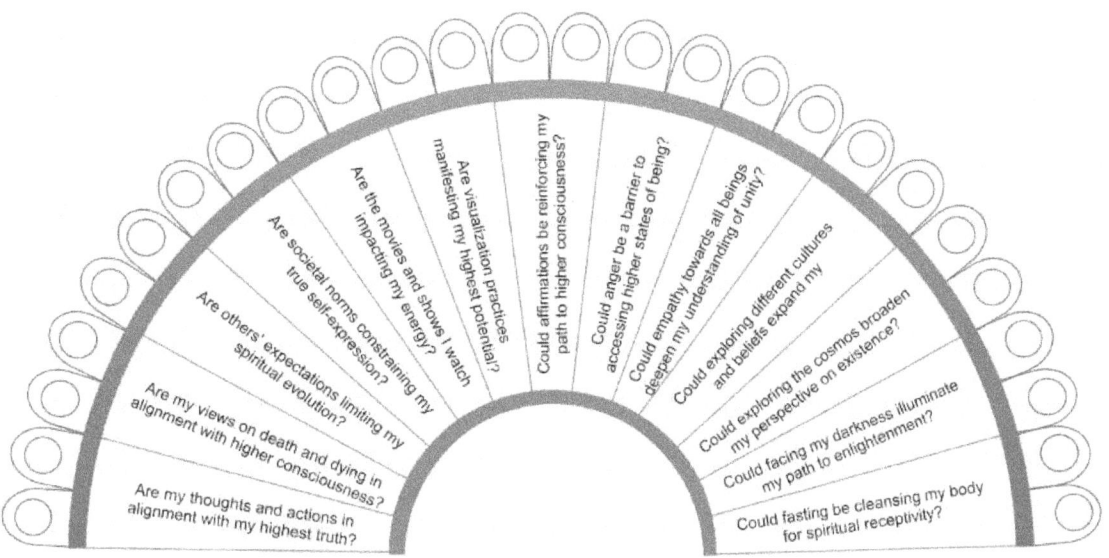

Meditation Topics, Chart 3

The questions around the fan read:

- Are my thoughts and actions in alignment with my highest truth?
- Are my views on death and dying in alignment with higher consciousness?
- Are others' expectations limiting my spiritual evolution?
- Are societal norms constraining my true self-expression?
- Are the movies and shows I watch impacting my energy?
- Are visualization practices manifesting my highest potential?
- Could affirmations be reinforcing my path to higher consciousness?
- Could anger be a barrier to accessing higher states of being?
- Could empathy towards all beings deepen my understanding of unity?
- Could exploring different cultures and beliefs expand my
- Could exploring the cosmos broaden my perspective on existence?
- Could facing my darkness illuminate my path to enlightenment?
- Could fasting be cleansing my body for spiritual receptivity?

Royal Template 13

Diving Deep into the Pool of the Mind

Chart 413

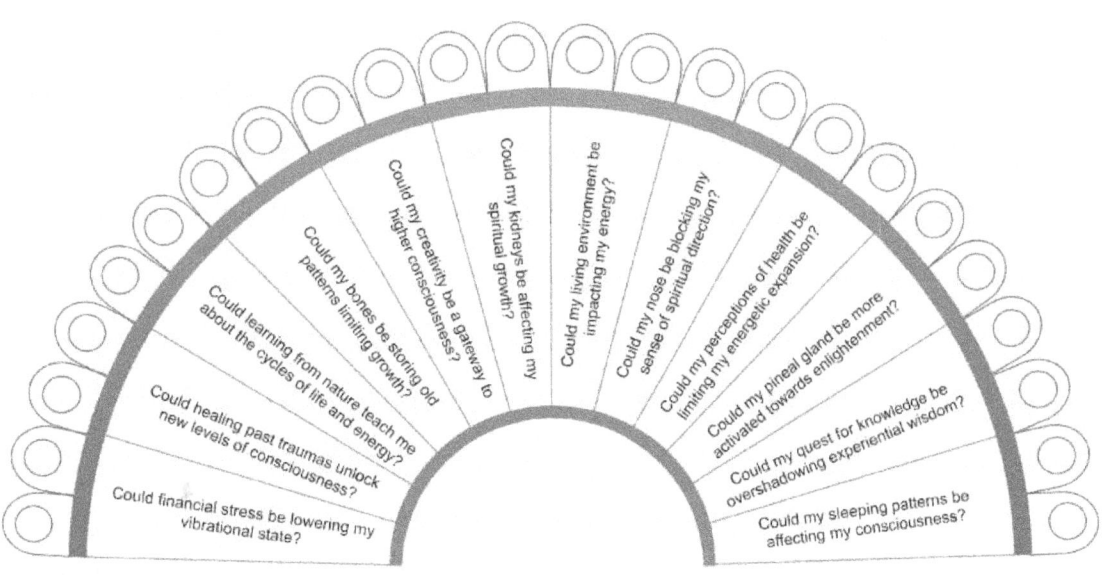

Meditation Topics, Chart 4

The questions around the fan read:

- Could financial stress be lowering my vibrational state?
- Could healing past traumas unlock new levels of consciousness?
- Could learning from nature teach me about the cycles of life and energy?
- Could my bones be storing old patterns limiting growth?
- Could my creativity be a gateway to higher consciousness?
- Could my kidneys be affecting my spiritual growth?
- Could my living environment be impacting my energy?
- Could my nose be blocking my sense of spiritual direction?
- Could my perceptions of health be limiting my energetic expansion?
- Could my pineal gland be more activated towards enlightenment?
- Could my quest for knowledge be overshadowing experiential wisdom?
- Could my sleeping patterns be affecting my consciousness?

Royal Template 12

Diving Deep into the Pool of the Mind

Chart 414

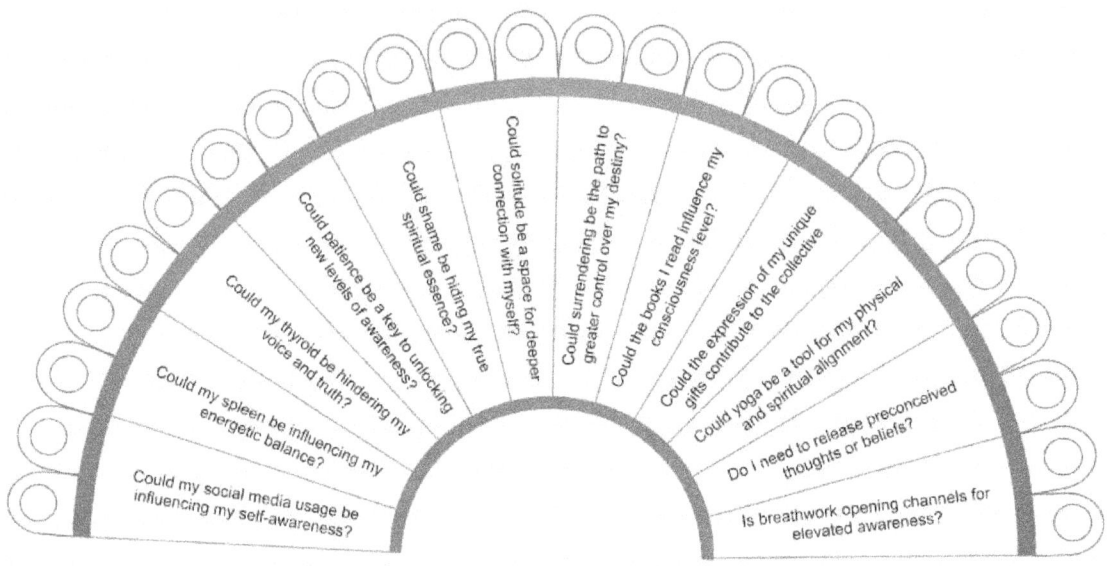

Meditation Topics, Chart 5

The questions shown on the chart:

- Could my social media usage be influencing my self-awareness?
- Could my spleen be influencing my energetic balance?
- Could my thyroid be hindering my voice and truth?
- Could patience be a key to unlocking new levels of awareness?
- Could shame be hiding my true spiritual essence?
- Could solitude be a space for deeper connection with myself?
- Could surrendering be the path to greater control over my destiny?
- Could the books I read influence my consciousness level?
- Could the expression of my unique gifts contribute to the collective
- Could yoga be a tool for my physical and spiritual alignment?
- Do I need to release preconceived thoughts or beliefs?
- Is breathwork opening channels for elevated awareness?

Royal Template 12

Diving Deep into the Pool of the Mind

Chart 415

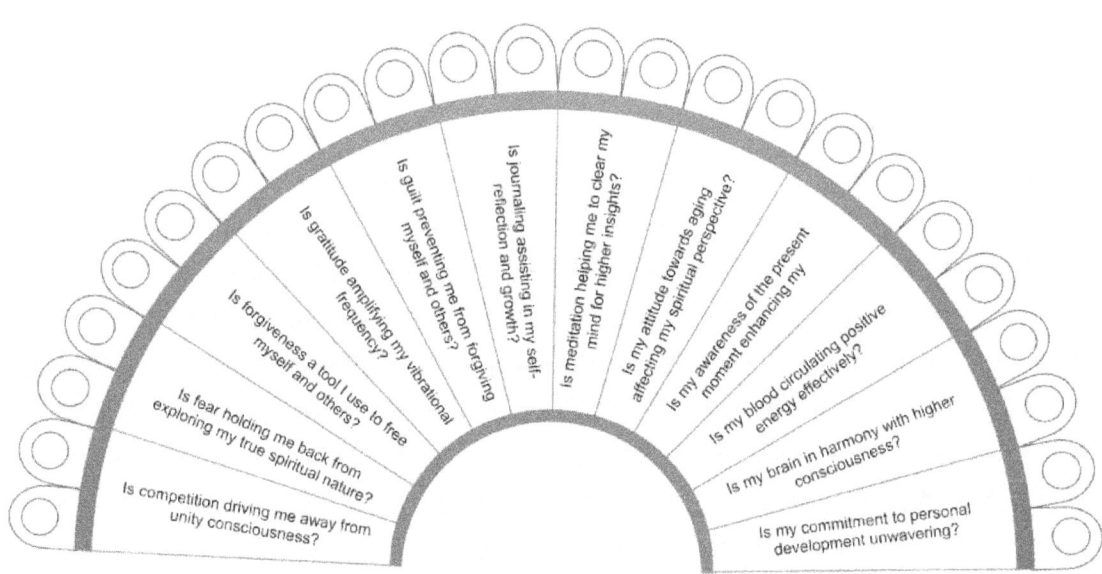

Meditation Topics, Chart 6

The questions shown on the chart:

- Is competition driving me away from unity consciousness?
- Is fear holding me back from exploring my true spiritual nature?
- Is forgiveness a tool I use to free myself and others?
- Is gratitude amplifying my vibrational frequency?
- Is guilt preventing me from forgiving myself and others?
- Is journaling assisting in my self-reflection and growth?
- Is meditation helping me to clear my mind for higher insights?
- Is my attitude towards aging affecting my spiritual perspective?
- Is my awareness of the present moment enhancing my
- Is my blood circulating positive energy effectively?
- Is my brain in harmony with higher consciousness?
- Is my commitment to personal development unwavering?

Royal Template 12

Diving Deep into the Pool of the Mind

Chart 416

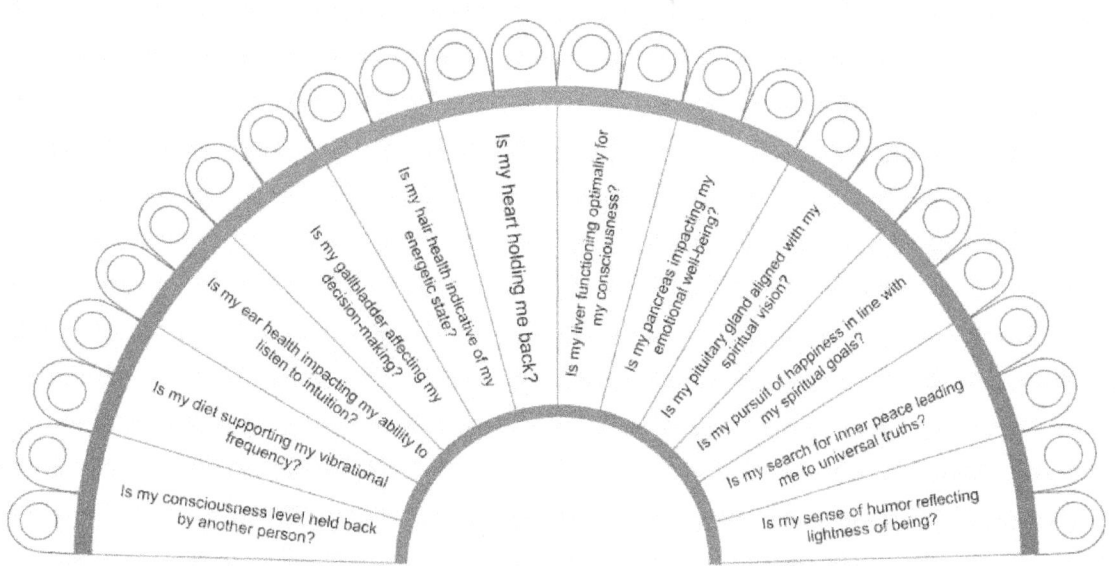

Meditation Topics, Chart 7

Is my heart holding me back?

Is my liver functioning optimally for my consciousness?

Is my pancreas impacting my emotional well-being?

Is my pituitary gland aligned with my spiritual vision?

Is my pursuit of happiness in line with my spiritual goals?

Is my search for inner peace leading me to universal truths?

Is my sense of humor reflecting lightness of being?

Is my hair health indicative of my energetic state?

Is my gallbladder affecting my decision-making?

Is my ear health impacting my ability to listen to intuition?

Is my diet supporting my vibrational frequency?

Is my consciousness level held back by another person?

Royal Template 12

Diving Deep into the Pool of the Mind

Chart 417

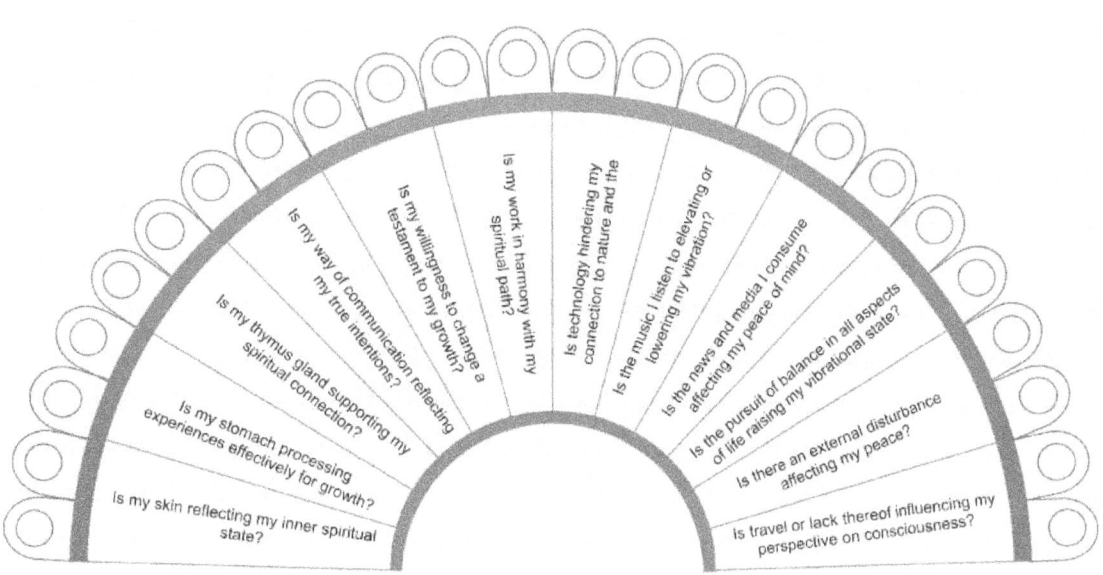

Meditation Topics, Chart 8

Is my work in harmony with my spiritual path?

Is my willingness to change a testament to my growth?

Is my way of communication reflecting my true intentions?

Is technology hindering my connection to nature and the

Is the music I listen to elevating or lowering my vibration?

Is the news and media I consume affecting my peace of mind?

Is the pursuit of balance in all aspects of life raising my vibrational state?

Is there an external disturbance affecting my peace?

Is travel or lack thereof influencing my perspective on consciousness?

Is my thymus gland supporting my spiritual connection?

Is my stomach processing experiences effectively for growth?

Is my skin reflecting my inner spiritual state?

Royal Template 12

Diving Deep into the Pool of the Mind

Chart 418

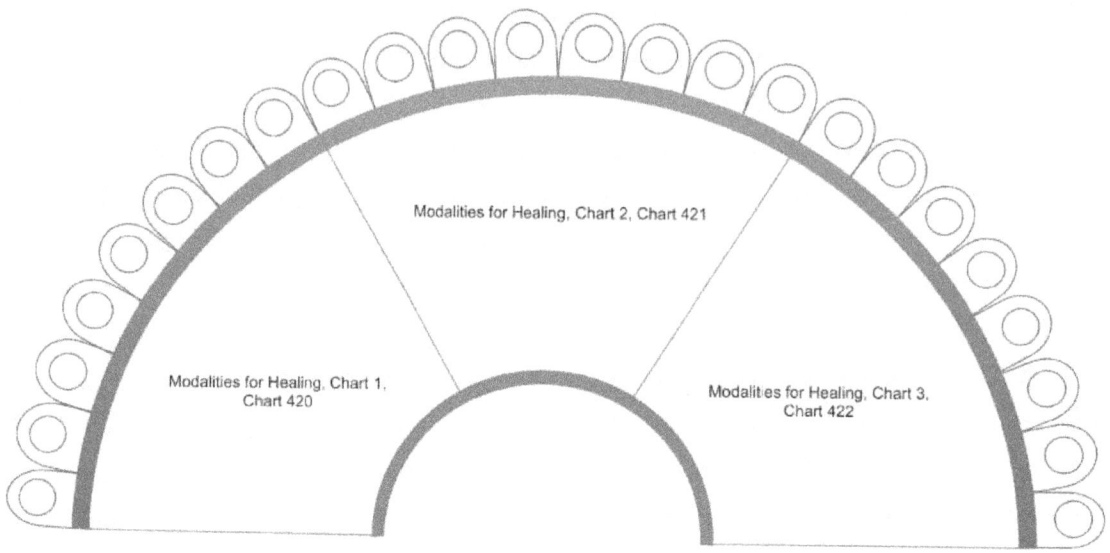

Modalities for Healing, Master Chart

Modalities for Healing, Chart 2, Chart 421

Modalities for Healing, Chart 1, Chart 420

Modalities for Healing, Chart 3, Chart 422

Royal Template 3h

Chart 419

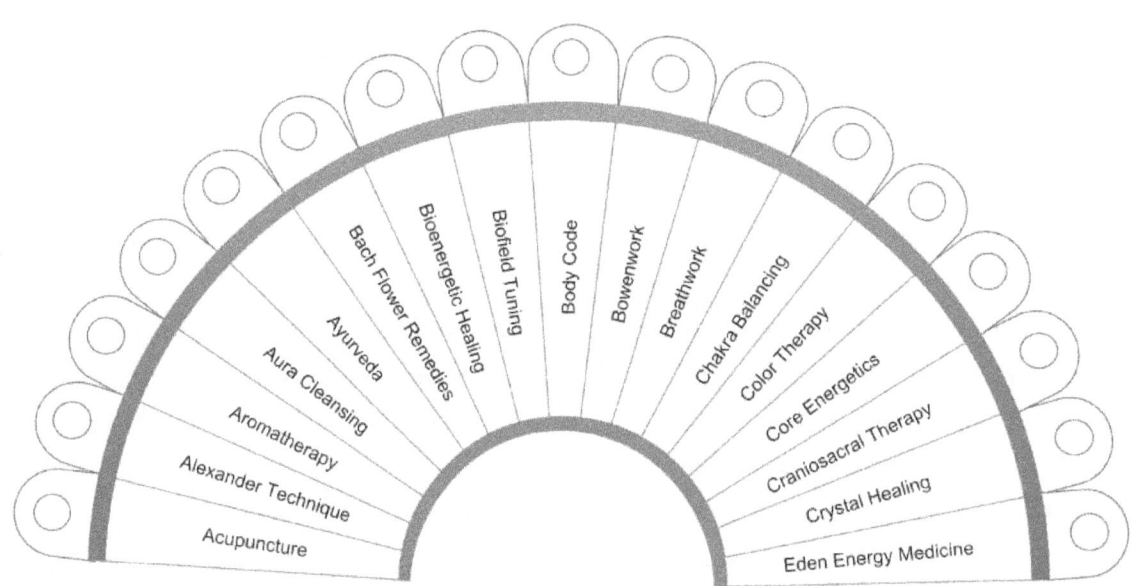

Bach Flower Remedies
Bioenergetic Healing
Biofield Tuning
Body Code
Bowenwork
Breathwork
Chakra Balancing
Color Therapy
Core Energetics
Craniosacral Therapy
Crystal Healing
Eden Energy Medicine
Ayurveda
Aura Cleansing
Aromatherapy
Alexander Technique
Acupuncture

Modalities for Healing, Chart 1

Royal Template 17

Chart 420

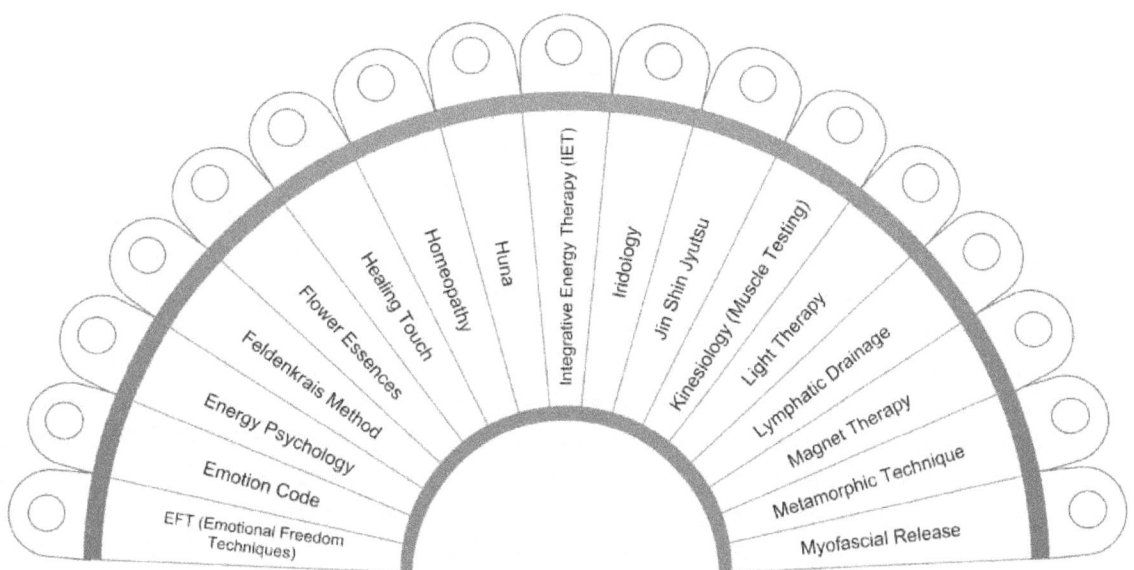

Modalities for Healing, Chart 2

Royal Template 17

Diving Deep into the Pool of the Mind

Chart 421

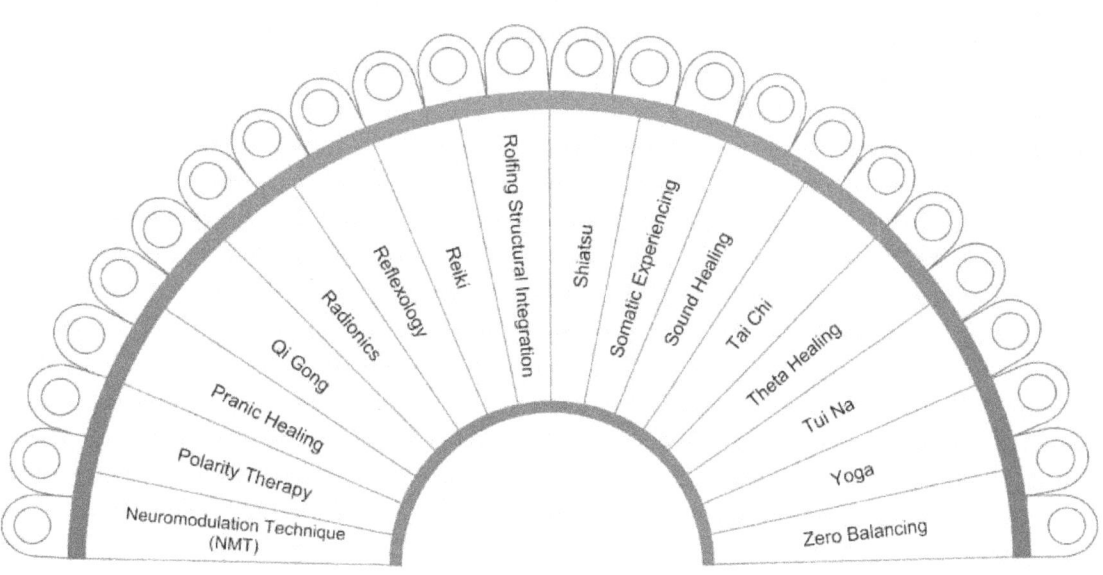

Modalities for Healing, Chart 3

Royal Template 16

Diving Deep into the Pool of the Mind

Chart 422

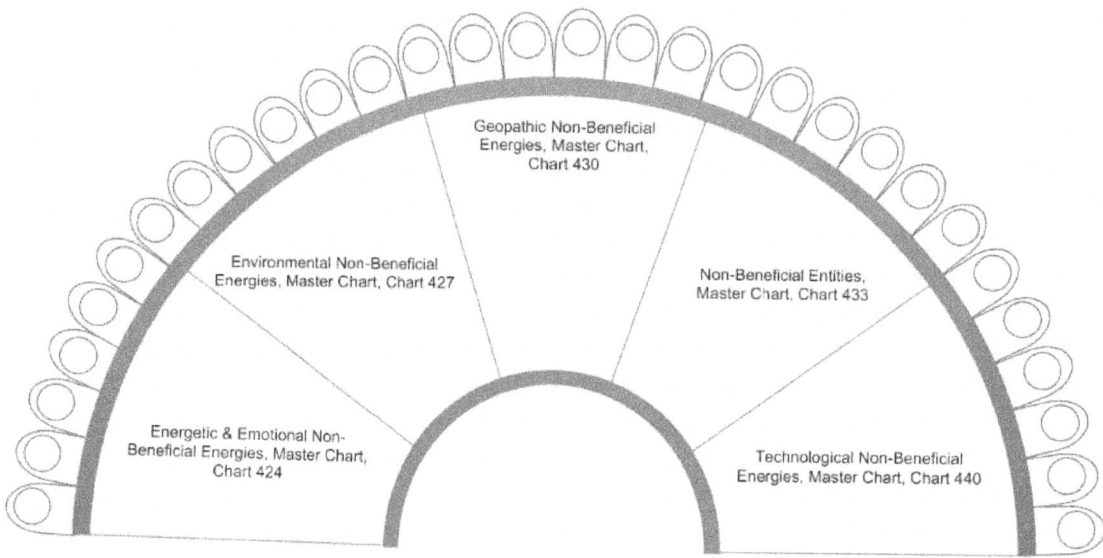

Non-Beneficial Energies, Grand Master Chart

Geopathic Non-Beneficial Energies, Master Chart, Chart 430

Environmental Non-Beneficial Energies, Master Chart, Chart 427

Non-Beneficial Entities, Master Chart, Chart 433

Energetic & Emotional Non-Beneficial Energies, Master Chart, Chart 424

Technological Non-Beneficial Energies, Master Chart, Chart 440

Royal Template 5h

Diving Deep into the Pool of the Mind

Chart 423

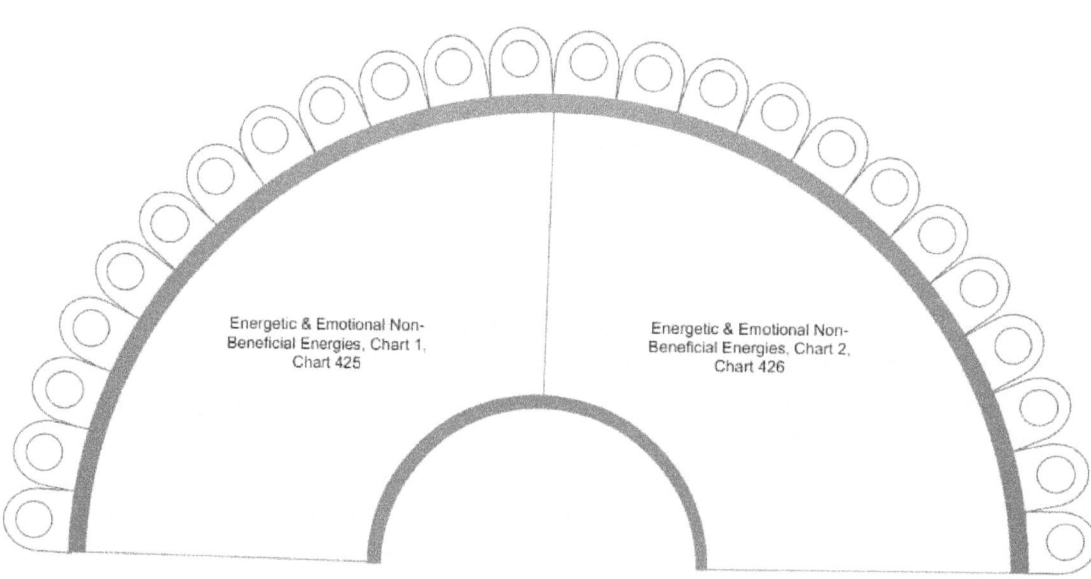

Energetic & Emotional Non-Beneficial Energies, Chart 1, Chart 425

Energetic & Emotional Non-Beneficial Energies, Chart 2, Chart 426

Energetic & Emotional Non-Beneficial Energies, Master Chart

Royal Template 2

Diving Deep into the Pool of the Mind

Chart 424

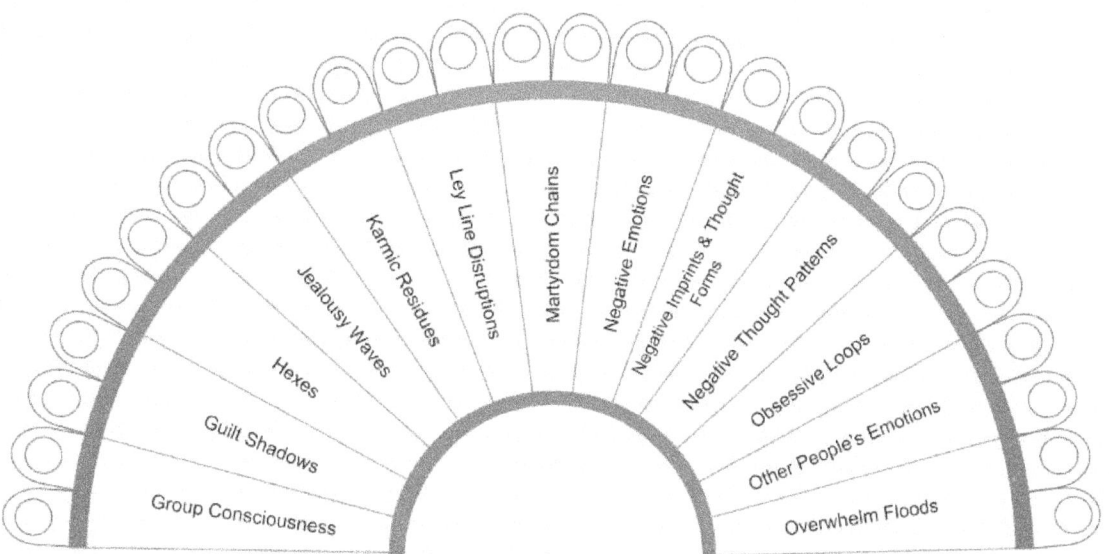

Energetic & Emotional Non-Beneficial Energies, Chart 1

Ley Line Disruptions
Karmic Residues
Martyrdom Chains
Negative Emotions
Negative Imprints & Thought Forms
Jealousy Waves
Negative Thought Patterns
Hexes
Obsessive Loops
Guilt Shadows
Other People's Emotions
Group Consciousness
Overwhelm Floods

Royal Template 13

Diving Deep into the Pool of the Mind

Chart 425

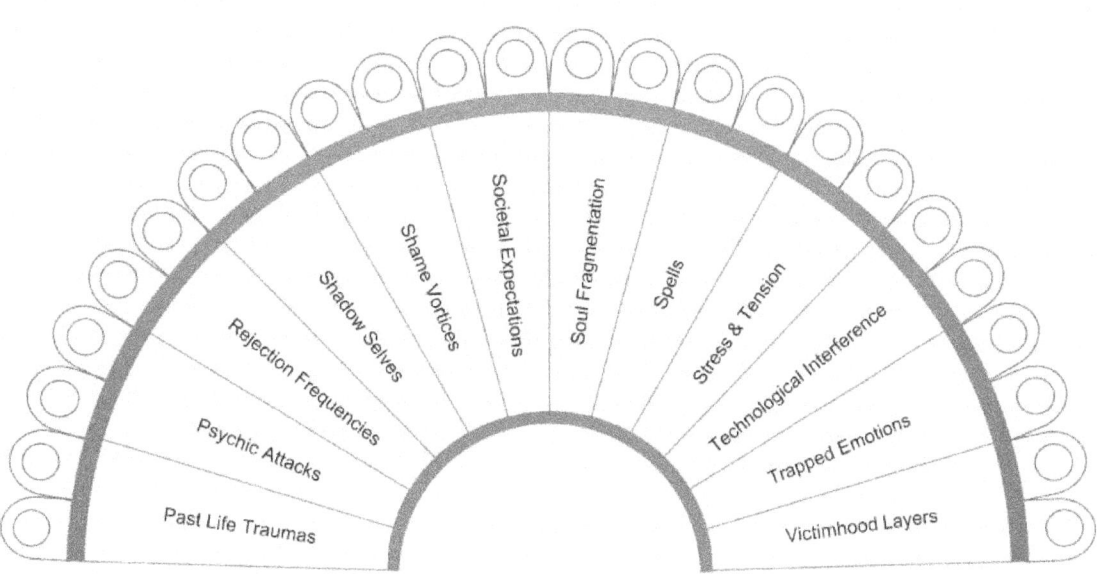

Energetic & Emotional Non-Beneficial Energies, Chart 2

Societal Expectations
Shame Vortices
Soul Fragmentation
Shadow Selves
Spells
Rejection Frequencies
Stress & Tension
Psychic Attacks
Technological Interference
Trapped Emotions
Past Life Traumas
Victimhood Layers

Royal Template 12

Diving Deep into the Pool of the Mind

Chart 426

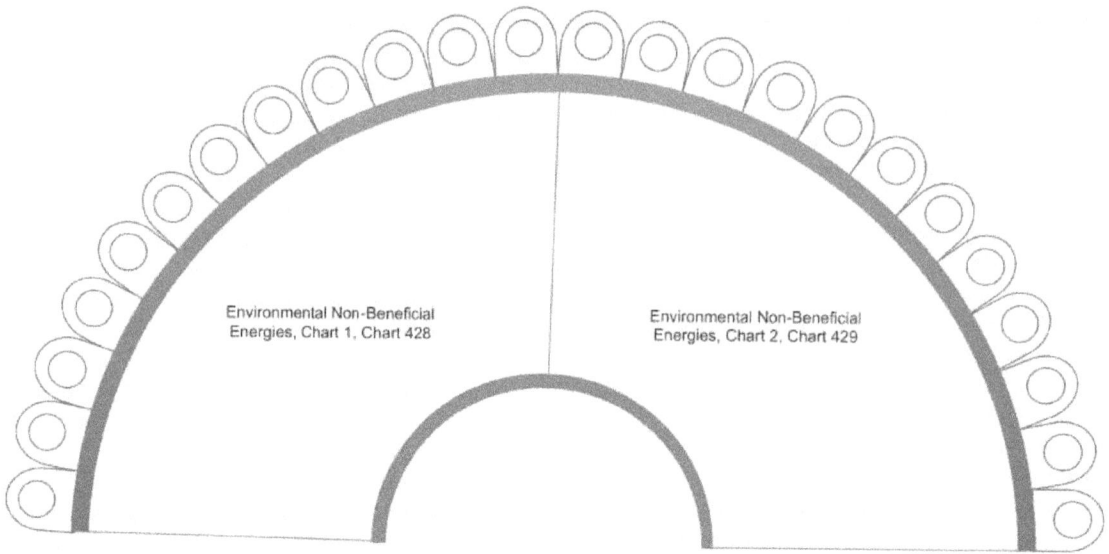

Environmental Non-Beneficial Energies, Master Chart

Environmental Non-Beneficial
Energies, Chart 1, Chart 428

Environmental Non-Beneficial
Energies, Chart 2, Chart 429

Royal Template 2

Diving Deep into the Pool of the Mind

Chart 427

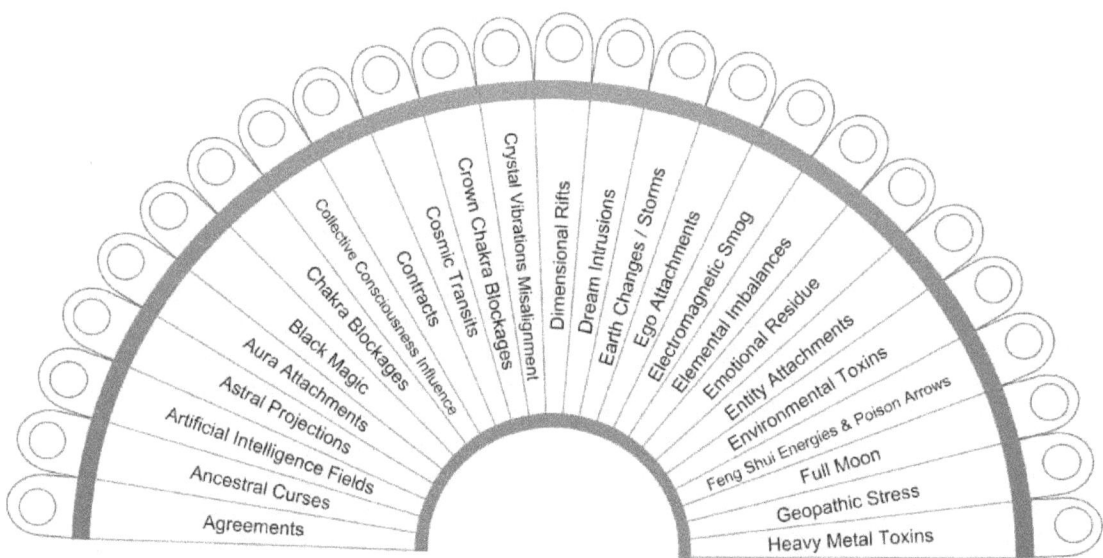

Environmental Non-Beneficial Energies, Chart 1

Labels (left to right):
- Agreements
- Ancestral Curses
- Artificial Intelligence Fields
- Astral Projections
- Aura Attachments
- Black Magic
- Chakra Blockages
- Collective Consciousness Influence
- Contracts
- Cosmic Transits
- Crown Chakra Blockages
- Crystal Vibrations Misalignment
- Dimensional Rifts
- Dream Intrusions
- Earth Changes / Storms
- Ego Attachments
- Electromagnetic Smog
- Elemental Imbalances
- Emotional Residue
- Entity Attachments
- Environmental Toxins
- Feng Shui Energies & Poison Arrows
- Full Moon
- Geopathic Stress
- Heavy Metal Toxins

Royal Template 25

Diving Deep into the Pool of the Mind

Chart 428

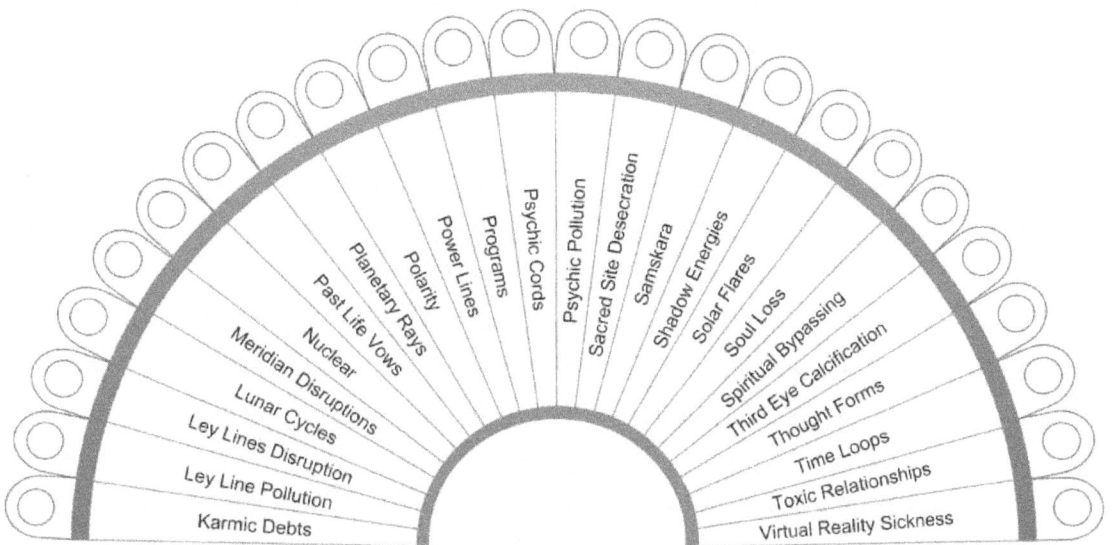

Environmental Non-Beneficial Energies, Chart 2

Labels (left to right):
Karmic Debts, Ley Line Pollution, Ley Lines Disruption, Lunar Cycles, Meridian Disruptions, Nuclear, Past Life Vows, Planetary Rays, Polarity, Power Lines, Programs, Psychic Cords, Psychic Pollution, Sacred Site Desecration, Samskara, Shadow Energies, Solar Flares, Soul Loss, Spiritual Bypassing, Third Eye Calcification, Thought Forms, Time Loops, Toxic Relationships, Virtual Reality Sickness

Royal Template 24

Diving Deep into the Pool of the Mind

Chart 429

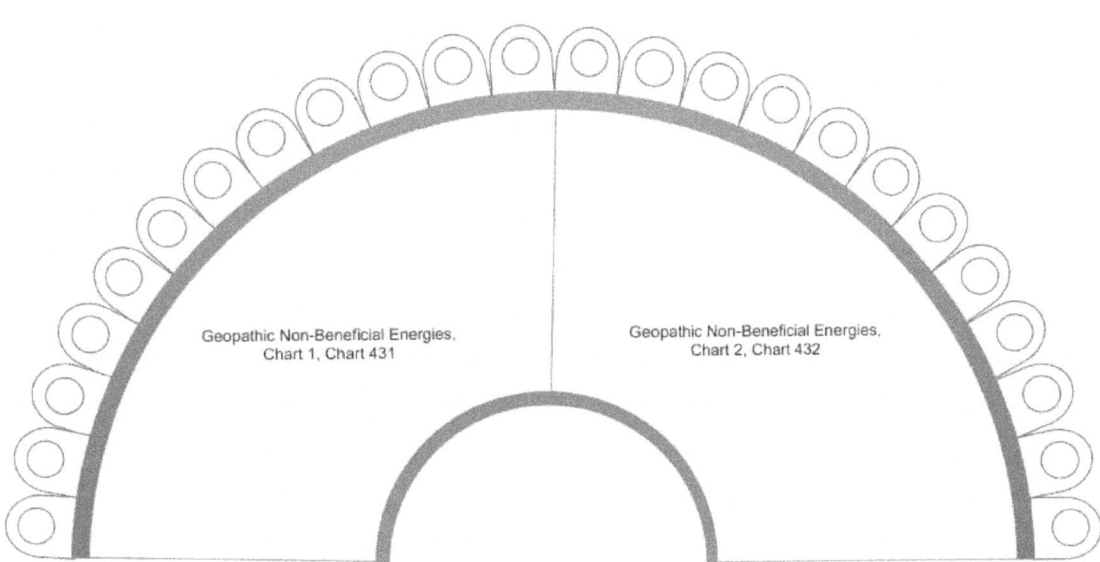

Geopathic Non-Beneficial Energies, Chart 1, Chart 431

Geopathic Non-Beneficial Energies, Chart 2, Chart 432

Geopathic Non-Beneficial Energies, Master Chart

Royal Template 2

Diving Deep into the Pool of the Mind

Chart 430

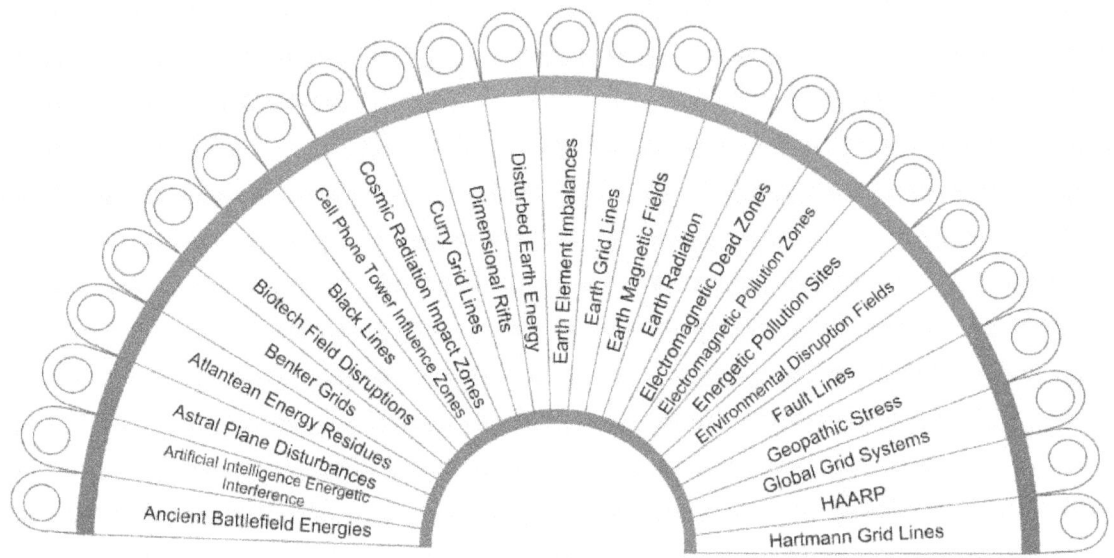

Geopathic Non-Beneficial Energies, Chart 1

Ancient Battlefield Energies
Artificial Intelligence Energetic Interference
Astral Plane Disturbances
Atlantean Energy Residues
Benker Grids
Biotech Field Disruptions
Black Lines
Cell Phone Tower Influence Zones
Cosmic Radiation Impact Zones
Curry Grid Lines
Dimensional Rifts
Disturbed Earth Energy
Earth Element Imbalances
Earth Grid Lines
Earth Magnetic Fields
Earth Radiation
Electromagnetic Dead Zones
Electromagnetic Pollution Zones
Energetic Pollution Sites
Environmental Disruption Fields
Fault Lines
Geopathic Stress
Global Grid Systems
HAARP
Hartmann Grid Lines

Royal Template 25

Diving Deep into the Pool of the Mind

Chart 431

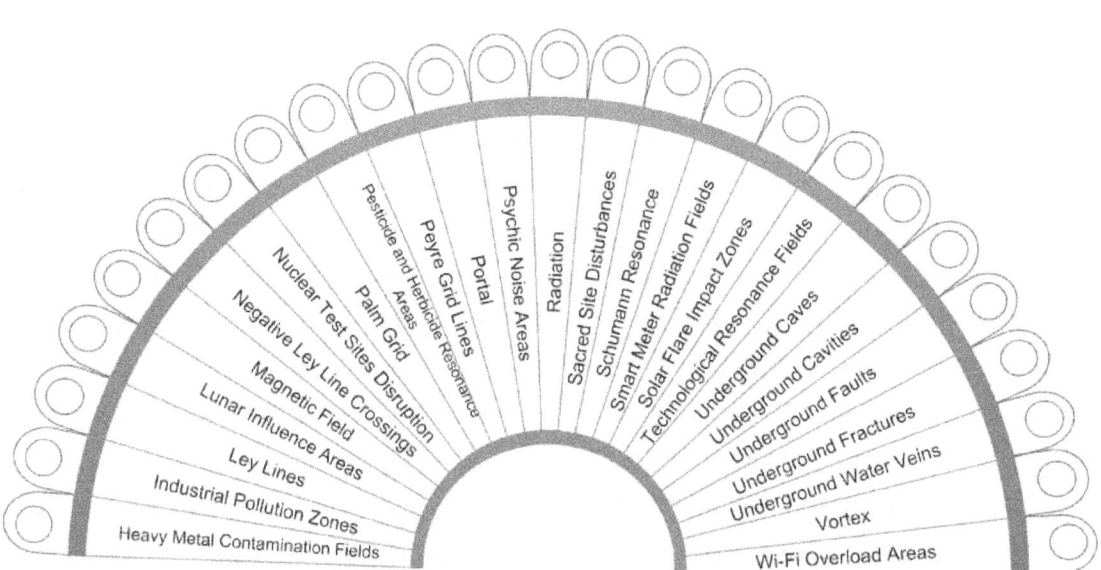

Geopathic Non-Beneficial Energies, Chart 2

Heavy Metal Contamination Fields
Industrial Pollution Zones
Ley Lines
Lunar Influence Areas
Magnetic Field
Negative Ley Line Crossings
Nuclear Test Sites Disruption
Palm Grid
Pesticide and Herbicide Resonance
Peyre Grid Lines
Portal
Psychic Noise Areas
Radiation
Sacred Site Disturbances
Schumann Resonance
Smart Meter Radiation Fields
Solar Flare Impact Zones
Technological Resonance Fields
Underground Caves
Underground Cavities
Underground Faults
Underground Fractures
Underground Water Veins
Vortex
Wi-Fi Overload Areas

Royal Template 25

Diving Deep into the Pool of the Mind

Chart 432

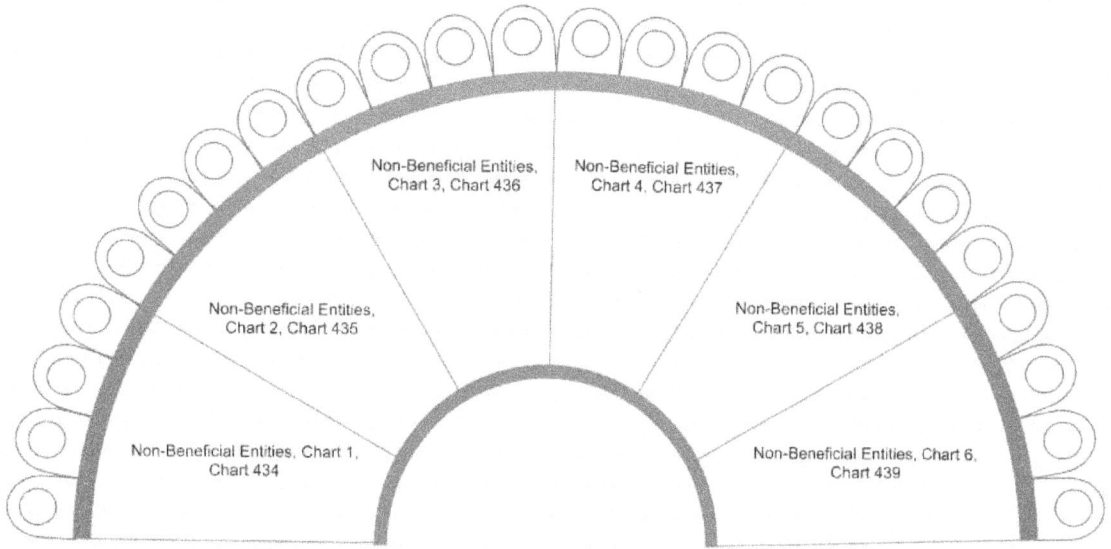

Non-Beneficial Entities, Master Chart

Non-Beneficial Entities, Chart 3, Chart 436

Non-Beneficial Entities, Chart 4, Chart 437

Non-Beneficial Entities, Chart 2, Chart 435

Non-Beneficial Entities, Chart 5, Chart 438

Non-Beneficial Entities, Chart 1, Chart 434

Non-Beneficial Entities, Chart 6, Chart 439

Royal Template 6h

Diving Deep into the Pool of the Mind

Chart 433

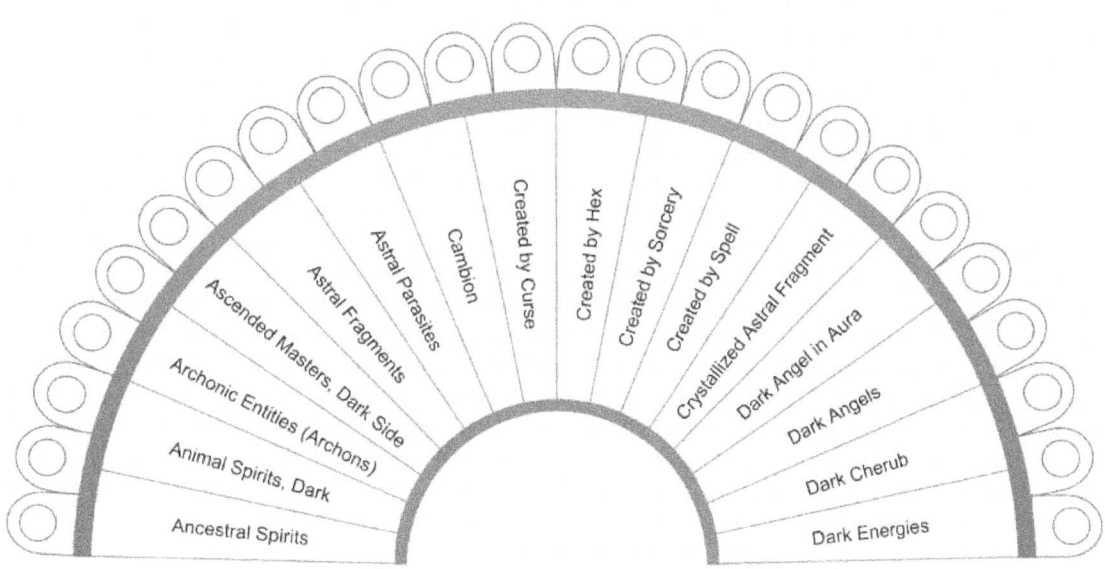

Non-Beneficial Entities, Chart 1

Ascended Masters, Dark Side
Archonic Entities (Archons)
Animal Spirits, Dark
Ancestral Spirits
Astral Fragments
Astral Parasites
Cambion
Created by Curse
Created by Hex
Created by Sorcery
Created by Spell
Crystallized Astral Fragment
Dark Angel in Aura
Dark Angels
Dark Cherub
Dark Energies

Royal Template 16

Diving Deep into the Pool of the Mind

Chart 434

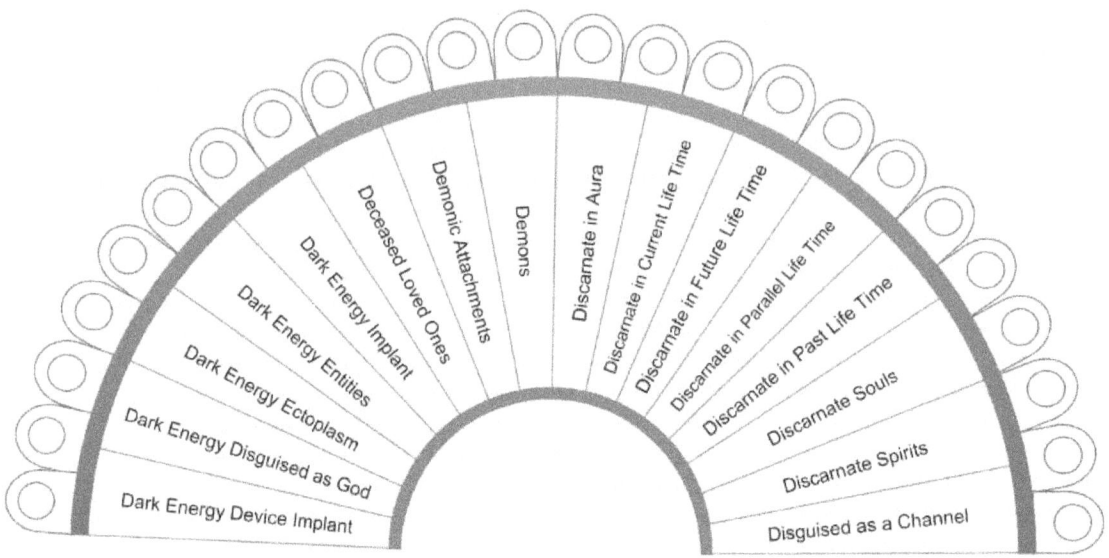

Non-Beneficial Entities, Chart 2

Demonic Attachments
Deceased Loved Ones
Dark Energy Implant
Dark Energy Entities
Dark Energy Ectoplasm
Dark Energy Disguised as God
Dark Energy Device Implant
Demons
Discarnate in Aura
Discarnate in Current Life Time
Discarnate in Future Life Time
Discarnate in Parallel Life Time
Discarnate in Past Life Time
Discarnate Souls
Discarnate Spirits
Disguised as a Channel

Royal Template 16

Diving Deep into the Pool of the Mind

Chart 435

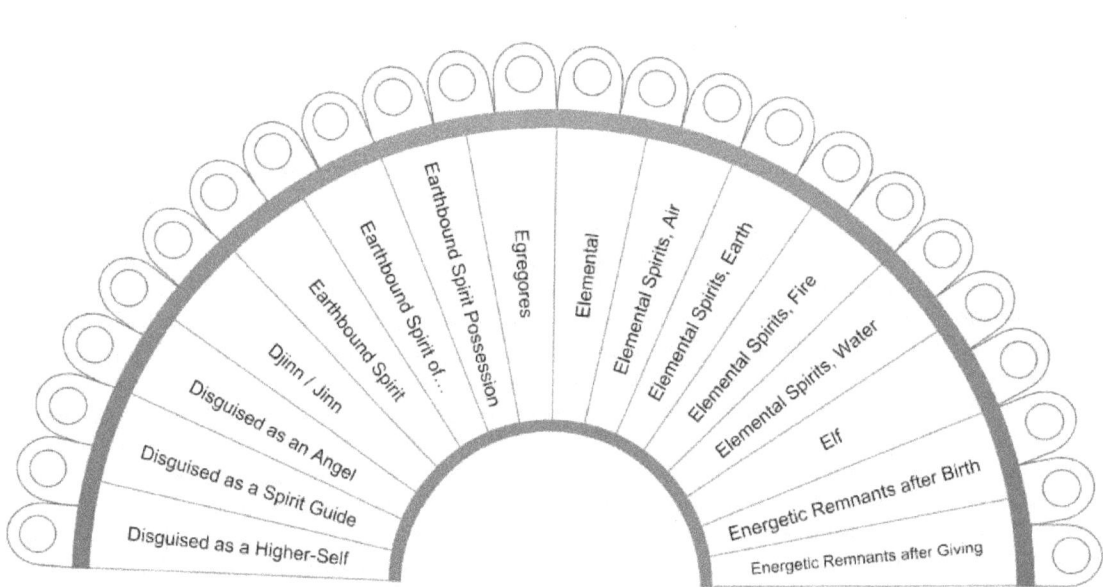

Non-Beneficial Entities, Chart 3

Earthbound Spirit Possession
Earthbound Spirit of...
Earthbound Spirit
Djinn / Jinn
Disguised as an Angel
Disguised as a Spirit Guide
Disguised as a Higher-Self
Egregores
Elemental
Elemental Spirits, Air
Elemental Spirits, Earth
Elemental Spirits, Fire
Elemental Spirits, Water
Elf
Energetic Remnants after Birth
Energetic Remnants after Giving

Royal Template 16

Diving Deep into the Pool of the Mind

Chart 436

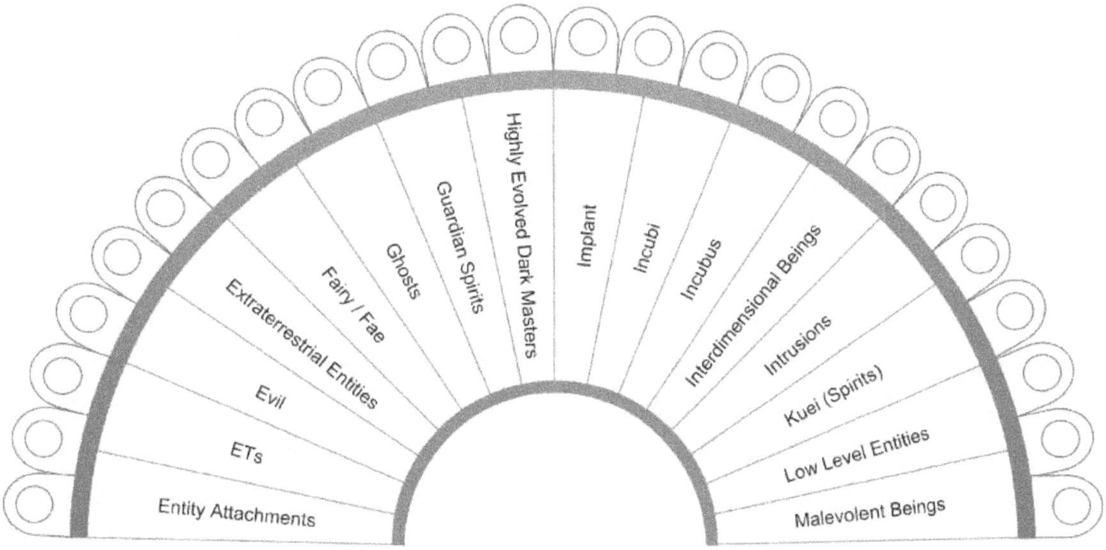
Entity Attachments
ETs
Evil
Extraterrestrial Entities
Fairy / Fae
Ghosts
Guardian Spirits
Highly Evolved Dark Masters
Implant
Incubi
Incubus
Interdimensional Beings
Intrusions
Kuei (Spirits)
Low Level Entities
Malevolent Beings

Non-Beneficial Entities, Chart 4

Royal Template 16

Chart 437

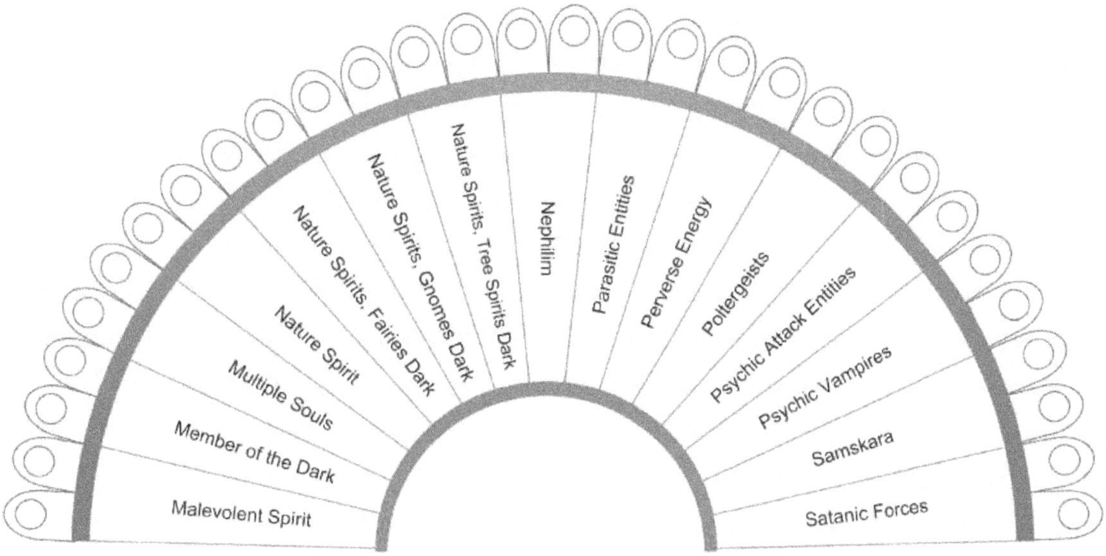
Malevolent Spirit
Member of the Dark
Multiple Souls
Nature Spirit
Nature Spirits, Fairies Dark
Nature Spirits, Gnomes Dark
Nature Spirits, Tree Spirits Dark
Nephilim
Parasitic Entities
Perverse Energy
Poltergeists
Psychic Attack Entities
Psychic Vampires
Samskara
Satanic Forces

Non-Beneficial Entities, Chart 5

Royal Template 15

Chart 438

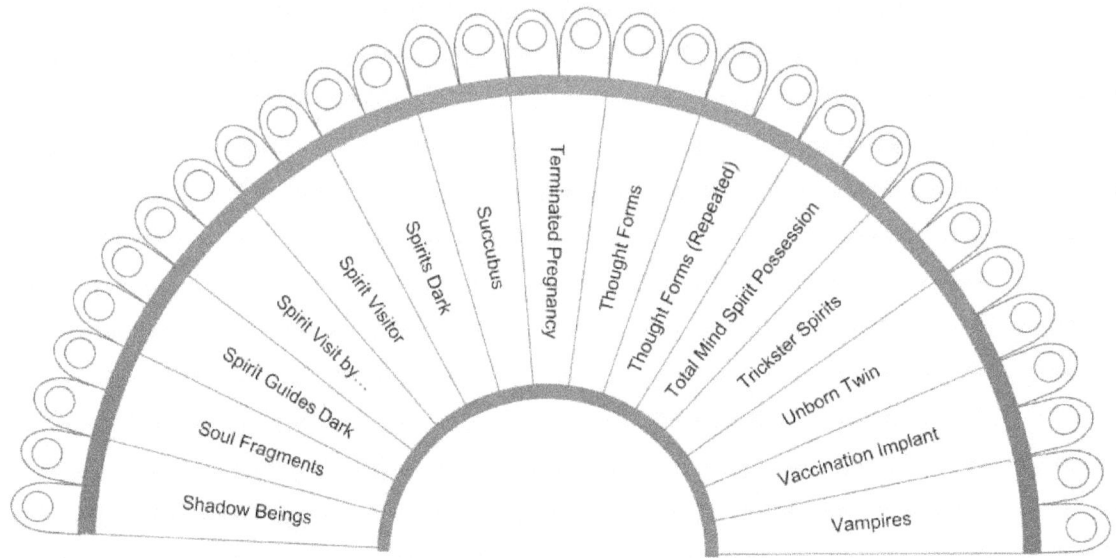

Non-Beneficial Entities, Chart 6

Spirit Visitor
Spirits Dark
Succubus
Terminated Pregnancy
Thought Forms
Thought Forms (Repeated)
Total Mind Spirit Possession
Trickster Spirits
Unborn Twin
Vaccination Implant
Vampires
Spirit Visit by...
Spirit Guides Dark
Soul Fragments
Shadow Beings

Royal Template 15

Diving Deep into the Pool of the Mind

Chart 439

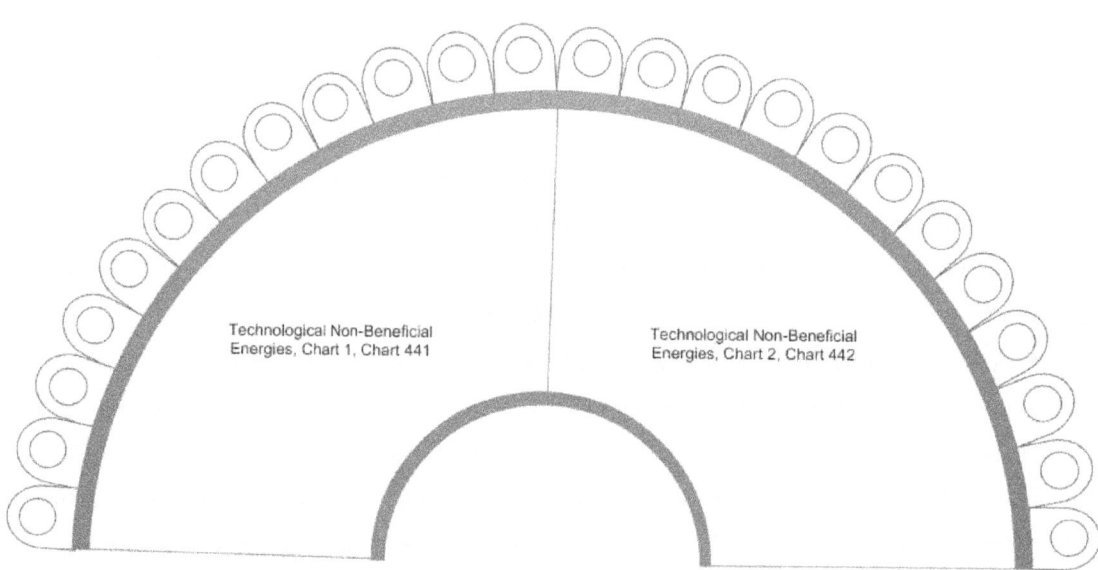

Technological Non-Beneficial Energies, Chart 1, Chart 441

Technological Non-Beneficial Energies, Chart 2, Chart 442

Technological Non-Beneficial Energies, Master Chart

Royal Template 2

Diving Deep into the Pool of the Mind

Chart 440

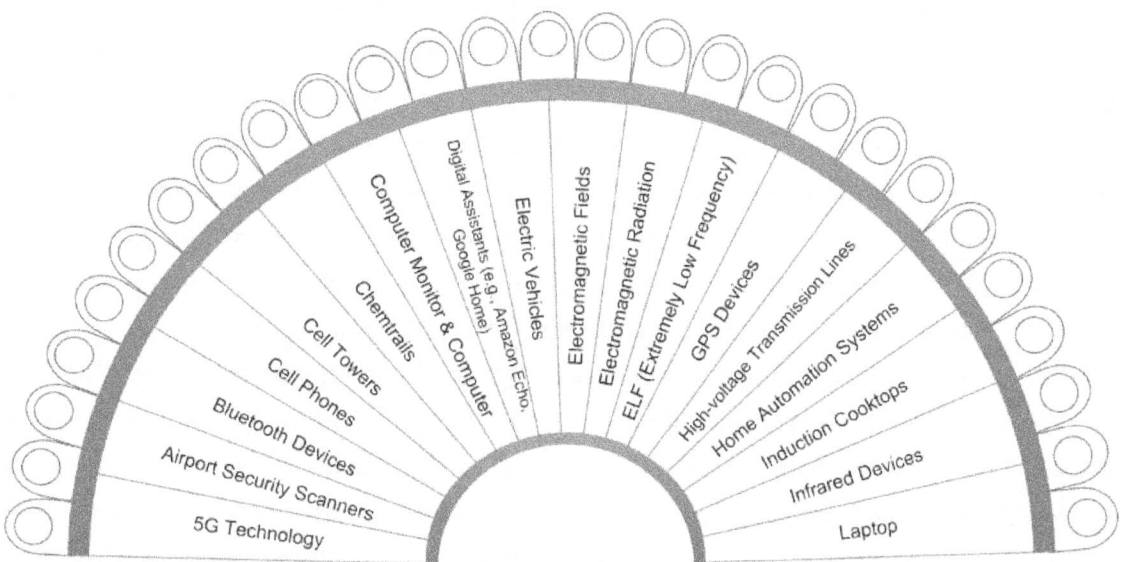

Technological Non-Beneficial Energies, Chart 1

Royal Template 18

Diving Deep into the Pool of the Mind

Chart **441**

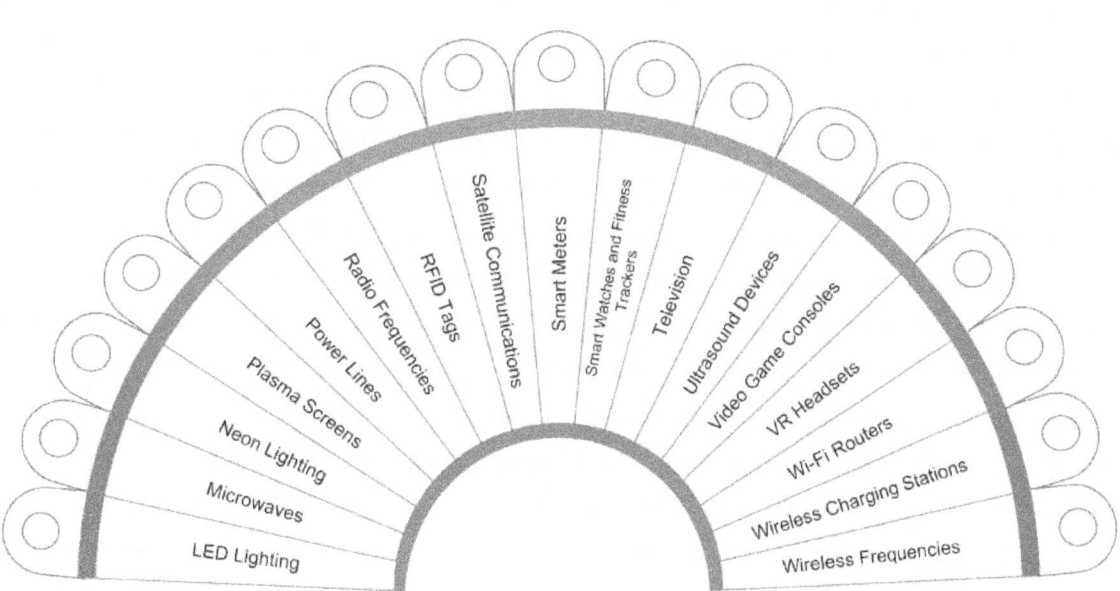

Technological Non-Beneficial Energies, Chart 2

Royal Template 17

Diving Deep into the Pool of the Mind

Chart **442**

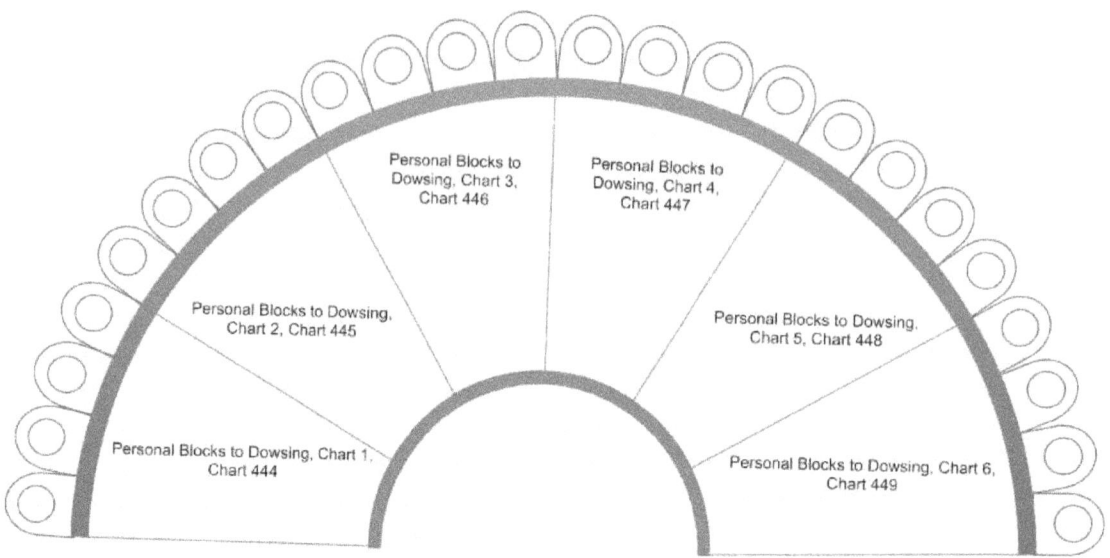

Personal Blocks to Dowsing, Master Chart

Chart 3: Personal Blocks to Dowsing, Chart 3, Chart 446
Chart 4: Personal Blocks to Dowsing, Chart 4, Chart 447
Chart 2: Personal Blocks to Dowsing, Chart 2, Chart 445
Chart 5: Personal Blocks to Dowsing, Chart 5, Chart 448
Chart 1: Personal Blocks to Dowsing, Chart 1, Chart 444
Chart 6: Personal Blocks to Dowsing, Chart 6, Chart 449

Royal Template 6h

Chart 443

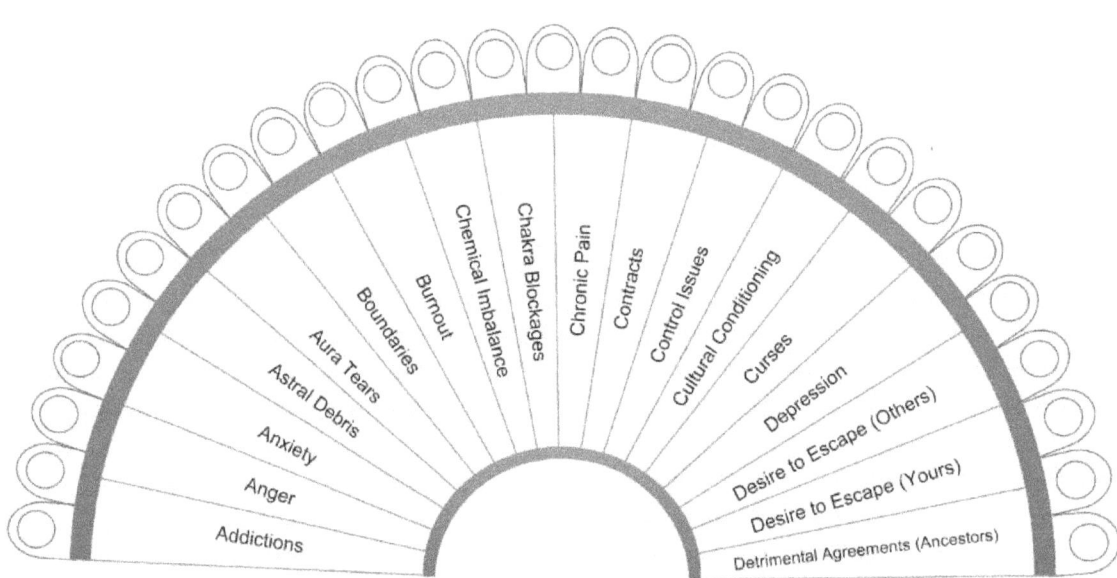

Labels (left to right): Addictions, Anger, Anxiety, Astral Debris, Aura Tears, Boundaries, Burnout, Chemical Imbalance, Chakra Blockages, Chronic Pain, Contracts, Control Issues, Cultural Conditioning, Curses, Depression, Desire to Escape (Others), Desire to Escape (Yours), Detrimental Agreements (Ancestors)

Personal Blocks to Dowsing, Chart 1

Royal Template 18

Chart 444

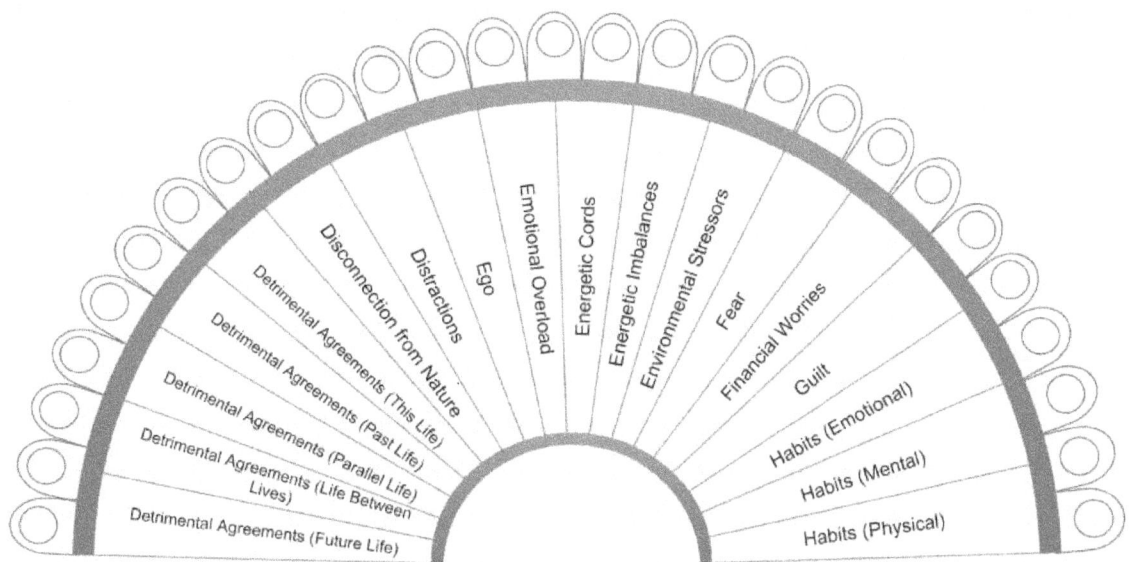

Personal Blocks to Dowsing, Chart 2

Royal Template 18

Diving Deep into the Pool of the Mind

Chart 445

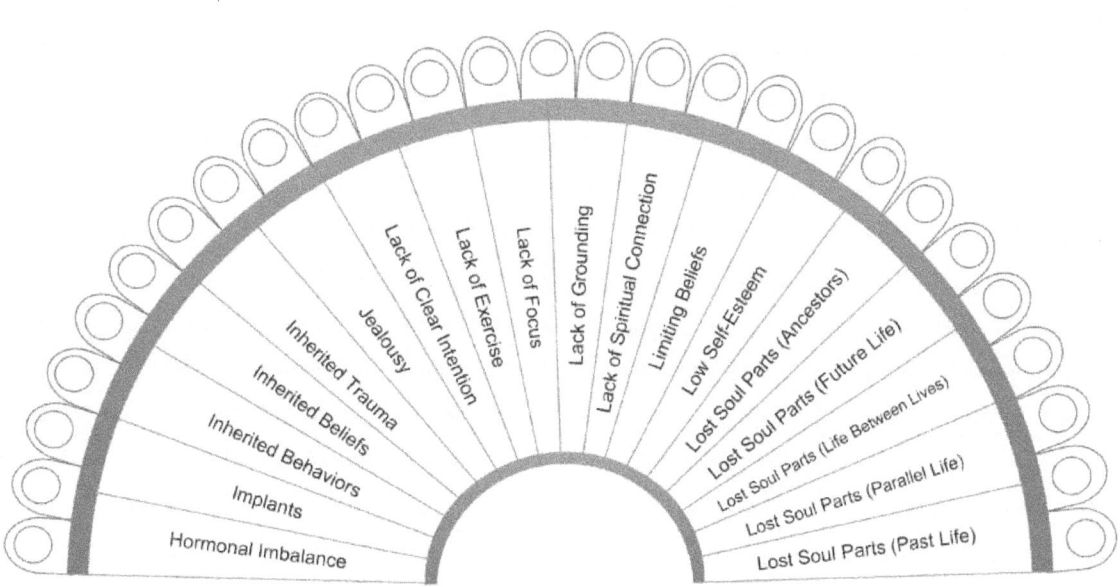

Personal Blocks to Dowsing, Chart 3

Royal Template 18

Diving Deep into the Pool of the Mind

Chart 446

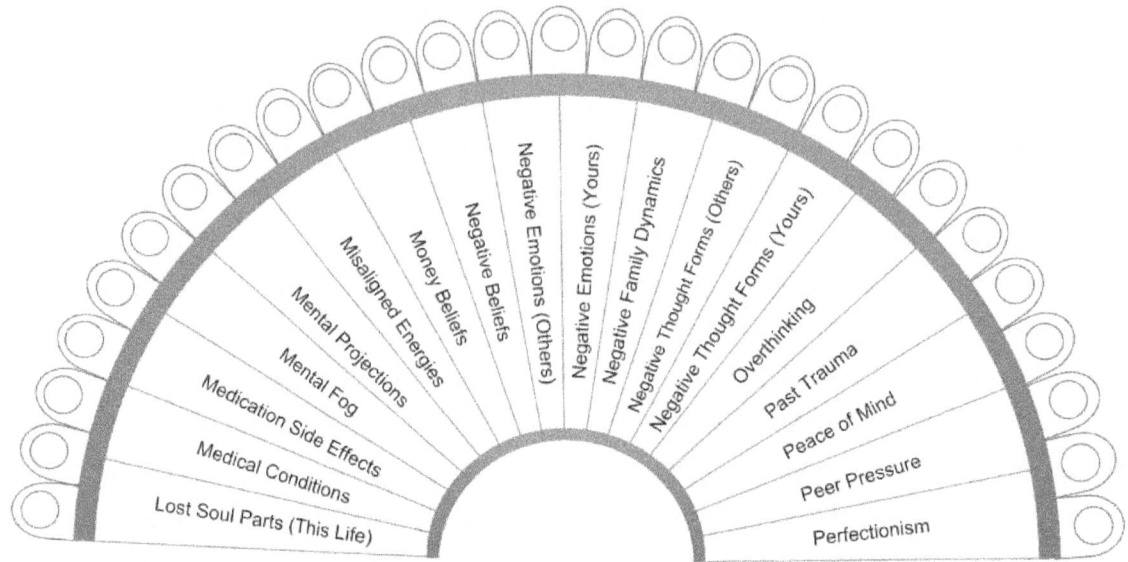

Personal Blocks to Dowsing, Chart 4

Negative Emotions (Yours)
Negative Emotions (Others)
Negative Beliefs
Money Beliefs
Misaligned Energies
Mental Projections
Mental Fog
Medication Side Effects
Medical Conditions
Lost Soul Parts (This Life)
Negative Family Dynamics
Negative Thought Forms (Others)
Negative Thought Forms (Yours)
Overthinking
Past Trauma
Peace of Mind
Peer Pressure
Perfectionism

Royal Template 18

Diving Deep into the Pool of the Mind

Chart 447

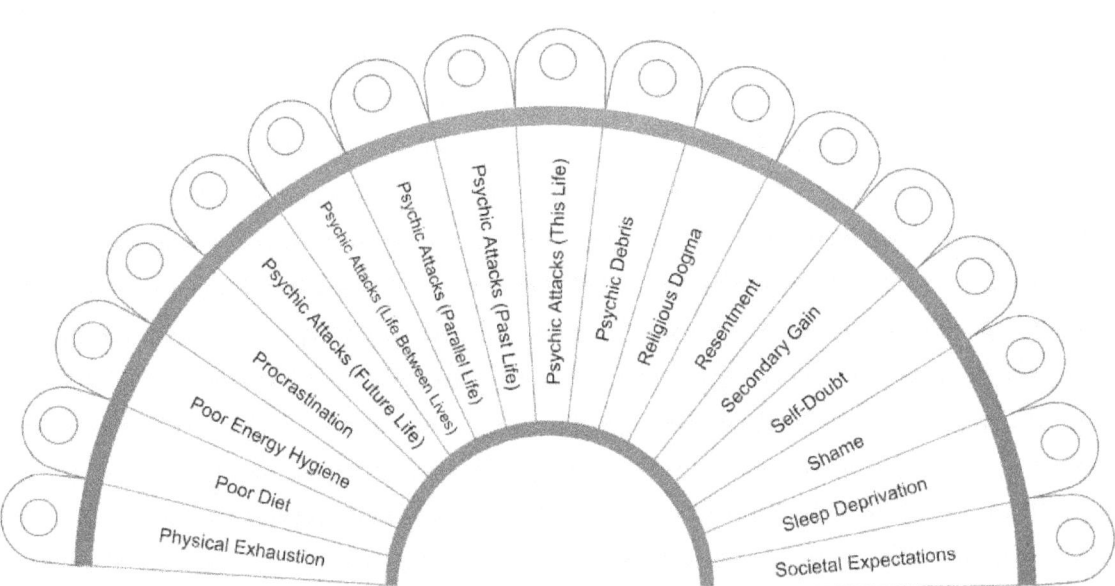

Personal Blocks to Dowsing, Chart 5

Psychic Attacks (This Life)
Psychic Attacks (Parallel Life)
Psychic Attacks (Past Life)
Psychic Attacks (Life Between Lives)
Psychic Attacks (Future Life)
Procrastination
Poor Energy Hygiene
Poor Diet
Physical Exhaustion
Psychic Debris
Religious Dogma
Resentment
Secondary Gain
Self-Doubt
Shame
Sleep Deprivation
Societal Expectations

Royal Template 17

Diving Deep into the Pool of the Mind

Chart 448

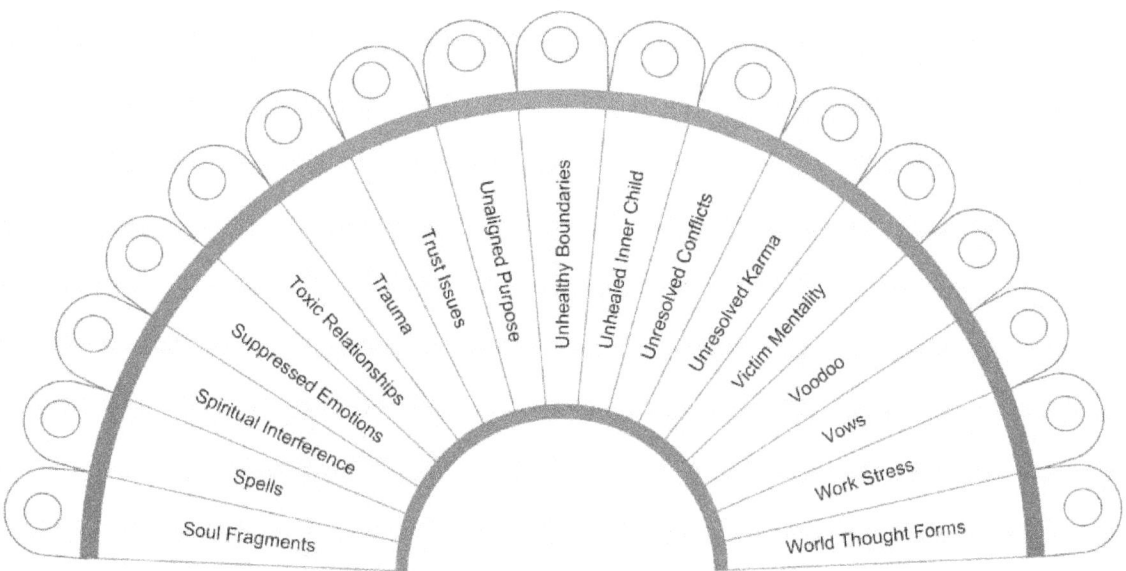

Personal Blocks to Dowsing, Chart 6

Toxic Relationships
Trauma
Trust Issues
Unaligned Purpose
Unhealthy Boundaries
Unhealed Inner Child
Unresolved Conflicts
Unresolved Karma
Victim Mentality
Voodoo
Vows
Work Stress
World Thought Forms
Soul Fragments
Spells
Spiritual Interference
Suppressed Emotions

Royal Template 17

Diving Deep into the Pool of the Mind

Chart 449

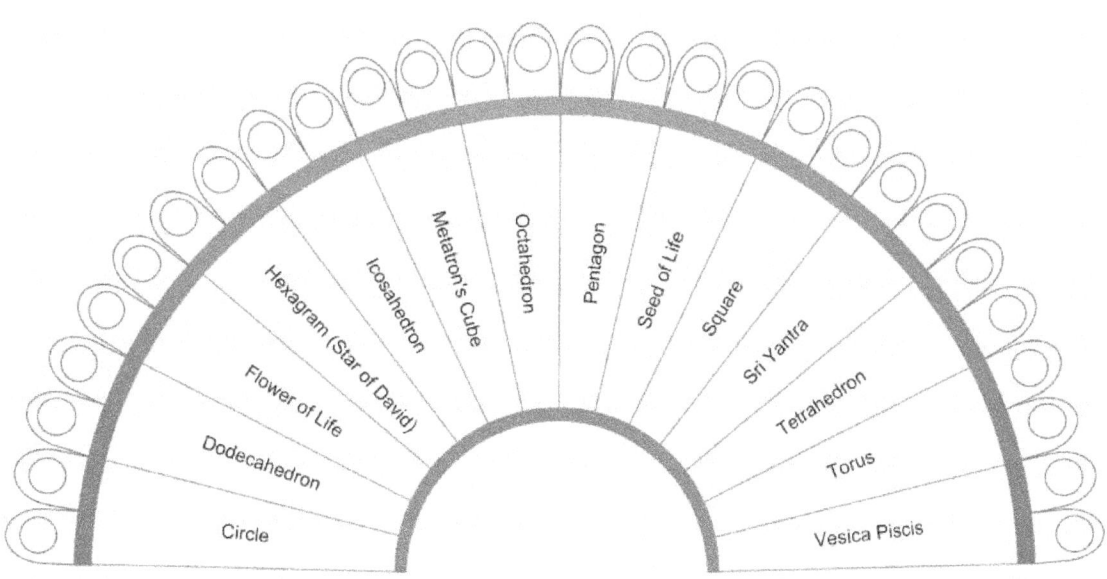

Sacred Geometry Patterns and Symbols

Hexagram (Star of David)
Icosahedron
Metatron's Cube
Octahedron
Pentagon
Seed of Life
Square
Sri Yantra
Tetrahedron
Torus
Vesica Piscis
Circle
Dodecahedron
Flower of Life

Royal Template 14

Diving Deep into the Pool of the Mind

Chart 450

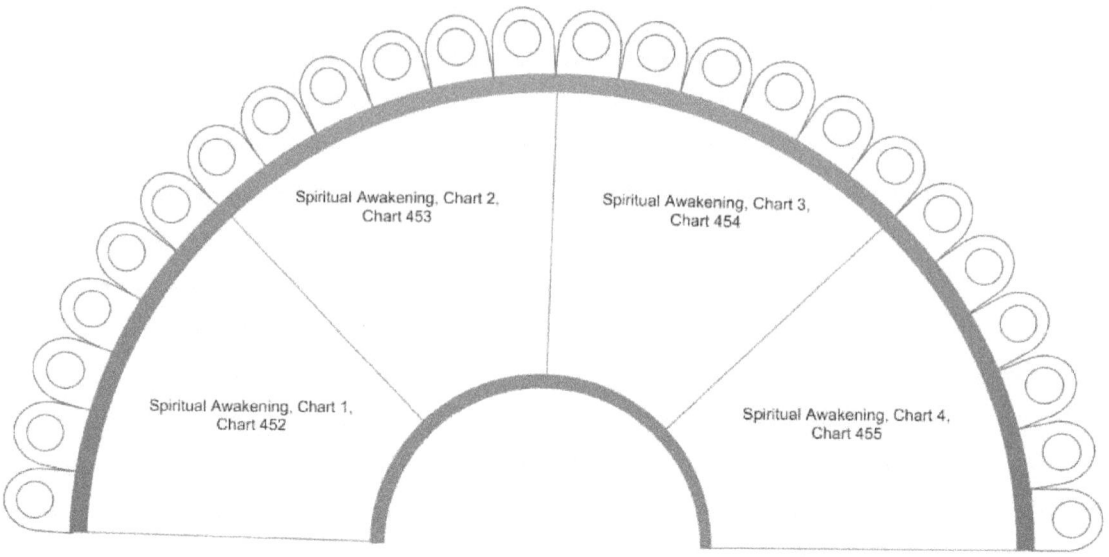

Spiritual Awakening, Master Chart

Spiritual Awakening, Chart 2, Chart 453

Spiritual Awakening, Chart 3, Chart 454

Spiritual Awakening, Chart 1, Chart 452

Spiritual Awakening, Chart 4, Chart 455

Royal Template 4h

Diving Deep into the Pool of the Mind

Chart 451

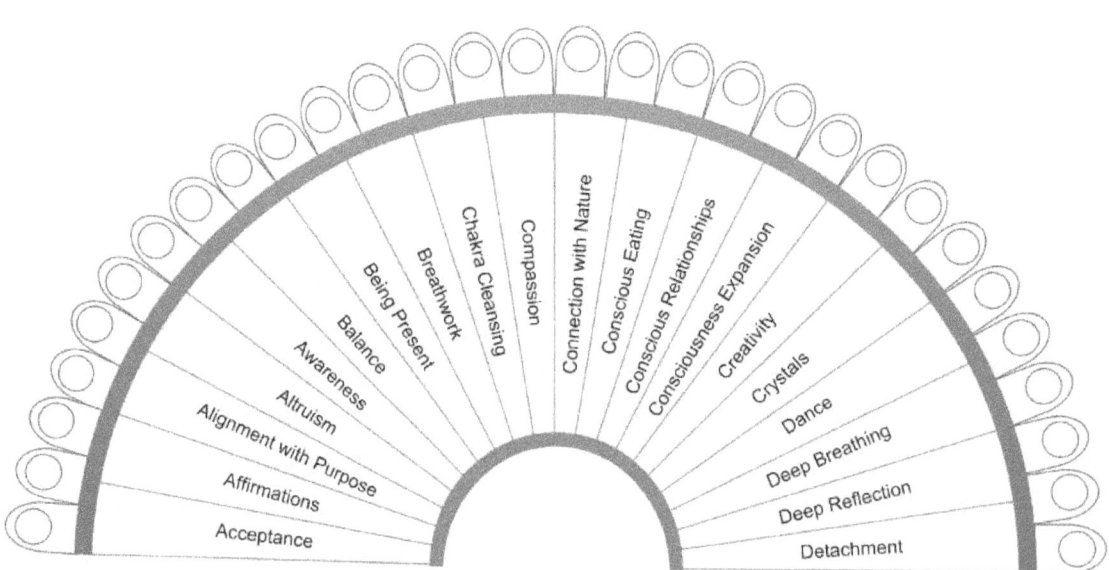

Chakra Cleansing
Compassion
Connection with Nature
Conscious Eating
Conscious Relationships
Consciousness Expansion
Creativity
Crystals
Dance
Deep Breathing
Deep Reflection
Detachment
Breathwork
Being Present
Balance
Awareness
Altruism
Alignment with Purpose
Affirmations
Acceptance

Spiritual Awakening, Chart 1

Royal Template 20

Diving Deep into the Pool of the Mind

Chart 452

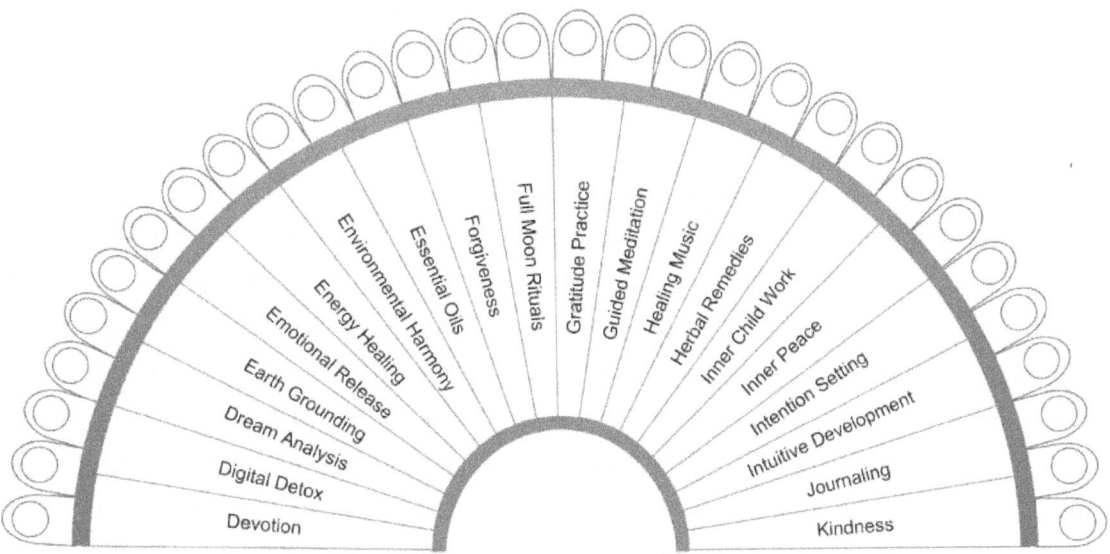

Spiritual Awakening, Chart 2

Full Moon Rituals
Forgiveness
Essential Oils
Environmental Harmony
Energy Healing
Emotional Release
Earth Grounding
Dream Analysis
Digital Detox
Devotion
Gratitude Practice
Guided Meditation
Healing Music
Herbal Remedies
Inner Child Work
Inner Peace
Intention Setting
Intuitive Development
Journaling
Kindness

Royal Template 20

Diving Deep into the Pool of the Mind

Chart 453

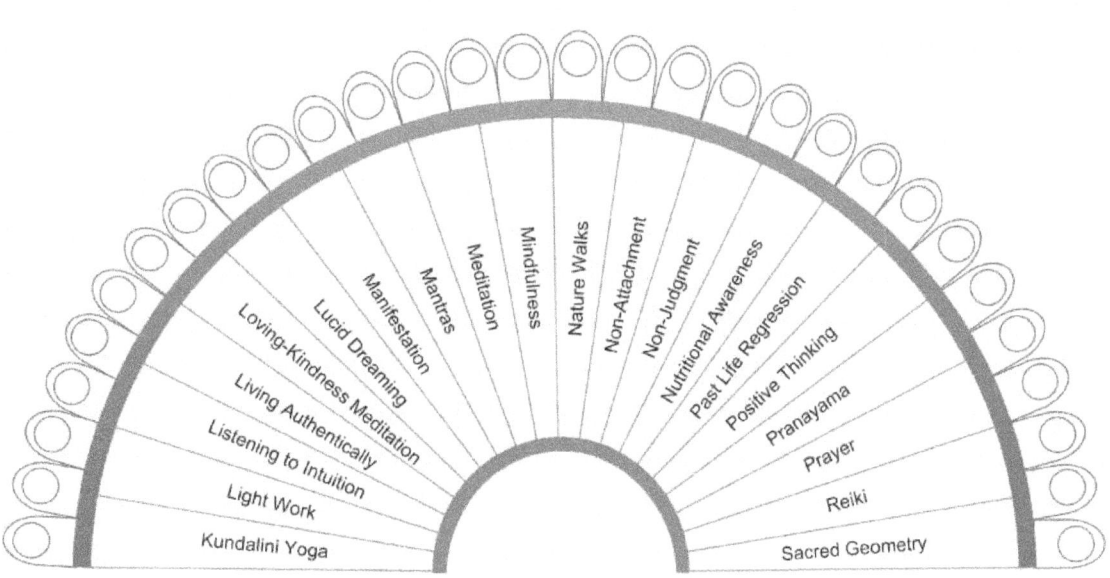

Spiritual Awakening, Chart 3

Mindfulness
Meditation
Mantras
Manifestation
Lucid Dreaming
Loving-Kindness Meditation
Living Authentically
Listening to Intuition
Light Work
Kundalini Yoga
Nature Walks
Non-Attachment
Non-Judgment
Nutritional Awareness
Past Life Regression
Positive Thinking
Pranayama
Prayer
Reiki
Sacred Geometry

Royal Template 20

Diving Deep into the Pool of the Mind

Chart 454

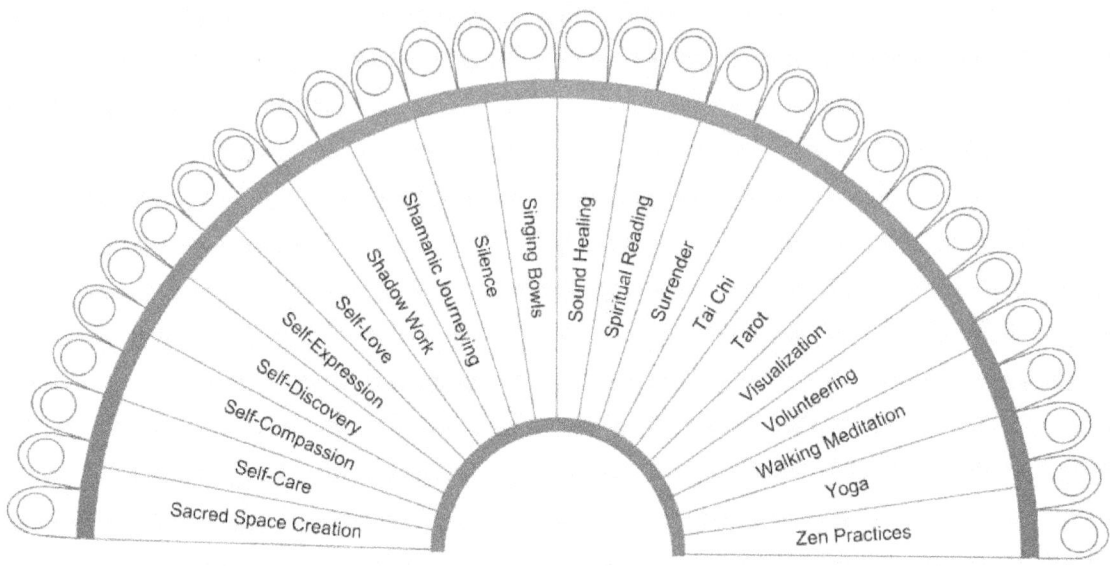

Spiritual Awakening, Chart 4

Shamanic Journeying
Shadow Work
Silence
Self-Love
Singing Bowls
Self-Expression
Sound Healing
Self-Discovery
Spiritual Reading
Self-Compassion
Surrender
Self-Care
Tai Chi
Sacred Space Creation
Tarot
Visualization
Volunteering
Walking Meditation
Yoga
Zen Practices

Royal Template 20

Diving Deep into the Pool of the Mind

Chart 455

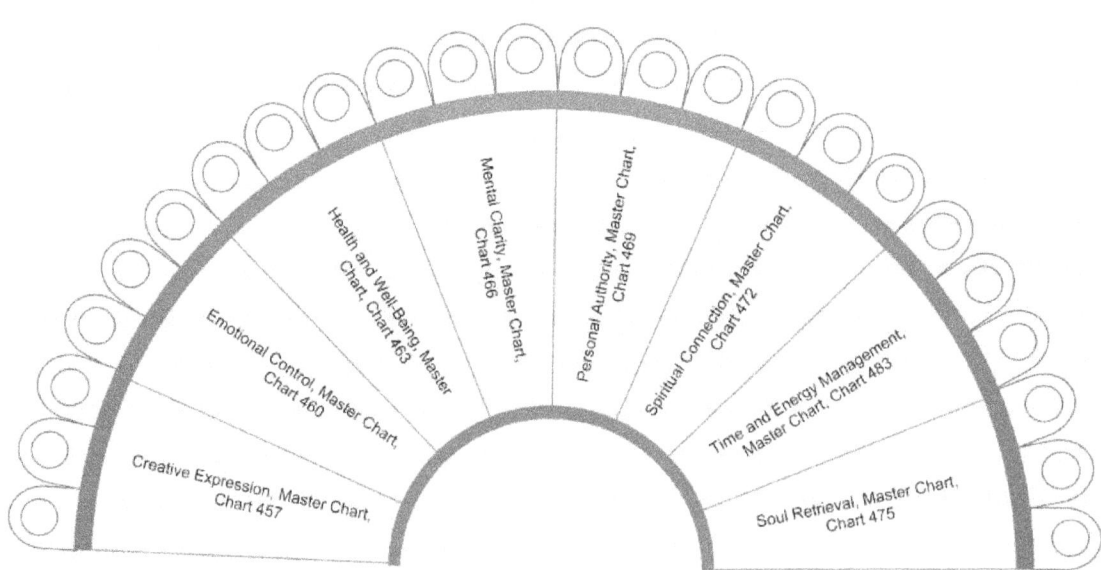

Things Lost, Taken, or Given Away, Master Chart

Emotional Control, Master Chart, Chart 460
Health and Well-Being, Master Chart, Chart 463
Mental Clarity, Master Chart, Chart 466
Personal Authority, Master Chart, Chart 469
Spiritual Connection, Master Chart, Chart 472
Time and Energy Management, Master Chart, Chart 483
Creative Expression, Master Chart, Chart 457
Soul Retrieval, Master Chart, Chart 475

Royal Template 8

Diving Deep into the Pool of the Mind

Chart 456

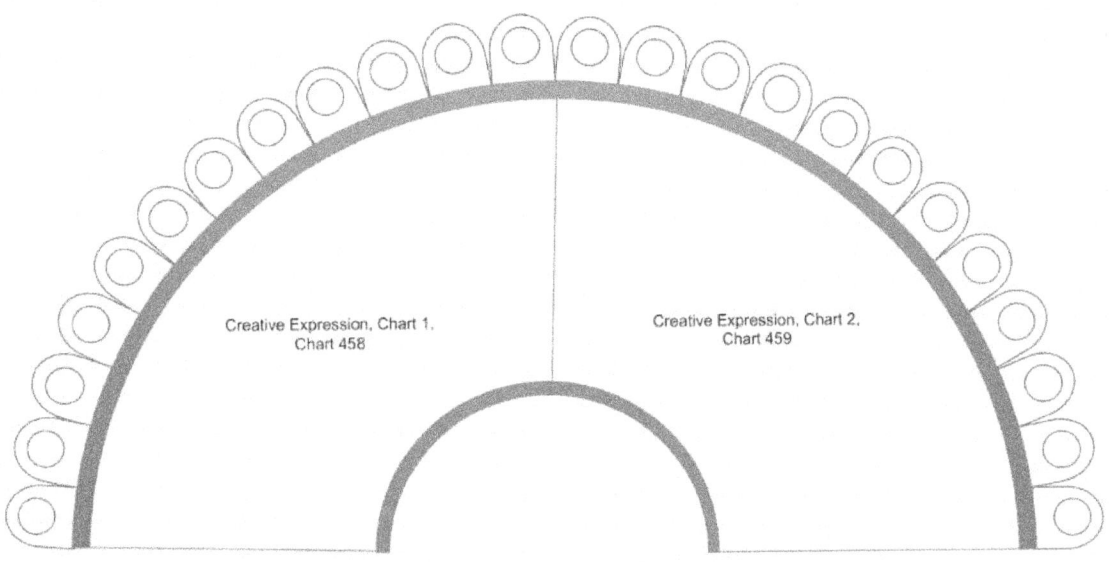

Creative Expression, Master Chart

Creative Expression, Chart 1. Chart 458

Creative Expression, Chart 2. Chart 459

Royal Template 2

Diving Deep into the Pool of the Mind

Chart 457

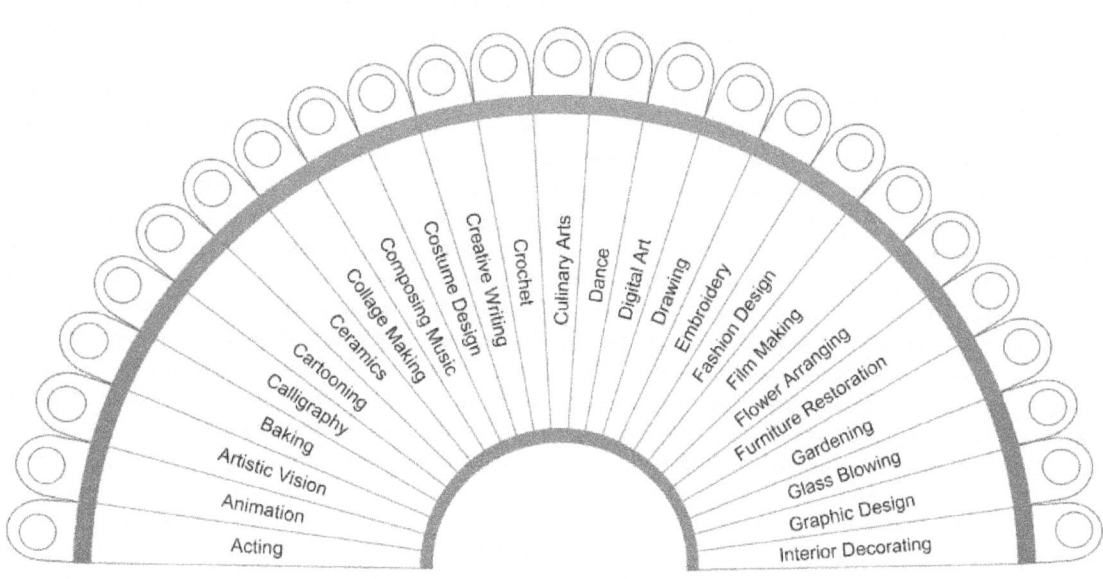

Creative Expression, Chart 1

Labels (from left to right): Acting, Animation, Artistic Vision, Baking, Calligraphy, Cartooning, Ceramics, Collage Making, Composing Music, Costume Design, Creative Writing, Crochet, Culinary Arts, Dance, Digital Art, Drawing, Embroidery, Fashion Design, Film Making, Flower Arranging, Furniture Restoration, Gardening, Glass Blowing, Graphic Design, Interior Decorating

Royal Template 25

Diving Deep into the Pool of the Mind

Chart 458

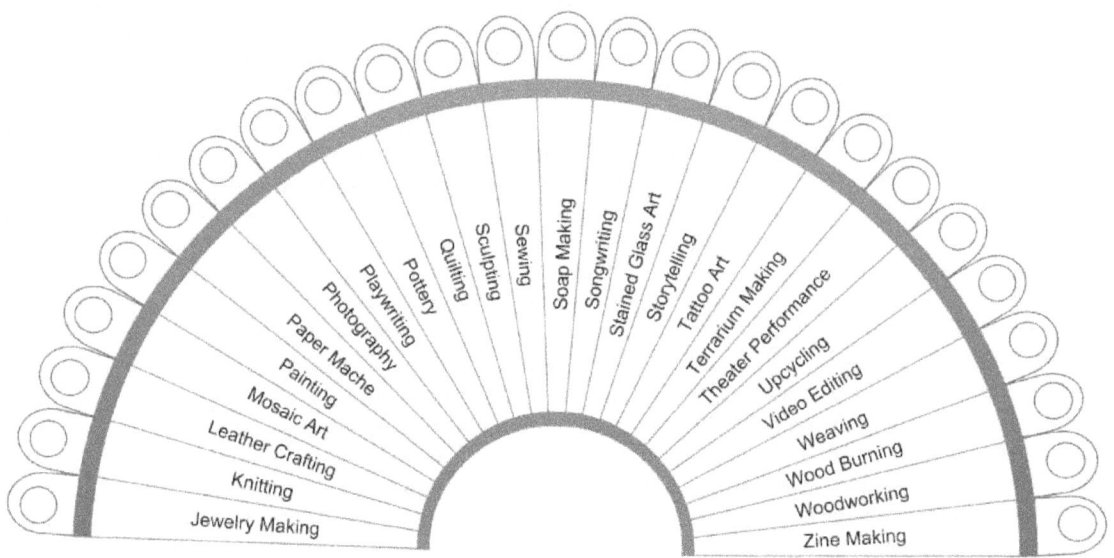

Creative Expression, Chart 2

Jewelry Making
Knitting
Leather Crafting
Mosaic Art
Painting
Paper Mache
Photography
Playwriting
Pottery
Quilting
Sculpting
Sewing
Soap Making
Songwriting
Stained Glass Art
Storytelling
Tattoo Art
Terrarium Making
Theater Performance
Upcycling
Video Editing
Weaving
Wood Burning
Woodworking
Zine Making

Royal Template 25

Diving Deep into the Pool of the Mind

Chart 459

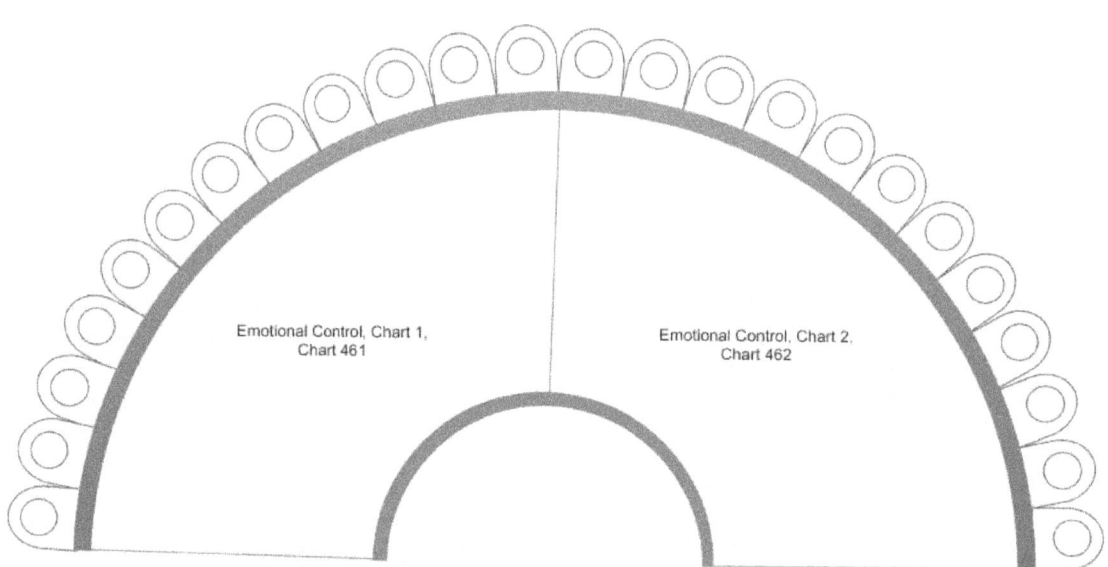

Emotional Control, Chart 1, Chart 461

Emotional Control, Chart 2, Chart 462

Emotional Control, Master Chart

Royal Template 2

Diving Deep into the Pool of the Mind

Chart 460

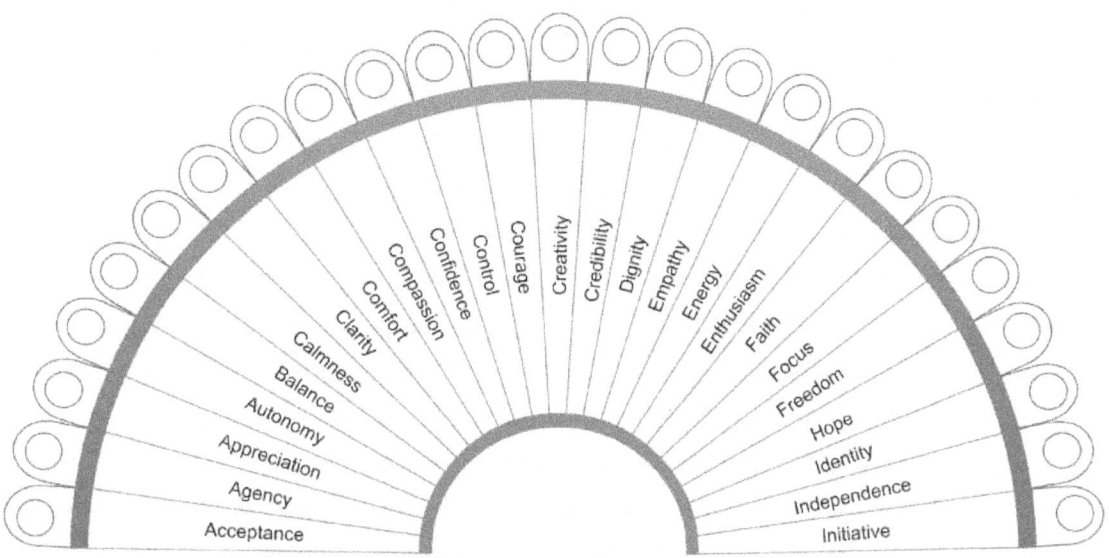

Emotional Control, Chart 1

Royal Template 25

Diving Deep into the Pool of the Mind

Chart 461

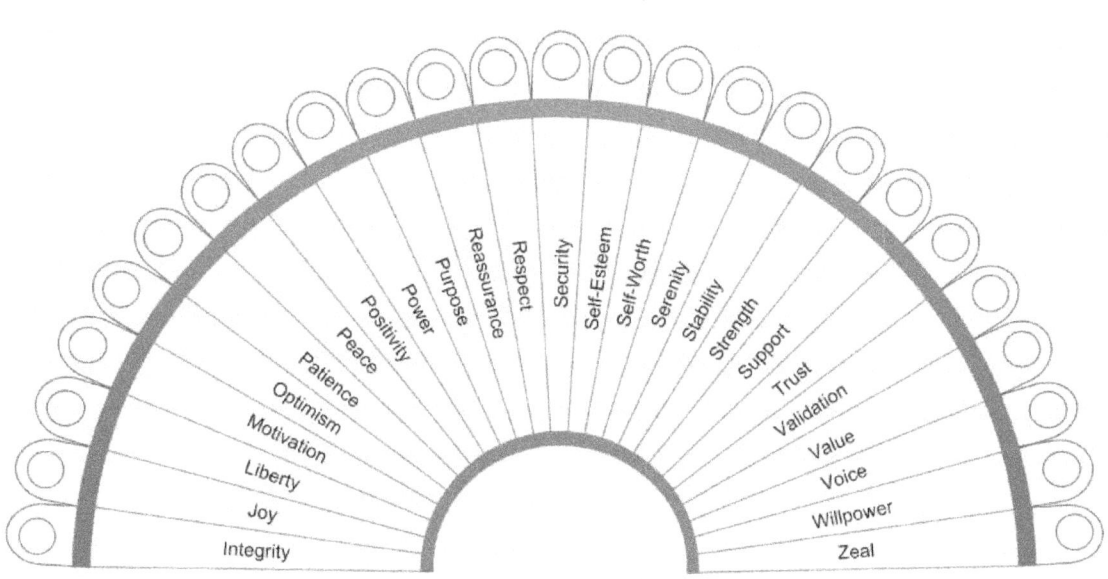

Emotional Control, Chart 2

Royal Template 25

Diving Deep into the Pool of the Mind

Chart 462

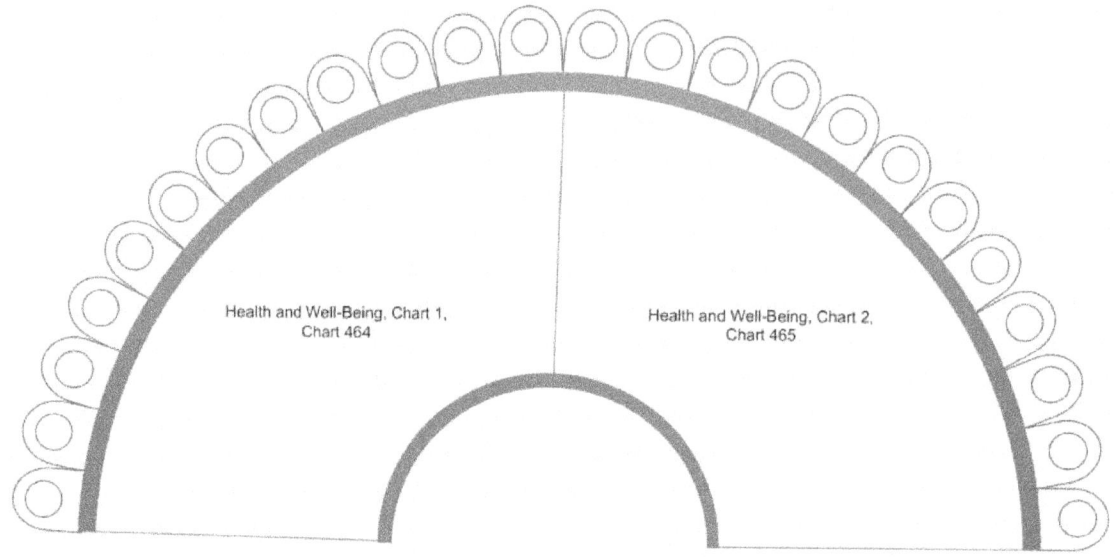

Health and Well-Being, Master Chart

Health and Well-Being, Chart 1,
Chart 464

Health and Well-Being, Chart 2,
Chart 465

Royal Template 2

Diving Deep into the Pool of the Mind

Chart 463

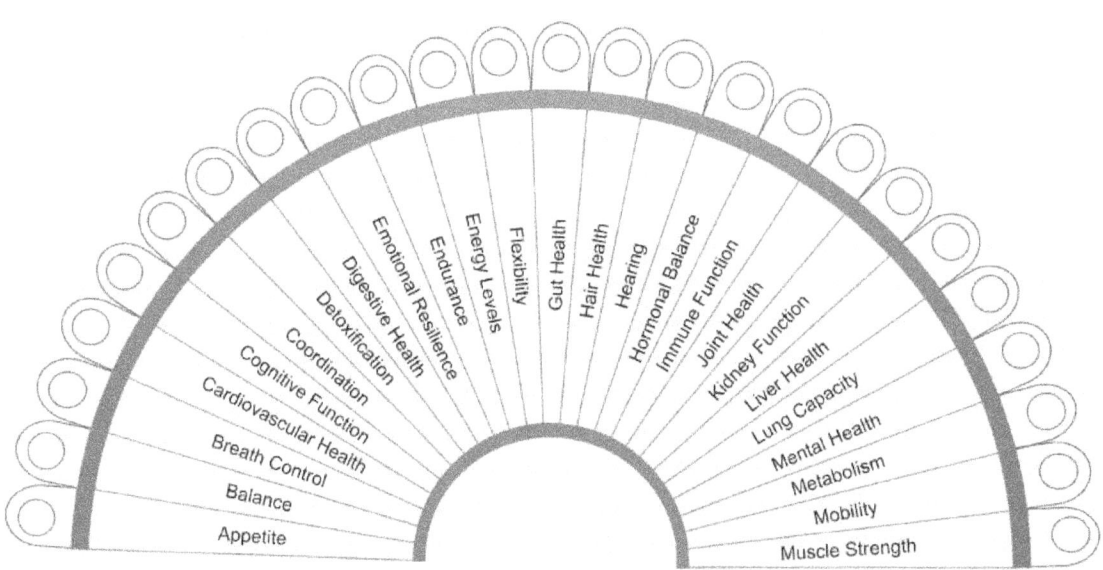

Appetite
Balance
Breath Control
Cardiovascular Health
Cognitive Function
Coordination
Detoxification
Digestive Health
Emotional Resilience
Endurance
Energy Levels
Flexibility
Gut Health
Hair Health
Hearing
Hormonal Balance
Immune Function
Joint Health
Kidney Function
Liver Health
Lung Capacity
Mental Health
Metabolism
Mobility
Muscle Strength

Health and Well-Being, Chart 1

Royal Template 25

Diving Deep into the Pool of the Mind

Chart 464

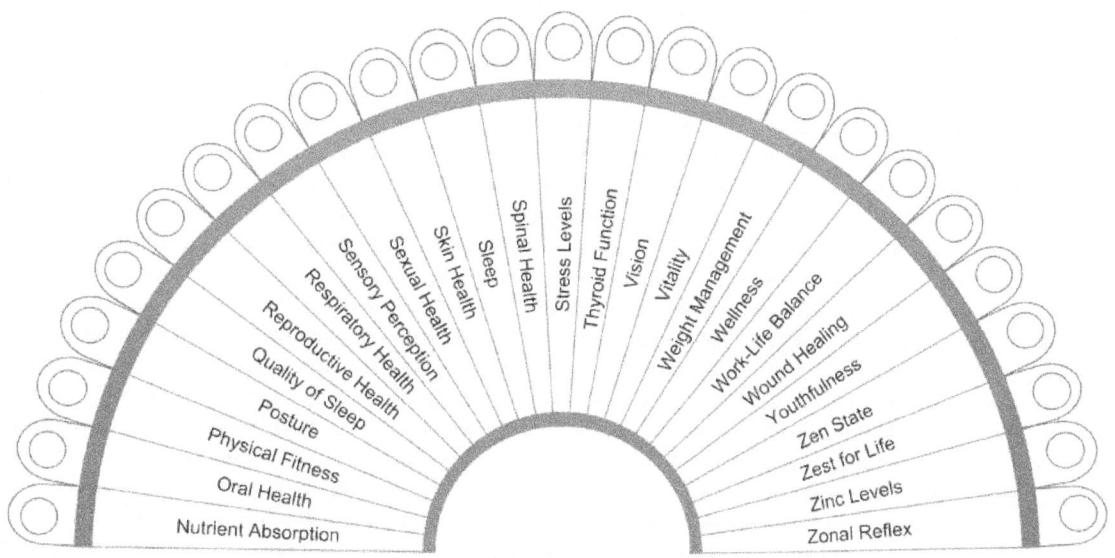

Health and Well-Being, Chart 2

The chart contains the following labels (left to right):

- Nutrient Absorption
- Oral Health
- Physical Fitness
- Posture
- Quality of Sleep
- Reproductive Health
- Respiratory Health
- Sensory Perception
- Sexual Health
- Skin Health
- Sleep
- Spinal Health
- Stress Levels
- Thyroid Function
- Vision
- Vitality
- Weight Management
- Wellness
- Work-Life Balance
- Wound Healing
- Youthfulness
- Zen State
- Zest for Life
- Zinc Levels
- Zonal Reflex

Royal Template 25

Diving Deep into the Pool of the Mind

Chart 465

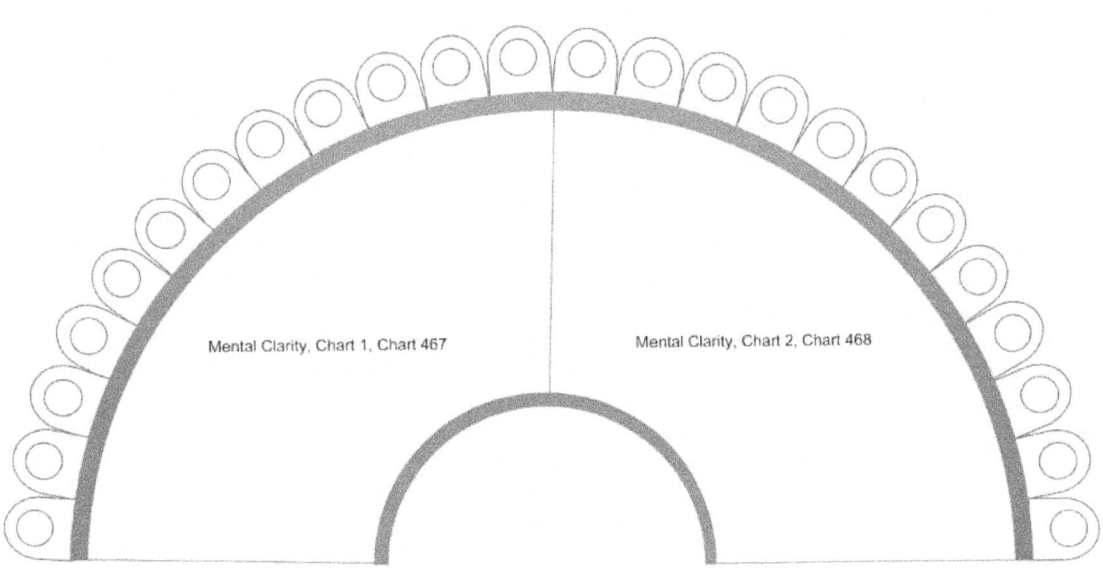

Mental Clarity, Chart 1, Chart 467

Mental Clarity, Chart 2, Chart 468

Mental Clarity, Master Chart

Royal Template 2

Diving Deep into the Pool of the Mind

Chart 466

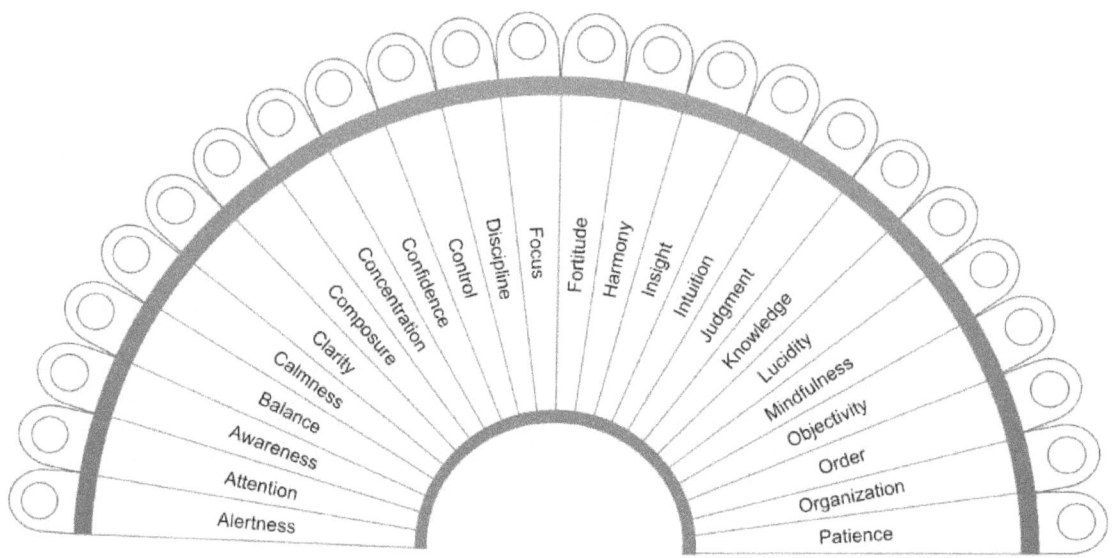

Mental Clarity, Chart 1

Alertness, Attention, Awareness, Balance, Calmness, Clarity, Composure, Concentration, Confidence, Control, Discipline, Focus, Fortitude, Harmony, Insight, Intuition, Judgment, Knowledge, Lucidity, Mindfulness, Objectivity, Order, Organization, Patience

Royal Template 24

Diving Deep into the Pool of the Mind

Chart 467

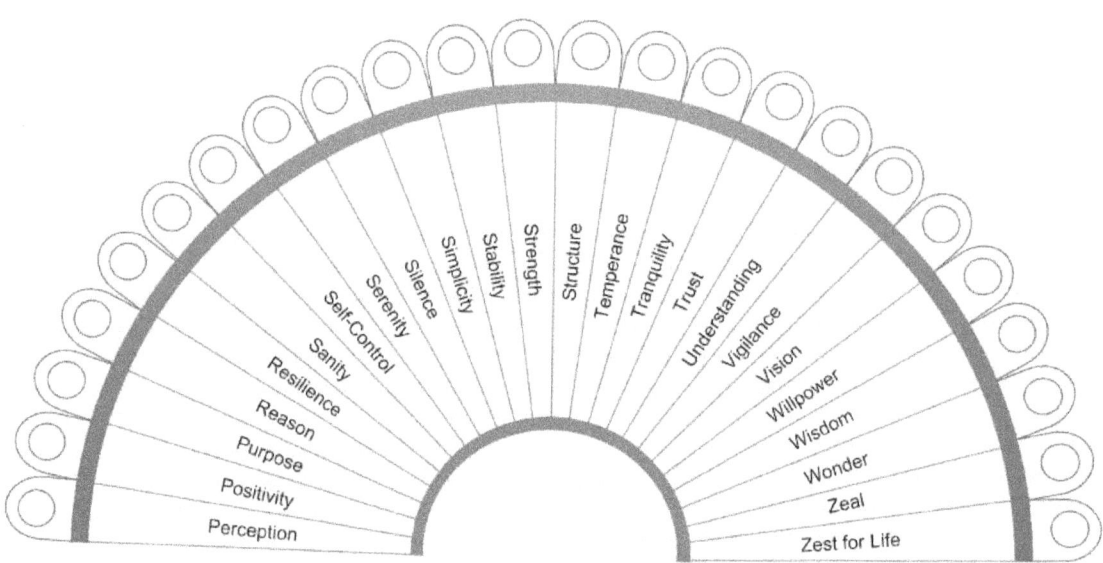

Mental Clarity, Chart 2

Perception, Positivity, Purpose, Reason, Resilience, Sanity, Self-Control, Serenity, Silence, Simplicity, Stability, Strength, Structure, Temperance, Tranquility, Trust, Understanding, Vigilance, Vision, Willpower, Wisdom, Wonder, Zeal, Zest for Life

Royal Template 24

Diving Deep into the Pool of the Mind

Chart 468

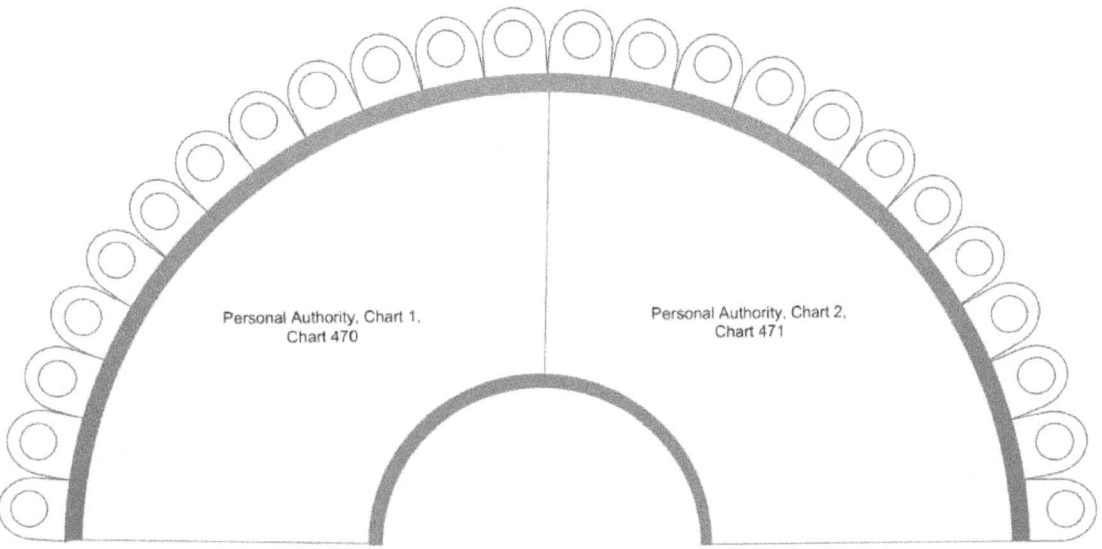

Personal Authority, Master Chart

Personal Authority, Chart 1,
Chart 470

Personal Authority, Chart 2,
Chart 471

Diving Deep into the Pool of the Mind

Chart 469

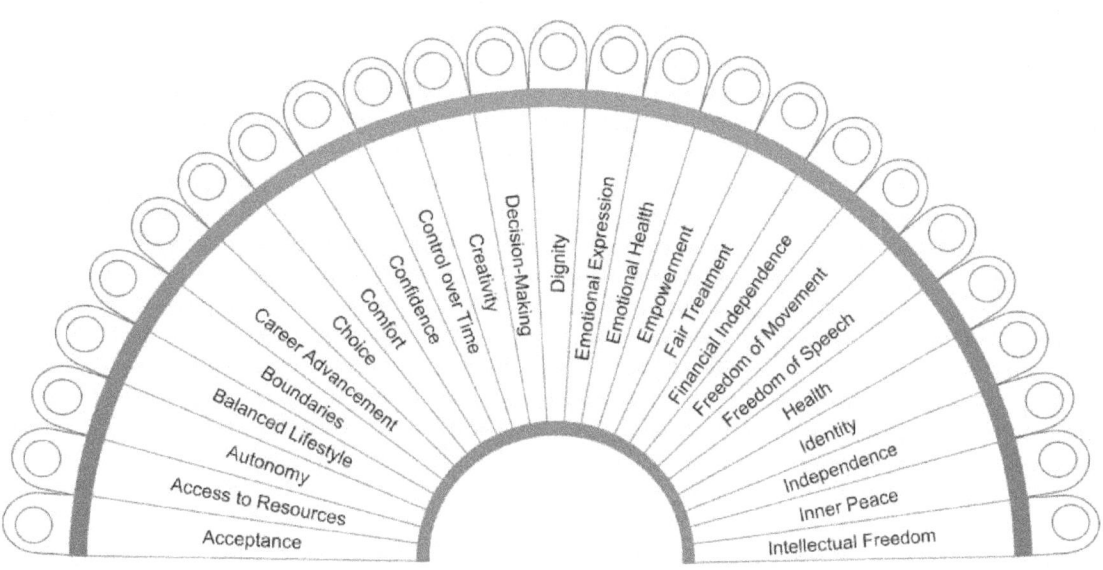

Labels (left to right):
Acceptance, Access to Resources, Autonomy, Balanced Lifestyle, Boundaries, Career Advancement, Choice, Comfort, Confidence, Control over Time, Creativity, Decision-Making, Dignity, Emotional Expression, Emotional Health, Empowerment, Fair Treatment, Financial Independence, Freedom of Movement, Freedom of Speech, Health, Identity, Independence, Inner Peace, Intellectual Freedom

Personal Authority, Chart 1

Diving Deep into the Pool of the Mind

Chart 470

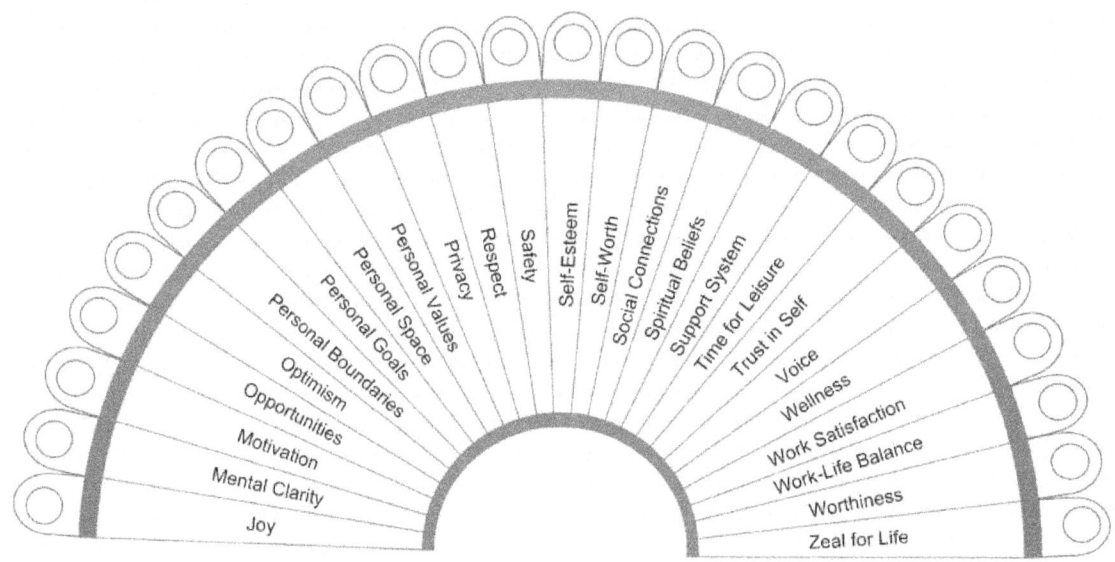

Personal Authority, Chart 2

Personal Values
Personal Space
Personal Goals
Personal Boundaries
Optimism
Opportunities
Motivation
Mental Clarity
Joy
Privacy
Respect
Safety
Self-Esteem
Self-Worth
Social Connections
Spiritual Beliefs
Support System
Time for Leisure
Trust in Self
Voice
Wellness
Work Satisfaction
Work-Life Balance
Worthiness
Zeal for Life

Royal Template 25

Diving Deep into the Pool of the Mind

Chart 471

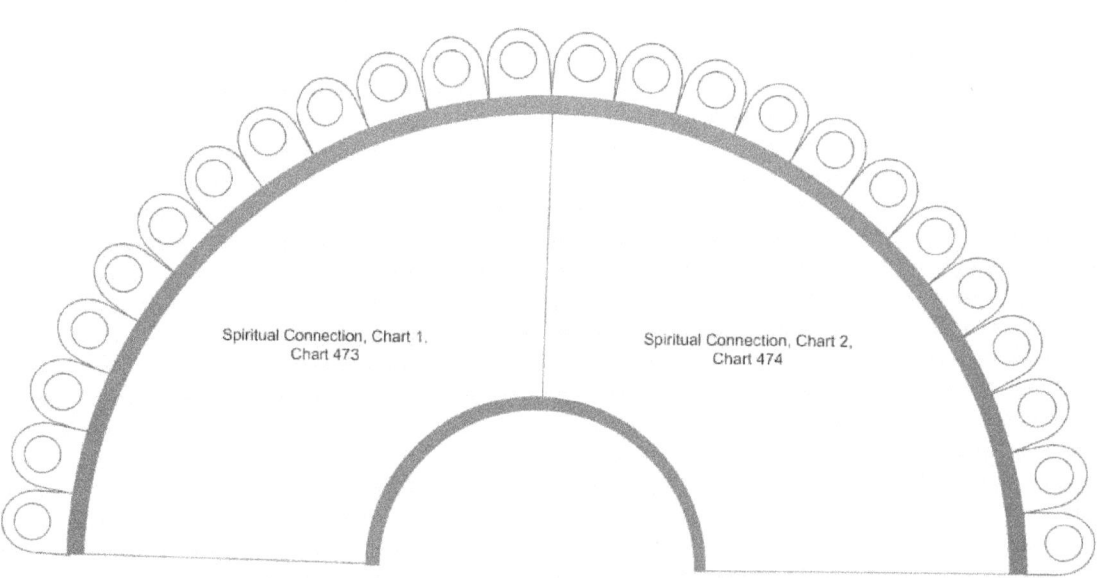

Spiritual Connection, Chart 1,
Chart 473

Spiritual Connection, Chart 2,
Chart 474

Spiritual Connection, Master Chart

Royal Template 2

Diving Deep into the Pool of the Mind

Chart 472

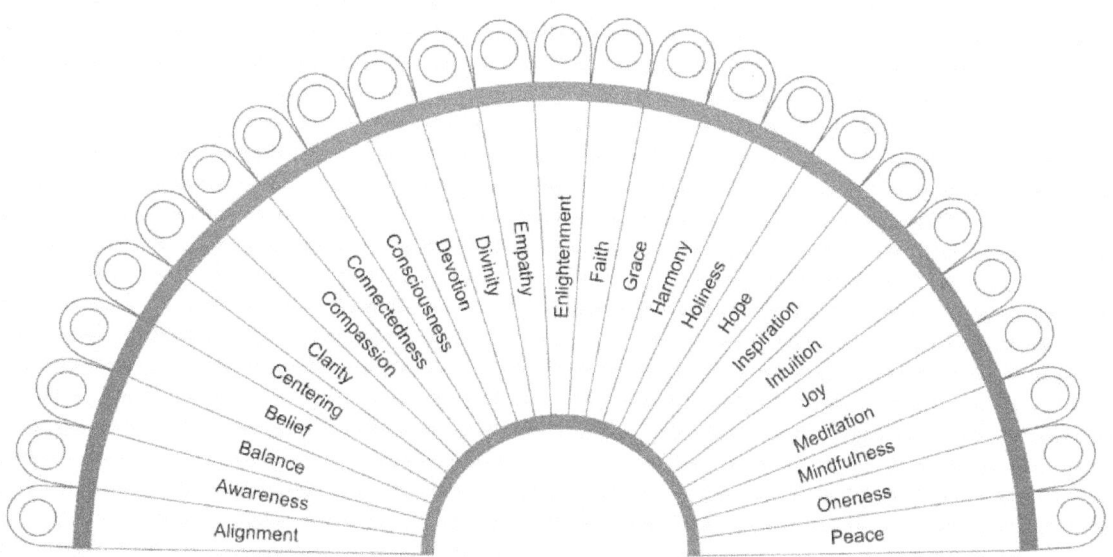

Spiritual Connection, Chart 1

Royal Template 25

Diving Deep into the Pool of the Mind

Chart 473

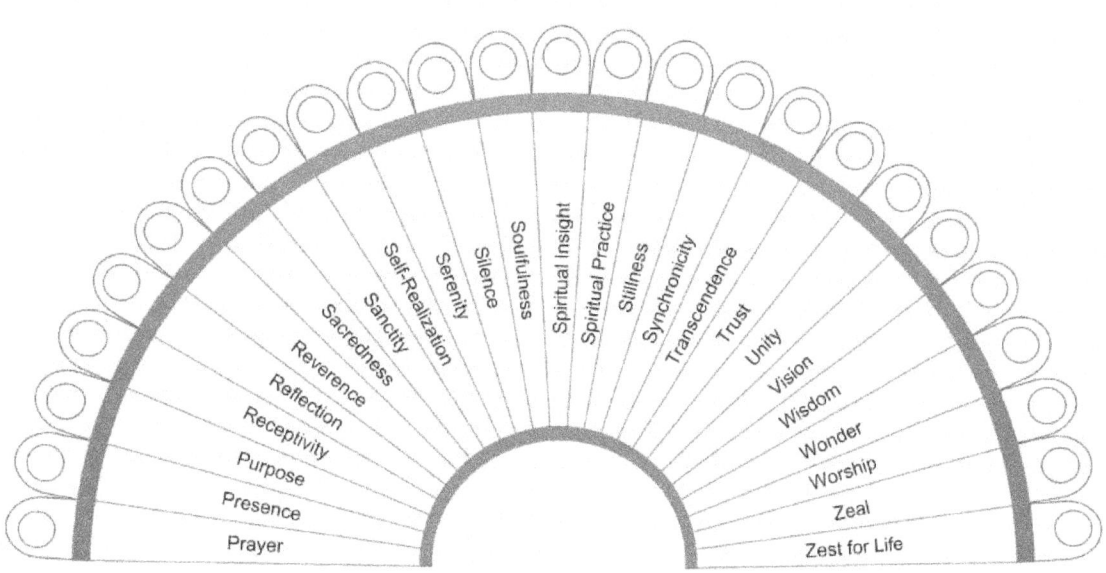

Spiritual Connection, Chart 2

Royal Template 25

Diving Deep into the Pool of the Mind

Chart 474

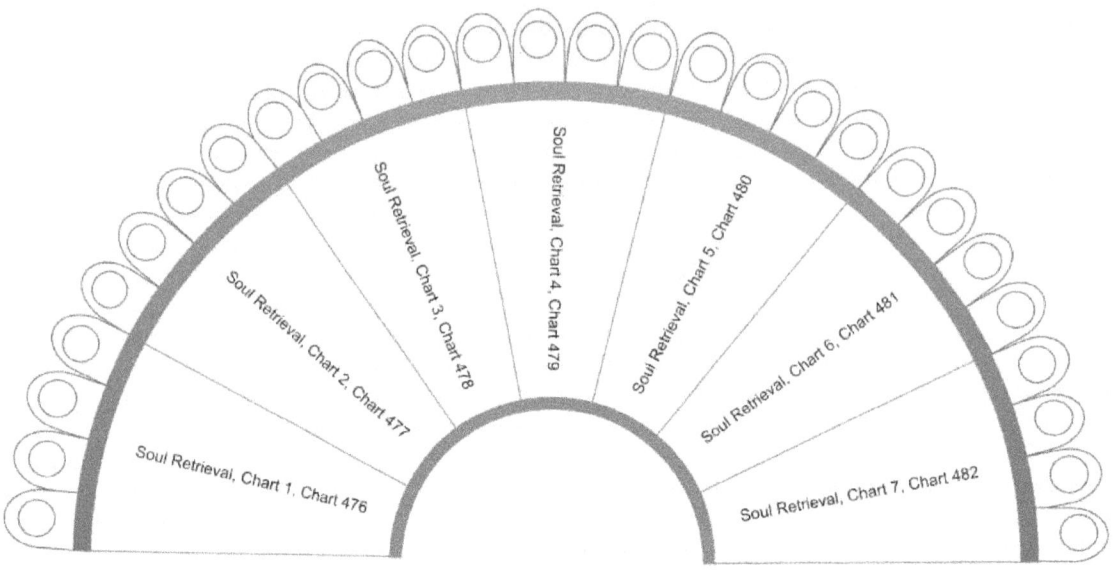

Soul Retrieval, Master Chart

The chart contains the following sections:
- Soul Retrieval, Chart 1, Chart 476
- Soul Retrieval, Chart 2, Chart 477
- Soul Retrieval, Chart 3, Chart 478
- Soul Retrieval, Chart 4, Chart 479
- Soul Retrieval, Chart 5, Chart 480
- Soul Retrieval, Chart 6, Chart 481
- Soul Retrieval, Chart 7, Chart 482

Royal Template 7

Diving Deep into the Pool of the Mind

Chart 475

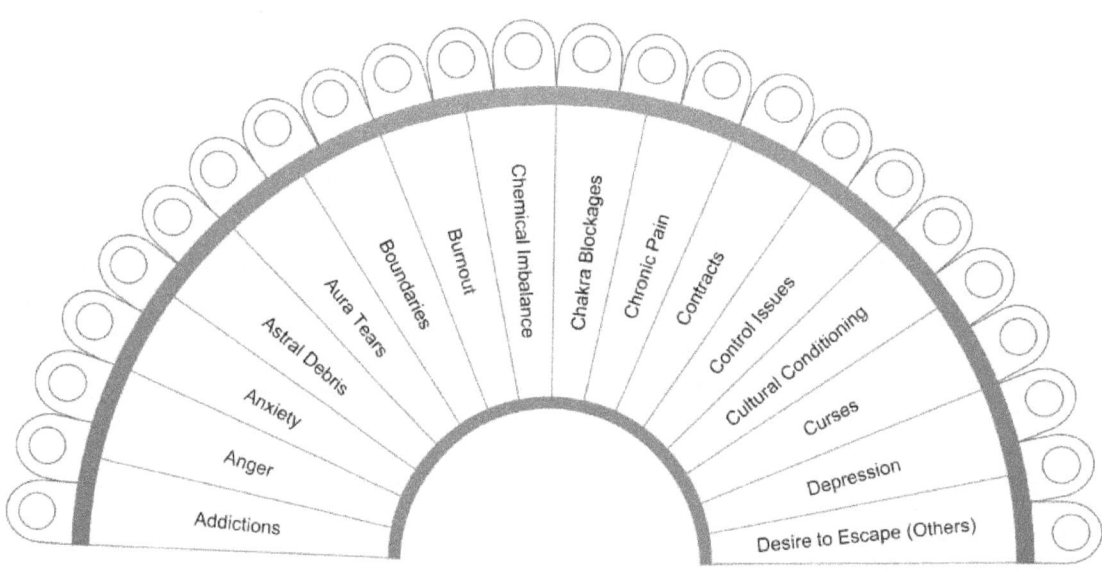

Soul Retrieval, Chart 1

The chart contains the following sections:
- Addictions
- Anger
- Anxiety
- Astral Debris
- Aura Tears
- Boundaries
- Burnout
- Chemical Imbalance
- Chakra Blockages
- Chronic Pain
- Contracts
- Control Issues
- Cultural Conditioning
- Curses
- Depression
- Desire to Escape (Others)

Royal Template 16

Diving Deep into the Pool of the Mind

Chart 476

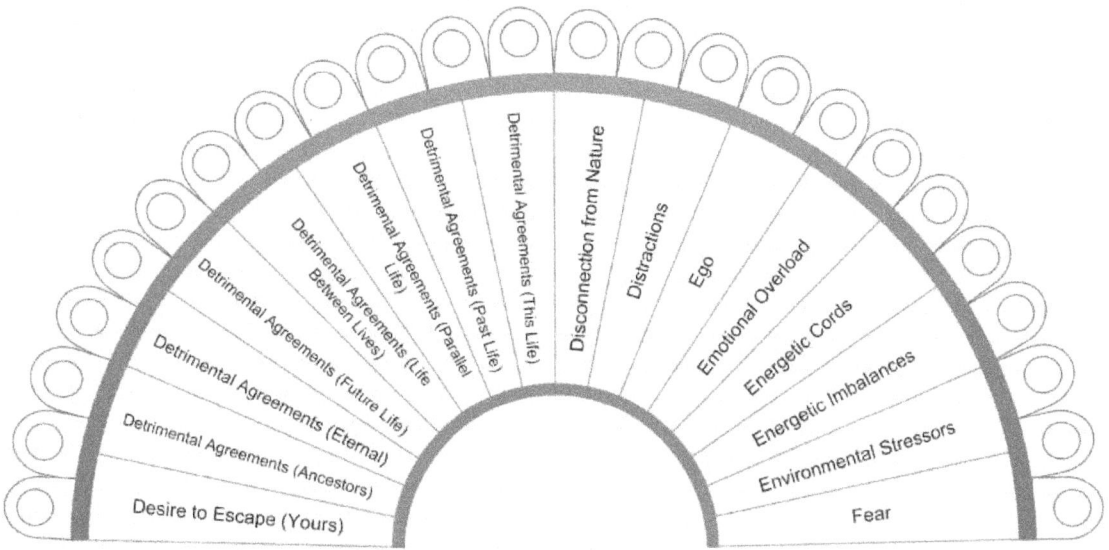

Soul Retrieval, Chart 2

Labels (clockwise):
- Desire to Escape (Yours)
- Detrimental Agreements (Ancestors)
- Detrimental Agreements (Eternal)
- Detrimental Agreements (Future Life)
- Detrimental Agreements (Life Between Lives)
- Detrimental Agreements (Parallel Life)
- Detrimental Agreements (Past Life)
- Detrimental Agreements (This Life)
- Disconnection from Nature
- Distractions
- Ego
- Emotional Overload
- Energetic Cords
- Energetic Imbalances
- Environmental Stressors
- Fear

Royal Template 16

Diving Deep into the Pool of the Mind

Chart 477

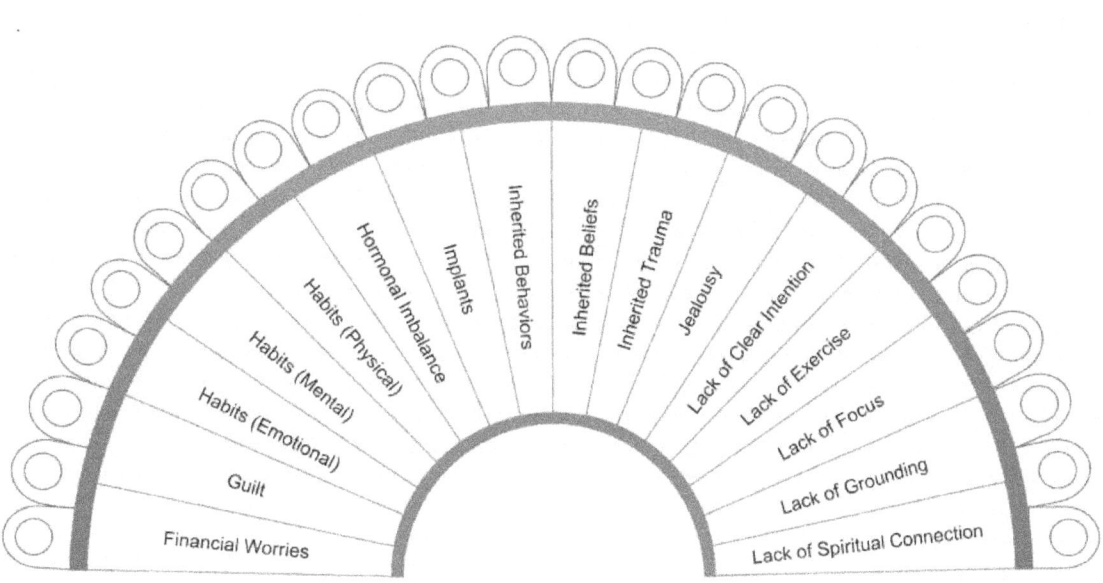

Soul Retrieval, Chart 3

Labels (clockwise):
- Financial Worries
- Guilt
- Habits (Emotional)
- Habits (Mental)
- Habits (Physical)
- Hormonal Imbalance
- Implants
- Inherited Behaviors
- Inherited Beliefs
- Inherited Trauma
- Jealousy
- Lack of Clear Intention
- Lack of Exercise
- Lack of Focus
- Lack of Grounding
- Lack of Spiritual Connection

Royal Template 16

Diving Deep into the Pool of the Mind

Chart 478

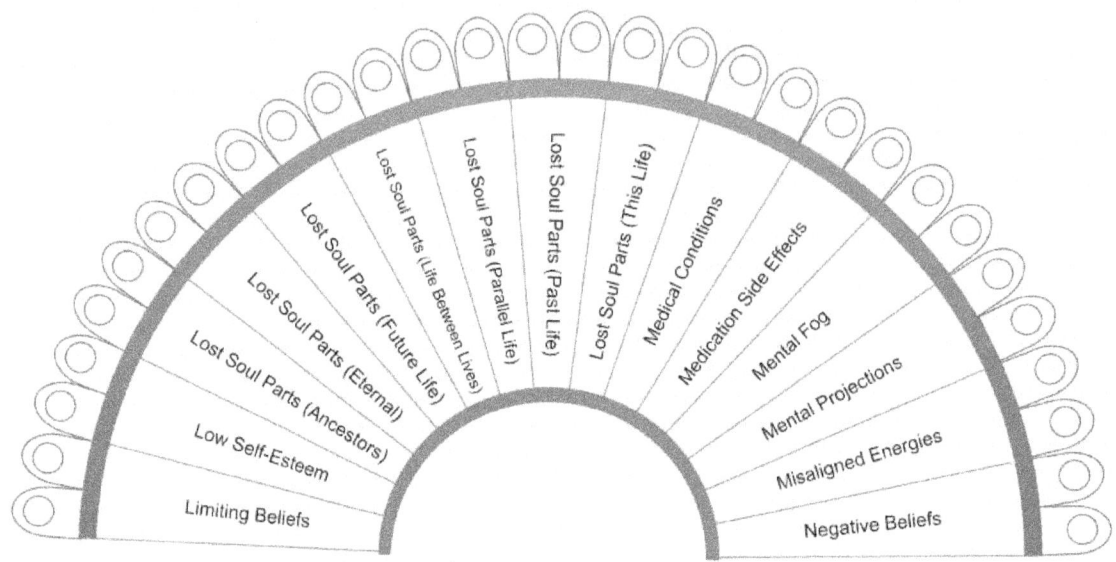

Soul Retrieval, Chart 4

The chart contains the following labels (from left to right):
- Limiting Beliefs
- Low Self-Esteem
- Lost Soul Parts (Ancestors)
- Lost Soul Parts (Eternal)
- Lost Soul Parts (Future Life)
- Lost Soul Parts (Life Between Lives)
- Lost Soul Parts (Parallel Life)
- Lost Soul Parts (Past Life)
- Lost Soul Parts (This Life)
- Medical Conditions
- Medication Side Effects
- Mental Fog
- Mental Projections
- Misaligned Energies
- Negative Beliefs

Royal Template 15

Diving Deep into the Pool of the Mind

Chart 479

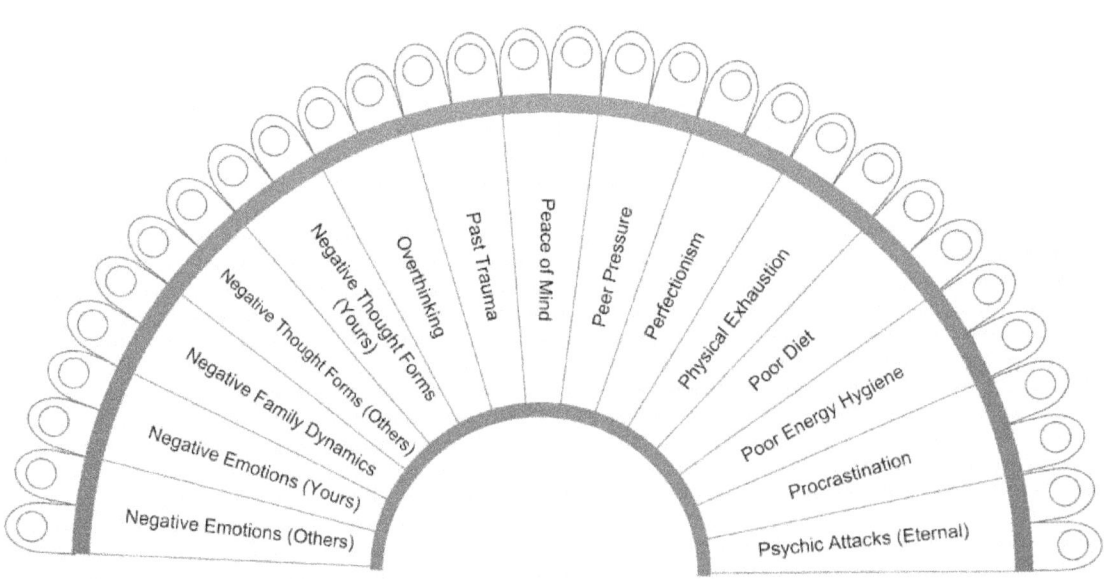

Soul Retrieval, Chart 5

The chart contains the following labels (from left to right):
- Negative Emotions (Others)
- Negative Emotions (Yours)
- Negative Family Dynamics
- Negative Thought Forms (Others)
- Negative Thought Forms (Yours)
- Overthinking
- Past Trauma
- Peace of Mind
- Peer Pressure
- Perfectionism
- Physical Exhaustion
- Poor Diet
- Poor Energy Hygiene
- Procrastination
- Psychic Attacks (Eternal)

Royal Template 15

Diving Deep into the Pool of the Mind

Chart 480

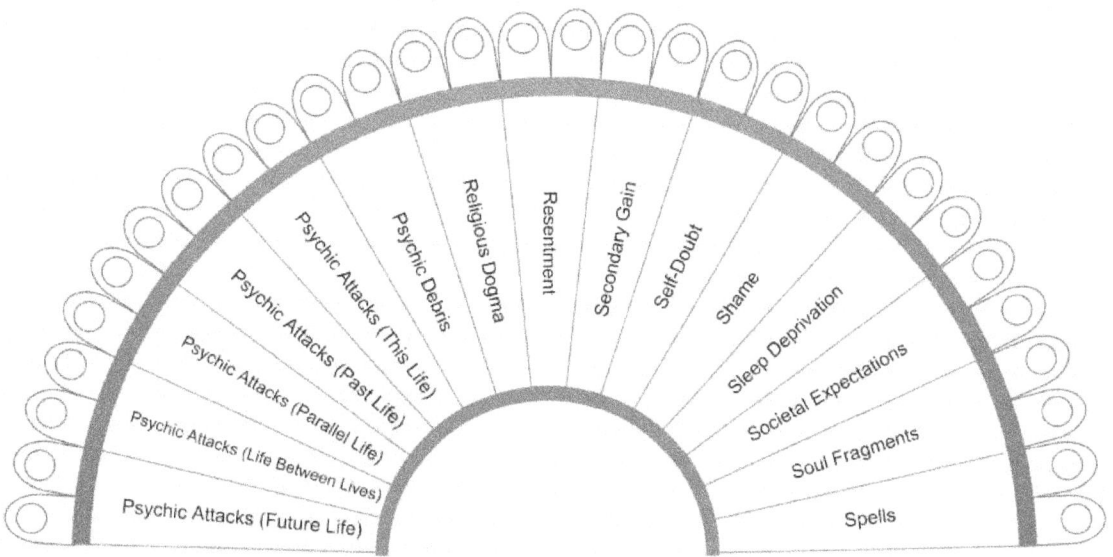

Soul Retrieval, Chart 6

The following labels appear around the chart (left to right):

- Psychic Attacks (Future Life)
- Psychic Attacks (Life Between Lives)
- Psychic Attacks (Parallel Life)
- Psychic Attacks (Past Life)
- Psychic Attacks (This Life)
- Psychic Debris
- Religious Dogma
- Resentment
- Secondary Gain
- Self-Doubt
- Shame
- Sleep Deprivation
- Societal Expectations
- Soul Fragments
- Spells

Royal Template 15

Diving Deep into the Pool of the Mind

Chart 481

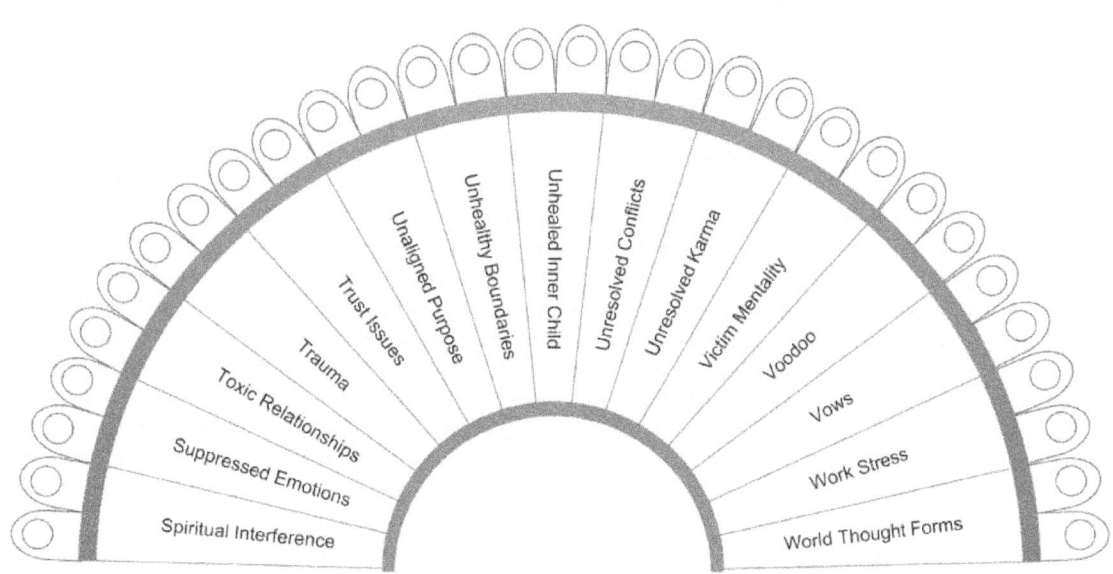

Soul Retrieval, Chart 7

The following labels appear around the chart (left to right):

- Spiritual Interference
- Suppressed Emotions
- Toxic Relationships
- Trauma
- Trust Issues
- Unaligned Purpose
- Unhealthy Boundaries
- Unhealed Inner Child
- Unresolved Conflicts
- Unresolved Karma
- Victim Mentality
- Voodoo
- Vows
- Work Stress
- World Thought Forms

Royal Template 15

Diving Deep into the Pool of the Mind

Chart 482

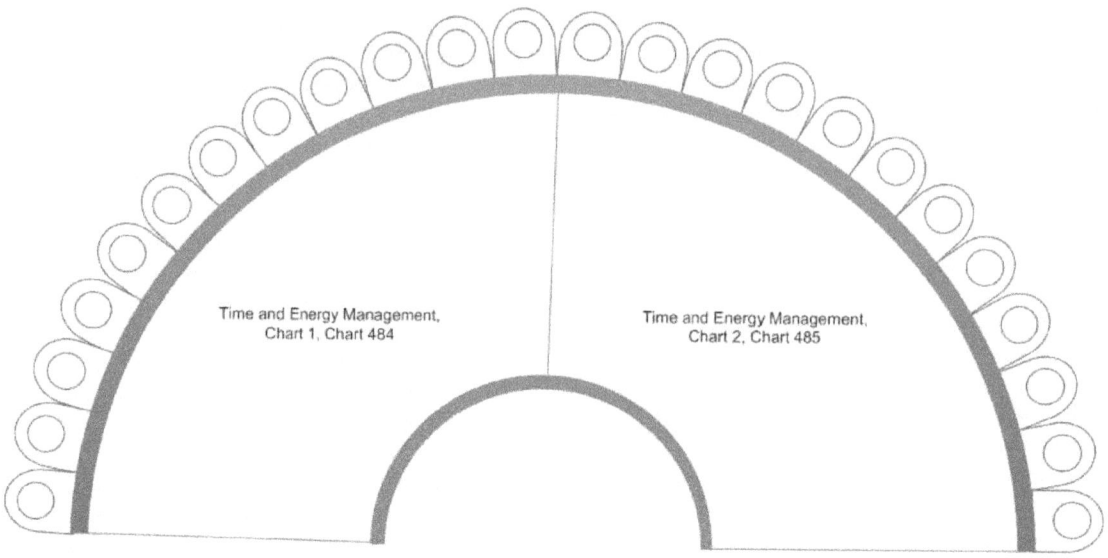

Time and Energy Management, Master Chart

Time and Energy Management, Chart 1, Chart 484

Time and Energy Management, Chart 2, Chart 485

Royal Template 2

Diving Deep into the Pool of the Mind

Chart 483

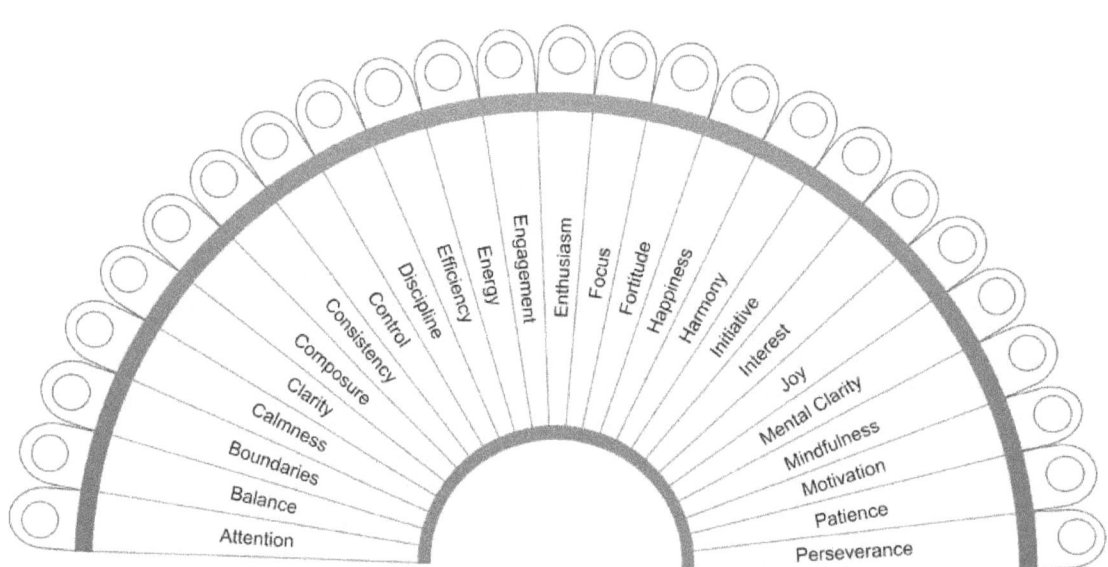

Labels (left to right): Attention, Balance, Boundaries, Calmness, Clarity, Composure, Consistency, Control, Discipline, Efficiency, Energy, Engagement, Enthusiasm, Focus, Fortitude, Happiness, Harmony, Initiative, Interest, Joy, Mental Clarity, Mindfulness, Motivation, Patience, Perseverance

Time and Energy Management, Chart 1

Royal Template 25

Diving Deep into the Pool of the Mind

Chart 484

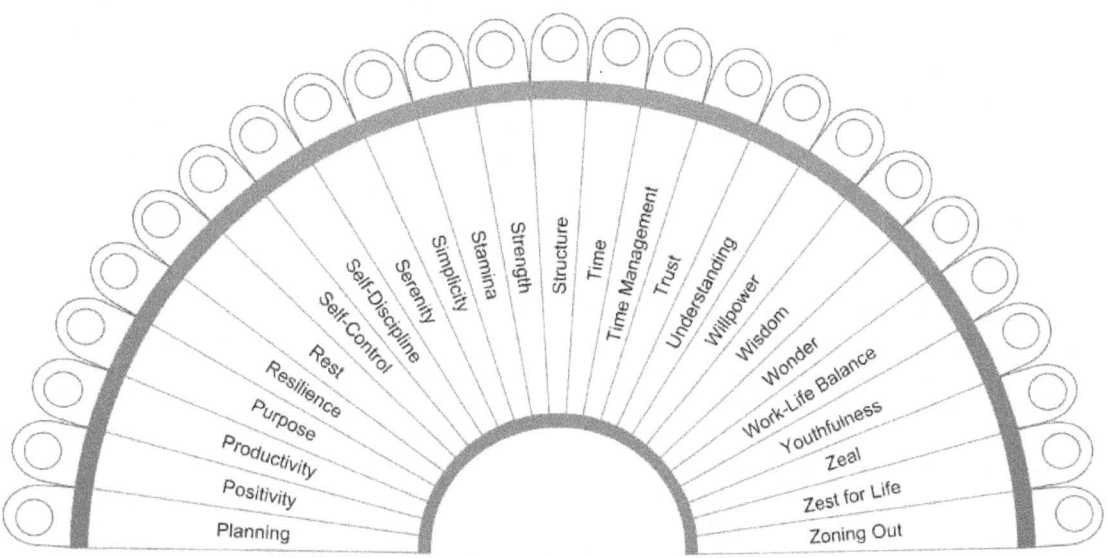

Time and Energy Management, Chart 2

Planning
Positivity
Productivity
Purpose
Resilience
Rest
Self-Control
Self-Discipline
Serenity
Simplicity
Stamina
Strength
Structure
Time
Time Management
Trust
Understanding
Willpower
Wisdom
Wonder
Work-Life Balance
Youthfulness
Zeal
Zest for Life
Zoning Out

Royal Template 25

Diving Deep into the Pool of the Mind

Chart 485

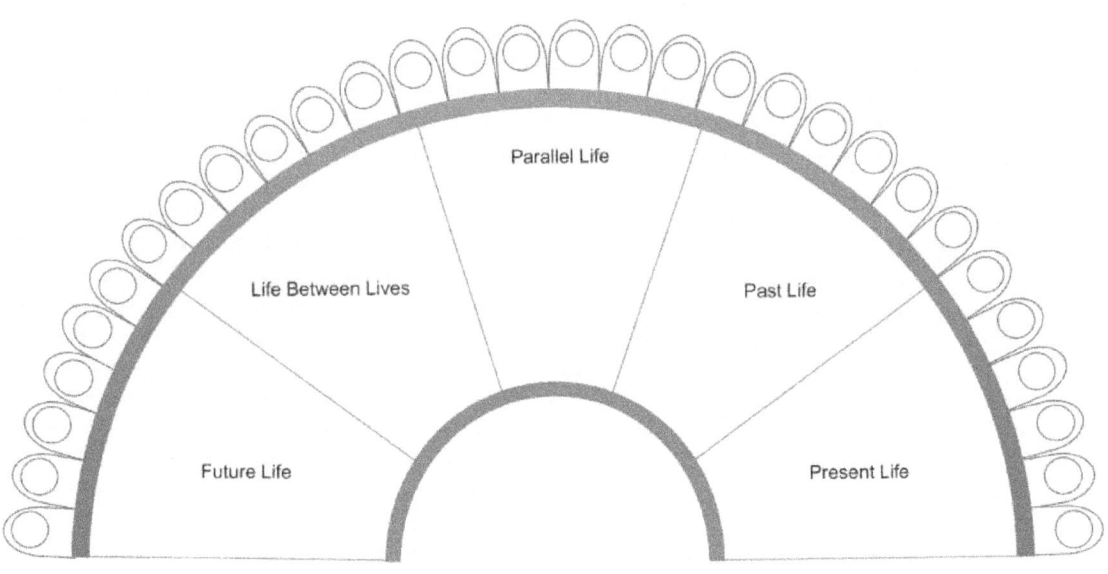

Parallel Life

Life Between Lives

Past Life

Future Life

Present Life

Time Line

Royal Template 5h

Diving Deep into the Pool of the Mind

Chart 486

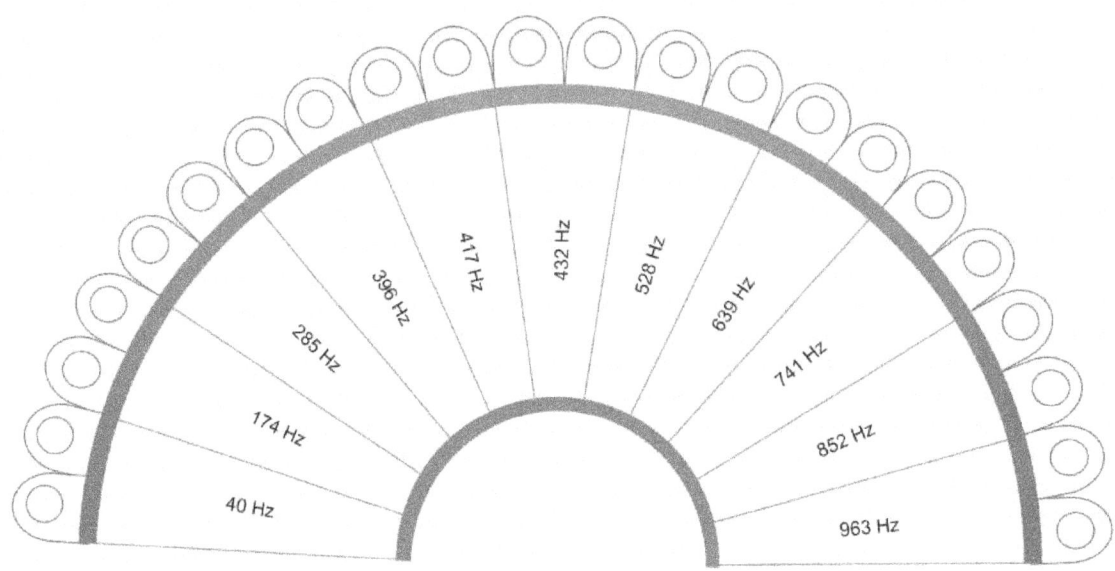

Frequencies

396 Hz
417 Hz
432 Hz
528 Hz
639 Hz
285 Hz
741 Hz
174 Hz
852 Hz
40 Hz
963 Hz

Royal Template 11

Diving Deep into the Pool of the Mind

Chart 487

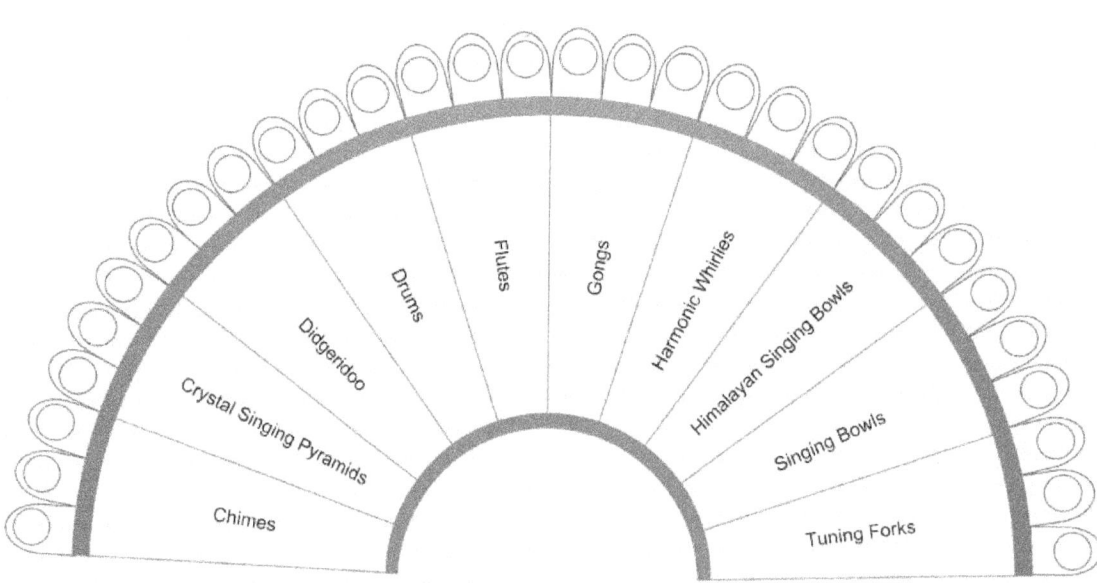

Sound Tools

Drums
Flutes
Gongs
Didgeridoo
Harmonic Whirlies
Crystal Singing Pyramids
Himalayan Singing Bowls
Chimes
Singing Bowls
Tuning Forks

Royal Template 10

Diving Deep into the Pool of the Mind

Chart 488

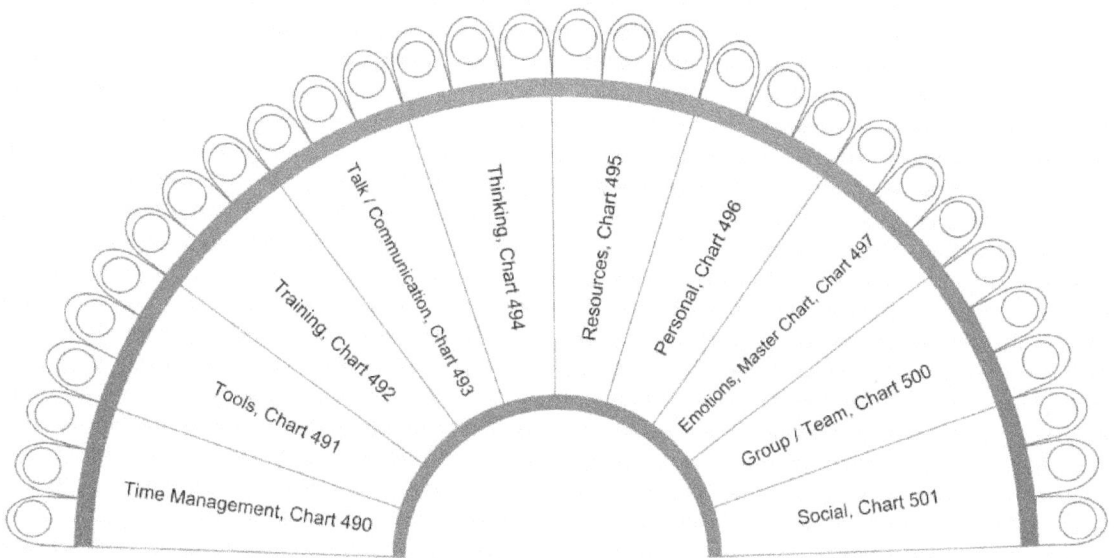

Obstacles & Impediments, Master Chart

Chart labels (clockwise):
- Time Management, Chart 490
- Tools, Chart 491
- Training, Chart 492
- Talk / Communication, Chart 493
- Thinking, Chart 494
- Resources, Chart 495
- Personal, Chart 496
- Emotions, Master Chart, Chart 497
- Group / Team, Chart 500
- Social, Chart 501

Royal Template 10

Diving Deep into the Pool of the Mind

Chart 489

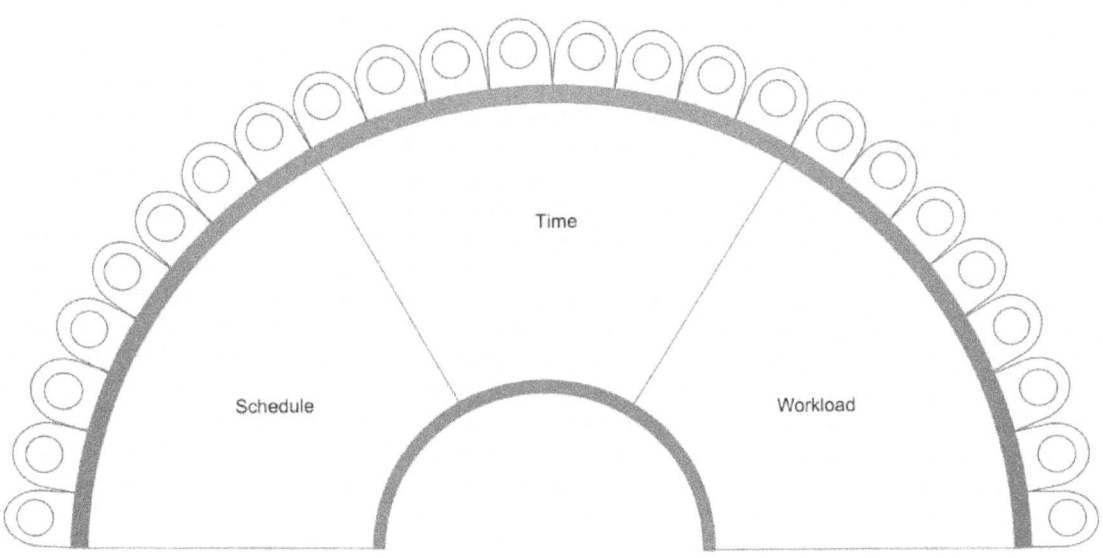

Time Management

Labels:
- Schedule
- Time
- Workload

Royal Template 3h

Diving Deep into the Pool of the Mind

Chart 490

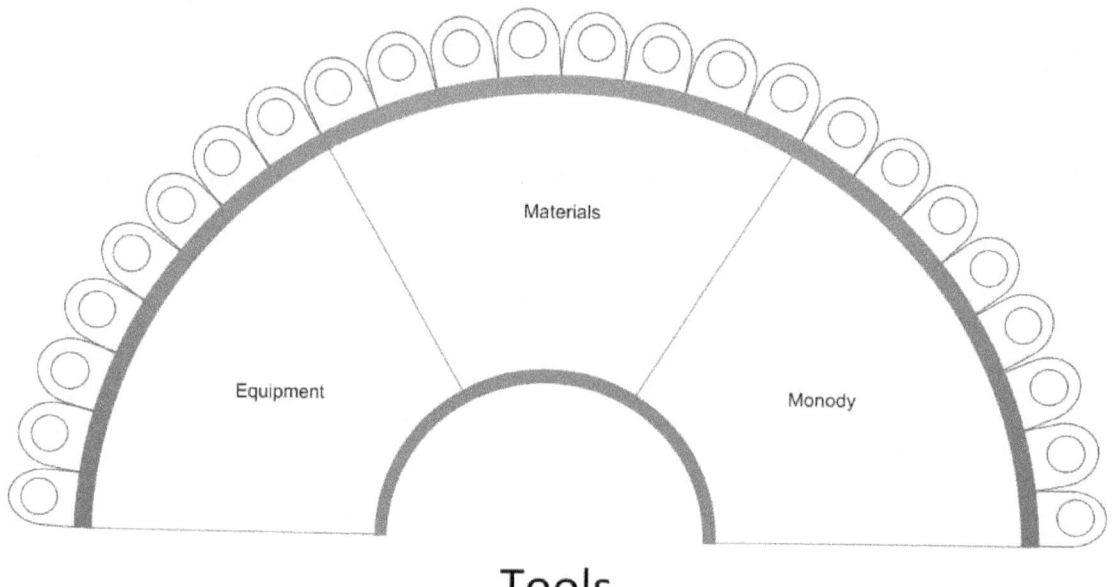

Tools

Materials

Equipment

Monody

Royal Template 3h

Diving Deep into the Pool of the Mind

Chart 491

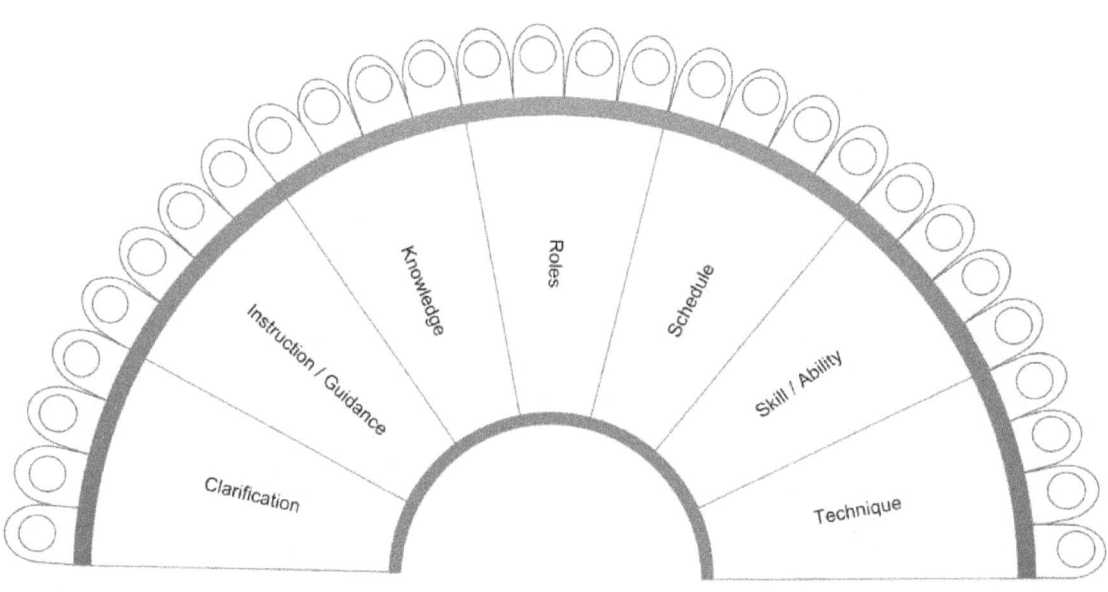

Training

Instruction / Guidance

Knowledge

Roles

Schedule

Skill / Ability

Clarification

Technique

Royal Template 7

Diving Deep into the Pool of the Mind

Chart 492

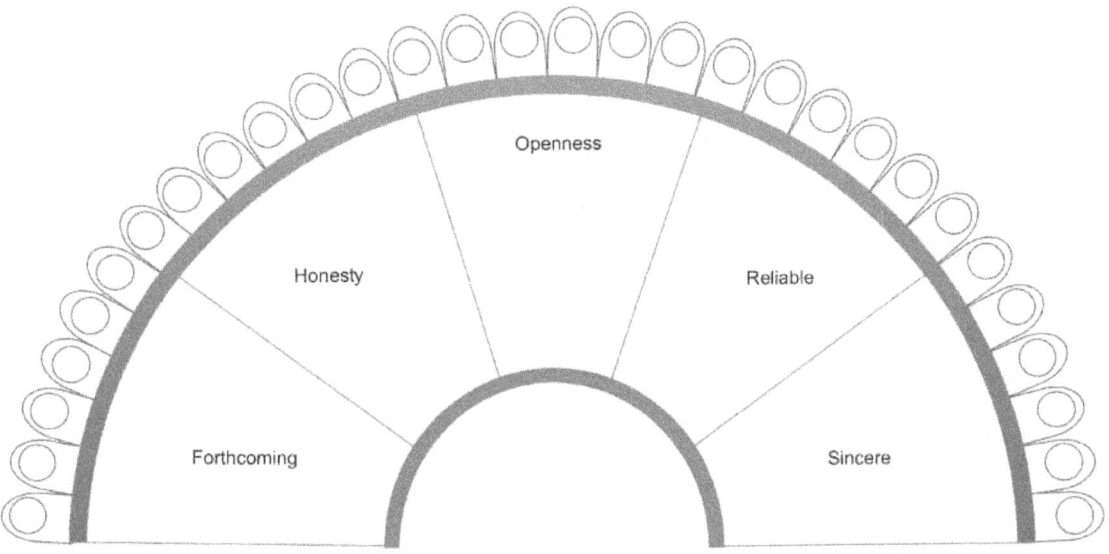

Talk / Communication

Royal Template 5h

Diving Deep into the Pool of the Mind

Chart 493

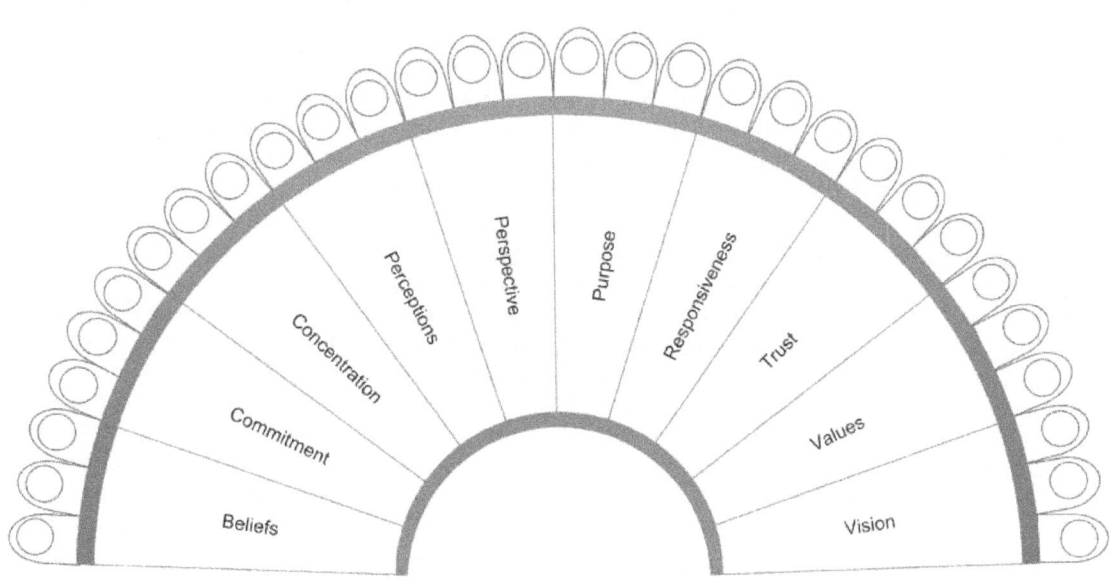

Thinking

Royal Template 10

Diving Deep into the Pool of the Mind

Chart 494

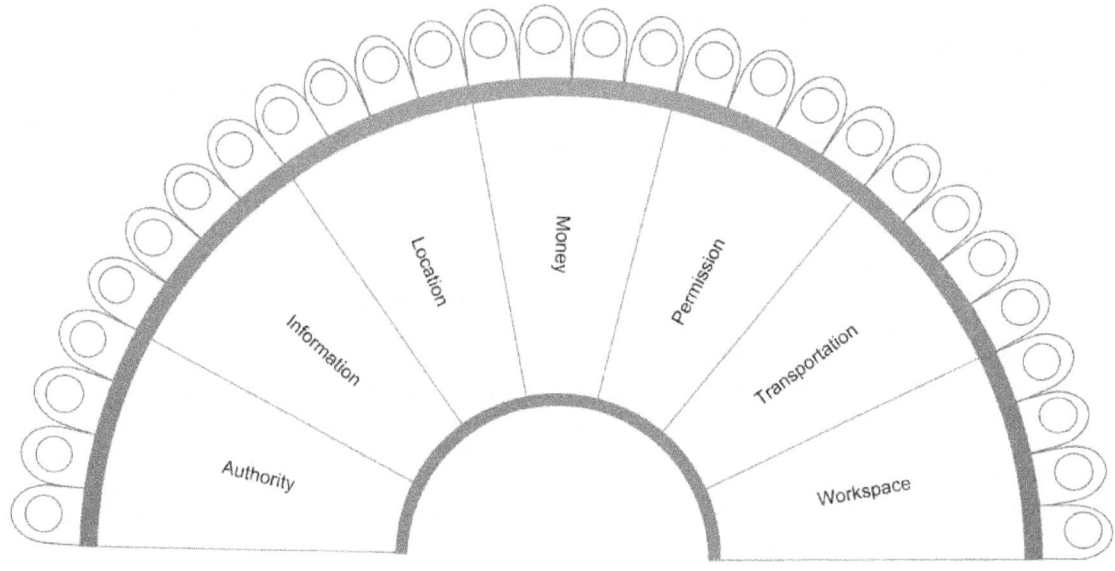

Resources

Royal Template 7

Diving Deep into the Pool of the Mind

Chart 495

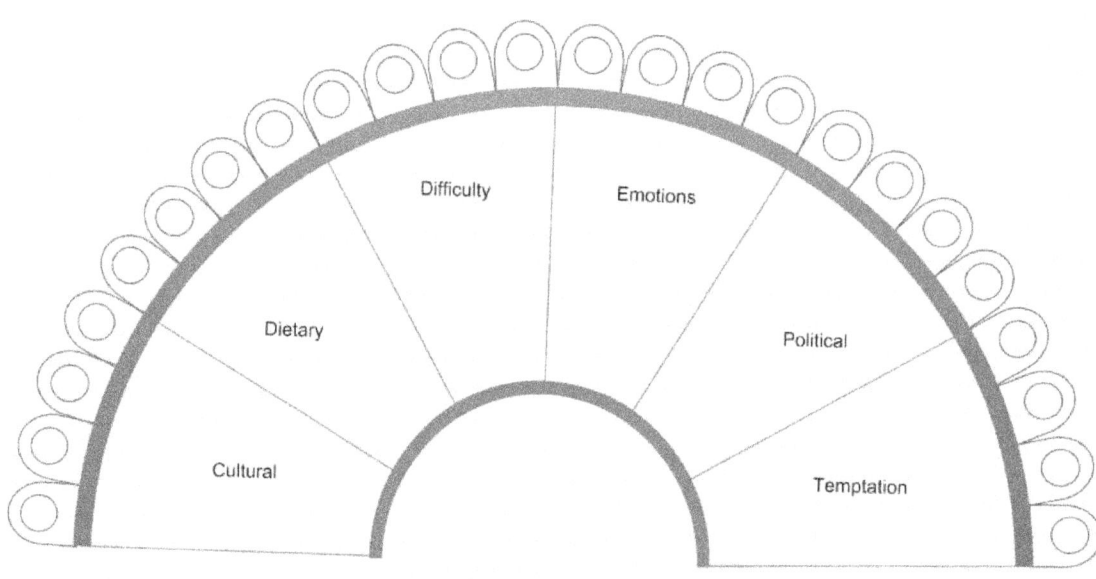

Personal

Royal Template 6h

Diving Deep into the Pool of the Mind

Chart 496

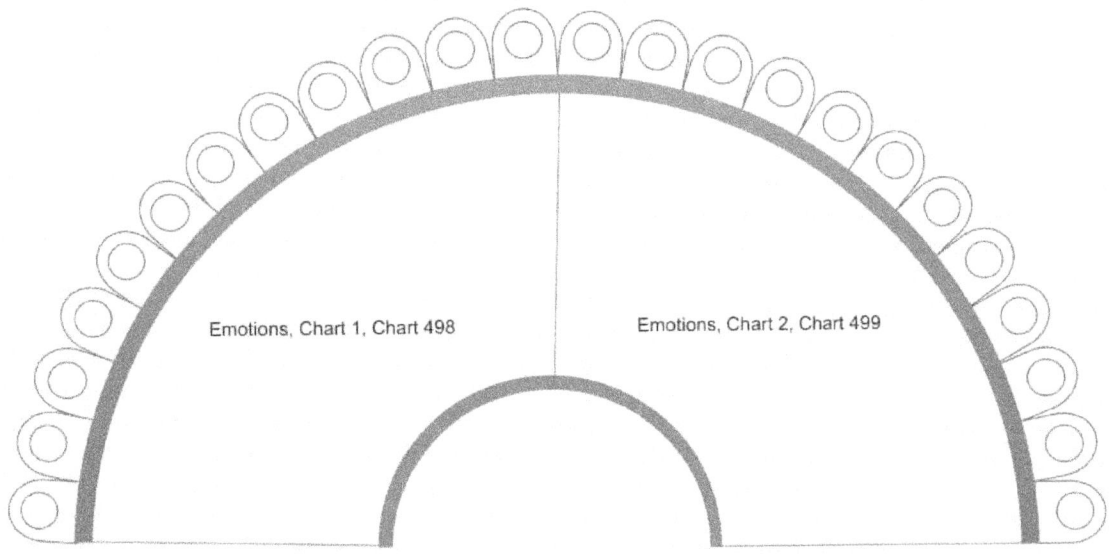

Emotions, Master Chart

Emotions, Chart 1, Chart 498

Emotions, Chart 2, Chart 499

Royal Template 2

Diving Deep into the Pool of the Mind

Chart 497

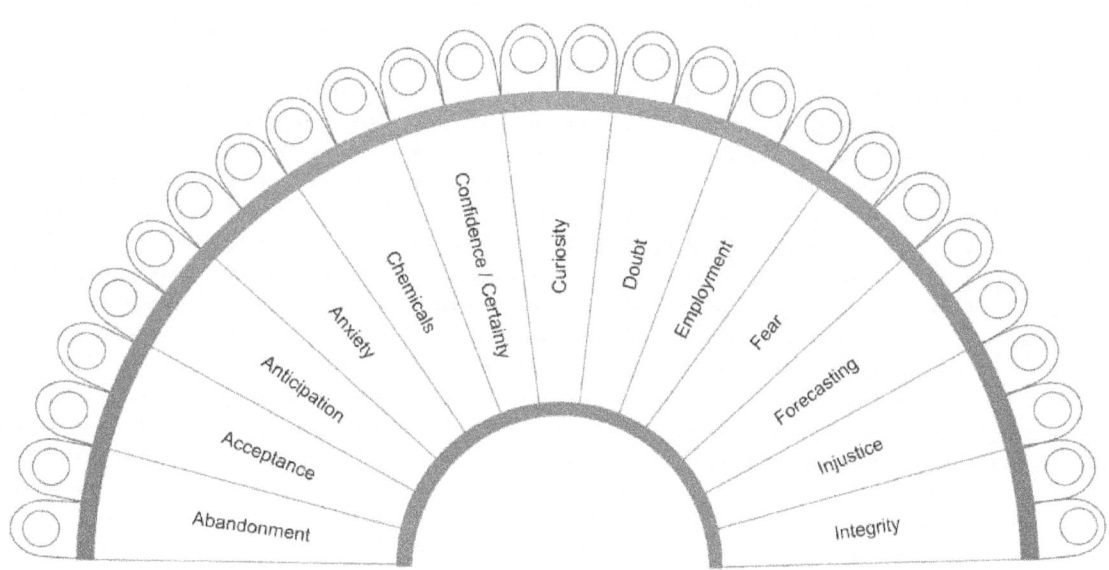

Confidence / Certainty

Chemicals

Curiosity

Anxiety

Doubt

Anticipation

Employment

Fear

Acceptance

Forecasting

Injustice

Abandonment

Integrity

Emotions, Chart 1

Royal Template 13

Diving Deep into the Pool of the Mind

Chart 498

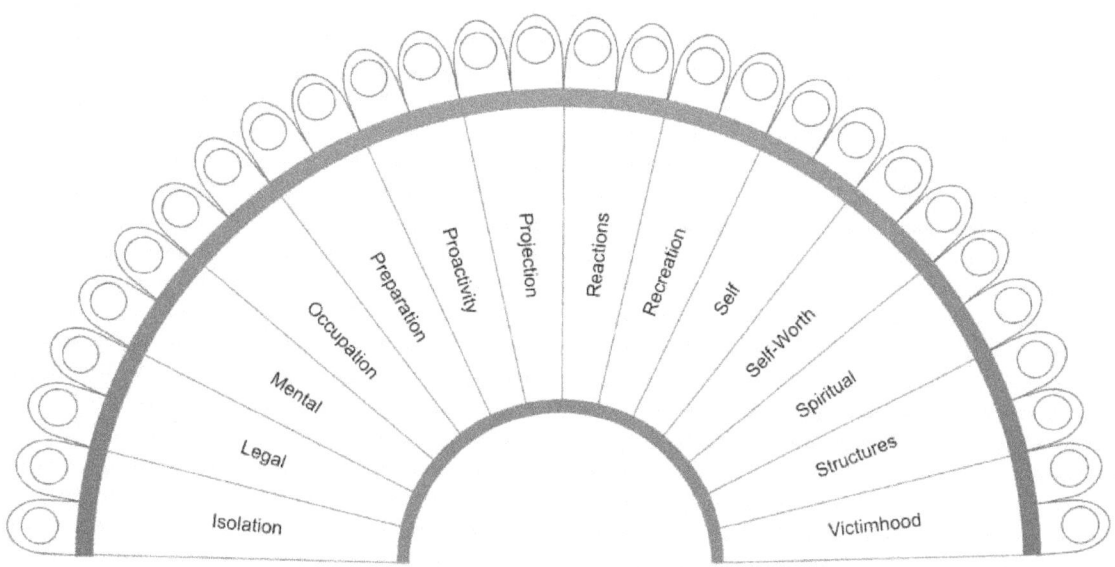

Emotions, Chart 2

Isolation · Legal · Mental · Occupation · Preparation · Proactivity · Projection · Reactions · Recreation · Self · Self-Worth · Spiritual · Structures · Victimhood

Royal Template 14

Diving Deep into the Pool of the Mind

Chart 499

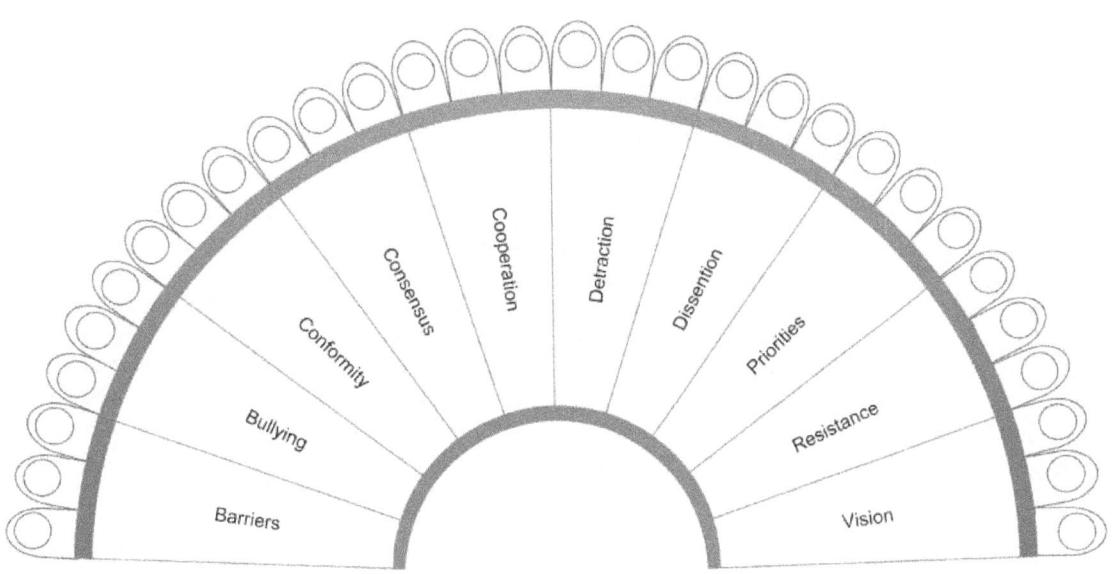

Group / Team

Barriers · Bullying · Conformity · Consensus · Cooperation · Detraction · Dissention · Priorities · Resistance · Vision

Royal Template 10

Diving Deep into the Pool of the Mind

Chart 500

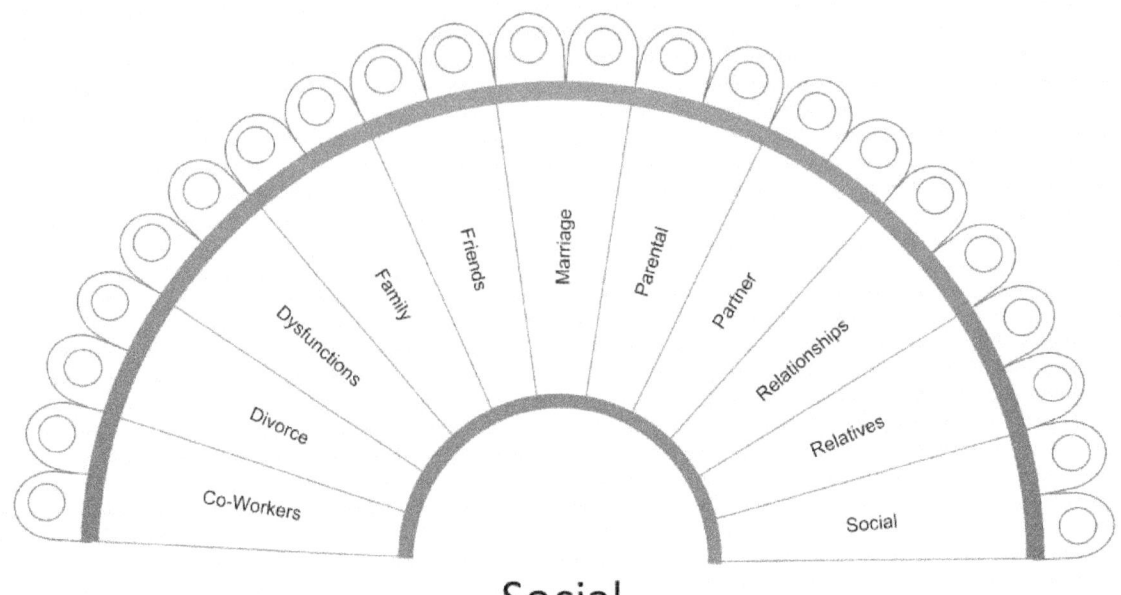

Social

Royal Template 11

Diving Deep into the Pool of the Mind

Chart 501

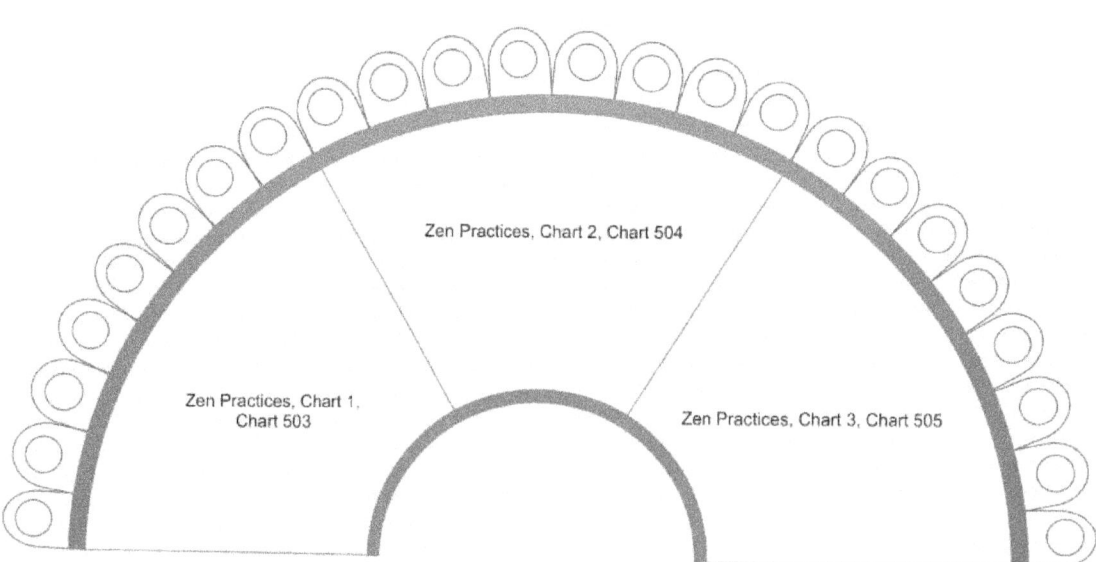

Zen Practices, Master Chart

Royal Template 3h

Diving Deep into the Pool of the Mind

Chart 502

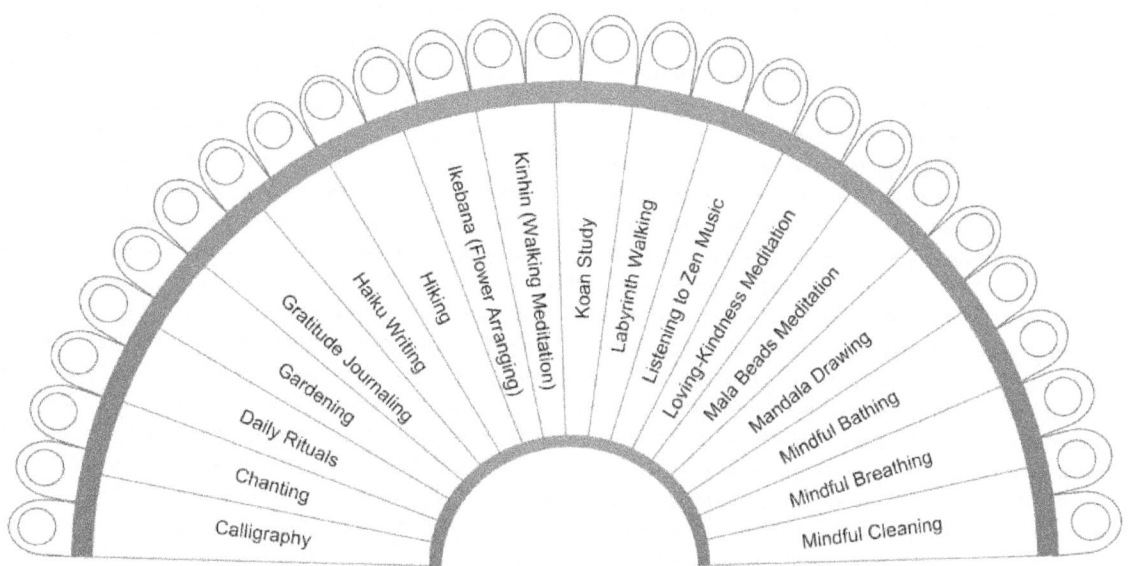

Zen Practices, Chart 1

Ikebana (Flower Arranging)
Kinhin (Walking Meditation)
Haiku Writing
Hiking
Koan Study
Labyrinth Walking
Gratitude Journaling
Listening to Zen Music
Loving-Kindness Meditation
Gardening
Mala Beads Meditation
Daily Rituals
Mandala Drawing
Chanting
Mindful Bathing
Mindful Breathing
Calligraphy
Mindful Cleaning

Royal Template 18

Diving Deep into the Pool of the Mind

Chart 503

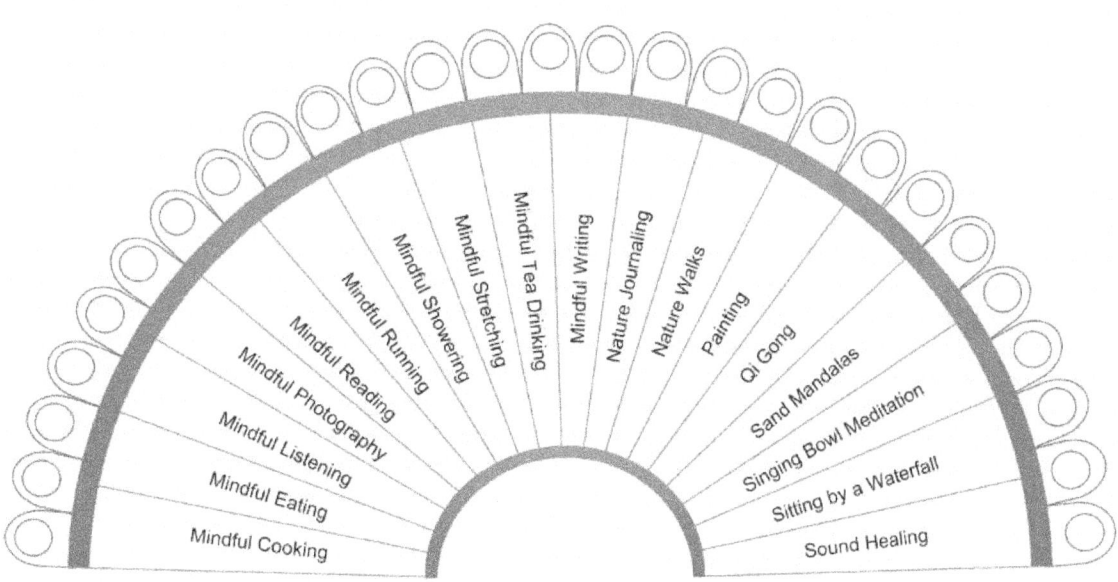

Zen Practices, Chart 2

Mindful Showering
Mindful Stretching
Mindful Running
Mindful Tea Drinking
Mindful Reading
Mindful Writing
Nature Journaling
Mindful Photography
Nature Walks
Mindful Listening
Painting
Mindful Eating
Qi Gong
Sand Mandalas
Singing Bowl Meditation
Mindful Cooking
Sitting by a Waterfall
Sound Healing

Royal Template 18

Diving Deep into the Pool of the Mind

Chart 504

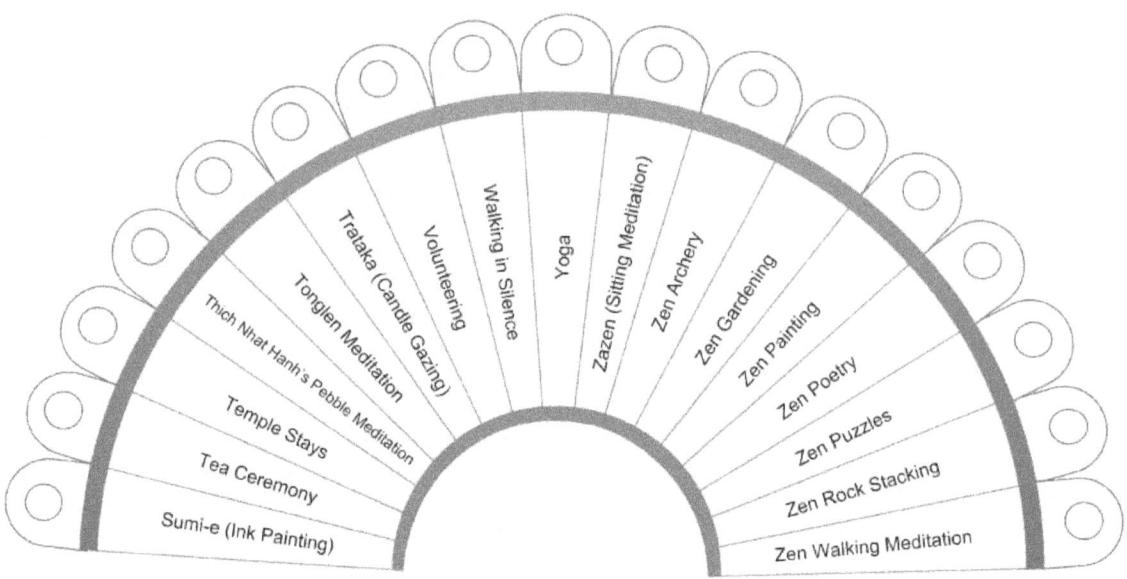

Zen Practices, Chart 3

Walking in Silence
Yoga
Zazen (Sitting Meditation)
Zen Archery
Zen Gardening
Zen Painting
Zen Poetry
Zen Puzzles
Zen Rock Stacking
Zen Walking Meditation
Volunteering
Trataka (Candle Gazing)
Tonglen Meditation
Thich Nhat Hanh's Pebble Meditation
Temple Stays
Tea Ceremony
Sumi-e (Ink Painting)

Royal Template 17

Chart 505

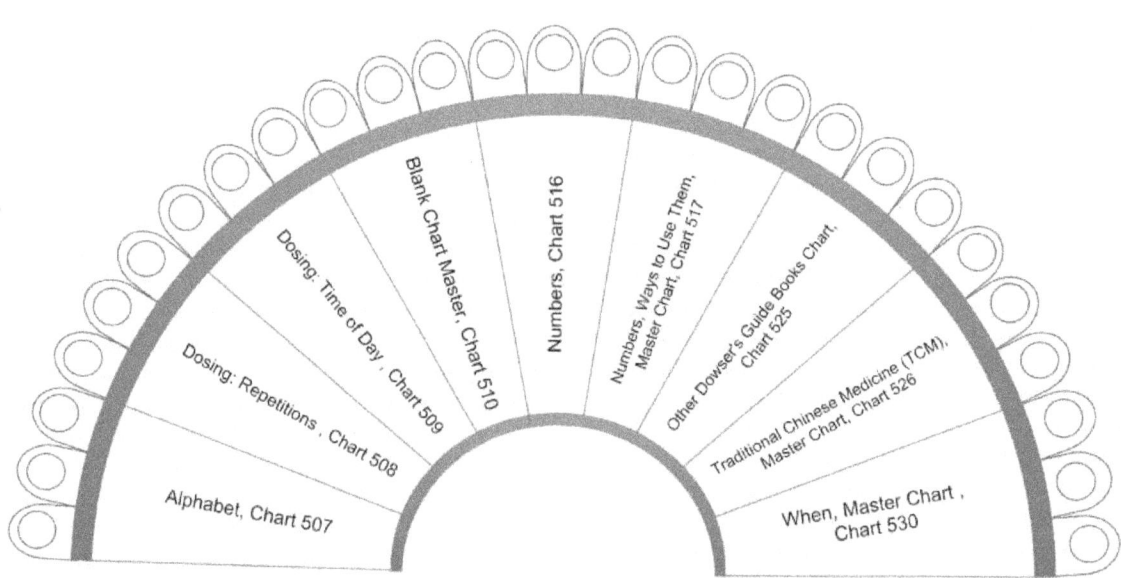

Diving into the Pool of Helpful Tools

Blank Chart Master, Chart 510
Numbers, Chart 516
Numbers, Ways to Use Them, Master Chart, Chart 517
Dosing: Time of Day , Chart 509
Other Dowser's Guide Books Chart, Chart 525
Dosing: Repetitions , Chart 508
Traditional Chinese Medicine (TCM), Master Chart, Chart 526
Alphabet, Chart 507
When, Master Chart , Chart 530

Royal Template 9

Chart 506

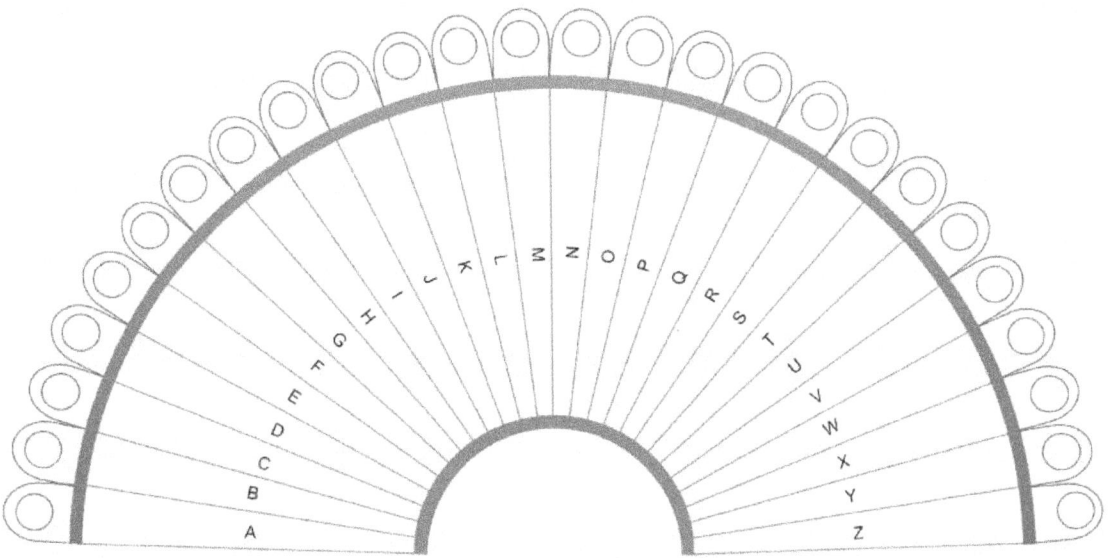

Alphabet

Royal Template 26

Diving Deep into the Pool of the Mind

Chart 507

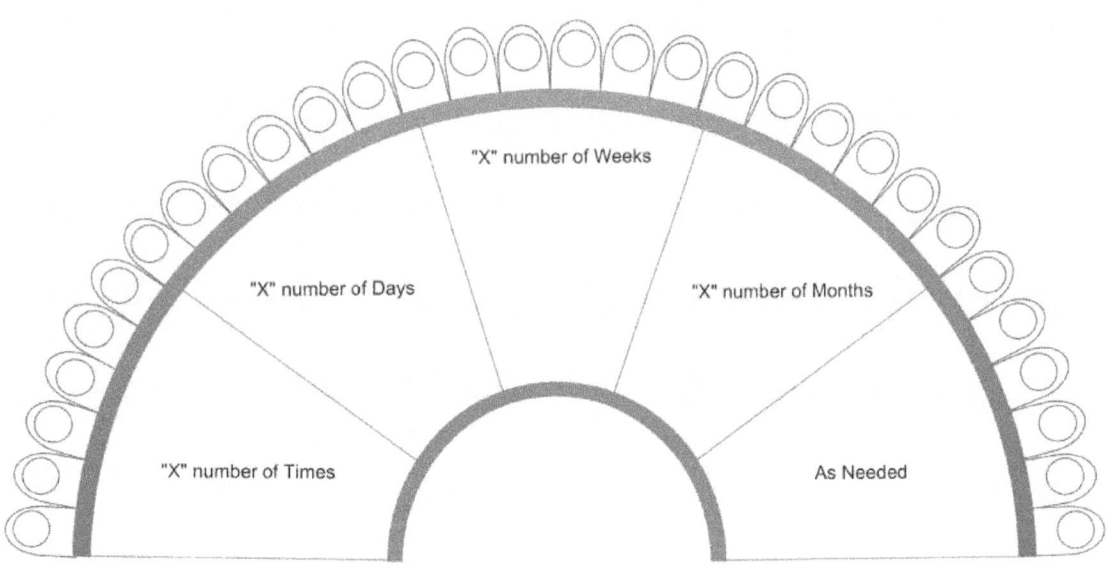

Dosing: Repetitions

"X" number of Weeks

"X" number of Days

"X" number of Months

"X" number of Times

As Needed

Royal Template 5h

Diving Deep into the Pool of the Mind

Chart 508

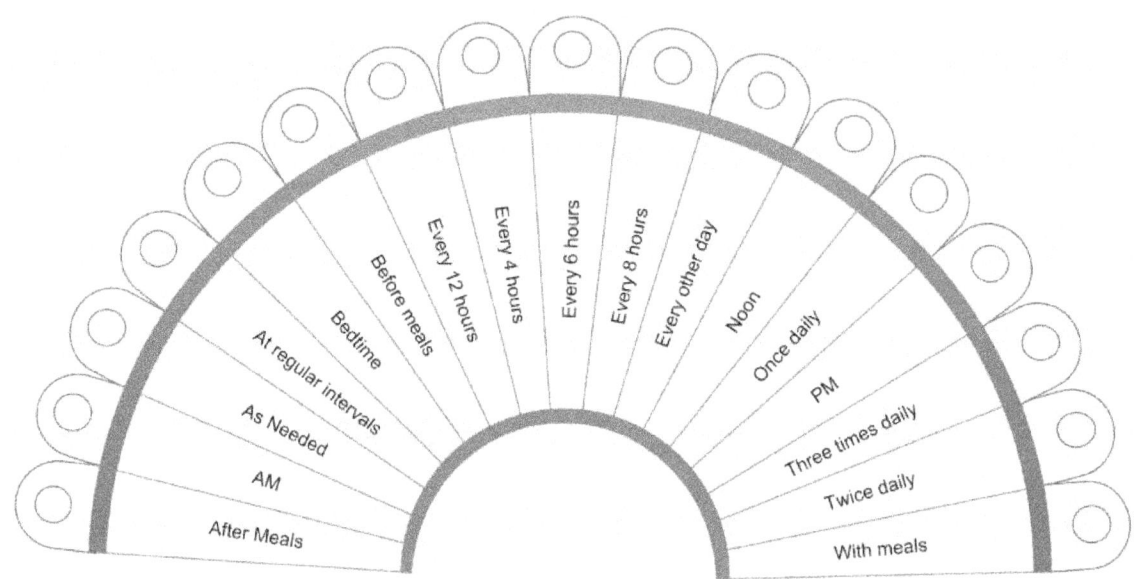

Dosing: Time of Day

The chart includes the following labels arranged radially:

- After Meals
- AM
- As Needed
- At regular intervals
- Bedtime
- Before meals
- Every 12 hours
- Every 4 hours
- Every 6 hours
- Every 8 hours
- Every other day
- Noon
- Once daily
- PM
- Three times daily
- Twice daily
- With meals

Royal Template 17

Diving Deep into the Pool of the Mind

Chart 509

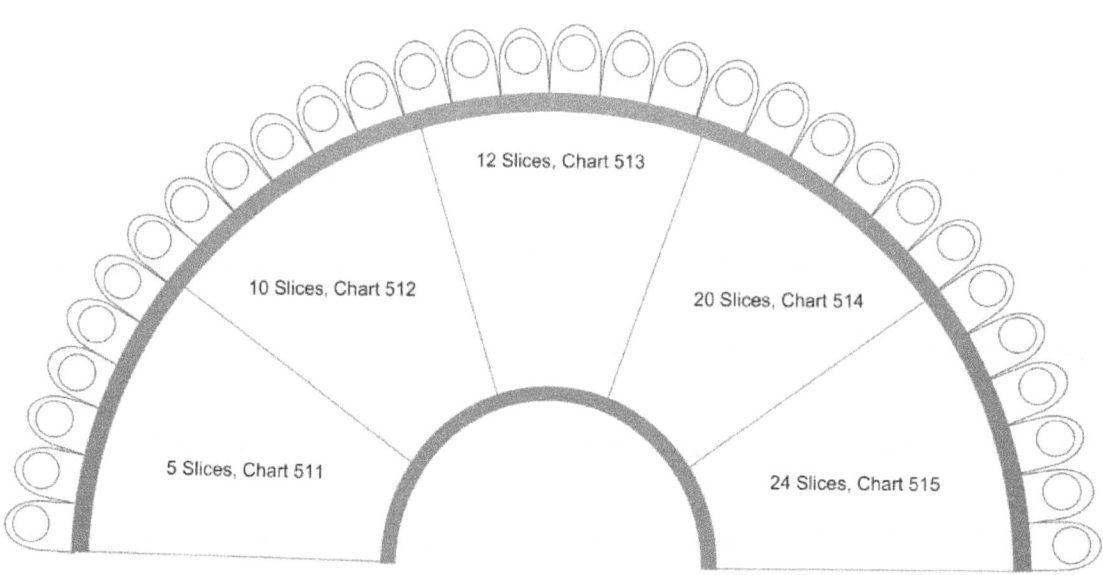

Blank Chart Master

- 12 Slices, Chart 513
- 10 Slices, Chart 512
- 20 Slices, Chart 514
- 5 Slices, Chart 511
- 24 Slices, Chart 515

Royal Template 5h

Diving Deep into the Pool of the Mind

Chart 510

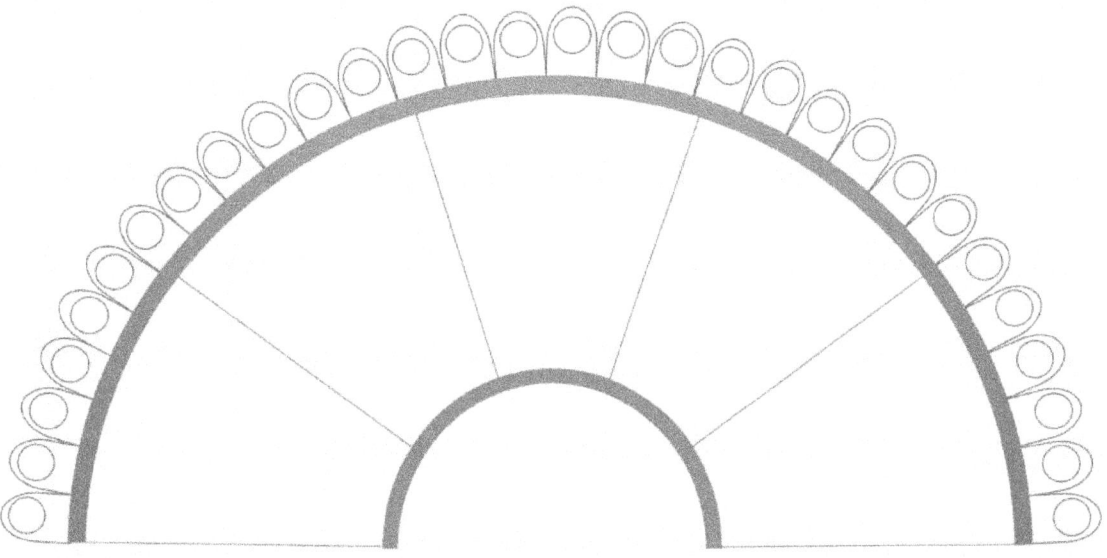

5 Slices

Royal Template 5h

Diving Deep into the Pool of the Mind

Chart 511

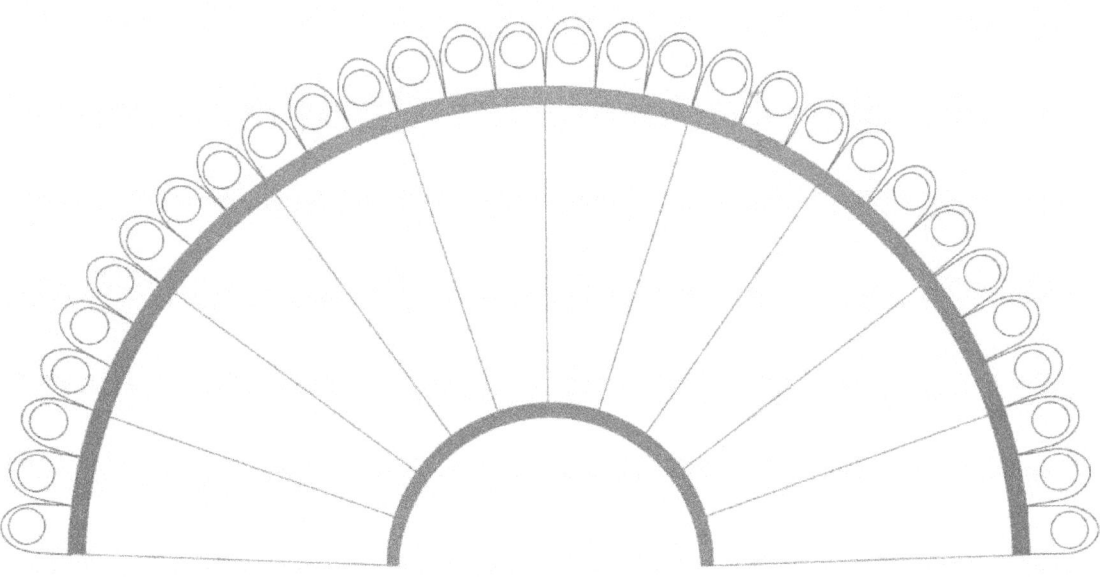

10 Slices

Royal Template 10

Diving Deep into the Pool of the Mind

Chart 512

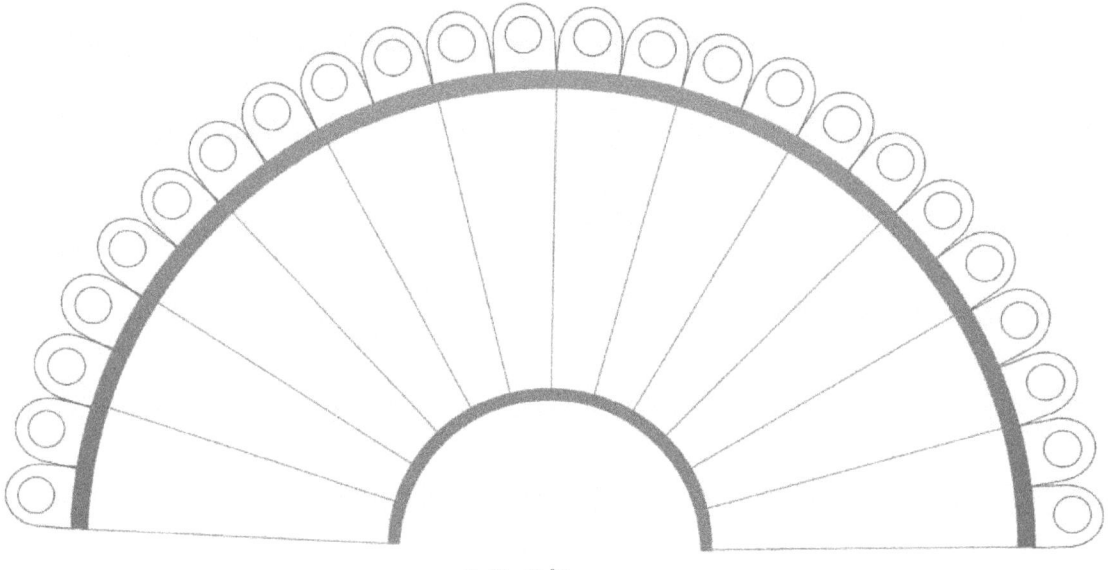

12 Slices

Royal Template 12

Diving Deep into the Pool of the Mind

Chart 513

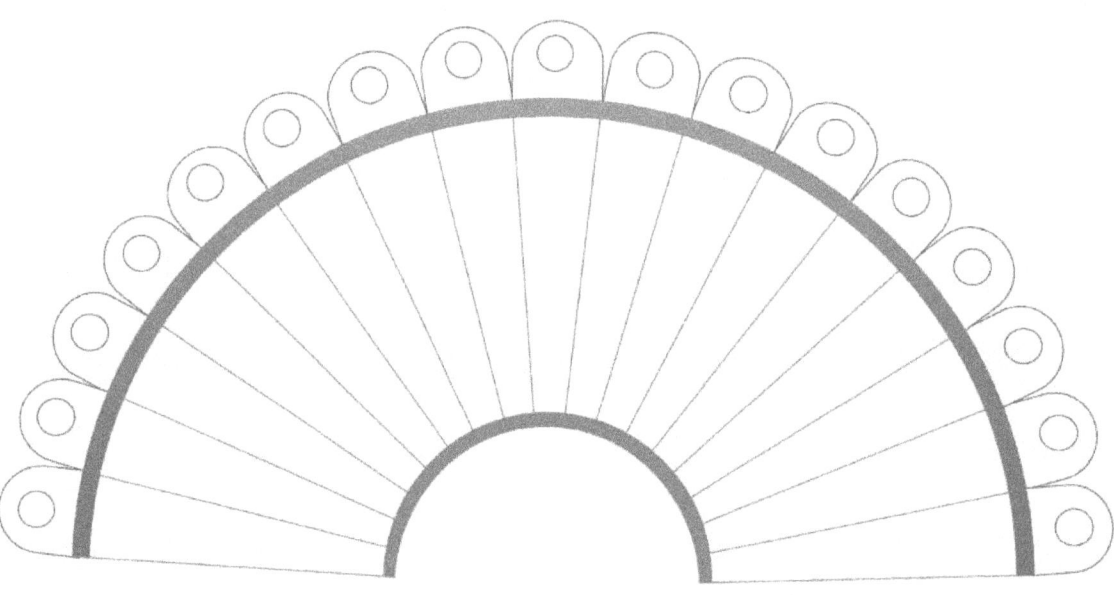

20 Slices

Royal Template 17

Diving Deep into the Pool of the Mind

Chart 514

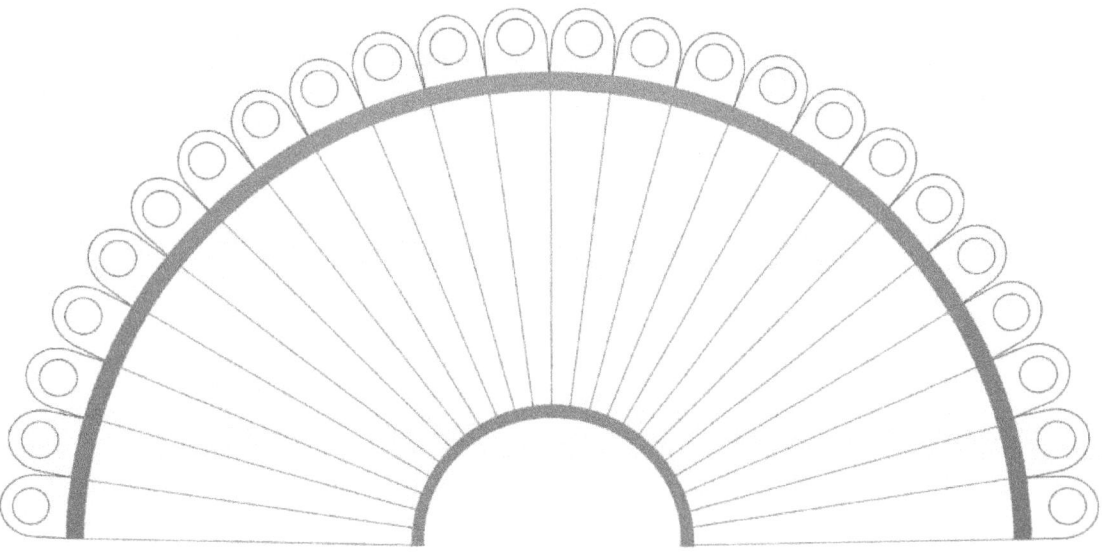

24 Slices

Royal Template 24

Diving Deep into the Pool of the Mind

Chart 515

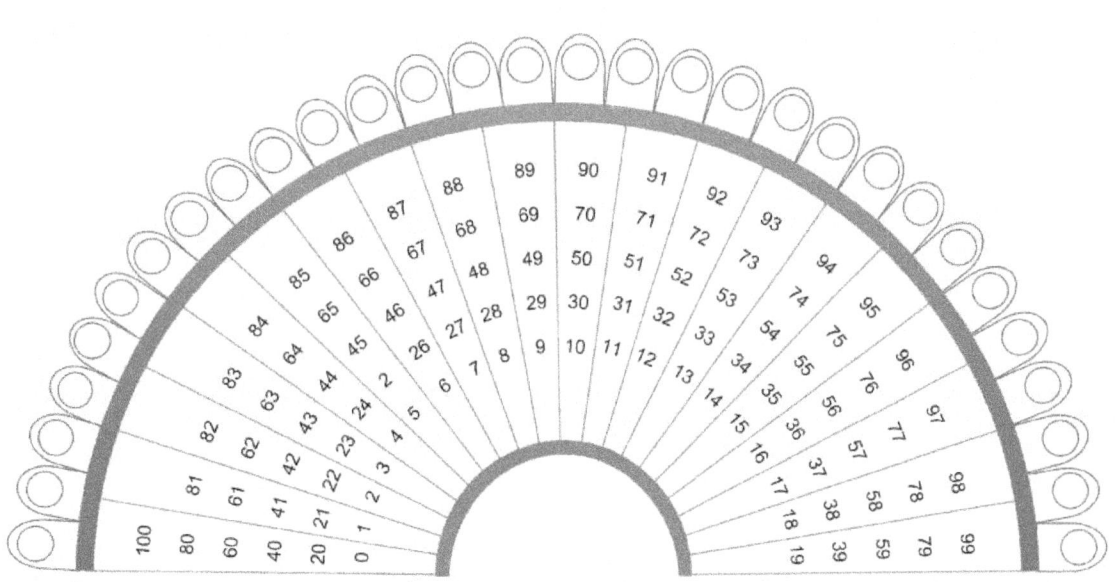

Numbers

Royal Template 20

Diving Deep into the Pool of the Mind

Chart 516

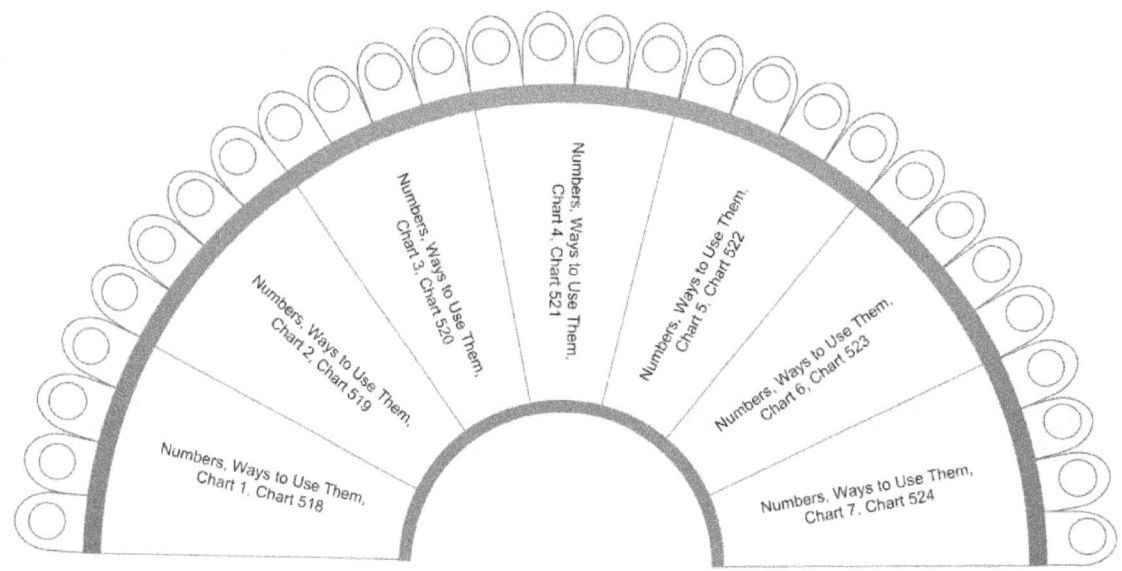

Numbers, Ways to Use Them, Master Chart

Chart labels (clockwise):
- Numbers, Ways to Use Them, Chart 1, Chart 518
- Numbers, Ways to Use Them, Chart 2, Chart 519
- Numbers, Ways to Use Them, Chart 3, Chart 520
- Numbers, Ways to Use Them, Chart 4, Chart 521
- Numbers, Ways to Use Them, Chart 5, Chart 522
- Numbers, Ways to Use Them, Chart 6, Chart 523
- Numbers, Ways to Use Them, Chart 7, Chart 524

Royal Template 7

Chart 517

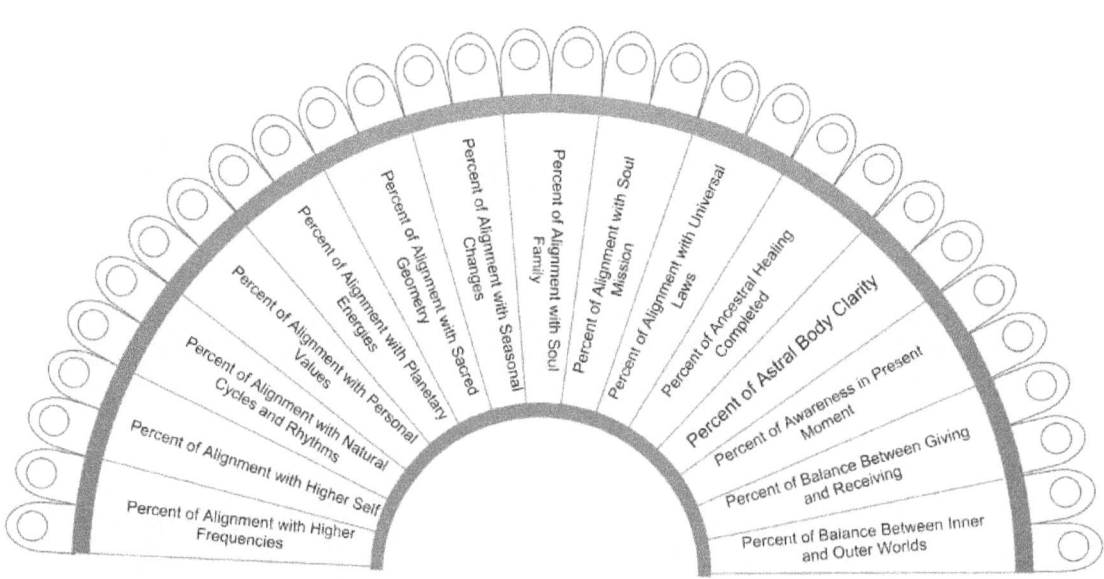

Chart labels:
- Percent of Alignment with Higher Frequencies
- Percent of Alignment with Higher Self
- Percent of Alignment with Natural Cycles and Rhythms
- Percent of Alignment with Personal Values
- Percent of Alignment with Planetary Energies
- Percent of Alignment with Sacred Geometry
- Percent of Alignment with Seasonal Changes
- Percent of Alignment with Soul Family
- Percent of Alignment with Soul Mission
- Percent of Alignment with Universal Laws
- Percent of Ancestral Healing Completed
- Percent of Astral Body Clarity
- Percent of Awareness in Present Moment
- Percent of Balance Between Giving and Receiving
- Percent of Balance Between Inner and Outer Worlds

Numbers, Ways to Use Them, Chart 1

Royal Template 15

Chart 518

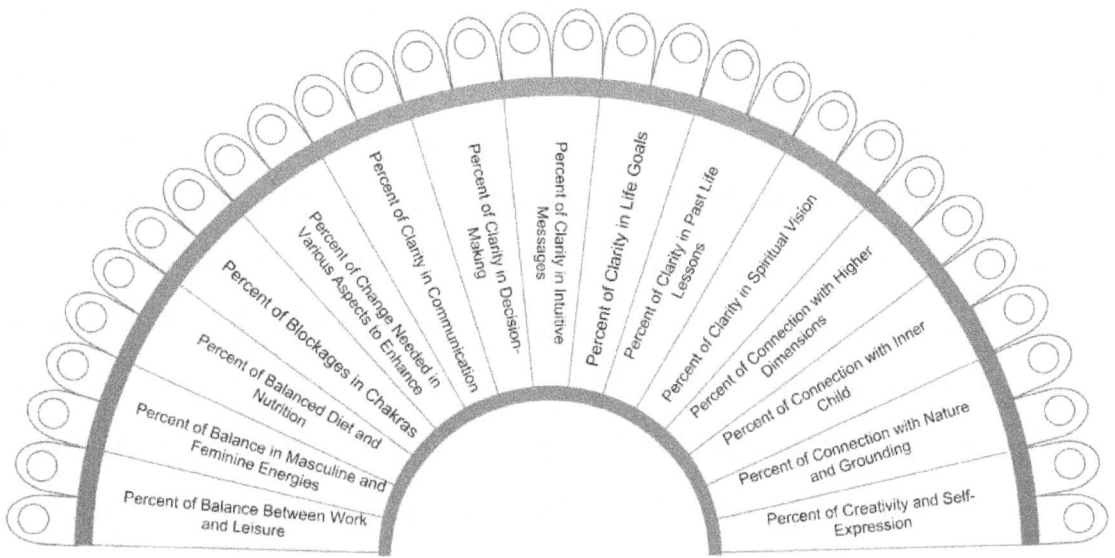

Numbers, Ways to Use Them, Chart 2

Percent of Clarity in Life Goals
Percent of Clarity in Intuitive Messages
Percent of Clarity in Communication
Percent of Change Needed in Various Aspects to Enhance
Percent of Blockages in Chakras
Percent of Balanced Diet and Nutrition
Percent of Balance in Masculine and Feminine Energies
Percent of Balance Between Work and Leisure
Percent of Clarity in Decision-Making
Percent of Clarity in Past Life Lessons
Percent of Clarity in Spiritual Vision
Percent of Connection with Higher Dimensions
Percent of Connection with Inner Child
Percent of Connection with Nature and Grounding
Percent of Creativity and Self-Expression

Royal Template 15

Diving Deep into the Pool of the Mind

Chart 519

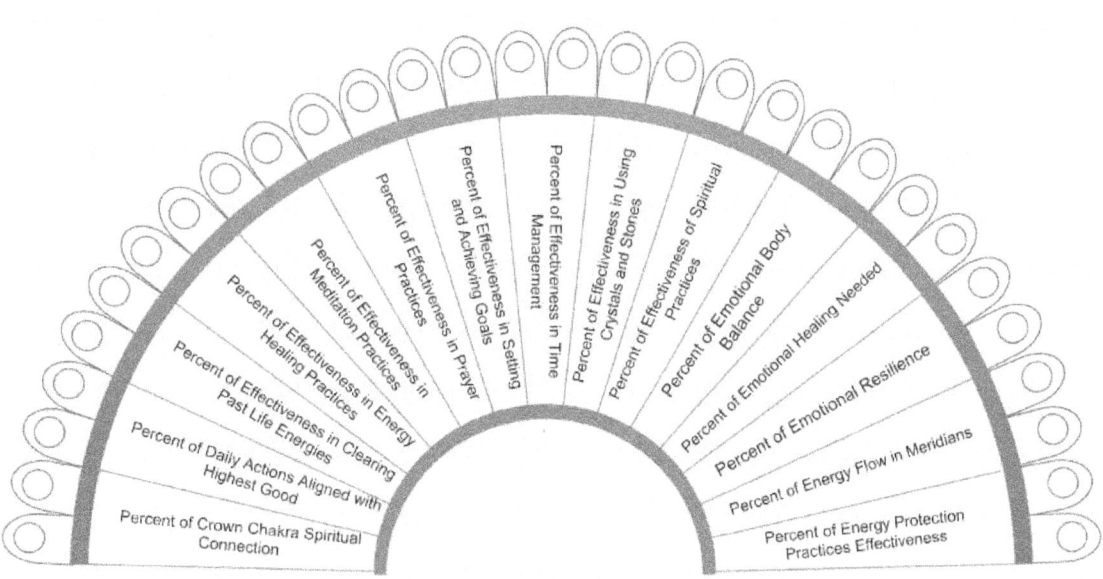

Numbers, Ways to Use Them, Chart 3

Percent of Effectiveness in Using Management
Percent of Effectiveness in Setting and Achieving Goals
Percent of Effectiveness in Prayer
Percent of Effectiveness in Meditation Practices
Percent of Effectiveness in Energy Healing Practices
Percent of Effectiveness in Clearing Past Life Energies
Percent of Daily Actions Aligned with Highest Good
Percent of Crown Chakra Spiritual Connection
Percent of Effectiveness in Time
Percent of Effectiveness of Crystals and Stones
Percent of Effectiveness of Spiritual Practices
Percent of Emotional Body Balance
Percent of Emotional Healing Needed
Percent of Emotional Resilience
Percent of Energy Flow in Meridians
Percent of Energy Protection Practices Effectiveness

Royal Template 15

Diving Deep into the Pool of the Mind

Chart 520

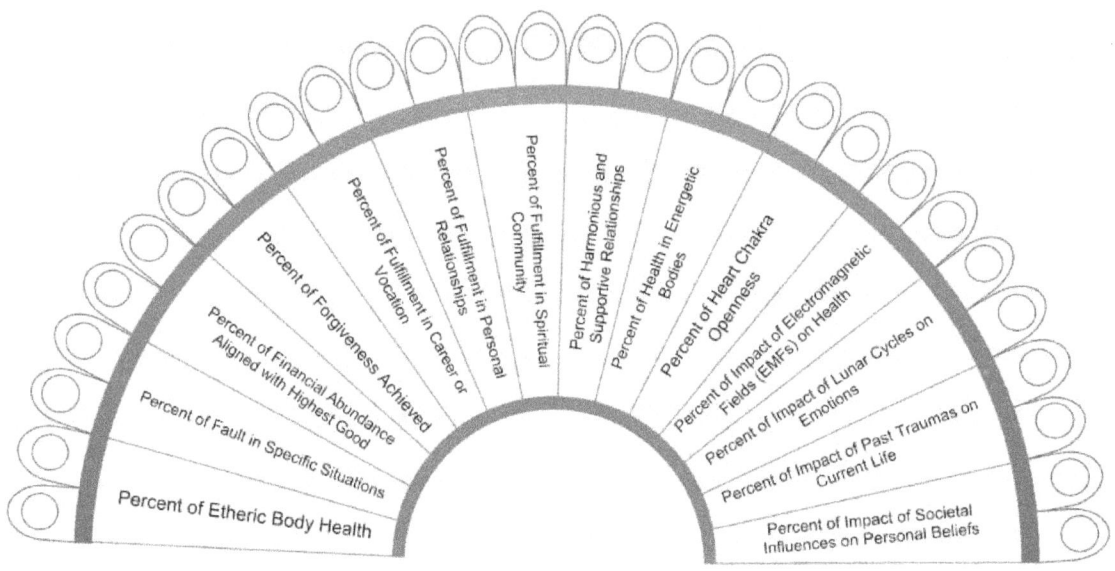

Numbers, Ways to Use Them, Chart 4

The fan chart contains the following labels (from left to right):

- Percent of Etheric Body Health
- Percent of Fault in Specific Situations
- Percent of Financial Abundance Aligned with Highest Good
- Percent of Forgiveness Achieved
- Percent of Fulfillment in Career or Vocation
- Percent of Fulfillment in Personal Relationships
- Percent of Fulfillment in Spiritual Community
- Percent of Harmonious and Supportive Relationships
- Percent of Health in Energetic Bodies
- Percent of Heart Chakra Openness
- Percent of Impact of Electromagnetic Fields (EMFs) on Health
- Percent of Impact of Lunar Cycles on Emotions
- Percent of Impact of Past Traumas on Current Life
- Percent of Impact of Societal Influences on Personal Beliefs

© 2025, Susan V Whittaker

Royal Template 14

Diving Deep into the Pool of the Mind

Chart 521

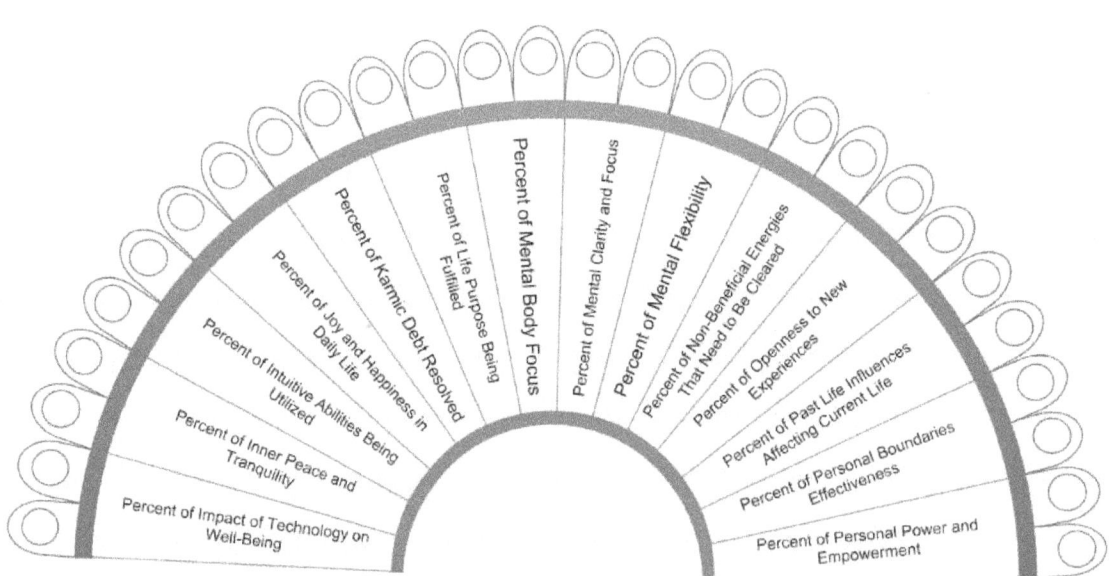

Numbers, Ways to Use Them, Chart 5

The fan chart contains the following labels (from left to right):

- Percent of Impact of Technology on Well-Being
- Percent of Inner Peace and Tranquility
- Percent of Intuitive Abilities Being Utilized
- Percent of Joy and Happiness in Daily Life
- Percent of Karmic Debt Resolved
- Percent of Life Purpose Being Fulfilled
- Percent of Mental Body Focus
- Percent of Mental Clarity and Focus
- Percent of Mental Flexibility
- Percent of Non-Beneficial Energies That Need to Be Cleared
- Percent of Openness to New Experiences
- Percent of Past Life Influences Affecting Current Life
- Percent of Personal Boundaries Effectiveness
- Percent of Personal Power and Empowerment

© 2025, Susan V Whittaker

Royal Template 14

Diving Deep into the Pool of the Mind

Chart 522

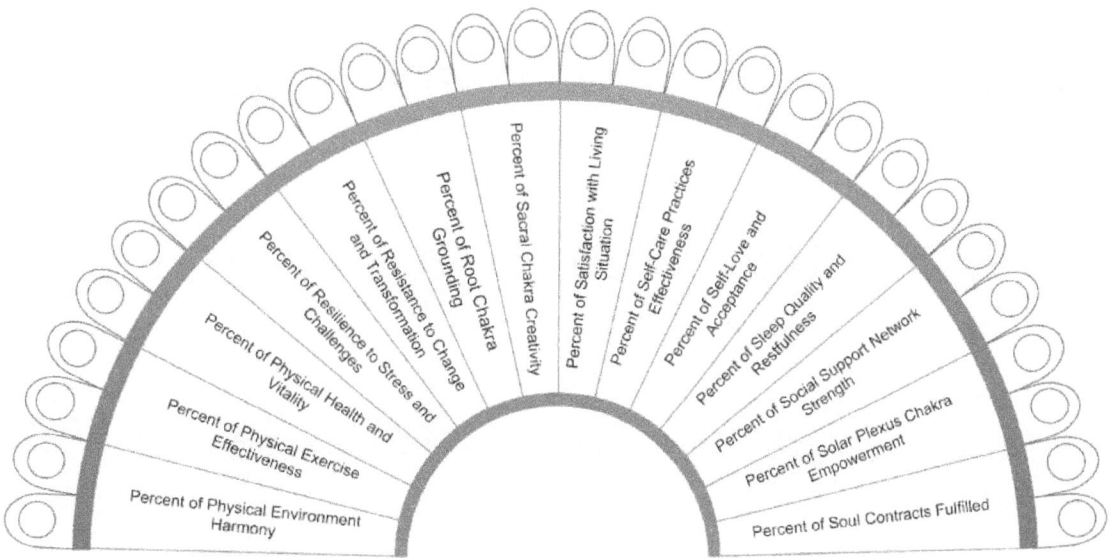

Numbers, Ways to Use Them, Chart 6

The fan chart contains the following labels (clockwise):

- Percent of Physical Environment Harmony
- Percent of Physical Exercise Effectiveness
- Percent of Physical Health and Vitality
- Percent of Resilience to Stress and Challenges
- Percent of Resistance to Change and Transformation
- Percent of Root Chakra Grounding
- Percent of Sacral Chakra Creativity
- Percent of Satisfaction with Living Situation
- Percent of Self-Care Practices Effectiveness
- Percent of Self-Love and Acceptance
- Percent of Sleep Quality and Restfulness
- Percent of Social Support Network Strength
- Percent of Solar Plexus Chakra Empowerment
- Percent of Soul Contracts Fulfilled

Royal Template 14

Diving Deep into the Pool of the Mind

Chart 523

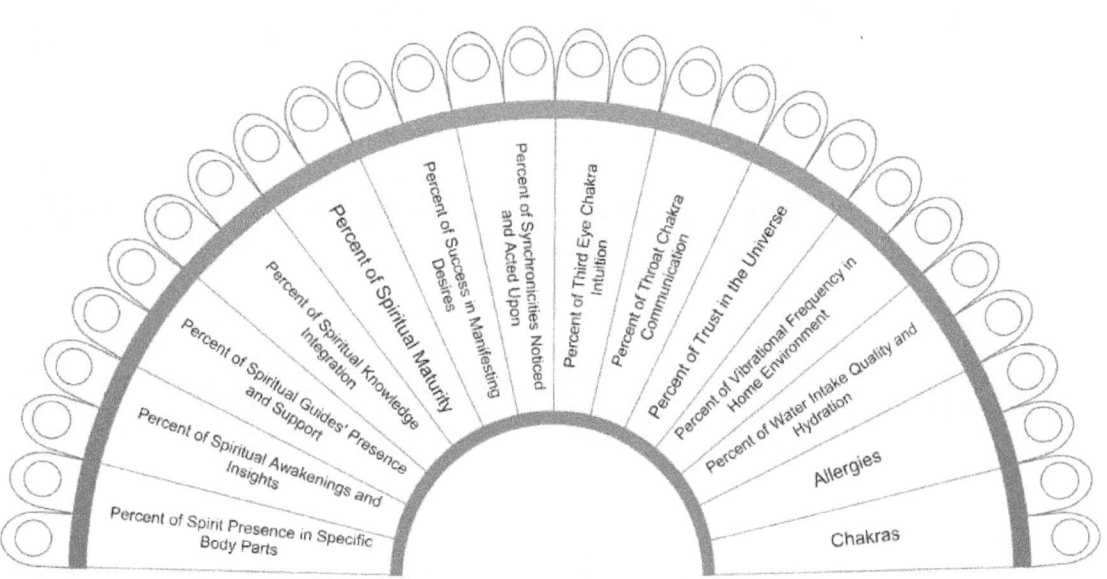

Numbers, Ways to Use Them, Chart 7

The fan chart contains the following labels (clockwise):

- Percent of Spirit Presence in Specific Body Parts
- Percent of Spiritual Awakenings and Insights
- Percent of Spiritual Guides' Presence and Support
- Percent of Spiritual Knowledge Integration
- Percent of Spiritual Maturity
- Percent of Success in Manifesting Desires
- Percent of Synchronicities Noticed and Acted Upon
- Percent of Third Eye Chakra Intuition
- Percent of Throat Chakra Communication
- Percent of Trust in the Universe
- Percent of Vibrational Frequency in Home Environment
- Percent of Water Intake Quality and Hydration
- Allergies
- Chakras

Royal Template 14

Diving Deep into the Pool of the Mind

Chart 524

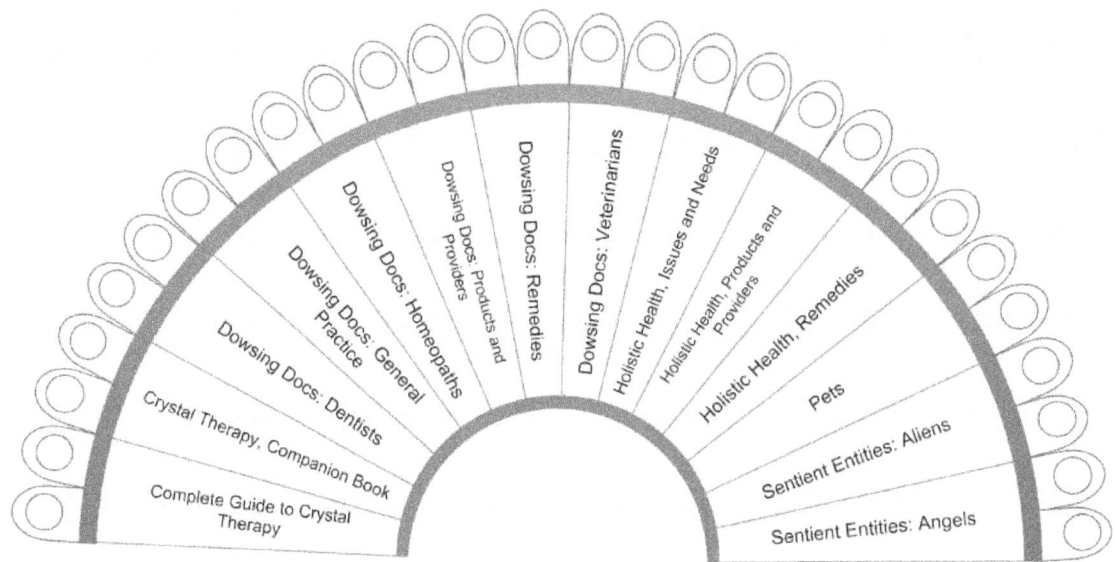

Other Dowser's Guide Books Chart

Complete Guide to Crystal Therapy
Crystal Therapy, Companion Book
Dowsing Docs: Dentists
Dowsing Docs: General Practice
Dowsing Docs: Homeopaths
Dowsing Docs: Products and Providers
Dowsing Docs: Remedies
Dowsing Docs: Veterinarians
Holistic Health, Issues and Needs
Holistic Health, Products and Providers
Holistic Health, Remedies
Pets
Sentient Entities: Aliens
Sentient Entities: Angels

Royal Template 14

Diving Deep into the Pool of the Mind

Chart 525

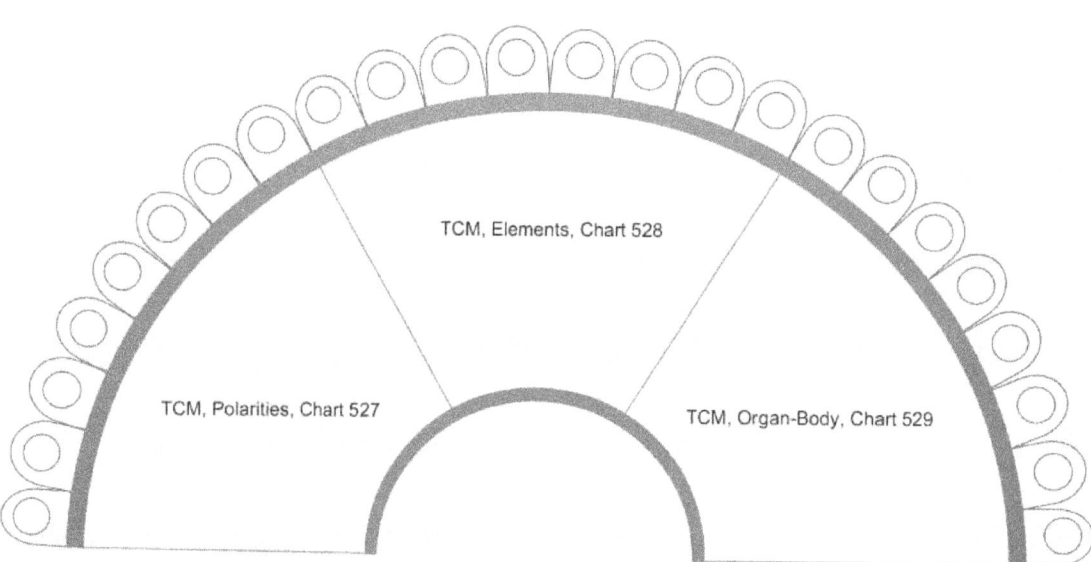

TCM, Elements, Chart 528

TCM, Polarities, Chart 527

TCM, Organ-Body, Chart 529

Traditional Chinese Medicine (TCM), Master Chart

Royal Template 3h

Diving Deep into the Pool of the Mind

Chart 526

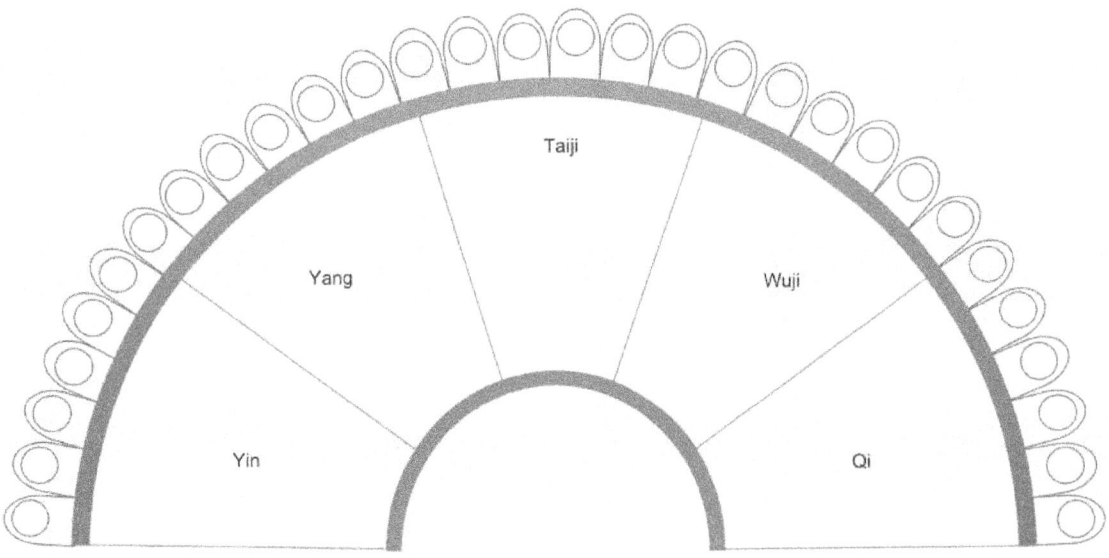

TCM, Polarities

Taiji

Yang

Wuji

Yin

Qi

Royal Template 5h

Diving Deep into the Pool of the Mind

Chart 527

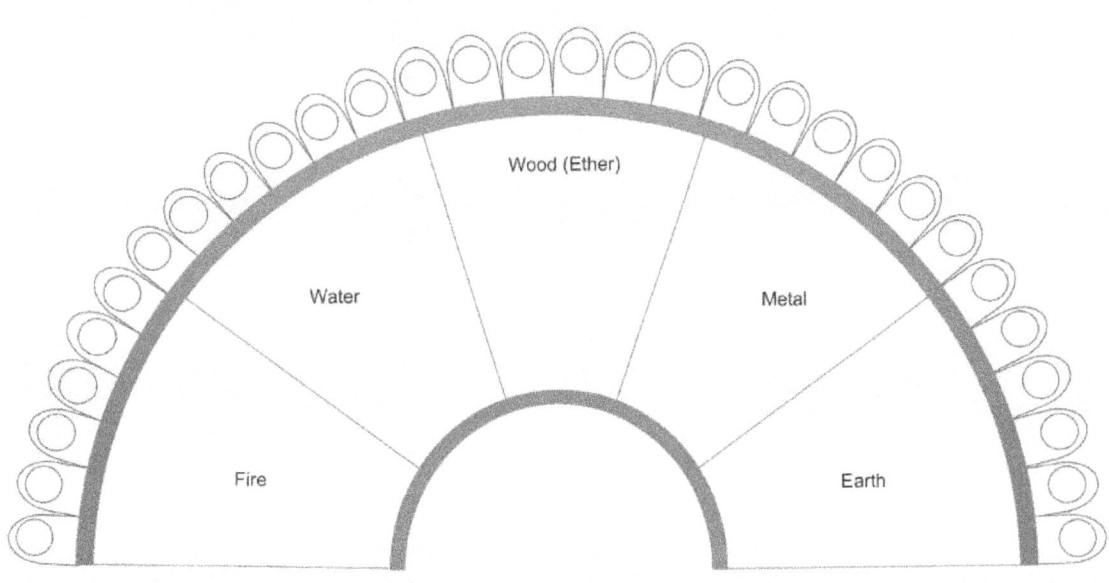

TCM, Elements

Wood (Ether)

Water

Metal

Fire

Earth

Royal Template 5h

Diving Deep into the Pool of the Mind

Chart 528

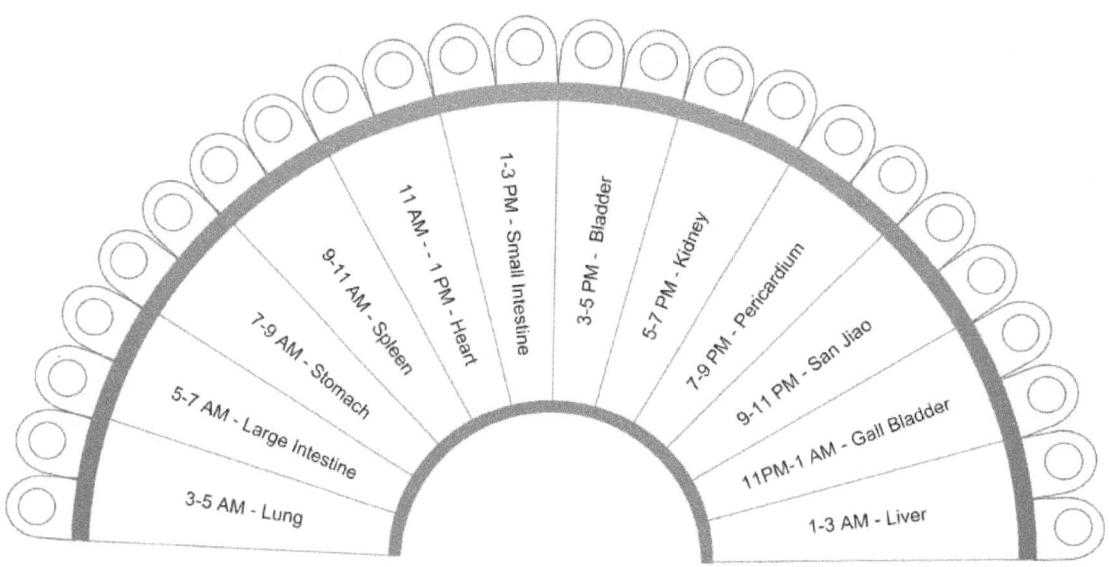

TCM, Organ-Body

The fan chart contains the following labels from left to right:

- 3-5 AM - Lung
- 5-7 AM - Large Intestine
- 7-9 AM - Stomach
- 9-11 AM - Spleen
- 11 AM - 1 PM - Heart
- 1-3 PM - Small Intestine
- 3-5 PM - Bladder
- 5-7 PM - Kidney
- 7-9 PM - Pericardium
- 9-11 PM - San Jiao
- 11PM-1 AM - Gall Bladder
- 1-3 AM - Liver

Royal Template 12

Diving Deep into the Pool of the Mind

Chart 529

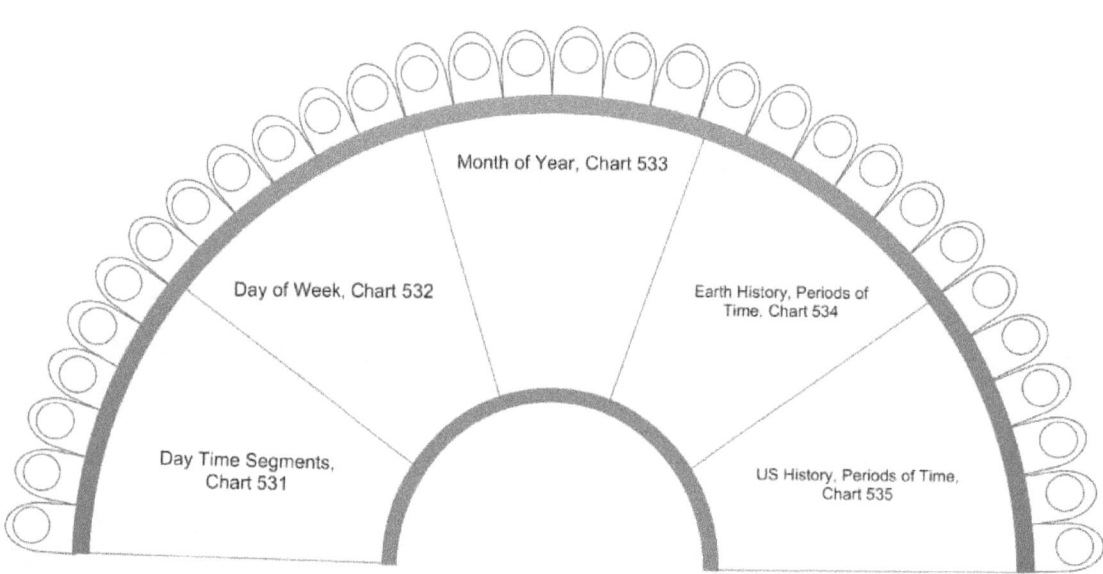

When, Master Chart

The fan chart contains the following labels:

- Day Time Segments, Chart 531
- Day of Week, Chart 532
- Month of Year, Chart 533
- Earth History, Periods of Time, Chart 534
- US History, Periods of Time, Chart 535

Royal Template 5h

Diving Deep into the Pool of the Mind

Chart 530

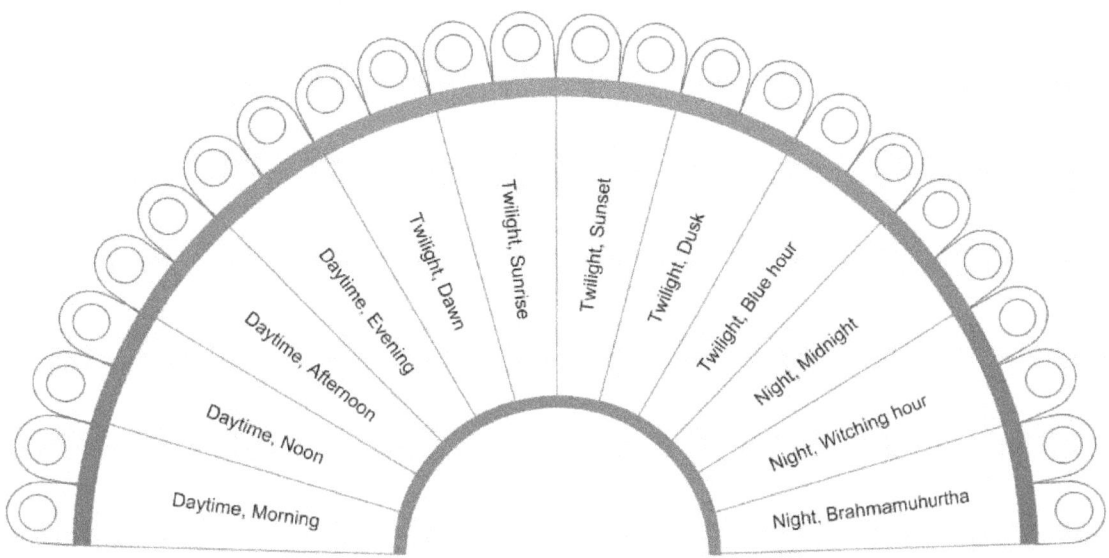

Day Time Segments

The segments shown, from left to right:
Daytime, Morning · Daytime, Noon · Daytime, Afternoon · Daytime, Evening · Twilight, Dawn · Twilight, Sunrise · Twilight, Sunset · Twilight, Dusk · Twilight, Blue hour · Night, Midnight · Night, Witching hour · Night, Brahmamuhurtha

Royal Template 12

Diving Deep into the Pool of the Mind

Chart 531

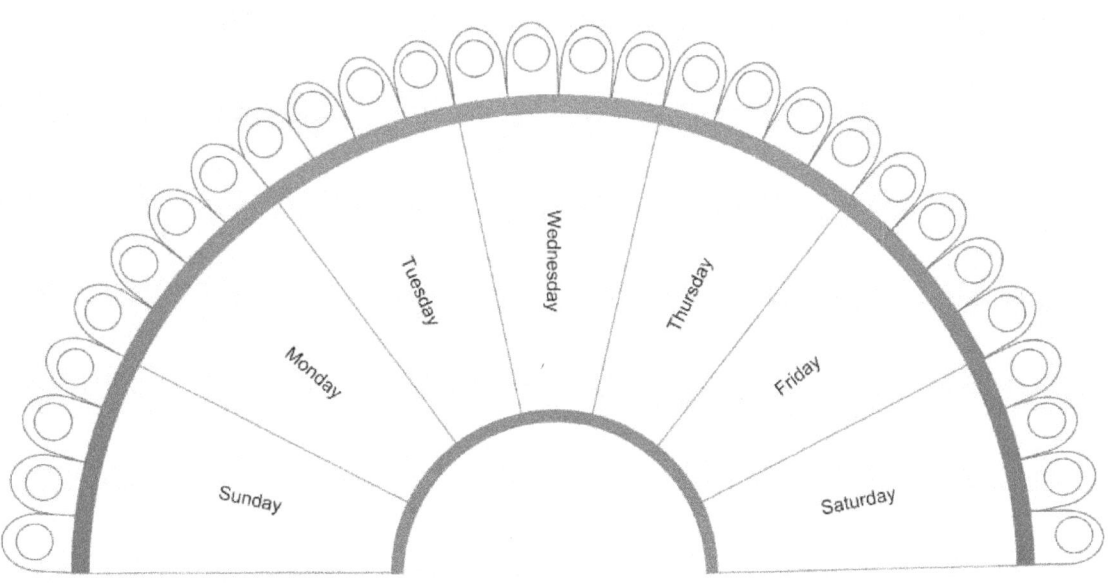

Day of Week

The segments shown, from left to right:
Sunday · Monday · Tuesday · Wednesday · Thursday · Friday · Saturday

Royal Template 7

Diving Deep into the Pool of the Mind

Chart 532

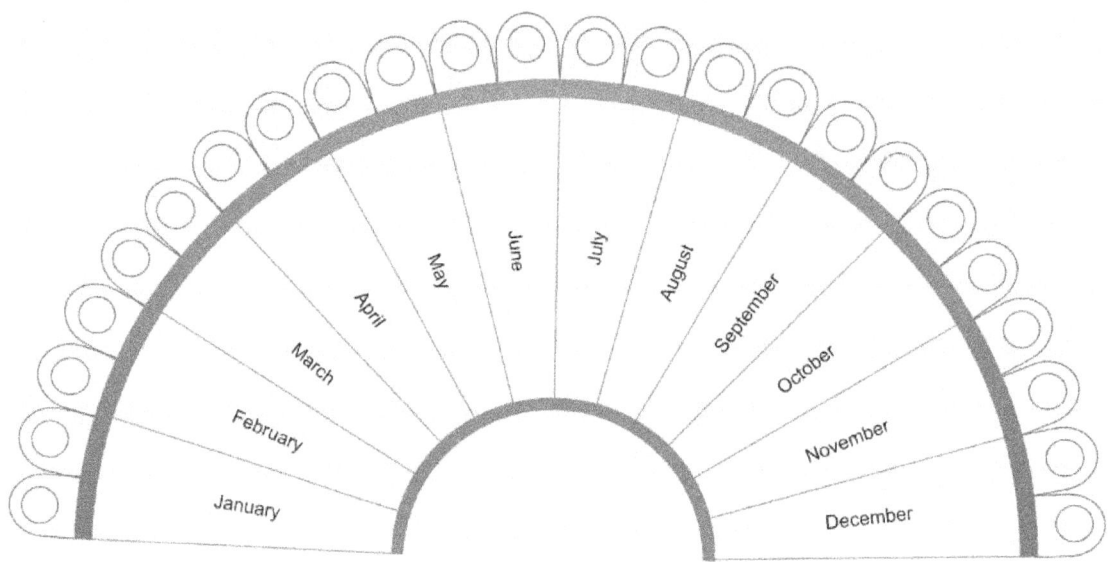

Month of Year

Royal Template 12

Diving Deep into the Pool of the Mind

Chart 533

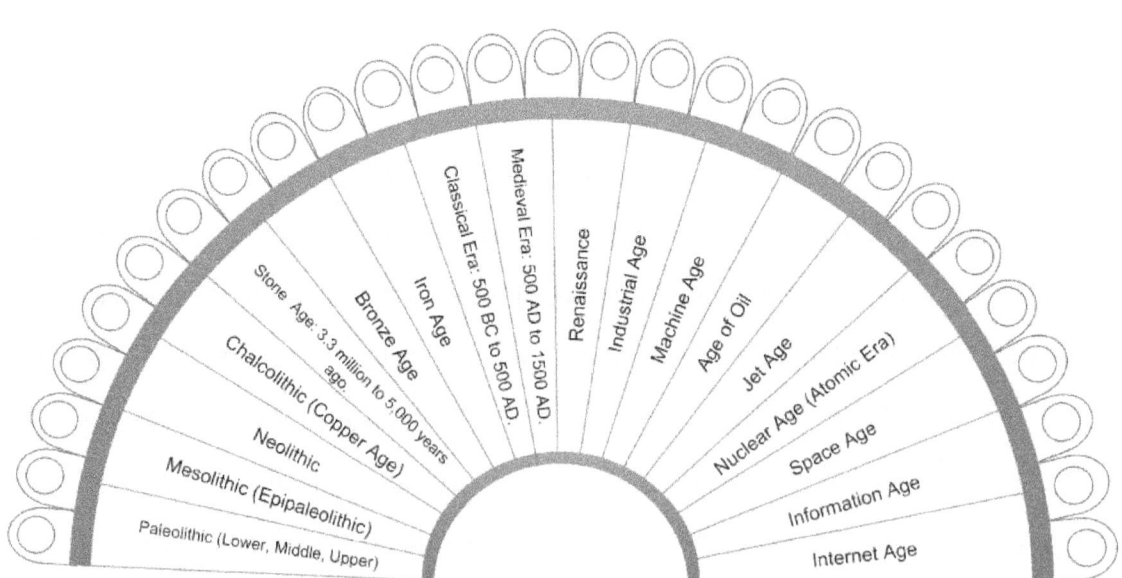

Earth History, Periods of Time

Royal Template 18

Diving Deep into the Pool of the Mind

Chart 534

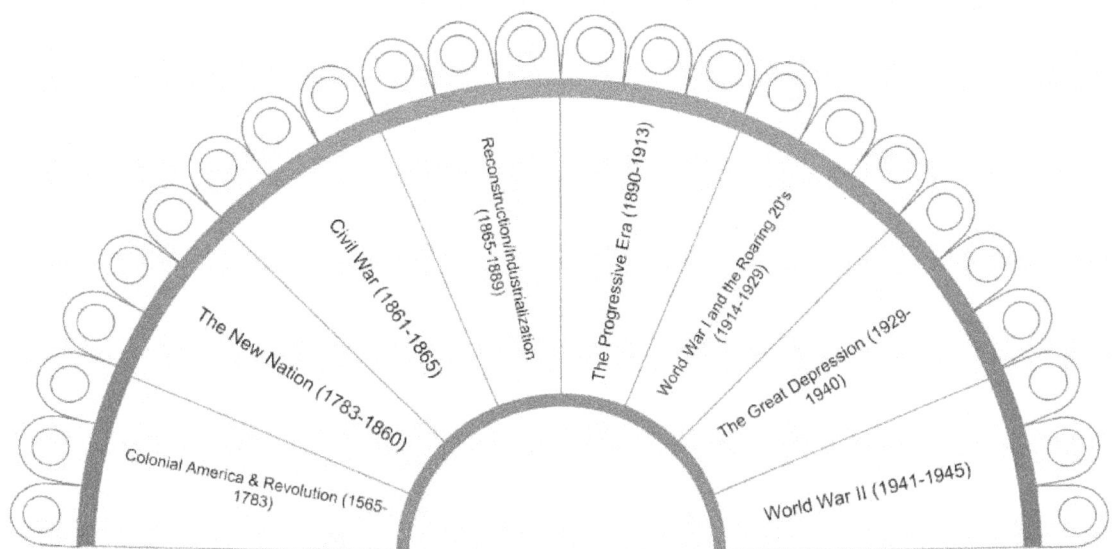

US History, Periods of Time

Colonial America & Revolution (1565-1783)

The New Nation (1783-1860)

Civil War (1861-1865)

Reconstruction/Industrialization (1865-1889)

The Progressive Era (1890-1913)

World War I and the Roaring 20's (1914-1929)

The Great Depression (1929-1940)

World War II (1941-1945)

Royal Template 8

Diving Deep into the Pool of the Mind

Chart 535

BOVIS LIFE FORCE (CHI) BIOENERGY UNITS DOWSING CHART

Divine Source, Universe, Central Sun, Regulus A Ascended Masters

Ref. dowsergary@comcast.net

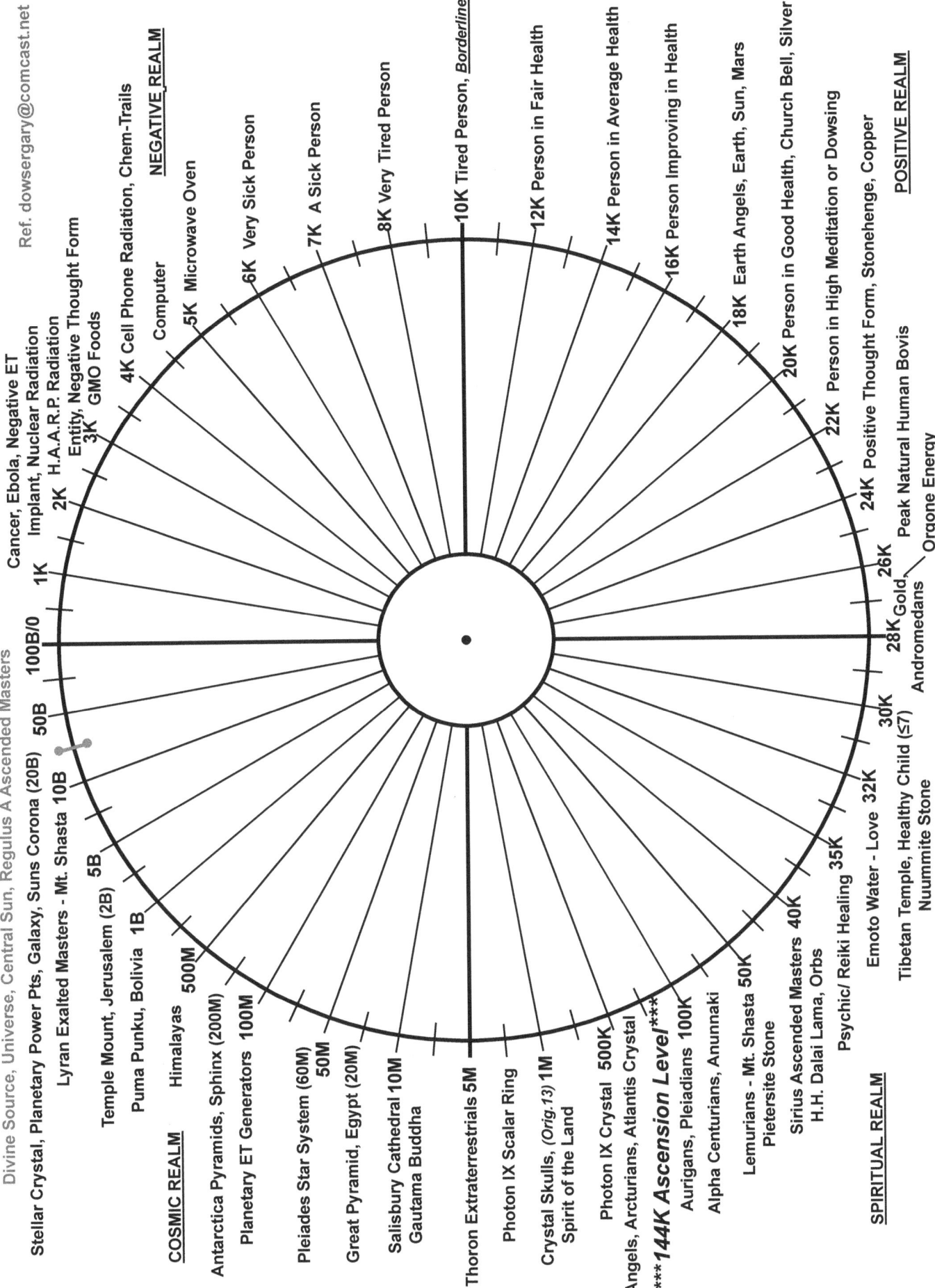

NEGATIVE REALM

Cancer, Ebola, Negative ET
Implant, Nuclear Radiation
H.A.A.R.P. Radiation
Entity, Negative Thought Form
GMO Foods
Cell Phone Radiation, Chem-Trails
Computer
Microwave Oven
Very Sick Person
A Sick Person
Very Tired Person
Tired Person, *Borderline*
Person in Fair Health
Person in Average Health
Person Improving in Health
Earth Angels, Earth, Sun, Mars
Person in Good Health, Church Bell, Silver
Person in High Meditation or Dowsing
Positive Thought Form, Stonehenge, Copper
Peak Natural Human Bovis
Orgone Energy

Scale markings: 1K, 2K, 3K, 4K, 5K, 6K, 7K, 8K, 10K, 12K, 14K, 16K, 18K, 20K, 22K, 24K, 26K, 28K, 30K, 32K, 35K, 40K, 50K

POSITIVE REALM

Gold
Andromedans
Healthy Child (≤7)
Emoto Water - Love
Tibetan Temple, Healthy Child (≤7)
Nuummite Stone
Psychic/ Reiki Healing
H.H. Dalai Lama, Orbs
Sirius Ascended Masters
Pietersite Stone
Lemurians - Mt. Shasta
Alpha Centurians, Anunnaki
Aurigans, Pleiadians
144K Ascension Level
Angels, Arcturians, Atlantis Crystal
Photon IX Crystal
Spirit of the Land
Crystal Skulls, *(Orig.13)*
Photon IX Scalar Ring
Thoron Extraterrestrials

SPIRITUAL REALM

Gautama Buddha
Salisbury Cathedral
Great Pyramid, Egypt (20M)
Pleiades Star System (60M)
Planetary ET Generators
Antarctica Pyramids, Sphinx (200M)
Himalayas

COSMIC REALM

Puma Punku, Bolivia
Temple Mount, Jerusalem (2B)
Lyran Exalted Masters - Mt. Shasta
Stellar Crystal, Planetary Power Pts, Galaxy, Suns Corona (20B)

Scale markings: 100B/0, 50B, 10B, 5B, 1B, 500M, 100M, 50M, 10M, 5M, 1M, 500K, 100K, 40K, 35K, 32K, 30K, 28K

Divine Source, Universe, Central Sun, Regulus A Ascended Masters

Expanded Scale 100 Billion Unit Bovis Life Force Biometer
May be copied for personal or chapter use. Revised 10/07/17, Gary R. Plapp

The Author

Many people know the author as the inventor of non-consumable supplements, a breakthrough technology for health and longevity used in the Broad Spectrum DeTOX program. Some may remember meeting her at road shows in any of 67 Costco stores where she sold Goal Zero's portable solar power generators as Suzie Solar.

Her path started in an isolated village of 80 to 100 people in Alaska where she grew up. Her father was an air traffic controller serving bush pilots. He taught her about technology and the value it has for helping others. She "talked" with people far away using Morse code before she could read. The village's three shamans shared their ancestral wisdom and taught her how to use the energy of plants to keep people healthy. They helped her develop metaphysical skills and psychic abilities and hold a deep love for the world, nature and people.

As she grew up, her parents took her on many rock hounding trips in the "Lower 48." She could feel the energy of the minerals and rocks. She sensed how they could help people with their vibrational energy in a way that is similar to how plants can make people healthy. This is the foundation for her astonishing discovery of non-consumable supplements that are homeopathic and consist of high mineral sand, crystals and copper. Her sense of nature's energy is shared with the world through a 1,500 page, 2-volume book, *The Complete Guide to Crystal Therapy*. This epic book lays out 2,700 ways to use 1,111 crystals for physical, emotional and spiritual issues and needs.

Later in life, she pondered the question about life after death and the concept of ascension. She integrated the stories of the shamans with religious beliefs and recognized the Biblical reference to 144,000 people being resurrected meant people with a high enough level of energy will ascend to the next plane or dimension.

As she worked in the Costco stores, she met and spoke with over 400,000 people and became an extraordinary resource and hub of useful information. This experience also led her to concern that the energy of many people was not high enough for ascension. Given her love for humanity, this was a burden. That issue, drove her to create this book. Because, if one's energies are not high enough and they believe they are the best they can be, what else can they do?

The answer came when she discovered the objective metaphysical wisdom of consciousness could be tapped through the use of dowsing charts and a pendulum. The universe is ready and willing to answer questions. She spent 10 years designing charts so no one should be left behind. This book can bring *enlightenment* through a heart-mind connection. Anyone can use it to take another step forward to a higher level of loving energy and a better self.

www.ingramcontent.com/pod-product-compliance
Lightning Source LLC
Chambersburg PA
CBHW041109120626
46547CB00019B/2638